The Oxford Companion to
Twentieth-Century British Politics

The Oxford Companion to
TWENTIETH-CENTURY BRITISH POLITICS

Edited by

John Ramsden

OXFORD
UNIVERSITY PRESS

OXFORD
UNIVERSITY PRESS

Great Clarendon Street, Oxford OX2 6DP

Oxford University Press is a department of the University of Oxford.
It furthers the University's objective of excellence in research, scholarship,
and education by publishing worldwide in

Oxford New York

Athens Auckland Bangkok Bogotá Buenos Aires Cape Town
Chennai Dar es Salaam Delhi Florence Hong Kong Istanbul Karachi
Kolkata Kuala Lumpur Madrid Melbourne Mexico City Mumbai Nairobi
Paris São Paulo Shanghai Singapore Taipei Tokyo Toronto Warsaw

with associated companies in Berlin Ibadan

Published in the United States
by Oxford University Press Inc., New York

First published 2002

British Library Cataloguing in Publication Data
Data available

Library of Congress Cataloging in Publication Data
Data available

ISBN 0–19–860134–4

1 3 5 7 9 10 8 6 4 2

Typeset in 8.5pt/10pt Minion
by Kolam Information Services Pvt. Ltd, Pondicherry, India
Printed in Great Britain
by T. J. International Ltd, Padstow, Cornwall

CONTENTS

PREFACE & ACKNOWLEDGEMENTS

Centuries as such do not excite historians very much these days, as viable units for analysis or for the meaningful periodization of the past. The 'long 18th century' of the historians' imagination lasts for up to 155 years, and other centuries have been correspondingly abbreviated. The 20th century has been less subject to such arbitrary redefinition, but not immune from it, and a particularly imaginative Oxford examiner once invited students to discuss the proposition that, 'The nineteenth century is generally taken to have ended in 1914, but it should be 1916'. Virginia Woolf was equally certain that the modern world began just *before* the Great War, when London saw its first exhibition of the post-impressionists.

Things are, however, a good deal easier when the focus is specifically on British political history, for 1900 was the year in which the Labour Party was founded. Although the biggest and most regular winners of the century's party battles were the Conservatives, Labour's arrival in its first decade did usher in a very different type of politics to what Britain had ever seen before, one more about economics and material well-being than about issues of status, civic rights, and morality. The 'New Liberalism' that flourished in the decade before 1914 was in its way a reaction to Labour's rise, though one that did not eventually head off Labour's thrust to replace the Liberals as the main party on the left. Between the wars and again in the 1950s and the 1980s, Conservative success rested to a significant extent on their ability to portray themselves as the most effective party of resistance to socialism and to the trade unions—both at home and abroad. In due course, the disappearance (whether permanently or not, we cannot yet tell) of British people's distrust of Labour in the 1990s goes far to explain the Conservatives' inability to prosper as the century ended. Even at the end of the century, the centrist Liberal Party had yet to recover beyond the point to which it had plunged as Labour first advanced during and after the Great War. So, as a 'Conservative Century' it may fairly be described, but it was in reaction to Labour's arrival in 1900 that 20th-century politics were made and progressively remade thereafter.

There are other continuities too, though many of these were under challenge as the century ended, more so indeed than at any other time since 1900. Britain still used, for example, the same system of election for the House of Commons in 1997 as it had done in 1900, and though the House of Lords lost in 1911 powers that it had rarely used, and then lost in 1948 powers that had been rarely used since 1911, its structure, membership, and manners had changed very little. And although Britain first applied to join a supranational European organization in the early 1960s, and succeeded in getting in at the third attempt in the early 1970s, its impact on the inner life and attitudes of Westminster and Fleet Street was far less than might have been expected.

Britain began the century as one of the world's greatest powers—as *the* greatest power if the criterion was the size of overseas empires—but was also already in the 1900s a country lamenting its relative economic decline. In the third quarter of the century, most British colonies were liberated, though with as little drama at Westminster as their acquisition had aroused during the previous century. But throughout the century, the political debate was periodically enlivened by echoes of arguments about British economic decline that first hit the hustings in Joseph Chamberlain's crusade for tariffs when it began in 1903. Insofar as this was a debate about the relative merits of free trade and protection for a world-trading economy, its echoes continue indeed within current debates about 'Europe', and with the same capacity to wreck the careful plans of party managers, bringing down John Major much as it had brought down Arthur Balfour. For the present then, the 20th century still seems a very viable period around which a reference work like this can sensibly be organized.

It is, though, a Companion to *Political* History in the century, and readers should bear this in mind when reading entries which would have been presented quite differently in a book with a different primary focus. Economists would find therefore that the discussion of economists, economic issues, and principles is weighted here towards the role that they have played in politics, just as military historians will find that wars and weapons are viewed from the same political perspective.

This angle of approach is most obviously the case geographically. Scotland and Wales are given, we believe, their due weight as separate political systems, though most of the rest of the book also of course describes political systems, parties, and events in which Scotsmen and Welshmen took active and often leading roles: Baldwin and Asquith were after all the only premiers who would have called themselves 'English' between 1906 and 1937. Ireland was inextricably tied up with British politics during the period of the Union, until 1921, and again in the last third of the century as violence in Ulster drew both Britain and Ireland into cooperative action; it would make little sense to ignore altogether Irish affairs only between 1921 and 1969, so there is some coverage of them here (if once again from a mainly United Kingdom perspective). If this were a Companion to the Political History of the British Isles, the balance in all these cases would have been different.

A work that aims to be as wide-ranging and as comprehensive as this one must rely on many people's efforts. It would not have been possible to set it up, to define an overall approach and structure, to arrive at the relative allocation of space between subject areas and the exact delineation of entries, or to recruit a team of qualified writers, without a great deal of effort from my team of associate editors. I am extremely grateful for their input at several stages of the project, and to the book's large numbers of authors (particularly, I must add, those who delivered on time and without a reminder, and those who gallantly took on additional entries when time was pressing). Oxford University Press has a long and distinguished tradition of producing such large reference works, and it has been a great reassurance for a general editor taking charge of his first such book to know that this experience was at my disposal when needed. Pam Coote, Wendy Tuckey, and Rebecca Collins have been a far better production team than this editor at least deserved.

John Ramsden

EDITORS

GENERAL EDITOR

JOHN RAMSDEN is Professor of Modern History at Queen Mary, University of London, author of *An Appetite for Power: A History of the Conservative Party since 1832* (1998) and of all three 20th-century volumes in the *Longman History of the Conservative Party* (1978, 1995, 1996).

ADVISORY EDITORS

Scotland, Ireland, Wales

GEORGE BOYCE is a Professor in the Department of Politics, University of Wales Swansea. His books include *Nineteenth Century Ireland: The Search for Stability* (1990), *Nationalism in Ireland* (1995), and *Decolonisation and the British Empire, 1775–1997* (1999).

International Policy

KATHLEEN BURK is Professor of Modern and Contemporary History at University College London. She is the author of a number of books including *Britain, America and the Sinews of War 1914–1918* (1985), *Morgan Grenfell 1838–1988: The Biography of a Merchant Bank* (1989), with Alec Caincross, '*Goodbye, Great Britain*': *The 1976 IMF Crisis* (1992), and *Troublemaker: The Life and History of A. J. P. Taylor* (2000). Her research interests include Anglo-American relations from 1607 to the present.

Political Sociology, Political Theory, the Study of Politics

JACK HAYWARD is a Fellow of the British Academy, Emeritus Professor of Politics at Oxford University, and Research Professor of Politics at Hull University. He is the author of a number of books including *The State and the Market Economy* (1986), *After the French Revolution* (1991), and editor-contributor to *The Political Science of British Politics* (1986), *Industrial Enterprise and European Integration* (1995), *Elitism, Populism and European Politics* (1996), and *The British Study of Politics in the Twentieth Century* (1995).

Civil Service, Public Administration, the Constitution

PETER HENNESSY is Attlee Professor of Contemporary British History at Queen Mary, University of London. His publications include *The Hidden Wiring: Unearthing the British Constitution* (1995), *Never Again: Britain 1945–1951* (1992), *Whitehall* (1989), and *The Prime Minister* (2000).

The Labour Party, Trade Unions, Groups of the Political Left

KEITH LAYBOURN is Professor of History at the University of Huddersfield. He is the author and editor of 28 books and numerous articles. These include *Britain on the*

Breadline (1990, 1997), *The Evolution of British Social Policy and the Welfare State* (1995), *Socialism in Britain 1881–1951* (1997), *Under the Red Flag: A History of Communism in Britain* (1999), editor with Dylan Murphy, *Representation and Reality of War: The British Experience* (1999), and editor with Keith Dockray, *A Century of Labour* (2000). He also edits the *Annual Bulletin of Historical Literature.*

Liberal and Central Parties, Social Policy

JOHN STEVENSON is Fellow and Tutor in History at Worcester College, Oxford. He is the author of a number of titles and works of reference including *British Society, 1914–1945* (1984), *Third Party Politics in Britain since 1945* (1992), and with C. P. Cook, *The Longman Companion to Britain since 1945* (2nd edn., 2000).

Business Groups, Industrial and Economic Policy

JOHN TURNER is Professor of Modern History and Politics and Vice-Principal at Royal Holloway, University of London. He has published *British Politics and the Great War* (1992), *Macmillan* (1994), and articles on the Conservative Party, civil society, and business–government relations.

CONTRIBUTORS

AB ANDREW BLICK is a research student at Queen Mary, University of London

ACM ALEX MAY is research editor for the *New Dictionary of National Biography*, and secretary, *The Round Table*

AD ALEX DANCHEV is Professor of International Relations at Keele University. His most recent books are *On Specialness* (1998), a collection of essays on Anglo-American relations, and *Alchemist of War* (1998), a biography of Basil Liddell Hart

ADe ANNE DEIGHTON is a Lecturer in European International Politics at the University of Oxford, and a fellow of Wolfson College, Oxford. She has written extensively on British foreign policy since 1945, the development of European integration, and on contemporary European security

AJC Dr A. J. CROZIER is Senior Lecturer and Jean Monnet Lecturer in History at Queen Mary, University of London. He has published work on the origins of the Second World War

AM Dr ANDREW MITCHELL lectures in History and Education at Basingstoke College, an associate college of Portsmouth University

AS ALAN SHARP is Professor of International Studies at Magee College, University of Ulster, and Head of the School of History, Philosophy, and Politics

---

BB BRIAN BRIVATI is Reader in Modern British History at Kingston University, and author of *Hugh Gaitskell* (1996) and *Lord Goodman* (1999)

BJE Professor BRENDAN EVANS is Pro-Vice-Chancellor, Academic Affairs, at the University of Huddersfield

BL Dr BRENDAN LYNN is a Research Fellow at the Institute of Irish Studies, Queen's University, Belfast, and author of *Holding the Ground: The Nationalist Party in Northern Ireland, 1945–1972* (1997)

BMW Professor BRIAN WALKER is Director of the Institute of Irish Studies at Queen's University, Belfast. He is the author of *Ulster Politics: The Formative Years* (1987) and editor of *Parliamentary Election Results in Ireland, 1918–1992* (1992)

BP Professor BEN PIMLOTT is Warden of Goldsmiths' College, University of London, the author of *Labour and the Left in the 1930s* (1977), *Hugh Dalton* (1985), and *Harold Wilson* (1992)

BPa BIKHU PAREKH is Professor of Political Theory at the University of Hull

---

CAB Dr CHRIS BRADY is the Director of MBA Studies at the City University Business School and has recently published *Rules of the Game* (2000), on business management, and *End of the Road* (2000), the story of BMW's ownership of Rover

CAM CATHERINE MACMILLAN is a Lecturer in Law at Queen Mary, University of London, and the author of a number of articles examining the common law

CC CARL CHINN is Senior Lecturer and community historian at the University of Birmingham and author of *Poverty amidst Prosperity: The Urban Poor in England, 1880–1939* (1995)

CH Professor COLIN HOLMES taught at the University of Sheffield, 1963–98, and is now Part-Time Research Professor at the University of Sunderland

CKSU COLIN SEYMOUR-URE is Professor of Government at the University of Kent at Canterbury, and has written extensively about the press and broadcasting

CL Dr CHAS LOFT recently completed a thesis on government and the railways, 1951–64; he has been a part-time Lecturer at Queen Mary, University of London, and Visiting Professor of History at Westminster College, Fulton, Missouri

CPS Dr CHRISTOPHER STEVENS is a Senior Lecturer in Politics at the University of Teesside; his recent publications include articles on grass-roots Conservatism and 20th-century voting behaviour

CRS CATHERINE SCHENK is Senior Lecturer in Economic History at the

University of Glasgow, and the author of a book and over a dozen articles on international monetary relations since 1945

DD David Denver is Professor of Politics at Lancaster University

DEB Dr David Butler has been a Fellow (latterly Emeritus Fellow) of Nuffield College, Oxford, since 1954, and the author or co-author of all thirteen Nuffield election studies since 1951, as well as numerous other works on British politics

DEM Dr David Martin is a Lecturer in Economic and Social History at Sheffield University; he is co-editor of *Ideology and the Labour Movement* (1979) and of *The History of the City of Sheffield* (1993)

DG Dr Dylan Griffiths is a Lecturer in Politics at the University of Newcastle upon Tyne and his research interests are Welsh politics and British territorial politics

DGB George Boyce, advisory editor

DHD Dr David H. Dunn is Senior Lecturer in International Studies, University of Birmingham, and author of *The Politics of Threat: American Security Policy in the 1990s* (1997)

DJD Dr David Dutton is Reader in History at the University of Liverpool, and Visiting Professor at the Bolton Institute. He has written biographies of Austen Chamberlain, John Simon, and Anthony Eden

DLM Dylan Lee Murphy is a Ph.D. student at Huddersfield University and co-author of *Under the Red Flag: A History of Marxism in Britain, 1918–1990* (1999)

DMM Donald McRaild is a Lecturer in History at the University of Northumbria at Newcastle

DRB Dr David Brooks is Lecturer in History at Queen Mary, University of London; he is the author of books on late Victorian and Edwardian history, including *The Age of Upheaval* (1995)

DRW David Wootton is Professor of Intellectual History at Queen Mary, University of London; he has published widely in the history of political theory

DWM Dr David Mayall is Principal Lecturer in History at Sheffield Hallam University and co-editor, with John Burnett and David Vincent, of the three-volume *The Autobiography of the Working Class: A Critical Annotated Bibliography 1790–1945* (1984–9)

ECP Edward C. Page is Professor of Politics at Hull University; his research interests include comparative public policy and administration, his latest book, *Governing by Numbers* (2001), is a study of delegated legislation and 'everyday politics' in Britain

EP Edward Pearce is a journalist and freelance writer, former panellist on *The Moral Maze*, and the author of *The Lost Leaders* (1997); he is the official biographer of Denis Healey

FHC Forest Capie is Professor of Economic History at City University business school; he is the author/editor of twenty books and 100 papers on money and banking and commercial policy; he recently served as editor of the *Economic History Review*

GA Geoffrey Alderman is Vice-President of Touro College, New York; his books include *The Jewish Community in British Politics* (1983) and *Modern British Jewry* (2nd edn., 1998)

GAP Dr Geoffrey Allen Pigman is Research Fellow at the Centre for International and European Studies, Coventry University, and is the author of 'The Sovereignty Discourse and the U.S. Debate on Joining the World Trade Organization', *Global Society*, Vol. 12, No. 1, 1998

GBM Dr Gary Bryan Magee is a Lecturer in Modern Economic History at the University of Melbourne

GC Gerard Crompton is a Lecturer in the Canterbury Business School, University of Kent, and has published in the areas of transport and business history

GG Gordon Gillespie is co-author of *Northern Ireland: A Chronology of the Troubles, 1968–1999* (1999)

GJ Professor Grant Jordan, University of Aberdeen, has specialized in empirical studies of British central government and interest group activity and membership; he has been active in debates on corporatism (against) and policy communities (supportive)

HJM HELEN MERCER formerly taught at the Department of History of the LSE

HOJ Dr HARRIET JONES is Director of the Institute of Contemporary British History, at the Institute of Historical Research, University of London

---

IM IAIN MCLEAN is Professor of Politics, Oxford University, and official fellow in politics, Nuffield College, Oxford. He has written widely on 19th- and 20th-century British politics

IMY IAN YEATS has taught law since 1966 at Queen Mary, University of London, and is a member of the editorial board, and current survey editor, of *Public Law*

IP INDERJEET PARMAR is Lecturer in Government at the University of Manchester, with a research interest in Anglo-American elites and foreign policy

---

JAJ Professor J. A. JOWITT is Principal of the Northern College for Residential Adult Education, and Professor of Continuing Education at Sheffield Hallam University

JAR JOHN RAMSDEN, general editor

JAT Professor JOHN TURNER, advisory editor

JD JON DAVIS worked as an investment banker and in the Cabinet Office, and is now the Burke Trend scholar, researching the machinery of government reforms of the 1960s and early 1970s, at Queen Mary, University of London

JDT Professor JIM TOMLINSON is Head of the Department of Government at Brunel University, and author of *Democratic Socialism and Economic Policy: The Attlee Years 1945–1951* (Cambridge, 1997)

JFM Dr JOHN MARTIN is Senior Lecturer in Agrarian History at the De Montfort University, Leicester, and the author of *The Development of Modern British Farming since 1931* (2000)

JGJ J. GRAHAM JONES is an assistant archivist at the Department of Manuscripts, the National Library of Wales, Aberystwyth, and is currently responsible for the Welsh Political Archive

JH JACK HAYWARD, advisory editor

JHB JONATHAN BROWN is the archivist at the Rural History Centre, University of Reading. His research interests include agricultural practice and politics and market towns and trade in the 19th and 20th centuries

JJN Dr JOHN NOTT, is a social historian and specialist on 20th-century British popular culture, particularly dance halls and the popular music industry

JMB Dr J. M. BOURNE is Senior Lecturer in Modern History at the University of Birmingham, currently working on a revisionist history of the British army during the Great War

JPG Dr JOHN GARDINER, formerly a research student at the University of Kent

JPSG Dr JOHN GEARSON is a Lecturer in War Studies at King's College, London, and author of *Harold Macmillan and the Berlin Wall Crisis* (London, 1999)

JR JOHN REDMOND is Professor of European Studies and Jean Monnet Chair of the Political Economy of European Integration at the University of Birmingham

JRVE JAMES ELLISON is a Lecturer in History at Queen Mary, University of London; his research interests are in the history of Britain and European integration, and post-war British foreign policy

JS Dr JOHN STEVENSON, advisory editor

JSS Dr JOHN SHEPHERD was formerly Principal Lecturer and Research Degrees Adviser at Anglia Polytechnic University, Cambridge, and is completing a book on George Lansbury for Oxford University Press

JTC JOHN CALLAGHAN is Professor of Politics at Wolverhampton University and author of *Socialism in Britain* (1990), *Rajani Palme Dutt* (1993), and *The Retreat of Social Democracy* (2000)

JWY JOHN YOUNG is Professor of Politics at the University of Leicester, the editor of *The Foreign Policy of Churchill's Peacetime Administration, 1951–1955* (1988), and author of *Winston Churchill's Last Campaign: Britain and the Cold War, 1951–1955* (Oxford, 1996)

KAH KEITH HAMILTON is a historian in the Foreign and Commonwealth Office and Senior Editor of *Documents on British Policy Overseas*; his publications include *Bertie of Thame: Edwardian Ambassador* (1990) and (with Richard Langhorne) *The Practice of Diplomacy* (1994)

KG KEITH GRIEVES is Reader in History at Kingston University; his recent articles on Britain in the Great War relate to the war economy and civil–military relations

KJ KEITH JEFFERY is Professor of Modern History at the University of Ulster at Jordanstown; he is the author of many books on military history, including *For the Freedom of Small Nations: Ireland and the Great War* (Cambridge, 2000)

KJL Dr KENNETH LUNN is Reader in Social History at the University of Portsmouth; he has published extensively on the histories of race, immigration, and the labour movement in Britain, and is currently an editor of the *Labour History Review*

KL KEITH LAYBOURN, advisory editor

KMT Dr KEIR THORPE lectures in European history and works for Luton University and the Public Record Office; he has written on British economic planning and the government's responses to emergencies

KT KEVIN THEAKSTON is Professor of British Government at the University of Leeds and author of *Leadership in Whitehall* (1999), *The Civil Service Since 1945* (1995), and *The Labour Party and Whitehall* (1992)

KTS Dr KEITH SURRIDGE is a part-time Lecturer at Queen Mary, University of London, and has published on the South African war of 1899–1902

KY KEN YOUNG is Professor of Politics at Queen Mary, University of London, and was previously at the Institute of Local Government Studies, University of Birmingham

---

LL LORNA LLOYD is a Lecturer in International Relations at Keele University; she has published on legal, diplomatic, and historical aspects of the Commonwealth, League of Nations, and the UN

MC MARTIN CRICK is Senior Lecturer in Arts and Education at the University of Leeds, and author of *The History of the Social Democratic Federation* (1994)

MCh MARTIN CHICK is Senior Lecturer in Economic and Social History at the University of Edinburgh; his publications include *Industrial Policy in Britain 1945–51* (1998)

MCJ Dr MATTHEW C. JONES is a Lecturer in Modern History at Royal Holloway, University of London, specializing in 20th-century international history, and is currently working on south-east Asia in the 1950s and 1960s

MDN Professor MICHAEL NEWMAN is at the University of North London, and is the author of *John Strachey* (1989), *Harold Laski, A Political Biography* (1993), and *Democracy, Sovereignty and the European Union* (1996)

MEC MARTIN CEADEL is Fellow in Politics at New College, Oxford, and the author of *The Origins of War Prevention: The British Peace Movement and International Relations* (1996)

MES MORAG SHIACH is Professor of Cultural History, School of English and Drama, Queen Mary, University of London, and editor of *Feminism and Cultural Studies* (1999)

MJK MICHAEL KEATING is Professor of Political Science at the University of Western Ontario, London, Ontario, Canada

ML MARK LUNNEY is a Senior Lecturer in the School of Law, King's College London

MLC MARK CONNELLY is Reuters' Senior Lecturer in Media History and Modern British History at the University of Kent and author of *Christmas: A Social History* (1999)

MWB Sir MICHAEL WHEELER-BOOTH was Clerk of the Parliaments in the House of Lords, 1990–7

MWK MAURICE KIRBY is Professor of Economic History at Lancaster University; he has published widely in the fields of modern British economic and social history

---

NC NICHOLAS CULL is Professor of American Studies at the University of Leicester and has published widely on the political use of film and the media

NJC Dr NICHOLAS CROWSON is Lecturer in History at the University of Birmingham, and author of *Facing Fascism: The Conservative Party and the European Dictators 1935–1940* (1997)

PAT PHILIP TOWLE is Reader in International Relations at the Centre of

International Studies in Cambridge; he is the author of *Pilots and Rebels* (1989), *Enforced Disarmament from the Napoleonic Campaigns to the Gulf War* (1987), and *Democracy and Peacemaking* (2000)

PC PATRICIA CLAVIN is Senior Lecturer in the Department of History at Keele University, and has published widely on international economic relations in the inter-war period

PH PAUL HENDERSON is a Lecturer in History at the University of Wolverhampton; his main interests are labour history and the economic and social history of Latin America

PJH PETER HENNESSY, advisory editor

PJRR PETER RIDDELL is the Political Editor of *The Times* and author of *Honest Opportunism, the rise of the career politician* (1993)

PM PETER MARTLAND is a Research Associate at Corpus Christi College, Cambridge, and College Lecturer and Director of Studies in History for Clare and Magdalene Colleges, Cambridge; he teaches papers in British economic and social history and the history of intelligence

PN PHILIP NORTON (Lord Norton of Louth) is Professor of Government and Director of the Centre for Legislative Studies at the University of Hull; he is author or editor of 26 books

PPC Dr PETER CATTERALL is a Lecturer in History and Fellow in the Centre for Public Policy, Queen Mary, University of London

PPM Dr PAUL MITCHELL is a Lecturer in the School of Law at King's College London

PR Dr PETER ROSE is a former political journalist and the author of *How the Troubles Came to Northern Ireland* (1999)

PRGR PATRICK RENSHAW was formerly Reader in Modern History at the University of Sheffield, and the author of *The General Strike* (1975)

PS PETER STEAD is former Senior Lecturer at the University of Wales, Swansea, a regular broadcaster, and author of a biography of Richard Burton

---

RB LORD BUTLER OF BROCKWELL was, as Sir Robin Butler, cabinet secretary, 1988–97

RCW RICHARD WHITING is a Senior Lecturer in History at Leeds University, and the author of *The View from Cowley: The Impact of Industrialization on Oxford, 1918–1939* and has subsequently published articles on labour and taxation

RD Revd ROBIN DENNISTON was a publisher, before entering the Anglican priesthood, and the author of many publications on intelligence and national security issues

RE Dr RICHARD ENGLISH is Reader in Politics at Queen's University, Belfast, and author of *Radicals and the Republic: Socialist Republicanism in the Irish Free State, 1925–1937* (1998)

RF Dr RICHARD FINLAY is a Lecturer in the History of Modern Scotland at the University of Strathclyde, and author of a history of Scottish nationalism, *A Partnership for Good* (1996)

RJQA Professor R. J. Q. ADAMS is Professor of History at Texas A and M University, College Station, and the author of *Bonar Law* (1999)

RJS ROBERT SHEPHERD is the biographer of *Iain Macleod* and *Enoch Powell*, an award-winning television producer, and former government special adviser

RKST RICHARD TAYLOR is Professor of Continuing Education at the University of Leeds; he has published three books on the British peace movement, and several others on the ideology and policy of adult and higher education

RM Dr ROGER MIDDLETON, Reader in the History of Political Economy, University of Bristol, publishes on British economic policy and performance since 1890 and on the history of the British economics profession

RNS Professor REBA SOFFER is the author of *Discipline and Power: The University, History, and the Making of an English Elite, 1870–1930* (1995)

RWDB ROBERT BOYCE teaches international history at the LSE; his publications include *British Capitalism at the Crossroads, 1919–1932: A Study in Politics, Economics and International Relations* (1987)

SB STEPHEN BIRD is assistant archivist at the Labour History Archives and Study Centre at the University of Manchester, looking after the archives of the Labour Party and the Communist Party of Great Britain

SC Dr STEPHEN CONSTANTINE is Senior Lecturer in History at Lancaster University; his publications include *Buy and Build: The Advertising Posters of the Empire Marketing Board* (1986) and *Emigrants and Empire: British Settlement in the Dominions between the Wars* (1990)

SJB SIMON BALL is Senior Lecturer in History at the University of Glasgow, author of *The Bomber in British Strategy* (1995) and *The Cold War 1947–1991* (1997)

SM STEVEN MOREWOOD is a Lecturer in International History at the University of Birmingham, and the author of *The British Defence of Egypt, 1935–1940* (2000)

SMcC SEÁN MCCONVILLE is Professor of Criminal Justice at Queen Mary, University of London; he is author of numerous books and essays on prisons and penal policy, including most recently *Irish Political Offenders 1848–1922* (2001)

SS Dr SHAMIT SAGGAR is Reader in Electoral Politics at Queen Mary, University of London, and a member of the British Election Study consortium

---

TGO Dr THOMAS OTTE is a Lecturer in International History at the University of the West of England, Bristol; he is the editor of *Military Intervention: From Gunboat Diplomacy to Humanitarian Intervention* (1995), *Personalities, War and Diplomacy* (1997), and *The Makers of British Foreign Policy: From Pitt to Thatcher* (2001)

TWH Dr THOMAS HENNESSEY is Lecturer in British and Irish History at Canterbury Christ Church College and author of *Dividing Ireland: World War One and Partition* (1998)

VT VICTOR TUNKEL is a barrister, Senior Lecturer in Law at Queen Mary, University of London, and secretary of the Selden Society for English legal history

---

WF WILLIAM FRAME is a curator in the Department of Manuscripts at the British Library, and recently completed a doctoral thesis on the Conservative Party in the 1930s

WG WYN GRANT is Professor of Politics at the University of Warwick and the author of *Business and Politics in Britain* (2nd edn., 1993)

WMK WILLIAM M. KUHN is the author of *Democratic Royalism* (1996) as well as a biography of Queen Victoria's private secretary, Henry Ponsonby, and his wife Mary Ponsonby; he is Associate Professor of History at Carthage College, Kenosha, Wisconsin

CLASSIFIED CONTENTS LIST

POLITICAL BIOGRAPHIES

Supporters and Organizers

Liberal and Allies

Prime Ministers

Politicians

Supporters

Communists

Extreme Right Wing Politicians

Scottish Nationalists

Welsh Nationalists

Independent Politicians

Irish Politicians

Northern Ireland Politicians

Royalty

Private Secretaries to Royal Family

Civil Servants

Prime Ministers' Staff and Political Advisers

Diplomats

Colonial Administrators

Judges

Publishers

Industry and Business

Industrialists

Trade Unionists

Finance

Pacifists

ISSUES AND POLICIES

Issues

Economic

Political

Social

Education

Health

Religion

The Monarchy

Business

Europe

International

THEORIES AND IDEAS

Ireland

Europe

International

ORGANIZATIONS AND GROUPS

Central Government

Local Government

Committees

Parties

Party Organizations

Policy and Research Organizations

The Forces

The Church

Charities and Voluntary Organizations

Pressure Groups

Trade Union Organizations

Business

Media

Education

Ireland

Europe

International

Other

PUBLICATIONS AND DOCUMENTS

Books

Newspapers and Periodicals

Reports and Reviews

White Papers

Sandys white paper

Policy Documents

Fair Deal at Work
Industrial Charter
Labour's Immediate Programme
Looking Ahead
Putting Britain Right Ahead
Right Approach, The
Right Road for Britain, The
Signposts for the Sixties
We Can Conquer Unemployment

Election Manifestos

Action Not Words
Britain Belongs to You
Let Us Face the Future
Let's Go With Labour for a New Britain

Film and Television

Braveheart
Death on the Rock
newsreels
Spitting Image
That Was the Week That Was
Yes Minister
Yesterday's Men

Other

Black Papers
Citizen's Charter
Focus
Framework documents
Hansard
Mosley memorandum
What the Conservatives have done for the British People

QUOTATIONS AND PHRASES

'appalling frankness'
'at a stroke'
'back to basics'
'bastards, the'
'best prime minister we have'
'blood, toil, tears, and sweat'
'blown off course'
'Bolshevism run mad'
'bomber will always get through, the'
'bonfire of controls'
'breaking the mould'
'business as usual'
'Chinese slavery'
'Conservative Party at Prayer, the'
'Crisis, what crisis?'
customary processes
'damn the consequences'
'east of Suez'
'economical with the truth'
'Falklands factor'
'filling the cup'
'five giants'
'free at the point of delivery'
'from the cradle to the grave'
'gnomes of Zurich'
'Gotcha!'
'hard-faced men who look as if they have done well out of the war'
'Hitler has missed the bus'
'homes fit for heroes'
'inevitability of gradualness'
Iron Lady
'jaw-jaw is better than war-war'
'Labour Isn't Working'
'Lady's not for turning, The'
'lame ducks'
'little local difficulties'
'lower than vermin'
'march towards the sound of gunfire'
'methods of barbarism'
Mr Balfour's poodle
'naked into the Conference Chamber'
'never had it so good'
New Labour
'new style of government'
'No, no, no!'
'no such thing as society, There is'
'Not a penny off the pay, not a second on the day'
'party's over, the'
'peace for our time'
'Peers v. People'
'plough my furrow alone'
'pound in your pocket'

PLACES

Prime Minister's Residences

Places in Britain

Abroad

ABBREVIATIONS

BMA	British Medical Association
BNP	British National Party
BSE	Bovine Spongiform Encephalopathy
BUF	British Union of Fascists
CB	Companion of the Order of the Bath
CBI	Confederation of British Industry
CIA	Central Intelligence Agency (US)
CND	Campaign for Nuclear Disarmament
CPGB	Communist Party of Great Britain
CPRS	Central Policy Review Staff
CSD	Civil Service Department
DEA	Department of Economic Affairs
DoE	Department of the Environment
DHSS	Department of Health and Social Security
DUP	Democratic Unionist Party
EC	European Community, formed in 1967 from the union of the ECSC, EEC, and Euratom, although the collective was sometimes still popularly known as the EEC; from 1993, known as the European Union (EU)
ECSC	European Coal and Steel Community
EEC	European Economic Community (see note under EC)
EMS	European Monetary System
EMU	European Monetary Union
ERM	Exchange Rate Mechanism
ESRC	Economic and Social Research Council
ETU	Electricians' Trade Union
EU	European Union (see note under EC)
FBI	Federation of British Industries (UK) Federal Bureau of Investigation (USA)
FO	Foreign Office
GCHQ	Government Communications Headquarters
GDP	Gross Domestic Product
GNP	Gross National Product
GLC	Greater London Council
HC	House of Commons
ICI	Imperial Chemical Industries
ILP	Independent Labour Party
IMF	International Monetary Fund
IRA	Irish Republican Army
KB	King's Bench
KC	King's Counsel
KCMG	Knight Commander of the Order of St Michael and St George
LG	David Lloyd George
LSE	London School of Economics and Political Science
MC	Military Cross
MFGB	Miners' Federation of Great Britain
MLR	Minimum Lending Rate
MoD	Ministry of Defence
MORI	Market and Opinion Research International
National Union	National Union of Conservative and Unionist Associations
NATO	North Atlantic Treaty Organization
NEC	National Executive Committee (of the Labour Party)
NF	National Front
NHS	National Health Service
NIESR	National Institute for Economic and Social Research
NUM	National Union of Mineworkers
NUWM	National Unemployed Workers' Movement
OECD	Organization for Economic Cooperation and Development
OEEC	Organization for European Economic Cooperation
OPEC	Organization of the Petroleum Exporting Countries
PAYE	pay as you earn
PRO	Public Record Office
PSBR	public sector borrowing requirement
QB	Queen's Bench
QC	Queen's Council
RAF	Royal Air Force
RPI	Retail Price Index
SAS	Special Air Service
SDLP	Social Democratic and Labour Party (Northern Ireland)
SDP	Social Democratic Party
SIS	Secret Intelligence Service (UK)
SNP	Scottish National Party
SOE	Special Operations Executive
SSRC	Social Science Research Council
TGWU	Transport and General Workers' Union
TUC	Trades Union Congress
UK	United Kingdom
UN	United Nations
USA	United States of America
USSR	Union of Soviet Socialist Republics
VC	Victoria Cross
$	US dollar

NOTE TO THE READER

This book is designed for easy use but the following notes may be useful to the reader.

Alphabetical arrangement

Entries are arranged in letter-by-letter alphabetical order following punctuation of the headword, with the exception that names beginning with Mc are arranged as though they were prefixed with Mac, and St is ordered as though it were spelt Saint.

Cross-references

An asterisk (*) in front of a word in the text signals a cross-reference to a related entry. Cross-referencing has been guided as far as possible by common sense and normally occurs only once within any given entry. This means that in some cases asterisks have been added to what are in fact slight variants of the actual headword; it also means that cross-references have been inserted where they seem most likely to assist the reader, rather than mechanically wherever a headword occurs in the text. Similarly, 'see' or 'see also' followed by a headword in SMALL CAPITALS is used to cross-refer when the precise form of headword to which the reader is being pointed does not occur naturally in the text.

Classified Contents List

The list of entries under major themes at the front of the book (see pp. xvii–xlvi) offers an alternative means of access to the material.

Contributors' initials

are given at the end of each entry and a key to these initials can be found in the List of Contributors at the front of the book (pp. xi–xvi).

Bibliographies

at the end of longer entries provide guidance to further reading.

Date of Ministries

A listing of dates of ministries from 1895 to 2001 can be found in Appendix 1.

Office Holders

A table showing prime minister, home secretary, foreign secretary, chancellor of the exchequer, lord chancellor, and other major offices with corresponding dates can be found in Appendix 2.

Results of General Elections

A list of general election results from 1895 to 2001 of all the major parties can be found in Appendix 3.

Government Commissions and Departments

In entries dealing with government commissions and departments which changed name frequently during the course of the century, the entry usually appears under the current name of the department with cross-references under the names of its most important predecessors; thus there is an entry under 'Defence, Ministry of' which is signposted under 'Admiralty' and the 'War Office'. Reports of major royal commissions may be found under the name of their chair.

abdication crisis (1936) occurred when the prime minister, Stanley *Baldwin, resisted Edward VIII's proposed marriage to Wallis Simpson, an American divorcée living in London. Baldwin told the king that he could not reconcile his position as supreme governor of the Church of England with the Church's disapproval of divorce. Baldwin, along with many others, also thought Mrs Simpson, a product of the jazz and cocktail age, unsuitable to be queen. The king's affair with Mrs Simpson and growing determination to marry her had been widely commented on in the press outside Britain, especially in the USA, but British newspapers voluntarily suppressed news of the gathering confrontation between king and ministers. This protected the king's privacy but it also gave the appearance of press and politicians colluding to keep the public in the dark and preventing them from expressing any sympathy with the king, who had been enormously popular, especially as prince of Wales. The king abdicated in favour of his younger brother who became George VI. The abdication crisis was, along with the death of Diana, Princess of Wales, one of the two great threats to the stability of the throne during the 20th century. The monarchy recovered from the abdication under the new king and queen, who set high standards of public service and helped to boost morale during the Second World War. *WMK*

Philip Ziegler, *King Edward VIII* (London, 1990).

Abercrombie, (Leslie) Patrick (1879–1957), town planner and one of the most influential planners of post-1945 reconstruction. Educated at Uppingham and articled to architects in Manchester and Liverpool, he practised in Chester from 1920, also pursuing from 1907 an academic career at the universities of Liverpool and London (where he was professor of town planning at University College, 1935–46). Abercrombie undertook a series of civic and regional planning studies from the 1920s, advocated a *'green belt' of undeveloped land around London, and was founder of the Council for the Protection of *Rural England, 1926. He was a member of the 1937 Barlow royal commission on the distribution of the industrial population, hailed as the 'planners' breakthrough' for its advocacy of controls to restrict the growth of London. Between 1941 and 1946, Abercrombie prepared a series of major plans for the reconstruction of British cities after the *Blitz, notably the *County of London Plan* (1943) and *Greater London Plan* (1944), as well as plans for Plymouth, Hull, Edinburgh, Clydeside, and the west Midlands. His London plans became the blueprint for post-war development and his plan for Plymouth with its pedestrianized shopping centre and ring roads contained many of the elements typical of developments after 1945. *JS*

Abingdon Street, London, SW1, the site of Liberal Party offices, 1910–34. *JS*

Ablett, Noah (1883–1935), militant south Wales miners' leader, syndicalist, *Plebs League organizer, and brilliant orator. Ablett went to Ruskin College, Oxford, on a miners' scholarship, and, in the true pit activists' tradition, honed his skills as a checkweighman and miners' agent. He served on the executive committee of the Miners' Federation of Great Britain (1921–6) but never broke into the union's mainstream, twice being beaten in elections for the post of secretary by what were seen as less militant candidates, including A. J. Cook. He published numerous articles and pamphlets, including, jointly, *The Miners' Next Step* (1912). Ablett remained true to his radical roots until his early death from cancer. *DMM*

abortion. The Abortion Act of 1967 was the first to legalize abortion in Britain, after centuries of illegality and religious and ethical opposition. The 1861 Offences against the Person Act made abortion at any stage of pregnancy subject to a maximum sentence of life imprisonment, though modification occurred in 1929 with the Infant Life Preservation Act, which made it an offence to destroy the life of a child 'capable of being born alive', deemed to be at about 28 weeks, except to save the life of the mother. In 1936 the Abortion Law Reform Association was founded to campaign on behalf of the estimated 500 women per year who died as a result of illegal 'backstreet' abortions, and landmark cases prior to the Second World War extended the range of circumstances in which abortion under medical supervision could be legal, such as where the mental or physical health of the mother might be seriously endangered. There remained widespread opposition, in particular from religious groups, notably the Roman Catholic Church, and amongst the more conservatively minded.

The Birkett committee, reporting in 1939, recommended a measure of reform and after the Second World War there were several attempts through private members' bills to alter the law. The eventual passage of the 1967 Act followed widespread pressure from liberal and women's groups, notably the Abortion Law Reform Association, who argued that illegality forced women to risk backstreet abortions from which many subsequently died or suffered grave injury. Opposition came from religious groups and conservatively minded MPs. Six attempts at reform through private members' bills were blocked between 1952 and 1965, but in July 1966 the newly elected MP for Roxburgh, Selkirk, and Peebles, David *Steel, introduced a bill with the assurance of support from sympathetic Labour and other MPs, as well as in the Lords. His bill passed into law on 26 October 1967, permitting abortion at up to 28 weeks in England, Wales, and Scotland, where it was necessary to preserve the mental or physical health of the mother, or where an additional child would adversely affect the health of the existing children in the family (known as the 'medico-social' clause). No time limit was applied where abortion would prevent grave permanent injury to the physical or mental health of the woman, where there was a substantial risk of serious foetal handicap, or where continuing the pregnancy would put the life of the mother at risk. The Act was widely seen as part of the permissive legislation of the sixties, but was highly contentious and could only be pursued on the basis of a free vote. Roman Catholic and conservative MPs subsequently sought to amend or limit the Act, achieving a limited result in the reduction of the statutory limit for abortion to 24 weeks under a clause in the 1990 Human Fertilization and Embryology Act. *JS*

Abraham, William ('Mabon') (1842–1922), Welsh miners' leader. Mabon (his bardic name) was the first effective organizer of Welsh miners, the first president of the South Wales Miners Federation, and MP for the Rhondda, 1885–1920. Elected first as a Lib-Lab, only reluctantly did he later join Labour. His legendary status was accounted for by negotiating skills, his girth, and a fine singing voice often deployed when tempers were frayed. His belief in industrial conciliation reflected his chapel values. *PS*

E. W. Evans, *Mabon* (Cardiff, 1959).

Abrams, Mark Alexander (1906–94), social science researcher who helped establish the use of market research in the UK. Abrams graduated from the LSE before working as a research fellow at the Brookings Institute in Washington DC. He returned to the UK to work for the London Press Exchange before establishing his own company, Research Services. His survey research was put to use in an influential and path-breaking book, *Must Labour Lose?*, a Penguin Special co-authored with Richard Rose and published in 1960, showing the extent to which Labour had lost touch with its electoral base. His skills were drawn on by Labour leaders Hugh Gaitskell and Harold Wilson. He subsequently took up an appointment as director of the survey unit of the Social Science Research Council. He was active in a range of organizations, including Age Concern. *PN*

Abse, Leopold (1917–), Labour politician, solicitor, and author. Leo Abse was MP for Pontypool, 1958–83, and the renamed Torfaen, 1983–7. An independently minded backbencher he sponsored private members' Acts on divorce, homosexuality, family planning, and legitimacy. In 1979, he fiercely opposed devolution. In an autobiography and subsequent studies of leading politicians, notably Mrs Thatcher, he divertingly applied Freudian analysis to British politics. Brother of the poet Dannie Abse, he remained a waspish extrovert with a love of flashy waistcoats and cars. *PS*

LEO ABSE, *Private Member* (London, 1973).

Abyssinian crisis (1935–6). This erupted in October 1935 when Italy attacked Abyssinia (now Ethiopia) and ended in May 1936 with the subjugation of Abyssinia and the subsequent termination of *League of Nations sanctions. Because of Britain's position in the League and of the state of British public opinion, a substantial portion of which subscribed to the principles of the League and adhered to the concept of collective security, the British government took the lead in imposing sanctions, with the French government reluctantly following. This, however, conflicted with a principal aim of British policy, which was to keep Italy out of Germany's orbit by preserving good Anglo-Italian relations and maintaining her in the *Stresa front with France and Britain. It was inevitable, therefore, that the British government would seek to end the conflict through compromise. This expressed itself in the Hoare-Laval pact of December 1935, which would have allowed Italy to realize the substance of her imperialist aims, while maintaining a nominal independence for a truncated Abyssinia. The details of the pact were, however, leaked; in the ensuing tumult it was abandoned and Hoare, the foreign secretary, was forced to resign. Mussolini, the Italian dictator, who might have accepted the proposals, now rapidly moved towards closer relations with Germany. Thus a European diplomatic revolution was effected, culminating in the announcement of the Rome-Berlin Axis in November 1936. Thereafter, it became a major objective of British policy to break the Axis by detaching Italy. League sanctions did minimal damage to Italy and minimal damage to Britain. Oil sanctions, had they been imposed from the start, could easily have been evaded because of the global cartelization of the oil industry. The denunciation by Neville Chamberlain of the continuation of sanctions as 'the midsummer of madness' marked the beginning of their demise. *AJC*

D. MACK-SMITH, *Mussolini's Roman Empire* (London, 1976). | E. ROBERTSON, *Mussolini as Empire-Builder: Europe and Africa 1932–1936* (London, 1977).

ACAS (Advisory, Conciliation, and Arbitration Service). The growing breakdown in industrial relations throughout the 1960s and 1970s led to the creation of the Conciliation and Arbitration Service in 1974. In 1975 it was renamed the Advisory, Conciliation and Arbitration Service in order to more accurately reflect the full range of its services. ACAS survived governments of very different ideological beliefs and by the end of the 20th century was more involved in helping companies to achieve efficiency with minimal workforce disruption. *JD*

ACAS website: *www.acas.org.uk*

Acland, Richard Thomas Dyke (1906–90), politician and founder of the *Common Wealth Party. Educated at Rugby and Balliol College, Oxford, Sir Richard Acland (he inherited a baronetcy in 1939) represented Barnstaple as a Liberal, 1935–42, then sat as a Common Wealth MP until 1945. He espoused radical proposals for 'common ownership', publicized in a best-selling Penguin Special, *Unser Kampf* (1940), an answer to Hitler's *Mein Kampf.* In 1942 he launched the Common Wealth Party to contest wartime by-elections against 'reactionary' candidates and in support of progressive policies. Three by-election victories against sitting Conservative MPs helped to establish the need for policies of social reform in the post-war settlement. When the party's 23 candidates were overwhelmed in the Labour victory of 1945, returning only one MP, Acland joined the Labour Party and served as MP for Gravesend from 1947 to 1955. In 1955, he resigned his seat over Labour's decision to support the hydrogen bomb programme. A principled idealist, he continued to write on political and moral questions until the last months of his life. *JS*

Acland-Hood, Alexander Fuller (1853–1917), Conservative politician and party organizer. He sat as MP for his county, Somerset, from 1892 until 1911. A bluff country squire known as 'the pink 'un' because of his devotion to hunting, he was an unimaginative chief whip, 1902–11. After three successive electoral disasters, party leader Arthur Balfour in 1911 reluctantly accepted reform of Central Office and Acland-Hood was relegated to the Lords as Baron St Audries and replaced by Lord Balcarres. *RJQA*

JOHN RAMSDEN, *The Age of Balfour and Baldwin, 1902–1940* (London, 1978).

Action Not Words, the Conservatives' campaign slogan and the title of their manifesto in the 1966 election. Ideas, however, were what they needed. The Tories failed to capture people's imagination with too many detailed promises, while Heath's uninspiring first aim was 'to run this country's affairs efficiently and realistically'. *RJS*

Adams, Gerry (1949–), Irish republican activist. Born into a staunch Republican family in west Belfast, Gerry Adams's father was a member of the IRA. Although never convicted of Provisional *IRA membership, Adams was alleged by the security forces to be head of that organization in the Ballymurphy area of west Belfast. He was interned in 1971 but released in 1972 to enable him to take part in talks between the Provisional IRA and the British government in London. Adams became vice-president of Provisional Sinn Fein in 1978. Following the hunger strikes in 1981, Adams was instrumental in advocating the abandonment of the traditional republican doctrine of boycotting elected institutions in Northern Ireland and Eire. In 1983, the same year that he became president of *Sinn Fein, Adams was elected MP for West Belfast but refused to take his seat at Westminster. He lost the seat in 1992, but regained it once more in 1997. In 1988, Adams began talks with the leader of constitutional nationalism in Northern Ireland, John Hume. These led to the 'Hume-Adams' agreement of 1993, which built a common position for Northern Irish nationalism. Adams and Sinn Fein were excluded from the multi-party talks process in Belfast because of British government doubts over the credibility of the IRA ceasefire of 1994 which collapsed in 1996, but Adams led Sinn Fein into multi-party talks in Belfast in 1997 following the restoration of the IRA's cessation. He committed his party to the Mitchell principles of non-violence and democracy which governed the talks process. Under his leadership Sinn Fein signed up to the Belfast agreement in May 1998 which formally recognized the partition of Ireland, and became a minister in the devolved all-party government. *TWH*

David Sharrock and Mark Davenport, *Man of War, Man of Peace? The Unauthorised Biography of Gerry Adams* (London, 1997).

Adams, William George Stewart (1874–1966), prime minister's secretary, 1916–19. An Oxford professor of politics who had advised the government on Irish affairs (1911) before working at the Ministry of Munitions (1915), Adams was head of the prime minister's secretariat, a small group of advisers established by Lloyd George in 1917 and known as 'the garden suburb'. Initially, Adams concentrated on labour and food policy. In 1917–18 he played a major role in efforts to achieve consensus in Ireland. He edited the war cabinet reports of 1917 and 1918. *CL*

Adam Smith Institute, influential independent policy unit established in 1978 and named after the 18th-century Scottish philosopher and economist, one of the leading advocates of free-market capitalism and author of *The Wealth of Nations* (1776). The institute played a key role in the free-market revolution, which characterized the Thatcher Conservative administration, and is a persuasive advocate of privatization, the sale of council houses, increasing parental choice in education, the Citizen's Charter, the use of private firms to provide public services, and the shift to funded pensions. Its policies are based on incentive, choice, opportunity, and the enhancement of the individual in the decision-making process. The institute is a non-party organization working in conjunction with policy makers, promoting practical public policies intended to solve economic and social problems from a free market and libertarian perspective. It advocates the power of self-interest epitomized by Adam Smith's 'invisible hand', which reconciled public benefit with individual pursuit of private gain. Its policies are disseminated through reports, advisory services, and seminars for influential figures. It is active not only in the UK but also overseas, where international donors including the European Union, the World Bank, the Asian Development Bank, and the US Agency for International Development fund it. *JFM*

Adamson, (William Owen) Campbell (1922–2000), industrialist and business leader. After a long career in the steel industry, Adamson was seconded to the Department of Economic Affairs as a deputy secretary coordinating industrial advisers, 1967–9. This background in a large publicly influenced industry, followed by civil service experience, made him a natural candidate for the post of director-general of the CBI, which he held from 1969 to 1976. This was a period when tripartite cooperation between government, industry, and the unions was at its height and the executive head of the CBI was a significant public figure. Adamson made his contribution to tripartism through the CBI's voluntary prices initiative in 1971–2 which saw him at the peak of his persuasive power. His authority never fully recovered after remarks made in the February 1974 election campaign which were construed as helpful to Labour and he left the CBI to resume a successful career in business. *WG*

Adamson, William (1863–1936), miners' leader and Labour politician. Adamson was one of those Labour movement figures who moved 'from pit to parliament'. He worked in the mines for 27 years, from the age of 11 until he became a full-time official of the Fife and Kinross Miners' Association. He was Labour MP for West Fife, 1910–31, and, in between Arthur Henderson and John Clynes, an uninspiring chairman of the Parliamentary Labour Party, 1917–21. As secretary for Scotland in the cabinets of both minority governments of Ramsay MacDonald, he favoured Scottish devolution. *DEM*

W. Knox (ed.) *Scottish Labour Leaders 1918–1939: A Biographical Dictionary* (Edinburgh, 1984).

Addison, Christopher (1869–1951), politician and progressive social reformer. Qualified as a doctor in 1892, he was professor of anatomy at Sheffield, 1897–1901, and Liberal MP for Hoxton, 1910–22. Adviser to Lloyd George on national health insurance in 1911, Addison served on the Board of Education, 1914, then in the Ministry of Munitions from 1915. He actively supported Lloyd George's bid for the premiership in December 1916 and became minister of munitions in his government, then minister of reconstruction from July 1917. As the first minister of health from June 1919, he sponsored the pioneering Housing and Town Planning Acts of 1919—the *Addison Acts—which provided state assistance for local authority housing but proved too costly to be sustained. Leaving health, Addison served unhappily as minister without portfolio, April–July 1921, before resigning altogether. After losing his seat in 1922 he joined the Labour Party, becoming MP for Swindon, 1929–31 and 1934–5, and was minister of agriculture, June 1930–August 1931, when he refused to support the National Government. He entered the Lords as Viscount Addison in 1937 and was Attlee's leader of the House, 1945–51, also serving as secretary for the dominions, 1945–7; lord privy seal, 1947–51; paymaster general, 1948–9; and lord president of the council, 1951. *JS*

Kenneth O. and Jane Morgan, *Portrait of a Progressive: The Political Career of Christopher, Viscount Addison* (Oxford, 1980).

Addison, Paul (1943–), historian. Educated at Pembroke College, Oxford, supervised in his research at Nuffield College by A. J. P. Taylor, Addison was a lecturer at Pembroke before assisting Randolph Churchill in editing the Winston Churchill papers. In 1968 he went to Edinburgh University, becoming in due course reader and director of the Centre for Second World War Studies. His interest in the war, in which his father was killed, focused on the testimony of survivors and resulted in *The Burning Blue* (with Jeremy Crank, 2000), a study of the battle of Britain. However, Addison's *The Road to 1945* (1975) changed perceptions of modern British political history. Now every student appreciated that Attlee's consensus replaced Baldwin's; readers saw that Churchill's coalition was the 'greatest reforming administration since the Liberal government of 1905–14', and that in a highly politicized wartime Britain both major parties were absorbing the ideas of the pre-war 'non-socialist intelligentsia'. His *Churchill on the Home Front* (1992) reflected a continuing interest in a statesman who has 'lived too long . . . to rank as a consistent figure in the history of social policy' but who nevertheless had been an energetic Liberal reformer before 1911 and always thereafter a paternalist. 'We were then', Addison had said of the post-war era, '*almost* all Butskellites.' *PS*

Addison Acts, 1919, housing legislation passed in fulfilment of Lloyd George's *'homes fit for heroes' promise in the 1918 election campaign and in the run-up to the 1918 general election. The principal Act, the Housing and Town Planning Act, was a landmark piece of legislation in enlarging the functions of the state. For the first time the government required local authorities to survey the housing needs of their areas and to draw up and carry out plans to meet them. Second, the government offered subsidies to aid local authorities in carrying out their schemes. The main Act guaranteed local authorities for any losses incurred on municipal schemes beyond the proceeds of a penny rate. As rents were fixed as a result of wartime measures, the subsidies involved were substantial—and essential for any practicable schemes of municipal housing to be undertaken. A further Act in 1919 provided a capital subsidy of £260 for each house built for sale or rent by private builders. However, with the onset of an economy campaign in 1921, the grants available were limited and in 1922 ceased altogether. Although truncated, the Addison Acts set a major precedent for state intervention in housing and were responsible for the creation of the first *council houses which were to become a ubiquitous feature of housing provision between the wars and after 1945. Some 213,800 houses were built in England and Wales under the Acts. More extensive building took place under subsequent Acts which were less generously funded by the exchequer. Politically, the suspension of the Acts proved disastrous to Lloyd George's reputation, since he had apparently reneged on his earlier promises. The author of the Acts, Christopher Addison, felt as minister of health personally aggrieved and left the department in April 1921. *JS*

Mark Swenarton, *Homes fit for Heroes: The Politics and Architecture of Early State Housing in Britain* (London, 1981).

Adeane, Michael Edward (1910–84), private secretary to Elizabeth II, 1953–72. He was the grandson of Lord Stamfordham, George V's longest-serving private secretary, a hereditary connection that assisted his promotion to the same post under George V's granddaughter. Adeane counselled the queen during the crisis in 1963 when she was forced to choose a successor to Harold Macmillan who was retiring due to ill health and she chose Lord Home, largely on the strength of Macmillan's advice. Some thought Adeane should have himself sought more guidance from leading Conservative politicians rather than allowing the queen to rely solely on the outgoing premier, whose advice she was not bound to accept. Adeane personified the tweedy and regimental set that surrounded the queen in the 1950s, justly criticized by John Grigg for making the queen sound like 'a priggish schoolgirl' in her speeches and for isolating her from other social circles. Adeane heeded Grigg's advice, although the most dramatic changes in presentation of the monarchy, including the television documentary *Royal Family* (1969), did not come until the late 1960s, at the end of Adeane's long, perhaps too long, term of office. *WMK*

Kenneth Rose, *Kings, Queens and Courtiers* (London, 1985).

administrative law, the legal principles regulating the exercise of governmental power; more narrowly, meaning judicial review, the process by which the superior courts are asked to determine the validity of decisions, actions, and inaction of public authorities except parliament. It was inhibited early in the century, but expanded rapidly from about 1960, a significant example of judicial activism. Its objectives include protecting citizens against government power and facilitating the discharge of governmental functions. Judicial review concerns not merits but legality; not whether an impugned decision was right or the best, but whether it was within the range of permissible decisions. Theorists debated the basis on which courts might interfere with decisions of other (often elected or democratically accountable) authorities. The traditional answer was the *ultra vires* doctrine: parliament confers powers (*vires*) on public authorities: the courts enforce its wishes by ensuring that the powers are properly exercised and not abused or exceeded. This theory derives from a particular view of the constitution and the centrality of parliament.

By the end of the century changes in the machinery of government affected judicial review. Public functions were 'hived off' to non-governmental, even private, agencies and 'self-regulation' was accepted. The courts tended to include in the ambit of judicial review other bodies exercising typically governmental functions and to review the exercise of functions not conferred by statute. This undermined the *ultra vires* basis of judicial review. Academic discussion (some by judges writing extrajudicially) sought a new basis: the courts were not just enforcing the parliamentary will but were imposing on decision makers explicitly judge-made principles of fairness and good administration. This theory attracts argument: the danger is politicization of the judiciary. The grounds on which decisions are reviewable are created and refined by the courts. In *Council of Civil Service Unions* v. *Minister for the Civil Service* (1985) Lord Diplock classified them thus: a decision could be vitiated by illegality, irrationality, or procedural impropriety. Irrationality means that the decision lies outside the range of possible conclusions to which any rational decision maker could come. The Diplock categories were neither mutually exclusive nor exhaustive: he contemplated adopting under European influence a test of proportionality (was the challenged decision a proportionate way of attaining its objectives?). This brings the courts closer to examining the merits of decisions. These changes in the judicial role accelerated in anticipation of the incorporation of the European Convention on *Human Rights in 2000. *IMY*

Peter Cane, *An Introduction to Administrative Law* (3rd edn., Oxford, 1996). | P. P. Craig, *Administrative Law* (4th edn., London, 1999). | H. W. R. Wade and C. F. Forsyth, *Administrative Law* (8th edn., Oxford, 2000).

Admiralty. See Defence, Ministry of.

adversary politics is characteristic of two-party Britain, polarized between a Commons majority supporting the government and a Commons minority supporting the opposition, the alternative government. It is the antonym of consensus politics which is characteristic of much multi-party continental Europe and achieves political accommodation with coalition government. Adversary politics has been associated with the 'first-past-the-post' electoral system for a century, whereas consensus politics is associated with proportional representation. The term was popularized in a book inspired and edited in 1975 by S. E. Finer, *Adversary Politics and Electoral Reform* (1975), which contended with rival analyses of what, in the wake of the two 1974 general elections, needed to be put right if the British political system was to be more effective. Equally popular 1970s alternatives (although they were not incompatible with it, as they focused on different parts of the political system as the source of Britain's problems) were overloaded government and pluralistic stagnation.

Whereas the British two-party system had been much admired and regarded as a model to be emulated, the preoccupation with relative economic decline and the conviction that successive British governments of both right and left had proved incapable of reversing this decline, undermined its status as a venerated pillar of the constitution. In the post-oil shock context of exacerbated government impotence, the search for a culprit turned to what had previously been considered to be a cause and not simply a correlate of prosperity: strong one-party government. It was argued that the alternation in office of ideologically polarized parties, committed to reversing enacted policies, and reorganizing the institutions of its predecessors, led to confusion and loss of any consistent sense of direction. Proportional representation and coalition politics would allow a stable centrism to assert itself, avoiding unrealistic, short-term promises that would have to be reversed within the lifetime of a government, under the pressure of circumstances beyond its control.

The major theoretical challenge to this adversary politics diagnosis of Britain's political ills came from Richard Rose's *Do Parties Make a Difference?* (London, 1980). Concentrating upon what parties in power did, rather than what they said they would do, Rose showed that consensus in practice predominated over the adversarial rhetoric of party manifestos. The advent of Margaret Thatcher as prime minister in 1979, whilst suggesting that party leaders do make a difference, had by the accession of Tony Blair in 1997 resulted in a resurgence in concern with electoral reform and consensus politics in Britain. *JH*

A. M. Gamble and S. A. Walkland, *The British Party System and Economic Policy, 1945–1983: Studies in Adversary Politics* (Oxford, 1984).

advertising, political. Paid-for advertising by political parties is not allowed on radio or television in Britain. For the most part, therefore, it takes the form of posters on hoardings or advertisements in the press. This began in a small way during the 1920s and 1930s as parties began to adopt the advertising techniques used by business. In the post-war period, however, with the Conservatives leading the way, advertising became a central element of national campaigning. The Conservatives were first to employ a professional advertising agency, in the late 1950s. Labour was much more suspicious and slow to take the issue seriously and, for the most part, the party relied on advice from volunteers working in the advertising world. By the 1980s, however, elections were almost as much a battle between rival advertising agencies as between rival parties. Agencies were employed by the major parties to design posters and newspaper ads, to devise slogans, to select and book hoarding sites, and to determine the outlets for press campaigns. Under the influence of the professionals, advertising became more sophisticated and aggressive and also, usually, negative. Perhaps the most famous British political poster, 'Labour Isn't Working', was produced by Saatchi and Saatchi for the Conservatives in 1978–9. Most advertising expenditure was formerly focused on the press but in the elections of the 1990s there was a switch to posters. In 1997, for example, the Conservatives spent about £13 million on advertising of which £11 million went on posters; Labour spent about £6 million out of £7.4 million on posters. In part this is because the launch of a poster campaign can bring useful additional free publicity. The vast sums that the parties now spend on advertising suggests that they are convinced that it pays electoral dividends, but there is little reliable evidence about this. *DD*

Advisory Committee on Policy, an informal body in the Conservative Party, set up in its modern form in 1949, but deriving indirectly from the wartime *Post-War Problems Central Committee. Chaired by the party leader or, more often, by the leader's nominee, it contained representatives from the National Union, the parliamentary party, and the front bench. It had no formal powers, hence 'advisory', but was important as a sounding board for the confidential discussion of policy initiatives prior to their promulgation as 'party policy'. *JAR*

Afghan War, Third (1919). In May the Afghan amir attempted to end British political interference by invading India. Despite early successes, the Afghans were soon defeated and forced to retreat, the RAF being used for the first time in frontier warfare, bombing the Afghan army and the capital city Kabul. Peace was signed in August when Britain agreed to abandon control of Afghan foreign policy, in return for the Afghans denying refuge to Indian nationalists. *KTS*

Anthony Clayton, *The British Empire as a Superpower 1919–1939* (London, 1986).

Agadir crisis. See Moroccan crisis.

Agar-Robartes, Thomas Charles Reginald (1880–1915), Liberal MP. It was Agar-Robartes who suggested on 11 June 1912 in the Commons the desirability of excluding the four most Protestant counties (Antrim, Armagh, Down, and Londonderry) from the operation of the Third Home Rule Bill. To have accepted the proposal would have meant that the Unionists had lost the battle to save the union between Great Britain and Ireland. They nonetheless supported it on tactical grounds. The proposal was defeated on 18 June by 69 votes. *DGB*

Age Concern, campaigning pressure group concerned with the rights of the elderly, originally formed in 1940 as the National Old People's Welfare Council, at a time of widespread agitation for increases in pension provision. It changed its name in 1971 to Age Concern, joining a group of sectional pressure groups such as *Shelter and the *National Council for One-Parent Families, which became prominent in lobbying on welfare issues affecting their constituencies. Age Concern has campaigned for increased pensions, for winter fuel payments for the elderly, and against age discrimination in employment. *JS*

agents, election, officials appointed by candidates to manage and be responsible for the conduct of their election campaigns. The agent has principal responsibility for authorizing and monitoring expenditure, and is under a statutory requirement to prevent any illegal expenditure. Until 1918, agents were also largely responsible for ensuring the registration of voters. Candidates are required by law to appoint agents (though it is possible for candidates to appoint themselves and they are deemed to have done so if no name is notified within a specified time to the returning officer) and an agent stays in post until the election result is declared and a return of the candidate's election expenses has been made. Political parties, especially the Conservative Party, used generally to appoint full-time agents, who ran the local party offices in between elections as well as running election campaigns, but financial constraints meant that by the 1990s full-time agents were very much the exception rather than the rule. Any irregularities in election expenditure may result in prosecution of a candidate and agent, though prosecutions are extremely rare. In 1999 the MP for Newark and her election agent were convicted of making false declarations, but the convictions were subsequently overturned. *PN*

R. J. Clayton (ed.), *Parker's Conduct of Parliamentary Elections* (London, 1990). | H. F. Rawlings, *Law and the Electoral Process* (London, 1988).

Agricultural Marketing Acts, 1931 and **1933**, the culmination of efforts by government between the wars to promote efficiency in marketing as a remedy for low prices received by farmers for their produce. Studies of the subject, both official, such as the Linlithgow committee of 1923–4, and unofficial, had concluded that farmers would better themselves if their marketing organization was stronger and more cooperatively based. The Agricultural Marketing Act, 1931, was the first serious attempt to give legislative support to these ideas. Under this Act producers of a commodity could propose a marketing scheme which, if approved by minister and parliament, would become compulsory for all producers. A two-thirds majority of producers in favour was needed before a scheme could be submitted for approval. The Act was not well received by farmers, who were suspicious of the Labour minister, Christopher *Addison, and the Hops Marketing Board was the only one established under this Act.

A new Agricultural Marketing Act, promoted by a new minister, Walter *Elliott, was passed in 1933. This extended the 1931 Act to grant the Board of Trade powers to restrict imports of commodities for which a marketing scheme was approved. Marketing boards for potatoes, milk and bacon pigs were established in the 1930s. After suspension during the Second World War they were revived, except for the Bacon Pigs Board, and new schemes were promoted for wool, eggs, tomatoes, and cucumbers. *JHB*

agricultural policy. British agricultural policy in the 20th century was inspired by a mixture of motives, strategic, social, and economic. These included greater self-sufficiency in time of war; maintenance of rural life and population; low food prices; reduction of instability in farm incomes; promotion of agricultural production and of efficiency and modernization in farming. These objectives were similar to those pursued by continental European governments, although the measures taken differed. The free-trade, free-market instincts of British governments limited the extent of their involvement in agriculture before the Second World War. Price support was introduced with the Corn Production Acts, 1917 and 1920, but then withdrawn in 1921. The abandonment of free trade and anticipation of war in the 1930s brought about a more active policy, with the introduction of the *Agricultural Marketing Acts, some limited tariff measures, and the reintroduction of price support.

The experience of the Second World War and the need to rebuild the economy afterwards brought about a major change in peacetime agricultural policy. The Agriculture Act, 1947, laid the basis for substantial support for agriculture, primarily to encourage increased home production of food. Objectives might change slightly in following years, but the principles of support did not. The main instrument of policy was price support through deficiency payments. The government set guaranteed prices at its annual review of agriculture in consultation with the *National Farmers' Union, and the deficiency between these and the market prices at which farmers sold their produce was made up by the Treasury. This satisfied the needs of international trade and kept prices to the consumer low. Additional measures of agricultural support through grants and direct subsidy were introduced during the 1950s and 1960s, and these came to take up a larger share of state spending on agriculture.

Entry to the European Community (EC) brought with it the adoption of the Common Agricultural Policy. Whereas Britain had supported farm incomes and agricultural production within the regime of world trade, Europe had sought to do this by self-sufficiency. The EC's market was, therefore, protected by tariffs. Within the EC, intervention buying maintained the guaranteed prices of farm produce, with the result that prices to consumers were higher. An effect of this strongly production-orientated policy was overproduction. By the 1980s the size of surpluses and the growing cost of EC support were becoming of political concern. International pressures for liberalization of world trade and concerns about the environmental effects of subsidized farming were also growing. Measures to limit both overproduction and the EC budget were introduced, including milk quotas in 1984 and *set-aside in 1988. Revisions to rules governing intervention buying made modest reductions to support prices. Grants and subsidies to support diversification of farm businesses, environmentally sensitive farming practices, and organic farming were introduced both by European and UK national measures. However, as the 1990s progressed, pressures for radical change to European agricultural policy remained. *JHB*

Agriculture, Fisheries, and Food, Ministry of, formed in 1954 by the merger of the Ministry of Food and the Ministry of Agriculture and Fisheries. Food's administrative history dates back to 1916 when the first ministry for food control was established. It was abolished in 1921 but reappeared in 1938 (as the Ministry of Food). Agriculture and Fisheries goes back even further: 1919 saw the creation of the Ministry of Agriculture and Fisheries, replacing the existing Board of Agriculture and Fisheries. Responsibility for food safety was hived off from the Ministry of Agriculture, Fisheries, and Food in 2000 with the creation of the Food Standards Agency. *JD*

Ministry of Agriculture, Fisheries, and Food website: *www.maff.gov.uk*

Ahern, Bertie (1951–), Irish politician, taoiseach from June 1997. A former accountant, Ahern made his mark politically as minister of finance, 1991–4. When the government collapsed in November 1994, he became leader of Fianna Fáil, in opposition. Success at the general election of June 1997 made him taoiseach, heading a coalition government which included the Progressive Democrats. Along with Tony Blair's arrival in office a month earlier, this imparted a stimulus to the Northern Ireland peace process. In January 1998, the British and Irish governments together endorsed balanced constitutional change in their two countries, including provision for a Northern Ireland assembly, a joint north–south ministerial council, and an intergovernmental British–Irish council. Along with much else, these recommendations were included in the Good Friday agreement of April 1998 and, on Ahern's initiative, through a referendum in May 1999 the republic abandoned its constitutional claim to jurisdiction over Northern Ireland. *DRB*

AIDS (Acquired Immune Deficiency Syndrome) became a cause of widespread public concern in Britain in 1986 following the discovery in Africa and America of a hitherto unknown viral disease which usually proved ultimately to be fatal. The disease is transmitted via the blood and bodily secretions and can be sexually transmitted, or passed on by drug users sharing needles or through blood transfusions. In 1986 the government mounted a major public education campaign through television, radio, the press, posters, and leaflets to every household, advocating 'safe sex' through the use of condoms. A follow-up campaign in 1988 targeted those going overseas and drug users. By the end of 1992 nearly 17,000 people (2,000 of them women) had been diagnosed HIV positive (the precursor of AIDS), over 5,000 had developed full-blown AIDS, and 3,000 people had died. By 1998, a total of 32,242 people were identified as HIV positive (5,300 of them women) and 15,565 cases of full-blown AIDS had been reported.

Though originally seen as primarily a 'gay plague', one in five of current HIV cases is a non-drug-using heterosexual, while a small group of haemophiliacs were inadvertently affected by AIDS before blood-screening became prevalent. HIV infection is found throughout Great Britain, with the highest rates in London. Transmission is still occurring amongst some homosexual and bisexual men, but also amongst injecting drug users and the heterosexual community. The 'leakage' of AIDS into the general population was recognized by the testing of all pregnant women in London for the HIV virus, revealing one in 550 screening positive in 1998.

The AIDS crisis provoked the largest public health campaign by the government outside the two world wars. Open discussion of varieties of sexual behaviour and 'safe sex' played a significant part in the liberalization of public debate on a range of issues, including not only homosexuality but also the drug culture. Attempts to bring the latter into contact with public health services formed one of the key elements in the government's HIV/AIDS strategy, by promoting needle-exchange facilities and improving access to HIV testing. Broadly, the government has moved from a strategy of mass advertising to targeting sections of the population deemed most at risk. As well as promoting public awareness, the government has funded voluntary groups such as the Terence Higgins Trust, London Lighthouse, and the National AIDS Trust. Total funding for HIV/AIDS treatment and care through health authorities in the UK amounted to over £330 million in 1998–9.

In political terms, the AIDS crisis was something of a nine days' wonder dominating public health debate for a relatively short period in the late 1980s. While still a major public health issue amongst sections of the population at risk, it has increasingly been overtaken by other public health debates, notably over food safety. Moreover, the AIDS crisis was combated on a largely non-partisan basis, with the only objections to the widespread public health campaigns coming from minority religious groups, such as Roman Catholics, whose opposition to the promotion of 'safe sex' was not expressed in party terms. *JS*

Aims of Industry, free enterprise pressure group. Aims of Industry was created in 1942 by industrialists to counter growing support for post-war collectivist policies and to advocate free enterprise. The group's opposition to state ownership of industry was immortalized by its 1949 'Mr Cube' campaign against Labour's plan to nationalize the sugar industry. Aims of Industry cultivated close links with the Conservatives, and Michael Ivens, its director, 1971–94, was involved in the work of other free-market think-tanks. *RJS*

aircraft industry. The reliance of aircraft manufacturers on military orders and government subsidies for civil projects has led successive governments to intervene in the industry. A collapse in the aftermath of the Great War was prevented by the government's decision to reserve defence contracts for a pool of British firms, in order to maintain production capacity. The decision that Britain should concentrate on fighter production, and the USA on bombers, during the Second World War, threatened to leave the British at a disadvantage in peacetime civil aircraft production. The coalition government established the Brabazon committee in 1943 to recommend a programme of designs, which the post-war Labour government then helped to fund. Although the subsequent Conservative administration emphasized the role of private manufacturers, it maintained pressure on the national air corporations to buy British. However, the potential for a British lead in passenger jet production was lost following the Comet disasters of 1953–4 and in 1960 the government used the prospect of 'launch aid' for civil aircraft production to encourage amalgamations and rationalization of the industry. The Plowden report of 1965 and the cancellation of several military projects signalled a move towards government-inspired cooperation with other European manufacturers, presaged by the *Concorde project. Government involvement reached its peak in the 1970s with the rescue of Rolls-Royce in 1971 and the nationalization of the airframe industry, as British Aerospace (BAe), in 1977. However, in 1980, 51 per cent of the state's holding in BAe was sold (more followed in 1985), though continuing government sensitivity towards the aerospace industry as a provider of British jobs was demonstrated in the following year by the controversy over the American acquisition of helicopters in the *Westland affair. *CL*

Keith Hayward, *Government and British Civil Aerospace: A Case Study in Post-War Technology Policy* (Manchester, 1993).

Aircraft Production, Ministry of (1940–6). Concerned by the slow production of aircraft in 1940, Churchill created the ministry in May and appointed his old friend Lord *Beaverbrook to its head. Beaverbrook ran the ministry for a year in his own maverick style, overcoming Air Ministry opposition to prioritize fighter production, achieving a major increase in fighter numbers—a significant factor in the battle of Britain—and dispersing aircraft factories to limit the effect of air raids. The ministry was merged into the Ministry of Supply in 1946. *CL*

Air Ministry, See Defence, Ministry of.

Aitken, Jonathan William Patrick (1942–), Conservative politician. Beaverbrook's great-nephew, excluded from his will as able to fend for himself, is now best known for the fending. A former liberal hero (he revealed British duplicity in the Biafran war), he was acquitted on a secrets charge and wrote *The Young Meteors* (1967). Defence procurement minister then chief secretary of the treasury under Major, he sued the *Guardian* over claims of a Saudi contact meeting, but when his perjury was demonstrated, he withdrew the case and was arrested. He confessed and was convicted. *EP*

Aitken, Max. See Beaverbrook, 1st Lord.

Akers-Douglas, Aretas (1851–1926), Conservative politician and party organizer. Akers-Douglas sat for East Kent, 1880–1911; was chief whip, 1885–95; and home secretary, 1902–5. He chaired the Unionist Organization Committee (1911) after the party's defeat in three successive elections, which recommended a thorough reform of Central Office. Akers-Douglas was an intimate adviser to Arthur Balfour but his influence declined sharply after Andrew Bonar Law succeeded Balfour as party leader in 1911. He became Viscount Chilston in 1911. *RJQA*

Viscount Chilston, *Chief Whip: The Political Life and Times of Aretas Akers-Douglas, 1st Viscount Chilston* (London, 1961).

Alamein, battle of. See El Alamein, battle of.

Alanbrooke, Viscount (1883–1963), soldier and staff officer. Commissioned in 1902, Alan Brooke was an outstanding artillery commander on the western front, later appointed instructor at Camberley in 1923 along with many other future leaders of the army. His promotion from major to brigadier in 1929, over the heads of nearly 100 more senior officers, demonstrated the army's capacity for self-renewal. Brooke was sent to France in command of II Corps in September 1939, but was consistently pessimistic about the military capability of the British Expeditionary Force (BEF), leading to friction with its commander Lord Gort. After Dunkirk, he was sent back to Brittany to form a '2nd BEF' but convinced Churchill that the adventure was futile. Appointed chief of the imperial general staff in December 1941 and chairman of *chiefs of staff (COS) committee in March 1942, he was Churchill's key wartime military adviser. Brooke visited Egypt in 1942 and played a key role in replacing Auchinleck with the Alexander/Montgomery team. He was a consistent advocate of the Mediterranean strategy and, as a result, distrusted by the Americans, but he also led the COS to the brink of resignation in fierce debate with Churchill on strategy in the Far East in March 1944. Ennobled as Alanbrooke, 1945, he remained in post until June 1946 under the new Labour government. His decision to allow Arthur Bryant to publish some of his papers in 1957 caused some ill feeling for puncturing the Churchillian 'myth'. A brilliant professional. *SJB*

David Fraser, *Alanbrooke* (London, 1997 edn.).

Albemarle report (1960). This followed wartime and immediate post-war reports on the Youth Service. It came at the time of a bulge in the adolescent population and rising concerns over the behaviour of teenagers. It advocated the strengthening of the service through a ten-year programme to make it available to all. It aimed for the establishment of youth leadership as a profession, the promotion of appropriate training, and the provision of facilities, particularly by local education authorities. *KMT*

Aldermaston, atomic weapons research establishment. The 'Aldermaston march' was the annual focal point in the late 1950s and early 1960s for protests in Britain against nuclear weapons. What rapidly became an annual Easter jamboree of protest began modestly in 1958 as the brainchild of the newly formed Gandhian Direct Action Committee (DAC). The DAC's march took place from London to Aldermaston in Berkshire, embodying its commitment to taking the moral issue directly to the workers on the site. Between 5,000 and 10,000 took part and, despite the misgivings of the more conventional *Campaign for Nuclear Disarmament (CND), the march was a success and attracted wide publicity. From 1959, CND organized the march, beginning at Aldermaston on Good Friday and culminating in Trafalgar Square in London on Easter Monday, thus neatly symbolizing CND's more orthodox, pressure-group view that lobbying those in power was the main aim of the campaign. By 1959, this was a mass protest: 20,000–25,000 attended the final rally. As the movement grew in 1960, so did the number of marchers, and their sense of their own collective power. Numbers at the final rally were estimated at near 100,000. The march had assumed a cultural and political life of its own and 'Aldermaston' became a symbol and rallying point for extra-parliamentary protest. Although the numbers marching continued to increase, reaching a peak of around 150,000 in 1962, the movement began slowly to decline as Labour slid away from the issue, and the ideological tensions and frustrations in the movement itself became more apparent. The march continued, in one form or another, until the late 1960s but its potency, reflecting that of the movement at large, had evaporated by 1964. *RKST*

aldermen in local government. The ancient office of alderman was reintroduced in the 19th century to provide continuity and stability in the new elected local authorities. A number of aldermen, proportionate to council size, were elected by the council for a period of six years. In urban authorities, aldermanic elections were often used to bolster or, on occasion, to restore a party majority, bringing the system into disrepute. Despite criticisms, the aldermanic system lasted until abolished, other than in the City of London, by the Local Government Act, 1972. *KY*

Aldington, Lord. See Low, Austin Richard Wilson ('Toby').

Alexander, Albert Victor (1885–1965), Labour politician. Sheffield-born, locally educated, and a Baptist lay preacher, Alexander was MP for Sheffield, Hillsborough, 1922–31 and 1935–50. He served in the Great War, reaching the rank of captain, and thereafter specialized in defence policy. After junior office in 1924, he held the Admiralty, 1929–31, and in Churchill's wartime ministry 1940–5, and became defence minister, 1946–50. As Viscount (later Earl) Alexander of Hillsborough, he was Labour's leader in the Lords, 1955–64. *JAR*

Alexander of Tunis, Earl ('Alex') (1891–1969), soldier and reluctant politician. Harold Alexander joined the Irish Guards in 1911, unsuccessfully offering resignation during the Curragh 'mutiny'. He had a glittering record on the western front, reputedly enjoying his time in the trenches, and then led a force of German-speaking Balts in a Lettish-Polish offensive to capture eastern Latvia from the Bolsheviks (1920), after which he commanded a battalion of Irish Guards in Turkey during the Chanak crisis (1922). Alexander led 1st Division to France on the outbreak of war in 1939 and commanded the rearguard at Dunkirk, taking the decision not to sacrifice British troops as a gesture to the French. Sent out to command British forces in Burma in February 1942, he extricated the army from Rangoon and supervised the retreat to India. In August 1942 he replaced Auchinleck as overall commander in the Middle East, whilst Montgomery took over the Eighth Army, but took direct command of the armies clearing Tunisia of German forces and commanded the Anglo-American invasion of Sicily in 1943. He personally landed at Salerno in September 1943 to avert failure of the invasion of Italy, planned the Anzio invasion, January 1944, failing to seize Rome, and authorized the bombing of Monte Cassino in February. Alexander became supreme allied commander, Mediterranean, in December 1944 and unsuccessfully advocated a major offensive to capture Vienna. His armies intervened successfully in the Greek civil war and defeated German forces in north-east Italy in April 1945. Alexander's often loosely defined role made his achievements difficult to evaluate. After the war he was a successful governor-general of Canada, 1946–52, and reluctantly served as Churchill's minister of defence, 1952–4, where he had little impact on British defence policy but did not oppose greater reliance on nuclear weapons. The *beau idéal* of an officer and a gentleman. *SJB*

Nigel Nicolson, *Alex* (London, 1973).

Aliens Act, 1905, the first modern legislation regulating immigration into Great Britain. Coming after the anxieties of the Boer war and prompted by a press- and trade union-induced xenophobia over the influx of Russian Jewish immigrants into Britain, a royal commission on alien immigration in 1902 recommended limitations on the ingress of foreigners. This led Balfour's government to pass the Act, which among other provisions required immigrants to verify their economic independence before admission to the country. *RJQA*

Colin Holmes, *John Bull's Island: Immigration and British Society 1871–1971* (London, 1988).

Allan, Alex (1951–), prime ministers' principal private secretary, 1992–7. A former treasury official, Allan became the key civil servant in John

Major's Downing Street. He was centrally involved in several constitutional issues, including the establishment of the Scott and Nolan inquiries, the prime minister's decision to sue over allegations of an affair, and talks with the Irish government on the future of Northern Ireland. He remained at Downing Street for a few months after the 1997 general election, helping to bed-in Tony Blair's administration. *CL*

Allen, (Reginald) Clifford (1889–1939), socialist activist and anti-war campaigner. A founder member and chairman of the No-Conscription Fellowship, he was imprisoned on three occasions during the Great War for refusing to undertake military service. During the 1920s a leading figure in the Independent Labour Party, Allen remained loyal after 1931 to Ramsay MacDonald and the National Government, being elevated to the Lords as Lord Allen of Hurtwood. During the 1930s he was actively involved in a range of movements which stressed democracy, internationalism, and cooperation amongst progressive elements across the political spectrum. *JAJ*

Arthur Marwick, *Clifford Allen: The Open Conspirator* (London, 1964).

Allen, Douglas Albert Vivian (1917–), civil servant. Allen counts as one of the most economically literate civil service permanent secretaries, achieving a first-class degree in economics and statistics at the LSE in 1938 and spending most of his Whitehall career at the Treasury dealing with economic policy issues. He moved from the Treasury to the new Department of Economic Affairs in 1964 as deputy secretary and then permanent secretary, 1966–8. As permanent secretary to the Treasury, 1968–74, he worked closely with Labour Chancellor of the Exchequer Roy Jenkins, but saw the Treasury lose some influence in the Heath government, when the prime minister relied more on William Armstrong for economic policy advice. Allen was never comfortable as permanent secretary of the Civil Service Department and head of the civil service, 1974–7. In the aftermath of William Armstrong's controversial high-profile role and fall from office, he was obliged to play a more modest policy role than he would have liked and to concentrate on the relatively humdrum issues of civil service management. He became Lord Croham in 1978. *KT*

Allen, Philip (1912–), civil servant. Allen entered the Home Office in 1934 and served most of his Whitehall career there, though he also served in the offices of the war cabinet, 1943–4; the Ministry of Housing and Local Government (deputy secretary, 1955–60), and the Treasury (a second secretary, 1963–6). He was permanent secretary of the Home Office, 1966–72, his regime being marked by a positive social reformism and by important changes in internal departmental style and culture. *KT*

Alliance (1981–7), centrist political grouping. The Alliance of the *Liberal Party and the *Social Democratic Party (SDP) was formed in September 1981, following the creation of the SDP in March of that year as a breakaway from the *Labour Party. In spite of the opposition of some Liberals and of some members of the SDP to the pooling of their efforts in an alliance, support from David *Steel and Roy *Jenkins was important in winning over both parties to the acceptance of the principle, ratified at the respective party conferences in autumn 1981.

A string of spectacular by-election successes, notably at *Crosby and Glasgow *Hillhead, promised a major breakthrough for a 'third force', propelling it at one point to an opinion poll rating of over 40 per cent, ahead of both Labour and the Conservatives. In a period when the Labour Party appeared to be dominated by the Left and Thatcher offered a particularly intransigent version of Conservatism, there was serious speculation that the Alliance might displace the Labour Party as the major opposition party to the Conservatives. This prospect was marred by a number of factors. The agreement to share local and parliamentary seats equally between the two partners in the Alliance caused ill feeling on both sides. Many local Liberals were reluctant to give up what had at last become possibly winnable seats, in which they had campaigned fruitlessly for years, while some members of the SDP felt that the new party was making unnecessary concessions to an older, 'failed' party. Moreover as inter-Alliance bickering took some of the novelty off the appeal of the party, the *Falklands factor completely transformed Thatcher's electoral prospects. Hence, although the Alliance campaigned relatively effectively in the 1983 general election on a joint manifesto, its 26 per cent of the vote was too low and too evenly spread to bring it a large haul of seats. Only 23 Alliance MPs were returned, the majority of them Liberals. Only five sitting SDP MPs retained their seats and two of the *'Gang of Four' (Shirley *Williams and William *Rodgers) were amongst the casualties. Another casualty was Jenkins's leadership of the SDP since his immediate and unopposed replacement by David *Owen followed the election.

Faced with an overwhelming conservative majority, Steel and Owen struggled to maintain the momentum of the Alliance. Fuelled by occasional by-election victories, as at Portsmouth South (14 June 1984), Brecon and Radnor (4 July 1985), and Ryedale (8 May 1986), the Alliance sustained support but was seriously embarrassed by differences within the party over defence policy, where a hawkish David Owen aroused hostility from the anti-nuclear sections of the Liberal Party. At the Liberals' Eastbourne Assembly in September 1986, an anti-nuclear amendment passed against the wishes of the leadership prompted the Alliance poll ratings to slump. The nuclear issue was patched up following the *Ettrickbridge conference at David Steel's home in October and a relaunch of the Alliance in early 1987 permitted it to campaign effectively in the general election of that year. But the 'two-leaders' strategy of Owen and Steel failed to convince the electorate and proved vulnerable to questions on the nuclear issue. The Alliance obtained 23 per cent of the vote in the general election of June 1987, but only won 22 seats. The result repeated the pattern of 1983 in so far as the Alliance had secured a substantial minority of the popular vote but had failed to register a proportionate share of seats because the level and distribution of its support severely disadvantaged it under the prevailing electoral system.

Steel now called for a merger of the two parties immediately after the election, precipitating the creation of a new party, the Social and Liberal Democrats. A group of former SDP members led by Owen remained separate, maintaining a 'continuing' SDP. Similarly, a group of Liberals, led by Michael *Meadowcroft, set up the *Liberal Party (Continuing) to continue traditional Liberal policies. Although the Liberal Party survived as a minor force, mainly based in Yorkshire, the 'continuing' SDP was wound up in 1990. The Alliance's heirs, the Social and Liberal Democrats, were eventually to re-establish themselves securely as a third party under the revised title of *Liberal Democrats.

The Alliance provided the most serious attempt to set up a third force in British politics since the Second World War. Its attempt at *'breaking the mould' proved abortive for a number of reasons. Primarily the attempt to create a new party failed to secure sufficient defectors from the Labour or Conservative parties to damage fatally either of them. The Conservatives recovered from their low point of the pre-Falklands period, while the more vulnerable Labour Party retained sufficient of its core support and more centrist politicians to survive the defection of the SDP leadership and MPs. The level of support achieved in the general elections of 1983 and 1987 was too low and too diffused to secure a significant body of MPs, while the tensions of having two separate parties and leaders proved disadvantageous. Nonetheless, the Alliance laid the foundations for the most successful third party in late 20th-century politics, the Liberal Democrats, and maintained interest in a core of policies, notably proportional representation, regional government, devolution, and environmental and welfare reform which the successor party inherited. *JS*

Alliance Party of Northern Ireland. The Alliance Party is unique among parties in Northern Ireland in that it has drawn on support from both Protestant and Catholic communities. It supports the union as the wish of the majority, backs power-sharing at local and assembly level, and is happy with north–south cooperation. Founded in 1970 as a pluralist party to pursue reform and partnership, it achieved its greatest successes during the 1970s. It won 9.2 per cent of the vote in the assembly elections of 1973 and party leaders Oliver Napier and Bob Cooper, later chairman of the Fair Employment Commission, played a key role in the short-lived *power-sharing executive. The party increased its vote to 14.4 per cent at the 1977 council elections. Thereafter its vote failed to improve, due largely to the deepened polarization of Northern Ireland society. Despite Alliance's cross-community approach, the development of the peace process has not worked to the party's advantage and at the recent assembly elections support for Alliance had declined to less than 7 per cent. *BMW*

W. D. Flackes and Sydney Elliott, *Northern Ireland: A Political Directory, 1968–1999* (Belfast, 1999).

Alport, Cuthbert James McCall ('Cub') (1912–98), Conservative politician. A protégé of R. A. Butler's and the first director of the *Conservative Political Centre, Alport initiated the *One Nation group after becoming an MP in 1950. An enlightened imperialist, he was Commonwealth relations minister in 1961 when Macmillan appointed him high commissioner to the Central African Federation, with a life peerage. Two years later, however, his mentor, Butler, dissolved the federation. In 1984, Alport was deprived of the Tory whip in the Lords following his criticism of Thatcher. *RJS*

Mark Garnett, *Alport: A Study in Loyalty* (Teddington, 1999).

alternative vote, a preferential but non-proportional method of election. Each voter lists preferences on the ballot paper, indicating the first preference with a 1, the second preference with a 2, and so on. The first preference votes are then aggregated. If a candidate achieves 50 per cent + 1 of first preference votes, the candidate is declared elected. If no candidate reaches that threshold, then the candidate receiving the least number of first preference votes is eliminated and the second preferences of that candidate's voters are then allocated among the remaining candidates. The process is repeated, each candidate receiving the least number of votes being eliminated, until a candidate reaches the 50 per cent + 1 threshold. Supporters argue that the system ensures that each winning candidate has majority support and that candidates have to appeal widely, rather than simply to partisan supporters, in order to attract second preference votes. Critics claim that the system produces the least objectionable candidate, rather than the most preferred, as the winner. It is also a non-proportional system: it does not produce a strong correlation between the proportion of first preference votes cast for the candidates of one party and the proportion of seats won by that party. The system has been advocated at various times throughout the century and an unsuccessful attempt to introduce it was made by the Labour government in 1931. Variants of the system were proposed by a working group of the Labour Party in 1993 and by the independent commission on the voting system in 1998. *PN*

P. Dunleavy, Helen Margetts, Brendan O'Duvy, and Stuart Weir, *Making Votes Count* (Colchester, 1998). | David M. Farrell, *Comparing Electoral Systems* (Hemel Hempstead, 1997). | Labour Party, *Report of the Working Party on Electoral Systems* (London, 1993).

Altrincham, Lord. See Grigg, Edward.

Alverstone, 1st viscount (1842–1915), judge and Conservative politician. A highly successful advocate, Richard Everard Webster accepted Salisbury's offer to become attorney-general in 1885 and entered parliament the same year. He remained in the Commons until 1900, during that time serving as attorney-general on three separate occasions whilst continuing his legal practice and achieving notoriety as leading counsel for *The Times* in the Parnell commission. Although he held the high judicial offices of master of the rolls, 1900, and lord chief justice of England, 1900–13, his judicial career was only moderately successful. *ML*

Amery, Julian (1919–97), Conservative politician, son of Leopold *Amery. At Oxford, Julian Amery reversed the *'King and Country' Union resolution of 1933. A member of the Special Operations Executive, he parachuted into Yugoslavia with, unhelpfully, Randolph Churchill; he admired Mihailovic, the Serbian nationalist leader shot by Tito. Having failed to save his pointlessly hanged, unstable brother John, insignificantly present in Berlin during the war, Amery was a lifelong opponent of capital punishment. He was an imperial rather than a free-market right-winger, a dedicated anti-communist, cool towards the USA. Elected by just fourteen votes in Preston in 1950, he rebelled with the Suez Group against withdrawal in 1954 from the British-controlled Suez Canal bases. Subsequent events—the Egyptian canal-seizure and British invasion—were a watershed for old style British imperialists like Amery, for American-instructed withdrawal tore up his map of the world; this imperialist was a strong pro-European. The son-in-law of Harold Macmillan, who favoured Cecilian-style patronage, he held office from 1956, notably defence posts during a period of exponentially rising defence costs. He negotiated Cyprus bases and defended the Hola Camp killings before promoting successively Skybolt, TSR 2, and Bloodhound, independent patriotic weapon ventures but devourers of money, all eventually cancelled. Instructively, he preceded Tony Benn in promoting Concorde. Defeated at Preston in 1966, he returned for Brighton Pavilion in 1969, and was minister of works and junior minister at the Foreign Office under Heath, but, surprisingly was not included by the cautious Thatcher. He became best known as an international diehard, friend of Rhodesia, South Africa, and Pakistan's General Zia, typically seen by Amery as 'a last bulwark' against Soviet Russia. Yet, despite heavy drinking and the style of another age, Amery was liked. Courteous and consistent, without class malice, he was recognized as his own sort of (doomed) idealist. *EP*

Julian Amery, *Approach March* (London, 1973).

Amery, Leopold Stennett (1873–1955), Conservative politician, imperialist, journalist, and diarist. Ultimately Leo Amery's career indicates promise not fulfilled: it was once joked that if he had been half a foot taller and made his parliamentary speeches half an hour shorter he would have been prime minister, yet for over half a century he was at the heart of British politics. Elected to parliament in 1911 as MP for South Birmingham (later Sparkbrook) he retained his seat until 1945. He left behind him careers in the law and journalism, having worked on *The Times* for a decade. Throughout his political life, empire and his desire to strengthen economic ties between the mother country and the colonies were consistent themes. Influenced as a young man by *Milner, he became his under-secretary at the Colonial Office in 1919. This was followed by a period at the Admiralty before he became an active colonial secretary, 1924–9. Despite not supporting the Empire Crusade, he failed to achieve office under the National Government, and his criticism of the 1932 Ottawa agreements lessened the likelihood of a recall to office. He supported the 1935 India Bill, favoured the partition of Palestine (he had in 1918 helped draft the *Balfour declaration), but opposed colonial appeasement. He advocated rearmament, but during the late 1930s became increasingly uneasy about appeasement, abstaining in the Munich votes. Still a backbencher at the outbreak of war, he became increasingly critical of Neville Chamberlain's leadership and his economic strategy. His dramatic intervention in the Norway debate when he quoted Cromwell and urged Chamberlain's resignation was widely seen as providing a lead for the Conservative rebellion. Churchill sent Amery to the India Office, 1940–5. In the post-war years he remained a staunch supporter of imperial preference, criticized the economic domination of the USA, and championed closer European cooperation. *NJC*

L. S. Amery, *My Political Life*, 3 vols. (London, 1953–5). | J. Barnes and D. Nicholson (eds.), *The Leo Amery Diaries*, 2 vols. (London, 1981, 1988).

Amnesty International, international organization founded in 1961 by barrister Peter Benenson to campaign on behalf of political prisoners and prisoners of conscience. Based in London, it is entirely funded by private subscriptions and has over 50,000 members in over fifty countries. Its reports on human rights violations have been influential in securing the release—or improving the conditions—of thousands of detainees around the world. In the UK its criticism of the treatment of suspected IRA terrorists in Northern Ireland during the early 1970s led to restrictions being placed upon interrogation techniques. *JS*

Amory, Derick. See Heathcoat Amory, Derick.

Amritsar (1919), Sikh holy city, where Indian army soldiers massacred unarmed Indian civilians. On 13 April, following much civil unrest, Brigadier-General Dyer dispersed an illegal gathering of about 20,000 people by ordering his troops to open fire, killing 379 and wounding 1,500. Afterwards, an unrepentant Dyer was dismissed from the army, but gained widespread support in Britain. Amritsar hastened the process whereby Gandhi and other Indian nationalists were permanently alienated from British rule. *KTS*

Lawrence James, *Raj: The Making and Unmaking of British India* (London, 1998).

Amsterdam, treaty of (1997). Signed formally on 2 October 1997, the treaty was both a product and a tool of advancing European integration. As the third major revision of the treaty of Rome (see also Single European Act; Maastricht treaty), it attempted to improve the efficiency of European Union institutions, particularly by extending 'co-decision' between the Council of Ministers and the European Parliament. A limited success, it was one more stage in the evolution of the European Union. *JRVE*

anarchism, political doctrine advocating the abolition of organized authority and its replacement by some form of non-governmental co-operation between free individuals. Although agreed on the need to abolish the state, anarchists have disagreed over revolutionary tactics and the economic organization of the society which will replace it. Thus theories range from individualist anarchism through Proudhon's mutualism to the more familiar 20th-century variants of collectivism, anarchist communism, and anarcho-syndicalism.

In Britain there has been 'a recurrent libertarian itch' amongst writers ever since Godwin and Shelley (Woodcock, 371) but as a movement anarchism has always been ephemeral. It achieved some influence in the developing socialist movement during the 1880s and 1890s but its maximum impact came during that great period of working-class unrest 1910–19. As increasing numbers of militants rejected parliamentarianism and espoused direct action, so anarchist ideas gained more currency; the movement was particularly strong in the Welsh coalfield. The libertarian strand in British socialism was overwhelmed by the impact of the Bolshevik revolution but the idea of the millennial general strike as the means of transforming society attracted adherents until the debacle of 1926. Thereafter, it appeared to contemporaries that anarchism was dead. A brief revival of interest in anarchist theory occurred amongst left-wing intellectuals during the Spanish civil war, anarchists provided a centre of opposition to the Second World War, and Herbert Read offered libertarians a new philosophy of education with which to transform society, but the movement was essentially moribund until a resurgence in the 1960s. Seizing upon current issues and maintaining the theory of direct action, anarchists have been active in the Campaign for Nuclear Disarmament, the squatters' movement, feminism, environmental protests, and in educational experiments such as free schooling. *MC*

John Quail, *The Slow Burning Fuse: The Lost History of the British Anarchists* (London, 1978). | George Woodcock, *Anarchism* (London, 1986).

Anderson, John (1882–1958), civil servant, proconsul, wartime minister. Anderson was one of the great state servants of the century. A forbidding, austere character, he was a superb machine man—Churchill once dubbed him 'the automatic pilot'. As a civil servant, he had first made his mark at the national health insurance commission, becoming (permanent) secretary of the Ministry of Shipping in 1917 and serving as under-secretary in the Irish Office at Dublin castle during the Troubles. Permanent secretary at the Home Office, 1922–32, he put together the government emergency organization to defeat the General Strike. He was a successful governor of Bengal (1932–7) at a difficult and dangerous period in the province's history. Then, elected to parliament as an independent MP for the Scottish universities, he joined the Chamberlain government in 1938 as lord privy seal, in charge of civil defence and air raid precautions. On the outbreak of war, he became home secretary and minister of home security, before entering Churchill's war cabinet as lord president of the council (1940–3)—in which coordinating role he was virtually 'home front prime minister'—and then chancellor of the exchequer (1943–5). Anderson was also a key figure during and after the war in policy making on the atom bomb and atomic energy. *KT*

John Wheeler-Bennett, *John Anderson, Viscount Waverley* (London, 1962).

Andrews, John Miller (1871–1956), prime minister of Northern Ireland, 1940–3. Member of a prominent linen family, Andrews was elected to the Northern Ireland parliament in 1921. He served as minister of labour and then minister of finance, in which positions he showed considerable ability and compassion. At the age of nearly 70, he became prime minister, but made limited impact in this role during the following three years. *BMW*

Patrick Buckland, *The Factory of Grievances: Devolved Government in Northern Ireland, 1921–1939* (Dublin, 1979).

Angell, (Ralph) Norman (1872–1967), peace activist and pundit, born Ralph Norman Angell Lane. An unconventionally educated journalist, he won fame through his book *The Great Illusion?* (1910), which argued that financial interdependence made military aggression economically counter-productive for advanced states (but was commonly misinterpreted as saying that war was impossible). An isolationist in 1914 who helped to found the Union Democratic Control, he became a champion of collective security through the League of Nations during the 1930s. Briefly a Labour MP, 1929–31, he was knighted in 1931, and won the Nobel peace prize for 1933. *MEC*

Albert Marrin, *Sir Norman Angell* (Boston, 1979).

Anglo-American Council on Productivity (1948–52), established to share ideas on improving productivity in the two countries. The council arose from American government concern to demonstrate to the US Congress that, as a recipient of Marshall aid, Britain was determined to improve its economy by policies to raise productivity. In trying to be sensitive to British feelings, the council was publicly committed to ideas going in both directions across the Atlantic but, given the much higher levels of productivity in the USA, it was essentially about persuading the British to adopt American ideas. The council was enthusiastically embraced by Sir Stafford *Cripps, chancellor of the exchequer, who was already pressing on both unions and employers the need to raise productivity, but was received with hostility by many who regarded it as humiliating to be thought in need of lessons from the USA. But the Federation of British Industries and the TUC agreed to support the idea, helped by the government renouncing the taking of any direct role in the council itself. The most important activity of the council was organizing teams of workers, managers, and technicians to visit the USA. Forty-nine visits were made to plants in specific industries, and seventeen to investigate particular issues, such as management accounting. The reports of these missions were widely disseminated, but most commentators have been sceptical as to whether all this activity had much impact on British economic performance. Partly this was because many of the reports included vague rhetoric about the benefits of the 'American way of Life' which both glossed over the problems of the American economy and appeared of little relevance to 1940s austerity Britain. The council was replaced by the British Productivity Council in 1952. *JDT*

ANTHONY CAREW, *Labour under the Marshall Plan* (Manchester, 1987). | GRAHAM HUTTON, *We Too Can Prosper* (London, 1953).

Anglo-American relations. Throughout the 20th century Britain's most important international relationship, by far, was that with the USA. Financially and militarily, it was the USA which saw her through both world wars. Imperially, there was something like a passage of power in the same period—not an easy passage, but a remarkably peaceful one as successions go, for ideologically, despite superficial difference, there was a strong affinity between them. Diplomatically, no two great powers shared more secrets or cooperated more closely, in peace and war. Politically and psychologically, official Britain devoted countless hours to fathoming, influencing, mobilizing, wooing, and (quietly) castigating the USA. Instrumentally, the Anglo-American relationship became an end in itself, a matter of self-congratulation, a totem of virility in a detumescent time. Individually, the reputations of politicians and public servants of every stripe were made, and broken, by the success or failure of their personal Anglo-American relations. Churchill would not be Churchill without Roosevelt.

Churchill was indeed their Evangelist-in-Chief. 'The natural Anglo-American special relationship' was his coinage and his dream. It was he who advertised the benefits of the relationship and dramatized its possibilities in his own life. The very idea of a 'special relationship' is evangelical; the Churchillian notion of a 'natural relationship' even more so. Ever since the 1940s the British have swallowed these ideas like warm beer. As Martin Wight astringently remarked, 'there are associations between powers that seem to be deeper than formal alliances, to be based on affinity and tradition as much as interest, to be not so much utilitarian as natural.... Thus the British imagine their relationship to be with the United States (rather more generally than Americans imagine their relationship with England)' (*Power Politics* (London, 1986), 123).

The seminal Anglo-American experience of the century was the Second World War. Whatever was special about the special relationship was learned in the schoolroom of the Grand Alliance, 1941–5. Rhetorically, demobilization was extraordinarily long postponed. As late as 1962, Harold Macmillan could base a successful pitch for the Polaris missile on a manipulative appeal to a common past, an Anglo-American paradise pulsing with goodwill, good faith, and nuclear weapons. In the long run, however, the poor relation became the less special one. Anglo-American relations waxed fat on war, hot and cold. Notwithstanding some spectacular lapses (Suez, 1956), commonality on the sanction and application of force was basic to Anglo-American *raison d'être* and self-belief. Being willing and able to intervene globally, and to agree how, was the bedrock of the relationship from Adolf Hitler through Moscow Centre to Saddam Hussein. These wars worked, in Anglo-American terms, because the enemy was easily identifiable. For Britain, moreover, the alternative was unappetizing. Europe was a parochial place, and a mad project, studiously ignored. It is different now. The enemy is hard to define; the European project ready to mature. What price the special relationship? *AD*

ALEX DANCHEV, *On Specialness* (Basingstoke, 1998). | DAVID DIMBLEBY and DAVID REYNOLDS, *An Ocean Apart* (London, 1988). | ALAN P. DOBSON, *Anglo-American Relations in the Twentieth Century* (London, 1995).

Anglo-German naval agreement (1935). Effected by an exchange of notes of 18 June, Germany agreed to limit her surface tonnage to 35 per cent of the Royal Navy and was conceded submarine parity. This agreement had its origins in the efforts made by the British to bring Germany into an arms limitation agreement, following the collapse of the *disarmament conference. Although by February 1935 the British and French had conceded the case for the legalization of German rearmament in exchange for certain assurances, Hitler proceeded to a unilateral denunciation of the disarmament clauses of the treaty of Versailles the following month. This action was condemned by the British, French, and Italian governments at the Stresa conference of April 1935. Meanwhile, the British ministers Simon and Eden had visited Hitler on 25–6 March. While the talks were disappointing, Hitler did reiterate an earlier offer to limit the size of the German navy. As the Washington-London system of naval limitation was collapsing, it seemed prudent to take advantage of anything that might diminish the naval threat to Britain. An agreement was, therefore, speedily concluded;

it both angered the French and damaged the Stresa front. *AJC*

Eva Haraszti, *Treaty Breakers or Realpolitiker: The Anglo-German Naval Agreement of June 1935* (Boppard am Rhein, 1974).

Anglo-Irish agreement (1938), a partial settlement of differences arising from Eamon de Valera's challenge to the 1921 Anglo-Irish treaty following his return to power in 1932. De Valera had ceased land annuity payments, thereby provoking an economic war with the UK. He had removed allegiance to the crown from Eire's constitution, and had intensified the campaign against partition. Neville Chamberlain and Malcolm MacDonald, his dominions secretary, were anxious about Eire's stance in any European war, not least as she might influence other Commonwealth countries like South Africa. They saw de Valera, now apparently secure in office, as a man to do business with, and indeed as a barrier against republican extremism in Ireland. Chamberlain, a more energetic prime minister than his immediate predecessors, aspired to settle the Irish problem in a way that had eluded his father and his brother. For his part, de Valera wanted to end the trade war and he needed a diplomatic success to offset his lack of progress on partition. Accordingly, commercial hostilities between Britain and Ireland were concluded, and Eire paid a lump sum of £10 million as a final settlement of all financial claims. The *treaty ports were handed over by Britain in an attempt to ensure Eire's goodwill in a future conflict. This reinforced Irish sovereignty and gave de Valera some compensation for the continuation of partition. Indeed he used the latter as an excuse to refuse Britain's request for a mutual defence agreement. Chamberlain offered a formula, that Britain would not veto Irish unity once Northern Ireland concurred; but de Valera rejected this and any commercial concessions to the six counties. Ironically, remembering 1921, he feared extreme republican opposition. In Belfast, Craigavon strengthened his own and Northern Ireland's position by calling a snap general election and extracting further economic aid from Britain. *PR*

Robert Fisk, *In Time of War: Ireland, Ulster and the Price of Neutrality, 1939–1945* (Dublin, 1983).

Anglo-Irish agreement (1985). The agreement was signed by the British prime minister, Margaret Thatcher, and the Irish taoiseach, Garret Fitzgerald, at Hillsborough castle on 15 November 1985. For Mrs Thatcher, who had escaped assassination at the hands of the IRA only a year earlier, the aims of the accord were clear: to wean nationalists away from Sinn Fein, to secure better cooperation in the security field from the Irish Republic, and to retain US support. However, the Protestants never forgave her government for failing to consult them or their representatives.

The agreement comprised twelve articles and envisaged an intergovernmental conference headed by the secretary of state for Northern Ireland and Irish foreign minister which would meet regularly to promote cross-border cooperation and deal with security, legal, and political matters. The conference was to be serviced by a permanent secretariat of northern and southern civil servants based at Maryfield near Belfast. The document stated that both Britain and the Republic supported devolution on a basis which would secure widespread acceptance throughout the community. The reaction from both Republicans and Unionists was very hostile. Sinn Fein called it a disaster which copper-fastened partition while Unionists claimed that Thatcher had betrayed them by allowing Dublin to have a say in the affairs of the province and that the government was preparing to abandon them to the Republic.

The Unionists launched a campaign of protest and non-cooperation, hoping for a similar result to the action which had destroyed the *Sunningdale agreement in 1974. On 23 November, a vast crowd of Loyalists gathered in Belfast city centre to denounce the agreement. It was said that nothing like it had been seen since 1912. However, the agreement was soon winning international approval and its historic nature was becoming clear. For the first time since partition, a British government was accepting a role for Dublin in the running of the province. Also, the terms of the agreement encouraged the Republic to accept that a united Ireland was not an immediate objective but a long-term aspiration which must have the approval of a majority in Northern Ireland.

In January 1986 by-elections were held in fifteen constituencies where Ulster Unionist MPs had resigned in protest. Overall Unionist support fell short of their 500,000 target by 80,000 but Sinn Fein's share of the nationalist vote fell too, indicating that the Anglo-Irish agreement was producing the beneficial result desired by both Dublin and London. In April Unionist leaders announced a campaign of civil disobedience and a boycott of Westminster by their MPs, but this soon proved a dismal failure. Mrs Thatcher, years later, described the results of the agreement as disappointing, maintaining that it alienated

Unionists without gaining the level of security cooperation London had the right to expect. But its defenders argue that it has been vindicated by the steps which led to the 1998 Good Friday agreement. *PR*

JONATHAN BARDON, *A History of Ulster* (Belfast, 1992). | PAUL BEW, PETER GIBBON, and HENRY PATTERSON, *Northern Ireland 1921–1996: Political Forces and Social Classes* (London, 1996).

Anglo-Irish intergovernmental conference, a consultative forum for British and Irish ministers to discuss matters relating to political, security, and legal matters in Northern Ireland, established by the *Anglo-Irish agreement (1985). The British government committed itself to make determined efforts to resolve any differences which arose within the conference with the Irish government. The Irish government could put forward proposals for legislation and opinions on major policy issues. Ulster Unionists opposed the conference and any Irish influence in Northern Ireland. *TWH*

Anglo-Irish treaty (1921). The 'treaty' ('Articles of agreement for a treaty between Great Britain and Ireland') was signed after a terrorism and guerrilla war between the IRA and the crown forces which began in 1919 and ended when a truce was arranged in July 1921, negotiations beginning on 11 October 1921. The Irish delegation was led by Michael Collins and Arthur Griffith but lacked experience and was hampered by de Valera's refusal to attend the talks while trying to keep control of them from Dublin. The Irish hoped to manoeuvre the British on to their weakest ground, the partition of Ireland. Lloyd George, under pressure from Unionists in his coalition government who were restive about the negotiations, persuaded Griffith to give him a pledge that if Lloyd George were to stand against this Unionist pressure then Griffith would not break off the talks, providing Lloyd George were to offer a boundary commission rectifying the border between Northern Ireland and the Irish state. By the beginning of December neither Collins nor Griffith wanted to make the break on Ulster. They were both satisfied with the grant of dominion status to the Irish state and accepted the expedient of a boundary commission with Lloyd George's powerful hint that Northern Ireland would cease to be a viable state once the border was readjusted. Lloyd George now moved towards a conclusion, standing firm on dominion status, sweeping aside the last Irish attempt to make the break on Ulster, citing Griffith's pledge of 12 November, and demanding on 5 December that the treaty be signed—otherwise it would mean a war to the finish, 'and war within three days'. At 2.30 a.m. on 6 December the treaty was signed. Ireland became a dominion of the British Commonwealth of Nations with the same status as that of Canada. *DGB*

KEITH MIDDLEMAS (ed.), *Thomas Jones's Whitehall Diary, 3. Ireland, 1918–1925* (Oxford, 1971). | FRANK PAKENHAM, *Peace by Ordeal* (London, 1935).

Anglo-Japanese alliance (1902–21). The first Anglo-Japanese alliance was concluded in February 1902 and provided for mutual assistance in the event of either of the two countries being involved in a war against two other powers. It was Britain's first formal peacetime alliance since the Portuguese alliance of 1669, and part of its significance derives from this fact. The Japanese alliance was originally made to meet the looming crisis in northern China caused by the incessant growth of Russian power in the Far East. Earlier attempts (1898 and 1901) to form a combination with Germany to block Russia's further advance in China had ended in failure. The German option seemed preferable to a Japanese combination as the latter's military capabilities were untested against a recognized European great power. However, failing German support, Foreign Secretary Lord Lansdowne responded positively to Japanese overtures in April 1901, for the two countries had common interests. With her military resources already dangerously overstretched by the Boer war, Britain could not simultaneously defend India and her interests in China without assistance from another power. Japan was similarly concerned about the rapid growth of Russian influence in the region, but felt too weak to meet the Russian challenge on her own. From Britain's perspective the combination of British and Japanese naval forces in the China seas provided sufficient protection of her interests in China against either Russia on her own or even a Russo-French combination, without incurring any European obligations. Far from marking the end of isolation, as has traditionally been argued, the Japanese alliance on the contrary served to highlight Britain's relative aloofness from Europe.

However, rather than restraining Japan, the alliance emboldened her and led to the Japanese attack on Russia's Far Eastern possessions in February 1904. With that war, against all expectations, going in Japan's favour, the alliance was renewed in August 1905, two years before it was to expire. This second, revised alliance also had a poise against Russia since a future Far Eastern conflict with her could not be ruled out; but its provisions were now much tighter, stipulating mutual assistance in any war, with Japan's pledge of assistance extended to cover India. In the years following Japan's victory, relations between the two countries and Russia improved, and the character of the alliance thus began to change. At least in British thinking it was now no longer exclusively concerned with China. With another Far Eastern war increasingly remote, Britain could leave the safeguarding of her Chinese interests to Japan, permitting Britain to concentrate her naval forces against the 'German threat' in home waters. The alliance therefore developed a poise against Germany. The great value of the alliance for Britain's defence and foreign policy led to its renewal in 1912. Even so, Japan's growing ambitions on the Chinese mainland now clashed with Britain's desire to maintain the status quo there. Japan's 'twenty-one demands' on China in 1915 indeed seemed to undermine the alliance. Suspicion of Japan was now deep-rooted and, following strong American pressure, the British government decided not to renew the alliance in 1921. It was instead replaced by a looser four-power agreement, also involving France and the USA, which provided only for consultation in the event of disputes in the Far East. *TGO*

Ian H. Nish, *The Anglo-Japanese Alliance: The Diplomacy of Two Island Empires, 1894–1907* (London, 1966). | Ian H. Nish, *Alliance in Decline: A Study in Anglo-Japanese Relations, 1908–1923* (London, 1972).

Anglo-Welsh Review, magazine concerned with literature and the arts in Wales which first appeared as *Dock Leaves* in 1949 and which remained in existence until its 88th number in 1988. Its policy of bringing together Welsh-language and Anglo-Welsh writers and of dealing with all the arts in Wales largely reflected the ideas of Raymond Garlick (editor to 1961) and Roland Mathias (editor 1961–76). In its day it provided the major forum for the critical debate on Welsh artistic identity. *PS*

animal welfare. The Society for the Prevention of Cruelty to Animals was founded in 1824, changing its name to the Royal Society for the Prevention of Cruelty to Animals in 1840, and remains the largest voluntary body concerned with animal welfare. It was instrumental in promoting legislation against cruelty to animals in the 1911 Protection of Animals Act and its many subsequent amendments. Birds were first specifically covered by a Protection of Birds Act in 1925, subsequently added to by further specific Acts.

The principal legislation protecting animal wildlife in Great Britain is the Wildlife and Countryside Act of 1981 which produced an extensive list of protected species, restricted the introduction into the countryside of animals not normally found in the wild in Britain, and afforded greater protection for sites of special scientific interest (SSSIs), of which over 6,000 have been identified in Great Britain. Of the last, some have been designated for protection under the European Commission's birds and habitats directives. The list of protected species is reviewed by the three statutory nature conservation agencies, the Countryside Council for Wales, Scottish National Heritage, and English Nature, every five years. Animal welfare on farms is covered by a highly developed framework of rules. Where appropriate, these implement EU requirements which apply during the transport, slaughter, and maintenance of livestock. The State Veterinary Service carried out over 4,300 farm inspections in 1997, resulting in over 100 prosecutions for violations.

Animal welfare has only rarely aroused partisan political rivalries, with the primary exception of attempts, largely originating from within the Labour Party, to obtain a ban on deer- and fox-hunting. After several failed attempts to secure a majority for such a ban, a private member's bill seeking to ban hunting with hounds received a second reading in the Commons in 1997 with a substantial majority. The Labour government refused to find parliamentary time for the bill, but promised to prepare its own legislation following consultation with interested parties. In practice, the Conservative Party has always aligned itself with those opposing such a ban, and has made common cause with the Countryside Alliance which promotes the interests of field sports. A second area of concern has arisen over the treatment of animals being exported for slaughter to Europe. As a result of demonstrations at UK ports in 1997–8, the government has sought to improve the conditions under which animals are transported to the Continent.

A more long-standing issue has been that of animal vivisection and the use of animals in medical experiments. The Anti-Vivisection Society has campaigned since the 1920s on these issues. Concerns over the continuation of experiments have led to direct action campaigns by animal rights activists, including the freeing of animals from laboratories and breeding establishments. The use of direct action, including the actions of hunt saboteurs, has brought animal rights and animal welfare issues to the forefront over the past two decades. The development of direct action campaigns against animal experimenters represents a new departure, led by a younger generation of animal rights activists. In the meantime, organizations such as the RSPCA and the Royal Society for the Protection of Birds maintain a more general watch over animal welfare issues and advocate policies and legislation which protect animal rights. *JS*

Anschluss **(13 March 1938)**, historical shorthand for the union of Germany and Austria following the invasion of Austria by the German army. Hitler decided to proceed forcibly in this matter when the Austrian chancellor, Schuschnigg, announced on 8 March 1938 that there would be a plebiscite on the issue of Austrian sovereignty. The British government of Neville Chamberlain had accepted the inevitability of the *Anschluss* for some time. Nevertheless, its timing and manner created unease, coming as it did ten days after an initiative by the British to induce Germany into a general, European settlement that would have included the reinstatement of Germany as a colonial power. This scheme was now put into abeyance and on 24 March Chamberlain publicly warned of the dangers to world peace of a war that might start in central Europe. It remained, however, imperative to maintain contact with Berlin, as the *Anschluss* carried with it an immediate threat to another central European state; namely, Czechoslovakia. *AJC*

ANDREW J. CROZIER, *Appeasement and Germany's Last Bid for Colonies* (Basingstoke, 1988). | JÜRGEN GEHL, *Austria, Germany and the Anschluss 1931–1938* (Oxford, 1963).

Anstruther-Gray, William John (1905–85), Conservative politician. Anstruther-Gray was an MP for almost thirty years between 1931 and 1966 but spent only two months in office, as assistant postmaster general in Churchill's 1945 Caretaker Government. He personified the traditional 'knights of the shires' and as chairman of the 1922 Committee after 1964 seemed remote to younger MPs, but his communication of backbench concern to Douglas-Home influenced the latter to resign, whereupon Anstruther-Gray presided over the Tories' first leadership ballot. *RJS*

anti-Semitism, prejudice against Jews, has been a recurrent theme in 20th-century British politics. At the beginning of the century, it was fuelled by the immigration of mainly poor Jews from Russia and Austria-Hungary. A campaign by the British Brothers' League against this influx prompted A. J. Balfour's Conservative government to appoint a royal commission (1902–3) and then to pass the Aliens Act, 1905. At the general election of 1906, some Tory candidates ran anti-Semitic campaigns, but the incoming Liberal administration dared not repeal what it knew to be a popular measure. During and after the Great War, anti-Semitism and xenophobia remained closely aligned features of the political landscape, bolstered by anti-Zionism and anti-Bolshevism; these themes were to be found in successive general elections between 1918 and 1924. The Labour and Communist parties were periodically attacked by elements of the right as agents of an international Jewish conspiracy. But it was the decision of Oswald Mosley in 1934 to make anti-Semitism an official ideology of the *British Union of Fascists (BUF) which thrust prejudice against Jews once more to the forefront of the political agenda. Although the BUF remained a small, peripheral party, its anti-Jewish platform found support from elements within the Conservative Party. At Cheltenham (1937) the mayor, Daniel Lipson, was denied selection as the Tory by-election candidate on account of his Jewish identity. Thereafter, for well over a decade, professing Jews found it very difficult to be selected as Conservative parliamentary candidates. During the 1970s and 1980s the Labour Party, which a majority of British Jews had hitherto regarded as their natural political home, became associated with extreme left-wing anti-Zionism. Whilst anti-Zionism must be carefully distinguished from anti-Semitism, this distinction was not always maintained by 'the loony left', and it was not in any case a distinction which appealed to British Jewry. The damage done to Labour was significant, perhaps severe: incoming Labour leader Tony Blair put a very high priority on healing this wound. At the end of the century anti-Semitism remained a minor, largely submerged feature of the British political landscape. It had not, however, completely disappeared. *GA*

G. ALDERMAN, *Modern British Jewry* (2nd edn., Oxford, 1998).

Anti-Waste League (AWL), pressure group formed in 1921. Inspired by Lord Rothermere and supported by his newspapers, the AWL demanded lower taxes and substantial cuts in spending on the Lloyd George coalition government's social programmes. The league found much popular support for its campaign, and its independent candidates actually took three seats from government supporters at by-elections between February and June 1921, menacing several others. The threat led to the severe budget cuts dubbed the *Geddes axe. *RJQA*

An t Oglach, IRA journal, first published in August 1918 by the Irish Volunteers. This paramilitary organization was involved in the Easter Rising of 1916, and by 1919 it had evolved into the IRA. On 31 January 1919 *An t Oglach* stated that the Volunteers were entitled 'morally and legally to slay British police and soldiers'. Throughout the Anglo-Irish war of 1919–21 it articulated the views of the IRA leadership. *TWH*

apartheid, 'separateness' in the Afrikaans language. Apartheid was introduced in *South Africa in 1948, designed to preserve white rule and restructure South African society by building upon earlier segregationist policies. Apartheid stipulated that the four main races in South Africa—white, coloured, Asian and African—were to be kept rigidly apart. Thus various Acts classified the race of every individual, prohibited mixed marriages, and forced non-whites to use separate residential areas and amenities. From 1959, separate African homelands were established based on tribal identity. Africans were forced to leave the cities and live in often inhospitable regions; outside these areas they had no civil rights. Apartheid denied Africans an education and work skills, which by 1980 had, alongside international economic sanctions, undermined South Africa's economy. Consequently, apartheid began to be dismantled from 1991, and ended finally with the election as president of Nelson Mandela in 1994. *KTS*

LEONARD THOMPSON, *A History of South Africa* (London, 1990).

'appalling frankness', phrase used by Baldwin on 12 November 1936 during a Commons debate. Responding to criticisms from Churchill, Baldwin offered his 'own views with appalling frankness', explaining why in 1933 he could not have won an election on rearmament. The speech was considered by many parliamentarians a tour de force, but critics later claimed unfairly that Baldwin had admitted to having put party before country (Winston Churchill, *The Gathering Storm* (London, 1948), 607). *NJC*

appeasement, word used to describe the foreign policy of the government of Neville Chamberlain, 1937–40. Following the outbreak of war in 1939, appeasement was discredited and came to be equated with unrequited concession to German demands, with the Munich agreement of 1938 regarded as appeasement in its classic form. Appeasement, however, was not confined to the Chamberlain government and, furthermore, encompassed more than mere concession. Appeasement was the practice of all governments in inter-war Britain and at its core revolved around revision of the treaty of Versailles (see PARIS PEACE CONFERENCE) in such a way as to bring Germany into satisfactory treaty relations with all her neighbours. What was meant by appeasement was appeasement of the European situation, or the pacification of Europe, through a general settlement. In its earliest manifestation, appeasement was economically motivated. As a trading nation, Britain was interested after 1919 in an economically fully restored Europe of which Germany would be a critical part. There was, therefore, from the beginning an inclination on the part of British governments to promote modification and adjustment of the financial and economic aspects of the Versailles system. This was realized in the reduction of reparation payments that Germany was required to make under the Dawes and Young plans and their effective cancellation at the Lausanne conference of 1932.

By this time, however, even more far-reaching changes in the edifice of the Versailles system were under consideration in the Foreign Office. The tension in Europe promoted by the rise of Nazism, continued German demands for the revision of Versailles, French anxieties in respect of security, and the general background of the world economic crisis encouraged the promotion in the department of an 'all-in' settlement that at a minimum would require disarmament, guarantees of security, and rectification of frontiers. Hitler's accession to power did not give pause to these deliberations for, on the contrary, it was considered that comprehensive revision of the Versailles system might make Hitler a conventional statesman and Germany a stable element in a stable Europe. By spring 1936 a scheme for a general and European settlement, including colonial readjustment, had been outlined and received cabinet approval. It was endorsed by the foreign secretary, Anthony Eden, and also received the emphatic support of Chamberlain, then chancellor of the exchequer. German obstructionism and continued disturbance of the peace of Europe by the remilitarization of the Rhineland made it impossible, however, to make immediate progress. On succeeding as prime minister in 1937, Chamberlain was determined to elicit a German response to these proposals which were finally presented to Hitler on 3 March 1938. Hitler's fundamentally negative reaction was revealed ten days later in the **Anschluss*. In the succeeding *Munich crisis, British policy remained motivated by the search for a general settlement to which the settlement of the Czech question would be a prelude. German policy during the following months, however, revealed the futility of a general settlement and war ensued. *AJC*

Andrew J. Crozier, *Appeasement and Germany's Last Bid for Colonies* (Basingstoke, 1988). | Martin Gilbert, *The Roots of Appeasement* (London, 1966). | Keith Robbins, *Appeasement* (Oxford, 1988).

Apprentice Boys of Derry, organization that commemorates biannually in Derry the siege of the city in 1688–9 when Protestant defenders held out against the Catholic forces of James II. The first Apprentice Boy clubs were founded in the early 19th century but the main growth in numbers came after 1921. Besides clubs based in Derry, there are reckoned to be nearly 200 clubs elsewhere. In recent years both the main parade in Derry and some 'feeder' parades have been matters of controversy. *BMW*

B. M. Walker, *Past and Present: History, Identity and Politics in Ireland* (Belfast, 2000).

Arcos raid (1927). This was a police raid, on 12 May, on the offices of Arcos Ltd and the Soviet trade delegation in Moorgate, London. Authorized by Home Secretary Joynson-Hicks, the recovery of compromising material provided the pretext for severing diplomatic relations with the USSR and encouraged belief in the existence of a Soviet spy ring. The raid should be seen in the context of the 1927–8 rightward move of Baldwin's government following the 1926 General Strike and fear of Bolshevism. *NJC*

arms limitation. See SALT.

Armstrong, Robert Temple (1926–), secretary to the cabinet, 1979–88, and head of the civil service, 1981–8. A brilliant senior civil servant in a traditional 'establishment' mould, Armstrong glided to the top via the Treasury, the Cabinet Office, and ministerial private offices, including service as principal private secretary to two prime ministers, 1970–5, Heath and Wilson. Permanent secretary to the Home Office, 1977–9, he was selected by Thatcher as cabinet secretary in 1979, assuming the additional role of head of the home civil service after the dismissal of Ian Bancroft in 1981. He played a key backstage role in the negotiation of the Anglo-Irish agreement (1985). Unwillingly pushed into the public eye by a succession of crises, including the Ponting and Westland affairs, Armstrong was sent out to Australia to defend in court the government's banning of the *Spycatcher* book (which had alleged malpractice by the security services) and notoriously admitted to being 'economical with the truth'. A cautious and careful man, concerned to ensure the orderly conduct of government and to keep the machine running, he worked (sometimes against the tide of political leadership of the day) to maintain the integrity of the civil service and defend its traditional values. *KT*

Kevin Theakston, *Leadership in Whitehall* (London, 1999).

Armstrong, William (1915–80), head of the home civil service, 1968–74. A brilliant scholarship boy from a working-class, Salvation Army background, Armstrong entered the civil service in 1938. He was private secretary to the wartime cabinet secretary Edward Bridges and to three successive chancellors of the exchequer 1949–53 (Cripps, Gaitskell, and Butler). He rose unusually rapidly to be joint permanent secretary to the Treasury, on the economic side, 1962–8. A subtle Whitehall operator and influential adviser to ministers, he consciously broke the mould in cultivating a public profile, particularly as head of the civil service handling the post-Fulton reforms of civil service management and organization after 1968. He stands out as one of the great reforming heads of the civil service in the 20th century. But his role in the Heath government—as one of the architects of the government's economic policy U-turn, and the prime minister's closest confidant and right-hand man—was controversial. Critics unfairly dubbed Armstrong 'deputy prime minister', but he did become almost a political official who was over-identified with the prime minister and who unwisely strayed across the boundary between civil service and political roles. *KT*

Kevin Theakston, *Leadership in Whitehall* (London, 1999).

Arnold-Forster, Hugh Oakley (1855–1909), Conservative secretary of state for war (1903–5). Grandson of Thomas Arnold of Rugby and adopted son of Gladstone's Irish secretary, W. E. Forster, Arnold-Forster enjoyed a reputation as an expert on military affairs, but when Balfour turned to him to reform the army after the Boer war, his plans for two parallel (long- and short-service) forces proved to be expensive, unpopular, and in the end unsuitable. Rigid and uncompromising, his struggles in his short-lived ministry brought him no success. *RJQA*

Arts Councils. The Arts Council of Great Britain, the national funding body for the arts, was established and incorporated by royal charter in 1946, succeeding the Committee ('Council' from April 1940) for the Encouragement of Music and the Arts which was set up in January 1940. The Arts Council of Great Britain was in 1994 divided into three new bodies, the Arts Council of England, the Scottish Arts Council, and the Arts Council of Wales. The situation in Northern Ireland had always been different with the Committee for the Encouragement of Music and the Arts established in 1942 being followed in 1962 by the Arts Council of Northern Ireland. *JD*

Arts Council of England website: *www.artscouncil.org.uk*

arts policy. The UK has a strong voluntarist tradition in the arts which until relatively recently was an area of little direct concern to the government, apart from the administration of major national institutions such as the British Museum and National Gallery. Hence prior to the Second World War patronage in the arts was left primarily in private hands and even new cultural organizations, such as the BBC, were kept at arm's length by governments. As a result, much of the artistic, musical, theatrical, and film culture of the first half of the 20th century developed on a commercial and private basis. The Great War, however, witnessed the inauguration of an Official War Artists scheme modelled on one adopted by the Canadian government. From 1916, under the Ministry of Information, artists were commissioned to record the war, eventually producing several thousand paintings and prints. Following the Armistice, a number of artists were also engaged by the War Memorials Commission to produce works for a planned Hall of Remembrance. An exhibition of war artists' work at the Royal Academy in 1919 and in 1920–3 at the Crystal Palace attracted large audiences. Economic stringency prevented any extension of state subsidy towards the arts between the wars, but the Second World War saw a fresh initiative to commission works representing the experience of the nation at war. Under the auspices of the Ministry of Information, Kenneth Clark, director of the National Gallery, set up the war artists' advisory committee to appoint official war artists with officer rank and to commission work from individual artists. During the war, it commissioned over 5,000 paintings, many of which were exhibited widely in wartime Britain and abroad.

In addition to a revival of the war artists' scheme, the Second World War saw the establishment in January 1940 of the Council for the Encouragement of Music and the Arts (CEMA) as a further example of state sponsorship of the arts. Set up under the aegis of the Board of Education, headed by Lord De La Warr, and with funding from the Pilgrim Trust, its aim was to aid and maintain cultural life by encouraging amateur music and drama, as well as assisting unemployed professional performers at a time when many theatres and concert halls were closed. Amateur entertainment was assisted with grants, while tours by theatre groups and musicians to blitzed areas and munitions factories were undertaken.

Funding was eventually taken over by the Treasury and placed under a council organized by the Board of Education. The emphasis also shifted towards the maintenance and provision of high professional standards in the arts and their dissemination to a wider public. Under the chairmanship of J. M. Keynes from 1942, CEMA began to develop in a more professional and centralized direction, promoting a London Old Vic season, appointing regional officers, and setting up full-time paid directors of music, drama, and art, with advisory panels in each area. Plans were also laid for the Royal Opera House in Covent Garden to become the national home for opera and ballet after the war.

From 1943 Keynes and his colleagues were preparing CEMA to become a permanent peacetime organization which would supervise patronage of the arts and, acting independently of direct intervention from Westminster, channel state funding to them. The idea of permanent state funding for the arts was one which chimed with the collectivist mood of wartime and the sense of cultural renaissance which CEMA-inspired art exhibitions and concerts, as well as plans for post-war reconstruction, had helped to foster. On 12 June 1945, the chancellor of the exchequer announced the creation of an Arts Council to be funded by the Treasury. Its royal charter, granted in August 1946, constituted an Arts Council of sixteen members, selected by the chancellor of the exchequer, together with separate and autonomous committees for Scotland and Wales and a separate Arts Council for Northern Ireland. The Council had unpaid advisory panels for the major areas of artistic activity, responsible for making recommendations for funds.

Initial funding for the Arts Council totalled £235,000 in 1945–6, and was still under a million pounds (£820,000) ten years later. The 1960s saw a widening role for the Arts Council with the appointment of Jennie *Lee as first minister for the arts in 1964. A new charter was granted to the Arts Council in 1967 and there was an increasing trend towards the support of major regional companies for theatre, opera, and ballet, as well as the major institutions based in London and Stratford-upon-Avon. Although the tradition was maintained that ministers could not direct or even advise the Arts Council and governments have consistently declared that they will not interfere with the Arts Council's discretion, broad changes in political trends have been registered. During the Thatcher government, there was greater emphasis on private funding and commercial efficiency in arts organizations. Moreover, a concerted policy of developing regional arts culminated in 1991 with the creation of ten regional arts boards through which much Arts Council funding is now administered. Having risen to twenty members, the Arts Council of England has been reduced to eleven, and retains responsibility only for the four national companies—the Royal Opera House, the English National Opera, the Royal Shakespeare Company, and the Royal National Theatre—as well as for touring, publishing, and other organizations without a regional base.

Currently, arts policy falls within the remit of the Department for Culture, Media, and Sport (DCMS), headed by a secretary of state, which determines government policy and administers expenditure on national museums and art galleries, the British Library, other national and heritage bodies, and the Arts Councils of England, Wales, Scotland and Northern Ireland. In 1998–9, funding for the arts in England amounted to £209 million for museums and galleries, £99 million for broadcasting and the media (including film), £90 million for libraries, and £198 million for the visual and performing arts. The last amount was channelled through the Arts Council of England, with a further £48 million for the Arts Councils of Scotland, Wales, and Northern Ireland. In addition the Arts Councils distribute National Lottery proceeds, amounting to £250 million in 1998–9. By 1998 the Arts Council and Heritage Lottery Fund had announced since 1994 grants of over £1,645 million to arts projects. Millennium celebrations led the government to promote one of the largest and costliest arts initiatives in Britain with the Millennium Experience ('the Dome') on a reclaimed site at Greenwich with a budget of £758 million raised from government, the National Lottery, and private sponsorship.

Government arts policy continues to operate within a climate of financial restraint in so far as there are always more demands upon funding than can be met, even with the accession in recent years of major new sources of funds via the National Lottery. Successive arts ministers have had to compete for funds alongside the pressures from much bigger spending ministries whose budgets dwarf that of the DCMS. Central government funding has also to be set alongside that obtained from other sources, as in the case of the 'Millennium Experience' where Lottery and private business sponsorship were also involved. Private business sponsorship to the arts amounted to £95.6 million in 1997 and since 1984 there has been in existence a 'pairing scheme' to match government sponsorship with private funding. Local authorities are also responsible for maintaining a significant part of the national cultural heritage and supporting artistic activity, including about 1,000 local museums and art galleries, as well as orchestras, theatres, and opera and dance companies, and thousands of libraries. In 1997–8, net revenue support for the arts in England from local authorities amounted to approximately £194 million.

State funding for the arts remains controversial: though few have wanted to pursue the absolutist laissez-faire line, there has been persistent questioning of whether taxpayers' money is appropriately spent on minority cultural pursuits and whether state funding adequately reflects artistic merit. Many aspects of cultural life, including major festivals like summer opera at Glyndebourne, the commercial theatre, cinema, fine arts, and many forms of music, function with little or no government subsidy. Others, such as the BBC, operate in a grey area with government support, but without its direct involvement. Some major flagship organizations, such as the Royal National Theatre, the Royal Opera House, and the Royal Shakespeare Company, could not exist without government support. The network of regional theatres built up from the 1960s is also largely dependent upon state subsidy. Arts policy has remained essentially hybrid but with increasing emphasis upon commercial efficiency, regional development, and wider access by meeting the needs of ethnic communities, young people, and the disabled. *JS*

Ashdown, Jeremy John Durham ('Paddy') (1941–), Liberal politician and first elected leader of the *Liberal Democrats, 1988–99. Leading the party from shortly after the merger of the two *Alliance parties, the *Liberal Party and the *Social Democratic Party (SDP), he saw it develop from a nadir of support amidst post-merger bickering and the survival of a 'continuing' SDP under David Owen to the largest number of seats secured by a third party for over half a century when the Liberal Democrats obtained 46 seats in the 1997 general election. A former Royal Marine and civil servant, Ashdown joined the Liberal Party in 1976, working to build up a base of support in Yeovil where he was employed as a manager at the local Westland helicopter company. He took Liberal support from third place to win the Yeovil seat in the 1983 election, and was party spokesman on trade and industry from his election to the Commons, earning a wider recognition within the party for his opposition to *cruise missiles being sited in Europe, at the Liberal Assembly in 1984.

As education spokesman from 1987, he further enhanced his reputation and emerged as one of two candidates, with Alan *Beith, for leadership of the newly merged Liberal Democrats. Ashdown's more dynamic and professional campaign secured him the leadership in July 1988 with over 70 per cent of the vote. He inherited a demoralized and almost bankrupt party. The total number of votes cast in the leadership contest, just under 58,000, showed that core membership of the new party was very low. The failure to win the Richmond (Yorkshire) by-election in 1989, because of the intervention of an Owenite SDP candidate, was symptomatic of Ashdown's difficulties, further emphasized by continuing confusion over the new party's name, and brought home sharply when it crashed in support to fourth place behind the Green Party in the European elections of June 1989 with only 6 per cent of the vote.

Ashdown energetically rebuilt the party, though, spending as much time as possible outside Westminster, cultivating grass roots support, computerizing the party's membership lists (the first major party to do so), and securing its financial future. The unpopularity of the Thatcher administration's poll tax provided the opportunity for the Liberal Democrats to win their first by-election at *Eastbourne in October 1990 and to undermine seriously her prospect of remaining Conservative leader. He was also able to capitalize upon his former military experience in the Far East to speak with authority on issues such as Hong Kong, where he advocated UK passports for all Hong Kong citizens, following the agreement to hand the colony back to China.

Generally well regarded for his energy and commitment, the only serious difficulty for him in the run-up to the general election of 1992 was the revelation of an earlier affair with his former secretary, but the continuing support of his wife, Jane, allowed him to recover politically. Moreover, the party's continuing by-election and local government successes allowed it to campaign effectively under Ashdown's leadership in the April 1992 election, securing twenty seats and second place in another 154. The decay of the Major administration, especially following 'Black Wednesday', gave Ashdown further opportunities to re-establish the credibility of the party with a series of spectacular by-election victories in 1993–4. As well as campaigning actively for UN involvement in the former Yugoslavia, he manoeuvred the party skilfully towards cooperation with the Labour opposition under Tony Blair on constitutional issues. Following the return of 46 MPs at the 1997 general election, Ashdown continued cooperation with the Blair government via a policy of 'constructive opposition', leading to the setting-up of a cabinet committee to oversee the implementation of agreed constitutional reforms. Of these, the securing of devolution for Scotland and Wales, the adoption of proportional representation for European elections, and the airing of proposals for further constitutional reform have been tangible gains, but also a mixed blessing. From only two seats gained in the 1994 European elections on a first-past-the-post system, the Liberal Democrats moved to ten seats on an almost 13 per cent share of the vote in June 1999 under a regional list system. In the first elections for the Scottish parliament and the Welsh assembly, held on a proportional basis in May 1999, the Liberal Democrats were beaten into fourth place by the respective nationalist parties. Nonetheless, Ashdown's reputation was already secure as having established a viable third party when he announced that he would be retiring as leader with effect from July 1999 and giving up his Yeovil seat at the end of the 1997 parliament. *JS*

PADDY ASHDOWN, *The Ashdown Diaries, 1988–1997* (London, 2000). | JOHN STEVENSON, *Third Party Politics in Britain since 1945* (Oxford, 1992).

Asian politics in Britain. Casting an eye upon racial politics in Britain at the end of the 1990s, it would appear that Asian participation in political life has developed, from a low start, to maturity and strength. Electoral data confirms that in 1997 the registration and turnout rate of this large and varied group ranked alongside or even exceeded their white (and black) counterparts. Five Asians were successfully elected in that year's general election, all but one representing seats in which large numbers of Asian voters were concentrated. In local government, estimates from the mid-1990s revealed a fairly astonishing rate of improvement: over one hundred had been elected outside London, achieving a position very close to parity, with a similar picture emerging in several inner London boroughs. Lastly, the strong electoral alignment between Asians and the Labour Party meant that many independent commentators had begun speculating openly, perhaps naively, about the potential benefits that might be thought to accrue from this relationship. A generation previously, Asians had been few in number in elective politics, rarely successful as candidates, often confined to the terrain of single-issue 'homeland' politics, and generally undervalued by mainstream parties.

This amounts to a significant transformation by any standards. Furthermore, even though considerable progress can be charted, it remains the case that structural and other impediments exist on the community's chances of attaining greater influence. Three central factors have been behind the story of political maturation. First, Britain's electoral arrangements have placed weight on electoral strength derived from sheer numbers of voters. For Asians, this has been an opportunity in the sense that the combined size of the three largest Asian groups—Indians, Pakistanis, and Bangladeshis—had reached 1.5 million (based on outdated Census data from 1991). Estimates closer to the 1997 election suggested that growth of the order of a further third was likely by the following Census in 2001. One Asian media outlet reported some 36 'Asian marginals', where notional Asian voters were greater than defending majorities. Whilst this may have talked up the actual figure, it remained the case that a number of serving candidates felt that the importance of this would-be voting bloc could not be overlooked.

Second, the constellation of issues and interests that comprise mainstream parties' interest in Asian affairs has gradually shifted away from first-generation immigrant matters and toward the aspirations of British-born younger Asians (now a majority within the community at large). The upshot of this has been that interest has gravitated to mainstream educational, employment, and related policies in which it is increasingly conceded there is a legitimate 'Asian dimension'. For instance, distinctive though complementary arrangements aimed at boosting recruitment in areas such as policing, civil service employment, and higher education are now commonplace.

Finally, the face of Asian political involvement has not been divorced from the group's participation in British economic life. In this regard, recent Labour Force Survey evidence has shown wide divergence in the patterns of some groups of Asians as compared with others. However, in education, employment, and business start-ups decisive headway has been achieved amongst Indian Asians in particular. As part of a wider picture of advancement, such economic progress has been described by many as heralding a new era of weakening partisanship with the Labour Party. One of the interesting barkless dogs, therefore, has been the singular failure of Labour's opponents to build a sizeable following among Asians. Evidence from the 1997 British Election Study indicated that the problem has not stemmed from lack of effort (there has been plenty) but rather from a failure to exploit a growing social class division in the political outlook of middle-class Asians compared with their more numerous working-class peers. The secret of Asian politics may thus lie in first understanding traditional British class politics. *SS*

R. Ballard (ed.), *Desh Pardesh: The South Asian Presence in Britain* (London, 1994). | C. Holmes, *John Bull's Island: Immigration and British Society 1871–1971* (London, 1988). | S. Saggar (ed.), *Race and British Electoral Politics* (London, 1998).

Asquith, Herbert Henry (1852–1928), last Liberal prime minister and man who led Britain into the Great War. Asquith rose to prominence as home secretary from 1892 and then as chancellor of the exchequer under *Campbell-Bannerman. As leader of the Liberal Party, 1908–26, and prime minister, 1908–16, he presided over the party at its greatest electoral strength and witnessed its split into factions and demise as a potential governing party by the mid-1920s.

Asquith was born at Morley in west Yorkshire and educated at Balliol College, Oxford, becoming president of the Oxford Union. He gave up a Balliol fellowship for the Bar in 1874, and entered politics as member for East Fife in 1886, where he remained MP for 32 years. Following the death of his first wife, in 1894 he married Margot Tennant (see Asquith, Margaret), who brought him greater financial stability and a wider circle of political acquaintance. Success at the Bar led to becoming QC in 1890 and his talents in the

Commons brought him the position of home secretaryship in 1892, from which he emerged creditably, so much so that he was offered—but declined in order to concentrate on the Bar—the chance of opposition leadership in the Commons in 1898. He enhanced his reputation in defence of free trade during Joseph Chamberlain's *tariff reform campaign and was championed by the *Liberal Imperialists as a potential rival to Campbell-Bannerman for leadership of the party. An attempt to impose him as leader at the time of Balfour's resignation (see Relugas compact) was defeated and instead he became chancellor of the exchequer where he was responsible for extending the system of grants to local authorities, reducing the national debt, and providing the first old age *pensions.

Prime Minister

On 6 April 1908, he succeeded Campbell-Bannerman as prime minister and was almost immediately pitchforked into a struggle with the Lords occasioned by their rejection of Lloyd George's *'People's Budget'. Asquith's conduct of the campaign against the Lords proved effective, winning both the 1910 general elections, though with the Liberals reduced to dependence on Labour and Irish support, and pushing through the *Parliament Act, 1911, by which the powers of the House of Lords were reduced. With able lieutenants in Lloyd George and Winston Churchill, Asquith presided over an immensely fertile period of legislation which saw the introduction of national insurance, labour exchanges, trade boards, Welsh Church disestablishment, and land taxes. Faced with an almost unprecedented set of problems in trade union unrest, the *suffragette campaign, and Ulster opposition to Irish home rule, Asquith nevertheless remained virtually unchallenged as prime minister. He managed trade union unrest by a mixture of firmness and conciliation, allowed the suffragette campaign of violence to alienate even some of its supporters while adopting severe measures against them, and in spite of vehement Ulster protest and the threat of civil war enacted a Home Rule Bill which awaited implementation in 1914 at the outbreak of the Great War.

Wartime Leader

Asquith's hold on power was undermined by the war and this fatally compromised the future of the Liberal Party as a whole. Having carried a virtually undivided cabinet into war (no small achievement given Liberal divisions over the Boer war), the pressures of the 'shell scandal' on the western front and failures in the Dardanelles forced him into a coalition with the Conservatives in May 1915. Beset by personal problems, including the loss in action of his eldest son, Raymond, in September 1916, Asquith was increasingly seen as an obstacle to the efficient and dynamic conduct of the war. His promotion of Lloyd George to the key posts of minister of munitions and then secretary for war had already identified the heir apparent and in December 1916 he was ousted from the premiership in a palace coup led by Lloyd George and Law.

Liberal split

Asquith had resigned the premiership, but not the leadership of the Liberal Party. Unable to reconcile himself to his loss of power, he was faced in 1918 by Lloyd George's attempt to maintain the wartime coalition into peace. As a result the Liberal Party fought the 1918 *'Coupon' Election in two fragments, the stronger one being led by Lloyd George. Asquith and his followers were badly defeated and he lost his own seat. Returned at a by-election in February 1920 he led the *'Wee Frees' or Independent Liberals in opposition to the Lloyd George coalition. Even after the fall of the coalition in 1922, enduring bitterness prevented a wholehearted reconciliation and only an uneasy reunification was achieved for the 1923 general election. Even after again losing his seat in 1924 and taking a peerage as the earl of Oxford and Asquith, he retained the leadership of the party. It was only in October 1926 that he relinquished the leadership, allowing Lloyd George to emerge as undisputed leader.

Asquith's reputation is inevitably bound up with two larger questions: the downfall of the Liberals and the course and conduct of the Great War. Often seen as an upholder of traditional Liberal values, he has been seen as representative of an older, outdated style of politics which was hindering the Liberals in meeting the challenge of Labour or which, on some readings, was so outmoded by the rise of Labour that its survival was an irrelevance anyway, and a throwback to a bygone world of restricted electorates rather than mass democracy, and of denominational, deferential politics rather than those based on class allegiance. In practice, Asquith was a more complex political figure. A Liberal Imperialist who defended the Boer war and maintained the naval estimates, he also presided over the inauguration of the Liberal 'welfare state' prior to 1914. Although the latter was largely the work of younger colleagues such as Lloyd George and Winston Churchill, he gave them their head and oversaw a period of remarkable legislative activity including the enactment of home rule for Ireland. That these were achieved in the face of militant threats from trade unionists, suffragettes, and both Unionist and Republican forces in Ireland only enhances the achievement. Far from presiding over the 'crisis of Liberalism', revised views of his career suggest that many of the problems with which he was faced were managed effectively and gave the Liberal Party at least a fighting chance of dealing with its political rivals on the left and the right. Modern research has now largely discredited the idea that there was any certainty about the Liberal Party's decline as, even with the split with Lloyd George and the mass enfranchisement of 1918, it still took until 1924 and four post-war general elections for the party to cease to be a potential party of government. The greatest charge against Asquith is that having been deposed he failed to accept defeat. By retaining the leadership until 1926 and fighting the 'Coupon' Election of 1918 in rivalry to the National Liberals he fatally exacerbated the split within Liberalism at a time when it was most vulnerable to having its vote and a shoal of new voters poached by Labour or the Conservatives. Asquith's defence, and that of his followers, that Lloyd George was an unprincipled careerist who was betraying Liberal values and traditions sounded increasingly irrelevant as the party visibly declined in influence and support in the early 1920s.

Asquith could not be considered a great war leader, certainly not for the kind of war the Great War turned out to be. However competent he might be in private, his relaxed style and inherited assumptions about the conduct of war were overtaken in 1916 by the need for greater urgency, efficiency, and dynamism. Lloyd George was seen by many as the kind of man who could win the Great War; whatever his other qualities, Asquith was not. *JS*

Stephen Koss, *Asquith* (London, 1976). | George R. Searle, *The Liberal Party: Triumph and Disintegration, 1886–1929* (London, 1992).

Asquith, (Emma Alice) Margaret ('Margot') (1864–1945), second wife of Herbert Henry *Asquith, active Liberal, and political hostess. The sixth daughter of wealthy ironmaster and Liberal MP Sir Charles Tennant, Margot Tennant married Asquith in May 1894 when he was home secretary. Privately educated and with an interest in social reform, she was part of the cross-party group of intellectuals known as the 'souls'. Her wealth and personal contacts enhanced her husband's political career, allowing him to concentrate on politics, but was also well known for strong opinions expressed in ways which may not have assisted her husband in negotiating the difficulties which he faced as prime minister and wartime leader from 1914. *JS*

Assheton, Ralph Cockayne (1901–77), Conservative politician, party organizer, banker, and landowner. An MP from 1934 to 1955, Assheton held a number of junior posts, 1936–43, before becoming financial secretary to the Treasury, 1943–4, and party chairman, 1944–6. A right-winger and an ineffective speaker, he unsuccessfully attempted to use the position to press his own policy views. He chaired the select committee on nationalized industries, 1951–3, and sat in the Church of England assembly, 1930–50. *NJC*

Association of British Chambers of Commerce. See British Chambers of Commerce, Association of.

Astor, Nancy Witcher (1879–1964), Conservative backbencher, social hostess, and Christian Scientist. Virginia-born, she married Waldorf Astor in 1905, and became the first woman MP to sit in parliament, representing Plymouth Sutton, 1919–45. Regarded as a personality rather than a serious politician, ministerial office was never achieved. With a quick wit she became a celebrated hostess in the family seat of Cliveden, Buckinghamshire, and her weekend gatherings of the Cliveden Set gathered notoriety in the late 1930s for influencing government policy to appease Hitler. *NJC*

A. Masters, *Nancy Astor: A Life* (London, 1981).

asylum, political. The right to asylum for refugees fleeing from religious or political persecution has traditionally been regarded as a hallmark of the tolerant attitude of British governments to diverse political and religious opinions. High-profiled groups in the past, such as the Protestant Huguenots fleeing the persecution of Louis XIV, and French royalists exiled by the French Revolution, contributed to a policy maintained during the 19th century of sheltering refugees from continental Europe, including at various times, Mazzini, Marx, Herzen, and Kropotkin. The first restrictions on the 'open door' policy came with the *Aliens Act, 1905, primarily directed at the immigration of poor Jews from Eastern Europe, although political refugees were specifically excepted from its restrictions. Further restrictions were placed on immigration as a result of the Great War, although Belgian and, later, refugees from Fascist and Nazi persecution were admitted in significant numbers. Since 1945, the issue of political asylum has become closely bound up with that of race and immigration control. Although the UK follows the 1951 UN Convention and Protocol relating to the status of refugees once lawfully resident, ensuring that they should receive treatment at least as favourable as the indigenous population, as the number of asylum seekers has grown, UK governments have sought to distinguish genuine political refugees from economic migrants. From approximately 4,000 asylum seekers annually in the late 1980s, the number had risen to 46,000 in 1998. Attempts in the 1993 Asylum and Immigration Appeals Act to reduce the number of asylum seekers admitted to Britain by restricting those allowed 'Exceptional Leave to Remain' have still left Britain with the second largest number of asylum seekers in Western Europe. In 1998 over 31,000 asylum decisions were made, of which 17 per cent were grants of asylum. In addition, as an emergency measure, the UK admitted for a period of twelve months over 4,000 people from Kosovo whom the UN classified as vulnerable. Nearly 15,000 appeals against removal were made in 1998 and growing concern about delays and the position of asylum seekers led to a new Immigration and Asylum Bill in 1999, providing for 'fast-track' processing of asylum seekers, a single comprehensive right of appeal, and a national system of support separate from the benefits system in kind and offering accommodation on a 'no choice' basis. The temperature of the asylum debate was raised considerably by violence and disturbances involving asylum seekers, at the principal ports of entry in Kent in 1999, leading to a policy of enforced dispersal. Political claims over 'bogus' asylum seekers and concern from pro-asylum groups to protect the rights of asylum seekers have kept the issue of political asylum in the forefront of political debate. *JS*

'at a stroke', phrase linked with Heath's alleged promise in 1970 to cut prices. The words 'at a stroke' appeared in a party briefing paper, rather than a Heath speech, and actually referred to slowing the rise in prices. Nonetheless, Heath appeared to have pledged to reduce them. *RJS*

Atholl, duchess of (1874–1960), Conservative politician and philanthropist. Having entered parliament for Kinross and West Perthshire in 1923, her political career was typified by support for humanitarian issues: Russian slave labour, conditions for Indian women, and Spanish refugees. She opposed Baldwin's India policy and championed the Spanish republicans, earning her the label 'the Red Duchess'. These views and her growing concern at the threat of fascism meant she fell out with her local party and in 1938 resigned her seat to fight it as an independent. She lost. *NJC*

S. Hetherington, *Katharine Atholl 1874–1960: Against the Tide* (Aberdeen, 1989).

Atkin, James Richard (1867–1944), judge. Appointed to the King's Bench division in 1913, he progressed to the Court of Appeal in 1919 and the House of Lords in 1928. A compassionate and progressive judge, he was concerned that the law provided ordinary people with rights. Lord Atkin's judgements are legal landmarks. *Donoghue* v. *Stevenson* (1932) is a foundation of the modern law of negligence. His dissent in *Liversidge* v. *Anderson* (1941) strongly influenced legal conceptions of individual liberty in the face of executive action. *CAM*

Atkinson, Frederick John (1919–), government economist. Fred Atkinson was chief economic adviser to the Treasury and head of the Government Economic Service, 1977–9. He had joined the Cabinet Office's economic section in 1949, and his career as an economic adviser had taken him through posts in the Treasury, Foreign Office, Department of Trade and Industry, and Department of Energy. Atkinson was one of the five (out of six) surviving former government chief economic advisers who signed the famous letter to *The Times* in 1981 from 364 economists criticizing the Thatcher government's policies. *KT*

Atlantic, battle of the. Not a conventional engagement as such, since it took place over the whole length of the Second World War, the battle of the Atlantic (as Churchill called it) in essence marked the quest by German submarines to sink Allied ships supplying Britain from the USA, and Allied attempts to thwart them. Germany missed its best chance to starve Britain into submission, through lacking sufficient U-boats in the critical early period, 1939–41. Thereafter, although submarine production increased substantially, the increasingly active intervention of the USA, the breaking of the U-boat cipher system in mid-1941, the outstripping of sinkings by new shipping construction by autumn 1942, the closing of the 'air-gap' by long-range American Liberator aircraft, and technological (especially radar) and tactical developments rendered Allied victory inevitable over time. *SM*

G. Hessler, *The U-Boat War in the Atlantic, 1939–1945* (London, 1989). | David Syrett, *Defeat of the U-Boats: The Battle of the Atlantic* (Columbia, SC, 1994).

Atlantic charter (1941), declaration of common aims for the post-war world, issued by Prime Minister Winston Churchill and US President Franklin D. Roosevelt at their first wartime meeting, at Placentia Bay, off Newfoundland, in August 1941. The chief outcome of that historic, propagandistic encounter, the Atlantic charter was an Anglo-American contract of a kind, a prelude to co-belligerency, but also an international appeal, a rallying cry, a calculated inspiration: a rhetorical blend of principle and puffery. One article abjures 'territorial changes that do not accord with the freely expressed wishes of the peoples concerned'. Another invokes 'the right of all people to choose the form of government under which they will live'. A reference to 'a wider and more permanent system of general security' foreshadows the *United Nations Organization. Such a declaration was essentially Roosevelt's idea: self-determination, economic liberalization, and democratic mobilization were all part of the 'New Deal' war. The British, bounced, were less enthusiastic; the Soviets, derisive or suspicious. Both tried to qualify its provisions in defence of their own commercial and territorial interests. For Churchill, a declaration of peace was a poor substitute for a declaration of war, though he was glad enough of the Anglo-American association. To the Soviet ambassador in London, it sounded as if 'England and the USA fancied themselves as Almighty God, with a mission to judge the remainder of the sinful world, including my own country'. Yet the Atlantic charter earned its passage. A certain scepticism notwithstanding, it became a beacon of hope, and a benchmark of the post-war settlement. *AD*

Douglas Brinkley and David Facey-Crowther (eds.), *The Atlantic Charter* (New York, 1993). | Theodore A. Wilson, *The First Summit* (Lawrence, Kan., 1991).

atom bomb. See nuclear weapons.

Attack on Inflation, The (1975), white paper introduced when the inflation rate had soared to 26 per cent, following the removal of statutory wage controls in July 1974. It aimed to reduce the rate to under 10 per cent within eighteen months. Wage demands soared, prompting Jack *Jones of the Transport and General Workers' Union to call for capped flat-rate increases in May 1975. The measures introduced on 1 August 1975 involved a limit of £6 a week on all pay increases, and no rises at all for anyone on more than £8,500 per year. In the following year the rate of pay increase fell by more than half and the inflation rate declined to 12.9 per cent. *PPC*

Attlee, Clement Richard (1883–1967), prime minister and Labour leader. Attlee headed the first Labour government in power, not just in office, after the landslide 1945 election. He was an easy person to underestimate: a modest man 'who had much to be modest about' (as his rival Churchill quipped). In fact, his opponents' failure to perceive his formidable qualities helped him rise to the top. Laconic and diffident, Clem Attlee was also strong-minded and decisive, while his ability to manage men deemed superior to him was his greatest political gift.

Born in Putney, London, his father was a solicitor, and after Haileybury and Oxford he was called to the Bar in 1906, seemingly set to lead the life of an ordinary middle-class barrister. His move into Labour politics came via adult education, local government, and the Fabian Society. Secretary of Toynbee Hall, a social settlement house in London's East End, in 1910 he became lecturer at the trade-union Ruskin College, Oxford, in 1911 a lecturer and in 1913–23 a tutor at the influential LSE, which the Fabians Sidney and Beatrice Webb had helped found. Here he worked under William Beveridge, whose 1942 report was to provide the basis for the welfare state of social security and full employment Attlee's government later created after 1945. Attlee served with the Lancashire Regiment and the Tank Corps in 1914–18 and, though his role was later enhanced to make it seem more impressive, he did have 'a good war', was wounded at Gallipoli, and ended as a major in France. He entered politics on demobilization, becoming the first Labour mayor of Stepney in 1919–20. Long a Fabian, member of the National Union of Clerks and the Independent Labour Party (ILP), he was MP for Limehouse, 1922–50, and for West Walthamstow, 1950–5. He married Helen Violet Millar in 1922 (they had three daughters and a son), and took a big step upward the same year when he became parliamentary private secretary to Ramsay MacDonald. Under-secretary for war in Labour's first government in 1924, MacDonald made him chancellor of the duchy of Lancaster (succeeding Oswald Mosley) in 1929 and then postmaster general in 1930–1. That year, when MacDonald formed a *National Government in the depths of the Depression, hopelessly splitting his party, Attlee remained loyal and was re-elected as one of the Labour rump of 46 MPs. Following this debacle MPs, the ILP, constituency parties, and unions embarked on a bitter struggle to control the party. When Ernest Bevin used union power to help unseat the pacifist George Lansbury as leader, Attlee succeeded him in 1935, but Bevin and the unions never managed to control Attlee.

His principal task was to restore the morale of a defeated and disillusioned party, and eventually lead it back from the electoral wilderness, but there was hardly any chance that Labour would have won the election forestalled by the outbreak of war in 1939. Churchill's wartime coalition after 1940 changed all that. As deputy prime minister, Attlee, the complete opposite of his towering, grandiloquent boss, was keen on the kind of detail Churchill often impatiently brushed aside in his tireless quest for victory. Supported by key Labour men such as Bevin in the war cabinet, Attlee himself became an increasingly credible future prime minister as Labour at last became electable as a party. The war economy's acceptance of Keynesian methods, and the great attention given to post-war reconstruction based on the ideas of J. M. Keynes and Beveridge (ironically both former Liberals), helped all this, and partly explains Labour's huge and largely unforeseen victory at the polls when war in Europe ended in June 1945. With 393 seats, Labour had a majority of 180 over the Conservatives.

Prime Minister

Despite this, there was an abortive attempt to unseat Attlee and make Bevin or Herbert Morrison leader. Brushing this attempted coup aside, Attlee supervised one of the great periods of reform in British history, made all the more remarkable by the fact that the country was bankrupt, the world economy destroyed, and the terms of trade harsh. Yet Attlee's government brought public ownership, full employment, social security, free health care, wider educational opportunities, and much else, not only within this adverse economic context but also against a backdrop of Cold War, independence for India and Palestine, and the beginnings of decolonization. Throughout, he had to control a cabinet of contending political heavyweights, including Bevin, Aneurin Bevan, Stafford Cripps, Hugh Dalton, and Herbert Morrison. Severe shortages of fuel and other crucial raw materials meant deflation and further extension of unpopular rationing and controls in the 1947 sterling crisis. In 1949 the pound was devalued by about 30 per cent. Despite all this, his government lost no by-elections, and so was unprepared for the heavy losses suffered at the polls in February 1950. With its majority reduced to six, and further bereft by the deaths of Bevin and Cripps, Attlee's second administration faced further economic problems and crisis in the Korean war, during which he flew to the USA to secure President Truman's undertaking not to use the atomic bomb. Meantime, he embarked upon a £4.6 billion rearmament programme, partly paid for by health service cuts of £23 million. This was a defining moment. Charges for prescriptions and spectacles, trivial in themselves, were seen by socialists as a betrayal of principle, putting Cold War priorities before welfare. Bevan and Harold Wilson resigned, though for a decade the trade-union block vote enabled the party's right-wing leadership to defeat the Bevanite left. For a generation, Labour backed the USA more or less uncritically throughout the Cold War. Attlee's government staggered on until October 1951 when, despite winning more votes than the Conservatives, Labour won less seats and so lost power.

Elder Statesman

In opposition, Attlee outstayed his welcome. Instead of retiring at 68, he hung on, increasingly hostile and suspicious of possible successors like Bevan, Morrison (whom he hated for opposing him in 1935), and Hugh Gaitskell, only to lead his party to bigger election defeat in 1955. This failure to retire after 1951 exacerbated bitter party infighting over German rearmament and public ownership (which Attlee had long championed, but which was becoming unpopular), giving Gaitskell a tougher time when he succeeded him in 1955. When Attlee did step down in 1955 he became Earl Attlee (having earlier in his career said that 'Lord Love-a-duck of Limehouse' would be more appropriate) and died in 1967 aged 84, an increasingly lonely and forgotten man. Attlee's great achievement now looks clearer. It was to make Labour the Tories' chief opponent in British politics, prove that it could govern, and above all to create what later became known as 'the post-war settlement', or in Paul *Addison's phrase, 'Attlee's consensus'. Until the advent of Margaret Thatcher as prime minister in 1979, no Conservative government, however big its majority, tried to reverse the sweeping changes Attlee's government had made in 1945–51. His legacy stands comparison with that of any British prime minister of the century. Charming anecdotes abound about the laconic Attlee, often relying on his lack of ego for their point, although ego was not really something he lacked. He loved cricket and called the tape machine in 10 Downing Street 'my cricket machine' because it brought him the latest scores. His wife Violet (rumoured to vote Tory) drove him everywhere, but frequently went to the cinema while he made speeches. Of himself he wrote epigrammatically, 'Few thought he was even a starter | There were many who thought themselves smarter | But he ended PM | CH and OM | An earl and a knight of the garter.' *PRGR*

TREVOR BURRIDGE, *Clement Attlee: A Political Biography* (London, 1985). | KENNETH HARRIS, *Attlee* (London, 1982). | KENNETH O. MORGAN, *Labour in Power, 1945–1951* (London, 1984). | ROBERT PEARCE, *Attlee* (London, 1997).

Audit Commission (1983–). This has fifteen government-appointed members and took over the audit of local authorities in England and Wales from the District Audit Service which it absorbed. It also regulates local authority audits by private accountancy companies. Unlike the previous system, the commission is not only concerned with seeing that finances are being conducted legally but also that authorities are following the 'three Es': economy, efficiency, and effectiveness as outlined in its 1984 handbook. About half its time is spent on value-for-money work and the commission sees its task as raising awareness in local government of such concerns. In addition it has monitored local authority responses to initiatives such as competitive tendering for services. Aided by self-promotion, the Audit Commission has had a high profile. It has adopted an independent, often controversial approach to issues. In 1984 it strongly criticized the government's failure at trying to combine needs assessment and expenditure control leading to rising expenditure and uncertainty in local government which made planning difficult. A 1991 report revealed the failure of local authorities to respond effectively to European Community initiatives and in 1998 it reported on widespread fraud in local authorities. *KMT*

Audit of War, The. Correlli Barnett's *The Audit of War* (1986) was adopted by the Thatcherite right to lend historical justification to criticisms of the debilitating effect of the welfare state. Barnett argued that the Second World War had demonstrated the weakness of British industry and that policy makers, instead of addressing the problem immediately after the war, had instead squandered resources on welfare. Academic and other critics argued that Barnett had not demonstrated that welfare growth caused inefficiency. *JAT*

Auxiliary Division, Royal Irish Constabulary. See ROYAL IRISH CONSTABULARY, AUXILIARY DIVISION.

Avon, 1st earl of. See EDEN, ANTHONY.

'back to basics', policy aspiration used by John Major at Conservative conference, intended with no reference to sexual conduct. The phrase was taken by evidentially challenged commentators as a call to virtue. The subsequent sexual embarrassment (*sleaze) of several Tories was celebrated with cries of 'back to basics', a soundbite which did Conservatives serious damage. *EP*

Bacon, Alice (1911–93), Labour politician. Bacon was one of the most prominent female members of the post-war Labour Party. A party loyalist, she became the first female chair of the party, 1950–1. Representing the constituencies of Leeds North, 1945–55, and Leeds South-East, 1955–70, she served in government as junior minister for home affairs, 1964–7, and for education and science, 1967–70. A long-serving member of Labour's NEC, 1941–70, and a pro-European, she was a member of the consultative assembly of the Council of Europe, 1950–3. Bacon was made a life peer in 1970. *DMM*

Baghdad pact (1955). This regional security organization grew out of the mutual cooperation pact signed between Turkey and Iraq in Baghdad in February 1955. Britain, looking for arrangements that would help preserve its bases in Iraq, acceded to the pact in April, followed by Pakistan and Iran later in the year. Efforts to persuade Egypt and Jordan to join failed, and the pact intensified Nasser's hostility to Britain's continuing imperial presence in the Middle East, setting the stage for the Suez crisis. *MCJ*

Baird, John Lawrence (1874–1941), Conservative politician, party organizer, and governor-general of Australia 1925–30. An MP, 1910–25, Baird joined the Unionist Social Reform Committee and was a junior minister, 1919–24. Created Viscount Stonehaven, he returned from Australia to replace Neville Chamberlain as Conservative Party chairman, marking a return to the pre-1930 practice of appointing chairmen of non-cabinet status. From 1931 to 1936 he resisted moves formally to merge the parties of the National Government. There was a general perception of his second-rateness which Stonehaven reinforced by his tactlessness. *NJC*

Baker, Kenneth Wilfred (1934–), Conservative politician, organizer, and anthologist. Baker rose with Heath, over-adjusted to Thatcher, becoming a personal loyalist, and was rejected by Major. Ascending despite his (not entirely) loyal address speech, 1979, deploying technology expertise, Baker reached cabinet in 1986 during the struggle with the Greater London Council after drawing in debate with Ken Livingstone, but survived advocating the disastrous *poll tax—he suggested gradualism, 'dual running'. An interventionist education secretary, he was immortalized through teacher-release 'Baker days'. As home secretary, Baker improved prison conditions but a 'savage dogs' panic showed him fatally anti-dog in rushing to legislation. *EP*

Kenneth Baker, *The Turbulent Years: My Life in Politics* (London, 1993).

balance of payments, measurement of the flow of money in and out of a country, divided into the current account and the capital account. The current account includes visible *trade (imports and exports) and 'invisible payments', the latter including payments and receipts of royalties, interest, profits, insurance, transport, and tourism. The capital account measures outward and inward movements of short- and long-term investment. Investment overseas appears as a negative, while overseas borrowing generates a positive accounting. In equilibrium, the current account plus the capital account add up to zero: a surplus on the capital account implies a deficit on the current account and vice versa. Another way of viewing equilibrium is that expenditure equals revenue.

In theory, in a freely floating exchange rate regime, the exchange rate will adjust to keep the balance of payments in equilibrium. For example, if domestic goods are uncompetitive compared to foreign goods, demand for the country's currency will decline in the foreign exchange market and the exchange rate will depreciate until domestic prices are in line with foreign prices. When exchange rates are fixed, however, there are usually surpluses and deficits in the balance of payments. If a country's receipts are greater than their outflows, the balance of payments is said to be in surplus and the foreign exchange reserves increase. Conversely, if total outflows are greater than receipts, the foreign exchange reserves decline. In the 20th century, exchange rates have usually been inflexible and the balance of payments has attracted considerable political attention since a persistent deficit will eventually exhaust the nation's foreign exchange reserves. A persistent surplus will often generate inflation. Balance of payments deficits were an especially acute political problem from the Second World War until the advent of *North Sea oil in the 1980s.

The balance of payments is sometimes judged to be a constraint on domestic economic policy when exchange rates are inflexible. Macroeconomic policies aimed at expanding the domestic economy are often associated with inflation in the short term, which will erode the competitiveness of exports. Low interest rates designed to increase economic growth may also generate an outflow on the capital account. These two by-products of expansionary policy may generate a balance of payments deficit which is not sustainable in the longer term. In this case, the government will be unable to pursue expansionary policies without avoiding a balance of payments deficit if the fixed exchange rate is to be maintained. *CRS*

balance of trade, measurement of the net flows of goods in and out of a country. The balance of trade is calculated by the difference between total exports of goods and total imports. The balance of trade is in deficit when purchases abroad (imports) exceed sales of domestic products in international markets (exports). Conversely, the balance of trade is in surplus when exports exceed imports. The balance of trade forms part of the current account of the *balance of payments. *CRS*

Balcarres, Lord (1871–1940), Conservative politician and public servant. Balcarres looked every inch the bluff Lancashire aristocrat and sat in the Commons for his county from 1895, an effective chief whip from 1911 until he succeeded his father as earl of Crawford in 1913. In fact, he did not smoke, drink, or ride, he nurtured the family's magnificent private library, had a passion for the music of Wagner, and strove lifelong to preserve the nation's artistic treasures. His insightful diary tells much of what we know of the political men of his time. *RJQA*

John Vincent (ed.), *The Crawford Papers: The Journals of David Lindsay, Twenty-Seventh Earl of Crawford and Tenth Earl of Balcarres, 1871–1940, during the Years 1892 to 1940* (Manchester, 1984).

Baldwin, Peter Robert (1922–), civil servant. Baldwin served with the Foreign Office, 1942–5, and the General Register Office, 1948–54, before moving to the Treasury in 1954, where he was to spend the bulk of his Whitehall career. He was principal private secretary to the chancellor of the exchequer, James Callaghan, 1996–8, and an under-secretary and then deputy secretary (1972–6) dealing with public expenditure planning. He was briefly second permanent secretary at the Department of the Environment (1976) before becoming permanent secretary at the Department of Transport, 1976–82. *KT*

Baldwin, Stanley (1867–1947), Conservative politician and three times prime minister. The dominant political figure of the inter-war years, he remains something of an enigma. Despite leading his party for fourteen years, he found himself unable to impose his vision upon party policy but succeeded in capturing and dominating the political mood of the nation. He proved himself to be an articulate politician who, through a mastery of the wireless broadcast and the cinema newsreel, ensured that he was the first prime minister to be familiar in word, voice, and gesture to the electorate. His speeches invoked a sense of 'Englishness', provincialism, and ordinariness that appealed to the nostalgia of an increasingly urban electorate. After an early period in local politics, the family's Worcestershire iron business, and farming, he entered national politics when he was returned unopposed in the 1908 Bewdley by-election—a seat his father had held since 1892. Although inconspicuous in his early parliamentary years, his selection as parliamentary private secretary to party leader Law in 1916 began a steady, almost rapid, rise to the top. As president of the Board of Trade he clashed with Lloyd George, the coalition prime minister, over tariff reform. This encouraged him to speak passionately against the Conservatives maintaining the coalition at the 1922 *Carlton Club meeting. Law rewarded Baldwin with the Treasury and, whilst not very successful, this gained Baldwin vital press attention.

Prime Minister

In May 1923 Baldwin emerged as party leader over Curzon and succeeded in retaining the leadership until his decision to retire in May 1937. However, his opening spell as prime minister (only until January 1924) ended ignominiously when he called an unnecessary election over tariff reform and lost. The 1924 minority Labour government did not survive long and Baldwin returned to Number Ten in November. Of the five key features of Baldwin's 1924–9 ministry, the return to the gold standard, the Locarno treaty, the 1926 *General Strike, the 1926 imperial conference which led to the Statute of Westminster, and the Ministry of Health reforms of local government combined with an extension of social services, he was only centrally involved in one: the General Strike. This proved the high point of his second ministry. Motivated by his interest in industrial relations, owing to his own business experiences and his desire to conciliate, Baldwin was at the fore in rallying party and middle-class opinion against the strike. He skilfully utilized the radio, with the tacit assistance of John Reith, director-general of the BBC, to appeal to the sensibilities of the electorate, and illustrated a determination to win, but without provoking further confrontation. However, when the strike collapsed after nine days, Baldwin found it difficult to restrain the more reactionary voices in his party keen to impose retributive legislation. His position was weakened by defeat in the 1929 election, a defeat widely blamed upon Baldwin and his party chairman Davidson. In opposition Baldwin found himself under attack from right-wingers favouring tariffs and those opposed to Indian self-government. He was determined to maintain the cross-party cooperation over India, but was ill-suited to opposition because of his unwillingness to attack the Labour Party. The forces of the right were being marshalled by the combined media empires of Beaverbrook and Rothermere and their Empire Crusade campaign, and by Churchill, all intent upon removing Baldwin from the leadership. The internecine party warfare took its toll and, when combined with his own apathy, gave rise to serious thought about resignation. But the Conservative Party then possessed no formal mechanism for removing an incumbent leader, and an underlying stubborn streak in Baldwin obliged him to confront his critics at party rallies where he won resounding votes of confidence.

National Government

The politico-economic crisis of 1931 led in August to the creation of the *National Government. Baldwin was initially unhappy with the prospect of a coalition, but recognized that it offered an opportunity to exclude Lloyd George and pursue his preference for centralist politics. He was lord president from 1931 under the ex-Labour leader Ramsay MacDonald, a relationship that suited Baldwin for his subordinate position enabled him to deflect the government's critics but leave the substance of policy to others. From Baldwin's perspective the problem of India and the emergence of Nazi Germany were to dominate his remaining political years. Open warfare amongst Conservatives over the 1935 Government of India Act, led from the backbenches by Winston Churchill, once again threatened his leadership and the premiership to which he reverted in June 1935, but again Baldwin hung on and won in the end. The general election of November 1935 was intended as a new start, both in renewed party unity and in securing a mandate for rearmament. Baldwin had famously declared in 1932 that 'the bomber will always get through'; but on matters of substance he remained willing to leave the specifics to others, especially the chancellor, Neville Chamberlain. However, political controversy soon swamped his third administration, as the *Hoare-Laval pact (December 1935) and the German remilitarization of the Rhineland (March 1936) divided his party once more, called into question his abilities as leader, and exposed the vulnerability of his government to backbench critics. From 1935, Baldwin was thinking of retirement, and Chamberlain as his anointed successor was certainly keen for that event, but 1936's long *abdication crisis once more delayed matters. Ultimately it proved one of Baldwin's defining moments, as he successfully stage-managed the crisis and demonstrated shrewd political judgement. In May 1937 he retired to the Lords as Earl Baldwin of Bewdley, mentally and physically exhausted, but receiving as a retirement present a book of congratulatory telegrams from over 500 Conservative associations.

Although his active political career ended on that high note, the descent into war in 1938–9 and early British military failures in 1940 ensured that Baldwin was widely accused of failing to prepare Britain adequately for war. The longevity of Baldwin's leadership rested upon a reputation always stronger in the country than in his own party, and much of his value as leader lay in his ability to attract 'middle opinion' to the Conservatives, as no potential successor could be confident of doing. This was, though, also his weakness, since he failed to inspire awe amongst colleagues, and in private affected too much modesty. His leadership was typified by periods of impulsive, emotional, and exhausting spurts of nervous activity followed by prolonged periods of lethargy as he recouped his strength. After a nadir of obloquy in the 1950s, Baldwin's reputation began to recover as more favourable accounts of his career were written from the late 1960s, celebrating his role as a moderate who had helped to steer Britain through the constitutional crises of 1926, 1931, and 1926. *NJC*

Keith Middlemas and John Barnes, *Baldwin: A Biography* (London, 1969). | Sian Nicholas, 'The Construction of a National Identity: Stanley Baldwin, "Englishness" and the Mass Media in Inter-War Britain', in M. Francis and I. Zweiniger-Bargielowska (eds.), *The Conservatives and British Society, 1880–1990* (Cardiff, 1996). | Philip Williamson, *Stanley Baldwin* (Cambridge, 1999).

Balfour, Arthur James (1848–1930), Conservative politician and prime minister. As much as any person in British history, Balfour was bred to the premiership. The scion of a wealthy Scottish family whose prosperity was rooted in the India trade, his father died when Balfour was only 7. Greater influences were his Cecil relations: his mother, Lady Blanche, and her brother, Robert, 3rd marquess of *Salisbury and three times prime minister. His mother, a remarkable woman, encouraged her eight children to be intellectually curious, to take their religion seriously, and to understand that their birthright was at once a great gift and a grave responsibility. Balfour's uncle Robert agreed and added that politics was the natural sphere for a young man with Cecil blood in his veins.

Neither at Eton nor Cambridge did Balfour reveal the full power of his intellect, though at university, partly through the influence of the young dons Henry Sidgwick and John Strutt, he was drawn to both philosophy and science. Reconciling these great disciplines fascinated him, and a full political life did not prevent him from publishing such well-known works as *A Defence of Philosophic Doubt* (1879) and *Foundations of Belief* (1895). Interestingly, Sidgwick and Strutt married Balfour's sisters, and throughout his long life, no intellectual companionship inspired him as did the closed circle of his brilliant family and closest friends, gathered more often than not at the Scottish family seat, Whittingehame House. When the time came to choose an occupation, it was the advice of his admired uncle Salisbury that prevailed.

Rising Star

As his uncle's protégé in 1874 Balfour entered parliament, where he was at first better known for his wealth, hospitality, and the stylish figure he cut than for his intervention in House business. His prominent membership in London's most brilliant social circles certainly added to this image of the gilded dilettante. Only after his party went into opposition in 1880 did he begin to attract notice as a loose affiliate of Lord Randolph Churchill's 'Fourth Party' clique, which mercilessly and at every turn attacked the Liberal government and the feeble Tory leadership. In these years he dedicated himself to systematic study of the technique of parliamentary debate, a *métier* which he absolutely mastered. Balfour was given junior office in Salisbury's brief 1885 administration and, after Gladstone's failure to pass his Home Rule Bill in the following year, in his uncle's second government as the first ever Scottish secretary. His skilful handling of the Highland agrarian disturbances of the period proved his mettle, and in 1887 he accepted the greater challenge of the Irish chief secretaryship. For the next four years Balfour did battle with the Parnellite 'plan of campaign' against the agricultural landlords, combining a relentless policy toward lawbreakers with a series of social reforms to alleviate economic hardships, particularly the old evil of absentee landlordism. His successful tenure as Irish secretary wiped away memories of the languid young aristocrat, as he came to be seen as a courageous and innovative administrator, to the Irish Nationalists 'Bloody Balfour', and formidable front-bench debater. In 1891 he became leader of the Commons and first lord of the Treasury. He shone always in debate, but the regular mundane tasks of party management he found excruciatingly tiresome, and this distaste he never overcame. After the Liberal interlude of 1892–5, he returned as leader during the trying years of the Boer war, and this unhappy conflict made a great impression on his mind. For the remainder of his long career, he gave much of his attention to questions of national security and military preparedness.

Hesitant Leader

In 1902 Salisbury retired, and few questioned Balfour's right to the premiership. The inheritance was a troubled one, including unsolved economic woes and an army seemingly resistant to desperately needed reform. There were also successes: under Admiral Sir John Fisher the navy began a technological renaissance, Balfour himself created the Committee of Imperial Defence (CID), and the 1904 French *Entente Cordiale was concluded. Balfour's greatest difficulty came with the *tariff reform campaign begun in 1903 by colonial secretary Joseph Chamberlain. This protectionist movement reunited the factious Liberals, divided Balfour's own followers, and doomed his administration. He clung to power until December 1905, and led his party to disastrous electoral defeat a month later. In opposition he led a much-reduced party, profoundly divided between pro- and anti-tariff factions, and his efforts to reconcile their differences only antagonized both sides. His policy of destroying government legislation (including the 1909 budget) using the overwhelming Conservative majority in the Lords ultimately backfired, leading to an extended constitutional crisis, two election defeats in 1910, and the *Parliament Act, 1911, which broke for ever the power of the upper house. With his authority in tatters, he finally resigned the leadership in late 1911.

Elder Statesman

Over the three years of peace which remained, politics became consumed with the Irish question, and Balfour played a relatively small part in deciding the path his party followed. The Great War brought Balfour new political life. As father of the CID he regularly attended Asquith's war council, and when the first wartime coalition government was formed in May 1915, he became first lord of the Admiralty. In December 1916, he joined his fellow Tories in displacing Asquith in favour of another coalition under Lloyd George. Balfour now accepted the Foreign Office, an office which he found more congenial than the Admiralty had been. After America entered the war in early 1917, he conducted a triumphant tour of the USA and in the same year issued the *Balfour declaration which affirmed the right of the Jewish people to a national homeland (he had long been sympathetic to Zionism). As foreign secretary, he attended the *Paris peace conference, though his position was much diminished once the 'Big Four' heads of government took all major decisions into their own hands. The peace, though he loyally defended it, was not of his making, and in October 1919 he gladly embraced the role of elder statesman by handing the Foreign Office to Curzon and becoming lord president instead.

Though over 70, Balfour remained a great presence in public life, representing Britain at the Washington naval conference of 1921, and at the assembly of the League of Nations in Geneva. He remained loyal to Lloyd George and stood by him through the revolt of the Conservative backbenchers at the Carlton Club meeting. The rank and file wanted a Conservative government and prime minister, Law; and Balfour and his fellow coalition loyalists consequently found themselves in the political wilderness. Nonetheless, Balfour—by this time honoured with an earldom, the Garter, and the Order of Merit—would once again reconcile with his party, celebrating his eightieth birthday in office as lord president in Baldwin's second government. He helped to frame the constitutional forward path for the Commonwealth by developing the ideas later enshrined in the Statute of Westminster.

Among prime ministers, Balfour was the last of the brilliant aristocratic amateurs, to whom politics was a duty and not a profession. The necessary and mundane political tasks which fall to a modern party leader repelled him, and he did not do them well. Perhaps it was because he could be truly comfortable only among his own brilliant kind. This, and his natural posture of amused scepticism to worldly things, and his irresistible inclination to consider all sides of all questions were misread by many as snobbery, coldness, and irresolution. In fact they were the visible products of his insensitivity to ordinariness, his restless intellectual energy, and his absolute commitment to seeking what truth might be made to reveal itself. *RJQA*

Blanche Dugdale, *Arthur James Balfour*, 2 vols. (London, 1936). | Max Egremont, *Balfour: A Life of Arthur James Balfour* (London, 1980). | Ruddock F. Mackay, *Balfour: Intellectual Statesman* (Oxford, 1985). | Sidney Zebel, *Balfour: A Political Biography* (Cambridge, 1973).

Balfour committee on industry and trade (1924–9), set up under the chairmanship of the industrialist Sir Arthur Balfour to examine the reasons for Britain's sluggish economic performance after the Great War. It published reports covering such areas as overseas markets and industrial relations, as well as surveys of individual sectors such as textiles. In a final report in 1929 the committee argued that the most urgent need was for rationalization of the staple industries and for the losses in employment inevitable in this process to be made good by continued development of newer industries. It argued that rigidities in the economic system were preventing such rationalization from taking place through the normal mechanism of the market and, therefore, that industries such as cotton, coal, and steel must take active steps to rationalize themselves. As regards new industries, the committee argued for a greater awareness of the value of science and technology among managers. *WF*

Balfour declaration (1917), British diplomatic statement. On 2 November 1917 Arthur *Balfour, the British foreign secretary, wrote to Lord Rothschild, the leader of the British Zionists, explaining that the British government viewed 'with favour the establishment in *Palestine of a National Home for the Jewish people'. The declaration was motivated by a mixture of considerations, but mainly by wartime expediency and imperial ambition. Britain may have hoped to encourage world Jewish opinion, particularly in revolutionary Russia and in the USA, to greater enthusiasm for the Allied cause. Dr Chaim Weizmann, a chemist whose wartime work on acetone made him known to Prime Minister David Lloyd George, was a powerful advocate of Zionism. But Britain wished mainly to pre-empt the Germans and to safeguard its imperial ambitions in the undefeated Ottoman Empire, believing that a Zionist presence in Palestine was more likely to lead to British rather than French post-war protection of the area, and would help to undo any damage done by the 1916 Sykes-Picot agreement which had left Palestine's future unresolved. There were reservations. Earlier agreements between Sir Henry McMahon, Egyptian high commissioner, and Hussein, the sharif of Mecca, suggested that Palestine might be the 'twice promised land'. Edwin Montagu, secretary of state for India, himself a Jew, wished to ensure that Jews who had become assimilated in other states would not lose their rights. Curzon, lord president of the council, insisted that the Jewish national home should not prejudice the rights of other communities in Palestine, but this proved illusory. The 1922 League of Nations mandate for Palestine charged Britain with implementing the declaration. Its terms provoked severe riots and encouraged nationalism amongst the 700,000–strong Arab population which feared that Jewish immigration would overwhelm it. *AS*

Isaiah Friedman, *The Question of Palestine 1914–1918* (London, 1973). | Mark Levene, 'The Balfour Declaration: A Case of Mistaken Identity', *English Historical Review* (Jan. 1992).

Balfour Education Act. See Education Act, 1902.

Balfour of Burleigh committee (1916–18), a departmental committee of inquiry into post-war economic policy, emblematic of the impact of the Great War on economic thinking. The group of industrialists and other experts under Gerald Balfour (Arthur Balfour's cousin, and a former president of the Board of Trade) was set up after the signing of the *Paris resolutions. It recommended protection, with specific discrimination against enemy countries, and in its final report recommended the extension of some wartime state controls on industry into peacetime. It also favoured 'modernization', by which it meant larger productive units, vertical integration, and collective export marketing: the agenda of the protectionist heavy industrialists of the *Federation of British Industries. *JAT*

Balfour of Burleigh committee (1941–4). This committee investigated the economic problems facing upland sheep farmers in Scotland, Earl de la Warr chairing its counterpart for England and Wales. The formation of these committees marked a major turning point in the government's policy for the uplands in that it was the first official recognition that their problems were fundamentally different from those prevailing in the more prosperous lowlands. Its report, published in 1944, advocated an ordered programme of relatively high capital investment, stressing the need for a viable industry based on enterprises of a minimum economic size. In the case of single-family holdings, this was envisaged to be approximately 500 breeding ewes, 20 breeding cows, and ancillary enterprises, but farms of this type were significantly larger than the majority of holdings in the uplands. Its recommendations did not fully address the main underlying problem of how such a fundamental rationalization of the plethora of small units could be achieved in practice. The Scottish committee report was much more comprehensive than its counterpart for England and Wales but, together, they formed the basis of the Hill Farming Act introduced in 1946, which remained the cornerstone of the government's policy for hill farming until Britain's entry into the European Community. *JFM*

Report of the Committee on Hill Sheep Farming in Scotland (Cmd 6494, London, 1944). | J. F. Martin, *The Development of Modern Agriculture* (London, 2000).

Ball, Joseph **(1885–1961)**, Conservative organizer. War and post-war service with MI5 (possibly including involvement in politics through the *Zinoviev letter) brought him to the attention of politicians and he became Conservative director of publicity in 1927, soon placing a spy in Labour's printing works, and director of the *Conservative Research Department from 1930. Close to Neville Chamberlain, Ball was an important backstairs fixer in the politics of the 1930s. Characteristically, he burned all his papers shortly before his death. *JAR*

Balniel, Lord **(1927–)**, Conservative politician. After a spell in the Conservative Research Department, Robin Balniel won Hertford for the Tories in 1955, aged only 28. He became an opposition spokesman on foreign affairs in 1965 and principal spokesman on social security in 1967. Heath appointed him minister of state for defence in 1970 and for foreign and Commonwealth relations in 1972. Balniel lost his seat in October 1974 but succeeded his father as 12th earl of Crawford and Balcarres in 1975. *RJS*

Balogh, Thomas **(1905–85)**, Hungarian-born economist who fled to Britain in 1930, serving as a prominent member of Labour's economic and finance committee after 1943. In 1964–7 he was economic adviser to the Labour cabinet and from 1968, consultant to the prime minister. There the mercurial Balogh attracted the hostility of the press, ministers, and civil servants, and it has been suggested that he was largely excluded from policy making. He was, however, particularly associated with the development of *North Sea oil and gas, later serving as minister of state at the Department of Energy in 1974–5, and then as deputy chairman of the British National Oil Corporation, 1976–8. *PPC*

Bancroft, Ian Powell **(1922–96)**, civil servant. Bancroft entered the Treasury in 1947, serving as private secretary to three chancellors (Butler, Maudling, and Callaghan). In 1968 he moved to the Civil Service Department (CSD), heading the machinery of government division, and then played an important role in welding together the new giant Department of the Environment (DoE). After a spell as second permanent secretary at the CSD, 1973–5, he became the DoE's permanent secretary, 1975–7. His time as permanent secretary of CSD and head of the home civil service, 1978–81, was overshadowed by Thatcher's determination after 1979 drastically to cut the size of the civil service and improve its efficiency. Bancroft was a casualty of Thatcher's impatience with 'establishment' institutions and the traditional mandarin caste, and on a personal level he never really hit it off with her. Her decision to abolish the CSD in 1981 involved his early retirement. *KT*

Banham, John **(1940–)**. After a career which included fourteen years at McKinsey & Co., Banham entered public service as head of the Audit Commission, 1983–7, then becoming director-general of the CBI, 1987–92. He tried to move the CBI away from being a reactive industry lobby towards a more proactive and wider role. However, these efforts were overtaken by the onset of a recession which led to heightened tensions between the CBI and government. *WG*

bankers' diplomacy. This emerged in the 1920s when leading commercial bankers became heavily committed in both financing reconstruction and as government advisers on a range of issues, including *reparations, that extended beyond the financial sphere. Close cooperation between Morgan Grenfell & Co. in London and J. P. Morgan & Co. in New York, for example, underpinned the extension of commercial credits to Germany in the Dawes plan and *central bank diplomacy to reconstruct the gold standard. *PC*

'bankers' ramp' (1931), phrase invented during the August 1931 economic crisis by the editors of the *Daily Herald*. It implied that British and American bankers were acting politically in seeking to destroy MacDonald's Labour government by demanding cuts in unemployment benefit. It encouraged cabinet ministers to question the banks' advice. *NJC*

Bank for International Settlements (BIS), established in Basle, Switzerland, on 27 February 1930. It began operations in May and was designed to promote cooperation among central banks and to provide facilities for international financial operations. It acts as agent for international financial settlements and is a regular meeting place for governors of central banks. It also collects statistical data for the *G10 group. As the 'central bankers' banker' it accepts deposits and offers credits to central banks. *CRS*

Bank of England, central banking institution for the UK. The Bank of England was founded in 1694 as (then) the only joint-stock bank in England, and as the government's bank. There was no conception at that time of central banking, which had to wait until the late 19th century. But the function of the Bank was being scrutinized intensely, especially during the Napoleonic wars, and it began then to be appreciated that it had a central role to play in the monetary system. Quite what this role was became clearer in the course of the 19th century. After the 1844 Bank Charter Act, the Bank was constrained by a rigid gold standard rule; that is, apart from a fixed note issue, it could only issue new notes if they were backed with new holdings of gold. The Bank was still a private company and discussion continued on the responsibility it owed to its shareholders as against its wider public responsibility. By the late 19th century that was resolved, and the Bank accepted its role as manager of the monetary system. It had evolved as a 'lender of last resort' (sometimes seen as synonymous with central banking) and, coming to the rescue of the financial system in a liquidity squeeze and working alongside an increasingly prudent banking system, it produced remarkable financial stability.

The Great War changed all this: the gold standard was abandoned, the Bank's considerable independence was surrendered, and, following the war, difficult issues of debt and reparations meant the international monetary system was in disarray. The Bank, under its governor Montagu Norman (1920–44), played a major part in attempting to resolve the international issues and the domestic ramifications. Norman was a typical banker and has been criticized for not seeing a connection between interest rate-setting to defend the currency and activity in the real economy, but he took a number of initiatives to improve the public perception of banks (and the Bank particularly) in relation to financing industry. Although its independence was restored in principle after the war, by the 1930s it was becoming clear that the Bank had to respond to the wishes of the Treasury. Following the Great Depression of 1929–32, around the world banks and central banks were criticized for mismanaging monetary affairs.

In the Second World War central bank independence was again lost, while the Bank of England was nationalized in 1946, so formally taken under government control, like many other central banks. The Bank was directed to impose a range of controls on the banking system which proved in part ineffective and in other part distorting. Unfortunately, although economic performance was good after 1950, monetary stability began to wobble and as inflation started to soar in the 1970s questions were raised over whether this was the result of political influence over the central bank. As it became widely accepted that it was, calls for independence were made. When the new British Labour government was elected in 1997 it gave the Bank independence of a kind. The government would set the inflation rate and the Bank was asked to deliver that rate.

FHC

Bank rate, the rate of interest at which the Bank of England lent to the discount houses, the intermediaries between itself and the banking system. Bank rate dates back to the 19th century when the Bank was learning how to lend to the money market. Thus, in effect, it was the rate at which the Bank lent to the banking system, and for a long time it was a ritual that it was announced on Thursdays. One of the complaints against Montagu Norman, the governor 1920–44, was that he had the right to change this rate of interest without consulting anyone. If Bank rate was effective, then all other short-term rates of interest moved with it. For this reason, it is often used in historical studies as a good proxy for short-term interest rates. How was it made effective? By changing the quantity of money supplied in relation to demand. The Bank would engage in 'open market operations' in order to change the money supply and make Bank rate effective. That is, it would sell securities to the market to decrease the cash in the market if it wanted to see interest rates rise, and it bought securities if it wanted rates to fall. The markets thus began to look to Bank rate as a signal of the Bank's policy. Bank rate was almost unchanged during the period 1932–51. Then, as inflation was developing, it began to be used more actively. It was finally abolished in name in 1972, when different techniques for operating the system were introduced. It was replaced by 'minimum lending rate' and that in turn went in 1984. The Bank still meets to discuss through the Monetary Policy Committee the rate at which it will lend, and currently that figure is called 'base rate'. *FHC*

Bank Rate Leak Tribunal (1957), a key event in Harold Wilson's political career. Macmillan established the tribunal in November 1957 after shadow chancellor Wilson claimed that a Tory leak before the September Bank rate increase had prompted illicit profiteering in gilt-edge shares. The tribunal report of January 1958 dismissed these allegations, leaving Wilson exposed.

However, in the ensuing Commons debate, Wilson's impressive condemnation of City 'malpractice' saved his reputation and revealed his potential for party leadership. *AM*

Barber, Anthony Perrinnott Lysberg (1920–), Conservative politician and chancellor of the exchequer. Barber was a former RAF prisoner of war and barrister when he first fought Doncaster in 1950. Having won the seat in 1951, he became a whip in 1955 and was appointed parliamentary private secretary to the prime minister in 1958. Macmillan made him economic secretary to the Treasury in 1959 and financial secretary in 1962, and he entered Douglas-Home's cabinet in 1963 as health minister. Having lost Doncaster in 1964, Barber was elected MP for Altrincham and Sale in 1965 and joined Heath's team that fought the 1965 Finance Bill. He entered the shadow cabinet in 1966 and was made party chairman in 1967, becoming one of Heath's trusted advisers. In June 1970, he was appointed chancellor of the duchy of Lancaster to negotiate British entry into the European Community, but, following Macleod's death, became chancellor of the exchequer five weeks later. Barber implemented the party's tax reforms, but was seen as a political lightweight who was subservient to Heath. Ironically, he was less happy than the rest of the cabinet with 'the Barber boom', as the 1973 policy of all-out expansion became known. Inflation had also been fuelled by the 1971 removal of controls on bank credit, while floating the exchange rate removed the traditional constraint on expansion of a sterling crisis. But, after oil prices quadrupled in 1973, Barber cut public spending. In January 1974, he spurned an unexpected TUC offer not to use any miners' settlement in other pay negotiations, although the offer was explored for a further fortnight. He left the Commons in 1974, accepted a life peerage, and pursued a business career. He served on both the 1982 Falkland Islands Inquiry and the Commonwealth's 1986 eminent persons group on South Africa. *RJS*

Anthony Barber, *Taking the Tide: A Memoir* (Norwich, 1996).

Barker, Ernest (1874–1960), one of the few pioneers of the academic study of politics in the first half of the 20th century who bridged the widening gulf between the humanities, law, and the social sciences. He sought to reconcile the idealist philosophy he had imbibed as an Oxford disciple of T. H. Green with an enduring Whig reverence for national political institutions and culture, based upon a respect for individual rights and the rule of law. While Barker identified the institutions of local self-government and voluntary associations as formative of the British national character, he adopted a moderately pluralist position compared to those, such as Harold Laski and G. D. H. Cole, who sought to elevate the group into a rival to both the individual championed by Herbert Spencer and the state celebrated by Bernard Bosanquet. With a Whiggish concern for balance to avoid possible group tyranny, he preferred Maitland's advocacy of administrative courts to Dicey's reliance upon parliamentary sovereignty in the search to make both groups and governments legally accountable. Barker's appointment to the chair of political science in Cambridge did not enable him to develop the study of politics there, as it had in Oxford. However, his theoretical and empirical writings were staple reading well into the mid-20th century, but have since suffered the neglect shared by most of the founding fathers. In retirement, Sir Ernest Barker championed the British Commonwealth as a worldwide institutionalization of an exemplary pluralist voluntary association. It would continue after decolonization to spread Whig ideas of representative government and the common law adumbrated in the 1931 Statute of Westminster. *JH*

Julia Stapleton, *Englishness and the Study of Politics: The Social and Political Thought of Ernest Barker* (Cambridge, 1994).

Barnes, George Nicoll (1859–1940), trade unionist and Labour politician. George Barnes's early life saw him move trades and places on a number of occasions before he eventually arrived in London in the late 1870s. He then found work as an engineer and soon became active in socialist and trade union politics. He was elected to the executive of the Amalgamated Society of Engineers in 1889 and was general secretary from 1896. He was an unsuccessful Independent Labour Party parliamentary candidate for Rochdale in 1895, but in 1906 he defeated Andrew Bonar Law in Glasgow to become one of Labour's first 29 MPs; in 1910–11 he was briefly chairman of the parliamentary party. Immediately, Barnes began to campaign for a National Pensions Bill and supported welfare reforms. During the Great War he became pensions minister and in August 1917 replaced Arthur Henderson in the war cabinet (as minister without portfolio), remaining in Lloyd George's government until 1921, though most of his party had left at the 1918 election, in which Barnes was opposed by John Maclean as official Labour candidate. He decided to retire in 1921, partly due to growing discontent with the direction being taken by the Labour Party and a much-reduced chance of holding his seat. *DWM*

George Barnes, *From Workshop to War Cabinet* (London, 1923).

Barnett, Joel (1923–), Labour politician. MP for Heywood and Royton, 1964–83, and a Callaghan supporter, Barnett was chief secretary to the Treasury, 1974–9, and in Callaghan's cabinet after 1976. Responsible for managing the detail in the vital role of negotiating public expenditure, he supported Denis Healey in cabinet in the controversy over terms for the IMF loan in 1976, opposing Tony Benn's 'alternative strategy' to invest North Sea Oil revenue. He was thus part of the beleaguered Treasury team unpopular with the Labour Party after 1976. *BJE*

Joel Barnett, *Inside the Treasury* (London, 1982).

Barnett-Goschen formula. G. J. Goschen, the chancellor of the exchequer in Salisbury's government, produced a formula in 1888, according to which eleven-eightieths of British public expenditure would be allocated to Scotland. This was altered to 10 per cent in 1978 by the Treasury minister, Joel Barnett, calculating it on a population basis and thus discounting 'need'. He left the Scottish Office free to allocate its money. This constituted an effective reduction of 23 per cent in funding but was to be introduced incrementally. *BJE*

Barry, Brian Michael (1936–), political scientist. Barry played a major role in reorienting political theory in Britain since the 1970s. Following Peter Laslett's 1956 claim that 'political philosophy is dead', Barry argued that, whereas Isaiah Berlin, Michael Oakeshott, and Karl Popper had offered visions of political life, it was only with the appearance of John Rawls's *A Theory of Justice* (1971) that a narrative theory that could be chewed, rather than swallowed whole, allowed political philosophy to be reborn. Barry's own writings have focused upon developing a critical liberal theory of social justice that maintains a delicate balance between pluralism and universality in tackling everyday political problems that confront public decision makers. His pre-Rawlsian books on *Political Argument* (1965) and *Sociologists, Economists and Democracy* (1970) had already set the tone for what was to come by their analytical engagement with empirical evidence. Barry's writings have had a worldwide influence that has been facilitated by a criss-crossing Atlantic career, in which he taught in a variety of British (Oxford, Essex, and LSE) and American (Chicago, in California, and since 1998 Columbia) universities, as well as at the European University Institute in Florence. He was a founder and co-editor of the *British Journal of Political Science* and initiated the 1975 transformation of the Political Studies Association. *JH*

B. Barry, *Democracy and Power: Essays in Political Theory* (Oxford, 1991).

Bartlett, Vernon (1894–1983), writer and independent MP. A journalist of liberal views who specialized in foreign affairs, Bartlett contested the Bridgwater division of Somerset as an Independent Progressive candidate on 17 November 1938. On a platform of opposition to Chamberlain's Munich agreement, and supported by local Liberal and Labour party members, he took what had been a safe Conservative seat. Re-elected in 1945, he did not contest the general election of 1950. After further newspaper work, he retired in 1961 to a vineyard in Tuscany where he continued to write books (some 28 in all). *DEM*

Iain McLean, 'Oxford and Bridgwater', in C. Cook and J. Ramsden (eds.), *By-Elections in British Politics* (2nd edn., London, 1997).

Basnett, David (1924–89), trade unionist. Basnett was general secretary of one of Britain's largest unions, the General Municipal Workers' Union, 1973–82, and of its even larger successor, the General Municipal Boilermakers' and Allied Trades Union, 1982–6. He was, though, an indecisive chairman of the TUC general council, 1977–8. Basnett hankered after the consensus industrial relations of the 1960s and 1970s and actively opposed Thatcher's anti-trade union policies. Taylor argues that Basnett gained a 'Hamlet reputation for dithering', although the mid-1980s, when Basnett retired, were barren years for all the dinosaurs of the Labour movement. *DMM*

Robert Taylor, *The Trade Union Question in British Politics: Government and Unions since 1945* (Oxford, 1993).

'bastards, the', John Major's phrase, off-microphone after a broadcast, referring to leaking, sniping right-wingers in his government—but the microphone was on, and it became headline news. The original four bastards, Redwood, Portillo, Howard, and Lilley were reduced to three when Downing Street made clear Howard was not a bastard. The episode reflected the post-Thatcher qualified loyalty of Europhobic right-wingers to Major. *EP*

Bath commission, See Radnor report.

Bathurst, Charles (1867–1958), Conservative backbencher and agriculturalist. A Gloucestershire landowner, Bathurst represented his county in parliament, 1910–18, as a champion of the agricultural interest and the rural way of life. He supported tariff reform as a design for agricultural renewal and advocated a strain of 'forward' Conservatism dependent on voluntarism to improve conditions in the distressed districts. He became Lord Bledisloe, 1918; held junior office in 1924–8; was governor-general of New Zealand, 1930–5; and chaired a royal commission on the central African colonies in 1938–9. *RJQA*

BBC (British Broadcasting Corporation), Britain's national broadcasting organization. The BBC was chartered in 1926 as a public body to succeed the radio manufacturers' own creation, the British Broadcasting Company. Its first director-general, John *Reith, believed that the BBC had a duty to educate. The corporation's bias was socially conservative, hardly surprising when its controlling board was weighted by establishment figures. In 1932 the corporation branched into international broadcasting, inaugurating an English language Empire Service to promote imperial cohesion. The multi-lingual *BBC World Service followed, and television services began in 1936. During the Second World War, the BBC was an essential instrument of domestic propaganda and morale and of political cohesion. In 1955, the arrival of independent television ended the BBC's monopoly, but by way of compensation it acquired a second television channel in 1963. The BBC has never been far from political controversy. During the 1926 General Strike, its airwaves were commandeered to powerful effect by the government. In 1940, the wartime broadcaster J. B. Priestley used the BBC to advance ideas of the war as an opportunity for social reform, and the Churchill government successfully applied pressure to have Priestley silenced. Fear that the BBC might somehow usurp the role of parliament as the chief arena for national politics led to the adoption in 1944 of the 'fourteen day rule' requiring the BBC to wait two weeks before carrying political comment on any issue coming before parliament. This rule withered during the Suez crisis of 1956. Subsequently BBC programming became an essential part of the British political landscape, with long-running programmes such as BBC television's *Panorama*, *Newsnight*, and *Question Time* or BBC Radio 4's morning *Today* programme acting as key platforms for both political debate and journalistic enquiry. Politicians from all quarters have at times identified bias in BBC news coverage, and programmes have excited criticism over issues of taste and decency. Coverage of Northern Ireland proved particularly controversial. In 1985 the Thatcher government's attempt to squash a *Real Lives* documentary, 'At the Edge of Union', led to a one-day strike by broadcast journalists. Other programmes, such as the path-breaking 1966 docudrama on homelessness *Cathy Come Home*, have played a part in raising public consciousness on particular issues. The BBC continues to be funded by a licence fee, though the Peacock report of 1986 predicted a future of multiple cable and satellite channels in which this would no longer be the case. The Broadcasting Act of 1990 brought major changes to the BBC, including a requirement for 25 per cent of its programmes to be independently produced. *NC*

Asa Briggs, *The BBC: The First Fifty Years* (Oxford, 1985). | Ralph Negrine, *Television and the Press since 1945* (Manchester, 1998).

BBC World Service, overseas services developed from the short-wave Empire Service, launched in 1932. An Arabic Service followed in 1938 to counter the dictator powers in the Middle East. Broadcasts were funded and guided by the Foreign Office. During the Second World War the range of languages used expanded dramatically. The World Service, with its reputation for reliability, played a major role in Western propaganda during the Cold War. It is a testament to its potency that broadcasts were frequently jammed in the Eastern bloc. *NC*

Michael Nelson, *War of the Black Heavens* (London, 1997). | Andrew Walker, *A Skyful of Freedom* (London, 1992).

Beatty, David (1871–1936), admiral. Beatty commanded the battlecruiser squadron, 1912–16, playing major roles in battles at the Heligoland Bight (1914), Dogger Bank (1915), and Jutland (1916). As commander of the fleet he received the German navy's surrender in 1918. Dashing and charismatic, he fitted the Nelsonian image of the British naval hero better than his more cautious predecessor, Jellicoe. *JMB*

Stephen Roskill, *Admiral of the Fleet Earl Beatty: The Last Naval Hero* (London, 1980).

Beaverbrook, 1st Lord (1879–1964), newspaper proprietor and Conservative politician. Born in New Brunswick, Canada, Max Aitken early on demonstrated a gift for, and a delight in, making money. Before the age of 30, he was a millionaire and outgrowing the entrepreneurial possibilities of Montreal. In 1910 he moved to London and rapidly established a friendship with his lifelong political hero, the New Brunswick-born Conservative Andrew Bonar Law. Both were committed to tariff reform and Empire, and soon Aitken was an MP, 1910–16, while, with his encouragement, Law became leader of their party. In 1916 Aitken acted as go-between among the leaders who brought down Asquith and installed a Tory-dominated coalition led by Lloyd George and Law. His reward was that he became Lord Beaverbrook and, for a time, minister of information. In 1922, like most other Tories, he abandoned Lloyd George and successfully implored Law to abandon retirement and lead a Conservative government. With the coming to power in 1923 of an old enemy, Stanley Baldwin, for the remaining inter-war years Beaverbrook concentrated his genius on his growing newspaper empire, begun in 1916 when he bought the moribund **Daily Express*. This he made the most successful mass-circulation newspaper in the world, and used it to challenge Baldwin during the *Empire Crusade. Though his papers supported appeasement in the 1930s, Beaverbrook served brilliantly as Churchill's minister of aircraft production during the dangerous days of 1940–1. The two old friends frequently quarrelled, but Beaverbrook returned as lord privy seal later in the war. He spent his remaining years as a political gadfly, superintending his newspapers and writing the history of Great War Britain. A small, rather ugly man, with a perpetual and infectious grin, and a brilliant wordsmith, his histories are persuasive and sometimes self-servingly misleading. Throughout his long life, his almost boyish love of making mischief, he admitted, made him 'the man who liked to stir things up'. *RJQA*

Anne Chisholm and Michael Davie, *Lord Beaverbrook: A Life* (London, 1992). | Stephen Koss, *The Rise and Fall of the Political Press in Britain*, vol. 2 (London, 1972). | A. J. P. Taylor, *Beaverbrook* (London, 1972).

Beckett, John (1894–1964), socialist and fascist. After a chequered parliamentary career as an Independent Labour Party MP, 1924–31, Beckett became disillusioned with Labour over social policy cutbacks in 1931 and embraced fascism. He joined the British Union of Fascists (BUF) in 1934. A combative propagandist, Beckett was appointed BUF director of publicity and editor of *Action* and *Blackshirt*. He left in 1937 but was subsequently connected with several other extreme right-wing groups. Beckett was interned under Defence Regulation 18B, 1940–3. *AM*

Beckett, Terence Norman (1923–), industrialist. After a long career with Ford which culminated in his becoming its British chief executive, Beckett served as director-general of the CBI, 1980–7. These years of the Thatcher government were not easy ones for the organization as tripartism waned. A down-to-earth centrist, Beckett threatened a 'bare knuckle fight' with the government in 1980, but did not follow the threat through after meeting Mrs Thatcher. *WG*

Beeching, Richard (1913–85), railways manager. Dr Beeching left ICI in 1961 and became chairman (at the controversially high salary of £24,000) of the British Transport Commission and the British Railways Board, 1962–5. He introduced more managers from non-railway backgrounds, and produced the challenging but statistically fragile *The Reshaping of British Railways* (1963, often called 'the Beeching report'), advocating a smaller network and emphasis on profitable traffic flows. Almost 2,500 route miles (4,023 route km) disappeared during his chairmanship, but this failed to solve the railways' financial problems. *GC*

T. R. Gourvish, *British Railways, 1948–1973* (Cambridge, 1986).

Beef war. Inadequate hygiene standards in British, especially southern English, beef farming (cattle fed with cattle offal) was blamed for BSE ('mad cow disease'), more prevalent than in Europe. There was an EU ban on British beef sales after belated Commons admissions by Stephen Dorrell, health minister, 1995. Government and press rage subsided after bombastic lobbying against the European ban was flatly rejected. There was then a major programme of slaughter, heavy losses, and compensation, which generated resentment in the north, Scotland, and especially Northern Ireland whose clean herds were also barred from the EU market. The ban was lifted in December 1998. *EP*

Beer, Samuel (1911–), political scientist. Beer undertook pioneering work from the mid-1950s on British parties and pressure groups that were incorporated into his influential *Modern British Politics* (1965), bringing an American insight into the study of group representation in Britain. It was the juxtaposition of the two kinds of representation, functional representation of interest groups and electoral representation of political parties, that insightfully placed the workings of British politics in a new perspective. However, by 1982, he melodramatically argued in *Britain against Itself* that the defence upon which the civic culture had been based was not merely in decline but had collapsed. Abandoning the sober analysis of his earlier work, he now argued, reflecting the conventional wisdom of the 1970s, that there was a 'paralysis of public choice' owing to the convergent impact of a decomposition of social class hierarchy and a revolt against authority, leading to pluralist stagnation. While the lack of trust in British government subsequently became an increasing feature of the early 1990s, in seeking its causes Beer attributed an exaggerated cultural impact to both technocracy and populism. Technocracy has never had the place in amateur-led Britain that it acquired in countries such as France, its protagonists (such as the 1968 Fulton report on the civil service and Heath's flirtation with managerialism in the early 1970s) making little headway. As for 'new populism' (unduly associated by Beer with pop culture), it was under Margaret Thatcher to become a means by which political leadership was to impose its authority upon the bewailed pluralistic paralysis, undermining the plausibility of Beer's assessment at the very time he was expounding it. *JH*

Beith, Alan James (1943–), Liberal politician. A former university lecturer (Newcastle University) and Liberal councillor in the north-east, Beith was elected to MP for Berwick-upon-Tweed in a by-election in November 1973, capturing the seat from the Conservatives, and held the seat thereafter. A respected figure in the party, he was successively Liberal spokesman on home affairs, education, constitutional reform, and foreign affairs, also acting as chief whip, 1976–85, and deputy leader, 1985–8. Beith's reputation for decency and loyalty made it possible that he would be the natural successor should David Steel resign but, in the election for the leadership of the newly merged *Liberal Democrats, Beith was eclipsed in a series of hustings meetings by Paddy *Ashdown's more dynamic style, though little difference in policy emerged. Obtaining less than 30 per cent of the votes cast, Beith accepted his defeat with characteristic good grace, serving the Liberal Democrats in a series of high-profile portfolios, including the Treasury and home affairs. He has proved one of the long-serving former Liberals who have secured the position of the Liberal Democrats as a significant force since the ending of the *Alliance. He also, through his strong Christian and Methodist connections, has retained a claim upon the traditional link of the Liberal Party with its Nonconformist roots. *JS*

Bell, Martin (1938–), BBC reporter and independent MP. Admired for his integrity and bravery, especially when wounded in Bosnia, he impetuously resigned in 1997 to fight on an 'anti-sleaze' ticket the Conservative stronghold of Tatton, held by the disgraced Neil Hamilton. The other main parties stood down. In a skilfully managed campaign and wearing his trademark white suit, Bell overturned a 22,365 majority to win by 11,077 votes. He was the first independent victor at a general election since 1945. *CKSU*

Bell, Richard (1859–1930), trade union leader and MP. Bell was a member of the Amalgamated Society of Railway Servants (ASRS) and in 1897 appointed its servant secretary. He was elected MP for Derby in 1900 with the support of the Labour Representation Committee (LRC) but retained strong Liberal sympathies. He resigned as general secretary of the ASRS in 1909 and, having lost the LRC's support, intimated that he would not contest Derby. Bell then became a civil servant at the Board of Trade. *CH*

Bell, Thomas (1882–1944), trade unionist and Communist. Tom Bell became involved in secularism and radical politics from a young age, joining the Independent Labour Party (ILP) at the age of 18 and the Associated Ironmoulders of Scotland on completing his apprenticeship in 1904. He became increasingly frustrated with the theoretical naivety and reformist strategies of both the ILP and the Social Democratic Federation, having joined the latter in 1903 only to be expelled within twelve months. As a result he became actively involved in the formation of the more radical Glasgow socialist society and, in 1903, the Socialist Labour Party. During the Great War, Bell moved first to London and then to Liverpool before returning to Glasgow in 1916, where he became a leading figure in the shop stewards' movement. The revolution in Russia in 1917 had a profound impact on Bell and, convinced of the need for a single Communist party, he was active in the attempt to unite the radical members of the other socialist parties behind one flag. The Communist Party of Great Britain (CPGB) was eventually formed at a national convention held on 31 July 1920. Bell was chiefly involved in propaganda work for the newly formed party, working as editor of the monthly *Communist Review* and as head of the education department. Briefly imprisoned for sedition in 1925–6, Bell spent the next three years in Moscow. Throughout his later political career and activities Bell remained committed to the general policies of the CPGB, including its rejection of

Trotskyism, and its 'class against class' strategies of the late 1920s and early 1930s. *DWM*

Thomas Bell, *The British Communist Party: A Short History* (London, 1937). | Thomas Bell, *Pioneering Days* (London, 1941).

Bell, Timothy John Leigh (1941–), public relations consultant, now Lord Bell, trading as Lowe Bell. Tim Bell was a pioneer of the shift from autonomous politics to heavy employment of advertising and public relations men, and involved during the 1987 election in a semi-public struggle for favour with Saatchi and Saatchi. A rogue poll and David Young pushing Bell inspired Thatcher with panic fear of losing (on 'Wobbly Thursday'), so she substituted Bell's plans and embittered the rightly confident party chairman, Norman Tebbitt. *EP*

Belloc, (Joseph) Hilaire Pierre René (1870–1953), journalist, poet, and Liberal MP. Born in France and educated at Balliol College, Oxford, becoming president of the Oxford Union, Belloc was a naturalized British subject. In 1902 he wrote for the *Daily News* on military matters and was literary editor of the *Morning Post*, 1906–10. He was Liberal MP for South Salford, 1906–9 and again in 1910, but became disillusioned with party politics. In 1911 he launched *Eye-Witness*, a paper which exposed the *Marconi scandal in July 1912. In *The Servile State* (1912) he lamented the loss of individual freedom in the quest for security. Much of his subsequent writing was in the Roman Catholic cause, completing John Lingard's *History of England* (1915) and *Europe and the Faith* (1920). *JS*

Bellwin, Lord (1923–), Conservative politician. Irwin Bellow was originally a municipal leader, notable for running an economic and well-regarded Conservative regime in Leeds 1975–9. An early Thatcher supporter, he was co-opted to government and the Lords on the advice of his friend Sir Keith Joseph, a Leeds MP. Bellwin became a junior minister for local government, 1979–84. He is mainly remembered for the 'Bellwin formula' in local government finance, one of Mrs Thatcher's interim enthusiasms—and discards. *EP*

Benn, Anthony Wedgwood ('Tony') (1925–), Labour politician and diarist. An example of that rare phenomenon, a Labour leader who moved leftwards as he got older, Anthony Wedgwood Benn was born into a political family: his father, Viscount Stansgate, had been a Liberal MP and Labour cabinet minister under MacDonald and Attlee. After education at Winchester and Oxford and wartime military service, Benn was elected MP for Bristol South East in 1950. The death of his father in 1960 led to a struggle to renounce his title: he was disqualified from the Commons, headed the poll in the subsequent by-election, was again disqualified, campaigned successfully for an Act of Parliament to allow renunciation of hereditary titles, and then recovered his Bristol seat in 1963. The episode confirmed his belief in the need to modernize British institutions, an attitude that fitted in well with the rhetoric of Harold Wilson who in his first administration made him postmaster general. He held the post, 1964–6, when he joined the cabinet as successor to Frank Cousins at the Ministry of Technology, where he remained until Labour left office in 1970. Following Labour's 1970 defeat, he moved fairly steadily leftwards, becoming 'Tony Benn' in the process, and as chairman of the NEC's home policy committee he did much to commit the party to *Labour's Programme, 1973*. He returned to cabinet in 1974 as minister for industry but was fairly publicly demoted to energy in 1975. Following the resignation of Wilson he unsuccessfully stood in the leadership contest in which James Callaghan was elected; in 1981 he was just defeated by Denis Healey for the deputy leadership. By this time Benn was associated with the far left Campaign for Labour Party Democracy, but his defeat in the general election of 1983 deprived him of an attempt to succeed Michael Foot. In 1984 he returned to the Commons in a by-election as MP for Chesterfield and continued as a dissident voice, an advocate of constitutional reform and of the rights of the Commons against the executive. He stood against Kinnock for the leadership of the Labour Party in 1988, but lost decisively. In 1999 he announced his intention to retire as an MP, but not from political activity, at the next general election, by which time he would have completed 50 (not quite continuous) years in the Commons. His diary, extracts from which have been published in several volumes, provides a detailed source for the student of modern British politics. *DEM*

Jad Adams, *Tony Benn: A Biography* (London, 1992). | Robert Jenkins, *Tony Benn: A Political Biography* (London, 1980).

Bennett, Peter Frederick Blaker (1880–1957), industrialist and Conservative politician. Bennett inherited Neville Chamberlain's Edgbaston parliamentary seat in 1940 and retained it until 1953. A Methodist and teetotaller, Bennett spent much of his life working in the motor industry, and was their representative at the 1932 Ottawa conference. He was president of the Federation of British Industries, 1938–9, his industrial experience then being utilized by the supply departments during the war, later becoming parliamentary secretary at the Ministry of Labour. *NJC*

Berkeley, Humphry John (1926–94), liberal-minded politician. Berkeley achieved the rare feat of having fought elections for three parties. He was elected Conservative MP for Lancaster in 1959, stood for Labour in 1974, and was a Social Democratic Party candidate in 1987. His successful campaign to replace the 'customary processes' of selecting Conservative leaders by balloting Conservative MPs became his legacy to the Tories. Berkeley's championing of homosexual law reform contributed to his 1966 election defeat. *RJS*

Humphry Berkeley, *Crossing the Floor* (London, 1972).

Berlin, Isaiah (1909–97), probably the most remarkable of a group of Continental, mainly Jewish, intellectuals, who enlivened British intellectual life from the 1930s, although Berlin was not an exile from Nazi Germany but Soviet Russia. He spent his entire academic life in Oxford, where, apart from his wartime service as first secretary at the British embassy in Washington, he acquired an unrivalled reputation as a brilliant teacher and essayist. His pre-Second World War reservations about logical positivism's anti-metaphysical polemics, and the attempts of 'Oxford philosophy' to reduce problems to matters of linguistic confusion, led him to concentrate on the history of political thought, in which the thinkers were not abstracted from their ideas. His 19th-century liberalism and pluralism, verging on a romantic anarchism, derived its inspiration from Alexander Herzen, although his seminal distinction between negative and positive liberty (the subject of his 1958 inaugural lecture as professor of social and political theory at All Souls, Oxford) owed more to Benjamin Constant. The scattered nature of most of his writings (until they were collected by others) reflected Berlin's view that values were multiple, incommensurable, and conflicting, freedom being the resistance to constraint within the straitjacket of all-embracing monism. No single society, period of history, or ideology could offer a complete, demonstrable, final answer to ultimate moral questions. Each individual should be free to make a personal choice. Such an approach precluded acquiring disciples or founding a school of thought. Sir Isaiah held many influential positions, including that of founder-president of Wolfson College, Oxford, 1966–75, and the presidency of the British Academy, 1974–8. The reassertion of the value of individuality and human diversity against totalitarianism and intolerance are his enduring legacies. *JH*

I. Berlin, *Four Essays on Liberty* (Oxford, 1969). | I. Berlin, *The Proper Study of Mankind: An Anthology of Essays* (London, 1997). | M. Ignatieff, *Isaiah Berlin: A Life* (London, 1998).

Berlin crisis (1948–9), Cold War stand-off precipitated by Stalin's blockade of overland routes to west Berlin on 24 June 1948 and resolved on 4 May 1949 after the success of the Anglo-American Berlin airlift. At the close of the Second World War, Germany was temporarily dismembered into four zones of occupation (American, British, French, and Soviet). Also, deep within the Soviet zone, Berlin was divided with the west of the city controlled by the Americans, British, and French, and the east by the Soviets. The Potsdam conference confirmed this and stated that each occupying power would acquire reparations from its own zone, but that the USSR would receive 25 per cent of reparations from the western zones as a mark of its contribution during the war. Furthermore, Potsdam established a council of foreign ministers (CFM) whose principal task was to draw up post-war peace treaties.

Germany, and Berlin, became the focus of a dangerous heightening of tension as the Cold War set in. Within their respective zones, the Western powers and the Soviets took actions which were perceived as mutually hostile. From Moscow, Stalin spoke of a unified Germany but the merger of the east German social democrats with the communists in April 1946 looked to the West like the Sovietization of east Germany. In May 1946, the USA suspended reparations from the US zone to the Soviet Union. Soon after, in July, the Americans instigated a merger of its zone with the British zone creating Bizonia (the French zone was added in April/May 1948). To the Soviets, this suggested that the West, led by the Americans, had accepted the future division of Germany. Throughout 1947 and into 1948, Germany became the battleground of the Cold War in Europe. From Moscow's perspective, the Marshall plan's objectives for Germany—to rebuild its economy at the heart of a new Europe revitalized by American finance and trade—was final evidence of American expansionism. Consequently, in December 1947 the CFM failed in its last attempt to settle the disputes over Germany. Thereafter, the West worked towards the construction of a west German state. In response, from 1 April 1948 the Soviets made access for the Western occupiers to west Berlin increasingly difficult, culminating in a full blockade of land, rail, and canal routes from 24 June. Two days later, American and British planes began an eleven-month airlift which supplied over 1 million tons (1,016,000 tonnes) of aid to west Berlin.

The Berlin crisis raised fears of a third world war but brought a Cold War stalemate. Neither the Americans nor the British wished to shoot their way through to west Berlin, certainly not as long as the airlift succeeded, and Stalin had no desire to stop it by force. On 4 May 1949, Moscow backed down. By the end of the month, the West German state came into existence and the Soviets constituted an East German government. The crisis, alongside concurrent Cold War schisms, set West against East. For the British, it confirmed the need for collective security through NATO and the airlift strengthened Anglo-American military cooperation at its core. *JRVE*

John W. Young, *Cold-War Europe, 1945–1991* (2nd edn., London, 1999).

Bermuda conference (1953), summit meeting of the Western 'Big Three', America, Britain, and France, 4–8 December. The Bermuda conference was perhaps the most important meeting of Western leaders since the end of the Second World War. Not only did it concern itself with the greatest international issue of the day, relations with the Soviet Union and the question of détente, it also dealt with, among other problems, the future of Germany, West Germany's rearmament and European unity, diplomacy towards China, and the question of nuclear weapons and Western defence.

The conference was the result of Winston Churchill's search for a summit with the Soviets. Churchill had seen the death of Stalin in March 1953 as an opportunity to reduce Cold War tensions but in this he was very much alone. His foreign secretary, Eden, supported by the Foreign Office, doubted the sincerity of the Soviet 'peace offensive'. So, more importantly, did the American administration, the French, and the German governments. Consequently, US President Eisenhower suggested a meeting to avoid division within the Western alliance and to contain Churchill's personal diplomacy with the Soviets.

The conference, convened in December after postponements due to French governmental instability and Churchill's ill health, concentrated mainly on the Western reply to Soviet acceptance of a four-power foreign ministers' meeting on a German peace treaty. It also saw much heated discussion over the creation of the European Defence Community (EDC), a French-inspired organization designed to contain West German rearmament. Ultimately, the Bermuda conference did more to expose fault lines in the Western alliance than to bridge them as 1954 brought deadlock in East–West relations and a crisis in the Western alliance over the EDC. *JRVE*

John W. Young, *Churchill's Last Campaign: Britain and the Cold War, 1951–1955* (Oxford, 1996).

Berrill, Kenneth (1920–), economist and public servant. By background and training, Berrill was an academic economist of a Keynesian persuasion. His career was divided between Whitehall and the universities; he was always more the supremely effective 'committee-man' than the original thinker. He spent twenty years at Cambridge and was a businesslike chairman of the University Grants Committee (1969–73). His work as a Whitehall adviser included a spell in the Central Economic Planning Staff in the late 1940s, two years as a special adviser on public expenditure at the Treasury (1967–9), and a short stint as head of the Government Economic Service and chief economic adviser to the government (1973–4). From 1974 to 1980 he was head of the Central Policy Review Staff (CPRS). Berrill was a less flamboyant operator than the CPRS's first head, Lord Rothschild, but under him the 'think-tank' was influential in industrial policy making and in public spending discussions. *KT*

Bertie, Francis (1844–1919), ambassador. Bertie joined the Foreign Office in 1863, reached the rank of assistant under-secretary in 1894, and was instrumental in bringing about the Anglo-Japanese alliance of 1902. As ambassador in Paris, 1905–18, he became closely associated with the transformation of the Anglo-French Entente Cordiale into a quasi-alliance. Quarrelsome, industrious, and petulant, he was a relentless critic of German diplomacy, and a much-valued adviser of Sir Edward Grey. *KAH*

Keith Hamilton, *Bertie of Thame: Edwardian Ambassador* (Woodbridge, 1990).

Besant, Annie (1847–1933), early feminist and political activist, later espousing the cause of theosophy and Indian nationalism. Besant began her public career as a journalist and public speaker in the 1870s, supporting birth control, women's rights, the land question, and free trade. Her marriage to the Revd Frank Besant, a clergyman, ended in legal separation in 1873 and she developed a powerful working relationship with Charles Bradlaugh, president of the National Secular Society. She wrote a weekly column for the *National Reformer*, later becoming editor and joint proprietor. She and Bradlaugh were prosecuted in 1877 for selling an allegedly obscene pamphlet, *Fruits of Philosophy*, which contained suggestions for birth control methods. They were found guilty but the verdict was quashed on appeal. In 1885, she became a member of the Fabian Society and was one of the leaders of the 1887 'Bloody Sunday' demonstration in Trafalgar Square. In 1888, she joined the Social Democratic Federation and played a key role in the Match Girls' Strike of the same year. She also successfully contested a seat on the London School Board that year. However, by 1891, she had relinquished her political offices to concentrate on the theosophy movement. In this, she was greatly influenced by the work of the leader of the movement, Madame Blavatsky. This spiritualist philosophy was to have a marked impact upon her life. She settled in India, although returning frequently to Britain to speak for the suffragette campaigns. She became involved in Indian nationalism and was president of the Indian National Congress in 1918, having been briefly interned in 1917 by the British authorities for her activities. She continued to campaign for Indian home rule until her death. *KJL*

R. Dinnage, *Annie Besant* (London, 1987). | O. Taylor, *Annie Besant* (London, 1992).

'best prime minister we have'. This comment by R. A. *Butler about Anthony Eden in January 1956 is one of his most famous equivocal remarks, or 'Rabisms'. On this occasion, the words were put into Butler's mouth when he accepted a journalist's proposition that Eden 'is the best prime minister we have'. *RJS*

Betterton, Henry Bucknall (1872–1949), lawyer and Conservative politician. Betterton entered parliament in December 1918 for Rushcliffe, a seat he represented until 1934. Recognized as a moderate who was sympathetic to the Conservatives' social reforming wing, Betterton was considered a rising star. He was parliamentary secretary to the Ministry of Labour in 1923 and 1924–9 before becoming minister of labour in 1931. His major achievement was the *Unemployment Assistance Board (UAB) Act, 1934. He retired from the Commons to join the UAB. *NJC*

Bevan, Aneurin ('Nye') (1897–1960), Labour politician. Nye Bevan was one of the key figures in Clement Attlee's post-war Labour governments, being largely responsible for the free National Health Service in Britain, which came into existence in July 1948. His opposition to the attempts of Herbert Morrison and Hugh Gaitskell to impose prescription charges led him to resign from the government in April 1951 and to act as the centre for a loose grouping of the socialist left within the Labour Party that became known as the Bevanites, although he returned to the Labour front bench in the late 1950s.

Bevan was born in Tredegar, south Wales, becoming a miner, but won a scholarship to the Central Labour College, London, in 1919. Returning to Tredegar in 1921, he was involved in trade union affairs, acting as chairman of the Tredegar council during the General Strike of 1926. Yet Bevan was very much a political animal, and became MP for Ebbw Vale in 1929, a constituency which he represented until his death. In parliament, Bevan campaigned tirelessly in the interests of both the employed and unemployed members of the working class. He briefly supported Oswald Mosley's New Party in 1931, because Mosley seemed to offer policies to tackle unemployment, but he soon became disillusioned with him. He opposed the household means test and operated through the left-wing journal *Tribune*, begun in 1937, to attack the Labour leadership. It was in these years, in 1934 indeed, that he married Jennie *Lee who, in her own right, became an influential force within the Labour left. During the Second World War he rejected the political truce between the main political parties and fought the war on two fronts, against both the Tory Party and the Fascists, and was unflinching in his attacks upon Winston Churchill. It was during these years that he gained a reputation for being an orator reminiscent of his fellow Welshman David Lloyd George.

Yet Bevan's finest hour arrived when he was appointed minister of health and housing in Attlee's 1945 government. In that role, he cajoled the private doctors and the British Medical Association, who referred to him as a 'squalid nuisance', the 'Minister of Disease', and a 'Tito from Tonypandy', into working with the NHS. His remark that his Tory opponents were 'lower than vermin' caused great controversy at this time. Bevan's NHS went further than the wartime health reforms and much further than the Labour Party had outlined in its 1945 election manifesto, by effectively nationalizing the hospitals, creating a public general-practitioner service, and making the treatment of illness and provision of medical treatment entirely free. In *In Place of Fear* (1952), he explained that it was ludicrous to expect patients to await a vital operation because they lacked the right number of self-contributions. But the NHS proved to be expensive and both Attlee and Morrison sought to curb expenditure and introduce prescription charges. Bevan fought off these attempts at the 1950 general election but then, on 17 January 1951, was moved to the post of minister of labour and national service. The move coincided with the decision of Gaitskell, chancellor of the exchequer, to impose health charges. This provoked Bevan to resign from the government on 24 April 1951.

Between 1951 and 1955, Bevan was the figurehead of a loosely organized group of left-wing Labour MPs, based upon the Keep Left Group, who became known as *Bevanites. They advocated unilateral nuclear disarmament, and Bevan's decision to oppose the Parliamentary Labour Party line of supporting the manufacture of the hydrogen bomb almost got him expelled from the party in 1955. At this point, however, Bevan's position changed. Having been defeated by Gaitskell in the party leadership contest of December 1955, he appears to have come to an understanding with him, and became his shadow colonial secretary. From then onwards, he was patriotic (but very effectively critical of Eden) over the Suez crisis and was treasurer of the party between 1956 and 1960. He effectively divested himself of being 'leader of the Left' when, in 1957, he attacked unilateral disarmament at the 1957 party conference, in his *'naked into the conference chamber' speech. In 1959 he became Labour's deputy leader but died of cancer in 1960. *KL*

John Campbell, *Aneurin Bevan and the Mirage of British Socialism* (London, 1987). | Michael Foot, *Aneurin Bevan*, 2 vols. (London, 1962–73).

Bevanites (1951–7), Labour MPs who supported Aneurin Bevan after his resignation from government in 1951. The group rebelled against the party leadership mainly on foreign and defence issues. In 1952 Bevanites captured seven places on the NEC of the party and continued to be an effective ginger group until the 1957 conference, when their leader broke with them over unilateral nuclear disarmament. Estimates of the size of the group vary from 25 to 47, depending on the issue. *BB*

Beveridge, William Henry (1879–1963), economist and author of the *Beveridge report (1942). Born in India and educated at Charterhouse and Oxford, Beveridge was influenced by the progressive Liberalism associated with late 19th-century Oxford and, during his early career as a journalist on the *Morning Post*, he lived at the Toynbee Hall university settlement in East London. He became particularly interested in the question of unemployment, publishing *Unemployment: A Problem of Industry* (1909). His advocacy of *labour exchanges had already brought him to the attention of 'New Liberals' such as *Churchill. In 1908, he became a part-time temporary civil servant, acting as assistant to Churchill in planning labour exchanges. Beveridge's enquiries also convinced him of the need for a system of national insurance. He became a permanent civil servant in 1909, reaching in 1913 the rank of assistant secretary.

During the Great War Beveridge worked in the Ministry of Munitions and the Ministry of Food. He resigned from the civil service in 1919 and was appointed director of the LSE. Before he returned to Oxford in 1937 as master of University College, he had published a pamphlet, *Insurance for All and Everything* (1924), which outlined the basis for a comprehensive system of social security based upon an extended scheme of national insurance. As chairman of the Unemployed Insurance Committee from 1934, Beveridge was well acquainted with the muddled system of state and private insurance provision which had grown up between the wars. He was appointed under-secretary at the Ministry of Labour in 1940 and in 1941 was chairman of the interdepartmental committee which produced the 1942 Beveridge report. Its publication and its widespread publicity, attracting a sale of over 600,000 copies, turned Beveridge into a national figure.

Beveridge was, however, distrusted by many civil servants and politicians who saw his report as impracticable and inappropriate in wartime. As a result, Beveridge found himself sidelined from central policy making, although the substance of his proposals was enshrined in white papers in 1944 which committed post-war governments to maintain 'high and stable' levels of employment and to legislate for a comprehensive system of contributory national insurance. In the same year his *Full Employment in a Free Society* argued the use of Keynesian techniques to maintain high levels of employment, keeping welfare within bounds and state intervention to a minimum. Beveridge became Liberal MP for Berwick-upon-Tweed in 1944, but lost his seat at the 1945 general election. He entered the Lords as a Liberal peer in 1946, thereafter undertaking various public roles, none of which matched the importance of his work on his most famous report. *JS*

LORD BEVERIDGE, *Power and Influence* (London, 1953). | JOSE HARRIS, *William Beveridge* (Oxford, 1977).

Beveridge report (1942), the foundation document of the post-1945 *welfare state. Published in December 1942, the report entitled *Social Insurance and Allied Services* was the product of a civil service interdepartmental committee commissioned in June 1941 under the chairmanship of Sir William *Beveridge, on the recommendation of Ernest *Bevin as minister of labour. Although Beveridge was an acknowledged expert in the field of unemployment and national insurance, Bevin's initial purpose was to shunt Beveridge out of his current position in the Ministry of Labour. Beveridge's brief was 'to undertake, with special reference to the inter-relation of the schemes, a survey of the existing national schemes of social insurance and allied services, including workmen's compensation, and to make recommendations'. It was one he interpreted very widely, especially in the scope and implications of his recommendations about future social policy. Although the committee gathered considerable evidence from various bodies, including business, the trade unions, and pressure groups, much of the thinking behind the report was Beveridge's own. When published in December 1942 the principal recommendation of the report was for a universal system of comprehensive social insurance, covering all the emergencies and vicissitudes of life. A single, flat-rate contribution paid by all, with a subvention from the exchequer, would provide pensions, sickness and maternity payments, unemployment benefits, and burial grants. A safety net of *National Assistance would operate for those who fell outside the system for whatever reason.

Well-publicized by Beveridge himself, the 'Beveridge plan' with its offer of security *'from the cradle to the grave' proved an immensely popular success, selling large numbers of copies and generating widespread discussion. It undoubtedly captured a moment of national optimism, following victories in north Africa and the prospect of eventual victory after three years of war. It also capitalized on the spirit of wartime collectivism being fostered by progressive Liberals, labour, and left-wing groups. Beveridge was able to persuade *Keynes of the merits of the plan by agreeing to limit the costs to the Treasury to no more than £100 million, achieved largely by limiting the payments to pensioners to below subsistence levels, but the scheme's viability still depended on other factors over which Beveridge had little or no direct control. The Beveridge plan assumed full employment and the introduction of both a *National Health Service and *family allowances. The first was necessary to provide a large enough tax and contribution base to support the scheme and avoid the effects of mass unemployment which had wrecked the financial basis of pre-1939 national insurance. A free National Health Service meant that the national insurance system did not have to run a health insurance scheme with additional expense and complication. A curative health service, *'free at the point of delivery', would reduce the burden on the state. Finally, the provision of family allowances was intended to relieve a significant amount of child poverty while leaving the wage structure and labour market untouched.

In spite of its public popularity, the report met vehement opposition from many officials and Conservative politicians who thought its provisions unrealistic. Churchill himself anyway wished to postpone discussion of welfare spending until after the war. However, attempts to postpone its consideration were defeated by a backbench revolt by Labour MPs in a debate on the report in March 1943, ensuring that it would be implemented at least in part by post-war governments. Although some of Beveridge's proposals were eventually whittled down, the white papers of 1944 on employment and national insurance gave substance to the main thrust of the Beveridge report.

Although seen as the flagship of wartime planning for post-war collectivism, Beveridge enshrined in his proposals the principles of the original *National Insurance Act, 1911, in which benefits were paid in return for contributions from employees. He thus ensured the continuation of the voluntarist principle and was also concerned to reinforce the concept of *less eligibility, meaning that income from benefits should not exceed the lowest level of regular earnings. The radical gloss Beveridge gave to the report with his talk of abolishing the *'five giants' of want, squalor, ignorance, idleness, and disease, also masked the relative conservatism of aspects of his thinking in regard to issues such as working women and the treatment of the long-term unemployed. Thus in recurrent debates about the welfare state, the Beveridge report has been criticized for its somewhat ambivalent intellectual position, representing neither a fully worked-out and rationalized 'welfarist' position nor a free market approach as later advocated by the 'new right'. *JS*

Social Insurance and Allied Services (Cmd 6404, London, 1942). | Karel and John Williams (eds.), *A Beveridge Reader* (London, 1987).

Beveridge report (1951), from a departmental committee chaired by Lord Beveridge, was supportive of the BBC's monopoly and warned against broadcast advertising, particularly sponsorship. It did advocate more attention to the regions and the coverage of support. Selwyn Lloyd's minority report pressed for another channel and advertising. ITV was created in 1955 on a regional basis with spot advertising. *KMT*

Bevin, Ernest **(1881–1951)**, trade unionist and Labour politician. Bevin was the greatest British trade union leader of the 20th century, yet he is more often remembered as the minister of labour, 1940–5, overseeing the organization of labour resources in Winston Churchill's wartime government, and as foreign secretary in Clement Attlee's Labour government of 1945–51.

Born at Winsford, in Somerset, Bevin was the illegitimate son of an agricultural labourer. He was raised by his mother until he was 8 when, upon her death, he moved to Devon to be raised by his half-sister. He received little formal education, began working on a farm at the age of 11 and then, at the age of 13, moved to Bristol to live with his half-brother. Bevin became a soft-drinks roundsman, was an active lay preacher in the Baptist Church, and was soon attracted into the Bristol socialist society. Bristol was an important seaport at this time and Bevin helped to organize the dockers and carters as a result of his concern for the unemployed and his work on Ramsay MacDonald's right to work movement in 1908. In 1910 he was asked to organize the carters for the Dock, Wharf, Riverside, and General Labourers' Union, better known as the Dockers' Union, and by 1914 he had risen to become one of its three national organizers. Seeing that employers' organizations were uniting, he became convinced that trade unions needed to unite more effectively. He therefore advocated the formation of the general council of the TUC in 1920 and pushed forward with the amalgamation of fourteen different unions into the Transport and General Workers' Union in 1922.

Throughout the inter-war years, Bevin was the dominant British trade union leader. He organized the *General Strike of 1926 and attempted to influence the economic policy of MacDonald's second Labour government of 1929–31 by serving on the Economic Advisory Committee and the Macmillan committee, but found that his influence was limited and published his own expansionist policies for tackling unemployment in his pamphlet *My Plan for 2,000,000 Unemployed* (1932). This advocated raising the school-leaving age and lowering the retirement age as well as policies to generate immediate work. He had more success with the Labour Party. The National Council of Labour brought the executives of the Parliamentary Labour Party, the Labour Party, and the TUC together to attempt to coordinate the policies of the movement. Bevin steered this organization into discussing the need for public ownership in the 1930s. He believed in the need for rearmament, and pushed for it strongly during the Spanish civil war (1936–9).

Bevin saw himself as a trade union leader and not as a political figure, although he stood unsuccessfully in the general elections of 1918 and 1931. However, on the formation of Churchill's wartime coalition government, in May 1940, Bevin was offered the Ministry of Labour and National Service, a crucial wartime job. The MP for Central Wandsworth stood down and Bevin was returned to the Commons, retaining the seat until 1951. In his new role, Bevin attempted to organize the whole country behind the war effort. His scheme to increase the number of coal miners in the country by directing young men, some of them public school boys, to the mines gave rise to the term 'Bevin boys'. He also had some epic battles in government with Lord Beaverbrook.

For his loyal support, Attlee rewarded Bevin with the post of foreign secretary in 1945. He supported the Marshall plan of 1947, whereby financial assistance was given to Western Europe, and, through his pressure, helped secure the formation of *NATO in 1949. Indeed, in this role he sought to preserve Britain's status as a world power, to work with the USA, and to oppose the threat to both Eastern and Western Europe posed by the Soviet Union. In particular, he worked hard to defeat the Soviet Union's air blockade of Berlin in June 1948. Bevin was seriously ill in these later years and resigned as foreign secretary in February 1951, becoming lord privy seal, which involved no departmental responsibilities, but died two months later. *KL*

Alan Bullock, *The Life and Times of Ernest Bevin*, 3 vols. (London, 1960–83). | Peter Weiler, *Ernest Bevin* (Manchester, 1993).

Bevins, (John) Reginald **(1908–96)**, Conservative politician. Bevins personified Liverpudlian

Toryism in the 1950s. He had begun as a Labour politician but had joined the Tories by 1939 and became MP for Toxteth in 1950. Macmillan, with whom he had worked at housing, appointed him postmaster general in 1959, with responsibility for broadcasting. Bevins's refusal to be cowed by the commercial television companies ruffled feathers, as did his attacks on Tory snobbery after his 1964 defeat. *RJS*

Reginald Bevins, *The Greasy Pole* (London, 1965).

Biffen, (William) John (1930–), Conservative politician and wit, close to Enoch Powell on economics, MP for Oswestry from 1961, and known before Thatcher as an advocate of free markets and monetary control. As chief secretary, 1979–81, then trade secretary, 1981–3, he stumbled. A nervous temperament made him indecisive and he lacked paper-eating qualities. But as leader of the Commons, 1983–7, Biffen triumphed, charming Labour opponents and combining wit with a subversive tolerance, and was widely thought the best post-war floor leader. He opposed Thatcher over the *poll tax, his cabinet intervention supporting Geoffrey Howe provoking a shrill outburst, and an angered Biffen soon afterwards made a speech calling for 'consolidation', an easing of the government's dogmatic right-wing stance. Restrained from instant dismissal, Thatcher undermined him through press secretary Bernard *Ingham, 'the sewer, not the sewage'. Excluded from the 1987 election campaign, he was sacked after victory. As Biffen prophesied, the poll tax destroyed Thatcher. To the abolitionists' claim in 1991, 'It's the flagship', Biffen replied 'If the flagship blocks the fleet, sink the flagship.' From the backbenches, amid general rapture, he had greeted Nigel Lawson's calamitous 1988 budget with 'I smell inflation', while the 1997 election validated his consolidation speech. From a good-humoured free market stance, his revulsion at Thatcher's virulent style anticipated the great national alienation from the Tories. *EP*

Billing, Noel Pemberton (1881–1948), populist politician who was independent MP for Hertford, 1916–21. Billing fought in the Boer war, 1899–1901, and was founder and editor of *Aerocraft*, 1908–10; then a squadron commander in the Great War. He unsuccessfully contested Mile End in January 1916 in support of a stronger air policy, and was founder and president of the Vigilantes, a society for supporting purity in public life, a campaign characteristic of his ability to profit from the patriotic wartime appetite for extreme right-wing causes. Billing was not able to survive the return to normal politics after the war, though, nor to do as well in 1939–45 as he had in 1914–18, unsuccessfully contesting four 1941 by-elections. *JS*

bill of rights, constitutional mechanism used to safeguard civil rights. It is normally entrenched within a codified constitution, as in the USA, where it was incorporated as amendments 1–10, and overseen by the courts. It is therefore problematic within the UK system of government, where parliament cannot bind its successors and where it would be no more entrenched than any other piece of legislation. As a result, pressure for a bill of rights is often linked to pressure for a codified constitution. The alternative is a bill of rights entrenched not in law but by practice and custom. Such a measure would depend upon a bipartisan consensus; thus the bill would likely be based on political and legal rather than social rights. Pressure for a bill of rights and a codified constitution began in earnest in the 1960s, primarily as a Liberal project, with some support within legal and administrative circles. In contrast, the Labour Party has remained largely hostile, as it is feared such a bill would place too much power in the hands of judges. Conservatives, likewise, were generally hostile to the measure, seeing it as incompatible with constitutional practice and fearing it would entrench social rights. There are notable exceptions to that last trend, including the journalist Ferdinand Mount and Lord Hailsham when in opposition, 1974–9, though his enthusiasm dimmed somewhat once he became lord chancellor in 1979. In 2000, the European Convention on *Human Rights, to which the UK had been a founder signatory, was incorporated into UK law, offering the prospect of a bipartisan bill of rights grounded in custom and practice. *CPS*

Bingham, Thomas Henry (1933–), judge. After army service, Bingham practised at the Bar from 1959 and was a legal adviser to the Department of Employment, 1968–72. A Crown Court recorder, 1975–80, he became a High Court judge, Queen's Bench division, in 1980; a lord justice of appeal, 1986–92; and master of the rolls, 1992–6. Bingham achieved political prominence in 1977–8 when investigating the sanction-busting supply of oil to the illegal Rhodesian regime. He received a life peerage in 1996. *JAR*

Birch, Nigel (1906–81), Conservative politician. Birch's personal fortune, made in the City during the 1930s, afforded him an acerbic independent-mindedness. Elected in 1945, he had become air secretary by 1955 but in 1957 he accepted demotion to become economic secretary to the Treasury. Defeating inflation was his sine qua non, and in 1958 he resigned with Thorneycroft and Powell over government spending. Birch later savaged Macmillan in the Profumo debate, quoting Browning's bitter condemnation of Wordsworth in 'The Lost Leader'. *RJS*

Birkenhead, earl of. See SMITH, FREDERICK EDWIN.

Birmingham Six, Northern Irish men (Hugh Callaghan, Paddy Hill, Gerry Hunter, Richard McIlkenny, Billy Power, Johnny Walker) sentenced in 1975 to life imprisonment for the fatal IRA bombing of two Birmingham pubs in November 1974. They were freed in 1991, the appeal court considering that their convictions were no longer safe and satisfactory since neither the confessions nor the forensic, scientific evidence upon which the convictions rested, were reliable. The men's release prompted the establishment of a royal commission on criminal justice. *RE*

CHRIS MULLIN, *Error of Judgement: The Truth about the Birmingham Bombings* (London, 1990).

Birrell, Augustine (1850–1933), Liberal politician. Son of a Baptist minister, he was educated at Amersham School, Caversham, and Trinity Hall, Cambridge. Called to the Bar in 1875, QC in 1895, and professor of law in London, 1896–9, he also established a reputation as essayist and reviewer on art and literature. Liberal MP for West Fife (1889–1900) and North Bristol (1906–18), Birrell served as president of the Board of Education, 1905–7, promoting the unsuccessful Education Bill of 1906. As chief secretary for Ireland, 1907–16, he established the national university of Ireland by the Irish Universities Act, 1908, which gave Catholics access to higher education. His Land Act, 1909, modified Wyndham's Act of 1903, and made land purchase less expensive. Increasingly sidelined in the home rule negotiations after 1912, he failed to anticipate the Easter Rising and resigned office in May 1916. The longest-serving chief secretary since the Union, his career has been judged as the last attempt to resolve the Irish question by beneficial legislation. *JS*

AUGUSTINE BIRRELL, *Things Past Redress* (London, 1937). | LEON O'BROIN, *The Chief Secretary, Augustine Birrell in Ireland* (London, 1969).

Bishop, Frederick Arthur (1915–), prime ministers' principal private secretary, 1956–9. Having served Anthony Eden, Freddie Bishop played a central part in Harold Macmillan's close-knit Downing Street team. Macmillan found him invaluable in the uncertain early days of his premiership and sent him to Washington to discuss the Middle East with his friend, Secretary of State John Foster Dulles (1957). Bishop attended cabinet meetings, and his advice helped Macmillan to take the initiative in formulating policy. He was deputy secretary to the cabinet, 1959–61. *CL*

Black, Duncan (1908–91), Scottish economist and pioneer of mathematical political science. From his undergraduate days at Glasgow University, Black sought throughout his life to develop a 'pure science of Politics'. His first breakthrough came while fire-watching in Warwick castle in 1942, when he proved the median voter theorem. This states that if all voters can be arranged along one line, say from the 'leftmost' to the 'rightmost', then the favourite option (or candidate) of the median voter is unbeatable. Any defensible choice procedure will select it (him, her). The median voter theorem is a basic analytical tool in political science. However, Black also found that it failed if there was more than one dimension. If, say, 'Protestant' and 'Catholic' cross-cut 'left' and 'right', then there may be no median voter, and no option which would not lose to another in a straight vote. This result has been generalized into some alarming 'chaos theorems' which may seem to cast doubt on the meaning of majority rule. For the last two decades of his life, Black worked on Lewis Carroll, whom he recognized as a fellow misunderstood mathematician. Black proved that Carroll, under his real name of C. L. Dodgson, was one of the profoundest writers on the properties of voting systems and on proportional representation before this century. *IM*

IAIN MCLEAN et al. (eds.), *The Theory of Committees and Elections by Duncan Black* (2nd edn., Dordrecht, 1998). | IAIN MCLEAN et al. (eds.), *A Mathematical Approach to Proportional Representation: Duncan Black on Lewis Carroll* (Dordrecht, 1996).

Black and Tans were the main source of recruits to the *Royal Irish Constabulary (RIC) and formed part of the British determination to use the police rather than the army as the chief weapon in its fight against the IRA. Recruiting offices opened in Britain before the end of 1919 and the first recruits arrived in Ireland in March 1920. There were insufficient police uniforms available, and they were therefore clad in a mixture of military khaki and RIC dark green; this earned them their nickname of 'Black and Tans' after a pack of hounds in Co. Limerick. They were mainly ex-soldiers with a sprinkling of others. Their discipline was in many cases poor and only served to undermine the British cause in the war against the IRA. *DGB*

C. J. M. Townshend, *The British Campaign in Ireland 1919–1921: The Development of Political and Military Policies* (Oxford, 1975).

Black Friday (15 April 1921), the day on which the unions of the railwaymen and the transport workers refused to give their industrial support to the Miners' Federation of Great Britain which was, from 1 April, involved in resisting wage reductions. It led to the collapse of the Triple Alliance and had a bearing on the General Strike of 1926. *KL*

Black Monday (19 October 1987), term used to denote the unprecedented drop in world equity markets which took place when more than £50 billion was wiped off London share values. The collapse was particularly acute in Wall Street when the Dow Jones Industrial Average fell 508.32 points, amounting to 22.6 per cent of its total value. Similar but slightly less spectacular falls were evident in other equity markets. The fall was significantly greater than the one-day 12.9 per cent fall, which heralded the stock market crash of 1929, but in 1987 it was not followed by a major worldwide recession. Stock markets rebounded strongly in part due to interest rate cuts by the central banks and the Bank of England. When evaluating the causes of the crash, many analysts drew attention to the effects of programme trading by large institutions where computers had been automatically set to sell large blocks of shares at predetermined prices, thus accentuating the falls. *JFM*

Black Papers, name given to pamphlets or position papers on education (to distinguish them from government 'white papers') published in the late 1960s and attacking progressive educational ideas. The first, published in March 1969, was *Fight for Education*, as part of the campaign to prevent comprehensivization. The moving forces behind publication were Dr Rhodes Boyson and Professor Caroline Cox, but contributors came from a wide cross-section of the literate and literary classes: *Black Paper 1975*, for example, included contributions by Kingsley Amis, Max Beloff, Robert Conquest, Iris Murdoch, and H. J. Eysenck. They began the counter-attack on educational changes, principally comprehensivization and 'all-ability' teaching, which flowed into the early Thatcherite education policy and had already sparked off Prime Minister Callaghan's call in a speech at Ruskin College, Oxford, in 1976 for 'a great debate' on education. *JS*

Black Rod. See Lords, House of: Officers.

Black Sections (late 1980s–1990). Diane Abbott, Paul Boateng, Bernie Grant, and other black Labour MPs and constituencies demanded that the Labour Party should form an autonomous black section within the Labour Party, to promote the interests of ethnic minorities, at a time when there were also demands for a stronger women's presence in the party. Resolutions in favour of this were defeated at the 1989 and 1990 party conferences, but a Black and Asian Socialist Society was formed. *KL*

Blackshirts. See British Union of Fascists.

Black Wednesday (16 September 1992), the day on which sterling was withdrawn from the European Exchange Rate Mechanism (ERM). After the devaluation of the Italian lira on the previous Monday, speculative pressure grew against the exchange rate of sterling due to the belief that the sterling rate in the ERM was too high. On Wednesday, interest rates were raised to 15 per cent and $15 billion was spent to support the pound. By evening, however, the exchange rate was no longer supportable and the pound was allowed to depreciate. This palpable defeat for a central government policy had a devastating impact on the Major government's standing. *CRS*

Blackwell, Norman Roy (1952–), head of prime minister's policy unit, 1995–7. A professional management consultant and former member of Margaret Thatcher's policy unit (1986–7), Blackwell worked on taxation, public spending, economic, and European policy for John Major, but concentrated chiefly on presentation and electoral strategy. He drafted the 1997 manifesto, supervised policy groups, identified themes for rejuvenating the Conservative programme, and influenced the government's decision to attack 'New' Labour, rather than denying that the party had changed; a strategy which ministers found it difficult to adhere to. *CL*

Blair, Anthony Charles Lynton ('Tony') (1953–), Labour Party leader and prime minister. Blair, a public-school- and Oxford-educated barrister, joined the Labour Party in 1975 and has been Labour MP for Sedgefield since 1983. As a Kinnock loyalist intent on modernizing the party, he served as opposition spokesman on Treasury and economic affairs, 1984–7; trade and industry, 1987–8; and energy, 1988–9; before becoming shadow employment secretary, 1989–92, and shadow home secretary, 1992–4. Following John Smith's death and with the agreement of his chief potential rival Gordon Brown, Blair was easily elected Labour leader in July 1994. Thereafter, he accelerated the Kinnock-Smith modernization process under the slogan 'New Labour' to adapt the party to changing domestic and international circumstances and broaden its appeal. A key 'Blairite' objective was to eradicate Labour's negative image as a left-wing union-dominated 'tax and spend' party associated with public ownership and declining social groups. The successful revision of *Clause 4 (which ended Labour's commitment to nationalization) at a special conference in April 1995 signalled Blair's determination to reposition the party in the political centre. Under his leadership, *New Labour distanced itself from 'old style' socialism by accepting the market economy, promoting communitarianism, embracing the 'stakeholder society', and supporting radical constitutional reform. These ideological shifts were reinforced by Blair's 1997 manifesto pledges to contain public spending, maintain existing taxation rates, and retain Thatcherite industrial relations legislation in order to attract middle-class voters.

Blair also strengthened the power of the Labour leadership in relation to the NEC, conference, and parliamentary party by appealing directly to the members in the country to endorse the revised Clause 4 (1995) and the draft manifesto (1996) and by directly appointing the chief whip. Political opponents, including marginalized Labour left-wingers, claimed that Blair was autocratic and abandoning socialist principles. He launched several other initiatives, including a recruitment drive which increased party membership from 280,000 in 1994 to 420,000 in 1997, and fund-raising activities which produced £15 million in donations from the private sector between June 1996 and March 1997. Careful cultivation of Rupert Murdoch's News International Corporation provided the Labour leader with important backing from the *Sun* and the *News of the World* during the 1997 election campaign. Blair's modernizing strategy and insistence on strict party discipline was vindicated when Labour, aided by Tory divisions and the Major government's unpopularity, secured a huge 179-seat majority at the 1997 general election.

As prime minister, Blair has tightly controlled public expenditure, introduced controversial cost-cutting welfare reforms, and adopted a policy of cautious engagement in Europe. Furthermore, he has pressed ahead with Labour's promised 'constitutional revolution' by creating devolved assemblies for Scotland and Wales, establishing arrangements for a new London authority with an elected mayor, and removing hereditary peers' voting and speaking rights in the Lords. Blair also advanced the Northern Ireland peace process by brokering the 1998 Good Friday agreement but subsequent progress has proved elusive. In 1999 he took a leading role in mobilizing NATO's response to Serbia over the Kosovo crisis. Though like all premiers he had a sticky patch in mid-parliament, Blair continued to exert a remarkable hold on public opinion, to register historically high prime ministerial approval ratings, and was easily re-elected in 2001.

AM

J. Rentoul, *Tony Blair* (London, 1996). | Jon Sopel, *Tony Blair, the Moderniser* (London, 1995).

Blake, Robert Norman William (1916–), historian. Robert Blake was a fellow at Christ Church, Oxford; provost of Queen's; university pro-vice-chancellor; and for seven years a Conservative city councillor. He received many honorary degrees, fellowship of the British Academy, editorship of the *Dictionary of National Biography*, and in 1971 a life peerage. He was also a regular reviewer and broadcaster, and consulted on constitutional issues by Buckingham palace and the cabinet secretary. His first book was an edition of *The Private Papers of Douglas Haig* (1952), which brought him to the attention of Lord Beaverbrook who allowed him access to the papers of Andrew Bonar Law, whose first biography Blake published in 1955 as *The Unknown Prime Minister.* Conservative history proved to be his *métier*, for he went on to write the standard biography of *Disraeli* (1966) and to edit a study of Lord Salisbury. He also delivered in 1968 Oxford's Ford lectures which became *The Conservative Party from Peel to Churchill* (1970), regularly updated and now covering *The Conservative Party from Peel to Major* (1999). Blake was largely responsible for making respectable the academic study of the party which dominated Britain for most of the century. *JAR*

Blakenham, Viscount. See Hare, John Hugh.

Blaney, Neil (1922–95), Irish politician. Blaney was a Fianna Fáil cabinet minister dismissed in 1970 amid accusations of conspiring to import arms. The charges were dismissed but Blaney later confirmed the existence of a plot to import arms for militant nationalists in Northern Ireland. Despite expulsion from Fianna Fáil in 1977, Blaney topped the poll in North-East Donegal and remained an independent Fianna Fáil member of the Dáil. He represented Connaught-Ulster, 1979–84, in the European parliament. *TWH*

Blatchford, Robert (1851–1943), socialist journalist. Blatchford reputedly made more socialists than any other individual through his editorship of the *Clarion*, a socialist weekly, and of *Merrie England* (1893). *Merrie England*, a collection of articles from the *Clarion*, was republished in 1894 in a penny edition which subsequently sold more than two million copies worldwide and marked the high point of Blatchford's career. The *Clarion* also spawned the *Clarion movement. Previous to the formation of the *Clarion* he had served for seven years in the army and was then a journalist on the *Sunday Chronicle*, and it was his articles for the *Sunday Chronicle* on the Manchester slums that made him a socialist. Blatchford was not a public speaker and disliked party manoeuvring and organization. His crusading journalism and his romantic and utopian socialism often brought him into conflict with the leaders of the Independent Labour Party and later the Labour Party. In particular this was the case with his pro-war views on the Boer war, his campaign against orthodox religion, his espousal of a direct and undiluted socialism, his support for socialist unity, and increasingly his fears about German militarism. He published a number of books including *Britain for the British* (1902), *God and My Neighbour* (1903), *Not Guilty: A Defence of the Bottom Dog* (1905), *The Sorcery Shop* (1907), and an autobiography *My Eighty Years* (1931). He drifted away from the Labour movement in the years before 1914 with his espousal of rearmament and preparation for war. During the Great War and the inter-war years, he was a journalist on a number of national newspapers. *JAJ*

Laurence Thompson, *Robert Blatchford* (London, 1951).

Bledisloe, Lord. See Bathurst, Charles.

Bletchley Park. See Government Communications Headquarters.

Bligh, Timothy (1918–69), prime ministers' principal private secretary, 1959–64. A wartime naval hero and former Treasury official, who had been private secretary to Sir Edward Bridges (1949–54), Tim Bligh initially found Freddie Bishop a difficult act to follow, but his Whitehall contacts and political nous led him to become a trusted aide to Harold Macmillan. Like Bishop he attended cabinet. He concentrated primarily on Treasury matters, but had influence elsewhere; for example, he advised Macmillan on his infamous 1962 reshuffle. He was an important intermediary for the prime minister during the Profumo affair and the leadership crisis (both 1963). His close association with Macmillan, rewarded with a controversial knighthood, would probably have frustrated his official career had he not left the civil service soon after his departure from Sir Alec Douglas-Home's Downing Street in the summer of 1964 (having advised Douglas-Home on the best time for the Conservatives to call an election). He subsequently attempted to become a Conservative parliamentary candidate. *CL*

Blitz (1940–1). The term 'Blitz' is actually a shortened version of the German *Blitzkrieg*, meaning lightning war, but the British used 'Blitz' to mean the bombing raids against the country by the German air force from the late summer of 1940 to the spring of 1941. Most large British cities were hit but the image of the British people, especially Londoners, sheltering by night then carrying on with their work by day became a potent symbol of defiance, earning Britain tremendous respect in the still neutral USA. *MLC*

'blood, toil, tears, and sweat', famously offered by Winston Churchill in his first Commons speech as prime minister, 13 May 1940, repeated that evening in a BBC radio broadcast. The phrase derived from John Donne and had also been used by Byron. Its use illustrated both Churchill's combative war leadership and his ability to conjure a message of shared Englishness to his listeners in 1940. *NJC*

Bloody Sunday (30 January 1972), when thirteen men were shot dead and seventeen more wounded by the soldiers of the Parachute Regiment in Derry (another man died later). None of those who were shot appeared to have been armed. The shooting began after a civil rights rally when part of the crowd attempted to climb over a street barrier and were forced back by the army with rubber bullets and a water-cannon. Over a hundred youths threw stones and iron bars at the soldiers and a running battle ensued. The question of who fired the first actual shot, however, has remained a highly contested issue ever since.

Bloody Sunday brought a wave of criticism on Britain from around the world and fury among

Irish nationalists, John *Hume noting that for many people in the Bogside it was 'a united Ireland or nothing'. Bernadette *Macaliskey struck British Home Secretary Reginald Maudling in the House of Commons and on 2 February the British embassy in Dublin was attacked by an angry mob and burned down. In April 1972 a committee of inquiry, headed by Lord Widgery, criticized the actions of the army on Bloody Sunday but did not state clearly that those killed were unarmed. In August 1973 at the inquest into the deaths, however, coroner Hubert O'Neill described the killings as amounting to 'sheer unadulterated bloody murder'. In January 1997, demands for a fresh inquiry grew with the publication of Don Mullan's *Eyewitness: Bloody Sunday* which uncovered evidence contradicting the findings of the *Widgery report. Although rejected by earlier Conservative administrations, on 29 January 1998 Prime Minister Tony Blair announced a fresh inquiry into Bloody Sunday. The new inquiry, under Lord Saville, opened in April 1998. *GG*

DON MULLAN, *Eyewitness: Bloody Sunday* (Dublin, 1997).

'blown off course', phrase from a Commons speech by Prime Minister Harold Wilson on 20 July 1966. Following a seven-week strike by seamen, which had slowed down exports, Wilson decided against devaluation in favour of a prices and incomes policy and cuts in public expenditure to reassure holders of sterling. He claimed, unconvincingly, that the strike had been the only cause of the government's change of course. *BB*

Blue Streak, abandoned British surface-to-surface missile. With its emphasis on reduced military expenditure but not reduced military presence, the 1957 Sandys defence white paper committed Britain to nuclear deterrence. Blue Streak was to be Britain's own medium-range missile from the mid-1960s. Although boosted by increased Anglo-American nuclear collaboration after the July 1958 revision of the McMahon Act, Blue Streak was cancelled, mainly on grounds of cost, in March 1960 when the Americans agreed that Britain could purchase the US Skybolt missile. *JRVE*

Blunkett, David (1947–), Labour politician. Born into a Sheffield working-class family, Blunkett, despite his blindness, graduated with a degree in politics, became leader of Sheffield city council (1980–7), entered the Commons in 1983, and was appointed to Blair's cabinet in 1997 as secretary for education. Widely admired for his tenacity in overcoming obstacles, in the 1980s he moved away from the 'hard left' of the Labour Party but has retained some puritanical attitudes. Blunkett has published a memoir (with Alex MacCormick), *On a Clear Day* (1995). In the aftermath of the 2001 election he moved to the Home Office. *DEM*

Blunt, Anthony Frederick (1907–83), art historian and Soviet agent. Blunt was educated at Marlborough and Trinity College, Cambridge, where he gained a first in modern languages and became a fellow. As an undergraduate he joined the intellectually exclusive secret society, the Apostles, became a committed Marxist, and was recruited as a Soviet agent and talent spotter by Guy Burgess. Like many Apostles, Blunt was homosexual. In 1937 he resigned his fellowship to join the staff of the Warburg Institute and lectured at London's Courtauld Institute of Art. Blunt joined the British Security Service (MI5) in 1940, remaining with them for the duration of the war. During this time, he passed to Soviet controllers papers concerning every aspect of the service, together with many military secrets. Blunt's departure from MI5 ended his usefulness as an agent, though he kept in touch with Burgess till his defection: 'Kim' Philby, another of the Cambridge spies, used Blunt to tip off Donald Maclean about his impending arrest. In parallel with his life as a Soviet agent, Blunt enjoyed a career as one of the century's most important art historians. In 1945, he was appointed surveyor of the king's pictures, and in 1947 became the director of the Courtauld Institute and professor of art in the University of London. Clear evidence of his treachery emerged in 1964, and, with guarantees of immunity, he confessed. In 1979, the prime minister confirmed Blunt's role as a Soviet agent. As a consequence, he was subjected to a campaign of media vilification, losing many honours including his knighthood and honorary fellowship at Trinity. *PM*

Boardman, Thomas Gray (1919–), Conservative politician. Elected to parliament in 1967, Tom Boardman was appointed industry minister in 1972 and was closely involved as coal minister in the Heath government's dispute with the miners over their pay during 1973–4. He became chief secretary to the Treasury in 1974, only a month before the February election was called. He was defeated in October 1974 and pursued a business career. Having become a life peer in 1980, he was a party treasurer, 1981–2. *RJS*

Boer war (1899–1902), a conflict between the British Empire and the Boer republics of Transvaal and Orange Free State, precipitated by British determination to uphold the political rights of uitlanders ('foreigners') in Transvaal, but behind which lay the ambition of Lord Milner, British high commissioner in South Africa, to annex the Rand goldfields. Militarily, the war fell into two phases. There was a conventional war between October 1899 and June 1900, which began with a series of defeats for the outnumbered British forces, the situation retrieved after the appointment of Lord Roberts as commander-in-chief; this was followed by a guerrilla war during which the British, under Kitchener, resorted to ruthless scorched earth tactics and the use of 'concentration camps'. A peace treaty was concluded at Vereeniging in May 1902. Politically, the war enjoyed much popular support in Britain, especially during the first phase, culminating in the relief of *Mafeking (17 May 1900), but the guerrilla war alienated many and the Liberal Party was badly divided. Diplomatically, the war highlighted British weakness and initiated the search for a less isolationist foreign policy. *JMB*

Thomas Pakenham, *The Boer War* (London, 1973). | Iain R. Smith, *The Origins of the South African War of 1899–1902* (London, 1994).

Bogdanor, Vernon Bernard (1943–), political scientist. A fellow of Brasenose College, Oxford, since 1966, he has written widely on the history and structure of the British constitution. His first book was *Devolution* (1979). His second, *The People and the Party System* (1981), analysed the debate on the referendum and on proportional representation since 1832. His other books include *Multi-Party Politics and the Constitution* (1983) which explored the impact that proportional representation might have on British constitutional structure, *The Monarchy and the Constitution* (1995), and *Power and the People: A Guide to Constitutional Reform* (1998). Some of his essays were collected in *Politics and the Constitution* (1996): this title expresses his fundamental view of the British constitution, for he sees it essentially as a political constitution in that its working at any particular time depends as much upon political contingencies as upon any constitutional principle. Thus, to analyse the constitution, the skills of the political scientist are as important as those of the constitutional lawyer. He attributes the main influences on his thinking to the lucidity of Geoffrey Marshall, the pragmatism of David Butler, and the historical range of S. E. Finer. But, in his contribution to the British Academy study *The British Contribution to Political Science in the Twentieth Century* (1999), he concluded that the study of politics does not yield laws or law-like generalizations; it is, at bottom, an approach towards understanding one aspect of the history of a society. *DEB*

'Bolshevism run mad' (1931), phrase of abuse used by Philip *Snowden during the general election of 1931. He used it in a BBC radio broadcast on 16 October to contrast the 'revolutionary' politics of the Labour Party with his own 'sane and evolutionary socialism'. *KL*

'bomber will always get through, the', phrase used by Baldwin in a Commons debate, 10 November 1932. It was part of a warning of the impossibility of government protecting 'the man in the street' from air attack, and was typical of early 1930s expectations of a future war. *JAR*

Bombing School incident. In September 1936 three leading members of Plaid Cymru set fire to the RAF Bombing School which had been built in the Welsh-speaking community of Pen-y-Berth on the Llyn peninsula in Caernarfonshire. Saunders Lewis, the Revd Lewis Valentine, and D. J. Williams themselves informed the authorities of their actions. There was a degree of nationalist indignation in Wales when the government transferred the trial from Wales to the Old Bailey and when the three were then sent to Wormwood Scrubs for nine months after refusing to give evidence in English. *PS*

Bonar Law, Andrew. See Law, Andrew Bonar.

Bondfield, Margaret (1873–1953), trade unionist and Labour politician. Bondfield was primarily a trade unionist. She joined the National Union of Shop Assistants; was the only woman on the TUC in 1899; and was involved in the Women's Trade Union League, the National Federation of Women Workers, and the Standing Joint Committee on Women's Industrial Organizations. She supported women's suffrage but was president of the Adult Suffrage Society, which rejected the limited suffrage ideas of the Pankhursts. These interests drew her into the work of the National Federation of Women Workers and the War Emergency Workers' National Committee during the Great War. Thereafter she rose rapidly in Labour circles. Elected to the general council of the TUC in 1918, she became its first woman chairman in 1923. Returned as MP for Northampton in 1923, she became minister of labour in the first Labour government, thus becoming the first woman to enter the cabinet, and the first woman privy councillor. But her support for Ramsay MacDonald in 1931 led to the loss of her influence within the Labour Party and the TUC, along with her parliamentary seat. *KL*

Margaret Bondfield, *A Life's Work* (London, 1949).

'bonfire of controls' (1948). As president of the Board of Trade, Harold Wilson took advantage of an improving economy to remove many controls and rationing rules inherited from the war. With a good publicity sense, he chose Guy Fawkes's day, 5 November 1948, for the gesture, announcing that he was having a 'little bonfire' of controls, and was later photographed tearing up a clothes-ration book. The Labour left favoured the continuation of controls on planning and egalitarian grounds but Wilson's act better reflected the mood of business and the country. *BJE*

Bonham Carter, Lady (Helen) Violet (1887–1969), Liberal activist, daughter of H. H. *Asquith and his first wife, Helen Melland. Privately educated in Dresden and Paris, as a committed Liberal, she supported her father's career both in and out of office, and was later the self-appointed guardian of his reputation too. President of the Women's Liberal Federation, 1923–5 and 1939–45, and of the Liberal Party Organization, 1945–7, she was nevertheless a friend and strong supporter of Winston Churchill (whom she had first known well in his Liberal days) and, later, of his anti-appeasement campaign. A strong supporter of the League of Nations, she also in later life supported European union, becoming vice-chairman of the United Europe movement in 1947. She married her father's political secretary, Maurice Bonham Carter, in 1915. In her later career, she was known primarily as a frequent broadcaster on radio and television news and discussion programmes. *JS*

Mark Pottle (ed.), *Diaries and Letters of Lady Violet Bonham Carter, 1904–1969*, 3 vols. (London, 1988–2000).

Bonham Carter, Mark Raymond (1922–94), Liberal politician, victor of the *Torrington by-election which marked the beginning of the post-war Liberal revival. The son of Sir Maurice and Lady Violet *Bonham Carter, he was educated at Winchester and Balliol College, Oxford, before serving in the Second World War. He unsuccessfully contested Barnstaple in the 1945 general election, turning thereafter to a career in publishing. With the first symptoms of a possible Liberal revival under Jo *Grimond, he stood at Torrington in 1958, making the first Liberal by-election gain since 1929. Torrington was lost, though, in the 1959 general election and Bonham Carter then devoted himself to Liberal Party organization. In 1966 he became the first chairman of the Race Relations Board, and headed the renamed Community Relations Commission, 1971–7. Interested in European issues and the arts, he re-emerged as a strong supporter of the *Alliance and became a life peer in 1986 as Lord Bonham Carter of Yarnbury. In 1988, he became Liberal Democrat foreign affairs' spokesman, introducing a successful private member's bill to give British citizenship to non-Chinese ethnic minorities in Hong Kong. *JS*

Boothby, Robert John Graham (1900–86), Tory maverick. Born in Edinburgh but educated at Eton, Bob Boothby supported Lloyd George's coalition government while at Oxford and always regarded himself as a 'Lloyd George radical'. In 1923, he stood unsuccessfully for Orkney and Shetland, and afterwards worked in Baldwin's secretariat. He was elected MP for East Aberdeenshire in 1924 and became a tireless champion of its farmers and fishermen. He had, however, embarked upon a city career for which he was ill-suited, and begun an endless round of travel and socializing that brought him many friends, including the conductor Thomas Beecham, Noel Coward, and Somerset Maugham, but militated against a political career. Although he became in 1926 parliamentary private secretary to Churchill, the then chancellor of the exchequer, he criticized the government over unemployment and in *Industry and the State*, published in 1927, joined other Tory rebels, including Macmillan, to urge economic intervention. In 1929, Boothby began a long relationship with Dorothy Macmillan that further damaged his career. He was among the first to urge economic expansion and rearmament, and having met Hitler in 1932 was an early opponent of appeasement. In 1940 he became Lord Woolton's deputy at the Ministry of Food, but within a year his earlier failure to declare an interest in Czech assets prompted a Commons inquiry and he had to resign. An advocate of European unity, he played a leading part in the Council of Europe from 1949. He was bitterly disappointed at being overlooked for office by Churchill in 1951, but his iconoclastic views, gravelly voice, and sharp wit enriched post-war debate and made him a radio and television celebrity. Macmillan made him a life peer in 1958 and he sat as a cross-bencher. *RJS*

ROBERT BOOTHBY, *Recollections of a Rebel* (London, 1978). | ROBERT RHODES JAMES, *Bob Boothby* (London, 1991).

Boreham, (Arthur) John (1925–94), government statistician. Boreham served as a statistician in a number of government departments, including the ministries of food, agriculture, and technology, as well as the Central Statistical Office (CSO), where he was deputy director, 1972–8, before becoming its director and head of the Government Statistical Service (GSS), 1978–85. He took the full force of the Thatcher government's determination to impose swinging cuts on the GSS in the early 1980s, but worked to maintain the quality and integrity of official statistics. *KT*

borough councils. See LOCAL GOVERNMENT STRUCTURE.

borstals, prisons for young offenders, named after the village in Kent where the first such institution was sited. It was initiated by the Prevention of Crime Act, 1908, which provided for the training of young offenders between 16 and 21 years old in order to wean them away from a criminal life. Originally an American idea, the borstal became the hope of enlightened prison reformers such as Sir Alexander Paterson (1884–1947), who worked with ex-borstal boys and was a prison commissioner, 1922–47. Under his influence, borstals provided recreational and educational facilities, adopting some of the house and honour systems of the public schools. Initially successful at reducing recidivism rates, the success of the borstals came under pressure as the number of juvenile offenders rose and there were calls for harsher treatment of young offenders. With growing juvenile delinquency, increasing recidivism, and changing public attitudes towards the ethos of the borstals, they were supplemented from the 1950s by approved schools for offenders of school age and detention centres to administer a *'short sharp shock' to young offenders between 15 and 21 years. Gradually, the role of the borstal and its very name was squeezed out of the juvenile punishment system. Secure units are available for offenders under 14 years who require detention, 'young offender' institutions deal with young people between 15 and 17 years, while those over 18 years are dealt with in adult prisons. The borstal system was inaugurated in the heyday of *New Liberalism, much influenced by *Christian socialism and *progressivism. After initial success, the rising tide of crime since 1945 has increasingly pushed debate towards more effective forms of reducing juvenile offending. *JS*

BAILEY, VICTOR, *Delinquency and Citizenship: Reclaiming the Young Offender, 1914–1948* (Oxford, 1987).

Bottomley, Horatio William (1860–1933), journalist, Liberal and independent MP, and fraud. Orphaned at the age of 5, Bottomley was befriended by Charles Bradlaugh (1833–91). He was a director and chairman of the *Financial Times*, 1888–9, declared bankrupt in 1891 but acquitted on a charge of conspiracy. He founded a string of companies with a combined capital of over £20 million, from which he allegedly took over £3 million for himself, though all failed. Between 1901 and 1905 he was the subject of over sixty bankruptcy petitions and writs. Bottomley's most successful publishing venture was *John Bull*, a penny weekly with a populist style which appeared under the slogan 'politics without party—criticism without cant'. Elected as a Liberal for South Hackney in 1906 and again in 1910, another bankruptcy in 1911 forced him out of politics, but he retained assets in his wife's name and continued to make money out of sweepstakes and lotteries. Adopting a stridently jingoistic stance at the outbreak of the Great War, Bottomley earned great popularity as a patriotic speaker and assisted in the recruiting drives. He started to sell government Victory Bonds through *John Bull*, but characteristically retained the proceeds, almost £900,000. Elected Independent MP for South Hackney, 1918, he was expelled from the Commons in 1922 following his prosecution for fraud and sentenced to seven years' penal servitude. When embarrassingly spotted sewing mailbags in gaol by a former political friend who murmured, 'Sewing, Bottomley?', he replied, 'No, reaping.' *JS*

Bottomley, Virginia Hilda (1948–), Conservative politician and beauty, married to humorous independent-minded Peter, apostle of the seat belt. She was MP for Surrey South-West from 1984, but never a Thatcherite, having worked for the Child Poverty Action Group. Bottomley advanced to cabinet under Major, becoming secretary successively for health and heritage. Advised by Professor Tomlinson, she undertook, heroically but with doubtful political prudence, the reorganization of Greater London hospitals, involving intellectually sound central concentration and local closure, but hostility was reflected in great anti-Conservative swings in localities affected. *EP*

boundary commission, local government, generic term covering a succession of commissions established to provide for the adjustment, as distinct from the comprehensive review, of local government structure. Prior to 1972, adjusting local government boundaries in response to urban growth and population change had proved an intractable problem. In the early part of the century, expanding county boroughs, or lesser authorities seeking county borough status, applied to the local government board for boundary alterations, mergers, or promotion. The president of the board had the power to make an order under the Local Government Act, 1888, as did the county councils themselves, subject to confirmation by the board. The procedures were awkward, the issues conflictual, and the system was replaced under the Local Government Act, 1926, by a reversion to private bill procedure. Parliamentary opposition ensured that successful bills were few, and the local government structure remained largely frozen in the 19th-century pattern. The problem of modernization remained, and the device of an expert commission, independent of party politics, to establish boundaries was resorted to by the coalition government in 1945. This first local government boundary commission was set up under Sir Malcolm Trustram Eve. The commission clashed with Minister of Health Aneurin Bevan, and was dissolved in 1949 without its proposals being implemented. The local government commission set up in 1958 found the task no easier. Impatient of adjustment, the Wilson government abolished that commission in favour of a radical review of structure by the *Redcliffe-Maud commission.

The comprehensive reorganization of structure which followed under the Local Government Act, 1972, established local government boundary commissions for England and Wales, to undertake rolling programmes of reviews and to keep the structure up to date until they, too, were dissolved in 1992. In England, a successor body, the local government commission, conducted a series of local structural reviews with the remit to create unitary authorities wherever they matched the circumstances of the area. Meanwhile, Wales had been treated separately under the 1958 Act, with its own local government commission. That commission made a number of proposals for rationalizing Welsh local government but, following the election of a Labour government in 1964, the newly established Welsh Office undertook its own process of consultation, producing a new framework based, as in England, on a sharp reduction in the number of authorities, and on the demotion of county boroughs to district status. These changes were incorporated in the 1972 Act. The Major government's plan to introduce unitary authorities, while less than successful in England, was uniformly applied to Wales—without the impediment of a commission—in the reorganization of 1996. The advantage of the commission model was that it distanced ministers from detailed involvement in local boundary issues, while they retained the responsibility to lay orders before parliament. The disadvantage was that while they were effective as mechanisms of adjustment, they proved unsuitable vehicles for the pursuit of any wider ministerial ambition to reorganize local government. *KY*

Boundary Commission, Parliamentary, the body responsible for recommending the boundaries for parliamentary constituencies. A commission was first created under the Representation of the People Act, 1918, but was an ad hoc arrangement, and a permanent commission was only brought into being by the 1944 House of Commons (Redistribution of Seats) Act. It comprises four separate commissions, one each for England, Scotland, Wales, and Northern Ireland. Each is chaired by the Speaker of the Commons (a non-party figure who in practice never participates) and each has a judge as deputy chairman. Assistant commissioners, almost always lawyers, are appointed to supervise local inquiries, and the commissions are advised by specialists in population and geographic surveys. The commissions are guided by rules laid down by parliament. They are supposed to ensure that constituencies are as equal as possible in the size of their electorates but they may deviate from this equality if special geographic considerations (for example, the size, shape, and accessibility of a constituency) appear to make this desirable. They are expected not to cross local government boundaries in creating constituencies. The commissions also deal with different electoral quotas (the average electorate per constituency), the quota in Scotland and Wales in the latter half of the century being smaller than in England. Under legislation passed in 1992, there must now be a review of boundaries every eight to twelve years (previously it was every ten to fifteen years), though a commission may issue an interim report. Recommendations from each commission are presented to the appropriate secretary of state, who is then required to lay them before parliament. Sometimes the redistribution proves controversial, working for or against the advantage of a particular party. Boundary reviews were the subject of protests in 1948 and 1955. In 1969 the Labour home secretary, James Callaghan, advised his supporters in the Commons to vote against the commission's recommendations, which they did. A review in 1982 was challenged unsuccessfully in the courts by the Labour Party. MPs await the recommendations of the commission with sometimes greater trepidation than they await the verdict of the electors. *PN*

ROBERT BLACKBURN, *The Electoral System in Britain* (London, 1995). | H. F. RAWLINGS, *Law and the Electoral Process* (London, 1988). | D. J. ROSSITER, R. J. JOHNSTON, and C. J. PATTIE, *The Boundary Commission: Redrawing the United Kingdom's Map of Parliamentary Constituencies* (Manchester, 1999).

Bowden, Herbert William (1905–94), Labour whip and minister. Labour's chief whip in the long years of opposition, 1951–64, he was a disciplinarian who supported the attempt to expel Bevan in 1955 and campaigned with Gaitskell against the adoption of unilateralist candidates in winnable seats in the run-up to the 1964 election. Appointed leader of the House in 1964, he was dropped after the 1966 election and left the Commons in 1967 to head the Independent Broadcasting Authority. He took a life peerage as Lord Aylestone, and joined the Social Democratic Party in 1981. *BB*

Bow Group, Conservative voluntary group, devoted to policy discussion, research, and publications. Founded in 1950, its name derived from early meetings at the Bow and Bromley Conservative Club in East London, at which Conservative ex-students attempted to emulate what the Fabians provided for Labour. It was welcomed by Central Office but made little impact until relaunched in 1957 with the magazine *Crossbow*, and through the chairmanships of ambitious future front-benchers, notably Geoffrey Howe, who said that Bow Groupers wanted 'to make the Tory Party fit for Observer and Guardian readers to live in' (Ramsden, 54). The group ran speaker-meetings in Westminster, attempts to form regional branches having little lasting success; policy groups whose reports were published; Conference fringe meetings; and *Crossbow*. It encouraged policy debate, insisting that publications represented only their authors' views, but was nevertheless thought of as on the Conservative left, particularly when from the 1960s the Monday Club attracted younger right-wing activists. But while the youth of its membership meant that most Bow Groupers reflected contemporary acceptance of the mixed economy and the welfare state, many were also more sceptical. While tender on social issues, Bow Groupers were tough on defence and public finance, and, as these assumptions came increasingly into conflict, the group drifted towards the right of the party. In the early 1970s, dismayed by the performance of the Heath government, that trend accelerated, and by 1975 *The Economist* saw the group as 'a monetarist, free-market only shrine' (Ramsden, 419). After 1975, the group's place on the left was taken over by Pressure for Economic and Social Toryism and the Tory Reform Group. Since there was a plethora of factions and groups on the right, the Bow Group lost much of its distinctiveness, but remained an important training ground in politics for future MPs. *JAR*

JOHN RAMSDEN, *The Winds of Change, 1957–1975* (London, 1996).

Bowley, Arthur Lyon (1869–1957), statistician and social investigator. An academic mathematician who held chairs at the LSE, 1919–36, and at Reading University, he was later director of the Oxford Institute of Statistics, 1940–4. Bowley developed applied statistics for the field of social studies, especially sampling techniques, which contributed to the British empirical school of social science. Major social investigations included *Livelihood and Poverty* (1915) and the *New Survey of London Life and Labour* (1930–5). *JS*

Bowyer, George Edward Wentworth (1886–1948), Conservative politician, whip, and party organizer. Bowyer entered parliament in 1918 for Buckingham which he held until 1937. He was a party whip, 1925–35, during the critical Baldwin years, and was appointed to the newly created party vice-chairmanship in 1930 with the remit to interview prospective candidates and advise constituencies on suitable nominees. He secured a parliamentary secretaryship at the Ministry of Agriculture during the Chamberlain wartime administration. As Lord Denham, he was a whip in the Lords. *NJC*

Boyd, Alan Tindal. See LENNOX-BOYD, ALAN TINDAL.

Boyd-Carpenter, John Archibald (1908–98), Conservative politician. Elected in 1945, Boyd-Carpenter quickly emerged as a pugnacious debater. He became a minister in 1951, launching the motorway programme and introducing pay-related pensions before he entered Macmillan's cabinet as chief secretary to the Treasury in 1962. Sacked from the front bench in 1966, he masterminded Tory backbench opposition to Lords' reform during 1968–9 and was a vigorous member of the upper house from 1972. *RJS*

John Boyd-Carpenter, *Way of Life* (London, 1980).

Boyle, Edward Charles Gurney (1923–81), cabinet minister and liberal Tory. Heir to wealth and a baronetcy, and educated at Eton, Boyle was still at Oxford when he fought the 1948 Birmingham, Perry Barr by-election. In 1950, aged only 27, he won the Birmingham, Handsworth by-election. He became a junior supply minister in 1954, and a year later was appointed economic secretary to the Treasury. He felt, however, that Suez was dishonourable, and resigned. Macmillan quickly restored him to office at education, and in 1959 he became financial secretary to the Treasury, where he supported incomes policy and French-style indicative planning. As an admirer of Butler, it was appropriate that he entered the cabinet in 1962 as minister of education, and the following year he supported Butler for the leadership. After 1964, his liberalism made him ill-suited as shadow home secretary, and in 1965 he became shadow education minister. He left the front bench in 1969 and his replacement as education spokesman by Thatcher can be seen as the portent of a transformation in Conservative politics. Boyle sat in the Lords as a cross-bencher from 1970, was vice-chancellor of Leeds University, and chaired the top salaries review body. *RJS*

Boyson, Rhodes (1925–), Conservative politician, with a reputation before late political entry as an outstanding headmaster (Highbury Grove Comprehensive), and contributing editor of the education **Black Papers*, advocating stiffer standards in teaching, well ahead of later received wisdom and then highly unfashionable. From a Labour background, with strong Lancashire roots and accent, Boyson was characteristic of Thatcherite Tory politics. He was successively junior minister for education (often at diverting odds with St John Stevas, his secretary of state), social security, and Northern Ireland, 1979–86, and led the 1988 backbench revolt against John Moore's plans for social security reform, which effectively destroyed Moore. *EP*

Bracken, Brendan (1901–58), Conservative politician and newspaper proprietor. An illegitimate child of Irish descent with a mop of ginger hair (detractors speculated upon Winston Churchill being his father), Bracken was a live wire, tall, vigorous, and temperamental who grew up in Australia and sought to hide his Irish origins. After a career in newspapers, he entered politics in 1929, winning Paddington North. After defeat in 1945 he inherited Henry Page-Croft's safe Bournemouth seat and remained in parliament until 1951. In 1923 he first came into contact with Churchill, and during the 1930s he was one of the few MPs who allied himself with Churchill over India, rearmament, and appeasement. This loyalty to Churchill undoubtedly hindered the development of his career but was rewarded in September 1939 with a position as Churchill's parliamentary private secretary. His experience of the newspaper industry precipitated his move to the Ministry of Information, 1941–5, when the fledgling ministry had finally overcome its initial problems. He became first lord of the Admiralty in 1945, but only for a few weeks. Bracken continued to act as chairman of the *Financial Times* until his death. *NJC*

Richard Cockett (ed.), *My Dear Max: The Letters of Brendan Bracken to Lord Beaverbrook 1925–1958* (London, 1990). | Charles Lysaght, *Brendan Bracken* (London, 1979).

Bradbury, John Swanwick (1870–1952), civil servant. After education at Manchester and Oxford, Bradbury entered the Treasury and worked on the 1909 *'People's Budget'. He also helped to frame the financial aspects of the *National Insurance Act, 1911, and was insurance commissioner, 1911–13, before returning to the Treasury as permanent secretary, 1913–19. In the latter role, he was responsible for raising the huge sums required to fight the Great War, one part of which was the issue of paper currency, notes popularly known as 'Bradburies'. He was subsequently a British delegate to the international reparations commission, receiving a peerage in 1925, and strongly supporting the return to the gold standard in the same year. *JAR*

Braddock, Elizabeth Margaret ('Bessie') (1899–1970) and **Tom** (1893–1963), husband and wife team who were key figures in the Labour movement in Liverpool, both serving for more than 30 years on Liverpool city council. Although involved with the Communist Party in the 1920s they became increasingly hostile to the left of the party. Bessie was MP for Liverpool Exchange (1945–70), sat on the NEC, and was a large, flamboyant, and sometimes abrasive figure in the House of Commons. *JAJ*

Bessie and Tom Braddock, *The Braddocks* (Liverpool, 1963).

Brailsford, Henry Noel (1873–1958), Socialist author and journalist. Brailsford wrote regularly on international affairs for a variety of newspapers and journals, including the *Manchester*

Guardian, the *Daily Herald*, and the *New Statesman*. A lifelong internationalist, he was an outspoken critic of British foreign policy. In *The War of Steel and Gold* (1914) he provided a textbook for those on the left trying to formulate a socialist foreign policy. Although a severe critic of the treaty of Versailles and a strong supporter of the League of Nations, Brailsford was one of the first to recognize the growing menace of Nazism and to advocate a military alliance of the anti-fascist powers. He provided one of the strongest contemporary indictments of Chamberlain's appeasement policy. He was similarly outspoken in his attacks on British imperialism and a fervent supporter of colonial independence. Brailsford always considered himself a socialist but was never doctrinaire. Having joined the Independent Labour Party (ILP) in 1907 he transformed the party's newspaper, the *New Leader*, into the country's leading weekly review during his spell as editor, 1922–6. One of the authors of the ILP's policy statement *Socialism in Our Time* (1926), which was rejected by the Labour Party, Brailsford nonetheless opposed its secession in 1932, remaining within the Labour Party and helping to organize Stafford Cripps's *Socialist League. He supported left-wing unity whilst outraging others on the left by his condemnation of the Russian purge trials, was one of the founders of *Tribune* in 1937, and was active in the movement to support the Spanish republican government during the civil war. Although a prolific author on foreign affairs, Brailsford is best remembered for *The Levellers and the English Revolution* (1961), a solid work of historical research. He is widely regarded as one of the greatest journalists of his generation and one of the outstanding socialist political writers of the century. *MC*

Braveheart (1995), Oscar-winning film, directed by and starring Mel Gibson. It portrayed the life of the 13th-century Scottish patriot Sir William Wallace, who led a campaign of resistance against the English occupation under Edward I. Although the film was historically inaccurate, it did capture the imagination and emotions of many Scots and was used by the Scottish National Party to boost its support. The film's success in Scotland produced the phrase the '*Braveheart* factor', used to describe popular and emotional empathy with Scottish nationalism. *RF*

'breaking the mould', phrase widely used by the *Alliance in 1981 to denote the imminent break-up of the current electoral situation under the impact of the new grouping. The aim of the newly founded *Social Democratic Party and their partners, the Liberal Party, was to forge a powerful force in British politics which would supplant the Labour Party as principal opposition to the Conservatives or possibly establish themselves as a dominant party of the progressive centre-left. The phrase appeared in Roy Jenkins's *What Matters Now* (1972), but only achieved wide currency with the formation of the Alliance a decade later, and was referred to with increasing irony as their hopes collapsed after the 1983 general election. *JS*

Bretton Woods, small town in New Hampshire which gave its name in 1944 to the international agreements signed there between the non-Axis powers that set up the International Monetary Fund (IMF), the International Bank for Reconstruction and Development (or World Bank), and the International Trade Organization (ITO). These institutions established new rules of conduct for the post-war capitalist world to encourage monetary stability and international trade to flourish. Centre-stage in early negotiations was President Franklin Roosevelt's determination to promote freer trade. In theory, the British government was sympathetic to Roosevelt's determination to establish a *Pax Americana* based on the model of the free-trading *Pax Britannica* of the 19th century. In practice, Britain needed discriminatory trading practices and currency controls to rebuild its economy after the war. In the end, though, it was American politics that killed off the ITO in 1946 when congress refused to surrender its power to protect American producers. It was replaced by the less ambitious General Agreement on Tariff and Trade. Agreement on monetary questions was achieved more easily because Anglo-American experts were in agreement as to how best to 'manage' the international economy. The World Bank was given a treasury of $7.6 billion, mostly from America, to help rebuild war-torn Europe and to promote economic development in Africa, Asia, and Latin America. The IMF's mission was to help countries to control currency crises—by offering stabilization loans—that, otherwise unchecked, threatened to destabilize the international economy too. At first, however, these institutions were overwhelmed by the task of post-war reconstruction and it took until 1958 for them to make a real contribution to stability and globalization in the international economy. *PC*

Michael Bordo and Barry Eichengreen (eds.), *A Retrospective on the Bretton Woods System* (Chicago, 1993).

Bridgeman, William Clive (1864–1935), Conservative politician. MP for Oswestry, 1906–29, Willie Bridgeman was an ardent *tariff reformer. As a whip he eased his party through problems over Ireland, the 1911 Parliament Act, and conscription. He had an interest in industrial relations which was reflected in a succession of junior ministerial posts from 1916. A friend of Baldwin, in 1922 he became home secretary, and as first lord of the Admiralty 1924–9 he defended the navy against the cost-cutting proposals of the exchequer, even threatening resignation. *NJC*

Philip Williamson (ed.), *The Modernisation of Conservative Politics: The Diaries and Letters of William Bridgeman, 1904–1935* (London, 1988).

Bridges, Edward (1892–1969), secretary of the cabinet, 1938–46, permanent secretary to the Treasury and head of the civil service, 1945–56. Perhaps the greatest British civil servant of the 20th century, Bridges's influence on Whitehall's ethos and traditions was profound. Son of the poet laureate Robert Bridges, he joined the civil service in 1919. Rising through the inter-war Treasury, he was the crucial connecting link of the administrative machine as Churchill's cabinet secretary during the Second World War. After 1945, he worked to adapt the machinery of government and the civil service to meet the demands of reconstruction and the ambitious programme of the Attlee government. Bridges was a great exemplar, and the most distinguished exponent, of the generalist tradition of the gifted 'all-rounder' or 'intelligent layman' (later castigated as the 'amateur'). He was also a strong champion of the idea of the civil service as politically impartial and free from party entanglement, embodying and providing for continuity in government. A great unifying figure in the post-war civil service, his leadership consisted more in providing an example and upholding high standards than in pushing through innovation in policy or management. *KT*

Richard Chapman, *Ethics in the British Civil Service* (London, 1988).

Bridges review (1946–8), administrative non-reform conducted by Sir Edward Bridges. Readers of Attlee's pre-war work on the desirability of a streamlined cabinet organized on functional Haldanian lines, or the Whitehall insiders who had read the paper he circulated as deputy prime minister with its ideas for importing business skills to augment traditional civil service practices after the war (plus the creation of a special staff college to blend the two), might have expected an administrative revolution after 1945 to match the economic and social transformations to which the incoming Labour government was pledged. To a surprising extent, Attlee lost sight of this—referring outside suggestions for reform from the Fabian Society and rather isolated Labour backbenchers such as Geoffrey Cooper to the head of the civil service, Bridges. Bridges convened two meetings of his fellow permanent secretaries in early 1946 to consider the lessons of the Second World War in the light of the state's extended responsibilities in the economic, social, and industrial spheres. He set the tone for his review in a letter to his colleagues. 'It is true,' he conceded, 'that in this war we have made far better use of the industrialists and others who have come to our assistance . . . But have others—like myself—been working on the general expectation that Civil Service problems would in a year or so resume more or less the same general pattern which they took before the war?' With a few notable exceptions, such as Sir Oliver Franks at the Ministry of Supply, they had. The outcome was no widespread use of outsiders, and no staff college—only an internal paper circulated under Bridges's name in 1948 on 'The Conduct of Business in Government Departments'. No universal cure for the problems of efficiency was available from the business world, the document declared. The Treasury's own organization and methods division could be relied on to provide the spur to improvements. Attlee and his ministers left it to the Whitehall insiders to be judge and jury in their own cause. *PJH*

Peter Hennessy, *Whitehall* (London, 1989). | Kevin Theakston, *The Labour Party and Whitehall* (London, 1992).

Brighton bombing (12 October 1984). During the 1984 Conservative Party conference in Brighton, a bomb exploded at the Grand Hotel, killing five people including Roberta Wakeham, wife of the chief whip, John Wakeham, and Sir Anthony Berry, MP for Enfield, Southgate. Norman Tebbit, the party chairman, and his wife were severely injured. Claiming responsibility, the Provisional IRA regretted their failure to kill the prime minister, Margaret Thatcher, but added, 'Today we were unlucky, but remember we have only to be lucky once.' *PR*

Britain Belongs to You (1959), Labour general election manifesto. Drafted by Richard Crossman and the *Daily Mirror* journalists Hugh Cudlipp and Sydney Jacobson, this was the first manifesto since 1945 to abandon a 'shopping list' of nationalizations, calling for public ownership of only steel and road haulage, but it fell short of being a revisionist document because of a commitment to bring into public ownership industries which are 'shown, after thorough enquiry, to be failing the nation'. *BB*

Britain's Industrial Future (1928), book published by the Liberal Industrial Inquiry in February 1928, also known as the 'Yellow Book'. It was the product of *Lloyd George's attempt to revitalize the party in the run-up to the anticipated general election. The Liberal Industrial Inquiry had been set up in 1925, including E. D. Simon, W. T. Layton, J. M. Keynes, Ramsay Muir, Herbert Samuel, Philip Kerr, Hubert Henderson, and Lloyd George himself. The book offered far-reaching proposals to cure mass unemployment: the putting of industries of public concern under public boards; an economic general staff within the government; the expansion of the joint industrial councils ('Whitley councils') and other employer–worker organizations; the use of the Bank of England's powers to maintain investment; and a large programme of national development in roads, houses, garden cities, electricity, land reclamation, and afforestation. The proposals were worked up by a committee headed by Lloyd George, Lord Lothian, and Seebohm Rowntree. Its report, published in March 1929 as **We Can Conquer Unemployment*, provided the basis for the Liberal campaign in the 1929 general election. The results of the inquiry were significant in offering a planned solution to Britain's industrial problems in advance of their time and in terms which would only become commonplace from the 1930s onwards. *JS*

British Army of the Rhine (BAOR). This originated in the two divisions stationed in Germany in 1945 as part of the Allied occupation force. When Cold War set in, they remained in place, doubling in strength as part of the NATO rearmament programme of 1952. Their status was formalized in 1954, promising a British commitment of 55,000 men until 1994. By the late 1990s a progressive contraction left some 25,000 keeping a watch on the Rhine. *AD*

British Broadcasting Corporation. See BBC.

British Chambers of Commerce, Association of, the longest established but arguably the least effective of the 'peak organizations' which flourished in the first two-thirds of the century. Formed in 1860 as an umbrella organization for local chambers of commerce, it concentrated for 40 years on commercial legislation and on standing up for the merchant interest against the railway companies. In the first years of the 20th century it was drawn into the *tariff reform debate, which divided its membership, and into discussions about the Liberal government's welfare reforms. Even then, it was often frustrated because its legislation was not taken up by the major parties. During and after the Great War it came under attack from the National Association of British Manufacturers (see NATIONAL UNION OF MANUFACTURERS) and the *Federation of British Industries for failing to represent manufacturing as distinct from merchant interests and, although its published statements perceptibly shifted to adopt protectionist and thus pro-manufacturer positions, it never regained a position as the principal conduit of business views to the Board of Trade. *JAT*

A. R. Ilersic, *Parliament of Commerce* (London, 1960).

British Council, international organization for educational and cultural relations, and therefore the main arm of the UK's 'cultural diplomacy'. It has a worldwide network of 254 offices and teaching offices in 110 countries, administering programmes in English language teaching, education, the arts, science, and governance. The council was founded in 1934, receiving its royal charter in 1940, which was subsequently renewed in 1993. It receives a grant-in-aid from the Foreign and Commonwealth Office and supplements this with income from abroad teaching English, conducting British examinations, and managing development and training contracts. *JD*

British Council website: *www.britcoun.org*

British Election Study (BES), established in the 1960s by David *Butler and Donald Stokes. They undertook national surveys of the electorate at the 1964, 1966, and 1970 general elections and reported the results in their book **Political Change in Britain*. Similar studies have been conducted at every subsequent general election and these constitute the longest series of academic surveys in Britain. In the 1970s, the team responsible for the studies was led by Ivor Crewe and Bo Sarlvik of Essex University while the surveys at the four elections from 1983 to 1997 were directed by Anthony Heath, Roger Jowell, and John Curtice. Initially, data collection was confined to a simple cross-section, post-election survey of a national sample of the British electorate, conducted by face-to-face interviews. Over time, however, the study has become more complex, involving panel surveys between elections and during campaigns, telephone interviewing, and special surveys of Scottish, Welsh, and (in 1997) ethnic minority voters. Methodological innovation, in both data collection and analysis, has been an important feature of the series. The BES has generated a unique set of time-series of data, which constitutes an invaluable record of continuity and change among British voters. By replicating questions from election to election the surveys have enabled analysts to identify and chart long-term trends among voters, such as the changing relationships between social characteristics and party choice. In addition, however, they also provide authoritative data on specific elections relating, for example, to voter reactions to campaign issues and events or current party leaders. Data arising from BES surveys are deposited at the Data Archive at Essex and have been widely used by researchers and for teaching purposes. A major book-length report has been published by the BES team after each election (see bibliography, below) but the surveys have been the basis for a very large number of other publications. They are by far the major source of data for individual-level electoral analysis in Britain. *DD*

David Butler and Donald Stokes, *Political Change in Britain* (London, 1969 edn., 1974 edn.). | Ivor Crewe, Anthony Fox, and Neil Day, *The British Electorate 1963–1992* (Cambridge, 1995). | Geoffrey Evans and Pippa Norris (eds.), *Critical Elections: British Parties and Voters in Long-Term Perspective* (London, 1999). | Anthony Heath, Roger Jowell, and John Curtice, *How Britain Votes* (Oxford, 1985). | Anthony Heath, Roger Jowell, and John Curtice, (with Geoff Evans, Julia Field, and Sharon Witherspoon), *Understanding Political Change* (Oxford, 1991). | Anthony Heath, Roger Jowell, and John Curtice, (with Bridget Taylor) (eds.), *Labour's Last Chance* (Aldershot, 1994). | Bo Sarlvik and Ivor Crewe, *Decade of Dealignment* (Cambridge, 1983).

British Empire, collective term for all the territories classified as either dominions, crown colonies, or protectorates, and which by 1920 covered a quarter of the land surface of the globe. Although the term 'British Empire' was still widely used before the Second World War, it then referred more often to the *crown colonies and protectorates, because the white self-governing areas were generally known as the Dominions (see dominion status) or as the British *Commonwealth.

In the period 1900–14, the administration of the colonial empire was not given much thought, especially when compared to the efforts to integrate Britain and the dominions into either a political or economic federation. Earlier, Joseph Chamberlain had tried to bring public attention to the economic development of the colonies, which he regarded as Britain's 'undeveloped estates'. This idea of 'constructive colonialism' was not taken up, however, until after the Great War. From 1920, the Empire was promoted by imperialists as a vast potential market within which Britain's war-ravaged economy could recover. The dominions did not want closer ties, so Britain looked towards developing the colonial empire. Leo Amery was at the forefront of efforts in the 1920s to promote the Empire's potential to the British public and was instrumental in 1926, for example, in setting up the Empire Marketing Board. Yet the hopes of British imperialists were dashed by Britain's own economic weakness throughout the inter-war period; the Empire received little financial investment despite the passage in 1929 and 1940 of Colonial Development Acts designed to facilitate this. The sums put aside were far too little to achieve anything substantial.

Politically, the governance of the colonial empire was based on ideas of trusteeship, whereby native rights were held to be paramount. Thus British statesmen believed that through firm, but fair, government they looked after native interests. Self-government for crown colonies, particularly African ones, was not considered, although in some places such as Nigeria indirect rule had been established, whereby acceptable native chiefs were allowed to rule their areas according to traditional custom. In Kenya and Rhodesia, however, there were white settlers who complicated Britain's relations with the indigenous populations. In Kenya, which was still largely undeveloped, the whites were told that native interests came first; but in 1923 Rhodesia (now Zimbabwe) was granted virtual self-government after union with South Africa was rejected, because it was more developed and had already been dominated by the white settlers for many years.

The Second World War revealed many of these political arrangements to be near worthless, particularly in those areas under indirect rule which had proved inefficient and corrupt, while the economic management of the Empire helped some but enraged others. Consequently, the post-war Labour government focused its attention on the Empire because it wanted a greater imperial contribution to Britain's shattered economy, but at the same time looked forward to political development within the crown colonies.

However, while Labour decolonized India, Burma, Ceylon (now Sri Lanka), and Palestine, in Africa and Malaya financial considerations came first and not much thought was given to ideas of self-government although, under American pressure, ministers spoke again of 'constructive colonialism', of preparing the colonies for eventual self-rule, and of the necessity of building viable economies before this could be achieved.

Within some colonies, though, wartime experience had given many people the desire for immediate political change. In the Gold Coast, with its long-standing viable economy, political change came more rapidly than anyone had envisaged: in 1957, it became Ghana, the first independent African colony. Once *decolonization had begun, it achieved a momentum of its own, one which the Conservative governments of 1951–64 found difficult to cope with. In most cases they hoped to control the pace of decolonization, but economic and military weakness meant that the British pulled out sooner rather than later. In most cases the British withdrew after doing deals with the nationalists which seemed to uphold British interests, although before leaving Malaya, Kenya, and Cyprus, they first fought and defeated communist and nationalist insurgencies. During the 1960s and 1970s, the colonial empire was dismantled, though some territories still remained under British rule and were renamed dependent territories. Some still have British colonists, such as the Falkland Islands. The process of decolonization continues, however; in 1997 Hong Kong, British since 1841, was given back to China. The vast empire on which in 1900 the sun never set (since colonies were in every time zone) has shrunk to a few islands and territories scattered across the globe. Not all even want to sever the British connection; the Falkland-islanders certainly did not in 1982, and in 1995 Bermuda voted to remain under British rule rather than become an independent state. *KTS*

JUDITH M. BROWN and W. ROGER LOUIS, *The Oxford History of the British Empire*, vol. 4 (Oxford, 1999). | BERNARD PORTER, *The Lion's Share* (London, 1984).

British Employers' Confederation. See CONFEDERATION OF BRITISH INDUSTRY.

British Housewives' League, right-wing pressure group which flourished during the late 1940s period of post-war austerity, led by Mrs Dorothy Crisp. It used such tactics as rallies, petitions, and mass-lobbying of parliament to great effect, claiming to represent ordinary housewives disgusted by the continuation of rationing. Initially allied with the Conservatives, though always formally independent of all parties, it moved to the far right and was by 1948 denouncing all parties as equally bad. *JAR*

British Institute of Management, founded in 1946 at the instigation of Sir Stafford Cripps. An organization which never quite achieved the great future that was forecast for it, organizational reforms in 1974–6 allowed it to undertake a direct representational role on behalf of managers. It took a different stance to the more liberal Institute of Directors, endorsing tripartite reforms. In the different political climate of the mid-1980s it largely abandoned public policy and returned to its original focus on professional issues of concern to managers. *WG*

British Institute of Public Opinion. See PUBLIC OPINION, BRITISH INSTITUTE OF.

British Manufacturers, National Association of. See NATIONAL UNION OF MANUFACTURERS.

British Medical Association (BMA), principal regulatory body and organization of medical doctors, especially general practitioners (GPs). By the 1900s, the BMA had emerged as the largest body representing the bulk of the 20,000 medical practitioners in Britain. In 1905 its *Report on Contract Practice* showed an interest in greater state intervention in the provision of general medical care, foreshadowing the 'panel' system set up under the *National Insurance Act, 1911, which brought GPs in to provide medical treatment for the fourteen million workers covered by the scheme. Its report of 1930, *A General Medical Service for the Nation*, suggested an extension of national insurance to provide for dependants of insured workers and for the self-employed. The BMA remained committed, though, to defending the interests of doctors within any state-run health service, especially resisting the idea that they should become a 'salaried service'. As a result of negotiations with the Attlee government's minister of health, Nye Bevan, over the formation of a *National Health Service, the BMA won the right of GPs to remain at arm's length from the government as essentially private contractors, with the right to maintain private patients if they wished. As the principal body representing the medical profession, the BMA has been inevitably concerned with attempts by successive governments to reform primary health care. It has invariably stood up for the independence of GPs, whatever the changes to the NHS structure of primary care. *JS*

British Nationality Acts. British nationality was only loosely defined in the 19th century and in 1844 an Act granted certificates of naturalization to all aliens who had been resident for five years. During the 20th century, nationality has been more strictly defined. Under current legislation (2000), British citizenship is acquired automatically at birth by a child born in the UK if his or her mother or, if legitimate, his or her father, is a British citizen settled in the UK. A child adopted in the UK by a British citizen also becomes a British citizen. Children born abroad to British citizens are themselves British citizens by descent. Citizenship can be acquired by registration for certain children who do not automatically acquire citizenship at birth, after five years for citizens of specified overseas territories, and by naturalization. The last is at the home secretary's discretion, requiring five or three years' residence (the latter if the spouse is a citizen); some knowledge of English, Welsh, or Scottish Gaelic; a main home in the UK; and crown employment or employment by an international organization or company linked to the UK. In 1998, 54,000 people were granted British citizenship under these rules and nearly 4,000 refused.

The background to these stringent conditions lies in the tightening-up of nationality qualifications and immigration control during the course of the 20th century, especially since 1945. The 1905 Aliens Act was the first to restrict the entry of immigrants and further legislation in 1914, 1919, and after 1962 restricted the 'open-door' policy of access for immigrants and refugees. In turn, nationality rules were tightened in order to limit immigrant flows and, implicitly, to regulate the influx of coloured settlers from the Commonwealth. These restrictions stood in contrast to the British Nationality Act of 1948, which conferred the status of British subject on all Commonwealth citizens. Restrictions on immigration in 1962 were followed in 1968 by an Act depriving East African Asians holding British passports of the automatic right of entry to Britain. Immigration rules were further tightened in 1971 and 1979, but it was the 1981 British Nationality Act which superseded the 1948 Act with the current regulations. In effect, these revoke the automatic right to British citizenship of any child, including those born in the UK, unless at least one of his or her parents is a British citizen by birth. Children born overseas to parents of patrial or naturalized British citizenship could be refused entry to the UK. In 1989–90, the policy of greater restriction of nationality and access to Britain was illustrated by the refusal to grant residency to 3.25 million Hong Kong Chinese who did hold British passports, though British citizenship was extended to 50,000 residents in particular categories and, subsequently, to non-Chinese residents who had no other passport. Current controversy over political *asylum also rests upon concerns over immigrant flows and the liberality or exclusiveness of British nationality laws. *JS*

British National Party (BNP), launched on 7 April 1982 in London. A split between John Tyndall and Martin Webster of the *National Front led to Tyndall forming the New National Front from which the BNP emerged. By 1989 it had become the principal far right group in Britain emphasizing in its programme hostility towards immigrants. Despite local power bases as in East London, it has remained on the British political fringe. *CH*

N. Copsey, 'Contemporary Fascism in the Local Arena: The British National Party and "Rights for Whites"', in M. Cronin (ed.), *The Failure of British Fascism* (London, 1996).

British Social Attitudes Survey, an annual survey of social and political attitudes in Britain, initiated in 1983 under the auspices of Social and Community Planning Research (now the National Centre for Social Research). The aim of the series is to provide a solid and reliable empirical basis for assessments of popular attitudes. It is intended that authoritative facts and figures should replace impressionistic accounts which are frequently characterized by stereotyping, untested assumptions, and 'common sense'. Each survey is based on interviews with over 3,000 people in Great Britain and covers a wide range of subjects, always including some that are topical. The 1999 report, for example, includes an analysis of the extent to which the British public espouses the 'third way' in politics, as advocated by the Blair government, as well as details of attitudes towards traffic problems. Central issues feature regularly, however, and the series has enabled investigators to track the nature and extent of change in key social values. Subjects regularly covered include people's attitudes to crime, civil liberties, education, employment, health, local government, public and private morality, social security, and taxation. The series is an invaluable source of time-series data and has been described as 'the most trustworthy and comprehensive guide to British life available between hard covers' (*Guardian*, 30 November 1999). Since 1985, those responsible for the British Social Attitudes (BSA) Survey have cooperated with teams doing similar work in other countries. Each national team has included an agreed set of questions, thus enabling fruitful cross-national comparisons and the distinctiveness of social attitudes in Britain to be assessed. The results of the BSA Surveys are published in a series of detailed annual reports which generally attract a good deal of attention and comment in the quality press. *DD*

Roger Jowell, John Curtice, Alison Park, and Katarina Thomson (eds.), *British Social Attitudes: The 16th Report* (Aldershot, 1999).

British Socialist Party. See Social Democratic Federation.

British Union of Fascists (BUF), Britain's main Fascist organization in the inter-war years. 'The British Union of Fascists represented the mature form of the fascist phenomenon in British society, being the only organization with any pretension to significance in inter-war Britain' (Thurlow, 92). The failure of his *New Party encouraged Oswald *Mosley to play for higher political stakes and his resolve was strengthened by Mussolini's successes in Italy. In forming the BUF in October 1932, Mosley was responding to what he regarded as the repeated failures of British governments to cure the country's relative decline. He appealed predominantly to the young, especially to 'the Front Generation' who had endured the Great War and then been sold short. In that respect the BUF, which emphasized the need for economic planning within a corporate political structure, unimpeded by parliament, represented a new creed for a new age. As such, the BUF cut through class barriers although, with the exception of its younger recruits, the organization remained essentially middle class.

The movement initially attracted important sources of political sympathy, most notably from Viscount Rothermere's *Daily Mail* and wealthy industrialists such as Lord Nuffield. However, political opinion turned significantly against the BUF following the Olympia meeting on 7 June 1934, characterized by violent clashes between BUF supporters and antifascists. Moreover, the BUF's adoption of a more overt *anti-Semitism also lost it some support. The BUF's involvement in the East End in pursuit of its anti-Semitism, and the clashes this provoked led to the Public Order Act, 1936, which was designed to control political extremism, in part by banning political uniforms. It remains uncertain whether the Act did actually curb the BUF's activities. However, support had certainly dipped by the late 1930s. Mosley hoped that their peace campaigns (1938–9) would revive his fortunes, but in the event this activity did not lift the movement significantly. Opponents portrayed Mosley and the BUF as putting Fascist sympathies before patriotism.

Much interest has focused on the degree of support for the BUF. Figures remain elusive, but membership probably peaked, at the end of the period of Rothermere's support, at 50,000. Numbers fell drastically in 1934–5, but had recovered to almost half the peak figure by September 1939. Local studies suggest variations in this pattern. If numbers are difficult to compile, there is more agreement on the BUF's influence. 'It was merely a minor irritant for the government' (Thurlow, 117). This view is widely echoed. The outbreak of the Second World War, against which Mosley had always set his face, did not result in the immediate demise of the BUF, but on 10 July 1940 the British government declared it a proscribed organization. Mosley's political dream was finished, for the time being, but revived in the post-war *Union Movement. *CH*

Robert Skidelsky, *Oswald Mosley* (London, 1975). | Richard Thurlow, *Fascism in Britain: A History 1918–1945* (Oxford, 1987).

British Workers' League. See Fisher, Victor.

Brittan, Leon (1939–), Conservative politician. Younger brother of Samuel *Brittan, educated at Cambridge, Yale, and the Inner Temple, he was chief secretary (admired), Home Office (smeared—possibly by MI5), and trade secretary. Brittan took the blame in 1986 over leak of the attorney-general's letter in the *Westland affair, attributed to Thatcher, and was battered by John Smith in the Commons and by the 1922 Committee where there was a whiff of Tory anti-Semitism. A strong pro-European, later at odds with Eurosceptics, Brittan recovered with his appointment in 1988 as EU commissioner, later vice-president. He was thought to have handled the 'Uruguay round' talks on liberalizing world trade brilliantly. *EP*

Brittan, Samuel (1933–), economist and financial journalist who undertook pioneering work on the interaction between economic doctrine and political influences in British economic policy. His investigation focused in particular on a critical analysis of the left–right spectrum in relation to economic policy and a reinterpretation of free market doctrines. His books included *Works and Correspondence of David Ricardo*, 11 volumes (ed. with M. H. Dobbs (1951–73)) and *Production of Commodities by Means of Commodities: Prelude to a Critique of Economic Theory* (1960, 1975). His reputation was enhanced by his popularist text *The Treasury under The Tories* (1964), with the updated and expanded version issued as *Steering the Economy* (1969). He was assistant editor of the *Financial Times* in the early 1980s. *JFM*

Brixton riots. See RIOTS.

broadcasting. From its foundation in the 1920s, the *BBC was prohibited by its charter from any political partisanship. This restriction was itself interpreted narrowly by the BBC's own early managers (especially John Reith) and governors, so that in practice neither BBC radio nor television, when it began to attract a significant viewing public in the 1950s, even reported party politics, let alone took any proactive part. The BBC had in the 1950s a self-imposed 'fourteen-day rule', which prohibited the reporting and discussion on the air of any political issue that would be (or indeed might be) debated in parliament during the next fortnight. BBC news journalists found this impossibly restrictive, and in the mid-1950s both the rule itself and the attitude that it represented were irrevocably smashed. In the meantime, activist media involvement in politics took place through a partisan press and in the newsreels.

The arrival of independent television in 1955 was one factor that opened the way for broadcasters to become politically active: one of its first innovations, the creation of an independent television news company (ITN), provided the catalyst for change. In order to attract a viewing public, ITN steadily pushed back the boundaries of what was permissible, going for topical reporting, aggressive interviewing of public figures, and the reporting of election campaigns actually before they were over. This last took real courage, when the 1958 Rochdale by-election was made the subject of ITN coverage, for the broadcasters had to face down the legal threats of the attorney-general in order to do so. Once Rochdale had been reported, and the government reluctantly decided that it dare not go to court to prevent the flow of information in a democracy, the floodgates opened. In 1959, the general election campaign was covered by the BBC as well as ITV, with BBC radio (which still enjoyed a monopoly) now also able to exploit opportunities that had arisen through the demands of competition in television.

The second factor encouraging change was the Suez crisis of 1956 for, with the nation both highly excited and deeply divided on political lines, the BBC simply had to provide news and comment, though it gave a further example of its new-found courage by allowing Labour the right to make a party broadcast on the crisis in reply to one by the prime minister, even though the government tried to prevent it. Anthony Eden, convinced that the broadcasters were acting against the national interest in a near-war situation, took to referring to 'those Communists at the BBC', suspecting them even of shining studio lamps in his eyes to make him look ineffective. This was not the last time that broadcasters became involved in mutual recriminations with party leaders, as was demonstrated by such cases as **Yesterday's Men*, **Death on the Rock*, and the coverage of strikes and of Northern Ireland (the last leading indeed to a *broadcasting ban on the coverage of terrorists). The broader acceptability of criticizing public figures that emerged at the time of the Suez crisis, but then exploded into the early 1960s satire wave, ensured that ground won in 1956–9 could not subsequently be lost, as the BBC's **That Was the Week That Was* showed in 1963–4.

By 1960 then, with half the population able to watch a television set in the home, much of the pattern was set. Television was expected to provide news programmes covering political and parliamentary events; and in such investigative programmes as *Panorama* and *World in Action* offered quality discussion programmes too; and would report and interpret election campaigns. When the next election came in 1964, the overwhelming majority of homes were now able to view. Most electors now said to opinion pollsters that television had become their main source of information about politics, and with Labour's televisual leader Wilson easily outpointing the resolutely unphotogenic Douglas-Home, television could be even claimed to be the only media battleground that now mattered. Henceforth, serious politicians had to undergo training in TV studio skills, no party could pick a leader without thinking if s/he would be 'good on television', and it was routinely said that a few minutes of live TV could decide the next government (just as, it was alleged, Nixon's unshaven chin had cost him the US presidency, in contrast to Kennedy's shining features when they debated on television in 1960).

Such claims were much exaggerated. Only in 1983 (when Thatcher completely outplayed Foot) did one party leader have as great an advantage over the other on television as Wilson had enjoyed in 1964. And, though Heath's television performances could at times be the despair of his advisers and supporters, he nevertheless won in 1970 against the visually effective Wilson. Nor did it turn out to be the case that television could dominate politicians and their agenda, for the broadcasters needed party leaders' cooperation as much as the other way round. And, if broadcasters themselves showed preference for (or hostility towards) any one party, then party headquarters would soon be crying foul and threatening legal action (or, what was worse, veiled threats of financial discrimination against relevant companies when they returned to power). Politicians could also use such leverage to ensure a sympathetic interviewer, or even restrict appearances to non-political programmes. Here Thatcher led the way, preferring appearances on the *Jimmy Young Programme* and *Nationwide*, where she was interviewed by a former disc jockey and an ex-sports reporter, rather than facing Robin Day on *Panorama*. A decade earlier, Wilson had refused to be interviewed by Robert McKenzie, because he asked such difficult questions. For their own party political broadcasts (five in every general election campaign for each major party) the parties kept firm control, and legislated to oblige all television channels to provide them with studio facilities and free air time. In the interests of parity, it continued to be the rule that television advertising time could not be bought by a political party, even on commercial channels, unlike in the USA where television advertising became a key medium of electoral campaigning.

Broadcasters settled down then to be a part, but by no means the whole, of the media's coverage of elections and political life. Most television news reporters had prior experience working in the press, all of them read newspapers while trying to decide priorities for their own programme's coverage of the day's news (just as newspapermen also watched and were influenced by television), and politicians found it increasingly hard to hide from tough questions coming from the media as a whole, especially during election campaigns. Above all, the speed of the media's coverage of politics had increased immeasurably (and would no doubt continue to do so as the number of cable channels, commercial radio stations, and internet websites continued to expand). Whereas in 1924, MacDonald, campaigning away from London, could avoid questions about the Zinoviev letter for several days (if not quite wisely), by 1959 Macmillan was responding on the same day to an unwise remark by Gaitskell on taxation. So, by 1992 the parties traded opinions five or six times a day on an alleged scandal in the NHS, until within three days the media (and probably the public too) was so bored with the issue that the NHS rarely got a mention in the rest of the campaign. Television certainly allowed British voters in the 1990s to be better informed than any previous generation, but it had also reinforced the move downmarket, towards shorter and more simplified items of coverage (at least in programmes with large audiences) and to trivialization in general. It was not an outcome of which Lord Reith would have approved. *JAR*

Michael Cockerell, *Live from Number Ten: The Inside Story of Prime Ministers and Television* (London, 1988).

broadcasting ban (1988). In November 1988 the British home secretary, Douglas Hurd, announced that broadcasting organizations would no longer be allowed to broadcast direct statements by representatives of Sinn Fein, Republican Sinn Fein, and the Ulster Defence Association. In a celebrated comment the prime minister, Mrs Thatcher, had spoken of 'starving the terrorists of the oxygen of publicity on which they depend'. The response of the BBC and other broadcasters was to employ actors to speak the words of the banned spokesmen. *PR*

Brockway, (Archibald) Fenner (1888–1988), anti-war campaigner and Labour MP. An activist in the Independent Labour Party (ILP) before 1914, he came to prominence during the Great War through his work for the No Conscription Fellowship. He was sentenced on four occasions for refusing to undertake military service, serving 28 months in gaol, the last eight in solitary confinement. During the 1920s, he was a leading figure in the ILP and the left movement 'Socialism in our Time'. Elected to parliament for East Leyton in 1929, he was prominent amongst the left rebels who were refused party endorsement for the 1931 election. In 1932 he was chairman of the ILP when it disaffiliated from the Labour Party. During the 1930s he attempted to articulate a left socialism between that of the Labour and Communist parties, but after the Spanish civil war and the Second World War, both of which severely tested his views on pacifism, he rejoined the Labour Party. He was MP for Eton and Slough, 1950–64, and was prominently involved with the movements for colonial freedom and with the Campaign for Nuclear Disarmament.

His support for colonial independence was longstanding and he was involved in all the major movements in this area, which led to him being referred to as 'the Member for Africa'. He accepted a life peerage in 1964, but remained highly active in a range of radical movements. Brockway inherited from his father a missionary zeal and his breadth of interest reflected the mixing of the English radical tradition with a commitment to socialism. A prolific writer throughout, his life and the wide variety of his interests are fully articulated in his four volumes of autobiography: *Inside the Left* (1942), *Outside the Right* (1963), *Towards Tomorrow* (1977), and *98 Not Out* (1986). *JAJ*

Brodrick, St John (1856–1942), Conservative politician. His difficulties in high office were many: as war secretary, 1900–3, he proposed a reorganization of the army acceptable neither to the military nor parliament, while his administration of the India Office, 1903–5, was undercut by the contest for control of the Indian Army between Lord *Curzon and Lord *Kitchener. Brodrick succeeded to the family peerage as viscount Midleton in 1907, devoting much of the balance of his political life to the cause of southern Irish unionism. *RJQA*

Brook, Norman (1902–67), secretary of the cabinet, 1947–62 and head of the civil service, 1956–62. A provincial middle-class grammar school meritocrat, Brook entered the civil service in 1925 and spent his early career in the Home Office. One of the outstanding civil servants of the Second World War, he made his mark as personal assistant to John Anderson, lord president of the council (1940–2), moving on to be deputy secretary of the cabinet (1942–3) and then permanent secretary of the Ministry of Reconstruction (1943–5). Brook is best remembered as the great technician of cabinet government in mid-20th-century Whitehall, one of the chief architects of the post-1945 extended system of cabinet committees, and responsible for the elaboration and refinement of the procedures of the cabinet secretariat in facilitating collective ministerial decision taking. A consummate 'machine-minder' and oiler of wheels, he was also the personal confidant and indispensable adviser to successive prime ministers, and was particularly close to and influential with Churchill and Macmillan. Discreet, impersonal, disciplined, correct, and unflappable, Brook was the supremely effective engine-driver of government—the greyest of grey eminences and the most powerful civil servant of his age. *KT*

KEVIN THEAKSTON, *Leadership in Whitehall* (London, 1999).

Brooke, Basil. See BROOKEBOROUGH, LORD.

Brooke, Henry (1903–84), Conservative politician and home secretary. Educated at Marlborough and Oxford, Brooke became one of the original members of the *Conservative Research Department in 1930. He won the Lewisham West by-election in 1938 and during the war was a member of the party's Post-War Problems Central Committee that developed policies for peacetime. After he lost his seat in 1945, he was deputed to lead the Tories on the London County Council and helped in the party's internal reforms by chairing the subcommittee on finance. At his suggestion, the 1948 party conference approved, instead of simply considering, a ban on financial contributions by candidates, thereby entrenching a more fair selection procedure. He was elected MP for Hampstead in 1950, and became financial secretary to the Treasury in 1954. Macmillan promoted him to the cabinet in 1957 as minister of housing and local government, but he inherited from Sandys the controversial legislation to decontrol private rents and had to face fierce opposition attacks. In 1961, he became the first chief secretary to the Treasury, charged with the task of policing departmental spending plans. Macmillan's substitution of Brooke for Butler as home secretary in 1962, however, was a bad misjudgement, for Brooke seemed out of his depth and out of touch, and his pedantic manner and staid image made him the butt of satirists. Although one of very few ministers who were not subject to scurrilous rumours during the 1963 Profumo scandal, he considered resigning. He lost his seat in 1966 and became a life peer. His wife had entered the Lords in 1964, and they were the first couple to sit on a front bench together. Their elder son Peter *Brooke served under Thatcher. *RJS*

Brooke, Peter Leonard (1934–), Conservative politician. Peter Brooke was a tribal Conservative, son of Henry *Brooke. He was a Harvard Business School graduate, holding junior Treasury office before becoming party chairman, then Northern Ireland secretary, later replacing the disgraced Mellor as heritage secretary. Brooke had to apologize for joining a sing-song on Irish TV after a major Northern Ireland killing, but was a cultivated man without great party animus, pitched between earnest and wit, thought the type of candidate likely to succeed as Speaker. *EP*

Brookeborough, Lord (1888–1973), Northern Ireland prime minister. After military service in the Great War, where he won the MC, Sir Basil Brooke returned to Co. Fermanagh to run his family estate. In 1929 he was elected to the Northern Ireland parliament and in 1933 appointed minister of agriculture, a position which he filled with considerable energy and success. From 1941–3 he was minister of commerce and production, becoming prime minister of Northern Ireland in 1944. He proved an able Unionist leader in the face of challenges from both the Irish government with its strong anti-partition stance in the late 1940s and the IRA with its campaign of violence against the Northern Ireland state in the late 1950s. Although socially conservative, he oversaw the introduction of the measures of the welfare state brought in by the Attlee government. In spite of his landed background, his personality won him grass-roots popular support among the Unionist community. In the years of political stability after the end of the IRA campaign, however, Brooke failed to take the opportunity to establish a broader basis of support for the Unionist cause, and was replaced in 1963 by Captain Terence O'Neill. He became Lord Brookeborough in 1952. *BMW*

Jonathan Bardon, *A History of Ulster* (Belfast, 1992). | Brian Barton, *Brookeborough: The Making of a Prime Minister* (Belfast, 1988).

Brown, Ernest (1881–1962), Liberal and Liberal National politician. After briefly representing Rugby 1923–4, Brown won Leith in 1927, retaining it until 1945. He followed John Simon into the National Government as a Liberal National, and was rewarded with a number of junior ministerial positions. In May 1940 he became secretary of state for Scotland, despite being an Englishman. From 1941 he was minister of health with responsibility for evacuation. An active Baptist, Brown was a well-liked parliamentarian, though often the butt of others' jokes. *NJC*

Brown, George Alfred (1914–85), Labour politician. After working as a trade unionist, Brown's parliamentary career began in 1945 when he won Belper for Labour, representing it for the next 25 years. He rapidly progressed through the ranks from parliamentary private secretary and a junior post to minister of works by 1951. During Labour's opposition years, 1951–64, Brown was a member of the shadow cabinet and defence spokesman. In 1960, following the death of Aneurin Bevan, he became Gaitskell's deputy leader, a tribute to his acknowledged administrative skills and passionate debating powers. To his surprise and disappointment, though, he was defeated in the 1963 leadership contest, losing by 41 votes in the final ballot to Harold Wilson, his judgement being thought suspect (though many MPs still professed to prefer 'George drunk to Harold sober'). After Labour won the 1964 election, Brown became secretary for economic affairs and successfully developed a *National Plan, despite initial opposition from both employers and unions. But the plan made over-optimistic assumptions about economic growth and was dropped in favour of a prices and incomes policy in 1966. Deeply disappointed, and now steadily more prone to heavy drinking, Brown became foreign secretary and was soon instrumental in helping to secure a Middle East settlement following the 1967 Arab-Israeli war, being awarded the order of the cedar of Lebanon for his efforts. Such success was not to be repeated, however, and he eventually resigned from the cabinet (though only after many earlier late-night threats to do so) in 1968, on a point of democratic principle and as the result of many clashes with Wilson. He lost his seat in 1970 and became a life peer as Lord George-Brown in 1971. Brown took his last political stand in 1976 when he resigned from the Labour Party over the issue of the 'closed shop'. A much loved politician with an engaging personality whose later career was a sad anticlimax. *DWM*

George Brown, *In My Way: The Political Memoirs of Lord George-Brown* (London, 1971).

Brown, (James) Gordon (1951–). Labour politician and chancellor of the exchequer. Brown entered parliament for Dunfermline East in 1983 and quickly became the party's leading young modernizer. He managed to support the process of reforming the Labour Party while maintaining strong support at Labour's grass roots, through a revivalist speaking style. He rose rapidly in the shadow cabinet, deputizing as shadow chancellor after John Smith suffered a heart attack in 1988, and becoming shadow chancellor after the 1992 general election defeat. Brown regularly topped the shadow cabinet poll and was identified as a possible future leader. After Smith's death, however, he stood aside for his friend Tony Blair. As chancellor of the exchequer from 1997, he delivered economic stability in the first years in office and fulfilled New Labour's general election pledge to maintain the broad macroeconomic framework inherited from the Conservatives. Within these constraints he moved resources to an ambitious 'welfare to work' scheme and provided the political support needed for the introduction of a minimum wage. His attempt to combine 'prudence' with a rhetorical commitment to older democratic socialist values, such as equality of opportunity, ensured his position as both the hope of the left and the government's second most important modernizer after Blair. *BB*

PAUL ROUTLEDGE, *Gordon Brown* (London, 1998).

Bruce-Gardyne, John ('Jock') (1930–90), Conservative politician and journalist. Elected to parliament in 1964, Bruce-Gardyne's free-market radicalism put him at odds with Heath, whose government he excoriated in *Whatever Happened to the Quiet Revolution?* (1974). Defeated in 1974, he was more in step with Thatcher and returned to the Commons in 1979. A man of dash and independence, he was discomfited as financial secretary to the Treasury when his heretical views on the Falklands war became public. He was not adopted for his redrawn constituency but was raised to the Lords in 1983. *RJS*

Bruges speech (September 1988). This speech by Margaret Thatcher included an onslaught on developing European integration. Delivered in and at the heart of the European Community, she spoke of 'a European superstate exercising a new dominance from Brussels', so accelerating her alienation from Lawson and Howe, but also inspiring the formation of an ultra-sceptic 'Bruges Group'. *EP*

Brunner, John Tomlinson (1842–1919), industrialist, politician, and philanthropist. Both as an employer and as MP for Northwich in Cheshire, Brunner epitomized the new, socially responsible, industrial middle class of the Edwardian era. He was co-founder and chairman of Brunner, Mond, a chemical company noted for its paternalistic concern for the welfare of its employees. In parliament he was involved in the Liberal campaigns of the day for social and constitutional reform. Brunner also used his personal wealth to further the cause of education in Cheshire. *WF*

STEPHEN KOSS, *Sir John Brunner, Radical Plutocrat* (Cambridge, 1970).

Brussels pact (1948), treaty signed between Britain, France, Belgium, the Netherlands, and Luxembourg on 17 March 1948. The pact was negotiated following the overthrow of the Czechoslovakian government by Communists. It committed the signatories to mutual aid against external attack and included clauses on economic, cultural, and social cooperation. It paved the way in 1949 for the North Atlantic Treaty and the Council of Europe, and, in 1955, for the Western European Union. *JWY*

JOHN BAYLIS, *The Diplomacy of Pragmatism* (London, 1993).

Bryant, Arthur (1899–1985), journalist and popular historian. Bryant produced 40 patriotic books that sold over two million copies and the 'Our Note Book' column for 50 years in the *Illustrated London News.* In 1927 he became educational adviser, later a governor, and chairman of the council (1946–9) of the Bonar Law College, Ashridge, founded to disseminate conservative ideas. Bryant's first book was *The Spirit of Conservatism* (1929), but he also lectured unceasingly to Conservative groups all over Britain, wrote reams of conservative tracts and newspaper articles, and directed thousands of costumed volunteers in national historical pageants. Bryant was a party publicist close to Conservative leaders for four decades, beginning with Stanley Baldwin. Aiming for a conservative readership to rival the 50,000 subscribers to the Left Book Club, Bryant edited and produced books for the National Book Association, 1936–9, though never exceeding a subscription list of 3,000. An active and influential appeaser even in 1940, he worked for a negotiated peace with Hitler. Bryant's ideal was a sunny landscape of English gardens, stalwart men, and loving dogs. *RNS*

REBA N. SOFFER, 'The Long Nineteenth Century of British Conservative Thought', in George Behlmer and Fred Leventhal (eds.), *Singular Continuities: Tradition, Nostalgia and Society in Modern Britain* (Stanford, 2000).

Bryce, James (1838–1922), writer, Liberal politician, and diplomat. Bryce came to the study of comparative politics through comparative law. Appointed by Gladstone regius professor of civil law, he was a close friend of fellow Oxford Liberals Dicey and T. H. Green. He continued to hold his chair until 1893, long after his election to the Commons in 1880 and while he was briefly under-secretary for foreign affairs in 1886 in Gladstone's government. He taught Americans things they did not know about their political institutions in *The American Commonwealth* (1888), regarded as an invaluable work of implicit comparative politics by future president Woodrow Wilson. After serving as chief secretary for Ireland in the Campbell-Bannerman government, Bryce went as ambassador to Washington, 1907–13, before taking his seat as viscount Bryce in 1914. His report of the Lords' conference on the reform of the second chamber remains a relevant guide to the contemporary debate on post-hereditary bicameralism. His report on German 'atrocities' in 1914 was, however, a dangerously sloppy concession to the prejudices of the time.

Unlike latter-day political scientists, Bryce could credibly offer advice to statesmen because he had practised what he preached in his final work, *Modern Democracies* (1920): 'The best way to get a genuine and exact first-hand knowledge of the data is to mix in practical politics' (vol. 1, p. 19). This two-volume descriptive and analytical comparative study ranged from the Athenian republic to contemporary Latin American republics, at a time when most university teachers of the subject knew more about the political life of ancient Athens than of existing regimes. While Bryce's inductivist approach to political enquiry was to give pride of place to the collection of 'facts', which seems simplistic at the end of the 20th century, it is a healthy empirical corrective to a priori theorizing of a kind inspired by economics. Bryce's political experience ensured that he was not in danger of confusing the real political world with the abstractions from it to which a would-be political science sometimes lends itself. *JH*

E. Ions, *James Bryce and American Democracy, 1870–1922* (London, 1968).

Bryce report (1918) arose from an inter-party conference set up to consider the powers and composition of the second chamber. The Bryce commission agreed that the 1911 Parliament Act did not provide a permanent solution. It envisaged that the House of Lords should be a revising chamber, proposing that its members be partly elected by MPs and partly chosen by a joint committee of both Houses. But although government proposals similar to those of the Bryce commission were put forward at different times in the 1920s, progress with the proposed reforms petered out. *KT*

BSE. See Beef war.

B-Specials. See Royal Ulster Constabulary.

Buchanan report (1963). Professor Colin Buchanan's appointment as adviser to the Ministry of Transport in 1961 and his subsequent report on urban traffic problems reflected Whitehall's attempts to get to grips with the consequences of mass car ownership. Buchanan saw no prospect of limiting car use and, although the report drew attention to the role of public transport, it concentrated on accommodating the car through new roads and redesigned towns. Public opposition to this approach was not fully appreciated until the Greater London Council tried to build urban motorways later in the 1960s. *CL*

Traffic in Towns: The Buchanan Report (London, 1963).

Buchanan-Smith, Alick Laidlaw (1932–91), Conservative politician. A genial and youthful-looking Scot, Buchanan-Smith never faltered from his left-wing Toryism. Having served at the Scottish Office in the Heath government, he resigned as Scottish spokesman in 1976 when Thatcher abandoned the party's devolution commitment. He found a niche in government after 1979 as deputy to Walker at agriculture and energy, but in 1987 declined to serve at the Scottish Office and made clear his disagreement with Thatcher's policies. *RJS*

Buchan-Hepburn, Patrick George Thomas (1901–74), diplomat, Conservative politician, and whip. The Scots-born Buchan-Hepburn served in the British embassy in Constantinople before becoming personal private secretary to Churchill, the then chancellor of the exchequer, in 1927. In 1931 he was elected MP for Liverpool, East Toxteth, which he represented until he switched to Beckenham in 1950. Having served as parliamentary private secretary to Oliver Stanley at five departments, his appointment as an assistant whip in 1939 heralded a lengthy career in the Whips' Office interrupted only by war service. Buchan-Hepburn became deputy chief whip in 1945 and was made chief whip in 1948, although his promotion apparently owed more to the insistence of the rest of the front bench than to Churchill. By 1953 he was trying to persuade Churchill to retire and, when Eden finally succeeded him, he joined the cabinet as works minister. Buchan-Hepburn was among the doubters over Suez, and was the only cabinet minister who clearly wanted Butler to replace Eden. He retired when Macmillan became prime minister and took a peerage as Lord Hailes, but agreed to become governor-general of the Federation of the West Indies. The federation, however, was dissolved in 1962. *RJS*

Buckingham palace conference (1914). The Parliament Act, 1911, empowered the Commons to pass into law over the Lords' objection any legislation carried in three successive sessions. By July 1914 the Asquith government, backed by the irresistible majority composed of Liberal, Labour, and Irish Nationalist MPs, stood on the verge of passing the Third Home Rule Bill for the final time. In Ireland lines were firmly drawn: the Nationalists insisted on home rule for all of Ireland, and the Protestants of Ulster were equally adamant in their demand, if home rule passed, to be excluded from the authority of a Dublin parliament. In this fractious atmosphere the leaders of the contending parties met at Buckingham palace on 21–4 July 1914. With Speaker James Lowther presiding, these included, for the government, Asquith and Lloyd George and their Irish Nationalist allies, John Redmond and John Dillon; for the opposition, the Tories Andrew Bonar Law and Lord Lansdowne, and Ulster Unionists Sir Edward Carson and James Craig. The two sides parted without compromise and only the eruption of the Great War a few days later provided an irresistible reason to leave the matter unsettled for a further seven years. *RJQA*

R. J. Q. Adams, *Bonar Law* (London, 1999). | Patricia Jalland, *The Liberals and Ireland* (London, 1980).

Buckton, Raymond William (1922–95), trade union leader. Originally a railway engine cleaner, Ray Buckton joined the Associated Society of Locomotive Engineers and Firemen (ASLEF) in March 1940, and served as the union's general secretary, 1970–87. He was branded a militant by the national press in 1982 due to ASLEF's disruptive strike action over flexible rostering. Buckton firmly believed in the merits of public ownership and was a key left-wing figure on the TUC general council, 1973–86. *AM*

Budd, Alan Peter (1937–), economist. Budd served as chief economic adviser to the Treasury and head of the Government Economic Service, 1991–7. He made his reputation as an economic forecaster at the London Business School (LBS), where he was professor of economics, 1981–91. In the late 1980s he was an adviser to Nigel Lawson before succeeding his former LBS colleague Terry Burns as the Treasury's top economist. He was appointed a member of the Bank of England's monetary policy committee in 1997. *KT*

budget, annual announcement of government plans for public spending and taxation for the forthcoming financial year. This has become a major political and economic event, reflecting the increase in scale of that spending, and the taxation to pay for it, which has grown in leaps and bounds, from £265 million, approximately 13 per cent of GDP in 1900, to £400 billion and 40 per cent of GDP a hundred years later. Not only has the budget grown enormously, but since the 1940s it has, to varying degrees, been used to manage the economy. Thus the budget is not just about the volume and pattern of public spending, but has also become a key to the overall economic strategy of the government.

Budgets focus attention on the issue of how big government should be. Many have in consequence been highly contentious. For example, the *'People's Budget' of 1909 led to a crisis around the issue of how the social reforms associated with New Liberalism, as well as the expanding military effort, were to be paid for. The failure of MacDonald's Labour government to balance the 1931 budget formed an important step on the path which led to the collapse of that government, driven by its unwillingness to balance accounts by cutting unemployment pay. In 1951 the budgetary decision to cut health service spending led to the resignation of Aneurin *Bevan as minister of health, and symbolized the clash between those who gave an absolute priority to welfare spending and those willing to hold back such programmes to pay for Britain's world military role. In 1976, the decision to cut spending marked something of a watershed in policy, with a Labour government asserting the need to rein back spending, especially on welfare. Over the century the trend has been for welfare to be the main driver of budgetary expansion, though wars have played an important role in both highlighting welfare needs and accustoming the population to much higher levels of taxation. Welfare spending in the post-war period has been driven relentlessly upwards by the growth in numbers of claimants, especially pensioners, and from the 1970s by those unable to find work. The years since 1945 have also seen a politically irresistible trend to spend more on health and education, 'goods' for which demand grows fast as incomes increase. However, by the end of the century the willingness to pay tax to finance this growth was increasingly in question, which may put a cap on future growth unless governments find more politically congenial routes to raising money.

Before the Great War it was almost universally accepted that, while disagreements might occur on the scale of public spending and the pattern of taxes to pay for it, balancing the budget was an absolute necessity, at least in peacetime. In the 1920s, however, a minority of voices began to be heard which argued that balancing of budget should be a secondary issue to its possible use for managing the economy. In the 1930s such notions became particularly associated with the work of the economist J. M. *Keynes, who argued that manipulating the budget would have a major impact on the level of activity in the economy, and that temporary deficits at least should be accepted as a means of economic management. Keynes developed these doctrines in the context of inter-war unemployment, and therefore tried to justify budget deficits as a means to increase demand. The budget was first used to manage the economy in 1941, but with the aim of restraining wartime demand to counteract inflation. After the war the use of the budget to manage the economy was clearly evident, certainly from 1947, and for the next 30 years budgetary activism became the norm. In the 1950s and 1960s 'the budget judgement' was the centrepiece of 'activist' macroeconomic policy, trying to balance the level of employment against inflationary and balance of payments pressures. This so-called 'Keynesian era' did not, however, see sustained budget deficits; the buoyancy of the economy kept tax revenues high, and deficits were not needed to boost the economy. From the mid-1970s this approach to the budget came under challenge as the old relationship between inflation and unemployment broke down, and the growing level of public spending came into question. Rapid spending growth in the early 1970s, unaccompanied by tax increases, led to a sharp increase in the budget deficit, and therefore in the *Public Sector Borrowing Requirement (PSBR). As the PSBR had become a key measure of financial confidence, the 1974–9 Labour government cut spending hard, a policy reinforced by the conditions attached to the IMF loan of 1976.

The new Conservative government proclaimed in 1979 that 'Public spending is at the heart of Britain's economic problems' and committed itself to cutting it back. Ministers were also highly critical of using the budget to increase demand and employment, believing such policies only increased inflation, and the 1981 budget was therefore a landmark in the repudiation of such an approach, as it aimed to reduce spending and the deficit at a time of sharp recession. Since the mid-1970s the upward trend in level of public spending has levelled off, but without the 'rolling back of the state' promised by Thatcher. The budget is now less important than in the early post-war decades, because all recent governments have played down any major use of taxing and spending to manage the economy, in the name of providing more stability for the private sector. Policy at the end of the 1990s accepted deficits as appropriate in recessions, but stressed that budgets should be balanced over the economic cycle. But whatever the precise formulation of budgetary policy, the size of the budget (which shows no sign of shrinking) means that for the foreseeable future it is going to remain an important component of economic debate. *JDT*

Roger Middleton, *Government versus the Market* (Cheltenham, 1996). | Alan Peacock and Jack Wiseman, *The Growth of Public Expenditure in the United Kingdom* (2nd edn., London, 1967).

Budget Protest League, campaigning organization formed in June 1909 and led by Walter Long. The league was hastily organized to resist the unprecedented finance bill introduced weeks after Lloyd George's *'People's Budget'. Choosing not to align themselves with the social reform and fiscal schemes of the *tariff reformers, leaguers attacked the collectivist and crypto-socialist elements of the budget. Within a few months, they lost the leadership in their chosen fight to the more proactive Tariff Reform League and its allies in parliament. *RJQA*

Neal Blewett, *The Peers, the Parties and the People: The British General Elections of 1910* (London, 1972).

Bullock report (1977), result of an inquiry into industrial democracy by a committee headed by the historian and master of St Catherine's College, Oxford, Alan Bullock. The committee was appointed in December 1975 by the second Wilson government, trying to accommodate demands for better employer–worker relations as found in other European countries. Issued in April 1977, the report proposed a complex formula for the inclusion of worker representatives on company boards. Although supported by the Callaghan cabinet, there was little enthusiasm for such ideas from either the TUC or the CBI and it was shelved. *JS*

Burgess, Guy Francis de Moncey (1911–63), diplomat and Soviet agent. Burgess was educated at Eton, the Royal Naval College, Dartmouth, and Trinity College, Cambridge, where he read history. Whilst at Cambridge, he gained a reputation for his brilliance and charm, and also for his drunkenness, homosexuality, and later his dirty and dishevelled appearance. He also joined the intellectually exclusive secret society the Apostles and the Communist Party. His Cambridge career ended in 1934 when he abandoned his research, though by this point he was already a Soviet agent. Like 'Kim' Philby, he tried to establish right-wing credentials by renouncing his Marxist past; at one time he acted as secretary to a right-wing Conservative MP who was also a prominent member of the Anglo-German fellowship. In 1936, Burgess joined the BBC as a current affairs producer. Two years later the Secret Intelligence Service (SIS) recruited him in its sabotage and propaganda section and in 1940 he recruited fellow-spy Philby. In 1941 Burgess returned to the BBC where he worked on propaganda for occupied Europe and acted as liaison officer with SIS and Special Operations Executive. In 1944 Burgess went to the Foreign Office as a press officer, where he flourished, despite his drunkenness and lifestyle. After a variety of postings he was sent to Washington as a second secretary with special responsibility for Far Eastern affairs, just as the Korean war started. However, by 1951 his appalling behaviour caused the ambassador to ask for his recall. At this point, with the net closing around Donald Maclean (though against the wishes of Philby with whom he was living), Burgess defected to Russia. Thereafter he lived a lonely and bored life in Moscow. *PM*

Burma Office, created in 1937 when Burma became a separate colony (until then it had been dealt with by the India Office). The Burma Office remained in existence until Burma achieved independence from Britain in 1948. *JD*

W. David McIntyre, *Colonies into Commonwealth* (London, 1974).

Burns, John Elliot (1858–1943), labour activist and Liberal minister, the first working man to enter the cabinet. Born in London and largely self-educated, Burns joined the Marxist Social Democratic Federation in 1884, contesting Nottingham West as a federation candidate in 1885. He founded the Battersea Labour League and was imprisoned for his part in the London unemployed riots of 1885 and 1886. A prominent leader in the 1889 dock strike, Burns represented Battersea on the newly formed London County Council, 1889–1907, where he was active in municipalizing transport and water services, and was also elected for Battersea as an independent Labour MP in 1892, retaining his seat until 1918. He maintained a distance between himself and the *Independent Labour Party, refusing to join, and the new *Labour Representation Committee. Increasingly allying himself with the progressive (Liberal) group on the London County Council, both in terms of social policy and of his opposition to the Boer war, he accepted the presidency of the local government board in the 1905 Liberal government. Criticized by socialists for failing to take a more interventionist stance on social policy, he nevertheless oversaw the Housing and Town Planning Act of 1909. Appointed to the presidency of the Board of Trade in February 1914, as a lifelong pacifist he resigned from the government over the declaration of war with Germany in August 1914 and declined to contest his seat in 1918, retiring to private life. *JS*

Burns, Terence (1944–), permanent secretary to the Treasury, 1991–8. A monetarist academic at the London Business School, Terry Burns was appointed chief economic adviser to the Treasury in 1980 before—unusually—taking over as permanent secretary in 1991. He pushed through a major reorganization of the Treasury in 1994. One of the main architects of Conservative economic policy in the 1980s and 1990s, he never properly meshed with Labour ministers and advisers after 1997 and retired early. *KT*

'business as usual', phrase used by Winston Churchill in a speech at London's Guildhall, London, on 9 November 1914, expressing the Liberal government's view that it could sustain the Great War (which had broken out in August) with little disturbance to normal government. In practice the war would promote immense disruption to political life and encourage major changes in government, the economy, and society. Often cited as an ironic comment on Liberal failure to appreciate that the pre-war order was changing, though such a view was untenable in November 1914 without the benefit of hindsight. *JS*

businessmen in government. During the Great War the mobilization of materials and manpower led to the appointment of industrial managers in new ministries as unprecedented problems of production and supply were encountered. At the Ministry of Munitions Lloyd George appointed Eric *Geddes to create new shell-filling factories and by 1918 over fifty of his colleagues from the North Eastern Railway worked in Whitehall departments. These 'men of push and go', or leading hustlers, were celebrated in Lloyd George's *War Memoirs* (1934) for challenging Asquithian 'Dilly and Dally' and 'pennyworth' thinking. They gathered statistical evidence of production bottlenecks and enlarged output as semi-autonomous, technically educated improvisers who, as practical men, impatiently embodied the munitions crusade. On the creation of new ministries in December 1916, some businessmen assumed ministerial responsibilities and laid the foundations for the government's response to attritional war in 1917–18, usually by improving or circumventing the supply functions of the Admiralty and War Office. As minister of shipping, Sir Joseph Maclay supervised merchant shipbuilding and, as a shipowner, his presence in Whitehall reassured the industry that the Admiralty's resistance to convoys would be overcome. At the newly created Air Board the contractor Weetman Pearson asserted the priority supply needs of home defence squadrons and Andrew Weir, 1st Lord Inverforth, shipowner, organized stores and equipment as surveyor-general at the War Office. At the intersection of civil–military relations these appointments required flexibility, energy, and courage to withstand, unprepared, the political limelight, assisted by volatile support from Lloyd George and pursuit of the self-evident national interest. At the Armistice, Coalition rhetoric, urgent social questions, and the continuing relevance of managing material resources encouraged businessmen to remain in government. Their loyalty to Lloyd George became contentious when opportunities for centrist initiatives waned and they had departed by August 1921.

However, their wartime experience formed the basis of inter-war networks of politicians, civil servants, and businessmen which facilitated the development of public corporations and initiatives to protect the supply of vital war materials. Usually nominally Conservative in politics, they generally espoused the separation of politics and business unless rationalization required government intervention, such as the state subsidy for Imperial Airways, the North Atlantic Shipping Act, 1934, and the creation of the Lancashire Cotton Corporation. In 1940 Sir Andrew Duncan became president of the Board of Trade and, subsequently, minister of supply, having previously been secretary of the Merchant Shipbuilding Advisory Committee (1916) and chairman of the Central Electricity Board (1927) and of the British Iron and Steel Federation (1935). He supervised the productive capacity of war industries and resisted plans for the extension of state economic planning in peacetime. He personified the businessmen in government who participated in planning the Mulberry harbour for the Normandy landing, but voiced scepticism of designs for the post-war 'New Jerusalem'. As outsiders, the role of businessmen in government in two world wars highlighted the formidable organizational and logistical challenge of total war and the paucity of industrial expertise in high politics in that period. The later experience of John *Davies and David Young in Conservative cabinets of the 1970s and 1980s re-emphasized the difficulty of switching from business to politics in periods of normal, peacetime politics. *KG*

K. Middlemas, *Politics in Industrial Society* (London, 1979). | J. Turner, 'The Politics of Business', in his (ed.) *Businessmen and Politics: Studies of Business Activity in British Politics 1900–1945* (London, 1984). | J. Turner, '"Experts" and Interests: David Lloyd George and the Dilemmas of the Expanding State, 1906–1919', in R. Macleod (ed.), *Government and Expertise in Britain 1815–1919* (Cambridge, 1988).

business voters. Until 1949, a British elector could qualify for an additional vote in a second constituency if s/he owned business property in that constituency worth £10 a year (before 1918 these rights were more extensive and some electors with widely dispersed property holdings could in principle vote many times). By the 1930s, there were about a third of a million business electors on the registers, concentrated mainly in city centre constituencies (especially the City of London which had few actual residents but still retained two MPs entirely because of its business vote), and there the business vote tended greatly to assist the Conservatives—the business vote may have prevented Ramsay MacDonald from winning a parliamentary majority in 1929. It was drastically curtailed in 1945 and abolished in 1949, but remained in force for local government elections for another twenty years, a fine example of Britain's crablike crawl towards democracy. *JAR*

Butler, David Edgeworth (1924–), political scientist and pioneer of psephology. Butler has been connected with Nuffield College, Oxford, since 1948, and has worked on the 'Nuffield studies' of each UK General Election (*The British General Election of...*) since 1950; studies were conceived as a means of preventing instant myths (such as the supposed 'bankers' ramp' in 1931) from becoming received history. They have pioneered two main developments. One is an authoritative set of descriptive statistics for each general election in the series, which have become the main source of aggregate data about constituency voting in the UK since 1945. The other is a unique set of interviews, in the run-up to each election, with leading party figures, who have been willing to talk to Butler about their plans for the election. Butler's related work has included another 'Nuffield series' on the 1975 referendum on European Community membership and the subsequent elections to the European parliament; several editions of a handbook, *British Political Facts*; the journal *Electoral Studies*; and policy work on boundary drawing and electoral administration. With Donald E. Stokes, then of the University of Michigan, Butler instigated the

*British Election Study, which provides an unrivalled set of data about the attitudes of individual members of the British electorate since 1963. Butler's most original book, **Political Change in Britain*, introduced, among much else, the study of political cohorts. Butler and Stokes pointed out that electors' political attitudes are often formed when they are socialized into politics as teenagers, and that therefore the politics of eras up to 50 years before the present are embedded in strata exposed to the keen geologist's eye at each election. *IM*

Butler, Richard Austen ('Rab') (1902–82), Conservative politician. Butler's span of nearly 27 years as a minister was exceeded only by that of Churchill in the 20th century. He was born in the Punjab, where his father served in the Indian civil service, and was educated at Marlborough and Cambridge, becoming MP for Saffron Walden in 1929, having married into the Courtauld family which had given him financial independence and secured him the seat. Appointed under-secretary for India in 1932, he faced the wrath of Churchill and the Tory right over the Government of India Bill (see INDIA). He was moved to labour in 1937, but from the following February was again in the firing line at the Foreign Office. Since Halifax, the foreign secretary, sat in the Lords, Butler had to answer the attacks by Churchill, Macmillan, and others on Neville Chamberlain's appeasement of the dictators. Despite being an unapologetic appeaser, he survived Chamberlain's fall in May 1940.

Butler's opportunity to apply his reformist Toryism and political skill to good effect came when made president of the Board of Education in July 1941. Disregarding Churchill's instruction not to stir things up, Butler embarked upon major reform. His *Education Act, 1944, gave every child the right to a secondary education, and provided for nursery education, further education, and the raising of the school leaving age. Despite flaws in the tripartite system of secondary education, the Butler Act, as it rightly became known, was a cornerstone of the post-war welfare state.

After the Conservatives' disastrous defeat in 1945, Butler's vision of a liberal and pragmatic Toryism inspired his reshaping of party policy and prevented the Conservatives being sidelined. Appointed by Churchill as chairman of the Conservative Research Department and of the industrial committee, his influence was reflected in the **Industrial Charter* in 1947 and *The Right Road for Britain* in 1949, that endorsed full employment and the welfare state. As chancellor of the exchequer from 1951, he set Britain free from austerity by reducing physical controls and taxation. *The Economist*'s coining of the phrase, 'Butskellism' to describe policy similarities with his Labour predecessor, Gaitskell, obscured as much as it illuminated. Butler adhered to Keynesian policy, although the cabinet prevented him taking the radical step of floating the exchange rate. He was one of the ablest post-war chancellors, but in his last year damaged his reputation with 1955's electioneering budget, followed afterwards by tax increases. Such was Butler's standing by 1953 that, when Churchill and Eden were both ill, he took charge of the government. He became leader of the House and lord privy seal in 1955, but without a department he lost clout in Whitehall. His indiscretions and inspired sayings, known as 'Rabisms', also landed him in hot water, as when he agreed that Eden was 'the best prime minister we have'. During Suez, his half-hearted attempts to restrain Eden made him appear devious. When the prime minister was forced to rest, Butler again took charge and had to handle Britain's climbdown. In 1957, he assumed, as did most observers, that he would succeed Eden, but the cabinet backed Macmillan.

Butler became home secretary while remaining leader of the House, and in 1959 also became party chairman, holding the latter two posts until 1961. He courageously resisted strident demands from Tory supporters for the return of flogging, reformed the laws on charities and licensing, legalized betting shops, and facilitated Roy Jenkins's reform of the obscene publications law on to the statute book. Although he implemented the Wolfenden committee's recommendations on prostitution, he was deterred from attempting homosexual law reform by the strength of opposition. In 1962, he introduced the long overdue Commonwealth Immigrants Act. Handed the seemingly impossible challenge of central Africa in 1962, Butler skilfully negotiated the dissolution of the Central African Federation without conceding full independence to southern Rhodesia. Although Macmillan did all in his power to deny him the premiership in October 1963, Butler could still have become prime minister had he refused to serve Douglas-Home. However, it was not in his nature to do so. He was compensated with the Foreign Office. In 1965, he became master of Trinity College, Cambridge, and sat in the Lords as a cross-bencher. Butler occupied great offices of state with distinction and was a constructive, tolerant, and very human politician.

RJS

RAB BUTLER, *The Art of the Possible* (London, 1971). | ANTHONY HOWARD, *RAB: The Life of R. A. Butler* (London, 1987).

Butler, Robin (1938–), secretary of the cabinet and head of the home civil service, 1988–97. A classic Northcote-Trevelyan high-flyer, Butler combined deep experience at the heart of government (joining the Treasury in 1961 and serving in the Number Ten private office under Heath, Wilson, and Thatcher) with the confident and enthusiastic style of the top public school (Harrow) head boy he was. As head of the civil service, he tried to reconcile enormous changes in the management and organization of the Whitehall machine (including the creation of executive agencies, contracting-out, and privatization—and he fought off ideas for more radical change) with the traditional ethos and impartiality of the civil service, against the background of the stresses and strains building up over a long period of single-party rule. However, his assertion to the Scott inquiry into arms to Iraq that 'half the picture can be true' made him appear an apologist for dubious ministerial actions. Anxious to show that the civil service could still play its textbook role as the efficient and impartial instrument of the government of the day, whatever its political complexion, he prepared for the successful transition to a Labour government in 1997 with immense care. *KT*

Butler Education Act. See EDUCATION ACT, 1944.

Butler-Sloss, (Ann) Elizabeth Oldfield (1933–), judge. After practising at the Bar, 1955–70, Mrs Butler-Sloss was appointed registrar, 1970–9; judge of the High Court, family division, 1979–88 (its president from 1999); and chair of the high-profile Cleveland child abuse inquiry, 1987–8. She was for many years Britain's most prominent female judge, becoming a lord justice of appeal, 1988–99. A former Conservative parliamentary candidate, she was sister to Michael Havers and married to Mr Justice Butler-Sloss, judge of the High Court of Kenya. *JAR*

Butskellism. See BUTLER, RICHARD AUSTEN ('RAB').

Buxton conference (30 May–1 June 1923), important meeting of the National Liberal Federation in 1923 which failed to secure reunion of the Asquith and Lloyd George wings of the party. A crucial amendment calling on the disaffected Independent Liberals (largely Asquith's followers) to discuss with the *National (Lloyd George) Liberals the best means of promoting party unity was defeated. Bitterness over the 1922 general election, when rival Liberals had fought each other, and the personal antipathy between Asquith and Lloyd George, overcame the support for reunion from constituency resolutions and pressure from the Welsh Liberals. Failure to reunify the party earlier continued the decay of local organizations and of national policy formation, before the unexpected conversion of Baldwin to protection in September 1923 gave the warring factions of the Liberal Party the free-trade cause around which they could unite. *JS*

by-elections, elections held to fill casual vacancies. They are employed when a seat becomes vacant through death, resignation, or the expulsion of the incumbent; instead of waiting until the next regular election, a by-election is held. Several parliamentary by-elections are usually held each year, though the number has declined in the last quarter of the 20th century. In the third quarter of the century, by-elections were variously triggered because MPs were given offices of profit under the crown (which disqualified them from Commons' membership) or because they were elevated to the Lords (also disqualifying them). The incumbent party usually won the resulting by-election. With greater voter volatility in and since the 1960s, parties—especially the governing party, which has the patronage power to elevate MPs to various public offices—have been less willing to create vacancies for fear of losing the ensuing by-elections. In the six parliaments up to and including that of 1964–6 there were 243 by-elections (an average of 40 per parliament) and the defending party lost only 21 of them. In the subsequent seven parliaments, there were 155 (an average of 22 per parliament) with the defending party losing 51 (Norton, 114). By-elections are now the result predominantly of the death of sitting MPs. The year 1998 was unusual in that it was the first in the 20th century in which not one by-election took place. The procedures for by-elections are the same as in general elections, though candidates have a higher campaign expenditure limit. Turnout in a by-election is normally lower than in a general election, though the campaign may attract a high media visibility. A by-election result in the St George's constituency in 1930 is generally credited with saving Stanley Baldwin's leadership of the Conservative Party (when a pro-Baldwin Conservative defeated an anti-Baldwin Conservative) and a by-election in Hull North in January 1966—a Labour marginal seat held by the Labour candidate, Kevin McNamara—is believed to have prompted Prime Minister Harold Wilson to call a general election. *PN*

Chris Cook and John Ramsden (eds.), *By-Elections in British Politics* (2nd edn., London, 1997). | Pippa Norris, *British By-Elections: The Volatile Electorate* (Oxford, 1990). | Philip Norton, 'Parliament in the United Kingdom: The Incumbency Paradox', in Albert Somit et al. (eds.), *The Victorious Incumbent: A Threat to Democracy?* (Aldershot, 1994).

Byers, (Charles) Frank (1915–84), Liberal backbencher. Oxford-educated, Byers was MP for North Dorset, 1945–50; he unsuccessfully contested Dorset North in 1951 and Bolton East in 1960. Leader of the Liberal Party in the Lords from 1967, his elevation to the peerage in 1964 had followed a lifelong commitment to the party, serving as its chairman in 1950–2 and 1965–7. He was one of the stalwarts of the party during its period of near eclipse, acting as chief whip, 1946–50, and campaign manager in several general elections. Outside politics, he was a successful businessman as director of Rio Tinto Zinc, 1951–73, and a broadcaster. Father of Stephen Byers, member of Tony Blair's cabinet. *JS*

cabinet, development of. The modern British cabinet is the mechanism by which the two principles of the governmental system, ministerial and collective responsibility, are balanced. It has been described as 'the Board of Directors for Great Britain' (Jennings, 228; Home quoted in Hennessy, 5) and as the 'most senior Committee of government' (Mackintosh, 411). However, tracing its origins and development are notoriously difficult enterprises, not least because the cabinet does not exist in law but is rather a dynamic resultant of managerial and political expediency and constitutional practice. That dynamism began in the 17th century as the Commons acquired certain legal rights and with them a degree of confidence in its own validity, and as problems between parliament and the crown began to manifest themselves. After the execution of Charles I there was, of course, no need for royal approval. However, after the 1660 restoration of the monarchy, an uneasy relationship between crown and parliament returned. The king used only a small group of privy councillors as his advisers on policy issues; these were referred to variously as the foreign committee of the privy council, the *Junto*, the council, or the cabinet (its name deriving from its private meetings in the *cabinet* (private office) of the monarch, rather than ceremonially in an apartment of state). Membership of this elite was on the basis of an ability and willingness to serve the crown, so that the cabinet, even in its earliest manifestation, was a tool of political management. Constant wrangling over the next twenty years only confirmed the need for harmony between crown, ministers, and a parliamentary majority, and the cabinet was the instrument which performed that function. While the cabinet technically still owed its existence and power to the crown, after 1688 it was obvious that ultimately the crown (and therefore the cabinet) deferred to parliament.

Although in 1717 George I effectively ceased to attend cabinet meetings, leaving them to their own devices, it was the effects of the 1832 Reform Act which were the step-change in the relationship between cabinet and crown. By altering the relationship between MPs and their constituencies the Act virtually ended royal influence. Initially this actually weakened the cabinet because royal patronage was replaced by a reliance on MPs who in turn relied upon local constituency patronage, but the re-emergence of a two-party system re-established the power of the cabinet. As the mass parties became more organized, so the cabinet took on the appearance and actuality of the board of directors analogy. There had developed a natural mix of senior departmental ministers, the lord privy seal, lord president of the council, and chancellor of the duchy of Lancaster. The leader of the majority party became prime minister and the premier, in turn, was charged with selecting the cabinet. By the start of the Great War the cabinet had settled into an institution selected and led by the prime minister, tasked with making policy decisions or giving approval to policy proposals made by other members of the government. The prime minister had gradually achieved greater formal stature and the war merely accelerated the public's desire for the prime minister and his cabinet to be recognized as the nation's policy-making elite. The Haldane machinery of government report of 1918 merely confirmed this position.

In 1914, Asquith formed a war council of six powerful ministers. The plan was to meet only as necessary. However, very quickly this became unworkable due to the continual nature of the problems and the antagonistic personalities involved. The membership soon expanded to thirteen, which further diluted its effectiveness. When Asquith eventually fell in 1916 Lloyd George and Law forged a coalition and immediately streamlined the cabinet by forming a five-man war cabinet, its members divested of most departmental responsibilities (though Law retained the Treasury). This arrangement allowed Lloyd George effectively to run the war with a tight-knit unit generally perceived as successfully improving the efficacy of decision making. However, once the war was over, it was obvious that, while politicians could suppress their ambition during conflict, they were less inclined to do so in peacetime. By November 1919 it was formally decided to return to the structure of the 'ordinary' cabinet. The result was an initial cabinet of twenty. Throughout the inter-war years membership of cabinets hovered around that mark and by 1939 the figure was 23. Chamberlain reduced the number to nine for his initial war cabinet, which was criticized by both Churchill and Attlee as too large. When Churchill assumed the premiership in 1940, he immediately reduced its size. Churchill centralized power even more than Lloyd George had done, but like Lloyd George he included prominent opposition politicians in his cabinet with Attlee becoming a virtual deputy prime minister with responsibility for domestic affairs.

The Caretaker Government of 1945 reflected received wisdom concerning peacetime cabinets and returned to a larger membership: sixteen. Attlee viewed sixteen to eighteen as about the right size for a cabinet. He also attempted a major restructuring of the cabinet system which would enable the prime minister to resist calls for an increase in size of cabinet. He hoped that by expanding the number of cabinet committees business could be diverted away from full cabinet. Initially this seemed to work, but for the remainder of the 20th century the size of cabinets stabilized at around 22. Various experiments such as Churchill's 'overlords', Attlee's 'co-ordinating ministers', and additional ministers 'of cabinet rank' (but not in cabinet) have been tried, but the cabinet has always returned to what appears to be the natural mix of senior departmental ministers and ministers without portfolio. At the end of the 20th century the cabinet has settled in shape and has retained the basic role from the 17th century; that role is as a harmonizing agent —be it between the crown and parliament or between the pressures of collective and ministerial responsibility. *CAB*

Peter Hennessy, *Cabinet* (Oxford, 1986). | Ivor Jennings, *Cabinet Government* (Cambridge, 1969). | John P. Mackintosh, *The British Cabinet* (London, 1977).

cabinet committees. A cabinet committee is a notoriously difficult thing to define. No formal records exist for committees before 1915 and, even with the establishment of what was to become the Cabinet Office, there was no attempt formally to log committees until the establishment of a committee book in 1927. That book only covered those aspects of defence which came within the purview of the Committee of Imperial Defence. It was not until the Second World War that attempts at a more comprehensive guide to cabinet committees were made. Despite this innovation, even in the Cabinet Office it still was not always easy to tell what ought to be included. In 1946 William *Armstrong wrote that 'so far as I know there is no definition of what constitutes a Cabinet Committee and . . . I am far from certain that the distinction [between cabinet and non-cabinet committees] is worth making'. The distinction he nevertheless arrived at, to distinguish between cabinet committees and the throng of interdepartmental official committees, which at points during the Second World War approached 800 in number, was that cabinet committees were those where the Cabinet Office provided the secretariat.

Using this simple criterion at least permitted a method of identifying cabinet committees. These committees are divided into 'ministerial' and 'official' committees, and those committees are in turn divided into 'standing' and 'ad hoc' committees. For convenience the ad hoc (temporary) committees are numbered and prefixed by administration. Blair's government, for example, takes the prefix MISC (miscellaneous) and his successor will take the prefix GEN (general); the terms alternate by administration. The 'standing' committees are established with the perception that they will be as permanent as they need to be. 'Ministerial' committees are those which tend to appear on the Cabinet Office's website and are chaired by cabinet ministers. 'Official' committees generally parallel ministerial committees and provide the administrative support for the parent committee, mostly in the form of research and briefings. Terms such as 'generally' and 'tend to' are used deliberately because the precise constitution and function of any cabinet committee can be exactly as the prime minister, or even the cabinet secretary, decide it should be. Harold Wilson, for example, was in the habit of testing the political water with an ad hoc committee and then converting it into a standing committee. While the existence of cabinet committees in general is now admitted, this only happened in the 1990s, and the existence of all cabinet committees is still not in the public domain.

As the tasks of central government increased, so the establishment of some sort of system to relieve the burden on the centre became inevitable. The cabinet system with its integral use of committees is merely a solution to the workload generated by government. Allowing executive decision-making to reside with the committees as well as with the full cabinet itself can only alleviate the burden. *CAB*

Peter Catterall and Christopher Brady, 'Cabinet Committees in British Governance', *Public Policy and Administration* (1998), 67–84.

Cabinet Office (1916–), the totality of organizational support provided to cabinet which enables the prime minister, and ministers collectively, to produce and implement policy. During its existence the Cabinet Office has also garnered to itself other smaller units, as and when this is considered necessary. With the exception of the cabinet secretary (head of the Cabinet Office), who is appointed permanently, staff are seconded from other departments, usually for a period of two to three years. This is designed to dissuade the Cabinet Office from developing its own agenda since it is expected to be politically neutral.

In common parlance the terms 'cabinet office' and 'cabinet secretariat' have tended to be used synonymously. Such usage can be traced back to the Cabinet Office's official birth in 1916. It was during the Great War that the necessity for a more ordered administrative structure was recognized, Lloyd George forming a cabinet secretariat which was initially the secretariat of the Committee for Imperial Defence (CID) by another name. Maurice Hankey, the secretary of the CID, thus became the first cabinet secretary. In the immediate post-war years there was considerable antipathy towards this new office because it was claimed that it had become unduly, and unconstitutionally, powerful. The clamour for its abolition was so great that, during the run-up to the 1922 general election, Law threatened to do just that, though, after the election, he chose only to reduce its size, no doubt recognizing its utility. Law also ensured that from 1924 onwards the minutes of cabinet meetings would no longer be a record of the proceedings but would instead be a record of the decisions and actions taken at those meetings.

As head of the office the cabinet secretary is uniquely influential. He attends all cabinet meetings in addition to chairing many of the most important 'official' cabinet committees. Since 1981, he has also been the head of the home civil service which by many accounts can take up as much as 30 per cent of his time. Harold Wilson placed the cabinet secretary's position in perspective, arguing that he was not only the cabinet's servant 'but he is also my Permanent Secretary . . . He advises me, briefs me, not only for Cabinet meetings and other Cabinet Committees over which I preside but on the general running of the government so far as policy is concerned.'

To date, there have been only eight cabinet secretaries. To the current post-holder, Sir Richard Wilson, fell the task of reorganizing the Cabinet Office such that it now consists of nine separate entities, each of which have subunits of their own. Thus the secretariat is a federation of six secretariats and the public service delivery unit has five subunits. Number Ten has its own unit, and there is a ministerial group headed by a senior cabinet minister. Additionally there are agencies, linked through the ministers group. *CAB*

cabinet procedure. The main tasks of the cabinet are first to coordinate the activities of the governmental departments and committees such that the government at least presents the impression of coherence, and second, to generate policy initiatives consistent with the efficient running of the country. Cabinet procedure attempts to facilitate those aims as efficiently as possible. The most easily observable procedural element is the frequency of meetings. Although they tend to occur on a regular basis (currently once a week), they can, theoretically, be convened at any time the prime minister chooses. There is no quorum, and as such a minister may be absent and lose the opportunity to voice his feelings. Although junior ministers may represent their secretaries of state, they may only be heard on their own departmental issues.

It is through the departments that most issues come to cabinet. Forty-eight hours' notice is required to be given to all cabinet members, via the necessary briefing and memoranda, before an item can be placed on the agenda by the cabinet secretary, with the approval of the prime minister. Two obligatory items are always on the agenda. First is parliamentary business, which usually entails selecting spokesmen for debates and the general tactical stance to be taken in respect of the opposition's position on any particular issue. Second is foreign affairs which, in recent times, has included European issues. Other items appear only if they are considered of sufficient collective significance to warrant inclusion. For an issue to actually get to the cabinet it must have been found to have been insoluble either in the departments or in *cabinet committee. Harold Wilson established a precedent that only the chairperson of a cabinet committee could bring an unresolved issue from the committee to cabinet.

Issues which are dealt with by cabinet will have previously been processed through the cabinet system. Once initiatives have been formulated, data will be collected, interpreted, distributed, and prioritized. These actions can constitute a tortuous, iterative process where the donkey work remains primarily the province of the cabinet and departmental secretariats. When the cabinet has finally decided an issue, the decision will be recorded and disseminated by the cabinet secretariat, in the form of minutes and conclusions. Formally, the conclusions are contained in the summary of the issue presented by the chairperson. Because the secretariat is required to produce the minutes and conclusions within 24 hours of the meeting, it is imperative that the chairpersons' summations are as precise (or imprecise) as they require them to be. Cabinet conclusions are circulated only to cabinet members and selected members of the cabinet secretariat. Out of courtesy, they also go to the monarch (and currently also to the prince of Wales). What minutes and conclusions rarely show are the discussions and arguments which precede the conclusions, although reading between the lines can be instructive. Copies of all cabinet minutes and conclusions are held in the Public Record Office under the codes CAB 128 and CAB 129 respectively. *CAB*

cabinet secretariat. Prior to 1916, a cabinet secretariat did not formally exist. The pressures of war, however, precipitated the transference of Sir Maurice Hankey's Committee of Imperial Defence secretariat to service the war cabinet, and in 1918 the Haldane committee recommended the retention of this arrangement. Despite attempts to revert to pre-war arrangements, the cabinet secretariat prevailed and prospered. The secretariat is a federation of six individual secretariats: for central affairs; economic and domestic; defence and overseas; European; constitution; intelligence and security committee organization. Additionally, it includes the chief scientific adviser, ceremonial branch, and the joint intelligence organization. Its prime responsibility is to service the cabinet organization, including cabinet committees and subcommittees. The cabinet secretary, as head of the secretariat, is quite simply the most powerful permanent, unelected member of the government. He sits, literally in most cases, at the right hand of the prime minister during cabinet meetings, and is responsible for preparing the agenda, in consultation with the prime minister, and for providing the minutes. Consequently, he is able to control the flow of business around the machinery of government. Although theoretically the secretariat is responsible to all ministers, in practice it has tended to serve the prime minister and those ministers without portfolio designated by the prime minister. In a radio interview in 1967, Harold Wilson argued that, in addition to its formal role, 'the Cabinet Secretariat is the private department of the Prime Minister'. Naturally the secretariat also has close working links with all other units of the Cabinet Office and some subunits report directly to the cabinet secretary. *CAB*

Cable Street, battle of (4 October 1936). By 1936 the *British Union of Fascists (BUF) had become increasingly involved in the politics of East London and planned a major demonstration through areas of Jewish settlement. A large anti-Fascist crowd thwarted the BUF's plans. 'They shall not pass' was the cry. The events have been described as a defeat for the BUF, but it held successful meetings in East London after Cable Street. The potential for future clashes encouraged the government to pass the *Public Order Act later the same year. *CH*

T. P. Linehan, *East London for Mosley* (London, 1996). | R. Skidelsky, *Oswald Mosley* (London, 1975).

Cadogan, Alexander George Montagu (1884–1968), senior British Foreign Office mandarin who became permanent secretary, displacing Sir Robert Vansittart in 1939. Cadogan, a career diplomat with an impeccable pedigree and background, rose effortlessly in the civil service hierarchy, Like most senior officials he opposed Neville Chamberlain's determination to appease Hitler and Mussolini and thus postpone or avert the coming world war. He supported Anthony Eden, the foreign secretary, in facing up to the dictators, and served him loyally throughout the war, working immensely long hours and attending all the main Allied conferences when Churchill, Stalin, and Roosevelt mapped out the shape of the post-war world. His private diaries covering this period, an important historical source, reveal a sensitive and emotional man, with often blistering opinions on his political masters and vivid descriptions of his encounters with neutrals such as the Turks, at the time urged by both sides to join the war. Without Eden, he accompanied Churchill on a secret visit to the Turkish leadership in January 1943. His devoted, tireless, and effective implementation of British foreign policy was acknowledged by the award of the Order of Merit. *RD*

David Dilks (ed.), *The Diaries of Sir Alexander Cadogan, 1938–1945* (London, 1971).

Caine, Sidney (1902–91), distinguished educationalist who initially worked for 29 years as a civil servant, rising to the rank of third secretary to the Treasury. In 1952 he was appointed vice-chancellor of the University of Malaya before becoming director of the LSE (1957–67) during a period of intense turmoil. He helped to pioneer new developments more generally, being a member of the committees which proposed the appointment of ombudsmen, and the concept of subscription television. *JFM*

Cairncross, Alexander Kirkland (1911–2000), economist and civil servant. Alec Cairncross was a lecturer at the universities of Glasgow and Cambridge before wartime duty as a temporary civil servant, continuing to advise government into the late 1940s. He returned to academic life as professor of applied economics at Glasgow, 1951–61, but was then government economic adviser, 1961–4, and head of the Government Economic Service, 1964–9, retiring to be master of St Peter's College, Oxford, 1969–78. A tough Scotsman with a strong will but an always engaging personality, he published widely in applied economics, and latterly also in the history of post-war economic policy, editing for publication both his own diaries and those of Sir Robert Hall. *JAR*

Alec Cairncross, *The Wilson Years: A Treasury Diary, 1964–1966* (London, 1997).

Cairncross, John (1913–95), civil servant and Soviet agent. Born in Glasgow, Cairncross was educated in Scotland, at the Sorbonne in Paris, and at Trinity College, Cambridge, where he gained a first in modern languages. By then he was already a member of the Communist Party. His teacher, Soviet talent-spotter Anthony Blunt, introduced him to 'Kim' Philby, who encouraged him to join the Foreign Office and become a Comintern agent. Cairncross later worked at the Treasury and in 1940 became personal secretary to government minister Lord Hankey. These jobs gave him ready access to cabinet, intelligence and diplomatic documents, and the papers of the Scientific Advisory Committee, whose work included the 1941 decision to begin work on the construction of an atomic bomb; this he passed on to his Soviet controller. In 1942 he moved to Bletchley Park, from where he passed many important secrets (his information concerning German military dispositions, he later claimed, was critical in determining the outcome of the battle of Kursk). Cairncross ended the war as one of the Soviet Union's most important and prolific agents. Although Cairncross claimed he ended his Soviet links at the end of the Second World War, he in fact continued to pass information concerning atomic weapons, the Korean war, and other matters. After the disappearance of Burgess and Maclean in 1951, he was questioned by MI5: although no firm evidence was ever found, his career ended and he left Britain. He was identified as 'the fifth Cambridge spy' in 1990 and died in France in 1995, shortly after completing his memoirs in which he denied his treachery, which was confirmed by the publication of some of the contents of his KGB file in 1998. *PM*

Calcutt report (1992). This report on press self-regulation came at a time of public concern about press intrusion into private lives, particularly of the royal family. It traced the failure of the industry to fulfil the demands made by similar previous committees and identified the Press Complaints Commission's inability to provide an effective machine for people making complaints. The report advocated the outlawing of certain press surveillance techniques and a stronger commission to regulate what was published. *KMT*

Callaghan, (Leonard) James (1912–), Labour politician. Jim Callaghan was the only politician of the century to hold all four great offices of state (chancellor, foreign secretary, home secretary, and prime minister), though he did not win a general election as Labour leader. His father, a chief petty officer in the Royal Navy, died when he was a boy and his mother raised him a strict Baptist. He was educated at elementary and secondary schools before passing civil service examinations and entering the Inland Revenue as a tax officer in 1929. He joined the Labour Party the same year and his first steps in politics were taken as an active member of the Inland Revenue staff federation, which he served as assistant secretary, 1938–47, working under Douglas Houghton. During the Second World War he followed his father's example by serving in the navy, and when war ended was one of the large cohort of new Labour MPs elected in the 1945 landslide. This began a distinguished parliamentary career: he was MP for South Cardiff, 1945–50; for South-East Cardiff, 1950–83; and for Cardiff South and Penarth, 1983–7. He was elected to the party's NEC, 1957–80, and held the politically powerful post of party treasurer, 1967–76. Callaghan's ministerial career began under Attlee, who sent him to the Ministry of Transport as parliamentary secretary, 1947–50, followed by a short spell as parliamentary and financial secretary at the Admiralty, 1950–1. During the following thirteen years in opposition, Callaghan steadily increased his standing within the party. His reputation as a bluff, genial, utterly reliable politician whose ordinary background gave him the common touch—'Uncle Jim'—disguised the fact that he was a ruthless political operator. He also stood in sharp contrast to that formidable generation of Oxford-educated intellectuals like Anthony Crosland, Richard Crossman, Hugh Gaitskell, Roy Jenkins, and Harold Wilson who loomed so large in the party's counsels. When Wilson became party leader on Gaitskell's sudden death in 1963, Callaghan had stood for the leadership, got 41 votes, and come third behind Wilson and George Brown. He had, though, done enough to split the right-wing vote, letting in the more left-wing Wilson, and to ensure himself a major post in the next Labour government.

Front-Bencher

Wilson led Labour to a wafer-thin parliamentary majority in the following year, and Callaghan became chancellor of the exchequer. This would normally have been the key position, especially at a time of acute economic problems and with Labour's promise to end the sterile cycle of stop-go, aiming to reach a new age of steady growth which would bring rising prosperity—and so pay for social reforms designed to update the welfare state that Attlee had bequeathed. However, Callaghan's Treasury was now in contention with the new Department of Economic Affairs (DEA), headed by Brown. The hard decision facing the new administration was whether to jump-start the economy with a devaluation, which Wilson refused to do. The economy thus remained sluggish, and by 1966 Brown's DEA had been sidelined and, instead of 'creative tension' (generally more tense than creative), the Treasury was back in charge. The 1966 general election gave Labour a 100-seat majority, but within months there was further economic crisis, and in the following year Britain was forced to devalue the pound and Callaghan resigned, to be transferred to the Home Office. Here he was confronted in 1968–70 with burgeoning troubles in Northern Ireland and the start of an IRA bombing campaign. He took the decision to put troops into the province to aid the police, and their numbers eventually rose to 16,000. He also chanced his arm at this time in cabinet, opposing Barbara Castle's **In Place of Strife* proposals and earning himself a semi-public rebuke from Wilson.

Leader and Prime Minister

Against most predictions, Labour lost the 1970 election, but Callaghan had rebuilt his party standing and returned as foreign secretary when Labour regained power in 1974. He was thus well placed to become prime minister in 1976 when Wilson surprisingly retired. By then the government had lost its slim majority, was heading for another economic storm in the 1976 IMF crisis, and the party was beginning to show the lurch to the left, the onset of Militant, and the other internal difficulties that bedevilled it in the 1980s. Callaghan showed admirable nerve and coolness in keeping going against tremendous odds, but was forced into a parliamentary pact with the Liberals in 1978 in order to survive, and forced to make concessions on the Scotland Bill in order to get it through at all, which led to the bill's defeat in a 1979 *referendum and his government's consequent loss of a Commons vote of confidence. In autumn 1978, with the opinion polls equivocal, he had decided not to go to the country at the end of four years, but his government was then devastated by the industrial unrest of the 'winter of discontent', 1978/9, and badly beaten by the Conservatives under their new leader Margaret Thatcher when an election was forced on him in May 1979. He led the opposition until 1980 when Michael Foot replaced him, was Father of the Commons from 1983, and became Lord Callaghan in 1987, when he spent more time on his Sussex farm. He married Audrey Elizabeth Moulton in 1938 and had a son and two daughters, one of whom, Margaret, married the influential *Times* economic correspondent Peter

Jay and, as Lady Jay, became leader of the Lords, 1998–2001. *PRGR*

James Callaghan, *Time and Chance* (London, 1987). | Bernard Donoughue, *Prime Minister: The Conduct of Policy under Harold Wilson and James Callaghan* (London, 1987). | Kenneth O. Morgan, *Callaghan: A Life* (Oxford, 1998).

Cambridge Five. See Blunt, Anthony; Burgess, Guy; Cairncross, John; Maclean, Donald Duart; Philby, Harold Adrian Russell ('Kim').

Cameron commission (1969). This was established under the chairmanship of Lord Cameron in March, to determine the reasons for violence in Northern Ireland since October 1968. Published in September 1969, its report was highly critical of the Royal Ulster Constabulary's actions at the Derry civil rights march the previous October. The report also found that grievances in areas such as housing allocation, limitations on the local government franchise, and gerrymandering of local electoral boundaries had some justification. *BMW*

Disturbances in Northern Ireland (Cmnd 532, Belfast, 1969).

Campaign for Democratic Socialism. See Democratic Socialism, Campaign for.

Campaign for Homosexual Equality. See homosexuality.

Campaign for Labour Party Democracy (CLPD) (1973–83), hard left ginger group in the Labour Party. The CLPD was established to alter the way the Labour Party selected parliamentary candidates, campaigned for mandatory reselection so as to increase the representation of the left, and then moved on to argue for the election of leader of the party by an electoral college, removing this role from Labour MPs. It achieved most of its objectives at a special conference in 1981, after which the party split. *BB*

Eric Shaw, *Discipline and Discord in the Labour Party* (Manchester, 1988).

Campaign for Labour Victory (CLV) (1977–81), right-wing ginger group in the Labour Party. The group was established to challenge left-wing dominance of constituency Labour parties but was consistently outmanoeuvred by the left. In turn, CLV became divided after 1980 over whether it was a loyalist organization dedicated to fighting inside the Labour Party or the nucleus for secession. When the Social Democratic Party (SDP) was founded, the CLV disintegrated, with a section leaving to join the SDP and others remaining to fight the left within the party. *BB*

Gerard Daly, 'The Campaign for Labour Victory and the Origins of the SDP', *Contemporary Record*, 7/2 (1993), 282–305.

Campaign for Nuclear Disarmament (CND), peace movement formed in 1958 to give voice to the growing disquiet over the dangers of nuclear weapons testing and possible nuclear war. Although by definition a political campaign (albeit with a wide range of conflicting perspectives), it was fundamentally inspired by emotive, moral outrage. Formed as a single-issue pressure group by liberal, metropolitan, middle-class intellectuals of some prestige (Bertrand *Russell, J. B. Priestley, A. J. P. Taylor, and Michael Foot amongst them), it rapidly became a mass movement of extra-parliamentary protest, the largest in Britain since Chartism. CND's central policy aim was the unilateral renunciation of nuclear weapons by Britain, as the third nuclear power at that time, to exert moral and political pressure upon the USA and USSR to engage in multilateral nuclear disarmament. By 1960, however, this had been overlaid with additional demands for Britain to leave NATO and adopt a foreign policy of 'positive neutralism'. In 1960, the Labour Party conference passed unilateralist resolutions despite fierce opposition from the leadership. The 1960 *Aldermaston march was huge, with over 100,000 at the final rally in Trafalgar Square. CND appeared to be gaining increasing support. However, 1960 also saw the creation—by CND's president, Russell, and others—of the Committee of 100, explicitly committed to non-violent, illegal, civil disobedience. At least at national level this split the movement, always a somewhat frail coalition of disparate groups united only in their commitment to the single issue of nuclear disarmament. In 1961 the Labour Party reversed its nuclear defence stance and, although CND and its demonstrations continued to grow, CND in reality had entered into slow decline. By the time the new Labour government was elected in 1964, CND had ceased to be a major political force.

The campaign continued, however, as a small but effective pressure group and information service on nuclear issues through the 1970s. As the Cold War escalated alarmingly in the late 1970s, in both military and ideological terms, the peace movement once again erupted—this time on an international scale. In Britain CND became, almost overnight, and for the second time, a mass movement. By the mid-1980s membership exceeded 100,000 and the annual budget was over £1 million. The 'new' CND was more transnational, with a more politically experienced and sensitive leadership, and more attuned to both feminist and 'green' concerns. E. P. *Thompson and European Nuclear Disarmament were also influential in creating a vision of a nuclear-free Europe, committed in the longer term to a democratic and humanistic socialism. Influential though it was, this movement too declined suddenly, in the late 1980s, largely as a result of external factors: the Gorbachev era and the thawing of the Cold War, and changes in the domestic politics of the Labour Party.

CND has thus had a roller-coaster existence since 1958, sometimes a mass movement, sometimes a small pressure group. Its significance is hard to judge. Certainly, it has had an impact on raising public and media awareness of nuclear issues. Less obviously, perhaps, CND was the precursor of all extra-parliamentary social and protest movements in late 20th-century Britain: its eruption in the late 1950s signified the end of the post-war consensus, and inaugurated a period of extra-parliamentary politics and cultural questioning. The irony is, of course, that despite this political importance its substantive goal of nuclear disarmament remains as distant as ever.

RKST

Campbell, Alastair John (1957–), prime minister's press secretary since 1997. Tony Blair recruited Campbell on winning the Labour leadership in 1994. A journalist since 1980, Campbell was political editor at the *Sunday Mirror* and then *Daily Mirror* (1987–93), before joining *Today.* Campbell has set a new benchmark in news management at Downing Street, and, identified as Blair's closest adviser, he appears to exercise considerable influence on policy. This, together with his blunt manner, has prompted comparison with Bernard *Ingham. But Ingham did not attend cabinet meetings, and, uniquely, Campbell has continued to direct Labour Party staff since becoming a civil servant. He played a key role during the 1999 Balkan crisis, as one of a group of ministers and officials (also including Jonathan Powell) operating in the absence of an official war cabinet. A spin doctor's spin doctor, he has provided media advice to both NATO and the European Commission. *CL*

Campbell, Gordon Thomas Calthrop (1924–), Conservative politician. A former soldier and diplomat, Campbell was elected MP for Moray and Nairn in 1959. He was appointed Scottish whip in 1962 and under-secretary at the Scottish Office in 1963. As the Scottish secretary of state under Edward Heath, 1970–4, Campbell was responsible for piloting the contentious Wheatley reform of Scottish local government through parliament. He lost his seat in the February 1974 general election to the SNP's Winnie Ewing. *RF*

Campbell-Bannerman, Henry (1836–1908), Liberal politician and prime minister. Born at Kelvinside, near Glasgow, and educated at Glasgow and Cambridge universities, 'CB' worked in his father's drapery firm in Glasgow before entering parliament as Liberal member for Stirling in 1868, the seat he represented for the rest of his life. One of his early interests was universal elementary education, but he first occupied office in 1871–4 as financial secretary at the War Office under Cardwell, returning to the post in 1880–2. He was secretary to the Admiralty, 1882–4, and then had a formative period as chief secretary for Ireland, 1884–5. Campbell-Bannerman was secretary for war, February–June 1886 and again 1892–5, under Gladstone and then Rosebery. In June 1895, after a vote of censure was narrowly passed in the Commons over his not having provided the army with sufficient cordite—the so-called 'cordite motion'—he was the occasion of the Rosebery cabinet's resignation, though his administrative record was considered generally effective.

Liberals in opposition after 1895 were a divided party, and on the resignation of Sir William Harcourt (1827–1904), CB became leader in the Commons with Rosebery as leader in the Lords. His generally affable temperament and good administrative record put him into the position of leader-elect of the party, especially when he skilfully negotiated the passions aroused by events in South Africa and the Boer war. He never criticized the army directly but attacked the *'methods of barbarism' being used to subdue the Boers and advocated conciliation and 'rights of self-government' to the defeated Boer states. Although opposed by some of the *Liberal Imperialists who plotted in the *Relugas compact to replace him with Asquith as leader in the Commons, he was able to reunify the party in opposition to Joseph Chamberlain's policy of *tariff reform and exploit the antagonism felt by Nonconformists towards Balfour's Education Bill of 1902. His attacks on the importation of Chinese indentured labour into South Africa, advocacy of smallholdings, support for payment of MPs, call for restriction of the Lords, veto, and appeal for retrenchment in public expenditure helped to divert the Liberal Party from the divisive issue of home rule and also to consolidate a potential broad base of electoral support.

When Balfour's increasingly divided Unionists resigned in December 1905, Campbell-Bannerman was invited by Edward VII to form a minority government, which he duly did (and with the Liberal Imperialists all safely included in the team). The immediate dissolution of parliament and subsequent general election brought the Liberals a landslide and the largest electoral triumph in their history. In spite of previous faction-fighting, Campbell-Bannerman was able to construct a ministry which called on the wide range of talent available to the party, including Lloyd George, Asquith, Morley, Haldane, and Grey, but CB himself was by now a sick man. He was forestalled by his death in office in April 1908 from fulfilling his legislative ambitions in the field of educational and electoral reform, but he had set the party on a course which would eventually lead to the reform of the Lords, and he had achieved an important reform of trade union law in 1906 and a magnanimous settlement of the Boer war, enshrined in the formation of the Union of South Africa in 1910. *JS*

John Wilson, *CB: A Life of Sir Henry Campbell-Bannerman* (London, 1973).

Campbell case (1924), the incident which brought down the first Labour minority government. J. R. Campbell, acting editor of the Communist *Workers' Weekly*, was arrested and charged with incitement to mutiny by the attorney-general but subsequently released. The Conservatives accused the government of 'truckling to Communism' and the resulting debate and vote of no confidence in the Commons on 8 October caused the prime minister, Ramsay MacDonald, to call a general election at which the Conservatives won a landslide victory. *MC*

Campion, Harry **(1905–96)**, government statistician. Campion was the main architect of the Central Statistical Office (CSO), created during the Second World War, and its first director, 1942–67. An academic in the 1930s (at Manchester University), he had entered Whitehall in 1939, working in the offices of the war cabinet as part of Lord Stamp's team advising on the planning of the war effort. Through the CSO, he presided over a revolution in the collection and use of British economic statistics. *KT*

Canary Wharf bombing (9 February 1996), massive explosion at Canary Wharf in London's docklands which signalled the end of the Provisional IRA's 17-month *ceasefire and the resumption of attacks on the British mainland. A coded warning to Radio Telifis Eirean had initially been ignored. Two people were killed, another 100 injured, and damage was estimated at £150 million. The action followed several months of growing resentment among republicans who claimed that Britain was deliberately stalling the peace process (see Peace process, mark ii). *PR*

candidates, parliamentary, people who seek election to parliament by contesting constituencies in general elections or by-elections. With certain limited exceptions, any citizen aged 21 and over may seek election. To be a candidate, an individual has to obtain the signatures of ten electors in the constituency and submit a deposit. The number of candidates increased significantly in the latter half of the century. The 1951 general election was fought by 1,376 candidates, that of 1983 by 2,579 candidates (an average of 4 per seat), and that of 1997 by 3,724 candidates (an average of 5.6 per seat). Though candidates generally fight with a party label, most are standing for parties that are not contesting a majority of the seats: a total of 169 party labels was used in the 1997 general election. To be successful, candidates need usually to be selected by one of the principal parties. In England, that for most of the century has meant the Labour, Conservative, or Liberal (now the Liberal Democratic) party. In Scotland and Wales it has meant these three parties plus, since the 1960s, the Scottish National Party and Plaid Cymru respectively. Since 1950, only four MPs have been elected without the support of a major party: all four were incumbents who had split from their party. In 1997, Martin *Bell, an independent MP, was elected, though in a constituency (Tatton) in which Labour and Liberal Democratic candidates had stood down in his favour.

Candidates selected by the major parties—certainly those who are most likely to be elected—tend to be middle class, middle-aged, male, and white. Female and non-white candidates are exceptional, but not as exceptional as they used to be. In the 1997 general election, a record number of women were elected (120 MPs, 18 per cent of the Commons, and double the number elected in 1992), as were nine non-white MPs. Successful candidates are more likely than unsuccessful ones to be middle-aged, university-educated (and, in the case of Conservative MPs, products of public schools), and drawn from business and the professions. Recent decades have also seen the emergence of more career-oriented politicians, those who live for politics and seek election at an early age, intending if elected to make a career in the Commons. Candidate selection by the principal political parties has generally been left to local parties, though with the national party—especially in the case of the Labour Party since the 1980s—retaining the power to impose candidates in certain circumstances. Prior to the start of an election campaign, candidates are known as 'prospective parliamentary candidates', they only become candidates, and thus incur election expenses, once the campaign has formally begun. During most election campaigns in the century, candidates addressed public meetings but such meetings gave way by the 1990s to other means of campaigning. For many candidates, the principal activities during election campaigns are now the issuing of press releases and undertaking some door-to-door campaigning. *PN*

Philip W. Buck, *Amateurs and Professionals in British Politics 1918–1959* (Chicago, 1963). | Anthony King, 'The Rise of the Career Politician in Britain—and its Consequences', *British Journal of Political Science*, 11 (1981). | Peter Riddell, *Honest Opportunism* (London, 1993). | Michael Rush, *The Selection of Parliamentary Candidates* (London, 1969).

capital gains tax (CGT), introduced in 1965 as part of the Wilson Labour government's Finance Act, to tax gains arising from the disposal of any asset, whenever acquired. CGT replaced a tax on short-term gains introduced by the Conservatives in 1962, and was aimed at improving equity by removing the opportunity of taking as a tax-free capital gain what was more properly income, especially through stock exchange dealings. Tax rates were only equalized with those of income tax in 1988. *RCW*

capitalism, an economic system in which production takes place as a consequence of the accumulation of capital by those who privately own and control the means of production, with the result that the majority needs to exchange its labour for wages. Although capitalism has been fostered in some countries by state intervention, the essence of classical economics is a free and unconstrained market, allowing 'market clearing' through the price mechanism. The principle of market clearing led some to the assumption that there is no such thing as involuntary unemployment: merely a labour-force cartel demanding wages at a level too high for the price mechanism to clear, an argument dismissed by J. M. Keynes. Instead, Keynes suggested that unemployment was caused by the economic incapacity of sectors of the workforce, as a result of the structural deficiencies of capitalism. The adoption of *Keynesian policies after 1945 led to an economic tradition in which the state intervenes, both at the macro-level of the economy, to ensure that the level of effective demand within the economy produces a balance between levels of inflation and unemployment, and at the micro-level of the firm, through measures such as wages policies and indicative planning systems. An expansion of interventionist policies during the Wilson, Heath, and Callaghan years, led to economic analyses which argued that the regulation of capitalism and the institutions that surrounded it, especially the incorporation of the interests of the labour movement into the policy-making process, were responsible for the apparent economic downturn of the 1970s. Crucial here was the process of tripartitism, where government appeared to be bargaining with the peak associations of capital and labour in a way similar to Scandinavian neo-corporatism (see CORPORATISM AND NEO-CORPORATISM). Such concerns led to the emergence of the 'New Right' in UK politics in the 1970s and 1980s.

In general terms, capitalism has responded to repeated waves of technical changes: heavy industry in the 1890s, mass production in the 1930s, and information technology in the 1970s. This led to the regulation theory of the French Marxist Michel Aglietta, who argued that the particular nature of the economic base at each stage produced different market-clearing needs, these in turn requiring different state institutions and policies. Thus, the fordist structures of the 1930s required Keynesian state intervention to ensure the continued success of capitalism, through a supply of economically active labour as mass consumers; while the neo-fordist (as Aglietta called it) or post-fordist structures that followed it required a different system, producing neoclassical economics and Thatcherite politics. This argument is too deterministic to have much explanatory power, especially as most of its academic proponents lack Aglietta's theoretical Marxist framework. However, it became general currency in the 1990s among economic geographers and political economists as a means of analysing the changing nature of welfare state institutions. More recently, Michel Albert has contrasted the social-market Rhineland capitalism of France and Germany with what he saw as the inferior, free-market Anglo-American model, in *Capitalisme contra Capitalisme* (1991). This led to a debate about the competing merits of the two systems, popularized by Will Hutton in *The State We're in* (1995). *CPS*

capital levy, a once and for all progressive tax on private wealth, popular in socialist circles before the 1950s. The idea originated, in a modern form, in the aftermath of the Great War. A. C. Pigou and J. M. Keynes both advocated the introduction of such a tax to pay for the cost of the war and it was widely supported across the political spectrum for a short time. Hugh Dalton translated the idea of a capital levy from theoretical economics to practical politics in his 1923 polemic *The Capital Levy Explained* and it became Labour Party policy, but the minority Labour governments of 1924 and 1929–31 played down the significance of the commitment and it was never implemented. The inter-war idea that private fortunes would be taxed for specific purposes, such as the repayment of war debt, declined in influence after the Second World War. However, the underlying principle became linked to the use of direct taxation for the redistribution of wealth so as to promote equality. In turn the capital levy influenced Labour's post-war tax policies, most notably in the form of the capital gains tax which applied the tax on wealth in a progressive form, and the related increases in death duties. *BB*

capital punishment. Politically, capital punishment was at its most potent as a political issue during the 1950s and 1960s when a long campaign for abolition was finally concluded by legislation in 1965. The issue was resurrected, especially in the Thatcher period, as a response to rising crime and to deal with particular types of murder, such as the killing of policemen or of children.

Britain had a tradition of a harsh penal code, in which the so-called 'bloody code' contained over two hundred capital offences by the beginning of the 19th century. By the start of the 20th century, however, the number of capital offences had been reduced to four: murder, treason, piracy, and sabotage. The last person to be hanged for treason was William Joyce, also known as the Nazi propagandist 'Lord Haw Haw', in 1946. Between 1900 and 1949, 657 people were hanged for murder, approximately half of all those convicted of the crime. From 1921, the *Howard League for Penal Reform made abolition of the death penalty its primary objective and in 1925 the National Council for the Abolition of the Death Penalty began to act as a coordinating body for the interested pressure groups.

Calls for abolition increased in the post-war era at a time of growing liberalization of penal regimes, such as the ending of corporal punishment in prison in 1948. High-profile cases such as that of the execution of a backward 19-year-old, Derek Bentley, in 1952; the revelation that in all probability an innocent man, Timothy Evans, had been executed in 1949; and the outcry over the execution of Ruth Ellis in July 1955 (the last woman to be hanged in Britain), added fuel to calls for abolition. In 1955, a newly formed National Campaign for the Abolition of Capital Punishment used these cases to press for reform, leading to the compromise Homicide Act of 1957 which created separate categories of capital and non-capital murder. The 1965 Abolition of Capital Punishment Act suspended the death penalty for five years, but abolition was then made permanent in 1969.

While some sections, mainly of the Conservative Party, were never reconciled to abolition and calls for the restoration of capital punishment often received a sympathetic hearing at Tory conferences, the cause acquired more momentum from the 1970s. The growth of terrorism, concern about rising crime in general, and the 'New Right' agenda which had seen the restoration and extension of capital punishment in the USA, led to Commons motions in 1979, 1983, and 1988 to reintroduce capital punishment for specific offences, such as the killing of police officers. All of them failed, votes in parliament proving, as in the case of abolition itself, consistently more liberal than public opinion as a whole. Moreover, a fresh and telling argument against restoration of capital punishment came with the release in 1989–91 of those unsafely sentenced for the IRA bombings in Birmingham and Guildford in 1975, some of whom would almost certainly have been executed had the death penalty still obtained. *JS*

Louis Blom-Cooper (ed.), *The Hanging Question* (London, 1969).

Caradon, Lord (1907–90), colonial administrator and diplomat. Hugh Foot entered the colonial service in 1929 and after spells in the Middle East, Cyprus, and Nigeria, became governor of Jamaica in 1951. In 1957, he was transferred to Cyprus in a bid to end the Greek Cypriot insurgency (see Cyprus crises). Foot was considered a conciliator but his early attempts failed. He rejected partitioning Cyprus between Greece and Turkey and advocated Cypriot independence, which he helped achieve in 1960. Thereafter, as Lord Caradon, he held various posts within the UN including British ambassador, 1964–70. *KTS*

'care in the community', popular description of the policy of deinstitutionalized care of the mentally and physically disabled, the elderly, and some categories of young offender. This new turn of policy began in the 1970s with a general reaction against the effect of long-stay institutions on their inmates, and with the wider use of behavioural drugs to control some aspects of mental illness. During the 1980s, many large Victorian insane asylums were run down and emphasis placed instead on small, community-based units or council housing with support provided by outreach staff.

The shift away from long-term hospital care to care in the community was reflected in hospital statistics: average length of stay in the geriatric hospital sector declined by about 9 per cent per year between 1978 and 1990–1, effectively emptying the NHS hospitals of long-stay geriatric patients in favour of domestic, residential, or nursing home care. Meanwhile over the same period, it was estimated that the number of occupied-bed days had fallen by 30 and 50 per cent respectively in the mental health and learning disability sectors. Personal social work staff were increased by 25 per cent in the period 1978–9 to 1990–1 with the allocation of health authority resources devoted to community care increasing from 8 per cent to just over 13 per cent in the same period.

The policy of community care, however, came under much criticism. It was seen as contributing to crime, homelessness, and suicide, as many ex-mental hospital patients in particular found themselves unable to cope 'in the community'. Although most healthcare professionals continued to support the broad thrust of policy towards deinstitutionalizing where possible, there was a call for greater resources and improved structures. As a result of reforms in community-care provision in 1991 and 1993, a new financial and managerial framework came into force which was intended to enable vulnerable groups to live as independently as possible in their own homes. Local authorities are now charged with arranging social care in the community, including home helps and home care assistants. Moreover recognition that much of the care in the community given to the elderly and disabled is provided by families and individual carers has led to calls for greater provision to assist them. A National Carers' Strategy, *Caring about Carers*, published in 1999 set out a programme to provide support for the estimated six million informal carers in Great Britain. With a growing elderly population and a continuing policy of keeping people in the community where possible, questions of the funding and management of community care and the needs of carers are seen as major social policy issues for the future. *JS*

car industry. This encompasses the making of cars, lorries, and coaches and has been a major growth sector of the British economy in the 20th century, following the development of the internal combustion engine. In comparison with other major manufacturing countries, the emergence of the British car industry was relatively slow, until the inter-war period, when production overtook that of other European countries. During this period the industry was regionally concentrated in towns such as Coventry and Dagenham, enabling them to escape the Depression of the 1930s virtually unscathed in comparison with northern industrial centres still dependent on the old staple industries. The industry's capacity to generate demand for components and intermediate inputs from other industries made it a very significant sector of the economy not only in terms of employment but also in relation to the balance of payments. The state of the industry came to be regarded as a bellwether for the health of the economy overall. Successive administrations used the car industry as an economic regulator, with the size of the domestic market being manipulated through sales, motoring taxes, and credit controls on car purchases. The exceptionally favourable conditions which followed the Second World War established Britain's position as the world's second largest motor manufacturing nation and the biggest exporter of cars and commercial vehicles. In 1952 the British Motor Corporation was the fourth largest car company in the world and productivity was the highest in Europe. Car production formed an integral part of the *stop-go cycles that characterized the post-war economy, however, and this phase proved to be transitory. The British car industry was the first to experience a spectacular decline as an independent national enterprise, from the 1960s onwards. The post-war problems of the car industry have been commonly attributed to government policies. Even during the 1950s boom in the domestic and foreign markets, there were endemic problems of industrial strife, stagnating productivity, and duplication of similar models by numerous small manufacturers, while progressive mergers that led to the creation of British Leyland in 1968 were of limited value in remedying such problems. Concerns over the impact of the decline of such a pivotal sector of the economy resulted in its de facto nationalization in 1975. Thirteen years later, a restructured British Leyland (BL), which was the only remaining British-owned volume car producer, was sold by the government. Rover became a subsidiary company of British Aerospace before eventually being taken over by the German firm BMW. By the late 1990s, massive overcapacity in the European car industry necessitated an extensive rationalization of production within Britain. *JFM*

Roy Church, *The Rise and Decline of the British Motor Industry* (Basingstoke, 1994).

Carlisle, Mark (1929–), Conservative politician, who replaced Norman St John-Stevas as education spokesman, becoming secretary of state in 1979. Moderate and cautious, not a Thatcherite 'one of us', he retreated on charges for school buses after a Lords' revolt. Carlisle was sacked in 1981, partly for evident unhappiness at the slashing budget of that year. Though a painstaking rather than brilliant Commons performer, he annihilated Neil Kinnock's allegations of raffling of schoolbooks, quietly insisting on specific instances, which provoked noise but no answer. *EP*

Carlton Club and the **Carlton Club meeting (1922).** The Carlton Club is a Conservative social meeting place. Founded in 1832 to mobilize resistance to the 1832 Reform Act, it became the social focus in London for parliamentary Conservatives and their principal supporters in the country, offering rooms for dining, smoking, drinking, and cards. The original premises were in Pall Mall, but after bombing in 1940 it reopened post-war in St James Street. In 1900, it was the senior of half a dozen Conservative gentlemen's clubs in London. Nearly all Tory peers and MPs were members, its membership strictly limited to Conservatives: although party co-operation with Liberal Unionists flourished after 1886, no Liberal Unionist joined the Carlton until the parties merged in 1912. The club conveniently hosted party meetings, notably one on 19 October 1922, generally called 'the Carlton Club meeting', at which Conservative MPs voted by 185 votes to 88 to go to a general election as a separate party, effectively terminating both Lloyd George's coalition and Austen *Chamberlain's party leadership, launching twenty years of Tory dominance under Law and Baldwin. Towards the end of the century the club's fortunes, like those of other London political clubs, declined sharply: fewer and fewer MPs were members and its distinctiveness was lost. *JAR*

Charles Petrie, *The Carlton Club* (London, 1955).

car ownership, in an economic sense, is used to denote either the number of cars owned per 1,000 head of population or in relation to the number of people for every vehicle. As incomes have risen, particularly since the Second World War, car ownership and usage have increased substantially so that motoring is no longer the prerogative of the rich but part of a mass market. The low price elasticity of demand for motoring has meant that significant increases in the cost of petrol, for example, have led to only modest falls in the level of traffic. Similarly, the price competitiveness of alternative forms of transport has only had a minor impact on the use of the motor car for existing owners. Consumers regard car transport as a 'luxury good' compared with alternatives such as public transport, walking, or cycling. Considerations such as the degree of comfort and convenience have meant that increasingly large numbers of people have seen other forms of public transport as a poor substitute for travelling in one's own car. Car ownership has increased not only as a functional response to the desire for greater freedom of mobility but also because the car is a visible social status symbol epitomizing the success of the owner. Thus the numbers of cars with registered owners in Britain rose from about two million in the 1930s, to seven million in the 1950s, and over twenty million in the 1990s. *JFM*

Carpenter, Edward (1844–1929), poet, writer, socialist, anarchist, and homosexual. Carpenter was one of the great inspirational socialist writers of his day, before party politics replaced the idea of living the life of a socialist. Beginning first as a Christian Socialist, and then a Cambridge extension lecturer, he lived for many years at Millthorp, near Sheffield, with his male lover. He wrote the inspirational free-verse poem *Towards Democracy* and *Homogenic Love and its Place in Free Society* (1887). *KL*

Carr, Robert Leonard (1916–), Conservative politician and home secretary. Elected MP for Mitcham in 1950, Carr was a founder member of *One Nation who never wavered from moderate Toryism. His industrial experience impressed Eden, who made him his parliamentary private secretary. As a labour minister from December 1955, Carr encouraged best employment practices before temporarily returning to business in 1958. Appointed to Heath's shadow cabinet in 1967, he consulted on the **Fair Deal at Work* proposals before introducing the *Industrial Relations Act, 1971, as employment secretary, but any chance of his moderating union opposition ended in 1972 when he became instead leader of the House. Having succeeded his friend Maudling as home secretary he displayed courageous liberalism during the Ugandan Asian immigration crisis. In 1974 he became shadow chancellor and in 1975 was briefly acting leader between Heath's defeat and Thatcher's victory. He was dropped from the shadow cabinet when Thatcher became leader and in 1976 entered the Lords.

RJS

Carrington, 6th Lord (1919–), Conservative politician, *beau idéal*, and fall guy. Carrington held office under six Conservative leaders, 1951–82. He reached the cabinet under Douglas-Home, 1963–4, and had close relations with Heath, who made him minister of defence and party chairman. Claiming descent from an 'honest Nottingham grocer with whom people left their money till he became a banker', Carrington was seen in the first two years of Thatcher government (and in earlier opposition where she had not shone) as the leading traditionalist figure in Tory politics. The combination of grand manner, moderate Tory politics, and diffident wit—'A bus knock down Mrs Thatcher? It wouldn't dare'—appealed to liberal snobbery. He was, though, a strong foreign secretary who, with Ian Gilmour, negotiated a settlement and free elections in Rhodesia (see RHODESIAN CRISIS) against considerable Afro-sceptical Tory opinion, including Thatcher's. In negotiations for a British rebate on its Common Agricultural Policy contribution, he resumed negotiations privately with the German deputy finance minister, obtaining a much better than expected deal, and was roundly interrogated and abused by Thatcher at Chequers for his pains. Carrington was undone in his pride of day by Argentina's seizure of the *Falklands in 1982, taking the blame with his Foreign Office ministerial team and resigning, so exculpating Thatcher.

EP

LORD CARRINGTON, *Reflect on Things Past* (London, 1988).

Carron, William (1902–69), right-wing trade union leader. Bill Carron was president of the Amalgamated Engineering Union, 1956–67. A devout Roman Catholic who worked hard against Communist and fellow-travelling entryism in the union, he was also a key figure in CIA-funded anti-Soviet organizations. A staunch supporter of Hugh Gaitskell as Labour Party leader, he continued to deliver his block votes to the right at the annual party conference even after Gaitskell had been replaced by Harold Wilson in 1963. He retired in 1967, when his union swung to the left.

BB

Carson, Edward Henry (1854–1935), Unionist politician. Carson was born in Dublin of a typical Anglo-Irish family, his father an architect and civil engineer, and his mother from a landed background in Co. Galway. He read classics at Trinity College, Dublin, then studied at the King's Inns, Dublin, and was called to the Irish Bar. He became crown counsel to the Irish attorney-general in 1886 and soon caught the eye of Arthur Balfour, chief secretary for Ireland, who would not have been repelled by Carson's nickname, 'Coercion Carson'. In 1889 he was appointed a QC, and in June 1892 became solicitor-general for Ireland. In the same year he entered politics as one of the Unionist members for Dublin University (Trinity College). He was called to the English Bar by the Middle Temple in 1893, making his name in some celebrated cases, notably in the libel action brought by Oscar Wilde against the marquess of Queensberry in 1895, in which he appeared for the defendant.

Carson's political career was based on his firm belief that Ireland, and his own Anglo-Irish people, could only prosper within the union. In 1910 he became leader of the Irish Unionists at Westminster, about twenty in number. Carson flung himself into the fight against Asquith's Third Home Rule Bill of 1912, and sanctioned the Ulster Unionist rebellion against the bill. As the situation deteriorated, Carson found himself contemplating the possibility of some form of exclusion of Ulster counties from the bill, and the abandonment of the rest of Ireland to the nationalists. Although he advised for partition in the aftermath of the Easter Rising of 1916, he could never really reconcile himself to that eventuality.

Carson was, though, not just an Irish leader but also a major British political figure. He was already talked of as a possible Tory leader when Balfour resigned in 1911, and in May 1915 entered Asquith's reconstructed government as attorney-general but resigned in October over Gallipoli and other military fiascos. He led a Conservative ginger group, the Unionist War Committee, formed in June 1916 to push for a more vigorous prosecution of the war, and played a significant role in the fall of Asquith and his replacement by David Lloyd George in December 1916. Carson now became first lord of the Admiralty, but proved as ineffective in office as he was effective in opposition. In July 1917 he moved to the war cabinet as minister without portfolio, but resigned in January 1918 because Lloyd George was drafting a Home Rule Bill for all Ireland. Following the British government's signing of the Anglo-Irish Treaty with representatives of Sinn Fein, Carson launched a bitter attack in the Lords on the government. After partition, though, he urged the Ulster Unionists to give the Catholic minority in Northern Ireland fair treatment. In July 1933 he came to Ulster for the last time on the occasion of the unveiling of his statue in the grounds of the Stormont parliament, where it still stands, larger than life, showing Carson in defiant attitude. Powerful in resistance but weak when in office, he was probably the worst leader that the British Conservatives never had. *DGB*

Alvin Jackson, *Sir Edward Carson* (Dundalk, 1993).

cartoons, political. Cartoons suited the lively mass-circulation daily papers growing in the early 1900s. First came F. C. Gould (*Pall Mall Gazette*) and W. K. Haselden (*Daily Mirror*). Hitherto, cartooning had been dominated by the *Punch* tradition of 'comic ideas, seriously illustrated'. Two antipodeans, Will Dyson and David *Low, set new standards. Dyson, a socialist, drew with passion for the Labour *Daily Herald* (from 1912), while Low, at the *Star* from 1919, and later at the *Evening Standard*, drew 'serious ideas, comically illustrated' and insisted on generous space and editorial freedom. Low became the most celebrated cartoonist of the inter-war era, ridiculing the fascist dictators and getting the paper banned in Germany. During the Second World War, much cartooning was propagandist. This made more paradoxical Churchill's wartime attempt to close the *Daily Mirror* because of a supposedly unpatriotic cartoon by Philip Zec. Post-war, political cartoons continued most prominently in the middle-market broadsheets and the *Daily Mirror*. Illingworth, Emmwood, Cummings, Mansbridge, *'Vicky' (Viktor Weisz), and Giles (social more than political) were the familiar names, gradually supplanting stalwarts such as Strube and Whitelaw. From the 1960s, however, the quality broadsheets took over. The (*Manchester*) *Guardian* had published Low's later work, and it now promoted Papas and then Gibbard; while Garland, Jensen, Trog (Wally Fawkes), and later Riddell and Brookes, drew for other broadsheets. Steadman and Scarfe introduced a sharper style and caustic tone, fitting the politics of the period. *Punch*'s outmoded gentility, too, gave way to the ruderies of *Private Eye*. These trends continued strongly during the Thatcher era, with the Rabelaisian vulgarity of Bell and Rowson at the *Guardian*. Across the century, the cartoonist's essential method remained the ingenious use of metaphor to interpret and evaluate persons and events—by no means always with humour, nor with caricature. The best cartoonists, arguably, employed all three. *CKSU*

Casablanca conference (1943), wartime meeting of Churchill and Roosevelt in January 1943 from which their foreign ministers were, somewhat curiously, excluded. The main purpose of the meeting was to decide upon Allied military strategy for 1943. The decision not to make any definite plans for a full-scale cross-Channel invasion of France, as Stalin wished, but to concentrate upon Churchill's preferred Mediterranean strategy, reflected Britain's continuing authority within the Anglo-American alliance. An attempt to bring together the rival French leaders, Generals Giraud and de Gaulle, was only partially successful. *DJD*

Case for Conservatism, The (1947). Written by Quintin Hogg, this was commissioned by the Conservative Research Department and published as a Penguin Special. Hogg argued that the Conservative Party's main historical role lay in its scepticism, its opposition to other ideologies, rather than in its own beliefs: the party adopted a balancing role, opposing whatever 'idea' the current party of change happened to be advocating. It marked the beginning of a period of fashionably 'intellectual' Conservatism during the 1950s. *NJC*

Casement, Roger (1864–1916), British diplomat and Irish nationalist. Born in Co. Dublin, Casement first went to Africa in 1884, becoming British consul in Portuguese East Africa in 1895. Publicizing systematic exploitation (by European employers) of native workers in Africa and South America, he was knighted in 1911 for his public services. Becoming increasingly involved with Irish nationalism, in 1914 he went to Germany hoping to obtain German aid for an Irish rising against Britain. German support fell short of his hopes, and on his arrival in Ireland in 1916 he wanted to postpone the planned rebellion, the *Easter Rising. Arrested after landing in Kerry, he was tried in England for treason, and hanged in London in August 1916 (after converting to Catholicism). In 1965 his remains were returned to Ireland, receiving a state funeral. Controversy still surrounds British attempts to discredit him through use of diaries detailing years of homosexual activity; some still believe the diaries to have been at least partially forged. Casement's complex life contains numerous paradoxes. An Ulster-educated Protestant long loyal to the United Kingdom, he became famous as a traitor executed after a Catholic, Irish republican rebellion. Impulsive, idealistic, and ambiguous, he navigated Conradian territory by means of compartmentalizing his competing instincts. *RE*

Brian Inglis, *Roger Casement* (new edn., Belfast, 1993).

Castle, Barbara Anne (1910–), Labour politician. Barbara Castle was born in Chesterfield but her education was at Bradford Girls' Grammar School and Oxford. She displayed an early political awareness and became the youngest member of the executive of the Socialist League in the late 1930s. In this period she served on St Pancras borough council (1937) and engaged in journalism. During the war she worked in the Ministry of Food (1940–4) and also on the *Daily Mirror* (1944–5). In the 1945 Labour landslide she was returned at Blackburn which remained her political base until she retired from parliament in 1979, after which, until 1989, she represented Labour in the European parliament. During her years at Westminster she held various offices: minister of overseas development (1964–5), minister of transport (1965–8), first secretary of state and secretary for employment and productivity (1968–70), and, finally, secretary of state for social services (1974–6). Within the party she was elected to the NEC (1950–85) and served as its chairperson (1958–9). Some of her ministerial initiatives have assumed particular importance. At transport she introduced the breathalyser and promoted the use of seat belts. A bigger challenge came at employment where her white paper, **In Place of Strife*, was intended to transform industrial relations, but this commitment to modernize the economy was thwarted, in a major setback for Harold Wilson's government. Her career benefited in the early days from the patronage of Dalton and, over a longer period, from her friendship with Wilson for whom she worked as parliamentary private secretary when he was at the Board of Trade, and when in those days both were attached to the Bevanite group. Her career was also strengthened by the fact that she was a 'workaholic' who was 'obsessed with detail' and for whom politics amounted to a 'consuming passion' (Ben Pimlott, *Harold Wilson* (London, 1993 edn.), 337). Her published diaries became an important primary source for the Wilson period. *CH*

Barbara Castle, *The Castle Diaries 1974–1976* (London, 1980). | Barbara Castle, *The Castle Diaries 1964–1970* (London, 1984). | Barbara Castle, *Fighting all the Way* (London, 1993).

Catholicism, Roman. A Catholic hierarchy was legally restored to Britain in the 19th century indicating the increased acceptance of Catholics' rights but not all disabilities have been removed, and neither the monarch nor the lord chancellor can be a Catholic. Traditional suspicions of Catholics were already disappearing by 1900, but the cultural assimilation of Catholicism had to wait until the 1960s, encouraged by the extension of university education and the concomitant emergence of a Catholic middle class, the increasing ecumenism that followed the Vatican II conference (1962–5), and a decline in Catholic endogamy. However, its loyalty during the Great War and the firm line taken by Cardinal Bourne during the General Strike of 1926—in contrast to that of the archbishop of Canterbury, Randall Davidson—were already persuading establishment figures to view Catholicism with more sympathy. Divisions over religion became increasingly confined to places like Liverpool, where there was briefly a Continental-style centre party in the 1930s, Glasgow, and Northern Ireland. Catholic voters, however, remained significant. Before 1914, Irish home rule ensured that the majority of Catholics who were of Irish extraction voted Liberal. Its disappearance as an issue, and the Liberals' decline, encouraged both Labour and Conservatives subsequently to court the Catholic vote. It might have been supposed that the Conservatives would have a number of advantages: as early as 1900, Catholic bishops were supporting them over denominational education, and Conservative positions on matters like divorce and abortion have also tended to be closer to Catholic doctrine. However, an internal party document concluded in 1949 that the 1944 Education Act had done much to alienate Tory sympathies amongst the estimated four million Catholic voters (8 per cent of the electorate). Meanwhile, electoral surveys suggested that, of all the churches, Catholics were and still are the most inclined to vote according to social class. Throughout the 20th century they have also tended to be the most working-class of church memberships. Most Catholic MPs have accordingly sat for Labour. In 1931 Labour Catholics were instrumental in defeating the Education Bill, but they have tended to play a less distinctive role in the post-war years. *PPC*

ADRIAN HASTINGS, *A History of English Christianity 1920–1990* (2nd edn., London, 1991).

Catto committee. Chaired by the Scots-born former governor of the Bank of England Lord Catto, the committee was set up, in 1950, following a Scottish economic conference, by the Labour Scottish secretary Hector McNeil, in response to the apparent upsurge in Scottish nationalism. It was originally given the remit to explore the financial relationship between Scotland and England to show whether the Scots were being economically penalized. A number of nationalist and Tory critics had claimed that the Labour government's policies of nationalization had injurious effects on the Scottish economy as control was removed to London. The committee was also set the task of showing whether it was feasible to calculate the Scottish share of exports and imports. At the end of the day, the report was inconclusive but appeared to confirm that Scotland was not unduly short-changed. One major consequence of the committee's report was the development of the gathering of accurate statistical information on the Scottish economy. *RF*

Scottish Financial and Trade Statistics (Cmd 8609, London, 1952).

Cave, George (1856–1928), lawyer and Conservative politician. Cave's political career was coloured less by legislative accomplishments than by his acting as adviser, often on matters of law, to successive party leaders Law and Baldwin. Lloyd George made him home secretary, 1916–19, and lord of appeal, 1919–22, but he re-entered party politics to support Law at the *Carlton Club meeting. He ended his career as a viscount and lord chancellor, 1922–4 and 1924–8. *RJQA*

ceasefires in Northern Ireland. The announcement of a ceasefire by the IRA on 31 August 1994 was unexpected for, following the *Downing Street declaration in December 1993, the most that republican leaders had hinted at was a temporary end to the violence. However, it is clear that a crucial element in the ultimate decision was the peace process developed by Social Democratic and Labour Party (SDLP) leader John Hume and Sinn Fein's Gerry Adams. This was built upon the proposition that 'the people of Ireland as a whole have a right to self-determination'. Also Adams had convinced his supporters that their aims were more likely to be achieved through a political initiative with the SDLP, the Republic, and the USA than by continuing the violence. Loyalist paramilitaries then called a ceasefire too, on 13 October, following the promise of a referendum on the outcome of inter-party talks. However, hopes for a permanent end to the violence were dimmed by the claim from the republicans that the British government was deliberately stalling the establishment of all-party talks leading to a final settlement, and on 9 February 1996 a huge IRA bomb exploded in London's Canary Wharf, ending the seventeen-month ceasefire. It had been known for several months that the militants within the IRA were gaining the upper hand, and for them the appointment of the Mitchell commission on arms decommissioning was a major stumbling block, since their contention that arms could only be given up after a political settlement was not going to be acceptable to Mitchell. It was not until 19 July 1997, after Tony Blair had replaced John Major as prime minister, that the IRA agreed to the restoration of its ceasefire, so starting the process that led to the Good Friday agreement. *PR*

PAUL BEW, PETER GIBBON, and HENRY PATTERSON, *Northern Ireland 1921–1996: Political Forces and Social Classes* (London, 1996). | TIM PAT COOGAN, *The Troubles* (London, 1995).

Cecil, Lord Hugh Richard Heathcoat ('Linky') (1869–1956), Conservative politician. The fifth son of the 3rd marquess of Salisbury, Lord Hugh was Conservative MP for Greenwich, 1895–1906, and for Oxford University, 1910–37. Raised in the intellectually exciting and religiously orthodox atmosphere of Hatfield House, 'Linky' (as he was known to intimates) became a skilled and merciless debater and a lifelong and fiercely committed defender of the Established Church. Tall and gaunt, a lifelong bachelor, he was an unashamed reactionary, believing in and defending without unction an England led by a benevolent landed aristocracy and blessed with a national church embracing the sole true Christianity—an England which was quite inconceivable in his time. As a young MP he led in the Commons the undisciplined band of 'Hughligans' who cared little for the wishes of their leaders and elders. When he returned in 1910, he battled for individual freedom, free trade, and the Lords, and his tirades and unseemly scenes earned him often unflattering notoriety. In the Great War he unpredictably qualified as a pilot officer in the Royal Flying Corps. This living, charming, and rather lovable anachronism left politics in 1937 to become a legendary provost of Eton College.

RJQA

Kenneth Rose, *The Later Cecils* (London, 1975). | J. A. Thompson and Arthur Mejia (eds.), *Edwardian Conservatism* (London, 1988).

Cecil, Lord (Edgar Algernon) Robert (1864–1958), Conservative politician. The third son of the 3rd marquess of Salisbury, Lord Robert entered parliament in 1906. He was a true product of a Hatfield upbringing: independent-minded, steeped in classical conservative values, committed to the Established Church, and distrustful of the tastes and politics of the middle classes. In parliament he championed free trade, and his contempt for *tariff reform as potentially ruinous to all classes was equalled by his distaste for Joseph Chamberlain and his admirers. Defeated in 1910, he returned to the Commons in 1911, where his ultra-orthodox free trade views taxed the patience of his colleagues, though his equally strident defence of the Irish Union and of the Welsh Church perhaps balanced this. Cecil became under-secretary for foreign affairs and minister of blockade in the wartime governments of Asquith and Lloyd George, chaired the Allied Economic Council at the Paris peace conference, and became one of the architects of the *League of Nations. This became his life's work: he served as minister for League affairs in Baldwin's first two governments and as British delegate to the League under the second Labour government and the National Government. Cecil was also founder and president of the British *League of Nations Union, and framer of the controversial peace ballot of 1935. Created Viscount Cecil of Chelwood in 1923, he received the Nobel peace prize in 1937.

Tall, stooped, and corvine in appearance, he was a man of contradictions: he combined a deep-seated religious and moral conservatism with an internationalist outlook more typical of the political left; born to great privilege, he distrusted the effects of wealth; and, though a fierce defender of aristocracy, he was an outspoken champion of individual freedom and natural rights.

RJQA

Viscount Cecil of Chelwood, *A Great Experiment* (London, 1941). | Viscount Cecil of Chelwood, *All the Way* (London, 1949). | Kenneth Rose, *The Later Cecils* (London, 1975).

Celtic fringe. The so-called 'Celtic' parts of the UK—Ireland, Scotland, Wales, and the south-west—have frequently been classed together as possessing a distinctive political identity compared with the rest of England. A particular religious, social, and economic history has frequently been adduced to mark these areas off from the more metropolitan area dominated by London and the south-east of England. In the 19th century, this was reflected in the strong backing of the Celtic fringe for the Gladstonian Liberal Party. By the time of the 1885 general election, the party took all but twelve of the 104 seats in Wales and Scotland. This, combined with a tendency for the Irish Nationalist Party to support the Liberals in order to further the cause of home rule, made the Celtic fringe predominantly a 'Liberal fringe'. Nonconformist support which was strong in Wales, Scotland, and Cornwall was an important factor reflecting the denominational struggles of the past, still evident in issues such as education and Welsh disestablishment, while topics such as land reform, tenant rights, and eviction carried weight across a broad swathe of Highland and western Britain.

The Liberal Party's support from these areas was emphasized as its strength declined in the course of the 20th century. In the December 1910 election, 100 of the 270 seats won by the Liberals came from Scotland, Wales, and the south-west. When the party was driven down to only 40 seats in the 1924 election, almost half came from these areas, with Scotland and Wales providing in total almost as many seats as England. However, even here the predominant position of the Liberal Party was being undermined. Labour made huge advances into the industrial seats of south Wales and central Scotland, while the Conservatives strengthened their support in many agricultural areas and middle-class seats. In effect, between the wars, Scotland and Wales were beginning to behave electorally more like England. This was increasingly demonstrated by the two-party hegemony of the period after 1945 when most of Scotland, Wales, and the south-west conformed in their voting patterns to the rest of Britain. Liberal support itself became genuinely 'fringe' even in these areas, often based in the rural areas of north Wales and the Highlands. This support, however, was vital to the survival of the Liberal Party and formed the basis for its revival after the 1950s. At the lowest point of their support in the early fifties, four of the six seats held by the Liberals were in Wales and Scotland. Significantly, the first by-election breakthrough in 1958 was in *Torrington, in West Devon, while its leader during the revival, Jo *Grimond, sat for Orkney and Shetland. By-election successes and general election results continued to confirm Liberal dependence on Celtic seats: of the 22

Alliance seats won in 1987, fifteen still came from Wales, Scotland, and the south-west. Even the surge in Liberal Democrat support in the 1997 election to 46 seats was based upon a bedrock of support in Scotland and Wales and major advances in the West Country.

Paradoxically, though associated largely with the Liberal Party, the Celtic fringe was also crucially important for the Labour Party during the period of Conservative dominance in the 1980s. Labour had an overwhelming majority of seats in Scotland and Wales in the 1983, 1987, and 1992 elections, while remaining a minority party in England. In 1987, for example, Wales and Scotland accounted for a third of all Labour seats. Finally, the Celtic fringe has spawned its own parties, such as the Crofters' Party of the late 19th century, and latterly *Mebyon Kernow and the Welsh and Scottish nationalist parties. They, like the Liberal Party, have gained support because of the increasing tendency from the 1950s of Wales and Scotland to support nationalist candidates and to deviate electorally from the rest of Britain. *JS*

Michael Kinnear, *The British Voter: An Atlas and Survey since 1885* (London, 1981).

censorship in 20th-century Britain has frequently been a source of controversy, particularly in areas such as the censorship of the arts or interference with broadcasting on political or religious grounds. Parliamentary legislation grew in the first half of the century in order to deal with the growing number of broadcasting outlets, but the existing laws of libel and obscenity were considered to be sufficient to control publishing outside wartime. For example, the *lord chamberlain was able to censor plays under the Theatres Act of 1843. This required all new plays to be approved by the lord chamberlain who also had the power to forbid the presentation of any play 'for the preservation of good manners, decorum, or of the public peace'. New legislation was introduced at the beginning of the 20th century in the 1904 Wireless Telegraphy Act which gave the government power to license broadcasting. As a result, broadcasting in Britain has always operated within a regulatory framework overseen by the government. In practice, the *BBC, an independent, though government-owned monopoly, operated a remarkable degree of self-censorship. When commercial services were introduced in the 1950s, they also operated within a licensing regime laid down by the government, and public service obligations were imposed by the 1954 Television Act.

Film censorship began in 1912 with the appointment by the industry (so as to head off state control) of the British Board of Film Censors (BBFC), a self-regulating body. Up to and beyond the Second World War, the BBFC imposed restrictions on the type of films which could be circulated and excluded any explicit material which might arouse political or religious controversy or outrage public decency.

Sensitive official information was first covered by the wide-ranging Official Secrets Act of 1911 which prevented disclosure of virtually any material the government deemed important. Even more far-reaching censorship of news and opinion came with the two world wars. The Defence of the Realm Act (DORA) of November 1914 and its subsequent amendments provided for the censorship of the press and international communication with fines, imprisonment, or closure of newspapers as penalties. Although some criticism was possible, it was illegal to write or say anything which might disaffect the armed forces or affect recruiting. While most censorship was effectively self-imposed during the Great War, DORA placed heavy restrictions on what could be reported directly to the public on military matters—newspapers were only allowed to repeat official bulletins, for example, and the prominent pacifist Bertrand Russell was imprisoned under DORA for speaking out against the war. Similar restrictions were in force in the Second World War, but applied somewhat more discriminatingly. Conscious that it required popular support for the war effort and of criticism that war reporting in the previous war was thought to have been too restricted, the government allowed greater freedom of expression. The Ministry of Information still, however, censored photographs and news stories, bringing pressure to bear where it felt necessary (for example, banning the columnist 'Cassandra' from the *Daily Mirror* after his criticisms of the war leadership were deemed excessive). They also effectively silenced any potentially pro-Nazi views and suppressed the communist *Daily Worker* in 1940–1 because it was deemed to be subversive.

Relaxation of censorship laws began gradually in the 1950s for films, more generally in the 1960s in a cultural climate which was ready to accept or sanction a wider range of views. The satire boom (see SATIRE, POLITICAL) in the early sixties brought a greater irreverence in the depiction of politics. In publishing, the failure in 1960 of the prosecution under the Obscene Publications Act of Penguin Books for publishing an unexpurgated text of D. H. Lawrence's *Lady Chatterley's*

Lover, hitherto unpublishable in Britain, had a profound effect on writing and publishing in subsequent decades. The ending of the censorship of plays by the lord chamberlain in 1969 effectively opened up the theatre, while the Board of Film Censors (renamed the British Board of Film Classification (BBFC) in the 1980s) gradually widened what was accessible in the cinema and, latterly, on video in line with its perception of changing public taste, but still banned very explicit scenes of sex and violence, including entire films.

A framework of censorship in the arts still exists via the Obscene Publications Acts, the laws of blasphemy and libel, regulatory bodies such as the BBFC and the broadcasting authorities, and local authorities' control over licences for public performances. In the cultural sphere controversy has been as likely to be sparked by perceived liberality as illiberality. Pressure groups such as the National Viewers' and Listeners' Council have since 1964 campaigned against excessive sex and violence in broadcasting. In response to these pressures, a Broadcasting Complaints Commission was set up in 1981 to consider and adjudicate on complaints of unfair treatment or invasion of privacy and in 1988 a Broadcasting Standards Council was established to consider the portrayal of sex and violence, and matters of taste and decency on the TV, radio, and video. These two bodies were combined in the Broadcasting Standards Commission in 1997. From 1963 the Press Council was charged with considering complaints against organs of the press. These were handled from 1991 by the self-regulatory Press Complaints Commission charged with implementing a code of practice among newspaper editors. In film, public cinemas must be licensed by local authorities, which have a legal duty to prohibit the admission of children to unsuitable films and may prevent any film from being shown, though usually following the recommendation of the BBFC, to which all films must be submitted for viewing before release. It can require cuts to be made or refuse a certificate altogether, more usually granting certificates in four classifications graded by suitability for age groups.

Political controversy has also frequently surrounded the enforcement of the Official Secrets Act (a new version of which was passed in 1989), for example, in 1984 over the prosecution and imprisonment of Sarah Tisdall, a Ministry of Defence employee, for disclosing a document to the *Guardian*, and the halting by the government in 1987 of the BBC documentary on the Zircon spy satellite. Political censorship was also exercised very publicly from 1988 to 1994 in the *broadcasting ban imposed on IRA spokesmen on British television. *JS*

Tony Aldgate, *Censorship and the Permissive Society* (Oxford, 1995). | Philip Knightley, *The First Casualty* (London, 1975). | Nicholas Pronay and Derek Spring (eds.), *Propaganda, Politics and Film* (London, 1982). | Richard Thurlow, *The Secret State* (London, 1995).

central bank diplomacy, co-operation between leading central bankers to manage the international economy. Its heyday came in the 1920s when the Financial Committee of the League of Nations failed to initiate international economic and financial reconstruction after the Great War. With no other institutions to facilitate international economic cooperation, collaboration between the world's most important central bankers emerged on an ad hoc basis to cope with the task of reconstruction and financial crises as and when they arose. The big problem at the war's end was currency instability and inflation which in much of central and eastern Europe reached the giddy heights of over 2,000 per cent a year. At conferences held in Brussels in 1920 and Genoa in 1922, the governor of the Bank of England, Montagu *Norman, attacked the problem of European reconstruction with missionary zeal. But Britain's plans dominated the field, until 1924 when the Federal Reserve Bank of New York, led by charismatic Benjamin Strong, put its financial muscle behind the *Dawes plan. That plan marked the potent fusion of private loans—links with private banks extended the scope of *bankers' diplomacy—and gold standard membership that became the hallmarks of economic reconstruction. Together Norman and Strong promoted the reconstruction of the international gold standard, a fixed exchange mechanism, as the policy tool to cure the world's economic ills. Sterling returned to the gold standard in 1925 (the USA had never left it) and by 1928 44 other currencies, aided by the central bank diplomacy of the USA, Britain, and latterly France, had joined the gold standard. The reconstructed system was dependent upon continued and close cooperation between the central banks of the main powers. If a country experienced a run on its currency, then financial assistance from the world's most important bankers was essential to sustain gold standard membership. From the outset cooperation between the central banks was not easy and Norman and Émile Moreau, governor of the Banque de France, often expressed their frustrations in strongly personalized terms. Moreau claimed that in his first meeting with Norman, the British banker announced: 'I detest your Government and your Treasury. For them I shall do nothing' (Boyle, 198). Without formalized structures to facilitate diplomacy, animosities and friendships (like that between Norman and the German central banker Hjalmar Schacht) certainly shaped relations between central banks, but far more disputes were generated by differences in national policy than personality. For all their claims of 'independence', central bankers were highly susceptible to domestic political pressure. With the onset of the 1930s Great Depression their will to cooperate was tested to breaking point. Their failure to staunch the sterling crisis of September 1931 that forced Britain off the gold standard marked the beginning of the end for central bank diplomacy. It was further hastened by the new determination of governments to take a more 'hands-on' approach to managing their domestic economies. *PC*

Andrew Boyle, *Montagu Norman* (London, 1967).

Central Electricity Generating Board. This was the organization responsible for the generation and transmission of electricity in England and Wales between 1926 and 1989. Its monopoly was established by the Electricity Supply Act, 1926, as part of a policy to rationalize the electricity industry, which had previously consisted of a multiplicity of companies heavily dependent on steam, coal, or gas to generate power. The board focused its activities on exploiting economies of scale by concentrating production in a small number of stations linked to a *national grid of high-tension transmission cables. It evolved to sell electricity to twelve area distribution boards, each serving a closed area or franchise. The 1989 Electricity Act established the legislative foundation for the restructuring and privatization of the industry. *JFM*

centralization in local government. The creation of powerful county and county borough councils at the end of the 19th century established a framework for countering the tendency to centralized power. Thereafter, local authorities steadily gained responsibility for new services, hitherto provided by single-purpose boards and ad hoc agencies, although these gains were arguably balanced by the losses to nationalization. For two decades after 1945, the relationship between central and local government was based on partnership, and local authorities were seen as more than mere agents of central departments. New initiatives which impinged upon local government were generally subject to prolonged consultation with a view to agreement before action and, prior to the 1960s, it was accepted that the local authority associations effectively had a veto over any changes in structure. However, with the expansion of services and the growth in social expenditure, the share of local spending funded from national taxes increased. Central control accordingly tightened, and local government expenditure became a tool of macroeconomic management. By the 1970s, local government had become the deliverer, rather than the originator, of services. Central control was stepped up with each successive initiative, with local authorities now the implementers of nationally formulated programmes. The last vestiges of partnership between central and local government disappeared with Margaret Thatcher's premiership in 1979, but a sustained move towards centralization awaited the legislative reforms of her third term (1987–90), while under John Major a new financial regime further shifted the balance in favour of central government. The rhetoric of the Labour government elected in 1997 favoured a return to greater local autonomy in the guise of 'democratic renewal'. *KY*

Central Policy Review Staff (CPRS) (1970–83), unit providing strategic analysis for the cabinet and the prime minister. When Edward Heath came to power in 1970 he tasked the Cabinet Office mandarins with establishing a policy review unit, also described as a 'think-tank' or a 'central capability unit'. Such a unit would enable the cabinet to deal not only with 'events' but also with strategy. The resultant white paper, *The Reorganization of Central Government*, established the CPRS. The intention of the unit was to provide systemic analyses of strategic issues across departments by using the brightest minds from both within and outside government. The appointment of the larger-than-life Lord Rothschild as the CPRS's first director ensured its early high profile. For the first three years of its existence the CPRS was the darling of the political chattering classes, but the oil crisis of 1973, which ironically the CPRS had predicted, marked the beginning of its end by refocusing attention on 'events'. In 1974 Wilson replaced Heath and created the Downing Street Policy Unit which effectively signed the CPRS's death warrant, since it was impossible to operate with two advice centres, and the CPRS died at Thatcher's hands in 1983. There have been many criticisms of the CPRS but its demise actually lay in its mission. Each department praised the CPRS for its 'interventions' in the affairs of other departments but criticized it for its 'interference' in their own, which explains both why it was needed and why it failed. *CAB*

Tessa Blackstone and William Plowden, *Inside the Think Tank* (London, 1988).

Central Statistical Office (CSO) **(1941–96).** The early days of the Second World War saw the establishment of three organizations which were to provide economic and statistical information for the prime minister: the prime minister's statistical branch; the survey of economic and financial plans, commonly known as the Stamp survey; and the economic section of the war cabinet. The three offices overlapped to some extent and in 1941 the Central Statistical Office was formed to bring cohesion to the work. The CSO was part of the Cabinet Office until 1989 when it became a department in the Treasury, a first step towards it becoming an executive agency. In 1996 the CSO was merged with the Office of Population Censuses and Surveys to form the Office for National Statistics. *JD*

Public Record Office website: *www.pro.gov.uk/finding/coreexec/data/cab-d10.htm* | CSO website: *www.ons.gov.uk*

Centre for Policy Studies (1974–), political research institute formed after Tory defeat in 1974 on the initiative of Sir Keith Joseph. It was influential from its office in Petty France, in combination with the *Institute of Economic Affairs and the Adam Smith Institute, in promoting free market ideas, but since some of its staff, notably Sir Alfred Sherman, were closer to Joseph whose leadership candidacy it urged, than to Thatcher, it was sometimes more 'political' (in the conspiratorial sense) than academic, an early example of the intense factionalization of the Conservative Party in the fourth quarter of the century. *EP*

Chalmers, Robert **(1858–1938),** civil servant. Chalmers entered the Treasury in 1882. A brilliant and ruthless official, and a committed Liberal in his politics, he worked closely with Lloyd George as chairman of the Board of Inland Revenue, 1907–11, particularly during the 1909 *'People's Budget' struggle, becoming permanent secretary to the Treasury in 1911. However, he fell out with his chief and was 'exiled' as governor of Ceylon (now Sri Lanka), 1913–16, returning to be one of three joint permanent secretaries to the Treasury, 1916–19. *KT*

Chamberlain, (Joseph) Austen **(1863–1937),** Liberal Unionist and Conservative politician. The elder son of Joseph and half-brother of Neville, Austen Chamberlain was prepared from childhood for a career in politics. After Rugby, Trinity College Cambridge, and study abroad, he returned home just as his father was forging a Liberal Unionist party from the ranks of the anti-home rule Liberals. This became Austen's political inheritance. Closer to the heart he bore the burden of his mother's death in giving birth to him, and perhaps this is why he spent much of his life trying to satisfy what he perceived to be his father's expectations. His father was his only hero and, unfortunately, a political model unsuitable for the son. Austen lacked his force and ruthlessness and, unlike him, wished in all things to be thought a gentleman, which made him oversensitive and vulnerable. Beaverbrook was cruel to suggest that 'he always played the game, and always lost' (Churchill used almost the same words) but it was not without some truth. As it was, he could only copy Joe's appearance, the signature eyeglass and orchid buttonhole, and thereby make himself faintly ridiculous.

He entered parliament as MP for Worcestershire East (1892), bordering his father's Birmingham stronghold. His lineage served him well and in 1895 he gained junior office under Salisbury. In 1902 he entered Balfour's cabinet as postmaster general, and three years later, when his father abandoned the Colonial Office to campaign for tariff reform, Austen was made chancellor of the exchequer as a kind of guarantee (or hostage) for the Chamberlain interest. When the government was overwhelmed in the 1906 election, most Unionists who survived the debacle were Chamberlainite tariff reformers, and when his father's health collapsed immediately afterwards, Austen became titular leader of the movement. Yet when Balfour retired from the party leadership in 1911, the two principal candidates to succeed him, Chamberlain and Walter Long, shrank from a divisive fight, leaving the prize to a tariff-reform dark horse, Andrew Bonar Law. After this painful act of self-denial, Chamberlain could never quite forgive Law for making it possible.

During these turbulent pre-war years, he usually supported the most extreme diehard side of most political issues and particularly in demanding continued commitment to tariff reform and resisting until the end the *Parliament Act, 1911. Too old to fight in the Great War which began in August 1914, there was only frustration for him until he was given the India Office in Asquith's government in May 1915; there he remained after Lloyd George displaced Asquith eighteen months later. Chamberlain returned to the exchequer,

1919–21, in the post-war coalition and became lord privy seal when he finally achieved the leadership of his party after Law's retirement in 1921. By this time Lloyd George's once unassailable authority was sadly decayed, but the punctilious Chamberlain in 1921 begged the great Welshman not to retire, bequeathing him the premiership. At the *Carlton Club meeting, when the Conservative backbenchers rejected continued coalition, Chamberlain, repelled by any possible imputation of treachery toward Lloyd George, refused to put himself at the head of the revolt and again dashed his own hopes for the premiership. Law was lured briefly from retirement to lead a strictly Conservative government, and Chamberlain was left again to contemplate his sacrifice.

In 1924, he agreed to serve as foreign secretary under Stanley Baldwin in a reunited Conservative cabinet, setting the stage for his greatest moment in public life: in 1925 he and the French and German foreign ministers negotiated the *Locarno treaty, guaranteeing the western European frontiers laid down at Versailles. He enjoyed universal praise, receiving the Order of the Garter and a share of the Nobel peace prize. Alas, the satisfaction was temporary, for Hitler and appeasement, which reached its zenith during his brother's premiership, lurked just around the corner.

Following the Conservative defeat in 1929, Chamberlain was destined to hold office again only briefly, at the Admiralty for a few months in 1931, following the formation of the National Government, though Baldwin teased him with the hint of a return to the Foreign Office in 1935. Thereafter he denied any interest in cabinet office, accepting instead the role of backbench elder statesman, in which he became a respected and effective critic of the policies of that government. In that role, he gained a greater measure of esteem and affection in the House than he had known throughout his long career. *RJQA*

DAVID DUTTON, *Austen Chamberlain: Gentleman in Politics* (Bolton, 1985). | SIR CHARLES PETRIE, *The Life and Letters of the Rt. Hon. Sir Austen Chamberlain*, 2 vols. (London, 1939–40). | ROBERT SELF (ed.), *The Austen Chamberlain Diary–Letters, 1916–1937* (London, 1995).

Chamberlain, Joseph (1836–1914), Unionist politician. Chamberlain's commercial success in his adopted home Birmingham allowed him to pursue political causes, among them public education and municipal improvement. He retired from business and was elected to parliament as a radical Liberal in 1876. Impatient and ambitious, he led the reorganization of the Liberal Party machine. In 1880 'Radical Joe' entered the cabinet of Gladstone and soon became his likely successor. Chamberlain's radicalism was mixed with a strong commitment to patriotism and Empire, and he rebelled against the 1886 Home Rule Bill and led a minority of colleagues to form the Liberal Unionist Party. In 1895 he joined the Conservative (Unionist) cabinet of Lord Salisbury as a partner—almost as a co-premier—selecting the Colonial Office as his base. By this point he was convinced that any hope of meaningful social reform depended upon the greatness and unity of the Empire, as his energetic pursuit of the Boer war (1899–1902) demonstrated. By 1903, without seeking the agreement of Salisbury's successor, Arthur Balfour, he announced his scheme for domestic renewal and imperial cooperation: tariff reform, combining duties on foreign imports with trade preference for colonial goods. The plan divided Unionists into pro- and anti-tariff factions. While Chamberlain canvassed the nation for tariff reform, Balfour's government slowly expired and in 1906 suffered humiliating electoral defeat. Most of the surviving Unionists were tariff reformers, and Chamberlain became effective leader, dictating terms to Balfour in the *Valentine compact. Within months, however, he suffered a crippling stroke; his public life was over, while tariff reform continued to divide his party for another decade. Though vain about his appearance, he was a generous and kindly man. A great patriot who burned to guarantee his country's future, Chamberlain's brilliance and impatience guaranteed that he would be judged a political messiah to some but an unstable destroyer to many more. *RJQA*

J. L. GARVIN and JULIAN AMERY, *The Life of Joseph Chamberlain*, 6 vols. (London, 1932–69). | PETER MARSH, *Joseph Chamberlain* (London, 1994). | ALAN SYKES, *Tariff Reform in British Politics, 1903–1913* (Oxford, 1979).

Chamberlain, (Arthur) Neville (1869–1940), politician and prime minister. Although only prime minister for three years from May 1937, these were vital years for Britain and consequently Chamberlain has remained a controversial figure. To his many detractors he was the man who failed to stand up to Adolf Hitler; to others, and increasingly to historians, he realized the inherent weaknesses of Britain's defences and economy and sought to mediate with the dictators whilst rearming the nation. In his own eyes, his inability to save the peace made him a failure and he feared that history written by his successors would judge him harshly. He was always self conscious of his 'failings'; throughout his life he lived in the shadow of the political reputations of his father, Joseph, and half-brother, Austen, and it is ironic that the only Chamberlain to become prime minister was Neville. He came very late to national politics, only becoming MP for Birmingham Ladywood in December 1918 at the age of 49, and then representing Birmingham Edgbaston from 1929 until his death. Previously he had confined his political activity to Birmingham, including a period as lord mayor. This led to jibes that he viewed all political issues 'through the wrong end of the municipal drainpipe'. His initial foray into national politics ended in acrimony when he resigned in August 1917 as director-general of national service after only seven months in office. The experience soured his relationship with Lloyd George, both men ever afterwards reluctant to work with the other. With the collapse of the Lloyd George coalition, Law appointed him paymaster general, though he also had a brief period as chancellor in 1923.

Coming Man

After Baldwin's re-election in 1924, Chamberlain moved at his own wish to the Ministry of Health, an environment in which he revelled, since he could exploit his knowledge of local government when framing legislation; fellow Conservatives now recognized him as a true political professional. Since his entry into politics he had shown a willingness to participate in the formulation and initiation of policy decisions. He had drafted the party policy document *Looking Ahead* (1924) and had created a secretariat to support the party's policy committees. During the crisis years of Baldwin's leadership, 1929–31, Chamberlain occupied the pivotal positions of Conservative Party chairman and of the *Conservative Research Department (CRD). The CRD was widely perceived as his private office, giving him assistance with speeches and enabling him to forge a close relationship with its director, Joseph Ball, whose talents for media manipulation Chamberlain utilized to the full from 1937. By 1930 he was regarded as Baldwin's heir, but the party chairmanship restricted his options, and Baldwin may have given him the post as a deliberate means of tying his hands and reducing the likelihood of a leadership challenge. During the 1931 economic and political crisis, Chamberlain played a vital role in securing Labour's downfall and in creating the *National Government. This was vital in making him the number two Conservative, a position reinforced by his becoming chancellor of the exchequer, November 1931–7. As chancellor he found little favour with the new Keynesian ideas and in 1932 presided over the Ottawa agreement (see OTTAWA CONFERENCE) which introduced protection, a measure his father, Joseph, had long advocated. It is clear that he was very active in suggesting what should happen within the government, as with the cabinet composition after the 1935 election. Unfortunately, from Chamberlain's perspective, Baldwin kept postponing retirement, first because of the Abyssinian crisis, then the November 1935 general election, and finally due to the abdication. With the rise to power of Hitler, the British were obliged from 1934 to begin rearmament.

Appeasement and War

As chancellor after 1931 and then from 1937 premier, Chamberlain played a dominant role. Conscious of the weaknesses of Britain's defences, but anxious that rearmament must not be allowed to interfere with the recovering economy, he sought to prioritize the defence programme and make the economy the 'fourth arm of defence'. Development of the RAF was favoured in preference to building up the army for a continental role, while the direct defence of Britain was deemed of primary importance, followed by the preservation of her trade routes, and only then the defence of the Empire. When he took over as prime minister Chamberlain sensed the urgency in foreign affairs and was resolved to intervene actively, conscious that Britain was in no position to fight Germany, Italy, and Japan. Efforts were thus redoubled to ascertain the dictators' requirements. The desire to pacify the Italians—to offset a hostile Germany—ultimately lost Chamberlain his foreign secretary, Anthony *Eden, but 1938 marked the high point of his participation on the world stage. The September Munich agreement (see MUNICH CRISIS) averted imminent war and gave Britain a valuable breathing space in which developments in radar technology and fighter aircraft offered the opportunity of a viable air defence system for the first time. His personal diplomacy to Germany, flying for the first time at the age of 69, captured the world's imagination, but his ill-judged declaration of 'peace in our time' came to haunt him as Hitler seized Prague and then in September 1939 attacked Poland. Despite the huge personal blow of war, he drew some comfort from the morality of Britain's position, but he was unsuited to the rigours of war leadership, providing erratic leadership to the nation and his party. After disaster in the Norway campaign a parliamentary rebellion precipitated his resignation in

May 1940. Despite the shock of his sudden fall he remained in the war cabinet so as to help the new prime minister, Winston Churchill. After all, his family tradition was one of accepting responsibility, something he never shirked. He became lord president, whilst retaining the party leadership, for the sake of unity, until chronic illness forced him to resign in October 1940. Within weeks he was dead. His distinctive style of leadership, rather similar to Thatcher's in the tendency to lead from the front, dismissed opposition, personalized debate, and stressed loyalty. His parliamentary majority, marshalled by chief whip David Margesson, followed behind, stirred by appeals to their loyalty as well as to their fear of political isolation. He was the rare example of a major prime minister who neither won nor lost a general election. *NJC*

David Dilks, *Neville Chamberlain, 1869–1929* (Cambridge, 1984). | David Dutton, *Neville Chamberlain* (London, 2001) | Keith Feiling, *The Life of Neville Chamberlain* (London, 1946). | R. A. C. Parker, *Chamberlain and Appeasement* (London, 1993).

Chamberlain Housing Act. See Housing Act, 1923.

Chanak crisis (1922). The treaty of Sèvres with Turkey provided for the neutralization of the Turkish straits and their occupation by Allied forces. In August 1922 the British garrison at Chanak came under threat from the forces of Kemal Ataturk's national movement. Contrary to the inclinations of his Conservative partners, the premier, Lloyd George, wished to resist the Turks and also appeared to enlist the aid of the dominions, but without consulting them. For many Conservatives he had gone too far, and the *Carlton Club meeting on 19 October 1922 effectively brought Lloyd George down. *AJC*

Chandos, Viscount. See Lyttleton, Oliver.

Channel Tunnel. The Channel Tunnel was commissioned in 1986 and officially opened in May 1994 at a cost of £10 billion, the largest privately financed engineering project in Europe to date. Proposals for a tunnel under the Channel date from the Napoleonic wars and the coming of the railways attracted some exploratory workings from the 1870s. Considerations of finance and national security put these schemes in abeyance until an agreement was signed in 1966 between the prime ministers of France and Britain to embark on a fresh project. This also ran into financial difficulties and was cancelled, but under Margaret Thatcher the project was revived. Rival schemes for bridges and tunnels were considered, as well as whether provision should be made for road or rail services: a rail-only tunnel, for both passengers and freight, was decided upon. A particular emphasis from Thatcher was that the tunnel should be built without government subsidy and financed by the private sector. Although as an engineering project the scheme went ahead successfully, there was considerable political argument about the failure of the government to provide funds for a dedicated rail link from London to the tunnel and the consequent delay in providing a high-speed link similar to the one available on the French side of the Channel. After the official opening by the queen and President Mitterrand, the first travellers were able to use the tunnel from November 1994. The current terminal is at Waterloo station, but a permanent terminal at St Pancras will take the high-speed link due for completion in 2007 at a cost of £4.2 billion under a public–private partnership scheme, underwritten by the government. *JS*

Channon, Henry ('Chips') (1897–1958), Conservative backbencher, diarist, and socialite. Of American parentage but married into the Guinness family, Channon was ambitious both politically and socially. MP for Southend from 1935 until his death, he only ever achieved minor political office. He was friendly with Edward VIII and a staunch supporter of Chamberlain's appeasement policy. Known for his right-wing views, he expressed some sympathy with the Hitler regime, but felt betrayed by its behaviour after 1938. *NJC*

R. Rhodes James (ed.), *Chips: The Diaries of Sir Henry Channon* (London, 1967).

Channon, (Henry) Paul (Guinness) (1935–), Conservative politician. Son of 'Chips' Channon, he was first noted for his sublime wealth and a Commons entry at 23 (for the Guinness family seat, Southend) and his mother's description of 'a colt from a stable the electors knew'. Parliamentary private secretary at 25 to R. A. Butler, he had mainly a subordinated career, with junior posts at housing and Northern Ireland under Heath and civil service and arts with Thatcher; finally in 1986 he became trade secretary after the Westland affair (embarrassed by a Guinness takeover, and in dispute with unconsulted juniors over a bid for Pilkington), then moved to transport, 1987–9. *EP*

Chaplin, Henry (1840–1923), Conservative politician and sportsman. Chaplin sat in the Commons for 48 years, 1868–1916. A true example of the ancient Tory county class, he tirelessly supported the agricultural interest in politics and was known universally as 'the squire'. He wooed and married a celebrated beauty, Florence Leveson-Gower, owned the famous racing stud Blankney Farm, and won the Derby in 1867. He became a keen tariff reformer in his hope that protectionism would revitalize country life. *RJQA*

Chapple, Francis Joseph (1921–), trade unionist. Frank Chapple, who joined the Electricians' Trade Union (ETU) in 1935 and the Communist Party in 1939, is most famous for then successfully taking the Communist executive of his own union to court for ballot-rigging, having himself left the Communist Party in 1958. He became general secretary of the ETU in 1966, remaining in that post as a staunch anti-Communist. He was a Social Democratic Party supporter until 1984, after which he became a life peer. *KL*

Charity Commission, a government-appointed body that supervises British charities, inspects their accounts, and reassures the public that such charities are being properly run. A charity must be registered with, and its purposes approved by, the commission in order to enjoy the benefits of 'charitable status', including exemption from taxation on its activities and on donations to its funds. *JAR*

Charles, Prince of Wales (1948–), heir to the throne since 1952. Charles was the first heir to be educated publicly, at boarding schools in Britain and Australia, as well as at Cambridge. After stints in the air force and navy, he took up a round of public duties. He established his own charity, the Prince's Trust, to help young people and businesses in the inner cities. Charles enraged professional architects but pleased the public with his condemnations of the excesses of urban modernism. His marriage to *Diana, Princess of Wales, after a promising start, ended in disaster for him personally and for the monarchy as an institution. He is only now beginning to recover from it, although training in self-sacrifice and grimly repetitive public engagements should give him the stamina both to survive and prosper as sovereign. *WMK*

Jonathan Dimbleby, *The Prince of Wales: A Biography* (London, 1994).

Charter 88, pressure group representing cross-party interests mainly from the Liberal and Labour ranks, advocating constitutional reform, including *proportional representation. The group was conscious of coming together on the tercentenary of the Glorious Revolution and proposed a new constitutional settlement, replacing that of 1688. It would be embodied in a written constitution, a new electoral system, an elected second chamber, a reformed judiciary, open government, and an 'equitable distribution' of power between local, regional, and national government. By 1991, the Charter had attracted 25,000 signatures and was able to draw upon the continuing frustration felt towards a constitutional and electoral system which seemed increasingly ossified. The group played an important part in persuading the Labour Party to take seriously the question of constitutional reform and influenced Neil Kinnock in setting up a working party under Professor Plant to look at electoral systems for regional assemblies and a reformed second chamber, later also including voting systems for the Commons. The Blair government has implemented part of the Charter 88 agenda, through reform of the Lords (though the elected element falls short of that suggested by the pressure group), devolution for Wales and Scotland, an Open Government Bill, and the incorporation of the European Convention on Human Rights into domestic law by the Human Rights Act of 1998. *JS*

Charteris, Martin Charles (1913–99), private secretary to Elizabeth II, 1972–7. He served in the queen's private office for nearly three decades, beginning as her private secretary when she was still Princess Elizabeth in 1950–2. Perhaps the most adept writer of modern private secretaries, he is remembered at court for the short and amusing speeches he composed for the queen to read. The queen's silver jubilee (1977), including informal walkabouts, processions down the Thames, and bonfires, was Charteris's masterpiece. His achievement was to demonstrate how small but apt innovations, or indeed revivals, could enhance the historical outlines of an institution sometimes suspected of having no capacity to change. After he left the household, he was an enormously popular and effective provost of Eton, showing once again his ability to adapt an ancient institution to late 20th-century requirements. *WMK*

Kenneth Rose, *Kings, Queens and Courtiers* (London, 1985).

Chartwell, country house in Kent, owned from 1922 by Sir Winston Churchill. Chartwell provided a haven in his 'wilderness years' of the 1930s, during which he often painted there and personally built a much-publicized wall around its rose garden. Churchill deeply loved Chartwell, its lake and its black swans, despite the heavy calls it made on his (frequently embarrassed) financial resources. Missing a ministerial income, he was almost compelled to sell the house in 1937 and again in 1946, but continued to use it as an alternative to Chequers when wartime premier. Seventeen friends collectively bought Chartwell for the nation as a historic site in 1946–7, stipulating that the Churchills could live there until their deaths, but when Winston died his widow allowed it to pass at once to the National Trust. It opened to the public in 1966, and continues to be one of the country's most-visited historic sites. *JAR*

Chataway, Christopher John (1931–), Conservative politician. An Olympic runner and television journalist, Chataway won North Lewisham in the 1958 London County Council election before becoming its MP the following year. He was an education minister for two years until 1964, but was out of parliament during 1966–9. Heath appointed him minister for posts and telecommunications in 1970 and for industrial development in 1972. He left politics for business in 1974 but continued to support campaigns for electoral reform. *RJS*

Chatham House (the Royal Institute of International Affairs (RIIA)), foreign policy think-tank. The RIIA was formed in 1920 to study foreign affairs scientifically so as to 'enlighten' public opinion and, thereby, buttress the position of official foreign policy makers. Founded by the prophet-like Lionel Curtis, rooted in the British elite, and funded by City institutions and American foundations, the RIIA continued the work of the *Round Table* movement which had sought to foster cooperation between Britain, the dominions, and the USA since the Edwardian period, through policy research and debate. It attempted to transform the Empire into a commonwealth of nations, to construct an Anglo-American alliance, and build a new liberal world order. By the Second World War, it had a highly reputable journal, *International Affairs*, and had become the most influential forum for the unofficial discussion of British foreign affairs. Attracting the patronage of prime ministers, foreign secretaries, senior civil servants, the RIIA mobilized, under the leadership of historians Arnold J. Toynbee and Charles Kingsley Webster, dozens of academics for post-war planning in the Foreign Office. Through its work in the Institute of Pacific Relations, it played a significant semi-official diplomatic role in Far Eastern affairs in its attempts to gain American support for British interests in the region. The RIIA has made a vital contribution to policy making, opinion mobilization, and informal diplomacy since its foundation. *IP*

Andrea Bosco and Cornelia Navari (eds.), *Chatham House and British Foreign Policy 1919–1945* (London, 1994). | Stephen King-Hall, *Chatham House: A Brief Account of the Origins, Purposes and Methods of the RIIA* (London, 1937). | Inderjeet Parmar, 'Chatham House and the Anglo-American Alliance', *Diplomacy and Statecraft*, 3 (1992).

Chelmer, Lord (1914–97), Conservative organizer. As Sir Eric Edwards, he was influential among Conservative Party members, National Union executive chairman (1957–65), party treasurer until 1977, becoming Lord Chelmer in 1963. His 1973 'Chelmer report' on the party organization called for more participatory democracy in the party machine and was intended to have an impact like that of Maxwell-Fyfe in the 1940s. At the time its effect was limited, though it prefigured reforms introduced after the party's 1997 defeat. *JAR*

Chequers, official country residence of the prime minister, bequeathed to the nation for that purpose by Lord Lee of Fareham in 1917. Chequers is a 16th-century country house located in the heart of the Chilterns, some 40 miles (64 km) from the centre of London. Lee reasoned that such a retreat would enable a degree of independence, especially for those not wealthy enough to afford additional residences, and part of the preamble to the bequest makes precisely this point: 'It is not possible to foresee or foretell from what classes or conditions of life the future wielders of power in this country will be drawn.' From its first prime ministerial resident, Lloyd George, to the current incumbent, Chequers has been much used as a weekend retreat, for informal political meetings, and for entertaining foreign guests. *CAB*

Chichester-Clark, James Dawson (1923–), Northern Ireland prime minister. He served in the Irish Guards during the Second World War and retired with the rank of major in 1960, in the same year that he was returned to the Northern Ireland parliament. In 1967 he became minister for agriculture, but in April 1969 he resigned from the government on the grounds that reforms were being pushed through too quickly. A month later, following the resignation of Terence O'Neill, Chichester-Clark defeated Brian Faulkner in a ballot of Unionist MPs to become Unionist leader and prime minister. As the security situation rapidly deteriorated in August 1969 Chichester-Clark was forced to ask for the introduction of British troops to support local security forces. With British troops directly involved in the security situation, however, power inevitably moved towards Westminster. The disbandment of the B-Specials (see ROYAL ULSTER CONSTABULARY) further undermined Chichester-Clark's support among Unionists and, with a lack of support from the British government for what he believed was the necessary security policy, he resigned in March 1971. He was later ennobled as Lord Moyola. *BMW*

SYDNEY ELLIOTT and W. D. FLACKES, *Northern Ireland: A Political Directory 1968–1999* (Belfast, 1999).

chiefs of staff (COS) (1923–). Senior military leaders had been regularly consulted by Lloyd George in wartime but as a formally constituted group the chiefs of staff first met in July 1923 to offer collective military advice to the government. Initially comprising the first sea lord, the chief of the imperial general staff (army), and the chief of the air staff, a chief of the defence staff (CDS) was added in 1957 and a vice-chief in 1984. Increasingly the CDS rather than the COS collectively has become the government's chief military adviser; in 1996 the traditional rotation of that post around the services was abandoned. *SJB*

child benefit, the principal social security benefit for families and children, the successor to *family allowances. It is tax-free, non-contributory, and is not means-tested. In 1999–2000 it was received by an estimated 7,036,000 families, covering 12,737,000 children. In attempts to reduce the social security budget, it has been suggested in the past that child benefit should be taxed, but such proposals have met opposition on the grounds that it is a benefit paid directly to the mother and represents part of a 'family friendly' policy. *JS*

Child Poverty Action Group, set up in 1965 to campaign for children in poverty. One of a number of single-issue pressure groups from the period, it highlighted the phenomenon that the percentage of children in poverty is always greater than that of the population at large. It has campaigned for the retention and increase of *child benefit and for extended assistance to poor families such as family credit, renamed the working families' tax credit from 1999. *JS*

Child Support Act, 1991. This set up a Child Support Agency to reassess and enforce maintenance payments for children after divorce or separation and to trace errant fathers. The workings of the Act aroused widespread protest because of financial hardship caused to second families, delays in producing individual assessments, and concern that the reform was merely a cost-saving measure because fathers' maintenance payments were deducted from benefits. A further Act in 1999 simplified the system of assessment and allowed mothers to receive up to £10 per week of any maintenance without reduction of benefit. *JS*

Chilston, Viscount. See AKERS-DOUGLAS, ARETAS.

'Chinese slavery', the popular cry raised in Britain after 1904 when it was learned that in South Africa the colonial administration under the leadership of the high commissioner, Lord *Milner (with the permission of the Colonial Office), had begun the importation of indentured Chinese labourers into the territory. Public outrage ignited as the newspapers reported the harsh conditions under which these bondsmen were housed, worked, and disciplined. The scandal contributed to the Conservative defeat in the 1906 election and much damaged Milner's reputation. *RJQA*

ALFRED COLLIN, *Proconsul in Politics: A Study of Lord Milner in Opposition and in Power* (London, 1964).

Chitnis, Pratap Chidamber (1936–), Liberal official and activist. Chitnis was head of Liberal Party organization, 1966–9. He was the organizer of the *Orpington by-election victory in 1962; the Liberal Party's first local government officer, 1960–2; its training officer, charged with recruiting and training agents, 1962–4; and then press officer. He played an important part in the revival of Liberal Party organization, but resigned in 1969 to become secretary of the Joseph Rowntree Trust, where he served for twenty years, also taking an active part in organizations concerned with race issues. A peer since 1977. *JS*

Christian Aid, charity which originated as 'Christian Reconstruction in Europe', in response to the social need and homelessness following the Second World War. In the 1950s, the focus of its work shifted towards Africa. By 1970, having been renamed Christian Aid, it was funding more than 100 development projects in 40 countries. More recently it has campaigned for an end to third world debt, fair trade, and against the exploitation of children in the third world. *PPC*

Christian Democracy, Movement for (MCD) (1989–). Britain has never had a Christian Democrat party akin to those in continental Europe, although the Conservative Party has had on and off links with European Christian Democracy since the 1960s. The MCD was not specifically designed to fill that gap, but to promote the importance of Christian perspectives to the whole of British politics. It was founded in 1990 after an initial meeting organized by the Roman Catholic Liberal MP David Alton in January 1989, and has sought to act as a broad movement to discuss the political operation of Christian principles. As such it bears resemblance to the 1934–5 Council of Action for Peace and Reconstruction, though it has avoided the close relationship with a senior politician which, in the shape of Lloyd George, proved fatal to the latter. *PPC*

Christian Socialism. There were a number of often short-lived 'Christian Socialist' societies from 1848 onwards. Several came together in 1924 to form the inter-denominational Society of Socialist Christians (SSC), which affiliated to the Labour Party the following year, though this link was to lapse in 1933. By then, SSC had become the Socialist Christian League (SCL). However, although a large number of Christian Socialists were elected in the Labour landslide of 1945, a parliamentary group proved ephemeral. And although individual Christian Socialists were influential in the Labour Party and the Campaign for Nuclear Disarmament, SCL itself remained small. In 1960 it was relaunched as the Christian Socialist Movement following a merger with the predominantly Anglican Society of Socialist Clergy and Ministers. Reaffiliating to Labour in 1986, it became much more prominent after John Smith's 1993 Tawney lecture, and even more so under Smith's successor as Labour leader, Tony Blair. *PPC*

Chris Bryant, *Possible Dreams* (London, 1996).

Church and State. In 1920, following a long parliamentary struggle, the Anglican Church in Wales was disestablished. The Church of Scotland, however, remains a self-governing established church, and the Church of England also remains established (and uniquely protected by the blasphemy laws), although its relationship with the state has changed substantially since 1900. The creation of the Church Assembly in 1919 (General Synod since 1970) gave it its own law-making body. The result has been to attenuate parliamentary oversight of the Church to the adoption or rejection of measures. Meanwhile, changes in 1977, whereby the Church would henceforth present two names from which appointees to senior ecclesiastical positions were to be selected, reduced prime ministerial interference in the appointment of bishops and Church affairs generally. Support for disestablishment has, however, at least within Anglicanism, been largely confined to its Anglo-Catholic wing. Outside pressure for disestablishment has meanwhile diminished. The Nonconformist-dominated Liberation Society was founded in 1844 and was very active in the late 19th century. Ecumenism, social change, and the altered status of the Church of England all, however, helped to ensure that disestablishment was rarely debated after 1919. The Liberation Society was disbanded in 1959, although subsequently figures like Tony Benn have sought to keep the issue alive. After they were linked to rates rather than cereal prices in 1920, clerical tithes proved a more serious issue. A tithe war followed in agricultural areas during the 1930s Depression as cereal prices plummeted. In 1936 the government sought to resolve the matter by redeeming tithes over 60 years. They were finally abolished in 1977. *PPC*

Church in Wales, disestablishment of. The Anglican Church in Wales was finally disestablished in 1920 after what had seemed an interminable period of parliamentary debate. The first of many bills had been introduced in 1870 but it was 1895 before any successful vote on the matter. Resolution of the issue was to be delayed, however, first by Unionist rule after 1895 and then by the Great War. The question had first arisen in the 1840s as pressure groups like the Liberation Society politicized the Nonconformist denominations which had begun to dominate public life in Wales. With the emergence of the Liberal Party as essentially the political wing of Welsh Nonconformity after 1868, the issue became a rallying cry of Welsh radicalism, a way of galvanizing the chapel-going masses. In 1920 Lord Hugh Cecil denounced the settlement as the 'robbery of God' but already disestablishment was a non-issue. The secularized endowments of the Church passed to the county councils whilst the disestablished Church flourished both financially and spiritually. Ironically the Church in Wales was to prove more able to survive in the 20th century than the Nonconformist denominations and it has had little difficulty in establishing a distinctive niche in the contemporary culture of Wales. *PS*

David Walker (ed.), *A History of the Church in Wales* (Cardiff, 1976).

Church of England, the established church in England since the 1530s. Defence of establishment and of the role of the Church in education lay at the root of the historic linkage between the Church of England and the Conservative Party. In 1900, there were seventeen bishops identified as Tories, six supported their Liberal Unionist allies, six the Liberals, and only four were without party labels. Episcopal partisanship was, however, to diminish rapidly in the early years of the century. The constitutional crisis of 1909–11 encouraged the view that bishops should avoid party strife, although controversies over religion, particularly over the levels of public support for the large percentage of schools that were of religious foundation, continued to dog educational legislation until at least 1959, a trend also fostered by other developments early in the century. One was the effect of the Great War in reducing the social gulf between Anglicans and Nonconformists and in encouraging post-war ecumenism. The other was the rising importance of class-based issues in the inter-war period, which cut across religious communities. And in the post-1945 years busier bishops were to be much less active or influential in a House of Lords swollen by life peerages. The Church, meanwhile, changed its stance on a number of social issues. Attitudes to divorce were already being moderated by 1920 by a growing awareness of, and desire to minister to, the misery caused by marital breakdown. The 1930 Lambeth conference gave tentative approval to the use of contraceptives. And in the post-war years concern about backstreet abortionists led to support, in certain circumstances, for abortion. By the 1980s, concern on the right that liberalization was promoting social malaise and family breakdown led to criticism of the apparent failure of the Church to act as a moral guardian on these issues. Thatcherites condemned the willingness of the Church, rather, to comment on social or defence policy during a decade of confrontation with a Conservative government. At the time it was quipped that the Church had switched from being 'the *Conservative Party at prayer' to 'the Social Democratic Party at prayer'. Whilst this may have been true of the clergy, however, it does not seem to hold true for the laity, who continued, as throughout the century, to be disproportionately Conservative. And although Anglican MPs can be found in all parties, a majority of them have usually been Tories.

PPC

Peter Catterall, 'The Party and Religion', in A. Seldon and S. Ball (eds.), *Conservative Century* (Oxford, 1994). | G. I. T. Machin, *Churches and Social Issues in Twentieth-Century Britain* (Oxford, 1998).

Church of Scotland ('the Kirk'), the established church in Scotland. In 1929 the Church of Scotland and the Free Church of Scotland reunited, bringing to an end the split between the two largest Presbyterian churches which had occurred in the Disruption of 1843. Politically, both the free and established churches supported the Conservative Party in the twenties, condemning the General Strike of 1926, and denounced the Labour Party as antichristian. Both churches were also responsible for fanning anti-Irish Catholic sentiment in Scotland and one of the key architects in the reunion of 1929, Dr John White, was at the forefront of this phenomenon. Undoubtedly, one of the key factors in the reunion was the belief that a more secular society was undermining the traditional authority of the churches. The appeal to anti-Catholicism can also be read as a means to promote the influence of the clergy by promoting Protestant bigotry. Such endeavours, however, largely fell on deaf ears and failed to retard secularization, although it was only in the 1960s that church attendance rates began to fall dramatically. The political stance of the Church shifted after the Second World War when the influential Church and Nation Committee, which reported on social and missionary affairs, began to posit more liberal policies on a whole range of issues ranging from African decolonization to penal reform. Although there was a scare in the fifties that ecumenicism was a way to introduce episcopacy into the Kirk, by and large, the political shift in Scotland towards Labour was reflected in the Church by a greater concern to promote social justice. In the 1980s, the Kirk played a prominent part in the campaign for a Scottish parliament.

RF

T. M. Devine and R. J. Finlay (eds.), *Scotland in the Twentieth Century* (Edinburgh, 1996).

Churchill, Randolph Spencer (1911–68), only son of Sir Winston *Churchill. Troubled by having to live up to his paternal expectations, there were many epic rows and tearful reconciliations. Randolph began with promise but his excitability and poor judgement, enhanced by heavy drinking, ensured failure to secure any winnable parliamentary seat, except when awarded one without a contest in wartime. He was an excellent speaker and talented journalist, late in life completing two early volumes of his father's official biography.

JAR

Churchill, Winston Leonard Spencer (1874–1965), dominant politician on the British right in the middle of the century, and major influence throughout his 65 years in politics. Churchill changed parties twice and was widely distrusted, but his unrelenting ambition and conviction of his own political worth ensured that he survived to become, in the words of A. J. P. Taylor, 'the saviour of his country' in 1940–5 (*English History 1914–1945* (Oxford, 1965) (n. 441)).

Churchill entered parliament in 1901, having won Oldham for the Conservatives in the 1900 'Khaki' Election as a Boer war hero. Initially he was the political heir of his father, Lord Randolph Churchill (1849–95), who had preached 'Tory Democracy', and whose two-volume life Winston filially published in 1906. A lifelong free-trader, he was soon disenchanted with Conservatism under Balfour, switching to the Liberals in 1904 and rising to the cabinet under Asquith.

Cabinet and Wilderness Years

Churchill brought the navy into the Great War in good shape, but association with *Gallipoli ruined his reputation and forced his resignation in 1915. Returning to office under Lloyd George, he became a centrist supporter of *coalitionism, but drifted back to the right as a hater of communism. With the end of coalition in 1922, he gradually rejoined the Conservatives, losing three successive parliamentary elections in the process, but was able in 1924 to win Epping (which he represented for the next 40 years, though the part he represented was renamed Woodford in 1945) and returned to cabinet as Baldwin's chancellor of the exchequer.

Churchill worked hard at the Treasury, but was no economist, and his reluctant decision to return Britain to the *gold standard in 1925 has been seen as a major contribution to Britain's economic difficulties until 1939. He was unduly confrontationist during the 1926 *General Strike, during which he edited the government's *British Gazette*. When the Conservatives lost office in 1929, he became disillusioned with policy on several issues, resigned from the shadow cabinet in 1930, and did not hold office again until war came in 1939. Initially, his 'wilderness years' were dominated by a failed attempt to halt the MacDonald government's modest proposal of responsible government for India, Churchill being both a strong opponent of Gandhi and a man unwilling to yield anything under duress. Despite early sympathy for Mussolini, once Hitler became German chancellor in 1933, he became a tireless advocate of British rearmament to meet the German threat and a regular (if not quite so regular as his own *War Memoirs* suggested) critic of British foreign policy. He became widely identified as the sternest critic of *appeasement and made a blistering attack on Neville Chamberlain after the 1938 Munich settlement (see MUNICH CRISIS). When appeasement failed, he had therefore a strong claim on office, returning to the Admiralty where he had been in 1914.

Finest Hour

Although Churchill shared blame for British feebleness in the 'phoney war' of 1939–40, and was personally culpable for disasters in 1940 such as the Norway campaign, he could not be blamed for inadequate pre-war rearmament. He had confessed in 1915 to being 'a war person', and he now flourished as never before. When Chamberlain was overthrown in May 1940, Churchill had become his inevitable successor as prime minister, forming a government more genuinely 'national' than its predecessor since all parties now took part. He was indeed more reliant on Labour and Liberal support than on Conservatives, many of whom continued to distrust him even after he became party leader in October 1940. As war leader, Churchill rose spectacularly to the occasion, inspiring the populace in 1940–1 with trenchant speeches that inspired people to face hard realities, and (as minister of defence) taking personal charge of the war effort. His interventions sometimes lacked judgement and many of his initiatives had to be talked down by the chiefs of staff, but his reiterated insistence on 'Action this Day' did much to keep Britain's war aggressive and effective.

The Anglo-American son of an American mother, he was able from 1941 to form a strong personal relationship with US President Roosevelt (though less close than he liked to believe), and also with Joseph Stalin. He thus appeared as one of the 'Big Three' who would settle the destinies of mankind when the conflict ended. Inevitably though, the catastrophic effect of war on the British economy and the fact that Britain had a relatively smaller population in a war whose armies needed millions, ensured that she was increasingly excluded from decisions in 1944–5. The last years of the war were therefore darkened for Churchill by fear of what might follow, though he remained convinced that, by 'punching above our weight', Britain would be able to remain a superpower after the war. He later emphasized this through the image of a 'three circles' concept of British foreign policy, whereby Britain alone was in Europe, the

Empire-Commonwealth, and the 'special relationship' with the USA, and through occupying this unique position would be able to influence all three worlds. Events such as the Suez crisis during his retirement exposed the frailty of such notions.

In order to concentrate on the war effort, Churchill had also neglected party planning of post-war policy, and anyway seemed not to want to return to party politics when the war ended. This was, however, the determined aim of Labour and the Liberals, so their 1945 withdrawal produced a partisan general election long before Churchill had wanted one, and for which he had not prepared. His barnstorming motorcade-campaigning, though it generated massive, cheering crowds, proved not to indicate much about the voters' intentions, and such misjudgements as his *Gestapo broadcast helped to derail what Conservative campaign there was. Churchill cannot be solely blamed for the massive Tory defeat in 1945, the causes of which had been building up for a decade—during much of which he had had little influence.

He was not a successful leader of opposition in 1945–51, frequently because he was not even there, and Conservative recovery in this period owed more to Eden, Woolton, and Butler. However, despite his declining health, Churchill did not reduce his determination to cling to the leadership and become prime minister again. He concentrated on writing memoirs and giving major international speeches on foreign policy, though the growing impact that these made did certainly help his party. The key events were the *'iron curtain' speech at Fulton, Missouri, in 1946, and subsequent orations at Strasbourg, Zurich, and The Hague. Churchill thereby appeared both as one of the earliest heralds of *Cold War against Russia and as godfather of *European integration. These two themes were more closely linked than was later remembered, since he saw European unity mainly as a bulwark of Western defence, and once the USA was again committed through NATO to defend Western Europe, Churchill's 'Europeanism' waned rapidly. In office from 1951, he did little to link Britain with the emerging European community, and did much to obstruct such ideas as a proposed European army.

Man of the Century

By 1951, Churchill was 76, increasingly frail (he had a third stroke in 1953) and rather deaf. His final government was therefore one in which central control was only fitfully exercised and speculation centred on how long he would be able to hang on. His own priority was to reduce the dangers of global war, fearing a Russian nuclear attack on Britain, and he sought therefore to promote an East–West summit (which eventually came about, but failed, just after he left office). Having had an eightieth birthday that was a massive national festival in his praise, Churchill was eventually cajoled into retiring in April 1955. In retirement he deteriorated in health and mental faculties, but did not die until over 90. His funeral was a huge state occasion, attended by world leaders and marked by memorial services all over the world, and numerous tributes to 'the man of the century' (as *Time* magazine put it). He is commemorated in statues and memorials around Europe and the English-speaking world, in funds collected for scholarships in half a dozen countries, in Churchill College in Cambridge and an International Churchill Society that became especially strong in North America, and in a multi-volume official biography which began to appear in 1966. Churchill's extraordinarily high reputation was barely dented by the few revisionist historians who appeared after his death (some of whom came in for great abuse from his admirers), and stood at the end of the century as high as in 1965.

Churchill was not, though, only a statesman and politician, having a great range of other interests at which he excelled. Already by 1900 he had been a soldier and become a major war correspondent; he wrote continuously for the press when not in office, and also completed works of serious history and autobiography, notably the four-volume life of his ancestor Marlborough (1934–8) and six volumes on the Second World War (1948–54); he exhibited paintings at the Royal Academy; he owned successful racehorses; and he was a considerable wit. Above all, and apart from his real services to the nation in 1940, this may explain his lasting appeal: he was for decades a larger-than-life public personality, a lovable rogue who made no attempt to disguise his ambition and his egocentricity. Since 1965, many British politicians have tried to associate themselves with Churchill's memory and quoted his words, but none has been thought to measure up to the man universally regarded in his last quarter-century as 'the greatest living Englishman'. *JAR*

RANDOLPH CHURCHILL and MARTIN GILBERT, *Winston S. Churchill*, 8 vols. (London, 1966–88). | NORMAN ROSE, *Churchill: An Unruly Life* (London, 1994).

Churchill, Winston, **and Secret Intelligence.** As home secretary from 1910, Churchill helped establish the Secret Service Bureau and encouraged its development. When war began in 1914, Churchill, as first lord of the Admiralty, chartered room 40, the navy's code-breaking and interpretive centre, but in 1915 the failure of his plan to force the Dardanelles cost him his job. Churchill blamed the Bolshevik revolution and the failure to win the civil war in Ireland on bad intelligence, and when the Great War ended he tried to ensure that Britain retained a strong intelligence capability. His interest in intelligence matters was enduring during the inter-war years, despite being party to the blundering revelation that Britain could read Russian codes, and whether in office or out he received regular intelligence analysis and briefings. When Churchill became prime minister in 1940 he found British intelligence in disarray. He restructured the organization, bringing it firmly under political control. He had the luck to come to power as the first enigma code was cracked, and he made the development of code-breaking at Bletchley Park a top priority. Bletchley Park in turn provided him with vital strategic intelligence, precious chips to bargain with Roosevelt and Stalin. *PM*

David Stafford, *Churchill and Secret Intelligence* (London, 1997).

Churt, Surrey, the home of David Lloyd George, 1921–45, was effectively the power base for the Lloyd George wing of the Liberal Party. *JS*

Chuter Ede, James **(1882–1965)**, Labour politician. Chuter Ede began a varied political life in the Liberal Party but by the 1920s had become a Labour man, serving the party faithfully and sensibly for more than 40 years. He held various public offices, both local and national, representing the parliamentary seats of Mitcham, Surrey, 1923, and South Shields, 1929–31 and 1935–65. He sprang to national prominence when in 1944, as parliamentary secretary to the Board of Education, he guided R. A. Butler's Education Act through the Commons. The high point of his career was reached in 1945 when he became home secretary, an office he held throughout the two post-war Labour administrations, 1945–51, making him the longest-serving home secretary since 1832. As home secretary he mostly displayed a common-sense touch but was neither sentimental nor soft. However, controversy over the issue of crime plagued him just as it has plagued every home secretary since. Chuter Ede framed the 1947 Criminal Justice Bill and was, at this stage, a staunch supporter of the death penalty. The bill had a rocky passage, and he was much criticized. He had wanted the capital penalty to be maintained but, in the end, had to accept the principle of each case being assessed on its merits. There was to be further embarrassment on the capital punishment issue, when Timothy Evans, whom Chuter Ede decided not to reprieve, was hanged. In later life, as a remorseful elder statesman, Chuter Ede softened his views on hanging and sponsored a bill to have Evans's remains transferred to the next of kin. Chuter Ede was also an accomplished leader of the Commons for seven months in 1951. He remained active in Surrey politics throughout his years of national standing. Following his death, Chuter Ede was described in *The Times* as 'one of the most sensible politicians of his generation'. His wartime diary is an important historical source. *DMM*

Kevin Jefferys (ed.), *Labour and the Wartime Coalition, from the Diaries of James Chuter Ede* (London, 1987).

Citizens' Advice Bureaux, a voluntary service supported by private donations and local government grants, seeking to give advice and information on consumer affairs and legal matters. There are over 700 Citizens' Advice Bureaux, manned by volunteers, and coordinated by a national association. *JS*

Citizen's Charter **(1991)**, personal crusade of John Major's, designed to transform both the quality and the culture of state-delivered public services, and to change 'the public face of the Conservative Party, as not caring about improving the public sector', according to an unusually passionate chapter ('Raising the Standard') in his *Autobiography*. Building on his 1989 speech to the Audit Commission as chief secretary to the Treasury, his Number Ten policy unit developed a programme whereby greater transparency, performance indicators, and the primacy of improved customer care would be applied across a whole range of public services including the NHS and transport. Major threw a great deal of his personal credit into pushing his new chartism which, he said, required the unique influence of Number Ten 'to shift reluctant colleagues, officials and state agencies'. It formed a central plank in his 1992 election campaign. He had originally wished to call it 'the People's Charter' but was persuaded by officials that this would lay a serious enterprise open to mockery. Though carefully designed to make sure charter requirements were not justiciable in the courts, and somewhat open to derision (the motorway 'cones hotline' entered the stock of standard national humour), by the time the Major government fell in 1997, 42 national charters and some 10,000 local ones were in existence. Major's chartism was central to his attempts to humanize Margaret Thatcher's legacy through a softening of ideology and a re-emphasis on what he called the 'compassion ... [which] ... the best of the Conservative Party has long lived by', underpinned by his own memory of the degree to which 'my family had depended on public services'. *PJH*

The Citizen's Charter: Raising the Standard (Cm 1599, London, 1991). | SARAH HOGG and JONATHAN HILL, *Too Close to Call: John Major in No. 10* (London, 1995). | JOHN MAJOR, *The Autobiography* (London, 1999).

Citrine, Walter (1887–1983), trade unionist, and general secretary of the TUC, 1925–46. Citrine was only 40 when he replaced Fred Bramley as general secretary in 1925. He was essentially an administrator and bureaucrat who viewed a possible confrontation with the coal owners, the most pressing industrial problem he faced when he took office, as a trial of strength and organization rather than a struggle for political power. His memorandum on the possibility of a general strike was thus a blueprint for TUC involvement of only a limited nature. Though he felt outmanoeuvred by Baldwin during the General Strike itself, he was also worried by the political implications of syndicalism during the strike and this hardened his already well-developed anti-communism. He greeted the end of the strike with relief. In the decade which followed, Citrine, in alliance with Ernest Bevin's Transport and General Workers' Union, kept the industrial wing of the Labour movement loyal to the Labour Party and parliamentary democracy during the Great Depression and a polarized international situation. He warned local trades councils not to take part in the hunger marches organized by the National Unemployed Workers' Movement from the late 1920s onwards. In the later 1930s, he supported calls for rearmament and Churchill offered him a post in the wartime coalition, but he refused and spent the war at the TUC. Though always loyal to the Labour Party and having helped ensure that Labour stayed democratic before the war, he was also a pioneer of a tripartist approach to industrial problems and he worked to position the TUC so that all governments would have to deal with it, an ambition that began to be fulfilled during the wartime coalition. After the war he worked in the nationalized sector, as chairman of the Central Electricity Authority, 1947–57. Citrine was the closest that one individual could come to being the personification of the collectivist age. His career, as trade unionist, democrat, anti-communist, and industrial bureaucrat, exemplified the mixed economy-corporatist 'consensus' created by the Attlee settlement and his performance in his various jobs reflected this. At the TUC he was used to getting his own way and ran the organization with a gentle authoritarianism. He found the nationalized industries and the managers from the old private companies much more difficult to deal with and was less successful in that phase of his career. *BB*

LORD CITRINE, *Men and Work* (London, 1964). | LORD CITRINE, *Two Careers* (London, 1967).

City of London, the UK financial services centre. The City, administered by the ancient Corporation of the City of London, covers 1 square mile (2.59 km^2) of the heart of the London business community, situated between EC1 and EC4. At the end of the 20th century its resident population consisted of just over 5,000 inhabitants, whilst more than 300,000 people came to work every day in its stockbroking and financial institutions. The corporation fulfils the same function as a London borough council in addition to exercising its historical powers, for example, to control all animal imports into Greater London and the running of the central criminal court (the 'Old Bailey'). The ruling body is the court of common council, which consists of the lord mayor and two sheriffs elected annually by a court of 25 aldermen and 130 common councilmen, who are themselves elected by occupiers and residents in the City's 25 wards. In the City, the lord mayor ranks immediately below the sovereign and acts as the capital's host in Guildhall and the Mansion House, his official residences. On behalf of the City he carries out engagements at home and abroad. The multitude of guild associations representing their respective trade and crafts which had flourished all over Europe for centuries are known in the City as the Livery, and are unique for their survival and diversity. These institutions are not simply archaic and picturesque leftovers of history but living organizations whose liverymen carry out important functions relating to the election of the government in the City and certain of its officers. The Livery has a long history of tradition, investments, lands, substantial charitable funds, and records which members are determined should continue. They support trade in a statutory or regulatory way by providing finance. As the financial centre of the country, the City of

London is one of Britain's most controversial institutions. It has operated for most of the 20th century as the world's leading financial centre in commodities, shipping, and insurance, a position derived from Britain's economic supremacy during the 19th century. Very close links have been forged with Westminster, which made the City a persuasive advocate of policies such as the return to the *gold standard after the Great War. At that time, its political influence over the government's management of the economy was substantial, a position which has become gradually eroded. Interpretations of the City's financial role vary from that of a national asset unrivalled anywhere else in the world to a sinister conclave of the high priests of finance whose policies have had an adverse effect on Britain's manufacturing economy. The City's overriding desire to maintain the strength and stability of sterling has, according to the latter school of thought, been responsible for inhibiting Britain's economic growth. The politics of the City of London tended to reflect the collective consciousness of the groups which operate within its confines rather than represent the dominating views of any single individual. *JFM*

David Kynaston, *The City of London* (London, 2001).

City of London bombing (24 April 1993), when the Provisional IRA exploded a 1-ton (1.02-tonne) bomb at Bishopsgate in London. One person was killed and over thirty were injured. It caused huge devastation among the buildings in the financial centre of the City. Damage was estimated at upwards of £1 billion. This included buildings, housing, and foreign and domestic finance groups such as Nat West bank, Hong Kong and Shanghai bank, Barclays bank, and Abu Dhabi investment bank. *TWH*

civil aviation. During the inter-war period, British civil aviation was characterized by excessive competition and lower subsidies than, for example, Germany or Holland. Initial government resistance to any subsidy ended when the fledgling British operators faced collapse in 1921. The creation of subsidized private monopolies in the form of Imperial Airways and British Airways helped reduce competition, but during the 1930s the Air Ministry's Civil Aviation Department (established in 1919) came under increasing criticism, in particular from the Maybury committee (1937) and Cadman committee (1938). In 1937 some of the department's functions were transferred to the Air Registration Board. In 1938, the Air Transport Licensing Authority was established to control competition, and the following year legislation was passed to establish the state-owned British Overseas Airways Corporation (BOAC). A Ministry of Civil Aviation was set up in 1945, and British European Airways and British South American Airways were established as public corporations in 1946 (the latter soon merging with BOAC). From the late 1960s, the state has taken a more arm's-length role in civil aviation. In 1967 the Ministry of Aviation (responsible for civil aviation since 1959) was wound up and, following the Edwards committee's report of 1969, the task of promoting and regulating civil aviation was handed to the Civil Aviation Authority, a quasi-independent body which acquired greater autonomy after 1980. British Airways was privatized in 1987, as was the British Airports Authority, and at the end of the century air traffic control seemed likely to follow. *CL*

Civil Aviation Authority (CAA), set up in 1972, absorbing part of the work of the former Ministry of Civil Aviation. Its main responsibilities include air safety, economic regulation, and consumer protection. The CAA also advises the government on aviation issues and conducts economic and scientific research, as well as representing consumer interests. *JD*

Civil Aviation website: *www.caa.co.uk*

civil defence. Civil defence had little relevance in Britain for much of the 19th century when her maritime supremacy meant that wars posed little direct threat to the domestic population. The development of 20th-century air power added a completely new dimension, realized for the first time in the Great War, by subjecting the civilian population to the threat of aerial bombardment and making some kind of civil defence structure necessary. Between December 1914 and June 1918 there were 106 attacks on Britain by German Zeppelins and *Gotha* bombers. The heaviest raid was in June 1917, when fourteen *Gotha* GIVs bombed London in broad daylight, causing 594 casualties, including 162 killed. This also brought a call for adequate civil defence. By the end of 1917, there was a sophisticated anti-aircraft defence for the London area, consisting of fighters, anti-aircraft guns, and balloons, coordinated from a headquarters in the Horse Guards.

The emphasis in 1914–18 was on deterring or shooting down enemy raiders rather than providing protection to civilians on the ground. Nonetheless with the cessation of hostilities it was increasingly recognized that in any future conflict considerable attention would have to be devoted to civil defence, especially given the prevailing military doctrine that 'the *bomber will always get through'. During the 1930s these fears were emphasized by the bombing of civilian targets in China, Abyssinia (now Ethiopia), and Spain, and by the added threat of the use of poison gas. As a result, in the 1930s Britain introduced air raid precautions (ARP) which included leaflets on dealing with blast and incendiary bombs and the issue of gas masks to the whole of the population. On the eve of the Second World War civil defence entailed the organization of the hospital and fire services into a unified national scheme, the provision of area and domestic shelters, and a system of ARP wardens responsible for enforcing a 'blackout' and providing services following raids.

This system, tested during the *Blitz on London and other major cities, was seen to demonstrate the utility of an organized system of civil defence, capable also of dealing with the new possibility of nuclear war. The Civil Defence Act of 1948 set up a volunteer Civil Defence Corps to provide rescue and welfare services in the event of attack. The corps was organized on a regional basis under the director-general of civil defence appointed by and responsible to the home secretary. In 1958 the Civil Defence Corps totalled 359,000 men and women with an additional 294,000 in the Industrial Civil Defence Service and auxiliary Fire and Hospital Services. The Civil Defence Corps was dismantled in the 1960s as nuclear tensions eased after the Cuban missile crisis of 1962. Although it had loyal support from those who saw it as an essential part of national defence, it was also criticized by those opposed to nuclear weapons on the grounds that civil defence was an illusion against nuclear attack and lulled the population into a false sense of security, believing that nuclear war would be simply 'the Blitz plus radioactivity'. Thereafter the civil defence system against nuclear attack rested upon the emergency plans prepared by local government and the public services. A UK Warning and Monitoring Organization was responsible for public warning of nuclear attack, estimating the location and strength of nuclear explosions, and the distribution and level of radioactive fallout. Apart from shelters for essential local authority personnel, the official policy for the general population was to 'stay-put', evacuation being seen as impracticable and the provision of shelters for the estimated 20–40 million at risk from a limited nuclear attack too expensive. In 1983 civil defence regulations required local authorities to make and keep up-to-date plans for a range of essential functions in the event of war, while expenditure under Thatcher rose steadily to £80 million in 1985–6.

As in the 1950s and 1960s, some political capital was made in the 1980s by anti-nuclear groups such as the Campaign for Nuclear Disarmament which argued that the inadequacy of any civil defence against nuclear weapons implied that Britain should give up its nuclear weapons and its role within NATO. The issue was often reinforced by depictions of the aftermath of nuclear attack, such as the banned Peter Watkins's documentary film *The War Game* and the BBC drama of the 1980s *Threads*. Even the government pamphlet *Protect and Survive* fanned the flames of debate by presenting an optimistic view of the survivability of a nuclear attack. The ending of the Cold War took the political steam out of the civil defence issue. Such provision as exists still rests upon the emergency plans of local authorities and the public services. *JS*

civil liberties. These arise from the belief that certain freedoms are basic to the working of a free society, and essential to the health of society as a whole. They are usually enshrined in law, and encompass such freedoms as the right to free speech, free association, and justice. Successful movements claiming that civil liberties have been denied, such as the civil rights movement in the USA in the 1960s, have based much of their success on appeals to the law or the constitution. In the UK, the National Council for Civil Liberties is an unofficial organization that keeps a watching brief on the actions of government and the law enforcement agencies; it was amongst the leading critics of the government of Northern Ireland in the 1930s. The term has also been extended to other liberties besides the legal and constitutional. L. T. *Hobhouse in 1911 defined liberties in wider social and economic terms, arguing that the citizen had the right to better opportunities in life. He based this on the idea of civil liberties as implying and requiring constraint: law was essential to liberty. But he argued that this constraint should also be applied to individuals whose desire it is to accumulate wealth and property. The notion that each man should have his own must be tempered by the acknowledgement that other members of society had a hand in producing that wealth, and enabling the acquisition of that property: 'At bottom it is the same conception of liberty and the same conception of the common will that prompts the regulation of industry and the severance of religious worship and doctrinal teaching from the mechanism of State control.' In recent British politics, the pursuit of this kind of civil liberty has led to a reaction against the consequences, which are the increasing power of the state over the individual. Government secrecy, restrictions, and controls are now seen as serious threats to the liberties of the citizen, and recent court cases, for example the *Birmingham Six and the *Guildford Four, have produced a scepticism about the belief that, in the UK, civil liberties are secure. It is likely that in the future, thanks to the UK parliament adopting the European Convention on *Human Rights and enshrining these rights into British law, the legal system will become much more rights-based, instead of one based on the securing of civil liberties in statute law and in certain Acts of Parliament (such as habeas corpus). However, it is also likely that the wider definition of civil liberties will be enhanced by this shift, and that Hobhouse's claim that liberty without equality was a name of noble sound but squalid result will take on a new lease of life. *DGB*

D. J. Manning, *Liberalism* (London, 1976). | K. R. Minogue, *The Liberal Mind* (London, 1963).

civil list, publicly funded royal finances. In the late 17th century, parliament determined to prevail in contests with the sovereign by taking over government finance. From this era parliament granted funds to the sovereign to pay for 'a list of civil charges', which over the next three centuries was gradually reduced to cover only those expenses necessary to carry out the duties of head of state. During the first half of the 20th century, parliament settled the amount of the civil list once and for all at the beginning of a new reign. Although this protected the dignity of the crown by preventing too many enquiries into private accounts, republican writers, like Philip Hall, have criticized this arrangement for surrounding royal finance with too much secrecy. Inflation in the late 1960s quickly rendered the civil list of Elizabeth II inadequate and her civil list settlement had to be reopened and increased repeatedly after 1972. From the 1990s, she gave up the concession whereby her private income was not taxed, in return for her relieving the civil list of a variety of charges and paying for these from her own resources. She lost the grace of the concession, however, as it occurred at a time of unpopularity following the fire at Windsor castle. Raising questions about royal finance has long been the most reliable way of arousing anti-monarchical feeling in Britain. *WMK*

Vernon Bogdanor, *The Monarchy and the Constitution* (Oxford, 1995). | Philip Hall, *Royal Fortune: Tax, Money and the Monarchy* (London, 1992).

Civil Research, Committee on, official committee appointed by the Treasury in 1925 and charged with investigating different aspects of non-military research. Reports compiled by its subcommittees included research into locusts (Cmd 3367), British Pharmacopoeia (Cmd 3101), the supply of radium (Cmd 3303), and the fishing industry 1929–30 (Cmd 3477), the last of which was chaired by Christopher Addison. Despite its grandiose all-embracing title, which implied it had been given a mandate to address research across a broad spectrum, its investigations were confined to a limited number of specialized areas. *JFM*

civil service. At the beginning of the 20th century the civil service as a profession and organization was highly fragmented and Balkanized: there were no standard pay scales or staff grading, and departmentalism ruled the day. In the aftermath of the Great War, under Warren Fisher as head of the civil service, a more homogeneous and efficient bureaucratic structure was developed, with service-wide classes (administrative, executive, and clerical) and greater central control and coordination by the Treasury. The scientific, technical, and professional classes were reorganized in the 1940s, and after the 1968 Fulton report 'specialist' and 'generalist' grades were unified at senior levels. The civil service was never monolithic, but from the 1920s to the 1970s it was a centrally managed and unified career service. The managerial reforms of the 1980s and 1990s, however ('next steps' executive agencies—employing three-quarters of all civil servants by 1997—'contracting-out', 'market-testing', the weakening of the Treasury's and the Cabinet Office's detailed control and supervision, and greater delegation to departments and agencies over pay, grading, and recruitment arrangements), put the clock back, recreating the old looser federation of different organizations and units. By the 1990s, it was argued, there was not one civil service, but a large number of separate civil services.

Data about the size of the civil service over time must be interpreted with caution because of changing official definitions and classifications. Nevertheless, the massive 20th-century expansion of government staff is clear: rising from 116,000 in 1901, to 172,000 in 1911, 317,000 in 1922, 387,000 in 1939, 740,000 in 1951, 643,000 in 1960, and 732,000 in 1979 (with totals swollen even higher during both world wars). Thatcher's determination to cut back on bureaucracy and waste saw numbers fall to 569,000 by 1989, and by 1997 the total was down to 472,000. Cuts have fallen disproportionately on the blue-collar industrial civil service which numbered over 300,000 in the 1950s, but was down to 180,000 by 1976 and only 34,000 in 1997. The service has also become geographically more dispersed: in 1931, 72 per cent of civil servants were based in London, but by the 1990s only 20 per cent. A 'two nations' civil service developed, with many younger and female staff concentrated in the lower grades and the giant 'clerical factories' of the big welfare state ministries, and a continuing strong 'Oxbridge' presence in the senior policy-making grades in Whitehall proper.

The power of the higher civil service and its role in the policy-making process has been a controversial issue. Some governments (Labour in 1964, the Conservatives in 1951 and in 1979) entered office suspicious of the civil service. From different ideological positions, left-wingers in the 1930s and 1960s/70s, and right-wing Conservatives and Thatcherites in the 1970s/80s, criticized civil service obstruction and sabotage of radical policies. In post-1945 consensus years, the civil service was a force for continuity. But ministers from all the main parties have generally established good working relations with their officials. The civil service and government departments have changed course when one party has taken over the reins of power from another. That successive governments have made major policy changes indicates either that civil servants have cooperated fully or that political will can in practice successfully overcome official resistance or sluggishness.

The long period of Conservative rule, 1979–97, put the established practices and conventions of government under considerable strain. The traditional 'departmental views' of the Whitehall ministries were overturned. Senior officials were put firmly in their (subordinate) constitutional place, and their role as managers of government services rather than as policy advisers was emphasized. There were allegations of the 'politicization' of the senior civil service or at least the emergence of a 'Conservative mind-set', and the devaluing or loss of Whitehall's ingrained 'institutionalized scepticism'. However, the successful transition to the new Labour administration in May 1997 showed the traditions of a permanent and impartial civil service remained deeply rooted.

The tradition of government secrecy was also remarkably durable throughout the century. The 'catch-all' 1911 Official Secrets Act reinforced the 'closed-government' culture of Whitehall insiders (ministers and officials). Pressure for more open government and for freedom of information reform built up from the 1960s. The Major government introduced a code of practice on release of Whitehall information in 1994 but only after 1997, with the Blair government, were plans introduced for full-scale *freedom of information reform of the sort seen in many other democracies around the world. *KT*

Peter Hennessy, *Whitehall* (London, 1989). | Kevin Theakston, *The Civil Service since 1945* (Oxford, 1995).

Civil Service Code (1996), the Major government's response to parliamentary dissatisfaction with the Armstrong memorandum of 1985, *The Duties and Responsibilities of Civil Servants in Relation to Ministers*, and following pressure from the top officials' trade union, the First Division Association. An obligation to observe it was accepted by Tony Blair and his incoming Labour ministers in 1997. A pre-election agreement between Labour and the Liberal Democrats to introduce 'a Civil Service Act to give legal force to the code's Report of the *Joint Consultative Committee on Constitutional Reform*, 1996, paragraph 84' was not fulfilled, however, in the early years of the Blair government. The twelve-point code required career civil servants to serve the 'duly constituted' government of the day 'with integrity, honesty, impartiality and objectivity'; advise ministers 'without fear or favour'; not to 'deceive or knowingly mislead Ministers, Parliament or the public'; keep ministerial confidences; avoid improper influences and the misuse of official information; treat the public sympathetically; disburse public money properly, efficiently, and effectively; comply with domestic and international law and treaty obligation; and uphold the administration of justice. If a civil servant believed he or she was being required 'to act in a way which is illegal, improper, or unethical; is in breach of constitutional conventions or a professional code; may involve possible maladministration', or was otherwise inconsistent with the code, they were to report the matter to their superiors. If satisfaction were not provided at departmental level or by the head of the home civil service, the affected official could report the matter in writing to the civil service commissioners who answer to the monarch, not to ministers (this final level of appeal outside the civil service loop is what particularly distinguished the code from the Armstrong memorandum). *PJH*

Civil Service Code (Cabinet Office, London, 1996). | PETER HENNESSY, *The Hidden Wiring* (London, 1995). | PETER HENNESSY, *Whitehall* (London, 1989).

Civil Service Commission and **Civil Service Selection Board**. After 1945, the Civil Service Commission (first appointed to oversee recruitment in 1892) organized a series of reconstruction competitions for admission to the administrative class. Intended to catch up on the cohorts of young men and women drawn into the armed services rather than the public service after 1939, a new method of recruitment was established alongside the written examinations that had been the staple of recruitment-on-merit since the 1870s. Based on the Second World War's War Office selection boards for officers, the new Civil Service Selection Board (CSSB, known as 'CIZBEE' to contrast it with the 'WOZBEES' of the War Office) relied upon a series of interviews, tests, and exercises to set alongside the intellectual calibre of the applicants as revealed in their university examination performances. The generation of senior civil servants 'for whom everything was possible', as one of their number, Ian Bancroft (later head of the home civil service), described them, who dominated the permanent secretaryships from the early 1970s until the late 1980s, was largely recruited by this so-called method II competition. Though the system had its critics, who claimed the CSSB allowed the existing senior civil service to select in its own image, it survived the century, in slightly modified form, as the chief supplier of the Whitehall mandarinate, the diplomatic service, and later the senior personnel of the secret services. *PJH*

PETER HENNESSY, *Whitehall* (London, 1989). | KEVIN THEAKSTON, *The Civil Service since 1945* (London, 1995).

Civil Service Department (CSD) (**1968–81**), set up following a recommendation of the *Fulton report as part of the overall drive to create better management of the civil service. The prime minister became minister for the civil service but day-to-day responsibility was handled by another minister. The new department took over the Treasury's pay and management group, along with the Civil Service Commission which attempted to ensure probity in public appointments. The CSD was involved in the Heath government's machinery of government reforms, having a role in the programme analysis and reviews and in the drafting of the 1970 *Reorganization of Central Government* white paper. The CSD's responsibilities meant it was also central to the civil service strikes in the 1970s and early 1980s. Almost thirteen years to the day after its creation, Margaret Thatcher abolished the department. Its staff and functions were scattered between the Treasury (which regained its manpower divisions) and the Cabinet Office which received the establishment duties (housed in its new management and personnel office). *JD*

PETER HENNESSY, *Whitehall* (London, 1989). | PETER KELLNER and LORD CROWTHER-HUNT, *The Civil Servants* (London, 1980).

civil service reforms (**1919**). See LLOYD GEORGE/BRADBURY/WARREN FISHER REFORMS.

Clarion movement. The Clarion movement began in December 1891 with the formation of the *Clarion* newspaper, a weekly journal produced in Manchester by the socialist journalist Robert *Blatchford. It was an unusual paper in that it combined explanations of the principles of socialism with a mixture of stories, poems, and humour, but was quickly taken up by socialist groups, particularly in Lancashire and the West Riding of Yorkshire, and thus became the focus of a movement which offered a cultural alternative to capitalist society. The movement was based upon fellowship and spawned many social groups and activities. Clarion glee clubs emerged in many areas of socialist activity, such as Keighley and Bradford, and there were Clarion bands and Clarion scouts, formed in 1894 by bodies of young socialist pioneers to spread the socialist message using leaflet raids by cyclists: they were encouraged to do so by the Clarion's supplementary sheet called 'Scout'. There were also Clarion camera clubs. In particular there were the Clarion man movement and the Clarion cyclists. Both organizations were committed to spreading the socialist gospel. Blatchford's book *Merrie England*, written under the pseudonym *Nunquam*, had sold many thousands of copies in the 1890s and early 20th century, offering explanations of socialism. Blatchford and Clarion took the message further by creating the Clarion van movement in 1896. Several horse-drawn vans, acting as speaker's platforms, were eventually in operation throughout England and Wales and in the early 20th century they were organized for many years by Edward Robertshaw Hartley, the famous Bradford socialist, and Gertrude Hartley, his daughter. It also attracted many prominent socialist speakers to its activities, most obviously Bruce Glasier. As for the Clarion cycling clubs, these partly emerged from the Clarion scouts and prospered in the first decade of the 20th century. Indeed, the *Clarion* advertised and offered cheap bicycle kits for sale which could be paid for in instalments; by 1910 about 10,000 had been sold. Clarion cycling club houses also appeared, and one survived on Otley Chevin, in Yorkshire, until the 1970s. In their heyday, during the early 20th century, the Clarion cyclists did immense propaganda work for the socialist movement and Philip Snowden, the first Labour chancellor of the exchequer, reflected in his *An Autobiography* the early days of the socialist movement when cyclists rode across Yorkshire and 'stuck on the backsides of cows posters proclaiming "Socialism the Hope of the World"'. Although the Clarion movement did survive the Great War, the zenith of its activity was between the 1890s and 1914. The war, the intense patriotism of Blatchford and his move to Conservatism, and the financial difficulties of the *Clarion* paper all undermined the influence of the movement. Like other cultural forms of socialism, the movement continued but was overtaken by the growth of the more overtly political activities of the movement and effectively faded into obscurity during the inter-war years. *KL*

Henry Pelling, *The Origins of the Labour Party* (London, 1954, and later edns.).

Clark, Alan Kenneth Mackenzie (1928–99), Conservative politician and walking controversy. Clark began as a controversial military historian, his *The Donkeys* (1961) partly inspiring *Oh What a Lovely War*. As a Conservative MP, 1974–92 and from 1997, and as a junior minister, he offended on race, referring to Africa as 'bongo-bongoland', and Europe, deliberately reading its regulations in the Commons in slow motion. An expansive millionaire, he sought office as an ultra-loyal Thatcherite, rising to be a useful minister of state, cynical and unfriendly to the military top brass. Mainly memorable for his published *Diaries* (2 vols., 1993 and 2000), important not for their omnipresent sexual obsessions, but as an immortal account of ambition, rivalry, enmity, ministerial preoccupations, and panic. *EP*

Clark, David George (1939–), Labour politician. A university politics lecturer, Clark was Labour MP for Colne Valley, 1966–70, and South Shields from 1979 to 2001. Shadow agriculture and defence spokesman under Kinnock, Smith, and Blair, he was chancellor of the duchy of Lancaster, 1997–8. He published white papers on freedom of information and better government but his efforts appear to have been frustrated by opponents in government and the civil service, and he was removed from office in the cabinet reshuffle of July 1998. *BJE*

Clark, William Donaldson (1916–85), prime minister's public relations adviser, 1955–6. A former diplomatic correspondent, Clark found his spell at Downing Street 'a story of disillusion' (Clark, 146). His relations with Eden, and Eden's with the press, were already declining when the Suez crisis broke. Subsequently, frustrated by his master's attacks on the press, and in particular the BBC, and unwilling to lie for the government, Clark began to doubt Eden's sanity and resigned when the ceasefire was announced. *CL*

William Clark, *From Three Worlds: Memoirs* (London, 1986).

Clarke, David Kenneth (1912–98), Conservative policy adviser. Clarke joined the Conservative Research Department in 1935 and following wartime work in government helped Henry Brooke to draft the 1945 manifesto. Afterwards he set up the parliamentary secretariat, to which he recruited Maudling, Macleod, and Powell. As director of the research department, 1945–51, he identified and developed the Conservative themes for the 1950s and beyond. He was principal of Swinton Conservative College, 1967–72. *RJS*

David Clarke, *The Conservative Faith in a Modern Age* (London, 1947).

Clarke, Kenneth (1940–), Conservative politician. The most effective Tory minister of recent years, Clarke was hated by anti-Europeans and his defeat for the leadership in 1997, despite large poll leads among the public and Conservative supporters, compared with Denis Healey's calamitous rejection by Labour in 1980. Son of a Nottinghamshire pit electrician turned shopkeeper, he passed through grammar school to Cambridge. At home as a whip under Heath, and candidly unattracted to Thatcherism, he was nevertheless unoverlookable, if his promotion slowed in her time. He was number two at transport, then health, before entering cabinet as paymaster general in 1984 where he worked surprisingly happily with David Young, his trade and industry chief in the Lords, among other things overlording the inner cities. As health secretary, Clarke succeeded anxious, imploded John Moore and showed opposite qualities, ignoring the scare of a possible nurses' strike from the Spanish mountain where he was birdwatching. Holding health in a period of Treasury stringency, he was reckoned to have got money for the NHS above expectation, while also annoying doctors and nurses. Refusing to serve further under her, during Margaret Thatcher's November 1990 ministerial consultation about her future, Clarke gave her a final nudge down the exit slide. After abrasive but inconclusive service at the Home Office, he became chancellor of the exchequer in 1993 after the devaluation of sterling, determined not to lose its competitive benefits. Confident in his own judgement that demand was already shattered, which was validated by later figures, he resisted all Bank of England pressure for deflationary interest rates, and was able to claim soaring exports, rising employment, and increased inward investment with only the mildest high street pressure. This did not offset the Major government's huge problems: Europe, the press, sleaze, and internal divisions. After 1997, in a small and more right-wing parliamentary party, despite an electoral deal with Redwood, he was defeated for the party leadership by Hague, remaining dominant in his party, more watched than written off. He was defeated again for leadership in 2001. *EP*

Malcolm Balen, *Kenneth Clarke* (London, 1994).

Clarke, Peter Frederick (1942–), historian. Clarke, professor of modern British history at Cambridge since 1991, is now master of Trinity Hall, Cambridge, and a fellow of the British Academy. Educated at Eastbourne grammar school and St John's, Clarke announced his arrival as a revisionist historian with *Lancashire and the New Liberalism* (1971), arguing that the pre-1914 Liberal Party, far from being in decline, was robust and adept at devising new policies, outstripping Labour in accruing working-class support. Subsequently, his major works were *Labour and Social Democrats* (1978) in which he traced the mutual influences and tensions in the crucial relationship between Liberal thinkers and Labour politicians in the early decades of the century, and *The Keynesian Revolution in the Making* (1988), which outlined in detail how Keynes was constrained by the political context in which he operated. Both that book and *The Keynesian Revolution and its Economic Consequences* (1998) were inspired by the way in which post-1979 Conservatism had undermined previous assumptions about the inevitability of Keynesian policies in a democracy. In *Hope and Glory: Britain 1900–1999* (1996) he ended his survey by regretting that Britain had missed the European bus. *PS*

Clarke, Richard William Barnes ('Otto') (1910–75), civil servant. Clarke was an unusual and controversial official, a man of strong character and views, and impatient with the traditional norms and style of the Whitehall mandarinate. A financial journalist and left-wing political activist in the 1930s, he entered the civil service as a wartime 'temporary' in 1939, joining the Treasury in 1945 where he was an active and influential figure in post-war economic policy making. Never exactly a 'safe pair of hands', Clarke was a forceful and innovative administrative entrepreneur. His great achievement was as the main architect of and the driving force behind the adoption of the public expenditure survey system (known as PESC in Whitehall—see Plowden report (1962) and Public Expenditure Survey (1959)) developed in the 1960s to plan and control government spending. He was perhaps less successful in the role of pulling together and running the giant Ministry of Technology, where he was permanent secretary, 1966–70. *KT*

Clark-Kerr, Archibald. See Inverchapel, Lord.

class-consciousness, the awareness of a collective self-interest shared with other members of the same social class. In Marxist thinking, the processes of capitalist industrialization inevitably sharpened social differences and produced classes whose economic interests clashed, and who would therefore move into class conflict, in the end to a class war in which the numbers of the working class must triumph. In practice, however, the class system in industrial and post-industrial societies like Britain was never so monolithic or so naturally conflictive. The middle class contained humanitarian reformers motivated by religion or ideology to act and vote against their own economic interests, and the working class included millions who were either natural individualists—and therefore did not feel much solidarity with other workers—or whose deference to the elite made them likely to choose the 'wrong' side in any conflict or voter-choice. At the borders between the social classes, there were in any case significant groups whose marginal status encouraged them to think in terms of mobility rather than class stasis: a lower middle-class clerk might be extremely conscious of the possibility of sinking to the level of the workers, while a well-paid skilled worker could entertain aspirations towards middle-class status, lifestyle, and gentility—for example, through *home-ownership. Nevertheless, there was a broad trend towards greater class-consciousness in the late 19th century, hard to measure with any exactitude but much remarked on by contemporaries, and this process helped to produce a political labour movement, the Labour Party of the 1900s.

Class-consciousness probably reached its peak in the middle years of the 20th century, as did *class voting, and was thereafter eroded by geographical mobility (moving town or region in search of employment would undermine social continuities), by growing overall affluence (which made ownership of 'status symbols' like cars and homes widely available across different social groups), by increasing educational opportunity (eroding geographical, employment, and attitudinal continuities across generations), and by the increasingly homogenous national culture of a television and internet system of communications. It would be foolish to suggest that class differentials and consciousness of them no longer existed at the end of the century, but there is also no doubt that they played a much lesser part in British people's lives and attitudes than over the previous 200 years. *JAR*

class-voting could only develop in Britain with the arrival of Labour as a party appealing especially (though even then far from exclusively) to working-class voters, who predominated in the British electorate after the 1884 Reform Act, and dominated it from 1918. Even before Labour's arrival, there had been a tendency from the 1880s for middle-class voters to drift to the Conservatives, and for the Liberals to seek compensation in the working-class vote. Indeed, much of the debate amongst historians of the Edwardian period, on the question of whether the Liberals could have survived as a governing party, revolves around the evidence of the Liberals' success in holding on to working-class votes in industrial areas like Lancashire (both sides in the debate apparently conceding that the middle class was by then flocking to the Tories). This is in the end a sterile debate, for unless there had been an open contest between Labour and the Liberals in industrial seats, which took place only in 1911–14 by-elections, there could be no unequivocal evidence about their relative appeal to the voters. In due course, the Great War and the *Representation of the People Act, 1918, provided Labour with the chance to overtake the Liberals by the early 1920s anyway, though once again historians have placed considerable emphasis on the additional working-class voters enfranchised in 1918 as a major explanation of this leap forwards.

Politics between the wars were thus more class-based than Britain had ever seen before, with the Conservatives apparently winning most middle-class votes and Labour a large share of working-class support; the Liberals, anchored in neither class, went into steep decline. We have to say that this is apparent rather than definite, for between the end of open voting after the 1872 Ballot Act and the advent of effective opinion polls in the 1940s, there is no hard evidence at all as to how any British people actually voted. What is quite certain is that the Tories won almost all of the most-middle class constituencies—better-off suburbs, seaside resorts, cathedral towns, and the like—while Labour had an equal sway in the inner cities (except where there were lots of middle-class *business voters) and mining and heavy industrial seats. Much of the political rhetoric of the time bewailed this polarization of the nation, blaming it on Labour's class appeal and the inevitable middle-class reaction to it, though Labour was in fact striving extremely hard (its own left-wingers said much too hard) to court the middle-class vote too, and to appeal as a 'national' party. There were some voices raised in the other direction, however, notably Stanley Baldwin, who remarked cuttingly that the middle class had no legitimate reason to complain about the class war, for they had started it themselves.

Labour's breakthrough to majority government in 1945, though it included improbable victories in middle-class constituencies like Dover, Wimbledon, and Winchester, was actually most significant for the fact that it took for the first time a majority of working-class votes. For whereas the suburbs returned to the Conservatives in 1950, Labour held its working-class majority without interruption for the next thirty years. The 1950s, for which clear polling and other survey evidence existed, were indeed the pinnacle of class voting in Britain: about four of every five middle-class voters went to the Conservatives, and about two of every three workers for Labour. The exceptions to this latter group, the 'working-class Tories', were the subject of exhaustive academic analysis: the size of the actual classes was so disparate, the middle class constituting only a third of the total electorate, that these working-class Tories were obviously the core explanation of the Conservatives' current success in 1951–64, and indeed of their survival as a party at all. Even with these exceptions though, class was clearly the overwhelming explanation of British political loyalties at this time. Peter Pulzer wrote that 'class is the basis of British party politics; all else is embellishment and detail'

(*Political Representation and Elections* (London, 1967), 98).

However, even as serious research took place, the pattern was changing. In 1959, and again in 1970, the Conservatives appeared to have improved their position by winning more votes cast by skilled workers, especially in the Midlands and South, though in between these victories Labour won two elections anyway. In 1974, the very fact that the Liberals and the nationalist parties in Scotland and Wales did so well (as 'non-class' parties) both reflected and in part explained a decline in class voting. Thereafter, the link of class and party allegiance 'dealigned', if rather unsteadily and discontinuously. The Conservatives took more working-class votes than Labour in 1983, mainly by winning over what Ivor *Crewe and others designated the 'new working class' (mainly in the South, working in the private sector, not members of trade unions, and owning their home). By then, in any case, de-industrialization was causing a sharp rebalancing of the classes themselves, with the middle class (if defined in the usual way as those in 'non-manual' work) moving steadily up to become a majority of all voters in the 1990s.

Those 1990s middle-class voters included, though, many whose fathers had been industrial workers, who still enjoyed aspects of the working-class lifestyle, and who in effect diluted the middle class by joining it, rather than being absorbed into and acquiring traditional middle-class loyalties. With the steadily increasing size of the social group that had provided their best support in the past, the Conservatives in 1979–92 actually did less well electorally than they 'should' have done (a fact largely disguised by the fact that they won four successive elections anyway). There was now a detectable Liberal class-vote, among public sector professional workers like teachers and doctors, while in 1997, Blair's Labour Party for the first time won more of the votes of the middle class than the Tories. By the 1990s too, the centre parties and nationalists were again present in sufficient overall numbers, with appeals that explicitly denied the centrality of class in politics, to erode further class itself as a correlation with voting. At the end of the century then, though there remained a lot of voters whose loyalty to class and party was intact, enough had become de-aligned from the traditional class–party link to make British elections considerably more volatile, unpredictable, and fragmented in their probable outcome. The disciplined class-voting battalions of the 1950s were no more. *JAR*

Jean Blondel, *Voters, Parties and Leaders* (London, 1963). | Anthony Heath, Roger Jowell, and John Curtice, *How Britain Votes* (Oxford, 1985). | R. T. McKenzie, *Angels in Marble* (London, 1968).

classical economics, a school of thought which dominated economic policy and thinking between approximately 1750 and 1870, its most famous exponents being Adam Smith, David Ricardo, Thomas Robert Malthus, and John Stuart Mill. The term 'classical economics' is in fact a rather nebulous one, and there remains to this day significant debate over its meaning. Most definitions of the term, however, stress the school's intellectual indebtedness to Adam Smith. To a large extent, then, the classical analytical system can be seen to have been erected upon Smith's equilibrium of supply and demand in competitive markets and on the labour theory of value. Furthermore, by accepting the Smithian notion of natural liberty, most classical economists also advocated freedom of action for business, small government, free trade, and the free movement of capital and labour. The main objective of classical economics was to explain the nature and causes of national wealth, and how that wealth was divided among the different sectors of society. Such an analysis was invariably carried out within the framework of a growing population, finite resources, and a free market. In terms of wealth generation, classical economics laid emphasis upon capital accumulation, market expansion, and the division of labour. In terms of distribution, it placed stress upon the costs of production. Prices were determined by the amount of labour embodied in the goods, rent by the scarcity and differential fertility of land in use, and wages by the cost of the means of subsistence. Profit was simply a residual. Another central feature of classical thought was the 'iron law of wages', which held that there was a natural tendency for population growth to force wages down to the subsistence level. The chief weakness of the classical approach was its inadequate treatment of aggregate demand and investment, detailed analysis of which really awaited the work of *Keynes. While few 20th-century economists have identified themselves with classical economics, the school has nevertheless remained influential. As their chosen names indicate, two prominent modern schools of economic thought—the neoclassical and new classical—see their intellectual lineage in classical economics. These modern schools accept the basic economic framework and policy prescriptions of the classical model. They differ first in their focus on the allocation of resources within a static economy, rather than on the long-run development of the economy as a whole; secondly, in their replacement of the labour theory of value with a subjective theory of prices; and thirdly in their acceptance of a marginal productivity theory of distribution in place of the classical school's socially determined income distribution. These differences, however, should be seen more as extensions and improvements to, rather than total rejections of, the classical framework. Indeed, if anything, interest in classical economics has intensified in recent years, as debate over the relationship between population, resources, capital accumulation, and economic growth—one of the great themes of classical economics—has once again come to the fore. *GBM*

Denis O'Brien, *The Classical Economists* (London, 1975).

Clause 4, part of Labour's constitution, symbolizing the socialist basis of the party. The Labour Party was dominated by Liberal radicalism until 1918, when Clause 4 of the new constitution committed the party to 'the public ownership of the means of production'. Although this appeared to commit Labour to a socialist basis it was not in fact Clause 4 which was important but the redistribution of power within the party in favour of the trade unions. Nevertheless, it assumed almost mythical significance, providing a vision of the future which appeared to be on the brink of fulfilment with the Labour government's nationalization programme, 1945–50. Clause 4 went unchallenged until, in response to three successive election defeats, Hugh Gaitskell unsuccessfully attempted to persuade the party conference to abandon it in 1959. Although Labour won further elections in the 1960s and 1970s, its electoral appeal was clearly declining. Revisionists felt that Clause 4 and nationalization were relics of a bygone age, vote-losers in the age of the 'affluent worker' but the left came to dominate the party, and the 1973 conference committed it to a substantial extension of public ownership. Many of the revisionists resigned to form the Social Democratic Party in 1981, but the electoral disasters of the 1980s caused a shift back to the centre, and in his first conference speech as party leader in 1994 Tony Blair signalled his intention to jettison Clause 4, regarding this as an important symbol of the party's modernization. A special conference in April 1995 finally buried the socialist myth, as 'New Labour' announced its intention to reform rather than transform society, to build an inclusive community based upon vague ethical values rather than a state socialist society. This pragmatic rather than ideological approach helped Labour to landslide electoral victories in 1997 and 2001. *MC*

Clay Cross, a Labour council that refused to implement the Housing Finance Act (HFA) of 1972. The eleven Labour councillors refused to raise municipal rents, as decreed by the HFA, and were surcharged and disqualified from office in 1973. Clay Cross looked back to the Poplarism of the 1920s as an example of municipal defiance to central government, and inspired Liverpool's Labour council in its confrontation with the Thatcher government during 1984–5 over rate-capping. *DLM*

David Skinner and Julia Langdon, *The Story of Clay Cross* (Nottingham, 1974).

Clean Air Act, 1956, the first major piece of legislation to control air pollution. Coming fully into force in June 1958, it made it an offence to emit 'dark smoke' or to fail to provide industrial premises with equipment to arrest grit and dirt, and empowered local authorities, subject to ministerial approval, to designate 'smoke control areas'. It came as a response to growing concern about the health risks associated with air pollution, highlighted by a series of severe London smogs in the early 1950s which had killed several thousand people. London had declared its first 'smokeless zone' in March 1955, coming into effect from October of that year. *JS*

Cledwyn, Lord, See Hughes, Cledwyn.

Clegg awards (1979–80). The leading member of the Oxford 'school' of industrial relations, Hugh Clegg (1920–95) was appointed in 1979 chair of a standing commission on pay comparability, after major public service disputes. Thatcher pledged to respect the awards in the 1979 election campaign and they therefore substantially increased public sector pay costs. A 20–5 per cent pay rise for teachers recommended in April 1980 was the last straw for the Thatcher government and the commission was then dissolved. *WG*

Clitheroe, Lord. See Assheton, Ralph Cockayne.

Cliveden set, phrase coined by left-wing journalist Claud Cockburn who alleged that leading politicians convened at Cliveden House, home of Waldorf and Nancy Astor, to pull strings generally, and especially to devise means of appeasing Nazi Germany. Although subsequently acknowledged as a myth, it entered the popular anti-appeasement vocabulary of the period. The Cliveden gatherings actually represented the diminishing 19th-century phenomenon of the political house party where sumptuous hospitality was mixed with opportunities to discuss politics but not to settle affairs of state. A later Lord Astor brought Cliveden back into public consciousness through its association with the Profumo scandal. *NJC*

NORMAN ROSE, *The Cliveden Set* (London, 2000).

Clore, Charles (1904–79), the epitome of the post-war tycoon, in the forefront of introducing the corporate takeover to Britain. He had started acquiring property before the Second World War and during the war built premises for government. His Sears Holdings Ltd. controlled a number of companies, particularly in retailing, with the most important single element being the British Shoe Corporation. Clore was an expansionist, profit-making capitalist at a time when this was not fashionable. *WG*

CLPV. See CAMPAIGN FOR LABOUR PARTY VICTORY.

CLV. See CAMPAIGN FOR LABOUR VICTORY.

Clydesiders, militant trade union group based in Glasgow, 1915–19. The group developed from opposition to changes in working practices which had resulted from the mobilization of British industry for total war. Most importantly unapprenticed workers, including women, were drafted into the engineering and other industries. This dilution of traditional craft-based trade-union closed shops led to industrial unrest. The 1915 Munitions of War Act stemmed the worst of this, but small groups of workers could still have an impact. In Glasgow, a militant shop stewards' movement grew up and set up a Clyde Workers' Committee which organized a series of strikes which continued throughout the war. When the government closed their paper, the *Worker*, in March 1916, it also arrested six members of this committee and dispersed them around the country. After the Bolshevik revolution in 1917 the temper of the agitation became more extreme. In 1918 the Clydesiders declared the creation of a Workers and Soldiers Soviet, which was suppressed by the government. The committee then organized a '40-hour' strike in January–February 1919 which led to the deployment of troops (including tanks) and more arrests. The improving economic situation and the reality that there would be no world Bolshevik revolution led, though, to a change in the emphasis of the group. Its lasting impact was in the militant shop stewards' movement which grew out of the strikes and influenced industrial relations down to the 1980s, both in the Glasgow area and nationally. However, in terms of being the cradle of a British revolution, the Clydesiders failed. In syndicalist terms they did not win support from other trade unionists across the country and therefore could not launch a general strike, and in broader terms they lacked the stimulus of military defeat or prolonged economic depression for their revolutionary aims to reach fruition. When Glasgow swung decisively to Labour in the 1922 general election, its slate of Labour MPs (including many who had been active industrially in the earlier disputes) proclaimed themselves 'the Clydesiders' (see also 'RED CLY-DESIDE'). *BB*

KEITH MIDDLEMAS, *The Clydesiders* (London, 1965).

Clynes, John Robert (1869–1949), trade unionist and Labour politician. J. R. Clynes was drawn to the cause of the underprivileged at an early age, contributing articles to the local Lancashire press on labour issues. He began his political career as district organizer for the National Union of Gasworkers and General Labourers in 1891 and was elected to parliament in 1906 as Labour MP for the North-East division of Manchester. Lloyd George brought him into government as minister for food control, 1917–18, and he was reluctant to leave when Labour resigned its ministerial posts in 1918. Having served briefly as party leader in 1921–2, Clynes was lord privy seal in 1924, but achieved his highest office in 1929–31 as home secretary. He refused the opportunity to resume the leadership of the party in 1931 and then lost his seat in the general election (but returned as MP, 1935–45). Generally respected for his moderation, humour, and reasonableness, Clynes was a widely liked member of the Labour Party and movement. *DWM*

J. R. CLYNES, *Memoirs*, 2 vols. (London, 1937). | J. R. CLYNES, *When I Remember* (London, 1940).

CND. See CAMPAIGN FOR NUCLEAR DISARMAMENT.

coal industry, one of an interrelated group of staple trades which propelled the expansion of the British industrial economy in the 19th and early 20th centuries. Though catering originally for the domestic market, by 1914 a third of total output was being exported. The industry's affairs rose to prominence over the divide of the Great War as a result of deteriorating labour relations, the product of the miners' desire for national wage bargaining and the determination of colliery owners to sustain decentralized wage settlements. The issue reached its climax in 1926 in the General Strike and miners' lockout, when the miners were forced to accept significant wage reductions in the face of a major contraction in trade. The industry's failure to recover in the later 1920s precipitated a move towards cartelization which achieved statutory form in the *Coal Mines Act, 1930. This legislation also provided for the compulsory amalgamation of collieries in conformity with contemporary views on industrial organization. Thus, the coal industry entered the Second World War as one of the most tightly regulated of private sector industries. It was this factor, in combination with the wartime system of state control, which paved the way for nationalization in 1946, independent of the Labour Party's constitutional and ideological commitment to public ownership. For the advocates of nationalization their hope and expectation was that the establishment of the National Coal Board (NCB) would introduce a new era of peaceful labour relations and also the means to raise productivity in response to ongoing programmes of capital investment.

In the period to 1970, nationalization may be judged a qualified success: the prospect of a postwar coal shortage was progressively ameliorated and efficiency gains were cumulatively of a high order. The industry also coped extremely well with demand fluctuations. This was especially the case in the 1960s, when the labour force displayed considerable adaptability in response to the changing direction of fuel policy in favour of oil and nuclear power. The succeeding decades, however, were marked by deteriorating labour relations and mounting financial problems. In the later 1950s and 1960s, the NCB's investment and pricing strategies had been subject to the vagaries of macroeconomic policy priorities. As inflationary pressure mounted after 1970, labour unrest was precipitated by the restrictive effects of government incomes policies and a leftwards shift in the balance of union power. National strikes occurred in 1972 and 1974, the latter providing the occasion for a general election on the theme of 'who governs Britain?'. Following the election of the Thatcher government in 1979, a determination to contain both inflationary pressure and trade union power acted in concert with changing energy priorities to provoke further labour unrest. The national strike of 1984–5 was fought mainly over the issue of pit closures: the defeat of the miners paved the way for the rapid rundown of the industry after 1990 and its progressive privatization. *MWK*

William Ashworth, *The History of the British Coal Industry*, vol. 5. *1946–1982: The Nationalised Industry* (Oxford, 1986). | M. W. Kirby, *The British Coalmining Industry, 1870–1946: A Political and Economic History* (London, 1977). | Barry Supple, *The History of the British Coal Industry*, vol. 4. *1913–1946: The Political Economy of Decline* (Oxford, 1987).

coalitionism. Coalitions are formed when two or more political parties come together formally to create a multi-party government in which portfolios are usually shared between them. In recent years this process has become the focus of systematic and comparative study, using techniques such as game theory, bargaining theory, and rational choice theory. It is distinct from consociationalism, where multi-party government is guaranteed by specific constitutional arrangements. Coalitions have become the norm in multi-party political systems where the voting system routinely prevents single party control of the legislature. This has not been the case in the UK, where two-party politics has been the overwhelming state of affairs in the Westminster parliament (though not necessarily in other British assemblies). At Westminster, coalitions have come about mainly as expressions of national solidarity (1915, 1931, and 1940), notwithstanding the existence of a majority party. Conversely, the dynamics of two-party government in the UK have meant that on those rare occasions where a third party has held the balance of power, the result has been minority government, supported conditionally by one or more opposition parties, pending withdrawal of support at a more opportune time, rather than coalition (1974 and 1977–9, for example). Minority government, rather than coalition, has also been the norm in UK local government when there has been no overall control. However, the use of proportional representation for the Scottish and Welsh assemblies first elected in 1999 has created the context there for formal coalitionism. In contrast, the arrangements in the Northern Ireland Assembly are consociational. *CPS*

David Butler (ed.), *Coalitions in British Politics* (London, 1978).

Coalition Liberals. See National (Lloyd George) Liberal Party (1918–22).

Coal Mines Act, 1930. The Act established a cartel system based upon the principal coalfields and provided also for measures of compulsory amalgamation of collieries. The cartel system was progressively refined and was instrumental in stabilizing prices in a declining market for coal. Drafting deficiencies in the original legislation, however, pre-empted compulsory amalgamations. The Act was representative of a general trend towards state intervention in industry and provided the framework for the wartime regulation of the coal industry after 1939.

MWK

Cockfield, (Francis) Arthur (1916–), tax expert and politician. A qualified barrister, Cockfield worked in the Inland Revenue from 1938 to 1952 before running the Boots Pure Drug Company during the 1960s. He held government posts under Heath and Thatcher, becoming a life peer in 1978. Appointed vice-president of the European Commission in 1985, Cockfield was supposed to guarantee the implementation of Thatcher's plans for the European single-market programme. Instead, he worked closely with the commission president, Delors, and famously fell out with Thatcher.

JRVE

Cod war, intermittent dispute between Iceland and the UK over fishing rights. The conflict began in 1953 when Iceland increased the extent of fishing limits in its coastal zone, in an attempt to replenish its depleted stocks of fish, principally cod. The effect was to undermine the British fishing industry, particularly in the north-east. At its worst, the dispute saw British frigates protecting British trawlers from Icelandic coastguard vessels.

JRVE

Cohen, Andrew (1909–68), colonial administrator. As head of the Colonial Office's Africa division in the late 1940s, Cohen was the driving force behind the policy of turning Britain's African colonies into self-governing nations. He was governor of Uganda, 1952–7; head of the department of technical co-operation, 1961–4; and permanent secretary of the Ministry of Overseas Development, 1964–8. A man of great dynamic enthusiasm, he was an intellectual elitist with a social conscience and a Fabian view of a dirigiste state.

KT

Cold War, state of international tension, 1945–89/91, in a bipolar system, in which the two superpowers, the USA and the Soviet Union, nevertheless avoided direct or 'hot war'. A short description fails to do justice to the complexity of the Cold War, and to the vast literature on it. Its main phases were 1945–55—dividing Germany, and bipolar institution-building; 1955–1963—discovering the 'rules of the Cold War game' especially in Berlin (see BERLIN CRISIS) and Cuba; 1963–78—détente; 1979–84—'Second' Cold War; 1985–9/91—end of the Cold War. Opinion is divided on the starting and ending dates: whether it began in Germany, and whether it ended in 1989, with the fall of the Berlin wall, or in 1991 with the collapse of the Soviet Union. The Cold War has influenced the domestic and international politics of every state since 1945; its principal features were bipolarity and alliance building, ideology, and weaponry.

A bipolar system emerged after the end of the Second World War. Institutionally, bipolarity was represented by the creation of the Organization for European Economic Cooperation (OEEC) to administer American Marshall aid to Western countries. In April 1949, the North Atlantic Treaty (see NATO) was signed between the USA, and Britain, France, Belgium, the Netherlands, Italy, Norway, Denmark, Iceland, Canada, and Portugal. Greece and Turkey joined in 1952, West Germany in 1955, and Spain in 1982. As the Berlin blockade of 1948–9 ended, the state of West Germany was created under Western tutelage. The Council of Europe came into being for democratic states in 1949. In the Eastern bloc, the Council for Mutual Economic Assistance (CMEA or COMECOM) was created in 1949, in response to the OEEC, between the USSR, Bulgaria, Czechoslovakia, Hungary, Poland, Romania, and later East Germany (Albania and three non-European communist states were members). The state of East Germany was also created in 1949, and the Warsaw Treaty Organization (WTO: USSR, Albania, Bulgaria, East Germany, Poland, Romania, Czechoslovakia) came into being in 1955, not least as a response to NATO's enlargement to include West Germany which the USSR had always resisted. Both superpowers found it hard to influence their allies' behaviour at all times.

The détente period from the mid-sixties to the late seventies was not the end of the Cold War, but witnessed greater levels of communication, with summits, superpower agreements on armaments, and the resolution of other issues of bipolar tension. Superpower détente was echoed in Europe, with national efforts, particularly with West Germany's Ostpolitik; and the beginning of the multilateral Conference on Security and Cooperation in Europe (See HELSINKI CONFERENCE/CSCE) process after 1972.

The institutionalization of the superpower blocs spread from Europe to the rest of the world, represented by pacts and alliances, informal coalitions, and hot wars. Intervention by both superpowers in nationalist and post-colonial conflicts also internationalized the impact of the bipolar conflict. Neither the non-aligned movement, nor neutrality options (for example, the Swiss, Swedish, Finnish, and Austrian models) were powerful enough to erode bipolarity.

The Cold War bipolar system had a strong ideological flavour, with roots in the Russian revolution. Despite debate over the extent to which ideology drove power-political considerations or was used as mask for power politics, the competing ideologies—communism/socialism versus capitalism/democracy—were very powerful. They represented collectivism versus individualism; the power of the state or the power of law; highly centralized market versus free market, and the rhetoric of Cold War politics was highly ideological. Both superpowers ensured that their dominant ideology was sustained by their key allies, with financial aid, propaganda, and through covert state agencies. Domestically, ideological dissidents received harsh treatment by the state (McCarthyism in the USA; repression of dissidents in the Soviet Union). Conflicts within both camps had ideological overtones (Soviet Union v. China; US support of neo-fascist regimes, particularly in South America). Ideology spilled into the ending of the Cold War, and Western efforts to reconstruct east-central Europe and the Soviet Union/Russia reflected the dominance of the Western, and particularly American, free market.

Weaponry, especially the nuclear technological revolution, reinforced the bipolar character of the Cold War. Superpower nuclear competition was intense, even when strategic arms limitation and non-proliferation talks were underway (NPT, SALT I, SALT II, START, INF). Nuclear weaponry was perceived to reflect the power and capability of its holders, even in space (Strategic Defense Initiative), despite its economic costs and destructive potential. It remains contentious whether the doctrine of nuclear deterrence actually prevented a direct superpower conflict.

Britain was a key player in the early Cold War. It helped successfully to entangle the USA in a new, global balance of power system with a permanent role in German and European politics. In the 1950s, Britain sought to play a role as mediator between the superpowers (Geneva summit, 1955; summit conference, 1960). Britain's Cold War role declined through the 1970s with superpower détente, which threatened to reduce the room for manoeuvre of all the Western European powers. In the 1980s, Margaret Thatcher sought to reinforce Britain as a hardline ally of the USA during the 'Second' Cold War; then recognized early on that the arrival of Mikhail Gorbachev in power in 1985 could give the West an opportunity to change the character of the Cold War standoff. The British only played a minor role in the diplomacy of the ending of the Cold War, reflecting its diminished diplomatic status, and remaining nervous about German power when Germany reunited.

The Cold War artificially enhanced the role of Britain as an international player. Britain had one of the four occupation zones in the defeated Germany, quickly acquired nuclear status, and was the Americans' most loyal global partner. Britain's Cold War diplomacy was complicated by problems of end-of-empire, relative economic decline, doubt about the importance of a supranational Europe as a Western power bloc, and the costs of its commitment to nuclear weaponry.

ADe

Anne Deighton, *Britain and the First Cold War* (London, 1990). | John Lewis Gaddis, *We Now Know: The Cold War as History* (Oxford, 1997). | Fred Halliday, *The Making of the Second Cold War* (London, 1986). | Martin Walker, *The Cold War and the Making of the Modern World* (London, 1994).

Cole, G. D. H. **(1889–1959)**, historian and socialist political theorist. (George) Douglas Howard Cole was the leading left-wing socialist intellectual of the first half of the century. His first major political allegiance was to the idea of guild socialism: workers' control of industries through trade unions. The idea was influential in trade-union, left-wing Labour Party, and Independent Labour Party circles long after the Russian revolution in 1917 which marked the point at which it ceased to be a practical political movement. Thereafter he became a prolific advocate of a set of left-wing positions, sometimes in tune with the direction of the Labour Party, as after the collapse of the MacDonald government in 1931, and sometimes on the fringes, as in 1945–51. In parallel to his writing and political involvement he made the occasional direct intervention in politics, as when he stood in the 1945 election as an independent. In his time, he was rivalled only by Harold Laski and R. H. Tawney as socialist intellectuals. However, his central idea, guild socialism, was superseded almost as soon as it gained a wide currency and few figures of such influence and reputation in their lifetimes have been relegated to such obscurity in the decades after their death. Cole himself showed some awareness of his fate and switched his writing from the contemporary analysis which had dominated the 1920s and 1930s—in works such as *Guild Socialism Restated* (1920), *Trade Unionism and Munitions* (1923), *The Next Ten Years in British Social and Economic Policy* (1929), *The Intelligent Man's Guide through the World Chaos* (1932), *The Intelligent Man's Review of Europe Today* (1933), and *Practical Economics* (1937)—to the history of the British Labour movement (often writing with his wife Margaret as co-author)—in works such as *British Working Class Politics, 1832–1914* and *Chartist Politics* (both 1941), and most importantly, in his five-volume *History of Socialist Thought* (1953–60). Aside from one contemporary advocate, Professor Paul Hirst (see *From Statism to Pluralism*, 1997), none of his works had much influence beyond the 1950s. *BB*

MARGARET COLE, *The Life of G. D. H. Cole* (London, 1971).

Coleg Harlech, an independent residential college for adult students spectacularly located on the Merionethshire coast. It was founded in 1927 by Thomas Jones who assured benefactors that it would produce a new generation of working-class leaders in Wales. Former students retain an enormous affection for the college and in particular for a teaching staff which has included many highly regarded Welsh writers. Inevitably it has lost some of its traditions within a more general era of continuing education. *PS*

Coleraine, Lord. See LAW, RICHARD KIDSTON.

Collins, Godfrey (1875–1936), Liberal politician. Returned as MP for Greenock in 1910, a seat he held until his death, Collins remained a loyal Asquith supporter throughout the 1920s. In 1931, he took the Simonite side of the Liberal split and was Scottish secretary from 1932 until he died in office. Collins had to deal with major social and economic problems in Scotland which had been left in the wake of the 1930s Depression. He also had to stave off increasing nationalist demands, which he did by setting in train plans to move the Scottish Office to Edinburgh. A successful publisher, Collins was regarded as a practical and non-partisan politician. *RF*

Collins, Michael (1890–1922), IRA leader and politician. Born in Co. Cork, Collins moved to London in 1906 where he worked as a Post Office clerk. There he joined the Irish Republican Brotherhood, a secret society dedicated to the violent overthrow of British rule in Ireland. Collins returned to Ireland in 1915 and participated in the Easter Rising of 1916. Following his release from an internment camp, Collins became director of organization and intelligence for the IRA. He proved a brilliant guerrilla strategist, disrupting the administration of British rule during the Anglo-Irish war, 1919–21. Following a truce between British and republican forces, Collins was persuaded by Eamon de Valera to go to London for negotiations between Sinn Fein and the British government. In December 1921, Collins was one of the Sinn Fein negotiators who compromised their republican principles by signing the *Anglo-Irish treaty. This created an Irish Free State within the British Commonwealth, which accepted the partition of Ireland, and Collins commented that he had signed his own death warrant. Back in Ireland, Sinn Fein and the IRA split over the question of the oath of allegiance to the British king. On 28 February 1922, under British pressure, Collins ordered Free State forces into action against anti-treaty forces which had occupied Dublin's law courts. This signalled the start of the Irish civil war. Collins was killed in an ambush on 20 August 1922 in Co. Cork. *TWH*

TIM PAT COOGAN, *Michael Collins: A Biography* (London, 1990).

Colombo plan (1951), originally drawn up by the Commonwealth to bring economic and social benefits to Asian and Pacific countries. In January 1950, seven Commonwealth foreign ministers met in Colombo, Ceylon (now Sri Lanka), to discuss how to prevent the spread of communism. Britain's foreign minister, Emest Bevin, hoped to further cooperation between Asian countries and helped promote the idea of resisting communism through economic aid. Consequently, a plan was drawn up which sought to foster economic cooperation and development amongst those countries joining the scheme, and in 1951 it was launched as the Colombo plan for cooperative economic development in south and south-east Asia. By the end of the decade 26 states were involved in the plan, including the USA and Japan. The Colombo plan has been seen as the Asian Marshall plan, and continues its work to this day in close association with the UN. In 1977, it changed its title and became known as the Colombo plan for cooperative economic and social development in Asia and the Pacific, reflecting the wide geographical diversity of those countries within the scheme. In 1986, the plan was made permanent, following the earlier practice of renewing it every five years. Since its inception, the plan has developed its own bureaucratic structures and the methods by which aid is provided: for example, in 1975 a staff college for technician training was created in Singapore, but moved to Manila in 1987. Much stress is placed on its cooperative aspects: general decisions are reached through consensus and individual countries tend to work together to construct aid packages. In essence, the plan facilitates the giving of aid, rather than providing it. *KTS*

W. D. McIntyre, *The Significance of the Commonwealth, 1965–1990* (Christchurch, New Zealand, 1991). | Andrew Walker, *The Commonwealth: A New Look* (Oxford, 1978).

Colonial Freedom, Movement for, pressure group formed in 1954 to bring together earlier bodies such as the Fabian Colonial Bureau and the British branch of the Congress of Peoples against Imperialism. Its objective was to increase the speed at which British decolonization took place. It soon came to dominate Labour thinking on colonial issues, but since British decolonization dramatically speeded up anyway before Labour returned to office in 1964, its impact on British official policy was limited. *JAR*

Colonial Office (1854–1967). As the nature of the British Empire changed out of all recognition in the course of the 20th century, so the Colonial Office mirrored its transformation. The century began with the Colonial Office having almost total authority over the Empire, the exception being the India Office (created in 1858). In 1925, a separate Dominions Office was created in order to deal with the rise of the self-governing dominions. When, in the late 1950s and 1960s, Asian and African colonies gained independence in a great rush, they therefore left the orbit of the Colonial Office to come under the jurisdiction of the Commonwealth Relations Office (CRO, created in 1947). In 1962 a single minister was appointed, becoming secretary of state for both commonwealth and colonial affairs, while in 1966 the Colonial Office came under the orbit of the CRO in a new Commonwealth Office. The Colonial Office was eventually abolished in 1967. *JD*

W. David McIntyre, *Colonies into Commonwealth* (London, 1974).

Colville, David John **(1894–1954)**, Conservative politician. Born into the Scottish steelmaking family, Colville was elected MP for North Midlothian in 1929. After a spell in the Treasury, he was appointed under-secretary for Scotland in 1935. The following year he was promoted to Scottish secretary and held this post until 1940, when he made way for Churchill's candidate, the Labour MP Thomas Johnston. Colville resigned his seat in 1943 when made governor of Bombay, a position he held until Indian independence in 1947, when he became Lord Clydesmuir. *RF*

Colville, John Rupert **(1915–87)**, private secretary to Princess Elizabeth (1947–9), and to Winston Churchill (1940–1, 1943–5, and 1951–5), and diarist. He also served in the private offices of Neville Chamberlain and Clement Attlee, as well as in the Foreign Office. The published extracts from his diary are feline, amusing, and attuned to social nuance. He was a natural courtier and, as his diary hints, also a favourite of Churchill's. *WMK*

John Colville, *The Fringes of Power: Downing Street Diaries, 1939–1955* (London, 1985).

Colville, Richard **(1907–75)**, press secretary at Buckingham palace, 1947–68. Before coming to the palace, Colville served in the navy. He brought the ex-naval commander's bluff, no-nonsense manner to his dealings with members of the press, whom he often treated with contempt. Throughout this period the monarchy consistently received favourable press coverage. Whether this was because or in spite of Colville's manner is not yet clear. *WMK*

Kenneth Rose, *Kings, Queens and Courtiers* (London, 1985).

commander in chief, sovereign as. One of the primary functions of the sovereign under Britain's constitutional monarchy is to serve as symbolic head of the armed forces. All members of the army, air force, and marines swear allegiance to the sovereign. The navy, which originates from the royal prerogative, is slightly different; but this service's ties to the monarchy are no less strong. All sovereigns of the century took special interest in the armed forces. Conservatives often point to this connection between sovereign and armed forces as useful in an emergency, for example, to thwart the claims to power of an anti-democratic politician. Such an emergency did not arise in the 20th century; nor does such a scenario seem likely when one remembers that more democratic constitutions have perished at the hands of armies than have been saved by them. *WMK*

Commercial and Industrial Policy, Committee on. See Balfour of Burleigh committee (1916–18).

Commission for Racial Equality. See Community Relations Commission; Race Relations Board.

Commons, House of, the popularly elected chamber of parliament which determines which party forms the government and to which the prime minister and other ministers are primarily accountable. The Commons only became fully democratic in 1950 after the abolition of multiple votes and the university seats. A series of reform measures in the 19th and 20th centuries extended the franchise. In particular, the 1918 Act extended the vote to all men, and to women over the age of 30, while women over 21 received the vote after 1928. The voting age for both men and women was cut to 18 in 1969. Nowhere are the powers or the functions of the Commons or Lords laid down in statute or in any single constitution document. They have developed over the centuries as the balance between the monarchy, the Lords, and the Commons has shifted in favour of the Commons as, first, the prerogative powers of the crown were assumed by the prime minister and cabinet and then the Commons limited the powers of the Lords. Yet many of these changes involve new conventions as much as new statutes. The prime minister exercises many prerogative powers over public appointments and may sign treaties in the name of the monarch without the approval of parliament being required. The Commons is, however, sovereign in that its Acts or decisions cannot be challenged or overruled in any court (with the exception of measures which conflict with European legislation). The dominance of the House of Commons was finally established during the 20th century following the battles between the Asquith government and the Conservative-dominated House of Lords in 1909–11, which resulted in a substantial limitation of the powers of the Lords. One sign of this shift of power was that a prime minister and most other heads of major departments were expected to be in the Commons, rather than the Lords (as often occurred in the early 20th century). The 3rd marquess of Salisbury, who left office in 1902, was the last prime minister to sit in the Lords, and membership of the upper house was cited by Lord Halifax as a reason why he could not become prime minister in 1940. The Commons performs several functions. Walter Bagehot in 1867 set out the classic definition of its roles: the provision and maintenance of the executive, the expressive function (reflecting the mind of 'the English people in all matters that come before it'), the teaching function ('teaching the nation what it does not know'), the informing function (expressing the grievances of the governed to government), and the legislative function. This list curiously omitted the original, and most historic, function of granting supply to the executive by approving spending and tax proposals. Relations with, and scrutiny of, European institutions have been a further function since the UK joined the European Community in January 1973. The most important role is sustaining a government in office and supplying most of its members. This is achieved by the decision of voters at a general election by providing a ruling party with a majority of MPs, some of whom become ministers, and, rarely, the largest single party if no group has an overall majority on its own. Apart from the formation of the wartime coalitions in 1915, 1916, and 1940, and their break-up in 1922 and 1945, there were only two brief occasions during the 20th century when a change of party in government did not directly follow a general election. In 1905, Balfour resigned as prime minister in the hope that Campbell-Bannerman could not form a workable administration. He did, and the Liberals won a landslide victory at the general election the following month. In 1931, the disintegration of the Labour cabinet led to the formation of a Conservative-dominated *National Government which, against its original intentions, won a record victory two months later. The other ten changes of party in office all occurred after general elections, without exception in the seven cases following the Second World War. The Commons also became almost a closed shop for becoming a minister. Party was throughout the 20th century the dominant factor in the House of Commons, ensuring that governments could count on securing the approval of their expenditure and tax proposals and almost all their legislative measures. Virtually all MPs are elected to the Commons under a party label and that has remained their primary loyalty, even without the encouragement of the party whips, influencing the behaviour of backbenchers and the operation of select committees and standing committees. The social character and role of MPs changed during the century with an increasing number of full-time members who were professional politicians. This was linked with their growing activity in dealing with the grievances of their constituents as well as the ambitions of more members to become ministers. *PJRR*

Walter Bagehot, *The English Constitution* (London, 1867). | Peter Riddell, *Parliament under Pressure* (London, 1998).

Commons, House of: backbenchers. All MPs sitting on the benches behind ministers or opposition spokesmen are known as backbenchers. The expansion in the number of ministers and of shadow teams reduced the relative number of backbenchers from 90 per cent at the beginning of the century to less than 75 per cent at the end. This is even excluding parliamentary private secretaries who do not receive additional pay but are required to vote with the government. Becoming a backbencher is also the first step to becoming a minister in virtually all cases except peers. Backbenchers have extensive rights to raise issues on behalf of constituents and on general matters and to influence internal party debates and decisions. Backbench MPs can write to ministers (and their letters are given priority), can put down oral and written questions, can put down private notice questions (usually over a disaster of some kind in their constituencies), can apply for adjournment debates (ensuring a reply of at least ten to fifteen minutes from a minister, can put down early day motions (statements of view which are almost never debated), and can put forward private members' bills. They cannot, however, propose increases in public spending, only reductions. Apart from these formal opportunities, backbenchers can also try to influence decisions and policy informally through their contact with front-benchers of their own party as fellow MPs, both when they vote together and at party meetings. The main parties have weekly meetings of backbenchers: the Conservative backbench *1922 Committeé and the Parliamentary Labour Party. These meetings discuss the business and the whipping for the week ahead, as well as current policy issues.

PJRR

Commons, House of: Committee on Standards and Privileges, select committee created in 1995 to take over work of Privileges and Members' Interest Committees, to consider complaints over both privilege and the Register of Members' Interests. Privilege is defined by **Erskine May* as 'the sum of the peculiar rights enjoyed by each House collectively as a constituent part of the High Court of Parliament, and by Members individually, without which they could not discharge their functions, and which exceed those possessed by other bodies or individuals'. Such privileges amount to the law and custom of parliament and are reaffirmed by the Speaker at the beginning of each parliament. Only the House, and not the courts, can determine what is a matter of privilege. These privileges include the freedom of speech of Members (which cannot be questioned in any court), freedom from arrest (except on criminal matters), and freedom of access. Contempts of the House are defined as acts which impede members in the performance of their functions, refusal to attend the House or its committees when summoned or obstructing anyone having business before the House, assaults and insults against officers of the House, prematurely publishing a committee report, deliberately misleading the House, accepting bribes, bringing the House and its proceedings into disrepute. When an MP believes there has been an alleged breach of privilege or contempt, he or she writes to the Speaker, who then decides whether or not the matter should take precedence over other parliamentary business. If so, the MP who raised the matter then tables a motion the following day proposing that the issue be referred to the Committee on Standards and Privileges. The committee then holds an inquiry and, if it finds that a serious breach of privilege has occurred, the Member alleged to have committed the offence can use the subsequent debate to explain his or her actions. Members can be suspended, or even, in very serious cases, expelled from the House. Bribery of members, or acceptance of a bribe, has not been an offence under various Prevention of Corruption Acts and a series of reports from the royal commission on standards of conduct in public life (the Salmon commission) in 1976, the committee on standards in public life (the Nolan, then Neill, committee) in 1995, and the joint committee on parliamentary privilege (the Nicholls committee) all recommended that bribery and corruption of MPs should be brought within the criminal law. A series of scandals about MPs' outside business interests led to a gradual tightening in rules from the 1970s onwards. Allegations against a number of Members involved in the Poulson bankruptcy scandal led to the creation in 1974 of a register of members' interests (listing broad categories such as directorships, consultancies, sizeable shareholdings, overseas visits, and the like), which was monitored from 1976 onwards by a select committee on members' interests. However, serious shortcomings in the register emerged over the following twenty years, as ethical standards became more confused and some MPs became involved with the rapidly growing lobbying industry. A series of complaints were made about the failure of MPs fully to declare their outside interests, both in the late 1980s and particularly in 1994 when allegations were made that MPs were prepared to accept money for asking parliamentary questions and raising matters in the Commons. These exposed inadequacies in the systems of both registration and supervision and led to the appointment in October 1994 of the Nolan committee into standards in public life. Its first wide-ranging report in May 1995 (see NOLAN REPORT) was damning about earlier failures of self-regulation and recommended the appointment of an independent parliamentary commissioner for standards to maintain the register of members' interests and to receive and investigate complaints. The committee also proposed tighter disclosure requirements on outside interests and a ban on MPs working for lobbyists, later modified by the Commons into a ban on members taking on paid advocacy work. The new system came into operation in 1995–6, with the creation of the merged Committee on Standards and Privileges to decide on serious cases and to recommend penalties. *PJRR*

Commons, House of: confidence motions. Many types of motion put before the Commons are implicitly or explicitly regarded as questions of confidence which, if passed, lead to the resignation of the government or the dissolution of parliament and a general election. There were three occasions in the 20th century when a vote in the Commons led to a change of prime minister or the government. On 21 January 1924, the Baldwin administration, which had lost its overall Commons majority at the general election at the end of 1923, was defeated by 328 votes to 256 on meeting the new House. On 8 October 1924, the MacDonald government was defeated by 364 votes to 198 on a Liberal motion (backed by the Conservatives) calling for an inquiry into the Campbell case. Parliament was immediately dissolved. On 8 May 1940, following the debacle of the Norway campaign, the National Government survived a vote for the adjournment of the House by 281 votes to 200, but the scale of the rebellion by Conservative MPs (33 voting against and 65 abstaining) was followed by the resignation of Neville Chamberlain as prime minister and his replacement by Winston Churchill. Motions expressing confidence in the government, or no confidence when tabled by the opposition, have been put when administrations are in serious political trouble, either generally or over a specific policy, even when there is no serious prospect of a defeat. The only such motion carried against the government of the day was on 28 March 1979 when the Callaghan administration lost a no confidence motion by one vote—310 votes to 311—leading to the immediate announcement of a dissolution and an election. *PJRR*

Commons, House of: 'Crossman select committees', these were given impetus by the influx of new MPs in the 1964 and 1966 elections supportive of reform, and by reports of the procedure committee established in December 1964. Progress was slow until Richard Crossman became the leader of the House in August 1966. Six committees were established, each prompted by different motives: science and technology (1966), agriculture (1966), education and science (1967), race relations and immigration (1968), overseas aid and development (1969), and Scottish affairs (1969). The committees had to struggle to achieve the same rights as held by the nationalized industries committee and against government hostility. Their major success was in establishing the position of select committees for their successors. The committees were soon dissolved: agriculture, and education and science in 1970, overseas aid and development in 1971 (revived 1973–9), and Scottish affairs in 1972. The others were replaced in the overhaul of select committees in 1979. *KMT*

Commons, House of: debates. The House of Commons does its business by holding debates on motions of various kinds, both when it is considering legislation and when it is discussing other matters. The motions range from detailed amendments on the wording of a clause to substantive confidence motions to more procedural motions to take note of a document or statement, or for the adjournment of the House. Often, debates end without a vote being taken, particularly on procedural motions. Leaving aside the hour for parliamentary questions between Monday and Thursday, and any ministerial statements, a normal daily session will contain at least two types of debate, and often more. There are several broad categories of debate: second reading, report stage, and third reading on legislation; the roughly twenty days allocated each session to the opposition (mainly to the leading opposition party, but also some to the minor parties, depending on the balance of MPs), for discussing any topic they like; a flexible number of days when the government initiates debates on motions of its choosing (generally to discuss policy statements or foreign policy crises); three estimates days (for debates on reports of select committees); a number of Fridays for debates on private members' bills and half-hour adjournment debates at the end of each day's sitting (when a backbencher raises a topic). In addition, every year there is a roughly six-day debate on the Queen's Speech and a four-day debate on the budget. The government controls the allocation of business and the leader of the House announces the business for the following week, and often for the two weeks ahead, each Thursday in a statement. A debate is introduced by the member putting forward the motion (for instance, a shadow spokesman on an opposition day), though a minister always has the last word in closing a debate before the vote is taken (except where amendments are being considered at a report stage where the mover of the motion speaks last). There are no limits on the length of front-bench speeches, though, from time to time, limits have been placed on the length of backbench speeches (generally of ten minutes) in the middle of debates. *PJRR*

Commons, House of: devolution. The formation of the Irish Free State in 1922, the associated creation of the Stormont parliament in Belfast from 1922 until its suspension in 1972, and the proposals for legislative devolution for Northern Ireland, Scotland, and Wales in 1999 all had implications for representation at Westminster. In the first two decades of the century Irish Nationalist MPs played an important role at Westminster, particularly after the 1910 elections, in supporting the Asquith government and pressing for Irish home rule. Three-quarters of the members from Ireland were Nationalists in this period but Sinn Fein won three-quarters of the Irish seats in the 1918 election. The division of the island of Ireland in 1922 led to a reduction in the number of Irish MPs sitting in the Commons from 101 to twelve. Because of the existence of the Stormont parliament, the constituencies of Northern Ireland MPs were larger than the average in mainland Britain and its total number of members less. The convention also developed that ministers would not answer questions in the Commons within the remit of the Northern Ireland government (similar rulings were made after the launch of the Scottish parliament and Welsh assembly). Following the suspension of Stormont the number of Northern Ireland MPs rose after the 1983 boundary changes to seventeen. A select committee for Northern Ireland affairs was not set up until 1994. The inauguration of the Scottish parliament and the Welsh assembly in 1999 had few immediate implications for proceedings at Westminster, though a number of MPs had dual mandates. The Scotland Act also contained provisions to ensure that the average size of Scottish constituencies was the same as in England, thus reducing the number of MPs from Scotland. *PJRR*

Commons, House of: dual mandate of MPs. From time to time a number of MPs have also been members of other elected bodies. A large number of MPs have been local councillors when first elected, though they have usually not then stood for re-election as councillors. From 1973 until the start of direct elections in 1979, all UK members of the European assembly were members of the Commons or the Lords. In the first direct elections in June 1979, ten members of the Commons, and four peers, were elected. Since then, a number of MPs have also been members of the European parliament, though in virtually all cases after 1989, they have not then sought re-election to the European parliament. Of the fourteen dual mandate MP/MEPs, eight went on to become ministers. No sitting MPs after the 1984 election have then been successfully elected to the European parliament, with the exception of Ian Paisley, John Hume, and, from 1979 until 1989, John Taylor, who sat both at Westminster and Strasbourg. In addition, several members of the Commons elected from Northern Ireland have also served at the same time as members of Stormont or various elected bodies in Belfast. Moreover, 22 members of the House of Commons and four peers were elected to the Scottish parliament and Welsh assembly in May 1999—though virtually all then said they would not be seeking re-election to the Commons. *PJRR*

Commons, House of: emergencies. The Speaker has the power under Standing Order 12 to summon the House earlier than the previously agreed date if the public interest requires it—invariably in response to a national emergency or the commitment of British forces to military action overseas. Such military actions in Korea, Suez, Northern Ireland (twice), the Falklands, the Gulf, and Bosnia have accounted for half the emergency recalls in the second half of the century. Usually, the House is recalled for just one or two days to deal with just the pressing matter. On 22 occasions, the Commons met on Saturdays, mainly before 1914, and on one Sunday, 3 September 1939, when the Second World War began. *PJRR*

Commons, House of: EU Law. The UK entered the European Community on 1 January 1973, under the terms of the *European Communities Act, 1972. This gave the force of law in the UK to existing and future community legislation. A series of court cases, notably in the Law Lords ruling in the Factortame case of 1990, confirmed the principle that 'it is the duty of UK court to override any rule of national law found to be in conflict with any directly enforceable rule of community law'. This judgement involved ignoring or 'disapplying' the Merchant Shipping Act, 1988, establishing for the first time that the Westminster parliament is not absolutely sovereign and its Acts can be overruled or overturned if they conflict with European law. Community legislation is applied in two ways: regulations can be directly applicable though may need to be supplemented by UK legislation for full implementation, but in most cases implementation is usually achieved via statutory instruments or orders in council. Directives generally require UK legislation for implementation. The scope of European legislation has gradually been extended to cover a wide variety of areas, notably following the *Single European Act of 1987. Parliamentary scrutiny has mainly been through holding ministers to account in their capacity as members of various councils of ministers which decide actions to be taken by community institutions. This is both by traditional means, such as oral and written questions and statements, and by specifically European committees (both in the Commons and the Lords). The name of the committees changed over the years but their role has remained to scrutinize proposals and community documents before they are formally adopted by the various councils and, since 1987, by the European parliament under the co-decision procedure. This has involved both a European scrutiny committee to consider commission proposals and, if necessary, question witnesses, before reporting to the full house, and, since November 1998, three European standing committees in which debates of up to 90 minutes are held. The House of Lords select committee on the European Communities tends to conduct inquiries on subject areas rather than community documents. Ministers have agreed to enter a 'scrutiny reserve' so that they would not commit the government to decisions until a matter had been considered by the relevant Commons committee. Protocol 13 of the treaty of *Amsterdam of 1997 stipulated a six-week period between legislative and justice and home affairs proposals being made available by the European Commission in all languages and a decision being taken by the relevant council.

PJRR

Commons, House of: finance. The provision, and withholding, of finance has been parliament's oldest and most important power, yet it was only in the 20th century that the House of Commons established its absolute supremacy over financial matters. The rejection by the Lords of the Lloyd George *'People's Budget' of 1909 led to the passage of the Parliament Acts of 1911 and then of 1949 which specify that money bills passed by the Commons are allowed one month to pass the Lords. If the Lords do not give them a third reading within a month, they can be sent for royal assent without the approval of the Lords. The Lords cannot amend the annual finance bill after it has been sent from the Commons. Paradoxically, however, few finance bills qualify as money bills under the terms of the Parliament Act since they contain a much wider range of provisions. The House of Commons is more assiduous at examining the details of taxation measures in the finance bill than at expenditure since annual estimates and supplementary estimates are voted through virtually on the nod. The only debates and votes tend to be on the overall totals of public spending, though select committees do hold inquiries into particular spending programmes and a few reports are debated each year. For most of the century, apart from the 1993–6 period when spending, and taxation proposals were presented together in a unified budget in November, the annual *budget was delivered in the spring. May was common for the budget before the Great War, then April, until the 1970s when March became the usual date—with variations after general elections. Tuesday has been the normal, though not invariable, day for delivery, but Mondays were popular in the 1920s. Between 1641 and 1967, proposals for raising taxation originated in the Committee of Ways and Means; and, though the committee was abolished in 1967, the Deputy Speaker still has the title of chairman of Ways and Means and normally presides over the budget. The speech, one of the highlights of the parliamentary year, contains an account of the state of the economy and of financial measures. The length of the speech fell steadily during the century to little more than one hour by the 1990s, partly to meet the demands of the wider television audience. Tax proposals, usually changing excise duties, can take immediate effect, though the necessary budget resolutions covering all tax changes are voted upon at the end of the five- or six-day budget debate in the Commons. The finance bill is published two or three weeks later. Up to 1968, all the committee stage was taken on the floor of the House but since then only the most controversial and novel proposals are considered there with the rest considered in a standing committee. In the 19th century, each departmental estimate was voted upon separately, though in 1896 a limit was put on the number of days for debating them. The character of supply days gradually changed during the century from consideration of estimates to general discussion of policy on motions initiated by the opposition. In 1966, this change was formalized with the acceptance that there would be 29 supply days with debates on substantive motions or for the adjournment. In July 1982, the system was changed with the creation of nineteen, later twenty, opposition days, plus three estimates days for debates on reports by select committees chosen by the liaison committee. *PJRR*

J. A. G. Griffith and Michael Ryle, *Parliament: Functions, Practices and Procedures* (London, 1989).

Commons, House of: hours of sitting. See Commons, House of: procedure.

Commons, House of: Irish MPs in. See Irish Parliamentary Party.

Commons, House of: ministers in. The number of ministers and whips in the House of Commons rose sharply during the century from 33 in the Salisbury government of 1900 to 89 in the Blair government after 1997. The big increases occurred during the two world wars and during the Wilson government of the late 1960s as the state extended its role and took on new responsibilities in social and industrial areas and new ministries were created. This involved two associated changes: first, the appearance of ministers of state in virtually all departments and then the creation of parliamentary under-secretaries. Legally, decisions rest with the secretary of state or minister in charge of a department but ministers of state and under-secretaries have increasingly handled legislation and answered questions and adjournment debates. Since the creation of departmentally related select committees in 1979, ministers have faced increasing calls to appear in front of Commons' committees. In addition, all cabinet ministers and many ministers of state appointed parliamentary private secretaries, MPs who helped them maintain contact with backbenchers and often attended ministerial meetings. But they do not receive any additional payment above their salaries as backbench MPs and, while they do count as ministers, they are expected to vote all the time with the government, or face the sack. The number of such parliamentary private secretaries rose from the 1970s onwards to between 30 and 40. Moreover, the balance between Lords and Commons ministers shifted during the century. Nearly half the Salisbury cabinet came from the Lords: from the 1960s onwards, only two ministers, the leader of the Lords and the lord chancellor, were automatically members of the cabinet, though occasionally another peer was. The 3rd marquess of Salisbury was the last prime minister in the Lords, and the earl of Home renounced his title in 1963 when he entered Downing Street. Lord Carrington was the last peer to hold one of the major offices of state when he was foreign secretary from 1979 until 1982. *PJRR*

Commons, House of: officers and staff. The House of Commons has its own staff who are involved in advising members on procedure and in the work of standing and select committees, security, housekeeping, provision of information, reporting of debates, and cooking food. These staff are not civil servants (though pay is kept in line with comparable Whitehall grades), but are employed by the House of Commons Commission, a statutory body set up under the House of Commons (Administration) Act, 1978. This superseded the largely defunct House of Commons Offices Commission. The Speaker is chairman and the leader of the Commons is ex officio a member, one member is nominated by the leader of the opposition (usually the shadow leader of the House), while three further members are appointed by the House (normally a senior backbencher from each of the two main parties and a representative of the smaller parties). One of the non-ministerial members answers questions on behalf of the commission on the floor of the Commons. The commission has wide-ranging powers over staffing and expenditure and lays before the House the annual estimate for the costs of administration. Its work is supported by various domestic committees of MPs, covering such matters as catering, accommodation and works, information, administration, and broadcasting. The structure of the House has been reviewed and changed from time to time but revolves around six departments—Clerk of the House, serjeant at arms, library, finance and administration, official report (*Hansard), and refreshment. The Clerk, the senior permanent officer of the House and principal adviser to the Speaker on the privileges, procedures, and practices of parliament, is a crown appointment, made by the monarch, on the advice of the prime minister who first consults the Speaker, who may in turn consult the House of Commons Commission. The Clerk Assistant, the deputy, is also a crown appointment on the advice of the Speaker. One, and often two or three, of the senior clerks are always present, sitting at the Table in front of the Speaker in order to be able to advise him. Clerks advise members on the procedural aspects of the business of the House, and of committees, where they sit alongside the chairman. The serjeant's department is the next most senior and is also a crown appointment. The serjeant, usually a retired officer of the armed forces, and his department are responsible for order, security, ceremonial, communications, the allocation and booking of accommodation, building maintenance and repairs, and other administrative matters. *PJRR*

Paul Silk with Rhodri Walters, *How Parliament Works* (London, 1993).

Commons, House of: the opposition in. The opposition has a formal role in the House of Commons, as shown by the formal, and paid, role of leader of the opposition for the leader of the largest party not in government. The leader of the opposition sits opposite the prime minister in the Commons, each having their team on either side of them, and their supporters behind them. The leader of the opposition, or spokesman, is given the first opportunity to question the prime minister or other minister after an answer to a question or a statement, or following the opening speech of a debate. Leaders of the opposition have had their shadow cabinets and shadow teams of spokesmen—since the 1950s with specific shadow departmental responsibilities. Opposition parties have a number of opportunities to argue their case on the floor of the House, moving amendments to the Queen's Speech, on a number of specified opposition days when they have the choice of subject for debates, in (occasionally) moving motions of censure, in objecting or praying against statutory instruments or orders, in seeking emergency or adjournment debates, in raising private notice questions, as well pressing questions. Since 1975, opposition parties have also received public money for their parliamentary work, the so-called Short money after Edward Short (later Lord Glenamara), the then leader of the Commons—based on a formula related to the number of seats and votes won. The money has been used by shadow spokesmen to employ researchers and other staff. The total was substantially increased in 1999 as part of changes to the funding of parties. The opposition uses its opportunities in the Commons both to press the government on legislation and issues of the day and to generate media and public interest in order to build up its national position as an alternative government. Of the sixteen leaders of the opposition during the 20th century, ten were prime minister at some stage—Austen Chamberlain and William Hague were the only Conservative exceptions, while George Lansbury, Hugh Gaitskell, Michael Foot, Neil Kinnock, and John Smith failed to do so on the Labour side (Gaitskell and Smith died in office). *PJRR*

House of Commons: petitions to. Any individual has the right to petition the Commons via a Member on an issue 'in which the House has the jurisdiction to interfere'. Bills were originally based on petitions to the House and this procedure is still used by promoters of private bills such as local authorities or corporations. In the 19th century, petitions were numerous, but their number and prominence declined during the 20th century. However, petitions are still published in full in the Voters and Proceedings of the House and they are sent to ministers—who are not required to reply but often do so. The subject of petitions varies from personal and local grievances over a pension or a school closure to broader matters such as abortion. An MP tells the House who the petition is from, what it is about, and his or her own attitude, without making a speech. The petition is then presented, usually late at night after the end of the main debate. *PJRR*

Commons, House of: private members' bills. Bills promoted by backbench MPs on general public policy issues (distinct from private bills dealing with a specific local authority or corporate interest). The most common method by which MPs can hope to get a bill onto the statute book is the ballot held just after the beginning of each parliamentary session. The twenty members who are successful are in the front of the legislature queue and in order of being drawn can choose the six or seven Fridays, starting in January, set aside for the second reading of such bills. A further half-dozen Fridays are set aside in the late spring and summer for report stages and third readings. Quite often MPs on the government side of the House take up bills suggested by departments which have not been able to get into the Queen's Speech. Sponsors of such bills face a number of obstacles—notably having at least 100 members willing to support a closure motion to force a vote at the end of the second reading debate or on amendments at report stage. Consequently, many highly controversial measures can be blocked unless they receive government assistance to provide time. The other routes are the Ten Minute Rule procedure, under which backbench MPs can introduce bills on Tuesdays and Wednesdays after questions and any statements and before the main debate of the day. The main use of the Ten Minute Rule procedure is to attract attention to an issue. Members can also present bills without debates, known as presentation bills. But, as with Ten Minute Rule bills, they are not likely to come high up on the list for second reading Fridays and therefore, unless they are uncontentious, stand little chance of becoming law. However, a number of bills do overcome these difficulties and become law. On average, just under half of the top twenty in the annual ballot eventually become law, though a mere handful of those presented (less than 8 per cent) clear all the hurdles, and just ten Ten Minute Rule bills became law over fifteen years in the 1980s and 1990s. Nearly half the private members' bills first introduced in the Lords became law. *PJRR*

Commons, House of: procedure. Rulings and procedures govern the orderly conduct of business in the House of Commons and provide a structure to the balance between the executive and the legislature in the absence of a written constitution. The House is the sole determinant of its own procedures and these cannot be challenged in the courts. These procedures have built up over the centuries both through precedent (as recorded in **Erskine May*) and through the standing orders of the House. These cover everything from the rights and privileges of Members, to the habits and conventions determining Members' relations with each other, to the way that business is considered. The standing orders and resolutions of the House are treated as permanent unless amended by the House itself. These are augmented by rulings from the chair which are enforceable though are often amended to take account of changing circumstances and attitudes. In addition, the House requires resolutions to be passed after each budget statement authorizing tax changes before the necessary finance bill is passed. The existence of procedure provides a check on what any government can do by laying down the stages through which a bill has to pass before becoming law and the rights of the opposition and backbench members in proposing amendments. These arrangements can be curtailed but only after debates, and votes, on the necessary timetabling motions. Similarly, procedure lays out the opportunity for the government of the day to be questioned. In almost every parliament, particularly since 1945, a procedure committee has been set up, on either a permanent or an ad hoc basis, to consider whether the House can improve the way it conducts its business. These have focused on, for example, matters of conduct, the design of the order paper, the length and shape of the parliamentary day and week, as well as central questions about how to improve the way legislation is debated and scrutiny of the executive. There have been a number of major inquiries into scrutiny and a report by the procedure committee in 1977–8 led to the creation of the departmentally related select committees after the 1979 general election. After the 1997 election, a modernization committee was set up to look at major changes alongside a procedure committee to consider more detailed aspects. *PJRR*

Commons, House of: relations with the Lords. The House of Commons established its ascendancy over the House of Lords as the preeminent chamber, with sole jurisdiction over taxation issues, following a lengthy and bitter battle over the *'People's Budget' in 1909. The *Parliament Act, 1911, severely limited powers of the Lords, both on financial and other measures, removing its role from money bills and providing that any other public bill could become an Act of Parliament without the approval of the House of Lords once it had been passed by the House of Commons in three parliamentary sessions (provided there was a gap of at least two years between its initial second reading and its final passage by the Commons). The 1911 Act exempted from these provisions any bill extending the life of a parliament, whose maximum duration was then reduced from seven to five years. The *Parliament Act, 1949, reduced the number of sessions in which a bill must be passed by the Commons from three to two and reduced the period from the initial second reading and the final passage of the bill from two years to one. These provisions do not apply to bills originating in the House of Lords, bills extending the life of a parliament, and secondary or delegated legislation. These provisions have only been used rarely. In addition to these formal limitations, the Lords has accepted constraints on the use of its powers. In particular, following the Labour landslide of 1945, the Conservative leadership in the Lords decided, under what became known as the Salisbury rules, that it should 'not frustrate the declared will of the people' by voting against the second or third readings of bills which had appeared in the governing party's manifesto. The Conservatives reserved the right to move amendments but not to 'destroy or alter beyond recognition' any such bill. The line between amending bills and destroying them was at times subjective, though, in general, the Lords accepted the view of the Commons if the latter rejected an amendment passed in the upper house. The Lords also accepted that it would not vote against secondary or delegated legislation, with the exception of the rejection of the Southern Rhodesia (United Nations Sanctions) Order 1968. The preamble to the 1911 Act announced the intention to end the hereditary basis of membership: 'where it is intended to substitute for the House of Lords as it at present exists a second chamber constituted on a popular instead of a hereditary basis, but such substitution cannot be immediately brought into operation'. Several proposals for reform were subsequently debated and a bill was produced by the Wilson government in the late 1960s but foundered on opposition from backbench MPs. This was partly because of fears that a reformed second chamber would challenge the supremacy of the Commons. Legislation to change the composition of the Lords, removing most of the hereditary peers, only became law in late 1999.

PJRR

Commons, House of: Scottish Grand Committee. The committee consists of all MPs representing Scottish constituencies. From 1948 until 1994, it met several times a year in Westminster to consider matters, including estimates, which had been referred by the House, together with consideration of the principle of Scottish bills. However, in the 1994–5 sessions, the committee was expanded to include some kinds of business which could only be undertaken by the House and it was also authorized to sit more regularly in various parts of Scotland, usually on Mondays. The committee also conducts general debates and has periods for questioning of ministers from both the Commons and the Lords. Following the start of the Scottish parliament in 1999, the government initially decided to retain the Scottish Grand Committee.

PJRR

Commons, House of: select committees. Select committees are appointed to conduct a variety of tasks which the full House cannot do, including scrutinizing the work of government departments and advising on procedures and domestic administration of the House (such as accommodation and works, catering, information, broadcasting, liaison (consisting of the chairman of all select committees), standards and privileges, procedure, selection (choosing members to serve on committees), standing orders, modernization of the House of Commons (since 1997). Committees have from time to time been created to conduct scrutiny of subjects on a permanent basis such as deregulation, European legislation, statutory instruments, and consolidation of bills. The longest surviving committee is the *Public Accounts Committee, created as part of Gladstone's reforms of public finance in 1861 to examine 'the accounts showing the appropriation of the sums granted by Parliament to meet the public expenditure and other accounts laid before Parliament as the Committee may think fit'. Most of the committee's work involves considering reports from the *comptroller and auditor-general into not just the probity of spending but also value for money. Public evidence-taking sessions are held with accounting officers of departments, normally the permanent secretary, and reports are then made, to which departments are required to give a detailed response, including any remedial action being taken. In the 19th century, select committees were appointed from time to time to look at particular problems or scandals and often had a big impact. Their use declined in the first half of the 20th century, but from the late 1950s onwards there was a growing debate about the need for a permanent system of committees to scrutinize the executive, in addition to the work of the *Estimates Committee. From 1966 until 1979 a number of committees looked at particular subjects, though not on a comprehensive basis. The most important was the expenditure committee (set up in 1971 and operating through six subcommittees) which work alongside some existing committees on, for example, science and technology, race relations and immigration, and nationalized industries. Following a report by the procedure committee, the House agreed in 1979 to set up a system of departmentally related select committees 'to examine the expenditure, administration and policy' of specified government departments and associated public bodies. The total was originally fourteen, but has varied as a result of changes in the structure of government. A specific Northern Ireland committee was only created in 1994, while the public administration committee in 1997 absorbed the work of two previous committees dealing with public services and the *Ombudsman. Select committees occasionally meet in joint sessions to conduct inquiries on issues overlapping several departments. Joint committees are also occasionally appointed from members of both Houses to look at particular problems on a short-term basis. Committees report to the full

House, though only a few of their reports are ever debated. They are nominated for a full parliament and reflect the party balance in the House. The chairman is selected by each committee, though the choice usually reflects an informal agreement between the parties on the allocation of chairmanships. MPs sit round horseshoe tables and proceedings are more informal than on standing committees. Select committees have powers to 'send for persons, papers and records', but they cannot order the attendance of Members. The departmental committees have made their mark through public evidence-taking sessions with ministers, civil servants, and outside experts which on important occasions have been televised. The committees have undertaken a variety of work, from looking at big policy issues to regular monitoring of budgets, European summits, expenditure announcements, and appointments. Their effectiveness has, however, been undermined by a rapid turnover of membership as MPs appointed to the front bench (whether as ministers or shadow spokesmen) leave committees, as do parliamentary private secretaries.

PJRR

Commons, House of: select committees (1973–5). In addition to the surviving specialist ones, the mid-1970s saw the rise of sessional ad hoc select committees. By 1975 there were 40 with 291 MPs as members, meaning almost half the House of Commons was directly involved. They focused on individual issues such as John Stonehouse, 1974–5; violence in marriage, 1974–5; Cyprus, 1975–6; and the conduct of MPs, 1975–7. Alternatively they established the background for legislation, for example on tax credit, 1972–3; the Channel Tunnel Bill, 1974; wealth tax, 1974–5; and the Abortion Amendment Bill, 1974–5. As a result they acted as royal commissions or departmental committees had done previously, but their reports rarely led to legislation. These select committees lacked coherence and suffered from limited resources. They could only appoint part-time specialist advisers. The two elections in 1974 meant that many select committee posts were not filled throughout that year. *KMT*

Commons, House of: speakership. The Speaker is the public face of the Commons, presiding over debates in the Commons, calling MPs to address the chamber, and interpreting the rules and procedures of the House, but not choosing the subjects for debate or statements. He or she is elected at the beginning of each parliament, and dragged by fellow MPs to the chair. The Speaker, who presides except when the House is in committee, is assisted in the chair by the chairman of Ways and Means, a deputy chairman (an office created in 1902), and a second deputy chairman (created in 1971). Twelve MPs held the speakership during the 20th century. Two died in office (Fitzroy and Hylton-Foster), others have not sought re-election to the Commons, and those stepping down in mid-parliament have immediately left the House. Virtually all former Speakers have become peers. Most Speakers in the century had previously been Conservative MPs until Horace King became the first Labour member to become Speaker in 1965. Since then, the position has alternated between the Conservative and Labour sides of the House. The Speaker became a nationally known figure from 1977 when sound broadcasting of the proceedings began under George Thomas, with his mellifluous Welsh tones, and from 1989 when the television cameras entered the chamber under Bernard Weatherill. The election of Betty Boothroyd as the first woman Speaker in April 1992 made the speakership even better known.

PJRR

David Butler and Gareth Butler (eds.), *British Political Facts 1990–1994* (London, 1994).

Commons, House of: standing committees, are responsible for scrutinizing legislation on a line-by-line basis. The term is misleading since current standing committees are not permanent, but it dates back to the time when such committees were appointed to consider a series of bills on related subjects. However, the post-Second World War standing committees have had an ad hoc membership chosen by the committee of selection after taking account of the balance of parties in the full House. Standing committees operate as mini-versions of the chamber with MPs facing each other and the proceedings chaired by a senior backbencher from the chairman's panel. Standing committees consider the details of public bills, debating them on a line-by-line basis and considering amendments; they also deal with delegated legislation, European Union documents, and the territorial Grand Committees. Public bills are committed to a standing committee immediately after the vote on second reading. Major constitutional bills are still, by convention, considered by a committee of the whole House, as are some measures which need to be passed urgently or are non-contentious. Since the mid-1960s finance bills have no longer been debated solely on the floor of the House but are split between debates on more controversial clauses in a committee of the whole House with the rest being considered upstairs in a standing committee. At the end of the committee stage, bills are reported back to the full House for report stage and third reading. A bill can be referred to a 'special standing committee', which sits as a select committee hearing evidence for up to three meetings before the committee starts its line-by-line consideration. But this procedure, initiated in 1979, was only occasionally used over the following twenty years and mainly for less contentious measures which did not produce partisan divisions.

PJRR

Commons, House of: Welsh Grand Committee. The committee operates like the Scottish Grand Committee, though it consists not just of all Members representing Welsh constituencies but also not more than five other members. After January 1996, its work was expanded to include oral questions to ministers, ministerial statements, and short debates. Members of the Welsh Grand Committee are permitted to speak in Welsh during meetings of the committee held in Wales, but not in Westminster. The committee was retained after the inauguration of Welsh devolution in July 1999, even though the main political focus had shifted to the National Assembly in Cardiff. *PJRR*

Commons, House of: whipping. The Whips' Offices of the parties exist to ensure that members are present to vote according to the party line. They also act as information officers monitoring the state of opinion and warning of potential problems and rebellions. The government chief whip, formally parliamentary secretary to the Treasury, is often known as patronage secretary, harking back to the days when the whips were members of the royal household and their job was to mobilize a majority in the Commons in support of the monarch. The deputy chief is still known as the treasurer of the royal household. Each week, members of the parties receive a weekly statement known as the whip, setting out the business for the following week, as well as details of all party and other meetings. The most important information is about when MPs have to attend. If the government is not concerned about the result of a vote, members are simply requested to attend and there is a single black line. A two-line whip, with two black lines, says that a member's attendance is 'necessary' from a certain time. MPs can, however, be absent if they pair with a member of the opposing party, thus cancelling out the absence of the two MPs. A three-line whip, with three black lines, says 'your attendance is essential' and MPs have to be present to vote. In practice, enforcement depends on the size of the government's majority, but there were occasions when the governing party's majority was very small, in 1950–1, in 1964–6, in 1974–9, and towards the end of the 1992–7 parliament when ministers had to cancel overseas visits and return home, and even seriously ill members were rushed in ambulances to the precincts of the palace of Westminster, normally New Palace Yard. Their presence is noted by the party whips and they are nodded through without having to go through the division lobbies. The absence of an MP on a three-line whip, or a vote against the party line, is regarded as a serious offence which will invariably produce a reprimand from the party's chief whip, and, in extreme cases, the loss of the whip for a time. Any parliamentary private secretary who does not support the party line in any whipped vote is always dismissed.

PJRR

Commonwealth, head of the. The sovereign is symbolic and titular head of this association of independent states. There are no constitutional duties associated with the role, but the monarchy has probably had both a unifying and an emollient effect; privileged access to the sovereign may have soothed ex-colonial feelings of resentment among Commonwealth leaders. Elizabeth II has taken lively interest in the Commonwealth, where relationships with leaders can be intimate and informal. Unlike other 20th-century associations of states such as the UN or NATO, the Commonwealth has emphasized family feeling and historical ties. In the post-Cold War era, the palace struggled to sustain the Commonwealth, while many politicians lost confidence in the usefulness of continuing association between Commonwealth countries.

WMK

Vernon Bogdanor, *The Monarchy and the Constitution* (Oxford, 1995).

Commonwealth of Nations, collective term given originally to Britain and the white dominions, but now also including most of Britain's former colonies. The Commonwealth is a loose association of 54 member states, whose leaders meet every two years and which promotes political, economic, and cultural cooperation. Of these, Elizabeth II remains the head of state of sixteen members, while another five have monarchies of their own; the remaining 33 are republics. Although the Commonwealth's public persona is the secretary-general, the British monarch has the honour of being 'head of the Commonwealth'.

The idea of a loose 'commonwealth of nations' before 1914 reflected the dominions' desire to distance themselves from Britain and forego a closer union, such as a federation. Nevertheless, during the Great War Britain, the dominions, and India drew closer together to prosecute the war more efficiently. But because the dominions were recognized as belligerent powers and signed the treaty of Versailles, their sense of nationalism and independence increased. Eventually, Britain conceded greater constitutional freedom through the Balfour definition of 1926 and the Statute of Westminster of 1931, although the dominions continued to remain economically and militarily dependent. Economically, this was demonstrated during the Depression when at the Ottawa conference of 1932 Britain gave the dominions trade preferences to help sustain their economies.

Although the Second World War again united Britain and the dominions, it also led to much change thereafter. With India, Pakistan, and Ceylon (now Sri Lanka) becoming independent members in the late 1940s, the Commonwealth's character changed dramatically. In 1949 India became a republic but was allowed to remain in the Commonwealth. This meant that the British monarch was no longer the main link between member states; the Commonwealth was now simply a free association of nations. From 1951, the new grouping was referred to as the Commonwealth of Nations, or just the Commonwealth. This was already reflected in the new *Commonwealth Relations Office.

From the British point of view it was hoped that the Commonwealth would help maintain good relations with dominions and former colonies. There was a great deal of Commonwealth cooperation during the Korean war (1950–2), and a Commonwealth division served with distinction. However, tensions soon arose, particularly during the Suez crisis in 1956. This affair actually split the old dominions and enraged India and Pakistan. With Britain now giving independence to its African colonies, it found that the interests of Commonwealth members were either too diverse or focused on issues which Britain preferred quietly to avoid. This can be seen in the growing hostility towards South Africa's apartheid policies from the non-white members of the Commonwealth, joined in their condemnation by Canada in 1960. South Africa, realizing its pariah status, chose to leave the Commonwealth and declare itself a republic in 1961.

From 1960 Britain increased the pace of *decolonization but more often than not the newly independent states joined the Commonwealth. This positive aspect, however, tended to cause as many problems as it solved. During the 1960s, the British government was frequently criticized, particularly over the handling of the Rhodesian crisis, and over continuing links with South Africa. Moreover, Britain's commitment to the Commonwealth was called into question in 1962 when it abandoned the idea of 'common citizenship' and passed an Act which restricted immigration from Commonwealth countries. At the same time Britain's attempt to join the European Economic Community also caused Commonwealth concern. In 1965, any hope that the Commonwealth could be a truly united organization was shattered when India and Pakistan went to war over Kashmir. Both countries ignored the Commonwealth and preferred to forge closer ties with new allies, the Soviet Union and China respectively. After they went to war again in 1971 over East Pakistan (Bangladesh, as it became), Pakistan left the Commonwealth as Bangladesh joined, and would not return until 1989.

At the 1971 Commonwealth conference in Singapore, Britain was heavily criticized for selling arms to South Africa. The ensuing row led some members to draft a declaration of principles, a sort of Commonwealth charter, which pledged members to ensure that its citizens enjoyed democracy and basic human rights. It was meant to embarrass Britain over South Africa, but after much discussion the declaration was toned down and said nothing that had not already been said before. Moreover, the irony was that many of Britain's critics already, or subsequently, denied these rights to their own people. Britain's relations with the Commonwealth continued to falter, particularly after joining the European Community in 1973. Few members were completely dependent on Britain economically any more, but for some, like New Zealand, which did still have close ties, the shock was pronounced.

In 1979 Britain solved the Rhodesian crisis much to the Commonwealth's satisfaction. Nevertheless, this represented only a honeymoon period between Margaret Thatcher's government and the Commonwealth for before long they had fallen out over the issue of economic sanctions against South Africa. In 1989, Britain stood out alone against Commonwealth plans to increase pressure on South Africa's economy. The scale of the sanctions was impressive but they were not needed because soon apartheid was being dismantled, South African politics had taken a new turn, and eventually, in 1994, Nelson Mandela's democratically elected government rejoined the Commonwealth. Over apartheid the Commonwealth showed a unity of purpose rarely seen before. It highlighted the fact that when necessary common ground could be found, punitive measures, short of war, could be imposed. This was again demonstrated in 1995, when Nigeria was suspended from the Commonwealth for its abuse of human rights. As a body promoting economic and cultural exchange, the Commonwealth appears a success and is attracting both real and potential members from areas with little or no British connection. In 1995 both Mozambique and Cameroon joined and it seems likely that the organization will last well into the 21st century. *KTS*

Denis Judd, *Empire: The British Imperial Experience from 1765 to the Present* (London, 1996). | Andrew Walker, *The Commonwealth: A New Look* (Oxford, 1978).

Commonwealth Immigrants' Act, 1962, landmark piece of immigration legislation ending the 'open door' policy for former British colonial subjects as enshrined in the *British Nationality Act, 1948. Following on from large increases in the numbers of coloured immigrants from the Commonwealth since the mid-1950s, it required most immigrants to have a work permit or employment voucher to enter the UK. Further controls were imposed in 1968 and 1971. The Act was widely interpreted as marking growing government anxiety over the social tensions raised by coloured immigration, such as riots in Notting Hill in 1958. *JS*

Commonwealth Immigrants' Act, 1968, further tightened immigration controls and was enacted in March 1968 as a direct result of an expected wave of expulsions of Asian settlers expelled from East Africa, especially Kenya. The Act established a voucher system for entry, depriving East African Asians holding British passports of an existing automatic right of entry to the UK. *JS*

Common Wealth Party, wartime progressive pressure group. The party was founded by the Liberal MP Sir Richard *Acland in 1942. During the prevailing electoral truce due to the war and existence of a coalition government, its aim was to contest by-elections against 'reactionary' candidates—when it was not opposed by Labour or other 'progressive' candidates. It merged the Movement Forward March, formed by Acland, and the 1941 Committee of the playwright J. B. Priestley. Standing for greater state intervention and a more active democracy, it won three by-elections, *Eddisbury in 1943, Skipton in 1944, and Chelmsford in 1945. Although membership of Common Wealth was proscribed by the Labour Party, its success appeared symptomatic of the changed mood of the electorate compared with pre-war, especially the readiness of voters in safe Conservative seats to support non-Conservative candidates. These successes, however, were more readily capitalized upon by the Labour Party when the electoral truce ended for the 1945 general election. Only one of the 23 Common Wealth candidates was elected, at Chelmsford where no Labour candidate stood. The victor, Ernest Millington, subsequently joined the Labour Party, as did Acland, who called on its members to enrol too. Common Wealth contested no more elections, but survived for a time as a campaigning organization. Common Wealth's wartime successes have generally been interpreted as foreshadowing Labour's victory in 1945, though its own failure in 1945 also demonstrated the electoral vulnerability of minor parties in the 'first-past-the-post' system. *JS*

Paul Addison, *The Road to 1945* (London, 1975).

Commonwealth Relations Office (CRO) **(1947–68)**. Succeeding the Dominions Office, it was set up to deal with the changing nature of the Commonwealth as more former colonies achieved independence. The rapid growth by the 1960s of African and Asian independence led to a fundamental review in British administration, with a single minister being appointed secretary for both commonwealth and colonial affairs in 1962. As the number of colonies dwindled, the Colonial Office came under the authority of the CRO in 1966, forming an integrated Commonwealth Office. Two years later it merged with the Foreign Office to become the Foreign and Commonwealth Office. *JD*

Commonwealth Secretariat. Formed in 1965 and situated in London, the Commonwealth Secretariat draws its staff from all over the Commonwealth. Headed by a secretary-general, its original function was to organize Commonwealth meetings but it has since taken on numerous other responsibilities, such as providing educational, scientific, legal, and medical advice. So far there have been three secretaries-general: Arnold Smith of Canada, 1965–75; Sir Shridath

(Sonny) Ramphal of Guyana, 1975–90; and Chief Emeka Anyaoku of Nigeria, 1990– . *KTS*

ANDREW WALKER, *The Commonwealth: A New Look* (Oxford, 1978).

communism as a set of political beliefs first emerged in Britain during the mid-19th century but was never really a political force until the formation of the Communist Party of Great Britain (CPGB) in 1920. Although there have been many other communist organizations in Britain, it is the CPGB that has dominated communist activity until it ceased to exist as a Marxist-Leninist party at its 43rd congress in 1991. The CPGB has never been a mass political force in British politics. Throughout the 1920s it struggled to attain a membership of 3,000, except at the time of the 1926 General Strike. Indeed, it was only the rise of Hitler in 1933 that pushed the CPGB forward through its united (socialist) and popular (all anti-fascist) fronts against fascism. Indeed, opposing fascism at home and abroad, and particularly through its actions in Spain (1936–9), led to an increase of membership from 3,000 at the beginning of 1933 to more than 17,000 by the beginning of the Second World War. Nevertheless, it never became a mass political party, its support limited because it was affiliated to the Comintern (the Communist International), and its existence was very much dictated by this body based in Moscow. Indeed, it was Lenin who forced the formation of the CPGB and the Comintern dictated the changes in strategy throughout the inter-war years, be they the united front of the early 1920s; 'class against class', 1928–33; or the united and popular fronts of the 1930s. Indeed, though the CPGB had opposed fascism throughout the 1930s, the German-Soviet pact of 23 August 1939 changed matters and created confusion within the CPGB which first of all in September 1939 supported the war against Germany as a 'just war', until Stalin forced it to change its line and oppose the war. All this changed again with the German invasion of the Soviet Union in 1941: the CPGB then became a super-patriotic organization, its membership almost tripling to 56,000 by the end of 1942.

After 1945 the membership of the CPGB fell rapidly as a result of the Soviet invasions of Hungary in 1956 and Czechoslovakia in 1968. Conflict within the communist world between the Soviet Union and China, and the fragmentation of communism into many ideological strands in the 1960s and 1970s added to its decline. As a result CPGB membership fell from 34,000 in 1956 to only 20,000 by 1977. Trotskyist organizations, such as the Socialist Workers' Party (1976), lured away members and the emergence of Euro-communism in 1977, opposed to the leadership of the Soviet Union, led to deep divisions within the CPGB. Finally, with the collapse of communism in Eastern Europe and the Soviet Union in 1991, the CPGB decided that its 3,000 members would regroup from 1991 as the Democratic Left. *KL*

KEITH LAYBOURN and DYLAN MURPHY, *Under the Red Flag* (Stroud, 1999).

Communist Party of Great Britain (CPGB). It is generally accepted that it was Lenin's influence which persuaded a disparate and deeply divided British revolutionary movement to fuse into the CPGB in 1920. Most British Marxists welcomed Russia's October revolution, which endowed the Bolsheviks with enormous prestige. Historians have also regarded it as axiomatic that the CPGB was overwhelmingly subservient to Moscow from the outset. Lenin persuaded the CPGB to seek affiliation to the Labour Party, much against the inclination of many militants, and it relied heavily on Moscow for its funding until the late 1930s, and again from the early 1950s until 1979. The *Daily Worker* was launched at the Comintern's insistence and with its financial support. Moscow money meant Moscow politics. A revisionist view, however (Morgan 1989; Branson 1997), has argued that after its formative period the CPGB, with occasional aberrations, moved steadily towards popular-frontism and an accommodation with the British political tradition. An examination of the party's history does not bear this out.

The CPGB achieved some success in the mid-1920s and in the aftermath of the General Strike membership rose to 10,000. Yet having unsuccessfully sought affiliation to the Labour Party and influence within the trade unions, it switched abruptly in 1928 to the 'class against class' policy of the Comintern. The Labour left were now characterized as 'sham lefts' and the trade unions as 'social-fascist agencies in the service of capitalism'. Although some in the party opposed such sectarian stupidity, in public all danced to the Comintern's tune. As a result the membership had dwindled to 2,555 by 1930. Hitler's seizure of power in Germany in 1933 forced the Comintern to outline a new policy of a united front against fascism, and the CPGB's mood changed rapidly to align itself with the new strategy of working with social democratic parties. This and the later campaign for a popular front of all parties opposed to fascism led to a marked revival in Communist fortunes. Six years of hectic activity saw the party organize national unemployed marches, spearhead the fight against Mosley's blackshirts, and play a key role in organizing aid for republican Spain. The party claimed almost 20,000 members by 1939, weekend sales of the *Daily Worker* often reached 200,000, it had established strongholds in several unions, and Communist influence was also evident in the highly successful Left Book Club.

However, this revival in Communist fortunes came to an abrupt halt with the announcement of the Nazi-Soviet pact and the Comintern's denunciation of the Second World War as an imperialist conflict. Harry Pollitt and other CPGB leaders were shocked by the news and Pollitt opposed the new anti-war stance, losing his position as party secretary. Yet within six weeks, even he fell into line. Why, in 1927 and again in 1939, did the CPGB accept a policy which defied all logic? In part this reflects a western Communist mentality which placed total faith in the Soviet Union. Members who had identified themselves with the Russian revolution from the beginning were concerned not to break ranks, to betray the cause. Furthermore the cultural and economic successes of the Soviet state contrasted sharply with the dole queues of the 1930s in Britain, and Russia's anti-fascism compared favourably with the bankruptcy of appeasement. Once Germany invaded Russia, the CPGB's popularity soared. Membership reached a record 59,000 in June 1942, and by 1945 it had two MPs, many local councillors, and a considerable influence in the trade union movement. These successes, the dissolution of the Comintern in 1943, and the publication of *The British Road to Socialism* in 1951 have led Noreen Branson to suggest that the CPGB had become an independent party, responsible for its own decisions and tactics. This is implausible. Nothing better demonstrates the basic continuity of the CPGB's policy than the alacrity with which, in 1947, it accepted the 'two camps' theory which divided the world into imperialist and anti-imperialist blocs. The Labour Party was firmly identified with the former, and the CPGB mounted an all-out attack on the Attlee government. In the circumstances of the Cold War the Labour leadership therefore moved to neutralize Communist influence.

The CPGB squandered an enormous reservoir of goodwill in the post-war period; in effect committing political suicide. Both of its MPs lost their seats in 1951 and thereafter the party's history was one of decline. Its pro-Soviet attitudes isolated it from working-class institutions, and it suffered a major haemorrhage of members after the Soviet repression of the Hungarian uprising in 1956. Although it maintained a base in a number of trade unions, largely due to its members' reputation for protecting workers' interests, the ETU vote-rigging scandal further eroded its influence. The party had nothing to offer the student revolutionaries of the 1960s and found itself increasingly outflanked on the left by the various Trotskyist groupings. The final years of the party saw it degenerate into a myriad of squabbling factions, and in 1991 the remaining members, less than 5,000, voted to dissolve the party.

For some the CPGB's history is interesting but irrelevant, but that is unfair. The history of the 1930s would have been very different without it, it achieved some significant influence during its golden age in 1942–5, and it did some effective work within the trade unions. There are many reasons for the failure of the CPGB to build a mass party of the working class but the sense that it was somehow foreign, that it took its orders from Moscow undoubtedly damaged its prospects. To that extent perhaps it is fitting that the party was wound up alongside the collapse of the Soviet Union. *MC*

Francis Beckett, *Enemy Within: The Rise and Fall of the British Communist Party* (London, 1995). | Noreen Branson, *History of the Communist Party of Great Britain 1941–1951* (London, 1997). | Francis King and George Matthews (eds.), *About Turn: The Communist Party and the Outbreak of the Second World War: The Verbatim Record of the Central Committee Meetings, 1939* (London, 1990). | Kevin Morgan, *Against Fascism and War: Ruptures and Continuities in British Communist Politics 1935–1941* (Manchester, 1989).

community politics, phrase used to denote the local activism which came to play a dominant part in the Liberal Party revival from the 1950s. Its practitioners claimed that its costs lay in the municipal liberalism of the likes of Joseph Chamberlain in the 1870s, in the defence of local government and communities against *centralization, and in the desire to encourage direct participation in the political process by ordinary people. Liberals sought to become community activists, campaigning on local issues and bringing people into the political process. Its hallmark was the use of new campaigning techniques, preempting the complacency of existing parties, concentrating on even the most trivial issues, such as uneven pavements and potholes in the road. Sometimes unkindly dubbed 'pavement politics', it used **Focus* news-sheets to publicize issues, drum up support, and provide feedback on successful campaigns or ongoing concerns. *Focus* leaflets, coming out up to six times a year, and much more rapidly in the run-up to local elections, were used to revitalize areas left moribund and complacent by established political parties. This was combined with the targeting of one or two wards, from which activists sought to build up strength and then create a domino effect on other neighbouring wards, eventually bringing political rewards in the form of local council and, ultimately, parliamentary seats. Together with conventional meetings, advice surgeries, grumble sheets, demonstrations, and petitions, they provided a strategy for rebuilding the Liberal Party from the bottom up.

Initially supported by the local government officer of the party, based at the party headquarters, the Association of *Liberal Councillors came increasingly to the fore in providing advice and assistance for community activists. Community politics was credited with the party's revival in a number of constituencies. Its most famous exponent, Trevor *Jones, signalled its success in Liverpool, taking the Liberal Party from two councillors in 1968 up to 48 in 1973 and control of the city, the first major council to be controlled by the Liberals since the war. The Liverpool example was galvanizing, with the techniques of community politics being adopted up and down the country. They were also applied to by-elections, where the use of *Focus*-style leaflets and local issues were used to create barnstorming campaigns which brought a whole string of by-election successes in 1972–4.

The techniques of community politics were not without their critics. Seen as the Trojan horse for the radical Young Liberals and the increasingly independent Association of Liberal Councillors, they were distrusted by many of the party hierarchy whose attention was concentrated on Westminster. The crudely populist and local focus of much of the campaigning was also seen as a diversion from traditional Liberal values, adding up to little more than a series of incoherent one-off campaigns. On the other hand the community politics advocates pointed to the poor outcome of conventional party strategy which even in the 1970 general election saw only six MPs elected. The result at the 1970 Liberal assembly was the adoption of a 'dual approach', committing Liberals to act both inside and outside the institutions of the political establishment and establishing a commitment to community politics. Community politics remained in the 1970s a key part of Liberal revival, proving especially successful in seats such as Rochdale and Yeovil where long-term work yielded lasting results. It was less successful when attempts were made to apply the techniques as a quick fix in the run-up to other elections. Although by-election victories were won on the basis of intense *Focus* campaigning, the seats were often lost quickly at the next election. Nonetheless, the barnstorming techniques of the activists proved successful in the early *Alliance heyday, bringing by-election successes such as *Croydon North-West and *Crosby. Under Paddy Ashdown and the newly formed Liberal Democrats, community politics became somewhat less prominent. Many of its activists were older and the style of the new party gave greater emphasis to efficient, professional organization and to more deliberative policy formulation. Nonetheless, the structure of local news-sheets and campaigning has remained and has inspired imitation at local level from the Labour and Conservative parties. *JS*

Michael Rosenbaum, *From Soapbox to Soundbite: Party Political Campaigning in Britain since 1945* (London, 1997).

Community Relations Commission, set up under the *Race Relations Act, 1968, to 'promote harmonious community relations'. Its role was seen by some as a 'racial buffer', a quasi-governmental body designed to deflect contentious issues of race into a bureaucratic framework which would also involve activists from the coloured communities. It was replaced in 1976 by the Commission for Racial Equality which absorbed its functions and those of the Race Relations Board. *JS*

comparative politics, methodological approach in political science. It allows theoretical generalization about political phenomena on the basis of the systematic evaluation of comparable evidence from different jurisdictions, usually, but not invariably, different nations. Comparative methods can be found in classical political thought, most notably Aristotle's classification of different forms of city state in *The Politics*, Montesquieu's *L'Esprit des lois* (1748), and De Tocqueville's *Democracy in America* (2 vols., 1835 and 1840). However, systematic comparisons developed after the late 19th century with works such as A. Lawrence Lowell's *Governments and Parties in Continental Europe* (2 vols., 1896), Otto Hintze's comparative essays written in the early 20th century and subsequently published in his *Gesammelte Abhandlungen zur allgemeinen Verfassungsgeschichte* (1962), and James Bryce's *Modern Democracies* (1929). The 1960s 'behavioural revolution' in social sciences gave an important impetus to the development of comparative politics. Above all, the theory of 'structural functionalism' stimulated interest in the analysis of non-western societies (see Gabriel Almond, *Comparative Politics: A Developmental Approach*, 1966).

Comparative studies take different forms. The number of countries included can vary from two (as in Hugh Heclo, *Modern Social Politics in Britain and Sweden*, 1974) to over 100 (Philips Cutright, 'National Political Development', *American Sociological Review*, 32 (1963)). The goal of the comparison can be to explain variation (Arend Lijphart, *Democracies: Patterns of Majoritarian and Consensus Government in Twenty-One Countries*, 1984) or to point to general trends (Otto Kirchheimer, 'The Transformation of the Western European Party System', in J. LaPalombara and M. Weiner (eds.), *Political Parties and Political Development*, 1966). The features compared may be quantitative and measurable (such as voting behaviour in Arend Lijphart, *Electoral Systems and Party Systems: A Study of Twenty-Seven Democracies 1945–1990* (1994)) or based on qualitative interpretation (Barrington Moore, *The Social Origins of Dictatorship and Democracy*, 1966).

In Britain, comparative methods have made their greatest impact in the study of political behaviour and elections. Central to debates in this area is the question of the changing electoral support for political parties and its impact on the character of parties and the party system. Powerful theoretical approaches, such as those developed by Seymour M. Lipset and Stein Rokkan (*Party Systems and Voter Alignments*, 1967) have given rise to major works of comparison such as Richard Rose's *Electoral Behaviour* (1974) and Stefano Bartolini and Peter Mair's *Identity, Competition and Electoral Availability: The Stabilisation of European Electorates 1885–1985* (1990).

The comparative study of government institutions and public policies in Britain as elsewhere is more diffuse. Major comparative studies of governmental systems as a whole include Herman Finer's *Theory and Practice of Modern Government* (1932), Brian Chapman's *Profession of Government* (1959), and Samuel Finer's *History of Government* (3 vols., 1997). Specific works of comparison examining distinctive features of government institutions and public policy include Richard Rose's *Public Employment in Western Nations* (1985), Jean Blondel's *Government Ministers in the Contemporary World* (1985), and Vincent Wright (ed.), *The Politics of Privatisation in Western Europe* (1989). *ECP*

HANS DAALDER (ed.), *Comparative European Politics: The Story of a Profession* (London, 1997). | MATTEI DOGAN and DOMINIQUE PELASSY, *How to Compare Nations: Strategies in Comparative Politics* (2nd edn., Chatham, NJ, 1990). | RICHARD ROSE, 'Comparing Forms of Comparative Analysis', *Political Studies*, 39 (1991).

Competing for Quality (1991), white paper establishing a programme whereby 'departments and Executive Agencies will in future set targets for testing new areas of activity in the market to see if alternative sources give better service and value for money'. The policy was part of the Major administration's attempt to extend the Thatcher reforms in a fashion that would permanently alter the size of the central state apparatus, it being widely recognized that activities once transferred to the private sector could rarely return to the civil service since the in-house Whitehall teams which bid to retain their existing work would either be broken up or would move out with that work into the non-public sector. Over the first two years of the programme (1992–4), some £1.8 billion worth of state activity was subjected to the market testing process, 55 per cent of which was eventually shifted to the private sector. *PJH*

Competing for Quality: Buying Better Public Services (Cm 1730, London, 1991). | PETER HENNESSY, 'The British Civil Service: The Condition of Mr Gladstone's Legacy as the Century Turns,' *Stakeholder* (July 1999).

Competition Commission (1999–). The Competition Commission's predecessors date back to 1948 when the Monopolies and Restrictive Practices Commission was established by the Monopolies and Restrictive Practices (Inquiry and Control) Act. It ceased to be responsible for restrictive practices in 1956, when this was handed to the director-general of fair trading and the Restrictive Practices Court. In 1973, the commission was renamed the Monopolies and Mergers Commission (MMC) by the Fair Trading Act. The Competition Commission replaced the MMC in 1999 as part of the Competition Act, 1998. *JD*

Competition Commission website: *www.competition-commission.gov.uk*

competitive tendering, in local government. Local authorities have long been free to contract-out activities, rather than provide them through direct labour organizations (DLOs), but were under no compulsion or encouragement to do so until 1959. In that year, the Macmillan government, under pressure from the construction industry, required them to subject one in three of their contracts to competitive tendering, although this requirement had no statutory force. The one-in-three rule was lifted by Richard Crossman in 1965. Compulsory competitive tendering (CCT) first appeared in the Local Government, Planning and Land Act, 1980, but was limited to building construction and maintenance, and highway maintenance work. Local authorities were permitted to carry out the work themselves, through their DLOs, only if they won the right to do so through competition. Resistance by many Labour-controlled authorities led the government to tighten regulations and limit evasion, moves which culminated in the Local Government Act, 1988. This Act extended competition requirements to street cleaning and refuse collection, building cleaning, vehicle and grounds maintenance, schools and welfare catering. The Act also permitted the secretary of state to extend the list of defined activities, and in 1989 sport and leisure management were added. The Major government extended CCT to such white-collar activities as finance, computing, personnel, library, and architectural services, under the Local Government Act, 1992. Councils were also encouraged to externalize further services on a voluntary basis (VCT). The long-standing hostility of the Labour Party to CCT ensured that it would not survive a change of government. The post-1997 Blair government introduced a 'best value' regime, under which councils were required to demonstrate effectiveness and quality, not just economy and efficiency, for a wider range of services than those covered by CCT. Competitive tendering was expected to continue, but as a management tool, and is no longer compulsory, except where, on the advice of the Audit Commission, the central department required a council to expose services to competition on the ground that they had failed to meet required standards. *KY*

comprehensive schools, designed to provide a wide range of secondary education for children within the same institution. This differed from the tripartite division of schools for different abilities set up under Butler's *Education Act, 1944, with entry graded according to results after the *eleven-plus examination. Growing opposition to selection at eleven and the second-class education offered to the majority of children in the non-academic 'modern' schools led to experiments with 'multilateral' or 'comprehensive' schools in both London and some rural areas like the Isle of Wight. After initial hostility, the Labour Party supported plans to comprehensivize the secondary education system and phase out the grammar school—as an issue of social justice. In 1965, the newly elected Wilson government instructed all local education authorities to prepare plans for the introduction of comprehensive schools, either by amalgamation of existing sites or by new buildings. In consequence of the policies followed by both Labour and Conservative governments after 1965, most secondary schools were reorganized into comprehensives. The policy has remained controversial because of arguments about its effectiveness in raising educational standards and the greater social equality claimed for it. *JS*

comptroller and auditor-general, officer of the House of Commons responsible for auditing the accounts of central government and other public bodies. The comptroller took on this role as part of the 1860s reforms of public finance which also led to the creation of the Public Accounts Committee. He heads a staff of nearly 1,000 in what has been known since 1983 as the National Audit Office. His staff not only audit accounts for probity to ensure there has been no fraud but also undertake value-for-money examinations to look at the economy, efficiency, and effectiveness with which programmes are run. This involves looking both at cases of past waste but also broader-based studies of the efficiency with which programmes are run. National Audit Office reports are discussed with departments and form the basis for inquiries by the Public Accounts Committee. *PJRR*

Conciliation and Arbitration Service. See ACAS.

Concorde, supersonic civil aircraft. A triumph of technical genius over economic sense, Concorde had by 2000 cost the British taxpayer £1 billion (at current prices). Britain and France agreed to co-operate on the project in November 1962, a collaboration which the Macmillan government hoped would help with its bid to join the European Economic Community (EEC). Despite the persistence of technical and, in particular, economic problems, successive governments continued to support the project (rather than antagonize France and incur heavy cancellation charges). Escalating oil prices had dashed hopes of foreign sales by the time of its first commercial flight in 1976, but small numbers of Concorde aircraft operated (if only with British

Airways and Air France) until a crash in Paris in 2000 led to the grounding of the remaining fleet. *CL*

Confederacy, secret organization of perhaps 50 members formed by three young Conservatives, Henry Page Croft, Thomas Comyn Platt, and Bernard Wise, in 1906. Committed to Joseph Chamberlain's campaign for *tariff reform, they were dissatisfied by the tepid response by many in the party, especially the leader Balfour, and sought to pressure and bully Tory free traders into acquiescence or silence. Their campaign of propaganda and intimidation ceased when the pro-tariff Andrew Bonar Law became leader in 1911. *RJQA*

LANY L. WITHERELL, *Rebel on the Right: Henry Page Croft and the Crisis of British Conservatism 1903–1914* (Newark, Del., 1997).

Confederation of British Industry (CBI) (1965–). The CBI was formed from a merger of the Federation of British Industries, the principal predecessor body; the British Employers' Confederation, which dealt with industrial relations questions; and the National Association of British Manufacturers, whose members were mainly smaller firms. Its formation at that time was encouraged by the new Labour government, and in particular the secretary of state for economic affairs George Brown, which wanted an effective employers' body with which it could have a dialogue about the management of the economy. As the CBI's title implies, it was originally seen as principally representing manufacturing industry, but over time it has evolved into a de facto confederation of British business, including the financial sector, retailers, lawyers, and even universities among its membership. This broadening of membership has in some ways increased the problem of 'stifling breadth', of developing policies which have an impact on government without offending some section of the membership. The CBI's period of greatest influence was from 1965 to 1979. Successive Labour and Conservative governments believed in the merits of 'tripartite' management of the economy and the CBI was particularly successful, in alliance with the majority of Labour ministers, in moderating the initially left-inclined stance of the Labour government of 1974–9. The leadership of the organization, both in terms of presidents and director-generals, often fell to those of a tripartite inclination, but this sometimes produced tensions within the organization, leading to the formation of internal pressure groups such as the Industrial Policy Group or occasional resignations by member firms. Organizational problems were also caused by the CBI's organization of both firms (including nationalized industries) and a somewhat chaotic system of industry level associations. The CBI lost influence under the Thatcher government, which preferred to listen to the more ideologically compatible Institute of Directors. By the end of the 1990s, the CBI's staff had shrunk substantially, but the election of the Blair government offered hope of a more effective dialogue with government. *WG*

W. GRANT, *Business and Politics in Britain* (2nd edn., London, 1993).

confidence motions. See COMMONS, HOUSE OF: CONFIDENCE MOTIONS.

Connolly, James (1868–1916), Marxist thinker and Irish political activist. Connolly was born in Edinburgh of Irish extraction and joined the British army aged 14. He deserted in 1889 and turned his self-education towards political end, founding the Irish Republican Socialist Party in 1896 and the *Workers' Republic* newspaper in 1898. Connolly went to the USA in 1902 and returned to Ireland in 1910, having shown his commitment to the cause of the left by founding an Irish Socialist Federation in New York and co-founding the International Workers of the World. On his return to Ireland, he organized the Irish Transport and General Workers' Union (ITGWU) in Ulster but became disillusioned by the sectarian divisions in Belfast (which he liked to blame exclusively on the Protestant workers). He took over the Dublin ITGWU strike and lock-out in 1913 after James Larkin's imprisonment and became acting secretary in 1914. His commitment to the plans for a rising at Easter 1916 placed him firmly in the hands of those who saw national sovereignty as an end in itself rather than a means to the kind of end that Connolly intended. His last acts suggested that he was reverting to his instinctive ethnic roots, for under sentence of death for his part in the Easter Rising he not only died in the Catholic faith, but insisted that his wife embrace it also. He was executed on 12 May while strapped to a chair because of his wounded ankle. Connolly was of little or no significance in the politics of the new Irish state, but was adopted as something of an icon by the most extreme and violent terrorist organization, the Irish National Liberation Army, in the much later Northern Ireland troubles. *DGB*

OWEN DUDLEY EDWARDS and B. RANSOM (eds.), *James Connolly: Selected Political Writings* (London, 1973). | RUTH DUDLEY EDWARDS, *James Connolly* (Dublin, 1998).

conscientious objectors. Some obligations imposed by the state require individuals to violate deeply held beliefs, and as early as the Vaccination Act of 1898 the British government recognized the legitimacy of conscientious objection. After Britain belatedly introduced conscription in 1916, however, this term became synonymous with refusal to bear arms, mostly on pacifist but occasionally on voluntarist grounds. Although the Military Service Acts allowed unconditional exemption (rather than from combatant duties only) and non-religious claims (rather than those grounded on Christianity only), the local tribunals which applied them made sparing use of these remarkably generous provisions. In consequence the 16,500 conscientious objectors of 1916–19 (roughly 0.33 per cent of total recruits) often failed to secure the exemption they claimed. A hard core of nearly a thousand 'absolutists' underwent considerable suffering, attaining martyr status in the eyes of progressive opinion, particularly once a reaction against the Great War set in during the 1920s. Conscription was reintroduced in April 1939, and in the Second World War objectors were, at 60,000 (1.2 per cent of those called up), more numerous than a quarter of a century before. They were also better treated by their tribunals. But they were again far too few to influence government policy, and were painfully aware of being disapproved of by a public convinced of the justness of the war. Few of them took an absolutist stand, most quietly accepting alternative service; and although conscription continued into peacetime (being abolished in 1957 with effect from 1960), conscientious objection ran at a negligible level. *MEC*

RACHEL BARKER, *Conscience, Government and War: Conscientious Objection in Britain, 1939–1945* (London, 1982). | JOHN RAE, *Conscience and Politics: The British Government and the Conscientious Objector to Military Service, 1916–1919* (London, 1970).

conscription, the compulsory enlistment of citizens, usually into the armed services. Despite vociferous campaigns for conscription as war threatened after 1900, Britain, exceptionally amongst the larger European states, had no peacetime conscription before 1914 and fought the first year and a half of war by raising volunteers. After considerable controversy, especially amongst Liberals, and the use of schemes which fell short of compulsion, such as the *Derby scheme, the Asquith government was forced to introduce conscription under the Military Service Acts, 1916, first of unmarried and later of married men, in order to meet the demands for men in the great attritional battles of the western front. The attempt to extend conscription to Ireland, however, aroused intense opposition and when passed in 1918 could not be implemented. Conscription lapsed in 1919, but was reintroduced for the first time in peacetime in April 1939 to meet the anticipated demands of a coming war. Once war broke out, conscription of men became universal and was extended to unmarried women between the ages of 18 and 50 by 1943, either for war work or for service in the women's branches of the armed forces. The National Service Act, 1947, provided for the continuation of conscription, initially for one year, but raised to two in 1950. In 1957, in the *Sandys white paper, the Macmillan government announced the phasing out of conscription, which finally ended in 1960. *JS*

R. J. Q. ADAMS and PHILIP POIRIER, *The Conscription Controversy in Great Britain, 1900–1918* (London, 1987).

consensus. see POST-WAR CONSENSUS.

Conservative Central Office (CCO), national party headquarters opened in 1870 and housed successively at St Stephen's Chambers, Sanctuary Buildings, Palace Chambers, and Abbey House in Victoria Street, since 1958 at Smith Square in Westminster. The CCO operates under the personal authority of the party leader, and has been managed since 1911 by the chairman of the Party Organization chosen by the leader; it has also provided since 1911 offices for the National Union and for the party treasurers, since 1946 for the Conservative Political Centre, and since 1979 for the Conservative Research Department. Since the late 1920s, it has also had a candidates' department (run by a party vice-chairman who was also an MP, and whose task it was to screen potential parliamentary candidates before offering lists of applicants to constituency associations), a women's department, and units running the party's youth movement and its activities in local government and agent-training. The CCO is the centre of the professional arm of the party, in its organizational, educational, and electioneering activities. In that context it also supervises 'Central Office Area Agents' in a dozen regional offices, each of which is also locally responsible for organization and training, press management, women's political activities, and fund-raising.

The internal structure of the CCO has changed at regular intervals, but the professional head of the office, principal agent until 1930, general director from 1930 to 1976, director-general/director of organization since 1976, has almost invariably been a career professional agent. Increasing weight has been given though to the post of director of publicity, first created in 1927 and usually going since 1945 to a media professional. In the last decades of the century, these two figures, along with the treasurers and the research director, have constituted a board of management chaired by the party chairman. In periods of healthy party fund-raising in the 1920s and 1940s, CCO employed about 200 staff, but this could be halved in bleaker times, and from the 1970s there was usually an increase in staff as an election neared but a purge to save money once it was over. This hampered both continuity and effectiveness.

For much of its life, for example in the time of Sir Joseph Ball, CCO's activities, its relations with the party and its dealings with the press, some of which it subsidized and a part of which it covertly owned, were shrouded in secrecy. This tended to credit CCO with more power than it ever actually wielded. It has usually had little formal authority and only limited influence within individual constituencies. The conventional wisdom was that for an applicant for a parliamentary candidacy to be perceived as the 'Central Office man' weakened his chances of selection. During the Heath-Thatcher period, CCO became more politicized, and its staff frequently associated with one faction or other of the party's policy battles. This tended more to reduce its collective influence than to enhance it. *JAR*

Michael Pinto-Duschinsky, 'Central Office and "Power" in the Conservative Party', *Political Studies*, 20 (1970). | Anthony Seldon and Stuart Ball (eds.), *Conservative Century* (Oxford, 1994).

Conservative Group for Europe, factional group within the Conservative Party which argued the case for a closer integration of Britain within the European (Economic) Community. *JAR*

Conservative Party, the dominating political force in 20th-century Britain. Conservatives usually governed the country alone or in coalition, while single-party majority Liberal or Labour governments existed for only twenty of the hundred years. Until the Blair government reformed its composition in 1999, the Conservatives controlled the House of Lords, and for 65 years were the largest party in the Commons. As a result of this entrenchment, Conservatives predominated in developing constitutional practices, shaping the expectations by which all governments were judged, and making long-term appointments to the civil service and the armed forces. In the cricketing language of Baldwin's Conservatives, merely by occupying the crease, the Tories denied opponents opportunities to make runs. As Tony Blair argued in 1998, echoing the title of a recent book, the 20th century was a 'Conservative Century'. Despite this record, Conservatives themselves spent much of the century worrying that they would decline into oblivion, fears that resurfaced after defeats in 1906, 1945, 1966, and 1997. Much interest in Tory politics in the 20th century lies in this tension between the party's own self-identity as the 'natural party of government', its generational eclipses at the polls, and its regular need to modernize itself to regain power. The party has mainly operated pragmatically and reactively, adjusting policy to contemporary fashion, showing an unconservative openness to novel techniques in electoral campaigning, and generally behaving as if winning power was more important than anything done with it afterwards. Robert Blake and John Ramsden, as historians of 20th-century Toryism, have each portrayed a party in which ideology was of secondary importance. Against this pattern, the party was convulsed by deep ideological fissures when from 1903 it divided over Joseph Chamberlain's 'crusade' for tariffs and imperial preference. In the 1990s, a long-gathering dispute over Britain's relationship with the European Union had a similar effect, prompting the fall of Thatcher, irremediably weakening her successor Major, and hindering the party's recovery under Hague. Conservative pragmatism thus alternated with periodic bouts of deeply ideological behaviour in which latitudinarian tolerance of different strands of opinion yielded to the certainties of the radical right, and the party became as a result impossible to manage.

In 1900, the party seemed misleadingly strong. In alliance with Liberal Unionists it had dominated since the Irish home rule crisis of 1886, winning three out of four general elections and governing for seventeen of the next twenty years. Nevertheless, the ageing Salisbury was becoming over-complacent, the party organization which had been so effective under Akers-Douglas and Middleton until the mid-1890s then failed to modernize to meet the demands of an increasing electorate, while party policy failed to head off either a Liberal resurgence or the formation of a Labour Party. When Salisbury made way for his nephew Arthur Balfour in 1902, there was criticism of a *'Hotel Cecil'. The new leader did not have either Salisbury's authority or his sureness of touch, and within a year several ministers resigned to take the tariff battle to the country. Until he himself resigned in 1911, Balfour endured three successive election defeats, a party divided on economic and international policy, and considerable personal hostility. In opposition from 1906, he used the Lords to check the Liberals' Commons majority, so unleashing the 1911 Parliament Act crisis in which the Lords lost their veto and the Conservatives their democratic credibility. Balfour's retirement produced a bitter leadership contest between Austen Chamberlain, Walter Long, and Andrew Bonar Law, which Law won only because he was disliked less than the others. It was, however, the uniting choice of a staunch partisan: as Lloyd George allegedly put it, 'the fools have stumbled on the right man by accident'. Law directed a rowdy party battle in the Commons and a vigorous campaign in the country, buttressed by the delayed modernization of the party machine in the country by Steel-Maitland. The party had good hopes of winning the election due (but not held) in 1915.

The Great War enabled the Conservatives to return to office in coalition with Liberals from 1915 to 1922, and to recover their self-respect and patriotic credentials. It also produced various threats: the introduction in 1918 of manhood suffrage and votes for women; a feared socialist majority in parliament; unrest foreshadowing post-war anarchy in industry; the Russian revolution of 1917 offering a glimpse of civil war and the destruction of property rights. Conservatives were therefore mostly reconciled to staying in Lloyd George's coalition government when peace and an election came in 1918, so uniting anti-socialist MPs in a single force of resistance, and under that banner they won a Conservative parliamentary majority behind the Liberal premier. This was an unstable combination, and needed to be regularized, as Lloyd George and centrist Conservatives attempted by planning to fuse the Conservatives and Lloyd George Liberals into one party in 1920. This plan was scuppered by Liberals unwilling to lose their historic identity, but Conservatives might well not have agreed anyway. Once fusion had failed, however, there was no way forward and, as apparent threats from the trade unions, the Labour Party, and Russia all waned in 1921–2, Tory reasons for backing Lloyd George vanished too. In a tricky situation in October 1922, Conservatives voted at the *Carlton Club meeting to fight the next election as a separate party under Law. This 'slice off the top' removed most of the front-benchers who opposed the Carlton Club vote and allowed the rise of the relatively unknown Stanley Baldwin, who took over when the dying Law retired in May 1923. Baldwin was party leader for fourteen years, if not always comfortably, and put his personal stamp on what the press called 'the New Conservatism'. In this phase, the party turned away from the polemical and partisan manners of the previous decades, greatly expanded its membership and income (hence also the effectiveness of its electoral campaigning), and adopted a self-consciously moderate identity. With a remarkable gift for political communication through speeches, radio, and the newsreels, Baldwin built up a considerable personal following by the later 1920s, enabling him to overcome the 1926 General Strike, vicious criticism of his leadership by the right and the press when in opposition in 1929–31, the economic crisis that led to a *National Government in 1931, and the *abdication crisis in 1936. In 1924 the Conservatives won a huge majority, the largest single-party victory of the century, and in 1931 and 1935 won even more seats as the leading component of the National Government. The moderate right's massive electoral strength (no other party ever won a parliamentary majority in the inter-war years) helped to marginalize British Fascists and ensured too that Baldwin could override critics on the right of his own party like Winston Churchill. During the 1930s, Conservative voters, especially in the recovering south and Midlands, had good reason to be grateful to a party which had weathered the economic storm at home and the communist threat abroad.

Strength again bred complacency, for the party's domestic effectiveness was not matched by ministers' perspicacity when faced by Hitler's Germany. Most Conservatives backed the desire of Baldwin and Neville Chamberlain to avoid war at almost any price, and hence were supporters of appeasement. In 1937–8 small groups of critics gathered around Churchill and Eden, but were never in a position to threaten the government, until in 1939 Hitler himself disproved the credibility of appeasement by making war inescapable. When the war began in 1939, it was therefore the Conservatives who were blamed for Britain's unpreparedness, and when the adoption for war purposes of Keynesian economic policies appeared also to discredit the pre-war government's domestic policies, they were increasingly adrift from popular opinion, itself radicalized by the egalitarian effects of 'the People's War'. The party's position was not helped by Churchill becoming leader in October 1940, since many Conservatives still distrusted him as an egotistical maverick, while he harboured grudges against party foes for keeping him out of office since 1929. Hence he did little to call off such attacks as the book *Guilty Men* (1940) written by *Beaverbrook journalists to discredit pre-war Conservatives. Churchill's inspirational war leadership reduced his distance from his own party, but his concentration on the war, and his refusal to plan domestic policy for the future, ensured that peace found it unready for the resumption of party politics. During the war years too, its organization had vanished, its offices closed, and its fund-raising and social activities ceased. The party thus crashed to an election defeat by Labour in 1945, losing half the seats held since 1935 and reduced to its lowest total of MPs since 1906.

Even in 1945, though, the Conservatives and their allies (Liberal Nationals and National Labour) retained almost 40 per cent of the national vote and were only 10 per cent behind Labour. The rapid recovery of the Tory organization under Woolton, reaching its highest ever number of members in the early 1950s, merger with the Liberal Nationals in 1947, and the development of the party's policy through such efforts of R. A. Butler's Conservative Research Department as the **Industrial Charter*, ensured a party recovery. In 1950 Conservatives almost drew level with Labour and in 1951 returned to office for thirteen years under Churchill, Eden, Macmillan, and Douglas-Home. The party gained seats in the Commons at all four elections in the 1950s, peaking with an overall majority of 100 in 1959. Although there were setbacks in foreign and colonial policy, Conservative ministers delivered a considerable improvement in standards of living, a substantial increase in homeownership, and economic growth that allowed increases in public expenditure without much impact on taxation. As in the 1920s and 1930s, the redistributive threat from Labour was countered by Conservatives championing the consumer, the taxpayer, and the homeowning individual family. This was, however, hard to maintain in a period in which affluent families' expectations were constantly rising, notably when after 1960 the British economy performed less satisfactorily than its international competitors. Even so, these Conservative governments survived the fiasco of the Suez crisis of 1956, implemented the decisive phase of British *decolonization, and made Britain's first application to join the European Economic Community (EEC) in 1961–2, all of these without producing splits that did lasting damage to Conservative unity. This was then the generation in which the Tory Lord Kilmuir could complacently refer to loyalty as the Conservatives' 'secret weapon'. Complacency in office and a sea change of public mood as the conservative fifties gave way to the more rebellious sixties were, however, undermining the foundations of Conservative rule. Economic weakness invalidated Conservatives' claim to be the party of governmental competence, a claim weakened further by failure to enter the EEC and personal scandals revolving around Vassall and Profumo. Macmillan sought to improve the government's image with a purge of his cabinet in 1962's 'Night of the Long Knives' but, when an operation forced his retirement in October 1963, there was an open fight for the succession and then public refusal by Iain Macleod and Enoch Powell to serve under Douglas-Home. Even with these disadvantages, Douglas-Home came close to winning a fourth successive party victory in 1964. In opposition, the party mood darkened quickly and Douglas-Home was forced to retire from the leadership in July 1965, effectively closing the chapter of party history that went back to Baldwin, had been reasserted in modernized clothing in the late 1940s, and had informed most of what Conservatives had done in office since 1951.

Neither the new leader Edward Heath nor the man he beat Reginald Maudling seemed to offer a decisive turn away from the party's recent past, but each was much younger than Macmillan and Douglas-Home, and from a lower social milieu than Conservative leaders of the past. Henceforth, Heath, Thatcher, Major, and Hague would in their different ways each assert their opposition to Labour's statist plans to introduce 'socialism' in more embattled language than had been customary since the 1920s, and from Thatcher onwards this 'radical-right' identity in economic policy would be expressed in a populist language regarding foreign nations, law and order, immigration, and the federalizing direction of the European Union.

Heath's tenure of the leadership was a transitional phase, with the strident language used after the 1970 Selsdon conference coexisting uneasily with continuing commitment to state intervention, a tension that produced his U-turn over industrial and incomes policies in 1972, and a policy on industrial relations which both confronted the trades unions and sought to placate them—but ended up by doing neither. The party's consequent defeat in two elections in 1974 paved the way for Heath's fall in February 1975 and replacement by Thatcher who had no such inhibitions about pursuing the agenda of the radical right. Conservatives' move in that direction owed something to changed international economic and political thinking, especially the new popularity of Milton Friedman and Friedrich von Hayek. It owed a little to Conservatives' wish to appeal to social classes that had not been strongly pro-Tory in the past, hence drives to extend home- and share-ownership to skilled workers, and to reduce basic levels of income tax (which such groups now paid, as they had barely done in the 1950s). It owed much, though, to the general perception that Britain in the 1970s was a country in serious decline, riven by industrial battles, plagued by low economic growth as a result of excessive taxation, and despised abroad after constant retreats in the process of dismantling the Empire. Conservatives differed greatly in the emphases placed on these problems, but almost all agreed that they could not be dealt with by traditionally limited policy approaches. They therefore rallied strongly to the dramatic tone and dynamic lead given by Thatcher.

During Thatcher's leadership, her party won all three general elections, the second and third by large majorities, but its position was always more vulnerable than that suggested. For most of the time the Conservatives trailed in opinion polls, almost all the time they did badly in local elections, while by-elections were dreaded for the humiliations that they usually produced. Nevertheless, Thatcher remained exceptionally popular with the party rank and file outside parliament, and with most Tory MPs too, at least so long as she was able to keep winning and pursue an active programme of anti-socialism. Hence, the relentless tide of legislation that she and Major were able to pass, their restless restructurings of education, local government, and healthcare, their systematic dismantling of the power of the trade unions and the scope of the public sector, policies that seemed well beyond the power of government to achieve in 1975. As Kenneth Clarke put it, Thatcher 'gave us the courage of our convictions', by successfully recovering ground that Conservatives had thought lost for ever. Increasingly, though, Conservatives also suspected her of valuing the fight more than the victory, of trusting too few even in her own party as 'one of us', and so damagingly narrowing her personal power base, and of accepting social division and the provocation of foreigners as the normal and permanent consequence—rather than just the necessary and temporary cost—of pursuing any policy. Most damagingly, many also came to the conclusion that she could not win the election due by 1992. Several former ministers had resigned from her cabinet, notably Heseltine and Lawson, but it was Howe's resignation over her anti-European rhetoric that allowed Heseltine to challenge her for the leadership in November 1990 and bring her down. Tories had never liked the idea of any assassin enjoying the profits of disloyalty, and in any case the Thatcherite right could never have been reconciled to Heseltine as leader. He was therefore beaten in the contest that followed Thatcher's fall by Major, then seen as a uniting candidate with no strong footing on either wing. Major was able to maintain this position through to an unanticipated election win in 1992, though retaining only a slim majority that proved too small to sustain him when the going then got rough, as it did after Britain failed to maintain her position in the Exchange Rate Mechanism. Thereafter, the Major government fought a continuous battle against disintegration, while the European issue increasingly drove its two wings apart and Major himself altogether failed to impose himself as Thatcher had done. Divisions, and the loss of by-elections which then allowed free rein to mavericks on the backbenches, were compounded by the onset of repeated allegations of 'sleaze', so that the government sank steadily lower in the voters' estimation over five years in office. The scale therefore of the 1997 defeat, the party's worst since 1832, and with under a third of voters backing Conservative candidates, had an inevitability about it, the price of overconfidence in office, much as had occurred after most earlier periods of extended Conservative rule.

Major immediately resigned after the 1997 election, and Tory MPs rapidly opted for a shift to an entirely new generation. They therefore drew a line under recent memories by electing the 36-year-old William Hague as leader after only eight years in the Commons and two in the cabinet. The youngest major party leader since Pitt in 1783 and the most inexperienced Conservative leader since Law, he was also the first since Law to speak with a regional accent and the first ever to have attended a comprehensive school. He rapidly sought to capitalize on the demand for a new start by moving towards greater democracy in the party structure and by holding referenda of party members, first to endorse his own leadership and subsequently to select candidates and approve policy statements, so appealing directly to the members over the heads of his recently fractious parliamentary colleagues. These changes seemed to denote more than a century's-worth of movement from both the social world and the aristocratic leadership of the 'Hotel Cecil', but then the Conservatives' success ever since democracy began to seep into the British political system in 1832 has owed much to their ability to reinvent themselves in each generation. In the 20th century, that facility had stood them in good stead. *JAR*

JOHN RAMSDEN, *The Age of Balfour and Baldwin, 1902–1940* (London, 1978). | JOHN RAMSDEN, *The Age of Churchill and Eden, 1940–1957* (London, 1995). | JOHN RAMSDEN, *Winds of Change: Macmillan to Heath, 1957–1975* (London, 1996). | ANTHONY SELDON and STUART BALL (eds.), *Conservative Century: The Conservative Party since 1900* (Oxford, 1994).

'Conservative Party at Prayer, the', a jocular reference to the political loyalties of the Church of England, in a phrase apparently coined by a Chartist in the 1840s. Frequently applied, until about the 1970s, to emphasize the then apparently natural Anglican-Conservative alliance, especially on such issues as education. *JAR*

Conservative Party conference, autumn mass meetings of the *National Union of Conservative and Unionist Associations, increasingly stage-managed since the 1960s by Central Office for television (though party factions have also organized an increasingly uncontrollable fringe programme). Apart from wartime and election years, conferences were held annually since 1867, originally in large cities but, since 1950, only in a small number of seaside resorts. Conference had no formal power, though individual conferences were politically significant (for example in 1921 for the Irish treaty, or 1950 for housing policy), and attempts have been made since about 1970 to increase democratic participation by constituency representatives. The conference is actually the most important of an annual cycle, but women's, local government, and Scottish conferences, for example, attracted much less public and media attention. *JAR*

RICHARD KELLY, *Conservative Party Conferences* (London, 1989).

Conservative Party leadership. In a party which had until the 1990s no written constitution, much authority derived from the leader, who could be only informally checked. In 1900, it was not even clear how a party leader was chosen. Formally, Conservatives had two co-equal leaders, those 'elected' to lead parliamentarians with the party whip in Commons and Lords, though it was acknowledged that, if either had been prime minister, then he took precedence. Salisbury and Balfour between 1885 and 1911 therefore had clear authority, but Law, chosen only by MPs in 1911, had to regard Lord Lansdowne as co-leader. In practice, the declining influence of the Lords after the *Parliament Act, 1911, clarified the situation. The Commoner Baldwin became leader in 1923 at least partly because his rival Curzon was in the Lords, and when Home and Hailsham sought the leadership in 1963, each had to disclaim his peerage to become a candidate.

The Conservative leader 'emerged' from discussion, rather than in a contested ballot of an identified electorate (as the proposer of Austen Chamberlain for the leadership smugly put it in 1921), and only afterwards was there a formal election, at which point there was only one candidate. That tradition was damaged by the disputed contests of 1957 and 1963, and became difficult to defend against the claims of democracy. Proper elections were introduced in 1965, and Edward Heath was thus the first elected leader, with the actual electorate restricted to Conservative MPs, though in each of the contests of 1965, 1975, 1990, and 1997 they were informed of the views of Conservative peers, the National Union, and constituency associations (and latterly of Conservative MEPs too), before casting their votes. Rules ensuring a direct voice for all party members were then adopted after William Hague was elected in 1997. The informality of the earlier system fostered much misunderstanding, especially the appearance that a leader enjoyed the job for life once he had 'emerged'. Robert *McKenzie demonstrated in 1955, in *British Political Parties*, that Balfour and both Austen and Neville Chamberlain had each been driven from office. Churchill, Eden, Macmillan, and Douglas-Home might later have been added to that list, so that only Salisbury (through age), Law (through illness), and Baldwin (after lengthy party battles) could be said to have freely chosen their own retirement. Being party leader could in fact be a pretty bloody affair, and Baldwin likened leading the Conservatives to driving pigs to market. It was expected that the mandate conferred by open election would strengthen the leader's hand, but the 1965 rules and later amended versions also formalized rights to challenge incumbent leaders. Both Heath and Thatcher were toppled against their will, while Major used the system in 1995 to confront his critics but in 1997 had to resign before he could be pushed.

In practice then, Conservative leaders have had to be responsive to party opinion revealed through the National Union, the Conference, the (shadow) cabinet, and the 1922 Committee, but could always strengthen their position by tempering policy and patronage in response to criticism. Nevertheless, Conservatives' natural respect for authority, at least until the latter part of the century, still left much room for manoeuvre by incumbent leaders. The leader has generally set the agenda for Tory politics, focused the party's image and campaigning identity, and promoted like-minded people over time—for all of which Thatcher's tenure of office provided ample evidence. *JAR*

Conservative Political Centre (CPC), party forum created in 1945 following pre-war experiments in political education, initially under the direction of 'Cub' Alport, but under the general patronage of R. A. Butler. Its aims were to foster knowledge of Conservative policies among party activists and an awareness by the leadership of members' views. The CPC therefore acted as a party publishing house, and ran summer schools and weekend conferences, often at Swinton College. Its main activity was in discussion groups in areas and constituencies, and within two years there were already more than 500 such groups, each receiving the same CPC brief before holding its meeting and feeding back local opinions, which the CPC then summarized into reports for its national committee and the party leaders. This 'two-way movement of ideas', though rarely involving more than a few thousand activists, was a crucial tool of party management, enabling the parliamentary leadership to avoid getting too far out of step with the grass roots. As membership then steadily declined, the 1950s level of activity was not maintained, and in the great debate on joining the European Community in 1971 only 300 groups took part. The CPC remained, though, important in Conservative politics, foreshadowing the focus-group methods of the 1990s, and was reorganized after the 1997 defeat as the 'Conservative Policy Forum'. *JAR*

Conservative Research Department (CRD), the policy research and literature-drafting arm of the Conservative central organization, located until 1979 in Old Queen Street. The CRD was created after Conservative defeat in 1929, when the party came to recognize that, in order to compete with Labour as a national rival for power, it had to be more professionally prepared for policy debates. Neville *Chamberlain, the most policy-orientated of Baldwin's colleagues, was chairman from 1930 to 1940 and effectively shaped its method of working. It had only about four staffers in the 1930s, went out of existence in the war years, and so had to be re-invented after 1945. Initially, separate units were then created to support the parliamentary party, to deal with policy research, and for library activities, but these were reintegrated into a single unit as the CRD in 1948. Much of the fame of the CRD traces back to that period in opposition in 1945–51, when it had about 50 staff who contributed crucially to the party's modernization of its policy stances in such documents as the *Industrial Charter* of 1947. With the intellectually formidable trio of Macleod, Maudling, and Powell all working there, its reputation as a forcing house for future ministers was also forged. Under the long-term chairmanship of Butler (1945–65), and the management of Michael *Fraser (1951–75), the CRD was a major influence on the work of Conservative governments and the development of party policy. Its decline began under Heath, who did not nominate a senior colleague to be policy-impresario as Chamberlain and Butler had been. The CRD's association with the 'wet' side of the inner-party battles of the 1970s led to its being treated with reserve by Thatcher and merged into Central Office in 1979. *JAR*

John Ramsden, *The Making of Conservative Policy: The Conservative Research Department since 1929* (London, 1980).

constituencies, geographic areas which return members to parliament. The number has varied, but since 1997 there have been 659 constituencies, each returning a single MP. They are divided into borough (essentially urban) and county (rural) constituencies, the distinction being important nowadays principally for reasons of allowed election expenditure: there are different limits for the two types of constituency. Single-member constituencies have been the norm since 1885, but they have only been used on a uniform basis since 1950; in the period 1918–50, fifteen ordinary two-member constituencies survived, alongside four university constituencies that elected either two or three MPs. The boundaries for constituencies are drawn up by a boundary commission and approved by parliament. Each constituency is given a geographic name and as far as possible constituency boundaries are devised to reflect local communities. Though constituency boundaries within each part of the UK (England, Scotland, Wales, Northern Ireland) are drawn in order to try to ensure that the number of electors in each is roughly equal, demographic and other changes produce some notable disparities in size. The emphasis on the number of electors means that constituencies vary enormously in geographic size, some heavily populated urban seats being very small geographically while some sparsely populated rural seats are massive. Since 1918, MPs were all elected on the same day in a *general election, the method of election used in each seat being that of *first past the post. Once elected, each MP is expected to help all those who live in the constituency, regardless of whether or not those seeking help voted for the MP. *PN*

ROBERT WALLER and BYRON CRIDDLE, *The Almanac of British Politics* (5th edn., London, 1996).

constitution, British. The 'unwritten' British constitution has traditionally been conceived as a 'living structure' (in Leo Amery's words), its forms and processes the result of a continuous historical process of development and pragmatic adaptation, rather than being based upon fixed principles or an entrenched legal settlement. Precedent and convention have therefore been central features of constitutional understanding and behaviour, Sidney Low's famous comment that 'we live under a system of tacit understandings, but the understandings themselves are not always understood' (*The Governance of Britain* (London, 1904), 12) pointing to the ambiguities inherent in such an approach. James Callaghan once praised this 'back of an envelope' flexibility, which has been accompanied for much of the 20th century by an uncritical view of the constitution and an absence of sustained and systematic constitutional debate and analysis. The constitution has been widely described as simply 'what happens', the 'rules of the game' being driven by political forces and exigencies. The open-ended nature of the constitution came under attack in the 1980s and 1990s, with the emergence of groups like *Charter 88 calling for a comprehensive package of reforms and a written constitution. The traditional doctrine of parliamentary sovereignty (celebrated by A. V. Dicey) also came in for criticism as allowing for an untrammelled executive dominance, growing centralization, and the absence of effective constitutional constraint. The Labour government's post-1997 reform programme, including devolution to Scotland and Wales, House of Lords' reform, and the Human Rights Act, was designed to introduce checks and balances to counter what Lord Hailsham once described as a system of 'elective dictatorship'. But the new constitutional settlement was equally likely to be shaped by the dynamic forces released by Labour's reforms in ways which the government did not expect and could not control. *KT*

Constitutional Conference (17 June–10 November 1910), inter-party conference, an attempt to resolve the impasse over reform of the House of Lords, stemming from the Lords' rejection of Lloyd George's *'People's Budget' of 1909. Resolutions presented to parliament in early April 1910 by the recently re-elected Liberal government proposed three changes: that the House of Lords should no longer have the power to reject or amend a money bill; that bills passed by the Commons in three successive sessions of parliament should become law despite the opposition of the Lords, and that the maximum length of parliament should be reduced from seven years to five. A Parliament Bill containing these proposals passed its first reading in the Commons on 14 April. The controversial budget which had caused the crisis was duly passed by the end of April, but the wider constitutional issue remained to be resolved. The situation was complicated by the death of Edward VII on 6 May and it was agreed that a constitutional conference should be called to find a solution and alleviate pressure on the new king, George V. The Liberal and Unionist parties sent delegates to the conference which came close to a compromise, and there were even proposals for a coalition government to resolve all major political issues. These attempts broke down, however, and on the day the conference collapsed, Asquith asked the king for an immediate dissolution of parliament in order to secure a specific mandate for reform of the Lords. The king sought to delay in order to ascertain the Lords' reaction to the Parliament Bill, but when the Lords refused to accept the Liberal proposals, parliament was dissolved on 28 November and a general election called, which produced much the same result as in January. The failure of the inter-party conference ensured that the issue of Lords' reform would have to be tested in another election, which thus gave the Liberals both a mandate and a sufficient majority to press on with reforming the upper house. *JS*

Consumers' Association, private organization set up in 1956 to campaign for consumers' rights in the purchase and quality of goods. An important body in the growth of consumer consciousness during the affluent post-war years, it is funded by the subscriptions of more than a million members to its various *Which?* magazines. *JS*

***Continuity and Change* (1994)**, white paper. The document had the air of a deal between the Major government and the civil service: the principle of a permanent, career, politically neutral civil service would be preserved in exchange for a renewed emphasis on management reforms and still tighter control on running costs. It also created a senior civil service with explicit, written employment contracts for top officials. This aspect raised fears of a creeping politicization of the senior ranks. In response to concerns expressed by the all-party Treasury and civil service select committee, the government agreed to the promulgation of a civil service code to underpin the traditional recruitment and promotion on merit. Personal contracts and a further dose of the so-called 'new public management' were later described by a senior official as 'the price we had to pay to get those buggers [Conservative ministers] off our backs'. *PJH*

The Civil Service: Continuity and Change (Cm 2627, London, 1994). | *The Civil Service: Taking Forward Continuity and Change* (Cm 2748, London, 1995). | *Fifth Report from the Treasury and Civil Service Committee: The Role of the Civil Service*, HC (London, 1993–4). | Peter Hennessy, 'The British Civil Service: The Condition of Mr Gladstone's Legacy as the Century Turns', *Stakeholder* (July 1999).

contracting in/contracting out. As trade unions affiliated to the Labour Representation Committee and the Labour Party from 1900, they often raised a political levy on members to sponsor a trade union/Labour candidate and to pay for their upkeep in parliament. In the *Osborne case (1909), however, this was challenged. The main attack on the trade union political levy was that political activity was *ultra vires* for a trade union since political activity lay outside the purpose of the trade unions as defined by the legislation of the 1870s. However, the Trade Union Act of 1913 reversed the court's decision, but allowed individual members to 'contract out' of this particular part of membership of their union. And so it remained that trade unions could provide a political levy to the Labour Party until, following the General Strike, Baldwin's Conservative government introduced the Trades Disputes and Trade Union Act of 1927. Under this legislation it was no longer lawful for a trade union to make a political contribution on behalf of a member unless 'notice in writing' to do so was given by individual members. Effectively, trade union members now had to 'contract *in*', in writing, rather than contract out of the arrangement by writing. This meant that trade union members had to take a deliberate action to contract in, which many were too idle, apathetic, or simply conformist to do. In the event, trade unions organized campaigns to ensure that the political fund to Labour was not decimated and, in 1946, the Attlee Labour government repealed the Act of 1927, reinstating 'contracting out'. *KL*

convertibility crisis (1947), the situation where the convertibility of a currency at its fixed exchange rate becomes insupportable and convertibility is therefore suspended, so that the currency can no longer be exchanged for other currencies or gold. When the supply of a currency in the international economy is greater than the demand for it, countries will sell it in order to buy other currencies. Eventually, this will reduce a country's foreign exchange reserves to the point where sustaining convertibility is no longer feasible. At this point, convertibility will be suspended, or the currency will be *devalued. In the former case, the debacle is referred to as a convertibility crisis.

The most famous convertibility crisis of the century was the 1947 sterling crisis. In July 1947, Britain was required to make sterling convertible to the US dollar and other currencies as part of the terms of the Anglo-American financial agreement of 1946. At this time British and European economies were still recovering from war and there was an excess demand for American goods and therefore for dollars. Once it was known that sterling would be convertible to the dollar in July 1947, other countries accumulated sterling in order to exchange it for dollars once sterling was convertible. Sterling was duly made convertible on 15 July 1947 at its exchange rate of $4.06 to the pound, but there was a run on the Bank of England's foreign exchange reserves as other countries sought to exchange their sterling balances for dollars. During 1947, there was an outflow of $4,100 million from the Bank of England compared to a total of $900 million in 1946. During the last week of convertibility, this outflow reached $237 million. On 20 August, Britain was forced to suspend convertibility of sterling, not restored until December 1958. *CRS*

Cook, Arthur James (1883–1931), trade unionist. A. J. Cook was general secretary of the Miners' Federation of Great Britain (MFGB), 1924–31. He started work in the south Wales coalfield in 1901 and was a mining lodge official, 1906–18. In the period up to 1914, Cook was a leading figure in various rank and file movements such as the Unofficial Reform Committee and the Industrial Democracy League. In 1918, he was sentenced to three months' imprisonment for his anti-war activities. Cook was elected miners' agent for Rhondda no. 1 district in 1919 and gained a seat on the executive of the South Wales Miners'

Federation. A member of the Independent Labour Party from 1906, he was also a member of the Communist Party of Great Britain during 1921. Cook was appointed to the MFGB's executive in 1921 and served a further two months' imprisonment for his activities in the national miners' strike of that year. In 1923, he helped to launch the Miners' Minority Movement whose support played an important part in his election as MFGB secretary. As miners' secretary he campaigned for an industrial alliance of all the major unions. Cook led the MFGB during the General Strike of 1926 and subsequent seven-month lockout of the miners. Following the miners' defeat he devoted his efforts to rebuilding the MFGB's battered organization. In the late 1920s Cook was heavily criticized within the labour movement, for his campaign against the TUC's collaboration with the employers, through the Mond-Turner talks. An inspirational speaker and prolific socialist writer, he was a much-loved miners' leader. As his biographer Paul Davies has observed, Cook has been misconceived as a brilliant orator who lacked leadership qualities, yet he was a pragmatic union negotiator who was politically outmanoeuvred by the Baldwin government during the miners' strike of 1926. *DLM*

Paul Davies, *A. J. Cook* (Manchester, 1987).

Cook, Robert Finlayson ('Robin') (1946–), Labour politician, foreign secretary 1997–2001. Robin Cook was educated at Edinburgh University and was active in student politics, the Workers' Educational Association, and Edinburgh city council before becoming MP for Edinburgh Central, 1974–83, and for Livingstone since 1983. He held several front-bench portfolios in opposition from 1980, including finance, health, Europe, and trade, and was Labour's campaign coordinator, 1984–6. Initially a member of the Tribune group, he gravitated towards the right of the Labour Party during the Kinnock and Blair periods, though was thought to remain closer to Labour's socialist roots than many of Blair's cabinet after 1997. A keen pro-European, he had a frustrating time as foreign secretary after 1997, wishing to make the pro-European case more actively than was thought expedient by the government's public relations strategists. He became Leader of the House in 2001. *JAR*

Cooper, (Alfred) Duff (1890–1954), Conservative politician, diplomat, and author. Cooper's life and career was anything but dull, being a Great War guards officer, a regular fixture at the gaming and card tables, and married to the actress and society beauty Lady Diana Manners, a serial adulterer. He was propelled into politics, representing Oldham, 1924–9. Considered a rising talent during his early parliamentary years, he offered a lifeline to the beleaguered leadership of Baldwin when he won the 1931 St George's by-election, fending off the challenge of the *Empire Crusaders. Loyalty was rewarded with ministerial office, first as financial secretary to the Treasury then the War Office. Despite adopting the mantra 'never ask for anything, never refuse anything, never resign' (Crowson, *Facing Fascism* (London, 1997), 232) he broke two of these three golden rules. At the War Office, Cooper's persistent championing of the army's cause, against the tide of governmental thinking, had irritated Neville Chamberlain. As Chamberlain prepared to take over as prime minister in 1937 Lady Diana intervened, fearful that the new premier intended demoting Duff. Ultimately Cooper retained his cabinet status but was moved to the Admiralty, where the deteriorating international situation combined with Cooper's anti-Germanic tendencies taxed his loyalty. When Chamberlain triumphantly returned from Munich, Cooper, unable to stomach the surrender of the Czechs, resigned—the only cabinet minister to do so. During the Second World War Cooper, after a period at the Ministry of Information, was dispatched to the Far East, returning shortly before the fall of Singapore. In the final war years he acted as the liaison minister with the Free French in Algiers. This began a fractious relationship with De Gaulle which continued when Cooper became British ambassador to Paris, 1944–7. During this period he assiduously promoted closer European cooperation and played a not insignificant role in the treaty of *Dunkirk. *NJC*

Duff Cooper, *Old Men Forget* (London, 1953). | John Charmley, *Duff Cooper: An Authorised Biography* (London, 1986). | Artemis Cooper (ed.), *A Durable Fire: The Letters of Duff and Diana Cooper* (London, 1983).

Cooper, Frank (1922–), civil servant. After wartime service with the RAF, Cooper joined the Air Ministry in 1948, moving into the Ministry of Defence (MoD) in 1964, where he was deputy secretary, 1968–70. After a stint in the Civil Service Department (1970–3), he served as permanent secretary at the Northern Ireland Office, 1973–6, in which post he played a key role in organizing the 1975 *ceasefire talks with the IRA. He returned to the MoD as permanent secretary, 1976–82. Cooper was proud of his provincial roots (he was educated at Manchester grammar school) and was an unusual civil servant: blunt talking, a dominating presence, and a formidable Whitehall operator whose style was variously described as akin to that of an industrial tycoon or a politician. An effective manager of the MoD, staffing was cut by 55,000 during his time as departmental head. He was also a key official adviser during the 1982 Falklands war.

KT

Cooperative Party. The Cooperative movement emerged in the mid-19th century as a form of collective retailing and production, which brought together associations of members for trading purposes and the sharing of profits through dividends. Effectively, it began with the Rochdale Society of Equitable Pioneers in 1844, and by the 1930s had spread throughout Britain, reaching a peak of 12.5 million members. In the course of this development it created a number of cooperative bodies: by 1863 there was a Cooperative Wholesale Society, which was producing goods for the various regional retailing 'coops', and in 1869 the Cooperative Union was formed on a federal basis to bring these cooperative societies together and hold annual decision-making conferences.

Theoretically the movement was non-political, but in 1917 the Cooperative Congress decided to form a political arm to influence government and the Cooperative Party therefore emerged in 1918. At the 1918 general election, A. E. Waterson was elected as Cooperative MP for Kettering but immediately took the Labour whip. Under an agreement made with the Labour Party in 1927, local Cooperative parties became eligible to affiliate to divisional Labour parties, and from 1941 the party's representatives became eligible to attend the meeting of the National Council of Labour, a body which brought together representatives from Labour's main organizations. In the 1945 general election the party successfully returned 23 MPs. However, it has faced political problems since that period, with some infiltration by Communists in the late 1940s and the defection of four MPs to the Social Democratic Party in 1981. Despite these problems and the decline of the movement in the retailing sector, the party returned eight MPs in 1983 and there were still fifteen in 1992.

KL

T. F. Carbery, *Consumers in Politics: A History and General Review of the Cooperative Party* (Manchester, 1969).

Corn Production Act, 1917. In 1917, the Lloyd George government introduced a new food production policy under which control of production and distribution of food was placed in the hands of the new Ministry of Food, with the Ministry of Agriculture responsible for farming production. The Corn Production Act, 1917, gave legislative effect to this policy, incorporating powers to control farm production, including the dispossession of inefficient farmers, and introducing minimum wages for agricultural labourers and minimum prices for wheat and oats.

JHB

corporation tax, introduced by James Callaghan as part of the Finance Act of 1965, although a more modest version of it had operated in 1920–4. It showed the differences in party-political attitudes towards companies and industrial investment. The 1965 Act regarded companies as entities separate from their shareholders. Companies paid tax on their profits and then shareholders paid income tax on their dividends. This was strongly criticized as double taxation of the shareholder, for profits retained in the company had a preferential treatment compared to those distributed to the shareholder. Labour thought that profits were more justifiable if they were retained for fresh investment, rather than distributed to the 'non-producing' shareholder. It was hoped that the tax would help negotiations with the trade unions over wage restraint. There was no evidence to suggest that retained profits were a better way of financing industry than going to stock market. The Conservatives helped shareholders by a reform in 1973 which credited to them the tax already paid by the company to offset their liability to income tax, so removing 'double' taxation. The desire to tax companies clashed with the aim of stimulating investment through tax allowances, so that the actual yield of company taxation declined during the 1970s. In 1984, so as to achieve a more neutral tax regime, the tax rate was lowered but particular concessions removed.

RCW

corporatism and neo-corporatism have not found a congenial home in liberal and pluralist Britain, by comparison with countries with Social Catholic values and disciplined organized interests. Corporatism, such as was developed in Fascist Italy, in any case, involved the incorporation of the interests into a would-be totalitarian state, depriving them of the very autonomy that would have allowed a traditional society to create a purported non-coercive social consensus. The neo-corporatist theorizing that developed from 1974 in the wake of an influential article by Philippe Schmitter, did not reflect a normative and retrospective preoccupation with avoidance of class conflict in an organic and hierarchical society. Rather, it purported to project an empirical reality, allowing a circumspectly positive reply to the question 'Still the Century of Corporatism?' in terms of interest intermediation. Neo-corporatism implied that parliamentary institutions, while not being superseded by functional representation (as under pseudo-corporatism in Italy, Portugal, and Spain), were taking second place to the tripartite control over economic policy by an interlocking directorate of government, business, and labour in socio-economic partnership. This did not necessarily occur in the economic and social councils that institutionalized the recognized interest groups which never came into existence in Britain but might be achieved informally through committees that went beyond consultation to making contractual agreements.

Although there had been tentative inter-war explorations in this direction and close cooperation of government, business, and labour during the Second World War, it was still the case that the TUC resisted legislation regulating trade union activities, preferring in its general secretary George Woodcock's words to be treated as 'outlaws' once post-war 'normality' had returned. The nearest Britain approximated to even a highly diluted form of neo-corporatism was from the mid-1960s to the mid-1970s, when the National Economic Development Council was involved with the Wilson and Heath governments in seeking to concert the activities of government, business, and labour. However, between the failure of the 1965 National Plan and the success of the coal miners' strike that precipitated Heath's defeat at the February 1974 general election, via attempts at implementing a national incomes policy, the feeble venture into tripartism miscarried. 'Solemn and binding agreements' proved not to be worth the paper they were written on, because the leaders of the TUC and CBI were incapable for more than limited periods of securing even partial action by their members on wages and prices in line with the commitments made. While a Labour government might secure some wage restraint from its union brothers on a brief, bilateral basis, this was so clearly behaviour in conflict with the purpose of trade unions in a liberal market economy that it could not be more than an ephemeral expedient. Attacks on British neo-corporatism were therefore polemical onslaughts on a largely non-existent phenomenon, a figment of Thatcherite imagination to justify the anti-trade union legislation of the 1980s. *JH*

R. J. Harrison, *Pluralism and Corporatism* (London, 1980). | P. C. Schmitter and G. Lehmbruch (eds.), *Trends towards Corporatist Intermediation* (Beverley Hills, Calif., 1979).

corruption, political, unethical and/or illegal conduct by politicians intended to secure personal (generally financial) advantage, or unfair advantage for their party in the electoral process. Britain for the most part enjoyed a healthy self-identity as having a clean and honest political system, but there were individual cases that punctured this comfortably reassuring pattern: over the century, seven MPs were expelled from the Commons after formal censure of their political conduct, but only two or three of these could be regarded as corruption cases. Nevertheless, the determination that parliamentarians be seen to be behaving ethically fuelled increasingly insistent demands that MPs (and in due course peers too) should record their outside interests on a register.

There were also periods at both the beginning and end of the century when more general allegations of the corruption of standards in political life were made. Electoral bribery, corruption, and coercion were the stuff of 18th-century politics, and lingered on long after reform began in the 1830s. The 1880 general election was probably in real terms the most expensive of all time, and this helped to bring to a head demands for higher standards. Legislation in 1883 fixed cash limits for each candidate's allowable expenditure (generous at first but steadily eroded by inflation) and set up mechanisms for policing the system and ensuring that infringements were punished. By 1900, corruption of the old type was mainly a thing of the past, but judicial inquiries into such cases as Exeter in 1910 suggested that ethical standards below the surface were still not all that was by then being claimed; there were similar claims about 'treating' surviving into this period, with gifts of beef or beer in one place, half-crowns wrapped in party leaflets in another. The decisive change came not with legal measures but with the rapid increase in the size of the electorate (fewer than six million in 1880, rising to almost thirty million in 1930), which made manipulation of individual voters by dubious means simply impracticable. When politicians were accused of bribing the electorate in the second half of the century, it was generally with policies rather than cash, as when Harold Wilson promised to build the Humber bridge while awaiting a crucial by-election in Hull in 1966, or when the Conservatives announced in 1974 restrictions on the mortgage rate which would mainly benefit middle-class voters. Such claims could not be taken to the courts, and were left to the 'jury' of voters to decide in the election itself.

More sweeping allegations of corruption in the Edwardian period resulted largely from the polarization of political attitudes in debates over tariffs and home rule for Ireland. Liberals, and Conservative free-traders too, argued that decisions on specific tariffs would enmesh business in politics unhealthily, with money changing hands between industrialists and the parties, either to line a politician's pocket or to fill the party's war chest with money for a campaign in favour of a particular customs duty which would benefit the industry in question (as was not uncommon in the USA and Canada). Conservatives retorted that Liberals in office after 1905 were filling their own funds with cheques from 'radical plutocrats', self-made millionaires who all then mysteriously seemed to acquire knighthoods and peerages. In fact, the sale of honours had gone on under Conservative as well as Liberal governments for decades, and only when it was shamelessly practised on the open market and through dubious intermediaries, when Lloyd George was premier, did the scandal erupt and enforce remedial measures in 1922. In the mean time, the Conservatives were able to exploit in 1913 the biggest corruption charge of the century, the *Marconi scandal.

Nothing comparable was to be seen until the 1990s, when once again there were allegations from the press and opposition of sleaze among parliamentarians. Once again this centred not only on cases of dishonesty by individual politicians ('cash for questions' and 'cash for access' to ministers), but also on the general ethical assumptions within government and the Conservative party. This time, with no Commons majority, the Major government could not face down its critics; it was obliged to set up exactly the sort of inquiry that Asquith had managed to avoid (see NOLAN REPORT), was seriously damaged by its report, and had to concede the toughening-up of parliamentary controls and disclosures to prevent anything like it from happening again. *JAR*

G. R. SEARLE, *Corruption in British Politics* (Oxford, 1987).

Cosgrave, Liam (1920–), Irish prime minister, 1974–7, and Fine Gael leader, 1965–77. Cosgrave was the son of W. T. *Cosgrave, the first chief executive of the Irish Free State. Liam Cosgrave's career revealed the importance of the hereditary principle in southern Irish politics as he followed his father as member of the Dáil (1943–81) and member of various governments before he became taoiseach (prime minister). The British had suspended the Stormont parliament in March 1972 but were anxious to follow this up with a quick settlement plan. Cosgrave was a signatory of the communiqué which resulted in the establishment of a Council of Ireland to create an 'Irish dimension' to the power-sharing executive agreed between the Social Democratic and Labour Party and the Ulster Unionists. *DGB*

DERMOT KEOGH, *Twentieth-Century Ireland: Nation and State* (Dublin, 1997).

Cosgrave, William Thomas (1880–1965), Irish politician and head of government, 1922–32. Cosgrave was a delegate to the first Sinn Fein convention in 1905. Elected to Dublin corporation in 1909 he joined the Irish Volunteers, the forerunner of the IRA, in 1913 and later fought in the Easter Rising of 1916. In 1917, he was elected as a Sinn Fein MP for Kilkenny. From 1919, Cosgrave served as a minister in the first Dáil, the revolutionary underground government established by Sinn Fein. In 1922 he became the first president of the executive council of the Irish Free State. In 1923 he founded Cumann nGaedheal, becoming its first leader. When a new political party, Fine Gael, was founded in 1933, he stood down as leader of the main opposition to Fianna Fáil. In 1935 he returned as leader of Fine Gael and remained leader of the opposition until 1944. Father of Liam *Cosgrave, Irish premier in the 1990s. *TWH*

Costello, John Aloysius (1891–1976), Irish Fine Gael politician and taoiseach, 1948–57. Costello is best remembered for declaring Eire a republic and withdrawing from the Commonwealth in 1949. These were moves to outflank Eamon de Valera and to please his coalition partners, Labour and Clann na Poblachta. The main consequence was further to entrench partition. Britain responded with the Ireland Act, 1949, ruling out any waiving of sovereignty without the consent of Northern Ireland's own parliament. *DRB*

cotton industry. This industry, encompassing both spinning and weaving, was a leading growth sector in the early 19th century. Heavily concentrated in the Lancashire region, it prided itself on the excellent quality and design of its finished cloth manufactured from imported raw cotton. Dominating world markets, it accounted for 65 per cent of the international trade in cotton yarns and piece goods in the 1909–13 period. During the Great War the British cotton industry suffered severely due to its enforced loss of world markets and the emphasis on war production. Following the cessation of hostilities, the industry experienced a short-lived revival before the onset of the inter-war Depression, during which British exports were undermined not only by the return to the *gold standard at pre-war parity in 1925 but also by increasing international competition. Foreign producers, particularly Japan, were able to derive advantage from mass-production factories concentrating on long runs of the same design. In contrast, British producers, characterized by large numbers of small family-dominated companies, were unable to secure the same degree of cheapness in production and efficiency in marketing. In the 1930s there came the manufacture and marketing of cotton goods at substantially lower prices as a result of the economies of scale, and attempts to improve efficiency concentrating on government-funded measures to secure rationalization via the scrapping of surplus capacity. There was a brief revival in the fortunes of the industry after the Second World War but thereafter its decline continued virtually unabated with the loss of overseas markets and import penetration from developing countries. Its decline would have been even more rapid had it not been for the imposition of quotas and protection including a voluntary ceiling on exports by other Commonwealth producers. The popularization of synthetic materials, such as rayon, lycra, and other alluringly sheer and diaphanous fabrics, accentuated the relative and absolute contraction of the cotton industry in relation to the rest of the textile sector.

JFM

Cottrell, Alan Howard (1919–), government scientific adviser. Cottrell's academic training was in metallurgy, in which subject he held university professorships at Birmingham (1949–55) and Cambridge (1958–65). He was deputy head of the metallurgy division at the atomic energy research establishment at Harwell, 1955–8; deputy and then chief scientific adviser at the Ministry of Defence, 1965–7; deputy chief scientific adviser to the government, 1968–71, and then chief scientific adviser, 1971–4. After leaving Whitehall, he was master of Jesus College, Cambridge, 1974–86.

KT

Council for Encouragement of Music and the Arts. See ARTS POLICY.

Council for Security and Cooperation in Europe. See HELSINKI CONFERENCE/CSCE.

council housing, local authority housing, usually for rent. Although some small estates were built before 1914, the first large-scale local authority schemes were begun under the *Addison Acts, 1919, with government subsidy. Combined with a freeze on urban rents, the inter-war years saw a succession of Acts under which over a million homes for rent were built by local councils, many of them in new 'council estates' on the fringes of the large conurbations. Local authority housing received new impetus after the Second World War in the drive to solve housing problems left over from the pre-war years and to meet post-war demands for better housing. Over three million council houses and flats were built between 1945 and 1985 with the aid of government subsidies, raising the proportion of people living in council-owned accommodation to one in three by 1979. Under the Thatcher government there was a drastic reduction in council-house building. 'Right to buy' legislation was introduced in the *Housing Act, 1980, and taken up by over a million council tenants. In 1987 legislation also allowed the placing of council estates under a private landlord. As a result the number of people renting from local authorities has fallen to fewer than one in five, while the number of owner-occupiers has risen to record levels. Although much post-war housing was criticized for poor quality and its soulless architecture, particularly the *tower blocks built in the 1960s and early 1970s, many council houses provided a much higher quality of housing than the slums and rented accommodation they replaced. *JS*

councillors, local government. The completion of the modern framework of local government in the 1890s ensured that the population of England and Wales had the right to be represented by local councillors. In 1900, any male occupier of rateable property was qualified both to vote and to be elected. Not until 1945 was the occupational qualification removed, while women were not universally qualified for election to a local authority until 1919. Paupers—those in receipt of poor relief—were disqualified from voting and election until 1948, when the poor law was abolished. Today, any British or Irish citizen over the age of 21 who has lived or worked in the area for at least twelve months may be nominated as a candidate for local election, although an employee of a local authority may not be elected to its council. Bankrupts, those convicted of corrupt or illegal practices, those in receipt of a custodial sentence of three months' imprisonment within five years of the election, and persons subject to a surcharge for unlawful local government expenditure are disqualified. Local government officers holding politically sensitive posts (those that may bring them into contact with councillors) may not engage in political activity, such as standing for election.

The number of councillors on principal authorities (that is, other than parish councillors) fluctuated with boundary changes and local reorganizations, and by 1964 stood at 43,000 in England and Wales. The comprehensive reorganization of local government under the Local Government Act, 1972, reduced this to 21,000. The number of parish councillors, on the other hand, has steadily increased to a total of around 65,000. Parish government aside, Britain has many fewer councillors per head of population than any other Western democracy, with an average representative ratio of one councillor for every 2,600 electors. Councillors perform two main functions: representing their electors both individually and collectively, and making decisions on behalf of the authority in committee and council. The amount of time committed to these dual roles has steadily increased with the growth of local government functions, and there have been several attempts since the 1950s to reform the conduct of council business so as to reduce the time demands on councillors. Although council work is seen as a voluntary service, the Local Government Act, 1948, enabled local authorities to pay nationally determined rates of travelling expenses and subsistence allowances to members, and to compensate them for any financial loss incurred while performing an approved duty. A system of attendance allowances was introduced in 1972, and special responsibility allowances, to recognize the workload of leading councillors, in 1980. In 1991 the attendance allowance was replaced by a basic flat rate allowance, and in 1996 local authorities were given the freedom to establish their own remuneration schemes. The representativeness of the councillor body has been a constant concern since the absence of working men was first noted after the initial elections in the reformed counties (1889) and districts (1893). Throughout the 20th century, councillors have tended to be predominantly male, middle class, and older than the populations they represent. *KY*

Council of Europe, intergovernmental consultative organization founded in 1949 and located at Strasbourg. Called for famously by Winston Churchill in his Zurich speech of 19 September 1946, the Council of Europe was convened after The Hague congress of May 1948. It was expected to be the first real post-war advance in European integration but became the first real setback, dogged by divergent Anglo-French visions of European unity. Its inaugural year, 1949, was also the year when the British government began to base its foreign policy on Anglo-American relations and when the French government began to look towards Europe as the foundation of its policy. Consequently, the Council of Europe was thought to be little more than a talking shop in its early years as the development of European unity followed the supranational route.

In its modern form, the council has two main roles. First, it continues to provide a forum where representatives of European Union member states and non-European Union member states are linked together. The growth of the council from its original twelve members in 1949 (Belgium, Britain, Denmark, France, Greece, Ireland, Italy, Luxembourg, the Netherlands, Norway, Sweden, and Turkey) to its current 40 verifies this. Membership of the Council of Europe, due to the required standards of democracy, was regarded as a stepping stone for those former Soviet satellites interested in joining the European Union. The council's second main role is in the field of human rights, its most substantial and effective work being done in this area. Whilst it is not a law-making body, it does make recommendations to member states and formulates conventions, one of the most celebrated being the 1950 European Convention on *Human Rights. *JRVE*

councils of action (1935), David *Lloyd George's final attempt at a political comeback. Hoping to capitalize on the national mood following the silver jubilee of George V, Lloyd George called on 12 June 1935 for a National Council of Action for Peace and Reconstruction with local councils putting up parliamentary candidates in over three hundred constituencies. This attempt to rally all the political forces outside the *National Government together with non-party groups like the churches in favour of a more dynamic foreign and domestic policy was swiftly outmanoeuvred by *Baldwin, who returned to the premiership in August and comfortably won a general election on more normal party lines in November. *JAR*

counter-inflation policy (1972). Counter-inflationary rhetoric was at the heart of Heath's successful election campaign in 1970. What was less clear, even to him, was how he was to achieve it. The manifesto explicitly rejected wage controls as a mechanism that the outgoing Labour government had tried and found wanting. At most, there was a hope that measures such as the

*Industrial Relations Act, 1971, might do the trick. By 1972, it was already clear that this was not happening. The miners' success in securing a 27 per cent pay increase was felt likely to drive wage-push inflation. In practice, the rest of the public sector pay settlements averaged only 9 per cent, and there were plenty of other factors pushing inflation upwards, such as the recent decision to float sterling, rising world commodity prices, and the government's own spending. However, with little willingness, in the government or elsewhere, to contemplate the abandonment of full employment that a *monetarist policy was felt to entail, Heath turned naturally to prices and incomes policy to contain inflation and protect his target of 5 per cent economic growth. Talks to try to secure a voluntary agreement broke down on union leaders' insistence on the statutory control of prices, but not wages. Instead, a statutory system to control both was rushed on to the statute book in November. After the election rhetoric, this seemed to be the most blatant of Heath's *U-turns in 1972. *PPC*

county boroughs. See LOCAL GOVERNMENT STRUCTURE.

county councils. See LOCAL GOVERNMENT STRUCTURE.

'Coupon' Election (1918), general election named after the letter of approval (or 'coupon', as in wartime rationing) signed by *Lloyd George, prime minister and leader of the National Liberals, and *Law, leader of the Conservatives, to identify the candidates they wanted voters to support. 531 coupons were distributed, 150 to National Liberals, most of the rest to Conservatives. The effective electoral pact between National Liberals and Conservatives, worked out over the previous six months, confirmed the division in the Liberal Party between Lloyd George's followers and *Asquith's *Wee Free supporters. 468 'couponed' candidates were elected, 335 Conservatives and 133 Liberals, providing the basis for the post-war coalition government led by Lloyd George until 1922. But, although the outcome of the election appeared to vindicate the effectiveness of the electoral pact, it has also been seen as undermining the position of the Liberal Party by creating a false picture of strength, based largely on the absence of Conservative opposition to many of their coalitionist MPs elected in 1918. (It was notable, in contrast to this, that Conservatives could still win in 1918, for example in Manchester, even without coupons.) When the coalition broke up in 1922, the Liberal Party was forced to fight both Conservative and Labour opponents, precipitating its decline to only 40 MPs in 1924. *JS*

Court of Appeal (England and Wales). The Judicature Acts, 1873 and 1875, created the High Court and the Court of Appeal (CA), together designated the 'Supreme Court of Judicature'. In fact the CA never became supreme as was intended: the Acts' abolition of the appellate jurisdiction of the House of Lords was reversed before it could take effect. This double appeal structure remains. The CA was originally established for civil appeals only, from all divisions of the High Court and from the county courts. The lord chancellor and the heads of the three divisions are ex officio members, but its regular staff are the lords justices of appeal (LJJ), presided over by the master of the rolls. A normal court has three judges. At present there are over 30 LJJ, but some of these are assigned to the criminal division, added to the CA in 1966 to replace the unsatisfactory court of criminal appeal (which itself had replaced the even more unsatisfactory court for crown cases reserved in 1908). The criminal division hears appeals from the Crown Courts against conviction or sentence, raising questions of law or of fact. The prosecution cannot appeal against an acquittal, but the attorney-general has the power to refer an acquittal to the CA for clarification of a point of law; and may also refer an over-lenient sentence for the CA's review. The criminal division is staffed by the lord chief justice and LJJ, with High Court judges and, since 1995, circuit judges. A normal court consists of three judges. *VT*

Cousins, Frank (1904–86), trade unionist. Cousins became a national figure as general secretary of the Transport and General Workers' Union (TGWU) in 1955. The TGWU block vote, hitherto used against the Labour left, now backed socialist and CND policies. Yet Labour's 1961 vote for unilateralism was reversed in 1962. In 1964 Harold Wilson made Cousins minister of technology, but he was unhappy in office and left in 1966 to return to leading the TGWU. *PRGR*

GEOFFREY GOODMAN, *The Awkward Warrior: Frank Cousins, his Life and Times* (London, 1979).

Cowley Street, London SW1, headquarters of the *Social Democratic Party, 1981–8, and of the (Social and) Liberal Democrats from 1988. *JS*

Cowling, Maurice John (1926–), historian and leader of 'the Peterhouse school'. A Londoner (evacuated in wartime to Hertford), educated at Battersea grammar school and Jesus College,

Cambridge (fellow, 1950–3 and 1961–3), Cowling became in 1963 a fellow of Peterhouse in Cambridge, which he moulded into his spiritual home. Noel Annan spoke of his 'growls' from his 'lair in Peterhouse', but what was overlooked was the wealth of experience in an officer in the British and Indian armies, a potential ordinand, a Fleet Street journalist, and a Conservative parliamentary candidate. It was India that taught Cowling that politics was elitist, and the notion that British political life was essentially dominated by only 50 or 60 people inspired *The Impact of Labour, 1920–1924* (1975). But, for Cowling, all 'the actors' had a doctrine, and subsequently he was more concerned with identifying 'the individual conscience' and 'the Christian sensibility' in both his own and in public life. In a festschrift, *Public and Private Doctrine* (ed. Michael Bentley, 1993), Peter Ghosh argued that Cowling's contribution was 'ahistorical', but *Conservative Essays* (1978), which Cowling edited, demonstrated clearly that he was a major influence on the 'new right'. Michael Portillo is the latest Peterhouse politician to ensure that Cowling's influence endures. *PS*

Cozens-Hardy, Herbert Hardy (1838–1920), judge and Liberal MP. Cozens-Hardy entered parliament in 1885 and remained there until his elevation to the Bench in 1899 by Lord Halsbury, an unusual occurrence given the influence political affiliation normally played in the latter's choice for judicial office. Judicial promotion to the Court of Appeal (1901) and master of the rolls (1907) followed. His tenure on the Bench coincided with the first appeals under the Workmen's Compensation Act, 1897, which he was said to have dealt with satisfactorily. *ML*

Cradock, Percy (1923–), prime minister's foreign policy adviser, 1984–92. Ambassador to Peking (1978–83), Cradock continued to play a leading role in negotiations with China until the signing of the joint declaration on Hong Kong (1985). At Downing Street, he enjoyed better relations with the Foreign Office than private secretary Charles Powell, and favoured a more positive approach to Europe than Margaret Thatcher. From 1985 he also chaired the Joint Intelligence Committee. *CL*

Percy Cradock, *In Pursuit of British Interests: Reflections on Foreign Policy under Margaret Thatcher and John Major* (London, 1997).

Craig, James (1871–1940), prime minister of Northern Ireland (1921–40). Born into a wealthy Belfast distilling family, Craig served in the Boer war. In 1906 he was elected MP for Co. Down, which he represented until 1921, becoming a whip and junior minister. Under Carson's leadership, Craig took a highly influential role in the organization of Ulster Unionist resistance to home rule, 1911–14, succeeding Carson as Unionist leader in early 1921. He thus became the first prime minister of Northern Ireland and played a very important part in the setting up of the new state. In his early days he made a number of efforts to conciliate the Catholic and nationalist minority, such as the appointment of a Catholic lord chief justice and a deliberate distancing between himself and the *Orange Order. By the end of the 1920s, however, faced with little positive response from the Catholic community and divisions within Unionist ranks, he directed his appeal more exclusively to Orange and Protestant interests. During the 1930s, partly in response to strong opposition from the southern government, he emphasized Unionist unity as a priority. He became Lord Craigavon in 1927. *BMW*

Patrick Buckland, *James Craig* (Dublin, 1980). | Bryan Follis, *A State under Siege: The Establishment of Northern Ireland, 1920–1925* (Oxford, 1995).

Craig, William (1924–), Northern Ireland Unionist politician. Craig came to prominence in 1968 when, as Stormont's home affairs minister, he banned a civil rights march in Londonderry which nevertheless went ahead and ended in violence, on *Bloody Sunday. Later, in the 1970s, he led the hard-line Protestant *Vanguard movement and helped plan the Loyalist strike which, in May 1974, toppled the power-sharing executive established by the Sunningdale agreement. However, a year later he suggested temporary power-sharing with the Social Democratic and Labour Party, dismaying his supporters and effectively ending his political career. *PR*

Craigie, Robert Leslie (1883–1959), diplomat. Sir Robert Craigie was educated at Heidelberg before entering the Foreign Office in 1907. In 1935 he was promoted to assistant under-secretary, but the pinnacle of his career was his appointment as ambassador to Japan in 1937, where he arguably delayed the conclusion of a German-Japanese alliance by his skilful and patient diplomacy during the Tientsin crisis of 1939. He served on the United Nations War Crimes Commission, 1945–8. *AJC*

Cranborne, Viscount (1946–), Conservative politician, great-great-grandson of Victoria's prime minister, the 3rd marquess of Salisbury

('Viscount Cranborne' being the courtesy title held by successive heirs to the marquessate). Robert Cranborne, heir to the 6th marquess, was MP for South Dorset, but left the Commons by writ of acceleration to the Lords, 1987 (his father still living). Lords leader under Major and notably loyal despite his Euro-reservations, in opposition, he fell to a spectacular 'Cecilicide' (sacking) by Hague in autumn 1998, after his unauthorized negotiations with Blair to reprieve 91 hereditary peers in return for Tory peers' co-operation with the government's legislative programme. *EP*

Crane, Walter (1845–1915), artist and socialist. He became active politically from the 1860s, heavily influenced by William Morris, and joined the Democratic Federation (later the Social Democratic Federation), in 1884, before attaching himself to Morris's Socialist League and also the Fabian Society. Crane's work featured in many Socialist publications and a major collection appeared in *Cartoons for the Cause* (1896). In 1898 he became principal of the Royal College of Art, an appointment which reflected his standing in the world of decorative art. *CH*

W. Crane, *An Artist's Reminiscences* (London, 1907).

Crawford, earl of. See Balcarres, Lord.

Crawford report (1926) advocated a monopoly government-appointed public corporation to replace private concerns in broadcasting. It recommended ending broadcasting restrictions on news and controversial issues. The restrictions were lifted to allow coverage of the General Strike. The BBC was established as a corporation by royal charter in 1927. *KMT*

Crawfurd, Helen (1877–1954), suffragist, co-operator, internationalist, and perhaps the most prominent female Communist of the inter-war period. She joined the Women's Social and Political Union in 1910, led the Glasgow Rent Strikes (1915), and became honorary secretary of the Women's Peace Crusade. Crawfurd left the Independent Labour Party because it refused to affiliate to the Comintern, and joined the Communist Party of Great Britain, 1920. She was secretary of the Workers' International Relief Committee, 1922. Crawfurd was defeated as the Communist candidate in both Bothwell, Lanarkshire (1929), and Aberdeen (1931). *DMM*

Crewe, Ivor Martin (1944–), political scientist. Crewe was educated at Oxford but, after a short spell teaching at Oxford and Lancaster universities, since 1971 he has worked at the University of Essex, becoming in 1982 professor of government and in 1995 vice-chancellor. From 1974 to 1982 he acted as director of the ESRC Data Archive, the UK-wide collection of survey data. He was from 1977 to 1992 an editor of the *British Journal of Political Science.* His academic focus has always been on elections and parties. His major works have been *Decade of Dealignment* (with Bo Sarlvik, 1983) and *The SDP* (with Anthony King 1995, but he has edited important works on *Political Communications* after each election since 1983, as well as reference works on the boundary revisions of 1983 and 1997 and time series of *British Election Study data. He has also written prolifically about the social bases of voting choice and the causes of electoral change, as well as about opinion polls and election forecasting. He was one of the first political scientists to identify, measure, and explain 'partisan dealignment' (the weakening of party loyalties) from the late 1960s onwards. His work is characterized by a pragmatic quantitative, sceptical approach. *DEB*

Crewe, 1st marquess of (1858–1945), Liberal politician. Educated at Cambridge, Robert Crewe-Milnes succeeded his father, Baron Houghton, in 1885 (subsequently being promoted through the peerage to the marquessate in 1911). One of the few remaining Gladstonian peers after the defection of the Whigs over home rule in 1886, he was lord lieutenant of Ireland, 1892–5. He remained active in opposition in the Lords and became lord president of the council in 1905. As Liberal leader in the Lords after 1908, he combined his conduct of business in the upper house with being secretary for the colonies, 1908–10, steering the Union of South Africa Bill though parliament. He attended the *Constitutional Conference of 1910 and was a moderating voice in the Lords over constitutional reform. Crewe held the post of secretary of state for India, 1908–15, combined with lord privy seal, 1908–11 and 1912–15. He participated in the home rule negotiations and after the outbreak of war chaired the Manpower Committee in 1915 and was a delegate to the economic summit in Paris in 1916. In the Asquith coalition government of 1915–16 he was lord president of the council, moving later to the Board of Education. A friend and confidant of Asquith, he resigned with him in December 1916, leading the peers loyal to Asquith until 1922. Crewe acted as ambassador to France, 1922–8, and returned briefly and improbably to office as war minister in the National

Government, August–November 1931. Later he served as Liberal leader in the Lords, 1936–44. A capable administrator, he continued to advise the Liberal leadership after his official career was over. *JS*

James Pope-Hennessy, *Lord Crewe, 1858–1945: The Likeness of a Liberal* (London, 1955).

Criccieth, Caenarfonshire. Welsh home of David Lloyd George, 1880–1945, to which he moved when he was 17. He served as an apprentice to a law firm in the neighbouring town of Portmadoc and was first elected to parliament for the Caernarfon boroughs seat (which included Criccieth) in 1890 and held it until he went to the Lords in 1945. *JS*

Crichel Down (1950–4), administrative scandal. The Crichel Down case involved 725 acres (294 hectares) of agricultural land in Dorset, compulsorily purchased by the Air Ministry in 1938 for use as a bombing range. In 1950, the Ministry of Agriculture decided to let it as a single, efficient unit rather than grant the request from Commander Marten, the son-in-law of the original owner, that he be allowed to repurchase 328 acres (133 hectares) of it. The National Farmers' Union supported his case which became a cause célèbre and converted Crichel Down into the most famous piece of land in British constitutional history. An inquiry by Sir Andrew Clark QC reported in 1954 in a manner highly critical of the Ministry of Agriculture whose minister, Sir Thomas Dugdale, resigned after serious hounding from the Conservative benches. Home Secretary Sir David Maxwell-Fyfe laid down the expectations of ministerial accountability for the actions of civil servants which became the norms against which all future cases were tested. These were:

- where there is an explicit order [to an official] by a minister, the minister must protect the civil servant who has carried out his order;
- where the civil servant acts properly in accordance with the policy laid down by the minister, the minister must protect and defend him;
- where an official makes a mistake or causes some delay, but not on an important issue of policy, the minister acknowledges the mistake and he accepts responsibility for it even though he is not personally involved, he states that he will take corrective action, and he would not, in those circumstances, expose the official to public criticism;
- where action has been taken by a civil servant of which the minister disapproves and of which he has no prior knowledge, and the conduct of the official is reprehensible, then there is no obligation on the part of the minister to endorse what he believes to be wrong, or to defend what are clearly shown to be errors of his officials; the minister is not bound to defend action of which he did not know, or of which he disapproves.

PJH

John Griffith, 'Crichel Down, the Most Famous Farm in British Constitutional History', *Contemporary Record*, 1 (spring 1987). | J. F. Nicholson, *The Mystery of Crichel Down* (London, 1986).

Crick, Bernard (1929–), political scientist who made a critical contribution to the development of the study of politics in his 1959 doctoral thesis *The American Science of Politics*. Whereas transatlantic developments of the behavioural approach modelled methodologically on the natural sciences had largely been ignored in Britain, Crick tackled this approach head on. He rejected its six basic tenets: that there were discoverable uniformities in human behaviour; that they could be confirmed by empirical tests; that the methods by which data were acquired and analysed should be as quantitative as possible; that theory should be empirical and predictive rather than philosophical and historical; that value-free research was possible and desirable; that the search for a macro-theory common to the social sciences took precedence over applied research into issues of reform. Crick's critique has not really been improved much since then, when the behavioural revelation was at its most presumptuous. He went on normatively to reassert a liberalized Aristotelianism in his *In Defence of Politics* (1962) and a Laskian concern with *The Reform of Parliament* (1964) continued in the activities of the Study of Parliament Group. His *Life of George Orwell* (1980) and his commitment to political education in schools marked Crick's impatience with conventional academic writing and the urge to carry forward a concern with citizenship education. *JH*

B. Crick, *The American Science of Politics* (London, 1959).

crime, offences, mainly against persons or property, which are defined as criminal in law, and for which the offender is liable to punishment by the state through the courts. However defined, crime was at a relatively low level in Britain in the late 19th and early 20th centuries, international visitors frequently remarking on the peaceable nature of British society and reacting with surprise to the fact that the British police were unarmed. The popular and media interest in the occasional gruesome murder case, in violence originating from politics in Ireland (such as the murder of Sir Henry Wilson MP by the IRA in Eaton Square in 1922), or in the

Sidney Street armed battle with Russian anarchists in the east end of London in 1910, were testament to the rareness of such excitements. The popularity of crime novelists such as Agatha Christie, generally celebrating eccentric or elite amateur sleuths, a peculiarly British genre of 'snobbery with violence', was itself escapist evidence of the far less interesting reality. In 1930, a British population of 45 million people was generating less than 200,000 reported crimes and only 11,000 people serving prison sentences after conviction for criminal offences. By 1950, with little increase in population, reported criminal acts had tripled and the prison population doubled; by 1970, the number of crimes known to the police had tripled again and the prison population was up to 39,000; by the 1990s the number of reported crimes annually had passed six million—more than one for every ten citizens. Such global figures must be treated with great caution, especially over a period as long as a century. Changing definitions of particular offences, variable reporting systems in different areas and at different times, and increasing tendencies by the public actually to report offences (crimes such as rape or domestic violence, long hidden in shamed obscurity) were all factors that distorted the apparent trends. Nevertheless, the broad pattern was inescapable: Britain experienced in the period after 1945 an explosion in criminal activity.

Within the overall (and accelerating) upward trend, certain categories of offence may be singled out. Traffic offences (for parking, exceeding speed limits, driving while under the influence of drink, and so on) were virtually non-existent before 1910, but had by the end of the 1930s already become the majority of all offences for which defendants were found guilty in the courts (rising to three-quarters of all convictions by the 1980s, and an even higher proportion if thefts of vehicles were included). Few, however, regarded this as evidence of a 'crime wave', and the figures were themselves inflated by the adoption of effective tests for driving while 'under the influence' from the 1960s. There were probably no more drunks than in earlier generations, but they were now far more likely to be driving a car, and more likely to be caught doing so. The drug-offender was far more likely to be met in fiction than in fact before 1939 (along with the even more mythical white-slave trafficker), but from the 1960s changing social habits and the easier availability of especially soft drugs like cannabis effectively 'criminalized' at least a significant proportion of the younger population who did not regard smoking 'pot' as a 'crime'. There was much debate about this, not least because the illegality of possessing any 'controlled substance' (including the relatively harmless soft drugs, since they probably—but not provably—led addicts on to frequently fatal hard drugs). Illegality of possession drove all drug-taking underground and increased the leverage (and the profits) that organized, international crime syndicates could extract from the situation. Since the high retail cost of illegal supplies also encouraged other offences—blackmail, extortion, vehicle-theft, violent street crime, and prostitution among others—it could be argued at the century's end that the definition of the 'criminal' ought to be pragmatically revised (as had been done with the partial legalization of homosexuality in 1967, partly at least on the same grounds and achieving the same anticipated effect in reducing ancillary offences).

At the core of perceptions of crime, however, lay offences which could not possibly be redefined or decriminalized: the number of murders roughly doubled between 1900 and the 1980s (years in which the population had itself risen by half anyway), but then more or less stabilized at what remained a relatively low level by international standards. This, more than anything, undercut campaigns for the restoration of the death penalty, for it made the deterrence argument relatively unpersuasive. On the other hand, woundings, thefts, robberies and burglaries (up more than tenfold after 1960), and rapes (up eightfold) were the crimes that really fuelled the public's increasing insecurity as a peaceable kingdom appeared to give way to a violent society as the century wore on, and steadily increased the salience of *law and order issues in British politics. The stabilizing of crime rates, however measured, in the 1990s did not materially alter this political consequence. *JAR*

Criminal Cases Review Commission (CCRC), established in 1995 to investigate cases of alleged wrongful conviction or sentence. It refers these to the appropriate appeal court, but only if it thinks such reference will succeed. The reference must concern a matter not raised at the trial or appeal, and where an appeal was previously rejected. The Court of Appeal may itself refer a case to the CCRC. The CCRC consists of a chairman and eleven or more commissioners. At least a third must be legally qualified, and two-thirds have experience of the criminal justice system; three or more consider a case. The CCRC was the response of the Major government to the public disquiet after several high profile appeals in the 1990s, such as the *Birmingham Six. It replaced the little-exercised power of the home secretary to refer a case to the Court of Appeal. The CCRC has no investigative staff. It asks the police or other officials to inquire and report back. *VT*

Cripps, Charles Alfred. See PARMOOR, 1ST LORD.

Cripps, (Richard) Stafford (1889–1952), socialist and Labour politician. A scientist turned barrister, Cripps acquired a formidable legal reputation, becoming the youngest KC at the British Bar in 1927. He joined the Labour Party in 1929 and, the following year, was appointed solicitor-general. Cripps represented the Bristol East constituency as either a Labour (1931–9, 1945–50) or independent (1939–45) MP. Rejecting MacDonald's invitation to serve in the National Government, he became a leading Labour left-winger in the 1930s and frequently clashed with the party leadership. He was the intellectual and financial driving force behind the Socialist League, 1932–7, which advocated an Emergency Powers Act to counter financial interests, abolition of the House of Lords, and reform of parliamentary procedure to create a socialist society. Elected to Labour's NEC in 1934, Cripps resigned when the party supported League of Nations' sanctions against Italy. In 1936 he disagreed with Labour's support for the league's policy of non-intervention in Spain and proposed a British 'united front of the working class' to defeat the National Government. With Aneurin Bevan, Ellen Wilkinson, and others, he helped to launch *Tribune* in 1937. At the 1937 conference he unsuccessfully challenged Labour NEC decisions that belonging to the Socialist League or sharing a public platform with Communist or Independent Labour Party representatives would result in expulsion from the party. In autumn 1938 he began to advocate a popular front, including Liberals and dissident Conservatives, to remove the Chamberlain administration. He refused to withdraw the 'Cripps memorandum' on the popular front and was expelled from the Labour Party in January 1939.

Following a world tour in late 1939 to explain British war aims, Cripps served as ambassador in Moscow, 1940–2, a disillusioning experience which curbed his socialist zeal. He then entered the war cabinet as leader of the Commons and lord privy seal. The failure of the 'Cripps mission' to India, 1942, proved another sobering episode and also led him to adopt a more centrist position (he undertook another unsuccessful mission to India in 1946). In November 1942, Cripps was demoted to minister for aircraft production but performed this role efficiently until the war ended. Rejoining Labour in March 1945, he entered the Attlee cabinet four months later as president of the Board of Trade, promoting management–union partnership within industry. He was also instrumental in the formation of the economic planning council in 1947. After the financial crisis of mid-1947, he was appointed minister of economic affairs with extensive powers (October) and then took over as chancellor of the exchequer (November). As the 'austerity chancellor', 1947–50, Cripps benefited from the Marshall aid programme and popular respect for his integrity, competence, and Christian principles. He pursued broadly successful policies which promoted an export-led recovery, planned consumption, and wage restraint, although his growing reputation for sound economic management was dented by the forced devaluation of sterling in 1949. Illness compelled him to resign from office and parliament in October 1950. *AM*

CHRIS BRYANT, *Stafford Cripps: The First Modern Chancellor* (London, 1997).

'Crisis, what crisis?' With the government passive in the face of the 1979 winter of discontent, a sun-tanned Prime Minister Callaghan returned from a Guadeloupe summit, and unguardedly claimed at Heathrow that the preoccupation of the British press with the disruption caused by strikes was 'parochial'. The *Sun* headlined his comment 'Crisis, what crisis?' (which he never actually said) and thus deepened government unpopularity. *BJE*

Croft, Henry. See PAGE CROFT, HENRY.

Crookshank, Harry Frederick Comfort (1893–1961), progressively minded Conservative who represented Gainsborough, 1924–56. He held a number of junior ministerial posts in the 1930s, but threatened resignation several times during 1938 in criticism of appeasement. An irascible man, his ill-feeling towards Neville Chamberlain was fuelled by a belief that the premier had failed to acknowledge his role in guiding the Coal Bill through parliament. He was postmaster general, 1943–5, and cabinet status was achieved in the post-war years as minister of health, 1951–2, and lord privy seal, 1952–5. *NJC*

Crosby by-election (28 November 1981), famous *Social Democratic Party (SDP) by-election victory, just after the birth of the

Liberal-SDP *Alliance, which helped to propel the Alliance to record opinion poll ratings of over 40 per cent. In the third of a series of spectacular by-election performances, following *Warrington and *Croydon North-West, Shirley *Williams overturned a 19,272 Conservative majority, securing the seat with a majority for the SDP of 5,289. The seat was lost in the general election of 1983, one of the 23 (out of 28) seats lost by sitting SDP members, though major boundary changes played a part in this. *JS*

Crosland, (Charles) Anthony Raven (1918–77), Labour politician. Crosland served in the war, then became an economics don at Oxford, 1947–50, and was Labour MP for South Gloucestershire, 1950–5, and Grimsby, 1959–1977. He came to prominence by publishing the path-breaking case for social democracy *The *Future of Socialism* in 1956, much admired by the then Labour leader Hugh Gaitskell. In 1963 he was instrumental in persuading Callaghan to stand against both George Brown and Harold Wilson for the leadership as he questioned Wilson's politics and Brown's character. In the 1964–70 Labour government Crosland was successively junior minister for economic affairs; secretary for education and science, 1965–7; president of the Board of Trade, 1967–9; and secretary for local government and planning, 1969–70. His main impact was at education where he significantly advanced comprehensivization and the closure of grammar schools, and established the polytechnic sector of higher education. While critical of Wilson's leadership he had a detached admiration for his nerve. He was more unsympathetic to Roy Jenkins as a potential leader because he suspected Jenkins of being more pro-European than concerned with the unity of the Labour Party. Crosland also had a personal rivalry with Jenkins which was intensified in 1967 when Jenkins was preferred as chancellor of the exchequer. The competition increased further in 1972 when the Jenkinsites voted for Ted Short rather than Crosland as deputy leader. As secretary for the environment, 1974–6, he favoured the metropolitan authorities in the distribution of rate support grant, introduced security of tenure for furnished tenants, and stopped the construction of a third London airport. He contested the party leadership when Wilson retired in 1976, but polled badly. He strongly opposed the spending cuts imposed by the IMF in that year, but in his ministerial role informed the local authorities that 'the party's over' in public spending. As foreign secretary in 1976 Crosland strove to end the Cold War, during a period of détente. His loyalty to the Labour Party and scepticism about the Jenkinsites suggests he would have rejected defection to the Social Democratic Party in the 1980s. Crosland was internationally recognized as one of the leading exponents of the intellectual case for 'revisionist social democracy'. In *The Future of Socialism* he offered a positive alternative to the conservatism of both the established right-wing and the Bevanite left, asserting that Labour should base its electoral appeal on improved public services and the ending of poverty rather than public ownership. *The Conservative Enemy* (1962) developed the case that advanced social welfare and the more equal distribution of wealth, on the Swedish model, provided a better purpose for Labour than the class-ridden parochial politics of the traditional Labour left. His final work, *Socialism Now*, was published in 1974 and reflected a greater pessimism about the state of the British economy. He recognized the need to give priority to the battle against inflation, although through cooperation with the trade unions rather than confrontation. He also pointed to the new consciousness about the environment, arguing that while Labour could not advocate limiting economic growth, environmental factors should be built into every policy decision. His thesis can be summarized as 'socialism equals equality'. His sudden, early death in office robbed Labour of a major figure. *BJE*

Susan Crosland, *Tony Crosland* (London, 1982).

Crossman, Richard Howard Stafford (1907–74), writer and Labour politician. Dick Crossman was a leading member of that generation of Oxford-educated intellectuals, such as Gaitskell, Wilson, Crosland, and Jenkins, who were so important in shaping the Labour Party after 1945. Son of a judge, Dick Crossman was educated at Winchester and New College, Oxford, where he became a fellow, aged 23. In the 1930s he was a member of Oxford city council, leading its Labour group, 1934–40, and assistant editor of the *New Statesman*, 1938–42. *Plato Today* (1937) made his name as a political theorist, but his reputation during the Second World War came from his command of propaganda. Deputy director of psychological warfare at the Allied Headquarters in Algiers (where Harold Macmillan also served) in 1943, he was assistant at the chief psychological warfare division of Supreme Headquarters Allied Expeditionary Force, 1944–5, following the invasion of Europe. A member of the Anglo-American Palestine commission in 1946, when Palestinian Jews were struggling to establish the state of Israel, he was Labour MP for Coventry East, 1945–74, but not given office by Attlee, who did not trust him. Others shared Attlee's view, as the soubriquet 'Dick-Double-Crossman' revealed. In opposition after 1951 he also clashed with Attlee's successor Hugh Gaitskell, but was on the Labour NEC, 1952–67, chairing working parties on national superannuation in 1956 and science in 1963. Wilson, an old ally from party battles, made him minister of housing, 1964–6; leader of the Commons, 1966–8; and secretary for social services, 1968–70. He was a restless minister, always convinced that more interesting things were happening elsewhere. Out of office, Crossman edited the *New Statesman*, 1970–2. *The Diaries of a Cabinet Minister*, three large volumes published posthumously (ed. Janet Morgan, 1975–7), present a vivid picture of growing lack of purpose in the Wilson government, though their value to historians is diminished by the fact that he signed a contract with his publisher before writing them. *PRGR*

Anthony Howard, *Crossman: The Pursuit of Power* (London, 1990).

Crossman select committees. See Commons, House of: 'Crossman select committees'.

Crowe, Eyre (1864–1925), Foreign Office official. Crowe entered the Foreign Office in 1885 and established himself as its German expert. Best remembered for his 1907 memorandum on the principles of British diplomacy and the impending German danger, he was the target of virulent press attacks during the Great War because of his German family connections. At the Paris peace conference (1919) he was the linchpin of the British delegation. In 1920 he became permanent secretary at the Foreign Office, a position he held until his early death in 1925. For Stanley Baldwin he was 'our ablest public servant'; Georges Clemençeau esteemed him as 'un homme à part'. *TGO*

Sibyl E. Crowe and Edward T. Corp, *Our Ablest Servant: Sir Eyre Crowe* (Braunston, 1993). | T. G. Otte, 'Eyre Crowe and British Foreign Policy: A Cognitive Map', in Otte and Constantine A. Pagedas (eds.), *Personalities, War and Diplomacy: Essays in International History* (London, 1997).

crown colonies, term given to colonies administered directly by a governor who was responsible to the Crown through the Colonial Office. However, by 1900 a few colonies were being allowed legislative councils, with some native members. Some crown colonies were situated in the Caribbean, but mostly in Africa and the Pacific. After 1948, virtually all were given complete independence, those that remain being now known as dependent territories. *KTS*

Crown Court (England and Wales). The Crown Court was established by the Courts Act, 1971, following the recommendations of the report (1969) of the Beeching commission, rationalizing the organization and structure of the courts in England and Wales. The Crown Court, constituted as part of the supreme court, replaced the ancient system of assizes and quarter sessions as the court of trial for all the more serious crimes. The country is divided into six circuits, each with sittings of the Crown Court in centres of population. A presiding judge in each circuit oversees the work of the circuit. The allocation of business is by a circuit administrator. Trial is by judge and jury. Depending on the gravity or complication of a charge, the trial judge may be from the Queen's Bench division of the High Court, or a circuit judge (the full-time regular staff); or may be a part-time recorder or deputy. The Crown Court also has jurisdiction to hear appeals from *magistrates' courts (including some civil matters) but for this purpose it is composed of a circuit judge sitting with magistrates. *VT*

Crown Prosecution Service. See public prosecutions, director of.

Crowther-Hunt, Lord (1920–87), political scientist and politician. Norman (Crowther) Hunt was a fellow and lecturer in politics at Oxford, 1952–82, and the rector of Exeter College from 1982 until his death. In terms of his own involvement in politics, he had two major interests, the civil service and constitutional reform. He was a key member of the Fulton committee (see Fulton report) on the civil service, 1966–8, and a member of the civil service college advisory council, 1970–4; he recounted his impressions of the civil service in a book co-authored with Peter Kellner (1980). He was a member of the Kilbrandon royal commission on the constitution (see Kilbrandon report), 1969–73, established by Harold Wilson to examine the case for devolution and he was the principal author of a memorandum of dissent to that royal commission's report. This memorandum of dissent showed great foresight in advocating devolution for the English regions and pointing to the potential significance of the European community for the British constitution. He was an adviser to Harold Wilson on constitutional affairs between March and October 1974 and went on to serve as a junior minister in the Department of Education and Science and the Privy Council Office during Wilson's premiership, 1975–6. *DG*

Croydon North-West by-election (22 October 1981), important Liberal win shortly after the birth of the Liberal-SDP *Alliance, the second in a series of Alliance by-election victories which seemed to offer the prospect of *'breaking the mould'. Bill Pitt, describing himself as a Liberal-SDP Alliance candidate (and an 'ordinary' local candidate as opposed to the national celebrities who stood and did so well at Warrington and Crosby), turned a Conservative majority of 3,769 into a Liberal majority of 3,254, quadrupling his share of the vote from 11 per cent in 1979 to 40 per cent in 1981. It was the first Conservative by-election defeat since the 1979 general election and the first victory for the Alliance partners who worked harmoniously together, the Liberal by-election team being supplemented by the glamorous *'Gang of Four'. It confirmed that the earlier near-miss at the *Warrington by-election had not been a flash in the pan. The seat, however, was lost in the 1983 general election. *JS*

cruise missiles, American intermediate range low-flying guided missile. The Soviet invasion of Afghanistan in 1979 destabilized SALT II and gave birth to the 'Second Cold War' with President Reagan denouncing the USSR as the 'evil empire'. A product of this was to make Europe once more the main theatre of superpower rivalry. In December 1979, NATO updated its Intermediate Nuclear Forces (INF) with 464 cruise and 108 Pershing missiles. Whilst this development caused some differences amongst Western European members of the alliance, it was thoroughly embraced by Margaret Thatcher, a vehement anti-communist and proponent of deterrence, who agreed to the stationing of 160 American cruise missiles in Britain.

Thatcher's decision had a major impact on the domestic political situation in Britain. Under Michael Foot, the Labour Party fought the June 1983 general election on a platform of unilateralism and campaigned against both cruise and Trident. There was also a proliferation of anti-nuclear sentiment particularly through the Campaign for Nuclear Disarmament which had been largely dormant since the 1960s but now saw its membership increase significantly. The most prominent expression of anti-nuclear protest was the women's peace camp around the US airbase at *Greenham Common where cruise missiles were stationed from November 1983. The peace camp gained an international reputation and, together with the Labour Party's unilateralism and similar political movements throughout Western Europe, caused great concern in the USA about the stability of the NATO alliance.

Cruise missiles were stationed on British soil until August 1989 when they finally left the Greenham Common airbase. This was symbolic of the thawing of Cold War tensions after the arrival of Mikhail Gorbachev in the Kremlin. At the successful Washington summit of December 1987 the superpowers agreed on the elimination of all intermediate range missiles in Europe including cruise, Pershing, and Soviet SS-20s. *JRVE*

cube rule (sometimes miscalled 'cube law'), statistical regularity suspected by some bright Edwardians but first documented in 1950. In British national politics, at times when only two parties are in contention nationwide, the electoral system exaggerates the first party's lead in votes over the second. If the vote shares of the two parties are in the ratio A : B, then their seat shares are in the ratio $A^3 : B^3$ when the cube rule operates. Thus for example, if the Conservatory Party wins votes compared to the Laboratory Party in the ratio 53 : 47, it will win seats in the ratio 59:41 approximately. The cube rule depends on an even geographical distribution of the sorts of people likely to vote for each party and on no viable third parties, whether geographically concentrated or not. In the UK, the conditions for the cube rule have existed only from 1900 to 1910 (ignoring Ireland, and treating Labour as a faction of the Liberals) and from 1945 to 1970. Political scientists now subsume the cube rule into a class of indices of responsiveness. The index of responsiveness is the exponent to which the vote ratio is raised to reach the seat ratio. An index of 1 denotes pure proportionality. An index of 3 is the cube rule. In modern Britain, the index hovers between 1.5 and 2. 'Responsiveness' is not the same as 'bias', which is the ratio of seats that each party gets when their vote ratio is 1 : 1. British politics currently has a bias in favour of Labour and moderate responsiveness. In the 1950s it had a bias in favour of the Conservatives and high (cubic) responsiveness. *IM*

R. Taagepera and M. S. Shugart, *Seats and Votes* (New Haven, 1989).

Cudlipp, Hugh (1913–98), Labour-supporting journalist and chairman of *Daily Mirror* newspapers, 1963–8, and subsequently of the International Publishing Corporation (IPC) and deputy chairman of Reed International until

1973. He advised Labour on the presentation of its manifesto in 1959, and was a confidant of Wilson and press adviser to Callaghan when each was premier. Cudlipp helped to engineer Cecil King's removal as chairman of IPC in 1968 after King had campaigned to oust Wilson as prime minister. *BJE*

Culture, Media, and Sport, Department of (1997–). The Department of National Heritage, the predecessor to the Department of Culture, Media, and Sport, was set up in 1992. The handover of functions (national heritage) order provided for many transfers of responsibilities to the new department: the Department of the Environment lost its role in heritage; the Department of Trade and Industry ceded its film and export licensing of cultural property duties; the Department of Employment lost its responsibility for tourism; broadcasting and safety at sports grounds was taken from the Home Office; and the Department of Education and Science relinquished its sports role. The Office of Arts and Libraries, also responsible for museums, became part of the new department. In 1997 the department was renamed the Department of Culture, Media, and Sport and its duties increased further with the addition of music industry sponsorship and the promotion of creative industries. *JD*

Department of Culture, Media, and Sport website: *www.culture.gov.uk*

Cumann na nGaedheal (Community of Irishmen), Irish party. Established in 1923, representing supporters of the Anglo-Irish treaty of 1921, it provided the government of the Irish Free State, under the leadership of William Cosgrave, until 1932. At home it favoured caution and consolidation. Following the civil war of 1922–3, it sought to remove the gun from politics, the army was largely demobilized, and an unarmed police force established. Abroad it asserted Ireland's new status as a dominion and member of the League of Nations. In 1925 the border with Northern Ireland, provisionally agreed in 1921, was confirmed in return for British financial concessions, but this prompted Eamon de Valera to end his policy of abstention. His new party, Fianna Fáil, entered the Dáil in 1927, shortly after the assassination of the government's strong man, Kevin O'Higgins. Overtaken by economic depression, Cumann na nGaedheal lost the 1932 general election. Socially conservative, it had little to offer an impoverished electorate except military tribunals, introduced in 1931 against an alleged threat from communism and the IRA. Still, the peaceful handover of power showed that Irish democracy had come of age. In 1933 the party merged with others to become Fine Gael. *DRB*

Joseph Lee, *Ireland 1912–1985: Politics and Society* (Cambridge, 1989).

Cumming, Mansfield George Smith (1859–1923), first chief of the British secret service. Mansfield George Smith (he added the name Cumming on his second marriage) was born in British India, the youngest child of a Royal Engineers colonel. Educated at the Royal Naval College, Dartmouth, he saw service against Malay pirates and in Egypt. Ill-health forced his retirement in 1885. However, in 1898, whilst still on the retired list, he was posted to Nelson's ship *Victory* for 'special services', which included some intelligence work. In 1909 Cumming was appointed chief of the foreign branch of the Secret Service Bureau (the forerunner of MI6 and the Secret Intelligence Service (SIS)). Between 1909 and 1914, with few resources, he worked part-time agents, mainly keeping track of Germany's naval building programme. During the Great War, he ran a number of highly successful operations, including the 'La Dame Blanche' network, which had by 1918 400 agents reporting on German troop movements. Other operations in pre-revolutionary Russia, Italy, and the eastern Mediterranean had equal success. Cumming was less successful after the Bolshevik revolution, which provided espionage opportunities for his most colourful agents, including Sydney Reilly, but little by way of concrete results. The end of the war saw dramatic cutbacks in Cumming's resources. However, he succeeded in entrenching his agency's role in espionage and counter-intelligence outside Britain and the Empire. He also established under diplomatic cover a network of SIS station commanders. Cumming was an eccentric character who saw espionage as 'capital sport' and always used green ink, establishing a pattern followed by SIS chiefs down to the present. He also had a fascination with high-speed travel. One accident in his Rolls-Royce cost the life of his only son and his right leg. *PM*

Cunliffe Committee on Currency and Foreign Exchange (1918–19) investigated the position of British public finances after unprecedented levels of expenditure during the Great War, and its report (Cmd 464) recommended returning sterling to the gold standard, as soon as practicable, along with other orthodox currency policies. The government's acceptance of these recommendations, announced on 15 December 1919, strongly endorsed by the Treasury on the grounds that it would restrain inflation and restore confidence in the economy, set the scene for the dominance of orthodox public finance in the inter-war years (although there was no return to gold until 1925), with serious consequences for the British domestic economy and the level of unemployment. The report and its consequences were roundly attacked in J. M. Keynes's *A Treatise on Money* (1930). *JAR*

Cunliffe-Lister, Philip (1884–1972), Conservative politician. Entering politics in 1918, having won an MC on the Somme, he continued to represent Hendon until his elevation to the Lords in 1935 as Viscount Swinton. He was marked out for preferment early, Law making him president of the Board of Trade when only 38. There he formed a close working relationship with Neville Chamberlain. When moved to the Colonial Office in November 1931 he initiated the first survey of the economic position of the colonies. Promotion to the Air Ministry in June 1935 placed Cunliffe-Lister at the very heart of the National Government. At this crucial time in the British rearmament programme he oversaw the acceleration of air rearmament and made the development of radar a priority. However, the sensitivities of the post made him vulnerable to critics, especially when the job of explaining air policy to the Commons was left to a junior on 12 May 1938 after his move to the Lords, and shortly afterwards he resigned. In reality Chamberlain had sacked him, angered by his championing of conscription and economic controls to facilitate rearmament in cabinet. Swinton's tenure at the Air Ministry was crucial in preparing the RAF to fight the battle of Britain. In 1940–2 Swinton chaired the Security Executive which included responsibility for the 18B regulations (allowing the internment of Fascists). He held the duchy of Lancaster in 1951, but devoted more energies to party organization including the creation of the Conservatives' *Swinton College in his Yorkshire family home. Despite the longevity of his ministerial career, he was never a household name, in part because he never held a major office, but also because of his triple name change from Lloyd-Graeme, to Cunliffe-Lister in 1924 (the result of a bequest), to Lord Swinton in 1935. *NJC*

Lord Swinton, *Sixty Years in Power* (London, 1966). | Lord Swinton, *I Remember* (London, 1948). | J. A. Cross, *Lord Swinton* (Oxford, 1982).

Cunningham, Charles Craik (1906–98), civil servant and permanent secretary at the Home Office, 1957–66. Cunningham's early career had been in the Scottish Office, which he joined in 1929 rising to be in charge of the Scottish Home Department, 1948–57. He ran a very tight ship at the Home Office, all policy submissions to the home secretary being routed through him, and, though personally a man of liberal opinions, did not essentially challenge the inward-looking bunker mentality characterizing the department at that time. *KT*

Cunningham, John Anderson ('Jack') (1939–). Labour MP for Whitehaven, 1970–83, and Copeland from 1983, he was parliamentary private secretary to James Callaghan, 1974–6, and organized Callaghan's leadership campaign in 1976. Spokesman on a number of opposition portfolios, 1979–97, he became minister for agriculture in 1997, where he commenced negotiations to remove the post-BSE European ban on British beef. Appointed minister for the Cabinet Office in 1998 with the role of cabinet 'enforcer' to ensure coherence within government, he was considered to be ineffective in that post and replaced by Mo Mowlam. *BJE*

Cunninghame Graham, Robert Bontine (1852–1936), socialist, author, and traveller. In a life marked by many colourful incidents, this landowner espoused socialist policies while MP for North West Lanarkshire (1886–92), was involved in the Trafalgar Square riot in 1887, and sentenced (along with John Burns) to six weeks' imprisonment. He travelled widely in South America, criticized imperialism, advocated Irish home rule and supported Scottish nationalism (as president of the National Party of Scotland from 1928). *DEM*

Cedric Watts and Laurence Davies, *Cunninghame Graham: A Critical Biography* (Cambridge, 1979).

Curragh 'mutiny' (1914). By March 1914 the crisis over Unionist Ulster's opposition to the Third Home Rule Bill revealed that the Unionists and their as yet unarmed Ulster Volunteer Force were determined to push matters to the limit. The question facing the Liberal government was whether or not it should deploy military force to make recalcitrant subjects obey parliament. On 14 March, lieutenant-general Sir Arthur Paget, commander-in-chief of the forces in Ireland, was warned that attempts might be made by 'evil disposed persons' to raid government stores of arms and ammunition. On 18 March, the government decided to move troops into Ulster. Paget confessed that he foresaw difficulties, notably the unwillingness of officers who sympathized with the Ulster Unionists to take part in active operations in the north. He was told that officers who refused to obey orders must be dismissed; but that a special case might be made for officers whose homes were in Ulster. Paget informed his command on 20 March that officers domiciled in Ulster would be permitted to 'disappear' and that other officers who refused to obey orders might tender their resignations, but these would not be accepted and they would be dismissed from the service. On 20 March the War Office received news that some cavalry officers were resigning their commissions, senior officers amongst them. Asquith announced on 22 March that the movement of troops was a purely precautionary measure. General Hubert Gough, the ringleader of the army 'rebels' (and later a major British commander in the Great War), obtained a further concession from Sir John French that troops under the command of his colleagues who had refused to obey orders would not be called upon to enforce the present Home Rule Bill on Ulster. Asquith disavowed this note, but the episode drove a wedge between soldier and politician that had repercussions in the Great War; and it gave the Ulster Unionists a great propaganda victory. *DGB*

F. W. Beckett (ed.), *The Army and the Curragh Incident, 1914* (London, 1986). | A. T. Q. Stewart, *The Ulster Crisis* (London, 1967).

Curzon, Ist marquess (1859–1925), Conservative statesman. The eldest son of the 4th Baron Scarsdale, George Nathaniel Curzon amassed a brilliant academic record at Eton and Jowett's Balliol College (also elected a fellow of All Souls, Oxford, 1883) before becoming secretary to Lord Salisbury in 1885. His neat and elegant figure graced that remarkable circle of brilliant socialites called the 'Souls' (as did his future colleagues Balfour, Brodrick, and Lyttleton), and he pursued love affairs with a recklessness which only good fortune prevented from becoming ruinously scandalous. Few knew that a curvature of the spine left him in considerable pain throughout his life. Curzon entered the Commons in 1886, served Salisbury as under-secretary in the India and Foreign Offices, 1891–8, and in 1899, at the age of only 39, was created Baron Curzon in the Irish peerage and viceroy of India. Long fascinated by Asian civilization, his Indian record was mixed: he energetically attacked the racialism and injustice which often characterized the Raj and acted to conserve some of India's decaying architectural treasures; but he insisted on a 'forward' policy toward Russia which brought him into conflict with his old friends Balfour, now prime minister, and Brodrick, the Indian secretary. In 1905 he quarrelled with his handpicked army commander, Lord Kitchener, who (with cabinet support) insisted on full control over the Indian army. Curzon resisted clumsily, without tact or patience, and lost utterly. He resigned, returned home, and was denied the satisfaction of refusing any honour, as none were offered. He never fully recovered from the humiliation.

Unsuccessful in finding a parliamentary seat, in 1908 he was elected a representative Irish peer and set about reconstructing his neglected political career. With the dearth of front-bench Conservative talent after the 1906 election debacle, Curzon's eloquence and brilliance ensured that his political fortunes were again on the rise. Ignoring the tariff reform controversy, he chose Lloyd George's 1909 budget as his cause, fighting hard for its rejection by the Conservative peers. However, he seemingly reversed himself in the last stage of the controversy in 1911 when he abandoned the rejectionist ditchers and joined the moderate hedgers (see HEDGERS AND DITCHERS) in allowing the Parliament Act to pass. Right-wing Tories found it hard to forgive him and he gained a reputation as a 'rat' which he never completely escaped. The coming of world war found Curzon without useful work until the formation of Asquith's coalition in 1915, in which he became lord privy seal. In December 1916 he supported Lloyd George in forming a new coalition with a five-man war cabinet, which he joined.

With the continuation of the coalition into peacetime, Curzon was delighted to become foreign secretary. That joy often turned though to vexation as he frequently encountered what he considered interference by the prime minister and his many unofficial advisers. He finally could not accept Lloyd George's anti-Turkish policy, and he was one of the few Tory cabinet ministers to support the backbench revolt that at the Carlton Club meeting displaced the coalition with a Conservative government led by Law. He retained the Foreign Office and thought he had gained too, with all possible rivals out of office, the succession to the premiership. However, when Law resigned seven months later, despite Curzon's undeniable qualifications, opinion among rank and file Tories was strongly against him and in favour of keeping the premiership in the Commons. The king agreed and chose Stanley Baldwin to lead his government. The ambitious Curzon was inconsolable, thinking Baldwin a man 'of the utmost insignificance', but pulled himself together and served the new government until his retirement, shortly before his death in 1925. There was about Curzon an undeniable grandeur, characterized by the magnificent style in which he lived in his many beautiful houses, the restoration of which destroyed his fortune. His undoubted brilliance, however, was often obscured by his difficult personality. Self-absorbed, pedantic, and convinced that he was a great man born to govern lesser men, his hauteur and soaring arrogance made it difficult for others to follow him if there were any alternative. To intellectual equals like Balfour, his contribution was simply not worth the trouble; to popular statesmen like Lloyd George, he was a living caricature whose ambition and work ethic made him vulnerable to the humiliating baiting to which he subjected him purely for his own amusement. *RJQA*

David Dilks, *Curzon in India*, 2 vols. (London, 1969–70). | David Gilmour, *Curzon* (London, 1994). | Harold Nicolson, *Curzon: The Last Phase, 1919–1925* (London, 1934). | Kenneth Rose, *Superior Person* (London, 1968).

Curzon line, boundary between Poland and Russia proposed by the Paris peace conference in December 1919 but communicated to them by Lord Curzon, the British foreign secretary. In July 1920 Curzon tried, unsuccessfully, to end the Russo-Polish war on the basis of that frontier, but the 1921 Riga treaty boundary was much further east. The Curzon line divided Nazi- and Soviet-occupied Poland in 1939 and became the frontier between Russia and Poland in 1945. *AS*

customary processes, phrase used to describe the informal procedure by which Conservative leaders 'emerged' before leadership elections were introduced in 1965. Harold Macmillan spoke of beginning 'the customary processes of consultation' in 1963, but this indicates a misleading traditionality. Balfour, Neville Chamberlain, and Eden succeeded automatically in 1902, 1937, and 1955 respectively; Baldwin was preferred to Curzon after the king's consultations in 1923; and Macmillan was selected after a cabinet poll in 1957. Douglas-Home's controversial selection in 1963 prompted reform. *RJS*

Customs and Excise. Administration of customs, duties on imports and exports, and excise, taxes on essentially (but not exclusively) home-produced goods, was amalgamated in 1909. The work of the department was changed significantly when value added tax was introduced in 1973. The new tax covered a much greater range of goods and services than purchase tax. Other new taxes administered by Customs and Excise were passenger duty insurance premium tax (both introduced in 1994), and landfill tax (1996). The department's efforts to combat the rise in drug smuggling rose steadily towards the end of the century. *JD*

Customs and Excise website: *www.hmce.gov.uk*

Cymdiethas yr Iaith Gymraeg (lit. 'The Society of the Welsh Language') was founded in 1962 by a group of young people who were frustrated by Plaid Cymru's general lack of ambition and in particular its failure to halt the *Tryweryn reservoir project. It was directly inspired by a BBC lecture in which Saunders *Lewis recommended civil disobedience and legal challenges to ensure the use of the Welsh language in the everyday administration of Welsh affairs. The time was ripe for this clarion call, for not only was the language in crisis as reflected in every census, but now there was a new generation of young people in Wales, especially students, who, like their counterparts in France and America, were looking for issues to make their own. With intellectuals like J. R. Jones and Alwyn D. Rees providing ideas, the youth of Wales took to the streets and the courts and demanded that Welsh be used on official forms, on road signs, in the courts themselves, in broadcasting, and in universities. Direct action brought immediate results as the government and other bodies seemed prepared to accept the notion that Wales was a bilingual country. Moreover the hitherto rather staid Plaid Cymru was reinvigorated. When Gwynfor Evans won the Carmarthen by-election in 1966 it was evident that there were scores of young people who were now prepared to help out in the challenge to the Labour Party in Wales. By any standard Cymdeithas was a successful pressure group. Its achievements, not least in the sphere of broadcasting and education, gave the language a new lease of life and effectively politicized Welsh-speaking youth very much to Labour's detriment. *PS*

Ned Thomas, *The Welsh Extremist* (Cardiff, 1971).

Cyprus crises. Britain had controlled Cyprus since 1878 but it became a crown colony only in 1923. The population of Cyprus was split between the Greek majority and a Turkish minority, and although Cyprus had never been part of modern Greece, Greek governments had claimed the island and had been encouraging the idea of *Enosis* (union with Greece) among Greek Cypriots. All debate on the subject was quashed in July 1954 when the British government announced that, because of the island's strategic significance, no change to the status quo could be expected. Archbishop Makarios, the leader of the Enosis movement, then recruited a Cypriot-born Greek Army Colonel, George Grivas, to organize a military arm of the movement, EOKA, and in autumn 1954 EOKA struck from its bases in the Troodos mountains, launching a guerrilla campaign combined with civil disobedience. In September 1955, Field Marshal Sir John Harding was appointed governor, and by June 1956 he was ready to strike back, launching a series of cordon-and-search operations. Operations were temporarily interrupted by the Suez expedition (which used Cyprus as a major base) but were restarted in 1957. Harding then retired and was replaced by the more conciliatory Sir Hugh Foot (later Lord *Caradon), who feared the international repercussions of the situation. In 1959, a new plan was agreed: Britain would keep its bases, while Turkey and Greece both agreed to respect an independent Cypriot state. Trouble flared again in 1963, though, when President Makarios attempted to alter the Cypriot constitution. This provoked interracial violence, and British troops divided the island in order to segregate the two communities. The UN then stepped in to patrol the so-called 'Green Line'. Violence erupted once more in 1967, and again in 1974, when Makarios was the target of a coup. This provoked a Turkish invasion, establishing an occupation of the northern half of the island. Since then the 'Green Line' has been restored and is still patrolled by UN forces.

MLC

Daily Express. Arthur Pearson founded the *Daily Express* in 1900, to compete in the lower middle-class market tapped by Harmsworth's *Daily Mail.* Although the paper was first to put news on the front page, Pearson lacked Harmsworth's marketing and editorial flair. Only after Max Aitken (Lord *Beaverbrook) acquired it in 1916 did the *Daily Express* become the most popular Conservative daily, under the editorship first of Beverley Baxter and then of Arthur Christiansen. The paper reflected Beaverbrook's personal ambitions and idiosyncratic Empire enthusiasm. These were typified in the *Empire Crusade of 1929–33 and maintained until his death in 1964. The authentic voice of post-war middle England but widely read among all classes, the *Daily Express* lost its way in the 1970s. Sold to the Trafalgar House conglomerate in 1977 by Beaverbrook's son, and to United Newspapers in 1985, the paper steadily failed to replace its ageing readership. By the 1990s, it was owned by a Labour peer and inviting its readers to back Tony Blair. *CKSU*

Matthew Engel, *Tickle the Public* (London, 1996)

Daily Herald, newspaper. Originally published by London print-workers in 1911 as a halfpenny strike sheet, the *Daily Herald* was relaunched in 1912. Until 1922, under the owner-editorship of George Lansbury, it was an iconoclastic, crusading paper, open to all sections of radical thought and a thorn in the side of the Labour leadership. It attracted a galaxy of literary talent and, pre-war, the genius of cartoonist Will Dyson. The *Herald* always struggled to survive, and a boycott by newsprint suppliers and advertisers after the Great War forced Lansbury to relinquish control to the TUC and the Labour Party. The TUC linked up with Odhams press in 1930, and in 1933 it became the first daily to reach a circulation of two million. Nonetheless, its fundamental problems remained. A remarkably loyal readership, still 1.3 million on its demise, was largely ageing and heavily working class, and it was therefore difficult to attract advertising income. The TUC sold its shares in 1964, and the paper was renamed the **Sun*, but remained Labour-supporting until bought by Rupert Murdoch in 1969. Dubbed the 'miracle of Fleet Street', the *Herald*'s history illustrates the difficulties inherent in attempting to reconcile political and commercial objectives. *MC*

Huw Richards, *The Bloody Circus: The Daily Herald and the Left* (London, 1997).

Daily Mail. The popular national daily press is conveniently dated to the foundation of *Northcliffe's *Daily Mail* in 1896. The paper catered to the curiosity and leisure interests of the expanding educated lower middle class. Advertising revenue enabled it to sell as 'a penny newspaper for one halfpenny'. Circulation reached 1,000,000 about 1914 and 2,000,000 by the mid-1940s. Like its competitors, the *Daily Mail* printed also in Manchester and Glasgow, crippling the regional morning papers and making the London-based press truly national by the Second World War. Always Conservative, the paper's partisanship was rarely uncritical, notably in European and Commonwealth matters, in the 1990s as in the 1930s. Northcliffe was a nuisance to the government during the Great War. His brother Rothermere, who inherited the paper, was equally tiresome to Baldwin. Circulation trailed the *Daily Express* in the 1930s–1960s but surged ahead in the Thatcher era. *CKSU*

S. J. Taylor, *The Great Outsiders* (London, 1996).

Daily Mirror, founded in 1903 by Alfred Harmsworth, Lord Northcliffe, as a picture paper for gentlewomen, edited by gentlewomen. The latter were soon sacked. The paper's turning point came in 1935, when it was redesigned as a working-class tabloid, in consultation with an advertising agency, and it steadily outstripped the TUC-controlled 'official' Labour *Daily Herald.* In the Second World War, it championed other ranks and their families. After 1945, its brand of warm individualism, good writing and firm but independent support of the Labour leadership matched post-war economic and social developments well into the 1960s. Circulation peaked at 5,000,000 in 1965. From 1970 the paper's formula was increasingly superseded by the brash *Sun.* An unhappy period (1984–91) in the ownership of the maverick Robert Maxwell left it level-pegging with the *Sun* in the uncertain end-of-century tabloid market. *CKSU*

Matthew Engel, *Tickle the Public* (London, 1996).

Daily Record, Scottish newspaper. Since the early 1950s, when it converted to supporting the Labour Party, the *Record* has been the best-selling daily newspaper in Scotland, with sales of around half a million. A strong supporter of devolution since the 1970s, the *Record*, unlike other Scottish newspapers which attempt to camouflage their political bias, was open in its support of the Labour Party, especially at election times. *RF*

Daily Telegraph. Founded in 1855, its circulation as London's first penny daily was the largest in the world, reaching nearly 250,000 in 1877. The halfpenny *Daily Mail* and revived *Times* hit it badly in the 1900s. In 1928, William Berry (Lord Camrose) bought control and revitalized it. Sales doubled when the price was halved in 1930 and they reached one million after the Second World War. Camrose's younger son took over in 1954 and launched a sister *Sunday Telegraph* in 1961. The paper's overwhelming circulation leadership in the 'quality' broadsheet field, its comprehensive news service, and its role as the unofficial voice of the Conservative Party leadership, discouraged innovation. But by the 1980s the paper was old-fashioned and required new investment. Hartwell sold out in 1985 to Conrad Black, an ambitious Canadian press baron. The paper was redesigned and brightened up, and its partisanship became less predictable. *CKSU*

D. Hart-Davis, *The House the Berrys Built* (London, 1991)

Daily Worker, the Communist Party of Great Britain's daily newspaper. Founded in 1930, on Comintern instructions, it was subsidized, directly or indirectly, by the Russian government throughout its history. Consequently it displayed an almost slavish adherence to the 'Moscow line'. Banned for almost two years during the Second World War, its fortunes thereafter mirrored those of the party, with sales peaking at 120,000 in 1948 but then declining rapidly. It was renamed the *Morning Star* in 1967. *MC*

Dalton, (Edward) Hugh John Neale (1887–1962), Labour politician. With a brief exception, when he represented Peckham, 1924–9, Hugh Dalton's constituency lay in the working-class north-east, but his own roots lay elsewhere. His father had been a canon of St George's chapel, Windsor, and a tutor to monarchy. Dalton himself had been educated at Eton and King's College, Cambridge, and his early inclination had been towards an academic career. In 1911 he took up a Hutcheson research fellowship at the LSE and began a study of income inequalities. He also pursued another interest and was called to the Bar in 1914. However, the Great War interrupted his career, for he saw military service and wrote a memoir, *With British Guns in Italy* (1919). The post-war years witnessed an initial resumption of his academic interests, and he became reader in commerce (1920–5) at the LSE and then reader in economics (1925–36). In parallel, however, he was pursuing his political ambitions and, following his election at Bishop Auckland in 1929, he was appointed under-secretary to Arthur Henderson at the Foreign Office. He declined to serve in the National Government and lost his seat in 1931, but regained it in 1935. By now he possessed a substantial power base within the Labour Party which resulted in his membership of the NEC between 1928 and 1952.

Dalton had anticipated the Second World War and warned his party against the likely outcome of developments in Europe. He had a sound grasp of European issues and spoke several languages. With the outbreak of hostilities his political role increased, and he became minister of economic warfare in the Churchill government (1940) and also assumed responsibility for establishing Special Operations Executive (SOE), a role which he relished and much missed after his transfer to the Board of Trade in 1942.

In his post-war government Attlee appointed Dalton to the Treasury and as chancellor he introduced four budgets in difficult economic circumstances. The great fuel crisis of 1947 and the sterling crisis of the same year were among the more dramatic problems he faced. Personal disaster also intervened in 1947 when he passed budget secrets to a reporter, believing in the journalist's trust. Dalton resigned, to be replaced by Sir Stafford Cripps, but Dalton's career had not ended. He rejoined the cabinet in June 1948 as chancellor of the duchy of Lancaster and, following the 1950 election, he served as minister of local government and planning until 1951. In 1957 he intimated that he would fight no more elections, and he received a life peerage in 1960.

Dalton left his mark in a variety of ways. He took a keen interest in rambling and served as president of the Ramblers' Association, 1948–50. In line with this interest in the countryside he managed to achieve a substantial transfer of land and houses to the National Trust through his taxation policies. In addition, he purchased land on the state's behalf. Lovers of the country's heritage owe him an undoubted debt. So does the Labour Party. In his later career he acted as a talent scout, identifying the young, both within and outside parliament, who would help to build Labour's future. George Brown, Castle, Callaghan, and Crosland, were among those who had their careers lifted through his benevolent patronage. *CH*

Hugh Dalton, *Call back Yesterday* (London, 1953). | Hugh Dalton *The Fateful Years* (London, 1957). | Hugh Dalton *High Tide and After* (London, 1962). | Hugh Dalton *Diaries*, ed. B. Pimlott, 2 vols. (London, 1985–6). | B. Pimlott, *Hugh Dalton* (London, 1985).

Dalyell, Tam (1932–), Labour politician. Educated at Eton and King's College, Cambridge, Dalyell has been MP for West Lothian since 1962, becoming in 2001 the Father of the House. He served as Dick Crossman's parliamentary private secretary, but though not reaching ministerial office has had a colourful career as a backbencher, as in his harrying to Margaret Thatcher to give information about the sinking of the **General Belgrano*. An opponent of devolution in the 1970s, his constituency gave its name to 'the West Lothian question' when Dalyell pointed out the illogicality of denying English MPs a say in the post-devolution affairs of West Lothian while still allowing him to vote on all matters relating to England. A classic member of the parliamentary 'awkward squad' whose activities help to keep all governments on their toes. *JAR*

'damn the consequences'. Of Lloyd George's 1909 *'People's Budget', Lord *Milner told a Glasgow audience: 'if we believe a thing to be bad . . . it is our duty to try to prevent it and to damn the consequences'. So advised, the Tory-dominated Lords rejected the budget, precipitating the crisis resulting in the 1911 Parliament Act. *RJQA*

Dangerfield, George (1904–86), writer. The son of a clergyman, born at Newbury and educated at Hertford College, Oxford, Dangerfield was to provide one of the romantic mysteries of modern British historiography. He went to the USA in 1930 and was literary editor of *Vanity Fair* before wartime service in the American infantry, becoming an American citizen in 1943. After the war he received some acclaim as a historian in North America, winning a Pulitzer prize in 1953 for *The Era of Good Feelings*, but remained unknown in Britain until the 1966 reissue of *The Strange Death of Liberal England* which had appeared almost unnoticed in 1935. A new generation of history students fiercely debated what was now presented to them as 'the Dangerfield thesis'. The notion that the moderate, consensual, middle-class liberal values of the Victorian era were effectively destroyed in 1910–14 by the triple challenge of working-class protest, the suffragettes, and the Ulster crisis proved to be extremely seductive. Subsequently an array of English historians (Clarke, Cook, Phillips, McKibbin) challenged the thesis, but this 'beguiling classic' (David Powell) still demands attention, not least for its literary brio. The book and its author were celebrated in *Albion*, vol. 15 (1985). *PS*

Dardanelles. See Gallipoli.

Davidson, John Colin Campbell (1889–1970), Conservative politician and party organizer. Widely regarded as a grey eminence in the Baldwin regime, he forged a particularly close relationship with Baldwin as his parliamentary private secretary in 1921–2. Davidson's political career blossomed from 1910 when he became private secretary to Lord Crewe and he was also Law's parliamentary private secretary, 1922–4. That involvement with Law and Baldwin ensured Davidson's close proximity to the heart of inter-war Conservative politics. He entered parliament in 1920 for Hemel Hempstead and held it until he took a viscountcy in 1937 (when he was succeeded as MP by his wife). During his career he held a succession of minor ministerial posts: chancellor of the duchy of Lancaster, 1923–4 and 1931–7, and parliamentary secretary to the Admiralty, 1924–6, but his most important role was as party chairman, 1924–6. He had been identified as a potential chairman as early as April 1921 after only six active months in politics. His tenure at Central Office was a time of rapid change in the party machine. Some dispute would later arise over whether some of these reforms were initiated by his successor Neville Chamberlain, but it cannot be denied that he revitalized the party machine in both financial and organizational terms, introducing initiatives such as cinema vans. The party chairman is the personal appointee of the leader, and as a result of this patronage Davidson found his fortunes closely tied to Baldwin's. Failure in the 1929 general election, after a lacklustre fight by Baldwin campaigning on a slogan of 'safety first', ensured Davidson was the chief recipient of Conservative disappointment and dismay. In a matter of months, given the leader's parlous position, Baldwin felt it necessary to sacrifice Davidson to satisfy his critics. *NJC*

R. Rhodes James (ed.), *Memoirs of a Conservative: The Memoirs and Papers of J. C. C. Davidson* (London, 1969).

Davidson, Randall Thomas (1848–1930), archbishop of Canterbury, 1903–28. As archbishop, Davidson prided himself on his political connections and his links to the court forged when he was dean of Windsor (1893–91) and clerk of the closet (1891–1903). As such he was well placed to act as an intermediary for the king during the 1909–11 constitutional crisis. He was also to play a more public leading role when calling for reconciliation during the 1926 General Strike. *PPC*

Davies, (Edward) Clement (1884–1962), Liberal politician and leader of the Liberal Party from 1945 to 1956. Trained as a lawyer and a KC from 1926, he was MP for Montgomeryshire, 1929–62. Davies accepted the leadership of the Liberals largely by default, following the rout of 1945 which left it with only twelve MPs and in which the then leader, Archibald *Sinclair, lost his seat. Sinclair was expected to make a rapid return to the Commons, but failed to do so, and Davies proved the most acceptable leader for the dwindling group of Liberal MPs, reduced to only six at the 1951 election. Although he presided over the Liberal Party during the nadir of its fortunes, he made a crucial contribution to its survival by refusing the offer of a seat in the cabinet from Winston Churchill in 1951, thereby keeping the party alive as an independent force. Regarded as too elderly to engender a revival, the failure of the party to better its position in the 1955 general election led to his resignation and succession by Jo *Grimond. *JS*

Davies, David James (1893–1956), political economist. Dr D. J. Davies, who had started work at a colliery aged 12 and had served in the American navy, returned to Wales to take a doctorate in agricultural economics and became one of Plaid Cymru's foremost political thinkers. Very much influenced by Scandinavian (and especially Danish) models he and his Irish wife established a school for the unemployed. He urged Plaid Cymru to embrace decentralization and cooperation and in so doing armed the party for its opposition to Labour. *PS*

Davies, John Emerson Harding (1916–79), industrialist and Conservative politician. The first director-general of the CBI, 1965–9, he had previously worked in the oil industry, becoming managing director of Shell-Mex. A commercially oriented technocrat who acted as a classic chief executive, Davies successfully got the CBI on its feet as an organization. Although his views were not always clear, he nevertheless defended tripartism and industrial policy against resistance from within the CBI. He was also concerned about the chaotic state of business representation in Britain and a keen supporter of British membership of the European Economic Community. After leaving the CBI, he entered parliament and became secretary of state for trade and industry in the Heath government. Like many businessmen, he did not adapt well to political life and was not a conspicuous success in his third career. He was relegated to the post of minister responsible for Europe from November 1972, holding posts in opposition before his death. *WG*

Davies, Margaret Llewelyn (1861–1944), social reformer. From 1889 to 1921 she was the general secretary of the Women's Co-Operative Guild, which she organized from an office in her father's vicarage in Kirkby Lonsdale. Under her influence, guild members, who were mostly working-class women, both widened their recreational opportunities and became involved in a range of progressive causes. She was a pacifist, penal reformer, and (as chairman 1924–8) a supporter of the Society for Cultural Relations between the USSR and Britain. *DEM*

Jean Gaffin and David Thomas, *Caring and Sharing: The Centenary History of the Women's Co-Operative Guild* (Manchester, 1993).

Davies, Stephen Owen (1888–1972), Labour politician. 'S.O.' (as he was invariably known) was MP for Merthyr Tydfil, 1934–72. Earning his

BA whilst still a miner, he became a union official. Often referred to as a Marxist individualist, the constitutional status of Wales was his passion: he introduced a Home Rule Bill in 1955 and supported the Parliament for Wales petition in 1956. Deselected because of age in 1970, he held the seat as an independent Labour candidate. He remained part-romantic, part-gadfly. *PS*

ROBERT GRIFFITHS, *S. O. Davies: A Socialist Faith* (Llandysul, 1983).

Davison, Emily Wilding (1872–1913), militant *suffragist. Although a member of the Women's Social and Political Union from 1906 and arrested and imprisoned several times (once for whipping a baptist minister she mistook for Lloyd George), Emily Davison became notorious for one act. On 4 June 1913, Derby Day, she was fatally injured after running on to the Epsom racecourse and seizing the bridle of Anmer, the king's horse. Whether or not she intended to sacrifice her life—she had a third-class return ticket to London—her large and moving funeral service was that of a martyr. *DEM*

LIZ STANLEY and ANN MORLEY, *The Life and Death of Emily Wilding Davison* (London, 1988).

Dawes plan. SEE REPARATIONS.

Dawson (born Robinson), Geoffrey (1874–1944), editor of *The Times*, 1912–19 and 1922–41, archetypal establishment figure. After Eton and Oxford, Dawson joined, from the Colonial Office, Lord Milner's 'kindergarten' administering South Africa in 1901. He edited the Johannesburg *Star* and was called by Northcliffe to *The Times* in 1908, falling out with him in 1919. Recalled under J. J. Astor's ownership, he enjoyed complete sovereignty in editorial policy—arguably a misfortune, since he became principal apologist for the disastrous appeasement of the fascist dictators. *CKSU*

EVELYN WRENCH, *Geoffrey Dawson and Our Times* (London, 1955).

Day, Robin (1924–2000), broadcaster. After Oxford, Day read for the Bar, but his career took off in 1955 as a pioneer newsreader for the fledgling Independent Television News. His courteous but relentless interviewing style set new standards. As public affairs television grew, Day became an institution, with horn-rimmed spectacles and large bow tie. Sir Robin matured into a consummate and scrupulously impartial moderator, the epitome of 'public service' broadcasting practice, both on radio and television. *CKSU*

ROBIN DAY, *Grand Inquisitor: Memoirs* (London, 1989).

D-Day (6 June 1944), operational name given to the date of the Allied continental invasion. British, American, and Canadian forces landed on the Normandy coast supported by overwhelming air and naval power. Despite heavy (mainly American) losses, a foothold was established by nightfall. Confused by deception plans, German forces did not at first know whether the operation was a bluff and were then unable to counter the quick build-up of Allied logistical superiority. *MLC*

Deakin, Arthur (1890–1955), trade unionist. Deakin became acting general secretary of the Transport and General Workers' Union (TGWU) when Ernest Bevin entered the war cabinet in 1940 and general secretary when Bevin became foreign secretary in 1945. Even more anti-communist than Bevin, he ruled the TGWU with a rod of iron at a decisive time, banning Communists and ex-Communists from seeking union office. He used the union's large block vote to defeat the Labour left over economic and foreign policy, 1949–51, and helped American unions form the anti-communist International Confederation of Free Trade Unions. *PRGR*

dealignment, class, the proposition that British (or other) voters have become less attached to their social classes than formerly, and hence less predictably likely to vote for class parties. After Labour's third general election defeat in a row, in 1959, class dealignment was a popular explanation, as in **Must Labour Lose?* After Labour's fourth general election defeat in a row, in 1992, the class dealignment explanation was considered again, as in *Labour's Last Chance?* Labour's election victories in 1964 and 1997 therefore imperilled the class dealignment hypothesis. Considered more carefully, the class dealignment hypothesis breaks down into two statements: 'people are becoming more loosely attached to social classes' and 'therefore, they are less likely to support class parties'. The first is true, so long as 'class' is carefully defined; the second false. Karl Marx defined class in relation to the means of production. You either control them or you do not. Marxian class still exists and is still relevant to voting. For instance, the petty bourgeoisie, self-employed artisans and tradespeople, are the most Conservative of all social classes. However, most people's class is a poor predictor of their social attitudes. Most owners of the means of production do so through their pension entitlements and insurance contracts, not as top-hatted capitalists. Most sellers of their labour power sell it to service employers, many of them in the public sector. Therefore, neither the label 'capitalist' nor the label 'proletarian' tells us much about most citizens. Furthermore, what people often think of as 'classes' (the social grades widely used in advertising and market research) reflect patterns of consumption, not power relations in the workplace, and therefore are not, properly, measures of class at all. However, political parties are led by people who want to win elections. Therefore, if they see their class basis eroding, they need to appeal in a new way. The Conservative Party, the most successful class party in British history, has several times relaunched itself to appeal to new social groups. Successful relaunches took place between 1875 and 1892, between 1922 and 1929, and between 1950 and 1955. Unsuccessful ones took place between 1903 and 1910, and after 1992. The Labour Party has been much poorer at winning elections, but it too has had successful relaunches in 1945 and 1997. Some of these relaunches, especially Labour's in 1945, have emphasized class; most, including Labour's most recent, have downplayed it. As no one social class comprises a majority of the electorate, that is not surprising. *IM*

M. Abrams, *Must Labour Lose?* (Harmondsworth, 1960). | A. Heath et al., *Labour's Last Chance?* (Aldershot, 1994).

death duties attracted particular interest in the 1920s and in the 1970s, as a means of reducing inequality through inheritance. While they have had some effect on the distribution of wealth, the possibility of avoiding the tax by making gifts before death has weakened their impact. To deal with this problem Labour replaced estate duty with capital transfer tax in 1975, to deal with lifetime giving, but this was weakened by the Conservatives and replaced by an inheritance tax in 1986, which restored the traditional system. *RCW*

Death on the Rock **(1988)**, Thames Television documentary about the March 1988 SAS killing in Gibraltar of three IRA members then on a bombing mission (Mairead Farrell, Daniel McCann, Sean Savage). The programme questioned the government's version of the killings, asking whether the three could not have been arrested. Publicly criticized by Margaret Thatcher, the programme further fuelled debates about alleged Northern Irish-related shoot-to-kill incidents, and about media coverage of the Troubles. The September 1988 inquest into the killings found that they were lawful, though the 1989 independent Windlesham/Rampton report on the programme substantially vindicated its makers. *RE*

Roger Bolton, *Death on the Rock and Other Stories* (London, 1990).

death rate. See population change.

decolonization, process by which a colonial power divests itself of colonies. In 1900, Britain ruled an empire larger than the world had ever known, though the 'white dominions' of Australia, Canada, and New Zealand had each gained internal self-government, controlled by freely elected (white) assemblies, by 1900. South Africa's complex internal arrangements were rationalized in 1911, after which it moved along the same dominion path. But, although the Indian National Congress had been in existence since 1885 to seek a similar status for India, there was far less readiness in Britain to yield power to a non-white successor-regime, hence the bitter political debates that surrounded the grant of limited concessions to Indian aspirations in 1909–10 and in 1919. Though the 1935 Government of India Act finally granted internal self-government at the provincial level, it was fought tooth and nail by Conservatives led by Winston Churchill. Even supporters like Baldwin did not expect to see actual Indian independence for at least 30 years, though India had a substantial middle class of educated Indians, and was likely to be deemed ready for self-government sooner than the other colonies. All such perceptions changed dramatically during the Second World War, and especially with its extension to Asia in December 1941. British prestige in Asia plummeted after humiliating defeats by the Japanese, and Indian nationalists' aspirations rose accordingly. On a broader front official British rhetoric that portrayed the war as the defence of freedom had uncomfortable implications for colonial powers, as Churchill discovered when President Roosevelt interpreted their Atlantic Charter of 1941 as an anti-colonialist agreement. In the aftermath of war in 1945, it was impossible to restore British authority in the Indian subcontinent; by 1948, India, Pakistan, Burma, and Ceylon (now Sri Lanka) had all become independent states, and the same process of rationalization of overseas commitments had enforced withdrawal from Palestine.

At this point, and especially with the return of Churchill's Conservatives to power in 1951, the process slowed: the early 1950s were characterized more by the consolidation of remaining colonies (in some cases by grouping them into local federations for mutual support) than by hurrying them towards freedom. All the same, independence movements within most colonies were increasingly active and difficult to deny, so that withdrawal now became far more a matter of 'when' than 'if'. British military weakness revealed in the Suez crisis of 1956 may have been the crucial factor, though the bloody civil war in the (former Belgian) Congo in the early 1960s—evidence of what happened if withdrawal was left too late—certainly concentrated minds in Whitehall. After the 1959 election had been won, Macmillan sent Iain *Macleod to the Colonial Office to speed up the process, as part of his attempted reorientation of Britain's international policy towards Europe, so incurring bitter recriminations from white settlers in places like the Kenyan 'white highlands' and in southern Rhodesia. Macmillan himself told the unwilling white South Africans that the anti-colonial winds of change were now irresistible. Ghana had gained independence in 1957 and the other west African colonies followed soon afterwards; east African and Asian colonies almost all became independent during the 1960s, a process reaccelerated by Wilson's withdrawal of British garrisons from east of Suez in 1967–8 after a sterling crisis. By the 1970s, little remained, but those colonies that did continued to present problems, notably the long-running Rhodesian imbroglio, the Gibraltar dispute with Spain, and the Falkland Islands that involved Britain in war with Argentina. And yet, the process had been surprisingly uncontentious within British politics (even for West Indian territories that Britain had ruled for over three hundred years) and for the most part Britain retained friendly relations and Commonwealth links with her former possessions, the common language no doubt assisting that process. Britain's colonial empire ended without a bang and without much even of a whimper; it certainly disappeared more rapidly than any world empire had ever done before.

JAR

John Cross, *The Fall of the British Empire* (London, 1968). | John Darwin, *The End of the British Empire* (London, 1991).

decriminalization, changes in the criminal law so that certain prescribed types of behaviour are no longer deemed illegal. This is a controversial concept based on the idea that, in respect of certain prescribed behaviours, criminal law adds to social problems rather than acting as a means of controlling them. The dearth of conclusive, empirical evidence concerning the general deterrent effects of the criminal law has led to a review of its role in shaping the development of society. The origins of the concept can be traced back to the 1960s, when it began to be suggested that there was a category of crimes for which there were no victims or injured parties in the sense of those who would complain to the police if it were feasible. What was deemed to be victimless crime included actions such as homosexuality between consenting adults, personal drug abuse, gambling, pornography, and prostitution. The arguments for decriminalization focus on two arguments, moral and pragmatic. In the case of the former, libertarians argue that everyone has the right to individual liberty on condition that there is no infringement of other people's rights, which are intended only to encompass contraventions to which all participants have consented on a free and voluntary basis. Reforms in the law were not intended to apply to cases involving coercion, for example, in the case of children too young to know what they are doing or entailing obvious intrusions into other people's privacy. Pragmatic arguments for decriminalizing victimless crime focus on the views that such laws are difficult to enforce because there are no complainants or that it is expedient not to enforce the legislation. Supporters of the latter idea argue that there should be a high degree of consistency between the law and the legal consciousness of the population. Consequently when there is a widespread demand for illegal services such as drugs (particularly 'soft' drugs like cannabis), and prostitution, the inability to enforce the law is self-defeating, since it undermines public respect for the law itself. The long-term aim for those advocating specific types of decriminalization is full legal and social recognition of the behaviour, which would be achieved by a change of opinion about the role of the state. Giving discretion to the courts to impose only nominal penalties for contraventions constitutes an initial phase in this development.

JFM

Deedes, William Francis (1913–), Conservative politician and journalist, beginning his career on the *Morning Post*. Bill Deedes was a Churchill junior and Macmillan cabinet minister surviving as an editor to defend Thatcher, and as a *Daily Telegraph* columnist to mourn Princess Diana, and encourage Hague. He was the Bill of 'Dear Bill', *Private Eye*'s satire on the Thatcher years. He was not, as alleged, the model for 'Boot of the Beast' in Evelyn Waugh's *Black Mischief*, but as correspondent in Abyssinia, he did own the model for Boot's kit. Winning the MC in the war, MP for Ashford from 1950, *inter alia*, minister of state at the Home Office, he became minister of information in 1962, so inheriting in the best spirit of Waugh, the *Profumo case. He was present at the famous 2 a.m. inquisition of Mr Profumo. Long a contributor, he was editor of the *Daily Telegraph*, 1974–86, though, under an odd regime with its proprietor then under the thumb of a terroristic managing editor, Deedes only ran the leader page and certain features. The paper nevertheless enjoyed high sales and an outstanding reputation for new/old Conservatism, Thatcherite before Thatcher, ahead of the ideological game in the 1970s. Bill Deedes was also a good friend to journalists trying to write decently, and in his late eighties was still producing a deft and sardonic column. A rare politician who survived politics to enjoy himself. *EP*

W. F. Deedes, *Dear Bill: W. F. Deedes Reports* (London, 1997).

Defence, Ministry of (1947–) The institutions concerned with warfare have been continuously integrated throughout the 20th century. In 1900 there were two ministries, the Admiralty for the navy and the War Office for the army. These each had a secretary of state at cabinet level (the Admiralty's called its secretary 'first lord'). As a result of deficiencies during the Boer war (1899–1902), the coordinating Committee of Imperial Defence (CID) was created in 1904 to advise and consult above and between the two ministries. Upon the outbreak of the Great War in 1914, the CID's duties were taken over by first the War Council, then the Dardanelles Committee, and then by the War Committee, but the conflict's magnitude demanded greater cohesion between the departments, especially with the new and massive Ministry of Munitions. When Lloyd George became prime minister in December 1916, a war cabinet was formed with its own secretariat. The Air Ministry was created in 1918 to oversee the formation of the Royal Air Force from the amalgamation of the Royal Flying Corps and the Royal Naval Air Service. This further complicated effective coordination between the services. The CID was reconstituted in 1919 while the supply function was reintegrated into the individual ministries. In 1924 the chiefs of staff committee was established as a subcommittee of the CID in order to improve coordination. As the rearmament crisis grew, a minister for coordination of defence was appointed in 1936, with day-to-day responsibility for the CID. Another significant step was the creation of the Joint Intelligence subcommittee of the chiefs of staff committee in 1938. When war finally came in 1939, the war cabinet was advised by a military coordination committee headed by the minister for coordination of defence. When Winston Churchill became prime minister in 1940, he also assumed the role of 'minister for defence' (the first to hold that title) and was served by a defence committee (operations) and a defence committee (supply). With a growing need for integrated planning of operations involving one or more of the services, the joint planning organization (created in 1927) was significantly enhanced, and consequently orders were issued on the authority of the chiefs of staff committee, not through individual services.

It was acknowledged that the unity of purpose which had been developed during the war should be retained after it and should be constitutionally acknowledged. Therefore in 1947 the Ministry of Defence (MoD) was set up by statute, which saw the chiefs of staff organization transferred to the new ministry while the chiefs of staff committee remained as the government's professional military advisers. The secretary of state for defence became the sole representative of the armed forces in cabinet. It became apparent that the minister needed greater control and the chiefs of staff committee a leader, and in 1955 a chairmen of the chiefs of staff was appointed, who in 1957 became chief of the defence staff, to a more powerful minister with greater control over the formulation of policy and the coordination of the three services and of the Ministry of Supply. Further integration came with the 1963 defence white paper which retained separate services but sought, wherever possible, to organize the MoD on a joint rather than individual service basis. The rising costs and complexity of defence purchasing led in 1971 to another white paper, creating a procurement executive to combine the procurement roles of the Ministries of Defence and Aviation Supply. This was reformed again in 1981 when a major reorganization provided for a minister of state and an under-secretary of state for both the armed forces and defence procurement. Wider and deeper integration continued throughout the last years of the century. *JD*

Ministry of Defence website: *www.mod.uk* | Franklyn Johnson, *Defence by Ministry* (London, 1980).

defence intelligence. At the core of Britain's Cold War and post-Cold War defence planning and integrated intelligence system has been a defence intelligence capacity designed to understand and anticipate enemy plans, strength, equipment, and movements. However, continuing institutional conflicts between the ministry of defence and foreign office undermined defence intelligence and, starved of resources, it was consigned to a position significantly lower than it should have been. At the core of the problem were the Cold War prejudices of the Ministry of Defence and Foreign Office. Each sought intelligence to reinforce its own view, looking for 'worst case' scenarios in Soviet military strength assessments and in parallel deductions of Soviet political objectives. Nonetheless, despite these serious institutional problems Britain's defence intelligence since 1945 (building on its Second World War experience) has enjoyed important and continued successes.

As the Cold War developed in the decade after 1945, reliable information from the Eastern bloc and the Soviet Union was at a premium. In the absence of Western penetration agents and until the start of U2 overflights in the mid-1950s, the West and particularly British intelligence was reliant almost entirely on human intelligence (HUMINT) derived from Soviet defectors, Austrian and German prisoners of war, scientists, and refugees. Many hundreds of thousands of POWs and scientific workers were deported to Eastern Europe and the Soviet Union at the end of the war and after. Their gradual release and return to the West provided information critical to Western understanding of the developing Russian atomic bomb programme. For example, the British gained important knowledge of East German and Soviet uranium mining and manufacturing activities and reactor building programme. This intelligence proved decisive, enabling British intelligence to understand the kind of atomic bomb Russia was creating. Hundreds of thousands of returning Austrian and German POWs, refugees and former technical deportees were screened by the Scientific and Technical Intelligence Division of the Control Commission for Germany (STID) and, until the Berlin Wall ended the flow in 1961, their intelligence was exploited. In addition, between 1946 and 1990, the British Commander-in-Chief's Mission to the Soviet Forces in East Germany (BRIXMISS) provided information concerning Soviet hardware and tactics. However, during these years important new forms of defence intelligence became available to British political and military planners.

These new forms of defence intelligence emerged during the decade after 1945, a time when high-grade, high-quality signals and imagery (photographic) intelligence (SIGINT and IMINT) were at a premium. In the course of that decade, Britain's signals and photographic intelligence received a massive and continuing boost. This came first in the form of the post-war Anglo-American intelligence agreements, which from the late 1940s gave Britain access to Soviet codes, thus enabling *Government Communications Headquarters to access Soviet traffic. Critically, these agreements also gave British analysts access to American image intelligence derived from the mid-1950s onwards from Soviet overflights by U2 spy planes and later by satellite reconnaissance. As a consequence, when combined with signals intelligence and the work of Western penetration agents, defence intelligence helped in the critical assessment of the Soviet nuclear threat, which was a key factor in the stabilization of the Cold War, and it helped make for more realistic planning and decision making. *PM*

deliberative democracy, the theory and practice of democratic choice following reasoned argument among the choosers. The normative theory of deliberative democracy emerged in the 1980s in response to two things. First, mainstream democratic theory, heavily influenced by Joseph Schumpeter, had restricted its attention to elections as a negative control mechanism, an opportunity to 'throw out the rascals'. Schumpeter had argued that a more inclusive conception of democracy was not only impracticable (because of limits on citizens' information) but undesirable (because he associated it with fascist populism in the 1930s). In the 1980s it was argued that Schumpeter had underestimated citizens' level of information, and the fear of right-wing populism had faded. Second, the exponential growth of information technology seemed to make experiments in direct democracy feasible as never before. Perhaps we could recreate the direct democracy of the Athenian assembly or the New England town-meeting through citizen computer networks. The American political theorist James Fishkin has tried some practical experiments in deliberative democracy. Advocates of deliberative democracy say that it is not only good in itself but that it helps achieve better informed and more tolerant decision making. By splitting multidimensional issues into their component dimensions, deliberative democrats hope that they can avoid the fickleness and arbitrary nature of majority decision on complex matters. Sceptics say that intractable multidimensional questions do not necessarily become more tractable by means of deliberative democracy; that the paradoxes and impossibility theorems of social choice still pose insurmountable barriers; and that deliberative democracy is not so easy for people who lack computers and talking skills. *IM*

J. Elster, *Deliberative Democracy* (Cambridge, 1998).

Dell, Edmund Emanuel **(1921–2000),** Labour politician. Dell was a history lecturer at Oxford and then an executive with ICI, 1949–63, before becoming MP for Birkenhead, 1964–79. After serving in junior posts in the 1964 government he became paymaster general, 1974–7, and secretary for trade and industry, 1977–9. On Labour's right wing, he supported the abandonment of Keynesianism and worked for acceptance of the terms of the IMF loan in 1976. An early opponent of the European Monetary System from a Eurosceptical position, he resigned from the cabinet to work in the City during the 'winter of discontent'. He later joined the Social Democratic Party and in the 1990s published a number of valuable works in contemporary history. *BJE*

democracy, a system of government derived from the classical Greek words *demos* (people) and *kratos* (rule), is by far the most important concept underpinning modern liberal government. It is also one of the concepts that is invariably contested, and the diversity of values and processes encapsulated by the term is at the core of political debate in the UK. Throughout the 20th century, discussion of democracy is implicit in political discourse, rather than explicit. In reality, democracy is a multifaceted concept which appears in a variety of forms; although one form in particular, indirect, representative democracy, dominated the 20th-century political domain.

Democracy has divided into two types: direct and indirect democracy. Direct or primary democracy, where all citizens are involved in a decision, can take several forms. In small communities, there might be an assembly at which all citizens might attend. In the case of classical Athens, the most often cited example, this was a distinct subset of the economically active population. In larger communities, problems of size can be overcome by use of a pyramidal system, with delegation and mandating of members at each level to the tier above. Another mechanism for direct democracy involves the use of referenda for routine policy choice, with the prospect that new information and communication technologies could deliver what has been termed 'teledemocracy'. Indirect democracy uses elections to establish an assembly as the locus for decision making. Here the norm is for the members of the assembly to act as representatives, elected periodically to speak on behalf of their constituency, and held to account only at election time, rather than mandated delegates and thus 'bound blindly and implicitly to obey' (a distinction insisted upon by Edmund Burke in a celebrated speech to his Bristol electors, 3 November 1774), and perhaps instantly recalled should they cease to do so.

A more compelling distinction, however, is between democracy as a means of enabling the population to choose between alternatives developed by others, and as a mechanism to permit popular influence over every facet of the policy-making process. Here, referenda are less democratic than they might seem, as they allow only a choice between competing, preconceived outcomes; and the existence of representative government as such offers only limited democratic input. In this respect, general elections offer only a plebiscite on political choices conceived elsewhere by members of the political elite, the process of 'competitive elitism', welcomed by both the German sociologist Max Weber and the Austrian economist and politician turned Harvard academic Joseph A. Schumpeter as ensuring that the superior values of the social and economic elite continue to dominate.

Those engaging with competitive elitism tend to take one of two positions. The first group, in which the USA political scientist Robert Dahl was a prime mover, supported the notion of indirect representative democracy, but saw it as underpinned by a multiplicity of interest groups which act to bring democratic opinion to bear on policy formation. The second group, with which Carole Pateman is associated, argued that Dahl's pluralism was itself inadequate, as interest groups were likely to comprise the same class of individuals as the legislature. Crucial here are such issues as the nature of the underlying political culture, the extent to which individuals have the economic ability to participate, and the openness of interest groups. Instead, Pateman argues for a process of workplace and community participatory democracy to create a mechanism by which policy can be shaped democratically, and as a means of changing political culture away from a reliance on political elites. Echoing the ideas of *guild socialists, such as G. D. H. Cole, she argues for a pyramidal structure of direct democracy, alongside a parliamentary system for areas such as foreign policy.

Democratic critics have been concerned that democracy is not itself a guarantee of good or equitable policies. Just as Aristotle distinguished between democracy as the rule of the mob and polity as its virtuous variant, conservatives have argued that it is the political culture underpinning the democratic process rather than democracy itself which is a guarantee of good governance. Thus, the rise of mass democracy in the UK led to two distinct, but interrelated fears. The first, epitomized in the work of Moisei *Ostrogorski's *Democracy and the Organisation of Political Parties* (1902), was that the composition of the grass roots of political parties was changing from moderate, independently minded members to activists, who were seeking to turn representatives into delegates (see OLIGARCHY). The second was that the property-owning and wealth-generating classes would lose control of the political system, or that to retain power they would be forced to outbid each other by offering policies which redistributed wealth to the masses. In the event, neither appeared to come true. The continued success of the Conservatives, and the emergence of Labour as a broadly social democratic party which respected the traditional rules of the political game, acted to persuade critics of democracy that the institutional structures underpinning the operation of government would protect the polity from such 'democratic overload'. *CPS*

CAROLE PATEMAN, *Participation and Democratic Theory* (Cambridge, 1970).

Democratic Socialism, Campaign for (CDS) (1960–4), right-wing ginger group in the Labour Party. The CDS was founded to articulate a revisionist position on policy issues but was overtaken by the issue of unilateralism. It became a pressure group campaigning to reverse the vote in favour of unilateralism which had taken place at the Labour Party conference of 1960. After success in 1961, it loyally supported the leadership of Hugh *Gaitskell until it divided over Europe and closed down after Labour won the general election in 1964. The decision to close effectively handed constituency Labour parties to the left and no effective right-wing organization then existed until 1977. *BB*

Democratic Unionist Party (DUP), Northern Ireland political party. Founded in 1971 by the Revd Ian *Paisley and Desmond Boal, the Ulster Democratic Unionist Party was a successor to the Protestant Unionist Party which opposed the reformist policies of Northern Ireland's prime minister, Terence O'Neill. The DUP was described by Boal as being to the right on constitutional issues and to the left on social issues. Boal became the first chairman of the party but Paisley rapidly became the dominant figure. When the Northern Ireland parliament was suspended by the Westminster legislation in 1972, the DUP demanded the return of Protestant majority rule. In 1973–4 the DUP and Paisley were prominent in opposing the Northern Ireland Assembly and the Sunningdale agreement. The DUP supported the Ulster workers' strike which brought down the assembly's power-sharing executive, and in the 1979 general election gained two Westminster seats from the Ulster Unionist Party (UUP). The DUP forged an electoral pact with the UUP to oppose the Anglo-Irish intergovernmental conference established by the British and Irish governments in 1985. During the 1992 inter-party talks the DUP refused to discuss any matters of substance with the Irish government until it had made a unilateral commitment to withdrawing Eire's constitutional claim to Northern Ireland. When Sinn Fein was admitted to a revamped talks process in 1997, the DUP withdrew, while David Trimble's UUP remained in. The DUP unsuccessfully led the 'No' campaign in the subsequent Northern Ireland referendum to validate the Belfast agreement. In the Northern Ireland assembly established by the agreement, the DUP formed the main opposition within Ulster Unionism to power-sharing and cross-border bodies. *TWH*

STEVE BRUCE, *God Save Ulster! The Religion and Politics of Paisleyism* (Oxford, 1986).

Denham, 1st Lord, See BOWYER, GEORGE.

Denham, 2nd Lord (1927–). Son of George *Bowyer, Denham was Conservative chief whip in the Lords, 1977–91, successfully managing a House less reliably Conservative than supposed. With increasing numbers of active cross-benchers, a great part of the hereditary Tory element absentee, and enthusiasm for Thatcher undersubscribed among peers, Denham would manage his narrow majority among the activists, but keep a reserve of awayday backwoodsmen alertable for commando action. He did not, however, succeed in preventing a Lords' revolt against abolition of the Greater London Council in 1986. *EP*

Denning, Alfred Thompson (1899–1999), judge. Lord Denning was one of the most important and unorthodox judges of the century. He sat in the High Court (1944–8), as a lord justice of appeal (1948–57), a lord of appeal in ordinary (1957–62), and finally as master of the rolls (1962–82). His work was characterized by two features. First, there was his literary style: succinct, staccato sentences and an evocative depiction of the factual background to a dispute. Second, his conception of the duty of the judge to do justice: rather than waiting for parliament to remedy an injustice, Denning moulded the relevant legal materials in order to achieve the result he wanted. But whilst the techniques he used were radical, the values he used those techniques to uphold were conservative. He was, for instance, concerned to protect consumers against businesses and to ensure that promises were kept. He assumed that the police and executive acted in good faith, dismissing an action by the *Birmingham Six in which they claimed that their confessions had been induced by police beatings. There was even a suggestion of racism, which eventually forced him to resign. He also chaired the inquiry into the *Profumo case, producing a readable, racy, best-selling report. *PPM*

Denniston, Alexander Guthrie ('Alastair') (1881–1961), first head of the British code and cypher school. Born in Scotland, Alastair Denniston was educated privately in England and at the universities of Bonn and Paris. He became a schoolmaster in 1906, then taught languages at Osborne, the pre-Dartmouth naval college. During the Great War he helped found and became head of room 40, the Admiralty's organization for intercepting, decrypting, and interpreting enemy wireless and cable communications. Good luck in the form of captured German code-books helped room 40 achieve a series of spectacular successes, including the decrypting of the infamous Zimmermann telegram. In 1919 Denniston became head of the new interdepartmental code and cypher school (GC & CS). As such he was at the forefront of inter-war developments in cypher security. Despite shortages of money, he kept his team together and presided over its expansion and move to Bletchley Park at the start of the Second World War. Under Denniston's leadership, Bletchley Park's brilliant organization cracked the main German enigma cypher, which did so much to shorten the war. From 1942 until his retirement at the end of the war he headed Bletchley Park's military wing, thereafter returning to his career as a schoolmaster. *PM*

deposits, lost, sums forfeited by candidates who fail to achieve a specified proportion of the votes cast in a parliamentary election. In order to discourage frivolous candidates, the Representation of the People Act, 1918, required candidates to deposit the sum of £150 with the returning officer, the money to be returned if the candidate achieved one-eighth (12.5 per cent) of the votes cast. A substantial growth in the number of candidates in the 1970s and 1980s, many of them regarded as non-serious candidates, led to calls for a more substantial deposit to be required, some arguing for a deposit of £1,000. In 1985, the deposit was raised to £500, with the sum to be returned if the candidate achieved one-twentieth (5 per cent) of the votes cast. The deterrent effect of the new deposit was short-lived: in the 1987 general election the number of candidates was not much fewer than in 1983. In the 1997 general election, only 25 candidates from fringe parties retained their deposits. Candidates who poll a few votes short of the 5 per cent threshold will typically request a recount of the votes. Some writers press for an increase in the size of the deposit while others argue for its abolition. *PN*

Robert Blackburn, *The Electoral System in Britain* (London, 1995). | House of Commons Select Committee on Home Affairs, *Report on the Representation of the People Acts*, Session 1982–3, HC 32–I (London). | H. F. Rawlings, *Law and the Electoral Process* (London, 1988).

Derby, 17th earl of (1865–1948), Conservative politician. In 1908, 'Eddy' Derby inherited with his ancient title one of the great fortunes, in a time when his net annual income of £100,000 was little troubled by an income tax of one shilling in the pound. Scion of a great political family, he was briefly Conservative MP for Westhoughton, 1900–6, and postmaster general under Balfour. Through the long Conservative exclusion from office he struggled unsuccessfully to free his party of the influence of tariff reform and thereby earned the distrust of the Tory leader, Andrew Bonar Law. During the first two years of the Great War Derby swiftly earned a reputation as a great recruiter for the army, and with the advent of the Asquith coalition he became director of recruiting and presided over the *Derby scheme, the last gasp of voluntarism before the implementation of conscription. When the Lloyd George coalition displaced Asquith, Derby became war secretary and apologist for the senior generals. In 1918 he resigned and was rewarded with the Paris embassy, where he became enormously popular. In 1922, he backed Bonar Law in the latter's decision to overturn the coalition and returned briefly to the War Office, 1922–4. Thereafter, he gave his attentions instead to his county and to his own interests, primarily to the turf, which he loved. His stud produced two winners of the

Derby stakes (founded by the 12th earl) and six of the St Leger. His influence in party politics was assured by his lineage and wealth but also by his geniality and his legendary hospitality at Knowsley and his other houses. He was perhaps the last of his class to enjoy political power because of who he was rather than what he did and was rightly called the 'king of Lancashire'. The portrait of Derby by Sir William Orpen in the National Portrait Gallery is one of the finest of its time. *RJQA*

Randolph Churchill, *Lord Derby, 'King of Lancashire'* (London, 1959).

Derby scheme (1915), recruiting plan named after the 17th earl of *Derby, director of recruiting at the War Office, 1915–16. The scheme invited men to 'attest' voluntarily their willingness to serve in the armed forces if they were eventually needed, without requiring them actually to join up there and then. This was a halfway house between the voluntary recruitment which had characterized the first year of the war and compulsory military service. By mid-1915, voluntary enlistment had begun to tail off while heavy losses on the western front were beginning to make manpower shortages a major problem. Moreover, there was increasing pressure for the burdens of the war to be equitably distributed over the whole of the male population. In these circumstances, conscription seemed the answer, but was opposed by many sections of the public and of the Liberal Party, who saw compulsion as an infringement on personal liberty. The Derby scheme was a stop-gap measure which would either ensure that men were available as required or at least prove the inadequacy of voluntarism, paving the way for conscription. When fewer men attested than were required, the way was clear for the introduction of conscription in January 1916. Politically, the scheme allowed Asquith to buy time and stave off the consequences of compulsion, though there was a chance that the scheme, backed by Derby's enormous popular influence as a recruiter, might succeed where earlier efforts had failed. *JS*

R. J. Q. Adams and Philip P. Poirier, *The Conscription Controversy in Great Britain, 1900–1918* (London, 1987).

de Valera, Eamon **(1882–1975)**, Irish politician and head of government. De Valera dominated and shaped independent Ireland. He was born in the USA but brought up in Limerick. In 1908 he joined the Gaelic League. During the 1916 Easter Rising, de Valera commanded the third battalion of the Irish Volunteers. Following the suppression of the rising, he was tried by court martial and sentenced to death but reprieved, allegedly because of his American birth. He thus found himself the surviving figurehead from the rising. After his release from prison in 1917, he won the East Clare by-election for Sinn Fein and became president of both Sinn Fein and the Irish Volunteers. When Sinn Fein MPs met in Dublin to declare Irish independence from Britain in 1919, de Valera was elected president of the Irish Republic. In 1921, he declined to go to London for the Sinn Fein–British government talks, persuading Michael Collins to go instead. He then rejected the Anglo-Irish treaty signed by Collins and Griffith which established an Irish Free State within the British Commonwealth, remaining committed to the republic. In the Irish Civil War of 1922–3 he supported the anti-treaty IRA but was politically marginalized.

In 1926 de Valera left Sinn Fein to found a new party, Fianna Fáil, and in 1927 he and his supporters entered the Irish parliament, Dáil Eireann, and took the oath of allegiance to the British king. In 1932, Fianna Fáil won the Irish general election and de Valera began dismantling the Anglo-Irish treaty. He wrote a new Irish constitution, which in 1937 established a republic in all but name. When the Second World War broke out, de Valera declared Eire neutral. In May 1940, with the British facing defeat, he rejected Winston Churchill's overtures to enter the war on Britain's side in return for a vague promise of Irish unity. In 1945, on the announcement of Adolf Hitler's death, de Valera personally conveyed his government's condolences to the German embassy in Dublin. Neutrality proved popular domestically but left Eire isolated internationally. De Valera found himself out of power during 1948–51 and 1954–7, but returned to office in 1957. He resigned as prime minister in 1959 but was president of Ireland from 1959 to 1973. *TWH*

John Bowman, *De Valera and the Ulster Question 1917–1973* (Oxford, 1982).

devaluation, the deliberate reduction in the value of a country's currency as expressed in the currencies of other countries. The term usually refers to the movement from one fixed exchange rate to another. The equivalent reduction of the exchange rate during a period of flexible or floating exchange rates is usually called a depreciation of the currency. In the short term, devaluation makes exports relatively cheap in terms of foreign currency, and makes imports relatively expensive in terms of domestic currency. For this reason, governments often devalue their exchange rate in order to improve the *balance of payments. Repeated resort to devaluation, however, will shake the confidence of investors in the credibility of the exchange rate which may be destabilizing. Alternatively, if governments cling for too long to an inappropriate exchange rate, the amount of the eventual devaluation may be greater than would have been needed at an earlier adjustment. One further consideration is that in an inflationary environment, a devaluation may cause domestic inflation through increased import prices. If domestic prices rise, the competitiveness which exports gained from the devaluation may be eroded and the balance of payments problems which precipitated the devaluation will resurface.

The most famous cases of the devaluation of sterling in the 20th century were in 1949 and 1967. In each case, devaluation was preceded by balance of payments deficits and then by an exchange crisis as speculators came to believe that the sterling exchange rate was too high. This encouraged holders of sterling to sell their balances in the expectation that the value would fall in the near future. As more speculators then sold their sterling, this put increased pressure on the exchange rate and the Bank of England was required to buy up the excess supply of sterling. Eventually, this drained the British foreign exchange reserves to the point at which maintaining the value of sterling in terms of other currencies became unsupportable. In each case, sterling was finally devalued in order to stem speculation and to enhance the balance of payments.

At the end of the Second World War, sterling was pegged to an exchange rate of $4.06 = £1 with limited convertibility. Throughout the post-war recovery, the shortage of foreign exchange was mainly met through international borrowing, but the relatively low level of the British foreign exchange reserves tended to be a constraint on expansionist policies which might encourage inflation. It was popularly known that the government was considering devaluation and by August 1949 speculative pressure had built, draining the foreign exchange reserves. Finally, on 18 September the pound was devalued 30 per cent to $2.80 = £1. The balance of payments continued to suffer from persistent deficits through the 1950s and 1960s and pressure on the foreign exchange reserves began to mount from 1965. Despite the government's attempts to stem the drain through deflationary packages, speculators were convinced that devaluation was inevitable and confidence in the currency ebbed. Eventually, the pound was devalued from $2.80 to $2.40 on 18 November 1967. Sterling remained at this exchange rate until 1971, when the fixed exchange rate was abandoned. *CRS*

Devlin, Bernadette. See MacAliskey, Bernadette.

Devlin, Joseph (1871–1934), Irish nationalist politician, last leader of the rump of the Irish Parliamentary Party at Westminster, 1918–22. An Ulster Catholic, he revived the Ancient Order of Hibernians as a counterbalance to the Orange Order, and he retained his West Belfast parliamentary seat from 1906 to 1922, even beating off the challenge of Eamon de Valera. Strongly opposed to partition, he supported fiscal autonomy at the Irish Convention in 1917–18. After 1925 he served in the Northern Ireland parliament. *DRB*

Devlin, Patrick Arthur (1905–92), judge. Lord Devlin sat as a High Court judge (1948–60), a lord justice of appeal (1960–1), and as a lord of appeal in ordinary (1961–4). It was a brief, but influential, period as a senior judge. He then spent more than twenty years as a judge of the administrative tribunal of the International Labour Organization. Devlin is perhaps best known for his work in legal theory. In particular, his Maccabaean lecture (1959) argued that society could justify criminalizing some immoral acts that caused no harm to others. The lecture provoked responses from Hart and Dworkin, among many others, and reignited a debate that had been smouldering since the publication of Mill's *On Liberty* (1859). It remains a striking and persuasive antidote to the subsequent wave of pluralism. *PPM*

Lord Devlin, *The Enforcement of Morals* (Oxford, 1965). | Ronald Dworkin, *Taking Rights Seriously* (London, 1977). | H. L. A. Hart, *Law, Liberty and Morality* (Oxford, 1963).

devolution, the granting of powers to a lower tier of government, while preserving sovereignty to the granting tier. In theory (though less in practice), devolution is to be sharply distinguished from federalism or confederation, in which neither tier may prevent the other from doing something claimed to be beyond its powers (**ultra vires*). Thus the abortive schemes for Irish home rule (1886–1914); the Government of Ireland Act, 1920; the abortive Scotland and Wales Acts, 1978; the Good Friday agreement for Northern Ireland, the Scotland Act, and the Wales Act (all 1998) are schemes of devolution. Unlike the federal arrangements of countries such as Germany and the USA, these schemes reserve supreme power to the national parliament. The most explicit statement of Westminster supremacy is the Government of Ireland Act, 1920, section 75, which states, 'The supreme authority of the Parliament of the United Kingdom shall remain unaffected and undiminished over all persons, matters, and things in Ireland, and every part thereof'. Nevertheless, all pre-1998 schemes of devolution have been bitterly controversial, and the Irish home rule crisis at the start of the century led to constitutional confrontation and almost to civil war in Northern Ireland. Despite the expressed sovereignty of the imperial parliament, Unionists fought bitterly against any relaxation of control over Ireland for a mixture of reasons: imperial, strategic, perhaps economic, and to save the Protestants of Ulster from inclusion in an all-Ireland parliament. That opposition in turn fuelled nationalism on the periphery. When most of Ireland left the United Kingdom in 1921, it did so as an independent state and a reluctant member of the Empire (later Commonwealth), which it left on declaring itself a republic in 1949.

The distinction between devolution and federalism is more apparent than real. The Ulster Unionists had not wanted the Northern Ireland parliament and government imposed in 1920. But, once they got it, they saw the usefulness of 'a Protestant parliament for a Protestant people' as Sir James Craig, the first prime minister of Northern Ireland, called it. When the UK government threatened to use section 75 of the 1920 Act to prevent Craig from abolishing proportional representation (a device that had been inserted to protect the Catholic minority), Craig threatened to dissolve and be elected with as large a majority, or larger, than he already had. This threat was credible, so the UK government backed down. The only time that section 75 was actually used was to abolish the Stormont parliament altogether in 1972. Similar power plays could occur with the 1998 Scottish, Welsh, or Northern Irish parliaments. If the disputed measure is popular in the devolved territory, its leaders possess a credible threat against which the top tier is powerless.

Devolution to Scotland and Wales will bring in its train more extensive judicial review of the *vires* of legislation than the UK has previously known. The Scotland and Wales Acts, 1998, provide for the Judicial Committee of the Privy Council to settle disputes between Westminster and Edinburgh or Cardiff on the *vires* of Scottish and Welsh legislation. This necessarily puts a further dent in the already battered piece of furniture known as 'parliamentary sovereignty'. *IM*

Vernon Bogdanor, *Devolution in the United Kingdom* (Oxford, 1999).

Devonshire, 8th duke of (1833–1908), Liberal Unionist statesman. Appropriately for the son and heir of one of the great Whig houses (see Whiggism), Spencer Compton (styled marquess of Hartington, 1858–91) entered parliament on the right wing of the Liberal Party in 1857. There he remained, serving in Gladstone's first two cabinets (and leading the party during his post-1880 'retirement'), until the 'Grand Old Man' bound the Liberals to home rule. In an unlikely partnership, Hartington then made common cause with Joseph Chamberlain, taking the anti-home rule Liberals off to form the Liberal Unionist Party and allying with Salisbury's Conservatives. Devonshire agreed reluctantly to become lord president in 1895, continuing in this office under Balfour. The party alliance was shaken by Chamberlain's revelation in May 1903 of his plan for tariff reform. The Chamberlainites admitted that it was impossible to effect the ingenious plan without a short-term increase in the cost of living. It was all too much for Devonshire and, despite Balfour's desperate effort to retain him, the duke resigned in October. The wounded government clung to office only until 1905. Though a partner of the Conservatives, Devonshire never became one and died in 1908 still an impeccable Whig free trader (having never set foot inside the Carlton Club). He enjoyed great prestige and influence in and outside Whitehall, certainly because of his lineage and wealth but also because of his transparent honesty and (exaggerated) reputation for speaking good sense. He had enjoyed a rather raffish youth, earning him the soubriquet 'Harty-tarty'; he was never ambitious (rejecting opportunities to become premier on three different occasions), loved the turf more than politics, and treated all with a charming and old-fashioned courtesy. *RJQA*

Bernard Holland, *The Life of Spencer Compton, 8th Duke of Devonshire* (London, 1911).

Devonshire, 11th duke of (1920–). politician and landowner. After a distinguished war, Devonshire stood for the Conservatives twice before succeeding his father in 1950. A nephew of Macmillan's wife, Lady Dorothy, Devonshire's appointment in 1960 as a minister at the Commonwealth Office prompted charges of nepotism. His promotion in 1962 reinforced the damaging impression that Macmillan favoured aristocrats and was outdated, despite his talk of modernizing Britain. Devonshire held office until 1964. During the 1980s he joined the Social Democratic Party. *RJS*

Dewar, Donald (1937–2000), Labour politician. Elected MP at the Garscadden by-election of 1978, Dewar's victory was widely interpreted in Labour circles at the time as having stopped the advance of the Scottish National Party. Active in Labour politics since his student days at Glasgow University, where he honed his debating skills, Dewar was an early believer in the principle of devolution. As shadow Scottish secretary, he was largely responsible for making the Labour Party sign up to the Scottish Constitutional Convention in 1988. As secretary for Scotland after 1997, he was in charge of the campaign to secure a 'Yes' vote in the referendum on a Scottish parliament and the subsequent steering of the Scotland Act through parliament. On both counts he was successful and was rewarded with the post of Scotland's first minister after the Scottish elections in 1999, then dying in office. *RF*

de Zulueta, Philip Francis (1925–89), prime ministers' foreign affairs private secretary, 1955–64. De Zulueta was an influential member of Harold Macmillan's private office. Although his work was not entirely confined to foreign affairs, by providing advice independent of the Foreign Office he enabled Macmillan to act as his own foreign secretary. However, this undermined de Zulueta's own prospects in Whitehall and although he remained at Downing Street during Sir Alec Douglas-Home's brief premiership, he left the civil service in 1964. *CL*

Diana, Princess of Wales (1961–97). Diana's marriage to *Charles, Prince of Wales in 1981 heralded a revival of popular interest in the throne. Their separation ten years later led to an equally sharp drop in popularity as well as the most serious republican debate for more than a century. Her death in Paris provoked unparalleled scenes of public grief as well as angry demands for reform of the monarchy. As such she may be the most significant figure in the history of the monarchy of the century. *WMK*

Dilhorne, Viscount. See MANNINGHAM-BULLER, REGINALD EDWARD.

Dill, John Greer (1881–1944), soldier and diplomat, head of the British joint staff mission in Washington and senior British member of the combined chiefs of staff, 1941–4. Dill's finest hour was in wartime Washington, where he attained a remarkable and beneficial ascendancy in the councils of the Anglo-American alliance—the linchpin of that extraordinary combination—centred on an unexampled personal friendship with the US army chief of staff, General George C. Marshall. *AD*

ALEX DANCHEV, *Very Special Relationship* (London, 1986).

dilution, the government's attempt to increase the output of war materials by introducing less skilled men and women into jobs previously the preserve of craftsmen. Under the terms of the Treasury agreement of March 1915, subsequently given statutory force by the Munitions of War Act, the trade unions agreed to accept, amongst other measures, the temporary dilution of labour. Union members were not so compliant, however, and rank and file engineers saw dilution as the culmination of long-term industrial trends which threatened their privileged craft status, fearing that it would become permanent. Moreover, because the skilled men were paid by time-rate but the dilutees by piece-rate, there arose the wartime anomaly of craftsmen who set up the machines being paid less than the machine operators. The result was a wave of industrial unrest, notably on 'Red Clydeside', which Marxist historians such as James Hinton have interpreted as an embryonic revolutionary movement. However, the revolutionary shop stewards' movement only became established in a handful of centres such as Clydeside, where the status and privileges of the craftsmen had remained intact at the start of the war. Elsewhere, in Coventry for example, pre-war changes in technology and industrial organization had already effected the dilution of craft labour, and shop stewards were concerned simply to maximize rewards for their members during a period of labour shortage. The majority of workers were only willing to act for definite and immediate aims, not for a political programme. Although the patriotic press demonized shop stewards, they actually gained a permanently enhanced role in the engineering industry after the war, their position confirmed by the national shop stewards' agreement of 1919. Workshop collective bargaining became accepted practice with the introduction of dilution. *MC*

JAMES HINTON, *The First Shop Stewards Movement* (London, 1973).

Diplock, (William John) Kenneth (1907–85), and **Diplock courts**. Diplock was one of the great judges. He sat in the High Court (1956–61), as a lord justice of appeal (1961–8), and as a lord of appeal in ordinary (1968–85), consistently delivering judgements of the utmost analytical and linguistic clarity. His approach to legal problems was utterly logical, often drawing on his mastery of legal history. This quest for analytical clarity led him to formulate new, more precise technical terms and definitions, though these prompted what Lord Diplock himself sardonically called accusations of 'gratuitous philological exhibitionism' (*United Dominions Trust (Commercial) Ltd* v. *Eagle Aviation Ltd* [1964] 1 WLR 74). In addition to his judicial work, he chaired an inquiry into terrorist intimidation of witnesses and jurors in criminal trials in Northern Ireland. The inquiry recommended that certain serious criminal offences should be tried by judge alone. Its recommendations were immediately enacted in the Northern Ireland (Emergency Provisions) Act, 1973, section 2; the new type of criminal courts thereby created being known as Diplock courts. *PPM*

Report of the Commission to consider legal procedures to deal with terrorist activities in Northern Ireland (Cmnd 5185, London, 1972).

direct action, the belief that it is legitimate to use industrial action to achieve political ends, which gained particular currency in 1910–21. In 1920, for example, trade unions forced the government to abandon military intervention in Russia by imposing a ban on the export of munitions. Avowed syndicalists rejected the need for a working-class political party altogether. The collapse of the triple industrial alliance in 1921 signalled the demise of direct action as an alternative to the parliamentary road to socialism. *MC*

disarmament conference (1932–4). After the Great War, there was a strong desire to avoid any risk of repetition, a fear reinforced by the growth of extremist movements across Europe and by best-selling war books and films such as Erich-Maria Remarque's *All Quiet on the Western Front* (book (Eng. trans.) 1929; film 1931). There was also a growing belief among historians that the international arms race, rather than German malevolence, had caused war in 1914, which led naturally to hopes that disarmament would promote peace. Britain had already limited arms expenditure after 1919, and then adopted a 'ten-year rule' to limit expenditure further. Attempts were therefore made to bring about multilateral international disarmament, through a conference at Geneva, under the auspices of the *League of Nations and chaired by Arthur Henderson, who as foreign secretary had helped to start the process. The conference was a disappointment, with mutual recrimination and no country risking its own national interest. It lingered on, but its useful life came to an end when Nazi Germany withdrew in October 1933. *JAR*

Distribution of Industry Act, 1945, a measure driven through the war cabinet in 1945 by the president of the Board of Trade, Hugh Dalton. It can be taken as the classic example of how state-controlled planning was coming to the fore as increasing efforts were made to eliminate the industrial weaknesses and mass unemployment of the 1930s. The need for additional assistance for so-called 'special areas' had been accepted in the 1930s but now Whitehall was given additional powers to direct industry to 'development areas' which embraced 13.5 per cent of the population (the special areas figure had been 8.5 per cent). The general principle of regional planning had been advocated in the 1940 Barlow report but it still took all the energy of Hugh Dalton, who as MP for Bishop Auckland had special knowledge of the blighted north-east, to get the support of his coalition colleagues. Following the Labour victory in 1945 the provisions of the Act, taken in conjunction with the use of industrial development certificates, nationalization, the development of trading estates, and the redesigning of ordnance and armament plants, resulted in significant industrial growth in Scotland, south Wales, and the north-east. *PS*

Paul Addison, *The Road to 1945* (London, 1975). | Kenneth O. Morgan, *Labour in Power 1945–1951* (Oxford, 1984).

distributive justice. This is based on a great, central question: should the individual keep what is his or hers by property law or through earning wealth? Or should the needs of society, and of individuals in society (because they are members of that society), take precedence? If we accept that society exists, and that its members have mutual obligations, then, as the *New Liberalism of the early 20th century recommended, wealth must be redistributed, so that society is more equal (and therefore more 'just'). *Socialism accepted this in a more full-blooded way, and the redistribution process was to take place largely through taxation of wealth, unearned and earned. The problem lies in deciding on what basis this judgement should be made; for example, who or what is to decide what wealth is superfluous to our needs, and what is not? The 'what' was easily answered: the state would decide this and enact it. The 'why' was always more problematical, but both were challenged by the New Right in the 1970s, which held that what you earn you should keep, in an open market—and the open market was the only realistic and successful means of sustaining a society's wealth and economic prosperity. In the UK, Margaret Thatcher claimed that the taxation policy inherent in the redistributive justice notion was a disincentive to the individual, who worked hard only to see his or her wealth taken (and often squandered) by the state. Moreover, a wealth-producing society created a 'trickle down' phenomenon, as economic growth benefited all, whereas the redistributive principle penalized all through creating economic stagnation as a result of disincentives, these being the result of high taxation. At the heart of the argument is the question of private property, and so the argument has a more philosophical tone than most debates in modern British politics. *DGB*

D. D. Raphael, *Justice and Liberty* (London, 1980).

district councils. See local government structure.

divorce, the legal dissolution of marriage, which became increasingly common during the course of the 20th century in Britain, mirroring trends in the USA and to a lesser extent in Europe. In 1900, only 512 divorces were granted in England and Wales, a rate of less than 0.01 per 1,000 married couples. By 1940 there were 7,755 divorces, in 1975 120,522, and in 1981 146,000, representing a rate of divorce of 11.9 per 1,000 married couples. In recent years the increase in divorces appears to have levelled off, peaking in the mid-1990s at 167,000 divorces per year in 1995.

The rise of divorce has reflected liberalization of divorce law, but also important changes in the social position of women, attitudes towards marriage and sexuality, and the decline of religious and social sanctions on divorce. Parliament passed major pieces of legislation modifying the law of divorce in 1923, 1937, and 1969. Pressure for divorce law reform has come from different groups, including liberals, the legal profession, and women's organizations. A royal commission, appointed in 1909 and reporting in 1912, paved the way for the 1923 Matrimonial Causes Act which relieved a wife of proving other misconduct in addition to adultery in obtaining a divorce, and the 1937 Act which extended the grounds for divorce. The 1969 Divorce Act abandoned the principle of marital fault and introduced the concept of 'irremediable breakdown'. In addition, extensions of legal aid provision from 1914 have brought divorce proceedings within the reach of larger categories of people. Having in 1900 had the lowest divorce rate in Europe, the UK now has one of the highest.

Greater equality and increasing employment opportunities for women appear to have gone hand in hand with a rising divorce rate. Both world wars, for example, saw a noticeable increase in divorce rates accompanying the rise in status of women. In recent years there has been concern about the social and, ultimately, financial costs to society of divorce, notably the problem of impoverished single parents, mainly women, the impact of broken homes on juvenile crime and underachievement, and more general 'breakdown of the family'. As a result, there has been pressure to resist further liberalization of the divorce laws, to pursue 'family friendly' policies in terms of the tax and social security structure, and to assist lone parents back into the workforce. *JS*

Lawrence Stone, *Road to Divorce: England, 1530–1987* (London, 1990).

Dixon, Pierson ('Bob') (1904–65), diplomat. Dixon was principal private secretary to foreign secretaries Eden (1943–5) and Bevin (1945–8), ambassador to Prague (1948–50), permanent representative to the UN (1954–60), and finally ambassador to Paris (1960–5). These posts placed him at some of the most important events in post-war British history. He drafted the Potsdam communiqué; recorded the first British veto at the UN, in defence of Eden's actions over Suez; and witnessed de Gaulle's veto of Britain's application to join the European Economic Community. Dixon was one of the most influential diplomats of his generation. *JRVE*

D-Notices. The D (Defence)-Notice system provided discreet official guidance to editors about stories likely to be regarded as breaching the extremely sweeping Official Secrets Acts (1889 and later). The notices, around a dozen in operation at any one time, might be general or highly specific (for example, about individuals). Overseen by a committee of civil servants and service chiefs, the system's key figure was the secretary, usually a retired senior officer. *CKSU*

Docker, Dudley (1862–1944), industrialist. Docker became a major figure in the Midlands in 1902 by arranging the merger of five rolling-stock companies into the Metropolitan Amalgamated Carriage and Wagon Company (MCWC), and then collected a large portfolio of directorships and shareholdings in railway, engineering, and finance companies. He was also a generous but manipulative supporter of

Conservative politicians such as Arthur *Steel-Maitland and John ('Empire Jack') Norton-Griffiths. During the Great War he helped to launch the *Federation of British Industries and the British Commonwealth Union, a secretive and strongly protectionist organization which backed anti-Labour candidates in the 1918 election. In the twenties he arranged the merger of MCWC with Vickers Ltd (then run by Sir Vincent *Caillard) to form a powerful military-industrial cartel. Docker continued to back right-wing political movements in Britain until the late 1920s, and financed anti-Bolshevik activity in southern Russia in the early part of the decade. *JAT*

doctor's mandate, what the members of the *National Government appealed for in their 1931 manifesto, seeking the power to take whatever measures proved necessary, perhaps including tariffs, to resolve Britain's economic crisis. It was intended to be vague enough to keep the support both of free-trade Liberals and protectionist Conservatives. *NJC*

Dod's Parliamentary Companion, political reference work. A long-established compendium—1999 was its 167th year of publication—*Dod's* is published annually (sometimes more than once if there is a general election). It includes, among other material, biographical details of members of both Houses of Parliament, complemented since 1980 with photographs of Members (and of those peers who submit them), and as such is frequently consulted by officials and members in both Houses of Parliament. *PN*

Dogger Bank incident (21–2 October 1904), Anglo-Russian diplomatic crisis. This arose out of the sinking of British trawlers in the North Sea by the Russian Baltic fleet (which had mistaken them for Japanese torpedo boats) when on its way to take part in the Russo-Japanese war. Following strong pressure from Prime Minister Arthur Balfour, Russia expressed regret and promised compensation; but for a short while war with Russia had seemed a real prospect. *TGO*

KEITH NEILSON, *Britain and the Last Tsar* (Oxford, 1995).

dole. See UNEMPLOYMENT PAY.

dollar gap, the gap between the amount of US dollars held by countries and the demand for dollars to buy goods from the USA, 1945–51. While Europe recovered from the war, there was a large demand for dollars to buy American goods, but the USA did not import sufficient goods from Europe to allow them to earn dollars through trade. The dollar gap ended with the recovery of Europe and the Korean war which increased US imports and the international supply of dollars. *CRS*

Dominions Office, spun off in 1925 from the Colonial Office in order to deal with the emerging self-governed elements of the British Empire, with a separate secretary of state for dominions affairs appointed in 1931. The Dominions Office was reconstituted as the Commonwealth Relations Office in 1947 in order to cater for the expanding number of independent states. *JD*

dominion status. Constitutional status achieved early in the century—following the grant of complete self-government—only by colonies with an overwhelmingly white population (South Africa excepted). By 1923 the dominions included Canada, Australia, New Zealand, South Africa, the Irish Free State, and Newfoundland, their affairs looked after in Whitehall by a separate Dominions Office, 1925–47. In 1947 India and Pakistan became the first non-white dominions, but the term was soon dropped as more non-white areas achieved independence. *KTS*

JOHN DARWIN, 'A Third British Empire? The Dominion Idea in Imperial Politics', in Judith M. Brown and W. Roger Louis (eds.), *Oxford History of the British Empire*, vol. 4 (Oxford, 1999).

Donald, Robert **(1861–1933)**, newspaperman. Donald was a Liberal journalist who worked mainly on the Scottish and local government press before becoming managing editor of the Liberal *Daily Chronicle*, 1902–18. Though a friend and golfing companion of Lloyd George, Donald ensured that the *Chronicle* mainly supported Asquith in the Liberal split of 1916–18, but Lloyd George had the final word by getting the paper bought by some wealthy backers and Donald removed. *JAR*

Donaldson, John George Stuart **(1920–)**, judge. After wartime military service, Donaldson practised at the Bar from 1946, specializing in industrial and commercial cases. He became a High Court judge (1966–79), lord justice of appeal (1979–82), and master of the rolls (1982–92), with the difficult task of succeeding Lord Denning. He was prominent politically as the first (and only) president of the Industrial Relations Court (1971–4), set up by the Heath government and abolished by its successor, an impossible task, given the refusal of the trade unions to recognize his court, but made no easier by his own active past as a Conservative. *JAR*

Donoughue, Bernard (1934–), prime ministers' senior policy adviser, 1974–9. On his return to office in 1974, Harold Wilson established the Downing Street policy unit. As head of the unit, Donoughue, an academic political scientist, built good relations with Whitehall and had access to a wide range of papers and committees. With the exceptions of defence, intelligence, and foreign affairs, Donoughue's unit, linked to a network of departmental policy advisers, was involved in a range of policies under Wilson, in particular Europe, Northern Ireland, and resisting Treasury calls for a statutory incomes policy. Donoughue was retained by James Callaghan (1976–9) and joined the prime minister's secret economic seminar. During the IMF crisis (1976) the unit helped Callaghan to resist the Treasury on one side and Tony Benn on the other. However, the precise extent of Donoughue's influence is a matter of some dispute. *CL*

Bernard Donoughue, *Prime Minister: The Conduct of Policy under Harold Wilson and James Callaghan* (London, 1987).

Donovan report (1968). This report on trade unions and employers' associations was established against discontent over unofficial strikes. It recognized that factory-level deals had effectively superseded nationally negotiated agreements It opposed legal sanctions against unofficial strikes. The report recommended an industrial relations commission and that agreements be registered with the government. It advocated reform of trade union structures including shop stewards. Legislation in line with the report was promised in **In Place of Strife*, but trade union and backbench hostility led to its abandonment. *KMT*

Dorrell, Stephen James (1952–), Conservative politician, but a shine and fade figure. Dorrell, originally in 1979 a One Nation Tory scorning ingratiation with the right, rocketed under John Major. He was immensely diligent, loyal to junior colleagues, and likeable, but lacked flair or humour. As heritage secretary, he apparently disliked sport, art, music, and theatre, transferring to health where he met the BSE crisis. Regarded as a leadership candidate, his late attempt to woo Eurosceptics with an implausible rightward lurch decelerated his campaign. In the 1997 leadership contest, recognizing a low response, he withdrew in favour of Kenneth Clarke. *EP*

Douglas-Home, Alexander Frederick (1903–95), Conservative politician, foreign secretary, and prime minister. As the eldest son of the 13th earl of Home, Alec Douglas-Home was the last aristocrat to hold the highest office. After an Edwardian childhood in the Scottish borders, followed by Eton and Oxford, he fought Coatbridge for the Unionists (as Scottish Tories were known) in 1929 under his courtesy title of Lord Dunglass. It was a tough initiation, but in 1931 he was elected MP for Lanark. Dunglass served a four-year apprenticeship as Skelton's parliamentary private secretary at the Scottish Office. Appointed parliamentary private secretary to Neville Chamberlain, the chancellor of the exchequer, he continued when the latter became prime minister and in 1938 accompanied Chamberlain to Munich (see Munich crisis), an experience that gave him a lasting aversion to summitry. Personal tragedy struck in September 1940 when Dunglass was diagnosed with tuberculosis of the spine. After surgery, he had to spend two years in a plaster cast, but he emerged from his battle with ill-health a stronger character. Despite his criticism of the Anglo-American abandonment of the Poles at the Yalta conference, he became a Foreign Office minister in Churchill's Caretaker Government. However, he lost Lanark in the 1945 Labour landslide, and although he recaptured the seat in 1950 he succeeded his father as the earl of Home in 1951. After the Tories won the 1951 election, he accepted the role of minister resident in Scotland that he and James Stuart had proposed in 1949.

Unknown Aristocrat in the Cabinet

Home's duties gave him experience in domestic affairs but kept him away from London, with the result that when Eden appointed him to his cabinet in April 1955 as Commonwealth relations secretary, he was as a relatively unknown figure. During Suez his 'firmness and discretion' as a member of the cabinet's Egypt committee were valued by Eden, while Home had to use all his influence to prevent the Commonwealth splitting apart. His position in Macmillan's administration was enhanced in 1957 following Salisbury's resignation over the release of the Cypriot leader, Archbishop Makarios, when he became leader of the Lords and lord president of the council while remaining Commonwealth secretary. Home also became a member of Macmillan's Steering Committee for Tory strategy. The crisis in southern Africa dogged his final year at the Commonwealth Office. He hankered after much slower progress towards African rule than was politically realistic and never saw eye-to-eye with Macleod.

Home, however, enjoyed a good rapport with the prime minister, and in July 1960 he became foreign secretary, although his promotion was condemned by the *Daily Mirror* as 'the most reckless political appointment since the Roman Emperor Caligula made his favourite horse a consul'. Home, however, was the perfect foil for Macmillan. His calm advice and unflinching resistance to Soviet pressure were invaluable as the *Cold War threatened to turn fatally hot. During the 1962 Cuban missile crisis, he was often with the prime minister when President Kennedy phoned and helped Macmillan to become a trusted sounding board.

Unexpected Prime Minister

Macmillan was determined that Butler should not succeed him but, although he spoke favourably of Home, he opted initially for Hailsham as his preferred successor. Under legislation being passed during 1963, peers were to be allowed to renounce their titles and Home was urged to seek the leadership by senior officers of the *1922 Committee. When the cabinet discussed Macmillan's leadership in October, Home stated that he was not a contender but during the ensuing crisis he skilfully played the role of the reluctant candidate. He confirmed Macmillan's suspicion that Hailsham was temperamentally unsuited for the leadership and reported American unease at the prospect of Hailsham becoming premier, adding that he would take on the task if Macmillan asked him to do so, in order to prevent the party collapsing. Home's subsequent emergence as Macmillan's successor through the 'customary processes', in preference to either Butler or Hailsham, provoked a major row, but he was able to form an administration despite the refusal of Macleod and Powell to serve. Having renounced his peerage, he became Sir Alec Douglas-Home and was elected MP for Kinross and West Perthshire.

Douglas-Home was an efficient, businesslike chairman of cabinet, but totally lacked inspiration. Instead of reinforcing the government's modernizing appearance, his aristocratic background, diffident manner, and dated appearance confirmed the Tories' 'grouse-moor' image. His 1962 confession that, in order to understand economics, he had to use a box of matches and move them around, was especially damaging. He allowed his chancellor, Maudling, free rein to break out of *'stop-go', but by backing Heath's abolition of *resale price maintenance he antagonized natural Tory voters and party members who owned local shops. In the event, the expected Tory election defeat of 1964 was much narrower than predicted. In opposition Douglas-Home prevented any repetition of the 1963 controversy by introducing rules for electing the Tory leader (also supervising their revision in 1974), the new procedure being first used after his resignation in 1965. Douglas-Home served in Heath's shadow cabinet and also chaired a party inquiry into devolution that recommended a 125-member Scottish convention. In 1970 Douglas-Home again became foreign secretary, but his second spell in the post was initially marred by his determination to sell arms equipment to South Africa. In 1971 he expelled 105 Soviet spies from Britain. Otherwise, Heath kept charge of the negotiations for entry into Europe; US President Nixon was not very interested in Britain; and Rhodesia (see RHODESIAN CRISIS) was deadlocked, despite Douglas-Home's efforts to broker a settlement. In 1974, Douglas-Home returned to the Lords with a life peerage as Lord Home of the Hirsel. He was a courteous traditionalist with a strong sense of duty who, as his biographer D. R. Thorpe observed, saw politics as a choice between the unpalatable and the disastrous. *RJS*

LORD HOME, *The Way the Wind Blows* (London, 1976). | D. R. THORPE, *Alec Douglas-Home* (London, 1996).

Dowding, (Derek) Hugh Tremenheere (1882–1970), air marshal. As commander of Fighter Command, 1936–42, Dowding was the architect of victory in the battle of Britain. He had encouraged the designs of the Hurricane and the Spitfire fighters and the construction of the radar chain. Crucially he dissuaded Churchill from dissipating fighters in the struggle for France. Carefully husbanding his forces, he prepared for the coming German onslaught. A laconic man, nicknamed 'Stuffy', he did not encourage personal affection, and when he retired many tried to claim his laurels for themselves. *MLC*

Downing Street declaration (15 December 1993), joint declaration by the British prime minister, John Major, and the Irish taoiseach, Albert Reynolds. The declaration, which set out general principles for holding peace talks in Northern Ireland, followed proposals drawn up by Sinn Fein leader Gerry Adams and Social Democratic and Labour Party leader John Hume and intensive negotiations between the British and Irish governments. It stated that 'the ending of divisions can only come about through the agreement of the people, north and south, representing both traditions in Ireland'. The British government would uphold the democratic wish of a greater number of the people of Northern Ireland on the issue of whether they preferred to support the union or a sovereign united Ireland.

Britain confirmed that it had no selfish strategic or economic interest in Northern Ireland. The government's role was to 'encourage, facilitate and enable the achievement' of a settlement in the province. It was for the people of Ireland alone by agreement between the two parts respectively, to exercise their right of self–determination on the basis of consent freely and concurrently given, North and South, to bring about a united Ireland. For their part the Irish government accepted that the democratic right of self-determination by the people of Ireland as a whole must be achieved and exercised, with and subject to the agreement and consent of a majority of the people of Northern Ireland. Both governments reiterated that the achievement of peace must involve a permanent end to the use of, or support for, paramilitary violence. Democratically mandated parties which established a commitment to exclusively peaceful methods and which had shown that they abided by the democratic process, could join in the dialogue in due course.

There was widespread support for the terms of the declaration, but a predictably hostile response came from the Democratic Unionist Party which claimed that Major had 'sold out' Ulster. Sinn Fein would not endorse the statement because, it claimed, the principle of consent amounted to a Unionist veto on Irish reunification. *PR*

Paul Bew, Peter Gibbon, and Henry Patterson, *Northern Ireland 1921–1996: Political Forces and Social Classes* (London, 1996). | Tim Pat Coogan, *The Troubles* (London, 1995).

***Dreadnought*, HMS** (1906), a battleship of revolutionary design. An 'all-big-gun' ship, it could outrange and outpace any other type of battleship then afloat. However, this also made all other battleships obsolete and so wiped out Britain's existing naval superiority. A Dreadnought-building war between Britain and Germany thus began in earnest. The cost of the ships put great pressure on the national budget but Britain was determined to maintain its naval supremacy. By 1914 Britain had nineteen Dreadnoughts compared with Germany's thirteen. *MLC*

Driberg, John Edward Neil ('Tom') (1905–76), Labour politician. Tom Driberg was a larger than life figure, an upper-class maverick, who had departed from Lancing under a cloud and left Oxford without a degree. His early political commitment was to the Communist Party of Great Britain (CPGB). He worked as a journalist and wrote the William Hickey column in the *Daily Express*. He was dismissed from the CPGB in 1941 on account of his links with MI5, but won a spectacular by-election victory as a leftist independent at Maldon in 1942 and from 1945 his political career was pursued within the Labour Party. *CH*

Tom Driberg, *Ruling Passions* (London, 1977). | Francis Wheen, *Tom Driberg: his Life and Indiscretions* (London, 1990).

drugs. Many addictive substances were freely available prior to the 20th century. Growing concern about the use of opiates as sedatives, especially in young children, led to the Pharmacy Act of 1868, which permitted the sale of opium only through licensed pharmacists. By the Second World War most of the more dangerous drugs were controlled, but were considered a minor problem compared with drink—until the rise of the rock and pop culture of the 1960s. The fashionable use of cannabis, amphetamines, hallucinogenic drugs such as LSD, and 'hard' drugs such as heroin and cocaine, made the 'drug culture' a wider cause of concern. The Misuse of Drugs Act, 1971, tightened the law against drug-taking and drug-trafficking, while increasing effort began to be devoted to the rehabilitation of drug users and publicity against drug use. Under a relatively benign regime, drug addicts were allowed to register, gaining legitimate access to drugs and, hopefully, to treatment.

Increasingly, however, the rise of unemployment and inner-city deprivation during the 1970s created an epidemic of hard drug use amongst the young, fuelled by the targeting of Western Europe by international drug cartels. Between 1976 and 1990, the number of drug-related offences almost quadrupled, with new highly addictive substances such as 'crack' cocaine being blamed for contributing to rising *crime rates. Drug abuse was also implicated in the spread of the *AIDS virus through the sharing of needles. A series of government publicity campaigns have been run since 1985 to persuade young people not to take drugs. Further concern arose in the 1990s, especially about the widespread use of recreational drugs, such as ecstasy, as well as evidence from customs' seizures of large-scale trafficking in a range of soft and hard drugs. In 1998 an anti-drugs coordinator or 'drugs tsar' was appointed to coordinate the fight against the supply of illegal drugs. A ten-year national strategy has been drawn up to take action in four areas: channelling seized assets from drug dealers into anti-drugs work, providing drug education to all children from 5 to 16, imposing drug treatment and testing orders on drug offenders, and shifting resources from treatment into prevention. In pursuit of the last aim, the Drugs Prevention Advisory Service was launched in April 1999 to promote community-based drug prevention. Drug treatment services in England and Scotland were allocated £64.5 million in 1999–2000. *JS*

Drumcree, since July 1995 the scene of confrontations involving the security forces, Orange marchers, and nationalist residents. The core of the dispute has been over the right of Orangemen to march in the nationalist Garvaghy Road area of Portadown on their return from a church service at Drumcree parish church on the Sunday preceding 12 July. The conflicting rights and demands of marchers and residents have seemed irreconcilable and at times have threatened to undermine the entire peace process (see PEACE PROCESS, MARK II). *GG*

DOMINIC BRYAN, *Orange Parades: The Politics of Ritual, Tradition and Control* (London, 2000).

Drummond, (James) Eric, (1876–1951), diplomat and first secretary-general of the League of Nations (1919–33). A skilful administrator, Drummond created the first multinational secretariat. He also played a quiet but valuable political role at the league, many statesmen seeking his advice in the knowledge that their confidence would be respected. He resigned from the league amidst universal regret, and became British ambassador to Rome (1933–9) where he made the best of a trying job. He became 16th earl of Perth in 1937. *LL*

JAMES BARROS, *Office without Power: Secretary-General Sir Eric Drummond 1919–1933* (Oxford, 1979).

DSIR. See SCIENCE AND TECHNOLOGY, OFFICE OF.

dual mandate of MPs. See COMMONS, HOUSE OF: DUAL MANDATE OF MPS.

Dublin Employers' Confederation, founded in 1912 by William Murphy to counteract the influence of James Larkin's Irish Transport and General Workers' Union. The main trial of strength between the two came in 1913, with the mass lockout of all employees belonging to Larkin's organization. The confrontation threatened Dublin with widespread disorder and starvation, and seemed to show the irrelevance of the Irish Parliamentary Party. Eventually the enployers prevailed, aided by Larkin's alienation of both British labour and the Catholic Church. *DRB*

du Cann, Edward Dillon Lott (1924–), Conservative politician. Du Cann spent only two years as a minister but became influential at Westminster despite mainly pursuing a City career. He narrowly won the 1956 Taunton by-election and in 1962 became economic secretary to the Treasury before moving to the Board of Trade in 1963. Appointed party chairman in 1965 by Douglas-Home, du Cann's chairmanship marked the first drive to modernize the party machinery since the Tories were last in opposition in the 1940s. He and Heath, however, were ill-suited colleagues. In 1967 du Cann left Central Office, and when the promise of office failed to materialize in 1970 he became a dangerous critic. His November 1972 election as chairman of the *1922 committee (he held the post until 1984) was a warning to Heath. In late 1974 he was a possible leadership challenger until ruling himself out because of his business interests. In addition to his influence on the Tory benches, his position at Westminster was enhanced by his chairmanship of the Commons committees on public expenditure (1971–3), public accounts (1974–9), and the Treasury and civil service (1979–83). He left the Commons in 1987. *RJS*

EDWARD DU CANN, *Two Lives* (Upton-upon-Severn, 1995).

Dugdale, Thomas Lionel (1897–1977), Conservative politician and party organizer. Having entered parliament for Richmond, Yorkshire, in 1929, Dugdale was Baldwin's parliamentary private secretary, 1935–7. He held junior Treasury posts, 1937–42, before securing a cabinet position as minister for agriculture, 1951–4. During the Second World War Dugdale saw service in the Middle East but was brought back to London to serve as deputy chief whip during Churchill's critical years, 1941–2. Apparently he had been considered for the post of chief whip but Churchill passed him over upon the advice of Brendan Bracken. Dugdale became party vice-chairman in 1941 and then chairman 1942–4 during which time he sought unavailingly to reconcile the desire of Churchill to win the war with the need to prepare the party for the peace. Whilst he succeeded in not antagonizing Churchill,

ill-health ensured that his chairmanship was relatively low key. A brief post-war ministerial career was wrecked by the *Crichel Down scandal. Although constitutionally responsible for the actions of his civil servants, Dugdale was hardly to blame. *NJC*

Duncan, Andrew (1884–1952), industrialist. Duncan was one of the 'industrial politicians' who emerged from the government–industry collaboration in the Great War. He first came to prominence when he was appointed coal commissioner in 1919. In 1927, he was appointed chairman of the Central Electricity Board with the task of establishing the national grid. In 1935, he became chairman of the Iron and Steel Federation, to which he returned after the Second World War. During that war he held ministerial posts for trade and supply. *WG*

Duncan Smith, (George) Iain (1954–), Conservative politician and party leader from 2001. After education at military and business colleges, 'IDS' was a professional soldier (Scots Guards) and worked in industry before succeeding Norman Tebbit as MP for Chingford in 1992. A *Eurosceptic rebel during the Major government, he joined the shadow cabinet under Hague, covering social security and then defence. The unpopularity of other candidates provided him with an unexpected chance to win the leadership in 2001. *JAR*

Dungannon Clubs, Irish nationalist movement launched in 1905 by Bulmer Hobson and Denis McCullough, both members of the Irish Republican Brotherhood. The title referred to the late 18th century volunteer conventions of Dungannon, Co. Tyrone, which had been supportive of political reform and of Irish legislative authority. They promoted an advanced nationalism, opposed recruitment for the British army, merging with *Cumann na nGaedheal, in 1907, to become the *Sinn Fein League. *RE*

Dunkirk, evacuation from, and **'Dunkirk spirit'**. On 4 June 1940, Operation Dynamo, the evacuation of British troops from the beaches around Dunkirk, reached its climax: 338,000 Allied soldiers were taken off the beaches in the wake of the defeat of the Franco-British armies in France. The evacuation was made possible by an 'armada of little boats' that crossed and re-crossed the Channel under German air attack. In Britain, the sacrificial dedication with which the operation was carried out created a fierce sense of solidarity known as the 'Dunkirk spirit', much appealed to by post-war politicians. *MLC*

Dunkirk, treaty of (1947), treaty of alliance signed between Britain and France on 4 March. Later seen as a precursor of the anti-Soviet North Atlantic pact, in actual form the 50-year treaty was anti-German and thus similar to the 1942 Anglo-Soviet pact and the 1944 Franco-Soviet alliance. It committed the signatories to aid each other against German attack and consult against a German 'policy of aggression'. *JWY*

Sean Greenwood, *The Alternative Alliance* (London, 1996).

Dunnett, (Ludovic) James (1914–97), civil servant. Dunnett joined the Air Ministry in 1936, and after the war served also in the Ministry of Civil Aviation and the Ministry of Supply. Becoming a permanent secretary at the relatively young age of 45, he headed the Ministry of Transport (1959–62), Ministry of Labour (1962–6), and Ministry of Defence (1966–74). At his best, he was a problem-solver, not a detached mandarin—a managerial-type civil servant who got things done and drove business through. *KT*

Dunraven, Lord (1841–1926), Anglo-Irish politician. Windham Thomas Wyndham-Quin, a progressive Anglo-Irishman, hoped to foster reconciliation between England and Ireland and between unionist and nationalist, and was one of the prime movers behind the land conference of 1902 which made great progress in settling the Irish land question through the Land Act of 1903. He was president of the Irish Reform Association in 1904 and supported a measure of devolution of certain local government functions to financial and legislative councils in Ireland. *DGB*

Durbin, Evan (1906–48), Labour intellectual and minister. Durbin's premature death, in a swimming accident while on a family holiday in Cornwall, deprived the Labour Party of an able thinker and an attractive personality, possibly of a future leader. He was born in Bideford, Devon, the son of a Baptist minister, and although the family was not wealthy he attended a minor public school, Taunton, and in 1924 entered New College, Oxford, where he studied zoology and, after graduating, took a second degree in PPE. As well as abandoning the Gladstonian Liberalism of his family in favour of socialism, he formed a close and lasting friendship with a like-minded fellow student, Hugh Gaitskell. One of his tutors, Lionel Robbins, later appointed Durbin as a lecturer at LSE. In the 1930s he became involved in the activities of the New Fabian Research Bureau, the Society for Socialist Inquiry and Propaganda, and the XYZ Club. He wrote several books, the best known of which, *The Politics of Democratic Socialism* (1940), is in the tradition of the ideas later developed by Crosland and Hattersley. State intervention, he maintained, could take a form that was not only compatible with democracy but would also do more for the individual, by ensuring full employment and greater economic equality, than capitalism. During the war Durbin was a member of the economic section of the war cabinet secretariat and personal assistant to Attlee. After unsuccessfully contesting the general elections of 1931 and 1935, he was elected MP for the safe Labour seat of Edmonton in 1945. He was appointed a parliamentary secretary in March 1947, some eighteen months before his early death. *DEM*

ELIZABETH DURBIN, *New Jerusalems: The Labour Party and the Economics of Democratic Socialism* (London, 1985).

Dutt, (Rajani) Palme (1896–1974), British Communist leader. Palme Dutt was born at Cambridge, and family influences ensured that he was already a committed socialist and imbued with the ideas of Indian nationalism when he embarked upon a distinguished academic career at Balliol College, Oxford, in 1914. Before completing his degree his political activities brought expulsion from the university as well as a period of imprisonment for refusing conscription to the army. After a brief period in teaching, he joined the Labour Research Department in 1919 and became a foundation member of the Communist Party of Great Britain (CPGB) the following year.

Dutt quickly established himself as a powerful presence within the party through his editorship of *Labour Monthly*, for which he wrote the 'Notes of the Month' for over fifty years, and his drafting of the *Report on Organisation* (1922), which sought the 'Bolshevization' of the infant organization. He was one of the Communist International's experts on India and was for many years the main mentor of the Indian communist leaders. Above all, Dutt was custodian of the Moscow line within the CPGB and dominated the party in partnership with Harry Pollitt for almost three decades. Significantly, the only serious hiatus in this partnership occurred in the autumn of 1939 when Pollitt could not support Moscow's volte-face on the meaning of the Second World War. Dutt took over the general secretaryship until it was restored to Pollitt in 1941, when the line changed again after the Nazi invasion of Russia. The verbatim record of the central committee debate which preceded Pollitt's resignation reveals Dutt's ruthless opportunism in the service of the Soviet Union.

Dutt's undoubted erudition and his capacity for subtle, persuasive, and logical reasoning was at its most creative and commanding during the years up to the end of the Second World War, the years when Lenin's foundation-myth for the Communist International—the theses contained in *Imperialism: The Highest Stage of Capitalism* (1916)—provided a compelling framework for his analyses. Thereafter his prodigious energies were increasingly consumed by mere polemic and apologetics for Stalinism. Even after his retirement from party office in 1965, Dutt saw fit to publicly intervene in defence of a cause that was more and more discredited within the Communist Party itself. *JTC*

JOHN CALLAGHAN, *Rajani Palme Dutt* (London, 1993).

Duverger, Maurice (1917–), almost the only French political scientist to make an impact outside France as the subject was developing in the mid 20th century. A public lawyer by training, he proceeded via a comparative study of French constitutions (1944) to writing the book that made his reputation, *Political Parties* (1951, translated into English in 1954). Although he subsequently published numerous books and essays, as well as being a prolific journalist in *Le Monde*, it was this book that prompted a great deal of research on the typology of political parties (notably his distinction between parliamentary-centred cadre parties and extra-parliamentary mass parties), as well as on the link between electoral systems and party systems. Duverger's emphasis upon the threefold correlation between the simple majority, single ballot electoral system tending to produce or sustain a two-party system; the simple majority, two ballot system tending to a flexible, interdependent multi-party system; and proportional representation tending towards a rigid, mutually independent multi-partyism, acquired the status of a law. Although it was quickly criticized and qualified both inside France (George Lavau's *Partis politiques et réalites sociales*, 1953) and elsewhere (Douglas Rae, *The Political Consequences of Electoral Laws*, 1967), it has stood the test of time well, although it is usually presented simply as an opposition between proportional representation and first-past-the-post electoral systems. Given that there are few social science 'laws' that have survived empirical tests unscathed, Duverger's book deserves its landmark status. *JH*

E

Eastbourne by-election (18 October 1990). Following the murder of Ian *Gow by the IRA, the Liberal Democrats overturned a secure Conservative majority on the basis of widespread opposition to the *poll tax and growing discontent with Thatcher's leadership. The most important consequence of the by-election was to convince many Conservatives that the poll tax would have to be revised, if not scrapped, and that Thatcher was becoming an electoral liability. In the following month, a leadership election was launched which brought about her resignation. For the Liberal Democrats, Eastbourne was a return to electoral credibility with the new party's first by-election victory, once again demonstrating the centre's ability to capitalize upon anti-government feeling in times of mid-term crisis.

JS

Easter Rising (April 1916), Irish nationalist rebellion against British rule. The rebellion was planned by members of the Irish Republican Brotherhood (IRB), Irish Volunteers, and Irish Citizen Army. The IRB Military Council with which the rebellion originated comprised Thomas Clarke, Seán Mac Diarmada, Patrick Pearse, Éamonn Ceannt, Joseph Mary Plunkett, Thomas MacDonagh, and James Connolly. The conspirators originally envisaged a widespread Irish rising, but confusion of organization and the failure of arms procurement combined to limit the scale of actual events. By the commencement of the rising on Easter Monday, 24 April, the aim appears to have been less that of military victory than of revitalizing nationalist fortunes through a sacrificial, redemptive gesture. The rising was in the event largely confined to Dublin, where buildings were seized and a proclamation read (on the steps of the General Post Office) in the name of the provisional government of the Irish republic, the seven military council members being the signatories to this subsequently iconic document. Fighting with British forces continued until the rebel surrender on 29 April. Fatal casualties in Dublin numbered 64 rebels, 132 members of crown forces, and approximately 230 civilians. Other violence occurred in Wexford, Galway, and Co. Dublin. Post-rising action by the authorities intensified nationalist sympathies in Ireland, and led to enhanced status for the rebels among Irish nationalists. Sixteen leaders were executed, including Roger Casement and the seven signatories to the proclamation. These latter figures became martyrs within Irish nationalist tradition, their quasi-religious status contributing towards that regeneration of feeling which the rising was intended to produce. Although celebrating the continuity of Irish rebellion through the centuries, the rising was very much a function of the Great War. It was held that a better opportunity for rebellion existed during wartime than would otherwise be the case. Moreover, the blood sacrifice of young, romantic patriots fitted the wider pattern of the 1914–18 period, and the rebellion contributed to the gradual process of wartime disaffection from the state experienced by much of Catholic Ireland. The poetic Easter gesture was part both of a Catholic nationalist struggle against Britain and of a struggle within Catholic Irish nationalism between constitutional politics (which the rebels rejected) and the more militant republicanism which they embodied. The rising helped (in the short term) to undermine the constitutional Irish

Parliamentary Party, and (over a longer period) to sustain aggressive Irish republicanism. *RE*

Máirín Ní Dhonnchadha and Theo Dorgan (eds.), *Revising the Rising* (Derry, 1991).

East Fulham by-election (23 October 1933) famously saw Labour's John *Wilmot defeat A. J. Waldron (Conservative ex-mayor of Fulham) by gaining a 29.1 per cent swing from the 1931 result. Contemporaries saw this as an indicator of popular pacifism that ultimately delayed the National Government's rearmament programme, as Baldwin later claimed. Nevertheless domestic issues, housing and unemployment, had also impacted upon the result. Polling day saw a high Labour turnout, a poorly mobilized Conservative vote, and Liberal defections to Wilmot. Labour lost the seat to the Conservatives in 1935. *NJC*

Martin Ceadel, 'Interpreting East Fulham', in C. Cook and J. Ramsden (eds.), *By-Elections in British Politics* (London, 1997).

'east of Suez', Kipling phrase from 'The Road to Mandalay', evocative of Britain's historic role in the Far East. Up to 1947, the defence of India spawned a network of colonies, protectorates, and bases maintained 'east of Suez'. After Indian independence, new justifications had to be found for such draining defence commitments, and these symbols of British power were looked on with increasingly sceptical eyes by the Treasury. Harold Wilson's Labour government arrived in office in 1964 with an expansive view of Britain's world role that stretched to the foothills of the Himalayas. However, in January 1968, under the pressure of successive sterling crises, and despite the American displeasure it would (and did) incur, the cabinet took the contentious decision to pull all British forces out of Malaysia, Singapore, and the Persian gulf by the end of 1971, marking an end to Britain's 'east of Suez' role. *MCJ*

Eccles, David McAdam (1904–99), Conservative politician. Elected in 1943, Eccles helped to produce the **Industrial Charter*. Appointed minister of works in 1951, he entered the cabinet as minister of education in 1954. He became Macmillan's president of the Board of Trade before returning to education in 1959. A notable victim of the *'Night of the Long Knives', he resigned his seat in 1962 and took a viscountcy. Heath made him paymaster general with responsibility for the arts, 1970–3. *RJS*

Eccleston Square, site in London of the headquarters of the Labour Party and the TUC, 1918–28, after which both moved to Transport House, Smith Square. *KL*

Economic Advisory Council, set up by Ramsay MacDonald in January 1930, deriving from an earlier, more informal grouping of government advisers. A small unit, it had a staff of only five, three of them economists, but met monthly under MacDonald's own chairmanship, along with outsiders such as R. M. Tawney, J. M. Keynes, G. D. H. Cole, and some sympathetic industrialists. It achieved little in the short term as the Labour government struggled to find a basis on which to cope with rocketing unemployment. It limped on through the 1930s, weakened by its lack of any central position in the Whitehall machine, and was from 1939 incorporated into the wartime systems that eventually became the economic section of the Cabinet Office in 1941. It can also reasonably be seen as some sort of ancestor of the corporatist creations of the 1960s, such as the National Economic Development Council, so may be more significant in the development of British government than in the evolution of economic policy. *JAR*

Economic Affairs, Department of (DEA) (1964–9), established with the aim of encouraging faster and more sustained economic growth in the British economy. The traditional all-powerful role of the Treasury in the economic sphere was to be limited: the DEA was to modernize and plan the economy in order to achieve a fundamental improvement in competitiveness. The new secretary for economic affairs (combined with the title of 'first secretary of state') was George Brown, second in influence and power only to the prime minister, Harold Wilson. The DEA was set up under the Ministers of the Crown Act, 1964, which abolished the posts of economic secretary to the Treasury and secretary of state for industry, trade, and regional development. Brown also became chairman of the National Economic Development Council. The main product of the DEA was the *National Plan, published in 1965, a coordinated cross-departmental initiative to foster faster growth with particular focus on industry, the regions, and prices and incomes. The recurrent economic troubles of the 1960s put paid to the DEA's plans. In 1966, administration of prices and incomes policy passed to the relevant departments, while in 1967 Brown quit, to be replaced by the prime minister (with Peter Shore assuming day-to-day responsibility as secretary of state at cabinet level), and the industrial preparations for Britain's application to join the European Economic

Community passed to the Board of Trade. Responsibility for prices and incomes policy, along with many staff, were transferred to the new Department of Employment and Productivity in 1968. The DEA was eventually dissolved in 1969. *JD*

Peter Hennessy, *Whitehall* (London, 1989). | Public Record Office website: *www.pro.gov.uk/finding/coreexec/data/EW-main.htm*

'economical with the truth', phrase from Mark Twain used by Sir Robert *Armstrong, cabinet secretary, when being cross-examined in an Australian court, on 18 November 1986, over the government's attempt to ban the book *Spycatcher*, which revealed classified information about the British security services. Armstrong denied that he had lied, but accepted that he had not told the whole story, having been 'economical with the truth'. *JAR*

economic appeasement, motivation that effectively underlay the entirety of *appeasement, although often treated as an element of it. After the Great War it was a primary objective of British governments to return to pre-war normality, by which was implied the centrality of Britain in the world's financial and economic system. This could only be achieved by the revival of trade. Peace, though, was Britain's most compelling interest for, as Stanley Baldwin articulated it, 'trade and commerce . . . flourish best in conditions of peace'. During the 1920s the British government sought to promote peace and trade by reducing the burden of Germany's reparation payments, which were finally abandoned at the Lausanne conference in 1932. This coincided very much with a stream of British opinion that by 1931 was articulated in the following way: world economic recovery would be contingent on European economic recovery and European recovery on German recovery. It was also felt that the revival of Germany's economic fortunes might diminish political extremism in that country. To achieve this goal, some favoured the creation of a German sphere of influence in central Europe; another group a revision of Britain's Empire-oriented economic policies of 1931–2 in Germany's favour; others colonial concessions and the provision of credit to make raw materials more accessible to Germany; finally, there were those who wanted to bring Germany back into a multilateral trading system, which found expression in the Van Zeeland mission and report of 1937–8. In general, though, there was a willingness to assist German economic recovery right up until the outbreak of war (as witness the Leith-Ross–Rüter discussions of November 1938) that would function both as reward for and encouragement to political moderation. *AJC*

Martin Gilbert and Richard Gott, *The Appeasers* (London, 1963). | Keith Robbins, *Appeasement* (London, 1988). | Gustav Schmidt, *The Politics and Economics of Appeasement: British Foreign Policy in the 1930s* (Leamington Spa, 1986).

Economic Planning Board was set up after the Second World War to carry forward wartime lessons in economic management into peacetime. It was serviced by Central Economic Planning staff, and chaired by Edwin Plowden, 1947–53, producing in 1948 a four-year plan for the economy, but its semi-detachment from broader government machinery and the return of the Conservatives to office in 1951 committed to the reduction of state control made it of limited significance, except as a precursor to similar machinery more seriously set up in and after the 1960s. *JAR*

economic war with Ireland (1932–8), dispute between Britain and Eire which began when Eamon de Valera started dismantling the *Anglo-Irish treaty of 1921. He removed the oath of allegiance to the British king from the Irish constitution and refused to pay land annuities to the British government (repayments for loans advanced to Irish tenant farmers to purchase land under the Land Acts, 1891–1909). The British imposed special duties on Irish imports, particularly cattle and dairy produce, and the Irish replied with duties on British coal, iron and steel, and manufactured goods. The economic war was concluded with the *Anglo-Irish agreement (1938). There were three parts to this relating to defence, finance, and trade. De Valera failed to move the British towards Irish unity. The defence agreement returned naval bases retained by the British under the terms of the Anglo-Irish treaty. Financially, the Irish government paid a £10 million lump sum as a final settlement of claims made under the treaty and subsequent agreements. Both countries ended tariffs on each other's goods and Commonwealth preference was restored to Irish goods, which also had free entry into the British market. *TWH*

Economist, The (1843–). The roots of *The Economist*'s position as probably the world's most influential business weekly, now with total sales well over 500,000, go back to the editorship of the Liberal Walter Layton (1925–38), who also owned the paper. Geoffrey Crowther, Layton's successor, raised the circulation from 10,000 to more than 55,000 over the next twenty years. By

1974, under a non-specialist editor, Alastair Burnett, circulation had doubled to 100,000, and it doubled again by 1980. In the Thatcher years the magazine continued to boom. The conglomerate Pearson, by now its owner (and owner of the *Financial Times*), developed it as an international magazine, where formerly it was a British one with large sales abroad. The American edition sold far more copies than the British, and the majority of advertising revenue came from overseas too. The magazine's content was accessible and wide-ranging and its political viewpoint independent but centrist. *CKSU*

Ruth Dudley Edwards, *The Pursuit of Reason: The Economist, 1843–1993* (London, 1993).

Eddisbury by-election (7 April 1943). The hitherto safe Liberal National seat of Eddisbury in Cheshire was the first win for the *Common Wealth Party. John Loverseed, a former RAF pilot, who campaigned with the slogan 'Hitler is watching Eddisbury', secured the seat and held it until defeated in July 1945 (when he fought as a Labour candidate—agricultural Eddisbury had never previously seen a Labour candidate). Common Wealth's victory, with subsequent ones at Skipton and Chelmsford, was widely interpreted as expressing the electorate's desire for change and foreshadowing Labour's victory in 1945. Eddisbury, however, returned to the Conservatives, who had not held the seat since losing it to a Liberal at an earlier by-election in 1929. *JS*

Eden, (Robert) Anthony (1897–1977), Conservative politician, foreign secretary and prime minister, whose name is inseparably linked with Suez. Eden was born into the landed gentry in Durham and educated at Eton and Oxford, but fighting alongside men from all backgrounds during the Great War led him to abhor class divisions. He had planned a diplomatic career, but fought Spennymoor for the Conservatives in 1922 and became MP for Warwick and Leamington in 1923. Eden's debonair good looks, clipped accent, and enlightened views marked him as a rising star. He served as parliamentary private secretary to the foreign secretary, Sir Austen Chamberlain, strongly supported Baldwin, and was influenced by the progressive Toryism of Skelton. In 1931 Eden became a Foreign Office minister, enhancing his reputation at the world disarmament conference of 1932–4. He entered Baldwin's cabinet in 1935 as minister for League of Nations affairs and, following the resignation of Hoare six months later, became foreign secretary, aged 38. Eden received a baptism of fire, as Mussolini triumphed in Abyssinia (now Ethiopia), Hitler reoccupied the Rhineland, and Spain was plunged into civil war. Initially he welcomed the more active role taken in foreign affairs by Baldwin's successor, Neville Chamberlain. However, when Chamberlain rejected a secret peace proposal from President Roosevelt without consulting him and overruled his insistence on an assurance from Mussolini before negotiations in early 1938, Eden resigned.

Long-serving Heir Apparent

Although Eden was not fundamentally against *appeasement, his resignation distanced him from the 'guilty men' of Munich (see Munich Crisis). On the outbreak of war he accepted the Dominions Office, and in May 1940 Churchill appointed him war secretary. By the end of 1940, Eden had returned to the Foreign Office and joined the war cabinet. As the wartime emphasis shifted to planning for peace, he balanced Churchill's faith in the Anglo-American alliance, arguing the importance of working with the Soviets, and finally convinced his boss of the need for a strong post-war France and of de Gaulle's key role in its creation. In opposition after 1945, he respected Bevin and adopted a broadly bipartisan approach to foreign policy, but criticized Morrison over *Mossadeq's nationalization of British oil installations in Abadan. He played little part in reshaping Tory domestic policy, although he reiterated Skelton's idea of a *property-owning democracy. Churchill had designated Eden as his successor in 1942, but over the years Eden became increasingly frustrated by his leader's stubborn refusal to retire. In 1951 Eden returned to the Foreign Office. Among a series of diplomatic triumphs, he saved NATO by proposing a more realistic alliance (the western European union) than the flawed European defence community, though promising to station British troops in Europe. In Indochina, he prevented a major escalation of the conflict. He also seemed to have repaired Anglo-Egyptian relations by negotiating the evacuation of Britain's Suez base, despite the *Suez Group's anger.

Flawed Leader

Despite Churchill's doubts about whether Eden was up to the job, his long-serving deputy became prime minister in April 1955 with high hopes, and the fresh mandate won by Eden was the first occasion in the century that a sitting government had increased its majority. Within months, however, the economy started to overheat, prompting a deflationary autumn budget. Eden's flaws also emerged. He delayed a major reshuffle and irritated ministers by meddling, while press criticism riled him, notably an article that called for 'the smack of firm government'. His scepticism towards European integration caused him to miss the opportunity to shape Europe's future when he sent only an official, instead of a minister, to the *Messina conference that created the European Economic Community (EEC). Eden's greatest folly, however, was to equate Nasser with Hitler. The cabinet reacted to Egypt's nationalization of the Suez canal company (see SUEZ CRISIS) in July 1956 by sanctioning the use of force in the last resort, but ministers assumed that Eden was uniquely qualified to resolve the crisis diplomatically. Eden, however, hoped not only to 'internationalize' the canal but to topple Nasser. He was less than frank with his cabinet and tended to present ministers only with the stark choice of pressing ahead or failing. When diplomatic efforts failed, Eden was tempted by a French scheme to use an Israeli attack on Egypt as the pretext for an invasion, ostensibly to bring peace and keep the canal open. At Sèvres on 24 October, British, French, and Israeli representatives signed a secret protocol. Eden intended that the only other ministers who were to know about it, in addition to Lloyd as foreign secretary, were Heath, the then chief whip, Macmillan, and Butler. The cabinet were not informed but endorsed a contingency plan for Anglo-French intervention in the event of an Israeli attack on Egypt.

After Israel invaded Egypt, RAF planes eliminated the Egyptian air force and on 5 November the Anglo-French landings began. Parliament was in uproar and the country was deeply divided. Two ministers, Boyle and Nutting, resigned. The queen was deeply concerned. The Commonwealth was split. The Americans were appalled and, following a massive run on the pound, it became clear that they would not help unless Britain accepted a UN solution. On 6 November Eden ordered British troops to halt. Having sought to reassert British influence in the region, he had all but destroyed it.

Finally, Eden's health failed. A botched operation in 1953 had made him susceptible to fevers, and on 23 November he flew to Jamaica to recuperate. On his return his party failed to rally to him. In the Commons on 20 December he denied any 'collusion' with Israel, and then ordered the cabinet secretary, Brook, to destroy the evidence. Eden resigned on medical grounds on 9 January 1957. He became the earl of Avon in 1961 and published his memoirs but never commented upon collusion. In the early 1960s and later, he opposed British entry to the EEC. The paradox of Eden is that a consummate diplomat came to grief as prime minister over foreign policy. *RJS*

DAVID CARLTON, *Anthony Eden* (London, 1981). | DAVID DUTTON, *Anthony Eden: A Life and Reputation* (London, 1997). | ROBERT RHODES JAMES, *Anthony Eden* (London, 1986).

Education, Department for (1992–5). The first of the Department for Education's predecessors, the Board of Education, was created in 1900 following the publication of the Bryce report, which recommended the establishment of a central authority to coordinate the development of secondary education. The board suffered from a lack of power and direction and was eventually replaced in 1944 by a Ministry of Education. In April 1964, following the recommendations of the Trend committee on civil science and the Robbins committee on higher education, the Ministry of Education and the office of the minister of science were merged. The new Department of Education and Science had extended responsibilities over science and the financing of higher education. In 1988, the Education Reform Act increased the powers of the central department at the expense of the local education authorities. Reorganization continued when in 1992 the department lost its responsibilities over science and became the Department for Education. In 1995 the department was merged with the Department of Employment. This ended the artificial division that had hitherto existed between education and employment and academic and vocational courses. *JD*

RICHARD ALDRICH, 'From Board of Education to Department for Education and Employment' *Journal of Educational Administration and History*, 32/1 (2000).

Education Act, 1902, usually known as the Balfour Act, after its chief sponsor, the Conservative Arthur *Balfour. School boards were abolished and responsibility for education, including higher or secondary education, vested in 140 local education authorities (LEAs), consisting of elected committees of county councils, county borough councils, and some of the larger county districts. Provisions were also made for rate support for voluntary schools. Grammar schools were established where required. A central Board of Education coordinated the system on a national scale, its president usually a member of the cabinet. The Act was important for placing responsibility for all sectors of education on local authorities and widening provision of secondary education. *JS*

Education Act, 1918, often known as the Fisher Act, after the president of the Board of Education, H. A. L. *Fisher. Part of the *reconstruction legislation after the Great War passed under the Lloyd George coalition, it raised the *school leaving age to 14 and abolished any remaining fees for elementary education. Plans to provide part-time 'continuing education' for 14–18-year-olds were shelved due to government economies in 1921. *JS*

Education Act, 1944, often known as the Butler Act from the responsible education minister, R. A. *Butler. It mainly implemented recommendations from pre-war reports, raising the *school-leaving age to 15 and providing free secondary education for all children. Secondary schools were divided into three types, grammar, technical, and modern, for children of different abilities, with entry usually determined by an *eleven-plus examination. Although the tripartite division of secondary education was subsequently criticized by supporters of *comprehensive schools, the Act was hailed at the time as a major example of progressive social legislation embodying the egalitarian sentiments of wartime society. *JS*

Education Act, 1979. This act of the newly elected Thatcher government removed the requirement placed upon local authorities by Labour's 1976 Education Act to submit plans for comprehensive reorganization of schools. It also enhanced parental involvement in the choice of schools for their children in participation on schools' governing bodies, a process carried much further by later legislation, notably the Education Act, 1980. *JS*

Education and Employment, Department for (1995–). See Education, Department for; Employment, Department of.

Education Reform Act, 1988. Despite a decade of regular legislation by the Thatcher government, the education secretary, Kenneth Baker, introduced his 'great education reform bill' (dubbed the 'Gerbill' by its critics), creating a *national curriculum to be followed by all pupils between the ages of 5 and 16. The governing bodies of all secondary schools, and of larger primary schools, were given direct responsibility for their own budgets. Secondary schools and larger primaries were also given the right to 'opt out' of local authority control, subject to a parental ballot. Funding of non-university higher education was transferred from local authorities to a Polytechnics and Colleges Funding Council and the University Grants Committee was replaced by a University Funding Council (these latter two bodies later merged into a Higher Education Funding Council overseeing a single higher education sector). The Act also abolished the Inner London Education Authority and transferred responsibility for inner London education to the boroughs. *JS*

Edward VII (1841–1910), sovereign 1901–10. Edward had one of the longest apprenticeships of any modern sovereign and did not come to the throne until the age of 60. Queen Victoria and Prince Albert subjected him to a rigorous education for which he was unsuited. He nevertheless acquired a charming manner perfectly attuned to the world of small talk and light banter in which he was required to perform most of his duties. He was the first prince of Wales to travel extensively outside Europe, including trips to Canada and India. This heightened the monarchy's connections to the Empire and raised expectations for world travel that the 20th-century royal family has been obliged to fulfil. Unlike his mother Victoria, he loved ceremonies, formalities, and dressing up. He also took an active interest in reform of the army after the Boer war, and in Anglo-French diplomacy. As king he was conservative in his political instincts, though friendly with Liberals and even radicals, especially in his youth. He played an important role in keeping the monarchy visible during his mother's long retirement and his own reign became a byword for splendour and display. Edward married a Danish princess, Alexandra, with whom he had five children. He also had a series of semi-public mistresses. However, his generation celebrated him neither as an adulterer nor a friend of big-spending plutocrats, which he was, but as an imperial paterfamilias. *WMK*

Simon Heffer, *Power and Place: The Political Consequences of Edward VII* (London, 1998). | Philip Magnus, *King Edward the Seventh* (London, 1964).

Edward VIII (1894–1978), sovereign for less than a year after his father's death in 1936. His abdication of the throne was unprecedented and caused one of the most serious crises for the monarchy in the century. Edward had a naval education, spent two years at Oxford, and acquired the easy but powerful magnetism of his grandfather, Edward VII. He joined the Grenadier Guards during the Great War, but was frustrated in his attempts to fight at the front. His war record and good looks inspired scenes of adulation among the crowds who came to see him on his travels after the war, but he disliked such work, which he dismissed as 'stunting'. He was (however unfairly) thought to sympathize with fascism, while his popularity with the political classes was not improved by ill-judged public remarks during his short reign, notably the statement that 'something must be done' on a tour of unemployment black spots in south Wales, which was naturally seen as criticism of his own government. But crucially he fell in love with Wallis Simpson, an American divorcée. The prime minister, Stanley Baldwin, opposed the king's proposed marriage on the grounds that a divorced woman would be unacceptable as queen, whereupon Edward VIII decided to abdicate. The ex-king, created duke of Windsor by his brother, married Mrs Simpson in France in 1937. He visited Hitler, whom he admired, but was British governor of the Bahamas during the Second World War. Afterwards they lived mainly in France and attended parties in the USA. A mixture of charm and selfishness is not uncommon among princes. The peculiar mix of these qualities accounts not only for his early popularity but also his later unhappiness and inability to serve the country as he wished.

WMK

THE DUKE OF WINDSOR, *A King's Story* (London, 1951). | PHILIP ZIEGLER, *King Edward VIII: The Official Biography* (London, 1990).

EEC, treaty of accession to. On 22 January 1972, the treaty of accession to the EEC (European Economic Community) was signed in Brussels by Britain, Denmark, Ireland, and Norway. This was a great personal achievement for Edward Heath who had given priority to securing EEC membership on taking office in June 1970. Whilst the treaty of accession had been agreed in Brussels, it still had to be voted into law in Westminster before Britain could formally join the EEC (see EUROPEAN COMMUNITIES ACT, 1972).

JRVE

egalitarianism, a concept central to modern politics, and even in a sense one that defines its very modernity. If we start from the assumption that all men (and women) are created equal, then we enter a sea of controversy: does this mean absolute equality? Or equality of opportunity? How does the search for an equal, or a more equal, society sit beside the classic freedoms enshrined in liberal thought, especially the right to pursue your life as you see fit? These questions arose in British politics as the *New Liberalism of the early years of the century sought to tackle the inequalities in society which various individuals and philanthropic bodies had exposed. New Liberals sought to square the circle by claiming that the state's role should be increased, and yet remain to some large extent limited. This would be done, for example, by the state helping the individual to help himself; the state would not provide work, but would provide the means (*labour exchanges) whereby the individual might find work for himself. State education would also create more equality of opportunity. Nowadays the debate is concerned with ethnic, religious, gender, and racial issues, and Northern Ireland is a kind of laboratory for equal rights legislation to prevent discrimination on the grounds of religious (and therefore political) belief. This is a tricky area: the question arises as to how equal treatment can be applied to those whose customs and beliefs are inimical to the ordinary laws of the land. In India, for example, Hindu Nationalists claim that the state's recognition of the Muslim law (sharia) contravenes the state's claim to treat all citizens equally, and is against the majority point of view. The general consensus amongst those who subscribe to egalitarianism is that, while all are not the same, all have equal claims. But the making good of these claims raises further problems: should positive discrimination be used to promote these claims (for example, to ensure more women MPs and more from ethnic minorities)? Should ordinary areas of employment have quotas made up from the ethnic or racial minorities, or the disabled? Unsurprisingly, modern British governments often fall back on the 'equality of opportunity' principle, claiming that through improved educational facilities equality of opportunity is best achieved. Some extreme modernists claim that mastering the new technology is the best way forward. Certainly, few politicians would want to exclude some concept of egalitarianism from their agendas, since political action is seen as central to the equality issue: laws can achieve this goal.

DGB

J. C. REES, *Equality* (London, 1971).

Eight Hours Act, 1926, passed by the Baldwin government in June in an attempt to end the lockout in the coal industry precipitated by the colliery owners' demand for wage reductions. The Act failed in its immediate objective and proved of limited effectiveness in restoring the industry's market position. On the expiration of the Act in July 1930, the then Labour government enacted a 7.5-hour day in partial redemption of its pledge to legislate for seven hours.

MWK

Eire, official title of the Irish state. In December 1937, the Constitution of Ireland—Bunreacht na hÉireann—supplanted the Irish Free State created by the Anglo-Irish treaty. The official name of the independent Irish state was now 'Eire', or in the English language, 'Ireland'. The Republic of Ireland Act, 1948, passed by the Irish parliament, made the status of Eire a republic but did not alter the title of the state itself. *TWH*

El Alamein, battle of (1942). Marking a critical turning point in the Mediterranean war for the Allies, the battle of El Alamein (23 October–4 November) was hard fought but its outcome was inevitable given the terrain; critical Axis fuel shortages; and massive Allied superiority in tanks, aircraft, troops, and field guns. Mersa Matruh had formed the linchpin of British defences in the western desert, but could be outflanked. This was not true of El Alamein, an Egyptian coastal town some 50 miles (80 km) west of Alexandria, which fronted a narrow 40-mile (64-km) front between the sea and the Qattara depression, impassable even to tanks. It was here that Rommel's spectacular final advance was halted as the eighth army made a successful stand in July 1942 (often referred to as the first battle of El Alamein). The respite afforded allowed the British to bring in substantial reinforcements (and a new commander, *Montgomery), including American Grant and Sherman tanks, which were superior to Rommel's staple tank, the Panzerkampfwagen III. Rommel tried once more to break through at Alam Halfa, only to be pushed back. When it finally came, the British offensive, focused on a narrow front, was decisive, marking the end of the Axis threat to Egypt as their forces were pushed back to Tripoli and beyond. *SM*

John Strawson, *El Alamein: Desert Victory* (London, 1981).

election expenses. See general elections.

election petitions. See general elections.

elections, local government. See local government elections.

elections, national. See general elections.

elective dictatorship, term coined in the 1976 Dimbleby lecture by Lord Hailsham (see Hogg, Quintin McGarel) to characterize the contemporary political system. He argued that the constitutional framework created by the Glorious Revolution of 1688 had allowed party to dominate the political system, but that in parliament there was now only one chamber, the Commons, which was dominated increasingly by the government, and the government was controlled by the cabinet, which itself was often dominated by a few of its members. The cabinet had at its disposal the civil service, providing it with resources and information that could not be matched by parliament. The consequence was an all-powerful cabinet, introducing measures which parliament did not and could not challenge or consider effectively. 'So the sovereignty of Parliament has increasingly become, in practice, the sovereignty of the Commons, and the sovereignty of the Commons has increasingly become the sovereignty of the government, which in addition to its influence in Parliament, controls the party whips, the party machine, and the civil service. This means that what has always been an elective dictatorship in theory, but one in which the component party operated in practice to control one another, has become a machine in which one of those parts has come to exercise a predominant influence over the rest' (Hailsham 1976: 8). Hailsham argued the case for a *bill of rights and a written constitution to counter the elective dictatorship, but later abandoned or qualified these proposals (Hailsham 1990). The term entered common currency and has been used especially to denote a powerful or overly powerful premiership, notably so during the premierships of Margaret Thatcher and Tony Blair. *PN*

Lord Hailsham, *Elective Dictatorship* (London, 1976). | Lord Hailsham, *A Sparrow's Flight* (London, 1990).

Electoral Reform Society (1958–), pressure group founded in 1884 as the Proportional Representation Society. Its aims, which have changed little since its inception, are to ensure that all votes have equal value, that all significant views within the electorate are given effective representation, that electors are permitted to vote for their preferred candidates without fear of wasting their votes, and that individual representatives are accountable to their electorates. To achieve these aims the society supports the introduction of the single transferable vote for all public elections in the UK. Throughout the century, it has had an active publications and lecture programme, and an associated educational charity, the McDougall Trust, founded in 1948, publishes the journal *Representation*. A subsidiary, Electoral Reform (Ballot Services) Ltd, conducts ballots on behalf of a number of outside organizations, such as trade unions. Another subsidiary, Electoral Reform International Services, founded in 1992, provides assistance to emerging democracies. In 1983 the society was recognized by the UN Economic and Social Council as a non-governmental organization with consultative status. Its director from 1960 to 1979, Enid *Lakeman, achieved a notable public profile as champion of proportional representation. *PN*

Electoral Reform Society, web page: *http://www.gn.apc.org/ers* | ENID LAKEMAN, *Power to Elect* (London, 1982).

electorate and **electoral register**, citizens having the right to vote, their names being formally recorded for that purpose. The number of citizens entitled to vote has grown enormously during the course of the 20th century, because of population growth and a widening of the franchise. At the beginning of the century, the electorate was 6.7 million; in 1997, it was just over 43.7 million. By 1970, virtually all citizens aged 18 and over were entitled to vote. In order to exercise the right to vote, citizens have to register as voters. The practice of registration was reformed under the provisions of the Representation of the People Act, 1918, and has been modified by subsequent Acts. Each year a form is mailed to the head of every household, requiring that person to record the names of all those ordinarily resident in the property on 10 October (15 September in the case of Northern Ireland) and eligible for inclusion, including those who will attain the age of 18 years during the period of the new electoral register. The form is then returned to the electoral registration officer for the constituency. About a third of households fail to respond and have to be chased up by mail or, if that fails, in person. An electoral register for each constituency is then compiled and is open for inspection: it takes effect the following February and is in force for one year. Electors who move to another constituency during this period, are away working, or are otherwise unable to vote in person, may apply for a postal vote. There are problems with ensuring the accuracy of the electoral register. It has been estimated that anything between 5 and 10 per cent of adults fail to register. Some voters fill in registration forms incorrectly or, for a variety of reasons, fail to complete them. There have been problems especially in registering people who have no fixed address. Various attempts have been made to improve the accuracy of the electoral register. One proposal is for a rolling electoral register, allowing for continuous updating. *PN*

ROBERT BLACKBURN, *The Electoral System in Britain* (London, 1995). | DANIEL DORLING, C. PATTIE, D. ROSSITER, and R. JOHNSTON, 'Missing Voters in Britain, 1992–1996: Where and with What Impact?', in D. M. Farrell, D. Broughton, D. Denver, and J. Fisher (eds.), *British Elections and Parties Yearbook 1996* (London, 1996). | H. F. RAWLINGS, *Law and the Electoral Process* (London, 1988).

eleven-plus examination, taken by children aged 11 to determine whether they attended the grammar, technical, or modern secondary schools set up under Butler's *Education Act, 1944. The examination was foreshadowed in the Spens report of 1938 which suggested that intelligence tests could be used to distinguish which children would benefit from each type of secondary education. As a result, almost all schoolchildren after 1945 sat the eleven-plus examination, increasingly seen as a pass or fail examination for entry into the grammar school. Growing concern in the 1950s about the efficacy of the tests, the problem of 'late developers', and the influence of social background on the results contributed to a campaign to remove the eleven-plus and adopt a system of *comprehensive schools. Following the Labour Party's support for comprehensivization after the 1964 election, the eleven-plus examination was largely phased out in the drive to make comprehensive schools the universal system of secondary education. In turn, with growing disquiet over educational standards from the late 1970s and the provision for the 'opting out' of schools from local authority control, there have been new calls for the reintroduction of selective testing of schoolchildren entering secondary education. *JS*

Elgin, 9th earl of (1849–1917), Liberal politician. Born in Canada and educated at Oxford, Elgin succeeded to the earldom in 1863. He served in the Liberal government of 1886, was viceroy of India, 1893–8, during a period of famine and political unrest, and chaired a royal commission into the military preparations for the Boer war, 1902. Elgin was colonial secretary in *Campbell-Bannerman's government, 1905–8, and hence Winston Churchill's first ministerial chief. *JS*

Elibank, Master of (1870–1920), Liberal politician and chief whip, implicated in the *Marconi scandal. Alexander Murray was styled the Master of Elibank as heir of the 10th Lord Elibank. Educated at Cheltenham and Sandhurst, he was MP for Midlothian, 1900–6 and 1910–12, and for Peebles and Selkirk, 1906–10, serving as Scottish whip, 1905–9. Briefly under-secretary of state for India, his organizational talents were recognized when he was appointed chief whip and patronage secretary in February 1910. Elibank maintained the Liberal majority in the Commons at a difficult time with skill, and revamped the party machine, but was criticized for the scale of his honours lists and peerage creations in 1910–12. He left office on grounds of ill health in August 1912, taking the title of Lord Murray of Elibank. In 1913 he was revealed to have bought shares on his own and the party's behalf in the American Marconi Company but remained on business in Bogota, refusing to answer allegations, and was censured by a Lords select committee in 1914 for a 'grave error'. He continued to play a role in Liberal politics, and acted briefly as director-general of recruiting at the Ministry of Munitions in 1915–16. *JS*

Elizabeth II (1926–), sovereign since 1952. The first decade of her childhood passed in relative obscurity, and she only entered the spotlight as heiress presumptive when her parents unexpectedly came to the throne following the abdication of Edward VIII. Elizabeth spent the Second World War in Windsor, away from the heaviest bombing of London, but joined the battle by doing a course at Aldershot and becoming a member of the auxiliary transport service. She married in 1947 her third cousin, Prince Philip of Greece, who became a British citizen and was created duke of Edinburgh. They lived happily for two years after the marriage in Malta where he was serving in the navy, but were obliged to return home to help undertake duties for her father whose health was beginning to fail. Although she has sometimes, especially in the 1990s, been labelled a rigid traditionalist, when she and her husband were young they did much to make the monarchy less formal and more accessible. For example, major royal ceremonies, including her coronation, were televised at her insistence. Garden parties at Buckingham palace, to which throngs of people were invited, replaced the exclusive society presentations of debutantes. There have been no political innovations, but neither have there been episodes where anyone could accuse her of extreme partisanship. This must be considered an achievement in so long a reign. She takes a greater interest in Commonwealth affairs than most contemporary politicians do; she also maintains strong contacts with the Church of England and the armed forces; she scrutinizes those proposed for honours. These are the areas where Downing Street has most often needed to heed palace opinion. Reverses in the 1990s in the monarchy's popularity brought on by the fire in Windsor, the question of who should pay for its repair, and the break-up of her children's marriages, took her by surprise at an age when most people of her generation were beginning to enjoy retirement. Perhaps the only just criticism that could be made of this period of her reign is that she continued to employ a private secretariat that struggled fruitlessly to find an adequate response. Still, her personal popularity has remained intact and this is a remarkable feat for someone who has been on the throne for more than four decades. *WMK*

Sarah Bradford, *Elizabeth: A Biography of Her Majesty the Queen* (London, 1996). | Ben Pimlott, *The Queen: A Biography of Elizabeth II* (London, 1996).

Elizabeth, the Queen Mother (1900–), the daughter of a Scottish peer, Elizabeth Bowers-Lyon married the future George VI in 1923 and was a tenacious supporter of her husband following the abdication crisis in 1936. She also charmed two important constituencies: she established connections with working people during the bombing of London in the 1940s and became friends with theatrical men like Noel Coward, Cecil Beaton, and Roy Strong. This secured the monarchy's hold on pillars of the arts world, who in turn set out through theatre, photography, and historical writing to glorify the monarchy. *WMK*

Elliott, Walter (1888–1958), Conservative politician. Born in Lanarkshire, Elliott retained a lifetime association with Scotland. He won Lanark in 1918 but was defeated in 1923. This was followed by capturing the marginal Glasgow division of Kelvingrove in 1924 and holding it until defeated in 1945, regaining it 1950–8. Despite voting to continue the coalition in 1922 he was rewarded with junior office. He returned to the Scottish Office, 1924–9. With the National Government, advancement to the Treasury as financial secretary was followed by appointment as minister of agriculture, secretary of state for Scotland, 1936–8, and minister of health, 1938–40. Although uncertain about Neville Chamberlain's appeasement policy, and especially Munich, he remained in office. With the fall of Chamberlain he never held cabinet office again. This enabled him to pursue a career as a journalist and broadcaster and to follow his interests in education, Empire, and defence. *NJC*

Colin Coote, *A Companion of Honour* (London, 1956). | N. A. Rose (ed.), *Baffy: The Diaries of Blanche Dugdale, 1936–1947* (London, 1973).

Elwyn-Jones, Lord (1909–89), lawyer and Labour politician. (Frederick) Elwyn Jones was educated at Aberystwyth University and Cambridge, before pursuing a distinguished legal career. He was Labour MP for Plaistow, 1945–50, and for Newham South, 1950–74, receiving a life peerage in 1974. His most important political and legal roles were as attorney-general in Harold Wilson's Labour government of 1964–70, and lord chancellor under Wilson and Callaghan, 1974–9. *KL*

LORD ELWYN-JONES, *In My Time: An Autobiography* (London, 1983)

emigration. Britain has a long tradition of emigration and it is estimated that approximately 25 million people emigrated from the British Isles, including Ireland, between 1815 and 1945. Emigration in the 19th century was particularly heavy from the poorer parts of the UK, especially from Ireland and the Scottish Highlands, and has absorbed a large proportion of the potential population increase of both countries until well into the 20th century. Ireland, for example, showed an absolute loss of population in every decade from the 1840s including, as the Irish Republic, every decade in the 20th century until the 1970s.

Rapid population increase, the opening up of the American West, and the development of the Empire greatly increased emigration from the UK as a whole in the late Victorian and Edwardian period. Emigration peaked in the years immediately before the Great War, averaging over 400,000 per year in 1909–13, over two million people, of whom only 150,000 were drawn directly from Ireland. Even with substantial immigration, mainly from Europe, the UK showed a net loss of population by migration of a quarter of a million per year by 1910. The USA, Canada, and Australasia were the destinations of almost 90 per cent of emigrants before 1914, with the USA taking the largest share.

Emigration slowed substantially after the Great War, Britain showing a net surplus of immigrants and returned migrants by the 1930s, as economic depression and stricter immigration controls in the USA had an effect. Even so, over two million emigrants left between 1920 and 1938, with Canada and Australia as the favoured destinations. Emigration became significant again after the Second World War. The continuation of sponsored emigration schemes begun before the war, offered families passage to Australia for as little as £10. As a result, the balance of population once again showed a net outflow, a situation which was maintained until the 1980s. Thereafter a small yearly surplus of immigrants over emigrants in the period 1988 to 1997 produced a total population increase by migration of about 300,000. By the end of the 1990s, emigration was running at around a quarter of a million per year. In contrast to the previous pattern, the European Union was now the biggest recipient of British migrants, followed by the Commonwealth and the USA.

Emigration has primarily been on a voluntary basis, though there was some government assistance and private philanthropic initiative in the 19th century. Assisted passages to the Empire were introduced after the Great War for ex-servicemen and their families. The Empire Settlement Act of 1922 allowed for up to £3 million per year to be spent upon assisted passages for emigrants and on land resettlement schemes. Between 1922 and 1936 the Act provided assisted passages for 405,000 people, the majority to Canada and Australia, representing about a third of all emigrants to the Empire in these years. Renewed in 1937 and in subsequent post-war legislation, the assisted places scheme was only finally allowed to expire in 1972.

Emigration had support from imperial visionaries from the late 19th century who saw the emigration of 'surplus' population from the UK as a means of relieving poverty and social tension at home, developing colonial territories, and strengthening imperial links. The existence of still underdeveloped parts of the Empire in the inter-war years was particularly attractive with the rise of mass unemployment at home, leading both trade unions and employers to support emigration. Emigration was also seen as appropriate for 'problem' groups such as orphaned or deprived children. On the other side, there were also fears expressed around the turn of the century of *national deterioration to which emigration contributed. Britain, it was alleged, was exchanging its youngest, healthiest, and most energetic 'stock' for poor, non-British migrants from Europe, many of them Jews. In a more general form such issues resurfaced after the Second World War with concern about the changing racial, skill, and age balance of the country caused by continued emigration, for example in fears of a 'brain drain'. *JS*

STEPHEN CONSTANTINE (ed.), *Emigrants and Empire: British Settlement in the Dominions between the Wars* (London, 1990).

Empire. See BRITISH EMPIRE.

Empire Crusade, movement championed by the media moguls *Beaverbrook and *Rothermere. It advocated free trade between Britain and its empire with tariffs imposed upon the goods (especially food staples) of other nations when imported into Britain. Dubbed a 'crusade' by the **Daily Express*, the movement contested a number of by-elections: Twickenham, East Islington, South Paddington, and St George's. The outcome was usually to split the Conservative vote, enabling the left to win the seat; but in South Paddington Vice-Admiral Taylor won for the Empire Free Traders. Unfortunately Taylor's success was overshadowed by an uncharacteristically successful speech by Baldwin to the party faithful at Caxton Hall. The publication of Beaverbrook's pamphlet *Empire Free Trade* (1929) elevated the campaign from being merely a newspaper stunt to an active propagandist organization. Between November 1929 and February 1930 the movement oscillated between this stance and that of a fully fledged single-issue political party. It was formally established as a political party on 18 February 1930, disbanded 8 March after Baldwin appeared to concede their demands, but relaunched on 3 April. Initially it received both covert encouragement and restraining direction from pro-tariff Conservative MPs, and one contemporary claimed that as many as 85 per cent of Conservatives supported the cause. Certainly it provided a vein for disgruntled Conservative activists, especially in southern England and the agricultural east Midlands, to vent their frustrations with Baldwin's leadership. The secondary aim behind creating a party was to gain the support of Rothermere. Motivated by an almost pathological distrust of Baldwin, Rothermere was only too keen to champion a cause that would undermine him. Ultimately Baldwin overcame the challenge when Duff Cooper won victory in the 19 March 1931 St George's by-election. Thereafter the campaign petered out. *NJC*

STUART BALL, *Baldwin and the Conservative Party: The Crisis of 1929–1931* (London, 1988). | A. J. P. TAYLOR, *Beaverbrook* (London, 1972).

Empire emigration. In the 19th century most British emigrants settled in the USA, but the new century opened with a sustained shift towards Canada, Australia, New Zealand, and to a lesser extent South Africa. (Few moved to India or the colonial empire except temporarily on business or for official duties.) The total number of emigrants in the decade 1901–10 was around 1.8 million, of whom about half went to the Empire. Approximately the same number of emigrants left Britain in the 1920s, but by then over two-thirds headed for the Empire. Emigrant numbers were thereafter never as high, but in the 1950s, when about 1.3 million emigrants departed, about four-fifths went to Empire destinations, especially Australia. The shift reflected greater imperial sentiment early in the century, the funding by British and Empire governments of assisted passage schemes, and the increased opportunities in fast-developing and economically diversifying Empire countries, especially for skilled workers and young families. *SC*

Empire Industries Association, backbench organization of Conservative MPs in the 1920s, which was the principal vehicle of protectionist argument within the parliamentary Conservative Party. Organized largely by W. A. S. *Hewins, it claimed over 200 members in the 1924–9 parliament, and was a thorn in the side of the cabinet, which Baldwin was trying to hold together by avoiding the issue of a general tariff. Although it included many of the survivors of the *'hard-faced men who look as if they have done well out of the war' who had entered parliament at the 1918 election, it was more significant as an organization of ideologically driven politicians than as a business lobby—a role taken up by the 'peak organizations' of the *Federation of British Industries and the *National Confederation of Employers' Organizations. Although its *raison d'être* was significantly diminished by the adoption of tariffs after 1932, it was still active until the 1950s, under the influence of Leo *Amery. *JAT*

Empire Loyalists, League of, right-wing pressure group associated with the magazine *Time and Tide*, which flourished in Britain from the mid-1950s. The league seriously embarrassed the Conservative government over its decolonization policies. Its role was effectively taken over in the 1960s by the *Monday Club. *JAR*

Empire Marketing Board (EMB) (1926–33). Baldwin's Conservative government set up the EMB in lieu of tariff protection with imperial preferences which the electorate had rejected in the 1923 election, and it was duly abolished after such a system was introduced. The board was modestly successful in encouraging trade between Britain and the Empire by scientific research into ways of increasing Empire production and by using advertising posters, publicity stunts, radio talks, and even films to persuade British consumers to 'buy Empire goods from home and overseas'. *SC*

Employment, Department of (1970–95). The Ministry of Labour was the antecedent to the modern Department of Employment. Created in 1916, it was a response to the labour requirements of the Great War and a reflection of the increasing influence of the Labour movement. There had been a labour department at the Board of Trade since 1893 and the ministry soon assumed responsibility for a number of responsibilities previously exercised by the Board of Trade and the Board of Education, for example industrial relations, labour exchanges, employment statistics, and youth employment. During the inter-war period, the ministry concentrated upon unemployment issues, and evolved into one of the largest departments of state. Nevertheless, it was the Second World War that had the greatest impact upon the ministry. The need to provide military training resulted in 1939 in the Ministry of Labour being transformed into the Ministry of Labour and National Service. In 1959, the ministry reverted back to the Ministry of Labour until in 1968 it became the Department of Employment and Productivity, streamlining to the Department of Employment in 1970. In 1995 the department merged with the Department of Education to form the Department for Education and Employment, a move to integrate the converging worlds of education and training.

JD

Employment Acts, 1980–90. During the 1980s the Conservative government of Margaret Thatcher introduced eight Acts, including the Wages Act of 1986 and the Public Order Act of 1986, which brought about radical changes to the employment laws of Britain and threw trade unions onto the defensive. The introduction of new legislation designed to make trade unions more accountable was central to the new government's economic philosophy, which aimed to deregulate and 'free' the economy in order to achieve the economic renaissance of Britain. In other words, the attack upon trade union power was part of the process of rolling back the modern welfare state and state control which was perceived to be the cause of Britain's post-war economic decline. It was also a deliberate attempt to restore the upper hand to management in British industry.

The Employment Acts of 1980, 1982, 1988, 1989, and 1990, and the Trade Union Act of 1984 imposed this Conservative approach in a step-by-step manner, at first gently through Jim Prior then more toughly through Tebbitt, Howard, and others. To the Thatcher administration these Acts have ensured that all workers have basic rights in dealing with trade unions, but to trade unionists they have appeared to remove basic rights from employees under the banner of deregulation and the 'freeing' of market forces. Indeed, the 1980 Act limited picketing rights and made secondary picketing illegal; the 1982 Act limited the right to a closed shop; the 1984 Act introduced ballots on political funds and for strike action; the 1988 Act allowed trade union members to ignore a trade union ballot decision on industrial action; the 1989 Act further undermined the rights of individual workers; and the 1990 Act further attacked closed shop by making it illegal for an employer to refuse to employ a worker on the grounds of s/he not being a member of a trade union. All these measures remain on the statute books. *KL*

Employment Protection Act, 1975. The second Wilson government (1974–6) repealed Heath's Industrial Relations Act of 1971 and replaced it with the Trade Union and Labour Protection Act of 1974 and this Employment Protection Act of 1975. These two Acts gave legislative support for improving the voluntary system of industrial relations and providing the broader employment rights previously suggested by the *Donovan commission and the TUC. There were measures guaranteeing payments during short-time working and maternity and leave rights.

KL

enabler, local government as, concept of the role of local government associated with the reforms of the third Thatcher government. Nicholas Ridley's 1988 Centre for Policy Studies pamphlet *The Local Right: Enabling Not Providing* (Policy Study No. 92) and the Adam Smith Institute's *Wiser Counsels* (1989) are generally credited with the notion that local authorities should no longer provide services directly, but should secure their provision through a process of commissioning from private, voluntary, and other bodies. Their provider role, if any, would be essentially residual. The concept of enabling was manifested in the post-1987 legislation in housing, education, and social services and was continued by the Major government. Despite its neo-Liberal origins, the concept of enabling has been adopted in Labour circles to express a more expansive view of local government's civic leadership role in meeting community needs by orchestrating the full range of available resources. *KY*

energy policy. An energy policy in the sense that it could be conducted in the national interest became possible in the UK following the nationalization of the coal, gas, and electricity industries in the later 1940s. To the end of the 1950s, the overwhelming policy priority was to encourage the National Coal Board to increase coal output through the creation of new capacity. However, the industry's inherent tendency to rising costs, together with underpricing, led to a domestic coal 'gap' which could only be closed by imports. In the recession of 1957–9, therefore, the government began to encourage a movement towards oil at the very time when new coal capacity was coming on stream. Thus, during the 1960s surplus capacity was kept in check only by a planned programme of pit closures.

In 1967, the government proclaimed a 'four fuel' policy for energy. This entailed swingeing reductions in coal output and an increasing commitment to oil, indigenous natural gas, and nuclear power for electricity generation. Until the early 1970s, oil was the fastest grower in the energy sector mainly because of its low relative cost. Major refining capacity was developed in Britain after 1950, both for strategic and for balance-of-payments reasons. In the 1970s, however, the industry was subject to the inflationary consequences of the Arab-Israeli war of 1973 when the OPEC cartel raised the international price of oil fourfold. In response, the major oil importers, including Britain, curtailed their consumption dramatically in order to contain the adverse macroeconomic impact of the OPEC decision. The consequences for UK energy policy were profound: with long delays forecast for the completion of nuclear power stations and uncertainties concerning the ultimate cost of electricity generated by this means, the government was obliged to reverse the rundown of the coal industry. Preparations were therefore made for re-expansion on the basis of low-cost production capacity in Yorkshire and Warwickshire.

After 1979 the direction of energy policy underwent further radical change following the election of a Conservative government committed to giving greater emphasis to market forces. In this setting, the national coal strikes of 1972 and 1974 were viewed as having enhanced trade union militancy and an inflationary wage spiral, to the detriment of overall economic performance. Governmental concerns over the security of coal supplies were writ large during the national miners' strike of 1984–5. Although by that time the supply of oil from the North Sea was the overwhelming factor in domestic consumption, continuing price variations at the world level focused attention on the expansion of nuclear generating capacity. Environmental concerns, however, acted in concert with mounting awareness of the true cost of nuclear energy, to downgrade the nuclear option by the end of the decade.

The policy record indicates that post-war British governments failed to devise a long-term energy strategy. The short-run horizons generated by the electoral cycle provide one explanation, as does the sector's subordination to macroeconomic policy priorities. The deleterious effects were registered in continuing inconsistencies in investment planning and poor forecasting of future energy demand. *MWK*

William Ashworth, *The History of the British Coal Industry*, vol. 5. *1946–1982: The Nationalised Industry* (Oxford, 1986). | D. R. Helm, J. A. Kay, and D. P. Thompson (eds.), *The Market for Energy* (Oxford, 1988). | G. L. Reid, *The Nationalized Fuel Industries* (London, 1973).

Enniskillen bombing (8 November 1987), when a bomb planted by the IRA in a disused school exploded as marchers were assembling for the annual Remembrance Day ceremony at Enniskillen in Co. Fermanagh. The building collapsed on those standing nearby, killing eleven people and injuring more than 60 others. Ironically, the bombing did much to improve community relations in the area and also damaged support for the IRA's political wing, Sinn Fein. *GG*

Denzil McDaniel, *Enniskillen: The Remembrance Day Bombing* (Dublin, 1997).

Ensor, Robert Charles Kirkwood (1877–1958), journalist and historian. Robert Ensor was the unusual but inspired choice of Sir George Clark to write the volume *England 1870–1914* (1936) for the original *Oxford History of England* series. With a background in Liberal journalism and Fabian politics, Ensor was no conventional academic, yet his historical instincts were sharpened by this close engagement with contemporary affairs, and when he came to write *England 1870–1914* he was able to draw upon personal communications from individuals such as Lloyd George. His journalistic expertise and wide, cultivated mind impart *England 1870–1914* with a stylistic verve, range of reference, and acuteness of judgement even when assessing figures whose political sensibilities did not accord with his own. He praises, for example, Salisbury's 'massive wisdom and calm temper' (p. 201). Ensor's sympathies were nevertheless more strained when it came to political extremism, and here *England 1870–1914* bears the imprint of the Liberal crisis, at home and abroad, of the 1930s. Irish home rule he considered one of the great missed opportunities of recent history. Ensor also wrote about the outbreak of the Great War from a distinctly anti-appeasement stance. His point was registered by readers when the book appeared in 1936; one wrote to Ensor noting that 'it knocks the bottom clean out of Hitler's case'. *JPG*

Entente Cordiale (1904), Anglo-French agreement. The agreement of 8 April 1904, negotiated by foreign secretary Lord Lansdowne and French ambassador Paul Cambon, settled a series of unresolved colonial disputes between the two countries ranging from Newfoundland fisheries to the independence of Siam (now Thailand). At its core, however, was French recognition of Britain's control over Egypt in exchange for British support for France's ambitions in Morocco. For Lansdowne, the Entente was a rational compromise, safeguarding vital imperial interests whilst reducing the risk of conflict with France. More importantly even, by extension, it also lessened tensions with France's ally and Britain's traditional imperial rival, Russia.

The European implications of this colonial agreement became apparent when Germany challenged France in the Morocco crisis of 1905. Failure to support France meant risking the collapse of the Entente and would have led to Britain's renewed diplomatic isolation. The Entente therefore entailed the tightrope walk of continually reassuring France of Britain's support against Germany, without encouraging her to provoke Germany into an act of aggression. In this way the *Moroccan crises (1905 and 1911) transformed the Entente from a purely colonial agreement into a virtual diplomatic alliance. Reassurances of diplomatic support, however, were accompanied (increasingly after 1911) by staff talks, resulting in a series of agreements on military and naval cooperation in the event of a Continental war. Arguably, though these agreements were not binding, they nonetheless entailed a moral commitment to France. At any rate, when Germany took the calculated risk of a Continental war in August 1914, the majority of the Asquith cabinet decided that Britain had to come to France's assistance. France was still too weak; and her defeat would have meant Germany's hegemony in Europe. Only now was the Entente turned into a full military alliance. *TGO*

T. G. Otte, 'The Elusive Balance: British Foreign Policy and the French Entente', in Glyn Stone and Alan Sharp (eds.), *Discordant Neighbours: Anglo-French Relations in the Twentieth Century* (London, 1999). | K. M. Wilson, *The Politics of Entente* (Cambridge, 1987).

entryism, the tactic of infiltrating rival political organizations. The concept has been usually associated with the far left and was initially used by the Communist Party as it sought affiliation to the Labour Party. More recently Trotskyist groups adopted the tactic, the most successful being the *Militant Tendency (Revolutionary Socialist League). This group dominated the Labour Party's youth movement and its Merseyside organization, and a number of members were elected as Labour MPs in the 1980s. Its members were eventually expelled from the party. *MC*

environmentalism. Concern about the environment stretches at least as far back as the industrial revolution. Controls over industrial waste and pollution were largely left to local authorities prior to the 19th century, but there was growing concern about the encroachment of buildings and development on the countryside. A private body, the *National Trust, founded in 1895, began to purchase or accept bequests of areas of natural beauty, including the coastline, to protect them from development. The foundation of the Council for the Protection of *Rural England in 1926 was another response to the encroachment of new development on the countryside, seeking to highlight the threat posed not only by buildings but also by the impact of roads and traffic. A particular cause of disquiet was the untrammelled growth of London in the inter-war years and its sprawl into the home counties. One solution advocated before the Second World War was a *green belt of land around major conurbations which would be protected from further building and development. This concept, enshrined in wartime plans by *Abercrombie for London and its environs, was implemented for Greater London and other major towns and cities by the 1950s. Another major conservationist move was the creation of *national parks by the National Parks Act of 1949, where development would be restricted. Pressure to abate pollution concentrated on the problem of smoke from domestic and industrial fuel, emphasized by the London smogs, one of which in 1952 was estimated to have caused the deaths of 4,000 people. Local acts were followed by the *Clean Air Act of 1956 which allowed smokeless zones to be established. With subsequent amendments and reinforcements, the issue of controlling air pollution became a major element in environmental politics, focusing increasingly on the effects of traffic upon air quality in urban areas rather than domestic or industrial fuels. A further dimension of environmental concern accompanied the development of nuclear weapons and civil nuclear power. By 1962 it was recognized that nuclear tests had left ineradicable traces of radioactivity in the environment, while a radioactive leak in 1957 at the Windscale plant in Cumbria was the first to indicate the potential hazards of the civil use of nuclear power.

Sensitivities were heightened in the 1960s on a variety of issues. The collapse of a coal tip at Aberfan in south Wales in 1966, killing 118 children, revealed a still large and dangerous backlog of industrial dereliction. Scientific products, such as the chemical pesticide DDT, once thought of as harmless, were now found to have toxic side effects. Moreover, spectacular pollution disasters. such as the wreck of the oil tanker *Torrey Canyon* in 1967, also brought to prominence the pressures on the natural environment from modern industry. Environmental concerns were given governmental recognition by the creation of a Department of the Environment in 1970 and the appointment of a royal commission on environmental pollution. The 1974 Control of Pollution Act was the first comprehensive attempt to tackle pollution problems by giving new powers and duties to local and river authorities. Marine pollution was also covered by specific Acts in 1971 and 1972.

In 1981, the Wildlife and Countryside Act established protection for a wide range of animal and plant species and two years later another royal commission recommended the adoption of lead-free petrol (progressively implemented from 1986). Conservation issues were publicized by pressure groups such as *Friends of the Earth (founded 1970) and the Ecology (later the Green) Party was founded in 1975 specifically to raise consciousness on environmental issues. 'Green' issues became of international significance in the 1980s with concerns about transnational and global problems. These included the effects of acid rain caused by sulphur dioxide—often in other countries, fears of global warming and the effect of so-called greenhouse gases, and the depletion of the ozone layer. These resulted in growing government involvement in and compliance with international and European agreements for action to reduce sulphur dioxide output, encourage renewable energy sources and to cut the harmful chlorofluorocarbons (CFCs) which affect the ozone layer.

The *Green Party was launched in 1985 when alarm over some of these issues was at its height. For a time, mirroring the impact of green parties on the Continent, the Green Party enjoyed immense publicity and gained 15 per cent of the vote in the 1989 European elections. Although its prominence declined thereafter, it has maintained a presence in local government and had a considerable knock-on effect on other parties, forcing them into a more explicit stance on the environment. For example, though frequently seen as a 'left' issue, Mrs Thatcher took a leading interest in the global consequences of climate change highlighted in the 1980s and the Conservative government passed the Environmental Protection Act, 1990, consolidating and extending anti-pollution controls. The fuel-cost 'escalator' was also adopted by the Conservatives as a means of reducing vehicle emissions and complying with internationally agreed targets. As a result environmentalism has moved increasingly from a fringe issue into the mainstream of politics, marked by UN-sponsored 'earth summits' such as those at Rio de Janeiro (1992) and Kyoto (1997) and an increasing range of initiatives by the European Union. In addition to the now long-standing areas of concern, fresh issues have emerged over food safety in the 1990s. The link between the cattle disease BSE and the fatal human infection new variant Creutzfeldt-Jacob disease, led to a mass slaughter programme in 1996–7 affecting several million animals and the virtual extinction of British beef exports. In 1999 controversy arose surrounding the introduction of genetically modified (GM) crops into Britain, leading to direct action by *Greenpeace to disrupt GM plantings. *JS*

Environmental Protection Act, 1990, passed to strengthen the existing system of protection against pollution. The Act was both part of an evolving process of legislation against various forms of environmental hazard and a response to the rise of *environmentalism as part of the political agenda in Britain, the EU, and worldwide. The legislation extended the powers and duties of central and local government over all types of pollution. These included greater controls over air and river pollution, improved waste disposal, compulsory recycling schemes, and stronger measures against litter. *JS*

Equal Opportunities Commission, created in 1976. It was given three main tasks: to work towards the end of sexual discrimination; to promote equal opportunities for both sexes; and to review the Sex Discrimination Act, 1975 (revised 1986), and the Equal Pay Act, 1975 (revised 1984). *JD*

Equal Opportunities Commission website: *www.eoc.org.uk*

equal pay. For much of the 19th and 20th centuries women have not enjoyed equal pay to men, even for identical work or that of similar skill. Women's work was traditionally seen as secondary to that done by men as the assumed heads of households and families. Women were expected to leave work when they married and had children, reinforcing a stereotype of women working only for part of their lives, in cases of individual hardship or preference, such as widows or spinsters, or in times of exceptional emergency, as in the two world wars. Although equal pay was part of the agenda of 19th-century feminists and received support from the TUC as early as 1888, there was little progress. Lobbying by women teachers and civil servants resulted in a royal commission on the civil service recommending equal pay for equal work in 1914, but it was not implemented.

The high wages received by women during the Great War proved only temporary and with the onset of mass unemployment women's claims for equal pay were given low priority. Recommendations by the Commons for equal pay for female civil servants were vetoed in 1936, as were proposals in 1944 for equal pay for women teachers. Another royal commission appointed by Churchill in 1944 was effectively neutered by not being allowed to make any positive recommendations under wartime conditions. Nonetheless, the equal pay issue was pursued by feminists in the Equal Pay Campaign Committee and a trade union coordinating committee on equal pay. By 1949 the Labour Party programme proposed equal pay and was supported by the TUC annual conference in 1951. In 1954 two petitions to parliament for equal pay, and the knowledge that Labour was likely to implement equal pay if elected, led the Conservatives to introduce equal pay in the public sector.

But equal pay remained unusual in private industry until Barbara Castle took up the issue when raised by striking women workers at the Ford plant at Dagenham in 1969. This led to the Equal Pay Act of 1970, ensuring women equal pay for 'the same or broadly similar work'. Further legislation followed in 1984 as an amendment to the Sex Discrimination Act of 1975, bringing UK equal pay legislation into line with European Community regulations by assuring women equal pay for work of equal value. In spite of the legislation, studies continue to show considerable disparities in the actual earnings of men and women. These reflect the distribution of the female workforce in low-paid sectors of employment, often in part-time work, and usually with lower levels of unionization than male workers. The Minimum Wage Legislation of 1999 was intended to assist many low-paid women workers to achieve higher wage rates. *JS*

Michael Rubenstein, *Equal Pay for Work of Equal Value* (London, 1984).

Erroll, Frederick James (1914–2000), Conservative politician. Elected to parliament in 1945, Erroll's industrial experience shaped a ministerial career that began at supply in 1955. Between spells at trade, he was economic secretary to the Treasury, 1958–9, and entered Macmillan's cabinet as president of the Board of Trade in 1961. He supported his friend Maudling during the 1963 leadership battle, but served in Douglas-Home's cabinet as minister for power. He stood down after the 1964 election, taking a hereditary barony. *RJS*

Erskine-Hill, Alexander (1894–1947), lawyer and Conservative politician. After an initial unsuccessful attempt to enter parliament as a Liberal in 1918, Alec Erskine-Hill was elected as a Conservative for Edinburgh North, 1935–45. He never held ministerial office, but during his chairmanship of the 1922 Committee in 1940–4 it became the focus for party discontent. He led the criticism of Churchill's wartime leadership 1941–2 in a series of public speeches following the reverses in Crete and north Africa. *NJC*

Erskine May, guide to the rules, practice, and procedures of the House of the Commons, named after a 19th-century Clerk of the House, Sir Thomas Erskine May. The first edition appeared in 1844 and it is revised every few years subsequently under the editorship of the Clerk of the House. Rulings based on *Erskine May* are accepted as definitive and the Speaker, or whoever is in the chair, will normally take advice from the Clerks at the Table on rulings from *Erskine May*. The contents range from minor points of etiquette, such as how members should address each other, to key issues of procedure affecting what is or is not in order. *PJRR*

Erskine May's Treatise on the Law, Privileges, Proceedings and Usage of Parliament (18th edn., London, 1998).

establishment, term given to the social, political, and administrative elite at the core of 20th-century British political life; usually said to comprise members of the aristocratic, upper middle, and professional classes, and dominating the upper reaches of the civil service, the legal profession, industry, and government; dissected by Anthony Sampson in *The Anatomy of Britain*

(1962) and by C. P. Snow in his *Strangers and Brothers* sequence of novels (1940–70), Snow arguing that any member of the establishment either knew any other member or knew someone who did.

The establishment is deemed by some to be a repository of right-wing political views and thus acts as a brake on radical reform (a view much advocated by Tony Benn), but Thatcherites have argued that it in fact came to support the post-war settlement and was thus equally resistant to right-wing radicalism.

While its members continued to dominate political life throughout the 20th century, a debate exists as to whether the establishment comprises a power elite or a ruling class, the latter seeing the power elite as linked to the capitalist class (see MARXISM). The crucial issue here is the extent to which the establishment has common consciousness, cohesiveness, and ability to act together.

The sociologist C. Wright Mills argued in *The Power Elite* (1956) that the USA possessed three elites, industrial, military, and political, which acted as a single power elite, and whose members were bound together by psychological similarity, social intermingling, and common interest, rather than wilful coordination. The Marxist Ralph Miliband came to a similar conclusion in his analysis of the British ruling class. Sampson, in contrast, basing his work on interviews and empirical analysis, argued that the establishment was relatively open to newcomers and had no single centre of power. Whereas the degree of openness of the elite does not directly affect its capacity to wield power, analyses such as Sampson's suggest that the establishment might be politically inchoate, or at least comprise a plurality of elites. Elitism is notoriously difficult to analyse empirically, as showing that any given elite does not have a single centre of power leaves the possibility that there is an inner elite pulling the strings. However, it seems unlikely that the UK establishment could ever cohere around a simple set of common interests. There are obvious conflicts, for example, between the interests of finance capitalism and the interests of industrial capitalism. The argument that these interests, although apparently contradictory, are a smokescreen behind which an inner elite plots its core interests, demands organizational capacity for conspiracy at odds with both power elite and Marxist analysis. *CPS*

W. L. GUTTSMAN, *The British Political Elite* (London, 1963). | HUGH THOMAS, *The Establishment* (London, 1959).

Estimates Committee. First appointed in 1912 and suspended in 1914–21, the Estimates Committee then ran until 1971, when it was replaced by the *Expenditure Committee. Its task was to scrutinize annual expenditure estimates and consider how policies could be carried out more effectively. During the Second World War a national expenditure committee was appointed, and afterwards the Estimates Committee's role was strengthened and it established a number of subcommittees. The committee was supposed to focus solely on administrative aspects rather than policy; however, after 1945 it began to probe into these wider areas. Its work was hindered by limited staff resources and the amount of information that government made available. Following the reports of the Procedure Committee of 1965, the committee began to reform. A steering subcommittee and one covering supplementary estimates were established. The others focused on economic affairs, social affairs, defence and overseas affairs, technological and scientific affairs, and building and natural resources. However, with the rise of the specialist Crossman select committees there were problems of membership and overlap of work. Consequently the Estimates Committee's membership was reduced from 43 to 36 and the subcommittees gave up their specialist areas and once again became subcommittees A to G. *KMT*

ethical socialism. The socialist revival of the 1880s and 1890s, which spawned organizations such as the Fabians and the Independent Labour Party, reflected as much an ethical rejection of the perceived social, economic and spiritual failings of capitalism as it did enthusiasm for public ownership. The latter, for many, was at most a means to an end. However, with the rise of the Labour Party, socialism increasingly ceased to be a faith to be proselytized, becoming instead a programme to be implemented. The pendulum was swinging back by the end of the 1950s and concern that the means, such as nationalization, were being confused with ends began to be voiced. In the 1980s and 1990s, helped by a growing tendency to doubt collectivism's economic efficiency and to regard it as undermining the personal responsibility which is the basis of an ethical society, ethical socialism began to revive. *PPC*

Ettrickbridge conferences (1983, 1987). Ettrickbridge was Liberal leader David Steel's home in the Scottish borders, and the scene of two significant meetings or summits. The first, during the 1983 election campaign, on 29 May, was ostensibly a meeting of the joint Alliance Campaign Committee to discuss strategy in private. It witnessed fierce Liberal criticism of Roy Jenkins's performance as Alliance prime minister-designate. Although largely kept from public attention, it paved the way for his resignation as leader of the Social Democratic Party (SDP) and his replacement by David Owen after the election. The second meeting, on 22 November 1987, between David Steel and Robert Maclennan, then SDP leader, sought to work out a policy document for a merged party, particularly on the difficult issue of defence. The meeting produced no final result but eventually, after much controversy, paved the way for merger to go ahead in March 1988. *JS*

Eucharistic Congress (1932). This took place in the Irish Free State and was the 31st in a series of international congresses organized by the Roman Catholic Church for the promotion of devotion to the Blessed Sacrament. It was presided over by the papal legate. The centrepiece was an open air Mass in Phoenix park in Dublin attended by over one million people. The congress represented Ireland's Catholic and national awareness and was a symbol of national reconciliation following the civil war. *TWH*

eugenics, 'science' of improving human and social quality by altering the genetic make-up of the population. A eugenics movement developed in nearly all industrial societies at the end of the 19th century, influenced by the discoveries of eugenicists such as Francis Galton about the role of genes in producing the racial 'stock' of societies. Eugenicists were also influenced by *Social Darwinists who were concerned about mechanisms which could lead to the improvement or deterioration of the national character through evolution and selection. Eugenics was immensely influential, providing a justification for a range of interventions to ensure the betterment of the national stock.

Positive eugenics included the encouragement of births amongst the 'most desirable' elements in the population, pro-natalist policies such as *family allowances, free *school milk and *school meals, and the *school medical service. It could also encourage birth control (see FAMILY PLANNING), to ensure smaller but adequately resourced families, more widely available health care for pregnant and nursing mothers, and a wide range of environmental and social improvements in areas such as pollution, town planning, and housing. Negative eugenics discouraged those with 'undesirable' traits from reproducing. Policies such as birth control and, in extreme cases, sterilization, might be deployed to limit the reproduction of those seen to reduce the quality of the national stock.

The first vogue for eugenics in Britain coincided with concerns about *national deterioration around the turn of the century. Awareness that fertility rates were falling amongst the upper classes while remaining high within the poorest sections of the population, concerns about alien *immigration, and the revelation that large numbers of recruits for the *Boer war were unfit for military service, produced something of a panic with the appointment of a committee to investigate the problem of national deterioration, which reported in 1904, and the introduction of a variety of measures to improve the health of mothers and young children. A Eugenics Society was founded in 1907 and the *Eugenics Review* became the mouthpiece for its proposals, including the passage of the 1913 Mental Deficiency Act. Eugenic ideas and the language of eugenics remained a commonplace into the inter-war years, influencing the birth control and family allowance movements, and broader movements for social betterment, such as housing and town planning.

By the 1930s though, eugenic ideas were being tainted by their extreme use by racist groups such as the Nazis. The failure of the campaign by the Eugenics Society to achieve the legalization of sterilization in the 1930s demonstrated the decline in the direct influence of eugenic ideas on British legislation, while revelations of the Nazis' behaviour in the Second World War rendered the use of eugenic language virtually taboo after 1945. *JS*

DANIEL J. KEVLES, *In the Name of Eugenics: Genetics and the Uses of Human Heredity* (London, 1985). | RICHARD A. SOLOWAY, *Demography and Degeneration: Eugenics and the Declining Birthrate in Twentieth-Century Britain* (London, 1990).

Euro-elections until 1979 were indirect, members of the European parliament (MEPs) belonging to their national parliaments, as they still do in some countries. Thereafter, they have been held every five years, almost simultaneously (some voting like the UK on Thursdays, most on Sunday) but have remained essentially national rather than transnational contests and are treated as such by political parties, the media and voters. The low turnout (see Table 1), especially in the UK, reinforces the view that they are secondary elections, more analogous to local than to

Table 1. Turnout in European parliament elections, 1979–1994 (%ages)

	1979	1984	1989	1994	Average
UK	32.3	32.6	36.2	36.4	34.4
EU	65.9	63.8	62.8	58.3	62.7

Source: adapted from J. Smith, appendix on the 1994 European Elections, in J. Hayward (ed.), *The Crisis of Representation in Europe* (London, 1995), 210.

general elections. Euro-elections do not lead to a change of government, although they may offer opportunities to the opposition and to minor protest parties to exploit the mid-term unpopularity of the government, depending upon the timing of the national and EU political cycles.

While there is no uniformity of EU electoral rules, until 1999 the UK was unusual in using 'first past the post' (except in Northern Ireland), rather than some form of proportional representation. There is little transnational campaigning by the major-party EU federations (the Confederation of Socialist Parties, the European People's Party (mainly Christian Democrat), and the Federation of European Liberals, Democrats, and Reformers), their rather bland manifestos being guidelines rather than substitutes for national manifestos preoccupied with national issues. The candidates selected by parties tend to be successful local politicians who have failed to be selected or to win national elections, or those who have lost their seats, a composition not calculated to promote the standing of the European parliament.

Because of the electoral system used in Britain until 1999 and the tendency of voters in mid-term elections to register their disenchantment with government, the results of the four elections shown in Table 2 indicate the decline in support for the Conservative Party from 1979 and the rise in the Labour vote, disproportionately reflected in the massive switch in seats. The Green Party won 14.9 per cent of the vote in 1989 without securing any seats. Despite the increase in the powers of the European parliament, there is little sign that the hope that direct elections would arouse cross-national public electoral support for the EU will materialize for the foreseeable future, especially in Britain. *JH*

D. Butler and M. Westlake, *British Politics and European Elections, 1994* (London, 1995). | J. Lodge (ed.), *The 1994 Elections to the European Parliament* (London, 1996). | J. Smith, *Citizens' Europe? The European Elections and the Role of the European Parliament* (Royal Institute of International Affairs, London, 1994).

European Coal and Steel Community (ECSC). On 9 May 1950, the French foreign minister, Robert Schuman, called for the pooling of Franco-German production of coal and steel to establish common foundations for economic development as the first step in the federation of Europe. This Schuman plan was the basis of the ECSC whose membership was comprised of 'the Six' (Belgium, France, Italy, Luxembourg, the Netherlands, and West Germany). With its supranational structures and its mixture of free market and dirigiste economic policies, the ECSC was the founding stone of the European Union. Whilst Britain was invited to join the ECSC, it has been suggested that the offer was not serious and that the Labour government's rejection fulfilled French hopes. The ECSC's supranationalism clashed with British priorities in 1950, signalling the parting of the ways between Britain and the Six which was widened when Britain failed to accept the *Messina conference proposals in 1955. *JRVE*

European Communities Act, 1972. Whilst the Heath government had signed the treaty of accession to the *EEC (European Economic Community) in January 1972, Britain could not formally become a member state until the treaty had been voted into law. To assure the safest passage through parliament, the government drew up a European Communities Bill of only twelve clauses which accepted the treaty of

Table 2. Euro-Election results by seats won and %age vote in Great Britain, 1979–1994

	1979		1984		1989		1994	
Parties	Seats	Vote	Seats	Vote	Seats	Vote	Seats	Vote
Conservative	60	50.6	45	40.8	32	34.7	18	27.6
Labour	17	33.0	32	36.5	45	40.1	62	44.0
Lib Dem	0	13.1	0	19.5	0	6.7	2	16.6
SNP	1	1.9	1	1.7	1	2.7	2	3.2

Source: adapted from T. Bainbridge with A. Teasdale, *The Penguin Companion to European Union* (London, 1995), 187.

*Rome, all EEC regulations, and Heath's terms of entry. The bill was voted into law in February 1972 by a majority of eight. *JRVE*

European Community. See EUROPEAN UNION.

European Court of Human Rights, institution of the *Council of Europe dedicated to the administration and implementation of the Convention for the Protection of Human Rights and Fundamental Freedoms. In December 1948 the general assembly of the UN adopted the Universal Declaration of Human Rights which was a comprehensive and historic statement on basic human rights but created no means to enforce them. It is this which primarily distinguished the convention adopted by the Council of Europe in November 1950 which created institutions to defend the rights of citizens in its member states. The institutions comprise the European Commission of Human Rights and the European Court of Human Rights. It is the commission which receives human rights complaints and decides whether there is a case to be heard. Through the writing of a report it endeavours to reach a solution which is acceptable to the complainant, and only if this is not possible will cases go to the European Court of Human Rights. The court hears the case in public and reaches a decision by majority from the panel of nine judges. Its decision is final, since a case cannot be heard by court unless all legal processes in the relevant member state have been exhausted. The court has become an authoritative, successful, and internationally renowned institution. It provides a public service which is not offered by the institutions of the EU, whose legal body, the Court of Justice, deals purely with the interpretation and application of European Community law. The work and influence of the European Court of Human Rights has grown as the Council of Europe has increased the range of its human rights activities by amendments to the 1950 convention and the creation of new conventions, such as the 1989 convention on torture and punishment. *JRVE*

European Defence Community (EDC), pact between the original six members of the European Union, agreed in 1952 to accommodate American demands for West German rearmament but never implemented because of French unease about German rearmament under any circumstances and concern about the lack of British involvement. The void was filled by the Western European Union created in 1954 (firmly based on intergovernmental rather than supranational lines). *JR*

EDWARD FURSON, *The European Defence Community: A History* (London, 1980).

European Free Trade Association (EFTA), an economic organization established by the Stockholm convention of May 1960. Located in Geneva, EFTA was originally designed to foster trade between those European countries who were not members of the European Economic Community (EEC). It has only one institution, the EFTA Council, which holds ministerial meetings twice a year and official meetings twice a month. In December 1958, the British-inspired proposal to attach an all-European industrial free trade area around the core of the EEC failed. This left the British government without a European policy and Europe divided between the six EEC states and the non-six members of the *Organization for European Economic Cooperation (OEEC). Receiving encouragement from the Swedish and Swiss governments and from business organizations, in May 1959 the Macmillan cabinet agreed to the idea of an EFTA including Austria, Denmark, Norway, Portugal, Sweden, Switzerland, and the UK. This policy had three goals; first, to prevent the non-EEC states gravitating towards the EEC, so making that institution dominant in Europe; second, to protect British trade with the EFTA states; and third, to act as a stopgap to a multilateral European organization bridging the EEC and EFTA. From its inception, though, EFTA lost much of its impetus as Britain, its most powerful member, and Denmark sought EEC membership as early as 1961. Their eventual accession to the EEC in 1973, together with that of Portugal in 1986, and Austria, Finland (associate member in 1961 and full member from 1986), and Sweden in 1995, reduced EFTA's membership to Iceland, Norway, and Switzerland (including Liechtenstein). EFTA–EU relations were formalized in May 1992 with the creation of the European Economic Area (EEA) which constituted a free trade area between the fifteen EU states and Iceland, Liechtenstein, and Norway; Switzerland's membership of the EEA was rejected by referendum in December 1992. *JRVE*

European integration, catch-all term used to describe the various processes of unification amongst European states, mainly in the post-war period. It encompasses the fundamental dichotomy between the prevailing form of supranational integration, the lineage of which runs from the *European Coal and Steel Community (ECSC) through to the present-day *European Union, and the non-supranational cooperation of institutions such as the *Council of Europe, the *European Free Trade Association, and the *Organization for Economic Cooperation and Development. In its effect on the government of European states, both at the international and national levels, and on the lives of European peoples, European integration has become the most dominant development in the history of Europe since the Second World War.

European integration has its modern origins at the beginning of the 20th century. The rise of Germany brought with it ideas of imposing unity on Europe. This would take the form of an economic union, or *Mitteleuropa*, described by one adviser to Kaiser Wilhelm II as the creation of a 'central European customs and economic union, a settlement of the colonial question on generous lines, the humiliation of England, the preservation of peace with [Germany's] allies Austria-Hungary and Italy and the containment of the powerful Russian influence' (Stirk, 11). Such plans remained prevalent in Germany during the Great War as a means of perpetuating and strengthening German domination of the Continent, and it was fear of this development which brought more peaceful proposals for integration in the inter-war period. In 1923, an Austrian aristocrat, Count Richard Coudenhove-Kalergi, published a now famous book entitled *Pan-Europa* which called for the creation of a United States of Europe. Kalergi was a critic of the Versailles peace settlement of 1919 and believed that only European unity could save the European peoples from a future war due either to aggressive German nationalism or an expansionist Soviet Russia. In *Pan-Europa* he wrote that 'history gives Europe the following alternatives: either to overcome all national hostilities and consolidate in a federal union, or sooner or later to succumb to a Russian conquest. There is no third possibility' (Stirk, 27). In comparison with later blueprints for European integration, *Pan-Europa* was striking in that it excluded Britain. Kalergi saw the British Empire as an extra-European organization whose economic power would make it a competitor with a future united Europe.

Pan-Europa was a concept which was bedevilled by the advance of inter-war history. It was proposed at a time of Franco-German hostility over the implementation of the Versailles peace settlement and the issue of repayments. Perhaps its greatest legacy was its promotion of European unity and the encouragement it gave to the Briand plan, the first governmental plan for European integration discussed by European states at an international forum. In a speech to the League of Nations in September 1929, the French foreign minister, Aristide Briand, suggested a union of European states with new institutions and in May 1930 submitted a memorandum on these lines to the League inviting responses from European governments. Whilst the Briand plan was stillborn for many reasons, the actions of the British government were critical to its failure. Setting a benchmark for later British diplomacy, MacDonald's second Labour government sent its official reply to the Briand memorandum a day late. This symbolized British negativity towards the plan which at heart was the result of a clash between Britain's global free trade economic policies and France's preferred regional, protectionist policies. This, together with political opposition to submerging Britain in a European organization, lay behind the government's rejection of the plan; similar proclivities would keep Britain out of post-war supranational institutions in the 1950s.

Mutual motives behind *Pan-Europa* and the Briand plan, mainly the attempts to deal with German power in a European economic framework and to present a strong Europe to external threats, lay behind post-1945 initiatives for European integration. Despite its later reputation as the awkward partner of Europe, Britain did not immediately reject Europe but during Ernest Bevin's foreign secretaryship in 1945–8 worked towards increased cooperation, even considering a European 'third force' between the two superpowers. Cold War priorities, economic policies, and a fundamental opposition to the French-inspired supranational form of integration embodied in the ECSC, however, kept Britain outside the embryonic European Community during the 1950s, evolving at the *Messina conference and in the treaty of *Rome. The crucial period 1955–61 saw two vital and parallel developments: rapid and successful creation of the European Economic Community (EEC) and slow and troubled British acceptance of the need to join it.

The progress of European integration since the 1950s has not followed the route which its post-war architects, notably the French Europeanist Jean Monnet, wanted. This was much to do with the indomitable presence of the French leader Charles de Gaulle, to whom the EEC was only a means to restore French grandeur by securing leadership of Europe, rapprochement with West Germany, and power over Britain. The process of integration has nevertheless always been highly complex and greater than the influence of any one personality. Despite crises in the 1960s and sclerosis in the 1970s, integration was revived with the Single European Act. In its modern form (see AMSTERDAM, TREATY OF; EUROPEAN PARLIAMENT) the European Union is the product of 'completion, deepening [and] enlargement', goals first propounded at The Hague summit in 1969 but which have persisted thereafter. Completion refers to such milestones as the creation of a common agricultural policy, a single market, and most recently European monetary union (EMU). Deepening suggests the extension of EU competencies in areas such as foreign policy, justice, and home affairs. Finally, enlargement, which began in 1973 with Britain, Denmark, and Ireland, has seen the number of member states rise to fifteen with the prospect of that number nearly doubling if all current applicants meet the membership criteria. *JRVE*

A. S. MILWARD, *The European Rescue of the Nation-State* (London, 1992). | P. M. R. STIRK, *A History of European Integration since 1914* (London, 1996). | H. YOUNG, *This Blessed Plot: Britain and Europe from Churchill to Blair* (London, 1998).

European Monetary Union (EMU), single currency, or irrevocably fixed exchange rates with free movement of capital and a common monetary policy. EMU has been a policy objective of the European Economic Community (now European Union) since the 1969 Werner report. The ill-fated 'snake-in-the-tunnel' of the 1970s was doomed from the onset as its launch coincided with the demise of the international system. It was followed in 1979 by the rather less ambitious European Monetary System (EMS) which sought to establish 'a zone of monetary stability' which it eventually did in the second half of the 1980s; indeed, Britain was eventually tempted to join. However, internal pressures built up and led to a near-collapse of the system in 1992–3. Nevertheless, by this time, the *Maastricht treaty had set out a three-stage timetable for EMU which maintained its momentum and the third stage began in 1999 with eleven member states participating, the 'outs' being Denmark, Greece, Sweden, and the UK. The Euro was therefore created as the embryonic single currency, initially only as a parallel currency alongside national currencies, but it was intended that from mid-2002 Euro coins and notes would be introduced and the Euro then replace the separate national currencies (which would cease to exist) in the states making up the Euro-zone. The third stage would also introduce a common monetary policy for the Euro-zone to be managed by the European Central Bank (ECB).

The main advantages of EMU relate to the removal of transaction costs which facilitates trade and is particularly important in the context of the EU's internal market. In addition, EMU is also seen by some as a political project, paving the way for European political union. The argument against EMU centres on two controversial economic issues: first, EMU implies the loss of the exchange rate as a policy weapon which, in the absence of alternatives, may leave individual member states unable to adjust their economies effectively, thereby leading to higher unemployment. Secondly, EMU requires a single monetary policy which has to fit all member states simultaneously, which could be inappropriate in situations where external shocks are asymmetric. Thus, for example, a recession in the Far East might affect European economies to different extents (and even in different directions), depending on the nature and closeness of their links with that region. At the end of the century, Britain had decided to exercise its opt-out and chose not to participate yet in the third stage of EMU. However, the pressures to do so rapidly built up. For example, the significantly lower interest rates in the Euro-zone were extremely attractive to a nation in which a large proportion of the population has sizeable debts in the form of mortgages. Under John Major, official British policy was 'to wait and see', while under Tony Blair it became to 'prepare and decide' (facilitating technical planning to join, but leaving the main issue still open), ambiguities that reflected the sharp divisions on Europe in both major political parties. *JR*

DAVID CURRIE, *The Pros and Cons of EMU* (London, 1997). | D. GROS and N. THYGESEN, *European Monetary Integration from EMS to EMU* (2nd edn., London, 1998).

European Movement, all-party pressure group promoting *European integration founded in 1949. In the spring of 1947, Winston Churchill convened in Britain an informal organization of influential politicians and leading social circles known as the United Europe Movement (UEM). Its aim was to promote Anglo-European contacts and the creation of a European community. At the same time, inspired by French and other western European federalists, a similar grouping was formed on the Continent: the Union Européene des Fédéralistes (UEF). The

UEF had as one of its platforms the creation of a European 'third force' and was inspired in this by strong French and Italian socialist factions. Both of these new Europeanist movements developed plans to widen support for unity and in December 1947 they agreed that a congress should be held to discuss what form Europe's future should take and how it could be achieved. The result was The Hague Congress of May 1948 which marked the first post-war show of unity by politicians throughout Britain and Europe and was the most influential event in the European Movement's history. The congress was a heavyweight affair with 800 delegates including twelve former premiers and other dignitaries under the leadership of Churchill. A political resolution was passed which called for a common market, a convention on human rights, an assembly, and a transfer of sovereign powers to a new body, the Council of Europe. In October 1948, the various groups promoting European integration were joined and adopted the name of the European Movement under the honorary presidencies of Léon Blum, Winston Churchill, Alcide de Gasperi, and Paul-Henri Spaak. This body has since worked throughout its 29 member states to raise support for European unity. *JRVE*

European parliament, the assembly of the European Union representing its 370 million citizens. Direct elections have been held every five years since June 1979. By the late 1990s, the parliament was composed of 626 Members (MEPs) who convened in Brussels and Strasbourg and had legislative, budgetary, and supervisory powers. The European parliament had its roots in the parliamentary assembly created as part of the European Coal and Steel Community (ECSC) which met for the first time in September 1952. It was established formally by the treaty of Rome when 142 representatives from the six member states were delegated by their national parliaments. With enlargement in 1973, pressure built up within the European Community to democratize the European parliament through direct elections. In July 1979 after direct universal suffrage throughout the nine member states, 410 MEPs met in Strasbourg. With each enlargement, the number of MEPs has increased.

Originally, the treaty of Rome provided for the European Commission to propose and the Council of Ministers to decide after consulting the European parliament. The parliament thus had little more than a watching brief. With the development of the European Community/Union, however, its competencies have been widened and strengthened significantly through legislative evolution (see the AMSTERDAM, TREATY OF; MAASTRICHT TREATY; SINGLE EUROPEAN ACT). In essence, the parliament has three fundamental powers: the power to legislate; power over the European Union (EU) budget; and power of supervision over the executive. It has control over legislation through co-decision with the Council of Ministers in certain areas and power of sanction over the annual budget and EU expenditure. The appointment of a European Commission president and commissioners must be approved by the parliament and the resignation of the entire Santer commission in March 1999 symbolized the parliament's power in this area. *JRVE*

European referendum (1975). Officially, the 1975 referendum was designed to give the British people an opportunity to take a decision on membership of the European Community after Wilson's 1974–5 renegotiation of Heath's terms of entry. In effect, it was more of a strategy to outmanoeuvre the left within Wilson's cabinet and Labour Party whose leading figures, such as Tony Benn, had pressed for a referendum. On 5 June 1975 the British electorate were asked: 'Do you think that the United Kingdom should stay in the European Community (Common Market)?' A high turnout of 64.5 per cent cast their votes, of whom 67.2 per cent voted in favour and 32.8 per cent against. This had much to do with the great disparity in expenditure and impact of cross-party organizations prior to the referendum. Whilst the 'yes' vote was 'unequivocal... it was also unenthusiastic' and was, at heart, 'a vote for the status quo' (David Butler and Uwe Kitzinger, *The 1975 Referendum* (London, 1976), 280). *JRVE*

European secondary legislation, select committee on, first appointed in 1974 following recommendations of the ad hoc Foster select committee and Britain's accession to the European Community in 1973. It scrutinizes directives and draft legislation after they have been prepared by the European commission and can recommend that approval can be withheld under scrutiny reserve which means there must be parliamentary debate before the measures are adopted. From 1976 its scope expanded to include all documents submitted to the council of ministers. *KMT*

European Union (EU) (1993–), formerly the European Community (EC) (1967–93), an evolving international organization designed to promote European cooperation and integration with elements of pooled sovereignty. The EU was created by the Maastricht treaty in 1992 and has three elements: pillar 1 was the existing EC, which was formed in 1967 by the merger of the European Coal and Steel Community (ECSC), the European Economic Community (EEC), and the European Atomic Energy Community (Euratom); pillar 2 was the embryonic common foreign and security policy (CFSP); and pillar 3 was cooperation in the fields of justice and home affairs. Whilst pillar 1 retains and extends its element of supranationality, pillars 2 and 3 involve mainly intergovernmental cooperation. However, the term the 'European Union' has been increasingly used loosely to describe European integration in all its manifestations since 1958.

The ECSC (1951), EEC (1958), and Euratom (1958) had six members: France, West Germany, Italy, Belgium, the Netherlands, and Luxembourg. The EU has expanded continually since then: in 1973 (Britain, Ireland, and Denmark), 1981 (Greece), 1986 (Spain and Portugal), and in 1995 (Austria, Finland, and Sweden). In the late 1990s there were applications pending from ten central/eastern European countries (Poland, Hungary, the Czech Republic, Slovakia, Bulgaria, Romania, Slovenia, Latvia, Lithuania, and Estonia) and three from the Mediterranean (Turkey, Cyprus, and Malta) of which six had reached the stage of beginning negotiations for accession. Despite its underlying political agenda, the EU remained primarily an economic organization in terms of its actual policies. The centrepiece of the EU is the single market which was largely completed (albeit with notable gaps) in 1992. In addition, there are well-developed common policies for agriculture and fisheries and extensive involvement in a range of economic activities through the EU's regional, social (training), competition, industrial, and research and development policies. The EU also has trade agreements with virtually every country in the world. The only overtly political policy of the EU has been the EPC (European political cooperation) framework (which has been transformed into the CFSP), dating back to 1970, but this has amounted to little more than rather mixed efforts to coordinate political positions; in fact, it has largely failed in its more important applications (to Cyprus and the former Yugoslavia).

The EU has four principal institutions. The European Commission is based in Brussels with twenty commissioners and represents the European interest. Its main functions are to initiate new policies and to administer existing ones. The Council of Ministers consists of one minister from each member state and represents the national interest. Its primary purpose is to take decisions on proposals made to it by the commission. The European parliament is directly elected and currently has 646 members. It scrutinizes and puts forward amendments to policy proposals and has limited powers of co-decision with the council of ministers, particularly with regard to budgetary matters. The European Court of Justice has one judge from each member state and has two main functions: to interpret the EU's treaties and to settle any disputes which arise with regard to EU matters. In addition, the European Council, which consists of the heads of state, meets twice a year, usually in the member state currently holding the presidency, to debate and determine the overall direction of the European Union.

At the end of the century, the agenda of the EU was dominated by three objectives: first, the completion of economic and monetary union; second, the enlargement of the EU to absorb the new democracies of central and eastern Europe; third, the extension and development of the political aspects of the EU, notably the common foreign and security policy. However, there remained internal tension within the European Union between those who favoured the extension of the use of supranationality, possibly to the point of creating a European federation (loosely, the original members and later members from central Europe and the south) on the one hand, and those of an intergovernmental persuasion (Britain and the Scandinavians) on the other. Indeed, Britain's relationship with the EU has always been a troubled one, particularly with regard to the British contribution to the EU budget. This culminated in a prolonged dispute in the early 1980s which resulted in a rebate being paid to the British which still continues. However, there remains within Britain substantial opposition to further development and, to some extent, even membership of the EU. *JR*

J. D. Armstrong, L. Lloyd, and J. Redmond, *From Versailles to Maastricht: International Organisation in the Twentieth Century* (London, 1996). | D. Dinan, *Ever Closer Union* (London, 1994). | Derek Urwin, *The Community of Europe* (2nd edn., London, 1995).

Eurosceptic, a term which became common currency in the 1990s to describe a particular breed of British politician, mainly but not exclusively Tory, to whom the European Union (EU) and often Germany are a dangerous threat to Britishness. In its most visceral form,

Euroscepticism demands British withdrawal from the EU. The activities of backbench Eurosceptics like William Cash and Sir Richard Body largely paralysed John Major's government after 1992, and competition from Eurosceptic bodies like the Referendum Party helped to precipitate its landslide defeat in 1997. *JRVE*

evacuation. The evacuation from the cities of vulnerable groups, especially children, during the Second World War has achieved almost mythic status as one of the driving forces behind the creation of the post-war *welfare state. Faced with the threat of aerial bombardment, pre-war governments had set in train extensive programmes for the evacuation of schoolchildren, mothers with pre-school children, the blind, and the handicapped, from areas vulnerable to bombing. The first wave of evacuation took place from 1 September 1939, two days before the declaration of war, involving approximately 1.5 million people. Many of these drifted back during the 'phoney war' in the autumn and winter of 1939–40, but the beginnings of the *Blitz saw widespread evacuation from vulnerable towns and cities. Again, as the Blitz receded, many children returned to their former homes, though others remained as evacuees for the duration. A final wave of evacuation from London and the south-east came with the German V1 and V2 offensives in 1944–5.

In all, approximately four million children were affected by evacuation, although only a minority of all children were ever involved. The incidence of evacuation, even from ostensibly vulnerable industrial targets, was also very patchy, ranging from as low as a quarter of eligible children in some areas to as high as four-fifths in others. The most potent feature of evacuation politically was the outcry that arose almost immediately over the condition of many of the evacuees. Widespread concern was expressed about their evident poverty, poor clothing, lack of cleanliness and hygiene, and general behaviour. These reactions were alleged by writers such as Richard Titmuss, in *Problems of Social Policy* (1951), to have helped to encourage middle-class support for the welfare state and for the Labour Party in the run-up to the 1945 general election.

In practice, as no detailed investigations were carried out on groups of evacuees, much of the discussion about their conditions and behaviour remained anecdotal. It was sufficiently widespread, however, to be the cause of renewed debate about urban conditions and to contribute to pressure for measures to alleviate child poverty, such as *family allowances. Some reactions, such as those outlined in the study edited by Margaret *Bondfield, *Our Towns* (1943), suggested that attitudes towards evacuees were often shaped by class prejudice, exacerbated by the genuine problems faced by evacuees adjusting to a strange environment. *JS*

Angus Calder, *The People's War* (London, 1969). | John Macnicol, 'The Effect of the Evacuation of Schoolchildren on Official Attitudes to State Intervention', in Harold L. Smith (ed.), *British Society in the Second World War* (Manchester, 1986). | Ben Wicks, *No Time to Wave Goodbye* (London, 1990).

Evans, Gwynfor Richard (1912–), Welsh nationalist politician. Born and raised in Barry in south Wales, Gwynfor Evans grew up in a strongly Nonconformist, culturally Welsh but English-speaking, household. A Welsh learner himself, his commitment to Wales and the Welsh language has been the touchstone of his political life. President of Plaid Cymru, 1945–81, and honorary president thereafter, Evans was a more conventionally Welsh Nonconformist figure than his Roman Catholic predecessor Saunders Lewis. He was Plaid Cymru's first MP, capturing Carmarthen from Labour in July 1966. Labour regained the seat in 1970 but Evans recaptured it for Plaid Cymru in October 1974 before losing it to Labour again in 1979. In 1980 he threatened to fast unto death unless the Conservative government honoured its manifesto commitment to establish a fourth Welsh television channel, S4C. His protest and the campaign of civil disobedience and direct but non-violent protest that it inspired was eventually successful in causing the government to execute a U-turn and implement its election promise. The campaign for a Welsh television channel displayed his lifelong commitment to pacifism and non-violence; during the Second World War he was the secretary of the Welsh Pacifist Movement (Heddychwyr Cymru). During the 1980s and 1990s his concern has shifted to the consequences for the Welsh language of English migration into Welsh-speaking communities. His numerous books in both Welsh and English display his passionate commitment to Wales, his deep Christian faith, and a profound respect for history and learning. *DG*

Gwynfor Evans, *Pe Bai Cymrun Rydd* (Cardiff, 1989).

Evans, Harold (1911–83), prime minister's public relations adviser, 1957–63. On becoming prime minister, Harold Macmillan sought out the best public relations officials in the civil service and found Evans, who became arguably the most successful press secretary, and part of Macmillan's Number Ten 'family'. Working with the government's publicity ministers (Charles Hill until 1962, then William Deedes), he was influential and effective but uncontroversial, although his official neutrality did not survive his appointment (he advised Macmillan on a party political broadcast in 1962). His impassive appearances before the lobby helped build Macmillan's 'unflappable' image. A successful news-manager, Evans established the pattern of regular lobby briefings which his successors have generally followed, and made the most of Macmillan's tours and summits. Rewarded with a hereditary baronetcy from Macmillan and a silver plate from the lobby, he left Whitehall after helping to present Sir Alec Douglas-Home to the nation. *CL*

Harold Evans, *Downing Street Diary: The Macmillan Years 1957–1963* (London, 1981).

Evershed, (Francis) Raymond (1899–1966), judge. Evershed was called to the Bar in 1923 and appointed KC in 1933, but his career really took off in the war years: he was regional controller for the east Midlands from 1942, became a judge in Chancery in 1944, promoted to the Court of Appeals in 1947, and was master of the rolls, 1945–62, and a lord justice of appeal in ordinary, 1962–5. He sat on numerous government commissions and enquiries, and was vocal in criticizing parliament's increasing tendency to legislate in too much detail, leaving less and less discretion to the courts. *JAR*

exchange controls have been purportedly used to influence the exchange rate. The term is often used synonymously with capital controls. They can be applied to the current account transactions of the balance of payments or to the capital account. They have been used since time immemorial but for modern Britain they were introduced at the outbreak of the Second World War, were formalized in the Exchange Control Act of 1947, and then went through various amendments in extending their coverage, and then gradually reducing it, before finally being abolished in 1979. Exchange controls persisted elsewhere and in some countries have been introduced in the 1990s. One reason they lasted quite so long is that in the international monetary system which was designed in the war years (at *Bretton Woods, an adjustable peg system) capital controls were essential to its operation, and this was explicit in the original design. But in the post-war world which was generally characterized by increasing liberalization in international trade and payments, some problems arose when recommendations for 'convertibility' of currencies were made. When the Bretton Woods 'system' broke down in the early 1970s, the case for exchange controls was in some ways weakened and yet they continued in existence. There are always some gainers and losers under controls and the gainers are frequently the more coherent groups who can lobby successfully, which may account for the persistence of exchange controls. Controls on capital distort international trade and payments, and so damage efficiency. They restrict the choices individuals can make and suffer from all the disadvantages of protectionist measures. Currently, there is even less likelihood of them working than in earlier years, for in a world with increasingly integrated markets they have become almost impossible to enforce. *FHC*

Exchange Equalization Account (EEA), system operated by the Bank of England for counteracting, by purchases and sales, temporary fluctuations in the exchange rate. First established in 1932 in response to Britain's departure from the *gold standard, it provided a relatively effective means of maintaining a given level for sterling in the foreign exchange markets. During the 1940s, the EEA managed the dollar pool developed as an instrument of a common war effort to ensure the convertibility of sterling for sterling area members. After the war it was responsible for holding and managing the country's external reserves and for managing the exchange rate. *JFM*

excise duties were levied from medieval times on domestically produced goods, and therefore depended upon consumption or outlay rather than directly upon price. The items yielding the most revenue have been tobacco, alcohol, and petrol. Before 1939, the incidence of the first two was a class issue, since the majority of the population did not pay *income tax but were responsible for most of the revenue from indirect taxation. This simple division ended with the spread of income tax during and after the Second World War. They have been convenient to collect, have not affected family living standards directly, and even though they became heavy they did not encourage switching to other forms of consumption. Moreover, it seemed worthy to tax items which damaged people's health. After 1945, when income tax was high and there was concern about its effect upon incentives, it was argued that indirect taxes were preferable because they were less visible. A high tax on cigarettes or beer should have deterred effort as much as income tax because of the similar effect on purchasing power. Trade unions, too, were as keen to compensate for taxes on cigarettes as they were for other tax changes. What probably counted more for chancellors was to have a roughly balanced set of taxes—direct or indirect—rather than be committed to a narrow reliance on one or the other. *RCW*

U. K. Hicks, *British Public Finances* (London, 1954).

exit poll, a survey of how people have voted, conducted as electors leave the polling station. Such polls are used to predict the outcome of elections before the votes are counted and the results declared. Because of this, they tend to be popular with the broadcast media, keen to anticipate the outcome on the evening of general elections. Exit polls tend to be more accurate than conventional opinion polls. Whereas conventional polls usually survey voting intentions, and therefore have to correct for possible non-voting, exit polls survey the actions of those who have actually voted. They also have the advantage over other post-election surveys in that those questioned are likely to have an accurate recall of how they have just voted. It is also easier in exit polls than in other surveys relying on a quota sample to ensure that the sample is socially representative. Even so, exit polls exhibit the same limitations as other quota samples and, though having a good track record, do not always predict accurately election results. Exit polls in 1992 overestimated the support for the Labour Party, and underestimated support for the Conservatives, though not to the same extent as conventional polls. *PN*

Expenditure Committee (1971–9) consisted of six highly autonomous subcommittees: general; trade and industry; defence and external affairs; education and arts; environment and Home Office; and employment and social services which took over Home Office issues in 1974. Each worked on a few particular projects of its own, guided by the chairman's interests, rather than producing an integrated scrutiny of annual expenditure plans. Additionally, members tended to lack expertise. The committees were superseded in 1979 by the departmental select committees. *KMT*

export drive, the commitment to increased levels of exports. As a specific and coherent policy, its origins can be traced back to 1940 when, in order to earn foreign exchange, export groups were established at the instigation of the Board of Trade. These were coordinated through the Export Council, which encouraged the preferential allocation of raw materials by statutory limitation of inland sales and other devices. Following the implementation of Lend-Lease and Mutual Aid, exports were restricted to the essential needs of other belligerents and to those goods which had to be sold to neutrals in order to purchase essential imports. The termination of Lend-Lease in 1945 necessitated a drive to increase levels of exports in an effort to deal with the balance of payments. The Attlee government directed resources into investment and exports while holding back domestic consumption, by intensifying wartime austerity measures. The instruments of this policy were rigorous control and the allocation of imports by the government to ensure a switch in sources of overseas markets. After the war, export controls and detailed targets agreed with all the major industries were used to redirect production to the export markets. In the case of the car industry, allocations of steel were subject to at least 50 per cent of the finished vehicles being exported. Industries such as agriculture and textiles, which could contribute to import substitution, received preferential treatment. Export licences covered the whole range of exports, sometimes to prevent the export of machinery needed by British industry, sometimes to prevent the export of raw materials required for the war effort. Exchange controls and fiscal policy were also used extensively, particularly after 1947. Exports increased in real terms by 77 per cent between 1946 and 1950. By encouraging a switch in the sources of imports from dollar to sterling areas, the programme led to significant reductions in the current account dollar deficit. *JFM*

extradition, procedure by which one state secures the return from another of a fugitive accused or convicted of crime. Extradition to foreign countries is governed by treaties, given effect under statute. Surrender to Commonwealth countries was originally distinct but assimilated to extradition in stages. The processes were combined and the law consolidated in the Extradition Act, 1989, but surrender to Ireland is wholly separate. Extradition combines political and judicial decision making. The courts decide whether surrender is permissible under statute and relevant treaties, but cannot order it. Extradition cannot lawfully be effected outside the statutory framework and there are safeguards limiting it. Notably, there is no surrender for 'an offence of a political character'. This expression has proved difficult to define: the case-law is reviewed in *T* v. *Home Secretary* (1996). The trend in the later part of the century was to remove the political offence protection from crimes associated with terrorism. *IMY*

Eyres-Monsell, Bolton Meredith ('Bobby') (1881–1969), Conservative politician. Entering parliament in 1910 for Evesham, Eyres-Monsell's political career revolved around the Whips Office and the Admiralty. His most testing period was as chief whip, 1923–31, during which time he sought to restrain the anti-Baldwinite elements of the party, especially from 1929. As first lord of the Admiralty, 1931–6, he defended the navy's corner during debates over defence priorities and oversaw the 1935 Anglo-German naval treaty. *NJC*

Fabian Society (1884–). Formed in London in 1884, the Fabians achieved prominence as a source of socialist ideas with the publication of *Fabian Essays in Socialism* in 1889. During its first thirty years Fabianism was defined by the ideas of Sidney Webb and George Bernard Shaw. The leading Fabians subscribed to a gradualist, democratic, and parliamentary form of socialism. They believed that liberal individualism had been giving ground before the advance of collectivism for many decades, as the state took collectivist measures in response both to the dysfunctions of capitalism and to the growth of democracy. They wished to make more people conscious of this allegedly inevitable process by supplying ideas and principles of social reconstruction to each of the great parties in turn. It was not until they became disillusioned with this strategy of 'permeation' of the established party elites, around 1912, that they began to take the Labour Party seriously, though the society had been affiliated to it since its inception in 1900.

During the Great War, Fabian influence in the Labour Party derived chiefly from the work of Webb who helped to clarify Labour's position on post-war reconstruction and co-authored, with Arthur Henderson, a new party constitution and the manifesto *Labour and the New Social Order*, with its demands for nationalization and the introduction of a national minimum standard of life. The war also saw the first serious secession from the Fabian Society in 1915 when G. D. H. Cole led a revolt in favour of a more decentralized and participatory form of guild socialism. When some of the leading Fabians wrote approvingly of Stalin's Russia in the 1930s, the priority which they had always attached to bureaucratic planning and state paternalism was starkly revealed.

It was left to Cole, ironically, to revive the near-moribund Fabian Society in 1939 and it was at this point that the society adopted the 'self-denying ordinance' forbidding the expression of a collective Fabian viewpoint. Of the 394 Labour MPs elected in 1945, 229 were Fabians, including the prime minister, Attlee, and nine of his cabinet. Though there could be no common Fabian programme binding these individuals together, the society was at the peak of its prestige. The Labour government pursued policies both at home and abroad (in its colonial development programme) that members of the society had long campaigned for.

The publication of *New Fabian Essays* (1952) marked the beginning of a 25-year period when Fabianism was dominated by the Keynesian 're-visionism' associated with Hugh Gaitskell and Anthony Crosland. Important research continued to be done by individual Fabians—particularly in the field of social policy—but as a source of radical ideas the society had lost ground by the 1960s and today it competes with many rival and stronger influences on Labour policy.

JTC

JOHN CALLAGHAN, *Socialism in Britain since 1884* (Oxford, 1990). | JOHN CALLAGHAN, 'The Fabian Society since 1945', *Contemporary British History*, 10 (1996). | MARGARET COLE, *The Story of Fabian Socialism* (London, 1961). | A. M. MCBRIAR, *Fabian Socialism and English Politics 1884–1918* (Cambridge, 1962).

Fair Deal at Work (1968), Conservative policy document on trade union reform. Conservatives eschewed interventionist industrial relations policies during their thirteen-year rule, 1951–64, but in opposition planned sweeping changes. Published before the *Donovan report on the subject, *Fair Deal at Work* proposed a new legal framework for all union activities. Union reform was a popular policy, but its enactment in the *Industrial Relations Act, 1971, provoked furious union protests and proved to be unenforceable.

RJS

Fair Employment Acts (Northern Ireland), 1976 and **1989**. The 1976 Act established the Fair Employment Agency (FEA) to promote equality of opportunity in employment and make discrimination on the grounds of religious or political opinion illegal. In 1989, in the light of statistics showing that Catholic males were still more than twice as likely to be unemployed as Protestant males, a new Fair Employment Act introduced compulsory monitoring of the 'perceived religion' of the workforces of companies with more than ten employees. The Act also gave greater scope to schemes aimed at countering imbalances in the workforce and replaced the FEA with a strengthened Fair Employment Commission. In 1998 the Fair Employment and Treatment Order made it unlawful to discriminate on the grounds of goods, facilities, and services and permitted employers to recruit specifically from and offer religion specific training to, the unemployed. *GG*

PAUL BEW and GORDON GILLESPIE, *Northern Ireland: A Chronology of the Troubles 1968–1999* (Dublin, 1999).

Faith in the City (1985), report by the archbishop of Canterbury's commission on urban priority areas. The report marked a new low in the often fraught relations between the Church of England and the Thatcher government. Its views on the policies required for inner city renewal were famously described as 'Marxist' by an unnamed cabinet minister, although its recommendations were directed more at the failings of the Church's ministry in blighted urban areas. *PPC*

'Falklands factor', overdone journalistic phrase, purporting to explain reviving Tory popularity in 1982–3. Thatcher's Conservatives polled badly in 1979–81, causing doubt about survival, so Thatcher was widely discounted as unemployment rose, climaxing in 1981's riots. Victory in the *Falklands war, though raising Conservative morale and Thatcher's own standing, probably did not turn the tide, nor win the 1983 election for the party, but it did give Margaret Thatcher a new authority, which she proceeded furiously to use. *EP*

Falklands war (1982). Argentina invaded the Falkland Islands, 'that little ice-cold bunch of land down there', as Ronald Reagan described them, on 2 April 1982. Overnight, Las Islas Malvinas were transformed from a postage stamp to a political reality. To the astonishment of the world and the mortification of the inhabitants, plain old Port Stanley, the capital, took on a new identity as Puerto Argentino. Spanish was once again the language of the streets, belying the English signposts. An Argentine soldier reflected afterwards: 'When we first arrived in the Malvinas, the general feeling was that the war—such as it was—was over; it had been won for Argentina on 2 April.' In Buenos Aires, joy was unconfined. The Junta led by General Leopoldo Galtieri had executed a daring and successful *coup de main.* After waiting 150 years they had regained possession of what was rightfully theirs; the British garrison had been expelled; the British lion had been declawed. Prime Minister Margaret Thatcher, the Iron Lady, had been humbled.

In London this impertinence triggered a profound political crisis. 'One felt they might do it,' William Whitelaw subsequently remarked, 'but one never really believed they would.' Lord Carrington, the much-admired foreign secretary, resigned, speaking resonantly of 'great national humiliation'. British sovereign territory and British citizens had been seized by force—by upstart, unelected, unwashed, and unwanted interlopers. For Thatcher, 'the reputation of the Western world' was at stake in the Falklands, not to mention the fate of her government. A hastily assembled naval task force inched implausibly out of Portsmouth on its way to the South Atlantic.

Subsequent events by no means fulfilled Argentine expectations. An intensive round of shuttle diplomacy by the US secretary of state, Alexander Haig, failed utterly—except to give the British task force time to reach its destination. There was a war. It was short and in its own terms decisive. Shockingly and controversially, the venerable Argentine cruiser **General Belgrano* was sunk on 2 May, with heavy loss of life; the British destroyer HMS *Sheffield*, as if in retribution, two days later. British landings at San Carlos on East Falkland began on 21 May. After some bloody fighting at Darwin and Goose Green, and on the mountains overlooking Port Stanley, the Argentines surrendered on 14 June. Some 655 Argentine and 255 British servicemen perished.

Many others suffered, and continue to suffer, post-traumatic stress disorder: the war did something to bring this epiphenomenon to public consciousness. Nothing remained of Las Islas Malvinas but a gleam in the eye.

On both sides the political consequences were severe. Galtieri and his Junta were disgraced and imprisoned: in 1983 democracy returned to Argentina. Britain was not so lucky: Thatcher and hers arguably surfed to victory on the strength of the Falklands factor and a buoyant economy. Diplomatic relations were resumed in 1990, but the issue of sovereignty remains stubbornly unresolved. *AD*

Alex Danchev (ed.), *International Perspectives on the Falklands Conflict* (Basingstoke, 1992). | Lawrence Freedman and Virginia Gamba-Stonehouse, *Signals of War* (London, 1990).

family. The family was the central focus of social policy for much of the century. Social reformers have seen the well-being of the family as the basis of a healthy and productive society. At the beginning of the 20th century a primary issue was family poverty: social investigators had demonstrated by the end of the 19th century that almost a third of working-class households were in poverty, and an even larger proportion of children. Humanitarian concern was reinforced by the large number of volunteers for the Boer war who failed their medical inspections, arousing fears about *national deterioration caused by poor living conditions, amongst other factors. As a result there was a concerted effort from the Edwardian period to improve social conditions for families. The *school medical service and the provision of milk and meals were directed at improving the health of children, while the raft of legislation brought in before the Great War to provide national insurance, labour exchanges, and wage boards was intended generally to raise living standards and prevent interruption of earnings. The acceptance of responsibility for families by the state was confirmed in the Great War with allowances for servicemen's dependants. The extension of state responsibility into *council housing in the *Addison Acts, 1919, and subsequent *slum clearance and housing legislation were witness to a major investment by central and local government in improved housing as the basis for a healthy family life. In a similar vein, Conservative articulations of the ideal of the *property-owning democracy from the 1920s onwards had as its centrepiece the respectable, settled domesticity of family life.

State responsibility for maintaining family incomes was demonstrated between the wars by adjusting dole payment according to the number of dependants. By the Second World War, the advocates of family allowances and a minimum wage were effectively arguing that government had a responsibility to maintain families at a minimum level of subsistence. In its reintroduction of servicemen's allowances for dependants during the war, the government tacitly accepted this responsibility, ensuring a minimum income for families. In the *Beveridge report (1942), Beveridge proposed a comprehensive system of welfare based on the assumption of the traditional family in which married women were not expected to work and in which the major objective was to provide insurance against interruption of earnings. He assumed that a system of family allowances would be in place to provide minimum family incomes in accordance with the number of children in the family. The Family Allowances Act of 1945, granting a payment of 5 shillings a week (25p) for every child after the first, was the most direct intervention by the state on behalf of family maintenance. Accepted as part of the post-war consensus, it demonstrated immediate concerns about family poverty. By the late 1950s, however, social surveys revealed that neither full employment nor the welfare state had eradicated poverty measured in relative terms, especially amongst one-parent families, the disabled, and the elderly. Pressure groups such as the Child Poverty Action Group, founded in 1965, and Gingerbread, founded in 1970, maintained pressure for improvements to family welfare. In 1975 the Child Benefit Act provided an updated version of family allowances, now applying to all children.

Under the Conservative government of Margaret Thatcher there was renewed emphasis on individual and household responsibilities for family welfare and betterment. Strong support for owner-occupation and tax reliefs on private wealth and pensions were seen as part of a return to 'Victorian values'. Universal benefits came under criticism and there was increasing emphasis upon more 'targeted' benefits, such as family income supplement, from 1971, and its replacement family credit from 1988. This, in turn, was replaced by the working families' tax credit from October 1999, a tax-free but means-tested benefit payable to low-income working families with children. Along with childcare tax credits, these policies have formed part of a declared 'family friendly' policy by the Blair government. Growing concern at the levels of divorce, juvenile delinquency, drug abuse, and truancy led in November 1988 to a government green paper, *Supporting Families*, outlining proposals for strengthening family life. The welfare of children is envisaged as the core of the policy. *JS*

Michael McCarthy, *Campaigning for the Poor: CPAG and the Politics of Welfare* (London, 1986). | Susan Pedersen, *Family, Dependence, and the Origins of the Welfare State: Britain and France, 1914–1945* (London, 1993).

family allowances had been long advocated as a means of relieving poverty in large families and were regarded as a significant part of the creation of the *welfare state in the *Beveridge report (1942). The Family Allowances Act, 1945, introduced payments originally of 5 shillings (25p) a week for all children except the eldest. Granted as a universal benefit without a *means test, they were paid direct to the mother, to help ensure that they were spent on the children for whom they were intended. Later renamed child benefits, they were distributed on the same basis, with regular increases to keep pace with inflation. Whether child benefits should remain universal and untaxed has excited much controversy in recent years. *JS*

family planning. Limiting the number of children to what a family could afford to raise properly had been advocated during the 19th century by social reformers such as Francis Place and Annie Besant, but religious disapproval of birth control by artificial means had made it virtually impossible for open discussions of birth control methods before the Great War. Demographic evidence, however, shows that some middle- and working-class families were already practising some forms of family limitation from the end of the 19th century. Groups influenced by *eugenics, such as the Malthusian League, produced some three million pamphlets between 1879 and 1921 advocating birth control as part of a programme for a fitter and healthier race. Somewhat highbrow in their influence, they none the less proposed in 1919 the first British birth control clinic to be set up in the East End, though it was not actually established until 1922. In the interim, the Great War had increased the use and knowledge of condoms amongst the troops as a means of combating venereal disease.

Much the most influential pioneer of family planning, however, was Dr Marie *Stopes whose book *Wise Parenthood* (1918) had sold over 300,000 copies by 1924. Although artificial birth control remained opposed by some influential religious groups, such as the Roman Catholic Church, family planning clinics were developed under the auspices of what became known by 1939 as the Family Planning Association, while, from 1930, maternity and child welfare clinics could also advise married women on birth control. Family planning became a progressive cause too, advocated as a means of reducing overcrowding.

A royal commission reported in 1949 (Cmd 7695) that increasing numbers of couples of all classes were practising some form of family planning, using either artificial means, principally condoms, or natural means of abstinence, the 'safe' period, or coitus interruptus. A new dimension to family planning was, though, introduced in the 1960s with the widespread availability of the oral contraceptive, becoming one of the most common means of contraception by 1970. Liberalization of *abortion also brought into prominence the possibility of legal means of terminating unwanted pregnancies as an adjunct to family planning. The Family Planning Act of 1967 authorized the provision by local authorities of family planning advice to married or single women, at cost, under National Health Service (NHS) auspices, taking over the role hitherto largely provided by voluntary birth control clinics. In 1974 a free, comprehensive programme of family planning advice was set up under the NHS. In recent years the *AIDS scare has focused attention once more on 'safe sex' (using condoms), and concern about young teenage pregnancies has led to debate about the extent and role of sex education, including birth control advice, in schools and for younger people within the NHS. The issues have been highlighted by the availability of the 'morning after' pill as an emergency form of contraception and a high abortion rate of over 185,000 per year in mainland Britain in 1998, with some of the largest increases in the under-20 age group. *JS*

Audrey Leathard, *The Fight for Family Planning: The Development of Family Planning Services in Britain, 1921–1974* (London, 1980).

Farquhar, Horace Brand (1844–1923), Conservative Party treasurer and courtier. Briefly an MP, 1895–8, he became Baron Farquhar in 1898. He served in the royal household, 1907–22; was Conservative Party treasurer, 1912–23; and in 1912 president of the National Union. Late in his life his mind failed, and after the discovery of fiscal discrepancies he was sacked by Law. Farquhar was thought a financial genius and enormously wealthy, but the generous legacies he bequeathed turned out to exist only in his mind. *RJQA*

LORD BEAVERBROOK, *The Decline and Fall of Lloyd George* (London, 1963).

fascism, political ideology on the extreme right with a strong racial identity and a totalitarian approach to government. The name derived from the *fasces* (bundles of sticks wrapped around an axe) carried by magistrates in ancient Rome, symbols of their power to impose chastisement or execution on citizens, and adopted as a fascist symbol in Mussolini's Italy, his supporters therefore becoming known as Fascisti. The generic term 'fascist' was widely applied to all the extreme right-wing movements of the 1930s (and afterwards), though this conceals many fundamental differences between them. It was, however, deliberately adopted in the party name *British Union of Fascists by Oswald *Mosley in 1932. Fascism attributed overwhelming importance to the nation, and sought to explain its failings by scapegoating minority groups that could be identified as racially impure; this was very often linked, as in Britain, with *anti-Semitism, Jews being fascists' favourite scapegoats, and other forms of racism. Fascists indeed often argued that the nation was in serious peril and/or dangerous decline, and used this as justification for extreme countermeasures, including the abandonment of democratic processes (which were anyway portrayed as mere diversions, compromising avoidance of major issues). The creed also, however, exulted authoritarian leadership for its own reasons, arguing that the will of the powerful leader was itself the essential embodiment of national will, and could not be expressed except in action, frequently in war. Fascism in Britain originated ideologically in fragmentary groupings during the 1920s which sought to emulate Mussolini's alleged achievement in rejuvenating Italy. They failed, though, to produce any charismatic figure who could attract the public attention, until Mosley deserted the Labour Party in 1931 and needed a new vehicle for his political ambitions. Briefly, the British Union of Fascists became politically significant in the mid-1930s, but was already in serious decline before war came in 1939. After 1945, when Britain emerged from a war of survival against fascist regimes, it was unlikely that it would flourish further. The post-war history of British fascists has indeed been mainly a story of the fragmenting, infighting, and regrouping of tiny fringe groups. Apart from brief upsurges, for example in the 1960s, when coloured immigration was hotly debated, post-war fascist groups came nowhere near emulating even Mosley's levels of support in the mid-1930s. *JAR*

Father of the House of Commons. The honorary title of Father of the House goes to the member with the longest continuous service. By convention, the Father presides at the first meeting of the House after a general election, sitting in one of the clerks' chairs until the Speaker is elected (or if a vacancy for the Speakership occurs through death or resignation). A total of nineteen MPs have served as Father during the 20th century, including five serving or former prime ministers (Campbell Bannerman, Lloyd George, Winston Churchill, Callaghan, and Heath). Lloyd George was Father of the House for the longest period, from November 1929 until December 1944, and he had the longest total service in the House of 54 years and 8 months. Churchill had a total of 62 years' service but it was broken twice and his longest continuous service was 40 years. The Father of the House at the end of the century was Sir Edward Heath who was elected to the Commons in February 1950 and became Father in April 1992. *PJRR*

Faulkner, (Arthur) Brian Deane (1921–77), Northern Ireland prime minister. Faulkner was an ambitious Unionist politician whose frequent changes of front marked him out as either a statesman or a very adept trimmer. He was born into a typical Unionist family in Co. Down, working in the family textile business, becoming the youngest-ever MP elected to Stormont as member for East Down in 1949. He proved an able and efficient politician, becoming chief whip of the Ulster Unionist Party, 1956–9, minister for home affairs, 1959–63, and of commerce, 1962–9. His hope of assuming the leadership of the Ulster Unionists was dashed when Terence O'Neill replaced Lord Brookeborough in 1963 and he was suspected of harbouring a grievance. Faulkner seemed finally to have come down as a hardliner when he resigned over O'Neill's decision to appoint the Cameron commission into the disturbances in Northern Ireland on the grounds that the result of this move would be to give the impression that reform was being forced from the government. He was too ambitious and important to remain in the wilderness, and after O'Neill's departure he became minister of development, 1969–71, and then gained the leadership of the Unionist Party and the premiership in March 1971.

As premier, Faulkner set as his main priority the introduction of a more vigorous security policy, but he also offered the mainly Catholic and nationalist Social Democratic and Labour Party (SDLP) the chairmanship of two new functional committees at Stormont. Following the deaths of two Catholics in Derry in July, the SDLP stated that they would withdraw from Stormont unless the killings were investigated by an inquiry. Faulkner, who had earlier cautioned against internment as a key weapon in the counter-terrorist campaign, now decided that it must be introduced, and on 9 August 1971 army and police raids were made, but on the basis of out-of-date and inaccurate lists. The immediate consequence was an upsurge in violence. When the parachute regiment shot fourteen Catholics in Derry in January 1972, Edward Heath, the Conservative prime minister, decided that Westminster must take over responsibility for security in Northern Ireland. Faulkner resigned, but he welcomed the March 1973 British government proposals for Northern Ireland and he accepted a power-sharing executive. At the *Sunningdale agreement in December 1973, he accepted a Council of Ireland consisting of members of the Northern Ireland and Irish Republic executives. Faulkner now suffered, though, a steady erosion of Unionist support, which forced his resignation as leader of the Unionist Party in January 1974. In May 1974 a new Loyalist group, the Ulster Workers' Council, launched a strike, and Faulkner, besieged by the strike and given only doubtful support by Harold Wilson's government, resigned on 28 May.

Brian Faulkner was an optimistic man who never inspired trust, but who can be said to have played a role in trying to re-educate Ulster Unionism from its 'no surrender' mentality. He died in a riding accident in March 1977. *DGB*

JOHN HOUSTON (ed.), *Brian Faulkner: Memoirs of a Statesman* (London, 1978).

Fawcett, Millicent (1847–1929), suffrage campaigner. Born Millicent Garrett, and the sister of Elizabeth Garrett Anderson (1836–1917) who campaigned as a doctor for better medical services for women, she married Henry Fawcett in 1867. After lobbying for women's educational rights in the University of Cambridge, Fawcett began work at the very beginning of the women's suffrage movement in 1867–8. A born activist, she also campaigned for the property rights of married women and for the protection of girls in employment—and equally forcibly against Irish home rule and British policy towards civilians in the *Boer war, when she led a ladies' commission of inquiry that produced a report most hostile to the army. In the heyday of the suffragette campaigns, she was president of the National Union of Women's Suffrage Societies, 1905–14, opposing the more militant tactics of the *Women's Social and Political Union. Fawcett retired from active work once the vote was won in 1918, becoming something of an establishment figure, with a DBE (1925). *JAR*

***Fearless* talks**. See RHODESIAN CRISIS.

Feather, Victor Grayson Keir Hardie (1908–76), trade union leader. Vic Feather was, as his full name suggests, born into a socialist household, and he himself became a well-known Independent Labour Party activist and journalist in Bradford. In 1937 he was appointed as an assistant in the TUC's organization department. He built his reputation in the fight against Communist infiltration of the trades councils and played a crucial part in the overthrow of the corrupt leadership of the Electricians' Trade Union in 1961. Feather was also active in the international union arena and is credited with creating a new trade union structure in post-war Germany, which was to prove one of the most successful in Europe. He finally reached the summit of the trade union movement in 1969, but his four years as TUC general secretary coincided with the worst period of industrial strife since the war. Feather was a natural conciliator and negotiator, popularly known as 'Mr Fixit', and he opposed the use of legislation in the field of industrial relations. Thus he found himself confronting Harold Wilson's Labour government when it introduced its **In Place of Strife* white paper in 1969. The defeat of this scheme contributed to Wilson's defeat in the general election of 1970. Although Feather's negotiating skills failed to persuade Edward Heath's Conservative government to abandon its own industrial relations legislation, under his leadership the TUC mounted an effective campaign of non-cooperation which made the restrictive aspects of the 1971 Act largely inoperative. Despite being preoccupied with these conflicts with government, he strengthened the TUC by creating industrial committees which brought together the leaders of unions in the same industry. Feather's struggle with the Labour government did not shake his loyalty to the Labour Party and he swung the TUC to more open Labour support, compared to the non-partisanship of his predecessor George Woodcock. *MC*

Fed, the. See SOUTH WALES MINERS' FEDERATION.

federalism. The notion of federalism has developed in two distinct ways. In its constitutional sense, it refers to a federated political system.

Here federalism is, as defined by Sir Kenneth *Wheare, 'an association of states which has been formed for certain common purposes, but in which the member states retain a large measure of their independence' (Wheare, 1). In practice, following the example of the USA, this has come to be seen as the division of sovereignty between the central and the state tiers of government with a constitutionally embedded legal mechanism to prevent either from impinging on the law-making autonomy of the other. The extent to which areas of sovereignty are defined by the constitution and the nature of the legal safeguards varies from system to system. The USA and Switzerland are examples of countries with strong federalist arrangements; in Germany and Austria, federalism is closer to regional government. In this sense, federalism can be distinguished from unitary government, where all sovereignty resides in a single authority, such as the UK and France, and confederal government, where transfers of power from states to a central government are not deemed to have amounted to a critical loss of sovereignty. In a confederal system, the central government would not be expected to have tax raising powers, and its control over foreign and defence policy, the likeliest reason for its existence, would be incomplete, with states retaining a large degree of autonomy over the use of force. By these definitions, the European Union would seem to be a developing confederal, rather than a federal, system. An alternative understanding of federalism, derived in part from the work of the 'English pluralists' G. D. H. Cole, J. N. Figgis, and Harold Laski, sees federalism as an organizational form which uses institutions, structures, and political culture to ensure political diversity, through a series of checks, balances, and decentralizations in general and a strong local government in particular. Thus, it has a lot in common with the practice of subsidiarity underpinning the German federal state. The institutional framework needed to underpin this organizational form need not involve federation and is therefore compatible with what might otherwise be seen as a unitary state. Indeed, this view of political organization dissolves the notion of a unitary state embodying sovereignty. Instead, the potential power of the state is seen as something threatening the pluralist nature of society. *CPS*

K. C. Wheare, *Federal Government* (4th edn., London, 1963).

Federation of British Industries (FBI), founded in 1916 as a representative organization of industrial producers, under the leadership of Dudley *Docker of Metropolitan Carriage and Wagon Co. and Vincent Caillard of Vickers Ltd. Docker, Caillard, and their fellow manufacturers of munitions and other heavy engineering goods were anxious to defend the position of manufacturers against increasing government control during the Great War. The FBI espoused tariff protection, export cartels, and the establishment of a ministry for industry (which it expected to influence). It favoured tripartite relationships between 'peak organizations' of employers, trade unions, and government to manage economic policy after the war. It drew its first staff from the ranks of former civil servants, and sought to become the sole voice of capital in Whitehall. In this it was not encouraged either by Christopher Addison, the minister of reconstruction, or by other businessmen's organizations such as the *National Union of Manufacturers or the *Engineering Employers' Federation.

Between the wars the FBI strove to sustain its claim to be the main channel of communication between industrial employers and the government. Though largely in favour of tariff protection, it was hampered not only by the suspicions of free-trader businessmen and bankers, but also by the hostility of the National Union of Manufacturers (later the National Association of British Manufacturers), made up largely of smaller businesses, which regarded it as too soft on the trade unions and too ready to concede on tariffs. Much practical business was done between government departments and industry-specific trade associations, rather than with the FBI. Nevertheless the FBI was invited to discussion at key moments, such as when it joined with the TUC and the National Confederation of Employers' Organizations (NCEO) to discuss economic policy options from 1930 to 1932, and when it engaged with the government over defence policy in the later 1930s. During and after the Second World War it was accepted as the voice of manufacturing industry, though it could never constrain the actions of its member companies and could not therefore commit them to tripartite agreements with government and the unions. In 1965 it merged with the British Employers' Confederation (formerly the NCEO) and the National Association of British Manufacturers to form the *Confederation of British Industry.

JAT

Federation of Small Businesses. Originally the National Federation of Self-Employed and

Small Businesses, the Federation of Small Businesses is the principal organization representing smaller firms in Britain. In 1998, it had 110,000 members, of which 37,000 were small traders and 39,000 companies with fewer than four employees. Since its formation when it had the reputation of being an 'outsider' group, it has shifted towards an 'insider' strategy of influencing government policy through well-argued policy papers. *WG*

Fellowes, Robert (1941–), private secretary to Elizabeth II, 1990–9. He grew up on the royal estate at Sandringham as the son of the land agent and married a daughter of the 8th earl Spencer, who also grew up in the neighbourhood. He arrived at Buckingham palace as assistant private secretary in 1977, via Eton, the Scots Guards, and a brokerage in the City. Thus, cocooned in the establishment, he was caught unawares by the world of media manipulation and Thatcherite rebellion from the status quo that hit the palace with such force in the 1990s and adversely affected the monarchy's popularity. He had uneasy relations with his sister-in-law, Diana, Princess of Wales, and with younger members of the royal family whose conspicuous consumption turned many habitual monarchists into critics of the cost of the throne. The queen, however, remained devoted to him. As she pointed out at his retirement, he was the only private secretary she had held in her arms—when he was a baby. *WMK*

feminism is concerned with advancing the place of women in society, who, it is held, have been excluded from fair share of its benefits due to their gender alone. Feminism originated in the 18th century under the influence of the Enlightenment, and was taken up by advocates such as John Stuart Mill, though the first significant feminine voices in Britain were heard in the early 20th century, as the *suffragette movement led by Mrs Pankhurst succeeded in drawing attention to the exclusion of women from participation in political life. But the idea is not narrowly political: feminists have moved the debate on to other questions, such as, is there in the state a fundamental sexism that sets itself against a woman's right to be a person and to be in control of her own destiny? Does pornography degrade women? Are women automatically seen by men as inferior, even if they are in theory equal before the law, and have equal rights in work and career opportunities? Those who feel that women can never get equal treatment from men sometimes advocate a whole separate state in society for women. They hold that men will always think that women must derive their status from their relationship with men, and so such relationships must be severed. In politics, socialists have argued that the problem lies in the capitalist system which forces women to be a kind of underclass, tied to family life, or certain kinds of work. This belief calls for political action to end this system, and in Marxist thought it is held that the Marxist system, once established, will bring about the end of discrimination against women. The debate moves to the biological question: are women essentially different from men because of their childbearing capacity, their different physical strength, and the like? Feminists would deny this, and of course modern science can allow women to bear children without a male partner, and thus women can live together without being childless. Politicians are wary of either endorsing or rejecting feminist claims. New Labour points out that it has more female MPs (labelled 'Blair's Babes' by the popular press) than any other party. This, feminists would say, is to miss the point. *DGB*

Simone de Beauvoir, *The Second Sex* (London, 1953). | Barbara Caine, *English Feminism, 1780–1980* (Oxford, 1997).

Fianna Fáil, Irish political party. In May 1926, Eamon de Valera formed Fianna Fáil, or 'soldiers of Ireland', following his break from Sinn Fein over the issue of abstention from the Irish parliament. Fianna Fáil took its seats in parliament in 1927 and formed the government in Eire, 1932–48. Between 1948 and 1957, it alternated in government with anti-Fianna Fáil coalitions but began another sixteen-year period in office in 1957. De Valera retired from office in 1959 and was replaced by Sean Lemass, leader until 1966. Jack Lynch, 1966–79, succeeded him but was hampered by party divisions over Northern Ireland; Charles Haughey, 1979–90, was implicated in supplying weapons to Northern Ireland in 1970; Albert Reynolds, 1990–4, played a key role in the Northern Ireland peace process; and Bertie Ahern, 1994– , negotiated the Belfast agreement in 1998. *TWH*

Richard Dunphy, *The Making of Fianna Fail Power in Ireland 1923–1948* (Oxford, 1995).

Field, Frank (1942–), Labour politician. After directing the Child Poverty Action Group he became Labour MP for Birkenhead in 1979. As minister of state for welfare reform from 1997, he contributed to the 1998 green paper *A New Contract for Welfare*. A strong supporter of 'welfare to work', he disliked dependency and encouraged lone mothers and the disabled to work, opposing the means-testing of welfare benefits because it encouraged fraud, but recognizing that universal welfare provision could only survive if voters supported it out of self-interest. An iconoclastic thinker on welfare policy, he became frustrated and left office in 1998. *BJE*

Figgures, Frank Edward (1910–90). Having joined the Treasury in 1946, Figgures began a distinguished career in international economic relations as director of trade and finance at the *Organization for European Economic Cooperation in 1948–51. He later followed his involvement in the free trade area proposals of the 1950s by becoming first secretary-general of the *European Free Trade Association in 1960–5. Latterly internal disputes were to make this an unhappy position. He was to suffer similar problems when serving at the height of Heath-style corporatism as director-general of the National Economic Development Office, 1971–3, and as first and only chairman of the Pay Board, 1973–4, which was wound up by the incoming Labour government. His publication of statistics on miners' pay (the 'Figgures figures') also helped to undermine Heath's government during the February 1974 election. *PPC*

'filling the cup', policy adopted by the *Campbell-Bannerman government in face of obstruction by the House of Lords, 1906–8. Rather than abandon their programme the Liberals would keep passing measures in the elected Commons and send them to the Lords, where, if they continued to be wrecked, the Lords themselves would 'fill the cup'—the case for reform of the upper house which duly overflowed in 1910–11. *JAR*

Financial Facilities, Committee on, appointed by the government in November 1917 to consider the provision of financial facilities for the resumption of trade following the war. Unlike its better known and more influential counterpart the Cunliffe Committee, the majority of its members were from industry and commerce. Chaired by Vassar-Smith, its 1918 report similarly recommended the restoration of the gold standard, an end to state borrowing, and a reduction in wartime credit inflation. *JFM*

Financial Management Initiative. See RAYNER SCRUTINIES AND FINANCIAL MANAGEMENT INITIATIVE.

Finer, Samuel Edward (1915–93), political scientist. In an academic world where prudent specialization has tended increasingly to predominate, Sammy Finer stood out for his imaginative breadth of conception and the panache of his execution. His swashbuckling style expressed innovative thoughts and stimulated those of others. He was a key figure in the British political science of the second half of the century, his work on interest groups, the military, and adversary politics, as well as more generally on comparative politics, being especially influential. The rapturous reception of his posthumous *The History of Government from the Earliest Times* (1997) was a recognition of the breathtaking boldness of his conception of comparison and of his sustained focus upon the core activities of government.

At the beginning and end of his career in Oxford, Finer devoted much attention to British government. *The Life and Times of Sir Edwin Chadwick* (1952) was a penetrating study of Benthamism applied to the reform of Victorian administration and public policy, following on from his *A Primer of Public Administration* (1950). Installed as the professor of political institutions in the new Keele University, in 1954 he published *Local Government in England and Wales* (with Lord Radcliffe-Maud). However, he broke new ground with his study of lobbying *interest groups in *Anonymous Empire* (1958), discussed analytically and not through descriptive case studies, many of which followed in the wake of his pioneering work. Having in 1956 published a celebrated article on 'The Individual Responsibility of Ministers', debunking the view that British ministers resigned whenever they seriously blundered, Finer collaborated in *Backbench Opinion in the House of Commons* (1961), a methodologically innovative if controversial book. After studying the political role of the military (*The Man on Horseback*, 1962) and publishing a frequently reprinted textbook (*Comparative Government*, 1970), Finer returned to British concerns in *Adversary Politics and Electoral Reform* (1975) and *The Changing British Party System, 1945–1979* (1980). In the latter, he argued that the party system had become dysfunctional, leading to an 'elective autocracy' requiring primary elections, the referendum, and popular initiative to open up the 'closed shop for party politicians' (pp. 229, 212). *JH*

S. E. Finer, *The Changing British Party System, 1945–1979*, American Enterprise Institute (Washington, 1980). | S. E. Finer, *The History of Government from the Earliest Times*, 3 vols. (Oxford, 1997). | *Government and Opposition*, 29/5 (1994), special issue on S. E. Finer.

Finer report (1974), investigated the rise of one-parent families and identified their tendency to low incomes and housing difficulties. It advocated the creation of family courts. It particularly argued that lone parents should not be forced to work and instead should be given a guaranteed maintenance allowance. This would be sufficiently flexible to allow part-time work and provide a reasonable income. In contrast to the Child Support Act of 1991, it saw maintenance from absent fathers as less important. *KMT*

Finlay, Robert Bannatyne (1842–1929), lawyer and Conservative MP. Trained first as a physician, Finlay became a distinguished barrister. He entered parliament in 1885, was attorney-general under Salisbury and Balfour (1900–5), and was much respected in Tory councils. Finlay provided Law with a legal case when he considered amending the Mutiny Act in 1914. In 1916 he became lord chancellor in Lloyd George's coalition and during 1921–8 was a judge of the International Court of Justice at the Hague. *RJQA*

first past the post, popular name used for the system of election in which the candidate winning the largest number of votes is declared elected, there being no requirement that a winning candidate achieves an absolute majority of the votes. This system has been used consistently, though not universally, for elections in the UK (to the House of Commons, local government, and—from 1979 to 1999—the European parliament). The system has the advantage of simplicity: it is easy to understand. It is also transparent: electors can see what happens to their votes. Critics argue that the system results in some candidates being elected on a minority of the votes cast and that there is not a close relationship between the proportion of votes cast for the candidates of one party and the seats won by that party in the Commons. *PN*

P. Dunleavy, Helen Margetts, Brendan O'Duffy, and Stuart Weir, *Making Votes Count* (Colchester, 1998). | Lord Norton of Louth, *Power to the People: The Case for Retaining our Voting System* (London, 1998).

First World War. See Great War.

Fisher, Herbert Albert Laurens (1856–1940), historian and Liberal politician. Educated at Winchester and Oxford, H. A. L. Fisher taught history at Oxford before becoming vice-chancellor of Sheffield University, 1912–16. He was then recruited to government by Lloyd George and was president of the Board of Education, 1916–22, where he introduced the Education Act, 1918, as part of Lloyd George's scheme of post-war *reconstruction. Principally known for raising the school-leaving age to 14, its plans for 'continuing education' for 14–18-year-olds were shelved because of economic difficulties. Fisher was MP for Sheffield, Hallam, 1916–18, and for the combined English Universities, 1918–26. *JS*

Fisher, John Arbuthnot (1841–1920), naval administrator and reformer. As first sea lord, 1904–10, Fisher prepared the Royal Navy for war against Germany by effecting a revolution in warship design, introducing the *Dreadnought class of battleships and the battlecruiser. Recalled from retirement in 1914, his resignation the following May over the conduct of the *Gallipoli campaign contributed to the political crisis which resulted in the formation of Asquith's coalition government. *JMB*

Ruddock Mackay, *Fisher of Kilverston* (Oxford, 1973).

Fisher, (Norman Fenwick) Warren (1879–1948), head of the civil service, 1919–39. Fisher was a dominant and controversial figure in inter-war Whitehall, serving as permanent secretary to the Treasury and head of the civil service for twenty years, and doing more than anyone else to modernize and unify the civil service in the years after the Great War. Educated at Winchester and Oxford, his early career was in the Inland Revenue, and he won prominence for his work with the national health insurance commission in 1912–13. He owed his appointment as the first 'head of the civil service' to Lloyd George's patronage. Fisher did not play a significant role as an economic or financial policy adviser between the wars, but introduced important reforms to the system of Treasury control and entrenched its power as the central department of government. He played a leading part in the reorganization of the civil service, key threads in its development in the 20th century leading back to him, including the system of civil service classes (administrative, executive, and clerical), the philosophy of the generalist (Fisher controlled top appointments and switched senior officials between departments on what he called the 'musical chairs' principle), and the designation of permanent secretaries as accounting officers responsible for economy in departmental management and spending. He also operated as a wide-ranging policy adviser to successive prime ministers and was particularly active in defence planning and foreign policy in the 1930s. *KT*

Eunan O'Halpin, *Head of the Civil Service: A Study of Sir Warren Fisher* (London, 1989).

Fisher, Victor (1870–1954), journalist and political organizer. Of middle-class antecedents, Fisher joined the Fabian Society and later the Social Democratic Federation, but abandoned socialism in 1914, opposed to its pacifism. With the support of Lord Milner, he formed the British Workers' League to challenge the Labour Party as a suitable organization for patriotic working men. In 1918, this became the National Democratic Party (Fisher was an unsuccessful parliamentary candidate in 1918 and 1923) which supported Lloyd George's peacetime coalition. *RJQA*

Fisher Education Act. See EDUCATION ACT, 1918.

Fitt, Gerard (1926–), Northern Ireland politician and civil rights leader. Gerry Fitt, already a Stormont MP in Ulster, rose to prominence in Britain after the 1966 general election in which he stood as a Republican Labour candidate, winning the Westminster seat of West Belfast. He immediately breached the convention that Ulster's domestic affairs could not be raised in parliament, describing discrimination against Catholics in the province. He and a number of backbench Labour MPs founded the Campaign for Democracy in Ulster at Westminster to demand civil rights for Northern Ireland's Catholics. Fitt was a founder and leader of the mainly Catholic *Social and Democratic Labour Party (SDLP) set up in 1970 and, during the brief life of the power-sharing executive in Northern Ireland in 1974, he was deputy chief executive. He was always an implacable foe of the Provisional IRA, some of whom attacked his home in 1976. In 1979 Fitt, who believed in dialogue with Unionists, resigned as SDLP leader after his party opposed proposals for a new devolutionary solution to the province's problems. He was created a life peer in 1983. *PR*

W. D. FLACKES, *Northern Ireland: A Political Directory 1968–1979* (Dublin, 1980). | PETER ROSE, *How the Troubles came to Northern Ireland* (London, 1999).

Fitzalan, Viscount. See TALBOT, LORD EDMUND.

FitzGerald, Garret (1926–), Irish politician. As minister for foreign affairs in a Fine Gael-led coalition government, he helped negotiate the 1973 *Sunningdale agreement. He underestimated the impact which a powerful council of Ireland and the failure to delete the Irish Constitution's territorial claim to Northern Ireland would have on Ulster Unionist opinion. In 1981 he took office as taoiseach, and launched a 'constitutional crusade' to make Eire more attractive to Ulster Protestants. The loss of a 1986 referendum on liberalizing the divorce law was a severe setback. In 1981 he and Margaret Thatcher established an Anglo-Irish council to consult on a range of matters, and in 1985 FitzGerald agreed the Anglo-Irish intergovernmental conference, giving Eire a formal consultative role—the Irish had pushed for joint British-Irish authority—in Northern Ireland's affairs. FitzGerald's coalition fell from power in 1987. *TWH*

GARRET FITZGERALD, *All in a Life: An Autobiography* (London, 1991).

'five giants', identified by William *Beveridge in his 1942 report *Social Insurance and Allied Services* as the evils against which society was battling: idleness, ignorance, disease, squalor, and want. The original reference was from Bunyan's *Pilgrim's Progress* (1678) where Pilgrim confronts giants of evil and temptation. *JS*

floating voter, a voter who does not consistently vote for one party but rather 'floats' between parties. The term became popular in Britain in the 1950s and such voters were portrayed as discerning electors, choosing between parties on the basis of their performance or election programmes. Later studies suggested that those who frequently switched their votes tended to be apathetic and less well informed than those voters who voted consistently for one party. This analysis has itself been challenged by further research, some studies finding little difference between consistent and floating voters in their interest in, and knowledge of, politics. Research by Hildet Himmelweit and others, focusing on the period from 1959 to 1974, found that consistent voters could easily become floating voters. There is a relationship between party identity and consistent party voting; the weaker the identity the greater the likelihood of becoming a floating voter. Greater electoral volatility in the period since the 1970s has been attributed to partisan and class *dealignment. Though parties have had to work harder to attract the support of a more volatile electorate, the term 'floating voter' is now rarely used. *PN*

ROBERT J. BENEWICK, A. H. BIRCH, H. BLUMLER, and A. EWBANK, 'The Floating Voter and the Liberal View of Representation', *Political Studies*, 17 (1969). | HILDET HIMMELWEIT, P. HUMPHREYS, M. JAEGER, and M. KATZ, *How Voters Decide* (London, 1981). | WILLIAM L. MILLER, H. D. CLARKE, M. HARROP, L. LEDUC, and P. F. WHITELEY, *How Voters Change* (Oxford, 1990).

flying pickets, strike tactic first effectively used in the miners' dispute of 1972, organized by Arthur Scargill, when the unexpected arrival of highly mobile groups of trade unionists from Yorkshire persuaded police to close down the Saltley coal depot in Birmingham. It was effective again in the 1973–4 miners' strike and in other disputes, and in 1984–5 thousands of miners from coalfields on strike were sent to persuade working miners in the Midlands to join the NUM strike, and to try to prevent coke leaving depots or coal reaching power stations. The tactic was this time rendered ineffective through the use of the police on a massive scale, for example at *Orgreave. *DLM*

Focus, common name for Liberal Party newssheets and campaign literature produced as part of the *community politics strategy from the 1960s and prominently used in by-election campaigns. Mass-produced by litho-offset printing, they have remained part of the characteristic infrastructure of Liberal Democrat politics at ward and constituency level. *JS*

Fontainebleau summit (1984), meeting of the European Council of Ministers which began on 25 June 1984. The main conclusion of the summit was the settlement of a long-term dispute between Margaret Thatcher and other European Community (EC) members over British contributions to the EC budget. The dispute was resolved by allowing the UK to receive a rebate on the part of its contribution based on value added tax. The resolution of this issue liberated the EC to renew its momentum toward economic and monetary union. *CRS*

Food, Ministry of (1938–54). See AGRICULTURE, FISHERIES, AND FOOD, MINISTRY OF.

Food Standards Agency. The crisis of BSE ('mad cow' disease) and the growing consumer concern over food hygiene and overall standards prompted the creation of the Food Standards Agency in March 2000, following the royal assent in November 1999 of the Food Standards Bill. The agency was the result of joint consultation between the Ministry of Agriculture, Fisheries, and Food; the Department of Health; the Cabinet Office; the Scottish Office; the Welsh Office; and the Northern Ireland Office along with other Whitehall departments. *JD*

Food Standards Agency website: *www.foodstandards.gov.uk*

Foot, Hugh. See CARADON, LORD.

Foot, Michael (1913–), author and Labour leader. Michael Foot was one of the sons of the Liberal MP Isaac Foot, his siblings (the 'feet') including Lord *Caradon, the lawyer Lord Foot, and Sir Dingle Foot who was solicitor-general under Harold Wilson. His own career took him into journalism, and into a more left-wing brand of politics than the family had usually professed. Foot worked on various newspapers in the 1930s, running the 'William Hickey' gossip column in the *Daily Express* and for a short time editing the *Evening Standard* in 1942. It was with *Beaverbrook's encouragement that he and others wrote the polemical *Guilty Men* (1940), very effectively castigating the appeasers for the way in which they had let the country drift into war unprepared. By then, he was also taking a more activist role, as managing director of the weekly **Tribune* newspaper, 1945–74, (of which he was also assistant editor, 1937–8, and editor, 1948–52 and 1956–9). Having unsuccessfully contested Monmouth in 1935, he represented Devonport for Labour from 1945, but lost the seat in 1955. As a Bevanite, Foot was a keen supporter of Nye *Bevan in his 1950s battles with Gaitskell (not least through his regular *Daily Herald* column), inheriting Bevan's seat at Ebbw Vale when Nye died in 1960, and representing it until 1992 (the seat was renamed Blaenau Gwent in 1983). In a wider sense too, Foot was Bevan's heir, for no other Labour politician of his generation could match Bevan's platform oratory and few were as firmly attached to Bevan's left-wing causes, including unilateralism, while the memory that Harold Wilson had resigned alongside Nye in 1951 made Foot a Wilson supporter whenever the going got rough during the 1964–70 Labour government. Foot's final homage to Bevan came with the publication of a superb (if somewhat uncritical) biography (*Aneurin Bevan*, 2 vols. (London, 1962) 1973).

Up to 1970, Foot seemed a born backbencher, a staunch defender of the rights of parliament and a man unlikely to move into the executive. All that changed with the party's shift to the left during the 1970s. In order to manage a fractious parliamentary party, Wilson made Foot secretary for employment in 1974, with the difficult task of unscrambling the Conservatives *Industrial Relations Act, 1971. His solution, the *Employment Protection Act, 1975, pleased the unions but paved the way for the militancy of the later 1970s and was itself repealed by the Thatcher government after 1979. Foot had not shone as a departmental minister, and was moved by Callaghan in 1976 to the more congenial role of leader of the Commons.

Michael Foot was thus well placed to succeed Callaghan when he retired in 1980, and was narrowly elected to do so. As leader of the opposition, he seemed often out of his depth, unable either to resist or to ride out the party's civil strife and leftward gallop. The loss of Labour MPs to the new *Social Democratic Party in 1981–2, a *Falklands factor that did not cause but helped to sustain Tory recovery from 1982 onwards, and a new policy package for the 1983 election that was aptly described by a shadow cabinet colleague as 'the longest suicide note in history', were all features of his leadership. His platform oratory seemed out of place in a world where politics was now presented by spin-doctors and advertising men, and his judgement was sometimes suspect (for example, wearing a 'donkey jacket' for a Remembrance Day parade, mercilessly derided by critical newspapers). He therefore presided in 1983 over an election campaign in which the party at last offered the left (and indeed Foot himself) a programme that it had always wanted, but produced Labour's worst result for 40 years. Pausing only to ensure that he would be succeeded by Neil Kinnock, then a fellow Welsh MP on the left and a unilateralist, he stepped down as soon as decently possible. Thereafter, Foot was a staunch supporter of Kinnock's leadership, perhaps more through loyalty than conviction since Kinnock led it remorselessly back to the right, but he spent more and more time reviewing and writing historical and literary works, for example studies of H. G. Wells and of Jonathan Swift, radical intellectuals like Foot himself, but also men who had mainly succeeded when staying on the sidelines of political life. *JAR*

football hooliganism emerged as part of a problem of youth crime in the 1960s, associated with vandalism and violence between rival groups of supporters both inside and outside football grounds. By the 1970s, clashes between groups of football supporters had become virtually endemic, requiring a large policing presence at most football matches, the routine separation of rival fans, and arrangements outside grounds for the safe arrival and departure of visiting fans. These measures reduced the number of serious incidents, though violence away from the immediate vicinity of grounds (and abroad) remained a problem. In May 1985 a football supporter was killed in a riot between Leeds and Birmingham supporters, then in the same month, at the Heysel Stadium, Brussels, 38 people were killed and 250 injured following the collapse of a wall during rioting between Liverpool and Juventus fans. Margaret Thatcher condemned the incident as bringing 'shame and dishonour' on the country and a ban was imposed on British clubs playing on the Continent. Further efforts to eliminate hooliganism at football grounds followed, including the widespread use of video cameras to identify troublemakers and build up a register of known offenders. Complacency at the success of these measures at home was shattered by the difficulty of restraining the behaviour of British fans abroad. Outbreaks of violence by English fans at the 1998 football world cup in France and during the European championship in Belgium and Holland in 2000 led the Labour government to introduce new legislation. This allows the police to prevent known troublemakers from travelling abroad. Although criticized by civil liberty groups, these powers were put into operation for the first time in 2000. *JS*

football sectarianism in Scotland. The earliest Scottish football clubs emerged from local charitable and community organizations, reflecting ethnic/religious divisions between Catholic Scots-Irish and Protestants. In Edinburgh Hibernians was Catholic and Heart of Midlothian Protestant; Glasgow Celtic was founded by Catholic interests while Rangers emerged from Protestant, Masonic, and Unionist circles. As religious tensions increased in the first part of the 20th century, football rivalry reflected them. Glasgow Celtic was less obviously sectarian and fielded Protestant players, although flying the Irish tricolour above its ground. Rangers, which never selected a Catholic player until Maurice Johnston was signed in 1989, provided a focus for Protestant loyalty which helped cement the Protestant working-class subculture until sectarianism declined in the 1970s. Confrontations at 'old firm' games between the Glasgow clubs have been controlled over the years by vigorous policing and separation of supporters, while both groups of fans support the Scottish national team. *MJK*

Foreign and Commonwealth Office (1968–). The creation of the Department of Overseas Trade in 1917 was the first of several administrative reforms to amend the functions of the Foreign Office (FO) (which had itself existed since the 18th century). The year 1919 saw the commercial diplomatic service established within the FO, along with its amalgamation with the diplomatic service. In 1934, an economic relations section was added to the FO. The weakened state of Britain in the post-war period and the rapidly changing nature of empire continued the administrative changes; during Harold Wilson's first government in 1965 the foreign, commonwealth, and trade commission services were amalgamated to form the unified diplomatic service. Integration was complete with the merger of the FO and the Commonwealth Office to become the Foreign and Commonwealth Office in 1968. *JD*

Ruth Dudley Edwards, *True Brits: Inside the Foreign Office* (London, 1994). | Foreign and Commonwealth Office website: *www.fco.gov.uk*

Foreign Office. See Foreign and Commonwealth Office.

Forestry Commission, set up in 1919 to replenish the timber supply that had been felled during the Great War, coupled with the realization that Britain was far too dependent on imported timber. Prior to the commission's establishment, Britain had no state forestry policy as such, though special commissions were sometimes appointed and various Acts were passed dealing with the management of the relatively limited crown forests. Its mission at the end of the 20th century was described as being to 'Protect and expand Britain's forests and woodlands and increase their value to society and the environment.' *JD*

Forestry Commission website: *www.forestry.gov.uk*

Forgan, Robert (1891–1976), Labour and Mosleyite politician. Forgan was one of the 'front generation', attaining the rank of captain in the Great War and being awarded an MC. His early political attachment was to the Labour Party, becoming MP for West Renfrewshire, 1929, but he then came under Oswald Mosley's influence. Forgan followed Mosley into the New Party and then the British Union of Fascists (BUF), where he became director of organization and deputy leader. His departure from the BUF in 1934 marked the end of his political career. *CH*

Forsyth, Michael Bruce (1954–), Conservative politician. Forsyth was MP for Stirling, 1983–97, first known as a zealot for monetarism, privatization, hanging, and other right-wing enthusiasms, deriving from rightist groups at St Andrew's University. He rose through the Scottish Office on genuine ability and the steady disappearance of other Scottish Conservative MPs. A factionalist, he was at one stage of Thatcher-induced paranoia seen as the office reporter on the soundness of his secretary of state, Rifkind. Forsyth survived on a tiny majority to become secretary of state himself in 1992, when more admired for astute management than overt extremism, but lost his own seat in 1997. *EP*

'Forty Thieves, the', derogatory term applied in the 1920s by their critics on the party left to Conservative diehard backbenchers with banking and industrial interests. These politicians were generally very right wing, inarticulate, and poorly regarded by their contemporaries. The equivalent MPs in the 1940s were known as the 'Industrials'. *NJC*

Fowler, (Peter) Norman (1938–), Conservative politician. A journalist with *The Times*, 1961–70, and MP from 1970, Fowler, despite resigning during terminal Thatcherism to 'spend more time with [his] family', returned as party chairman under Major. At transport he began privatization of buses, nearly resigned as secretary at the Department of Health and Social Security but his resistance to social services economies was appreciated after the enthusiasm of John Moore. The model of safe politics, Fowler, managing the fight against AIDS, campaigned for safe sex. Surviving 1997 in Sutton Coldfield, he returned as uncle to Hague's shadow cabinet, the family man spending ever more time with his party. *EP*

Norman Fowler, *Ministers Decide* (London, 1991).

Framework documents. Two documents, 'Frameworks for the Future', were released by the British and Irish governments on 22 February 1995. Part I outlined 'A Framework of Accountable Government in Northern Ireland', and proposed a single-chamber assembly of about 90 members elected by proportional representation and serving for a fixed term of four or five years. All-party assembly committees would oversee the work of the Northern Ireland government departments. The work of the assembly would itself be overseen by a directly elected panel of three individuals. Part II dealt with North–South relations. The 'New Framework for Agreement' stated that the guiding principles for achieving cooperative government were the principle of self-determination, the consent of the governed, the pursuit of political goals by non-violent means, and the respect for both Nationalist and Unionist traditions in Northern Ireland. There would be North–South institutions to promote agreement amongst the people of Ireland, which would aim at harmonization in certain areas of government, such as trade, health, and education. The Irish government also agreed to support new proposals to change the state constitution to meet Unionist objections to its territorial claims. The Framework was met with a sceptical Unionist response and an enthusiastic response from the Social Democratic and Labour Party. Republicans sought solace in the documents' cross-border dimension. The documents were taken by all sides as containing messages of change, though arousing fears as well as hopes. *DGB*

PAUL BEW and GORDON GILLESPIE, *The Northern Ireland Peace Process: A Chronology* (London, 1996). | JAMES LOUGHLIN, *The Ulster Question since 1945* (London, 1998).

franchise, term denoting eligibility to cast a vote in an election. At the beginning of the 19th century, the franchise was limited to a small proportion of the landed, adult male population. Demands for change led to the passage of Acts extending the franchise in 1832, 1867, and 1884—after the passage of the last, a majority of adult males had the vote—with further extensions taking place in the 20th century. The Representation of the People Act, 1918, extended the vote to women aged 30 and over, more than doubling the size of the electorate, and a further Act in 1928 lowered the age to 21. The Representation of the People Act, 1969, reduced the voting age from 21 to 18 years. The franchise was also extended in 1985 to British citizens living abroad (for up to five years of absence, extended under the Representation of the People Act, 1989, to twenty years). Only very limited categories of British citizens are not eligible to vote. These include members of the House of Lords (though only for elections to the House of Commons; they can vote in other elections), certified lunatics, and people convicted of certain offences. In order to exercise the right to vote, citizens have to be on the electoral register (see ELECTORATE AND ELECTORAL REGISTER). *PN*

ROBERT BLACKBURN, *The Electoral System in Britain* (London, 1995). | H. F. RAWLINGS, *Law and the Electoral Process* (London, 1988).

Franks, Oliver Shewell (1905–92), philosopher and public servant, don, mandarin, diplomat, banker, provost, pillar of state. Profoundly reasonable and publicly austere, a figure of immense moral authority, Oliver Franks was a philosopher-king with a Nonconformist conscience. Between the wars he studied and plied his trade as a disciple of John Locke, in 1937 becoming (at 32) professor of moral philosophy at Glasgow; but he was not long for the life of the mind, for war service in the Ministry of Supply launched him into a new orbit. In spite of his amateur status—a lifelong refrain—he became permanent secretary. In official circles his reputation was made, yet he refused all entreaty to remain in public life, and accepted the only position he ever really wanted (he said): provost of Queen's College, Oxford, his alma mater (1946–8). He was, though, summoned back to the outer life by his patron Ernest Bevin—an unbeatable if unlikely combination—to chair the Committee of European Economic Cooperation (CEEC, later OEEC, later still OECD) preparing the collective response to the Marshall plan (1947): what became the European Recovery Programme. No sooner was that done than he was offered the plum of the Washington embassy (1948–52), where he played a crucial part in negotiating the North Atlantic treaty (1949). Departing the diplomatic life, he settled on being chairman of Lloyds bank (1954–62) and provost of Worcester College, Oxford (1962–76)—not to mention under-labourer in the college garden—meanwhile developing his practice of adjudication: characteristically, a public inquiry, followed by a report. Soon there were Franks reports on everything from official secrets to Oxford University and the Falklands war. They were improving documents. As for their author, a natural exemplar, in the end he offered no lesson to others except that of a life well led. *AD*

ALEX DANCHEV, *Oliver Franks* (Oxford, 1993).

Franks report (1972), investigated the Official Secrets Acts of 1911 and 1920 which were still in force. It advocated replacement by an official information Act with tighter definitions of what was secret and ending the offence of receiving secret information which had particularly affected journalists. Despite Labour's manifesto promise to fulfil these recommendations, no new legislation had been passed by the time Thatcher came to power and unsuccessfully tried for stricter laws. Prosecutions of journalists continued under the old Acts. *KMT*

Fraser, (John) Malcolm (1878–1949), newspaperman and political organizer. Fraser had been day editor of the *Daily Express* and editor of the *Evening Standard* before becoming the Conservatives' press adviser in 1911. After war service he returned to Central Office and became principal agent, 1919–23, from which position he helped to stage-manage the 1922 end of Lloyd George's government. His report on the Junior Imperial League in 1939 recommended the reorganization carried out in 1945 when the Young Conservatives were created. *JAR*

Fraser, (Richard) Michael (1915–96), Conservative organizer. After war service, Michael Fraser joined the refounded *Conservative Research Department (CRD) in 1946, working there with Macleod, Powell, and Maudling. Unlike these future cabinet ministers, however, he sought no parliamentary seat, staying on at the CRD to become its director, 1951–64, after which he was given a widened remit as deputy chairman of the party organization until 1975, though still retaining special responsibility for policy. In these roles he was for quarter of a century the effective head of the Conservatives' policy-making machinery, secretary to the Steering Committee, the advisory committee on policy, and the shadow cabinet. The confidant of Harold Macmillan and Edward Heath in particular as party leaders and prime ministers, he was able to move in and out of government departments when the party was in power, becoming one of the most influentual men in Britain, though never elected to any post and holding no public position until he entered the Lords as Lord Fraser of Kilmorack. *JAR*

Fraser, (William) Kerr (1929–), civil servant. A veteran of the Scottish Office, Fraser entered the Scottish Home Department in 1955; he was private secretary to the secretary for Scotland, William Ross, 1966–7; assistant secretary in the regional development division, 1967–71; under-secretary in the Scottish Home and Health Department, 1971–5; deputy secretary, 1975–8; and finally, permanent secretary of the Scottish Office, 1978–88. In retirement, he became principal of the University of Glasgow, 1988–95. *KT*

'free at the point of delivery', phrase used to describe the underlying philosophy of the *National Health Service (NHS) as implemented in 1948. It referred to a service in which all consultations with GPs, dentists, opticians, and hospital staff were free, as were all prescriptions and treatment. It was of course paid for through taxation—but by all citizens and not only the sick. Although charges were introduced in some areas of medicine from 1951, and prescription charges have risen steadily at or above the rate of inflation, the phrase is still invoked to resist such policies as charging for GP consultations or 'hotel' costs in hospitals. Others argued that a completely free service produced irresponsible consumer demand and contributed to escalating and, ultimately, insupportable costs. In practice, only part of the NHS is still 'free at the point of delivery', though there remain strong arguments about eliminating those elements which remain. *JS*

Freedom Association, right-wing pressure group, originally the National Association for Freedom, but the title dropped because of the acronym NAFF. It was created by the sports-statistical McWhirter brothers (Ross being later murdered by the IRA) advised by former Communist and Sheffield University academic, Ken Watkins, and young Graham Mather, later of the Institute of Directors and MEP. It fought union power, especially closed shops, during the Foot era at employment. Taylor Woodrow-financed, it backed the *Grunwick lawsuit over non-union labour and the 'Three Clerks' action for wrongful dismissal of railwaymen non-unionists. It also published a vigorous, sometimes shrill, fortnightly, *Free Nation.* *EP*

freedom of information (FoI). The basic principle of a freedom of information regime, is that of a legal 'right to know': a formal right of access for citizens to government records and information. This is related to, but not quite the same as, 'open government' (which implies the generous release of information by government, rather than rights of access by citizens). Britain's traditions of 'closed government' have been buttressed by the draconian and catch-all 1911 Official Secrets Act, the veil of cabinet secrecy, civil service discipline rules, and a Whitehall culture equating secrecy with good government. Pressure for a more open style of government built up from the 1960s and the 1972 *Franks report proposed that criminal sanctions should apply only to defined categories of information, but the Heath government took no action. Labour's 1974 manifesto promise to scrap the Official Secrets Act was also abortive, and the 1977 'Croham directive' did not result in significantly increased voluntary disclosure of background factual and analytical information used in policy making. While secrecy was being reduced in other parts of the public sector in the 1980s (with legislation on access to local government information and access to personal files), the Thatcher government resisted FoI reform at the Whitehall level. The 1989 Official Secrets Act narrowed the scope of the criminal law to protect defined categories of information, but did not satisfy FoI campaign groups who were also dissatisfied by the exemptions built into the Major government's 1994 code of practice on the release of background information. The Blair government introduced a radical FoI white paper in November 1997, but its draft legislation, introduced in 1999, was heavily criticized by outside reformers for tilting the balance too far in favour of government and for the limitations it proposed to keep on openness. *KT*

Free-Fooders. With the advent in 1903 of Joseph Chamberlain's protectionist tariff reform campaign, many among Chamberlain's Unionist allies dreaded the political impact of a policy which would levy duties on imported food and raise the cost of living. Led by such luminaries as the duke of Devonshire and the Cecil brothers, Lords Hugh and Robert, through their Free Food League, these tariff sceptics battled their pro-tariff colleagues right through until the coming of the Great War. *RJQA*

Free Presbyterian Church, Scottish sect. Formed in 1893 in protest against liberalizing tendencies within the Free Church of Scotland, this sect has been mainly confined to the western Highlands of Scotland. The Free Presbyterians are strict sabbatarians and are even opposed to the running of public transport on Sundays. In spite of the prevalence of religious fundamentalism, it appears to have had little impact on the politics of the Highlands in the 20th century. *RF*

free trade, economic philosophy articulated most notably by the 18th-century economist Adam Smith (1723–90). Free trade became the dominant British economic policy in the 19th century and remains, in modified form, highly influential today. The efficacy and boundaries of free trade have frequently been the cause of political dispute and significant in determining party lines and realignments. In the course of the 19th century Britain removed most of the restrictions on its international trade built up in the earlier mercantilist era. The repeal of the Corn Laws in 1846, the ending of the Navigation Acts, and a general lowering of duties and tariffs, created a largely unrestricted international trade on Britain's part. Under the influence of proponents such as Richard Cobden (1804–65), it was assumed that the liberalization would maximize both trade and output. A system of laissez-faire applied internationally would bring universal benefits of growth and development to all countries, promoting not only economic well-being but a regime of peace and harmony between nations. These views seemed vindicated by the rapid expansion of first the British and then subsequently other economies under the free trade regime from the mid-Victorian period.

Free trade began to come under challenge intellectually from socialists and Marxists who questioned the distribution of the wealth created, as well as from conservatives who feared the disruption of traditional practices and communities under the impact of free trade. Although at a political level both the Liberal Party and the Conservatives had come to espouse free trade by the end of the 19th century, there were beginning to be doubts raised about its benefits. The rise of foreign competition and the imposition of tariffs by newly industrializing countries such as France, Germany, and the USA, to protect their developing industries, produced calls within Britain for consideration of tariff reform in the form of protection. First articulated in the 1880s, tariff reform was powerfully advocated by Joseph Chamberlain's Tariff Reform League from 1903. Free trade sentiment remained predominant, however, especially within the Liberal Party whose success in the 1906 election confirmed them as the party of free trade.

Although temporarily suspended for the duration of the Great War, Britain mainly readopted free trade with the cessation of hostilities, including in agriculture. Amidst a widening economic depression, Baldwin advocated protection in the 1923 election, but failed to capture public support. Only with the onset of the world economic crisis following the Wall Street crash of 1929, did Britain eventually yield its position on free trade. In 1932 the National Government introduced a limited scheme of protection and also one of imperial preference which allowed trade from the Empire to escape some tariffs. The rise of protectionism and economic nationalism during the 1930s was regarded by the time of the Second World War as counter-productive. Liberal economists, increasingly influenced by Keynesianism, sought to rebuild the post-war world under the influence of a revival of free trade.

In 1944 the *Bretton Woods conference produced agreements for an international framework based upon the IMF, the World Bank, and the General Agreement on Tariffs and Trade (GATT). As an agency of the UN, GATT promoted the reduction of tariffs and liberalization of trade and successive GATT agreements have lowered tariff barriers worldwide. Within this system Britain maintained elements of tariff preference for goods from the Commonwealth until entry into the European Community (later European Union) in 1973 when these became subject to transitional arrangements and many were discontinued. Membership of the EU implies some restrictions on complete free trade, but the EU negotiates collectively as part of the GATT cycle. Arguments over further centralization and unification of the EU and debates about possible secession from Europe are still conducted in terms of the losses or benefits Britain might gain from a free trade regime outside the EU. *JS*

Free Wales Army, best-known of the fringe nationalist groups set up in the 1960s, led by Julian Cayo Evans. Although it had a core membership of only about twenty, it received much attention in the Welsh and British press, 1965–9, from journalists attracted by the uniforms, drills, and weapons of its members. It was responsible for many explosions which rocked dam sites and public buildings in Wales. Nine men were brought to trial between April and July 1969, and on 1 July—the day of the investiture of the prince of Wales at Caernarfon—six were sentenced to terms of imprisonment. *JGJ*

French, John Denton Pinkstone (1852–1925), general. After success in the Boer war, French led the British Expeditionary Force to France in August 1914, presiding somewhat ineffectually over the early encounter battles and the onset of trench warfare before his replacement in December 1915 by Douglas Haig. French's publicizing of a 'shell scandal' in May 1915 contributed to the political crisis, resulting in the formation of the Asquith coalition and the creation of the Ministry of Munitions. *JMB*

Richard Holmes, *The Little Field-Marshal: Sir John French* (London, 1981).

Friedman, Milton (1912–), American economist whose theories have been influential on British New Right thinking. The youngest child and only son of an eastern European Jewish family, Friedman trained at Chicago and Columbia universities. In 1938 he married fellow economist Rose Director, and although Milton is often given the credit, many of his publications are the fruit of their extraordinary intellectual partnership, based primarily at the University of Chicago. Friedman's career has been devoted to the promotion of free market economics and individual freedom. He was a founding member of the Mont Pelerin Society in 1947, serving as its president in 1970–2. He was briefly a Fulbright scholar at Cambridge in 1952–3. Friedman gained public notoriety because of his popular evangelizing on behalf of neo-liberalism, winning the Nobel prize for economics in 1976. Between 1966 and 1984 he was a columnist with *Newsweek* magazine. A key influence on British New Right thinkers and politicians throughout this period, he published frequently through the *Institute of Economic Affairs (IEA) in the 1970s. The IEA assisted him in preparing the television series which accompanied one of his best-known books, *Free to Choose* (1980), which made a large impact on the popular understanding of the *monetarist case. As a monetarist, he advocated the elimination of inflation by gradually reducing the targets for key monetary indicators over a period of years. His belief in floating exchange rates fuelled the arguments of many Conservatives as early as the 1960s to set the pound free, while Friedman's opinions on a wide range of issues, from negative income tax to free trade, were central to the policy debates of the Thatcher years. *HOJ*

Richard Cockett, *Thinking the Unthinkable: Think Tanks and the Economic Counter-Revolution, 1931–1983* (London, 1994). | Abraham Hirsch and Neil de Marchi, *Milton Friedman: Economics in Theory and Practice* (London, 1990).

Friends of the Earth, environmental pressure group founded in 1971; somewhat overshadowed by the more activist *Greenpeace in recent years. *JS*

'from the cradle to the grave', phrase used to describe the comprehensive system of social insurance envisaged by the *Beveridge report (1942)—though never actually used there. It was originally from Shelley's 'Prometheus Unbound' and was applied to the promise of social insurance by Churchill in a radio broadcast on 21 March 1943. *JS*

FTSE index and **FT-30**, numerical indices of a basket of leading British shares, used to measure changes in the performance of the UK stock market. The FT-30 encompasses the top 30 shares and was first calculated in 1935 with a base of 100. In 1962 the *Financial Times* in conjunction with the Institute of Actuaries developed the FT Actuaries share indices. The most important of these was the All-share index covering around 740 equity prices. Other indices include the FTSE-100, FTSE Mid 250, and the FTSE Small Cap. In 1999 a fourth index, the FTSE fledgling, was introduced which included newly listed and other listed companies not part of the other indices. *JFM*

Full Employment in a Free Society (1944), book by William *Beveridge, outlining the need for a commitment by the state to full employment and demonstrating how it could be achieved. Published on his private initiative, Beveridge saw his 'report' as complementary to the 1942 royal commission report on social insurance and allied services. The ending of mass unemployment was an underlying assumption of that earlier *Beveridge report (1942). Full employment was necessary to a comprehensive system of social insurance, both to create a large enough tax base to fund it and to prevent its bankruptcy by having to support long-term, mass unemployment. Beveridge believed that the adoption of *Keynesian methods would allow the 'elimination of idleness' without resort to draconian planning and state control. *Full Employment* went to press in May 1944, shortly before the coalition government white paper on *Employment Policy*, which accepted the primary aims of the government to maintain 'a high and stable level of employment'. Beveridge was, if anything, more wholeheartedly Keynesian than the white paper, putting him on the more liberal wing of post-war reconstructionists. *JS*

Jose Harris, *William Beveridge: A Biography* (Oxford, 1977).

***Full Employment* white paper (1944)**, historically seen as enshrining the application of *Keynesian demand-management to the maintenance of full employment. Recent scholarship has instead emphasized the vagueness and contradictions of this wartime document. Whilst an optimistic belief in Keynesian counter-cyclical techniques informed the academics from the economic section who drafted chapters 1 and 2, Treasury officials responsible for much of the rest of the document were less convinced of their likely efficacy, or that unbalanced budgets would be without unpleasant side-effects. Vagueness also characterized the target of a 'high and stable level of employment'; what this meant in practice, an appendix hinted, was around 8 per cent unemployment. However, beyond some suggestions on regional policy to meet Treasury officials' concerns about the revival of the structural unemployment of the inter-war years, it gave little indication as to how this was to be achieved. The significance of the white paper lies less in its limited role as a policy instrument, and more in its political importance in the aftermath of the *Beveridge report (1942) and in the expectations it helped to fuel. *PPC*

Fulton report (1968) (Cmnd 3638), by a departmental committee of inquiry into the civil service which sat under Lord Fulton (vice-chancellor of Sussex University and fellow temporary civil servant with Harold Wilson during the Second World War). Described by its secretary, Richard Wilding, as 'the last of the great Fabian documents', the Fulton inquiry was set up after critical reports from the Fabian Society on the alleged amateurishness of a generalist mandarinate and from the House of Commons Estimates Committee on the need for an examination of the structure and management of the civil service. Wilson took a close interest in the committee's progress and Number Ten files confirm his direct personal input through both Fulton and Norman *Hunt, Oxford don, and moving critic of Whitehall among the committee's membership. Wilson was particularly keen that managerial virtues should be emphasized and that Fulton be 'stiffened' to persist in the recommendation of a unified, classless civil service against the wishes of senior officialdom and their sympathizers on the committee. Wilson, however, declined to back Hunt in his desire that future top recruits to Whitehall should have been schooled in 'relevant', as opposed to classical or traditional subjects. When published in June 1968, the report opened with an attack on an institution 'still fundamentally the product of the nineteenth-century philosophy of the Northcote-Trevelyan Report', and made 28 recommendations to bring the civil service in line with 'the needs of the second half of the twentieth century'.

Of the 28 proposals, some were implemented by Wilson (the splitting-off from the Treasury of a new civil service department with the prime minister designated henceforth 'minister for the civil service'; the creation of a civil service college; and a start on unified grading—though this was not completed until the 1980s). Edward Heath accepted the Fulton recommendation of hived-off agencies, creating the weapons procurement executive and the property services agency—though not until Margaret Thatcher began the process which eventually put three-quarters of the civil service into *Next Steps Executive Agencies was the Fulton recommendation of 'accountable units' of management implemented fully. The returning Wilson established a Fulton-style policy unit in 10 Downing Street in 1974 which has been maintained and adapted by all his successors. Heath followed up the Fulton plea for a diminution of official secrecy by establishing the Franks inquiry into section 2 of the Official Secrets Act in 1971. But not until the Major government's 1993 *Open Government* white paper and the resultant code of practice on access to government information (1994) were serious dents inflicted on the carapace of administrative secrecy. Other Fulton reforms such as a warmer place in the bureaucratic sun for scientists and other professionals, and a greater two-way flow between Whitehall and other professions, were achieved to a limited extent over the ensuing 30 years. Thatcher abolished the Civil Service

Department in 1981 and dispersed its functions between the Treasury and the Cabinet Office.

PJH

GEOFFREY FRY, *Reforming the Civil Service: The Fulton Committee on the British Home Civil Service 1966–1968* (Edinburgh, 1993). | 'Fulton 20 Years On', *Contemporary Record*, 2/2 (1988). | PETER KELLNER and NORMAN CROWTHER-HUNT, *The Civil Servants: An Inquiry into Britain's Ruling Class* (London, 1980). | RICHARD WILDING, 'The Fulton Report in Retrospect', *Contemporary Record*, 9/2 (1995).

Funding Agency for Schools, established in April 1994 under the 1993 Education Act, in order to support grant-maintained schools. The Schools Standards and Framework Act, 1998, provided for the ending of grant-maintained status in September 1999 and the cessation of the agency's principal school-related functions on 31 March 1999. The agency finally closed on 31 October 1999. *JD*

Fussell, Paul (1924–), American literary historian. After war service, which provided background for *Wartime: Understanding and Expriencing the Second World War* (1989), Fussell's career was spent mainly at Rutgers University and the University of Pennsylvania. He first researched 18th-century literature, the Augustans and Samuel Johnson, but was also active in public debate, as contributing editor to *Harper's* and *The New Republic.* Fussell's later work centred on the 20th century, with studies of Kingsley Amis (1994) and British literary travellers (1980). His most influential book, however, was *The Great War and Modern Memory* (1975), which shaped perceptions for a generation. Fussell argued that war experience had forced the birth of all that was culturally 'modern', the cheerfulness with which soldiers marched to war in 1914 never being possible again in a century whose characteristic was irony rather than innocence. Latterly his view has been widely challenged, by cultural historians who point out both the ferment in the arts before 1914 and the survival of patriotic traditionalism after 1918. Military historians have observed that Fussell took the world-view of a few over-emotional poets for the entire British war experience of 1914–18.

JAR

ROBIN PRIOR and TREVOR WILSON, 'Paul Fussell at War', *War in History* (1994).

Future of Socialism, The (1956), key left-wing political text. Published by Tony *Crosland, this work was the most important theoretical work produced by the Labour Party in the post-war period. Crosland argued that the nature of capitalism had been altered by the Second World War and the rise of the managerial class, and that therefore the question of ownership was now less important than the question of distribution. The implications for the Labour Party were that nationalization was no longer a prerequisite for a socialized society and that equality, the goal of socialism, could be achieved by such economic interventions as indicative planning, demand management, and progressive taxation. Crosland also pressed for a more flamboyant image for socialism, arguing that a managed economy could be one in which people enjoyed better design and a higher standard of living. The book was influential in introducing new American sociological findings to a British audience. The central assumption of the work, that capitalism was permanently altered by the existence of the public sector, has not been substantiated, nor has the idea that, the problem of production having been solved, the remaining problem was now only how to distribute the fruits of economic growth more fairly. Crosland brilliantly described the conditions of the 1950s and the long post-war era of full employment, high growth, and low inflation, but his model of economic change was flatly contradicted by the economic conditions of the 1970s and the resurgence of market-capitalism in the 1980s. However, the values Crosland espoused, and his message of an egalitarianism that lifted people up rather than brought everyone down to the lowest common dominator, have remained relevant and were still influencing key figures in New Labour in the 1990s. *BB*

G7 and **G5**. G7 identifies the group of seven major industrial countries (Canada, France, Germany, Italy, Japan, the UK, and the USA). The group originated from informal meetings between the finance ministers of France and Germany in the early 1970s. In 1975 they invited the government leaders of Italy, Japan, UK, and USA to meet at Rambouillet in France. Canada was added at the first formal summit at Puerto Rico in 1976. The finance ministers and heads of government of the G7 meet regularly to exchange information and to set an economic and political agenda each year. Under the Plaza agreement of 1985 they agreed to promote favourable economic performance, to achieve balanced growth, and to stabilize exchange rates. This was reinforced by the Louvre accord of 1987 where they agreed to maintain currency stability. When the group meets without Canada and Italy, it is known as the Group of Five (G5).

CRS

G10, international economic grouping. G10 includes the UK, USA, Canada, Japan, Germany, France, Italy, Belgium, Netherlands, and Sweden. Switzerland joined in 1984. In 1962 these countries agreed to lend the IMF a total of $6 billion on request under the general arrangements to borrow. This marked a shift in global economic policy-making away from the USA and the IMF, and toward Europe. Sometimes known as the Paris Club, these countries play a leading role in international monetary reform. *CRS*

Gaitskell, Hugh Todd Naylor (1906–63), Labour politician, chancellor of the exchequer (1950–1), and leader of the Labour Party (1955–63). In the inter-war period Gaitskell was an Oxford don, one of a small group of economists who introduced the ideas of J. M. Keynes to Labour politicians like Hugh Dalton. After wartime service on the home front, he reached the Commons in 1945 and was minister of fuel and power (1947–50), before becoming Attlee's last chancellor. He delivered only one budget, which was dominated by the need for rearmament and which split the cabinet and contributed to the defeat of the government in 1951. In opposition, Gaitskell campaigned effectively for the leadership, which he won on Attlee's retirement in 1955, and led the party with a zealous belief in its need to modernize.

His leadership was thus characterized by a series of bruising internal conflicts. He initially went some way to reconcile the left and worked closely with Bevan on Suez in 1956, but his revisionist policies led to confrontations over nationalization and *Clause 4. He was also committed to the Atlantic alliance and collective security which in turn led to more divisions over unilateralism. His belief in the Commonwealth led to a break with his own right-wing supporters over membership of the European Economic Community (EEC). These divisions resulted in the three great crises that summed up his period as leader. Following a crushing defeat in the 1959 general election, Gaitskell proposed the updating of Clause 4 of the party constitution to reflect modern concerns as revealed in the work of pioneering pollsters like Mark *Abrams. Despite pinning his personal prestige to a new statement of party aims, he was defeated. This led to a concerted attack on his position as leader and the defeat of his defence policy by resolutions inspired by the Campaign for Nuclear Disarmament

(CND) at the Scarborough conference of 1960. He responded to defeat with his famous 'fight and fight and fight again to save the party we love' speech, which rallied supporters of NATO and began the processes that saw CND defeated at the 1961 conference. At the 1962 conference he dismayed many of his supporters by opposing British membership of the EEC in an equally electrifying platform performance.

His attempt to change Clause 4 and his two great conference speeches were typical of his style of leading from the front and his faith that the party could be persuaded to adopt his positions by the force of rational argument. This didacticism was matched by his faith in economic intervention as a means of improving society. He chose to be a socialist because he believed that it was right, rather than having been born into it, and he was impatient with those who did not share his faith. Though an inspirational leader for those who agreed with him, he inspired passionate dislike amongst his political opponents. In the final analysis his ability to hold the Labour Party together was questionable, though the substance of the policy differences between the two wings of the party in the 1950s appears much less profound in hindsight than it did at the time. For example, his revisionism was conducted within strict intellectual and emotional limits that rejected market economics in favour of Keynesian demand management and planning. Though he was convinced of the need to transcend nationalization as the main means of achieving greater equality, he remained dedicated to the ends of social justice and retained a deep-seated faith in state action. Moreover, he did not believe that the historical Labour Party needed to be abandoned to achieve a modern and relevant approach and was very much of the 1931 generation in his suspicion of pacts with other parties. He was wedded to the Labour Party and had a strong belief in its ability to change. His sudden death in early 1963 probably robbed him of the opportunity of being prime minister, and thus his career had an unfinished quality about it. Moreover, he made a major tactical mistake in the 1959 campaign when he pledged that the Labour Party would not increase taxation. This focused the campaign on Labour as a tax and spend party and raised doubts about its honesty. While his next campaign might have been more effective, he would not have been in as good a position as Wilson to exploit Conservative problems over Profumo and other scandals, because of the nature of his own private life and his affair with the socialite Ann Fleming. He had undoubted qualities of leadership and revealed himself in the great struggles of his career as a man of the highest integrity and courage, but his single-mindedness, which could often appear as stubbornness, must leave a question mark over the claim frequently made for him as being 'the best prime minister we never had'. *BB*

Brian Brivati, *Hugh Gaitskell* (London, 1996). | Philip Williams, *Hugh Gaitskell* (London, 1979).

Galbraith, Thomas Dunlop **(1917–81)**, Conservative politician. 'Tam' Galbraith came to national prominence in 1962 when he resigned from the Scottish Office over allegations about his relationship with *Vassall. While civil lord of the Admiralty between 1957 and 1959, Galbraith had written letters to Vassall, an admiralty clerk and homosexual, who was later convicted of spying for the Russians. Galbraith resigned following the publication of these letters in an interim inquiry, but he was subsequently exonerated by a judicial tribunal. *RJS*

Gallacher, William **(1881–1965)**, Communist. Willie Gallacher was chairman of the Clyde Workers' Committee, 1915–50, and participated in the campaigns that laid the basis for the shop stewards' movement that emerged in Scotland during the Great War. At the second congress of the Communist International in July–August 1920 Lenin persuaded him to join the newly formed Communist Party of Great Britain (CPGB). He was elected to its executive in 1921, and to the Comintern executive in 1924 and in 1935. He was also a CPGB delegate to the national council of the National Unemployed Workers' Movement. In 1925 he was sentenced to twelve months, with eleven other Communist leaders, under the Incitement to Mutiny Act of 1797, and so was incarcerated while the 1926 General Strike took place. In 1935 he was elected as Communist MP for West Fife, visiting the International Brigades in Spain in 1937 in that capacity, and was the only MP to protest against Chamberlain's visit to Hitler at Munich in 1938. He lost his parliamentary seat in 1950 but remained an active Communist, chairman of the CPGB until 1956 and president of the party until 1963. A loyal party man, he did, however, oppose the Comintern on several key issues. He initially opposed their 'class against class' policy, which labelled social democrats as 'social-fascists'; in May 1939 he voted against their directive to support the National Government's conscription measures; and in early October 1939, he objected to their policy of opposition to the war. However, rather than be expelled, he always accepted Moscow's new line in the end. Socialist pioneer, shop stewards' leader, agitator, and propagandist, he was imprisoned four times for his trade union and Communist activities. *DLM*

William Gallacher, *Revolt On The Clyde* (London, 1936). | William Gallacher, *Last Memoirs* (London, 1966).

Gallipoli, a rocky peninsula in European Turkey guarding the entrance to the Dardanelles, the site of landings by British and dominion troops on 25 April and 6 August 1915, designed to knock the Ottoman Empire out of the Great War and turn the flank of Germany and Austria. Characterized from the outset by poor planning, inadequate resources, and inept leadership, the campaign incurred heavy losses in a series of fierce battles before its abandonment in December 1915–January 1916. *JMB*

Gallup, George ('Ted') (1901–84), opinion pollster. Gallup is regarded as the father of the art to which his name is so often attached. A professor of journalism from Iowa, he applied the principles of agricultural sampling to market research and then to political behaviour. He founded his company, the American Institute of Public Opinion, in 1935 and achieved a spectacular triumph in 1936 when, in his syndicated column, he predicted the comfortable re-election of Franklin Roosevelt in defiance of the forecast of the well-established but unscientific *Literary Digest* poll. His techniques were then copied worldwide, often by direct affiliates of his Princeton, New Jersey, corporation, as in the case of the British Institute of Public Opinion. He seemed to face disaster in 1948 when he predicted that Dewey would beat Truman, although his error (4 per cent) was less than in 1936 when he underestimated Roosevelt's triumph by 7 per cent. But his general record of accuracy and the enormous potential of sample surveys for commercial market research guaranteed the continued success of his operations and their widespread imitation. There were academic critics of the *simplisme* of his quota sampling techniques but polls, and often 'Gallup polls', now flourish throughout the democracies of the world. He edited many volumes, archiving poll findings, and in an early work, *Public Opinion in a Democracy* (1939), he advocated the use of polls as a systematic instrument of direct democracy. *DEB*

Gallup poll. See Public Opinion, British Institute of.

gambling as a social phenomenon has a long history in Britain, but the 20th century has seen the addition of new forms of gambling to traditional areas such as horse racing and card games. The inter-war years witnessed the widespread introduction of betting on football matches, via the football pools, and the development of greyhound racing. The post-war era involved the rise of Bingo halls, especially popular amongst women, and the licensing of casinos in a number of major towns and cities. American-style fruit machines also became a common feature of pubs, clubs, and amusement arcades. The most notable recent addition was the National Lottery, introduced in 1994 with government support, to provide money for charitable and other causes. Franchised to a private consortium, Camelot Group plc, the National Lottery has become the biggest lottery in the world with ticket sales of over £5 billion in 1997–8. In 1998 a National Lottery Act provided for changes to the lottery's funding of good causes and reformed the system of regulatory control so as to ensure that money is allocated fairly across all regions of the UK and among different groups. The lottery was originally regulated by the director-general of the National Lottery, but he was replaced by a new National Lottery commission in spring 1999.

Gross expenditure on all forms of gambling, including the National Lottery, was estimated in 1998 at over £40 billion a year. The largest proportion of this was spent on horse racing and at greyhound tracks, where gambling can take place on-course or at 8,500 licensed off-course betting offices. A form of pool betting is organized on racecourses by the Horserace Totalizer Board (the 'Tote') which also has off-course betting offices. Betting on other events, football, cricket, and more general issues, including the outcome of political events such as elections, has also attracted a growing following.

Gambling was heavily regulated until the 1950s when off-course betting on horse racing was legalized and the first betting shops were licensed. The government regulates the Tote and off-course betting and ensures that there is a return to the racing industry through an annual levy, based on an annual agreement between the bookmakers' committee and the horse-race betting levy board, with the home secretary as ultimate arbiter. Gambling and its associated bodies are thus a significant industry and sections of it, especially those concerned with horse racing, have often enjoyed close contacts with the establishment. It is also a significant source of state revenue: duties are charged on off-course betting, pool betting, gaming in casinos, and on fruit machines, while a 12 per cent duty is taken from gross stakes in the National Lottery. This yield has been dwarfed recently by the distribution to charities available from the National Lottery, which will by 2001 have raised more than £10.5 billion for good causes and supported over 31,000 separate projects. Social disapproval of gambling, strong into the post-war period amongst religious groups such as Nonconformists, has now largely been replaced by tolerance. Various measures have been taken in recent years to provide new opportunities for the betting and gaming industry and for their consumers, such as permitting the advertising of commercial bingo, the encouragement of new National Lottery outlets, and the relaxation of regulations governing the facilities in betting shops. *JS*

game theory, mathematical theory of the interaction of rational actors. Their interaction produces one of several possible outcomes, and to each outcome is attached a pay-off for each player. If players try to maximize their pay-off, game theory predicts what they would do if they were rational and fully informed. In recent years it has expanded to make predictions about people (and animals) who are not fully rational or fully informed. The great mathematician John von Neumann (1903–57) invented game theory between the 1920s and the 1940s. Treated at first as a mathematical curiosity, it did not find a niche in social science until the 1970s, and in political science more recently. There are two main classes of games: zero-sum and non-zero-sum (the latter sometimes wrongly called positive-sum or negative-sum). In a zero-sum game such as chess, the total pay-off available to all players together is the same in all outcomes; the players are therefore in outright competition and have no incentive to cooperate. In non-zero-sum games such as 'the prisoners' dilemma', some outcomes yield a total pay-off higher than others: players have a joint incentive to maximize the game pay-off, but they also have an individual incentive to maximize their own. That is what makes non-zero-sum games interesting, and more useful models of political processes than zero-sum games. Another important distinction is that between 'normal-form games' and 'extensive form games'. In the former, players choose simultaneously in ignorance of each others' choices, or are treated as if they did. In the latter, they choose in a sequence, knowing the history of the game and at least something about one another's preferences at each decision point. The most important development in the 1980s was in the theory of evolutionary games. Animals are not rational beings, but natural selection may select those whose genes play successful strategies. Therefore animal (or any other non-rational) behaviour may be modelled by game theory. *IM*

J. D. Morrow, *Game Theory for Political Scientists* (Princeton, 1994).

'Gang of Four', ironic description of the far from revolutionary leaders of the *Social Democratic Party formed in March 1981: Roy *Jenkins, David *Owen, William *Rodgers, and Shirley *Williams. As signatories to the *Limehouse declaration, announcing the establishment of a Council for Social Democracy on 26 January 1981, they precipitated the defection of twelve Labour MPs which led to the formation of a separate party on 26 March. The original gang of four was a Chinese opposition group led by Mao Tse-tung's widow, openly criticized in 1977 and brought to trial in 1981. *JS*

garden city movement, name given to the ideas associated with the town planning pioneer Ebenezer *Howard, who aimed to combine the advantages of urban living with those of the countryside, advocating relatively small urban communities, separated by green spaces, and laid out at a low density. His views were encapsulated in pioneer *new towns such as Letchworth and Welwyn Garden City. Translated into a style of suburban layout, his ideas underpinned the design of many of the council estates and private housing developments built in the 20th century. *JS*

Gardiner, Alfred George (1865–1946), Liberal author and journalist. Gardiner worked on the *Northern Daily Telegraph* from 1886 and edited the *Daily News*, 1902–19. A passionate supporter of Liberal political and social causes, campaigning effectively against the use of Chinese labour (see 'Chinese slavery') in South Africa and in favour of South African self-government, he raised the circulation of the paper to 800,000 a day by 1915, gathering around him a glittering array of journalistic talent including H. W. Massingham, H. W. Nevinson, and G. K. Chesterton. Gardiner supported the declaration of war on Germany in 1914 and Asquith's conduct of the war thereafter. Siding with Asquith against Lloyd George in 1916, he also severely criticized the treaty of Versailles (see Paris peace conference). His attacks on Lloyd George led to the owners of the *Daily News* bringing pressure on him to resign the editorship, though he continued to write as a freelance journalist and author thereafter. *JS*

Garvin, James Louis (1868–1947), journalist. Born in Birkenhead, the son of an Irish labourer, a virtual autodidact, the youthful 'Jim' Garvin aspired to and secured posts in provincial newspapers, leading to appointment in 1899 as leader writer for the *Daily Telegraph*. After briefly editing the *Outlook*, in 1908 he became editor of Lord Northcliffe's **Observer* and quickly revivified the moribund Sunday newspaper, making it the voice of the twin causes of imperialism and tariff reform (eventually also writing much of the official life of Joseph Chamberlain). Garvin's influence grew with his success: he became a confidant of the Conservative leader Arthur Balfour, inspired his 1910 tariff referendum pledge, and suggested the 1910 Buckingham palace conference. He battled against the *Parliament Act, 1911, and during the Great War became an influential supporter of Lloyd George. In the inter-war years he advocated Chamberlainite social reform and international conciliation through the *League of Nations. Championing rearmament, he nonetheless supported appeasement as a policy of realism. Following a disagreement with his proprietor, Viscount Astor, Garvin left the *Observer* in 1942 but continued to write for the Beaverbrook press until his death in 1947. A demanding and creative editor, he reinvented the quality Sunday newspaper. *RJQA*

David Ayerst, *Garvin of the Observer* (London, 1985). | A. M. Gollin, *The Observer and J. L. Garvin 1908–1914* (London, 1960).

GCHQ. See Government Communications Headquarters.

Geddes, Auckland Campbell (1879–1954), physician and Conservative minister. A professor of anatomy in Canada before the Great War, Geddes returned to Britain to become one of Lloyd George's 'men of push and go'. He was rushed into a safe parliamentary seat before becoming the first minister of national service, 1917–19, and later headed the Ministry of Reconstruction and local government board, 1919–20. In 1920 he left parliament to become ambassador to the USA, 1920–3, and became a peer in 1942. An extremely effective wartime administrator without the patience for peacetime politics. *RJQA*

R. J. Q. Adams and Philip P. Poirier, *The Conscription Controversy in Great Britain, 1900–1918* (London, 1987). | Lord Geddes, *The Forging of a Family* (London, 1952).

Geddes, Eric Campbell (1875–1937), politician and businessman. After labouring work in the USA and managing tramways in the Himalayan foothills, Eric Geddes joined the North Eastern Railway in 1904. On the outbreak of war he was deputy general manager and in May 1915 his expertise was mobilized by Lloyd George, minister of munitions. Improvement in gun ammunition output was followed by the reorganization of military railways on the western front in 1916. In 1917 his relish for statistical analysis and coordinated planning proved relevant at the Admiralty, where he encountered obstruction and drew hostility from Conservative colleagues on the dismissal of Admiral Jellicoe. As head of a fighting department he had become a politician against his better judgement, but at the Armistice his imagination was captured by the prospect of designing a consensual, indeed depoliticized, integrated transport system. However, as the first minister of transport he became preoccupied with railway decontrol during the rapid return to financial orthodoxy. He left the Commons in 1922, but the demise of reconstructionist ideals was confirmed in a final service to his beleaguered political master, Lloyd George, as wielder of the *Geddes axe in 1921–2. As chairman of Dunlop after 1922 he perceived the spheres of politics and business as quite separate, but he knowingly transgressed this ideal as chairman of Imperial Airways, after 1924, as he steered the government's chosen instrument on civil air policy through years of financial stringency. His persistence eventually secured intergovernmental agreement for the introduction of the Empire Air Mail Scheme in 1934. *KG*

P. K. Cline, 'Eric Geddes and the "Experiment" with Businessmen in Government, 1915–1922', in K. D. Brown (ed.), *Essays in Anti-Labour History* (London, 1974). | K. Grieves, *Sir Eric Geddes: Business and Government in War and Peace* (Manchester, 1989).

Geddes axe (1921), economy drive. In August 1921, Lloyd George's response to Conservative- and press-backed anti-waste agitation, in the quest for electoral survival, was the appointment of a committee on national expenditure, which would confirm the dissolution of residual reconstructionist ideals by instigating public economy. It was chaired by Sir Eric Geddes and was comprised of businessmen who had improvised administrative change in wartime supply departments. It was the last service undertaken by self-conscious 'outsiders' (see businessmen in

GOVERNMENT) during Lloyd George's premiership, who now appeared to be handed responsibility for fiscal policy. The Economy Committee depended on Treasury briefings and often expressed the rigorous budgetary objectives of officials, who were determined to regain control over spending departments. In three reports, published up to February 1922, massive cuts of £87 million were proposed in overall supply estimates of £528 million (Sir Robert Horne, chancellor of the exchequer, had demanded cuts of £130 million). The Economy Committee played no part in ensuing cabinet meetings, which eventually endorsed savings of £52 million. The suggestion of a ministry of defence to replace the three service ministries was bitterly contested by a review committee, under Winston Churchill's chairmanship, in January 1922. He also defended costly plans for the naval base at Singapore, and only one-half of the projected savings of £86 million in service estimates was eventually agreed. Consequently, the Board of Education was subjected to close scrutiny. Plans for the part-time education of 14-year-old school leavers were curtailed, as savings amounting to £18 million were sought by businessmen antipathetic to the state provision of post-elementary education. This 'distancing' approach to managing retrenchment exemplified Lloyd George's indirect approach to policy making. Ultimately, however, budgetary priorities could not be determined by non-ministerial visiting businessmen without a secretariat. In their attempts to wield the economy 'axe', on behalf of the executive, most members of the committee concluded that politics and business should become, once more, quite different spheres. *KG*

K. GRIEVES, *Sir Eric Geddes: Business and Government in War and Peace* (Manchester, 1989). | A. McDONALD, 'The Geddes Committee and the Formulation of Public Expenditure Policy, 1921–1922', *Historical Journal*, 32 (1989).

General Agreement on Tariffs and Trade (GATT) (1947), multilateral treaty and rulebook for liberal international trade. A core component of the post-1945 international economic architecture envisioned by British, American, and other non-communist industrialized countries' negotiators at the 1944 *Bretton Woods international economic conference, the GATT established rules for open international trade based upon principles of non-discrimination, national treatment, and tariff reduction. The initial GATT was signed by 37 industrial countries which then represented 80 per cent of world trade. US failure to ratify the 1948 Havana charter meant that the *International Trade Organization envisaged to manage GATT did not enter operation, which left GATT rules and undertakings to be administered by a skeletal Geneva-based secretariat that grew incrementally in response to GATT's expanding responsibilities and number of signatories.

The principal activities of GATT have been to reduce tariffs and liberalize other barriers to trade through a series of multilateral negotiating rounds, and to resolve trade disputes between participating countries. Additional states acceded to GATT steadily, until by the mid-1990s there were well over 100 signatories. In the 1960s, it paved the way for developing countries to join it and accept its trade-liberalizing disciplines by agreeing to temporary exceptions for developing states from the most stringent liberalization provisions. Following overall success in reducing tariffs on manufactured goods, GATT from the 1970s tackled the more difficult task of reducing non-tariff barriers to trade. In the 1986–94 Uruguay Round multilateral negotiations, GATT negotiators significantly strengthened their dispute-resolution procedures, expanded their purview to include trade in services as well as goods, and for the first time established a framework for liberalization of agricultural trade. The Uruguay Round also succeeded in creating a World Trade Organization, which, upon commencing operations in 1995, subsumed the GATT secretariat and took over administration of GATT rules. *GAP*

JEFFREY SCHOTT and JOHANNA W. BUURMAN, *The Uruguay Round: An Assessment* (Washington, 1994). | G. R. WINHAM, *International Trade and the Tokyo Round Negotiations* (Princeton, 1986).

General Belgrano, formerly *USS Phoenix*, the aged Argentine cruiser sunk by the British submarine *Conqueror* on 2 May 1982, with the loss of 368 men (one-third of the crew). In demonstration, this was the opening engagement of the Falklands war. A shocking and controversial action, reprehensible to some, sensible to others. An effective deterrent to the Argentine navy, but a certain provocation; a target of opportunity, but a deliberate escalation of the war, on which Margaret Thatcher and her ministers faced relentless questions later. *AD*

MARTIN MIDDLEBROOK, *Task Force* (Harmondsworth, 1987).

general elections, held at regular intervals to return Members to the House of Commons, and in effect to choose the next government.

Elections to the Commons must be held within a period of five years from the meeting of a new parliament. The five-year limit was introduced by the 1911 Parliament Act: previously, the limit had since 1713 been seven years. The country is divided into constituencies, each of which returns an MP on the first-past-the-post system. Though general elections are held throughout the nation, elections fought by parties on a national, as opposed to a regional or sectional, basis are essentially 20th-century phenomena: the general election of 1906 was the first election to be fought on a national basis, and 1918 was the first time that all contests were on the same day.

The basic framework for national elections in the inter-war years was set by the Representation of the People Act, 1918. This established residence rather than property ownership as the essential qualification for voting and also extended the vote to women aged 30 years and over: the effect was to more than double the size of the electorate. The Act reformed the process of electoral registration, lowered the level of permitted campaign expenditure, and transferred the administrative cost of elections from the candidates to the taxpayer. The effects of the Act were summarized by David Butler (1963: 12): 'Elections became calmer; petitions became much rarer; registration procedure became much more efficient; party machines became stronger; and the administrative machinery worked more smoothly.' The rise of the Labour Party also placed greater stress on the concept of the mandate and the inter-war years saw the publication of party election programmes in the form of manifestos. Elections were conducted largely on a local and labour-intensive basis. During the election campaign, a candidate—variously supported by leading party figures—would address a series of public meetings in the constituency. Party workers would campaign vigorously to get out the vote on the day. Campaign posters were heavily used. Though the Labour Party was able to form two minority governments, general elections were heavily dominated by the Conservative Party.

The nature of elections changed after the Second World War. The electoral process was changed by the provisions of the Representation of the People Act, 1948, which removed the six-month period of residence necessary to qualify to vote, extended postal voting to civilians, abolished plural voting, and abolished university seats. There were also more frequent reviews of constituency boundaries. The quarter-century after 1945 witnessed the form and properties of two-party competition. The Labour Party competed for office with the Conservatives, the Liberal Party maintaining at times a fairly minimal representation of only six seats in the Commons. In the 26 years from, and including, 1945 the Labour and Conservative parties were each in office for thirteen years. The period also witnessed a change in campaigning: there was a greater emphasis on the use of the broadcast media. Television was important initially as a medium for broadcasting the results on election night: the 1950 general election was the first to have the results broadcast, and between 1945 and 1955, the only broadcasts during the campaign were party election broadcasts. The 1959 election was a watershed in terms of the use of television, which thereafter became the main focus of party attention and the principal medium through which electors received news about the campaign. The use of television also served to give elections a more national focus, giving greater attention to party leaders. The parties also introduced more central campaign management.

The period since the 1960s has witnessed greater volatility in electoral behaviour, with elections being characterized by more multi-party competition and each of the two principal parties making inroads into their opponent's traditional class support: the Conservatives attracting support from skilled workers in the 1983 and 1987 general elections and Labour achieving substantial middle-class support in the 1997 general election. The 1980s also saw greater professionalization in the running of election campaigns and elections geared more to the needs of a 24-hour news service. Parties competed each day through early morning press conferences to set the news agenda for that day. Local campaigns became subservient to the national campaign. They also changed in nature, with a shift from a labour-intensive to a technology-intensive campaign. There was less emphasis on door-to-door canvassing and a much greater use, especially by the Labour Party, of telephone canvassing and direct mailshots. The Labour Party in 1997 proved highly effective in directing the campaign from a national election headquarters (distinct from the party headquarters), providing clear lines for candidates to take and using a computerized database to respond to opponents' claims. The Labour Party also targeted campaign resources in key seats. The Conservatives—regarded in the 1950s and 1960s as the most highly efficient of the parties in terms of campaign organization—failed to adopt the same highly centralized campaign organization. Research has shown that in 1997 they tended to devote more resources to safe than to marginal seats. *PN*

DAVID BUTLER, *The Electoral System in Britain since 1918* (Oxford, 1963). | DAVID BUTLER and DENNIS KAVANAGH, *The British General Election of 1997* (London, 1998). | DENNIS KAVANAGH, *Election Campaigning* (Oxford, 1995).

General Strike (1926), the greatest industrial confrontation in British history. Facing an economic downturn, coal mine-owners threatened a cut in wages in 1925, the latest incident in a long-running confrontation between militant trade unionists in the miners' unions and the owners who were still smarting from the wartime control of their industry. The TUC decided to back the miners and a triple alliance of miners, railway, and transport workers threatened to stop all movement of coal. Baldwin's Conservative government backed down, agreeing to pay the difference between coal owners' cuts and current levels of pay with a nine-month subsidy and set up a royal commission, under Herbert Samuel, to investigate the mining industry. This victory became known as Red Friday and was seen as a major victory for militant trade unionists and trapped the TUC into supporting the miners. The Samuel commission published its report in March 1926: it rejected state subsidy, thereby ensuring a cut in wages, but the mine-owners now increased the stakes by proposing an increase in hours and new working conditions. The miners refused these terms and from 1 May were locked out of the pits. Last-minute talks between the TUC and the government collapsed when printers refused to work on the *Daily Mail* (an edition highly critical of the unions) and a general strike was called on 3 May. The government was far more prepared than the TUC for a prolonged confrontation. J. H. Thomas, a moderate union leader, set up a negotiating committee and a deal was done behind the backs of the miners. The strike ended on 12 May. The miners stayed out for six months but were eventually forced to accept cuts in wages and longer hours. The symbolic and political significance of the strike was immense. In simple terms the revolutionary potential of the British trade union movement was shown to be non-existent (at least at the nationally organized level—the local pattern showed much more militancy). The role of the TUC caused thus prolonged bitterness in the more militant sections of the miners' unions, but the effect was not altogether negative for the union movement. The general strike was discredited as a political weapon, but the TUC had demonstrated the potential for unity of action. The consequences of the strike were both legislation which restricted general and sympathetic strikes, and the *Mond-Turner talks which opened up more channels of helpful communication between unions and business. *BB*

KEITH LAYBOURN, *The General Strike* (Manchester, 1993).

General Theory of Employment, Interest and Money (1936), ground-breaking study by the economist J. M. *Keynes. The *General Theory* set out in detail the ideas which Keynes had elaborated since the 1920s on the use of 'deficit financing' and 'demand management' to regulate the economy. Its publication was a landmark in the history of economic ideas in Britain because it elaborated an alternative political economy to both the orthodox 'Manchester system', which stressed balanced budgets and free markets, and state socialism, with its stress on public ownership, planning, and control. Keynes argued that it was possible for the state to regulate economic activity and to alleviate unemployment without jeopardizing individual freedom. This could be accomplished through programmes of investment and spending, which would in turn stimulate economic activity and maintain maximum productive capacity. While the ideas set out in the *General Theory* would involve a large extension in the traditional functions of government, Keynes argued that by stabilizing the operations of the market his approach would strengthen rather than weaken liberal capitalism as an alternative to communist and socialist models. The text should therefore be understood in its historical context, as a response to the social and political consequences of mass unemployment and the decline of staple industries which had plagued Britain's economy since 1921. Although its critics warned that the proposals of the *General Theory* would tend towards inflation, the book was widely acclaimed, and would prove to be increasingly influential on the British intellectual and policy-making elites of the following two decades. *HOJ*

PETER CLARKE, *The Keynesian Revolution in the Making* (Oxford, 1988). | RICHARD KAHN, *The Making of Keynes' General Theory* (Cambridge, 1984).

Geneva conference (1954), international conference on Korea and Indochina. The conference, which opened on 26 April 1954, was held against the background of the imminent fall of the French fortress of Dienbien Phu and the determination of the American secretary of state, Foster Dulles, to organize a system of collective security against communism in the Far East. But the British foreign secretary, Anthony Eden, who acted along with Soviet foreign minister Molotov as co-chairman of the conference, was determined to resist an anti-communist coalition even if this meant a deterioration in Anglo-American relations. In particular, believing that a third world war was a real possibility, Eden wanted to end the war in Indochina without giving America a pretext to intervene.

By the beginning of June it was clear that no agreement would be reached on the reunification of Korea, but over Indochina progress proved possible, especially after Dulles returned to the USA on 3 May. Eden was at his best in the detailed discussions which followed and he patiently strove to build bridges with the communist leaders of China and the Soviet Union. On 20 July the Vietminh agreed to a partition of their country at the 17th parallel and the following day three months of negotiations were rewarded by the decision of the French and the Vietminh to agree to a ceasefire. Though this proved very far from being a long-term solution to the problems of south-east Asia, the immediate crisis had been overcome and the settlement stands as one of the most considerable diplomatic achievements of Eden's career. As one member of the British delegation has put it, this turned out to be 'the last example of an independent British policy exercising significant influence in the resolution of a major international crisis' (Cable, 3). *DJD*

J. Cable, *The Geneva Conference of 1954 on Indochina* (London, 1986).

Geneva protocol (1924), draft international instrument sponsored by Ramsay MacDonald, then prime minister and foreign secretary, and his French counterpart, Herriot. It attempted to enhance security through the League of Nations by supplying a satisfactory test of aggression: in essence, refusal to accept the verdict of arbitration. Baldwin's Conservative government declined on 12 March 1925 to ratify the protocol on the grounds that the application of sanctions would fall disproportionately on the shoulders of Britain and the dominions, and sought instead to deal with security issues at *Locarno. *AJC*

George V (1865–1936), sovereign, 1910–36. Privately educated by a clergyman and as a cadet in the navy, the unexpected death of his elder brother in 1892 put him in line to inherit not only the throne, but also his brother's fiancée, Princess Mary of Teck (see Mary, Queen Consort of George V). Their arranged marriage proved an unusually happy one and they had six children. In 1901, he began a series of tours or progresses through the colonies. The travels his father, as prince of Wales, had taken out of boredom or curiosity, his son was now obliged to make as a duty and a tradition. On these travels abroad his real education began under Arthur Bigge, later Lord Stamfordham, whom he inherited as private secretary on the death of Queen Victoria. Stamfordham helped to steer his charge through events as different as the opening of the first parliament of the commonwealth of Australia in 1901 as well as the Delhi durbar of 1911, the first and only imperial coronation attended by a reigning sovereign in India. As king he tried unsuccessfully to mediate disputes between Unionists and home rulers over Ireland, but his sympathies were probably too evidently on the side of the Unionists—he was better as a symbol of grim endurance during the Great War. He showed a keen nose for the survival of the monarchy by renouncing his German titles, renaming his family as the house of Windsor, and denying asylum to his Russian cousin, the tsar, at a time of rising war-weariness and republican feeling in Britain. His Christmas radio broadcasts to the nation and empire, begun late in his life, made creative use of a new medium and handed on a new duty to his descendants. Neither imaginative, nor well read, nor particularly enthusiastic about many of his duties, he became the model of an unenquiring country squire, whose true passions were shooting and stamp collecting. This image and his quarter-century of service appealed to British people who gave him a welcome that surprised him by its warmth at his silver jubilee in 1935. *WMK*

Harold Nicolson, *King George the Fifth* (London, 1952). | Kenneth Rose, *King George V* (London, 1983).

George VI (1895–1952), sovereign, 1936–52. Like his father, George V, he was educated privately and as a cadet in the navy. Also like his father, he was not at first expected to come to the throne. The *abdication of his brother, Edward VIII, thrust him suddenly into the limelight. A nervous and shy man, he was strengthened by his wife (see Elizabeth, the Queen Mother), who combined an easy, charming manner with an iron will to support her husband. The king's two biggest accomplishments were the restoration of confidence in the monarchy following the unprecedented departure of his brother, and his symbolic leadership during the Second World War. Though known as Albert (or Bertie) before the abdication, he took the name George to emphasize continuity with his father. The continuities were real as well as manufactured: he was happily married and the couple had two daughters to whom they were close. They avoided the fashionable yacht-and-nightclub society favoured by his brother and Mrs Simpson, preferring instead the invariable routine of Windsor, Sandringham, and Balmoral favoured by his parents and grandparents. He and the queen also provided useful wartime leadership by making an American visit in 1939 that helped diminish American resistance to entering the European war. Their insistence on staying in London during the war and their repeated calls on those who suffered bomb damage inspired devotion to them in Britain. Though opposed to Labour plans to enact a welfare state following the war, the king did not interfere and this was typical of the caution and political restraint that a good constitutional sovereign, which he was, needs to exercise. He passed on these traits to his daughter, Elizabeth II, with whom he had a warm and communicative relationship, breaking the tradition set by Queen Victoria, Edward VII, and George V of cool and distant relationships with their heirs. His widow remained to the end of the century the royal family's most popular member, celebrating her own centenary in 2000. *WMK*

Sarah Bradford, *King George VI* (London, 1989). | John Wheeler Bennett, *King George VI* (London, 1958).

Gestapo broadcast (4 June 1945), Winston Churchill's first radio broadcast of the general election campaign. He argued that Labour ministers, his recent wartime colleagues in office, would not be able to introduce socialist measures without recourse to a secret police to enforce them. Generally thought to have seriously harmed his credibility in the election. *JAR*

Gibb, Andrew Dewar (1888–1974), Scottish politician. A former Conservative candidate in the 1920s, Gibb gravitated towards Scottish nationalism in the early 1930s. He played a prominent part in the merger of the Scottish Party and the National Party of Scotland which formed the Scottish National Party (SNP) in 1934 and was party chairman, 1936–40. A professor of law at Glasgow University, Gibb was a vociferous anti-Catholic and anti-socialist. His right-wing views alienated him from the bulk of the SNP and he ceased to play a part in active politics after the outbreak of war in 1939, although he continued to publish widely on the question of Scottish nationalism and politics. *RF*

Gibbon, Hugh Grassic (real name James Leslie Mitchell) (1901–35), Scottish novelist and literary critic. Gibbon is best known for his trilogy *A Scots Quair* which charted the impact of the Great War and the inter-war Depression on a fictitious north-east family. Gibbon was prominent in the Scottish literary renaissance of the inter-war years and in 1934 collaborated with Hugh MacDiarmid to produce the journal *Scottish Scene.* He was a committed Marxist, although some of his ideas veered towards an anti-industrial, romantic utopianism. He denounced Scottish political nationalism which put him at odds with some of his literary contemporaries. He died in poverty at the age of 34. *RF*

Gibraltar, British colony and one of the classical 'pillars of Hercules' at the western mouth of the Mediterranean. Gibraltar was captured by an Anglo-Dutch force in 1704, during the War of the Spanish Succession, confirmed in British possession by the treaty of Utrecht, 1713, and in 1830 given the status of a crown colony. During both world wars, Gibraltar functioned as an important strategic base. By 1964, Britain was ready to relinquish control over internal affairs, which resulted in tension in Anglo-Spanish relations. The Spanish government now contended that under the treaty of Utrecht sovereignty should revert to Spain. In 1967, however, the people of Gibraltar voted overwhelmingly in a referendum to remain under British rule. This was followed in 1969 by Spanish closure of the border, which denied access to the colony to 5,000 Spanish workers. Following the death of Franco, the Spanish position became less rigid and in February 1985 the border was fully reopened. *AJC*

Gilmour, Ian Hedworth John Little (1926–), Conservative politician and writer. After owning and brilliantly editing the *Spectator*, then a liberal Tory paper, Gilmour became an MP in 1962. Junior defence and Home Office posts under Heath preceded a brief defence secretaryship in 1974, but he became lord privy seal 1979–81, deputy to his close ally, Carrington, and helped negotiate the end of Smith's regime in Rhodesia and the European Economic Community (EEC) rebate. Sacked by Thatcher in 1981, he remained a dangerous critic, the most open and contemptuous of the non-Thatcherites, later producing *Dancing with Dogma*, a sardonic memoir and a reasoned case for Keynesian 'wet' Toryism. *EP*

Gilmour, John (1876–1940), Conservative politician. Following military service in the South African war, Gilmour entered local politics. In 1910 he was elected to the Commons where he remained until his death. He was the Tories' Scottish whip, 1919–22, and secretary of state for Scotland, 1924–9. Under the National Government he held a succession of posts including home secretary, 1932–5. Outside politics he contented himself with breeding livestock, foxhunting, and golf. *NJC*

Gilmour report on the Scottish Office (1935), report of the committee set up under former secretary of state for Scotland Sir John Gilmour to examine Scottish administration. Gilmour recognized the emergence of the secretary of state as 'Scotland's minister', with a general brief to look after Scottish interests in cabinet, and recommended the consolidation of the various Scottish boards and departments under an administration based in Edinburgh. The recommendation was largely carried out by the *Reorganization of Offices (Scotland) Act, 1939. *MJK*

Gladstone, Herbert John (1854–1930), Liberal politician. Youngest son of the prime minister W. E. Gladstone, Herbert Gladstone was educated at Eton and University College, Oxford. Liberal MP for Leeds, 1880–1910, he served as Liberal whip in his father's 1880–5 government, followed by his appointment as financial secretary to the War Office in 1886. The most notable event in his early career came in December 1885 with his 'flying the Hawarden Kite': an indiscreet revelation of his father's conversion to Irish home rule. Immediately taken up by the press, his action prematurely committed his father to the cause and had profound consequences in splitting the Liberal Party. He served as under-secretary at the Home Office in 1892–4 and in Rosebery's government as first commissioner of works. In 1899 Gladstone became chief whip while the Liberals were in opposition and, although pro-Boer in sentiment, sought to preserve party unity during the Boer war when serious divisions opened up in its ranks. In 1903 he negotiated the 'Gladstone–MacDonald pact' (see LIB-LAB PACT (1903)) with the secretary of the infant Labour Party, Ramsay *MacDonald. From December 1905 Gladstone served as home secretary under *Campbell-Bannerman and *Asquith, supervising the passage of the Workmen's Compensation Act, 1906, the Eight-Hours Act, 1908, and the Trade Boards Act, 1909. He also instituted the *borstal system and children's courts in 1908, and reorganized the Court of Appeal in 1907. Criticized for his handling of a Roman Catholic procession in 1909, he left the Home Office in December. In 1910 he took a viscountcy and became the first governor-general of, and high commissioner to, the Union of South Africa. Gladstone supported strongly the principle of responsible government, working in close cooperation with General Louis Botha. He returned to Britain in July 1914 but did not resume a ministerial career, concentrating on public work during the Great War and working at Liberal headquarters in 1922–3 to reunify the party. In 1928, his memoir *After Thirty Years* was a powerful defence of his father's reputation and career as well as his own. *JS*

Gladwyn, Lord. See JEBB, GLADWYN.

Glasgow Govan by-elections. See GOVAN, GLASGOW, BY-ELECTIONS.

Glasgow Herald, the leading quality newspaper of the west of Scotland. The *Herald* reflected the political views of its middle-class readership and was staunchly Conservative. It opposed devolution in the 1960s and 1970s and only began to adopt a more liberal and pro-devolutionary stance after 1981 under the editorship of Arnold Kemp. *RF*

Glasgow Hillhead by-election. See HILLHEAD BY-ELECTION.

Glasier, (John) Bruce (1859–1920) and Katherine (1867–1950), socialist evangelists and propagandists who were key figures in the development of the Independent Labour Party (ILP) and the Labour Party. Neither sat in parliament, their involvement with the movement being as speakers, writers, and organizers. Although from very different backgrounds, Bruce's socialism being forged in late 19th-century Glasgow, whereas Katherine's was much more the product of the late 19th-century middle-class conscience, both were committed to a socialism that was rooted in ethics rather than economics. Neither contributed much to socialist theory, their teachings being primarily ethical and increasingly anti-Marxist. Bruce was first elected to the national administrative council of the ILP in 1897, where he remained, with one brief interval, until his death 23 years later, and he was also editor of the *Labour Leader.* A prodigious contributor to the Labour press, he wrote *The Meaning of Socialism* (1920) and *William Morris and the Early Days of the Socialist Movement* (1921). After Bruce's death, Katherine continued on the socialist lecture circuit, later becoming involved with the Save the Children Fund and the establishment of pit-head baths. *JAJ*

LAURENCE THOMPSON, *The Enthusiasts: A Biography of John and Katherine Bruce Glasier* (London, 1971).

globalization of markets, phrase which describes the process that has allowed access to financial markets on an international basis. This process is largely due to the reduction in protective national regulation of capital flows, and to advances in technology. Since the 1960s most governments have gradually relaxed exchange controls on international capital flows: in 1979, the final controls were relaxed in Britain. After this deregulation, investors were free to invest their money abroad, and foreign investors had a wider choice of investments in Britain. Technological advance such as the application of computers and more efficient clearing systems has made it easier to move capital between financial centres at any moment in response to marginally higher returns in different parts of the world. Since the 1980s the globalization of markets has been blamed for increasing the volatility of capital flows and for interfering with the economic sovereignty of national governments. Floods of short-term capital outside the control of the state can quickly destabilize an economy in response to speculative rumours. Conversely, freedom from regulation has been credited with increasing the efficiency of the global distribution of capital and the returns on investments, which have benefited private investors. *CRS*

Glorious Glosters, plaudit awarded by the press and newsreels to the first battalion of the Gloucestershire regiment for its heroic stand against overwhelming odds, after being cut off during a Chinese offensive on the Imjin river, 22–5 April 1951, in the Korean war. All but five officers and 41 men were either killed or taken into a brutal and degrading captivity. This was the most celebrated and remembered British event of the war. *JMB*

'gnomes of Zurich', phrase used by 1960s Labour politicians for international financiers who speculated against the pound. Such foreign holders of sterling were important in 1964–7 when they were concerned about inflation and the levels of public expenditure. The autumn budget of 1964 led to a run on the pound and subsequently the Wilson Labour government tried to pacify the bankers and speculators even while being critical of their power. The July 1966 crisis budget which cut public expenditure was introduced to appease the 'gnomes', but speculation continued until the pound was devalued in November 1967. *BJE*

Goddard, Rayner (1877–1971), lord chief justice, 1946–58. His unexpected appointment followed a long judicial career (High Court judge, 1932–8; lord justice of appeal, 1938–44; and lord of appeal, 1944–6). Goddard held strong beliefs regarding the punishment of wrongdoers and was a vigorous supporter of both corporal and capital punishment. His conduct of certain trials has attracted criticism, notably the 1952 trial of Derek Bentley for murder. Bentley was hanged, but the Court of Appeal quashed his conviction in 1998 as unsafe. *CAM*

Godley, Wynne (1926–), economist. Godley started his career at the Treasury before being seconded for two years to the National Institute for Economic and Social Research in 1962 where he undertook a number of key econometric studies. By the mid-1960s he was in charge of short-term economic forecasting in the Treasury, was responsible for the statistical system on which selective employment tax was based, and carried out the calculations which underlay the devaluation of sterling in 1967. In 1970 he became the director of the department of economics at Cambridge, where he maintained a pro-Keynesian position. *JFM*

P. ARESTIS, *A Biographical Dictionary of Dissenting Economists* (Aldershot, 1992).

gold reserves, the term used to denote the amount of gold retained, along with foreign currency reserves, as official national reserves to underpin the currency and as a contingency against an adverse *balance of payments. Banks have also retained gold reserves as a legal minimum reserve against their own note issue and deposit liabilities. Such stocks were particularly important prior to the Great War, when Britain like most industrialized nations was on the *gold standard, and all forms of legal tender could be converted on demand into fixed quantities of fine gold, as legally defined. Under the emergency Currency and Bank Notes Act, 1914, the Treasury was authorized to allow the Bank of England to exceed the prescribed limit, and since then the gold reserves, as opposed to other types of currency reserves specifically required for the same purpose, have been less significant. Historically, official gold reserves were one of the measurements of the UK's economic well-being. Until 1914, the prevalent policy was to maintain large holdings, a strategy based on experience rather than theory, for the authorities did not have a clear idea of the causes of gold movements or the ways in which the remedies worked. During the Second World War, the entire gold holdings of the Bank of England were transferred to the *Exchange Equalization Account. The abandonment of internationally fixed prices for gold in the 1970s, coupled with floating currencies, enabled gold to become a quasi-currency in its own right. In the late 1990s, following the growing preference for interest-bearing assets at a time of continuing falls in the price of gold and preparations to meet EMU entry criteria, the European central banks announced plans to sell off a large proportion of gold holdings, and in May 1999, the British Treasury announced the reduction of British gold reserves from 715 to 300 tonnes (704 to 295 tons), moves that were (naturally) heavily criticized by the gold-exporting countries. International concern led to the announcement of a five-year moritorium on Bank of England sales, to prevent a further collapse of the commodity's price. *JFM*

gold standard, the device for maintaining currency stability involving free convertibility of banknotes into or out of gold and freedom to export gold, which functioned continuously in Britain from 1821 to 1919 and in most of the developed world from 1880 until the Great War, but only briefly thereafter, despite British-led efforts to reintroduce it. The Cunliffe Committee on Currency and Foreign Exchanges after the war recommended the return to the gold standard as the surest way of regaining economic prosperity. This became official policy in December 1919, but post-war dislocation delayed implementation for the next five years. The brief appearance of a Labour government in 1924, however, lent urgency to the argument that, as Lord Bradbury put it, the gold standard made the currency 'knave-proof', and the next Conservative chancellor of the exchequer, Winston Churchill, announced the immediate return to gold in his first budget speech on 28 April 1925. This made Britain the first major European country to return to gold convertibility and the only one fully to restore its pre-war parity (£1 = 0.23558 oz (6.679 g) of fine gold or $4.86). The decision was welcomed in parliament, the press, and particularly the City, which faced a growing challenge from New York for international supremacy as a financial capital. But hopes thus raised soon proved ill-founded. Industrial unrest, culminating in the General Strike of May 1926, pointed to the dangers of adopting a high and fixed exchange rate. Unemployment remained high and overseas trade failed to regain pre-war levels, leaving Britain economically depressed by the conventional criteria of the day. Nor did the City benefit. Churchill, embarrassed by the consequences of his decision, pressured the Bank of England to ease industry's plight by refraining from interest rate rises, which led the Bank to reintroduce informal overseas lending controls so as to keep sterling above its gold export point. The predicament became acute in July 1931 when sterling, undermined by a negative balance of payments, came under speculative attack. Despite the formation of a National Government determined to restore confidence by drastic public economies, and emergency assistance from France and the USA, sterling was forced off the gold standard on 21 September. The humiliation was intensely felt, and aggravated relations with France and the USA who were accused of failing to play by the rules of the gold standard game. With many other countries following Britain off gold, post-war efforts to restore a global integrated economy abruptly ended. The National Government itself used the occasion to introduce imperial trade protection while leaving sterling to find its own level. By the time the next round of post-war planning began, it was clear that dollars rather than gold would form the basis for a new monetary standard. *RWDB*

Robert Boyce, *British Capitalism at the Crossroads, 1919–1932: A Study in Politics. Economics and International Relations* (Cambridge, 1987). | Barry Eichengreen, *Golden Fetters: The Gold Standard and the Great Depression, 1919–1939* (New York, 1992).

Gollan, John (1911–77), Communist leader. Gollan was a party apparatchik, whose career took place within the Communist Party of Great Britain (CPGB). From the Edinburgh working class, he joined the youth section of the party in 1927. He became assistant editor of the *Daily Worker* in 1949 and in 1956 succeeded Hany Pollitt as general secretary of the party. He argued increasingly that socialism could be achieved without civil war, through pressures within and beyond parliament. Gollan retired in 1975 but remained influential within the ranks of the party. *CH*

Gollancz, Victor (1893–1967), publisher. Gollancz was a tireless worker for socialist and humanitarian causes and through his publishing business provided an outlet for socialist writers. Born in London into an Orthodox Jewish family and educated at St Paul's School and Oxford, Gollancz entered publishing after a brief spell as a schoolmaster. His initial contact with the publishing world came through involvement in Ernest Benn, of which firm he became managing director, but he went on to found Gollancz in 1928. In the late 1930s one of his major initiatives involved the launch of the *Left Book Club, which published some of the major socialist works of the 20th century. At this time, Gollancz hoped that war with Germany could be avoided. He was disappointed by events but engaged his energies at the end of the war in relieving distress within Germany. He also worked assiduously in the cause of Israel, while recognizing the serious problem of Arab refugees. Other issues also captured his interest: he campaigned vigorously against the death penalty and served on the National Campaign for the Abolition of Capital Punishment, and participated in the Campaign for Nuclear Disarmament. *CH*

R. Dudley Edwards, *Victor Gollancz: A Biography* (London, 1987). | John Lewis, *The Left Book Club: A Historical Record* (London, 1970).

Gordievsky, Oleg (1938–), spy. Gordievsky was the Secret Intelligence Services' (SIS) most successful penetration officer inside the KGB. An experienced first chief directive officer, he completed his training in 1963, then spent the years before 1982 both at KGB's Moscow headquarters and the KGB residency in Copenhagen. The invasion of Czechoslovakia by Soviet forces in 1968 and the crushing of reformist ideas across Eastern Europe alienated Gordievsky from the Soviet system, and in 1974 he began working for SIS. His main importance was in alerting Britain and the USA to Soviet fears of a NATO first strike, which reached their climax during the NATO 'Able Archer' exercise in November 1984. He reported on the bizarre methods used by the Soviet Union to monitor developments, which included changes in stocks held by British blood banks and the number of meetings between the queen and Mrs Thatcher. Gordievsky also passed to SIS vital information concerning KGB agents in Western capitals, as well as crucial information about the workings of the Soviet system and the apparatchiks running it. Between 1982 and 1985, Gordievsky was in London as deputy KGB resident. In that post he provided daily briefings for Mikhail Gorbachev, when, as a rising Soviet political star, Gorbachev visited London three months before becoming general secretary of the Soviet Communist Party. In 1985 Gordievsky was promoted to KGB resident in London but was almost immediately recalled to Moscow, where he was interrogated as a suspected British spy. Unable to find evidence, Gordievsky was released and eventually escaped to the West. In 1990 he published a history of KGB foreign operations jointly with Christopher Andrew. *PM*

Gordon Walker, Patrick Chrestien (1907–80), Labour politician. Gordon Walker was for years an influential intellectual, but became notorious for losing elections. Labour MP for Smethwick, 1945–64, he held junior government office, 1946–51. Despite defeat (on race) at *Smethwick in 1964, Wilson made him foreign secretary and found him a safe seat at Leyton, but he lost that too and had to resign office. He recaptured Leyton in 1966 and became minister without portfolio and then secretary for education and science, 1967–8. He was a member of the European parliament, 1975–6. *PRGR*

Robert Pearce (ed.), *Patrick Gordon Walker: Political Diaries* (London, 1991).

Gorell Barnes, William Lethbridge (1909–87), prime minister's personal assistant, 1946–8. A former Foreign Office, War Cabinet Office, and Treasury official who had been Clement Attlee's personal assistant when the latter was lord president of the council (1943–5), Gorell Barnes provided Attlee with advice on both international relations and the economy, and informed him on the progress of Britain's atomic programme. He was subsequently deputy secretary at the Colonial Office (1959–63) and a member of the UK team at the unsuccessful negotiations over membership of the European Economic Community in 1962. *CL*

Gormley, Joseph (1917–93), trade unionist and president of the National Union of Mineworkers (NUM), 1971–82. He joined the NUM in 1932 and was elected on to the executive in 1957. In 1960, Joe Gormley became secretary of Lancashire area NUM and in 1971 NUM president. A pragmatic leader who preferred negotiation to confrontation, he nevertheless led the miners' strikes of 1972 and 1974 most effectively, and so helped bring down the Heath government. *DLM*

Joe Gormley, *Battered Cherub: The Autobiography of Joe Gormley* (London, 1982).

'Gotcha!' A moronic headline in the *Sun* celebrating the sinking of the Argentinian cruiser **General Belgrano* in the Falklands war, an expression of the jeering jingoism fanned by the gutter press, savagely curtailed by the sinking of the British destroyer HMS *Sheffield* two days later. *AD*

ROBERT HARRIS, *Gotcha* (London, 1983).

Gould, Bryan Charles (1939–), Labour politician. Gould tried to revive the Labour Party by making neo-Keynesian economic ideas relevant in the 1990s. Born in New Zealand and educated there and at Oxford, he worked at the Foreign Office in London and Paris, 1966–8, and was law fellow at Worcester College, Oxford, 1968–74, when he was MP for Southampton, Test. Losing this seat in 1979, he was MP for Dagenham, 1983–94. He quit the shadow cabinet when Labour's NEC rejected the idea of a referendum on the 1992 Maastricht treaty, which treaty he had opposed. The same year he was trounced by John Smith (he got less than 9 per cent) and Margaret Beckett when running for party leader and deputy leader. He left the Commons in 1994 to become vice-chancellor of the University of Canterbury, New Zealand. *PRGR*

Goulding, Edward Alfred ('Paddy') (1862–1936), businessman and Conservative politician. A barrister, Goulding rose through London local politics to become an influential backbencher, 1895–1922. An enthusiastic tariff reformer, he allied himself with the Tory social reformers and the secret *Confederacy. Universally known as 'Paddy', Goulding was a close friend of Lord Beaverbrook and Law, supporting the latter in his two successful bids to become party leader. Due to Beaverbrook's intervention, he was for many years chairman of Rolls Royce Ltd. *RJQA*

Govan, Glasgow, by-elections (1973 and 1988). Following the publication in October 1973 of the Kilbrandon report on the constitution which highlighted the issue of devolution, the Scottish National Party (SNP) were able to win this safe Labour seat on 8 November. In addition to the growing prominence of constitutional issues, the nationalists had been building up an increasing head of steam which took the Labour Party by surprise. In March the nationalists launched the 'It's Scotland's Oil' campaign which took advantage of the discovery of North Sea oil at a time when the price of oil was escalating due to the effects of the Arab-Israeli war. The SNP candidate, Margo MacDonald, whose charismatic and energetic performance contrasted favourably with a lacklustre and complacent Labour showing, was an important factor in the nationalist victory. MacDonald lost the seat to Labour in February 1974, but, in a remarkable twist of fate, almost fifteen years later than the previous by-election to the day, MacDonald's husband, Jim Sillars, won Govan for the SNP in a by-election on 10 November 1988. A poor performance by the Labour candidate and disillusionment with the seeming impotence of Scotland's 50 Labour MPs to stop the implementation of Thatcherite policies north of the border were the major contributors to Sillars's victory. *RF*

Government Communications Headquarters (GCHQ). Like SIS, the British government's Cheltenham-based communications headquarters has never released historical documents concerning its past and so any accounts of its history rely heavily on conjecture. GCHQ has a continuous history dating back to the creation of the Royal Navy's room 40 as a signals intelligence centre during the Great War. In 1919, the British government, anxious to retain a code-breaking capacity, created an interdepartmental code and cypher school (GC & CS) that, despite serious shortages of money, maintained a lead in inter-war developments in cypher security. As a result of its integration into the Foreign Office, GC & CS maintained its integrity and developed important links to French and Polish code and cypher experts. Shortly before the outbreak of the Second World War, these links helped it obtain a German enigma machine, which was at the time considered capable of producing unbreakable codes. In 1938, GC & CS acquired Bletchley Park, an estate north of London, where, at the start of the Second World War, the rapidly expanding organization relocated. During the war, Bletchley Park succeeded in cracking the main German enigma codes and built the world's first electronic programmable computer, *Colossus.* Through their efforts, they provided Churchill, the chiefs of staff and operational heads with the 'ultra' secret, critical information which helped shorten the war. In 1940 and 1941 when Britain fought on alone, these decrypts provided Churchill with the few cards he had during his negotiations with Roosevelt and Stalin. Churchill recognized the central importance of Bletchley Park and gave it top priority: for him it was 'the goose that laid the golden eggs, but didn't cackle in the night'.

By the end of the war, Bletchley Park had around 7,000 personnel and was the world's leading and most successful code-breaking and signals intelligence centre. To maintain this vitally important function, the British government moved the by-now renamed Government Communications Headquarters to Cheltenham in 1948, having changed its priorities from German to Soviet communications and signals intelligence. In the circumstances of the Cold War, GCHQ played a vital role breaking Russian codes and in the development of new signal intelligence methods. These provided clues leading to the unmasking of atom spy Klaus Fuchs in 1950 and the attempt to arrest Donald Maclean a year later, foiled by his escape to Moscow with Guy Burgess.

The Second World War's great legacy was the link with the USA. American cryptographers worked at Bletchley Park and data was communicated on a daily basis during the critical battle of the Atlantic. The BRUSA agreement to share signals intelligence became the basis of this collaboration, and in 1947 the UKUSA agreement extended this collaboration to include Canada, Australia, and New Zealand. Between them these nations divided the world up into cryptographic spheres of influence. During the war Britain had been the dominant partner in the intelligence alliance; thereafter, the US with its vast resources quickly took over this role, particularly in the field of computer-based resources, together with photographic and satellite intelligence. However, so long as GCHQ's successes in the Cold War remain classified, it is impossible to assess its contribution. To date, the only decrypts declassified are those concerning Verona, which played a crucial role in the unmasking of spies in Britain and the USA: especially the atom spy Klaus Fuchs and Donald Maclean. In addition, GCHQ provided decrypts from Arab and other Middle East states during Suez and the Six Day War.

Until the 1980s, government denied the existence and function of GCHQ, in the same way it denied the existence of the Security Service (MI5) and the Secret Intelligence Service (MI6). However, it did not remain that way because, following a damaging industrial dispute at Cheltenham in 1981, Margaret Thatcher banned GCHQ employees from membership of trade unions. This decision and the way it was handled proved a public relations disaster, with GCHQ and its intelligence functions in the public gaze for months and years after. This and other revelations concerning Britain's intelligence community, not the least the publication of Bletchley Park's wartime role, forced the government to review its attitude to the service. The result was the 1994 Intelligence Services Act, which placed GCHQ and the other agencies on a statutory footing complete with parliamentary oversight. GCHQ's policy of open recruitment has also been matched by the declassification of most of its historical wartime documents. *PM*

Gow, Ian Reginald Edward (1937–90), Conservative politician. Gow was a libertarian rather than hard right-winger, and a provocative wit, resigning over Irish developments, but also unhappy in office: housing, 1983–5, and Treasury minister of state, 1985. He was an outspoken Unionist, killed by an IRA car bomb in 1990, ironically thus creating the Eastbourne by-election whose result destroyed Thatcher. Gow had been an outstanding parliamentary private secretary to Thatcher, making detailed study for her of trends of political opinion, but privately, shortly before his death, expressed the view that 'In view of her mighty services to the party, for her own sake, she should go'. *EP*

grammar schools, secondary schools usually of relatively old foundation, many of them dating back to the Tudor period, intended to give pupils a basic grounding in the classical languages, hence their name. Many foundations were originally charitable, providing places for non-fee-paying scholars. Over the centuries, most became primarily schools for the better-off, with some developing into *public schools. Most others were gradually absorbed into the state secondary education system during the 20th century. In many parts of England and Wales local education authorities created grammar schools either as new foundations or based upon older ones, as the most academic tier of secondary education. Their place in this regard was enshrined in the *Education Act, 1944, which established the grammar school as the destination for the academically orientated section of the school population which had passed the *eleven-plus examination. The grammar school system became the target for those who attacked the eleven-plus as socially divisive and discriminatory, especially towards working-class children. Implicit in advocacy of the system of comprehensivization from the 1950s was the abolition of the eleven-plus and so of grammar schools as a distinctive tier of education. In 1953, the Labour Party conference adopted comprehensivization as official party policy and in 1958 called for the abolition of the eleven-plus. By the 1964 general election some more rural councils were already operating 'all-in' comprehensives and others had set up sixth-form colleges to cater for academic education beyond 16. Labour's victory in 1964 was followed by the issue in July 1965 of circular 10/65 by the education secretary, Anthony Crosland, requiring all local authorities to draw up schemes for the comprehensivization of their secondary schools.

Although Heath's Conservative government withdrew circular 10/65, grammar schools continued to be closed in large numbers when Margaret Thatcher was education secretary, 1970–4, and its proposals were reimposed by the next Labour government's 1976 Education Act. Although, in turn, the Thatcher government sought to reverse the trend towards comprehensivization, the great majority of local education authorities had by that time either absorbed their grammar schools into an overall 11–16 comprehensive provision, turned them into sixth-form colleges, or allowed them to become independent schools. Hence one of the effects of the comprehensivization programme was to cause some of the most prestigious civic grammar schools, such as Manchester grammar school, to move into the independent sector.

By the late 1960s, defence of the grammar school system had become a major feature of the debate over education. The *Black Papers on education argued that the destruction of the grammar schools, the adoption of comprehensivization, and new teaching methods had contributed to declining educational standards. As a result, support was expressed for those Conservative local authorities which had retained grammar schools and there were calls for their return. Under Conservative government in the 1980s and 1990s, the remaining hundred grammar schools were given a reprieve and there was a shift towards 'opting out' and new types of school, such as city technology colleges, which sought to reproduce features seen to be associated with the grammar school system such as selection and high academic standards. The 1997 Labour government initially indicated its desire to remove remaining grammar schools, but proceeded cautiously. In 1999, legislation was passed giving parents the right to petition for ballots over the retention of grammar schools in their local authority area, but these provisions proved extremely hard to activate in practice. In contrast to England, Northern Ireland has retained the eleven-plus and a system of selective grammar schools throughout the post-war period (for half of which it has been directly ruled from Westminster). *JS*

Grayson, Victor (1881–?1922), socialist politician. Victor of the 1907 Colne valley by-election, Grayson was a firebrand socialist and the best platform speaker of his generation. In 1907 he won Colne Valley as an unofficial Labour candidate, breaking Labour's pact with the Liberals and in the face of opposition from the party leadership, then took his demand for a right to work bill to the Commons. In January 1910, however, he lost the seat and disappeared in mysterious circumstances after the Great War, a victim of drink and of a feud with Maundy Gregory, the salesman of honours. *BB*

Greater London Council. See LONDON LOCAL GOVERNMENT.

Great Illusion, The. See ANGELL, (RALPH) NORMAN.

Great Strike, Penrhyn Quarry. See PENRHYN STRIKE.

Great War (1914–18), conflict between the Allied and associated powers, principally the British Empire, France, and Russia, later joined by Italy (May 1915) and the USA (April 1917), and the central powers, principally Austria-Hungary and Germany, later joined by the Ottoman Empire (November 1914) and Bulgaria (July 1915). The war's origins lie in the spread of Slav nationalism in the Balkans, following the decay of Ottoman power, and the threat which this posed to the security of Austria-Hungary. The assassination of the Austrian Archduke Franz Ferdinand by a Serb nationalist at Sarajevo on 28 June 1914 set in train a series of diplomatic events which erupted into a European war on 1 August when Austria's ally, Germany, declared war on Russia, following this two days later with a declaration of war on Russia's ally, France. Great Britain declared war on Germany on 4 August. The ostensible cause of British belligerency was German violation of Belgian neutrality, but behind this lay British strategic determination to maintain the balance of power in Europe and concern for the long-term security and prosperity of the British Empire.

The architects of Britain's entry into the war, notably the Liberal foreign secretary, Sir Edward Grey, expected a 'traditional' British war, in which Britain's role would be largely naval and her military effort confined to the despatch of a small expeditionary force to support France. These comforting assumptions were immediately dispelled by the eruption onto the British political scene of the imperial proconsul Lord *Kitchener, who was appointed secretary of state for war on 5 August. Kitchener believed that the war would be long and require full national mobilization. He also believed that the war could not be concluded in a way satisfactory to British interests unless Britain raised a mass army and took a full (and preferably a final) part in the defeat of Germany. The immediate decision to raise a mass army was made with virtually no cabinet, parliamentary, or public debate, but the consequences were profound. Within less than two years from the outbreak of war, the strain of raising, equipping, and supplying Kitchener's 'new armies', numbered in millions, had resulted in the fall of Britain's last Liberal government (May 1915), the formation of a Ministry of Munitions (May 1915), which (under Lloyd George) was given unprecedented powers to transform the output of Britain's war industries, the introduction of compulsory military service (January and May 1916), the large-scale employment of women in transport and manufacturing industry, the acceptance of organized trade unionism in the highest councils of state, the suspension of the gold standard, and massive increases in taxation. From 1 July 1916, the beginning of the battles of the Somme, Britain's new armies also began to suffer the mass casualties for which the war is now principally remembered. The British army fought major wars against the Ottoman Empire at *Gallipoli, in Mesopotamia, and in Palestine, the outcome of which did much to shape the 20th-century Middle East. Substantial British contingents also fought against the Austrians in Italy and the Bulgarians in Macedonia. But what makes the Great War unique in British history is that the main part of the British army, the British Expeditionary Force (BEF), was engaged from start to finish with the main forces of the main enemy (Germany) on the main battlefield. This was the western front in France and Belgium, characterized from September 1914 by the development of opposing systems of trench fortifications and concrete strong points, defended by dense masses of barbed wire, interlocking arcs of machine guns, and masses of quick-firing artillery. The difficulties and human costs of fighting this war of attrition (leaving some 600,000 British Empire dead) have cast a permanent shadow over British perceptions of the war and especially over the BEF's principal commander, Douglas Haig. This has disguised the achievement of Haig's armies, deploying awesome firepower directed by leading edge technologies of sound ranging and flash spotting, tanks, ground attack aircraft, and gas, in bringing about the German surrender in November 1918.

The Great War, contrary to later impressions brought about by post-war disillusionment, enjoyed a very high degree of popular support. German violation of Belgian neutrality and subsequent 'atrocities' meant that British belligerency camped throughout the war on the moral high ground. Despite this, the war was politically divisive at the highest levels and has been seen by many as instrumental in the decline of Liberalism and the rise of Labour. Prime Minister Asquith's apparent unwillingness to win the war at all costs gradually undermined his authority among his cabinet and coalition colleagues and led to his replacement by Lloyd George in December 1916. The Liberal Party suffered a split from which it was never to recover. This was not the only important political change associated with the war, for there was a mass extension of the franchise in 1918 embracing all males aged 21 and over and, for the first time, women also had the vote (if aged 30 and over). Mass working-class electorates proved, perhaps, even more damaging to the Liberal Party than the leadership split. The enfranchisement of women (from 1928 on the same terms as men) eventually produced an electorate with a female majority, proportionately more sympathetic to the Conservative Party than male voters. Male and female perceptions of the role of women changed, though the employment of women in 'male' industrial occupations did not survive the return to peacetime conditions. Perceptions of the appropriate role of the state were also changed, if not quite transformed. The trade union movement achieved a degree of political respectability and power, which it retained until the 1980s.

The most important long-term political effect, however, was probably the feeling, soon common to public and elite opinion, that the war had been just too costly in blood and treasure, a view re-emphasized in the 1960s with the growing popularity of war poets like Siegfried Sassoon and Wilfred Owen, and the writings of Paul *Fussell. After 1918, though, the dominant opinion came to be just that the experience was one that ought not to be repeated, and this helped to provide the background to appeasement in the 1930s. *JMB*

J. M. Bourne, *Britain and the Great War 1914–1918* (London, 1989). | John Turner, *British Politics and the Great War* (London, 1992).

Greek civil war. See Truman doctrine.

green belt, areas of land deliberately left open and protected from development. They are intended to check the sprawl of large built-up areas, safeguard surrounding countryside from encroachment, discourage the merger of neighbouring urban communities, preserve the character of historic towns, and encourage urban regeneration by prioritizing the rescue of derelict and other urban land rather than greenfield sites. The idea of green belts was a characteristic feature of British town and country planning from the end of the 19th century. They were an intrinsic part of Ebenezer *Howard's influential and visionary scheme for *garden cities, publicized in his book *Tomorrow: A Peaceful Path to Real Reform* in 1898. Moderately sized urban communities of about 30,000 people would be separated from each other by areas of farmland and woods. The idea was taken up by town and country planners such as Raymond Unwin and Patrick *Abercrombie as a means both of restricting urban growth and of providing a 'green lung' of recreational space around urban areas. In 1938, the first prototype green belt was established around the fringes of Greater London under the London and Counties Green Belt Act, but it was only with the wartime plans of Abercrombie for London and its environs that it received definitive shape. The *Greater London Plan* of 1944 envisaged a heavily restricted zone of development contiguous to the existing urban area of London, in which new housing and commercial development would be prohibited. Beyond this a zone designated for development was to be established with a ring of *new towns providing nodal points for growth. The green belt around London was established after 1945 and in August 1955 the idea became part of general government planning policy when the housing minister, Duncan Sandys, ordered 140 local authorities to set up green belts similar to London's. Since then, green belts have provided the blueprint for local development, although subject to the discretion of local authorities. Concerns about erosion of the green belts by new development have surfaced regularly since the 1960s, prompting planning disputes between local authorities, developers, and local conservation groups. Recent concern has focused on the trend towards the use of green belt land for a new generation of out-of-town superstores and leisure facilities. In 1999, 3,706,500 acres (1.5 million hectares) were designated as green belt in England and a further 385,476 acres (156,000 hectares) in Scotland. *JS*

Green Book. See *Land and the Nation*.

Green Party, founded in 1973 as the People's Party and renamed the Ecology Party in 1975, the Green Party adopted its current name in September 1985. The party campaigns to raise public consciousness about environmental and peace issues and to promote an 'ecological' or 'green' perspective on economic matters. By 1987, the Green Party had an estimated 6,000 members and almost a hundred parish or community councillors, plus three district councillors. It fielded 133 candidates in the 1987 general election, compared with 53 in 1979, polling 89,854 votes, but losing its deposit in every contest. The Green Party's influence extends, though, much more widely than its electoral performance, with the activities of the *Greenpeace organization to alert public attention to environmental hazards. The party achieved a breakthrough in the 1989 European elections, when it achieved its best results, with 14.9 per cent of the vote, and took second place in six Euro-constituencies, though obtaining no MEPs. It benefited from growing environmental concerns aroused by Chernobyl, acid rain, the greenhouse effect, and pollution. Party membership also rose rapidly, making it an effective force in local politics. The party retains a loose structure and has no leader, only spokespersons. It consistently achieved over 4 per cent of support in national opinion polls in 1989–90 but fell thereafter. In the 1992 general election the Green Party polled only 170,000 votes and was subsequently plagued by a period of infighting. In 1997, it fielded only a third of the candidates it had in 1992 (95 as opposed to 254) and again failed to secure any MPs. It has had some continuing success, however, at local level and secured a number of council seats. Under the regional list system it won two seats in the 1999 European elections on 6.8 per cent of the vote, and had earlier obtained a seat in the new Scottish parliament. *JS*

Greene, Sidney Francis (1910–), trade unionist. Sid Greene was general secretary of the National Union of Railwaymen, 1957–75, and was also a prominent member of the TUC, acting as chairman of the TUC general council, 1968–70, in the critical period of *In Place of Strife*. A staunch moderate, he was knighted in 1970, made a life peer in 1974, and fulfilled many other national duties in retirement. *KL*

Greene, Wilfred Arthur (1883–1952), judge. A man of many talents, Greene dedicated much of his life to the service of the law. Before his appointment to the Court of Appeal (1935), he chaired a number of committees dealing with company law, trade practices, and telecommunications. He was promoted to master of the rolls (1937) and to a lord of appeal in ordinary (1949). Much of the modern law of judicial review of the actions of central and local government can be traced to his decision in *Associated Provincial Picture Houses Ltd* v. *Wednesbury Corporation* ([1948] 1 KB 223). *ML*

Greenham Common (US Cruise Missile Airbase, Newbury). The women's peace camp at Greenham was established in 1981. Despite prosecution by civil and military authorities, hundreds of women remained encamped through the early 1980s to protest against the installation of *cruise missiles. In December 1982, 30,000 women encircled the 9 mile (14.5 km) fence, and in 1983 women invaded the base and danced on the missile silos. Protests continued intermittently until, with the end of the Cold War, the base closed. Despite widespread hostile publicity, Greenham remained a potent international symbol of women's rejection of war and violence. *RKST*

Greenpeace, activist environmental pressure group. Formed in 1971, it is notable for its pro-active stance to protect the environment and conserve animal life. For example, Greenpeace protesters have attempted to interfere with Japanese whaling operations and deliberately sailed into sea areas where nuclear testing was scheduled. The group achieved worldwide publicity in 1985 when the Greenpeace ship *Rainbow Warrior*, sent to protest against French nuclear testing in the Pacific, was sunk by French secret service agents in Auckland harbour with the loss of two lives. A high profile campaign was also mounted in 1996 against the dumping at sea of a disused UK oil exploration platform. The organization had an estimated membership in 1991 of 410,000, in 210 groups. *JS*

Greenwood, Arthur (1880–1954), Labour politician. Greenwood was a political organizer and one of a handful of politicians who provided the Labour Party with solid backbone when its future seemed in doubt between 1931 and 1940. Educated at Leeds University, he lectured there in economics, contested Southport for Labour in 1918, and was MP for Nelson and Colne, 1922–31, and Wakefield from 1932 until his death. He was minister of health in MacDonald's second government, 1929–31, contested the leadership and became deputy to Attlee in 1935. He spoke powerfully in the 1940 debate that brought down Neville Chamberlain ('Speak for England, Arthur!' he was urged) and served in the war cabinet, 1940–2, when he became acting leader of the party and held the post of party treasurer, 1943–54. He was lord privy seal, 1945–7, paymaster general, 1946–7, and minister without portfolio, 1947–51, under Attlee. He was the father of Tony *Greenwood. *PRGR*

Greenwood, Arthur William James ('Tony') (1911–82), Labour politician. The son of Labour minister Arthur *Greenwood, he was MP for Heywood and Radcliffe, 1946–50, and Rossendale, 1950–70. Greenwood served continuously as a Bevanite member of the NEC of the Labour Party, 1954–70, becoming party chairman in 1963–4, and contesting the party leadership in 1961. Widely considered an ineffective cabinet minister, 1964–70, Wilson then persuaded him to run for the general secretaryship of the party. After his defeat he was created Lord Greenwood of Rossendale. *BJE*

Greenwood, Hamar (1870–1948), Liberal and subsequently Conservative politician. Born in Canada, Greenwood moved to England in 1895 and was called to the Bar in 1906. He served as Liberal MP for York, 1906–10, Sunderland, 1910–22, and as a Conservative for East Walthamstow, 1924–9. After serving in France, 1914–16, he was secretary to the Overseas Trade Department, 1919–20. As a tough chief secretary for Ireland in the Troubles of 1920–2, he reinforced the Royal Irish Constabulary with the *Black and Tans, whose dubious conduct he stoutly defended. Given a peerage in 1929, he was treasurer of the Conservative Party, 1933–8. *JS*

Gregory, (Arthur John) Maundy (1877–1941), conman and salesman of honours. The son of a Southampton clergyman, Gregory was first an actor and theatrical stage manager, though his entire life remained an act long after he gave up the stage. He made many friends in high places, including reigning European monarchs (he himself claimed descent from no fewer than eight English kings), and was for a time involved in running a magazine, itself very close to fraud, but he came to political prominence as the middleman used by Lloyd George's chief whip, Freddy *Guest, when raising money for the National (Lloyd George) Liberals after 1916. Gregory had a palatial Westminster office (Colin Coote thought it seemed a cross between Downing Street and MI5) and may have earned as much as £30,000 a year in commission for the sale of political honours (see HONOURS SYSTEM). When the 1922 *honours scandal made further work of this kind impossible, he turned to other deceptions which eventually exiled him to France. He died near Paris, in a German military prison—by then posing as 'Sir' Arthur Gregory. *JAR*

TOM CULLEN, *Maundy Gregory* (London, 1974).

Grenada incident (1983). US intervention in the Caribbean island of Grenada (a member of the Commonwealth) caused a squall of mutual Anglo-American exasperation in October 1983, even between Margaret Thatcher and Ronald Reagan, so compatible in ideology and bellicosity. But Grenada was not the Falklands (despite Reagan's reminder 'When she needed us, we were there'); there was no consultation, just bare notification, which meant British humiliation. Taunted by the opposition as 'Reagan's poodle', Thatcher swallowed hard: 'Britain's friendship with the United States must on no account be jeopardized.' *AD*

Grey, Edward (1862–1933), Liberal politician. Sir Edward Grey (he was already a baronet and a substantial landowner in Northumberland) was the youngest MP in the Commons when elected for Berwick-upon-Tweed in 1885, representing it until he took a peerage in 1916 as Viscount Grey of Falloden. In his early political career, Grey supported Irish home rule and land reform. He was under-secretary at the Foreign Office, 1892–5, and, siding with the *Liberal Imperialists, he supported Britain's cause in the Boer war. Appointed foreign secretary in December 1905 he inherited the 1904 Anglo-French Entente Cordiale and made the defence of France against German aggression the principal feature of British foreign policy while avoiding a binding alliance. He supported France in the two *Moroccan crises of 1905–6 and 1911. He also renewed the 1902 Anglo-Japanese alliance in 1911, and one of his major achievements was the Anglo-Russian entente of August 1907. Radicals accused Grey of secret diplomacy and covert pledges to France, but these went no further than military conversations (which did, however, increase Britain's moral obligations to her allies). Although he sought agreement with Germany over the Baghdad railway in 1913, his outrage over German violation of Belgian neutrality in 1914, and determination to fulfil Britain's 'obligations of honour' towards France, led him to support Britain's entry into the Great War and to defend it most persuasively in the Commons.

Grey could achieve little in diplomacy once war broke out and when the government was reconstructed in December 1916 he lost office with other Asquithian Liberals. His reflections on the origins of the war led him to support a league of nations as an arbiter of international disputes. When the actual *League of Nations was founded in 1919, Grey became president of the *League of Nations Union, and, as temporary ambassador to Washington in 1919, he attempted unsuccessfully to bring the USA into the league. Some fanciful attempts were made to entice Grey back into politics to lead a new centre party in 1919–21, but he declined due to failing eyesight. In 1923–4, however, he led the Liberals in the Lords and served from 1927 to 1933 as president of the Liberal Council which attempted to preserve Liberal values. *JS*

Keith Robbins, *Sir Edward Grey: A Biography of Lord Grey of Falloden* (London, 1971). | G. M. Trevelyan, *Grey of Falloden* (London, 1937).

Grieve, Christopher Murray. See MacDiarmid, Hugh.

Griffith, Arthur (1871–1922), Irish nationalist. A Dublin-born printer, writer, and journalist, Griffith was educated by the Christian Brothers, and was a founder-member of the Celtic Literary Society in 1893. He was also a member of the Gaelic League and Irish Republican Brotherhood. Working in gold mines in South Africa during 1896–8, he edited, on his return to Ireland, radical nationalist newspapers (the *United Irishman* and subsequently *Sinn Fein*). Griffith espoused independence for Ireland under a dual monarchy (ingeniously set out in his *The Resurrection of Hungary: A Parallel for Ireland* (1904)), and also a Listian protectionist economics. His ideas were central to Sinn Fein, established in 1905. Griffith joined the Irish Volunteers in 1913, and participated in their Howth gun-running in the following year. However, his emphasis was essentially non-violent. He took no part in the 1916 Easter Rising, but was arrested afterwards because of his perceived influence. Vice-president of the post-rising, revitalized Sinn Fein, he was elected Sinn Fein MP for East Cavan in 1918. Though not truly a republican, Griffith was a leading figure in the Irish republican movement of 1919–21; he was acting president of the Dáil in 1919, and was imprisoned during 1920–1. He was the leading Irish negotiator of the 1921 Anglo-Irish treaty (which led to the establishment of the Irish Free State), a leading pro-treaty politician in 1922, and president of the Dáil in the latter year. Griffith's ideas have been profoundly influential in Irish nationalist thinking, self-reliance and self-sufficiency in economics and mentality becoming key features of subsequent nationalist philosophy. *RE*

Brian Maye, *Arthur Griffith* (Dublin, 1997).

Griffith (or Gruffydd), Moses (1893–1973), agriculturist and Welsh nationalist. Griffith was born on the Llyn peninsula and briefly served in the wartime Veterinary Corps before studying agricultural botany at Bangor. He subsequently combined farming with pioneering work on grasslands as project director, government adviser, and consultant. He was Plaid Cymru's first treasurer, 1925–32, and did much to shape its agricultural policy which emphasized self-sufficiency as a means of regenerating the essentially rural culture of Wales. He was for many years a benefactor both of Saunders Lewis and his party. *PS*

Griffith-Boscawen, Arthur Sackville Trevor (1865–1946), Conservative politician. Griffith-Boscawen was MP for all but four of the years 1892–1922. A tariff reformer, he achieved office under Lloyd George and became agriculture minister in 1921. He ultimately grew disenchanted with the coalition and joined Stanley Baldwin in overturning it at the *Carlton Club meeting which brought Andrew Bonar Law to the premiership. Appointed health minister in October 1922, he unfortunately lost his seat in the 1922 election and at a subsequent by-election and was never able to restart his career. *RJQA*

Arthur Griffith-Boscawen, *Fourteen Years in Parliament* (London, 1907). | Arthur Griffith-Boscawen, *Memories* (London, 1925).

Griffiths, Brian (1941–), head of prime minister's policy unit, 1985–90. An academic economist, Griffiths advised Thatcher on economic matters in opposition. At Downing Street he supported the views of her economic adviser Alan Walters, but did not enjoy good relations with the Treasury. A committed Christian, interested in family issues, he took the leading role in framing the Education Reform Act, 1988, and influenced the policy behind the Broadcasting Act, 1990, and the introduction of the internal market to the NHS. *CL*

Griffiths, James (1890–1975), trade unionist and Labour cabinet minister. A former coal miner and miners' agent, he was elected Labour MP for Llanelli in 1936. Griffiths served in the Attlee government as minister of national insurance, 1945–50, when he implemented the proposals of the *Beveridge report (1942) with measures for national insurance, national assistance, and industrial injuries compensation. He was also chairman of the Labour Party, 1948–9, and secretary of state for the colonies, 1950–1. A fervent devolutionist, Griffiths was the first secretary of state for Wales, 1964–6. *JGJ*

James Griffiths, *Pages from Memory* (London, 1969).

Grigg, Edward William Macleay (1879–1955), colonial administrator and politician. Initially a journalist, Grigg was profoundly influenced by the ideas of the 'kindergarten', the forcing house of young administrative talent that gathered around *Milner in South Africa. This career was followed by a period in the army, rising to lieutenant-colonel. Upon return to civilian life he became private secretary to Lloyd George, who encouraged his entry into politics as a Liberal representing Oldham, 1922–5. In 1925 he was appointed governor of Kenya, although he failed to achieve his object of unifying Kenya, Tanganyika, and Uganda. Against the perceived wisdom he placed his trust in tribal self-government and provincial autonomy. He returned to England in 1930 and re-entered politics in 1933 as Conservative MP for Altrincham. Concerned at the rise of Nazi Germany, and especially because of the weaknesses of British armaments, he campaigned for the introduction of national service. He nevertheless remained loyal to the leadership. During the Second World War he held junior ministerial posts and became Lord Altrincham in 1945. *NJC*

Grigg, (Percy) James (1880–1964), public servant. With the patronage of Sir Warren Fisher, Grigg became principal private secretary to the chancellor of the exchequer, 1921–31. During this time he was at the heart of British economic policy, attending for example the 1923 Washington war debt conference. This was followed by a period at the Inland Revenue and service in India. His organizational skills earned him the secretaryship of state for war, 1942–5, which obliged him to take a parliamentary seat as a National MP. *NJC*

Grimond, Joseph (1913–93), leader of the Liberal Party, 1956–67, and a principal figure in its recovery after 1945. Educated at Oxford, Grimond trained as a barrister, then served as MP for Orkney and Shetland, 1950–83. He took over the leadership from Clement *Davies in 1956 at the nadir of the party's fortunes, and gave it fresh vision and drive. His leadership saw the party achieve its first by-election success since 1929 at *Torrington in 1958, further success at *Orpington in 1962, and a doubling of its MPs from six in 1956 to twelve in 1966. His aim to create an effective radical, non-socialist party of the left had achieved only partial success by the time of his resignation in 1967, with the Liberals still only a minor parliamentary force. Succeeded by Jeremy *Thorpe, he served as interim leader in May–June 1976 after the latter's resignation. Although he opposed the *Lib-Lab pact (1977–8), he proved sympathetic towards the *Alliance and was a respected elder statesman during the difficult transition of the Liberal Party into the Liberal Democrats. His support for such ideas as Scottish devolution and support for the

European Community left a lasting imprint on Liberal and later Liberal Democrat policy. *JS*

Grosvenor Square riot. See RIOTS.

Groundnut scheme. Groundnuts are a high protein, extremely nutritious legume grown extensively in temperate climates as a source of edible oil. They are not a true nut, but the pod of *Arachis hypogaea* which has the peculiar habit of ripening underground. During the worldwide food shortages of the late 1940s, the Labour government initiated a Groundnut scheme to encourage their commercial production, mainly in Tanganyika, east Africa. The scheme, promoted initially by John Strachey, minister of food and managing director of the United Africa Company, entailed the clearing of millions of acres of scrubland. Generally regarded as an embarrassing fiasco, it cost more than £40 million over five years. *JFM*

Gruffydd, Moses. See GRIFFITH, MOSES.

Gruffydd, William John (1881–1954), poet, critic, and politician. W. J. Gruffydd was the foremost Welsh scholar of the first half of the 20th century. The son of a north Wales quarryman, he was educated at Jesus College, Oxford, before an almost thirty-year tenure of a professorship at Cardiff. He was a prolific author, a brilliant editor of the journal *Y Llennor*, and Liberal MP for the University of Wales, 1943–50. He was first elected in a famous 1943 by-election in which he defeated Saunders Lewis of Plaid Cymru, a party to which he had previously belonged. *PS*

Grunwick (1976), violent industrial dispute. Grunwick was a badly equipped mail order film-processing laboratory in Willesden, where, in order to compete, it employed a predominately black and female labour force as casual labour. The pay was low, the workforce compelled to work overtime, and employers denied any right to unionization. The workforce struck against this in August 1976 but despite Lord Scarman's inquiry the law could not force the employers to recognize a unionized workforce demanding better conditions of employment. There were much-publicized violent clashes on the picket line, in which some Labour ministers became damagingly involved. *KL*

Guardian, Liberal- and subsequently Labour-supporting newspaper. First appearing in 1821 as the *Manchester Guardian*, it was edited by a series of extremely influential journalists, notably C. P. *Scott, who was editor, 1872–1929, and A. P. *Wadsworth, 1944–56. Always the voice of the Liberal- and Labour-inclined middle-class conscience, the *Manchester Guardian* had firm roots in northern Nonconformist and Liberal politics. Under pressure from the more competitive world of mid-20th-century publishing, the newspaper changed its name to the *Guardian* in 1959 and was published from London from 1961, doubling its circulation to about 400,000 by the 1990s. It still retains a distinctive anti-establishment stance and a strong support for civil liberties causes. *JS*

DAVID AYERST, *The Manchester Guardian: Biography of a Newspaper* (New York, 1971).

Guest, Frederick Edward (1875–1937), politician and promoter of aviation. Freddy Guest acted as private secretary to his cousin, Winston Churchill, and served as a Liberal MP, 1910–22 and 1923–9, then as a Conservative MP, 1931–7. He was secretary for air, 1921–2, but was most prominent as Lloyd George's chief whip and main political fixer, 1917–21, using Maundy *Gregory to sell honours and so raise the *Lloyd George fund, to finance a coalition Liberal organization. Cynical, lightweight, and a corrupter of political ethics, Herbert *Gladstone thought Guest to be 'Lloyd George's evil genius'. *JS*

Guildford Four, Paul Hill, Gerard Conlon, Carole Richardson, and Patrick Armstrong, gaoled for life in 1975 for the fatal IRA Guildford and Woolwich pub bombings of late 1974. They were released in 1989, the Court of Appeal deciding that the police had lied about the confessions on which the convictions rested, and which the accused had retracted. The four were found not guilty after a retrial in 1990. In 1993 three former detectives were cleared of the charge of conspiracy to pervert the course of justice, in relation to interview notes in the Guildford case. *RE*

guild socialism, utopian leftist principle that flourished during the 1910s and 1920s. It offered an alternative to the dominant statist conception of socialism in Britain, drawing on pluralist theory to offer a vision of a society characterized by industrial democracy and the dignity of labour. In this society power would be shared between producers, organized into industrial unions, and consumers, represented by the state. There would be no conflict of interest because everyone would be both consumer and producer. These ideas, first presented in A. R. Orage's *New Age* by S. G. Hobson and later developed by G. D. H. *Cole reflected a growing concern, shared with the syndicalists, about the nature of state socialism. Hilaire Belloc in *The*

Servile State had suggested that workers would become little more than 'well fed instruments of production' whilst 'wage slavery' would continue. Cole pointed out that the state was shaped by economic forces over which it had little control, and therefore any attempt to transform society by parliamentary means would fail. Guild socialists, however, rejected the syndicalist general strike in favour of a gradual encroachment upon managerial prerogatives by the unions. Guild socialist ideas gained credibility because of growing support for the notion of workers' control during the war years. In practical terms, however, they achieved little. The National Guilds League, formed in 1915, never had more than a thousand members. Its only significant success came in 1920 with the national building guild, which flourished briefly in the post-war property boom before collapsing in 1923. Guild socialist ideas were eclipsed by the increasingly monolithic post-war Labour Party and by the emergence of the Communist Party. They enjoyed a brief resurgence in the 1930s and the 1960s but in essence they made too many assumptions about the goodness and reasonableness of human behaviour. *MC*

Margaret Cole, *The Life of G. D. H. Cole* (London, 1971).

guillotine. See Commons, House of: procedure.

Guinness, Walter Edward (1880–1944), Conservative politician. Irish-born, Guinness entered parliament as MP for Bury St Edmunds in 1907. He was under-secretary of state for war, 1922, followed by two periods as financial secretary to the Treasury, 1923 and 1924–5, before securing cabinet status as minister of agriculture, 1925–9. As Lord Moyne (1932) he returned as agriculture minister in 1939 before becoming colonial secretary and leader of the Lords. As minister in the Middle East in 1942, he was assassinated by terrorists in Palestine. *NJC*

Gulf war (1990–1). On 2 August 1990 the Iraqi president, Saddam Hussein, began an invasion of the tiny neighbouring country of Kuwait, a long-standing British ally and important source of oil. It was also feared that Iraqi forces might attempt to invade other pro-Western nations in the area, particularly Saudi Arabia. A quick deployment of American troops to Saudi Arabia thus followed and was soon supplemented by further contingents from the UN, including a large British force, While the build-up of forces in the Gulf continued, the hope of a diplomatic solution was maintained, but when those efforts stalled the UN demanded an unconditional Iraqi withdrawal from Kuwait and threatened military action to enforce compliance. Maintaining a joint stance among the allies proved difficult, since it involved inter-Arab/Muslim questions of loyalty, and also provoked reactions from Russia and China. By December, though, the military build-up was complete and the American General ('Storming Norman') Schwarzkopf, overall commander of the UN forces, prepared to launch his campaign, aiming to make full use of considerable technological superiority over Iraqi forces.

On 17 January, the first stage of the operation began. For ten days, aerial assaults overwhelmed Iraq's command and control centres, smashed communications links, and grounded the Iraqi air force. It was also a period of controversy, due to the fact that many so-called 'smart weapons' missed their intended targets or hit targets which proved to be of no military value, incurring loss of Iraqi civilian lives in the process. The Iraqi government attempted to make propaganda value out of these mistakes (all this by now easily visible to Western viewers on cable television). Iraq also attempted to draw Israel into the conflict by launching a series of rocket strikes on Israeli cities, hoping that an Israeli response would shatter delicate Arab unity against Iraq. Frantic diplomatic efforts were made to keep Israel out, including the US Patriot missile system delivered to Israel to fight off the threat from Iraq's Scud missiles.

Allied land forces moved into action on 24 February. Schwarzkopf had decided to avoid the Iraqi defences dug in on the Kuwait–Saudi Arabian frontier. Instead, his forces attacked the Iraq frontier itself and then wheeled round to attack the exposed western flank of Kuwait. Iraqi troops, poorly equipped and poorly led, surrendered in droves or withdrew rapidly. Casualties to the allies were minimal (not so the Iraqi forces, which suffered very heavy losses). One great tragedy, though, was the loss of British soldiers, thanks to a 'friendly fire' incident. By 28 February, Kuwait City had been liberated. The retreat of Iraq's forces had fulfilled UN resolution 678, which empowered UN forces to use all necessary means to eject Iraq from Kuwait—but nothing more. Political controversy therefore now broke out as to whether allied forces should continue their pursuit of the Iraqi army, so as to neutralize it completely and (hopefully) bring down Saddam too. Caution won the day, however, when allied forces were brought to a halt and then withdrawn from Iraq. Since the end of the war, UN sanctions against Iraq have been maintained, as have two 'no-fly' zones designed to stop persecution of Iraqi's minority groups. *MLC*

LAURENCE FREEDMAN and EFRAIM KARSH, *The Gulf Conflict 1990–1991: Diplomacy and the New World Order* (London, 1993).

Gulland, John William ('Jack') (1864–1927), Liberal politician. Gulland was an active local politician in Edinburgh before entering the Commons for Dumfries in 1906. He was a Liberal whip from 1909, and *Asquith's chief whip, 1915–16, during the period in which his party moved inexorably towards Asquith's overthrow. He then went into opposition with Asquith and remained Liberal chief whip until losing his seat in 1918. *JAR*

Gummer, John Selwyn (1939–), Conservative politician. Originally a partisan, spoilt youth politician, rebuking women priests, at environment he was a serious force. Briefly party chairman, 1984–5, after Parkinson's sex crisis, Gummer was then down-ranked. Ardently pro-poll tax, he became minister of agriculture (1989), notoriously feeding his daughter hamburger on-camera during the beef crisis, but at environment, 1993–7, he became critical of cars and rural supermarkets. A pro-European and Major loyalist, Gummer's status on the Tory left emphasized the party's shift. *EP*

Gunn, Neil (1891–1973), Scottish novelist. Gunn was an active member of the Scottish National Party (SNP) in the mid-1930s. He was involved in the merger of the National Party of Scotland and the Scottish Party to form the SNP in 1934. The party's lack of electoral success and its interminable infighting left him disillusioned by the late 1930s, by which time he played little role in nationalist politics. *RF*

Gun-running (1914). In January 1913 the Ulster Unionist Council authorized the formation of the *Ulster Volunteer Force (UVF) as a formal paramilitary army, to consist of 100,000 men aged between 17 and 65. The political leaders of Ulster Unionist resistance showed some reluctance to authorize arming, but Major Fred Crawford produced a scheme of running in 20,000 to 30,000 rifles with ammunition into Ulster. While the Liberal government was still reeling from the shock of the *Curragh 'mutiny', Crawford was buying the weapons, which were then landed at Larne harbour, Bangor, and Donaghadee on the night of 24–5 April 1914. This gun-running had two important effects: it was a Unionist propaganda coup; but it encouraged the Irish Volunteers (IVF), formed in 1913 in imitation of the UVF but in order to defend home rule, to try to emulate the UVF and run guns into Ireland. The IVF sought to raise a loan to buy arms and succeeded in purchasing some 1,500 obsolete Mauser rifles and 45,000 rounds of ammunition. They ran these into Howth harbour on 26 July 1914 in a yacht owned by the Anglo-Irishman Erskine Childers. In Bachelors Walk an angry collision occurred between soldiers, who were being taunted by the crowd, and the marchers, which resulted in the troops opening fire, killing three people and wounding 38. The upshot of these two gun-running episodes was to weaken respect for law and order, and arm two paramilitary forces which, however militarily weak, might sooner or later confront each other, and thus plunge Ireland into civil war. *DGB*

ALVIN JACKSON, 'Larne Gun-Running in 1914', *History Ireland*, 1 (1993). | A. T. Q. STEWART, *The Ulster Crisis* (London, 1967).

Gunter, Raymond Jones (1909–77), Labour politician. Ray Gunter was Wilson's minister of labour, 1964–8, a post he described on his appointment as 'the bed of nails'. From the beginning he found himself in conflict with the trade unions by angering them in an article in *Socialist Commentary*, in which he threatened government action if they failed to reform themselves. In April 1968 he became minister of power but resigned in July 1968, complaining of general dissatisfaction with government policy. He voted in favour of entry to the European Community in 1971 and resigned the Labour whip in the following year. *KL*

H

Hacking, Douglas Hewitt (1884–1950), Conservative politician and party organizer. Representing Chorley, 1918–45, Hacking served his early parliamentary years as parliamentary private secretary to Craigavon and Worthington-Evans, before a junior ministerial post at the Home Office, 1925–7. This secured his reputation as a Commons performer, but his initial promise was not fulfilled for he never advanced beyond under-secretary (Home Office, 1933–4; War Office, 1934–5; Dominions, 1935–6). In fact Hacking's role was developing in terms of the party's organization. From being appointed vice-chairman of the National Union in 1930, he rose to party chairman, 1936–42. He began a series of reviews of party organization, including parliamentary candidates' financial obligations and London area organization, that prefigured the post-1945 Conservative Party recovery. He advised Chamberlain against calling a snap election in the aftermath of the Munich agreement, fearing it would antagonize the trade unions with potentially dire consequences for the rearmament programme. He reluctantly agreed to remain at Central Office under Churchill but found that his calls for the party to adopt a social reform programme were ignored. Elevated to the Lords in 1945. *NJC*

Hague, William Jefferson (1961–), Conservative party leader, 1997–2001. He was described as 'the next Conservative leader but 14', after a conference speech in 1977 when aged 16 and an assured if insufferable encomium of Thatcherism and Thatcher, neither then ascendant. After an Oxford first, Union presidency, and McKinsey recruitment, he squeaked into parliament at the Richmond by-election, 1988. Junior office followed, then cabinet (secretary for Wales) at 34, in 1995, the vacancy following the previous Welsh secretary Redwood's pitch at the leadership. Hague, though, learned Welsh, travelled the country meeting people, in contrast with the Anglocentric Redwood; Hague also became engaged to Ffion Jenkins, herself Welsh. He stood for the 1997 leadership succession in the parliamentary party, a mechanism he promptly replaced, but was assisted by the inability of Lilley, Redwood, or Howard to win, Portillo being unavoidably absent, and the shift of Dorrell's support to Clarke, which concentrated all the non-left-wing vote upon Hague. Insisting that there would be 'No leadership honeymoon', an early visit to the Notting Hill carnival involved Hague in the demotic wearing of a baseball cap back to front—mocked as a public relations ploy, and as cover for Hague's premature baldness. Pressing hard in the Eurosceptic direction, Hague closed off Tory acceptance of the Euro for ten years, involving the resignation of junior front-benchers Ian Taylor and David Curry and the public displeasure of Heseltine and Clarke, but the ploy appeared to play well with Tory voters. He recovered ground with parliamentary performances, especially at Prime Minister's Questions where he was quicker, better informed, and cleverer than Tony Blair—also funnier. But the crisis over the future of the Lords, involving the sacking of Viscount *Cranborne in 1999, suggested the continuing difficulty of party management for any new Conservative leader out of government office. Both his own and his party's poll-ratings stubbornly refused to rise, and after the 2001 election defeat he resigned at once. *EP*

Haig, Douglas (1861–1928), soldier. After a successful pre-war career, during which he contributed to R. B. Haldane's military reforms, Haig served on the western front throughout the *Great War and commanded British forces, 1915–19. On the Somme (1916), at Arras and third Ypres ('Passchendaele') (1917) and during the epic retreats and advances of 1918, he commanded Britain's largest ever armies in the greatest and most costly battles the country ever fought. Revulsion at the human costs of victory, post-war disillusionment, and the poisonous assault on Haig's humanity and professional competence by Lloyd George turned him into one of the most controversial and reviled personalities in modern British history, often portrayed as a stupid butcher with no more idea how to win the war than piling corpse upon corpse. His smaller band of admirers have emphasized his immense achievements in organizing, training, and supplying British armies of unprecedented size while in constant contact with the main forces of a powerful enemy in a complicated coalition war, his openness to new ideas, and his post-war work for the welfare of veterans. *JMB*

Gerard De Groot, *Douglas Haig 1861–1928* (London, 1988). | John Terraine, *Douglas Haig: The Educated Soldier* (London, 1963).

Hailsham, Lord. See Hogg, Quintin McGarel and Hogg, Douglas McGarel.

Haines, Joseph Thomas William (1928–), prime minister's chief press secretary, 1969–70 and 1974–6. A former *Daily Mirror* journalist, Joe Haines provided a more partisan service than his predecessor, Trevor Lloyd-Hughes. He served Wilson in opposition (1970–4) and became the prime minister's closest confidant after 1974, writing Wilson's public speeches and acting as more of a policy adviser than a press secretary. His press relations, although conducted in accordance with Wilson's wishes, were generally bad, particularly after he abandoned regular lobby briefings in June 1975. *CL*

Joe Haines, *The Politics of Power* (London, 1977).

Haldane, Richard Burdon (1856–1928), Liberal politician and lawyer. Educated at Edinburgh Academy and the Universities of Göttingen and Edinburgh, Haldane was called to the Bar in 1879. He was Liberal MP for East Lothian, 1885–1911, and lord chancellor, 1912–15, when he increased the number of lords of appeal and raised the prestige of the Judicial Committee of the *Privy Council. As secretary of state for war, 1905–12, he inaugurated a series of major army reforms, including the creation of a general staff, a British Expeditionary Force, and a volunteer force, the Territorial Army, which together laid the foundations for British military participation in the Great War. Created a viscount in 1911, and having many German friends (a factor which was an embarrassment in 1914), he was sent on an unsuccessful peacemaking mission to Germany in 1912. He also supported the establishment of civic universities and chaired a committee in 1904 which was the effective predecessor of the University Grants Committee. Haldane provided support both for a vigorous defence policy and for the social reforms of *New Liberalism. On the formation of the coalition government in 1915 *Asquith allowed him to be dismissed because of Conservative suspicions of his pro-German feelings. Disillusioned with the Liberals, he accepted Ramsay MacDonald's offer to lead Labour representation in the Lords. He also served again as lord chancellor and chairman of the Committee of Imperial Defence in 1924, remaining Labour's leader in the Lords until his death. *JS*

Dudley Sommer, *Haldane of Cloan: His Life and Times, 1856–1928* (London, 1960).

Haldane report (Cd 9230) (1918), on the machinery of government. Commissioned by the wartime coalition as part of its planning for reconstruction, it enshrined the enduring notion 'that in the sphere of civil government the duty of investigation and thought, as preliminary to action, might with great advantage be more definitely recognised'. R. B. *Haldane, Hegelian, army reformer, and Liberal (later Labour) politician, placed philosophical flesh on the bones of the Lloyd George–Hankey cabinet reforms. It concentrated on the cabinet as 'the mainspring of all the mechanism of Government', fulfilling three main functions: the final determination of policy to be submitted to parliament; the supreme control of the national executive in accordance with the policy prescribed by parliament; and the continuous coordination and delimitation of the activities of several departments of state. Cabinet should be small (ten to twelve members), meet frequently, be kept supplied with all necessary material in a form that would facilitate expeditious decisions, consult all other ministers affected by its decisions, and employ a systematic method for ensuring that its decisions were carried out effectively. Beneath the cabinet, the structure of departments should reflect the themes and tasks of government, each possessing an intelligence and research branch with a central ministry of research led by a senior minister to pull such thinking together. Special parliamentary committees should be created to shadow the functions of government. Very little immediate use was made by the Lloyd George coalition of the output of what Haldane called his 'Great Reform Committee'. However, the Treasury reorganized its financial and personnel relationships with other departments in 1919, five research councils were created over the period 1918–65, and there was a touch of the Haldanian about the departmentally related select committee structure created as part of the St John-Stevas reforms of 1979. The Haldane nostrums continued to exercise an exemplary influence over several generations of Whitehall officials. As cabinet secretary, Sir Burke Trend tried (and failed) to persuade Harold Wilson to use his spring 1968 reshuffle to reorganize Whitehall's economic departments to reflect the needs of managing a modern economy in the Haldanian manner. Trend, a great admirer of Haldane, used his 1918 report directly when helping Edward Heath construct his *Central Policy Review Staff in 1970 (which might be regarded as Haldane's ministry of research by another means) and in his last years called for 'a comprehensive job on the Haldane' model to tackle the 'conceptual problem' of preparing the machinery of government for the 21st century. *PJH*

Peter Hennessy, *Whitehall* (London, 1989).

Halifax, Lord. See Wood, Edward Frederick Lindley.

Hall, Robert Lowe (1901–88), economist and civil servant. As one of the few professionally trained economists to remain in Whitehall after the war, he was the Keynesian voice in many of the most important economic policy decisions of the late 1940s and early 1950s. Hall headed the economic section of the Cabinet Office, 1947–53, and served as an economic adviser until 1961. He received a life peerage, as Lord Roberthall, 1969. *HOJ*

Alec Cairncross (ed.), *The Robert Hall Diaries* (London, 1991). | Kit Jones, *An Economist among Mandarins: A Biography of Robert Hall* (Cambridge, 1994).

Hall, (William) Reginald ('Blinker') (1870–1943), director of naval intelligence. The son of Britain's first director of naval intelligence, Hall received a naval education and was commissioned in 1890. His forceful personality marked him out and by the outbreak of war in 1914 he was captain of a battlecruiser. Thereafter Hall became director of naval intelligence; his interrogation of captured German officers exaggerated a facial twitch, giving rise to his nickname. As director of naval intelligence, Hall took control of room 40, integrating its decrypting functions with his own interpretive section. By intercepting German communications with Mexico and the USA, Hall obtained vital information forewarning of German activities like the Roger Casement affair. His most important success was the infamous Zimmermann telegram, in which the German foreign minister proposed an alliance with Mexico should the USA enter the war on the Allied side. Hall passed the telegram to the US government in such a way as to preserve the integrity of Britain's code-breakers. The ruse worked brilliantly, making America's entry into the war easier. Hall was honoured by the CB and KCMG, and also achieved the rank of admiral. Retiring from the navy in 1918, Hall entered the Commons as a Conservative MP and was briefly principal agent at Conservative Central Office. Whilst his role is unproven, the *Zinoviev letter stunt, which was widely (though probably wrongly) blamed for helping bring about the first Labour government's defeat in 1924, bears his hallmarks. *PM*

Halls, Michael (1915–70), prime minister's principal private secretary, 1966–70. Harold Wilson brought Halls, who had been his private secretary at the Board of Trade (1948–50), to Downing Street against civil service advice, in the hope that he would ease the tension that had existed between his own advisers and Halls's predecessor, Derek Mitchell. In this sense the appointment succeeded, but although loyal to, and trusted by, Wilson, Halls was out of his depth at Downing Street. He died in office in 1970. *CL*

Halsbury, 1st earl of (1823–1921), jurist and Conservative minister. Hardinge Stanley Giffard was called to the Bar in 1850, and built a reputation as one of the greatest litigators of his generation. He successfully defended Governor Edward Eyre throughout the latter 1860s, and his spirited if unsuccessful appearance for Arthur Orton, the notorious Tichborne claimant, 1871–2, bolstered his renown. Giffard enthusiastically entered Conservative politics: in 1875 he became Disraeli's solicitor-general and was elected MP for Launceston two years later. In 1885 he was appointed lord chancellor by Salisbury and went on to hold that office in every Conservative government until 1905. His stance in law was steadfastly conservative, upholding individual liberty over modern collectivism and traditional over reformist values, of which his celebrated decision in the Taff Vale case in 1901 is but one example. Despite his age, Halsbury became a Conservative icon of resistance to change by leading the diehard stand in the Lords against the Parliament Act of 1911, the Liberal government's legislation which guaranteed the destruction of the political power of the upper house, and a 'Halsbury club' briefly flourished in his honour. Halsbury lived to be 98 and continued occasionally to hear cases as late as 1916. *RJQA*

GREGORY D. PHILLIPS, *The Diehards: Aristocratic Society and Politics in Edwardian England* (Cambridge, Mass., 1979). | R. V. F. HEUSTON, *The Lives of the Lord-Chancellors, 1885–1940* (Oxford, 1964). | ARTHUR MEJIA and J. A. THOMPSON (eds.), *Edwardian Conservatism* (London, 1988).

Hamilton, Edward Walter (1847–1908), civil servant. Eddie Hamilton entered the Treasury in 1870 and was Gladstone's devoted private secretary, 1873–4 and 1880–5. A keen Liberal and socially well connected, he left a noted diary covering the period 1880–1906 (3 vols., ed. Dudley Bahlman). A Treasury budgetary and financial expert, he rose to be joint permanent secretary, 1902–7, and was centrally involved in the controversy over the imposition of the corn duty and the question of tariff reform which split the Balfour government in 1902–3. *KT*

Hamilton by-election (2 November 1967). The victory of the Scottish National Party (SNP) at Hamilton sent shock waves through the Scottish political establishment. The seat had been Labour's sixth safest in the UK and few expected that the SNP, a party which had no MPs, would win. Yet, in retrospect, there were signs before Hamilton that the SNP were on the move. In March the nationalists had won almost 30 per cent of the vote in the Glasgow Pollok by-election, and in May the SNP won over 60,000 votes in the Glasgow council election. Furthermore, voter dissatisfaction with the Wilson government was growing. Devaluation of sterling, poor Scottish economic performance, rising unemployment, and standards of living which trailed behind the rest of the UK were the major causes of voter discontent with the government's performance. Also, the Labour Party had become ossified in central Scotland, with local branches containing few members whose main concerns revolved around local government. The dynamism of the youthful SNP, and in particular their colourful candidate, Winnie Ewing, contrasted favourably with Labour. *RF*

Hammersmith South by-election, (24 February 1949). After big by-election swings against the Labour government in 1948, the Conservatives pinned their hopes on gaining Hammersmith South in February 1949, investing huge efforts in a highly publicized campaign. The seat was, however, no longer marginal because of social change, and when Labour won, the Tories suffered a crisis of confidence. There was criticism that they offered only vague promises, which prompted work on detailed policies, allowing the publication of *The Right Road for Britain*. *RJS*

Hankey, Maurice Paschal Alers (1877–1963), secretary to the cabinet, 1916–38. A royal marines officer by background, Hankey permanently shaped the machinery of British government as the creator of the *cabinet secretariat. Secretary to the Committee of Imperial Defence from 1912, during the Great War he was secretary of key ministerial committees before Lloyd George appointed him as the first-ever cabinet secretary in December 1916. Hankey introduced businesslike procedures to the work of the cabinet, with a prepared agenda and a record of decisions, seeing off moves to abolish the secretariat in 1922. A man of tireless industry and large and precise memory, he also carved out a place as an indispensable aide and adviser to successive prime ministers (being particularly active on defence and strategic issues). Made a peer in 1938, he served in a number of ministerial posts 1939–42 until sacked by Churchill. *KT*

STEPHEN ROSKILL, *Hankey: Man of Secrets*, 3 vols. (London, 1970–4).

Hannington, Walter (1896–1966), Communist activist and organizer of the unemployed during the inter-war years. 'Wal' Hannington is famous for organizing the *National Unemployed Workers' Movement (NUWM) in April 1921 and for representing their interests through the six great hunger marches of the inter-war years. He was also a member of the Communist Party of Great Britain (CPGB) from its foundation in 1920, and often on its central committee. The association between the NUWM and the CPGB was not an easy one, though, for the CPGB was often opposed to the palliative measures that Hannington envisaged for the unemployed. The conflict was most obvious in 1932 when, after a hunger march, he was arrested and imprisoned for three months. The CPGB leadership felt that Hannington should have been more cautious in the statements he made at the time of his arrest and felt that he operated the NUWM almost as a dictator. Hannington simply ignored the criticism. He wrote several books, the most notable being *Unemployed Struggles* (1936) and his autobiography *Never on Our Knees* (1967).

KL

KEITH LAYBOURN, *Britain on the Breadline* (2nd edn., Stroud, 1998). | JOHN STEVENSON and CHRIS COOK, *The Slump* (London, 1977).

Hansard, the official report of the proceedings in the chamber of the House of Commons and its standing committee is universally known as Hansard after Thomas Curson Hansard, son of the printer to the Commons, who began 'Hansard's Parliamentary Debates' in 1829. In 1909, the operation was taken over by the House of Commons itself. Hansard reporters sit in the Press Gallery immediately above the Speaker's chair, recording what is said via shorthand, machine shorthand on stenograph machines, and from tapes. The report is full but not strictly verbatim since repetitions and redundancies are removed and obvious mistakes corrected. However, nothing is left out and members are not allowed to make alterations of substance or subsequently write-in material to add to the record. The whole operation is fully computerized and linked to the Stationery Office as printer. Reports of debates up to 1 a.m., and occasionally beyond, are available at breakfast time. The official report has been available on the parliamentary web site (*www.parliament.uk*) from 12.30 p.m. on the day following the sitting: from October 1996 for Commons debates and from November 1998 for standing committee debates. *PJRR*

Hansard Society for Parliamentary Government, an independent and non-partisan charity. It was founded in 1944 by Stephen King-Hall MP to publicize the proceedings of parliament and to educate the young about how parliament works. Over 50 years the society has worked in various ways to fulfil the founder's intentions. It has arranged a large number of sixth-form conferences and organized mock elections for schoolchildren at the time of national and European elections. It has helped in international programmes to spread education about parliamentary procedures in the newly emergent democracies of Eastern Europe. It has run a sustained programme for interns, mainly from the USA, to be attached to MPs' offices. It has sponsored commissions to explore in detail various aspects of government. The most notable of these have been on *Electoral Reform* (chair, Lord Blake, 1976), *Equal Room at the Top* (Lady Howe, 1990), *A Level Playing Field for Elections* (Christopher Chataway, 1991), *The Legislative Process* (Lord Rippon, 1993), and *Regulation of Utilities* (John Flemming, 1997). It has published a series of *King-Hall Papers* on issues of public importance and it holds regular public meetings, 'Democracy Forums', in London. Its major publication is *Parliamentary Affairs*, a journal, issued quarterly since 1948. *DEB*

'hard-faced men who look as if they have done well out of the war', phrase quoted in J. M. *Keynes's *Economic Consequences of the Peace* (1919), alleging that post-war MPs included too many war-profiteering businessmen. The phrase was quoted from a 'friend' (actually Stanley Baldwin, who took a dim view of the moral quality of many of his political contemporaries). *NJC*

Hardie, (James) Keir (1856–1915), socialist politician. Hardie was a miner who led the first strike in the Lanarkshire coalfield, in 1880. He was fired and became a journalist and full-time political activist and union official. He combined these careers, becoming secretary to the Ayrshire miners' union while running a newspaper called *The Miner*, and later *Labour Leader*. In 1892 Hardie was elected as the independent labour candidate for West Ham South, entering parliament defiantly wearing a cloth cap. His political position was essentially that of an advanced liberal, his beliefs based on Christianity rather than Marxism, but he was not at home with the ethos of the Liberal Party and his rhetoric, in contrast to other early Labour representatives, remained stubbornly confrontational. He advocated progressive taxation, constitutional reform, and the creation of a welfare state, and was passionately in favour of women's suffrage, a political commitment reflected in his long affair with Sylvia Pankhurst. Primarily, he wanted to see an increase in working-class representation in parliament and helped found the Independent Labour Party (ILP) in 1893 to promote labour representation. Largely because of his anti-royalist views, the Liberals ran a candidate against him in 1895 and he lost his seat. He then agitated through *Labour Leader* and other channels to secure ILP seats. He believed in the unity of working-class action and strongly supported the formation of the Labour Representation Committee in 1900. Returned to parliament for Merthyr Tydfil in 1900, he extended his view of cooperation to support for a pact with the Liberals which secured an increase in Labour representation to 29 in 1906, and Hardie became the fledgling party's leader. He was never very comfortable as leader and was soon replaced by Arthur Henderson, later by Ramsay MacDonald. His pacifism at the outbreak of the Great War reduced his influence, but by the time he died he was already firmly placed at the head of Labour's pantheon of heroes. His politics were simple, spiritual in tone and inspiration, but his personality was complex and driven. His lasting contribution was neither exactly ideological nor organizational, but almost emotional: he represented a self-confident and independent Labour movement that did not need the coat-tails of the Liberal Party nor the blessing of the establishment to be part of the body politic. While not really advocating a detailed form of industrial socialism, despite his friendships with Frederick Engels and Eleanor Marx, Hardie inspired a belief in the possibility of a separate path for the British working-class movement. *BB*

Caroline Benn, *Keir Hardie* (London, 1997).

Hardinge, Alexander Henry Louis **(1894–1960)**, private secretary to Edward VIII and to George VI, 1936–43. Hardinge had served in the royal household throughout the Victorian era and this assisted his promotion to the private secretariat. He clashed with Edward VIII, who saw himself as a reformer and associated Hardinge with his father's traditionalism. Hardinge alienated his chief by writing a frank letter opposing his proposed marriage to Mrs Simpson. George VI employed him after the abdication, but also disliked him because Hardinge's invariable reply to anything he suggested was 'no'. Hardinge resigned early partly due to ill health, partly due to friction with his deputy, Alan Lascelles. If they were content to see him go at the palace, he nevertheless served the monarchy during a particularly daunting era that included not only abdication but also world war. *WMK*

Helen Hardinge, *Loyal to Three Kings* (London, 1967).

Hardinge, Charles **(1858–1944)**, diplomat and colonial administrator. Hardinge entered the diplomatic service in 1880. Equipped with a well-honed sense of where power lay, and aided by his royal connections, his career flourished under Edward VII. In 1904 he accompanied the king to Paris, which visit facilitated the conclusion of the Entente Cordiale. As ambassador at St Petersburg he made it his personal mission to bring about an Anglo-Russian rapprochement, a mission accomplished in 1907, by which time Hardinge had already moved on to become permanent secretary at the Foreign Office (FO) (1906–10). He worked well and closely with Foreign Secretary Sir Edward Grey, although he was later rumoured to have exercised an unduly pro-Russian influence over Grey. Both men were concerned about Germany, and were committed to containing Germany's growing power. Lest relations with France and Russia be compromised, Hardinge strongly opposed a naval and political agreement with Germany in 1909.

In 1910 he was appointed viceroy of India, throwing himself into social and educational reforms in the colony which had initially been made possible by the reduced Russian threat to India, but which were ultimately rendered impracticable because of the outbreak of the Great War. Turkey's entry into the war led to the ill-fated Mesopotamia expedition of 1915–16, for which Hardinge (along with Austen Chamberlain) was censored by a parliamentary commission. Still, never out of luck or out of favour, Lord Hardinge returned as FO permanent secretary (1916–20), though he was now no longer equal to the task. Intimidated by Northcliffe press campaigns, and on bad terms with Foreign Secretary Lord Curzon, he was unable to halt the decline of FO influence on policy making. In 1920 he retired to the Paris embassy where he remained until 1922. As the title of his eponymous memoirs indicated, Hardinge was in every respect a representative of the old (pre-1914) diplomacy. *TGO*

Lord Hardinge of Penshurst, *Old Diplomacy* (London, 1947). | Lord Hardinge of Penshurst, *My Indian Years* (London, 1948). | Brinton C. Busch, *Hardinge of Penshurst: A Study in the Old Diplomacy* (New York, 1980).

Hare, John Hugh **(1911–82)**, Conservative politician. Elected to parliament in 1945, Hare became a Conservative Party vice-chairman in 1951 and from 1955 served at the Colonial and War Offices before entering Macmillan's cabinet in 1958 as agriculture minister. Appointed labour minister in 1960, this unassuming son of an earl made written contracts of employment statutory, giving workers rights beyond their pay packet. As party chairman from 1963, when he was created Viscount Blakenham, his organizational effort minimized the 1964 Tory defeat. *RJS*

Harlech, Lord **(1885–1964)**, Conservative politician and banker. William Ormsby-Gore, later Lord Harlech, entered parliament in 1910, remaining in the Commons until 1938 when he became a peer. His career was dominated by imperial posts. From 1936 until 1938 he served as colonial secretary. A notable critic of Nazi Germany, he was a staunch opponent of colonial concessions to Germany. From 1944 until 1957 he served on the board of the Midland bank and led the consortium bearing his name which won one of the first commercial television franchises. *AJC*

Harmsworth, Alfred. See NORTHCLIFFE, LORD.

Harris, Arthur Travers ('Bomber') (1892–1984), air marshal. As commander of Bomber Command, 1942–5, Harris will for ever be associated with the British policy of 'area bombing' German cities. Though this policy was decided on by the British government before Harris took command, he was an outspoken advocate of the strategy and Bomber Command achieved maturity under him, which meant that he has often been wrongly described as its architect. Harris was thus rather shamefully made a scapegoat when the British people and government later reacted against the destructive bombing campaign. *MLC*

Harris, Charles Joseph William (1901–86), assistant to chief whips. From 1919 to 1961, Harris was private secretary to successive chief whips, serving governments of different complexions and personally embodying the so-called 'usual channels' through which parliamentary business and party deals are fixed. Harris was a Conservative Party official, 1917–19, and when the Conservatives were out of office in 1924 and 1929–31 worked for the opposition chief whip. But he subsequently became an established civil servant, acceptable to and working for both main parties. *KT*

Harrod, Roy Forbes (1900–78), economist and biographer. A fellow of Christ Church and Nuffield Colleges, Oxford, Harrod was influenced primarily by Keynes and Edgeworth. He is remembered for his role in developing the one-sector growth or 'Harrod-Domar' model, which attempts to explain the relationship to macroeconomic characteristics of long-term economic growth. After the war, he championed the use of fiscal and monetary expansion to stimulate maximum economic growth. His best-known non-economic work is the official *Life of John Maynard Keynes* (1951). *HOJ*

Hart, Judith Constance Mary (1924–91), Labour politician. A former sociology lecturer, Hart was Labour MP for Lanark, 1959–83, and Clydesdale, 1983–7, becoming Lady Hart of South Lanark in 1988. She held several junior ministerial posts in the 1964–70 and 1974–9 governments. On the left of the party, she was difficult to keep in line with government policy, and successive leaders had their differences with her. Her main interests were overseas development and social security. She supported Michael Foot for the leadership. *BJE*

Hartshorn, Vernon (1872–1931), trade unionist and Labour politician. Born in Monmouthshire, Hartshorn worked in the mines in his early life before becoming a full-time union official at Maesteg in Glamorgan. A member of the Independent Labour Party, he was one of those young men who challenged the rather conservative leadership of the South Wales Miners' Federation, although he was to become a more pragmatic figure during the Great War, when he adopted a patriotic position. Hartshorn became MP for Ogmore in 1918, and mainly spoke in parliament on behalf of the miners. He was postmaster general in Ramsay MacDonald's Labour government of 1924, and in 1930–1 he was briefly lord privy seal in the second Labour government, eventually taking over, rather ineffectively, the responsibility for unemployment. *KL*

Harvey, Ian Douglas (1914–87), Conservative politician whose promising career was destroyed by scandal. Elected to parliament in 1950, Harvey was a Foreign Office minister in 1958 when charged with indecency after an incident with a guardsman in St James's Park. Homosexual acts between men were then a criminal offence, and Harvey resigned from office and from parliament. He later wrote about the scandal's devastating effect and advocated equality for homosexuals. *RJS*

IAN HARVEY, *To Fall like Lucifer* (London, 1971).

Harvey, Oliver (1893–1968), diplomat. Harvey entered the diplomatic service in 1919 and served as private secretary to foreign secretaries Eden and Halifax, 1936–43. He was appointed deputy secretary in the Foreign Office in 1946, enjoying then with Ernest Bevin the same close relations he had previously enjoyed with Eden. In 1948–54, he was ambassador in Paris. His published diaries are an essential source for the study of British foreign policy, 1937–45. *AJC*

JOHN HARVEY (ed.), *The Diplomatic Diaries of Oliver Harvey*, 2 vols. (London, 1970, 1978).

Hastings, Patrick (1880–1952), lawyer and Labour politician. After becoming one of the greatest courtroom advocates of his generation, Hastings was Labour MP for Wallsend, 1922–6. As attorney-general in Ramsay MacDonald's 1924 government, he authorized the prosecution for treason of John Campbell but then withdrew the prosecution, after protests in the Labour Party, citing as his reason Campbell's excellent war record. A successful opposition censure motion, alleging political impropriety in this *Campbell case, precipitated the fall of the government.

BJE

Hattersley, Roy Sidney George (1932–), Labour politician and author. A stalwart of the centre-right of the Labour Party, in the tradition of Gaitskell and Crosland, the best years of Hattersley's political life were spent in opposition. He was born into a working-class family in the Hillsborough area of Sheffield (near the ground of Sheffield Wednesday, of which he has been a lifelong follower). His parents (he was their only child) were unusual: his father had been a Roman Catholic priest and his mother was an ardent Labour Party member who went on to become lord mayor of the city. A bright child who got to grammar school, he developed an early interest in politics; his memoir *A Yorkshire Boyhood* (1983) gives an account of his support for A. V. Alexander in the general election of 1945. After studying economics at Hull University, he too won a seat on Sheffield city council at the age of 24 and cast around for a parliamentary constituency. At the general election of 1964 he was elected MP for Sparkbrook, Birmingham, which he represented until 1997. He held junior posts in the Wilson government, 1967–70. When Labour returned to power in 1974, he was made minister of state at the Foreign Office and reached the cabinet in September 1976 as minister for prices and consumer protection. As such, he had a close view of the decline of the Callaghan government and its collapse in 1979. Always a pro-European, he was a Labour loyalist who had no truck with those who left to form the Social Democratic Party in 1981. Hattersley served as a front-bench opposition speaker from 1979 to 1992, although it was as a broadcaster and contributor to newspapers and magazines that he most came before the public; in 1982 he received the Granada columnist of the year award. His case for equality, *Choose Freedom: The Future for Democratic Socialism* (1987), if less widely noticed, had some influence in anti-Bennite circles. Between 1983 and 1992 he was deputy leader of the Labour Party. He retired from the Commons in 1997 and was made a peer. He continued to write, often with a self-deprecating wit but also—with an irony not lost on him—from a position well to the left of the Blair government.

DEM

Roy Hattersley, *Who Goes Home? Scenes from a Political Life* (London, 1995).

Havers, (Robert) Michael Oldfield (1923–92), lawyer and Conservative politician. A friendly indiscreet figure, not Mrs Thatcher's natural chum, and the actor Nigel Havers's father, he rose via law offices to the lord chancellorship, long denied him by the crustacean Hailsham. He held the post for a year, when he was ill and subsequently dying. He was author as attorney-general of a Contempt of Court Act, widened by judges; he stopped Mary Whitehouse's prosecution of the National Theatre's *The Romans in Britain*; and threatened resignation, with solicitor-general Patrick Mayhew, whose legal opinion was leaked in the *Westland affair.

EP

Hawtrey, Ralph (1879–1975), economist and Treasury official. Hawtrey, a mathematics scholar at Cambridge, spent virtually all his working life at the Treasury, but contributed actively to academic debate on monetary theory and published a stream of highly regarded treatises. His proposals for reforming the *gold standard were adopted at the 1922 Genoa financial conference, but gained only qualified acceptance among ever-cautious central bankers. While sustaining fruitful links with academics including J. M. Keynes, his influence at the Treasury diminished after the abandonment of the gold standard in 1931 and the ascendance of other talented officials.

RWDB

Hayek, Friedrich von (1899–1992), Austrian economist and philosopher. The key theme of the Austrian school of economics is spontaneous order. Money exists and has value not because the state creates it but because people find it convenient to have a medium of exchange. The intellectual roots of the Austrian school are utterly different to those of mainstream neoclassical economics in Chicago, but that does not matter for the purposes of this *Companion*, because busy politicians have noticed not their differences but their similarity. Both Austrian and Chicago economists object fiercely to state intervention either in the market or in personal freedoms. Hayek was born and educated in Vienna, where he was immersed in Austrian economics. He came to Britain in 1931, not intending to stay, but had to when the Nazis took over Germany and Austria. He burst on British politics with *The Road to Serfdom* (1944), dedicated to 'The Socialists of All Parties'. Hayek argued that planning, then at its wartime peak of popularity, was never a benevolent process. The road of planning (of anything) was the road to serfdom. He seemed a man out of his time, even more so with his huge *The Constitution of Liberty* (1960, described at the time as a 'magnificent dinosaur'), which aimed to delineate the minimal state necessary to promote personal and economic freedom. The first politician to take Hayek seriously was Sir Keith Joseph, the intellectual leader of the Conservatives' revolt against the state in the 1970s. He put Hayek on his reading list for civil servants on becoming a minister. Margaret Thatcher 'banged *The Constitution of Liberty* down on the table', saying 'This is what we believe' at the start of her fight against the 'wets' in the Conservative Party. Hayek's views on the market economy, if not his way of expressing them, are now accepted by leading politicians of all parties. *IM*

Andrew Gamble, *Hayek: The Iron Cage of Liberty* (Cambridge, 1996).

Hayward, Jack Ernest Shalom (1931–), political scientist. A graduate of the LSE and the Sorbonne, he taught at Sheffield, Keele, and Hull universities before becoming professor of European politics at Oxford, 1992–8. From an initially free-market point of view he moved to the left or centre-left under the influence of Ralph Miliband and Andrew Shonfield, among others. He started with research into *solidarisme* in France, but switched to a focus on French planning and was inspired by the writing of Crozier and Hoffmann. His fascination with France led to *The One and Indivisible French Republic* (1973) and, much later, *After the French Revolution* (1991). His works, often with colleagues, include *Planning, Politics and Public Policy* (1975), *Planning in Europe* (1978), and *State and Society in Contemporary Europe* (1979). He went on to write *The State and the Market Economy: Industrial Patriotism and Economic Intervention in France* (1986) and, in a wider vein, to edit *Governing in the New Europe* (1995) and *Industrial Enterprise and European Integration* (1995). One of the great influences on Hayward was S. E. *Finer and, after Finer's death, he put the finishing touches to Finer's monumental *History of Government from the Earliest Times* (1997). Hayward' s great contribution to the study of politics, apart from his activities in the British Political Studies Association and the British Academy, has been to use his intimate knowledge of the French political economy to throw light on the wider politics of bureaucracy. *DEB*

H-blocks, cell blocks, so called because of their shape, built at the Maze prison to accommodate terrorist prisoners with the ending of special category status. This was the status accorded to prisoners who were members of paramilitary organizations. These prisoners were not required to do prison work, could wear their own clothes, were allowed extra visits and food parcels, and were grouped together in large prison compounds reminiscent of Second World War prisoner-of-war camps. In 1975, the Gardiner committee criticized special category status, claiming that it meant virtually the loss of disciplinary control by prison authorities. As a result, Merlyn Rees, for the Labour government, announced the phasing out of special category status in 1976. Prisoners who would normally have been placed in compounds were now put in H-block cells at the Maze prison. Republican prisoners resisted the changes and this led to the *hunger strikes. *TWH*

Head, Antony Henry (1906–83), soldier and Conservative politician. Head saw active military service during the Second World War. A delegate to the Potsdam conference he entered parliament as MP for Carshalton in 1945. He established his parliamentary reputation on defence matters and Churchill sent him to the War Office in 1951. He was minister of defence during the 1956 *Suez crisis and was privately disquieted at the failure to complete the invasion. When Macmillan decreased the emphasis on conventional military forces, Head retired to the backbenches. He became Britain's first high commissioner to independent Nigeria in 1960. *NJC*

Healey, Denis Winston (1917–), Labour politician. Healey became one of the most influential Labour personalities of his generation. Aloof, arrogant, and a bit of a bully, he made his name in the 1950s as a specialist in defence questions, not the most likely route to power in the party of the left. Born in Keighley, he went to Bradford grammar school and Balliol College, Oxford, where he became a Communist, but by 1940 had reverted to the Labour Party. He was in the Royal Engineers, 1940–5, serving in North Africa and Italy where he was mentioned in dispatches. As Major Healey in uniform, he startled the 1945 party conference with a powerful speech calling on Labour to promote socialist revolution throughout Europe. Narrowly failing to win Pudsey and Otley, he was secretary of the Labour Party international department, 1945–52, making many friends abroad—he always had a bigger reputation abroad than at home. He was MP for South-East Leeds, 1952–5, and for Leeds East, 1955–92. An early supporter of Ernest Bevin's foreign policy, he took a tough, unsentimental post-Marxist view of international and strategic power and developed a dominance in defence thinking unique in British political life.

Healey became a close friend of President Kennedy's defence secretary Robert McNamara, and Harold Wilson made him minister of defence in 1964, a post he held right through to Labour's defeat in 1970. Wilson's 1964 campaign had implied he would scrap Britain's 'so-called independent, so-called deterrent', but nothing of the sort happened. Yet mindful that Britain could no longer act as world policeman, Healey's overriding objective was to give value for money. His £56 million defence cut in 1965 was the first real reduction since 1951: he scrapped the TSR2 aircraft, ended carrier construction, and aimed at real reductions of £400 million by 1970. What he avoided (until devaluation forced it in 1967) was ending the east of Suez defence commitment that the country could no longer sustain.

Out of office from 1970, Healey consolidated his position at the centre of party politics and in 1974–9 was chancellor under Wilson and Jim Callaghan. The economic position was much worse and unions less biddable than in the 1960s, yet, unlike Callaghan, Healey enhanced his public standing. The 'oil shock' and union pay demands helped create 'stagflation' and destroy the Keynesian consensus which had underpinned the world economy since the 1945 Bretton Woods agreement. Healey's 1976 'letter of intent', which the IMF demanded as the price for supporting sterling, was crucial. It not only led to public spending cuts of around £4 billion in 1976–8, but opened the way for the Thatcherism which dominated policy making in the 1980s. Thanks to North Sea oil revenue, Healey brought in an expansionist budget in 1978, but the left cast him as the villain of the 1970s economic drama, and when Labour was crushed at the polls in 1979, Michael Foot narrowly beat him to the party leadership in 1980 (he beat Tony Benn, though, by 1 per cent to become deputy leader). Healey never held office again, but continued most effectively in the fight against the left within the party and the Conservatives at elections. When he retired from the Commons in 1992, he could claim to have been Labour's most powerful policy maker and one of its most potent communicators over two decades. *PRGR*

DENIS HEALEY, *The Time of My Life* (London, 1989). | KENNETH O. MORGAN, *Labour People: Leaders and Lieutenants, Hardie to Kinnock* (Oxford, 1987).

Health, Department of (1988–). See HEALTH AND SOCIAL SECURITY, DEPARTMENT OF.

Health and Safety Executive (HSE). Conceived as a tripartite body encompassing government, trade unions, and employers (and hence an example of so-called corporatism), the HSE was established in 1975 as a result of the Health and Safety at Work Act, 1974. The three main organizations that dealt with occupational safety prior to its creation—Her Majesty's Agricultural Inspectorate (from the Ministry of Agriculture, Food, and Fisheries) and factory and mines inspectorates (both from the Home Office)—were subsumed into the new HSE. Two other inspectorates joined on its creation in 1975, the explosives inspectorate from the Home Office and nuclear installations inspectors from the Department of Energy. *JD*

Health and Safety Executive website: *www.hse.gov.uk*

Health and Social Security, Department of (1968–88). Health and social security administration underwent tremendous evolution throughout the 20th century. The century began with the medical department of the local government board administering health issues, and this was spun off in 1919 to create a Ministry of Health. As concern over poverty deepened, so did the administrative measures undertaken to alleviate it. Having previously presided over groundbreaking welfare reforms as chancellor, David Lloyd George when prime minister established a Ministry of Pensions in 1916. This was followed in October 1944 by the creation of the Ministry of Social Insurance (renamed National Insurance in November 1944). The two ministries were merged in 1953 to form the Ministry of Pensions and National Insurance, and it was renamed the Department of Social Security in 1966. In 1968 a single Department of Health and Social Security was formed, existing until 1988 when they were separated once more. *JD*

Department of Health website: *www.doh.gov.uk* | Department of Social Security website: *www.dss.gov.uk* | PETER HENNESSY, *Never Again* (London, 1992).

Healy, Timothy Michael (1855–1931), Irish politician. A prominent nationalist and skilful parliamentarian, famous for his savage wit, Tim Healy had contributed notoriously to Parnell's overthrow in 1890–1. Thereafter he was a restless, controversial figure, quarrelling bitterly with successive Irish leaders. Opportunistically, he argued that Ireland's religious and agrarian interests could be better served by cooperating with Unionist governments. He attacked John Redmond's subservience to the Liberals, especially over the 1909 'People's Budget', with its increased taxation of Irish land and whiskey. With William O'Brien, Healy formed an independent nationalist grouping, the All-for-Ireland League, which won eight seats, mainly in the south-west, in January 1910. His harsh criticism of Redmond's willingness to compromise over partition in early 1914 contributed to Irish disillusionment with constitutionalism and the Irish Parliamentary Party. Healy welcomed Sinn Fein's emergence and, with Andrew Bonar Law's concurrence, was rewarded with the governor-generalship of the Irish Free State in 1922. *DRB*

Heath, Edward Richard George (1916–), Conservative politician and prime minister who took Britain into the European Community. As the son of a skilled carpenter and former maid in Broadstairs, Heath's achievement in becoming Conservative leader was exceptional. From grammar school he went to Oxford and during the city's 1938 by-election supported the anti-Munich candidate, A. D. *Lindsay, the master at Balliol, against the Conservative candidate, Hogg. After wartime service in the artillery, he passed equal top into the civil service in 1946 but a year later became a Conservative candidate. Elected MP for Bexley in 1950, Heath acted on the beliefs that shaped his career by becoming a founder-member of the One Nation group and using his maiden speech to advocate British involvement in the European Coal and Steel Community. He became a whip in 1951, and as chief whip from 1955 was instrumental in preventing the Conservative Party from destroying itself over the *Suez crisis.

The Rise of a New-Style Tory

A close ally of Macmillan's, Heath entered the cabinet as labour minister in 1959 but the following year became deputy to Home at the Foreign Office as lord privy seal with special responsibility for relations with Europe. Given charge of Britain's negotiations to join the European common market in 1961, he emerged with his reputation enhanced, despite de Gaulle's veto. Having supported Douglas-Home as Macmillan's successor, Heath became president of the Board of Trade with an expanded role covering industry and the regions. However, his abolition of resale price maintenance angered many local shopkeepers who traditionally voted Tory. After the 1964 Tory defeat Heath was put in charge of policy, but he made his reputation when he replaced Maudling as shadow chancellor and savaged Callaghan's 1965 budget. Heath's combative persona won him the first Tory leadership election on 27 July 1965, when he received 150 votes to Maudling's 133 and Powell's fifteen. Heath personified a new, less class-bound Toryism, but his managerial approach to politics was uninspiring and he lacked popular appeal. On television, he looked wooden, while speechmaking seemed to him a foreign art. As a bachelor with interests in classical music and sailing, he was further set apart. Nobody, however, could have prevented the heavy Tory defeat in 1966. Although Heath's warnings about Labour's bogus claims for the economy were soon vindicated, his sacking of Powell from the shadow cabinet over the *'rivers of blood' speech angered many Tory supporters. But when he defied the pundits to win the 1970 election he seemed finally to have established his authority over his party.

From High Hopes to 'U-Turns'

Heath planned to modernize Britain with a 'new style of government', while upholding the post-1945 commitment to a mixed economy, full employment, and the welfare state. Nothing, however, was allowed to stand in the way of his overriding ambition to take Britain into the European Community (EC). He removed the final obstacles in private talks with President Pompidou and secured parliamentary approval despite opposition from around 40 Tory MPs. British entry into Europe in 1973, however, contributed to Heath's abandonment of his 'quiet revolution' of lower taxes, lower spending, and less intervention. In early 1972 unemployment rose to one million, then a post-war record, and the rescue of *Upper Clyde Shipbuilders reversed government policy on *'lame ducks'. Heath's main aim, however, was to enter Europe with an expanding economy and enable British industry to seize its opportunity. The 1972 budget boosted demand while state aid to industry was increased. In February 1972, however, the miners won a 27 per cent pay award, and Heath therefore sought agreement with the TUC and CBI for policies to control wage inflation without restraining the economy. Relations with the unions were, however, soured by the 1971 Industrial Relations Act, and when tripartite talks failed in November 1972 Heath imposed a statutory pay and prices freeze in contradiction of his manifesto pledge. With the cost-price spiral under control, the 1973 budget was designed to sustain high economic growth (the so-called 'Barber boom').

Crisis and Downfall

Heath's attempts to accommodate the miners' wage demands in 1973 within his pay policy were damaged by a combination of negotiating errors and the miners' increased bargaining power as a result of the fourfold rise in world oil prices. Heath responded to the miners' overtime ban by putting industry on a three-day week, and when the miners voted to strike in February 1974 he finally called an election. By polling day, however, 'Who governs?' was no longer the sole issue. Although the Tories won most votes, they were not the largest party in the Commons and fell well short of an overall majority. By trying to form a coalition with the Liberals, Heath seemed a bad loser. Despite his government's mounting problems, Heath had also devoted great effort to resolving the crisis in Northern Ireland. Having introduced direct rule from Westminster in 1972, he negotiated the 1973 *Sunningdale agreement with representatives of both communities and the Irish government. Tragically, however, the power-sharing executive was short-lived. Although Heath's call for national unity in October 1974 minimized Tory losses, his third election defeat as leader made a leadership challenge inevitable. His defeat by Thatcher in the first ballot on 4 February 1975 indicated his unpopularity among Tory MPs. Heath remained a trenchant critic of monetarism and Euroscepticism, and he was a leading 'Yes' campaigner in the 1975 referendum, but he never allayed the suspicion that he was acting out of pique against Thatcher. In 1992, he received the Order of the Garter and became Father of the House (in which position he presided controversially at the election of a new Speaker in 2000). He left the Commons in 2001.

As prime minister, Heath was ahead of his time in seeing the need for radical change. However, the strains on Tory loyalty caused by entry into Europe and his U-turns were exacerbated by other controversial reforms, including the wholesale restructuring of local government, and he could ill afford to treat his party with such apparent disdain. In this latter respect he brought his troubles on himself, but the tide of events had made him an unlucky prime minister. *RJS*

Sir Edward Heath, *The Course of My Life* (London, 1998). | John Campbell, *Edward Heath* (London, 1993).

Heath, Thomas Little (1861–1940), civil servant. Heath entered the Treasury in 1884, becoming joint permanent secretary, 1913–19. One chancellor said of him that he was 'regarded by the other departments as the special incarnation of all that is most angular and pedantic in treasury traditions and practices' (E. O'Halpin, *Head of the Civil Service* (1989), 30). Pushed to one side when Warren Fisher was made head of the Treasury, Heath became comptroller-general and secretary to the commissioners for the reduction of the national debt, 1919–26. *KT*

Heathcoat Amory, Derick (1899–1981), Conservative chancellor of the exchequer and industrialist. After Eton and Oxford, Heathcoat Amory entered the family textile business in Devon and became a councillor in 1932. He probably would not have entered national politics, but his cousin, who was MP for Tiverton, was killed in action and he stepped into the vacancy in 1945. He served on the committee that produced the **Industrial Charter*, was appointed pensions minister in 1951, and moved to the Board of Trade in 1953. He entered the cabinet as agriculture minister in 1954 following Dugdale's resignation. He was one of three cabinet ministers to abstain on capital punishment in 1956, and was a doubter over Suez. When the Treasury team resigned in 1958, his reassuring presence was a godsend for Macmillan who made him chancellor of the exchequer. His 1958 budget was cautious but, under pre-election pressure from Macmillan and also because of Treasury misjudgement, he reflated too much in 1959. In his post-election budget, he wanted to deflate, but again at Macmillan's urging he was less restrictive than he wanted. In 1960 he retired from politics, as he had planned, and became Viscount Amory. *RJS*

hedgers and ditchers, the colourful designations given to two Conservative party factions who battled over the question of how to deal with the Parliament Bill of 1911. 'Ditchers', led by Lords *Halsbury and Willoughby de Broke, and Austen Chamberlain and F. E. Smith, demanded that the Tory peers 'die in the last ditch' and reject the Liberal bill. The majority of the party, including the leader, Balfour, supported the 'hedger' argument for accepting a bill which could not realistically be stopped.

RJQA

Gregory D. Phillips, *The Diehards: Aristocratic Society and Politics in Edwardian England* (Cambridge, Mass., 1979).

Heffer, Eric Samuel (1922–91), Labour politician. Eric Heffer was Labour MP for Liverpool, Walton, 1964–91, serving as industry minister in Wilson's government, 1974–5. Elected to Labour's NEC in 1975, he was party chairman in 1983. He stormed off the platform at the party conference in 1985 in protest at Kinnock's speech that attacked the Militant-led council in Liverpool. An outspoken champion of socialism in the Labour Party and supporter of working-class militancy. *DLM*

Eric Heffer, *Never a Yes Man* (London, 1991).

Heiser, Terence Michael (1932–), civil servant. Lacking the conventional education and background of top mandarins, and joining the civil service as a clerical officer aged 16, Terry Heiser rose through the ranks, winning a reputation as a gritty and effective 'can-do' official. An expert on local government in the Department of the Environment (DoE), he was Tony Crosland's private secretary in the mid-1970s, and as permanent secretary of the DoE, 1985–92, played a major role in the development of the poll tax. *KT*

Help the Aged, pressure group formed in 1961 to campaign on behalf of the elderly. One of a number of single issue pressure groups formed at about the same time in response to growing concerns about the persistence of poverty amongst specific sections of the population. *JS*

Helsby, Laurence Norman (1908–78), civil servant. Helsby was a university lecturer in economics in the 1930s, becoming a temporary senior clerk in the House of Commons in 1940 and from 1941 a civil servant in the Treasury. He was principal private secretary to Prime Minister Attlee, 1947–50, first civil service commissioner, 1954–9, permanent secretary at the Ministry of Labour, 1959–62, and then a surprise choice (by Macmillan) as joint permanent secretary of the Treasury and head of the civil service, 1963–8. *KT*

Helsinki conference/CSCE. The conference on security and cooperation in Europe (CSCE) began in 1973 and culminated in the Helsinki final act in 1975. Part of the general process of détente, it was a multilateral counterpart to West Germany's Ostpolitik. Comprised of 33 European states (all except Albania), the USA, and Canada, it was the only truly pan-European forum. Proposed by the USSR as a means of endorsing the inviolability of existing frontiers in Europe, by conceding to these concerns the West and the neutrals were able to establish commitments to non-governmental contacts and cooperation on humanitarian issues. These were used to pressurize the Eastern bloc over human rights. The final act contained three 'baskets' of specific measures. Basket One dealt with security issues and included confidence-building measures, the exchange of observers, and prior notification of military manoeuvres. Basket Two concerned scientific, technological, and environmental cooperation and greater East–West trade. Basket three dealt with humanitarian cooperation and contained provisions for the free flow of people, information, and ideas. By agreeing to the last and by the establishment of periodic review conferences on the implementation of these undertakings 'the CSCE process' extended beyond the initial conference as an important vehicle for concern over human rights. After the revolutions of 1989, the CSCE became a forum for discussing the political and strategic changes. At one stage it was even seen as a pan-European successor organization to both the Warsaw Pact and NATO. In 1992, the CSCE underwent a major reorganization when it became an agency of the UN with peace monitoring duties. In 1994 it changed its name to the Organization on Security and Co-Operation in Europe (OSCE), With a membership of 53 states its main value now is as a forum for dialogue on broader European security issues. *DHD*

Henderson, Arthur (1863–1935), Labour Party leader. A former Liberal Party organizer, Henderson was a delegate to the conference which established the Labour Representative Committee in 1900 and was elected its treasurer in 1903, leading the parliamentary party, 1908–10. When Ramsay MacDonald resigned as leader at the outbreak of the Great War, Henderson reassumed the leadership and became the first member of the Labour Party to hold cabinet office when he was invited to join Asquith's coalition government. He was president of the Board of Education, 1915–16, and paymaster general, 1916–17. When his proposal that he attend an international peace conference in Stockholm was rejected by the war cabinet, he resigned from office. From that 1917 resignation until 1924, his political career suffered a series of reverses as he won and lost seats in parliament, before settling in at Burnley after 1924. He was chief whip when the party was in opposition, 1920–4 and 1924–9, refusing to challenge MacDonald for the leadership. He served as home secretary in 1924 and foreign secretary in 1929–31, resigning with Lansbury and Clynes in 1931, rather than accept Snowdon's proposed cuts in public expenditure. In the election that followed the formation of the National Government, with Henderson now again briefly Labour leader, he again lost his seat, but was returned at a further by-election at Clay

Cross in 1933. His major concerns in foreign policy were peace and disarmament. He was chairman of the international disarmament conference of the early 1930s, and was awarded the Nobel peace prize in 1934.

Henderson's long and distinguished career in the Labour movement is best summed up by one particular moment. He was elected treasurer of the emerging Labour Party in 1903 and immediately the Independent Labour Party members objected because he was a Liberal rather than a socialist. However, Henderson was more responsible than any other individual for welding the trade unions and the Labour Party together. He was, in other words, the representative figure of moderate, sensible parliamentary socialism. His work in structuring the party and the conference around the power and control of the trade unions was to have long-term consequences for the nature of the Labour Party, but he was also capable of being more than merely a bureaucrat. He was a tireless campaigner for peace, perhaps reflecting on his wartime service in the coalition government (in a war in which his eldest son had been killed at the battle of the Somme) but also from his direct experience at the Foreign Office. The most significant feature of his tenure at the Foreign Office was the recognition by the British government of the Bolshevik regime in the Soviet Union, but he also secured the treaty at the *London naval conference which suspended the building of new warships for six years. Though ultimately irrelevant, the treaty was a rare piece of successful disarmament and diplomacy in a dark era. Much more than merely a time-server, Henderson was rather less than a world statesman. His most memorable comment concerned the experience of holding office, 'The first 48 hours decide whether a new Minister is going to run his office or whether his office is going to run him.' Henderson, masterful in running the Labour Party, was generally felt to have been a 'good' minister by his departments. *BB*

F. M. Leventhal, *Arthur Henderson* (Manchester, 1989).

Henderson, Hubert (1890–1952), economist. A Liberal reformer, Henderson was invited by Keynes to edit the *Nation* in 1923, and together they wrote the pamphlet *Can Lloyd George Do It?* in 1929. But Henderson and Keynes grew apart intellectually from this time, it being first noticeable when both served on MacDonald's Economic Advisory Council in 1930. Henderson hated Keynes's **General Theory of Employment, Interest, and Money*. This unease remained apparent during the war, when he served as an economic adviser in Whitehall. *HOJ*

Henderson, Neville Meyrick (1882–1942), diplomat. Henderson entered the diplomatic service in 1905, and after a series of disappointing posts, he was surprisingly appointed ambassador in Berlin in 1937. A competent diplomat, he nevertheless was beset by a weakness for too easily identifying himself with the states to which he was accredited, and he soon developed a reputation as an apologist for Nazi Germany. This verdict is now regarded as harsh, although he clearly misunderstood the ideological imperatives of Nazism. *AJC*

Neville Henderson, *Failure of a Mission* (London, 1940).

Henderson, Nicholas (1919–), diplomat and diarist. 'Nico' Henderson did everything there is to do in post-war diplomacy. He served Ernest Bevin, he attended Oliver Franks, and was ambassador in Bonn (1972–5), Paris (1975–9), and Washington (1979–82). He became generally famous during the Falklands war for his acute grasp of the message and the medium—his effortlessly dishevelled appearances on prime-time American television made a great impression—and for his prescience, his tolerance, and his unstuffy savoir faire. *AJC*

Nicholas Henderson, *Mandarin* (London, 1994).

Hennessy, Peter John (1947–), 'Whitehall watcher', historian, and constitutional commentator. Hennessy worked for many years as a journalist in the 1970s and 1980s, reporting mainly on Whitehall, with spells on *The Times*, the *Financial Times*, and *The Economist*, and was a columnist for the *Independent* and the *New Statesman*. He was a regular presenter of the BBC Radio 4 *Analysis* programme, 1986–92. Co-founder of the Institute of Contemporary British History (in 1986), he became professor of contemporary history at Queen Mary, University of London, in 1992. His publications include: (with Keith Jeffery) *States of Emergency* (1983); (with Michael Cockerell and David Walker) *Sources Close to the Prime Minister* (1984); *What the Papers Never Said* (1985); *Cabinet* (1986); (edited with Anthony Seldon) *Ruling Performance* (1987); *Whitehall* (1989); *Never Again: Britain 1945–1951* (1992); *The Hidden Wiring: Unearthing the British Constitution* (1995); *Muddling Through: Power, Politics and the Quality of Government in Post-War Britain* (1996). In 2000, he published a major survey of prime ministerial government, *The*

Prime Minister. A professional demystifier of the secret codes of state power in Britain, Hennessy's best work combines investigative tenacity, nuggets from government files in the PRO, incisive 'insider' interview evidence, and great narrative drive and enthusiasm. *KT*

Herbert, Alan Patrick (1890–1971), independent politician, author, and wit. After Great War service which generated the critical novel *The Secret Battle* (1919), he joined the staff of *Punch* in 1924, his initials A.P.H. becoming synonymous with the magazine's brand of humour. Through his journalism he emphasized social and political causes that he would later champion as MP for Oxford University (1935–50). He successfully introduced the private member's Matrimonial Causes Act, 1936, liberalizing *divorce law. The abolition of the university franchise in 1950 obliged his retirement from active politics, and in the post-war years he enjoyed considerable success with a run of musical plays but still retained his interest in public life, campaigning for a Thames barrage, for a public lending right for authors, and against bureaucratic and business jargon. *NJC*

Reginald Pound, *A. P. Herbert: A Biography* (London, 1976).

Herbert, Jesse (1851–1916), Liberal Party organizer. Herbert was secretary to the Liberal chief whip in the Edwardian period and so occupied a linking position between the parliamentary party and the party organization. His responsibilities included working out the constituency details for the *Lib-Lab pact (1903). *JAR*

Heritage, Department of National (1992–7). See Culture, Media, and Sport, Department of.

Heseltine, Michael Ray Dibdin (1933–), Conservative politician, and leadership contender, guyed by the running commentary of his friend, Julian Critchley: Heseltine was planning his career at Oxford on a cigarette packet with 1988 pencilled in for his premiership. Curtailing national service with a hopeless parliamentary candidacy, he flourished through property deals, then the Haymarket press, specialist advertisement-heavy trade publishing. His abrasive and partisan style, a South American balcony manner of speechmaking, which earned him the nickname 'Tarzan' and made him from 1975 the darling of the party conference, masked a lack of capitalist triumphalism. Heseltine was MP for Tavistock, 1966–74, for Henley, 1974–2001, holding junior posts at transport and aerospace under Heath. He was much criticized for threateningly seizing the Commons mace in 1976, something last done by Mosleyite John Becken in 1931 when Labour sang 'the red flag'. Ironically, Heseltine was actually a Tory left-winger, favouring the role of the state, opposing much-loved punishments, but may have voted for Thatcher in the first ballot, 1975. If so, this was not a lasting relationship, since he backed Whitelaw in the run-off. At environment, he freely used listing notices, as for Billingsgate Fish Market, he met Merseyside riots in 1981 with a public funding project, and a garden centre. Heseltine also claimed in 1988 that his office, examining the poll tax in 1981, had dismissed it in a morning. At defence, he hired a contractor to fight cost-plus deals—and contractors. For a businessman, Heseltine was illusionless about businessmen but always hard line on defence—support for Trident and bombast about *Greenham common counterbalancing his inadequate right-wing credentials elsewhere. He was a casualty of the *Westland affair in 1986, a modest deal liberating pent-up hatreds, and an early clash of European-American prejudices. Heseltine now became a steady Thatcher enemy, observing the civilities but building his reputation at conference and the local party circuit, abominated by Thatcherites. In this pre-campaign for the leadership, he stressed Europe, unemployment, and the environment. The crisis opportunity, ignited by Geoffrey Howe's biting resignation speech, allowed Heseltine to challenge Thatcher in November 1990, getting enough votes to end her reign but not enough to win for himself. He then served under Major, his first pleasurable duty being to kill the poll tax, replacing it with banded council tax, but eventually was deputy prime minister, spurning a widely proclaimed succession chance in 1995. Under Hague's leadership, Heseltine continued to proclaim the pro-European case but also announced in 2000 that he would not stand again for re-election. *EP*

Michael Heseltine, *Life in the Jungle* (London, 2000).

Heseltine, William Frederick Payne (1930–), private secretary to Elizabeth II, 1986–90. An Australian, he was the first and only non-UK national to serve as the sovereign's private secretary in the century. He provided greater press access to the monarchy family and contributed to the production of a TV documentary, *Royal Family* (1969). This film broke with tradition by making the monarchy seem more human and less mysterious. It also led to greater curiosity about the royal family's private life and a press that was bolder about intruding on their privacy. *WMK*

Hewart, Gordon (1870–1943), judge and Liberal politician. Hewart entered parliament in 1913 and became solicitor-general (1916–19) and attorney-general (1919–22). He was appointed lord chief justice in 1923, retiring in 1940. A brilliant advocate, he is remembered primarily for his book *The New Despotism* (1929), which warned of the dangers of delegated legislation and increasing bureaucracy (whose impact was such that it was rumoured that Whitehall considered an attempt to boycott it) and for his dictum: 'it is important not only that justice should be done; but that it should be manifestly seen to be done'. *ML*

Lord Hewart, *Not Without Prejudice* (London, 1937). | Robert Jackson, *The Chief: The Biography of Gordon Hewart, Lord Chief Justice of England, 1922–1940* (London, 1959).

Hewins, William Albert Samuel (1865–1931), economist and Conservative politician. Hewins campaigned tirelessly throughout his political career for a Britain committed to tariff reform and Empire. The first director of the LSE, 1895–1903, he went on to hold chairs in economic history and economics at the University of London and King's College, London. An MP for six years, 1912–18, he was a leader of the Unionist business committee which helped to force a coalition government in 1915, under-secretary at the Colonial Office, 1917–19, under Lloyd George, and a strong voice for the 'diehard' right wing of his party. *RJQA*

W. A. S. Hewins, *The Apologia of an Imperialist: Forty Years of Empire Policy*, 2 vols. (London, 1929).

Hicks, John (1904–89), leading British economist, Nobel prizewinner, and author. Prior to the Second World War, Hicks established the foundations of economic analysis which subsequently dominated teaching in the West. Chronologically, his interests incorporated wages, money, general equilibrium, social accounting, cycles, international trade, consumer theory, growth theory, methodology, and capital theory. His investigations using mathematical methods utilized historical applications of economic concepts. Hicks was professor of economics at the University of Oxford until his retirement in 1965. His publications included *Theory of Wages* (1932), *Value and Capital* (1939), *A Contribution to the Theory of the Trade Cycle* (1950), *Capital and Growth* (1965), and *The Crisis in Keynesian Economics* (1975). *JFM*

Hicks, Ursula (1896–1985), British economist. Ursula Webb read history at Oxford, where she was awarded an MA in 1918. In 1929 she embarked upon a degree in economic history at the LSE where she stayed on to become a graduate student and later a lecturer. She co-founded the *Review of Economics*, which became a leading scholarly journal. Her first book, *Finance of British Industry 1920–36*, written with her husband John Hicks, established her reputation as an important economic theorist, particularly in the area of mathematical modelling. After 1950, they played a key role in advising many of the Commonwealth countries how to deal with economic difficulties that they faced in the transition to independence. *JFM*

Hicks Beach, Michael Edward (1837–1916), Conservative politician. 'Black Michael' (so-called for his considerable temper and swarthy appearance, allegedly making him resemble a character in Anthony Hope's *The Prisoner of Zenda*) sat continuously in the Commons, 1864–1906. Success came early: he gained junior office under Lord Derby (1868) and in Disraeli's second ministry became chief secretary for Ireland and then colonial secretary in time to inherit from his predecessor the unfortunate Zulu war, 1878–9. In the period of opposition which followed, Hicks Beach laboured hard to keep the party, and particularly the rivals Lord Randolph Churchill and Salisbury, united. His efforts led to his chairmanship of the National Union and in Salisbury's short 1885 government to his appointment as chancellor of the exchequer and afterwards as opposition leader in the Commons (1885–6). In Salisbury's second administration, Hicks Beach made way as chancellor and leader of the House for Churchill and returned to the Irish Office in the midst of the uproar following the failure of Gladstone's Home Rule Bill, but was forced to resign almost immediately due to a severe eye infection which for a time threatened to blind him. He recovered in time to serve with distinction as president of the Board of Trade, 1888–92. In 1895 Hicks Beach returned to the exchequer. The South African war in 1899 demanded a sharp increase in government income, and this led even this staunch free trader in 1902 to reimpose the lapsed registration duty on imported corn as a purely revenue measure. With Salisbury, he retired from office in 1902, unhappy that his corn duty had become the centre of controversy in the Conservative quarrel over Joseph Chamberlain's tariff reform plan. In

1906 he became Viscount St Aldwyn, and earl in 1915. *RJQA*

Victoria Hicks-Beach, *The Life of Sir Michael Hicks Beach, Lord St. Aldwyn* (London, 1932).

High Court (England and Wales), established in 1876 as the normal trial court for all important civil cases. It now has three divisions: the Queen's Bench Division, the Chancery Division, and the Family Division. The Queen's Bench Division (QBD) (about 70 judges headed by the lord chief justice) hears contract and tort actions, with specialized courts hearing commercial matters (such as insurance, agency, banking) and shipping cases (negligent navigation, rights over ships and cargoes). Juries are occasionally used, mostly in libel cases. The QBD also has the judicial review jurisdiction over lower courts and tribunals, officials, government ministers, local authorities, and other public bodies, to see they are acting as required by law. The Chancery Division (about seventeen judges headed by the vice-chancellor) hears property disputes, trusts, mortgages, wills, estates, company and partnership matters, insolvency, and tax; a specialized court hears matters concerning patents, trade marks, designs, and other intellectual property claims. The Family Division (about sixteen judges headed by the president) deals with all the more complicated family matters, defended divorce and nullity petitions, legitimacy, validity of marriage, matrimonial property, and various matters concerning children: custody, maintenance, wardship, adoption, and so on. High Court hearings may be held outside London in major provincial centres where this is more convenient to litigants. *VT*

higher education. The sector expanded only slowly in Britain in the first half of the century. The numbers of those receiving some form of higher education at universities, teacher training colleges, and other forms of further education rose from 25,000 in 1900–1, to 61,000 in 1924–5, and 69,000 in 1938–9. The number of university students, 42,000 in 1924–5, was double the figure of 1900–1 and had risen to 50,000 by 1938–9. Most of this expansion took place in England and Wales, with the founding of new 'red-brick' university colleges, initially awarding London University degrees, at Nottingham, Southampton, Exeter, Hull, and Leicester, and of the University of Reading. The creation of the University Grants Committee in 1919 provided a means of channelling state finance to the universities, and brought them into a more coherent but arms-length relationship with central government. Total government expenditure on higher education rose from £3.9 million in 1920–1 to £9.8 million in 1937–8, while that from local sources, mainly rates, grew from £4.2 million to £10.3 million. English university expenditure rose by over 90 per cent between 1924 and 1937, though in Scotland by only a third of this, resulting in a decline of student numbers there from 10,400 to 9,900. The higher education sector, however, remained small: only 13,200 of those entering employment in 1934 were from universities out of a total of 554,500, and the total higher education sector only accounted for 27,700. As late as 1938 only 2 per cent of 19-year-olds were receiving full-time education.

Nor did higher education figure very prominently in plans for reconstruction after the Second World War. During the 1950s, however, there was a growing climate of opinion that Britain was lagging behind in the provision of higher education, especially in comparison with the USA. The only expansion in provision since 1945 had been at Keele in north Staffordshire, founded in 1949. As a result, in 1954 still only 3.2 per cent of the relevant age group were attending university in the UK. In 1959 the University Grants Committee invited applications for new university sites, from which six were selected. Sussex, already approved in 1958, opened in 1961 and was followed by York, East Anglia, Essex, Lancaster, Kent, and Warwick. Stirling and Ulster were also founded by 1967. The *Robbins report of 1963 encouraged expansion beyond the limits originally envisaged; Sussex, for example, doubled in size between 1964 and 1967. A common feature of these 'new universities' was experiment with new groupings of subjects, typically into 'schools' where interdisciplinary combinations of subjects could be studied. By 1967, the percentage of the age group entering university had risen to 6.3. Although the new universities were the flagship of the expansion of the higher education sector, the bulk of the increase in student numbers actually occurred at Oxbridge and the existing civic universities. By 1972 there were 45 universities compared with 17 in 1945. The Robbins target, however, remained unattained as late as 1980, though much of the shortfall was taken up by students taking courses at the 30 polytechnics set up since 1967. In 1989 education minister Kenneth Baker called for a doubling of numbers in higher education; in 1992 the abolition of the Council for National Academic Awards (CNAA) signalled the end of the polytechnic sector. Polytechnics and large higher education colleges were now allowed to call themselves universities, effectively creating a fresh tier of 'new' universities.

There were in 1999 89 universities in the UK, one of which, the University of London, itself comprised over forty separate institutions, together with nineteen colleges and institutes of higher education with the power to award their own degrees. In addition the *Open University provides part-time higher education. By 1997 there were an estimated 1.3 million full-time higher education students and another 900,000 part-time. *JS*

Highlands and Islands Development Board, created in 1965 and succeeded in 1991 by the Highlands and Islands enterprise network. They were established in order to support the people of the Highlands and Islands of Scotland to strengthen their communities, develop skills, foster business competitiveness, and attract inward investment. *JD*

Highlands and Islands Enterprise Network website: *www.hie.co.uk*

Hill, Charles (1904–89), doctor, politician, and broadcaster. Hill made his mark as the wartime 'radio doctor', broadcasting folksy chats about healthy living on rations. As secretary of the British Medical Association when Labour introduced a free health service, Hill spoke for the medical profession and drove a tough bargain. In 1945, he stood as an independent for Cambridge University, but in 1950 was elected MP for Luton as a 'Liberal and Conservative'. In 1951, he revived his homespun radio persona in Tory election broadcasts that attracted more listeners than any other politician except Attlee and Churchill. The 'radio doctor' became a food minister in 1951 and was made postmaster general in 1955. At the end of the Eden government, Hill became responsible for government presentation and continued in this role after he entered the cabinet in 1957 as chancellor of the duchy of Lancaster. In 1961, Hill became minister of housing and local government, but in 1962 he was sacked in the *'Night of the Long Knives'. As Lord Hill of Luton he was chairman first of the independent television authority and then from 1967 of the BBC. *RJS*

LORD HILL, *Both Sides of the Hill* (London, 1964). | LORD HILL, *Behind the Screen* (London, 1974).

Hill, Jonathan Hopkin (1960–), Conservative political adviser. A public relations expert and former special adviser to Kenneth Clarke (1986–9), Hill joined John Major's policy unit in February 1991, developing a troubleshooting role. As Major's political secretary from the start of the 1992 general election campaign, he increased the policy influence of the political office. After leaving Downing Street (1994), he advised Major during the Conservative leadership campaign (1995) and general election (1997). *CL*

SARAH HOGG and JONATHAN HILL, *Too Close to Call: Power and Politics—John Major in No. 10* (London, 1995).

Hillhead by-election (25 March 1982), Alliance by-election victory in Glasgow which returned Roy *Jenkins to the House of Commons. Jenkins overturned a safe Conservative majority, taking the seat with 10,106 votes to 8,068 Conservative and 7,846 Labour, completing the return of all the Social Democratic Party's *'Gang of Four' to Westminster. *JS*

Hilton Young, Edward (1879–1960), politician. Hilton Young was a barrister, Liberal MP for Norwich, 1912–23 and 1924–9, and Conservative MP for Sevenoaks, 1929–35, when he became 1st Lord Kennet. He was a junior minister under Lloyd George and, following his change of party, minister of health in the National Government, 1931–5. *JAR*

hire purchase, a common form of credit agreement for retail sales. Under the system, the purchaser acquires an item from a retailer who has sold goods on to a finance house, which in law is classified as the seller. Finance houses make available to the customer finance which is paid back in instalments. In contrast with consumer credit, which has become increasingly popular since the 1970s, the customer does not become the legal owner until the last instalment is paid. *JFM*

'Hitler has missed the bus', words uttered by Neville Chamberlain in a speech of 4 April 1940. Britain had increased her fighting strength considerably and, in not attacking Britain and France earlier, he believed that Hitler had lost the opportunity to win the war. When Germany's blitzkrieg in the west actually erupted five days later, the phrase was then much quoted to show Chamberlain as out of touch with the realities of the war. *AJC*

HMS *Dreadnought*. See DREADNOUGHT, HMS.

Hoare, Samuel John Gurney (1880–1959), Conservative politician and ambassador. Representing Chelsea, 1910–44, Hoare's role in helping destroy the Lloyd George coalition in 1922 was rewarded by Law with the Air Ministry. Hoare had been an early exponent of the importance of air power and would hold the post three times during his career: 1922–4, 1924–9, and 1940. In 1922, the RAF was still in its infancy and it fell to Hoare to help shape its future role. In this task he drew upon the expertise of Hugh *Trenchard and between them they envisaged wide possibilities, both civilian and military, for *The Empire of the Air* (title of book by Hoare himself, 1957). With the formation of the National Government, Hoare became India secretary, having been a party representative at the first round table conference, and it fell to him to draft the new Indian constitution after the second round table talks failed to reach agreement. In April 1934 Churchill alleged that Hoare had manipulated evidence presented to the joint select committee that was considering his own India white paper. Hoare successfully guided his India Bill through parliament by 1935, a task aggravated by the guerrilla warfare from his own backbenches and right-wing party activists. He was seen in certain circles as potential successor to Baldwin, and clearly he was an ambitious man, enjoying the tacit support of the Beaverbrook press empire. Unfortunately his fortunes were severely dented when shortly after becoming foreign secretary he was obliged to resign over the *Hoare-Laval pact. Only a few months earlier Hoare had committed Britain to collective security; but his secret negotiations with the French over Abyssinia (now Ethiopia) appeared to disregard this commitment and reward Italian aggression. Abandoned by Baldwin's cabinet and pilloried by many in his own party, his resignation speech actually won him widespread sympathy. He quickly returned to cabinet in 1936, in May 1937 becoming a liberalizing home secretary (he was a Quaker), and was one of Neville Chamberlain's inner cabinet during 1938–9. He joined the war cabinet in 1939 but a decade in office had taken its toll and when the Chamberlain government fell in 1940 his ministerial career was over. Churchill sent him as ambassador to Spain, 1940–4, where he helped to keep fascist Spain neutral throughout the Second World War. Made Viscount Templewood, 1944. *NJC*

J. A. Cross, *Sir Samuel Hoare* (London, 1977). | Lord Templewood, *Nine Troubled Years* (London, 1954).

Hoare-Laval pact (1935), secret Anglo-French agreement to deal with Mussolini's invasion of *Abyssinia (now Ethiopia). The pact was once seen as a typical example of British appeasement policy in the face of fascist aggression. The reality, however, was more complex. British policy makers were caught in an unenviable dilemma between the need to uphold the country's obligations as a member of the *League of Nations and a desire not to drive Italy into the arms of the infinitely more dangerous Nazi Germany. For much of 1935 Britain attempted to negotiate a settlement which would be acceptable to all sides. On 19 June the cabinet decided that a solution might be possible if landlocked Abyssinia were offered access to the sea at the port of Zeila in exchange for territorial concessions to Italy in the Ogaden desert. Such a settlement was not, however, acceptable to Mussolini who began military operations in October.

Britain's scope for manoeuvre was circumscribed by a speech by the new foreign secretary, Samuel Hoare, to the League Assembly on 11 September which committed Britain to honour its obligations under the Covenant. To a large extent, however, Hoare's line was dictated by the forthcoming general election and the need to pay lip-service to the continuing popular faith in the League. With the election safely won, the cabinet on 2 December authorized Hoare to continue the quest for a negotiated settlement. Discussions in Paris with his French opposite number, Pierre Laval, led to a proposed deal involving territorial concessions by Abyssinia in excess of anything discussed hitherto. At first the cabinet backed this plan, but the proposals, leaked to the French press, provoked popular uproar and threatened a Conservative rebellion in the Commons. The government decided that it would have to abandon the pact, and Hoare, disgraced, now resigned. His place was taken by Anthony Eden, whose popular image was of an ardent champion of the League of Nations. *DJD*

Hobhouse, Leonard Trelawny (1864–1929), Liberal journalist and writer. Following education and teaching at Oxford, Hobhouse was on the staff of C. P. *Scott's *Manchester Guardian*, 1897–1902, and continued to write for the paper for many years afterwards. Though a philosopher by training, he became London University's first professor of sociology, from 1907 until his death. Hobhouse was a prolific author and a lucid interpreter of complex philosophical and academic principles for a popular readership. He is generally regarded along with J. A. *Hobson as the principal intellectual advocate of the *New Liberalism of the Edwardian period, with its recognition of the need for greater state intervention (and hence of higher taxes) in the pursuit of social justice, as he argued in *The Elements of Social Justice* (1921). The basic tenets of this approach to politics were classically set out in his

Liberalism (1911), a book that was characteristically written for the 'home university library'. *JAR*

Hobson, Bulmer (1883–1969), Irish nationalist. Born in Co. Down, of Quaker background, Hobson was nevertheless a convinced Irish nationalist from his schooldays. He was co-founder of the nationalist youth movement, Fianna Éireann, of the Ulster Literary Theatre, and of the Dungannon clubs. Having been vice-president of Sinn Fein, he left the movement in 1910 and became more devoted to the Fianna and the Irish Republican Brotherhood (IRB). During 1911–14 he edited the IRB paper, *Irish Freedom.* A founder-member of the Irish Volunteers in 1913, he co-organized their 1914 Howth *gun-running. Hobson broke with the militants behind the 1916 Easter Rising, and opposed that rebellion. He subsequently withdrew from revolutionary politics, interesting himself in a variety of artistic and social projects. *RE*

Hobson, John Atkinson (1858–1940), economist and writer. Hobson was an economist who, somewhat unusually, approached his subject from the perspective of a sociologist, and was much concerned with the popularizing of his views in the political arena, notably through articles in the Liberal weekly *Nation.* In the 1880s and 1890s, in such books as *The Physiology of Industry* (co-authored with A. F. Mummery, 1893) and *The Evolution of Modern Capitalism* (1894), he developed the idea of 'under-consumption' as a fundamental characteristic of industrial capitalism which was central to his later writings. This interpreted capitalism as an inherently exploitative system from which workers deserved and required the regulation and protection of the state. He thus advocated progressive taxation so that the profits made from industrial capitalism could be redistributed to its victims. Internationally, a similar approach in Hobson's *Imperialism* (1902) led to an unusually negative (for that time) portrayal of the impact of Western states on their colonies, again described as inherent in the very economic system of developed capitalism rather than attributed to the vices or failings of individual capitalists or colonizers. This deterministic approach to the impact of economic principles on political action influenced Lenin's writings on imperialism, and within Britain was much cited by peacemaking opponents of the arms race that preceded the outbreak of war in 1914. However, Hobson's more lasting influence in Britain was in the provision of a serious basis of economic theory to reinforce the more advanced Liberal thinking of the early part of the century. Along with L. T. *Hobhouse, Hobson helped to shape the *New Liberalism of the 1900–14 period. *JAR*

Hodge, John (1855–1937), Labour politician. Hodge was a prominent trade union activist and Great War coalition minister. He was a steelworker and founder member of the Steel Smelters' Association in 1886 and later president of the Iron and Steel Workers' Confederation. He was a Manchester city councillor, MP for Gorton, the first minister of labour, 1916–17, and of pensions, 1917–19. The epitome of compromise and moderation, he opposed his union's involvement in the General Strike of 1926. *KL*

Hogg, Douglas McGarel (1872–1950), lawyer and Conservative politician. Following commercial experience with the family sugar business and a period of military service during the South African war, Hogg began a legal career specializing in commercial and common law. In 1920 he was appointed attorney-general to the prince of Wales. By nature a Conservative he was invited by Law to become attorney-general in 1922, only then entering parliament as MP for St Marylebone, but he led the Conservative attack on the Labour government's handling of the *Campbell case which prompted its downfall. In March 1928 he became lord chancellor as Lord Hailsham, and from 1931 was war secretary during a period when Britain's defences were in a parlous position after many years of limited defence spending. Hogg championed the military services' cause and won the respect of the army council. When the unity of the *National Government was threatened by the issue of protection it was Hailsham who proposed that its members should 'agree to differ', a compromise which suspended the normal practice of cabinet collective responsibility and thus kept the Liberal free-traders in office until after the 1932 Ottawa conference. Ill health obliged his retirement in 1938. *NJC*

Hogg, Douglas Martin (1945–), Conservative politician and butt. The son of Quintin *Hogg, he inherited the family oddity, and was MP for Grantham from 1979. Hogg, like his father, was not illiberal, but his virtues could easily be missed. He had early unpopularity—as a whip physically obstructing a deserter, dismissing the Commons as the price of office, with an insulting despatch-box style, and he described Labour, when opposing renewed anti-terrorist legislation, as supporting the IRA. At agriculture, charged with the BSE crisis (see BEEF WAR), he claimed subsequently to have advised earlier drastic action, but was obliged to treat with the European Commission at its most implacable, and therefore took the blame—lots of it. *EP*

Hogg, Quintin McGarel (1907–), Conservative politician and lawyer. Hogg was a fellow of All Souls College, Oxford, and a barrister when he won the 1938 Oxford by-election, but in May 1940 he was among the Tory MPs whose revolt led to Neville Chamberlain's resignation. After war service, he joined the progressive Tory reform committee and in 1945 was an air minister in Churchill's Caretaker Government. In *The *Case for Conservatism* (1947) Hogg stylishly advocated a blend of tradition and pragmatism, and he was involved in drafting the policy document *The Right Road for Britain*. In 1950, however, he succeeded his father, 1st viscount Hailsham, and reluctantly entered the Lords. During the *Suez crisis in September 1956, Eden appointed him first lord of the Admiralty, but Hailsham had to insist on being told about the invasion plan and had to prevent Mountbatten, the first sea lord, resigning. In 1957, he entered Macmillan's cabinet as education minister and in the autumn became party chairman and lord president of the council. Hailsham's exuberance, exemplified by his bell-ringing at the 1957 Tory conference, revived party workers. Following the 1959 landslide victory, he became lord privy seal and science and technology minister, retaining the latter post until 1964, then becoming leader of the Lords in 1960 and assuming responsibility for sport in 1962 and for the north-east in 1963. By 1963 Macmillan wanted Hailsham to succeed him and made him head of the British delegation to negotiate the nuclear *test-ban treaty in Moscow. Hailsham's excitable behaviour, however, caused others to have doubts. Macmillan, having decided to resign the following October, was persuaded of Hailsham's temperamental unsuitability as his successor, a view reinforced by Home's passing on reported American unease about Hailsham. Unaware that Macmillan had abandoned him, Hailsham declared his intention to renounce his peerage so as to fight for the leadership. When Butler prevaricated in the campaign to stop Home, however, Hailsham agreed to serve in the Douglas-Home cabinet, and as Quintin Hogg was elected MP for St Marylebone. In 1968, as shadow home secretary, he rebuked Powell for his inflammatory language in the 'rivers of blood' speech. In 1970 he was appointed lord chancellor, the post that his father had held, and became a life peer. He served in Thatcher's shadow cabinet and was again lord chancellor, 1979–87. *RJS*

LORD HAILSHAM, *A Sparrow's Flight: Memoirs* (London, 1990). | GEOFFREY LEWIS, *Lord Hailsham* (London, 1997).

Hogg, Sarah Elizabeth Mary (1946–), head of prime minister's policy unit, 1990–5. A former journalist, Hogg was John Major's key adviser, particularly on economic policy, poll-tax reform, and Europe. After 1992, and in particular following the 'back to basics' debacle (1994), she was criticized for poor long-term strategy, a failing she saw as inevitable given the government's short-term problems. After leaving Downing Street, she joined Major's team in the Conservative leadership campaign (1995). *CL*

SARAH HOGG and JONATHAN HILL, *Too Close to Call: Power and Politics—John Major in No. 10* (London, 1995).

holidays with pay. Before 1900, few working-class families could afford annual holidays. The TUC, in 1911, was the first public body to call for holidays with pay. Collective bargaining secured 1.5 million paid holidays by 1925, rising to 4 million in 1937. It was not until 1938, however, that parliament produced legislation on holidays with pay. By 1945, four-fifths of Britain's workforce were entitled to paid holidays and rising prosperity in the post-war period encouraged even more to take longer holidays, cheap flights making these increasingly likely to be abroad. *JJN*

Holme, Richard Gordon (1936–), Liberal and Liberal Democrat activist. Holme acted as senior adviser to David *Steel and Paddy *Ashdown, and chaired the 1997 general election campaign which gave the Liberal Democrats the largest third-party support in the House of Commons since the 1920s. He has fought several constituencies himself, but failed to secure a seat. His former positions included president of the Liberal Party, 1980–1, senior adviser to Steel during the *Alliance with the *Social Democratic Party, and membership of the Labour/Liberal Democrat Cabinet Committee set up in 1997. He has a long-standing interest in electoral reform as founder director of the National Campaign for Electoral Reform from 1976, director of the Electoral Reform Centre from 1983, and founding co-chair of Charter 88. He took a peerage in 1990. *JS*

Holmes, John Eaton (1951–), prime minister's foreign affairs private secretary since 1996, and principal private secretary since 1997. A career diplomat, Holmes was centrally involved in negotiations surrounding the peace process in Northern Ireland under John Major. Following Alex Allan's departure, Holmes combined his foreign affairs role with the job of principal private secretary (which was to have gone to Jonathan Powell) to become a key figure in Tony Blair's Downing Street. *CL*

Holt, David ('Tim') (1943–), statistician. Professor of social statistics at the university of Southampton since 1980, Holt was brought in to Whitehall in 1995 as head of the Government Statistical Service and director of the Central Statistical Office—since 1996 the Office for National Statistics (ONS). Against the background of failing public confidence in the integrity and reliability of official statistics, Holt acknowledged the importance of the ONS being independent and being seen to be independent, the Blair government preparing plans for its major reform. *KT*

Holy Loch, nuclear base set up in October 1960. A memorandum of understanding was signed between the USA and Britain for the basing of American Polaris nuclear submarines at Holy Loch, near Glasgow. British proposals for a dual control arrangement and for the base to be located at Loch Linnhe, away from Scotland's population centres, were rejected. Although it was often assumed to have been a quid pro quo for American supply of *Skybolt nuclear missiles to Britain, the link between the two was ambiguous, which proved crucial at the *Nassau conference. *JPSG*

Home, earl of. see DOUGLAS-HOME, ALEXANDER FREDERICK.

homelessness. Shortages of accommodation were not unusual during the huge 19th-century growth and movement of population, producing a major problem of vagrancy. By the 1914–18 Great War this had largely disappeared, apart from tramps and 'casuals' who used the wards of the workhouse. The private rented sector had sufficient flexibility to absorb even the poorest tenants—though often in very inadequate conditions.

During the post-1945 period there was a growing problem of homelessness amongst specific groups, such as coloured immigrants, single mothers, and casual workers. From the 1970s and through the 1980s, rising unemployment, a growing divorce rate, and the pressure of housing costs precipitated a larger crisis of homelessness, seen in the increasing numbers of families placed in bed-and-breakfast or other temporary accommodation, reaching a peak of over 60,000 by the early 1990s. By 1990 over 140,000 families were designated homeless by local authorities. Clearly visible, too, were signs of homelessness amongst the young with an increasing number of 'rough sleepers' appearing on the streets of the capital and other cities.

Local authorities were given duties to assist certain categories of the homeless under the 1985 and 1996 Housing Acts, and have legal duties to provide housing assistance for families and vulnerable people who are eligible for assistance, unintentionally homeless, and in priority need. The priority need group includes households with children or containing a pregnant woman, those made homeless by an emergency, and those vulnerable as a result of old age, mental or physical illness or disability. Latterly, these groups have been added to by a growing number of political *asylum seekers. In 1998–9, local authorities in England accepted more than 105,470 households as meeting the conditions of homelessness, with an additional 43,118 in Scotland. Various attempts have been made by recent governments to tackle the high profile issue of homelessness on the streets of London and other large cities. A Rough Sleepers Initiative was launched in 1990 in central London, later extended to 27 other areas. In London this was replaced in 1999 by a London Rough Sleepers Unit with a budget of £145 million over three years to provide temporary and longer-term accommodation. The government in 1999 declared that its aim was to reduce the number of people sleeping rough in England and Wales by two-thirds between 1999 and 2002. Funding to this end is now channelled through a Homelessness Action Programme and voluntary organizations. *JS*

Home Office, one of the oldest offices of state. The grand reorganization of 1913 divided the Home Office into six sections: industrial; liquor licensing, nationality, by-laws, and private bills; criminal, police (given a separate division in 1914), and the probation service (created in 1907); children, white slave traffic, and obscenity laws; royal and ceremonial, explosives, vivisection, and many miscellaneous functions; metropolitan police, Channel Islands, Isle of Man, finance, wild birds, and aeroplanes. The Great War brought many changes. The defence of the realm regulations empowered the Home Office to control the movement of aliens and the internment of 30,000 enemy aliens (a tightening of the law after the ineffective 1905 Aliens Act which only controlled those on large boats). Intelligence was a growth area for the Home Office during the war but it was not until 1952 that it was clarified that the head of the Security Service, MI5, was personally responsible to the home secretary—but with a right of access to the prime minister. Issues relating to trading with the enemy passed to the Board of Trade and troubles in the mines led to the creation of the Mines Department in 1920. The 1920 Government of Ireland Act, which created Northern Ireland, made the Home Office the coordinating department between Westminster and the new government in Belfast (this was to bring great stress between the recrudescence of the Troubles in 1968 and the creation of the Northern Ireland Office in 1972). The Home Office also gained new functions with much League of Nations involvement through commissions, the international labour office, and the control of narcotics.

The decision to make the Home Office responsible for air raid precautions (ARP) in 1923—the ARP department of the Home Office being set up in 1935—was the first towards preparations for the possibility of another war; fire-fighting was another element. Responsibility for ARP services on the ground was handled by local authorities, which had been brought in as partners with the Home Office in 1935, but the incendiary bomb attacks of 1940–1 betrayed the ineffectiveness of the fire services and the National Fire Service (Emergency Provisions) Act, 1941, led to the creation of a national service under the authority of the Home Office until 1947. On the outbreak of war in 1939, the Ministry of Home Security was set up as a sister department to the Home Office and sharing a minister, Anderson; it was abolished on 31 May 1945. There was also a tremendous expansion of activity in the Home Office proper. A substantial regional organization was created. The increased duties of the police were augmented by the police war reserve. The emergency regulations and defence regulations demanded interference in almost all aspects of life. Just as in 1914–18, the control of refugees and detention of enemy aliens was a Home Office responsibility. It also dealt with the émigré governments and soldiers of Europe, along with the vast armies of the USA and Commonwealth which arrived in Britain.

The years after 1945 saw a considerable fluctuation in the functions of the Home Office. The mass Commonwealth immigration produced the 1962 Commonwealth Immigrants Act, the 1965 Race Relations Act, and the creation of the Race Relations Board, which was followed in 1968 by the Community Relations Commission. This led to the Home Office becoming responsible for anti-discrimination legislation and in 1975 the Equal Opportunities Act set up the Equal Opportunities Commission while the 1976 Race Relations Act amalgamated the Community Relations Commission and the Race Relations Board into the Commission for Racial Equality. Other accretions to Home Office duties included the integration of the prison commission in 1963 after a separate existence of 86 years, the big expansion and renaming of the probation service to the probation and after-care service in 1966, and, upon the break-up of the Ministry of Posts and Telecommunications in 1974, the addition of the broadcasting and radio regulatory departments. Several functions were also taken away from the Home Office. The wartime practice of the Ministry of Labour and National Service administering factory inspection was made permanent in 1945, the Ministry of Pensions and National Insurance gained workmen's compensation in 1946, responsibility for conditions in shops and offices transferred to the Ministry of Labour in the 1960s, authority for explosives and petroleum safety left for the newly created Health and Safety Executive in 1972, and the children's department was moved to the Department of Health and Social Security in 1971. *JD*

Home Office website: *www.homeoffice.gov.uk*

homeownership has undergone considerable expansion in Britain since the beginning of the 20th century. In 1914, owner-occupiers made up only a tenth of the housing tenures in England and Wales. The introduction of rent controls during the Great War, a general rise in affluence for those in work, and low interest rates saw owner-occupation expand substantially between the two world wars, especially in the 1930s. By 1939, almost a third of tenures were owner-occupation, mainly financed by mortgages on the newly built properties which made the 'inter-war semi' a feature of the suburban fringe of almost every town and city in the British Isles. Politically, there was also support from the 1920s in Conservative circles for a *property-owning democracy as a bulwark against socialism and political instability.

Owner-occupation continued to rise in the post-1945 period, reaching a half of all housing tenures by 1977. Encouragement was given through the granting of tax relief on mortgages, though this was limited to a £25,000 ceiling in 1974 (later raised in 1983 to £30,000). A major boost was given to owner-occupation by the *Housing Act, 1980, which gave council tenants the right to buy their own houses at heavily discounted rates. In 1993, a rent-to-mortgage scheme gave a million tenants the right to purchase their homes gradually. In spite of serious downturns in the housing market, resulting in nearly one million repossessions during the early 1990s, these measures have combined to raise owner-occupation to almost four-fifths of all tenures in England and Wales by 1999 and to just over two-thirds in the whole of Great Britain (the Scottish dependence on 'council housing' remaining stronger than further south). Having largely achieved a property-owning democracy in which (alongside the Netherlands and Ireland) Britain has one of the highest densities of owner-occupation in Europe, governments have first limited and then ultimately removed the tax relief available on mortgages. The Conservative Finance Acts of 1993 and 1994 limited relief available and it was finally phased out by the Blair government in 1999. *JS*

'homes fit for heroes', popular version of a pledge given by Lloyd George on 24 November 1918, during the *'Coupon' Election campaign: 'What is our task? To make Britain a fit country for heroes to live in.' The 1918–22 government's failure to carry through on its plans for social reform, notably on housing, and the high level of unemployment (especially among ex-soldiers) during the 1920s and 1930s, ensured that in 1945 such phrases could be recalled to great political effect by Labour. *JAR*

Homosexual Law Reform Society. See HOMOSEXUALITY.

homosexuality. For most of the 20th century male homosexuality was illegal. It was restricted by a series of laws dating back to the 12th century and the 1885 Criminal Law Amendment Act which specifically criminalized male homosexual acts. Lesbianism was excluded from such restrictive laws. Little progress was made on legal reform until the 1960s. A rapid increase of the number of men prosecuted for homosexual acts after 1945 led to a government review of existing laws. The Wolfenden report (1954–7) recommended a relaxation of the law and in 1967 the Sexual Offences Act enforced these recommendations, making homosexual acts between consenting adults in private legal in England and Wales. Later this was extended to Scotland (1980) and Northern Ireland (1982). No further significant legislation was passed until the 1980s. Fuelled by the *AIDS scare and the influence of so-called 'loony-left' councils, Margaret Thatcher's government introduced 'Section 28' (of a Local Government Act) in 1988. This barred local authorities from 'promoting' homosexuality in schools. It became a symbol of homophobic discrimination and precipitated a decade of protest led by two groups formed in its wake: Stonewall (1989) and *OutRage (1990). In 1994 the campaign achieved the lowering of the age of consent for gay sex to 18. Tony Blair's election in 1997 saw progress towards equal rights for homosexuals, but this was opposed by the House of Lords: equalization of the age of consent and removal of Section 28 were approved by the Commons in 1999 but rejected by the Lords. The existing ban on homosexuals in the armed forces was lifted in 2000 and in Scotland Section 28 was overturned. At the end of the century, the legal fight for homosexual rights remained a contentious issue. The more radical gay and lesbian movement of the 1970s and 1980s, however, brought with it a rapid growth in a gay urban subculture. A host of gay bars sprang up in London, notably 'Heaven' which opened in 1979. In the 1980s, Soho rapidly assumed the status of London's 'gay district' and by the 1990s most larger towns throughout Britain could boast at least one gay bar. *JJN*

Hong Kong. This unique colonial outpost was the hub for Britain's commercial operations in east Asia, but with the 99-year lease of the New Territories due to expire in 1997, the Thatcher government was forced to negotiate a withdrawal agreement with Beijing in 1984. China would recover sovereignty over Hong Kong, but allow a significant degree of autonomy for 50 years after the handover. Nevertheless, the democratic reforms introduced by Chris Patten, the last governor, soured Sino-British relations and highlighted the lack of such changes in the past. *MCJ*

honours scandal (1922). Honours and peerages had been systematically exchanged for donations to party funds (both Liberal and Conservative) for several decades before the issue came to the political surface in the dying days of the Lloyd George coalition government. Lloyd George himself was suspect from the viewpoint of his critics because of his implication in the 1912 *Marconi scandal. He was also in an unusual position when he became prime minister in 1916, famously described by Beaverbrook as 'a prime minister without a party'. Lloyd George did have a party of sorts, the Coalition Liberals, but, since the official Liberal organization had mainly followed Asquith when the party split after 1916, Lloyd George's supporters had no party fund, no reserves built up over time. Lloyd George had therefore little option except to fall back on traditional methods, but to use them more riskily than in the past. Through his chief whip Freddy *Guest, and the middleman Maundy *Gregory, he set out to raise a large capital sum quickly.

Already by January 1918, he was coming under fire for his patronage: having seen the New Year's honours list, Neville Chamberlain wrote that 'I never cease to congratulate myself that I did figure among that rabble'. For the most part, though, while in alliance with Lloyd George, Conservatives remained diplomatically silent, complaining only when he 'poached' one of their own wealthy supporters in order to raise money for his own party. By 1921–2, with more Conservative critics about anyway and Lloyd George unsure how long he could remain in office and therefore more urgent in his need for cash, he was becoming even less discriminating. The issue finally came to the boil in June 1922, when the birthday honours list appeared, containing the name of Sir Joseph Robinson as a new baron. Robinson's business practices barely stood up to a moment's scrutiny—he had traded with the enemy during the Great War and been fined for fraud only a few months earlier—while three others of Lloyd George's nominations were also heavily criticized, in a Lords debate in which a price list for honours and bargaining letters from the government's agents were read out. There was uproar in the press, and it became clear that the premier had now gone much too far; he had also incensed George V. The government had to concede that there would be an independent vetting system for future nominations (see HONOURS SYSTEM) but the damage to Lloyd George's reputation was irreparable. For critics like Baldwin who gave political ethics a high priority, the honours scandal in June helped to push them into overthrowing Lloyd George in October. *JAR*

honours system. The sovereign is the 'fountain of honour'. This means that all recognition of public service comes from the monarch, though in fact almost all honours are awarded on the recommendation of the government of the day. The practice is to issue two annual lists, one on New Year's day and one on the monarch's official birthday (currently in June). Hereditary peerages, once considered the greatest honour, were largely discontinued after the Second World War, especially after life peerages were introduced. Exceptionally, Margaret Thatcher recommended hereditary peerages for William Whitelaw and George Thomas (but neither had heirs to inherit their peerages). Other senior honours are membership of the Privy Council, or knights of one of the orders of chivalry. The oldest is the Order of the Garter, with the Order of the Thistle for those connected with Scotland. There are also the Order of the Bath and the Order of St Michael and St George. Knights bachelor, though historic, do not belong to an order of chivalry. The Order of the British Empire, created after the Great War to recognize distinguished civilian service, was later opened to take up the overflow caused by the limitation of many of the other orders. It now accounts for most honours awarded and those at OBE (Officer of the Order of the British Empire) and MBE (Member of the Order of the British Empire) dominate every list.

There are a variety of other awards, some highly coveted, including the Order of Merit and Companion of Honour. Edward VII instituted the Order of Merit to honour men and women who had made unusual contributions either in state service or in the arts and sciences. The order, restricted to 24 persons, has been given to military men (such as Lord Roberts), painters (Augustus John), and politicians (Margaret Thatcher). The Order of Merit, along with the Orders of the Garter and the Thistle, as well as the Royal Victorian Order, for personal service to the sovereign, are the only awards that during the latter half of the 20th century remained within the personal gift of the sovereign. The Companion of Honour is, like the Order of Merit, limited in number but awards are recommended by the government of the day.

The honours system has sometimes been criticized, especially from the left, for perpetuating a hierarchical society attuned to social distinction. The use of titles for awards of knighthood and for life peerages gives strength to this claim. The sale of honours by the Lloyd George government after the Great War led to the Honours (Prevention of Abuses) Act of 1925, which set up a committee that investigates all nominations for honours on political grounds. A longer-term difficulty, which fuelled a movement toward House of Lords reform at the end of the century, was that life peerages have not diminished the habitual hostility of the upper house to Labour and Liberal measures. Names on specific honours lists have also been questioned, as for example Harold Wilson's list when he retired as prime minister, on the grounds that some were unworthy.

The modern honours system retains features that Burke saw as distinctive of the 18th-century constitution. Recent creations jostle next to ancient survivals. Devices of medieval origin have often been adapted to pay homage to the principle of merit on which the modern state recruits and rewards its servants. There is a self-deprecating humour that has grown up around the honours system in which the MBE is said to stand for 'my bloody effort' and the OBE for 'others' bloody effort'. In the Order of St Michael and St George most often awarded to civil servants, the companion's CMG becomes 'call me God' while the dizzy heights of the grand cross GCMG translates as 'God calls me God'. *WMK*

Michael De La Noy, *The Honours System* (London, 1985).

Hood, Christopher Cropper (1947–), political scientist. Hood has made major contributions to the field of public policy and public administration. His work is characterized by the development of innovative typologies which order existing knowledge and explore relationships between their different components. *The Limits of Administration* (1976) diagnoses and classifies implementation problems; *The Tools of Government* (1983) sets out the instruments by which government seeks to shape its environment. A second characteristic of Hood's work is the identification of underlying trends and movements in administrative thought and practice (*Administrative Analysis*, 1986; *The Art of the State*, 1998). His seminal 'Public Management for all Seasons?' (*Public Administration*, 1991) set out the changes introduced to the public sector in Britain after the 1980s, linked them to international developments, and introduced the term 'new public management' which structured subsequent discussions of administrative reform. A third characteristic of Hood's work is an inventive, often-witty use of language and metaphor to develop penetrative points and make them stick in the mind, including 'contrived randomness' as a form of administrative control, 'multiorganizational suboptimization' as a form of implementation problem, and his physiognomic presentation of data on government ministries in *Bureaumetrics* (1981, with Andrew Dunsire). *ECP*

Hopkin, (William Aylsham) Bryan (1914–), government economic adviser. Hopkin was chief economic adviser to the Treasury and head of the Government Economic Service, 1974–7. His long career as a Whitehall economist included service in the Ministry of Health, the prime minister's statistical branch (1941–5), the Cabinet Office economic section, the Ministry of Overseas Development, the Department of Economic Affairs, and the Treasury—his career covering the years of Keynesian ascendancy. He was professor of economics at the University of Wales, Cardiff, 1972–82. *KT*

Hopkins, Richard Valentine Nind (1880–1955), civil servant. Hopkins was chairman of the board of Inland Revenue, 1922–7, before transferring to the Treasury to head the finance and supply branches, becoming second secretary in 1932 and permanent secretary to the Treasury and head of the civil service, 1942–5. The Treasury's leading expert on financial matters, he also worked closely with the Bank of England and its powerful governor, Montagu Norman. He clashed with Keynes in the 1930s, but during the Second World War ensured that the Treasury utilized Keynesian tools of macroeconomic management. *KT*

Hopkinson, Henry Lennox d'Aubigné (1902–96), Conservative politician. Hopkinson was a diplomat who subsequently entered the Conservative organization as joint director of the Conservative Research Department, 1946–50, becoming a Conservative MP, 1950–6, when he was made Lord Colyton. As junior minister at the Colonial Office he had to resign after making an unfortunate remark about the non-decolonization of Cyprus. *JAR*

Hore-Belisha, Leslie (1893–1957), politician and cabinet minister. A formative career in journalism ensured that when he became a minister Belisha was adept at cultivating the media. In 1923 he was elected Liberal MP for Devonport. In 1931 he took a leading role in forming the *Liberal National Party to support the National Government and secured junior office at the Treasury. He caught the eye of chancellor Neville Chamberlain, ensuring promotion in 1932 as financial secretary to the Treasury. Moved to the Ministry of Transport in 1934, he introduced the 'Belisha beacon' pedestrian crossings, the driving test for new motorists, and a revised highway code. In 1937 he was moved to the War Office where he embarked upon an extensive programme of reforms, though his reliance on the eccentric Basil Liddell-Hart as an adviser and his reforming zeal alienated the conservative military establishment. Controversy dogged his tenure of the post and in January 1940 Chamberlain 'sacked' him amid acrimony and claims of anti-Semitism in high places. *NJC*

R. J. Minney, *The Private Papers of Leslie Hore-Belisha* (London, 1960).

Horne, Robert Stevenson (1871–1940), Conservative minister. After a brief time as university lecturer in philosophy at Bangor, Horne was called to the Bar and practised with great success in Glasgow and London. Keenly interested in politics, he entered wartime government service in 1916 and became one of Lloyd George's 'men of push and go' from the world of business. Remarkably, he entered the Commons and sat on the coalition front bench on the same day in December 1918; his rise in the post-war coalition crested when he became chancellor of the exchequer in 1921. His loyalty to Lloyd George remained firm at the *Carlton Club meeting, and he refused office under Law. Baldwin, who thought the wealthy bachelor too fond of London night life, did not welcome him back to office, and Horne then built yet another extremely successful career as a company director. *RJQA*

Horner, Arthur (1894–1968), Communist and trade unionist. A leading figure in the *South Wales Miners' unofficial reform committee by 1914, he went to Ireland in 1917 to avoid military service and joined the Citizen's Army. On his return to Britain in August 1918, he was arrested and imprisoned until May 1919; whilst there he was elected checkweighman at Mardy colliery, which began his career as a union official. A foundation member of the Communist Party of Great Britain (CPGB) he was co-opted to its executive in 1923. During the 1920s he played a formative role in the development of the Miners' Minority Movement (MMM); and in 1927 helped organize the South Wales hunger march to London. In 1929, he was forced to resign as MMM secretary because of his opposition to the new sectarian policies of the Communist International, and in 1931 he was censured by the CPGB for leading an ideological deviation, 'Hornerism', from the Comintern's 'class against class' line, but this was viewed as only a tactical mistake and allowed him to remain a party member. In 1933 he helped set up the South Wales Miners' rank and file movement, and edited its paper the *South Wales Miner.* During 1934–5 he led the South Wales Miners' Federation (SWMF) campaign that successfully pushed out the South Wales Miners' Industrial Union from the South Wales coalfield. Gaoled four times for his political activities, he was the first CPGB member to lead a major national union, becoming president of the SWMF, 1936–46, and general secretary of the National Union of Mineworkers (NUM), 1946–59. A leading figure in the miners' rank and file movements up to 1936, he later played a crucial role in bringing about the unification of the district mining unions to form the NUM in 1945. *DLM*

Arthur Horner, *Incorrigible Rebel* (London, 1960).

Horrabin, James Francis ('Frank') (1884–1962), artist, writer, and politician. Born in Peterborough, he started work as a metalwork designer, and then worked as a journalist in Sheffield and London. Horrabin was Labour MP for Peterborough, 1929–31, and though he never returned to parliament, maintained his interest in politics, particularly imperial matters, and was chairman of the Fabian Colonial Bureau, 1945–50. He published a number of works but he is most well known for his political atlases, such as the *Plebs' Atlas* (1926) and the *Atlas of Current Affairs* (1931). These were written for the National Council of Labour Colleges, with which he had a long connection. Throughout his life Horrabin maintained a successful combination of interests in politics, art, and workers' education. *SB*

Horsbrugh, Florence Gertrude (1889–1969), Conservative politician. Elected to parliament in 1931 Horsbrugh served as a health minister from 1939 until 1945, when she became a food minister in Churchill's Caretaker Government. Defeated in the 1945 election, she was re-elected in 1950 and appointed education minister in 1951. On the inclusion of this post in the Churchill cabinet in 1953 Horsbrugh became the first woman to serve in a Conservative cabinet. She left office in 1954 and entered the Lords in 1959. *RJS*

Hoskyns, John Austin Hungerford Leigh (1927–), head of Downing Street policy unit, 1979–82. A former army officer and successful businessman, appalled by Britain's apparent decline in the 1970s, Hoskyns, who had no previous attachment to the Conservative Party, became a key 'Thatcherite' thinker. His 1977 'Stepping Stones' policy paper (co-written with Norman Strauss) identified union reform and financial stability as strategic priorities for a future Conservative government, although its blueprint was not fully adopted. Hoskyns' policy unit devised and advocated a strategy for taking on the National Union of Mineworkers and offered strong support for the deflationary measures pursued by Chancellor Geoffrey Howe. Frustrated by what he saw as politicians' lack of strategic thinking, and ultimately too radical for Thatcher, Hoskyns left Downing Street believing that his primary task had been largely accomplished but that his ideas on civil service reform would not be realized from within Whitehall. *CL*

PETER HENNESSY, *Whitehall* (London, 1989). | JOHN RANELAGH, *Thatcher's People* (London, 1991).

Hotel Cecil, the large town house of the marquesses of Salisbury, sometimes used as a meeting place for Conservatives when Salisbury was party leader, 1885–1902, more occasionally on later occasions. Used more generally as a shorthand description of the Cecil family's domination of Conservative politics until the end of Balfour's leadership in 1911. *JAR*

Houghton, (Arthur Leslie Noel) Douglas (1898–1996), Labour politician. Organizing secretary of the Association of Tax Clerks from 1921, and a revered figure in clerical trade unionism, Houghton became secretary of the Inland Revenue Staff Federation in 1936, with James Callaghan as his assistant secretary, and together with the Inland Revenue they set up the PAYE (Pay-As-You-Earn) system. He was Labour MP for Sowerby, 1949–74, chancellor of the duchy of Lancaster, 1964–6, and minister without portfolio, 1966–7. He was on the party's right wing, though he opposed incomes policy. As chairman of the Parliamentary Labour Party, 1967–70, he allied with Callaghan in opposing Barbara Castle's proposed reform of industrial relations. He used his position in 1969 to encourage opposition to Wilson's leadership, but by supporting Callaghan he alarmed the supporters of Roy Jenkins who then hesitated about advancing Callaghan. After the coup failed Wilson carpeted Houghton, but could not remove him, since he had been elected by Labour MPs. In opposition after 1970 Houghton rejected voluntarism in industrial relations, criticized Britain's 'nineteenth-century trade unionism', and voted with Heath's government in favour of entry into the European Community. He became Lord Houghton of Sowerby in 1974 and chaired the committee which in 1975–6 introduced state aid for political parties. *BJE*

House of Commons. See COMMONS, HOUSE OF.

House of Lords. See LORDS, HOUSE OF.

Housing Act, 1919. See ADDISON ACTS, 1919.

Housing Act, 1923, also known as the Chamberlain Act after Neville *Chamberlain, the then minister of health in Baldwin's Conservative government. The Act modified the system of open-ended subsidy seen in the *Addison Acts, 1919, offering a flat-rate subsidy of £6 a year for twenty years for each house built to a specified standard either by local authorities or by private enterprise. Some 436,600 were built under the Act before the subsidy was withdrawn in 1929, the great majority of them by private enterprise and for sale to white collar workers. *JS*

Housing Act, 1924, known as the Wheatley Act after the Labour minister of health, John *Wheatley. Following Labour criticism of the Conservative *Housing Act, 1923, the state subsidy on housebuilding was raised to £9 to be paid annually for 40 years for houses built to rent at controlled rents. Largely designed to meet the needs of local authorities, it formed the basis for a very substantial increase in municipal housing or *council housing: 521,700 houses were built under the Act by the time that the subsidy was abolished in 1933. *JS*

Housing Act, 1980, major housing Act of the Thatcher administration, giving local authority tenants of three years' standing the right to buy their houses at discounts ranging from 33 to 50 per cent according to length of tenure. *JS*

housing associations, voluntary charitable bodies that became popular from the 1970s as a means of low-cost house purchase, allowing purchasers the opportunity to buy a part-share of a property, the balance being retained by association. The 1974 Housing Act provided for the registration of and assistance to housing associations in designated housing action areas. Housing associations became especially important in deprived areas in the inner cities and schemes have been developed in Wales, Scotland, and Northern Ireland to meet similar needs. Housing association building has therefore come to play a significant part in urban regeneration schemes. *JS*

housing benefit, an income-related but untaxed benefit to assist those on low incomes to meet the cost of rented accommodation. Introduced in the Social Security and Housing Benefits Act of 1982, it replaced existing rent rebates, allowances, and rate rebates by a single consolidated benefit. *JS*

housing policy in Britain has undergone progressive and substantial change over the course of the century. For almost all governments since the end of the 19th century, the state's housing policy has formed a significant part of the attempt to provide better conditions for the population at large through improved housing. Although part of this policy has been secured through the encouragement of local authority housebuilding for rent and the development of a substantial *council housing sector, it has also involved encouragement of private house-purchase through the subsidization of housebuilding for private purchase, the granting of mortgage tax relief for house purchase, and, at various times, rent controls over the private rented sector.

The first major steps by the government to interfere with the housing market came during the Great War. Fears of inflationary rent rises caused by the relocation of workers—and rent strikes in 1915 in Glasgow and elsewhere—led the government to introduce rent controls on smaller houses. As the great majority of housing tenure in 1915 was in the rented sector, this affected a substantial proportion of the working-class population. During the inter-war period, rent controls were modified but substantially retained. Rent controls were again extended in 1939 and 1947, but faced challenge from the Conservative governments elected after 1951, leading to the Rent Act of 1957 which decontrolled many rented properties. The Labour government's Rent Act of 1965 reintroduced controls, providing for the fixing of 'fair rents' through a system of 'rent tribunals'. These were extended in the 1974 Housing Act, which also increased security of tenure. This package of policies was substantially reversed by the Thatcher government's 1980 and 1988 Housing Acts. Security of tenure was reduced and 'fair rent' assessments for future tenancies abolished. However, by the 1990s rented provision only accounted for a small proportion of total housing tenure in Great Britain, some 14 per cent in 1996.

One consequence of the introduction of rent controls in the early 20th century was to swing the balance of housing tenures and government initiatives towards the two other main sectors: local authority or 'council houses' and owner-occupation. The provision of more and better-quality housing for lower income groups became a major preoccupation of governments between the wars, starting with the *Addison Acts, 1919, and the substantial programmes of municipal housing inaugurated under the *Housing Act, 1924, and the major *slum clearance campaigns begun in the 1930s. The Second World War interrupted these programmes and, with damage for the *Blitz adding to the problems of an ageing housing stock, drives to rehouse the population became a principal feature of policy under both Labour and Conservative post-war governments. The Conservative government in 1954 carried housebuilding to new heights, reaching a total 354,000, 262,000 in the public sector. This total was subsequently outstripped by Wilson's Labour government when a record total of 426,000 houses were constructed in the UK in 1968, though only half were in the public sector. As these figures indicate, there was already a substantial shift towards the private housebuilding sector, continuing a trend towards *home-ownership begun in the inter-war period.

With over a half of all housing tenures owner-occupied by 1980 and growing criticism of some aspects of local authority housing, there was considerable political support for the encouragement of house purchase undertaken by governments in the provision of mortgage tax relief. The *Housing Act, 1980, giving local authority tenants the right to buy their homes, often with substantial discounts, brought about a substantial fall in public sector housebuilding, reaching in 1992 its lowest peacetime level since 1921, when only 17,000 public-sector homes were built. Under the Blair government there has been some revival in public-sector housing, principally by allowing local authorities to utilize the capital receipts from previous sales, a practice tightly restricted until 1997.

In addition to their actions over rents, housebuilding, and the encouragement of home-ownership, governments have accepted responsibility for assistance to low-paid tenants through systems of rent and rate rebate, consolidated in 1982 as means-tested *housing benefit. Concern at inner-city decay, highlighted by events such as the riots of 1981, have also led to a series of initiatives, such as Housing Action Trusts (HATs), to run some of the poorest local authority estates; since 1991 HATs have attracted £650 million of public funding. A further initiative in 1995 was the Estates Renewal Challenge Fund, attracting £525 million in public and private funds to regenerate rundown estates. In addition, government housing policy has extended to the problem of *homelessness, seen as an increasing problem from the 1970s and for which new responsibilities have been placed on local authorities. The 1977 Housing (Homeless Persons) Act made local authorities more fully responsible for providing accommodation for the homeless, responsibilities which were extended in 1995. Moreover, central government initiatives have also been in place since 1990 to tackle the problem of 'rough sleepers' in London and other cities. *JS*

Howard, Ebenezer (1850–1928), visionary town planner, author of the hugely influential idea of the *garden city. A parliamentary shorthand writer by profession, Howard's book *Tomorrow: A Peaceful Path to Real Reform* (1898) became the most dominant influence on British town and country planning. He sought to combine the advantages of urban and rural life in self-contained communities of around 30,000 people, planned at a low density and separated by *green belts. As well as being influenced by an earlier generation of model *new towns built by enlightened philanthropists, Howard sought to alter profoundly the national pattern of settlement, stemming the tide of rural depopulation and reducing the scale of the conurbations. He also envisaged land reform as a basis for general reform with dividends from Garden City Development Limited and any surplus applied to the benefit of the community, a principle applied to the prototype garden city at *Letchworth. *JS*

D. MacFadyen, *Sir Ebenezer Howard and the Town Planning Movement* (London, 1970).

Howard, Michael (1941–), Conservative politician. Howard was a product of the 1960s 'Cambridge mafia', but a late entrant to politics after a legal career, quickly making his name in 1984 by supporting a freeze on purchased council house receipts. He was one of three ministers who promoted the *poll tax for Thatcher, and, as home secretary from 1993, made many enemies with his hard line so combatively drawn. Having removed liberal advisers, he became a hate object among middle-class liberals and the press, and was regularly overruled in the courts, but could claim a serious fall in the crime figures. An opponent of the death penalty, Howard made a notable speech noting trial errors, and was 'grateful not to be issuing posthumous pardons'. His candidature for the party leadership after the 1997 election defeat did not get far, his standing far from enhanced by a difficult cross-examination about his record as home secretary, and by the declaration that there was 'something of the night about him' by his own junior minister, Anne Widdecombe. *EP*

Howard League for Penal Reform. Named after the 18th-century penal reformer John Howard, the league was set up in 1921 to campaign on behalf of more humane and liberal prison conditions. It has particularly campaigned against excessive severity in the treatment of prisoners, especially for the abolition of corporal punishment, achieved in 1948, and against *capital punishment. Other achievements have included the introduction of shorter sentences and the diagnosis of mental illness amongst prisoners. *JS*

Howe, (Richard Edward) Geoffrey (1926–), Conservative politician and late-developing assassin. Never flashy, Howe recorded a fine career of useful, unrelenting work, assisting at the creation of the Bow Group. He was a mild advocate with a cerebral approach, affectionately mocked for flat style and masochistic loyalty, but ended with a dazzling demolition of Thatcher in a speech occasioned by his resignation, and precipitating hers.

Proud of his Welshness, despite his English name and Somerset antecedents, and of his tinplate-worker grandfather, Howe represented the breakthrough of the Conservative meritocracy—Port Talbot fashioned by Winchester and Cambridge rather than Hatfield or Blenheim. Briefly in the 1964 parliament, he returned for Reigate (later East Surrey), was solicitor-general in 1970, and drafted Heath's trade union legislation. Howe was also instrumental in implementing Heath's 1972 *U-turn, becoming minister responsible for price control and in the process discovering his own scepticism about such interventionist methods, so that he moved towards the Joseph camp of free marketeers when in opposition in 1974.

Having recorded sixteen votes in the party leadership poll of 1975, 'putting down a marker' for the future, he was Thatcher's chancellor for four years. His 1981 budget, removing £3 billion from a shrinking economy, was the watershed for free-market radicalism. But Howe will be remembered with Thatcher for maintaining a dear pound when sterling was treated as a petro-currency—disastrously for exports. Upon the government's political survival of the consequent three million unemployed and equally consequent fall in trade union power, would rest the 'Thatcher revolution', a shift of control to management in the workplace and to new corporate power nationally. How far this was willed, how far inadvertent is unclear but Howe, unlike Thatcher, had, despite his earlier rough handling, no desire for revenge. Foreign secretary from 1983, he evolved away from the prime minister's circle, notably over Europe, though loyal and long-suffering as Thatcher grew offensively Eurosceptic. An outburst against Howe in cabinet provoked Biffen's rebuke and dismissal. Howe had supported her against Heseltine during Westland, but affronted and resisting her anti-European and anti-German stand at summits, he was finally demoted in 1990 to a non-departmental deputy prime ministership. His resignation swiftly followed and was marked by a Commons speech in which he spoke of going out to bat only to find that the captain has damaged the bat in the pavilion. Acknowledging that he had stayed silent too long, he went public in exquisite time for the challenge season, firing-up the Heseltine candidacy which destroyed Thatcher. Denis Healey had once mocked his attacks as 'like being bitten by a dead sheep', but this bite was fatal. *EP*

Geoffrey Howe, *Conflict of Loyalty* (London, 1994).

Howell, David Arthur Russell (1936–), Conservative politician. Howell shot to fame as one of the most technocratic of Heath's technocratic advisers and ministers. His energy secretaryship ended in 1981 with responsibility for the first (usually forgotten) miners' strike under Thatcher, fought without adequate stockpiled coal and with a press primed for customary capitulation; the column was dodged by Thatcher at her most pragmatic. At transport, Howell lost face over indecision on the road weight of juggernauts, and was removed in 1983. Unusually loyal to parliament, he found satisfaction as long-term chairman of the foreign affairs select committee. *EP*

Howell, Denis Herbert (1923–98), Labour politician. Howell was MP for Birmingham constituencies, 1951–9 and 1961–92. As a supporter of Gaitskell's attempt to redefine the Labour Party as social democratic, he joined the '1963' group of committed Gaitskellites who remained unreconciled to Wilson's leadership. While minister for sport, 1964–70 and 1974–9 (he was a former football league referee), he also achieved greatest popular fame as the ad hoc minister for disasters, for example, minister for drought during the arid summer of 1976 and minister for snow in 1979. He was vice-president of the European Movement from 1979 and a life peer, 1982. *BJE*

Howth gun-running. See Gun-running.

HTV, operating name of Harlech Television which was awarded the independent television franchise for Wales and the west in 1968 in succession to the TWW company which had held the ITV franchise in Wales since the start of independent broadcasting. The original bid was made by a group who, under the leadership of Lord Harlech and of broadcaster John Morgan and boasting the support of the actor and Welsh icon Richard Burton, promised to make a significant contribution to Welsh culture. The enormous cost of renewing the franchise in 1991, declining revenues, and the need to maintain parallel facilities in Bristol and Cardiff have restricted opportunities. The parent company was United News and Media. *PS*

Hudson, Robert Arundell (1864–1927), Liberal political organizer. Hudson worked for the National Liberal Federation in Birmingham from 1882, staying on when it moved to London in 1886 and becoming its secretary in 1893. He was thus the key party organizer in the Edwardian Liberal revival, and was knighted in 1906—effectively for having helped the Liberals to win that year's election. *JAR*

Hudson, Robert Spear (1886–1957), Conservative politician. After a career in the diplomatic corps Hudson secured the parliamentary seat of Whitehaven, 1924–9, before holding Southport, 1931–52. He held a succession of junior ministerial posts during the 1930s and was associated with the 1938 under-secretaries' revolt against Neville Chamberlain. Churchill appointed him minister of agriculture in 1940, and during wartime difficulties Hudson helped the industry overcome its malaise and ensure increased production and the adoption of new methods and approaches. *NJC*

Hughes, Cledwyn (1916–), Labour politician. Cledwyn Hughes was a solicitor who was MP for Anglesey, 1951–79, and in the cabinet as secretary of state for Wales, 1966–8, and minister of agriculture, 1968–70. However, it was after his ennoblement as Lord Cledwyn in 1979 that he became one of the most powerful and respected politicians in Wales. He was opposition leader in the Lords, 1982–92, but it was his position as president of the University College of Wales, 1976–84, and subsequently pro-chancellor of the University of Wales which placed him at the centre of Welsh affairs. Cledwyn was the grey eminence of Welsh public life in the 1980s and was consulted over a wide variety of appointments. He was undoubtedly one of the most influential people in preparing the way for the new constitutional dispensation for Wales that emerged at the end of the century. *PS*

Hughes, Emrys (1894–1969), Welsh pacifist and rebel Labour MP. A close associate of Keir Hardie, Hughes edited the Scottish socialist newspaper *Forward*, 1924–48, and was Labour MP for South Ayrshire, 1946–69. In the Commons, as both Churchill (whose critical biography he wrote) and Macmillan conceded, he excelled at asking witty and difficult supplementary questions. However, his uncompromising, often emotional left-wing views twice led the Labour leadership to withdraw the party whip (1954–5, 1961–3). On the second occasion, Hughes was also temporarily suspended from the Parliamentary Labour Party. *AM*

Human Nature in Politics (1908), Graham Wallas's attempt to put human beings back into political science. It was based not on the rationalist behaviouralism of the utilitarians but on the non-rationalist psychology of William James. His experience as a London county councillor had given him an empirical understanding of the everyday motivations of the public. The book's publication in 1908 did not win Wallas appointment to the Gladstone chair in Oxford but he did become the first professor of political science in the Fabian LSE. The book's reception was far more favourable in the USA, which was willing to utilize the quantitative method, whose use Wallas preached rather than personally practised. His book was speculative and anecdotal in style, relying upon arresting assertion rather than systematic evidence. However, one should not demand the survey research results of the second half of the 20th century in a pioneering 1908 book. In his foreword to the fourth edition of Wallas's frequently republished book in 1948, A. L. Rowse described it as 'the most important contribution to be made to political thought by an Englishman in this century', going on to regret how little progress had subsequently been made since the appearance of his 'classic'. This was to come much later, especially from the 1980s, when information technology and SSRC/ESRC funding, as well as the establishment of *Electoral Studies* in 1982 and the Elections, Public Opinion and Parties (EPOP) group of the Political Studies Association in 1990 (with its *Yearbook* from 1992), made it possible to carry out Wallas's ambitious programme in Britain. As Weiner put it, Wallas was 'Moses rather than Joshua: he showed the way out of the desert but he did not himself enter the land of modern political science' (Weiner, 96). *JH*

M. J. Weiner, *Between Two Worlds: The Political Thought of Graham Wallas* (Oxford, 1971).

human rights, probably the most important concept of the 20th century. This belief is based on the notion that human beings have inherent, inalienable rights, simply because they are human, and not as the product of 'grace and favour' legislatures. The universalism of the claim, that all men and women are born with natural rights, is seen by its enemies as its fundamental defect: what use—or even meaning—can, say, the 'right to work' have in a tribal African society which has no modern economy to provide the kind of work that is envisaged in the concept? What does the right to so many days' holiday every year have in a society where any work is itself a luxury? Defenders of the cause point out that the fact that some of these rights do not apply everywhere, does not disqualify many, perhaps most, from applying. The pressure for the recognition and defence of human rights increased after the Second World War, which saw the manifest abuse of individuals and groups on an unprecedented and organized scale. The *United Nations Charter endorsed such human rights as freedom of speech, worship, and association, and the agenda is ever widening. It can indeed apply to almost anything, and encompasses the rights to freedom from fear and from persecution, to positive rights such as the right to justice, equal opportunity in life, the possession of economic goods, work, holiday and the like. Thus the categorization of human rights is sometimes misleading. Some rights would seem to require constraint on the state (such as the right to privacy); others require state intervention (the right to a job). The latter might contradict the former. If there is a human right to property, then how does this sit beside the right to a more equal distribution of economic goods? If a family has the right to live according to its philosophical or religious beliefs, then can the law override parental wishes with regard to the fate of twins joined together at birth, both of whom it is held will die if one is not sacrificed? Should human rights set aside the Roman Catholic teaching on abortion or contraception? The growing recognition of the pluralist character of modern British society has increased the concern for group as well as individual rights, but again there is potential conflict here: should a community have the right to arranged marriages or compulsory dress codes for women when the state is devoted to liberal goals and the protection of the rights of individuals? Whatever the problems, however, the vocabulary of politics will still revolve around the concept that there are human rights and that it is the business of politics to secure them, both at home and internationally. *DGB*

Maurice Cranston, *What are Human Rights?* (London, 1973).

Human Rights, European Convention on. On 4 November 1950 the *Council of Europe drew up the Convention for the Protection of Human Rights and Fundamental Freedoms, which demanded that its member states recognize an individual's rights under international law. The Convention did not replace national human rights legislation but provided recourse to international institutions should national systems fail to produce a solution. The Convention is administered in Strasbourg by the European Commission of Human Rights and the European Court of Human Rights. *JRVE*

Hume, John (1937–), Ulster nationalist politician. Prior to his entry into active politics, Hume had first come to prominence in his native city Derry by way of his involvement in the local credit union movement and the unsuccessful campaign to ensure that Northern Ireland's second university would be sited in the city. By the late 1960s, however, frustrated with the apparent lack of political progress, he became associated with the civil rights campaign and in doing so made sufficient impact to win a seat in the Stormont parliament following the election of February 1969. Along with others he sought to establish a new and vibrant opposition to Unionism which led to the formation of the *Social Democratic and Labour Party (SDLP) in August 1970. As a leading member of the party Hume was closely involved in the *Sunningdale agreement which helped to establish a power-sharing executive to govern Northern Ireland, and he became minister of commerce. The subsequent Loyalist strike which brought down this administration was to leave a lasting impression on him. In particular, he now firmly believed that a purely internal settlement would not work and that the only alternative was to try to bring outside influences to bear. On assuming the leadership of the SDLP in 1979, along with his other roles as a member of the European parliament and a Westminster MP, he pursued this policy, with closer ties being forged with the Irish government as well as efforts being made to attract international opinion. The approach was successful in helping to produce the *Anglo-Irish agreement (1985), but within Northern Ireland problems continued to mount. In particular, the ongoing republican terrorist campaign in association with the growing electoral support for its political wing *Sinn Fein, ensured that little progress was made. To try to overcome this Hume began a series of discussions with the Republican movement which by the early 1990s began to come to fruition with the commencement of what is widely termed the *peace process. Out of this emerged the Good Friday agreement and, as attempts continue to ensure its implementation, John Hume is still closely involved. *BL*

Barry White, *Statesman of the Troubles* (Belfast, 1984).

hunger strikes in Northern Ireland (1978–81). Republican prisoners in the *H-blocks at the Maze prison refused to wear prison clothing, considering themselves prisoners of war rather than ordinary criminals. Wearing only blankets, they refused to wash, leave their cells, or use toilet facilities, and covered the walls of their cells with excreta. In March 1981 prisoners, led by Bobby *Sands, began fasting. The prisoners listed five demands: the right to wear their own clothes, no prison work, freedom of association, extra recreational facilities and more letters and visits, and the return of remission lost on protest. Prime minister Margaret Thatcher refused to give in to their demands and Sands died on the 66th day of his fast, the first of ten hunger strikers to die, the last dying on 20 August 1981. Francis Hughes, serving a life sentence for murder, died on the 59th day of his protest; Raymond McCreesh died after 61 days; Patsy O'Hara after 61 days; Joe McDonnell, after 61 days; Martin Hurson after 46 days; Kevin Lynch, after 71 days; Kieran Docherty, elected to the Irish parliament in Cavan-Monaghan, after 73 days; Thomas McElwee after 65 days; and Michael Devine after 66 days. Sixty-one other people died in violent incidents during the hunger strikes. Fifteen police officers, eight soldiers, and seven members of the Ulster defence regiment died in bombings and shootings, and 34 civilians were also killed. The hunger strikes finally ended on 3 October 1981. While the Thatcher government would not concede 'political status', the prisoners nevertheless won substantial concessions on several issues, such as prisoners being allowed to wear their own clothes at all times, but only after their fasting had ceased. *TWH*

Hunt, John Joseph Benedict (1919–), cabinet secretary, 1973–9, subsequently company director and chairman of government-appointed committees. Hunt had a cool, courteous, distinguished, no-nonsense air and effectively advised cabinet and particularly prime ministers. He has been portrayed as making the post of cabinet secretary under Wilson and Callaghan the strongest civil service position since the 16th century. Once ennobled (as Lord Hunt of Tamworth) he worked on Lords' committees and chaired the departmental committee on cable television. *KMT*

Hunt, Norman (Crowther). See Crowther-Hunt, Lord.

Hunt report on the RUC (1969). Lord Hunt's report led to far-reaching reforms in

Northern Ireland's local security forces. Hunt recommended that the *Royal Ulster Constabulary should become an unarmed force, that the Ulster Special Constabulary, the 'B-Specials', be replaced by a new part-time force under British army control, and a police reserve be set up. The B-Specials held a special position within Unionist mythology, as the personification of the Northern Ireland state's ability to protect itself from internal and external attack. At Downing Street talks with Harold Wilson, Northern Ireland Prime Minister James Chichester-Clark agreed to the suggestion that the general officer commanding Northern Ireland should be director of security operations. Wilson had given a television interview in which he indicated that the B-Specials would be phased out. The Northern Ireland government was forced to admit that it was bowing to London pressure, when Chichester-Clark revealed it had hoped to 'modernize' the Specials but had been frustrated by the decision of the Hunt committee to set up the Ulster Defence Regiment in its place. Many Unionists saw the B-Specials' demise as undermining Northern Ireland's status within the UK. *TWH*

Hunt report (1982), supported the rapid development of cable television, but also addressed concerns over programme quality and monopolies. It was keen that cable television develop on a local basis with appropriate franchises and favoured a relative hands-off regulation of standards under a new authority. Cable television was launched in 1983 with the cable authority awarding eleven regional franchises. Development was far slower than had been anticipated even though the 1990 Broadcasting Act allowed the rise of cable telephone services. *KMT*

Hurd, Douglas Richard (1930–), Conservative politician. Originally a Foreign Office career civil servant, Hurd, son and grandson of Tory politicians and first noticed as political secretary to Edward Heath, 1968–74, ironically entered parliament as Heath was falling in 1974. He was slow rising but his worth was gradually acknowledged by Thatcher with whom he was never then estranged, if never close. Hurd seemed at times a perpetual minister of state (Foreign Office, 1979–83; Home Office, 1983–4) but was also a light novelist, writing *Palace of Enchantment* (1984) which described, rather plaintively, a high-quality politician left frustrated as perpetual minister of state by unperceptive superiors. There were, though, no novels for twelve years after promotion to cabinet (Northern Ireland, 1984; home secretary, 1985–9; foreign secretary, 1989–95). At Northern Ireland, he called the IRA 'a dwindling force' ahead of major explosions, and met Adams and Morrison, helping to prepare the *Anglo-Irish agreement (1985). A brave opponent of capital punishment, Hurd once privately described the rejection of hanging as the test that mattered. He appointed Marmaduke Hussey chairman of BBC with all its consequences and was allegedly limp in dealings with Thatcher over the very philistine Broadcasting Bill. His amendment of the Official Secrets Act in response to a Liberal private member's bill effectively ended the absurdities of the old Act, but abolished the public interest defence. As foreign secretary, he combined with John Major in 1989 to nudge Thatcher into the Exchange Rate Mechanism—though at too high a parity. Though consistently a loyalist in Major's government, he sustained the pro-European case with Kenneth Clarke. He reached his apotheosis with Major in the corridors of *Maastricht, negotiating the treaty and the opt-outs intended to soothe sceptics. He then returned home for the real test, putting the treaty into law through the clenched teeth of the Eurosceptic faction backed by most of the Tory press. Never a hero to the right which remembered his time in Heath's private office, Hurd was happy to leave the Foreign Office to Rifkind in 1995. He published a memoir of the Heath government, *An End to Promises* (1975), and kept a diary, publication of which is awaited. *EP*

Hyndman, Henry Mayers (1842–1921), pioneer British Marxist and founder of the *Social Democratic Federation (SDF). He was its parliamentary candidate for Burnley on four occasions, coming within 400 votes of winning the seat in 1906. His support for the Great War caused the party to split in 1916 and effectively ended his political influence. H. M. Hyndman has been much maligned by Labour historians, who have accused him of leading the SDF into sectarian isolation and of importing an alien tradition into British politics. Paradoxically, he has also been disowned by Marxists, who have suggested that his reformism, jingoism, and authoritarian personality were responsible for preventing the emergence of a socialist alternative to the Labour Party. Yet he was an indefatigable propagandist who did much to popularize what Tsuzuki has called 'Anglo-Marxism' and enjoyed a considerable reputation amongst European socialists. *MC*

C. Tsuzuki, *H. M. Hyndman and British Socialism* (London, 1961).

I

Ibbs, (John) Robin (1926–), industrial and government adviser. Joining ICI in 1952, Ibbs rose to be head of corporate planning of the industrial giant and a director of the company. In the 1980s he was recruited into Whitehall, first as head of the Central Policy Review Staff (CPRS), 1980–2, and then as adviser to the prime minister on efficiency and effectiveness in government, 1983–8. He left to join the board of Lloyds Bank (becoming chairman, 1993–7). Ibbs did not operate in the freewheeling style of the first CPRS head, Lord Rothschild, and under him the 'think-tank' concentrated on industrial policy issues and the nationalized industries. He consolidated and extended the work of Thatcher's first efficiency adviser, Derek Rayner, addressing the shortcomings and lack of follow-up at the implementation stage of the 'scrutiny programme'. Ibbs also set in motion the efficiency unit work which led to the path-breaking *Next Steps report of 1988 and the drive to introduce a system of executive agencies to deliver most government services. *KT*

ICI, chemical company. Imperial Chemical Industries was formed in 1926 as the merger of Britain's four largest chemical companies and was designed as a British counter to foreign giants such as the German I. G. Farben. As its name suggests, ICI was especially keen to control the Empire chemical market, and regarded itself as performing a quasi-public duty in so doing. Perhaps for this reason the company's fortunes have remained politically important in the 70 years since its formation. *WF*

'I counted them all out and I counted them all back', reassuring formula used by the television reporter Brian Hanrahan, on the aircraft carrier *Hermes*, observing a raid on Argentine positions in the Falklands war, so indicating without breaching security that no British planes had been lost. Redolent of the battle of Britain and the stiff upper lip, it became a popular catchphrase. *AD*

ideology is a debated concept, but in essence it can be defined as a system of beliefs and assumptions which are to some extent logically ordered and which thereby offer a means of explaining individual and social experiences and present a prescription for political action. An ideology is therefore more than an aggregation of ideas. Some see ideology as structured around explicit political belief systems, such as Marxism, socialism, feminism, and fascism; others use it more widely to refer to a set of ideas, shared by a group, such as a class, a political or social movement, an elite, or a society. In general, ideologies tend to view their opponents' position as ideological and their own as natural. For Marx, ideology had a negative connotation. It hid the contradictions whose concealment was essential for the continuation of capitalist society. In contrast, Marx claimed a scientific basis for his own analysis. Antonio Gramsci argued that the bourgeoisie controlled capitalist society both through economic power and through the creation of an 'ideological hegemony'; but he saw ideology in a positive sense, in that it offered a means of embodying the interests of the working class. More recently, Karl Popper encapsulated the conservative fear of ideology, by arguing that it created closed systems of thought which acted as a 'secular religion'. The term ideology can also be used, as, for example, by Karl Mannheim, to denote a series of ideas which reinforce the existing social and political structure. In this way, it is much harder for ideas which are at odds with the prevailing ideology to find their way on to the political agenda than those which reinforce it (see POWER). As ideologies, liberalism and conservatism both offer particular problems of analysis. Liberalism is an open system of thought, rejecting a monopoly of truth, and welcoming free speech and an open competition between ideas. Conservatism likewise lacks an organized and agreed philosophical content. Mainstream conservatism is explicitly pragmatic and anti-ideological, so that some, such as Michael *Oakeshott, treated with hostility Margaret Thatcher's attempt to present conservatism as having a coherent philosophical foundation. An alternative viewpoint, however, sees both liberalism and conservatism as ideologies, as both comprise a set of ideas which offer the basis of organized social and political action. *CPS*

Illingworth, Percy Holden (1869–1915), Liberal politician. Illingworth was a Cambridge-educated Yorkshireman and MP for Shipley from 1906. He worked mainly as a whip, becoming a respected chief whip, 1912–15, so managing the difficult home rule debates and the first six months of the Great War. His death in office weakened the party, and so contributed to the ending of the last Liberal government a few months later. *JAR*

IMF (International Monetary Fund), an organization designed to facilitate the operation of international economic relations, located in Washington DC. It was created by representatives of 44 countries at the *Bretton Woods conference in July 1944. The IMF is comprised of a fund of currencies and gold contributed by members and available for short term loans to allow countries to overcome balance of payments deficits without resorting to exchange rate adjustments. The IMF board is authorized to impose conditions on loans from the fund in order to ensure that structural problems in the debtor economy are resolved, and to avoid further calls on the fund's resources. These conditions have often included devaluation and reductions in government debt.

Although the IMF began operations in 1947, the inconvertibility of national currencies and the supply of liquidity from Marshall aid and the European Payments Union meant that it did not operate as planned until European currencies were made convertible at fixed exchange rates in 1958. By this time the USA was running persistent balance of payments deficits and the activities of the IMF in the 1960s were overshadowed by efforts of the *G10 nations to resolve global payments imbalances. In this period, the resources of the fund were increased and the Special Drawing Right was introduced in 1967 as an alternative reserve asset to the US dollar. In 1971–2 the fixed exchange rate which the IMF was designed to protect collapsed, and the fund's activities became more focused on the support of less developed countries, especially in the context of the large oil price increases of 1973 and 1979. The UK was forced to draw on the IMF during the balance of payments crisis of 1976. Since the 1980s, the IMF has become increasingly involved in assisting countries during financial crises, and in negotiations to reschedule less developed countries' sovereign debt. *CRS*

IMF crisis (1976), sterling (and political) crisis of the Callaghan government, culminating in an IMF loan of £3 billion, the largest hitherto made in the history of that organization. The origins of the crisis lie in the international economic turmoil of 1973. But while most developed countries were recovering from the ensuing depression by 1976, the British position continued to deteriorate. As confidence in the pound drained away, a run on sterling began in March 1976, which seemed unstoppable. In 1976 as a whole, some £2.5 billion in short-term funds were withdrawn from London, which could not be met by current foreign reserves. The value of the pound declined by nearly 25 per cent against the dollar in nine months, effectively a massive and uncushioned devaluation. A short-term loan from the Netherlands Bank in June only postponed the decision of the government to open negotiations with the IMF in the autumn. After 26 meetings during October and December, the cabinet agreed to a £3 billion loan in three instalments from January 1977, in return for spending cuts totalling £2.5 billion in 1977/8 to 1978/9 and £500 million raised from selling government shares in British Petroleum. In fact, Denis Healey had already put into place successful policies to control wages and cut spending. But internationally, the damage was already done, and the IMF imprimatur on British economic policy was necessary to restore confidence.The episode was traumatic both at home and abroad, reinforcing perceptions of Britain's 'lame-duck' economy and ignominious decline. Most significantly, the IMF episode was a turning point in the history of economic ideas, because it fatally damaged the confidence of Keynesians and boosted the credibility of the monetarists, who controversially blamed the crisis on the expansion of the money supply in the mid-1970s.

HOJ

KATHY BURK and ALEC CAIRNCROSS, *Good-Bye Great Britain: The 1976 IMF Crisis* (London, 1992).

immigration. During the 19th century Britain received substantial immigration, the largest group being Irish but greatly added to by European migrants seeking economic advancement or political *asylum. Black and Asian immigrants were also present by 1914, but in relatively small numbers compared with the Irish or the Europeans who already made up substantial communities. Concerns were expressed about the impact of immigration before 1914 in terms of *national deterioration and the replacement of white Anglo-Saxon stock by Celts, Jews, and other 'inferior' groups. In fact Britain had a net outflow of population because of very heavy *emigration in the period up to 1914. But, although the majority of Irish immigrants were working class and gravitated towards particular occupations such as the building trades and domestic service, a number of immigrants or people of immigrant stock had made a prominent contribution to public life by the early 20th century.

Population outflows and inflows largely balanced each other between the wars, but a substantial body of liberals, intellectuals, and Jews entered Britain during the inter-war years fleeing from European fascism. Although figures are imprecise, an estimated 50,000 Jewish refugees came to Britain during the 1930s, adding to a large Russian-Polish immigration in the years before 1914. The Second World War saw further immigration to Britain, many as displaced persons from eastern Europe. These included persons of Polish, Ukrainian, and Baltic nationality who preferred settlement in Britain to a return to the Soviet-dominated east after 1945.

A much larger immigration occurred after 1945 as Afro-Caribbean and Asian citizens of the Commonwealth took advantage of their rights under the *British Nationality Acts, 1948, to emigrate to Britain, and often responding to job advertisements placed in the West Indies and elsewhere by British public bodies and firms. Britain thus experienced a major influx of coloured Commonwealth immigrants. According to the global figures available, Britain between 1948 and 1962 still underwent a small outflow of population because of the substantial emigration to Australia, New Zealand, and Canada by Britons seeking a new life abroad. Prior to their restriction by the *Commonwealth Immigrants Act, 1962, immigrant flows from the coloured Commonwealth averaged around 50,000 per year between 1955 and 1960, peaking at over 100,000 per year in 1961 and 1962, after which controls were introduced. Immigration continued during the 1960s as dependants and those with work permits continued to enter the country.

Further groups of refugee immigrants came in 1972 with the expulsion of 30,000 Ugandan Asians and in 1990 when rights of entry were given to 50,000 Hong Kong residents prior to the handover of Hong Kong to China. Because immigration statistics are imprecise, a full census of the impact of immigration on the population of Britain is hard to produce, particularly as many 'immigrants' are now second, third, or older generations of an effectively indigenous population. But, according to one calculation, in 1997, the Afro-Caribbean immigrant population in Britain numbered over 300,000 and the Asian population over 700,000. This immigration has contributed to a non-white ethnic population of 3.6 million in 1997, making up 6.4 per cent of the total British populace. Of that 3.6 million, approximately 1.7 million are south Asian and another 1.2 million of Black Caribbean or African origin. The Chinese population in 1997 was estimated at 157,000. In 1981 it was estimated that the number of Irish in Britain who had come from the Irish Republic since 1922 was over 600,000.

As ethnic minority groups, immigrants have traditionally concentrated in particular communities. Liverpool and the north-west of England, along with Glasgow and west Scotland, have particularly high levels of Irish immigrants. Traditionally, the East End of London has had a large Jewish population, although this has increasingly given way to newer Asian communities. London, in general, has some of the largest concentrations of ethnic minority populations, including Brent with over 44% in 1991, Tower Hamlets at 42% and Hackney at 35%. Outside London, the highest concentrations in 1991 were in Leicester (28%), Slough (27%), and Birmingham (21%).

Immigration has frequently produced tension and political controversy. *Riots against racial minorities have occurred in the 19th and 20th centuries, including in south Wales in 1919 against black seamen and clashes between fascist demonstrators and Jews in the East End during the 1930s. Anti-coloured riots at Notting Hill and Nottingham in 1958 were followed by the inner city race riots in Bristol in 1980 and then in Brixton, Toxteth, and Manchester's Moss Side in 1981, when coloured youths played a prominent part. Concern about relations between ethnic minority youth and the police has also continued to cause unease, as in Oldham in 2001.

Immigration has also entered the political arena much more overtly through the activities of groups such as Oswald Mosley's anti-Semitic *British Union of Fascists in the 1930s, and in the post-war period through groups such as the *National Front and the *British National Party. Concern over immigration has led to two major policies: tighter restrictions on entry to Britain and the development of policies to foster good race relations, including legal protection against discrimination. Immigration into Britain was unrestricted until 1905 when concern about immigration from Russian Poland produced the first legislation. Other legislation followed in 1914 and 1919 restricting the entry of alien immigrants and refugees. The first restriction on Commonwealth immigration came with the Commonwealth Immigrants Act, 1962. In 1968 East African Asians holding British passports lost their automatic right to stay in the UK. The 1971 Immigration Act tightened controls still further, allowing 'patrial' entry, that is entry only to those born in the UK or whose parents or grandparents were of British origin. Further restrictions followed in 1979, through the British Nationality Act of 1981 and the Immigration Act of 1988. In 1989 Britain refused residency to 3.25 million Hong Kong Chinese who currently held British passports.

As a counterweight, as early as 1936 legislation was passed in the *Public Order Act to counter racial abuse and manifestations of direct anti-immigrant violence are routinely condemned (see also RACE RELATIONS ACTS). *JS*

Immigration Act, 1971, sought to rationalize controls on entry to the UK for both aliens and Commonwealth subjects. Anyone who could not establish a patrial link with the UK (through having had parents or grandparents born there) was denied automatic entry as an immigrant. Further controls, as in 1979, have reaffirmed the principle, removing the automatic right of husbands or fiancés of women settled in the UK to join them. Restrictions have also been placed on the entry of parents, grandparents, and children over the age of 18. *JS*

Imperial Chemical Industries. See ICI.

imperialism, advocacy of colonial control over subject peoples by a metropolitan power. It was joked that Britain had acquired an empire 'in a fit of absence of mind', without a fully fledged debate or commitment to the concept. It was for example, an almost accidental consequence of Victoria becoming empress of India (1876) that made her descendants king-emperors and Britain truly an empire. There was, though, massive satisfaction at all levels of society in contemplating the extent of British power in an empire 'on which the sun never sets' (because it extended to every time zone), and in the assertion of British rule over so much of the globe. By the start of the 20th century, however, those easy assumptions of British imperial power, so largely displayed during Victoria's diamond jubilee in 1897, had been shattered by the Boer war. On the right, Joseph Chamberlain sought protective tariffs and imperial preference to bind together economically an empire that no longer seemed so obviously a source of security. On the left, J. A. *Hobson published *Imperialism: A Study* (1902), presenting empire not as a sacrificial act of shouldering 'the white-man's burden' to better the lives of childlike Africans but as economic exploitation determined by domestic capitalism. From this point, imperialism was a contentious theme in British politics, broadly backed on the right on grounds of great-power status and realpolitik, if uneasily disguised as a service and obligation. The left now saw only a transitional phase during which Britain would economically develop colonies and educate natives for 'nation-building' self-government.

The Empire reached its greatest geographical extent only after 1919. Though colonial administrators and governments were by then more impressed by Britain's economic weakness than her imperial strength, there was a determined effort to persuade the British people of the virtues of imperialism. There were parades on 'Empire day', patriotic book prizes for school essay competitions, advertisements for Empire-grown foods, imperial exhibitions such as those at Wembley in 1924–5 and Glasgow in 1938, endless cheap reprints of imperial-minded novelists like Kipling, John Buchan, and A. E. W. Mason, and (for the first time in that generation) feature films about imperial heroes like *Clive of India* (1935). All these combined in a flood of propaganda.

It remains unclear how far this changed perceptions below the surface. Was imperial razzmatazz soaked up more for its entertainment value than for its message? Certainly, when *decolonization began, hesitantly in the 1940s, then rapidly from about 1960, it occasioned less agonizing debate even than the onset of Victorian imperialism had done a century earlier, as the brief, inglorious life of the League of Empire Loyalists demonstrated. Nevertheless, there clearly did-exist a popular consciousness of Britain's exceptionality as an imperial nation with world trading links and the status to go with it, mobilized for action by Churchill through his war speeches of 1940, and still discernible in Britain's collective inability to settle for a European role since joining the European Community in 1973. Rudyard Kipling had asked in 1892, 'what should they know of England, that only England know?' Salmon Rushdie more recently argued that the British have lived so much of their history abroad (in their empire—at least in the mind) that, now that it has gone, they do not know who they are. *JAR*

J. M. MacKenzie, *Propaganda and Empire* (London, 1985). | A. P. Thornton, *Imperialism in the Twentieth Century* (London, 1978).

imperial preference, a system of preferential trading arrangements among countries of the British Empire/Commonwealth. Different preferences were extended by different Commonwealth countries from as early as the late 19th century, and Joseph Chamberlain's tariff reform crusade campaigned from 1903 (unsuccessfully) to turn this into the core of Britain's trading policy. Britain extended some small preferences to the Empire in 1919, though as an essentially free trade country the extent was limited. Britain also gave preferential treatment to Empire countries in the capital market in the 1920s. It was after Britain adopted protection in its commercial policy in 1931/2 that a large extension of the preferential system became possible and was made. A general *protective tariff of 10 per cent was introduced in April 1932, and raised later in the year, but Empire countries were given reduced tariffs—lower by 30 per cent. At the 1932 *Ottawa conference, Empire countries extended preference to goods such as meat which were not covered by the tariff, and a system of quotas gave them better treatment than foreign countries. The impact of imperial preference on trade was not large but the principle greatly annoyed Britain's biggest trading partner, the USA. At the beginning of the Second World War, when the USA was providing 'Lend-Lease' to Britain (and others), they made it a condition that Britain would remove imperial preference after the war. Such conditions are difficult to enforce but, when negotiations on the *General Agreement on Tariffs and Trade were taking place, Britain agreed to phase out preferences. Thereafter they were in decline, although at the beginning of the 1960s around 30 per cent of Britain's exports still went to Commonwealth countries and half of these exports had preference granted to them. They thus presented an obstacle in Britain's negotiations to join the European Economic Community. *FHC*

Import Duties Act, 1932, although not the first inroad on free trade, symbolized the end of an era. Along with the abandonment of the gold standard the previous September, it marked Britain's retreat from economic internationalism and the introduction of a new strategy in which domestic producers received priority, followed by those of the Empire and finally foreign producers. To the disappointment of Empire enthusiasts, it remained only half developed and was replaced by a Europe-first strategy in the 1960s. *RWDB*

incomes policies. See wage freezes.

income support, a means-tested benefit payable to people over 16 years who are not required to be available for work and whose income and savings fall below set levels. Recipients include single parents, pensioners, carers, and long-term sick and disabled people. In 1999/2000, over 3,900,000 people were claiming income support. *JS*

income tax, the core of the British tax system and the main source of its progressive (bearing more heavily on the wealthier) character. It has given taxation its democratic form and appropriately has had a major role, both in the funding of government and in expressing political views urging that the growth of the state should be restrained. An income tax had existed to finance wars after the French Revolution, and was reintroduced as a temporary measure by Peel in the 1840s. But modern income tax properly developed just before the Great War, with differentiation between unearned and earned incomes and the introduction of a supertax on higher incomes in 1909. The war showed a dramatic increase in its force, from a maximum marginal rate of 8 per cent in 1914 to 50 per cent by 1919. Although the income tax receipts as a proportion of GDP fell back in each post-war period, they never returned to pre-war levels. The Second World War turned it into a popular tax, with the inclusion of the better-paid manual worker taxed at source through the new PAYE (Pay-As-You-Earn) scheme, involving deductions by employers prior to the payment of salaries and wages. There were 3.4 million income tax payers before 1939, rising to 12 million by 1945, and to 25 million by 1982/3. The threshold had also fallen: in 1955 a couple with two children had to earn 96 per cent of average manual earnings before they paid tax, but only 46 per cent in 1979. The failure of allowances to be fully adjusted for inflation also increased tax receipts. Politicians have been more convinced of the damaging effect of marginal tax rates on incentives than economists, and the 83 per cent top marginal rate under the 1974–9 Callaghan government did not yield its proper revenue. In the 1970s there was alarm that it was possible to be both in officially defined poverty and still liable to income tax, often at some of the highest marginal rates amongst all income tax payers. Reductions by Geoffrey Howe at the onset of the Thatcher government signalled a new tax regime which Labour had to accept when it came into office in 1997. *RCW*

ROGER MIDDLETON, *Government versus the Market: The Growth of the Public Sector, Economic Management and British Economic Performance, c.1890–1979* (Cheltenham, 1996).

independent broadcasting. Concerted pressure for competition in broadcasting in Britain began with Selwyn Lloyd's minority report for the Beveridge broadcasting committee of 1949 (see BEVERIDGE REPORT (1951)). In 1954, the Television Act established the Independent Broadcasting Authority (later Independent Television Authority) to license channels; oversee standards of taste, decency, and political impartiality in independent broadcasting; and regulate advertising on the air. The first independent station, Associated Rediffusion, went on the air in 1955. By 1960 independent programmes occupied every slot in the top ten of national viewing, prompting fears that entertainment would force out Reith's standards of public service broadcasting that still underpinned the BBC. By the 1970s, programmes such as Thames Television's *World At War* (1975) had demonstrated that the BBC had no monopoly on quality programme making. Two further independent channels followed in 1982 and 1997. The Broadcasting Act, 1990, tightened the control of independent television, establishing the Independent Television Commission to regulate satellite and cable services, and conduct competitive tendering for regional third channel franchises, including an annual review of output. Like the BBC, independent broadcasters sparked controversy for their coverage of Northern Ireland. In 1988 a Thames Television documentary, **Death on the Rock*, dealing with a terrorist incident in Gibraltar was broadcast despite the objections of the foreign secretary. Thames lost its franchise shortly thereafter. *NC*

RALPH NEGRINE, *Television and the Press since 1945* (Manchester, 1998). | B. SENDALL, *Independent Television in Britain* (London, 1983).

Independent Labour Party (ILP), socialist party founded in 1893. The ILP was founded by Keir Hardie, Robert Smillie, George Bernard Shaw, Tom Mann, George Barnes, John Glasier, H. H. Champion, Ben Tillett, Philip Snowden, Edward Carpenter, and Ramsay MacDonald in 1893, after Bradford's Manningham Mills strike. The objective was to secure working-class parliamentary representation separate from the Liberal Party. But the ILP also supported a socialist ideology and was not tied to the trade union movement. It existed as a separate political party for seven years before forming part of the Labour Representation Committee, in 1900–6, and the Labour Party from 1906. Thereafter it retained a separate, left-wing, and internationalist ethos throughout its history, best illustrated in the party's emphatic opposition to the Great War. Its manifesto against the war stated simply: 'German Workers Our Comrades'. The ILP gradually became organizationally much more part of the Labour Party, with some leading members leaving the ILP to join the Labour Party proper after it was formally launched in 1906, though the ILP held its own conferences and ran its own candidates. By 1927 the ILP was seriously at odds with the gradualism of the Labour Party and in that year published its own policy document, *Socialism in Our Time*. It stayed in the Labour Party until 1930, when the ILP conference voted to oppose the actions of the Labour government which did not accord with ILP policy and Labour then disaffiliated the ILP in 1932. In the years after 1932, the ILP ran 82 candidates in elections up to 1970, peaking with 139,577 votes and four MPs (all in Glasgow) at the 1935 election. Overall, eleven MPs took an ILP whip in these years, but most voted for and supported the Labour Party on key issues, and gradually rejoined it. The key figure in the ILP's history after the Great War was James Maxton and it was after his death in 1946 that the party declined. The ILP continued to field candidates until the 1970 general election, when its single candidate, in Halifax, lost his deposit. The logic for the existence of the ILP as a separate socialist party not tied to the trade union movement was ideologically strong but organizationally weak. At times the ILP served as the socialist conscience of the Labour movement, but the personality of

Maxton was perhaps too strong for the party to grow and develop as a separate entity. Most importantly, a separate doctrinaire socialist party was a non-starter in the context of the first-past-the-post electoral system. As the main Labour Party grew and became either the dominant party nationally or the main opposition, there was little scope for a smaller socialist grouping unless the Labour Party allowed its candidates to run unopposed (which it rarely did), or unless they, like Maxton, had immense personal followings clustered in particular areas. These factors caused the decline of the party, but some figures, like Jennie Lee, retained affection for the socialist purity that Maxton and the ILP represented. *BB*

R. E. Dowse, *Left in the Centre: The Independent Labour Party, 1893–1940* (London, 1966).

Independent Orange Order, a breakaway movement from mainstream Orangeism (see Orange Order (ulster)), founded in June 1903, with T. H. Sloan and R. L. Crawford prominent among its members. In particular they attacked the constructive Unionist policies of George Wyndham, Irish chief secretary 1900–5, for allegedly appeasing Catholics while neglecting Protestants. Official Unionism became sufficiently alarmed to found a new organization, the Ulster Unionist Council, in 1905. The order flourished while home rule was in abeyance; but this began to change, gradually from 1906, rapidly from 1910. *DRB*

independents. Britain's two-party system and first-past-the-post electoral system has made life extremely difficult for independents. At the local level, where the reputation of a neighbour, a landlord, or a popular doctor may override political allegiances, independents have done rather better, though mainly in the earlier years of the century. In practice, many such councillor independents were actually Conservatives in disguise, their numbers shrinking dramatically after the Conservatives decided to fight local government elections with a party label, though they remained widespread in such areas as Cornwall. In national elections, independents thrived in only three sets of circumstances, each of which was essentially abnormal. First, there were independents elected until 1949 for university constituencies, drawing their votes from an unusually discriminating electorate and chosen by proportional representation. The best-known was Sir Alan Herbert, whose non-party status helped him in getting through a liberalization of the divorce law that none of the parties wished to promote officially. Second, the world wars each led to suspension of normal political activity: a pending general election was postponed, and the main parties avoided contesting one another's seats at by-elections, so as not to divide the country at war. This provided openings for independents to stand and garner votes that would otherwise have gone elsewhere. During the Great War and in 1939–41, these were mainly mavericks of the right, but in 1942–5 they were mostly surrogate Labour candidates, who, if they survived, took the Labour whip in 1945. The respectable showing of an independent at the Oxford by-election of 1938, and Vernon *Bartlett's success a few weeks later at Bridgwater, in what were called the 'Munich by-elections', was a near-war situation of a similar type. Third, candidates who stood as independents after a noisy estrangement from their own party have sometimes done surprisingly well (Dick Taverne at Lincoln in 1972, and S. O. Davies at Merthyr in 1970), when the electors could be persuaded to back 'their' representative against the party machine. The successes of Martin Bell as an independent 'anti-sleaze' candidate in Tatton in 1997, and of Richard Taylor, defending the National Health Service at Wyre Forest in 2001, indicates that the opportunities remain—in the right place and time. *JAR*

India. From about 1900, and particularly after 1919, Indian affairs impinged continually on British politics. Increasing nationalist protests, mainly centred on the Congress Party, alongside growing economic and military weakness, forced British politicians to concede to Indians more say in India's constitutional development. Concessions were made in order to encourage moderates and undermine nationalists. The Indian Councils Act of 1909 gave Indians greater access to both local and central government, while the Government of India Act of 1919 went further and introduced a dual system of local government (or dyarchy) in which the provincial governors and the mostly elected legislatures dealt with separate matters. These measures were undermined by the massacres in Amritsar in 1919. The following year, General Dyer's actions were debated heatedly in parliament during which the whole nature of Britain's rule in India was discussed. Although Dyer's removal from India was upheld, nationalist protests increased.

British attempts to find an acceptable system of government for India, first through an investigative parliamentary commission under Sir John Simon, 1927–9, and then the Round Table conferences (1930–2), failed. Consequently, in 1935 the National Government introduced its own Government of India Bill, which met with sustained opposition, particularly from Winston Churchill, who with others in the India Defence League felt Britain was surrendering India and betraying Indian princes who had been British allies. Basically, the Act gave the provinces full autonomy, thus ending provincial dyarchy.

In 1942, following the loss of Malaya and Burma to the Japanese, Sir Stafford Cripps failed to gain nationalist support for Britain with the promise of dominion status after the war. Instead, Congress called on Britain to 'quit India', forcing the British to imprison Gandhi and the Congress leadership until near the war's end. However, the Attlee government was committed to Indian independence and in 1946, a cabinet mission which included Cripps went to India in an attempt to find a solution: it failed. In 1947, a settlement was achieved by partitioning the country into the separate states of India and Pakistan, after Mountbatten was appointed viceroy with far-reaching powers. By then Britain's withdrawal from both was considered inevitable. *KTS*

JUDITH M. BROWN, *Modern India: The Origins of an Asian Democracy* (Oxford, 1994). | LAWRENCE JAMES, *Raj: The Making and Unmaking of British India* (London, 1998).

India Office, created in 1858, administered the vast territories of the Indian subcontinent. In 1937, the Burma Office was hived off when Burma was made a separate colony, the secretary of state for India becoming the secretary of state for India and Burma. The India Office was closed in 1947 following Indian independence. *JD*

individualism, 19th-century term, used at first to describe the consequences of the American and French revolutions, stressing individual rights over the values of tradition and community. The classic account of the consequences of individualism is thus Alexis de Tocqueville's *Democracy in America* (1835). Individualists stress the idea of human dignity, which requires opportunities for privacy, autonomy, and self-development, and judge society by its ability to satisfy the wants and needs, and respect the rights, of individuals. Against individualism it may be argued that wants and needs are themselves social constructs, and that too much stress upon the individual is liable to dissolve those ties which hold society together and sustain it over time. Individualism is closely linked to political and economic liberalism. Ethical, political, and economic individualism is sometimes grounded in methodological individualism (as in the work of *Hayek and *Popper; methodological individualism is sometimes traced back to Hobbes). Methodological individualists stress that institutions and societies would not exist if they were not made up of individuals, and claim that any true statement about an institution or society must be capable of being reformulated as a statement about individuals within that institution or society. Thus there is, in Margaret Thatcher's words, 'no such thing as society'. Such an approach would appear to deny the significance of institutional and social structures, which may result in individuals acting in ways quite different from the ways in which they would act if they did not find themselves in a specific location or performing a specific role: a lawyer may argue his client's innocence while believing him to be guilty, and a judge may dismiss the charges against the accused while feeling certain that he committed the crime. *DRW*

STEVEN LUKES, *Individualism* (Oxford, 1973).

Industrial Charter (1947), Conservative Party policy document. It evolved from the demands of the activists at the 1946 Blackpool party conference for a clear statement of party policy and subsequent discussions in the party's Industrial Policy Committee chaired by R. A. *Butler. It was accepted by the 1947 party conference and provided the basis for much of the party's post-war domestic policy. In fact the Conservative Research Department had already been evaluating the party's industrial policy in light of Labour's nationalization plans. The Industrial Policy Committee comprised a mix of front- and back-bench Conservatives including Harold Macmillan, Oliver Stanley, and Derick Heathcoat Amory. Taking evidence from industrialists, businessmen, and trade unions as well as undertaking visits to provincial industrial centres, the committee's canvassing was intended both to give gravitas to the report and to provide a means of promoting its centrist idea to the wider party and its industrial supporters. Some committee members like Macmillan hoped the report would illustrate how far the party had developed since 1932 in the light of Beveridge and proposed nationalization. The *Industrial Charter* combined elements of free trade with interventionism, accepting that nationalization could not be reversed, and embraced Keynesianism with commitments to demand-management policies and full employment. The final section contained a 'workers' charter' which called for firms to adopt consultation procedures and codes of practice.

Whilst some have dismissed the *Industrial Charter* as pure propaganda that proved politically impracticable when the party regained power in 1950, others have pointed out that its publication enabled the Conservatives to regain the political middle ground and should be seen alongside Peel's Tamworth manifesto, Disraeli's 1872 Crystal Palace speech, and Baldwin's speeches of 1924, all of them intended as much for the party as for the floating voter. *NJC*

John Ramsden, *The Making of Conservative Party Policy: The Conservative Research Department since 1929* (London, 1980).

industrial derating (1928), budget measure. This was developed by Winston Churchill with the help of Harold Macmillan and was designed both as an antidote to industrial decline and as an answer to the protectionist lobby within the Conservative Party. The aim was to stimulate recovery by cutting business rates and replacing the lost local government revenue with a central government grant. This was argued to be especially applicable to depressed areas, where rates were inflated by the cost of providing for the unemployed and thus had a particularly unfortunate impact upon recovery. To finance the measure Churchill advocated a reduction in naval construction and this brought him into conflict with William Bridgeman, first lord of the Admiralty. Churchill's scheme was also opposed by Neville Chamberlain, the minister of health, who had his own plans for the reform of municipal government and regarded the replacement of business rates by a central government subsidy as a threat to the principles of local accountability and sound finance. While Churchill's scheme was modified in cabinet it nevertheless formed the centrepiece of the 1928 budget, and was prominently featured in the Conservatives' 1929 election campaign. *WF*

Martin Gilbert, *Winston S. Churchill: Prophet of Truth, 1922–1939* (London, 1976).

industrial relations, the way in which employers, employees, and increasingly governments have attempted to regulate the wages, conditions, and powers of industrial production. The rising fortunes of *trade unions, at least until 1979, and the increasing scale of industry have ensured that government intervention has become more overt in the 20th century. At the turn of the century British trade unions were still relatively weak and many employers did not recognize their claims. However, in some industries, most particularly in mining and steel, unions were recognized and sliding scale agreements, arbitration, and conciliation arrangements emerged. Government legislation played an increasingly important part in shaping the pattern of industrial relations. Though the Taff Vale judgement (1902) threatened the funds of striking unions, the Trades Disputes Act of 1906 exempted unions from liability for strikes in most cases. The Great War formed a turning point from voluntary to regulated arrangements. The need for increased war production led the government to curb trade union and managerial rights and shop-floor practices. The voluntary system of industrial relations was restricted by the Defence of the Realm Act, the Munitions of War Acts, and the Military Services Acts. In the extreme case of engineering the government introduced women 'dilutees', which provoked the outbreak of industrial unrest on Clydeside in 1915–16.

After the war governments sought to withdraw from direct involvement in industrial relations, though some of the wartime controls imposed upon industry remained. In many cases, as in the steel industry, good industrial relations prevailed. Nevertheless, in the wake of the General Strike of 1926, the Trades Disputes and Trade Union Act of 1927 affected industrial relations again by making sympathetic strike action illegal and preventing some public service groups organizing strike activity. Nevertheless, trade unions remained a powerful force in British society and trade union membership recovered in the mid- and late 1940s; the 1927 Act was withdrawn in 1946. From the start of the Second World War, the British trade union movement became deeply involved in operating the wartime economy. A schedule of reserved occupations was in operation and agreements were forged in some industries, such as engineering where the Amalgamated Society of Engineers and the Engineering Employers' Federation arranged for the 'relaxation of customs'. When Ernest Bevin became minister of labour in 1940 he created a joint consultative committee of seven employers and seven trade union leaders, asked for their support for the duration, and was given extra powers to control labour through the Emergency Powers (Defence) Act and defence regulation 58A. Soon afterwards a national arbitration tribunal was created to make decisions binding upon both parties. Strikes were thus effectively illegal and were formally made so under order 1305.

Although these wartime regulations were withdrawn after 1945, it is clear that government has continued to interfere in industrial relations, fearful of the threat that strikes presented to the

British economy, particularly in the late 1940s and early 1950s when alleged communist-inspired dock strikes convulsed the nation. By 1956–7 the Conservative government was actively intervening to limit wage settlements, as it did in 1957 in overruling the rather modest wage agreement negotiated for employees in the National Health Service by their own Whitley council. Civil service unions were also informed that all pay increases would have to be offset by corresponding economies. When faced by the more excessive wage demands of miners and railwaymen in 1958, the government compromised, but it was clear that government was moving towards some form of incomes policy, and an independent National Incomes Commission was formed in the early 1960s. This was superseded by the National Board for Prices and Incomes in 1964 and George Brown's formal acceptance of an incomes policy under Harold Wilson's Labour government in the economic crisis of 1966.

The conflict between the demands of government and the trade unions in the late 1960s led to the Donovan report (1968) which suggested that collective agreements between employers and trade unions should be extended. However, Barbara Castle opted for more government intervention in her white paper *In Place of Strife* (1969), which suggested that industrial relations should no longer be a voluntary activity, but be controlled and regulated by the state. The opposition of the trade unions ensured that Castle's policy was defeated but this was followed by Edward Heath's Conservative government introducing the Industrial Relations Act, 1971, which created the National Industrial Relations Court (NIRC) which could impose a 'cooling off period' in disputes and impose fines for 'unfair industrial practices'. The TUC and trade unions demanded the maintenance of the voluntary system, refused to register under the Act, and would not recognize the NIRC. The dockers refused to comply with the Act and five of them, the 'Pentonville five', were arrested and then hastily released after the outbreak of a national strike. Thus, the 1971 Act was effectively dead.

Since 1974 there has been more successful government intervention in industrial relations. The Wilson/Callaghan Labour governments tried to operate a 'social contract', effectively a voluntary incomes policy, which broke down when the government failed to redistribute income and wealth on an annual basis and led to the strikes of the 'winter of discontent' in 1978/9. Since then, the Thatcher and Major Conservative governments, and even the Blair Labour government, have introduced and operated seven major employment and trade union Acts which have weakened trade union power through limiting the rights of picketing, enforced ballots, and threats to unions funds. The balance of industrial relations power was moved from the unions to the employers, through government intervention, and that is where it currently resides. *KL*

Keith Laybourn, *A History of British Trade Unionism c.1770–1990* (2nd edn., Stroud, 1997). | C. J. Wrigley (ed.), *A History of British Industrial Relations*, 2 vols. (Brighton, 1982–7).

Industrial Relations Act, 1971. Edward Heath's Conservatives had decided to put legal teeth into industrial relations while planning policy in opposition, and this became the Industrial Relations Act of 1971, introduced by Robert Carr. It established a National Industrial Relations Court, which was to have jurisdiction over most industrial disputes, could advise the secretary for employment to impose a cooling-off period in industrial disputes, and could require a ballot in cases where strike action would be a serious threat to the economy. Despite private assurances to Carr that laws enacted with an electoral mandate would be respected, the TUC refused to work within the Act and employers were therefore reluctant to invoke its protection. Its weakness was further exposed when five dockers, the 'Pentonville Five', had to be released in July 1972 after refusing to comply with the court. The Labour government of 1974 brought the legislation to an end. *KL*

Industrial Relations Court. See National Industrial Relations Court.

Industrial Reorganization Corporation, announced in the Queen's Speech of 1966, and operated under temporary powers pending the passage of the bill which received the royal assent in 1967. This statutory body was created by the Wilson government in order to promote rationalization, mergers, and restructuring of industries, and to support exports and pool resources in advance of technological advances. In 1969 it was transferred to the Ministry of Technology but was abolished almost immediately by the incoming Conservative administration in 1970. *JD*

Industrial Reorganization League, formed in 1934 by Harold Macmillan and the 2nd Lord Melchett to promote a Self-Government for Industry Bill to solve problems in industries such as coal, steel, and textiles where efforts to negotiate voluntary rationalization had foundered on the obstruction of minorities. The league drew upon corporatist ideas of industrial planning and had supporters among both Conservatives and big business. In 1935 it unsuccessfully lobbied the National Government, the TUC, and the Federation of British Industries.

WF

Industrials, the, an informal group of Conservative backbenchers. Initially sometimes referred to as 'the Forty Thieves', these MPs had banking and industrial interests, were of a narrow disposition, and were poorly regarded by their contemporaries. Generally right-wing, there was some overlap of personnel with the Edwardian 'die-hards'.

NJC

industry, the collective term used either specifically to denote a group of firms producing identical or similar products, or in a more general sense to describe the productive capacity of the economy. In the narrow definition, the term was traditionally used to imply a group of firms in a single branch of trade or manufacture. These firms were closely related and in competition because of the great substitutability of their products and distinguished from other firms by a gap in the range of substitute products. Such a definition has become increasingly problematic. In a monopoly or nationalized industry, for example, the firm and the industry may be one and the same. Conversely, a single firm may be multidivisional or multinational, producing several different products each belonging to a different 'industry'. To define industry as one branch of production making a single product is not always accurate, as there is often a considerable degree of overlap between the various sectors. It is conventional to discern primary, secondary, and tertiary sectors within industry. The primary sector consists of agriculture, mining, and fishing, and is dependent on producing or extracting natural products from the land or sea. The secondary sector includes manufacturing industries which produce items from raw materials. It is this group which, according to some definitions, may best be regarded as industry. The tertiary or service sector encompasses the non-manufacturing industries such as insurance, banking, and retailing. The shape of the industrial sector changed substantially during the 20th century, due to the continuing decline in the importance of the primary sector in favour of manufacturing industries, and more recently their contraction in response to the proliferation of the service industries. The structure of industry was also transformed in the 20th century by a concentration of production in larger business units, benefiting from the technical and economic advantages of size, a trend marked initially in the manufacturing sector. In industries such as cigarettes, petrol, alcohol, and food processing, five companies accounted for more than 70 per cent of sales by the mid-1990s. Innovations have had a huge impact upon complementary fields in terms of merchandizing, advertising, packaging, retail selling, and consumer credit.

The 20th century witnessed fundamental changes in the government's relationship with industry. State intervention, which was introduced by necessity in the Great War, has gradually assumed a better-defined and permanent character. With market forces being superseded and supplemented by state direction, coordination through the public-sector control of key sectors of the British economy steadily advanced. Britain was the first country to pioneer industrialization in the early 19th century, but industry has declined relatively since the 1870s. Prior to 1914, the staple industries, export-orientated growth sectors, had continued to expand but at a slower rate than their overseas competitors. Dislocation of the international economy during the Great War initiated a contraction in Britain's lucrative foreign markets, a situation temporarily obscured by the short-lived post-war boom. Britain's poor export performance in the 1920s reflected the monetary policies pursued by her government and the economy's overt concentration on old staple industries for which demand was stagnating. The inter-war expansion of new light industries geared towards the needs of the domestic markets was unable to alleviate sufficiently economic depression and mass unemployment which engulfed the northern industrial areas of Britain. Mechanization, rationalization, and standardization were partly induced by the Second World War. Although the overall growth of British industry since 1945 has been very impressive in historical terms, it has failed to match the growth rates of its competitors. A decline was particularly evident during the post-war boom of the 1950s and 1960s, when increasing levels of import penetration prevailed. Since the 1970s there has been an ongoing process of de-industrialization in the manufacturing sector. Following the recession of the early 1980s, the expansion of Britain's industrial sector exceeded that of her competitors, but substantial differences in efficiency between one sector and another remained. Explanations for the long-term uncompetitiveness of British industry have focused on low levels of investment, technological conservatism, poor industrial relations, its fragmented industrial structure, the role of government policies, and sociocultural factors such as the failure to focus on the economic benefits of formal and systematic education and training, a debate much enhanced by the writings of Martin *Wiener. *JFM*

S. Pollard, *The Development of the British Economy 1914–1980* (London, 1983).

Industry, Department of (1974–83). See Trade and Industry, Department of.

Industry Act, 1972. See U-turns.

'inevitability of gradualness', phrase used by the Fabian Society founder Sidney Webb, which became a guiding principle of the evolutionary socialism which the Fabians advocated. As a pioneering social scientist, he was less advocating a style of politics than asserting that the progressive tide of history was inevitably gradual in character. *BJE*

infant mortality has shown a rapid decline in the 20th century as a result of improved nutrition and immunization against diseases of childhood which were still major killers in the first part of the century. Measured as the number of infants under 1 year dying per 1,000 live births, the figure for England and Wales fell from 110 in 1911–15, to 76 in 1921–5, to 58 in 1935–7, and in 1998 reached 6.3 for boys and 5.0 for girls. On the nutritional front, higher levels of affluence had a decisive impact, assisted by *school milk and *school meals in the immediate post-1945 period. Improvements in the environment played a part, including reductions in pollution and better housing, but other major factors have included the reduction of deaths through diseases such as measles, scarlet fever, whooping cough, and diphtheria—substantial killers in the Edwardian period, but declined to almost negligible levels today. Traditionally, infant mortality has not been evenly spread across the classes, recorded rates showing substantial differences between the social classes right up to the Second World War. Although the gap has narrowed, these have not been entirely eliminated, with higher rates of infant mortality still prevalent amongst the poorer sections of the community and ethnic minorities. *JS*

inflation, defined as 'a process of continually rising prices, or equivalently, of a continually falling value of money' (Parkin, 394), and commonly measured by the retail price index. This represents as an index number the price of a typical basket of goods and services purchased by an average consumer. It was first compiled, in its present form, in 1962 but has an earlier history, and can be linked statistically as a chained series, as the cost of living index which had been produced since 1914. Annual movements in this chained index, together with the cumulative effect of price changes (predominantly increases) on the purchasing power of £1 in 1914 (worth less than 2 pence by 1998), are shown in Figure A.

While inflation has been a characteristic of economic life as long as there has been money, in Britain, as elsewhere, it has been particularly prevalent in the 20th century. Until the 1930s the

Figure A. Annual movements in RPI and purchasing power of £1 in 1914

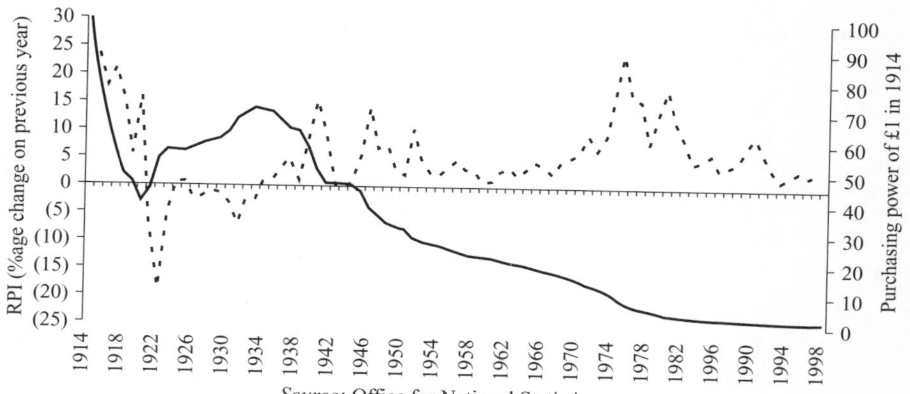

Source: Office for National Statistics.

- - - left-hand scale —— right-hand scale

normal pattern was of intermittent inflations followed by deflations, but thereafter price movements have been unidirectional and reached a crescendo in the 1970s with double-digit inflation rates, the peak being 1975 at 24.2 per cent. Indeed, the eightfold rise in prices, 1935–75, was quite unprecedented in British history; the previous eightfold rise had taken not four decades but four centuries. While high inflation continued into the 1980s (averaging 7.4 per cent for the decade), peaking at 18 per cent (in 1980), by the 1990s low single-digit rates were the norm.

Economists do not agree about the causes of inflation. Their disagreements were at their rawest and most public during the 1970s when, led by Milton *Friedman, monetarists (see MONETARISM) attacked the *Keynesian conventional wisdom. This had held, first, that there was a trade-off between unemployment and inflation (known as the Phillips curve) and, second, that inflation was not a monetary phenomenon but instead derived either from cost-push forces, principally trade unions pushing up wages, and/or demand-pull pressures, whereby inflation results when aggregate demand exceeds productive capacity.

In 1970s Britain the coincidence of rising unemployment and high inflation with rapid money supply growth and high public borrowing appeared to vindicate the monetarist interpretation of inflation. This established the conditions for the subsequent monetarist policy experiment pursued by the 1979–83 Conservative government, the era in which maintaining price stability as against full employment became the principal objective of macroeconomic policies. Hitherto, efforts to contain inflationary pressures had forced recourse to limited demand deflations and to various prices and incomes policies, but after 1979 it was unemployment that was allowed to rise as Conservative politicians and many economists became more preoccupied with the welfare costs of high and variable inflation. The process of privileging stable prices over low unemployment was completed in 1997 when operational independence in monetary policy was granted to the Bank of England who were charged only with meeting an exacting inflation target. *RM*

J. M. PARKIN, 'Inflation', in P. Newman, M. Milgate, and J. Eatwell (eds.), *The New Palgrave Dictionary of Money and Finance* (London, 1992), vol. 2.

Ingham, Bernard (1932–), prime minister's chief press secretary, 1979–90. A journalist before joining the civil service in 1967, Ingham spent almost all his official career dealing with the media. A Labour supporter in the 1960s, he became one of Margaret Thatcher's closest advisers, attaining a higher profile and greater influence than any previous press secretary. He introduced several centralizing changes to Whitehall's public relations machine, and was appointed head of the government information service in 1989. His abrasive treatment of the press arguably influenced the public's perception of Thatcher, and his news management (for example, stage-managing her visit to the Falkland Islands in 1983) was an important contribution to her success. Ingham was Thatcher's briefer, not the government's, as several ministers found to their cost. The *Westland affair (1986) thrust him into the public eye and led to calls for his dismissal, as the official accused of ordering a leak designed to damage Defence Secretary Michael Heseltine. However, Thatcher regarded him as indispensable. Her reliance on Ingham and Charles *Powell was seen by some as isolating her from her colleagues, backbenchers, and public opinion, thereby contributing to her fall, which precipitated Ingham's retirement. *CL*

BERNARD INGHAM, *Kill The Messenger* (London, 1991). | ROBERT HARRIS, *Good and Faithful Servant* (London, 1990).

Inland Revenue, government department managed by a board of commissioners appointed by royal warrant. The Inland Revenue is directly accountable to the chancellor of the exchequer through its chairman. Its purpose is the efficient administration and collection of taxes and duties. In 1999 it merged with the Contributions Agency. *JD*

Inland Revenue website: *www.inlandrevenue.gov.uk*

inner cabinets. In all governments, there is an identifiable elite within the elite of the cabinet, usually referred to as the 'inner cabinet'. Unfortunately this term has come to encompass virtually any group which meets for decision-making purposes which includes the prime minister but is less than the full cabinet. More accurately this term should only be assigned to groups which consist of a selection of prime ministerial confidants whose role is to provide advice and permit consultation on an intimate and unrecorded basis. It is precisely the unrecorded, informal, nature of the group which differentiates it from any other subgroup of the full cabinet. Using this definition, Chamberlain's 1938 group of himself, Halifax, Hoare, and Simon would be excluded on the grounds that their meetings were recorded and as such became a de facto cabinet committee. Similarly, Wilson's 1968 parliamentary committee was a formal cabinet committee and would also not be designated as an inner cabinet. Of course, purists would argue that they constituted the only real inner cabinets. War cabinets, including the 1956 Egypt committee, and small issue-specific gatherings, would also be excluded. Inner cabinets exist for the sole purpose of providing prime ministers with honest and private advice—and loyal support—throughout their premierships. They will be composed of those whom a prime minister decides to be either necessary or reliable, ideally both. *CAB*

In Place of Strife **(1969)**, white paper proposing changes in trade union law. Proposed by Barbara Castle, employment secretary, in response to a sharp upsurge in industrial action, it aimed to curb unofficial strikes. The plan provoked massive opposition from the Labour movement that resulted in a split in the Wilson cabinet, which then dropped the plan in June 1969. This mishandled trade union reform came close to forcing Wilson's resignation as prime minister, and contributed to Labour's defeat in the 1970 general election. *DLM*

Inskip, Thomas Walker Hobart (1876–1947), lawyer and Conservative politician. Inskip is best remembered for organizing parliamentary rejection of the revised Anglican Prayer Book, 1927–8, which he considered threatened the fabric of the Church of England. His critics later likened him to Caligula's horse (Cato, *Guilty Men* (London 1940), 74) for his alleged failings as minister for the coordination of defence, 1936–9, an appointment which surprised many, while Inskip found that he lacked both authority and resources to coordinate the three service departments. *NJC*

Institute of Economic Affairs (IEA), free enterprise think-tank. Created in 1955, the IEA was the brainchild of Anthony Fisher, the founder of Buxted chickens, who had been inspired by *Hayek's *The Road to Serfdom* (1944). The IEA was for many years a lone voice advocating economic liberalism through the unceasing efforts of Ralph (later Lord) Harris and Arthur Seldon, and its publications and seminars were important in the revival of free-market economics. *RJS*

Richard Cockett, *Thinking the Unthinkable* (London, 1994).

Institute of Fiscal Studies (IFS), independent research unit. The IFS was founded in 1969 to provide analysis of the tax system after the major reforms of the Labour government's 1965 Finance Act were introduced without any prior public debate; its provision of informed comment was resented by the revenue authorities in its early years. It has undertaken major enquiries into the tax system, examined the proposals of the political parties at general elections, and put forward alternative budgetary strategies. *RCW*

institutionalism, new. See NEW INSTITUTIONALISM.

interest group, a term that has had to contend with many competitors over the last 40 years, since when the phenomenon—first investigated in the USA—came into common use in Britain. The pioneering study in Britain was S. E. *Finer's *Anonymous Empire: A Study of the Lobby in Great Britain* (1958), but even then the more popular term was 'pressure group'. Finer rejected this term because it implied both that all groups would apply a sanction if their demands were rejected and that they had no other purpose than to exert pressure. However, lobbying is only one type of group activity (by extension from the lobby in parliament), so it was necessary to find a more comprehensive term. Others that have circulated (such as sectional group or cause group, promotional group or attitude groups, insider or outsider group) are limited to subcategories, so interest group has come to be accepted despite its somewhat selfish connotation. Provided it is understood that the 'interest' pursued may be 'disinterested', that the group may only seek to influence public policy intermittently, and that it does not, like political parties, seek to occupy political office directly, terminological controversy can give way to a consideration of the phenomenon itself.

Britain played a pioneering role from the 18th-century, through organizations such as the Committee for effecting the Abolition of the Slave Trade, in the form of pluralistic action which proliferated in the 20th century into an elaborate interest group system in which most interests are organized. Where they have been able to recruit as members a high proportion of their potential constituency, they acquire democratic legitimacy through their representativeness. While their relationship with the relevant parts of Whitehall may be formalized into a recognized right to be consulted, this is combined with attempts to influence parliament and public opinion directly and through the media. So, it is not primarily in the constellation of advisory committees that surrounds each ministry, but in the bilateral negotiations by which information and cooperation is exchanged for modifications in public policy, that the insider interests play their part in a consensual policy process. Where the relations are sufficiently close and continuous, the group-government network can become a stable policy community.

These cosy arrangements began to break down in the 1970s, notably through the failure of 'social contracts' between Labour governments and the TUC. The relationship between trade unions and successive governments became one of bitter confrontation and endemic conflict rather than cooperation and concertation, as trade unions were blamed for Britain's relative economic decline. The Thatcher government not only successfully challenged the veto power of the National Union of Mineworkers but weakened the position of producer groups generally in public services such as education and health, in the professions, and in industry. Established policy communities were deliberately destabilized in favour of competitive or imposed solutions.

However, as the old style producer groups, such as trade unions, lost members, other groups, notably in the environmental field, went from strength to strength. Groups for the protection of rural England, for the protection of birds, for clean air, rapidly increased their membership and range of activities. Furthermore, as the activities of the European Union impinged ever more intimately on most aspects of national life, interest groups increasingly turned their attention to Brussels, where they often received a far more favourable reception than they were accorded in Britain. By the late 1990s, the Blair government was more willing to adopt continental 'social partnership' practices, but without allowing interest groups to retrieve their former standing. *JH*

W. GRANT, *Pressure Groups, Politics and Democracy in Britain* (London, 1989). | R. KIMBER and J. J. RICHARDSON (eds.), *Pressure Groups in Britain* (London, 1974). | J. J. RICHARDSON, 'Interest Group Behaviour in Britain: Continuity and Change', in Richardson (ed.), *Pressure Groups* (Oxford, 1993).

International Brigades (1936–8), army units, made up of volunteers from over fifty countries who went to defend republican Spain against the fascists in the Spanish civil war. Organized by the Communist International, over 40,000 volunteers fought in five International Brigades; 20,000 were killed or wounded. There were some 500 British volunteers in Spain when the British battalion of the fifteenth International Brigade was formed in January 1937. Recruitment was carried out by the Communist Party of Great Britain (CPGB), from whose ranks came between a third and a half of the British volunteers. The British government declared enlistment to the International Brigades illegal in January 1937, but the CPGB continued its recruitment, the majority of volunteers being industrial workers and trade unionists. In 1936–8, over 2,200 British volunteers saw action in Spain, of whom 526 were killed and over 1,200 wounded. In June 1937 the International Brigade's dependants' aid committee was established, and by November it had raised over £43,000 for volunteers' families and those that had been invalided home. The International Brigades participated in most of the major battles, most notably in the defence of Madrid during the autumn of 1936 and at the battle of Jarma in February 1937. In 1938, they helped slow down fascist counter-attacks at Teruel and Gandesa, and fought in the last major republican offensive of the war, across the River Ebro. In September 1938, the republican government announced the withdrawal of the International Brigades and the British battalion returned to London in December 1938. Besides their military contribution to the Spanish republic, the International Brigades were a source of inspiration, both to the Spanish people and the worldwide Aid Spain movement. *DLM*

BILL ALEXANDER, *British Volunteers for Liberty: Spain 1936–1939* (London, 1982). | WILLIAM RUST, *Britons in Spain* (London, 1939). | K. W. WATKINS, *Britain Divided: The Effect of the Spanish Civil War on British Opinion* (London, 1963).

International Development, Department for. (1997–). Responsibility for international development was first accepted by the British government in 1929, with the Colonial Development Act. The Department of Technical Cooperation (DTC) was then established in 1961 as the aid programme expanded. In 1964, the Ministry of Overseas Development was set up to bring cohesion to the aid programme, integrating the DTC and the aid policy functions of the Foreign, Commonwealth Relations, and Colonial Offices. The ministry was dissolved and the functions transferred to the Foreign Office in 1970, only to be re-created in 1974. In 1979 it was once again moved to the Foreign Office, but again hived off in 1997 with the creation of the Department for International Development. *JD*

Department for International Development website: *www.dfid.gov.uk*

International Monetary Fund. See IMF.

International Socialists. See SOCIALIST WORKERS' PARTY.

International Trade Organization (ITO), unrealized post-war multilateral international trade surveillance and liberalization body. Signatories to the 1948 Havana Charter approved an ITO constitution that would have empowered the body to integrate free trade and full employment objectives, but opposition from both left and right in the US prevented the charter's ratification there. Thus the ITO did not come into operation, leaving its rulebook, the 1947 *General Agreement on Tariffs and Trade, to be administered on an ad hoc basis. *GAP*

internment, the legal detention without trial of terrorist suspects. In both world wars, for example, the British government interned for the duration of the war German and other enemy citizens resident in the UK, through fear of espionage and sabotage of the war effort, and because it felt unable to distinguish effectively between refugees and enemy agents. This led to considerable hardship and unfairness, as refugees from Hitler in the 1930s found themselves imprisoned instead by Britain.

Internment has been used with varying degrees of success in the Irish context. It was used by the British authorities following the 1916 Easter Rising and during the Anglo-Irish War, 1919–21. More successfully, in Northern Ireland, internment was employed under the Special Powers Act to undermine IRA activity. In 1922–4 728 men, nearly all nationalists, were detained and around 320 during the Second World War. During the IRA's unsuccessful border campaign, 1956–62, around 150 men were interned by the Northern Ireland government. Internment spectacularly failed in 1971 during the latest phase of the 'Troubles'. Brian Faulkner, Northern Ireland's prime minister, in making the decision to implement internment, felt that the decision was one which was virtually forced upon him. The Provisional IRA campaign had reached an unprecedented level of ferocity in the summer of 1971, so on 9 August 1971, in a series of dawn raids, the British army attempted to arrest 452 men, but only 342, mainly from the Official IRA, were captured, since the intelligence used was hopelessly out of date and many arrested had not been involved in violence since the 1920s. The immediate result was an upsurge in violence. By 12 August, 22 people had been killed and 7,000 people, mostly Catholics, were left homeless after their homes were burned. In the year prior to internment, 34 people had been killed, but after internment 140 died in 1971. Nationalists were angered by allegations that those arrested during the internment operation had been ill-treated, and the Unionist government was forced to set up a committee of inquiry: the Compton report concluded that individuals had not suffered physical brutality but there had been 'ill-treatment'. For the IRA the value of internment was most striking of all in its effect on its own personnel strength, for it claimed that only 56 of its members had been interned. In response to internment, even moderate nationalists called on Catholics to withdraw from all aspects of public life in Northern Ireland. The alienation of the Catholic population was almost complete.

TWH

interviewing, political. The broadcast interview developed slowly. BBC programmes were cramped by the requirement to be strictly non-partisan and to avoid editorializing. Technology made both live and filmed interviews stressful for leaders such as Churchill, Attlee, and Eden, reared in a pre-electronic age. Party managers kept tight control over whom, apart from leaders, could be interviewed. From 1955, ITV, learning from the USA, introduced courteous but more probing and less deferential practitioners (Robin *Day, Chris Chataway, George Ffitch). As channels proliferated and programme formats diversified—including phone-ins (from the mid-1970s), and exchanges on trains and planes, at summits, and outside Number Ten—the conventions about 'balance' too became more flexible. The advantage progressively shifted to the broadcasters. Interviewers such as Brian Walden, John Humphrys, David Dimbleby, and Jeremy Paxman acted as tribunes for the people, putting politicians under persistent pressure. Equally, politicians such as Macmillan, Wilson, and Thatcher saw the medium's potential. The resulting tensions produced periodic rows, generally off air and involving claims of bad faith about deviations from the line of questioning agreed in advance, or about the participation of other interviewees, or even who would have the last word. At their worst, interviews seemed futile sparring encounters or attempts at entrapment. At best, they drew out a politician's personality, knowledge, and ideas, and they advanced public understanding. The long, formal interview retained its place, but politicians were as likely to turn up in programmes about gardening or about children. *CKSU*

MICHAEL COCKERELL, *Live from Number Ten* (London, 1988).

Inverchapel, Lord (1882–1951), diplomat. Archibald Clark-Kerr entered the diplomatic service in 1905, achieving ambassadorial rank in Baghdad in 1935 and serving thereafter as ambassador to the Kuomintang government in China, 1938–42. From 1942 until 1945 he was ambassador in Moscow, a posting he found most depressing. Nevertheless, he established a good rapport with Stalin, whose high esteem he retained until the end, and ended his career as ambassador in Washington, 1946–8. *AJC*

Invergordon 'mutiny' (14–16 September 1931), amongst men of the Atlantic fleet on exercise, reacting against proposed pay cuts. The Admiralty quelled the unrest by cancelling fleet exercises and returning ships to their home ports with the promise to review the policy. The press labelled the unrest 'mutiny' although it was really little more than passive disobedience, but military disquiet was treated with the utmost concern by the National Government who therefore imposed only a temporary 10 per cent pay cut. *NJC*

IRA, 'Official', Irish paramilitary organization deriving from the *Irish Volunteers and which from 1918 took the lead in the republican campaign for Irish independence. The IRA as an organization never accepted the *Anglo-Irish treaty of 1921, and both during the inter-war years and after 1945 mounted campaigns to put pressure on the Northern Irish government, but with declining effect as time passed. Following the collapse of the IRA's border campaign, 1956–62, Sinn Fein began to consider constitutional options and adopted left-wing policies to broaden its electoral appeal, but many IRA traditionalists were alienated by the turn to politics. The idea for a civil rights campaign in Northern Ireland originated from a conference of Wolfe Tone societies, which were offsprings of the republican movement. The IRA leadership now believed that the uniting of Catholic and Protestant workers would break Ulster Unionism but, when a Northern Ireland civil rights association emerged, the IRA, which had revolutionary aims, was in a minority and Catholic moderates dominated. The outbreak of communal violence in Northern Ireland during 1969 found the IRA unprepared. At the 1969 IRA extraordinary army convention there were two critical resolutions: first, that the IRA should enter a 'National Liberation Front', in close connection with organizations of the 'radical left'; and second, that the republican movement should end its policy of parliamentary abstention from the Dublin, London, and Belfast parliaments. When both these resolutions were passed, a number of delegates left the convention to form the Provisional IRA (PIRA), the 'Official' IRA (OIRA) representing those militant Republicans who remained loyal to Cathal Goulding, the IRA chief of staff. The PIRA, however, soon outstripped the OIRA, building their strength from local defence committees in Belfast, and being widely perceived as defenders of the Catholic community from Protestant mobs. The tension between the OIRA and the PIRA was intense in 1970–1, often leading to violence between the two. In 1972, however, Goulding led the OIRA into declaring a *ceasefire, and was strongly critical of the PIRA bombing campaign, calling it inhuman in moral terms and provocative politically. *TWH*

Henry Patterson, *The Politics of Illusion: Republicanism and Socialism in Modern Ireland* (London, 1989).

IRA, Provisional (PIRA). Irish paramilitary organization. The Provisional IRA was formed in 1969 when a Provisional IRA Army council broke from the Official IRA over the issue of recognizing the parliaments in London, Dublin, and Belfast, and from 1969–70 onwards the PIRA took part in defensive actions against Protestant mobs in Belfast. Gradually the PIRA moved into offensive bombing and shooting operations against the British army. In 1972 a PIRA delegation, including Gerry Adams and Martin McGuinness, held secret but fruitless talks with the British government. In 1974–5, the PIRA announced a ceasefire in the mistaken belief that the British were prepared to disengage from Northern Ireland. During the late 1970s, particularly because of confessions extracted from terrorist suspects, the PIRA geared itself towards a 'long-term armed struggle', based upon putting unknown men, and new recruits, into a cell structure. Prestige targets included the killing of the British ambassador to Eire in 1976 and the murder of Lord Mountbatten in 1979. Twice, in 1984 and 1990, it almost wiped out the British cabinet, but the main focus of its violent campaign became off-duty members of local security forces in Northern Ireland. In 1994 the PIRA declared a total cessation of military operations which broke down in 1996 with the bombing of *Manchester and of London's *Canary Wharf, but in 1997 it renewed its ceasefire to allow Sinn Fein's entrance to political talks on the future of Northern Ireland. *TWH*

M. L. R. Smith, *Fighting for Ireland? The Military Strategy of the Irish Republican Movement* (London, 1995).

IRA Army Council. According to republican theology the IRA's army council considers itself the direct descendant of the last all-Ireland parliament of 1918 and the 'legal and lawful government of the Irish Republic'. The supreme body of the provisional IRA (PIRA) is the general army convention made up of delegates from the brigades and other sections of the IRA. It elects a PIRA army executive, which in turn elects a PIRA army council of seven members to take overall charge. This appoints a chief of staff and is supported by the general headquarters (GHQ) staff with eight departments, comprising a quartermaster, and directors of engineering, publicity, operations, finance, intelligence, security, and training. Below the army council and GHQ staff, the PIRA breaks into two sections, southern command and northern command. Under southern command are the Dublin brigade with its ASUs (active service units), and a scattering of rural ASUs. It mainly operates in a quartermaster role for northern command which has contained at least five brigades: Belfast, Derry, Donegal, Tyrone/Monaghan, and Armagh, each with their own ASUs. Selected teams are put together by the army council for specialist operations such as the attempted bombing of Gibraltar in 1988. *TWH*

Ireland Act, 1949, Britain's reaction to Eire's decision to leave the Commonwealth and declare a republic. It gave a guarantee that Northern Ireland would not cease to be part of the United Kingdom without the consent of the northern parliament. The Irish government and opposition alike denounced this guarantee given to Stormont and John Costello, the Irish prime minister, effectively declared a cold war on Britain for perpetuating partition. However, the British prime minister, Clement Attlee, pointed out that Eire considered the cutting of the last tie which united Ireland to the British Commonwealth as a more important objective than ending partition. At second reading in the Commons on 11 May, the Ireland Bill passed by 317 votes to 12 but at the committee stage many Labour backbenchers withheld their support in protest against the guarantee. *PR*

David Harkness, *Northern Ireland since 1920* (Dublin, 1983).

Irish Boundary Commission (1925) arose out of article 12 of the *Anglo-Irish treaty of 1921, which established a commission to determine the border between Northern Ireland and the Irish Free State. Due to the outbreak of the Irish civil war it was not established until late 1924. The three commissioners were the Northern Ireland representative J. R. Fisher, the Free State representative Eoin *MacNeill, and the chairman, South African judge Richard Feetham. During 1925 members of the commission toured existing border areas to receive opinions about a new boundary. Shortly before publication of their proposals, however, a newspaper carried a leaked report suggesting that very little territory would change hands due to their recommendations. This leak caused the southern representative to resign from the commission and the report was suppressed. In December 1925 the three governments of Northern Ireland, the Irish Free State, and the United Kingdom agreed to recognize the existing border. *BMW*

Jonathon Bardon, *A History of Ulster* (Belfast, 1992).

Irish Citizen Army, founded after the clashes between the Dublin Metropolitan Police and striking workers of the Irish Transport and General Workers' Union in the summer of 1913. The rough handling of strikers by the police persuaded a former British Army captain, Jack White, to suggest that the locked-out men should be formed into a small force (200 men) and given elementary military training. The army also attracted such exotics as Countess Markievicz (née Gore-Booth). James Connolly moved the army from a defensive to an offensive force, and planned to use it to strike a blow for freedom in the Great War, when England was distracted by the world conflict, but the army was destroyed in the fighting of the Easter Rising, and never reconstituted. *DGB*

Charles Townshend, *Political Violence in Ireland: Government and Resistance since 1848* (Oxford, 1983).

Irish conscription crisis (1918). Ireland was exempted from Military Conscription Acts that had applied in Great Britain since 1915, despite Unionist calls for them to be applied to Ireland. The German offensive of March 1918 renewed, this time irresistibly, the call that conscription must be applied in Ireland and the British government resolved to do so, taking power by order in council to implement this measure. At the same time Lloyd George agreed to introduce a Home Rule Bill, but maintained, somewhat unconvincingly, that there was no connection between the two. A mass protest involving all nationalist groups and the Roman Catholic Church followed. The British government backed down, abandoning the conscription plan and launching a campaign for more volunteers. The Home Rule Bill was also abandoned by May

1918 under the claim that there was a new German plot to become involved in treasonable conspiracy with Sinn Fein. The crisis gave a much-needed boost to the forces of revolutionary nationalism in Ireland. *DGB*

J. Ward, 'Lloyd George and the 1918 Conscription Crisis', *Historical Journal*, 17 (1974).

Irish Constitution (1937). Primarily the work of Eamon de Valera and passed by a referendum in July 1937 and enacted in December 1937, the Constitution of Ireland—Bunreacht na hÉireann—supplanted the Irish Free State. The official name of the state was now Eire, or in the English language, 'Ireland'. The effect of these changes was to establish an Irish republic in all but name. The constitution created the position of a non-executive president, gave the Roman Catholic Church a 'special position', and defined a traditional role for women in Irish society. Article 2, defining the Irish nation, declared that the 'national territory consists of the whole island of Ireland, its islands and the territorial seas'. Article 3 stated that pending the 're-integration of the national territory', the right of the Eire parliament and government to exercise jurisdiction over the whole of that territory remained. However, the constitution limited the area and extent of laws enacted by the parliament to the area of what had previously been called the Free State. Articles 2 and 3 were a territorial claim to Northern Ireland. According to the Irish Constitution, Northern Ireland was a part of both the Irish nation and the Irish state; it was not part of the United Kingdom. In British law, however, Northern Ireland was part of the United Kingdom, so the constitution formally challenged the right of British sovereignty in Northern Ireland. *TWH*

Basil Chubb, *The Government and Politics of Ireland* (Harlow, 1987).

Irish Convention (1917–18). This represented the British government's desire to remove, at least temporarily, the Irish issue from British politics and pass it over to Irishmen to settle for themselves. The convention included representatives of all the major Irish political parties, with the notable exception of Sinn Fein, and also representatives of business, trade, labour, and the churches, as well as prominent individuals. It debated from July 1917 until April 1918, and made surprising progress: the Southern Irish Unionists took the initiative in working for an all-Ireland settlement that would preserve the British connection and provide safeguards for Irish Unionists. The control of customs and excise would be decided by the imperial parliament after the war. The scheme was supported by nationalists who were prepared to dilute home rule for the sake of a united Ireland solution; but the Ulster Unionists and some nationalists opposed it. Any hope that the majority report might form the basis of a settlement was dashed by the *Irish conscription crisis of March 1918. *DGB*

R. B. McDowell, *The Irish Convention, 1917–1918* (London, 1970).

Irish Emergency. In Eire, the period of the Second World War was known as the 'Emergency'. When Britain declared war against Germany in 1939, Eire announced her neutrality. Eire demonstrated her independence from Britain while Northern Ireland's Unionists demonstrated their loyalty to Britain, but an estimated 43,000 men and women from Eire also enlisted in British forces. While there was low-level cooperation between Eire and Britain, especially in the repatriation of downed Allied airmen, Winston Churchill never forgave Eire's neutrality nor forgot the vital role of Northern Ireland's ports in the battle of the Atlantic. Northern Ireland supplied munitions, ports, and airfields, and was a base for troops, while in 1941 Belfast was bombed with the loss of over a thousand lives. Eire's neutrality drove yet another psychological wedge between it and Northern Ireland. *TWH*

Irish Free State, title of the Irish state established by the Anglo-Irish treaty of 1921. The treaty created an Irish dominion within the British Commonwealth. The Irish Free State was to apply to the 26 counties of Ireland termed 'Southern Ireland' in the Government of Ireland Act of 1920. Unlike Southern Ireland, the Free State was to exist within the Commonwealth but outside the United Kingdom. The Free State had the same constitutional status as the other British dominions—Canada, Australia, New Zealand, and South Africa—and the Free State's status was to be that used in Canadian law and practice. The establishment of the Free State led to the splitting of the IRA and to the Irish civil war of 1922–3 in which those who supported the treaty were victorious. Thereafter, the ruling party in the Free State, *Cumann nGaedheal, set about demonstrating that dominion status allowed the Irish to determine their own affairs. The Free State helped to redefine the relationship between the dominions and the United Kingdom towards one of equality. *TWH*

Nicholas Mansergh, *The Unresolved Question: The Anglo-Irish Settlement and its Undoing 1912–1972* (London, 1991).

Irish Labour Party, Irish political party. In 1912 the Irish Trade Union Congress voted to form a Labour party, but no formal party organization was established, and during the 1918 and 1921 general elections the Labour movement opted out. This was the period of the Troubles. In 1922 the Irish Labour Party contested the general election, winning 21.3 per cent of the vote, but in 1933 recorded its lowest vote, 5.7 per cent. Labour struggled in a conservative rural society, but socio-economic changes in the 1960s helped the party's fortunes. In 1973–7, Brendan Cornish took Labour into government for the first time, forming a coalition government with Fine Gael. The party was then out of power until 1982, when Dick Spring took over as leader and he formed another coalition government with Fine Gael. Spring became *tanasite*, or deputy prime minister, and was involved in the negotiations for the Anglo-Irish intergovernmental conference. In 1987 the Labour Party pulled out of the coalition in a dispute over the budget. In 1992 it polled a record 19.3 per cent of the vote and formed another coalition government, now with Fianna Fáil. In 1995 Spring led the party into a 'rainbow' coalition with Fine Gael and Democratic Left. Spring played a key role in the evolving Northern Ireland peace process until the coalition's fall from power in 1997. *TWH*

MICHAEL GALLAGHER, *Political Parties in the Republic of Ireland* (Dublin, 1985).

Irish Literary Theatre (ILT), arguably the most enduring legacy of the Irish literary revival of the 1890s, not only to Irish but to British culture. The idea of an Irish theatre took root in 1898 in the minds of W. B. Yeats, Lady Gregory, Edward Martyn, and George Moore, and was part of the grand project of creating a modern Irish literature and drama in the English language. Productions, such as Synge's *The Playboy of the Western World* and Sean O'Casey's *The Plough and the Stars*, aroused virulent and sometimes violent opposition as they pushed against the nationalist canon. Despite its sometimes uneven quality of production, the ILT and its successor, the Abbey Theatre (1904), succeeded in its aim of establishing Irish themes given authentic treatment in the English language. *DGB*

VIVIEN MERCIER, 'Literature in English, 1891–1921', in W. E. Vaughan (ed.), *A New History of Ireland, 6. Ireland under the Union, II, 1870–1921* (Oxford, 1996).

Irish National Liberation Army (INLA), Irish paramilitary organization. Established in 1975 as the paramilitary wing of the Irish Republican Socialist Party, it originated from disaffected members of the Official IRA who rejected that organization's 1972 ceasefire and then recruited Provisional IRA dissidents during the latter's 1975 ceasefire. The INLA began a series of attacks on Northern Ireland's security forces, its greatest success being the 1979 car bomb murder of the Conservative Northern Ireland spokesman Airey Neave. In December 1982 the INLA bombed the Dropping Well pub disco, killing seventeen people including eleven off-duty soldiers. The INLA was prone to murderous internal feuding. In 1986 a breakaway group, the Irish People's Liberation Organization (IPLO), was formed. Periodic INLA/IPLO attacks on one another became a feature of Northern Ireland's paramilitary life. *TWH*

Irish Office. Until 1922, the Irish Office had a lord-lieutenant of Ireland, based in Dublin, responsible for the administration of most Irish affairs. The chief secretary was a member of the Commons and was accountable for the parliamentary side of business. In 1922, the partition of Ireland took effect with the creation of the Irish Free State, and the posts of lord-lieutenant and chief secretary lapsed, but it was not until 1924 that the Irish Office was wound up. The remaining functions were split between the Home Office, coordinating with the newly established Northern Irish government in Belfast, and the Colonial Office, which handled relations with the Irish Free State. *JD*

Irish Parliamentary Party (1874–1918), the dominant electoral force in Ireland after 1874. Its position, except in Protestant north-east Ulster, remained virtually unchallenged until the rapid expansion of Sinn Fein in 1917–18. Its principal demand, Irish legislative autonomy within the United Kingdom, enjoyed Liberal support from 1886, but faced determined opposition from Unionists and the Lords. The party used its position at Westminster to extract economic and social reforms, but rejected the offer of administrative devolution in 1907 as inadequate. John Redmond, leader after 1900, faced criticism from colleagues, especially Tim Healy, for being subservient to the Liberals; but the ending of the Lords' absolute veto in 1911 offered him his chance. Holding the balance of power at Westminster following the 1910 general elections, he insisted on the introduction in 1912 of a Home Rule Bill scheduled to become law by 1914. However, intense opposition within Ulster forced the Liberal government to consider compromise and possible partition. Following the outbreak of the

Great War, the Third Home Rule Bill was formally enacted, with the provision that its implementation be postponed until one year after the termination of hostilities. Believing that he had won, Redmond urged Irishmen to enlist in Britain's army, but this proved a fateful miscalculation. Expectations had been aroused in Ireland; but the war showed no sign of ending soon, and at Westminster Redmond's position was weakened by the formation in 1915 of a coalition government including Unionists. Impatience, and a sense that 'England's danger was Ireland's opportunity', found expression in the 1916 Easter Rising, which proved a body blow to the Irish Parliamentary Party, Martial law ruined its claim to have established a new Anglo-Irish relationship, and in mid-1916 it became clear that home rule would only be implemented, if at all, at the cost of permanent partition. Nationalist Ireland began to shift its allegiance to Sinn Fein, whose candidates won four by-elections in 1917. Sinn Fein proposed to cease participation at Westminster, and instead to obtain international recognition for Ireland's claim to sovereignty. The *Irish Convention of 1917–18 witnessed a last attempt by the Irish Parliamentary Party to achieve a compromise with Unionism. It was frustrated, not least, by the British government's attempt to extend conscription to Ireland in April 1918. Sinn Fein gained most credit for resistance, and subsequently triumphed in the December 1918 general election, when the Irish Parliamentary Party was reduced from 78 seats to six. Irish independence would now be achieved by non-parliamentary means. *DRB*

Alan O'Day, *Irish Home Rule, 1867–1921* (Manchester, 1998).

Irish Reform Association, founded in 1904 by the Irish home ruler William O'Brien and the Anglo-Irish earl of Dunraven, out of the new spirit of 'conference plus business' which arose from the virtual settlement of the land question in a conference between landlords and tenants in 1903. The association suggested in September 1904 a scheme of devolved government less ambitious than home rule, but this was denounced by Irish Unionists and nationalists alike as a sell-out of their principles. As a direct consequence, the *Ulster Unionist Council was formed in March 1905. *DGB*

Irish Republican Army. See IRA, 'Official'; IRA, Provisional.

Irish Trade Union Congress. Established in 1894, it became the Irish Trade Union Congress and Labour Party in 1912 and in 1918 the Irish Labour Party and Trade Union Congress. In 1930 there was a formal separation between party and unions, and the title Irish Trade Union Congress (ITUC) was resurrected. Following the creation of the Irish Free State, a large number of Irish trade unionists remained members of British trade unions. In 1944, members of these British based unions accounted for 108,000 trade unionists affiliated to the ITUC, compared to 80,000 from Irish-based unions. The Irish Transport and General Workers' Union (ITGWU) was opposed to the influence of British unions in Ireland. In 1945 the ITGWU led the secession of ten unions which joined with other non-affiliated unions to form the Congress of Irish Unions, but in 1959 the rival unions united as the Irish Congress of Trade Unions. *TWH*

Irish Unionist Alliance (IUA), an organization opposed to home rule, founded in 1891. Composed principally of Anglo-Irish Protestant landowners, its interests came to diverge from those of Ulster Unionism, with its securer urban and industrial base. Thus the IUA opposed the partition proposals of 1912–14 and 1916 as liable to abandon southern Protestants in a Catholic sea. In 1917–18, at the Irish Convention, a substantial number accepted domestic self-government in principle, but disagreed with nationalists as to whether this should include fiscal autonomy. *DRB*

Irish Universities Act, 1908. This settled a contentious issue which had troubled Irish politics since the 1880s. It established Queen's University in Belfast and the National University of Ireland, a federal body comprising colleges in Dublin (UCD), Cork, and Galway (Maynooth being added shortly afterwards). Trinity College, Dublin, remained separate. Augustine Birrell, the chief secretary, was accused of favouring concurrent endowment and denominationalism; but argued that he was repairing a serious deficiency in Irish higher education. *DRB*

Irish Volunteers, a substantial paramilitary force which played a significant role in Ireland's destabilization during the Great War. Founded, with echoes of 1782, in November 1913 in Dublin, the Irish National Volunteers, as they were originally called, were a response to the striking success of the Ulster Volunteer Force. Their leaders, Professor Eoin MacNeill of the Gaelic League and Patrick Pearse, among others, of the Irish Republican Brotherhood, were out of sympathy with John Redmond's brand of constitutional nationalism. In July 1914 they organized the Howth gun-running, which led to a bloody confrontation with the British army at Bachelor's walk, Dublin. Redmond had claimed control of the organization in June 1914, and at the outbreak of war in 1914 he offered to merge the Irish National Volunteers with the Ulster Volunteer Force for the common defence of Ireland's shores. The offer was rejected, and when Redmond went on to urge Irishmen to enlist in the British army he provoked a split in the 180,000-strong force: 11,000 broke away to form the Irish, as opposed to the National, Volunteers, asserting that Ireland should take no part in the war so long as the Home Rule Act remained suspended and partition still threatened. Irish Volunteer units provided most of the men who participated in the Easter Rising in Dublin in 1916, though divisions within the leadership, especially following Britain's seizure of a German arms shipment, inhibited the spread of rebellion in other areas. In October 1917 Eamon de Valera became president of the Volunteers, with Michael Collins as director of organization. Sinn Fein's electoral victory in December 1918 apparently vindicated the principles of Easter 1916. The Volunteers assumed the role of army of the Irish republic and, with the murder of two policemen, they began the Anglo-Irish war in January 1919. *DRB*

THOMAS HENNESSEY, *Dividing Ireland: World War I and Partition* (London, 1998).

Irish Women's Franchise League (IWFL), Irish feminist organization. Founded by Hanna Sheehy-Skeffington and Margaret Cousins on 11 November 1908, the IWFL saw the culmination of its efforts during the 1918 general election, which was the first in which women (then only if over 30) were able to stand for parliament. The IWFL threw itself behind Sinn Fein's only woman candidate, Countess Markievicz, who became the first woman to be elected to parliament, though she then refused to take her seat. *TWH*

Irish Worker, a newspaper founded on 27 May 1911 and edited by James Larkin as the organ of the Irish Transport and General Workers' Union. It enjoyed a remarkable success, with sales averaging 20,000 per issue, was suppressed in December 1914, but then replaced in May 1915 by the *Workers' Republic*, edited by James Connolly at trade union headquarters in Liberty Hall. It experienced another revival in 1930–2 when edited by James Larkin junior. *DGB*

Iron and Steel Federation, British. The Iron and Steel Federation was set up with government encouragement in 1934, after the introduction of a high tariff on imported steel. It was given wide powers to coordinate the firms in the industry, to a greater extent than in any other privately owned industry. During the Second World War federation staff became the main component in the control board which ran the industry. This influential association was dissolved following the renationalization of steel in 1967. *WG*

'iron curtain' speech (5 March 1946), address given by Winston Churchill at Westminster College, Fulton, Missouri, officially entitled 'The Sinews of Peace'. He argued that 'from Stettin in the Baltic to Trieste in the Adriatic, an iron curtain has descended across the continent', dividing East from West. This, and the positive reaction to the speech, was a key moment in the emergence of the *Cold War. The term 'iron curtain' had been first used by the queen of Belgium in 1914, but Churchill's speech did include the first public use of the phrase 'special relationship' (see ANGLO-AMERICAN RELATIONS). *JAR*

Iron Lady, Soviet press epithet for Thatcher when, as opposition leader, she showed a harsher anti-Communist attitude than Heath had done. She gloried in the label anyway, but it was delightfully auto-recycled by journalists to 'iron maiden', a primitive Scottish instrument of torture, given her relations with colleagues. *EP*

iron law of oligarchy. See MICHELS, ROBERT.

Irwin, Lord. See WOOD, EDWARD FREDERICK LINDLEY.

Isaacs, Rufus Daniel (1860–1935), Liberal politician, lord chief justice, ambassador to the USA and viceroy of India. Son of a Jewish fruit merchant in Spitalfields, Isaacs joined the family business aged 15. He then worked as a jobber on the stock exchange before studying law and becoming a leading commercial advocate. A Liberal MP, 1903–13, he became solicitor-general and then attorney-general, 1910–13. Implicated in the *Marconi scandal of 1912–13, he was lucky to escape formal censure and even became lord chief justice, 1913–21 (Lord Reading from 1914, and eventually a marquess). Isaacs undertook the securing of loans in the USA during the Great War, serving as ambassador, 1918–19. As viceroy of India, 1921–6, he supervised the application of the Montagu-Chelmsford reforms and adopted a conciliatory attitude to Indian concerns. He was briefly foreign secretary in the *National Government, August–October 1931. *JS*

Isserlis, Alexander Reginald ('Sandy') (1922–86), prime ministers' principal private secretary, 1970. Following the death of Michael Halls, Harold Wilson again overruled official advice to appoint Isserlis. However, he had been at Downing Street for only a few weeks when Edward Heath's Conservatives came to power. Isserlis was soon replaced, having served just three months in all, leading briefly to accusations of a Conservative purge, but in fact reflecting a reassertion of the traditional process of civil service appointment to Downing Street. *CL*

Jackson, (Francis) Stanley (1870–1947), sportsman, administrator, and politician. Following a successful cricketing career as captain of Yorkshire and England, Jackson was Conservative MP for Howdenshire, 1915–27. In 1922–3 he secured junior ministerial office at the War Office and in 1923 became chairman of the Conservative Party. He was responsible for advising Baldwin to fight 1923's unnecessary general election on tariffs, an election the Conservatives lost. In 1927 he was appointed governor of Bengal, narrowly surviving an assassination attempt in 1932. *NJC*

Jackson, Thomas (1925–), trade union leader. Formerly a Post Office messenger, Tom Jackson ascended the Union of Post Office Workers (UPW) hierarchy to become general secretary, 1967–82. The disastrous 1971 postal strike almost bankrupted the UPW but subsequently the union's finances and membership level improved under his leadership. A pro-incomes policy 'moderate', Jackson remained on good terms with the ex-Labour founders of the Social Democratic Party. An attractive personality with an outsize moustache, his political influence on the TUC general council, 1967–82, was negligible. *AM*

James, Howell Malcolm Plowden (1954–), prime minister's political secretary, 1994–7. As adviser to Lord Young (1985–7), James was involved in the Conservatives' 1987 general election campaign team. He became one of the closest of John Major's aides during the troubled second half of his premiership, acting as chief of staff on Major's team during the 1995 Conservative leadership contest. A public relations expert who worked on electoral strategy before and during the 1997 general election, he played little part in policy making. *CL*

Janvrin, Robin Berry (1946–), private secretary to Elizabeth II since 1999. He first came to the palace as press secretary in 1987 after spells in the navy and the diplomatic service. Although he was at a public school (Marlborough) and married a French woman with two particles in her maiden name, journalists have labelled him as a modernizer, especially in comparison to his traditionalist predecessor, Robert Fellowes. This remains to be seen. *WMK*

Jarrow march (1936), symbol to a generation of the failures of the British economy during the inter-war years. Jarrow had once been a prosperous shipbuilding town but the closure of Palmer's shipyard in 1934 led to unemployment rising to 72.9 per cent by September 1935. A scheme to build an integrated steelworks never materialized, and so Ellen Wilkinson, who had become MP for Jarrow in 1935, encouraged the formation of a committee in July 1936 to organize a march of 200 men to London. Its purpose was to present two petitions to parliament, demanding work for Jarrow. The march began on 4 October 1936 and was joined at many points by Wilkinson herself, who received the marchers in London at Hyde Park and in the Memorial Hall on 31 October, coinciding with the opening of parliament. The men then returned home by train to a hero's welcome and, though the march did not bear immediate fruits, a smaller integrated steelworks was opened in Jarrow in 1939. *KL*

P. Kingsford, *The Hunger Marchers in Britain 1920–1939* (London, 1982).

'jaw-jaw is better than war-war', phrase used by Harold Macmillan in Australia in 1958, urging a continuing dialogue between East and West. Often wrongly attributed to Sir Winston Churchill, who similarly argued that 'Talking jaw to jaw is better than going to war' in Washington, 1954. *JAR*

Jay, Douglas Patrick Thomas (1907–96), Labour politician. Jay was MP for various London seats, 1946–83; an economist, democratic socialist turned liberal Keynesian; economic and later financial secretary to the Treasury, 1947–51. At the Board of Trade, 1964–6, his opposition to the 1964 surcharge on imports was ignored. A passionate anti-Common Marketeer, he opposed the Wilson government's application in 1966 to join the European Economic Community and was dismissed. His 'moderate' allies in the party were unmoved because of his fierce anti-Europeanism. He coined the phrase 'the gentleman in Whitehall really does know better', for which patronizing view his party was much attacked. Life peer, 1983, and father-in-law of Margaret Jay, Tony Blair's leader in the Lords. *BJE*

Jebb, Gladwyn (1900–96), diplomat. Jebb entered the diplomatic service in 1924, and during the Second World War had a key role in framing British policy towards the UN. He later served as permanent representative to the UN (1950–4) and ended his career as ambassador in Paris (1954–60). Promoted to the House of Lords as Lord Gladwyn, he became a leading exponent of British membership of the European Community. *JWY*

Lord Gladwyn, *The Memoirs of Lord Gladwyn* (London, 1972).

Jellicoe, John Rushworth (1859–1935), admiral. Despite his superb seamanship and tactical acumen, Jellicoe failed to deliver at Jutland (31 May–1 June 1916) the victory of annihilation over the German fleet expected by British public opinion, though he did maintain British command of the sea. As first sea lord, in 1917, his perceived lack of vigour in combating the dangerous German submarine menace alienated his political superiors and led to his dismissal. *JMB*

John Winton, *Jellicoe* (London, 1981).

Jenkin, (Charles) Patrick Fleming (1926–), Conservative politician. Churchill's successor as MP for Wanstead and Woodford, Jenkin was a Treasury minister under Heath, remembered for an unwise call to clean teeth in the dark during the 1974 three-day week. Supporting Thatcher, he became secretary for social security, 1979–81, economizing but cutting tobacco advertising, for industry, 1981–3. At environment, 1983–5, Jenkin was undermined by the battle between Thatcher and the Lords over abolition of the Greater London Council, resulting in a year's delay, for which he took terminal blame. *EP*

Jenkins, (David) Clive (1926–), trade unionist. An articulate Welshman, Jenkins was one of the most flamboyant trade union leaders of the 1960s, as general secretary of the Association of Supervisory Staff, Executives and Technicians, 1960–8. A prominent figure in the political Labour movement he found himself on many committees between the 1960s and 1980s, most notably being a member of the National Research Development Corporation between 1974 and 1980 and a member of the Bullock committee on industrial democracy in 1975. *KL*

Jenkins, Roy Harris (1920–), Labour, Social Democrat, and Liberal Democrat politician; founder member and first leader of the *Social Democratic Party (SDP). Son of a Welsh miner who was a Labour MP, but Oxford-educated, Jenkins entered parliament in 1950. He rose to prominence as home secretary under Harold Wilson in 1965–7, when he oversaw the liberalization of the law on *abortion through the Abortion Act and facilitated other liberalizing reforms. He became chancellor of the exchequer on Callaghan's resignation in 1967 following the devaluation debacle, and by pursuing a deflationary policy achieved a trade and revenue surplus. His neutral budget in April 1970 has, in retrospect, often been seen as playing a part in Labour's defeat in the election of June of that year. In opposition, 1970–4, his pro-European views were increasingly at odds with the party's policy.

Jenkins returned as home secretary, 1974–6, and was responsible for passing the Anti-Terrorism Act following the Birmingham bombings. Defeated by Callaghan in the 1976 Labour leadership election, he resigned from parliament to become president of the commission of the European Community from 1977 to 1981, but also, when delivering the Dimbleby lecture in November 1979, launched the campaign for a new centre party in Britain. In March 1981, he was one of the co-founders of the SDP, becoming its first leader. He enthusiastically went into the *Alliance with the Liberal Party with whose leader, David *Steel, he had already formed a strong working relationship. His near-miss at the *Warrington by-election launched a run of spectacular Alliance by-election victories including his own election at Glasgow *Hillhead in March 1982.

Named the Alliance's 'prime minister designate' in the 1983 election campaign, criticism of his performance led to his resignation as SDP leader in favour of David *Owen in June 1983. Jenkins strongly supported the merger of the two parties of the Alliance after the 1987 election. Having lost his own seat in the Commons in 1987, he accepted a peerage and became leader of the Liberal Democrats in the Lords, a position he held until 1998. He also formed a good relationship with the new Labour leader, Tony Blair, and encouraged the collaboration of the Liberal Democrats and the Labour Party in constitutional talks both before and after the 1997 election. In 1998, Blair appointed Jenkins to head a commission on changes in the voting system which reported in 1999.

In addition to his political career, Jenkins has been a prolific writer and biographer (for example *Asquith*, (1964), and studies of Baldwin and Gladstone), and since 1987 chancellor of the University of Oxford. *JS*

Roy Jenkins, *A Life at the Centre* (London, 1991). | Ivor Crewe and Anthony King, *SDP: The Birth, Life and Death of the Social Democratic Party* (Oxford, 1995).

Jennings, Ivor **(1903–65)**, distinguished academic and constitutional lawyer, whose work on the constitution was extensively used in the middle years of the century. He was an outstanding student at Cambridge, and then taught law before being appointed vice-chancellor of Ceylon University College, later the University of Ceylon. He advised ministers in Ceylon (now Sri Lanka) on independence and on the constitution, and was to advise other countries, notably Pakistan and Malaya, in drawing up constitutions. He returned to the UK to become master of Trinity Hall, Cambridge, and in 1961–3 was vice-chancellor of Cambridge University. A prolific writer, he authored 26 books, including three major works on the British system of government, *The Law and the Constitution* (1933), *Cabinet Government* (1936), and *Parliament* (1939), and several works on public administration (his first book, in 1930, was on the Poor Law Code) and on constitutions. He served on various public bodies, held several honorary doctorates, was made QC in 1949, and knighted in 1948. *PN*

Jewish community. During the mid-19th century, when the battle for Jewish political emancipation was being fought, Anglo-Jewry was largely Liberal in its politics, because the Liberal Party fully supported the right of professing Jews to exercise political liberties. Later, however, Anglo-Jewish voters began to turn to the Conservatives. This was partly because of the perceived anti-Jewish prejudice of Gladstone at the time of the Russo-Turkish war (1876–8) but also because the business classes in general had begun to turn in a Tory direction and because the Conservatives favoured state financial aid for denominational schools. Between about 1880 and 1906, a 'native' Anglo-Jewry of some 60,000 persons was swamped by about twice that number of mainly poor immigrants from eastern Europe. These brought with them vibrant trade-unionist and socialist traditions, expressed through a lively Anglo- Yiddish press. During the Great War, as immigrants became naturalized and as their children came of age, this demographic revolution impacted inevitably upon the politics of Anglo-Jewry. In areas such as Stepney, in London's East End, Jewish voters supported Labour and later Communist candidates. A residue of Jewish support for the Tories persisted throughout the inter-war period. However, during the 1930s this loyalty was put under considerable pressure as a result of the support given by individual Conservatives to the *British Union of Fascists, and as a by-product of the manner in which the governments of Stanley Baldwin and Neville Chamberlain interpreted the Balfour declaration (1917), designed to facilitate the establishment of a Jewish national home in Palestine. It is dangerous to infer the political preferences of British Jews simply from the number and affiliation of Jewish MPs. Nonetheless, it is significant that at the general election of 1945, and for the first time since 1874, no Jew was returned to the Commons as an official Conservative MP, whereas one of the two Communist MPs was Jewish.

In 1945 Anglo-Jewry was probably as socialist as it was ever to become. Over the next three decades this loyalty was to be dramatically eroded. British Jews became more prosperous and more middle class, moving from decaying city centres into the suburbs. Their Zionist loyalties were sorely confronted by a Labour Party seen as increasingly hostile to the very idea of a Jewish state—a tension which culminated in a bitter war of words between London Jewry and the Labour-led Greater London Council in the 1980s. Moreover, in Mrs Thatcher Britain's Jews found a kindred spirit and a champion; at one time Mrs Thatcher had no fewer than five professing Jews in her cabinet—a record. Under Tony Blair's leadership, Labour has made a determined effort to re-establish its credentials in Jewish eyes. But the evidence of the 1997 general election suggests that, although many Jews did not vote Tory, comparatively few actually switched to Labour. It remains to be seen, therefore, whether, as a whole, Anglo-Jewry has indeed returned to its left-wing roots. *GA*

G. Alderman, *Modern British Jewry* (2nd edn., Oxford, 1998).

job centres. See LABOUR EXCHANGES.

Johnson, Hewlett (1874–1966), socialist dean of Canterbury, 1931–63. Unlike many left-wing clergymen, Johnson was on the evangelical wing of the Church of England. Active in the Left Book Club in the late 1930s, he gained the sobriquet 'the Red Dean' for his unstinting defence of communism and the Soviet system in works such as *Christians and Communism* (1956). *PPC*

Johnson Smith, Geoffrey (1924–), Conservative politician. A television journalist and former London county councillor, Johnson Smith was elected to parliament in 1959. Having lost his seat in 1964 he was soon re-elected and became a whip in 1965 before serving as a party vice-chairman, 1965–71. An army and civil service minister in the Heath government, this Tory centre-left stalwart was elected to the 1922 Committee's executive in 1979 and became its vice-chairman in 1997. *RJS*

Johnston, Thomas (1881–1965), writer and Labour politician. Johnston was a leading figure in the Scottish Labour movement in the first half of the 20th century. He founded the journal *Forward* in 1906, and entered parliament in 1922 as part of the *Clydesiders group. He was a moderate, pragmatic politician and did not succumb to the revolutionary rhetoric of some of his colleagues. He lost his seat in 1931 but re-entered parliament in 1935. He was appointed secretary for Scotland in 1941 and used his organizational abilities to channel as much state intervention as possible for the Scottish economy. Johnston was for long credited as the Scottish secretary who did most for Scotland. *RF*

G. Walker, *Thomas Johnston* (Manchester, 1988).

Joint Intelligence Committee (JIC), set up in 1936 and tasked with setting Britain's national intelligence priorities and assessment of its results. It is the only body in Whitehall, outside the cabinet itself, where senior Foreign Office, inter-service, and intelligence service representatives come together to formulate risk assessments for government. The JIC produces regular intelligence assessments for the prime minister, government ministers, and officials on a range of international military, political, and economic problems and issues. It meets weekly and its members are drawn from senior officials of the Foreign Office, the Ministry of Defence, the Department of Trade and Industry, and the Treasury, together with the heads of the three security and intelligence agencies and the JIC intelligence coordinator. It is currently chaired by a Cabinet Office nominee, who has direct access to the prime minister.

The JIC was created in 1936 as a joint services committee. Its purpose was to assess intelligence reports for the chiefs of staff. Initially the JIC achieved little. This was partly because for the first three years of its existence the Foreign Office refused to participate: it joined only when it realized just how bad its own system of intelligence assessment and coordination had become. Furthermore it took until 1940 for the directors of the three service intelligence branches to all attend the same meeting. Thereafter the JIC remit was extended to include the receiving and assessment of all intelligence reports and improving the workings of British intelligence. These changes laid down the JIC's future guiding principles. Unfortunately JIC's integration and reorganization had barely begun when war broke out, and during the first year and a half of the war, which included the period of the 'phoney war', Dunkirk, the battle of Britain, and the start of the Blitz, its defence assessments proved to be largely worthless. As a consequence, during the course of 1941, the whole organization underwent a major reformation. Thereafter the JIC became charged with the coordination, assessment, and dissemination of all strategic intelligence—a task it succeeded in undertaking for the rest of the war.

The JIC had a good war and emerged as the most important body providing government with intelligence and risk assessments. The Cold War brought with it new problems. In retrospect the threat assessments made by the JIC during the early Cold War years proved balanced rather than alarmist. For example, when the Chinese intervened in the Korean war the JIC recognized the dangers and advocated a programme of rearmament. There have been many JIC reorganizations since 1945. One important structural change took place in 1957, as a consequence of the Suez and other intelligence debacles. Since that date the JIC has functioned within the Cabinet Office as a part of its interdepartmental structure under the cabinet secretary. Further changes to the structure of the JIC occurred in 1968, when Sir Dick White became the JIC's first intelligence coordinator. The task he and his successors undertake is to provide the cabinet secretary (and when necessary the prime minister) with advice on matters of coordination within the various intelligence agencies, together with their resource needs and activities. In line with the largely informal lines of communication running through the higher echelons within Whitehall, the intelligence coordinator also chairs various formal and informal groups responsible for intelligence management and advises on the allocation of resources. In line with other senior intelligence posts, the intelligence coordinator is appointed by the prime minister. Another development of the late 1960s was the creation of a joint-intelligence secretariat. A part of the Cabinet Office, the personnel making up this body are either seconded from other departments or are permanent Cabinet Office staff. As the JIC operates 24 hours a day, it is supported round the clock by duty intelligence officers.

An assessment staff was created at the same time as Dick White's 1968 appointment, comprising senior- and middle-ranking interdepartmental and service officers and responsible for preparing JIC papers derived from overt and covert intelligence sources relating to matters of current concern. The work of the assessment staff is subject to scrutiny by a current intelligence groups subcommittee of the JIC, which brings together government departments, services, and intelligence agencies. Thereafter, reports and papers are considered by the JIC before being circulated to ministers and other intelligence consumers. In addition to its executive head, the JIC has a non-executive chairman, who has broad supervisory functions and is responsible for ensuring that the JIC's warning and monitoring role is discharged effectively; he too has direct access to the prime minister. Following the 1983 Franks report on the Falklands war, the JIC chair passed from the Foreign Office to the Cabinet Office and was initially combined with the post of intelligence coordinator. However, since 1985 the duties have been divided; Thatcher, reflecting the high priority she gave to such matters, appointed Sir Percy Cradock, her own foreign policy adviser, as JIC chairman. At the time she clearly trusted the opinions of the JIC over those of the Foreign Office. Since that time a constant traffic of information has flowed between the chairman of the JIC in the Cabinet Office and Downing Street, making the JIC just about the best model there is for the dissemination of intelligence and policy formation. *PM*

***Jolly George* incident** (10 May 1920), celebrated example of direct action by British workers. The *Jolly George* was a ship chartered to take munitions from London to the anti-Bolshevik 'white' forces in the Russian civil war. Refusing to load it, the London dockers launched a 'hands off Russia' campaign which helped persuade the government against further intervention in Russia. *JAR*

Jones, Arthur Creech (1891–1964), Labour politician and trade unionist. During the Great War, he was a member of the No-Conscription Fellowship, and was imprisoned from September 1916 to April 1919 for failure to undertake military service. After the war, he was secretary of the National Union of Docks, Wharves and Shipping Staff which amalgamated with the Transport and General Workers' Union in 1922, in which he became national secretary of the administrative, clerical, and supervisory group. He first became interested in colonial issues in the 1920s through his trade union connections. Creech Jones unsuccessfully contested Heywood and Radcliffe in 1929, but was MP for Shipley, 1935–50, and became a key figure in the party on colonial affairs, sitting on the party's advisory committee on imperial questions and on the TUC colonial affairs committee, and was a co-founder of the Fabian colonial bureau. From May 1940 to June 1944 he served as parliamentary private secretary to Ernest Bevin at the Ministry of Labour. In 1945 he was appointed junior minister in the Colonial Office, becoming in October 1946, colonial secretary, which enabled him to play a key role in the movement from colonialism to independence in South Asia in that period. Defeated at the 1950 general election, he was subsequently elected for Wakefield, 1954–64. *JAJ*

Jones, Aubrey (1911–), Conservative politician and public servant. Elected to parliament in 1950, Jones personified the new, socially mobile Tory MP, having been born in Merthyr Tydfil and had a state education. He became minister of fuel and power in 1955 and was the last minister of supply, 1957–9. He resigned his Birmingham seat in 1965 following his controversial appointment as chairman of the Wilson government's *Prices and Incomes Board, where he served until the board's abolition by Heath. *RJS*

Jones, Elwyn. See ELWYN-JONES, LORD.

Jones, Frederick Llewellyn (1866–1941), solicitor and Liberal politician. He served as HM coroner for Flintshire, and was closely associated with the administration of health and education in Wales. A former Labour supporter, Jones was the Liberal MP for Flintshire, 1929–35, initially as an avid follower of David Lloyd George, thereafter as a Simonite Liberal, 1931–December 1932, and subsequently as a mainstream Liberal. He was a member of a huge number of public and professional bodies in England and Wales, including the Central Council for Health Education, 1923–40. *JGJ*

Jones, James Larkin ('Jack') (1913–), trade union leader. Originally employed in the engineering and dock industries, 1927–39, Jones became a Labour councillor in Liverpool at the age of 23 and fought for the International Brigade during the Spanish civil war. As Coventry district secretary of the Transport and General Workers' Union, 1939–55, he raised the local membership from 3,000 to 40,000. He was subsequently appointed Midlands regional secretary, 1955–63, and executive officer, 1963–9, before being elected general secretary, 1969–78. Jones retained tight control over the union despite being a longtime champion of 'shop stewards' power'. He became the most important British trade union leader in the 1970s, providing the main impetus for the Labour–TUC liaison committee (1972) which rapidly developed into an important industrial and economic policy-making forum within the movement. He was also the chief architect of the social contract which underpinned Labour–TUC relations during the Wilson and Callaghan governments, 1974–9. Jones remained resolutely opposed to any form of incomes policy and instinctively favoured free collective bargaining, but in the mid-1970s he advocated wage restraint to counter the destabilizing effects of inflationary pay settlements. Indeed, mainly due to his efforts, the TUC agreed to accept a £6 per week flat-rate increase, in a voluntary wage policy in 1975, although this redistributive approach to pay bargaining helped to fuel the worker grievances which erupted in the 'winter of discontent', 1978–9. During this period, right-wing opponents dubbed him 'Emperor Jones' and opinion polls revealed that he was regarded as the most powerful man in Britain. His retirement in 1978 not only removed a major constructive influence from the TUC but also deprived the Labour government of one of its most valuable allies. In retirement he was a ceaseless campaigner for pensioners' rights. *AM*

Jack Jones, *Union Man* (London, 1986).

Jones, Thomas (1870–1955), assistant (later deputy) secretary to the cabinet, 1916–30. A Welsh academic economist, Jones was the most significant and durable of the cronies Lloyd George employed on becoming prime minister in 1916. He helped cabinet secretary Maurice Hankey to establish the cabinet secretariat and was a vital intermediary during the Anglo-Irish treaty negotiations (1921). Having survived Lloyd George's fall (1922), he became a trusted confidant to his successors, Andrew Bonar Law (1922–3) and Stanley Baldwin (1923–4 and 1925–9). During the 1926 General Strike he persuaded Baldwin not to introduce anti-trade union legislation. A Labour Party member, Jones's relationship with Baldwin was so good that Ramsay MacDonald suspected him of Conservative sympathies and sidelined him in 1924 (but did not do so in 1929). From 1924 Jones played an important part in developing government economic planning, in particular after 1929. *CL*

Keith Middlemas (ed.), *Thomas Jones' Whitehall Diary*, 3 vols. (London, 1969–71).

Jones, (Owen) Trevor (1927–), Liberal activist. A self-made businessman, Jones led the political campaigns in Liverpool which made the Liberals the largest party on the council by 1973. An exponent of *community politics, Jones exported the tactics learned in Liverpool to by-election campaigns in the early 1970s. Triumphantly dubbed 'Jones the Vote', he invigorated Liberal morale and was elected president of the party in 1973. He remained leader of the Liverpool Liberal council group from 1976 until 1988. *JS*

Jopling, (Thomas) Michael (1930–), Conservative politician. Thatcher's chief whip, 1979–83, handling her modest majority in revolts, as over admission of Asian fiancées, Jopling obliged Labour by denying pairing status to the Social Democratic Party. Then having worked the berth as deputy in opposition, he was minister of agriculture, 1983–7. Jopling was friend and neighbour of William Whitelaw but lacked his gentlemanly blarney. He had serious problems over milk, accepting as fair a European Community cut of 9 per cent in production. Physically attacked in Wales, he had also reckoned the grain regime as too generous. *EP*

Jordan, Colin (1923–), racial nationalist. A prominent activist of the 1950s and 1960s, Jordan served his political apprenticeship within the League of Empire Loyalists. He founded the White Defence League in 1956 and then helped in 1960 to establish the British National Party and in 1963 the National Socialist Movement. He engaged in numerous confrontations with the authorities. A disciple of Arnold Leese, Jordan has argued for the preservation of the Nordic race and for a Britain free from Jewish domination. *CH*

C. Jordan, *Fraudulent Conversion* (London, 1954).

Joseph, Keith Sinjohn (1918–94), Conservative politician and prophet. Arguably Keith Joseph was the most creatively intelligent politician of his time and one of the most attractive, but few have suffered so much derision. He was the son of a lord mayor of London and founder of Bovis, Sir Samuel Joseph, at a time when the only other Jewish Tory MP was also a baronet. He entered parliament in 1956 just in time to oppose Suez, but was holding junior office at housing within three years, and by 1962 he was in cabinet as minister of housing. Despite praising capitalism for providing bankruptcies as well as millionaires, he accepted Macmillan's interventionism and had no affinity with punitive or militarist right-wingers in those days. He opposed capital punishment, supported legislation decriminalizing homosexuality, and in 1966, almost alone among Tory front-benchers, declined to oppose Labour's first race relations legislation. He had outstanding intellectual credentials—an Oxford first in law and fellow of All Souls—and was linked with Edward Boyle in support of humanitarian reforms which, enacted under Harold Wilson, became an emerging liberal mood. Since he would also become chief advocate of the free market, Joseph stood early behind the two distinct sorts of liberalism sustaining the present political consensus, but in the way of prophets, he would be short of honour. Under Heath's leadership for which he had voted, Joseph would shadow successively social services, labour, and trade, engaging in the overheavy policy blueprinting of that opposition. In 1970, Joseph was sent to social services rather than industry, and was notably generous towards the disabled and elderly, a big spender generally who resisted expenditure cuts. He also, to his later candid chagrin, increased the NHS bureaucracy.

Joseph's 'conversion' to true Conservatism (his own self-description in 1974) flowed from the frustrations of the Heath government, too much easy credit, rampant demand, and trade union power. His pamphlets and speeches in 1974–5 proclaimed the case for free markets, and he established the *Centre for Policy Studies. He might have stood against Heath, but diffidence, his wife's advice, and hostile reactions to an untypical Joseph speech at Birmingham, alluding to the growth in 'inferior human stock', ruled out an attempt. Joseph then supported Thatcher's candidacy. Coarser, illiberal, and nationalistic, Thatcher had the punch for a right-wing takeover, but Joseph, whom she deeply admired, became her inspiration and was relieved to be out of the front-line fight. This was just as well, for his moral candour, which acknowledged being wrong, broke the meaner rules of politics and was widely, insultingly derided. The 'mad monk' epithet stuck and his sensibility, thoughtfulness, and doubt seemed offensive to journalists. His ministerial career under Thatcher, at industry and then education, looks in retrospect rather creditable. Joseph separated the Post Office from telecommunications, opening the way to British Telecom's success, hired Ian MacGregor to run British steel, but sensibly pulled back from a Rolls Royce closure. At education, he declined the doctrinaire voucher scheme, annoying a right wing where he belonged only intellectually. Joseph believed in a social market system, but was sympathetic to the lower end of society, not Thatcher's style. No politician, his anxious concern and belief in market mechanisms was a civilized mix and his qualities more important than his killer-instinct deficiency. The overused phrase 'seminal influence' is in Joseph's case the truth. *EP*

Andrew Denham and Mark Garnett, *Keith Joseph* (London, 2001).

Jowett, Frederick William (1864–1944), socialist pioneer and parliamentarian. One of a handful of socialists in Bradford in the 1880s, Fred Jowett played a significant role in the Manningham Mills Strike and was a founding member of the Bradford Labour Union, subsequently the Independent Labour Party (ILP), and the Bradford Labour Church. As a councillor he was a key figure in the development of municipal socialism with his work in the fields of public health and housing, school meals, and the provision of municipal milk and coal supplies. He was MP for Bradford West, 1906–18, and for Bradford East, 1922–4 and 1929–31, and first commissioner for works in the 1924 Labour government. A prominent member of the ILP in the period before the Great War, Jowett was a member of its administrative council and on a number of occasions, chairman. He was a vigorous opponent of the Great War and during the 1920s increasingly a critic of the Labour Party. He, somewhat sadly, supported the disaffiliation of the ILP from the Labour Party in 1932. *JAJ*

Fenner Brockway, *Socialism over Sixty Years: The Life of Jowett of Bradford* (London, 1946).

Joynson-Hicks, William ('Jix') (1865–1932), Conservative politician. In 1908 Hicks successfully took Churchill's seat at a by-election, a well-publicized result which earned him the nickname 'Jix'. As a backbencher he championed the causes of the motor car, aviation, and the telephone. No supporter of Lloyd George, Jix played his part in the 1922 *Carlton Club meeting, and there followed a rapid succession of ministerial posts leading to his becoming home secretary, 1924–9. He established a diehard reputation for cracking down on communists and undesirables and on issues of morality, but also as a reformer for his borstal policies. *NJC*

judicial review. See ADMINISTRATIVE LAW.

Judicial Studies Board, responsible for the training of magistrates and judges. The board was set up to improve the specific skills of those in judicial authority (for example in civil rights law and European Community law, both now more important than when senior legal figures began their own careers). Training is mainly done by practitioners who already hold equivalent posts, and the board has an arms-length relationship only with its official sponsor, the lord chancellor's department. *JAR*

Junior Imperial League (JIL), the Conservative Party's youth wing before the Second World War. The JIL originated in the early 1900s but was not formally adopted by the party until 1911 and really flourished only from the 1920s. The under-30 'Imps', an important part of the Baldwin Conservatives' appeal to younger voters, claimed 300,000 members by 1929, together with Young Britons' branches for younger children. The organization declined in the 1930s, leading to the 1939 Fraser report and the JIL's replacement by the Young Conservatives in 1945. *JAR*

Justice, legal pressure group, the British section of the International Commission of Jurists. An independent research, discussion, and publication agency, Justice enables practising and academic lawyers to propose reforms to the legal system, as for example in its 1970 report which led in due course to the creation of a crown prosecution service. *JAR*

K

Kahn, Otto (1867–1934), American financier of German descent who was a partner in the banking firm of Kuhn Lieh, second only to Morgans. During the Great War he was strongly pro-British, offering his house St Dunstan's to the government free of charge to be used as a headquarters for blind ex-soldiers. After the war he wrote several influential articles and pamphlets on key financial issues. He argued that America's reluctance to cancel the Allied debt reflected internal disillusionment and the belief that it would not lead to peace in Europe. *JFM*

Kaldor, Nicholas (1908–86), economist and government adviser. Kaldor was, with Thomas *Balogh, one of Harold Wilson's Hungarian economic gurus. Born in Budapest, he was economics professor in Cambridge, 1966–75, after previously teaching at the LSE. A Labour supporter, he was special adviser on taxation, 1964–8 (when he devised the ill-fated selective employment tax), and again when Wilson returned to office in 1974. *JAR*

Kaufman, Gerald Bernard (1923–), journalist and Labour politician. A Labour MP from 1970, Kaufman had been parliamentary press liaison officer for the Labour Party, 1965–70, and became a junior minister for industry, 1975–9. As a right-wing Labour MP he was under threat of deselection for a period after 1983, but as shadow foreign secretary, 1987–92, he worked with Kinnock to remove the party's commitment to unilateralism in May 1989. He was later an active and vocal chair of the Commons' culture, recreation, and sport select committee. *BJE*

Keep Left (1947–51), both a publication and a Labour left grouping, which became part of the Bevanite revolt of the 1950s. The Keep Left group was a 'soft' left body within the Labour Party which emerged under the leadership of Ian Mikardo, Richard Crossman, Richard Acland, and Benn Levy in the winter of 1946–7, although it did not officially declare its existence until 1949. It believed that a third world war could be avoided by the creation of a 'third force' based upon an alliance between Britain and France, effectively 'a regional European security system', which would encourage disarmament and use the money saved to develop the economies of the third world. It was believed that this policy would encourage economic prosperity throughout the world and avoid war. The group's name was based upon a short pamphlet *Keep Left*, mainly produced by Mikardo and Crossman, and Michael Foot, which first appeared in May 1947 but was extended and updated to *Keeping Left* in 1950. By and large the group was a small body of friends, rarely more than a dozen in number, who frequently disagreed with each other. It developed into a discussion group but increased its number to more than 40 when Aneurin Bevan resigned from the Labour government in April 1951 and joined Keep Left. Eventually it became absorbed within the Bevanite group, which focused more upon day-to-day political matters than the long-term socialist planning which Keep Left supported. The 'salutary gadfly' of British politics was swallowed up into a broader groundswell of Labour left opposition to the Attlee-led Labour Party. *KL*

Keith Laybourn, *The Rise of Socialism in Britain* (Stroud, 1997). | Jonathan Schneer, *Labour's Conscience: The Labour Left 1945–1951* (London, 1988).

Keep Sunday Special Campaign (KSSC), interdenominational body founded to oppose the 1986 Shops Bill. Since the 1930s, the legal protection of the sabbath has been steadily reduced by increases in Sunday trading. Although Tory backbenchers rejected the 1986 bill, the only defeat suffered by Thatcher on a government bill in the Commons, it proved a hollow victory, and a compromise measure allowing limited hours of Sunday trading was eventually passed in 1993, since when KSSC has been less active. *PPC*

Kell, Vernon George Waldegrave (1873–1942), first head of the British Security Service (MI5). The son of a distinguished imperial soldier and an exiled Polish noblewoman, whose linguistic skills were inherited by her son, Vernon Kell was educated privately and at Sandhurst. In 1894, he joined his father's old regiment, where he honed his skills as a linguist and participated in several imperial campaigns including the Boxer uprising. In 1909, as assistant secretary to the Committee of Imperial Defence, Kell became the first head of Britain's Secret Service Bureau: the forerunner of MI5 and today's Security Intelligence Service (MI6). Between 1909 and the outbreak of war in 1914, Kell, a calm, modest, secretive man with an eye for detail, together with a handful of employees and scant resources, identified the 24 German agents operating in Britain. When war was declared all but one were rounded up, depriving Germany of knowledge of Britain's initial military dispositions. By the end of the war, Kell had accounted for more than 35 other German spies and created an organization of more than 800. In 1931, the year Kell's organization severed its War Office link, the Security Service took over many of Special Branch's counter-subversion functions. The 1930s saw the service suffer the consequences of out-of-date management and inadequate resources. That said, it had its successes, placing agents in the German embassy in London, monitoring Soviet penetration of trade unions and the Communist Party of Great Britain. However, by the time war broke out, Kell had lost any sense of direction and the agency was unable to cope with the demands made on it. As a consequence, during the early phase of the war the organization experienced a functional breakdown. This and other failures resulted in Kell's dismissal in June 1940. *PM*

Kennedy, Charles Peter (1959–), politician and leader of the Liberal Democrats, 1999– . The son of a crofter, Kennedy was the Social Democrat MP for Ross and Cromarty by 1983. He supported the merger of the Alliance parties into the *Liberal Democrats after the 1987 election and subsequently held several portfolios, though better known to the public as a humorist and regular broadcaster, and thought something of a lightweight by political commentators. He was, though, elected to lead the Liberal Democrats when Paddy Ashdown stood down in 1999 and led it to an increase in the numbers of its MPs in 2001. *JAR*

Keynes, John Maynard (1883–1946), the leading economist of the century. Although he maintained an academic position at King's College, Cambridge, from 1909, Keynes took an active role as both critic and adviser to successive governments throughout his career until his sudden death at the age of 63. Keynes took up a post in the Treasury during the Great War, taking responsibility for external financial policy. He became a figure of public importance upon the publication of his critique of the treaty of Versailles with Germany, *The Economic Consequences of the Peace* (1919), in which he argued against the imposition of harsh reparations. A critic of orthodox Treasury policy during the inter-war period, he warned against a return to the *gold standard in 1925, and his alternative proposals for cutting unemployment through public investment were the centrepiece of the Liberal manifesto of 1929. Keynes's attempts to promote such strategies as chairman of the committee of economists of the Economic Advisory Council during the 1929–31 Labour government foundered, however, as policy makers were overcome by the onset of deep economic crisis. He spent the following years producing his seminal work, *The *General Theory of Employment, Interest and Money* (1936), which was to have a revolutionary impact on the discipline of economics. During the Second World War, Keynes returned to the Treasury where he served as an economic adviser until his death. His energies were devoted increasingly to post-war planning, and he played an important role in the establishment of the *Bretton Woods system of international finance. In 1945 he negotiated the controversial dollar loan from the USA which was necessitated by the termination of USA Lend-Lease aid. *HOJ*

Peter Clarke, *The Keynesian Revolution in the Making, 1924–1936* (Oxford, 1988). | Robert Skidelsky, *John Maynard Keynes*, 3 vols. (London, 1983–2000).

Keynesianism, the approach to economic policy inspired by the work of J. M. *Keynes. Keynesianism became increasingly dominant among intellectuals and policy makers in Britain during the Second World War and this dominance lasted until the 1970s, when its failure to develop a satisfactory theory of inflation led to the rise of new schools of economic theory, in particular, *monetarism. Just as Marxism should not be confused with the ideas of Marx alone, Keynesianism should not be taken as synonymous with the work of Keynes. Loosely defined, however, Keynesians shared a belief that macroeconomic policy can and should be used by governments to manage the cyclical fluctuations of the market in order to control the level of employment and to maximize productive efficiency. Thus governments, by planning for a surplus at times of boom, and planning for deficits in a slump, could regulate demand in the economy, stimulating growth when necessary and discouraging overheating when economic activity threatens to overwhelm capacity. This approach originated in the inter-war years, when mass unemployment was the principal concern of policy makers and economists. From the late 1920s, Keynes himself called for programmes of public investment to alleviate unemployment and stimulate demand. He developed his proposals further in the *General Theory of Employment* (1936). But although Keynes's ideas attracted much attention at that time, the state response to unemployment and depression was conditioned by the 'Treasury view' orthodoxy.

Paradoxically, Keynesian approaches were not tested in Britain until during and after the Second World War, when mass unemployment was not problematic. In the 1950s and 1960s, this fed public assumptions that Keynesian policy making was responsible for what were in fact international trends favouring growth and full employment. Meanwhile, the more serious post-war problem of inflation was not adequately addressed. According to Keynesian economists, inflation bore a direct relationship to the level of unemployment: full employment would tend to drive up wages which in turn drove levels of inflation. This relationship between wages and unemployment was expressed as the 'Phillips curve' in 1958. Keynesians thus accepted that inflationary pressures would inevitably build in conditions of full employment, but wage-push inflation could not be addressed by macroeconomic policy without jeopardizing employment levels. This led them to an emphasis on the compulsory control of wage levels, an approach which increasingly dominated the policy making of British governments from the early 1960s, with limited success and at the cost of increasing social conflict. Critics of Keynesianism argued with increasing force that in its attempt to solve the problem of unemployment it was inherently inflationary, and that the controls necessary to contain inflation in such circumstances were incompatible with a free society. Thus, the neo-liberal economists could allege that Keynesianism was ultimately as problematic as socialism in its limits on the freedom of the market and the individual. The failure of Keynesian theory to confront these allegations undermined its credibility in the 1970s, particularly as both unemployment and inflation began to rise simultaneously: the condition known as *stagflation. The Callaghan government turned to the control of the money supply as an alternative device to control inflation from 1976, an early sign of the monetarist approaches adopted under Margaret Thatcher after 1979.

Historians disagree on the extent to which the broad intellectual acceptance of Keynesianism from the 1940s was mirrored by a 'Keynesian revolution' in policy making. Traditionally, the elite acceptance of this approach in Britain was associated with the publication of the 1944 white paper on employment, which accepted that the state bore a responsibility to maintain 'a high and stable level of employment', through the use of macroeconomic instruments. The first Treasury experiment of this kind, however, was with the 1941 budget, which deliberately reduced the projected deficit in an attempt to control inflationary pressure during the war. Some authors have focused on the 1947 budget, the first in peacetime to plan deliberately for a surplus, as marking a decisive shift from the use of direct controls towards fiscal policy in the Keynesian sense. The latest research has been more cautious, questioning the whole idea of a Keynesian revolution in Whitehall after the war, as a concept that exaggerates the influence of theory on the formulation of policy. In particular, while the Treasury was happy to plan for a budget surplus, which coincided with its desire to maintain its domination over high-spending departments, it was unwilling to budget for deficits to stimulate demand. It is now widely accepted that the political implementation of Keynesian approaches in post-war Britain was fatally flawed, leading to a 'stop-go' tendency in economic policy from the 1950s which impaired the smooth functioning of the economy. Supporters of Keynesianism thus argue that government policies were never a fair measure of their approach. Its detractors respond by alleging that Keynesian theory is politically naive, and does not take into account the inevitable reluctance of policy makers to risk votes in the short term in order to protect the long-term stability of the economy. *HOJ*

Peter Clarke, *The Keynesian Revolution in the Making* (Oxford, 1988). | David Marquand and Anthony Seldon, *The Ideas that shaped Post-war Britain* (London, 1996). | G. C. Peden, *The Treasury and British Economic Policy* (Basingstoke, 1988). | Jim Tomlinson, *British Macroeconomic Policy since 1940* (London, 1985).

'Khaki' Election, the general election of October 1900, which gained this soubriquet because of the decision of Lord Salisbury to seek an electoral mandate to press to conclusion the Boer war, some government candidates then campaigning in their khaki army uniforms. Despite a disastrous beginning, the war had turned in Britain's favour, and it was hoped to take advantage of the patriotic mood of the time. The decision proved successful and the government secured an overall majority of 134. *RJQA*

Kilbrandon report (Cmnd 5460) (1973), commissioned by Labour Prime Minister Harold Wilson in April 1969 following the success of the Scottish National Party (SNP) in winning a by-election in Hamilton in 1967 and securing 30 per cent of the vote in the local elections of 1968. A further incentive to take constitutional affairs seriously was the Declaration of *Perth made by Heath, the leader of the Conservative opposition in 1968, which committed his party to a programme of devolution for Scotland. Although the commission under Lord Crowther-Hunt was ostensibly designed to report on the constitution, it was, in Wilson's own words, 'designed to spend years taking minutes' and give the appearance that the Labour government took constitutional matters seriously, while the lengthy process would allow for breathing space, and it was hoped that by the time the report was finished, the problem would have disappeared. One problem with this strategy was that the original chair, Crowther-Hunt, died before it was completed and his place was taken by Lord Kilbrandon. The commission took evidence from various bodies and reported in October 1973. Although containing much information on the attitudes of various political organizations, trade unions, churches, together with public opinion surveys on the role of government in Scotland, the report did not endorse devolution and many of its recommendations were vague and woolly. Its main significance, however, was to draw public attention back to constitutional issues just in time for the elections of 1974. *RF*

James Kellas, *The Scottish Political System* (Cambridge, 1989).

Kilmuir, Viscount. See Maxwell Fyfe, David Patrick.

King, Cecil Harmsworth (1901–87), press baron. King was a director of the *Daily Mirror* from 1929, chairman of Mirror newspapers, 1951–63, and of the International Publishing Corporation (IPC), 1963–8. A propagandist through the *Daily Mirror* for Labour, he was a director of the Bank of England, 1965–8, and a member of the National Coal Board, 1966–9. He later became disillusioned, and by 1968 was using his newspaper to demand Wilson's resignation, flirting with the idea of a government of national unity, led by businessmen, to revive the economy. This led to his ousting by the IPC, when he had further brief fame by publishing his diaries. *BJE*

Cecil King, *The Cecil King Diaries, 1965–1974*, 2 vols. (London, 1972–5).

King, Thomas Jeremy (1933–), Conservative politician. Popular as a straight, unstand-offish minister, unrealistically fancied in small corners as leader, Tom King was a solid Northern Ireland and defence secretary. Rightish in opposition, opposing Rhodesian sanctions, he was admired as Michael Heseltine's legman at environment (local government) in 1979–83, was secretary for employment, 1983–5, Northern Ireland, 1985–9, and defence 1989–92, figuring in the homicidal fantasies of his deputy, Alan Clark's *Diaries*. He continued in the Commons after leaving office, in demand as a backbench uncle. *EP*

'King and Country' debate. On 9 February 1933 the Oxford Union passed a resolution by 275 votes to 153 stating that it would not under any circumstances fight 'for King and Country' (a phrase associated with patriotic attitudes during the Great War). This suddenly received world-wide notice, out of all proportion to its significance, as an indication of Britain's pacifist decadence that could only encourage the dictators. It was, in fact, an expression of loyalty to world peace, rather than an active act of disloyalty, and proved a very poor prediction of how Oxford students acted when war did come in 1939. *AJC*

Kinnock, Neil Gordon (1942–), Labour Party leader and European commissioner. Kinnock was born and bred in the mining and Labour Party culture of Gwent, and had characteristically taken a degree in industrial relations (and history) at Cardiff (where he was also active in student politics, already committed to a political career). He then devoted himself to the workers' educational association, and by 1970, was already in the Commons, representing the rock-solid Labour seat of Bedwellty, as he continued to do until 1995 (it was renamed Islwyn in 1983). His early parliamentary performances were clearly on the left-wing and unilateralist side of the parliamentary debate, and he was rarely to be seen without a Campaign for Nuclear Disarmament badge. Such men rarely got promoted at that time, and indeed his only office in the Wilson–Callaghan governments of 1974–9 was a short period as Michael Foot's parliamentary private secretary in 1974–5, though he was also seen as enough of a coming man to be elected to the party's NEC in 1978.

All this changed in 1979, when Labour went into both opposition and a spiral to the left, several of its most talented front-benchers either retired or left the party for the Social Democratic Party (SDP), and Kinnock's patron Michael Foot became party leader. He entered the shadow cabinet, holding the education portfolio, 1979–83, a keen but not always effective critic of the Thatcher government's education policies (see Carlisle, Mark). He was, though, a staunch advocate of the party's leftist policies up to and including the 1983 election campaign, and when Labour then lost very heavily indeed and clearly needed to make a new start with a leader much younger than Foot (perhaps one who could sustain opposition through several parliaments), Kinnock was the popular choice. He thus became leader of his party at the age of 41.

If, however, the left had expected that Kinnock would carry on where Foot left off, they were to be cruelly disappointed, and the signs had in fact been there to be seen for some years. Kinnock was one of the leading 'soft left' MPs who switched their support from Tony Benn to Denis Healey in 1980 and enabled Healey just to win the deputy leadership, having decided that Benn in a position of authority would send all the wrong signals to the voters. Now leader, he faced the logic of that earlier choice, with the added evidence of the 1983 electoral disaster there for all to see. With his deep, fundamentalist loyalty to the Labour movement (rather than to its policies), and with an unshakeable conviction that Labour just had to claw its way back to power in order to protect those who depended on it, he set out to pull the party back from the brink of disaster. In 1983, Labour had polled only slightly ahead of the Liberals, and it was at least possible (though far from likely) that Labour would fall through the electoral trapdoor into third place next time, and minor-party status. Perhaps the most that could be done was to consolidate Labour's second place, as indeed he did in 1987, but these were difficult years within the party, with the London left, the Liverpool Militants, and Arthur Scargill's striking miners of 1984–5 all diverting attention away from Kinnock's steady pull on the party in the direction of good sense and sanity. He was still not, though, a very effective parliamentarian, letting Thatcher off the hook over the *Westland affair by asking far too many questions (and thus allowing her the choice of which to answer) and more generally tending to use a couple of paragraphs whenever a sentence would have done better. The deadly soubriquet 'the Welsh windbag', much used by the tabloid press, had its element of truth.

Having secured second place in 1987, Kinnock moved more positively to establish a firm hold on the party in the years 1987–92, expelling Militants, shifting the party's policy rightwards on defence, public spending, and privatization, in a series of stealthy stages. He also sought to project himself as prime ministerial material, wearing double-breasted suits, travelling in large black cars, and more generally submitting to the electors' expectations of a national leader, as revealed to him by Peter *Mandelson. The general election of 1992 was thus a cruel let-down, for although Labour fought an excellent, united campaign, and the polls—even the *exit polls on election day—prophesied a Labour win, John Major managed stubbornly to turn the tide over the final few days and retain a small Conservative majority. Though claims that Kinnock, 'the Welsh boyo', had thrown it, through his prematurely triumphalist behaviour at a pre-election rally in Sheffield, were far from the point, the polling evidence did suggest that Kinnock himself was now a liability; voters did not like his baldness and his verbosity (some indeed did not like his Welshness either), and many felt that he had shifted so many policy positions over the years that they did not know what to think about his real beliefs.

In any case, he would have been bound to stand down after nine such gruelling years, and Labour clearly needed the very different public images of John Smith and Tony Blair in order to complete its comeback (though neither could have succeeded in what they did for their party without Kinnock's decade of preparatory spadework). He was, however, still only 50, and needed a second career, finding it by following his wife Glenys (already an MEP) to Brussels, on his appointment as a European commissioner in 1995. There he seems to have flourished, doing very respectably with difficult portfolios, inspiring enough trust among his fellow commissioners to be given the crucial task of cleaning up the commission's own act after it was forced to resign collectively amid charges of corruption and nepotism. *JAR*

Eileen Jones, *Neil Kinnock* (London, 1994).

Kirk. See Church of Scotland.

Kirk, Peter Michael (1928–77), Conservative politician. Elected to parliament in 1955, Kirk was army minister, 1963–4, and navy minister, 1970–2. He believed passionately in European unity and was appointed by Heath in 1973 to lead the first delegation of Conservatives to the *European parliament. In his maiden speech, Kirk urged Strasbourg to become more effective by adopting Westminster procedures such as question time. He was a keen advocate of direct elections to the European parliament. *RJS*

Kirkpatrick, Ivone Augustine (1897–1964), diplomat. Kirkpatrick entered the Foreign Office in 1919, served in the British embassy at Berlin, 1933–8, and later as wartime controller of the BBC's European services. Authoritarian, combative, and incisive, he was high commissioner in Germany, 1950–3, and, after his return to London as permanent secretary at the Foreign Office, 1953–7, he became closely identified with Anthony Eden's style and outlook during the 1956 Suez crisis. *KAH*

Ivone Kirkpatrick, *The Inner Circle* (London, 1959).

Kirkwood, David (1872–1955), trade union activist, leading figure on Clyde Workers' committee, and Labour MP. Born and raised in Glasgow, Kirkwood left school at the age of 12 and eventually completed an engineering apprenticeship in 1892. He was an active member of the Amalgamated Engineering Union and was dismissed from Beardmore's engineering works in 1895 for involvement in a strike. After a series of jobs elsewhere, he returned to Beardmore's in 1910 and by 1914 was chief shop steward, helping to ensure a closed shop for skilled workers in the company. Just before the Great War, he became a member of the Socialist Labour Party but switched very quickly to the Independent Labour Party (ILP) to further his opposition to the war. In 1915, he became treasurer of the Clyde Workers' committee, formed to challenge industrial conscription and dilution. He was arrested in 1916 following strikes at Beardmore's and deported to Edinburgh until May 1917. He contested Dumbarton for the ILP in the 1918 general election. The following year, for his part in the disturbances in George Square, Glasgow, he was arrested but subsequently found not guilty. The same year, he became a Labour councillor in Glasgow. As part of the famous 'Red Clydesiders' contingent of Scottish Labour MPs, he was elected for Dumbarton in 1922. He opposed the ILP disaffiliation from the Labour Party in 1932 and resigned in 1933 to join the Labour Party. He held his seat through the 1930s and 1940s, although his later interventions in parliament were relatively few. His autobiography, *My Life of Revolt*, was published in 1935. He was awarded a peerage in 1951, becoming Baron Kirkwood of Bearsden. He was a lifelong teetotaller, a strong Presbyterian, and a supporter of Scottish nationalism. *KJL*

W. Knox (ed.), *Scottish Labour Leaders, 1918–1939* (Edinburgh, 1984).

Kitchener of Khartoum, Earl (1850–1916), general, imperial proconsul, and cabinet minister. Most of Herbert Kitchener's military career was spent on imperial service. In the 1880s he was successively governor-general of the eastern Sudan, adjutant-general of the Egyptian army, and from 1889 for ten years sirdar (commander-in-chief) of that force. In 1898, having won the battle of Omdurman, he was appointed governor-general of the Sudan. He served in the high command during the *Boer war of 1899–1902, where he was widely held responsible for the ruthless scorched-earth tactics which eventually broke the Boer resistance. He was commander-in-chief of the Indian Army, 1902–9, where he introduced some much-needed reforms, but also drove the viceroy Lord Curzon to resignation after a bitter row over their respective military and civilian spheres of influence. On the outbreak of the Great War in August 1914 (shortly after he had been appointed British agent and consul-general in Egypt) Kitchener was made secretary of state for war. His greatest success in office was to persuade the nation that the war would not be 'over by Christmas' and that Britain would therefore require a large-scale army on a Continental scale. The famous recruiting poster, 'Your Country Needs You', on which he featured, strikingly contributed to the mass mobilization required for modern war. But he was a wretchedly bad politician. Accustomed to having his own way as an autocratic imperial proconsul, he had contempt for civilian politicians and the needs of a democratic system. By the time he was drowned at sea in 1916, travelling to Russia on a war mission, his cabinet colleagues were seriously considering how to remove him from office without damaging the government's reputation, for the public still held him in the highest esteem. Margot Asquith cruelly remarked that Kitchener might not have been a great man, but he made a great poster. *KJ*

TREVOR ROYLE, *The Kitchener Enigma* (London, 1985).

Klugmann, (Norman John) James (1912–77), Communist. Throughout his working life Klugmann was an influential ideologist within British communism. He was head of the Communist Party of Great Britain's education department, 1959–60; editor of *Marxism Today*, 1963–77; and author of the authorized *History of the Communist Party of Great Britain* (1968–9). Prior to this post-war activity he had been born into a wealthy Jewish family in Hampstead, educated at Gresham's School, Norfolk, and Cambridge, and had worked abroad in the communist interest before a wartime career spent largely in the Intelligence Corps and Special Operations Executive. *CH*

J. KLUGMANN, *From Trotsky to Tito* (London, 1951).

Knapp, James (1940–), trade unionist. Jimmy Knapp was an old-style Scottish-born trade union leader and staunch opponent of rail privatization who became general secretary of the National Union of Railwaymen (NUR), 1983–90, and held the same post in its successor, the Rail, Maritime, and Transport Union. Knapp worked his way up through the ranks of the railway industry, from signalman and branch secretary for the NUR through the regional office of the west of Scotland to NUR headquarters. He became a member of the TUC general council and of the International Transport Federation executive board, 1983. *DMM*

Knollys, Francis (1837–1924), private secretary to Edward VII, 1901–10, and joint private secretary with Lord Stamfordham to George V, 1910–13. He came to the household, like many private secretaries, via family connections. Knollys began as the prince of Wales's private secretary in 1870. He managed the prince's trip to India in 1875, the first visit of a future king to the Indian subcontinent, and allied with Lord Esher to ensure that Whitehall departments produced more information for the palace under Edward VII than had been the case under Victoria. He resigned over political tensions with Stamfordham and George V, who both resented Knollys's advice that the king should provide the Liberal government with guarantees to ensure the passage of the Parliament Act in 1911. Like Henry Ponsonby, Victoria's longest-serving private secretary, Knollys combined friendliness to Liberal political reforms with his management of an ancient institution. This was key to the monarchy's survival in the early decades of the 20th century. *WMK*

Korean war (1950–3). British and Commonwealth soldiers and sailors fought alongside other UN forces to defend the Republic of Korea (ROK) against North Korean and subsequently Chinese troops. The British people had little reason to be sympathetic towards the Koreans who had provided some of the most vicious guards holding British prisoners in Malaya during the Second World War. Furthermore, Attlee's Labour government had no liking for the ROK government in Seoul but, once the USA committed itself to fight under the UN flag against the Northern attack, Attlee and his colleagues felt bound to give them support. They believed that the lesson of the 1930s was that aggression anywhere had to be resisted and they wanted American help in the event of a Soviet attack in Europe. If their long-term aim was to ensure US support outside Korea, their short-term objective was to encourage the Americans to limit the war to the peninsula itself and not expand it into another world war involving China and the Soviet Union. They saw Britain as exercising a restraining influence on the Truman and Eisenhower administrations in Washington. In fact their desire to limit the war was shared by US leaders, although they sometimes differed on the way this should be achieved.

Despite the impoverishment of the country in the Second World War, which meant that rationing was still in force, and the colonial struggles the British were waging in Malaya and elsewhere, ships and troops were quickly rushed to the Korean peninsula where hostilities began on 25 June 1950. On 2 July British frigates were in action against North Korean gunboats and the following day the aircraft carrier *Triumph* launched its aircraft against North Korean targets. Although Turkey and other states sent forces to join the UN in Korea, the British Commonwealth contribution to the war became the largest after that provided by the USA itself. The 27th Brigade was sent to Korea from Hong Kong in August 1950 and Britain's only reserve, the 29th Brigade, followed. Altogether, over the next three years, 32 Royal Navy warships participated in the war, firing tens of thousands of shells against communist shore targets. British carriers launched over 20,000 sorties and formed the core of UN naval forces on the western side of the Korean peninsula. Commonwealth land and sea forces enhanced their reputation for professionalism and fighting power (see GLORIOUS GLOSTERS). These were particularly needed during the precipitous month-long retreat by UN forces down the peninsula when Chinese forces joined the war in November 1950.

The Korean war was the first occasion on which Britain had been so obviously involved in a war as a junior partner. Large as the Commonwealth contribution was from the British point of view, it was dwarfed by its American counterpart. Control of the war effort was exercised in Washington or by the UN commander, General MacArthur, not by London. Inevitably this caused some disagreements; Attlee made a famous visit to Washington in December 1950 to emphasize Britain's reluctance to see nuclear weapons used, even to stem the rout of UN forces. London was concerned in 1951 by what it considered the loose rein on which Washington was holding the domineering MacArthur and it encouraged the USA to overthrow the dictatorial ROK leader Syngman Rhee. There was also friction from time to time between US commanders in the field and the officers commanding the Commonwealth division, for example, over US insistence in 1952 that the UN should stage constant offensives in order to obtain prisoners, a tactic which the British commander General Cassels regarded as wasteful of lives.

Despite such disputes, the war can be regarded as a success for British policy. Communist aggression had been rebuffed, the domestic consensus between the main political parties in support of the war effort had been maintained, Britain had demonstrated support for the US, and the struggle had been limited to the Korean peninsula. The fear of communist aggression which Korea evoked also led to the transformation of NATO into a permanent military bureaucracy, locking the USA into the defence of Europe until the end of the Cold War. Unfortunately, it also led to a greater increase in British defence expenditure than the economy could stand after the buffeting it had received from six years of war against the Axis powers. The economic sacrifices made by the British people had to be set against political, diplomatic, and strategic success. *PAT*

CALLUM MACDONALD, *Britain and the Korean War* (London, 1990).

L

Labour, Ministry of. See Employment, Department of.

Labour and the Nation (1928), Labour policy document. Agreed at the Birmingham party conference, following a year's preparation, and aimed at the middle ground in British politics, this was largely the work of Ramsay MacDonald and R. H. Tawney. It made the gradualist case for a socialist commonwealth, including the public ownership of land, coal, power, and transport; control of the Bank of England; and improved social services, but shunned specific strategy or commitments for a future Labour administration. *JSS*

labour exchanges. In the late 19th century some voluntary bodies began to provide labour exchanges on a local basis. They also began to appear in various countries, most notably Germany. William *Beveridge, who was to be the principal architect of the British scheme, was impressed by their operation there on a visit in 1907. He was also struck by the need to offer an alternative to Labour calls for the 'Right to Work' more effective than the Unemployed Workman's Act, 1905, which he had been involved in administering. In his 1909 publication, *Unemployment*, he argued that the public works of the 1905 legislation could never be more than palliative. Instead, he argued that the solution lay in a better organization of the labour market through the introduction of exchanges. This would help the demand and supply side of the labour market to meet and smooth swings in labour demand. Beveridge, however, did not just see exchanges as devices to improve the efficiency of the labour market. He also felt that in the process they would provide a way of 'dispauperization' more humane, less costly, and more effective than that of the 'workhouse test'—the way of 'making the finding of work easy instead of merely making relief hard'. Not least, they would discourage the tendency in certain trades for employers to keep large armies of surplus casual labour available and instead allow labour to be allocated more efficiently. Meanwhile, his hope was that exchanges would also help to deal with the widespread problem of under-employment. Duly persuaded, Churchill introduced the necessary legislation in 1909, and the first 83 exchanges were opened the following February, whilst Beveridge was appointed as director of the new service. They were renamed employment exchanges in 1916. Beveridge, however, felt that they soon became diverted from the intention of organizing the labour market by the exigencies of war or unemployment relief. In 1973 the Employment and Training Act therefore sought to separate off the unemployment relief function, and replace employment exchanges with brighter, more user-friendly 'job centres' aimed at white-collar as well as manual workers. Whilst this arguably reflected the changing needs of an increasingly service-oriented economy, some critics nevertheless argued that the result was a greater distance from the needs of the long-term unemployed. *PPC*

'Labour isn't Working', Conservative slogan, used in 1978–9 when unemployment reached one million. It appeared on a Saatchi poster accompanying a photograph of a long, snaking, tasteful queue, supposedly of unemployed, actually Young Conservatives, and was much admired professionally. Further rising unemployment after the Conservatives took power in 1979 gave the slogan an unintended irony. *EP*

Labour Leader (1889–1922), newspaper. The *Labour Leader* began life as *Miner: A Journal for Underground Workers*, which was formed as a socialist paper, advocating state-owned railways and the eight-hour day, by Keir Hardie in 1887, the title being changed in February 1889. Hardie owned the paper until 1903, when it was then taken over by the Independent Labour Party. In 1922 it became the *New Leader* and, in 1946, the *Socialist Leader*. *KL*

Labour Party (1906–). The party was formally established in 1906, with Keir Hardie as its parliamentary chairman, just after the general election, emerging out of the *Labour Representation Committee formed in 1900. It replaced the Liberals as the progressive party of British politics and formed governments in 1924, 1929–31, 1945–51, 1964–70, 1974–9, and from 1997. It was in office for 24 years in the 20th century, or 24 years out of 70 since 1924. In effect, then, it has been the second major political party in Britain, next to the Conservatives, although it won its largest majority only in 1997 under the leadership of Tony Blair, one of the most enduring of its five leaders who have become prime minister and the first to win successive clear majorities. Nevertheless, the Labour Party was constantly faced with internal conflict throughout the century, in which there were arguments over the power of the trade unions, the nature of its socialism, its welfare state policies, and the extent to which it abandoned its past in search of support from 'middle England'. The party in 2000 was a long way from the party of 1906.

With 29, soon to be 30, MPs in 1906, Labour picked up more trade union support and began to appear as a serious political challenge for the progressive vote. Nevertheless, the years 1906–14 were ones in which the party supported Liberal governments. As such, there have been serious debates as to whether or not the party was developing as a political organization of the working class, on class grounds, or whether it was still the tail of the Liberal Party. Certainly many historians, such as Henry Pelling and Keith Laybourn, would argue that it had developed its political power substantially before 1914. However, others, particularly Trevor Wilson and Peter Clarke, suggest that Labour did not develop fully until the Great War, when the war experience and the Asquith–Lloyd George split broke the Liberal Party and provided the opportunity for Labour to emerge into the vacuum that this left. The problem with this interpretation, however, is that the Great War posed equally serious divisions within the Labour Party, and obliged its leader Ramsay MacDonald to resign.

Nevertheless, the war was clearly a turning point for Labour in many respects. The party joined the wartime coalition government in May 1915 and Labour leaders, such as Arthur Henderson, gained invaluable ministerial experience. Also, in 1918, Labour adopted a new constitution with the commitment to socialism, or the socialization of industry, entailed in its Clause 4. The reason for this has been debated, with some historians maintaining that it was a product of the need to sift between the variety of socialism on offer to distinguish it from the Liberal Party, while others suggest that it was not meant seriously or was a convenient umbrella under which most socialist and labour groups could gather. Whatever the reason, the adoption of Sidney Webb's *Labour and the New Social Order* (1918) document for the 1918 general election emphasized the extent of that commitment to a form of gradualist state socialism long supported by the Fabians. Although the party was now unified in its commitment to socialism, this did not bring immediate political success. Lloyd George's 'Coupon' Election of 1918 ensured that many Labour candidates faced a contest against a single Liberal or Conservative governmental candidate, rather than two separate candidates. As a result, Labour's vote, beneficially affected by the 1918 Representation of the People Act, increased enormously to 2.4 million (from 0.37 million in 1910) but its number of MPs was not far above the prewar level at 63. Yet in a further surge forward Labour almost doubled its vote by 1922, raised the number of its MPs to 142, and re-elected Ramsay MacDonald as leader. It also established a very strong position in urban local government, for example in Glasgow and in east London. In December 1923 Labour became the second largest party in the Commons, with 191 MPs and, because Baldwin was not able to gain an overall majority for his protectionist policies, formed a minority government in January 1924. Though it was replaced by another Conservative government in November, during its ten months in office it introduced helpful measures on housing, showed that Labour could actually govern, and was only ejected because of the loss of Liberal support.

Defeated in the 1924 general election, Labour was out of power until June 1929, when it formed a second minority government, supported by 288

MPs and scoring 8.4 million votes. Its political success came at a period of relative economic improvement, but the Wall Street crash of November, and the resulting collapse of economic demand throughout the world, shattered its hopes. There was a rapid rise in unemployment in Britain, from just over one million to more than three million. Committed to the gold standard and free trade, and to the financial orthodoxy of balancing the budget, it was clear that Philip Snowden, Labour's chancellor of the exchequer, would attempt to force expenditure cuts and deflate the economy. More radical measures, such as those from Oswald Mosley, were never close to getting government (or party) support. Pressure from the May committee's report on public finance, which appeared in July 1931, forced the issue of substantial cuts in government expenditure, including unemployment benefits. These were scaled down, but Snowden and MacDonald still forced the issue of a 10 per cent cut in unemployment benefits. After much discussion, this led to the split in the Labour cabinet (voting 11 to 9 in favour of the proposed cuts), its resignation, and the formation of a multi-party National Government on 24 August 1931, amid accusations of betrayal by MacDonald. Indeed, the Labour Party raised the charges of scheming and betrayal to the level of a myth which was endorsed by L. MacNeill Weir's book *The Tragedy of Ramsay MacDonald* (London, 1938), although these charges have been demolished by David Marquand in a more recent biography of MacDonald, where it is shown that MacDonald went to great lengths to try to get the Labour government to accept the public spending cuts in order to gain opposition support for its continuance. Nonetheless, very many Labour activists then and since have seen MacDonald simply as the betrayer of the party he had done so much to create.

The formation of the National Government was followed by Labour's disastrous general election performance in October 1931, when it was attacked by its recent leaders for offering *'Bolshevism run mad' and reduced to 52 MPs. Labour's defeat led to a reassessment of its position during the 1930s, which saw the emergence of the trade union movement, under Ernest Bevin, as a more powerful force and the commitment to socialist planning, under the guidance of Hugh Dalton and Herbert Morrison. The end product of this latter development was Labour's commitment to a limited programme of public ownership which eventually emerged in the policy document *Labour's Immediate Programme* (1937), which provided the basis of the post-war work of the Attlee Labour government. Attlee became leader in 1935, and, faced with the rising threat of European fascism, Labour moved from opposing all war to supporting rearmament. Labour also recovered some of its lost political ground, returning 154 MPs and 37.9 per cent of the vote, its highest up to that date, in the 1935 general election.

The Second World War brought Labour into Winston Churchill's wartime coalition government in 1940. Attlee, Bevin, Arthur Greenwood, Herbert Morrison, and other Labour leaders played a prominent part in that government. This may partly explain the rising opinion poll support for Labour from 1941–2 onwards, though there also seems to have been a widespread belief that Labour, rather than the Conservatives, would honour the government's collective commitment to full employment and avoid the horrendous unemployment problems of the 1930s. At the 1945 general election this led to Labour winning 393 seats, a Commons majority of 146, and almost twelve million votes. Attlee's two post-war Labour governments, of 1945–50 and 1950–1, were among the most hyperactive governments in British history. On the home front, Aneurin Bevan, minister of health, pushed through a National Health Service Act in 1946, which led to the foundation of the NHS in July 1948. This was achieved in the teeth of opposition from the doctors and the Conservatives. There was also a National Insurance Act, which drew upon the Beveridge report of 1942 in introducing a contributory system to deal with problems such as unemployment. Morrison also pressed forward the nationalization of about one-fifth of British industry, starting with the Bank of England, coal, and civil aviation in 1946. These developments were blighted by economic crisis in 1947, occasioned by a shortage of coal but amplified by the fact that under the terms of the American loan of 1946 Britain was obliged to make her currency convertible. There were also other economic crises, most obviously in 1949, when sterling had to be devalued. On the international front, Bevin, now foreign secretary, pushed forward with the creation of NATO in 1949 and Britain began to decolonize, starting with the granting of independence to India in 1947.

The 1950 general election reduced Labour's majority to six and the new government was marked by internal divisions. Most obviously, there was the clash between Hugh Gaitskell, the new chancellor of the exchequer, and Bevan, now minister of labour, over the introduction of prescription charges. Faced with this possibility, Bevan, with Harold Wilson and John Freeman, resigned from the government on 22 April 1951 and joined the Keep Left group which later became the basis of the Bevanites. In October, the Labour government was defeated by fifteen seats, despite recording 48.8 per cent of the vote, slightly more than the Conservatives. Labour now entered thirteen years of opposition during which there were major battles between its left and right wings. Bevan, and the Bevanites, responding to immediate issues, demanded a less confrontational policy in foreign affairs and more socialist measures. On the other hand, Attlee, Gaitskell, and Morrison were associated with Anthony Crosland, whose book *The Future of Socialism* (1956) suggested that Western capitalism had been transformed and that socialism did not need to be so committed to public ownership. Labour's defeat in the 1955 general election did not help matters and the splits became even more overt when Gaitskell replaced Attlee as leader in December 1955 during a period in which Bevan was almost expelled from the party. Subsequently, Bevan and Gaitskell appear to have agreed to put aside their differences in the hope that Labour would be returned to power again, although those hopes were dashed in 1959, when Labour lost even more ground to the Conservatives. This prompted Gaitskell to attempt, unsuccessfully, to remove Clause 4 from the party constitution at the 1959 conference. In 1960 he was defeated again when the party endorsed a resolution in favour of unilateral disarmament, though he succeeded in getting this modified to support multilateral disarmament in 1961.

Gaitskell died in 1963 and was replaced as leader by Harold Wilson who won the general election in October 1964, but with a majority of only four. The new government was committed to the use of science and technology to boost Britain's industrial performance and also set up a national board for prices and incomes and a comprehensive planning framework. Wilson strengthened his moves in this direction by winning the 1966 election with 363 seats and 48.7 per cent of the vote. Yet the newly formed Labour government was soon torn by internal differences as it faced balance-of-payments problems. Instead of the long-term planning it envisaged, it was riven apart with trade union militancy, industrial conflict, wage pressures, and eventually devaluation in November 1967. The abandonment of Barbara Castle's white paper *In Place of Strife* (1969), designed to reorganize industrial relations, did further damage to government credibility. Despite these problems, the Labour government of 1966–70 did have some achievements, most notably the expansion of both higher education and housing. Yet, although its position in the opinion polls improved, Labour was defeated in the general election of June 1970.

In opposition between 1970 and 1974, the party attempted to restore good relations with the TUC, forming the TUC–Labour Party Liaison Committee which discussed the social contract and endorsed Labour's *Programme for Britain*, adopted at the party conference in 1973. It suggested that trade unions would accept voluntary wage restraint in return for the redistribution of income and resources in Britain on an annual basis. Yet there was dissension elsewhere for there was deep division on the issue of Britain's entry into the European Community, with the left, the NEC, and the trade unions generally opposing entry whilst most Labour MPs supported it. Nevertheless, the economic problems of Edward Heath's governments, most particularly connected with the coal-mining dispute, led to Labour's return to power in the two general elections of 1974. Labour formed a minority government under Wilson in February 1974 and turned this into a tiny majority in the general election of October 1974. Yet by any standards the 1974–9 Labour administration was a disaster, though it did call a referendum in which the British people voted decisively in favour of remaining in the European Community. The 'social contract' arrangements collapsed as the Labour government was unable to deliver the industrial growth necessary for its part of the bargain, and as inflation and unemployment rose. Denis Healey, chancellor of the exchequer, obtained a loan from the IMF in 1976, underpinned by a similar amount of cuts in public expenditure. Matters got worse as the left and the Tribune group argued with the Manifesto group of the right on practically every issue of foreign and domestic policy. It was at this point, in March 1976, that Wilson retired and was succeeded by James Callaghan. Under his stewardship the party continued to lose MPs in parliamentary by-elections and, as a result, Labour was forced to operate a Lib-Lab pact in 1977–8, based on a Liberal-Labour consultative committee, in order to survive. This did not please the Labour left or the trade unions, while rising industrial conflict in 1978 and 1979, dubbed the 'winter of discontent' and dominated by public-sector strikes, ensured the defeat of the Labour government in the May 1979 general election.

Labour was in opposition for the next eighteen years as Margaret Thatcher and John Major attacked both the trade unions, with restrictive legislation, and the universality of a 'nanny' welfare state. During this period Labour fought three more general elections (1983, 1987, and 1992) in which its results, if not its campaigning, were so poor that many members doubted whether it would ever be returned to power again. Divisions within the party made matters much worse. Left and right fought over issues such as the mandatory reselection of sitting MPs, while electing the leader of the party was made a matter for the party as a whole, not just the Parliamentary Labour Party. In this adverse climate Callaghan resigned and was replaced by Michael Foot. In January 1981 the new electoral college arrangements were agreed at a special conference, whereby the unions gained 40 per cent of the vote, with the constituencies and the parliamentary party 30 per cent each. It was at this stage, when there were also debates over the role of Militant Tendency within the party, that some prominent right-wing Labour MPs broke away to form the Social Democratic Party. In disarray, Labour fought a disastrous general election in June 1983, when it obtained a mere 28 per cent of the vote. Election defeat led to Foot being replaced by Neil Kinnock who gradually improved the party's position and ran effective general election campaigns in 1987 and 1992 (despite Labour's defeat on both occasions). From 1983 onwards, relations with the unions were improved and the left's power within the party greatly undermined. It appeared that Labour could win the April 1992 general election but this again proved illusory, and on defeat Kinnock resigned almost immediately.

Labour's new leader was John Smith, who continued the processes of changing and modernizing the party that Kinnock had started. Smith, however, died in May 1994, to be replaced by Tony Blair who began to offer an approach that was described as *'New Labour', a 'third way' approach which maintained that both the state and private enterprise could contribute to Britain's economic and social recovery. As part of this process he forced the Labour Party to drop Clause 4 in 1994. An efficient and effective political leader with a very good rapport with the voters, Blair courted the support of the middle classes for Labour rather than the trade unions whose influence he further reduced. Under his leadership, the Labour Party won in May 1997 with the largest parliamentary majority any party has enjoyed since 1935 and easily won again in 2001. *KL*

P. F. Clarke, *Lancashire and the New Liberalism* (Cambridge, 1971). | Keith Laybourn, *The Rise of Labour: The British Labour Party, 1890–1979* (London, 1988). | Ross McKibbin, *The Evolution of the Labour Party, 1910–1924* (Oxford, 1974). | David Marquand, *Ramsay MacDonald* (London, 1977). | Lewis Minkin, *The Contentious Alliance: Trade Unions and the Labour Party* (Edinburgh, 1991). | Kenneth O. Morgan, *Labour People: Leaders and Lieutenants* (London, 1987). | Henry Pelling, *A Short History of the Labour Party* (10th edn., London, 1993). | Eric Shaw, *Discipline and Discord in the Labour Party: The Politics of Managerial Control in the Labour Party, 1951–1987* (Manchester, 1988).

Labour Party, National Executive Committee (NEC). Elected annually at the party conference the NEC acts as Labour's ruling body. It is currently made up of representatives from the constituency parties, the trade unions, socialist societies, and the women's section. The party treasurer is also a member as are the party leader and the deputy leader. But it was not always so. The Labour Party was formed in 1900 as the Labour Representation Committee before formally assuming its better known title in 1906. From the start, and throughout the century, it was run by an NEC, although its composition has changed dramatically. In 1900 it was composed of twelve members, five from the socialist societies (two for the Social Democratic Federation, two for the Independent Labour Party, and one for the Fabians) and seven trade union members. If two of the trade union members were socialists, which was true in its early years, then the socialists would have a majority on the NEC. It was this socialist-dominated body which ran the Labour Party through its early, pioneering years. However, the 1918 party constitution did much to change the balance of the party: the NEC was increased to 23 members, with thirteen seats allocated to the trade unions, five to constituency parties, four for women, and one to socialist organizations. There have been minor amendments over the years, but it was not until 1997 that the whole focus and importance of the NEC was altered.

Its composition and the method of the NEC's election were fundamentally altered by the *Partnership into Power* policy document, adopted at the 1997 party conference. This removed the formulation of policy from the conference, placing it into the hands of a 175-strong National Policy Forum. The composition and election of the NEC was drastically changed. The women's section was abolished and trade union representation reduced from seventeen to twelve, although six of these were to be women. Three places were to be reserved for the Labour government (nominated by the prime minister), three for MPs (elected by the Parliamentary Labour Party), and one for the leader of the Labour group in the European parliament. Six were set aside for representatives elected by postal ballot of all members. The idea seemed to be to move powers away from the NEC, to make it a more representative body of party opinion, and to reduce the powers of the trade unions. *KL*

Labour Party in Perspective, The **(1937)**, publication of the Left Book Club. Victor Gollancz invited the newly elected Labour Party leader Clement Attlee to contribute to his successful left-wing publications list. Attlee's account set the evolution of the Labour Party in its British context, proclaiming his belief in a peaceful transition to socialism, by the public ownership of all the major industries, as the only alternative to the evils of capitalism. His book received generally favourable reviews and was translated into several languages. *JSS*

Labour Party Liaison Committee, organization which linked the Parliamentary Labour Party, the party organization, and the members of a Labour government when the party is in office. The Liaison Committee replaces the shadow cabinet when Labour takes office, its membership including the chief whip, the leader of the Commons, and three elected members—the chair of the Parliamentary Labour Party and his two deputies. Its role has been to deal with disciplining the parliamentary party, for example dealing with backbench dissent on the Vietnam war during the 1964–70 Labour government. *BB*

Labour Representation Committee (LRC) (1900–6). The LRC was formed at a meeting at the Memorial Hall, Farringdon Road, London, on 27 February 1900. It resulted from the joint efforts of the trade unions, the cooperative societies, and socialist groups, such as the Independent Labour Party (ILP) and the Social Democratic Federation (SDF) who agreed to the amendment 'That this Conference is in favour of establishing a distinct Labour group in the House of Commons, who shall have their own whips', in order to promote legislation for the working classes.

The LRC was something of a political compromise. The Liberal-dominated Trades Union Congress was concerned at the threat to the legal position of trade unions in the 1890s. At its 1899 congress, it passed a resolution in favour of calling the meeting that led to the formation of the LRC, and about a quarter of the total trade union membership was represented, though mainly from newer unions of unskilled and semi-skilled workers. The ILP was also concerned to broaden its appeal given that it had effectively ruled out a fusion with the SDF or a return to the ranks of the Liberal Party. The SDF hoped to press its demands for the 'class war'. In the end, however, Keir Hardie of the ILP stressed the need to keep the trade unions on board and the new organization was determinedly independent rather than socialist. This much was ensured by its secretary, Ramsay MacDonald, also a member of the ILP, who saw the LRC as a progressive development from Liberalism.

The LRC was not certain of success but was pushed forward rapidly by a number of external circumstances. In the first case, Hardie was returned for Merthyr Tydfil in the 1900 general election and the LRC group of MPs had increased to four by the end of 1903. Secondly, the Taff Vale judgement, in which the railway companies successfully sought compensation for a strike by the Amalgamated Society of Railway Servants, made all trade unions liable to financial damages. This action drove many trade unions to affiliate with the LRC. Indeed, the affiliated membership rose from 350,000 in 1901 to 850,000 in 1903. By 1905, of the major unions, only the miners were not affiliated. Thirdly, MacDonald entered secret talks with the Liberal chief whip, Herbert Gladstone, which produced the *Lib-Lab pact (1903) which allowed both parties a free run against the Conservatives. As a result, 29 LRC candidates were returned in the general election of 1906. Shortly afterwards, the LRC officially became the Labour Party and Hardie was elected as leader of the Parliamentary Labour Party, defeating D. J. Shackleton by fifteen votes to fourteen. *KL*

Frank Bealey and Henry Pelling, *Labour and Politics, 1900–1906: A History of the Labour Representation Committee* (London, 1958). | Philip Poirier, *The Advent of the Labour Party* (London, 1958).

Labour Research Department (1918–24), formed in 1918, out of the Fabian research department, to establish an information and research section for the Labour Party. It was organized into four sections, which dealt with all sections of the Labour movement. However, its activities soon became redundant once the Labour Party and the TUC developed their own research structures. Another body with the same name has functioned in the post-war years, but working for trade unions rather than for the Labour Party. *KL*

Labour revisionism, ideological position in the British Labour Party in the 1950s. Associated with the ideas of Tony Crosland and the leadership of Hugh Gaitskell, revisionism was self-consciously modelled on the much earlier revision of Marxism by Eduard Bernstein and others. Their central position was that the ends of democratic socialism, equality, and social justice were more important than the means, social ownership and nationalization. Therefore any policy which worked and produced greater equality should be considered by the party and not just the policies which had been traditionally followed. In practice, the 1950s revisionists operated within tight ideological constraints which rejected nationalization but did not stray far from a traditional belief in economic intervention and state control. *BB*

Labour's Immediate Programme (1937), Labour policy document. Adopted at the Bournemouth party conference, it set out the priorities for a future Labour government. The proposals included the nationalization of the Bank of England (but not the joint-stock banks), energy and transport, the planning of land, assistance for the distressed areas, and support for the League of Nations and collective security. Mainly Hugh Dalton's work, this was the last instalment of Labour's policy making in the 1930s, setting the party on the path towards the Attlee government of 1945. *JSS*

'Lady's not for turning, The', slogan suggested by Ronald Millar or Alfred Sherman (some dispute), and used by Thatcher to tell the 1980 Conservative conference that she would not make the predicted U-turn on tight money and rising unemployment. Effective as a pun on the title of Christopher Fry's play *The Lady's not for burning.* *EP*

Laird, Gavin (1933–), trade unionist. After working in the Clydebank engineering industry and in the merchant navy, Laird went on to become an official of the Amalgamated Engineering Union and served as general secretary, 1982–94. He will chiefly be remembered as one of the principal architects of the more flexible and pragmatic policies adopted by much of the trade union movement in response to the industrial relations legislation of the Conservative governments of the 1980s. *PH*

Lakeman, Enid (1903–94), tireless propagandist for electoral reform, and in particular for the single transferable vote (STV). She started life as an industrial chemist, but from 1945 she devoted herself wholeheartedly to the cause of proportional representation. From 1960 to 1980 she served as secretary of the Proportional Representation Society (founded 1884, renamed the Electoral Reform Society in 1958). Her major work was *How Democracies Vote* (4th edn. 1974) but she also wrote incessant letters and articles for the press. She stood unsuccessfully as a Liberal at four parliamentary elections, and she campaigned vigorously in two Irish referenda in which it was sought to abolish the STV in which she so devoutly believed. She delighted in her OBE, awarded in 1980, claiming it as the only award ever offered for services to proportional representation. She left money for an annual lecture given at Royal Holloway, her old college. *DEB*

Lambert, George (1866–1945), Liberal politician. Lambert was MP for South Molton in Devon, 1891–1924 and 1929–45. He held junior office at the Admiralty, 1905–15, but thereafter devoted himself to the backbenches and to business interests. He was reluctant to choose sides when the Liberals split after 1916, and was thus a popular choice to chair the parliamentary Liberal Party, 1919–21, but could not arrest the growing strife between Liberals. In the later Liberal split of 1931, he became a Liberal National. *JAR*

Lambton, Viscount (1922–), Conservative politician and writer. Elected to parliament in 1951, Lambton was parliamentary private secretary to the foreign secretary, Selwyn Lloyd, but resigned in 1957. He was critical of Macmillan and helped Maudling's 1965 leadership bid. Heir to the earl of Durham, he disclaimed his peerages but continued to use his courtesy title as an MP. Lambton became Heath's RAF minister in 1970, but resigned and quit the Commons in 1973 after being photographed in bed with two women. *RJS*

'lame ducks', phrase referring to the Conservatives' apparently uncompromising intention in 1970 to let uncompetitive firms go to the wall. Contrary to widespread belief, Heath's trade and industry secretary, John Davies, qualified his pledge not to support failing industries both at the 1970 conference and a month later in the Commons when he mentioned 'lame ducks'. None the less the phrase stuck and made the government's U-turn in 1972 over support for

*Upper Clyde Shipbuilders very politically damaging. *RJS*

Lamont, Norman Stewart Hughson (1942–), Conservative politician and minister. After early involvement with the Bow Group, he was MP for Kingston-upon-Thames from 1972, junior minister at energy, industry, defence, and the Treasury, 1979–89, before reaching cabinet in 1989 as chief secretary. As a defence junior, caught in gridlock, he anxiously asked policemen to make him a way through traffic as 'I am the rote Minister responsible for the British Nuclear button'. He was in 1990 the manager of the Major campaign for party leader, rewarded with the Treasury, a nuclear button in its own right. Lamont took a high line against devaluation, but speculation intensified. He then imposed extremely high interest rates, deepening the recession, which led to house repossessions becoming commonplace, and businesses failing, notably in the south, ending in September 1992 after a few hours at a 15 per cent base rate. This financial crash destroyed Conservative credit for the decade, but Lamont, failing to accept blame (and credit for taking it), remained in office as his unpopularity grew, and drove Major to dismiss him. His resignation speech attacking Major as being 'in office, not in power' damaged the prime minister, but destroyed Lamont, for, when his Kingston seat was redistributed out of existence, he had to make a pilgrimage through constituencies that yielded nothing until at the last minute Harrogate came up, where a 16 per cent swing to the Liberals showed Nemesis kicking him when down. He then went to the Lords and remained an awkward presence in the party. *EP*

NORMAN LAMONT, *In Office* (London, 1999).

Lancaster House agreement (1979). This agreement, brokered by Margaret Thatcher's newly elected Conservative government, ended the *Rhodesian crisis and paved the way for black majority rule. In 1979 the situation in Rhodesia now favoured British intervention. War between the white regime and nationalist guerrillas was causing disruption throughout the region, and forced Zambia and Mozambique to withhold support from the guerrilla forces of the patriotic front, led by Robert Mugabe and Joshua Nkomo. White Rhodesians, meanwhile, no longer wished to fight for the black government which had recently been elected in Rhodesia under Bishop Abel Muzorewa, and in which Ian Smith still played an active part. All sides, therefore, now welcomed British mediation. As a result, Lord Carrington, the British foreign secretary, called a meeting of all concerned at Lancaster House in London.

The conference began on 10 September 1979 and Carrington was quickly able to isolate Smith by getting Muzorewa's agreement to end white control of the army and the public services. Then, he was able to work on the patriotic front, with Nkomo being more ready to compromise than Mugabe. First of all, he obtained their agreement that 20 per cent of seats in the new parliament should be reserved for whites. Mugabe was less inclined to accept this, but under pressure from his backers he finally acquiesced. Next, Carrington persuaded Muzorewa to stand down and agree to an interim period during which Britain once again took over Rhodesia. The patriotic front were then convinced to accept this with the promise that a lightly armed Commonwealth monitoring force would oversee forthcoming elections. Finally, it was agreed that Lord Soames would be appointed as governor to administer the transition period and organize a ceasefire. For Britain, the Rhodesian problem was virtually at an end. *KTS*

M. TAMARKIN, *The Making of Zimbabwe: Decolonization in Regional and International Politics* (London, 1990).

Land and the Nation (October 1925), the report of the Liberal 'Land Inquiry Committee' set up on the initiative of Lloyd George. Also known as the 'Green Book', it proposed a variety of measures of land reform but especially aroused controversy over its proposal to end the private ownership of agricultural land by converting farmers into 'cultivating tenants' under the supervision of county committees. Lloyd George founded the Land and Nation League to campaign on behalf of the Green Book in spite of evident opposition. With the Yellow Book on industry (see *BRITAIN'S INDUSTRIAL FUTURE*), it formed part of a raft of new policy initiatives undertaken and funded by Lloyd George in preparation for a renewed Liberal assault on power in the late 1920s. *JS*

land campaign, Liberal. Liberal concern over the rights of tenant farmers and small proprietors had its roots in 19th-century radicalism and anti-landlord feeling. This was compounded in the *Celtic fringe by religious antipathy to the payment of tithes to the Anglican Church by non-Anglicans. The disestablishment of the Anglican Church in Ireland and the campaign for the disestablishment of the *Church of Wales, were both expressions of this. Taxation of the estates of landed proprietors was increased in 1894 when graduated death duties on both real and personal property were introduced. *Lloyd George, influenced by his background in north Wales, took an early and prominent part in protecting the interests of small farmers and opposing tithes. In 1913, as chancellor of the exchequer, he followed the upheavals caused by his *'People's Budget' and the introduction of the *National Insurance Act, 1911, by launching a land campaign to appeal to rural workers in the run-up to a potential general election. Designed to offer greater security to tenants it was aborted by the outbreak of the Great War in August 1914. The land issue was, however, revived in the post-war coalition administration when Lloyd George was able to pass in August 1919 a Land Settlement Facilities Act for ex-servicemen. *JAR*

Roy Douglas, *Land, People and Politics: A History of the Land Question in the United Kingdom, 1872–1952* (London, 1976).

land conference, Irish (1902), an attempt to settle agrarian problems by negotiation between landlords and tenants. Partly successful, the episode also illustrated the Irish question's cross-currents and complexities. Captain John Shawe-Taylor, a landlord, first suggested a conference in September 1902. Irish landowners, conscious of their diminished influence, especially following the Local Government Act of 1898, were keen to regain the initiative. George Wyndham, Irish chief secretary, was anxious to allay agrarian discontent, and was concerned also at landlord–tenant divisions within Ulster's Protestant community. Among leading nationalists, William O'Brien was particularly enthusiastic. Meeting in December 1902, the conference rapidly reached agreement on the basis that British Treasury loans and subsidies should fund what would prove to be the largest single piece of land purchase legislation, the Irish Land Act passed in 1903. All this exposed significant differences within the Irish Parliamentary Party, which would otherwise become increasingly apparent. Agrarian radicals like Michael Davitt deprecated any bargain with landlordism. John Dillon opposed cooperation with unionists, and anyway feared his party's marginalization once Irishmen of opposing views found it possible to reach agreement independently. O'Brien, however, saw the latter as the way forward, and increasingly distanced himself from erstwhile close associates like Dillon. *DRB*

Andrew Gailey, *Ireland and the Death of Kindness: The Experience of Constructive Unionism, 1890–1905* (Cork, 1987).

land settlement as a political issue had its roots in late 19th-century concerns over the pace of industrialization and the perceived imbalance between rural and urban populations. It was advocated in the 20th century both as a remedy for unemployment and as a means of increasing social cohesion in an era when many feared the rise of class-based urban politics. During the Edwardian period, the Small Holdings and Allotments Act, 1907, provided county councils with powers to purchase land for lease to tenants. Following the Great War, the Lloyd George coalition took up the idea as part of its reconstruction programme, and, under the terms of the Land Settlement Act, 1919, attempts were made to establish ex-servicemen on smallholdings. Despite the marked failure of these attempts the onset of the 1930s Depression gave renewed life to the issue with many major figures, including Baldwin and MacDonald, advocating settlement as a remedy for unemployment. The failure of Lloyd George's 'New Deal' campaign of 1935, which included a grandiose plan for placing half a million of the workless on the land, effectively marked the end of land settlement as a major political issue. *WF*

land taxes have been levied in Britain since the end of the 17th century, but were largely superseded as a revenue source in the mid-19th century by income tax and excise duties. Death duties were first introduced on property and goods (including therefore land) in 1894 by Sir William Harcourt. As part of the *'People's Budget', David *Lloyd George also proposed a duty of 20 per cent on the unearned increment of land value, payable on the transfer of the property. The 'unearned increment' was the increase in the value of land which could not be directly attributed to the work of the owner. Of all the measures proposed in the 1909 'People's Budget', it aroused the most controversy amongst the landed opposition entrenched in the House of Lords, leading to their rejection of the budget and provoking the constitutional crisis of 1910–11.

Death duties were subsequently increased in the course of the century on all property left at death. They have often been seen as a major contributory cause of the decline and break-up of the greater, and even more the lesser, landed estates, as sudden demands for capital payments could often only be met by sale of the property itself (on a very grand scale in 1919–21 for example). In 1975, what were formerly known as estate or death duties were replaced by capital transfer tax, subsequently known as inheritance tax. Tax is charged at a single rate of 40 per cent above a threshold (£231,000 in 1999–2000) with exemptions. Approximately 3 per cent of all estates become liable for inheritance tax. *JS*

Lane, Geoffrey Dawson (1918–), judge. After war service in the RAF, Lane was called to the Bar in 1946, becoming recorder of Bedford, 1963. He was a judge of the High Court, Queen's Bench Division, 1966–74, in the Court of Appeals, 1974–9, and a lord of appeal in ordinary, 1979–80, before becoming lord chief justice, 1980–92. On retirement he was not mourned as one of Britain's greatest jurists. *JAR*

Lane-Fox, George Richard (1870–1947), Conservative politician. MP for Barkston Ash, 1906–31, Lane-Fox was a moderate Conservative with a main interest in agriculture. He seconded the motion for the *Carlton Club meeting which destroyed the coalition and ended Austen Chamberlain's leadership, his support for the motion helping convince a number of waverers. He was minister for mines, 1922–4 and 1924–8, during a turbulent period in industrial history that culminated in the General Strike, and a member of the Simon commission, 1928–30, on India. *NJC*

Lang, Ian Bruce (1940–), Conservative politician. Privately sparkling former Cambridge footlight, publicly subdued and heliophobic, as a whip Lang formed ties with John Major. As a Scottish Office junior loyal to Rifkind, he became a Thatcher anxiety object, problems exacerbated by Michael Forsyth. Lang was secretary of state from 1990, an undeviating Unionist and entirely loyal to Major, a quiet, orthodox Tory who enjoyed interim triumph in Scotland after escaping the predicted disaster of 1992. He transferred to trade in 1995, but was engulfed by the Wagnerian election of 1997, consuming all Scottish Tory seats in fire. *EP*

Lansbury, George (1859–1940), Labour politician and Christian pacifist. Lansbury is mainly remembered as the 76-year-old pacifist who resigned the Labour leadership after the 1935 Brighton conference, following Ernest Bevin's savage speech accusing him of hawking his conscience around in public. However, he was for decades a major politician on the left of 20th-century politics, whose greatest contribution to democratic politics was his spirited leadership of 46 opposition Labour MPs after the Labour nadir of 1931. In his diary Hugh Dalton criticized Lansbury's ineffectiveness, but underestimated his part in maintaining Labour morale. Lansbury was always identified with the deprived East End of London, where the family home was a political haven to all. No politician was associated with as many causes or as deeply revered among ordinary people. He held every municipal office: councillor, county councillor, magistrate, and poor-law guardian, but sought neither wealth nor social status.

After a grim experience emigrating in 1884–5, Bessie and George Lansbury returned from Australia with their young family, and eventually took over the family timber business. He was first attracted to Gladstonian Liberalism, but a valuable party agent (who masterminded three election victories) was lost when he finally departed to the Social Democratic Federation (SDF) in 1892. Marxist ideas had brought disenchantment with Liberal capitalism and a conversion to socialism. For ten years he lost his Christian faith and joined the ethical movement in London, travelled widely as SDF national organizer and stood for parliament. A member of the royal commission on the poor laws, 1905–9, he contributed to the famous minority report. Moving to the Independent Labour Party and finally the new Labour Party, he became MP for Bow and Bromley, 1910–12 and 1922–40. On entering the Commons, he soon rebelled against Labour subservience to the Asquith government, but his resignation to force a suffragette by-election in 1912 cost him his seat. In the same year, Lansbury, whose socialism was derived from his simple Christian faith, became chairman of the Church Socialist League. With Ben Tillett, he launched the rebel *Daily Herald* and kept it alive as editor. Another venture was *Lansbury's Labour Weekly*, which supported the General Strike. Lansbury suffered imprisonment twice for his political beliefs, in 1913 for a suffrage speech and during the 1921 Poplar rates rebellion when the 30 Poplar councillors were committed to prison. In 1924 Ramsay MacDonald excluded Lansbury from his first Labour cabinet, on George V's objection, but made him first commissioner for works in 1929. The energetic Lansbury popularized the royal parks and created 'Lansbury's lido' on the Serpentine. He was in the minority of Labour cabinet ministers not prepared to accept the 10 per cent benefit cut that ended the government. He did, however, save his seat when so many of the front bench were defeated in 1931, and hence became party leader until 1935.

With his large frame, kind face, and white side-whiskers, George Lansbury was an instantly recognizable figure and a charismatic public speaker. He was staunchly anti-imperialist, associated with the Indian home rule movement, and spent his final years in peace crusades, including visits to Hitler and Mussolini in 1937. *JSS*

Jonathan Schneer, *George Lansbury* (Manchester, 1990).

Lansdowne, 5th marquess of (1845–1927), Conservative minister. Born into a great Liberal family with large holdings in Ireland, Lansdowne gravitated into alliance with the Conservatives along with the other Liberal opponents of Gladstone's home rule policy after 1886. He had served in junior office under Russell and Gladstone and as governor-general of Canada, 1883–8, and Indian viceroy, 1888–94, before entering Salisbury's cabinet as war secretary, 1895–1900. Though something of a scapegoat for the early failures in the Boer war, he then took over the Foreign Office, 1900–5, and in this post he played a significant role under Salisbury and Balfour in the reorientation of British foreign policy away from isolation, negotiating the Anglo-Japanese treaty (1902) and the *entente cordiale* with France (1904). Following the electoral debacle of 1906, as opposition leader in the Lords, Lansdowne commanded the massive Unionist majority which fought against home rule and emasculated the Liberal legislative programme. This policy led to the constitutional crisis of 1909–11, and consequently to the Parliament Act which for ever broke the power of the upper house. Lansdowne enthusiastically supported war in 1914 and, when Asquith formed his coalition in 1915, he accepted office as minister without portfolio. Distressed by the desire of Lloyd George and the Conservative ministers to press the war to final victory, he circulated a controversial cabinet memorandum in November 1916, outlining his anxiety that only a negotiated peace could prevent the collapse of European society and the triumph of Bolshevism. He took no part in the Lloyd George coalition government, and in November 1917 published in the press a call for a compromise peace and suffered repudiation by his party and former cabinet colleagues. From this controversy his reputation never fully recovered; he remained divided from many political friends, and his public life was at an end. *RJQA*

Lord Newton, *Lord Lansdowne: A Biography* (London, 1929).

Larne gun-running. See gun-running.

Lascelles, Alan Frederick ('Tommy') (1887–1981), private secretary to George VI, 1943–52, and Elizabeth II, 1952–3. He started in royal service as assistant private secretary to the prince of Wales in 1920 and travelled extensively with him, Lascelles's published letters showing him to have been increasingly disenchanted with the prince's carousing on tour. By the time of his accession as Edward VIII, Lascelles had lost any influence he once had. Under George VI, however, he had more productive years and founded the first press office at Buckingham palace. He also commissioned the first informal biography of George V and helped George VI prevent the duke of Windsor from returning to England after the abdication. They both feared that the former Edward VIII would steal the limelight from his younger, shyer brother. This rearguard action absorbed more time and energy than it should have, but is characteristic of the family dispute which was mistakenly assumed by the palace to present grave constitutional issues, and which private secretaries have to manage as a larger part of their daily business. *WMK*

Duff Hart-Davis (ed.), *End of an Era, Letters and Journals of Sir Alan Lascelles from 1887 to 1920* (London, 1986). | Duff Hart-Davis *Letters and Journals of Sir Alan Lascelles from 1920 to 1936* (London, 1989).

Laski, Harold (1893–1950), political theorist and socialist intellectual. *Studies in the Problem of Sovereignty* (1917) and *Authority in the Modern State* (1919) were completed while in North America, 1914–20, and quickly established Laski's reputation as a pluralist thinker, who favoured extensive decentralization. As an academic at the LSE from 1920 (as professor from 1926), he became convinced that firm state action was necessary to bring about radical change, and he tried to attain a synthesis between this position and pluralism in *A Grammar of Politics* (1925). By now he was actively involved in the Labour Party, but the failure of the Labour government of 1929–31, and the rise of fascism in Europe eroded his optimism about the possibility of peaceful change, and he subsequently adopted a form of Marxism. In 1936 he was a founder of the Left Book Club and in 1937 was elected to the NEC of the Labour Party (where he was to remain until 1949). In September 1939 he was committed to the war, but also saw it as an opportunity for radical change in both domestic and international policies. In June 1945, as chairman of the Labour Party, he publicly announced that Attlee should not be bound by any agreements made by Churchill at Potsdam. Attlee immediately rejected this demand and Laski became the *bête noire* for the Conservatives throughout the election campaign. His position was now substantially weakened and his isolation was reinforced at the end of 1946 when he lost a libel case against the allegation that he had advocated violent revolution. Laski wrote too much, and overestimated his influence. But he was a charismatic personality, an inspiring teacher, and a serious thinker who attempted to combine socialist analysis with liberal values.

MDN

Isaac Kramnick and Barry Sheerman, *Harold Laski: A Life on the Left* (London, 1993). | Kingsley Martin, *Harold Laski, 1893–1950: A Biographical Memoir* (London, 1953). | Michael Newman, *Harold Laski: A Political Biography* (Houndmills, 1993).

Law, Andrew Bonar (1858–1923), Conservative politician. Britain's only prime minister born outside the country, Law was born in New Brunswick, the son of an Ulster-born Presbyterian minister of Scottish stock. As a young child, his mother died and his father remarried; but his opportunities were immeasurably increased when he was brought to Glasgow by his mother's relatives, prosperous merchants without heirs. Carefully educated for a life in commerce, by his thirty-fifth birthday Law was a major factor in the booming Glasgow iron trade. His goal, however, was a political career, and by 1900 he was rich enough to indulge his ambition: in the 'Khaki' Election he won Glasgow, Blackfriars for the Conservatives. Law, despite financial security, a happy marriage and six children, and a successful political career, had to bear more than his share of personal loss. Like his mother, his beloved wife Annie died suddenly in 1909, after seventeen years of marriage, while two sons were killed in the Great War. Melancholy by nature, he struggled throughout his life against the terrible burden of depression. Beyond the love of family and close friends, he took little solace in the usual pleasures: he refused all honours, lived simply and abstemiously, and went out into society only when absolutely necessary. His pipe, tennis, golf, bridge, reading, and good conversation were his pleasures. He was happiest when surrounded by his children. Otherwise, he worked without stint, and work above all saw this grave man through his personal trials. He supported tariff reform and soon gained notice for his well-argued speeches on economic matters; this earned him junior office under Balfour 1902–5. After the Unionist debacle of 1906, he found a safe seat in Dulwich, and his star rose among the small opposition contingent in the Commons. Among his disheartened party, Law's hard and telling blows against the government marked him out as a fighting man when fighting men were needed.

Unionist Leader

Law's party loyalty and courage led him in December 1910 to accept the challenge of contesting a Manchester constituency, where his narrow and gallant defeat won him more Unionist admiration, he accurately concluded, than could a hundred victories. When Balfour resigned as leader in November 1911, Law, then MP for Bootle, took Balfour's place when the better-known aspirants, Austen *Chamberlain and Walter *Long, deadlocked. His commitment to tariff reform caused a serious setback in 1912, when he attempted to abandon Balfour's pledge, once in office, to hold a referendum before installing a tariff programme. A nervous party fought shy, and he backed down. The tariff question, however, was soon pushed aside by another which would for ever be linked with his name, the renewed battle against home rule, and his fighting skills were needed.

The Parliament Act had rendered it impossible for the Unionist-controlled Lords to stop home rule as in 1893. Law, the Ulsterman's son, planned a dangerous campaign to harry the bill at each step and to support the Ulster Unionists in their campaign of resistance against it. He fought his hand with a harsh and partisan ferocity seldom equalled in parliamentary history and has been much criticized for it. His reasons were several: he believed absolutely that Protestant Ulster would never accept subordination to a Dublin parliament; second, repeatedly favourable by-elections convinced him that if a general election could be forced on a reluctant government, the Unionists would prevail; and third, that by showing an unbending public stance while offering private consideration of compromise, he could force the government to retreat from their resistance to permanent exclusion of Ulster from home rule. The Great War intervened, however, but the Irish settlement reached in 1921 provided for Ulster exclusion, and Law supported it.

The Liberal government persevered for the first ten months of war, but in Asquith's May 1915 coalition Law accepted the Colonial Office, an appointment well beneath his status as Unionist leader. Over the next eighteen months, he came to share with his old adversary Lloyd George the conviction that the conflict had to be prosecuted with more ruthless energy if victory was expected. In December 1916, the two cooperated in displacing Asquith in favour of a war cabinet under Lloyd George and formed a political partnership unlike any other in the 20th century. Law became chancellor of the exchequer and parliamentary anchor of the new coalition, his reputation as a partisan warrior exchanged for that of political conciliator and statesman. The demands of his position taxed his health, and the stunning loss of his two eldest sons in combat in 1917 severely tried his spirit, but he struggled on and played a fundamental part in the ultimate victory—and his reputation accordingly soared.

The 'Unknown Prime Minister'

In 1918 when war ended, Law believed that if the socialism which he distrusted were to be staved off, then the Lloyd George coalition had to continue into the immediate future. Thus, he loyally supported continuing the government, dependent after the 1918 election largely on Tory MPs. Yet he never ceased believing in the supreme importance of an independent Conservative party. Consequently, though poor health forced his retirement in 1921, he improbably returned to centre stage in 1922 to lead the backbench revolt against a further prolongation of the coalition. At the *Carlton Club on 19 October, he reluctantly came out against his former partner, Lloyd George, and most of the official party leadership, calling for an independent Conservative effort at the next election. He thus at last became prime minister and led the party to victory in the 1922 general election, though it was a rather sad anticlimax. His health was broken, and he was an undistinguished premier for only a few months. He retired finally in May and died in October 1923. Though Asquith jibed that he was 'the unknown Prime Minister', Law's government became the training ground for a generation of Conservative ministers, and his monument was a party repeatedly elected by the people to rule Britain for most of the century. *RJQA*

R. J. Q. Adams, *Bonar Law* (London, 1999). | Robert Blake, *The Unknown Prime Minister: The Life and Times of Andrew Bonar Law, 1858–1923* (London, 1955). | John Ramsden, *The Age of Balfour and Baldwin, 1902–1940* (London, 1978).

Law, Richard Kidston **(1901–80)**, Conservative politician. Son of prime minister Andrew Bonar *Law, he entered parliament in 1931. He became an unremarkable backbencher, although he opposed the 1938 Munich agreement and then held ministerial office during the Churchill wartime government. His debating skills were limited, and he proved ineffective at opposing Labour over the National Health Service Act, but after 1945 became a leading Conservative 'intellectual' figure (author, as Lord Coleraine, of *For Conservatives Only*, 1970) and helped influence a whole generation of the party towards the right. *NJC*

law and order. The second half of the century saw a considerable increase in crime, a growing debate about policing, and an increasing tendency for politicians to urge tougher measures against lawbreakers during their campaigns for election. It was not always thus: in the general elections of the 1920s, parties had little to say about policing in their manifestos, and when law and order was debated at all it was in the context of subversion of law-abiding Britain by alien political creeds such as fascism and communism. There was from the 19th century onwards a difference of philosophical approach between the parties, with Conservatives placing more emphasis on the state's duty to maintain order and to punish offenders, Liberals (and subsequently Labour) concerned to prevent the infringement of civil rights by an overenthusiastic use of the police and the legal processes, and to secure recognition that crime often arose from social deprivation. That different emphasis became more marked when crime and fears for the public's safety both increased after 1945. For humanitarian reformers on the left, the removal of what were seen as barbaric penalties, capital and corporal punishment, were key causes in the 1950s, and both were achieved by the end of the 1960s, while to the right this would remove deterrents to violent crime. Although such reforms passed through parliament on unwhipped votes, they were mainly carried on Labour votes and against the objections of Conservative MPs and peers. The shift of the Conservatives to the right after 1965, in a period in which crime continued generally to rise, isolated moderate Conservatives within their own party, and provided the opportunity to exploit the issue to win votes. In 1970, Edward Heath informed the press that the next Conservative government would take a tougher stance on law and order; this was fairly untypical of what the Conservatives' new policies were actually about, but seemed to evoke a public response. In this, as in so much else, the Heath government was a severe disappointment to the right-wing activists who were coming to dominate the party (not least in the way in which he had to bow to trade union power on the streets in 1972–3), but in his successor Margaret Thatcher the law and order issue found an exponent who meant what she said. Disorder during industrial disputes opened the way for Thatcher to offer the electorate the smack of firm government in 1979. She waged the war on crime rhetorically, with regular denunciations of trade unions and the Labour left as 'the enemy within', and of violent criminals as deviants who must bow to the will of the majority. She also waged it administratively, with increases in police numbers and pay, increased backing for the police in cases where tough measures were needed to restore order, and in higher sentences for convicted criminals (which in itself required more and bigger gaols). The prison population stood in the 1990s at more than double the level of the 1960s. Opinion polls suggested that by no means everyone agreed with such an approach, and critics could point to examples of police overzealousness and to miscarriages of justice in the courts. Nevertheless, among the Conservative voters who kept Thatcher and Major in office in 1979–97, there was a steady approval both of the importance of the issue and of the Conservatives' decision to accord it a high priority. In due course, as the Major government disintegrated after 1992, and the Labour Party itself moved to the right in its desperate search for electability, the issue ceased to favour the Conservatives. Tony Blair's promise to be *'Tough on crime, tough on the causes of crime' (a neat combination of the tough but tender 'third way') was very helpful to Labour's cause. In office after 1997, Jack Straw was as tough a home secretary as Britain had had in the century, conscious that this was a pledge on which Labour had to deliver, and he therefore ratcheted the debate further towards the authoritarian side even than the Conservatives had dared, for example with proposals to limit the right of trial by jury in order to secure more convictions in criminal cases. *JAR*

Law Commission, set up by the Law Commissions Act, 1965. It took over responsibility for the maintenance of common law (decisions by judges) and statute law (enacted by parliament) revision, from the office of the parliamentary counsel. The commission is comprised of a chairman, alongside four other commissioners who are appointed by the lord chancellor. Their work is assisted by a full-time staff and temporarily appointed experts relevant to whichever profession is being looked at. The aim of the commission is to keep the law under review in order to develop and reform it where necessary. This entails accepting outside proposals and making its own proposals to the lord chancellor with reference to legislation which is obscure, anachronistic, or in any way unsatisfactory. It conducts wide-ranging research to make its proposals as thorough as possible and reviews foreign legal systems so that it may improve its own functions. The Law Commission does not have jurisdiction over Scotland, this being the responsibility of the Scottish Law Commission which was established at the same time. *JD*

Law Commission website: *www.lawcom.gov.uk*

Law Officers' Department. Throughout the 20th century, there were two main law officers: the attorney-general and the solicitor-general, in effect the attorney-general's deputy. The Law Officers Act, 1944, provided for the statutory interchangeability of functions between the two; previous legislation had given them distinct powers. The main function of the law officers was to advise government departments on major points of law, being ultimately responsible for all crown litigation (a further function, the hearing of appeals against the comptroller general's decisions, was ceded to the patents appeal tribunal in 1932). Subjects to be dealt with were submitted by the Treasury solicitor, the director of *public prosecutions (whom the attorney-general regulated), and legal sections of government departments. Until the 1970s, the advice of the law officers was conveyed as a formal 'opinion', whereas subsequently it was delivered by way of correspondence. Further to the law officer's legal counsel responsibilities, there were two other significant functions: service in parliament and advocacy in the courts. The parliamentary duties of the attorney-general included sponsorship of law reform legislation, advice regarding peerage claims, and ex-officio membership of standing committees, along with answering in the Commons for his own department. Prior to 1992, the attorney-general also answered for the lord chancellor in the Commons, but this was assumed by a new appointment, the parliamentary secretary of the lord chancellor's department. The attorney-general's responsibilities with regard to court proceedings were tremendously diverse. In his role as an advocate, the attorney-general appeared in some of the highest profile court cases of the century, perhaps most notably the International Court of Justice at The Hague and the war crimes trials following the Great War and the Second World War. The attorney-general formerly had sole responsibility for authorizing appeals in criminal cases to the House of Lords. This was removed under the Administration of Justice Act, 1960. *JD*

law of negligence. The fundamental principle is that an individual must take reasonable care not to injure his neighbour's person or property. A 'neighbour' is anyone whom the defendant ought to have foreseen as likely to be affected. Two major policy questions remain contentious:

to what extent should the law protect those who have suffered merely economic loss; and should the law of negligence be replaced by a system to compensate all accident victims regardless of another's fault? *PPM*

P. S. Atiyah, *The Damages Lottery* (Oxford, 1997). | *Report of the Royal Commission on Civil Liability* (Cmnd 7054, London, 1978).

Lawrence, Alfred Tristram. See Trevethin, Lord.

Lawson, John James ('Jack') (1881–1965), Labour politician. From initial involvement in the Independent Labour Party, Jack Lawson was elected to the Commons in 1919 as MP for Chester-le-Street, a constituency he represented until his retirement in 1949. After holding junior office for war and labour under MacDonald, Lawson was secretary for war in Attlee's cabinet, 1945–6. He was known for his moderate political stance and ended his career with a peerage (1950). *DWM*

James Lawson, *A Man's Life* (London, 1932, 1944, and 1951 edns.).

Lawson, Nigel (1932–), journalist and Conservative politician. Lawson was originally a financial journalist at the *Financial Times* and *Sunday Telegraph*, then editor of the *Spectator*, opposing incomes policy and the Vietnam war. He also worked as a Conservative speechwriter and policy draftsman in 1963–4 and again in the early 1970s. Entering parliament in 1974, he became financial secretary in 1979 and energy secretary from 1981, after the tribulations of David Howell in a miners' strike. Coal stockpiled by Lawson would defeat Arthur Scargill in the strike of 1984. As chancellor, 1983–9, Lawson demonstrated certainty, proclaiming the correct view at meetings and inviting challenge. Thatcher long deferred to his judgement until, over the shadowing of the German mark and ERM membership, relations became embittered and he was driven to resign. The tide turned against Lawson's career, and perhaps the Conservatives in office, with his 1988 budget. After a market fall, hailed as a crash, he lit a small fire under a warm economy, producing interim backbench Tory delirium. One Labour MP confided later that 'it seemed that the Tories had won for ever' but Lawson had miscalculated, and John Biffen, more correctly, 'smelt inflation'. Lawson had taken remedial action against a false alarm. The cure, a shot of reflation, did everything that Tory monetarists had earlier said it would. Thatcher would resign in 1990 with inflation at 10 per cent, where she had found it in 1979; their successors showed an understandable but morbid preoccupation with rising prices. Never popular, never seeking popularity, Lawson had, genuinely, ruled out any leadership aspirations. He was quietly sniped at, like Leon Brittan, for Jewishness, in phrases such as 'more Estonians than Etonians in the cabinet', and 'this Cabinet is too North London for me'. A liberal without Thatcher's social antagonisms, he had been, with Geoffrey Howe, the key minister for the early Thatcher era, but the 1988 budget and his (politically) unsuccessful exchange rate policy caused reputation-reversal, a sad fate for one of the ablest of post-war chancellors. *EP*

Nigel Lawson, *The View from Number Eleven* (London, 1992).

Lawther, William (1889–1976), trade unionist. Lawther was one of the left-wing, sea-green incorruptible miners' leaders who took their union from catastrophic defeat after the 1926 General Strike to nationalization of the mines, better wages and conditions, and more power and influence after 1945. Born in Northumberland, and a graduate of the Central Labour College, London, Lawther was Labour MP for Barnard Castle, 1929–31, member of the TUC general council, 1935–54, president of the TUC in 1949 (the year he was knighted), and of the National Union of Mineworkers in 1954. *PRGR*

Leader, newspaper founded on 1 September 1900 by D. P. Moran which attacked the idea of a pluralist Irish nation, dismissing anything that was not Gaelic or Catholic as non-Irish. The *Leader* continued as the gadfly of Irish political life into the 1930s, and retained its reputation as a well-informed if excoriating observer of the political scene into the 1950s. *DGB*

leadership, the process of organizing and directing the activities of a group of people towards desired ends. In theory, leadership can come from within the group and remain part of it, so that it is invisible and embedded in the ways in which the group defines its goals and structures its course of action. However, 20th-century notions of leadership tend to set the leader apart, so that he/she acts to define the group's goals and to take credit for their success and responsibility for their failure. The British political system of government, depending as it does on winning a majority in an electoral battle rather than post-election government formation through a process of consensus and negotiation, has a particular emphasis on strong and charismatic leadership. Sources of leadership may vary. Max

Weber offers three ideal types: traditional leadership, based on social status; charismatic leadership, based on the possession of particular personal qualities; and legal-rational leadership, derived from rationally established rules and procedures. Each offers means by which the leadership of an individual is legitimated. Leadership, itself, involves a number of styles, including forcefulness, persuasiveness, an ability to conciliate, and the capacity to produce a consensus. Success comes from the ability to adapt leadership style as the nature of the political environment changes. In addition, political leaders may need different styles depending on the political constituency they are addressing. Some of the most successful British leaders found that their leadership skills were particularly suited to some occasions, but inadequate on others. Churchill's style was successful in wartime, but less effective thereafter, and Margaret Thatcher's talents were unsuited to the period of policy conciliation demanded after 1987. Conversely, Clement Attlee's consensual, if firm, leadership style proved unable to give the party the decisive policy direction it needed after 1950. *CPS*

League of Nations (1920–46). The creation of this, the world's first general international organization, was ensured by the determined advocacy of the president of the USA, Woodrow Wilson, but the detailed ideas it embodied came almost wholly from Britain. She, however, had taken US membership for granted. Thus, when America failed to join, Britain was, in effect, left leading an organization that had suddenly become a possible liability rather than an asset. But not too much was lost, for the obligations of League membership were not onerous. The only specific ones of importance concerned the use of procedures for the pacific settlement of disputes, and the imposition of economic sanctions on any state which made war in defiance of certain of these obligations. However, it was up to each state to interpret for itself what steps, if any, it should take in these matters. And all substantive decisions of the League's organs had to be unanimous. That is, the League was based on the idea of cooperation rather than direction.

The League began with 42 members; twenty states were later admitted; seventeen withdrew; and one—the Soviet Union—was effectively expelled after it invaded Finland in 1939. The League's headquarters were at Geneva, where its first secretary-general, Sir Eric Drummond, created a multinational secretariat from scratch. It was based on the British principle of a non-political civil service. The secretariat served the two principal organs, the assembly and the council. All member states (each having one vote) were represented in the assembly, which met once a year for about a month. In addition to Britain, six Commonwealth countries were League members: Canada, Australia, South Africa, New Zealand, India, and from 1923 the newly independent Irish Free State. They each had separate delegations and cooperated closely, but they did not always accept British leadership. Through the assembly, they and other small states gained a voice in international relations, and assembly resolutions were deemed to be an important indicator of world opinion.

The council held three or four week-long meetings each year, and special meetings as required. It represented the institutionalization on a global scale of the 19th-century 'concert of Europe'. Permanent seats on the council were occupied by the great powers for as long as they participated in the League: Britain, France, Italy (until 1936), Japan (until 1933), Germany (1926–33), and the Soviet Union (1934–9). In addition, some non-permanent council seats, held for three years, were awarded by the assembly on a rotating basis. Like the assembly, the council was envisaged as a purely deliberative body. It had some specific tasks, such as keeping an eye on the administering of mandated territories and the well-being of national minorities in certain states. More generally, it was entitled to discuss any matter within the League's competence 'or affecting the peace of the world'. It was assumed that usually a public rebuke from the council would be sufficient to deter a wrongdoer; in turn this assumed the existence of a sense of community and common interest that in fact proved to be lacking (and is perhaps always lacking in a world of sovereign states). However, the League was right in recognizing that it could only act effectively when states were in agreement.

The experience of the League reflected its circumstances. During the 1920s, when the international climate was favourable, it was fairly successful; but in the 1930s its weakness was revealed. When Japan invaded the Chinese province of Manchuria in 1931, Britain felt unable to act firmly without American support. That was not forthcoming, and without British leadership the other League members would not and could not act. Following Italy's invasion of *Abyssinia (now Ethiopia) in 1935, fear of driving Mussolini into Hitler's arms led to half-hearted and ineffective sanctions. Discredited as a collective security organization, the League remained in shadowy existence until April 1946.

Although the circumstances of its decline resulted in the League generally being judged a failure, it was by no means a continuous or complete one. Moreover, its covenant represented certain important milestones in the development of ideas about how international relations should be conducted, notably its condemnation of aggression and its assertion that any war or threat of war was a matter of general concern. Perhaps most significantly of all, the League established the idea that the world needed such a body. Unsurprisingly, its imprint on the shape of its successor, the United Nations, was far-reaching. *LL*

Viscount Cecil of Chelwood, *A Great Experiment* (London, 1941). | F. S. Northedge, *The League of Nations, its Life and Times* (Leicester, 1986).

League of Nations Union (LNU) (1918–45), pressure group. The LNU achieved a truly remarkable place in British public life during the inter-war period. Formed to keep governments up to the mark in their attitude to the *League of Nations, the LNU was tirelessly led by some eminent figures, notably the philosopher Gilbert Murray and Lord Robert Cecil. Its committees included leading people from every sphere of activity; all premiers except Ramsay MacDonald accepted honorary positions in the LNU; in 1925 it was granted a royal charter. By 1931, when membership reached its peak, a million people had joined the LNU, of whom 400,000 were active members.

The LNU was thus well placed to test a basic idea espoused by some leading drafters of the League's covenant, that democratic public opinion could have a beneficial effect on foreign policy, and could persuade governments to uphold the League. Certainly the LNU could not be ignored by any government, but its multi-party membership meant that it could never be an electoral threat, and hence its influence over any government was also limited. This was illustrated in the LNU's most notable achievement, the peace ballot of 1934–5, when 11,640,066 people overwhelmingly expressed support for the League, collective security, and disarmament. This massive pronouncement affected the presentation of British policy during the League's attempt to handle the ensuing Abyssinian crisis, but it did not influence the substance of what Britain did, and in private the government could dismiss the LNU as a collection of do-gooders and cranks.

Thus the LNU inadvertently revealed the flimsiness of a major assumption of the League. It demonstrated how the British public's shock at the carnage of the Great War resulted in a considerable support for the abstract idea of peace, but at the same time, however, the LNU encouraged an unrealistic appreciation of what the League could do to maintain it. *LL*

Donald S. Birn, *The League of Nations Union, 1918–1935* (Oxford, 1981).

Leathers, Frederick (1883–1965), shipping expert and cabinet minister. Leathers entered shipping aged 15 and was promoted fast, during the 1914–18 war advising the government. He became acquainted with Churchill, again advised the government in 1940, and in 1941 was appointed minister of war transport, as Lord Leathers with a peerage. In 1951 Leathers was made *'overlord' for the coordination of transport, fuel, and power. Following the failure of the 'overlords' experiment, however, Leathers left office in 1953 and in 1954 became a viscount. *RJS*

Lee, Arthur Hamilton (1868–1947), Conservative politician and philanthropist. Born without financial prospects, Lee became a soldier and then tried his luck in North America. He became a British military attaché with the US Army in Cuba, befriended Theodore Roosevelt, and returned to Britain with a wealthy American bride. He entered parliament in 1900 and eventually joined the post-war cabinet of Lloyd George, who raised him to the peerage. Lee presented *Chequers to the nation for the use of the prime minister. *RJQA*

Alan Clark (ed.), *A Good Innings: The Private Papers of Viscount Lee of Fareham* (London, 1974).

Lee, Frank (1903–71), civil servant. One of the outstanding post-Second World War Whitehall officials, Lee's early career was in the Colonial Office (1926–40) and included a period as a district officer in Nyasaland which may have influenced his energetic and tough-minded 'hands-on' approach. He moved to the Treasury in 1940, later serving in Washington, where he worked closely with Keynes in negotiations over the end of Lend-Lease and the British loan agreement. He was permanent secretary of the Ministry of Food, 1949–51, and then of the Board of Trade, 1951–60, where he was a key figure in economic policy making in the 1950s. In 1960 he became joint permanent secretary to the Treasury in charge of economic and financial policy, retiring early after a heart attack. By the time he joined the Treasury Lee had become a committed

European and he played a crucial role in the reassessment of British policy towards the European Economic Community in 1960–2. *KT*

Lee, Janet ('Jennie') (1904–88), Labour politician. Jennie Lee, the daughter of a miner who was active in the Independent Labour Party (ILP), initially worked as a teacher after attending Edinburgh University. Elected ILP MP for North Lanark, 1929–31, she eventually left the party in 1942 because of its anti-war stance. In the 1930s, Lee combined journalism and lecturing, touring the USA, the USSR, and Europe. She married Labour MP Aneurin *Bevan in 1934 and thereafter became his staunch political ally. During the Second World War, Lee was employed as a *Daily Mirror* lobby correspondent and an administrator for the Ministry of Aircraft Production. Joining the Labour Party in 1944, she became Labour MP for Cannock, 1945–70, and sat on the NEC, 1958–70. As junior minister for public buildings and works, 1964–5, and for education and science, 1965–70, Lee established the arts as a serious governmental concern and ensured that central funding for this area doubled. Her major contribution, supported by Wilson, was to found the Open University. She lost her seat in 1970 but was then made a life peer. *AM*

Jennie Lee, *My Life with Nye* (London, 1980).

Left Book Club (LBC), established in May 1936, was an influential force in the movement to promote a popular front. At its peak in April 1939, it had 57,000 members who received a book and the journal *Left News* every month. Based on local study groups and buttressed by social and cultural activities, the LBC campaigned for international resistance to fascism in alliance with the Soviet Union, and its rallies were often far larger than those of the Labour Party. The LBC was created by the publisher Victor *Gollancz, in association with John Strachey, who was effectively a Communist at the time, and Harold Laski, who was on the left wing of the Labour Party. Gollancz and Strachey ensured that the overwhelming majority of the club's books were acceptable to the Communist Party of Great Britain (CPGB), and Communists played the leading role in its central organization. By autumn 1938, the LBC had published many of the most influential left-wing books of the era, but Gollancz was becoming increasingly worried by Communist domination of the LBC, and began to assert a greater degree of independence. Laski was now also highly critical of the CPGB, and in August 1939 threatened to resign from the club unless it distanced itself from the Nazi-Soviet pact. Gollancz managed to maintain unity when the CPGB appeared to support the war the next month, but in the December 1939 issue of *Left News* Strachey followed the CPGB's new line in denouncing the war, while Laski urged total support for it. Gollancz agreed with Laski, and in April 1940 Strachey also endorsed this position. Communists were now purged from the LBC's headquarters, and Gollancz used the club to rally support for the war. It subsequently declined in importance and had dwindled to 7,000 members when Gollancz finally closed it down in October 1948. *MDN*

Ruth Dudley Edwards, *Victor Gollancz: A Biography* (London, 1987). | John Lewis, *The Left Book Club* (London, 1970).

legal aid, system that funds defence lawyers for defendants unable to afford the cost from their own resources. Legal aid was introduced by the Attlee government in 1949, as a 'second arm of the welfare state'; previously, the poorest defendants had to rely on charity or on lawyers prepared to work only for low fees (often the most junior members of the profession, in search of experience). The original scheme covered only higher courts and criminal cases, but was successively extended to include all courts and every type of case, though the original intention to set the financial limits low, so that four-fifths of the population could use the scheme, was gradually eroded. Since the scheme was 'demand-led', its cost escalated dramatically, fuelled by such social trends as the increased number of divorces (the single most important source of income to legal practices specializing in legal-aid cases). By the early 1990s, the annual cost had risen to over £ 1 billion, and government sought to impose restrictions. By then, the scheme had also suffered adverse publicity after apparently wealthy defendants in complex (and therefore very expensive) commercial fraud cases were found to qualify for legal aid because of the way in which their personal resources were held, while less than half of the ordinary population would by then have qualified for assistance. From 1996, on the initiative of the lord chancellor, the administration of the scheme passed from the Law Society (representing solicitors) to a government-appointed legal-aid board which has the duty of approving expenditure through its regional committees, while the total sum available annually was capped. *JAR*

legal profession. The profession saw dramatic change during the course of the 20th century. In terms of composition, the major change was the admission of the first women to the profession in 1922. Men remained the dominant majority well into the century, but the last twenty-five years saw an increasing number of women enter the profession, though the majority of senior practitioners remain male. Ethnic minorities remain under-represented within the profession. Changes have also taken place in the profession's education: an entrant must now hold an academic degree, a reflection of the increasing intellectualization of the study of law throughout the century.

Although both solicitors and barristers had participated in limited schemes to provide legal services to the impecunious, a major state-funded legal advice and assistance programme was introduced in 1948, providing a major source of work for many practitioners. Increasing costs (especially legal aid in civil proceedings) led to major changes to the scheme throughout the last decade of the century. Conditional fees (whereby a solicitor/barrister accepted a case on the basis that if the case was lost they would charge nothing, but if it was won a premium over and above the usual fee would be charged) were successfully introduced in a limited number of areas in 1993. Partly as a result of this success, the Access to Justice Act, 1999, altered the legal aid scheme by drastically reducing the number of areas in which the state would pay for legal advice whilst at the same time increasing the areas in which conditional fees could be used. The Conservative government's Courts and Legal Services Act, 1990, and its commitment to increased competition in the market for legal services paved the way for much change in the last decade of the century. The Act provided a means to end barristers' exclusive rights of audience before the highest courts in England and Wales with the result that, in December 1993, solicitors in private practice gained equivalent rights. The 1990 Act also abolished the necessity to adopt many of the traditional forms of practice by barristers (that is, the necessity to have a clerk and to practice from chambers with other barristers) although most barristers continue to practise in the old way.

The century also saw advertising restrictions relaxed: both branches of the profession may now advertise in good taste and in relation to a limited number of matters. The size of legal practices also increased throughout the century, with London home to some of the world's biggest law firms. The legal profession has much to ponder going into the 21st century. The abolition of the conveyancing monopoly in 1985, the changes to the legal aid scheme, and the extension of rights of audience beyond barristers in independent practice have taken place at a time when there are more solicitors and barristers than ever before. The precise changes these pressures will produce remains uncertain, but the legal profession at the end of the next century is likely to be very different from the one at the end of the 20th. *ML*

R. Abel, *The Legal Profession in England and Wales* (Oxford, 1988). | S. H. Bailey and M. J. Gunn, *Smith & Bailey on the Modern English Legal System* (3rd edn., London, 1996).

Legge-Bourke, Harry (1914–73), Conservative politician. Elected to parliament in 1945, Legge-Bourke was one of the last of the 'knights of the shire' who entered politics from duty rather than ambition. An independent-minded, traditional Tory, he was a member of the *Suez Group and resigned the Conservative whip in 1954 over the Anglo-Egyptian agreement. In 1962 he called on Macmillan to resign. Elected chairman of the 1922 Committee in 1970, he resigned through ill-health in 1972. *RJS*

legitimacy, the characteristic from which a political regime derives its political authority and the basis of its monopolistic use of force within its territory. The consensual nature of the UK political system and the common acceptance of the liberal-democratic state has generally removed consideration of issues of legitimacy from political discourse. The UK political system, however, in common with other Western democracies, has required constant adaptation in the light of changing political and social circumstances to ensure continued political legitimation. The development of the welfare state consensus in the 1940s and 1950s and the remodelling of the role of the state in the 1980s and 1990s can be seen as responses to the changing needs of legitimation. In general, this process has been absorbed into the two-party system of government, with opposition pressure forcing a government to alter direction in the light of democratic pressure. The nearest 20th-century Britain came to the sort of crisis of legitimation which threatens the basis of the political regime was during the 1970s when the ability of government to satisfy all the pressures it faced, including the need to assert its own authority, led to some doubts as to the continued viability of the political system. The political scientist Jim Bulpitt, in a seminal piece ('The Discipline of the New Democracy: Mrs Thatcher's Domestic Statecraft', *Political Studies*, 34/1 (1986)), suggests that the attraction of New Right politics in the 1970s was primarily as a mechanism which would insulate the Conservative Party from these pressures and thus reassert its legitimacy as a governing force. *CPS*

Leith-Ross, Frederick (1887–1968), chief economic adviser to the British government, 1932–9; director-general of the Ministry of Economic Warfare and deputy director-general of United Nations Relief and Rehabilitation Agency, 1939–46. In common with most of his generation employed in the Treasury, Leith-Ross had no formal training in economics. He had little to do with the domestic policy, but played a central role in shaping Britain's economic appeasement of Germany and Japan, where his expertise in international finance led British policy in international negotiations on *reparations and commercial debts, British war debts to America, and, in 1935, a ground-breaking reform of China's monetary system, *PC*

Lend-Lease (1941–5), American aid to wartime allies. The Lend-Lease Act was signed into law by its inspirer, Franklin D. Roosevelt, on 11 March 1941, after bitter debate in the US congress. It authorized the president 'to sell, transfer, exchange, lease or lend' supplies to countries whose defence he considered 'related' to that of the USA. Repayment terms were left open, and no limit was placed on the supplies or the sums involved. This was a turning-point in the Second World War, a war in which Washington had as yet no part. The USA had become 'the arsenal of democracy'. For his domestic audience the president famously likened the international situation to that of a householder whose neighbour's house catches fire. In such circumstances it is only sensible for him to lend his neighbour a hose. He does not haggle over the transaction at the time; he expects that once the fire is out the hose will be returned or replaced. The moral was clear. The German fire had to be extinguished. The American householder does the right thing, but he does so out of prudence and self-interest. The draft presented for Congressional approval was entitled 'An Act to Promote the Defense of the United States'. If it was indeed 'the most unsordid act in the history of any nation', in Churchill's magniloquent phrase, then it was also a well-calculated one.

The bulk of supplies under Lend-Lease went to the British (whose dedicated importuning had provoked this legislation) and—despite persistent mutual suspicion—the Soviets. Its contribution to the British war effort was immense, though not immediate, for the US leviathan took time to limber up. Despite imminent bankruptcy, Britain continued to pay in cash for most weapons and materials throughout 1941. Washington expected and extracted a quid pro quo, in the form of a loosely worded undertaking to reduce tariffs and promote trade after the war. The situation was then transformed. In 1942–4, almost all raw material exports to Britain came under Lend-Lease. By 1943 about 25 per cent of British military equipment was supplied by the USA. In total, Britain received some $21 billion of aid by these means ($14 billion in military supplies, $7 billion in raw materials). These were huge figures, nearly equivalent to the annual British GNP, but traffic was not all one-way. Reciprocal aid—'reverse Lend-Lease'—from Britain to the USA amounted to some $5.7 billion in the same period. Expressed proportionately, the respective contributions were not so dissimilar. Lend-Lease to Britain accounted for 4 per cent of US domestic output; reverse Lend-Lease to the USA for 3 per cent of British domestic output.

Lend-Lease to Britain was terminated, without discussion, in August 1945 (and to the Soviet Union, likewise, in May 1945) by the fledgling president Harry Truman—a slap, and a shock, to both. The war had ended, but what Keynes called Britain's 'economic Dunkirk' had only just begun. *AD*

Warren F. Kimball, *The Most Unsordid Act* (Baltimore, 1969). | David Reynolds et al., *Allies at War* (New York, 1994).

Lennox-Boyd, Alan Tindal (1904–83). Conservative politician and colonial policy specialist. Lennox-Boyd was elected Conservative MP for mid-Bedfordshire in 1931. He flirted with fascism, supported appeasement, and from 1938 served as a junior minister at labour, home security, and food. After wartime naval service, he became a junior minister for aircraft production in 1943. After 1945, the wealth that had come from his 1938 marriage to a Guinness heiress enabled Lennox-Boyd to travel throughout the colonies. In 1951, he was appointed a minister at the Colonial Office and, after serving for two years as transport minister, became colonial secretary in 1954. His gradualist policy, however, by which progress towards independence varied between slow and imperceptible, soon became untenable. In 1959, the Macmillan government stood condemned of having run a police state in Nyasaland and allowed the murder of eleven African detainees at Kenya's Hola camp. Lennox-Boyd offered to resign, but reluctantly remained until the 1959 election. In 1960, he became Viscount Boyd of Merton. At Thatcher's request in 1979, he headed a Conservative mission to observe Rhodesia's election (see RHODESIAN CRISIS), and recommended unavailingly that a future Tory government should recognize the Muzorewa-Smith government. *RJS*

PHILIP MURPHY, *Alan Lennox-Boyd: A Biography* (London, 1999).

less eligibility, principle of poor relief policy, by which benefits should be paid at a level lower than the lowest wages commonly available, so as to deter dependency. *JS*

Lestor, Joan (1931–98), Labour politician who personified the committed, left-wing, party constituency member. She taught at nursery and infant schools and in 1949 joined the Socialist Party of Great Britain, in which her father had been active, but switched to Labour in 1955. She was MP for Eton and Slough (succeeding Fenner Brockway), 1966–83, and Eccles, 1987–97, and junior minister for education and science, 1969–70. Interests included international questions, children, and resistance to racism, and she was a member of the Campaign for Nuclear Disarmament, 1983–98. *PRGR*

Letchworth, pioneer *garden city founded in Hertfordshire by Ebenezer *Howard in 1903. Letchworth incorporated many of the idioms later to become prototypes for the British town and country planning movement, including a *green belt, low-rise housing, and the first roundabout in Britain. *JS*

Let Us Face the Future (1945), Labour election manifesto. Well drafted by Herbert Morrison, this programme committed a peacetime Labour government to the nationalization of fuel and power, inland transport, iron and steel, and the Bank of England. Also among the pledges which caught the mood of the electorate after their wartime experience, and contributed to the Labour landslide victory, were full employment, the National Health Service, housebuilding, improved social security, and implementation of the 1944 Education Act. *JSS*

Let's Go with Labour for the New Britain (1964), Labour election manifesto. Mainly based on 1960–1 policy documents, this lambasted the Tories for thirteen wasted years and outlined ambitious plans for a modernized Britain. At the 1963 Scarborough party conference the new party leader Harold Wilson struck a chord with his memorable phrase that the country would be forged in the white heat of the scientific revolution. After three defeats, Labour won the 1964 election with a five-seat majority. *JSS*

Levene, Peter Keith (1941–), defence industry businessman and government adviser. Levene built up United Scientific Holdings, a leading defence contractor. Special adviser to Defence Secretary Michael Heseltine, he was appointed chief of defence procurement in controversial circumstances (bypassing normal civil service commission rules) in 1985 (serving until 1991), but the reforms he made to the contracting process saved 10 per cent from the defence equipment budget. He was the prime minister's efficiency and effectiveness adviser, 1992–7, overseeing wider Whitehall management reforms. He was lord mayor of London, 1998–9. *KT*

Lever, Harold (1914–95), Labour politician. Lever was a wealthy socialist and financial wizard, but a Labour MP, 1945–79. Although he held several positions in the first Wilson government, entering cabinet as paymaster general in 1969, he is chiefly remembered for his role as chancellor of the duchy of Lancaster, 1974–9. With a small staff in the cabinet office and a roving brief in financial and industrial affairs, he became a 'universal fixer' and thorn in the side of the Treasury. *HOJ*

Lewis, Saunders (1893–1985), dramatist, poet, and Welsh political activist. Saunders Lewis is generally regarded as the greatest figure in 20th-century Welsh literature and also as the leader who did most to shape the nature of Welsh nationalism in the period before the 1960s. He was born in the Wirral, the son of a Welsh Calvinistic Methodist minister, and he interrupted his undergraduate career at Liverpool University to serve for three years as an officer in the South Wales Borderers in the Great War. In 1925 he helped to found *Plaid Cymru, becoming its president in 1926, and in 1936 was arrested following the Bombing School incident and was subsequently dismissed by University College, Swansea, where he had taught Welsh since 1922. A student of languages, a Roman Catholic convert, and very much influenced by the writings of Corneille and the politics of Maurice Barres, Lewis was essentially a European who gloried in the power and sophistication of medieval Welsh literature. He was a major dramatist of ideas whose great desire was to see Wales reassert its cultural distinctiveness. His unceasing message was that the language was all-important and that political independence would be worthless if it were to die. *PS*

BRUCE GRIFFITHS, *Saunders Lewis* (Cardiff, 1979).

Liberal Action Group, Liberal pressure group formed in 1941, later known as Radical Action. The group expressed discontent with the wartime electoral truce and advocated progressive policies. Led by Lancelot Spicer (chairman), Honor Balfour, and Everett Jones, the group grew by 1944 to include five MPs and 34 prospective candidates. Members started contesting seats as Independent Liberals, coming within 195 votes of winning a safe Conservative seat at Chippenham in August 1943 and within 70 at Darwen in November. Other Liberals resigned offices to contest elections in 1944. It was symptomatic of tensions within the Liberal Party caused by the electoral truce, which also led to the founding of the *Common Wealth Party by Sir Richard Acland in September 1942. *JS*

Liberal Councillors, Association of, campaigning organization of the Liberal grass roots, taken over in 1975 by Tony Greaves (1942–) and turned into an influential part of the *community politics movement. Its base moved to Hebden Bridge in West Yorkshire in 1977, with the assistance of a grant which allowed it independence from the central Liberal Party organization. By 1980 the organization had over 1,300 members and contributed substantially to the growth of Liberal representation at municipal level. *JAR*

Liberal Democrats, political party of the centre, formed in March 1988 as the Social and Liberal Democratic Party, from a merger of the *Liberal Party and the *Social Democratic Party (SDP). The Liberal Democrats were the heirs to the *Alliance which had been formed in 1981 by the Liberal Party and the newly formed SDP. Motions towards a formal merger of the parties began immediately after the general election of 1987, which was widely regarded as disappointing for the Alliance; not only had the Conservatives won a third majority in parliament, but the percentage vote of the Alliance was as far from establishing itself as the major party of opposition as ever. Moreover the dual leadership of David *Steel and David *Owen was widely regarded as a failure in terms of presentation, confusing the electorate and highlighting divisions on policy. A call for a merger of the parties rather than a continuation of the Alliance came from David Steel within days of the election and these proposals were ratified by special conferences of both parties early in 1988. Temporary joint leadership of the new party was provided by David Steel from the Liberal side and Robert *Maclennan from the SDP, David Owen having resigned from the leadership of the SDP when the party, against his advice, voted to open merger negotiations. Of the remaining four SDP MPs, only one, Charles *Kennedy, had supported the merger, but Robert Maclennan was prepared to accept the democratic vote of the party and act as interim leader. Steel and Maclennan led the two parties into the merger, but each then declined to contest the leadership of the new party. The two contestants were Paddy *Ashdown, initially seen as the outside candidate, and Alan *Beith, former deputy leader of the Liberals. At the hustings meetings there was little to divide the two candidates, but Ashdown's more professional campaign proved more attractive compared with Beith's known qualities of loyalty and competence, and Ashdown was elected by 41,401 votes to 16,202 on 28 July 1988.

The party Ashdown inherited from the merger was small, demoralized, and almost bankrupt. There remained bitter divisions over the speed with which the merger had been pushed through, with confusion and discontent amongst some Liberals at the adoption of the short name 'Democrats'. Most serious of all, the attempt to recapture the 'third party' vote was compromised by the refusal of a group of former SDP activists, led by David Owen, to join the new party. The 'Continuing SDP' divided the potential support for the merged party and was widely regarded as responsible for the failure of the party to perform well in 1989, when, desperately short of funds and still struggling to establish its identity, the party was placed fourth after the Greens in the European elections, obtaining only 6.2 per cent of the vote and failing to secure a single MEP.

Gradually, some issues clarified and improved prospects. The name of the party was settled at the Liberal Democrats, confirmed by a ballot of members in October 1989. A potentially damaging split in the radical wing of the party was contained when Michael *Meadowcroft, former MP for Leeds West, announced in early spring 1989 that he was refounding the Liberal Party. A sufficient number of disillusioned former Liberals, unhappy with the compromises of the Alliance which were now apparently enshrined in the newly merged party, gave support, allowing the party to fight several dozen council seats and to contest parliamentary elections. However, the heavyweight defections required to seriously damage the merged party were not forthcoming and the 'Continuing' Liberal Party remained marginalized. Meanwhile the 'continuing' SDP was finding it difficult to support a national organization and ceased campaigning in the aftermath of a by-election at Bootle in May 1990 in which the Owenite party trailed behind the fringe candidature of the Monster Raving Loony Party. In contrast, the Liberal Democrats performed respectably in the May 1990 local elections, confirming a substantial presence in local government.

By October 1990 the Liberal Democrats had recovered sufficiently to win the *Eastbourne by-election, precipitating the fall of Margaret Thatcher, and in March 1991 to secure a victory at *Ribble Valley that forced the Conservative Party to abandon the poll tax. Ashdown worked to modernize the party's organization and constitution, setting up a computerized membership scheme, and moderated its policies, effectively ending its ambivalence over unilateral nuclear disarmament and moving the new party towards a more centrist position on economic policy. The Liberal Democrats also took up a clear pro-European Union stance, supporting the Conservative government on the crucial vote to ratify the *Maastricht treaty in 1993. They also consolidated a position as a major force in local government, with over 4,000 councillors by the early 1990s. The 1992 general election, however, only yielded the party twenty seats, and its percentage share of the vote was smaller than the third-party vote in 1987 and in 1983, at 18 per cent.

Continued success in by-elections and the first election of two Liberal Democrat MEPs in June 1994 were overshadowed by the revival of the Labour Party under Tony *Blair, promoting renewed talk of the Liberal Democrats supporting Labour in a future 'hung' parliament. The run-up to the 1997 election somewhat diminished these prospects as Labour support in the opinion polls remained very high. One feature of the pre-election period, however, was a historic agreement between the Liberal Democrats and Labour on a joint approach to constitutional reform. The Liberal Democrats fought a professional and highly effective campaign in 1997, targeting marginal seats where their challenges were most likely to displace incumbent Conservatives, and emphasizing their party's commitment to higher education and health spending, even at the cost of increased taxes.

In what was seen as a personal triumph for Paddy Ashdown, the Liberal Democrats won 46 seats in the poll on 1 May 1997, more than doubling their parliamentary representation in the best result for any British third party since 1929, despite a slight fall in their overall share of the vote to 17 per cent. The new prime minister Tony Blair did not offer any cabinet seats to Liberal Democrats as had previously been mooted. Nonetheless, common ground was demonstrated in the referendums on devolution in Scotland and Wales, and Liberal Democrat participation in discussions about reform of the Lords and of the electoral system. In September 1997, referendums on constitutional reform brought devolution to Scotland and Wales with elections to their respective assemblies being conducted on a proportional basis, and the European elections of June 1999 were also the first such elections conducted using a proportional system. Having achieved the best third-party performance for more than half a century, and ensured a major long-term aim in Scottish and Welsh devolution, other issues remained unresolved. A committee under Roy Jenkins was charged with finding recommendations for reform of the voting system for members of the Commons, but it remained unclear whether the Labour government would ever alter the 'first-past-the-post' system which had brought it such large majorities in 1997 and 2001.

On 20 January 1999, Paddy Ashdown announced his resignation as Liberal Democrat leader with effect from July 1999 and at the end of the parliament in 2001 he stood down from his Yeovil seat at the general election. In the meantime, the party suffered some losses in the May 1999 local council elections, though these were not unexpected after especially good performances in the run-up to the 1997 general election, in part due to the extreme unpopularity of John *Major's Tories. Liberal Democrat support was also disappointing in the first elections for the Scottish parliament and Welsh assembly, where the main contest was between nationalists and Labour. However, the Liberal Democrats gained enormously from the introduction of a proportional system at the European elections in June 1999. Having secured only two MEPs on 17 per cent of the vote in 1994, they now had ten MEPs on the basis of 13 per cent.

Five candidates participated in the election for the Liberal Democrat leadership held in August 1999: Jackie Ballard, Malcolm Bruce, Simon Hughes, Charles Kennedy, and David Rendel. The leadership campaign established Kennedy as the clear favourite, largely because of his youth and high profile in the media, but with Simon Hughes as the strongest challenger. After three rounds of transferred votes, Kennedy was elected with 56 per cent of the vote as leader to succeed Ashdown. *JS*

CHRIS COOK, *A Short History of the Liberal Party, 1900–1997* (London, 1998). | JOHN STEVENSON, *Third Party Politics* (Oxford, 1992).

Liberal Imperialists, informal faction of late Victorian parliamentary Liberals which came together to resist the further radicalization of their party after the departure of the Whigs over Irish home rule in 1886. A major focus of their attention was international policy, hence their name, and they took the lead in opposing Pro-Boers in the party during the *Boer war of 1899–1902. The leading members, Asquith, Grey, and Haldane (once the ex-premier Rosebery had ruled himself out of that role), nursed ambitions to take the leadership of the party from the radical Campbell-Bannerman, and hence made the *Relugas compact between themselves. Once in office—and particularly with Grey himself at the Foreign Office, Haldane at the War Office from 1905 and Asquith prime minister from 1908—their worries about the policy direction of their party faded rapidly. *JAR*

COLIN MATTHEW, *The Liberal Imperialists* (Oxford, 1975).

Liberal Industrial Inquiry. See *BRITAIN'S INDUSTRIAL FUTURE*.

liberalism, political philosophy. The first clear formulation of liberalism is in the political philosophy of John Locke (1632–1704), though the term itself only appears in the early 19th century, and has since become particularly identified with the political philosophy of John Stuart Mill (1806–73), and with the defence of a broadly Millian liberalism in Isaiah Berlin's 'Two Concepts of Liberty' (1958). Locke's liberalism is founded in the claim that individuals are born equal and free, and that legitimate governments can only be established through consent. Certain rights, such as the right to freedom of conscience, must remain inalienable. Where governments deny individuals their rights, those governments cease to be legitimate and individuals are entitled to rebel against them and replace them by new forms of government. Revolutions can therefore be legitimate, and the decisions of our ancestors have no validity if they infringe our inalienable rights. No government can be legitimate if it lacks an independent judiciary, if it taxes without consent, or if it imposes religious uniformity. This theory of inalienable natural rights, limited government, the division of powers, and the right of revolution provided an intellectual underpinning for the American (1776) and French (1789) revolutions. It was grounded in the claim that the right to private property is natural, and it was thus soon linked to the economic theories of Adam Smith (*The Wealth of Nations*, 1776), and to the principle of laissez-faire or economic liberalism.

There is an inevitable tension within liberalism between its stress on liberty and its stress on equality. A liberal account of rights can be developed in a libertarian direction (as by Robert Nozick in his *Anarchy, State, and Utopia*, 1974), which tolerates sharp inequalities of personal fortune in order to entrench individual liberty and responsibility, while, since Tom Paine's *Rights of Man* (1791–2), other liberals have wanted to provide a safety net, particularly for the old, the sick, and the unemployed. Moreover, Paine's *Agrarian Justice* (1797) was one of the first works to argue that certain opportunities should be available to all, an argument later developed to justify universal state education. The most impressive derivation of egalitarian conclusions from liberal principles is John Rawls's *A Theory of Justice* (1971).

This tension is apparent within the work of John Stuart Mill, whose *On Liberty* (1859) is the most widely read liberal text. Mill favoured economic competition within a free market; but he also defended progressive taxation and admired enterprises founded on co-ownership and co-operation. He believed in representative government, but also wished to defend minorities against the majority's potential for intolerance and tyranny. Mill was particularly concerned to foster intellectual and cultural diversity, which he believed to be a precondition for progress, and thus to foster a society which tolerated difference and was committed to pluralism. Only within such a society could political and economic liberty be supplemented by intellectual and cultural freedom. A further tension within liberalism can be traced back to Locke's account of human psychology. Locke argued that human beings are profoundly shaped by their experiences, and that their understanding of the world is the result of what he called 'the association of ideas', that is the ways in which the mind organizes experience. This view implies that we are the product of our education and environment, and that the only way to change behaviour is to alter people's experience. This argument appears to be at odds with the stress on individual responsibility which lies at the heart of economic liberalism, for it implies that society, not the individual, is responsible both for virtuous and for wicked behaviour. These two tensions within liberalism, between liberty and equality, and between environmentalism and individualism, bedevil modern uses of the word 'liberal'. For some, liberalism is identical with a belief in individual liberty, private property, and the market economy, and thus overlaps with conservatism. For others liberalism implies a commitment to economic redistribution and the welfare state, and the extension of liberty to include new freedoms such as abortion and divorce. Liberalism is often now taken to imply the view that inequality lies at the root of social conflict, and that consequently crime is the result of injustice, so that punitive measures are not an adequate response. In short, there are liberalisms of the left and liberalisms of the right.

DRW

JOHN GRAY, *Liberalism* (Milton Keynes, 1986).

Liberal National Party, 'Simonites', faction that split from the main Liberal Party in and after 1931, over membership of the National Government and the introduction of tariffs, remaining in partnership with the Conservatives and eventually merging into the Conservative Party in 1947. Initially, 23 Liberal MPs led by Sir John *Simon formed a new 'Simonite' grouping in October 1931. Since at the election a month later few of their candidates were opposed by either Conservatives or Liberals, 35 Simonite MPs were elected. When Sir Herbert Samuel's free-trade Liberals left the National Government in 1932, the Simon Liberals took their place as 'Liberal Nationals' (LNs) and continued to play an active part in cabinet and governmental office throughout the rest of the decade, their leaders being Simon, Ernest Brown, Leslie Hore-Belisha, and Sir Godfrey Collins. Although not regularly opposed by official Liberal candidates until 1945, the LNs mainly owed their survival and prospering to the lack of Conservative opposition in their constituencies, for they and National Labour were useful evidence that the National Government was more than a Conservative government in disguise. This had less relevance when Churchill became prime minister in 1940 and brought both Labour and the orthodox Liberals into office with him, and LNs then became less and less distinguishable from their Conservative allies. When Labour swept into office in 1945, and with orthodox Liberals now seeking to unseat them, the LNs' anti-socialism propelled them into ever closer relations with Conservatives on whom their eleven MPs now entirely depended for survival and with whom they hardly disagreed on policy matters anyway. On the initiative of Lord Woolton, who hoped unavailingly to bring all Liberals into the Tory camp, the Woolton-Teviot pact of 1947 united the two parties and the LNs closed their separate office. About a dozen MPs continued to be elected as 'Conservative and National Liberal' at each election in the 1950s, while over fifty candidates used that label in 1950 and 1951. These MPs had their own whip and a separate room in the palace of Westminster until the surviving three gave up that privilege in 1966.

JAR

Liberal Party, one of the two alternative political parties of national government from the middle of the 19th century until its decline as a potential party of government in the 1920s. Having undergone splits and serious decline in the following three decades, reaching a low point in the 1950s when the party could muster no more than six MPs and only a fraction of the popular vote at general elections, the party then began a period of slow and modest revival into the 1970s, re-establishing itself as a significant minority party in parliament and a force in local government. With the formation of the *Social Democrats in 1981, the Liberals joined them in the *Alliance, raising the party's profile and vote in the general elections of 1983 and 1987. Calls for a merger of the two parties after 1987 led to the formation of the *Liberal Democrats into which the greater part of the existing Liberal Party was subsumed. A small breakaway body, the *Liberal Party (Continuing), retained a distinct identity.

The original Liberal Party represented a fusion of Whigs, Peelite liberal Tories, and radicals in the mid-19th century, its formation traditionally associated with the meeting at Willis's Rooms in 1859 when these groups agreed to serve under Palmerston. In government under Palmerston until 1865, then Russell, the Liberals forged an identity based upon the support of reformist groups, including Nonconformists, old Whigs, artisans, and the *Celtic fringe. Under W. E. Gladstone's leadership (for most of the period 1868–94) the party was firmly wedded to the doctrines of free trade, religious toleration, administrative efficiency, a pacific foreign policy, and franchise reform. Gladstone's first two governments of 1868–74 and 1880–5 have been regarded as the high point of Gladstonian Liberalism, due to the substantial reform programmes carried out. In addition, the party adapted to the new electoral conditions created by the Reform

Acts of 1867 and 1884 and the Ballot Act of 1872 by establishing a strong presence in major commercial and manufacturing cities such as Birmingham and Manchester, and setting up a National Liberal Federation in 1877 to coordinate the party on a national scale.

Divided in 1886 over the issue of home rule for Ireland, the party was then in opposition, except for three years, until 1905. In his last premiership, 1892–4, Gladstone again attempted unsuccessfully to secure home rule for Ireland, which also had the effect of marginalizing the party from large sections of the electorate. With Gladstone's successor, *Rosebery, the party was increasingly seen as faddist, representing a variety of unrelated single-issue causes such as temperance, disestablishment of the Welsh Church, and Irish home rule, which did little to enhance its appeal to the electorate at large. A substantial general election victory in 1906, however, came as a result of divisions in the Conservative Party caused by the campaign of Joseph Chamberlain for tariff reform. This allowed the Liberal Party to capitalize on its continuing support for free trade, discontent over the consequences for non-Anglicans of the Balfour Education Act of 1902, and issues arising out of the Boer war.

Under *Campbell-Bannerman, prime minister from 1905 to 1908, then under *Asquith, the Liberal Party entered a critical phase in its history. With Asquith as leader, the party embarked upon a series of major social reforms, including old age *pensions, wage boards, labour exchanges, and national insurance (see NATIONAL INSURANCE ACT, 1911). Accepting the principle that higher state spending would be necessary to meet the higher expectations of the electorate as well as to meet increased military expenditure, this *New Liberalism produced conflict with the House of Lords when it rejected David *Lloyd George's *'People's Budget' of 1909. In the two general elections of 1910 the Liberal Party's representation was drastically reduced, forcing it to rely upon Labour MPs and the Irish National Party for a majority. During the next four years the Liberals faced not only the constitutional conflict with the House of Lords, resolved by the Parliament Act of 1911, but major issues of suffragette militancy, industrial unrest, and the prospect of civil war in Ireland. Women's suffrage campaigners, frustrated by the lack of progress in granting the vote to women, mounted widespread terrorist campaigns directed mainly at property, countered by coercive action by the government. Major strikes and mounting industrial unrest appeared to threaten the ability of the Liberal government to maintain essential services, though these were largely contained. Dependence upon *Redmond's Irish MPs led Asquith to revive home rule legislation in 1912. A bill was successfully driven through the Commons and passed into legislation ready for enactment by 1914, but was then delayed by the outbreak of the *Great War. This was only done, however, at the cost of intense opposition from Unionists in Ireland, especially in the North, where armed resistance was prepared by Carson's Ulster Volunteers (see ULSTER VOLUNTEER FORCE (1913–14)) and backed by the Conservative opposition. By the summer of 1914, the Liberal government appeared to face the threat of ever-intensifying labour militancy and civil war in Ireland.

The outbreak of war in 1914 temporarily eased the pre-war crises faced by the Liberals, but the strains of modern industrialized warfare were to prove almost fatally disruptive. Asquith's leadership came increasingly into question and he was forced to form a coalition government in May 1915, with Conservative and Labour membership, and put his dynamic colleague and potential rival Lloyd George in charge of a newly created Ministry of Munitions. By late 1916, Asquith's lacklustre performance led to him being deposed as premier by Lloyd George with Conservative backing, dividing the Liberal Party in the process. Although Asquith remained supportive of the government, his followers formed a rival faction to that led by Lloyd George. Lloyd George's decision to fight the general election in 1918 under the coalition banner, and Asquith's renewed refusal to join that coalition, led to outright rivalry in the electoral battle by which Asquith's followers were reduced to a mere 22 seats. While the National Liberals (see NATIONAL (LLOYD GEORGE) LIBERAL PARTY (1918–22)) returned 133, they mainly did so through the absence of Conservative opponents.

Meanwhile, the Labour Party had revamped its constitution, organization, and programme, fighting as a national party for the first time, and beginning to feel the beneficial effects of the Representation of the People Act of 1918 which had virtually trebled the electorate. When Lloyd George was forced to resign over the *Chanak crisis in 1922, the divided Liberals faced the full impact of both Labour and Conservative opposition, falling to a combined total of 116 seats, and behind Labour. Although the party's factions reunited under Asquith in 1923 to fight another election on the favourable, uniting issue of free trade, they again came third and saw Labour form its first government. Yet another election in 1924 saw the party reduced to a mere 40 seats.

Although there was a flurry of policy initiatives after Lloyd George assumed undisputed control of the party in 1926, including a bold election manifesto in 1929 offering a cure for mass unemployment, the party could still only win 59 seats and was losing ground on almost every front. The crisis of the early 1930s saw the Liberals split further, a section of *Liberal Nationals under John *Simon eventually becoming virtually indistinguishable from the Conservatives. A small independent element led by Herbert *Samuel with few policies other than free trade and internationalism obtained a mere twenty seats in 1935, while Lloyd George headed an even smaller group, mainly of relatives.

Despite Liberal participation in Churchill's wartime coalition and goodwill from the prime minister, decline continued after 1945, when only twelve seats were held, and took the party to the brink of extinction during the early 1950s when it was reduced to a handful of parliamentary seats. Had the Liberal leader Clement *Davies accepted Churchill's offer of cabinet office in 1951, the remaining Liberals would probably have been absorbed by the Conservatives, as the *Liberal Unionists and Liberal Nationals had been.

A Liberal revival began, however, from 1956, under the new leadership of Jo *Grimond, marked by by-election victories at *Torrington in 1958 and *Orpington in 1962, where the party benefited from a substantial protest vote in times of Tory unpopularity. The Liberal share of the vote at general elections increased steadily (partly as a result of putting up more candidates), although the party was unable to win sufficient seats to threaten the position of Labour and the Conservatives. During the 1960s, the party also attracted an influx of activist *Young Liberals which assisted it to a stronger base in local government and more active election campaigning generally. The party expanded its range of issues, emphasizing electoral reform, regionalism, freedom of information, and 'community politics', and was the first British party to embrace membership of the European Community.

In the first general election of 1974, the party under Jeremy *Thorpe won sufficient seats to negotiate a possible coalition with *Heath, but this failed to materialize. Temporarily set back by the *Scott affair and Thorpe's consequent resignation as leader, David *Steel took the party into the *Lib-Lab pact (1977–8) with Callaghan to re-establish some credibility. Little advanced in the 1979 election, the party received an enormous boost with Labour's split and the formation of the *Social Democratic Party (SDP) in 1981. With Labour in disarray and the Conservatives deeply unpopular, the rapidly formed Liberal-SDP Alliance saw a meteoric rise in opinion poll support, in one case to over 40 per cent, and a series of sensational by-election victories. The Alliance obtained almost a quarter of all votes cast in the 1983 and 1987 elections. An even spread of support, however, meant that the party still got no more than a score of seats, and in 1987 it also suffered from confusion over the dual leadership of Steel and the SDP's David Owen. Steel's call for a merger of the SDP and the Liberals produced a breakaway 'Continuing SDP' led by Owen, but eventually secured the fusion of the two parties and the election of a new leader, Paddy *Ashdown. In effect the traditional Liberal Party had ceased to exist and, first as the Social and Liberal Democratic Party, later with the name Liberal Democrats, the party sought to re-establish the momentum of the Alliance in the 1980s.

The headlong decline of the governing party of Gladstone and Asquith into third-party status by the 1920s has remained one of the major controversies of early 20th-century political history. Various reasons have been put forward for the party's downfall. It has been argued that the party was in serious difficulties by 1900, with its somewhat incoherent collection of 'fads' and 'fringes' excluding it from office for much of the period from 1886 to 1905, and in 1936 George *Dangerfield published his influential *The Strange Death of Liberal England* which argued that it was already in irreparable decline by 1914. Others like Peter *Clarke, however, have pointed to the ability of the Liberal Party prior to 1914 to revitalize itself via 'New Liberalism' and make a more dynamic appeal to the working-class electorate. Local studies have suggested that Liberal decline was patchy and that the party was still strong in many localities. The rise of the Labour Party has also been seen as the accompaniment and cause of Liberal demise as a governing party. The *Lib-Lab pact (1903) has been seen as a fatal sign of weakness, permitting the Labour Party to enter the Commons in significant numbers and become the Liberals' effective successor as the dominant force on the left. Once the electorate was more fully democratized in 1918, Labour was able to capitalize on its appeal to the working class, especially the organized working class, and form its first government in 1924. Gradually, it mobilized the progressive and left-of-centre vote under its own banner, thus depriving the Liberals of mass support and making them seem ever more irrelevant, more and more subject to *third-party squeeze. From this class-orientated perspective, the issue of the replacement of the more 'confessional' politics of the 19th century with the class-based politics of the 20th century is seen as paramount. Other commentators have pointed to more contingent factors governing the decline of the Liberal Party, notably the impact of the Great War—the 'rampant omnibus' in Trevor Wilson's phrase—which fatally wounded a healthy party. Compounded by the continuing rivalry between two powerful political personalities into the 1920s, the Liberal Party can be seen to be as much a victim of avoidable events as of ineluctable forces. The still sizeable vote for the Liberal Party during the 1920s and the protracted nature of its decline have attracted the view that it was also a casualty of the *'first-past-the-post' electoral system which after 1918 persistently under-represented its support in terms of seats in the House of Commons.

Similarly, the question of Liberal survival and revival is much debated. Following the splits of the 1930s and the absorption of the Liberal Nationals into the Conservative Party in 1948, Liberal representation was so low that extinction was a real possibility. This was especially so in the early 1950s when the party had only six MPs, a handful of councillors and less than 3 per cent of the popular vote in the general elections of 1951 and 1955. The 'Celtic fringe' continued to offer a reservoir of potential support and a possible base for revival, while two electoral pacts with the Conservatives in the double seats of Huddersfield and Bolton provided the Liberals with a foothold in urban as well as rural Celtic Britain. Grimond's stimulating leadership from 1956 saw the party begin to capitalize upon these assets and upon disillusion with the Conservatives. Liberal by-election victories gave vital publicity to a party otherwise marginalized at Westminster. Although Liberal hopes for an electoral breakthrough proved elusive in the 1960s and 1970s, a route to power through a 'hung parliament' always seemed a possibility. Twice in the 1970s, in Heath's negotiations with Thorpe following the 1974 election, and in the Lib-Lab Pact of 1977–8, the Liberals had the opportunity to be the minor but decisive partner of a minority governing party. However, negotiations in 1974 proved abortive and the Lib-Lab Pact of 1977–8 brought little lasting benefit. More significantly, the party began to enjoy greater success in local elections, building up substantial support from its very low base in the 1950s via *community politics. These successes, evident for example when it became the largest party in Liverpool in 1974, were continued by the Alliance and the Liberal Democrats, giving the latter control of 24 English local government districts by 1999.

In terms of policy, the Liberal Party carved out a distinctive set of policies for itself as a non-socialist party of the left during the post-war period. The party could lay claim to two of the eminent founding fathers of the post-war consensus, *Beveridge and *Keynes, both of them Liberals. Laissez-faire and internationalism remained key issues into the post-war period, but the Liberal Party was also distinctive in promoting constitutional reform in the form of proportional representation, regional government, and devolution. Attempts by the 'young Liberals' to radicalize the party programme further in the late 1960s were largely fought off, but their commitment was channelled into the community politics strategy and a strong anti-nuclear and environmental thrust which remained a feature of Liberal Party politics until the 1980s. Broadly speaking, the formation of the Alliance and the need to cooperate with the SDP shifted the Liberal Party towards the centre. The party advocated support for Europe and greater state spending where necessary, as well as constitutional reform. In addition the adoption of elements of the SDP's system of policy formulation such as the use of green and white paper statements, began to appeal to those distrustful of the radicalism of the old Liberal Assembly. These features were carried over into the new merged party after the demise of the Liberal Party as an independent force. In 1997, the Liberals finally got back to the level of parliamentary representation that they had enjoyed in 1929 and held it in 2001. The way up has seemed a great deal steeper than the way down. *JS*

PETER CLARKE, *Lancashire and the New Liberalism* (London, 1971). | CHRIS COOK, *A Short History of the Liberal Party, 1900–1998* (London, 1998). | GEORGE DANGERFIELD, *The Strange Death of Liberal England* (London, 1936). | KENNETH O. MORGAN, *The Age of Lloyd George: The Liberal Party and British Politics, 1890–1929* (London, 1971). | JOHN STEVENSON, *Third Party Politics in Britain since 1945* (Oxford, 1992). | TREVOR WILSON, *The Downfall of the Liberal Party, 1914–1935* (London, 1966).

Liberal Party (Continuing), the party, officially relaunched in March 1989, of those dissident Liberals who refused to merge with the *Social Democrats and who have maintained an active independent existence. Its first president was Michael *Meadowcroft (former Liberal MP for Leeds West). In the 1992 election, it fielded 73 candidates and in the 1994 European elections polled over 100,000 votes. It still has a few councillors. *JS*

Liberal Reorganization Committee (1935–6), appointed under Lord Meston to reconsider the structure of Liberal Party organization in the wake of the disappointing results of the 1935 general election. Its aim was to reconsider the whole structure of the party with a view to rebuilding its central structure, produced in the *Meston report. *JS*

Liberal Summer Schools. discussion meetings in the inter-war period which provided an opportunity for Liberals to rearticulate policy in the wake of the decline of the party's parliamentary fortunes. Important figures were attracted to the Summer School movement including J. M. *Keynes, Ramsay Muir Lord Lothian, and William *Beveridge. *JS*

Liberal Unionist Party, faction of 93 disaffected Liberal MPs which split off from the official ('Gladstonian') Liberal Party over Gladstone's proposal to reform the Irish Union in 1886 and eventually merged with the Conservatives, an important bridge over which sections of Victorian opinion moved to the political right. The Liberal split was not at first expected to be permanent, while the Liberal Unionists themselves contained two mutually suspicious groups of *Whigs under Hartington and businessmen-radicals led by Joseph Chamberlain. Gladstone's determination to pursue home rule for Ireland, however, forced the Liberal Unionists (LUs) to ally with Conservatives, keeping Salisbury in office, 1886–92, then joining his government in 1895. They also had whips in parliament and created a single LU party office in 1889, but in both cases cooperated actively with their Conservative counterparts. The LUs still had 68 MPs after the 1900 election (though never afterwards more than half that number), and enhanced the Unionists' appeal to Nonconformist voters and in regions like Scotland and the West Midlands, while Chamberlain's activities buttressed their claim to be pursuing 'social reform'. LUs remained, however, a separate party, no LU joined the *Carlton Club, and when Chamberlain launched his tariff reform crusade in 1903 both parties were equally split. This fissure was one of many in Edwardian Conservatism, but the fact that he was an LU cost Austen Chamberlain the party leadership of all Unionists in 1911. The successful candidate, Law, held similar opinions and came from a similar background, but was a Conservative. In the drive for party unity that followed Law's election, it was quickly agreed to merge the two parties in 1912, and past suspicions soon disappeared, but Conservatives continued to call themselves 'Unionists' in Scotland for another half-century, and, even though he led the Conservative party from 1937 to 1940, Neville Chamberlain was always elected to parliament in Birmingham as a 'Unionist'. *JAR*

libertarianism, the notion that human endeavour is best organized outside formal state apparatus, and possessing both practical and theoretical strands. Libertarianism can be distinguished from liberalism in that it has a tendency to put freedom before order. Libertarianism is normally associated with anarchism, and in this regard its impact has been muted in 20th-century Britain, although it has influenced some left-wing conceptions of the post-capitalist state. More important perhaps has been the impact of right-wing libertarian ideas, especially on the 'New Right' in the 1970s. Although some, such as the anarcho-capitalist Murray Rothbard in *For a New Liberty: the Libertarian Manifesto* (1978), have rejected all state apparatus, the main influence here has been Robert Nozick, in *Anarchy, State and Utopia* (Oxford, 1974), whose entitlement theory of justice led him to argue for a minimalist, nightwatchman state to protect the rights of private property. Within the Conservative Party, libertarian influences have led to calls for personal freedoms (such as decriminalizing certain drugs) often at odds with the party's traditional stance on issues of morality. *CPS*

Liberty, private organization founded in 1934 as the National Council for Civil Liberties (NCCL) by a group of liberal and left-wing activists. Its initial purpose was to observe and report on police behaviour towards hunger marchers and anti-fascist demonstrators, following allegations of police brutality and infringements of civil liberties. The NCCL attracted a distinguished group of sponsors, including Attlee, and established itself after 1945 as a significant pressure group concerned with the encroachments of state or police powers upon the rights of the citizen. In recent years it has campaigned for a *freedom of information Act, a bill of rights, and for safeguards over the use of computerized data. It was renamed Liberty in 1990. *JS*

Lib-Lab pact (1903), electoral agreement. Herbert Gladstone, Liberal chief whip, and

Ramsay MacDonald, *Labour Representation Committee (LRC) secretary, made a secret arrangement, allowing a number of Labour candidates to run unopposed at the 1906 election, so helping to increase Labour representation at that election to 29. For Gladstone the pact avoided confrontations such as had occurred at Clitheroe in 1902 when local Labour groups had refused to withdraw a candidate not approved by the Liberal Party. For MacDonald, the LRC was given the room to allow it to grow into a new political party (and ultimately the replace the Liberals as the main anti-Conservative party). A later Liberal leader, Jeremy Thorpe, thought that the 1903 pact had let 'the socialist cuckoo' into 'the radical nest'. *BB*

Lib-Lab pact (1977–8), period of cooperation between the Liberal and Labour Parties to keep James Callaghan's Labour government in office. By January 1977, Labour's parliamentary majority had fallen to one, and in March the Conservatives threatened a 'no confidence' motion. Under the terms of the pact, Labour was guaranteed support in the Commons in return for allowing the Liberals to veto proposed legislation before it went to cabinet. Liberals were also promised consideration of the issue of *proportional representation, at least for European elections. In the event, Labour did not deliver on proportional representation in European elections and the Liberals withdrew from the pact in the autumn of 1978. *JS*

life expectancy has been increasing in Britain from the middle of the 19th century. A male had a life expectancy of 40.4 years at birth in 1871, but 58.7 years by 1931. At birth the expectation of life in 1998 was over 74 years for a man and 79 years for a woman. Since 1971, life expectancy in the UK has been increasing by around two years per decade for men and around one-and-a-half years for women. Increased life expectancy came about during the century largely because of a decline in mortality rates, especially a decline in *infant mortality. Rising standards of living and improvements in medical technology produced these changes, especially the assault on childhood infectious diseases through immunization. Also important were improvements in housing and the overall environment. In general, in all age groups, death rates are higher for men than women, producing the higher levels of life expectancy for women. Causes of premature death vary by age and gender. Deaths from accidents or violence account for three in every five deaths of men aged between 15 and 30, while deaths from cancer account for more deaths of women in this age group. Deaths from cancer and circulatory diseases, including heart attacks and strokes, are the most common causes of death among older people. There were 628,000 deaths in the UK in 1998, a death rate of just under 11 per 1,000 population. *JS*

life peerages. Although life peerages were well precedented in the Middle Ages, by the later doctrines of peerage law, it was held that the crown could create only hereditary peerages. In 1856, Palmerston sought to confer a life peerage on a judge (Wensleydale) but this initiative towards strengthening the House of Lords was rejected by it as illegal. The Appellate Jurisdiction Act, 1876, subsequently permitted the creation of salaried lords of appeal in ordinary (Law Lords) without hereditary peerages, to assist in the hearing of appeals. At present there are twelve such Law Lords who retire at 70 but remain members of the House for life. The number can be raised by order, subject to affirmative resolutions in both Houses. In 1958 the Life Peerages Act permitted life peerages to be conferred on men and women, with no limit on numbers. Between 1958 and 1998 945 life peerages were created. In December 1998, there were 484 life peers including 87 women. Life peers have always been treated like other peers, and not as second-class members. They have transformed the House: the range of occupations and interest has widened and made available an extensive expertise in debate, legislation, and select committees, and opened the door to a great increase in activity by the Lords. *MWB*

Lilley, Peter Bruce (1943–), Conservative politician. The underrated and likeable 1989 prophet of the Major government's main privatizations, a voter against capital punishment and for liberalizing official secrets, Lilley was also the Portilloid denouncer (if from a cadged phrasebook) of cadging foreigners. An expert social security secretary, respected trade secretary, and Thatcher devotee, disliking Maastricht, he wavered between loyalty and disloyalty. As a non-impactive shadow chancellor from 1997, he was soon dropped. *EP*

Limehouse, site of a polemical speech by David *Lloyd George on 30 July 1909 at the Edinburgh Castle public house in East London. He roundly attacked the House of Lords for its rejection of the *'People's Budget', upset the king and the Unionist Party, and helped to precipitate the constitutional crisis of 1909–11. For a time,

'Limehousing' was a popular shorthand for political vituperation. *JAR*

Limehouse declaration (25 January 1981), statement issued by the so-called *Gang of Four (Shirley *Williams, David *Owen, William *Rodgers, and Roy *Jenkins) proposing the formation of a Council for *Social Democracy as a protest against the Labour Party's newly introduced method of selecting a leader—and more generally against the party's shift to the left. 'We believe', the declaration said, 'that the need for a realignment of British politics must now be faced.' The declaration, made outside David Owen's house in Limehouse, East London, precipitated the defection of a group of Labour MPs from the party and the formation of the *Social Democratic Party on 26 March 1981. *JS*

Lindemann, Frederick Alexander (1886–1957), prime minister's personal assistant, 1940–2, and paymaster general, 1942–5 and 1951–3. An Oxford professor of physics, Lindemann became a friend of Winston Churchill in the early 1920s, sharing his views on the need for greater British airpower in the late 1930s. In 1939, Churchill, as first lord of the Admiralty, recruited Lindemann to establish and lead a statistical section. In 1940, 'the prof', as he was known, and his staff followed Churchill to Downing Street, where the statistical branch produced advice on a wide range of policy. Ennobled as Lord Cherwell in 1941, Lindemann became paymaster general the following year. An awkward personality who enjoyed feuds and hated Germans, Lindemann was by no means a popular appointment, but was nevertheless a vital one. Thoroughly loyal to Churchill, his advice on weapons was particularly significant. His great asset was the ability to explain complex scientific and economic information in terms the prime minister could understand. He served in Churchill's shadow cabinet (1945–51). As peacetime paymaster general (1951–3), his economic advice included successfully opposing the *ROBOT plan to float the pound, but he was chiefly involved in Britain's atomic programme and the establishment of the Atomic Energy Authority. *CL*

Lord Birkenhead, *The Prof in Two Worlds* (London, 1961). | Roy Harrod, *A Personal Memoir of Lord Cherwell* (London, 1959).

Lindsay, Alexander Dunlop (1879–1952), educationalist and socialist intellectual. Sandy Lindsay was educated at Glasgow and Oxford, becoming president of the Oxford Union, 1902. He was subsequently a classics tutor at Oxford and an outstanding master of Balliol, 1924–49 (influencing among others Denis Healey and Edward Heath). Lindsay was educational adviser to the TUC and the Labour Party, but in 1938 contested the *Oxford by-election as an independent anti-appeaser. After a term as Oxford's vice-chancellor, 1935–8, he was instrumental in the creation of the new University of Keele, and was its first vice-chancellor, 1949–52. *JS*

literacy. During the course of the 19th and 20th centuries almost universal literacy was thought to have been achieved in Britain, the provision of compulsory education from the 1870s and the steady raising of the *school-leaving age having provided the mechanism through which this was achieved. Complacency on the issue of educational standards came under question with the *Black Papers from the 1960s and opening of an education debate during the 1970s. One result has been the recognition that significant numbers of children were leaving school without functional literacy. The *national curriculum of 1988 included required attainment standards, including basic standards of literacy. In 1992, the Schools Act required schools to submit annual reports on children's progress and in 1993 school tests were required to concentrate on 'the three Rs'. Under the 1997 Labour government, a slimmed-down curriculum for primary schools in foundation subjects was introduced. These arrangements were intended to focus attention on improving basic literacy and numeracy. In England national numeracy and literacy strategies have been introduced, requiring all schools to have a literacy and numeracy study hour each day. Adult literacy has been addressed in a government paper published in 1999, which found unacceptably high levels of illiteracy amongst the adult population. Approximately 20 per cent of those surveyed were found to suffer from degrees of innumeracy or illiteracy. A Basic Skills Agency with a budget rising from £180 million in 1998–9 to £350 million in 2001–2 is proposed to double the number of adult learners from 250,000 to 500,000 a year. *JS*

'little local difficulties', words used by Macmillan in 1958 to play down the resignation of all three of his Treasury ministers, Thorneycroft, Birch, and Powell, over government spending. Macmillan's brilliantly dismissive (if rehearsed) phrase, uttered as he left for a major Commonwealth tour, displayed sang-froid while disguising his deep concern. *RJS*

'Little Moscows', initially a derogatory but perhaps later a somewhat affectionate nickname for those communities in which the Communist Party of Great Britain achieved a degree of organizational success, primarily in trade union affairs but also in local government. The classic 'Little Moscows' have been identified as Mardy in Wales, and Lumphinnans and the vale of Leven in Scotland. Sociological and geographical factors seem to have been as vital as political influences. *PS*

STUART MACINTYRE, *Little Moscows* (London, 1980).

Livingstone, Ken (1945–), Labour politician and independent mayor of London. He was demonized by the Conservatives and the media as 'Red Ken' when leader of the Greater London Council, 1981–6, but his 'fares fair' policy and genuine desire to involve local communities in politics made him popular with Londoners. An MP since 1987, his left-wing views irritated the New Labour leaders, yet paradoxically his popularity soared. He was voted one of the top ten men of the year in a newspaper poll in 1997, and went on to defy Tony Blair's opposition and become the first directly elected London mayor in 2000, as an independent, having been expelled from the Labour Party for not supporting its official candidate. *MC*

Llandudno assembly (14–19 September 1981), Liberal conference which gave approval to the formation of the *Alliance with the Social Democratic Party, only 112 out of 1,600 delegates voting against ratification. *JS*

Llanelli riots (18 August 1911), disturbances which occurred at Llanelli (then spelt Llanelly). They have largely been overshadowed in radical mythology by events at *Tonypandy in 1910, but in fact the Llanelli riots were both more serious and politically intriguing. During a national rail strike a train under military protection was attacked by a crowd as it passed through Llanelli station; troops of the Worcestershire regiment responded by firing shots and as a consequence two men were killed and one was injured. The casualties had been standing on an embankment and the army's defence was that they had been hit accidentally when shots had been fired above the heads of the crowd. What was undoubtedly true was that the government was greatly concerned at keeping the line to Ireland open at a time of the international *Moroccan crisis. The prime minister, Asquith, had warned the railwaymen that the strike would have serious consequences and home secretary Churchill had deployed the army with some alacrity. *PS*

Lloyd, Geoffrey William (1902–84), Conservative politician. Elected to parliament in 1931, Lloyd became Baldwin's parliamentary private secretary. As a pre-war Home Office minister he organized air-raid precautions, and from 1940 played a crucial role as minister in charge of petroleum warfare. Lloyd lost his Birmingham seat in 1945 but was re-elected in 1950 and became fuel and power minister, 1951–5, until Eden relegated him. As Macmillan's education minister, 1957–9, he enhanced technological training. Lloyd entered the Lords in 1974. *RJS*

Lloyd, George (1879–1941), Conservative politician and colonial administrator. Lloyd entered parliament in January 1910 but was a relatively obscure backbencher. During the Great War he saw service in the Middle East where he developed a lifelong empathy for the Arab cause. He was governor of Bombay, 1919–24, before becoming high commissioner in Egypt, 1925–9, his relations with the Foreign Office, and especially Austen Chamberlain, becoming strained during this period. During the 1930s he championed imperial causes, opposed the 1935 India Act, and advocated conscription. *NJC*

JOHN CHARMLEY, *Lord Lloyd and the Decline of the British Empire* (London, 1987).

Lloyd, (John) Selwyn Brooke (1904–78), chancellor of the exchequer, foreign secretary, and Speaker of the House of Commons. Selwyn Lloyd's Nonconformist background and family connection with Lloyd George led him to stand for the Liberals in 1929, but he was persuaded of the need for protective tariffs and became a Conservative. Elected to parliament in 1945 for his native Wirral, where he had been a councillor, he emerged as one of the most promising Tories. He could claim to be 'the father of commercial television', since his minority report to the Beveridge committee on broadcasting in 1951 (see BEVERIDGE REPORT (1951)) advocating a competitive television system financed by advertising was largely enacted in 1954. As a Foreign Office minister from 1951 Lloyd was an able deputy to Eden. In 1954 Lloyd became supply minister before entering Eden's cabinet at defence, but his promotion to foreign secretary in December 1955 mainly reflected bad blood between Eden and Macmillan, and the prime minister's wish to run foreign affairs. During the *Suez crisis Lloyd strove for a diplomatic solution, but when his efforts failed he overcame his doubts about collusion with the French and Israelis and loyally backed Eden. He remained at the Foreign Office, however, until Macmillan appointed him chancellor of the exchequer in 1960. Lloyd's 1961 pay pause (to hold down wage inflation, especially in the public sector) made him unpopular, while his cautious, downbeat style increasingly irritated colleagues and in July 1962 his dismissal triggered the *'Night of the Long Knives'. An influential supporter of Douglas-Home in 1963, Lloyd joined his cabinet as leader of the House. Lloyd served in the shadow cabinet during 1964–6. In 1971 he was elected Speaker of the Commons, despite the opposition of some 50 MPs to the choice of a former, senior cabinet minister. Lloyd entered the Lords in 1976. *RJS*

D. R. Thorpe, *Selwyn Lloyd* (London, 1989).

Lloyd George, David (1863–1945), Liberal politician and prime minister. After growing up in a poor north Wales background, he trained as a soldier, taking on and championing the causes of his part of the *Celtic fringe. Elected to parliament for Caernarfon Boroughs in 1890, 'LG' served as its MP until his elevation to the peerage in 1945. After an early radical phase in which he opposed the Boer war, he joined Campbell-Bannerman's government as president of the Board of Trade, 1905–8, then served Asquith as chancellor of the exchequer, 1908–15; minister of munitions, 1915–16; and secretary for war, 1916. Lloyd George was prime minister from 1916 to 1922, but then never held office again. He led the Liberal Party from 1926 to 1931 and in 1945 he was created Earl Lloyd George.

As chancellor, Lloyd George proved a radical social reformer, introducing the *'People's Budget', old age *pensions, and national insurance (see National Insurance Act, 1911).

Wartime and Post-War Leader

As minister of munitions and wartime premier he was an efficient and dynamic administrator and leader. His decision to oust Asquith from the premiership in 1916, and then to continue the wartime coalition with the Conservatives in the *'Coupon' Election of 1918 did irreparable harm to the Liberal Party and damaged its reputation permanently. He pursued a vindictive policy towards Germany in the run-up to the 1918 election but at the *Paris peace conference was concerned to moderate French demands. Even before the end of the war Lloyd George opened a reconstruction campaign to appease working-class discontent and fulfil his radical aspirations. Housing Acts were passed in 1919, education reform introduced, and social insurance extended, though these programmes were cut short by a round of economies in 1921, the *Geddes axe. LG brought the Irish situation to an apparent conclusion by the *Anglo-Irish treaty of 1921, setting up the Irish Free State. The Conservatives who made up the majority of the coalition grew restive at his leadership and he was forced to resign after the *Chanak crisis in 1922.

Liberal Leader

Although he made a temporary truce with Asquith to fight the 1923 election, Lloyd George retained his own organization and personal control of the *Lloyd George fund. In 1926, he finally assumed the leadership of a Liberal Party reduced to a mere 40 seats in the 1924 election. LG showed considerable interest in policies to solve the problem of mass unemployment between the wars through greater government spending, drawing upon the ideas of J. M. *Keynes. He was still considered a possible contender for office in 1931 but was ill at the time of the August crisis of the second Labour government and missed out on the chance to shape or join the National Government. LG continued to promote ideas for economic regeneration, even expressing admiration for what Hitler had done economically, and sought unavailingly to mount a dynamic British campaign in 1935 through *councils of action. He was offered office by Churchill in the war cabinet of 1940, but felt himself to be too old to carry responsibilities.

The Record

Lloyd George's career can be considered in a number of different ways. He is one of a handful of 20th-century British statesmen to play a major role in international affairs, and could be considered a world statesman. As leader of Britain in the latter phase of the Great War, Lloyd George was instrumental in decisions which affected many different parts of the world, though he failed ever to impose his will on the British generals. He presided over the expansion of the British Empire to its largest ever extent, led the government which issued the *Balfour declaration, dealt with the first stirrings in Indian nationalism, and authorized the Allied intervention against Bolshevism in Russia in 1919. He dealt with the aftermath of the Easter Rising, waged the Anglo-Irish war of the *Black and Tans, but also made the peace settlement, the 'treaty' of 1921, which brought Irish conflict to a temporary end at the price of partition.

As British war leader, he was complicit in the treaties and settlements which effectively destroyed the Austro-Hungarian Empire and was a major figure in the Paris peace conference. His contribution towards the handling of Germany must be regarded as yielding mixed results. Although he had advocated a harsh settlement with Germany, he sought to minimize the damage to the European economy that would ensue if Germany was penalized too harshly, though with little success. His fall over the Chanak crisis demonstrated the extent to which his career after 1918 was dominated by the backwash of events from the Great War.

Domestically, Lloyd George's greatest achievement was his successful leadership of the country to victory in 1918. He was dynamic and effective as minister of munitions in moving Britain towards total mobilization for war in 1915–16. As prime minister from December 1916, he saw the country through the darkest months of the conflict when military failures in 1917, the German U-boat campaign, and war-weariness and industrial militancy threatened Britain with defeat. He effectively rallied the home front with his skills as negotiator, the introduction of rationing, and promises of post-war reconstruction. Compared with Churchill in the Second World War, LG failed to resolve relations with the military and never had the same degree of control, but threw his influence behind innovations such as the convoy system and attempts to break the stalemate on the western front. His most significant contribution lay in ensuring that the military had the tools to do the job and were backed by as complete a mobilization of the domestic economy as was feasible—effectively the record that allowed him to campaign in 1918 as 'the man that won the war'. Lloyd George's initiative in bringing *businessmen into government, creating a larger secretariat at Downing Street, and expanding the instruments of government with new ministries and agencies, marked a unique departure and a crucial precedent for 20th-century British government.

Judged solely in terms of policies and legislative achievement, Lloyd George also occupies a decisive place in political history. The 'People's Budget' and the legislation which brought old age pensions, national insurance, and labour exchanges were significant landmarks in the evolution of state responsibility for the lives of ordinary citizens. Although Lloyd George was only part of the government which passed these measures, extensive social policies were also propounded in his reconstruction proposals from 1917 and enacted by the 1918–22 coalition government. Most famously dubbed the *'homes fit for heroes' campaign, Lloyd George promised an expansion of state intervention by subsidies for housing, plans for education reform, and an extension of national insurance. Historians have often debated whether Lloyd George's policies were simply an attempt to win votes or to stave off the threat of industrial militancy in 1917–19 by 'killing Bolshevism by kindness'. Both motives played a part, but the policies enacted in 1919–21 built upon pre-war *New Liberal thinking. Plans for a housing programme were being mooted before 1914 and extensions to national insurance and to education provisions were not unlikely whichever government emerged from the Great War. As it was the *Addison Acts, 1919, marked a decisive step along the road to the creation of a large local authority rented sector of *council houses. The Fisher *Education Act, 1918, proved the major piece of educational reform between 1902 and 1944, while the expansion of national insurance in 1920 brought millions more workers into the schemes initiated in 1911, giving Britain the most extensive system of contributory insurance in the world. The reduction of spending in 1921–2, including the termination of the Addison Acts and the truncation of the Fisher Act's provision for continuing education, left a legacy of bitterness towards Lloyd George which barely abated during the inter-war years. Reinforced by the experience of the Depression, the promises of a 'land fit for heroes' rang hollow.

In practice, Lloyd George responded in 1921 to conventional economic wisdom as the world economy moved from a hectic post-war boom into recession and Britain found herself overstretched both in her domestic and overseas commitments. More clear-cut was Lloyd George's failure to create a new non-socialist party of the centre out of the wartime coalition. He failed to recognize the intrinsic strength of the Conservative Party, especially after the 1918 election, and his own vulnerability to a backbench Conservative revolt, as occurred in 1922. His later attempts to revive the Liberal Party and his flirtation with the idea of a British 'New Deal' simply failed to materialize. Judged an untrustworthy adventurer, he remained a 'lost leader' for the rest of his life.

Lloyd George's effect on the Liberal Party was also decisive. The political *coup d'état* which deposed Asquith and Lloyd George's perpetuation of the coalition government into peacetime with himself at its head broke the back of the old Liberal Party. These divisions, which surfaced at a time when it was facing the challenge of the rise of Labour and, after 1918, a revitalized Conservative Party, were of critical importance in its demise as an effective party of government in the mid-1920s. Although Lloyd George had some success in creating a revival for the 1929 election, support for the party had already dipped too low for it to obtain more than a fraction of seats in the Commons. *JS*

John Grigg, *The Young Lloyd George* (London, 1973). | John Grigg, *Lloyd George: The People's Champion 1902–1911* (London, 1978). | John Grigg, *Lloyd George: from Peace to War, 1912–1916* (London, 1985). | Peter Rowland, *David Lloyd George: A Biography* (London, 1975).

Lloyd George, Gwilym (1894–1967), home secretary. Son of Liberal prime minister David *Lloyd George, he was first elected in 1922 but, unlike his father David or sister Megan, moved closer to the Tories. He held junior posts before being appointed Churchill's fuel and power minister in 1942. After the war he stood as a Liberal National and Conservative, becoming food minister in 1951 and home secretary and Welsh affairs minister in 1954. He was sacked by Macmillan in 1957. *RJS*

Lloyd George, Megan Arfon (1902–66). The daughter of David *Lloyd George, Lady Megan was Liberal MP for Anglesey, 1929–51, but then joined the Labour Party and was Labour MP for Carmarthen, from 1955 until her death. She was deputy leader of the Liberals, 1949–51, but her defection to Labour (brother Gwylim had gone to the Tories) seemed to many to symbolize the poverty of Liberalism in the 1950s. *JAR*

Lloyd George/Bradbury/Warren Fisher Reforms (1919), administrative reform. In the aftermath of the Great War, the Treasury, led by its permanent secretary, Sir John Bradbury, drew up plans to unify the home civil service by extending the Treasury's control over the organization, management, and pay of all other domestic departments. Ministers accepted the outcome in August 1919, keen to use extra Treasury powers as the instrument of their post-war economy drive. These powers were promulgated by a Treasury minute of 4 September. It fell to Warren Fisher, a Lloyd George protégé brought in from the Inland Revenue at the age of 39 to replace Bradbury, to drive through the reforms. The September 1919 changes had established that, henceforth, the top civil servant in the Treasury would also serve as 'permanent head of the civil service', and advise the 'first lord of the Treasury' (the prime minister) on civil service appointments. Henceforth the consent of the prime minister was needed for the appointment or removal of top civil servants in all departments. This was laid down in a second Treasury minute of March 1920 and fed suspicions that Lloyd George was bent on usurping a collective cabinet system of government with a prime ministerial alternative. A third Treasury minute of July 1920 promulgated the Treasury's right to 'make regulations for controlling the conduct of His Majesty's Civil Establishments, and providing for the classification, remuneration, and other conditions of service of all persons employed therein'. *PJH*

Peter Hennessy, *Whitehall* (London, 1989). | Henry Roseveare, *The Treasury* (London, 1969).

Lloyd George fund, a private political asset accumulated by David *Lloyd George while prime minister, 1916–22. The main source of income appears to have been the sale of honours. Its extent was unclear at the time and has not been much clarified since, estimates in 1922 ranging between £1 million and £2 million. During the 1920s, as he wrestled with Asquith for control of the bankrupt Liberal Party, Lloyd George found the fact that he had a large capital sum at his personal disposal quite an advantage. Other Liberals were torn between need for cash and their reluctance to touch such tainted money. *JAR*

Lloyd-Graeme, Philip. See Cunliffe-Lister, Philip.

Lloyd-Hughes, Trevor Denby (1922–), prime minister's press secretary, 1964–9. As political correspondent of the *Liverpool Daily Post*, Lloyd-Hughes became friendly with local MP Harold Wilson. However, he was not a success as Wilson's press secretary. The lobby resented the elevation of one of its junior members; and Lloyd-Hughes was so assiduous in observing civil service neutrality that Wilson soon began to bypass him. From 1965 political briefings were provided by Gerald Kaufman, and in 1969 Lloyd-Hughes was replaced by Joe Haines. *CL*

lobby. See parliamentary lobby.

lobbying, a term with two different uses. First, lobbying is specifically the activity of 'for-hire' or commercial policy advocates, but there is a wider use that sees the policy-influencing efforts of any organization (interest group, corporation, governmental agency) as lobbying. This first use sees the lobbyist as a particular occupation; the second defines the lobbyist by function rather than a fee. In Britain, there is more of a 'how to' literature (I. Greer, *Right to be Heard*, 1985; C. Souza, *So You Want to Be a Lobbyist*, 1998) than there is analysis of the impact of the activities. Partly this is a product of client confidentiality, but the far more substantial reason is the difficulty in discerning the impact. With lobbyists active on both sides of most issues, some lobbyists can claim to be influential, whether or not there is a direct connection between their contribution and results. Kevin Maloney's *Lobbyists for Hire* (1996) is an attempt to assess effectiveness. Public concern at the legitimacy of lobbying, particularly paid lobbying by legislators themselves, prompted the report by Lord Nolan's committee on standards in public life. In the USA, lobbying has rather outlived its pejorative associations, as in Kenneth Crawford's *The Pressure Boys: the Inside Story of Lobbying in America* (1939), to become the technical and neutral term denoting the impact of *interest groups on the policy process. This literature has wrested interest group studies from Olson-type analysis of what happens within groups to the external effects on policy. The recent controversy has centred on whether groups primarily approach legislators who already support them or whether they target those opposed (see the debate in *American Journal of Political Science*, 1996). *GJ*

William Browne, *Cultivating Congress* (Lawrence, Kan., 1995). | J. P. Heinz, E. Laumann, R. Nelson, and R. Salisbury, *The Hollow Core* (London, 1993). | Grant Jordan, *The Commercial Lobbyists* (Aberdeen, 1991). | Andy McFarland, *Common Cause* (Chatham, 1984).

local authority associations. Prior to 1974, the many distinct types of local authority in England and Wales were organized into separate associations, with the exception of the county and non-county boroughs, which had been combined in the Association of Municipal Corporations (AMC). The others were the County Councils Association (CCA), the Urban and Rural District Councils Associations (UDCA, RDCA), and the National Association of Parish Councils (NAPC). Additionally, the Association of Education Committees (AEC) and the National Association of Divisional Executives in Education (NADEE) brought together authorities with education responsibilities. London's local authorities were represented by the Metropolitan Boroughs Standing Joint Committee (MBSJC) and, after the reorganization of London government, the London Boroughs Association (LBA), which later split on party lines, spawning a separate (Labour-left) Association of London Authorities (ALA). The primary purpose of these associations was to represent their interests to the central departments, but they also provided advice and support to their member authorities. Nevertheless, the principal effect of this pattern was to institutionalize the divergent—even antagonistic—interests of different types of area, greatly complicating negotiations over, for example, grant allocations, and exercising a virtual veto over the reorganization of local government structure. Local government reorganization in 1972 abolished the distinction between rural and urban districts, prompting the formation of a unified Association of District Councils (ADC). At the same time, delegation in education was terminated, and the divisional executives ceased to exist. The AMC was reconstituted as the Association of Metropolitan Authorities, so as to admit the new metropolitan district councils, and the CCA as the Association of County Councils, to which the new metropolitan county councils affiliated. The continuation of separate associations foreclosed the possibility of a single organization to provide a combined front to central government. This came only in 1998, when a generic Local Government Association was formed, and the separate associations dissolved. *KY*

local government audit. The system of local government audit has developed progressively through the 20th century from one of local discretion and variation to one of uniformity and central control. District audit originated as a means of securing proper control over the expenditure of poor law authorities, but was progressively extended into the mainstream of local government with successive structural reorganizations; internal and professional audit gave way to the scrutiny of the district auditor, a centrally appointed official. The district auditor has the power, where an item of expenditure appears contrary to law, to apply to a court for a declaration to that effect, and the court can order repayment. Where the district auditor judges a loss to have been incurred through 'wilful misconduct', he has the power to surcharge (levy a financial penalty) upon councillors involved; upon local government officers for improper payments; and upon both for unreasonable expenditure. The purpose of district audit is to ensure that expenditure is both lawful and reasonable, but the powers of centrally appointed district auditors have from time to time been seen as a negation of proper local discretion, without any compensating ministerial accountability. Following the Poplar dispute in the 1920s, the Audit (Local Authorities) Act, 1927, provided

that any councillor surcharged for more than £500 (a figure that was subsequently raised to £2,000) would be disqualified from holding office for five years. The number of surcharges made annually fell from more than 3,000 at the beginning of the century to around three or four in the 1970s as the system settled down, and local authority decision makers and auditors adapted to one another. The sums involved were generally small, but in 1996 the district auditor levied spectacular surcharges on the Conservative leader and her associates on Westminster city council. Meanwhile, the role of district auditors as advisers and consultants on financial management had developed considerably, and in 1982 the district audit service was placed under the national Audit Commission, the remit of which was to promote efficiency, value for money, and good practice, as well as to ensure financial propriety.
KY

local government elections. The system of local elections in Britain is not uniform, the present arrangements representing a continuation of long-standing diversity within the local government structure. At present, county councils, London boroughs, and the new Welsh unitary authorities elect their whole council every four years. Metropolitan district councils have annual elections for one-third of their councillors in each of the non-county election years, that is, in three years out of four. Non-metropolitan (or county) districts and English unitary authorities may choose either system, and just over a third of them—generally the more urban—have opted for annual elections. For election purposes, all councils are divided into either single-member wards (in counties, divisions) or multi-member wards (on a figure divisible by three, where annual elections are held). The arguments for single-member wards is that they are smaller, provide a strong link between councillors and their electors, and encourage higher turnouts. Multi-member wards, on the other hand, are associated with a more frequent opportunity to vote in those authorities where annual elections are held, and may permit some load-sharing between councillors. All local government elections are held on the simple majority or first-past-the-post system, although the 1910 royal commission on electoral systems recommended the adoption of a form of proportional representation (PR), which was endorsed by the Speaker's Conference of 1918. A bill to give local authorities a permissive power to choose such a system was subsequently introduced into parliament, but was not passed by the Commons. The *Maud committee of 1964–7 considered, but rejected, putting local elections on a PR basis. The Labour government elected in 1997 committed themselves to consider weekend voting, together with different electoral systems—including proportional representation—and procedures.
KY

local government finance, the most intractable problem of local government, the solution to which has evaded governments for 100 years. For much of the 20th century, local government expenditure was financed from three sources: rates (a local property tax), grants, and public borrowing. Throughout this period, borrowing increased steadily to finance the expansion of the physical infrastructure, while the proportion of current expenditure met from government grant steadily increased. This shift was associated with the growth in local expenditure, from £76 million in 1900 (England and Wales) to £5,405 million in 1970, an increase in real terms of more than 900 per cent. The financial relationship between central and local government at the beginning of the century was based on assigned revenues, designed to give local authorities the benefit of certain national taxes in support of their general expenditure. The system was controversial. Agricultural interests were more in favour of financial aid than were business interests in developing urban areas, as the pressures on the rates, which gained buoyancy from development, were more strongly felt in the countryside. By 1929, assigned revenues had virtually disappeared, to be replaced by a new block grant to compensate for loss of rate revenue, while assigned revenues and a range of specific grants were terminated. The block grant was distributed on the basis of a formula which took into account the characteristics of the local area rather than the expenditure of the local authority, a principle which was confirmed in the 1948 Local Government Act as the Exchequer Equalization Grant (EEG) and continues to the present day. Specific, or percentage, grants were targeted on the development (or protection) of specific services, and their use increased with the growth of state intervention.

The period from 1948 to 1958 was the high tide of specific grants, but because such grants (hitherto favoured by Labour) tended to encourage expenditure, the Conservatives moved to restrict them. Henry Brooke's Local Government Act, 1958, recast exchequer support as a general rate deficiency grant, ostensibly to provide freedom from central control, but in practice tightening control through the annual grant settlement. By the time Labour took office in 1964, action on the rating system was urgently needed to soften the effects of the 1963 reassessment, and Richard Crossman's Rating Act, 1966, introduced rate rebates for low-income households. The Local Government Act of that same year provided progressive increases in domestic ratepayer support in the new rate support grant (RSG) through a subsidy element which increased year-on-year by the equivalent of a 5p rate.

Successive governments of both parties struggled to restrict the growth of local expenditure. In 1975, the Layfield committee was set up to inquire into the whole basis of local government finance, but the committee's penetrating analyses of the need for a new system—a local income tax was favoured—failed to convince Labour ministers. The Conservatives, meanwhile, were pledged to abolish the rating system, and their return in 1979 saw an accelerated study of alternatives, though to little effect. Meanwhile, the new block grant system introduced by the Local Government, Planning and Land Act, 1980, proved the most complex of all grant regimes. Based on a complex statistical exercise, it produced a single grant-related expenditure (GRE) figure for each authority, the intention of which was to equalize the rate poundage charged to ratepayers across the country. Higher levels of expenditure were discouraged by severe financial penalties. However, these proved ineffective, leading to the Rates Act, 1984, which sought instead to bear down upon rate levels through 'selective limitation' or rate-capping of individual authorities. The imminence of the Scottish rating revaluation due in 1985 precipitated a decision to replace rates with a flat rate per capita 'community charge', to which the negative term *'poll tax' soon came to be attached. The introduction of the community charge in the Local Government Finance Act, 1988, provoked a political upheaval and violent civil disorder, while self-defeating attempts to soften its impact in the shires produced a costly system of compensation. With Margaret Thatcher's replacement by John Major in 1990, the community charge was immediately abandoned in favour of a hybrid system, the council tax. This new tax, introduced in the Local Government Finance Act, 1992, combined an element of broad-band property valuation with a personal charge based on a two-person household. One of its effects was to shift the balance of financial responsibility still further, so that no more than one-fifth of total expenditure was met by locally raised taxes in the late 1990s. *KY*

local government officers, term used to distinguish the white-collar staff of local authorities from their manual workforce and from elected councillors. All local government officers are employed by, and serve, the council of their local authority to which they are responsible. Traditionally, local government has been organized on the basis of distinct professions or specialisms, embodied in the separate departments of a local authority, with each headed by a chief officer of standing in that profession. Chief officers brief and advise the appropriate committees of the council and often enjoy a close relationship with their chairman. The second half of the 20th century saw the gradual ascendancy of a generalist cadre of administrators. Since 1974, legally qualified town clerks have emerged as chief executive officers (CEOs), only to be gradually replaced by people drawn from a wider range of backgrounds. Scrupulously non-partisan in theory, many local government officers made their careers in authorities to which they felt politically sympathetic. During the 1980s, there was a trend to councils expecting greater political commitment and a number of openly partisan appointments were made, in some cases of officers who served as councillors in other neighbouring, politically similar, authorities ('twin-tracking'). The *Widdicombe report of 1986 criticized the politicization of local government, and was followed by greater statutory restriction on officers' political activities. *KY*

local government politics. Political conflict is universal in local government as in national, although for much of the 20th century party-political contests were suppressed. Party competition may operate on a number of levels, from contesting elections under party labels, through the formation of distinct groupings in the council chamber, to the allocation of political spoils on party lines, and finally to cohesive and disciplined voting on matters of council business. Party politics also progressed through a succession of stages, with the rise of the Labour Party prompting apparently 'non-party' alignments between Conservative and Liberal parties in many areas, resulting in 'ratepayer' or similar anti-Labour fronts. The overt entry of the Conservative Party into local elections after 1946 crystallized two-party competition, although genuinely non-partisan local politics still flourished in the more rural areas, at least into the 1970s. The reorganization of local government in 1974, which merged formerly separate rural and urban areas, led to an intensification of party competition, as the major parties sought to redefine their spheres of influence. In the late 1980s, the resurgence of the Liberal/Liberal Democrat party produced three-way competition, resulting in a substantial number of councils being 'hung' or 'balanced', without overall control by any one party. Only a handful of councils remain independent of party politics.

KY

local government structure. At the turn of the century, the structure of local government had just been completed by the 1889 and 1892 Local Government Acts and the London Government Act, 1899. Outside London, England and Wales was governed by a two-level system of county and districts (urban and rural), with some rural districts additionally having parish councils. In each, authority lay with elected councillors. Those older towns which had been granted charters, from the 12th century onwards, had the status of boroughs, with certain exemptions from county rule. The larger and more important of them, including the fast-growing towns of the industrial revolution, were granted the status of 'county boroughs' in 1889, so becoming all-purpose authorities independent of their surrounding counties. London, after many years of campaigning, was included in the 1888 Act which created the county councils; the powerful London County Council was complemented by 28 metropolitan borough councils in 1899.

Urban expansion, however, undermined the apparent stability of this structure. The growing towns encroached upon the smaller authorities on their periphery, leading to conflict between the county and county borough councils. The more important non-county boroughs sought, and many obtained, promotion to county borough status, further weakening their counties. In 1921 a royal commission was appointed under the earl of Onslow to investigate the relations between authorities. In the legislation which followed in 1929, the number of urban and rural districts was reduced and boundaries adjusted. A 1926 Act provided for the promotion to county borough status by private act procedure, but increasingly governments were reluctant to see the number of county boroughs increase further. Following extended wartime review, the coalition government in 1945 created the first of a series of local government boundary commissions to manage the process of structural change. Following the dissolution of the commission in 1949, a prolonged period of consultation with the local authority associations was instituted, culminating in three agreed white papers on structure, functions, and finance in 1956–7. A new local government commission was established in 1958 to bring about adjustments, but made slow progress. It was abolished by the incoming Labour government, which instead established the *Redcliffe-Maud commission in 1966. A drastic reduction in the number of authorities was proposed, with a single-tier system of 'unitary' authorities for England (outside London), apart from a limited number of metropolitan areas. Following the Conservatives' rejection of the commission's report, the new structure established in 1972 was based rather on a uniform two-tier system of counties and districts; county boroughs were abolished. A framework of metropolitan boroughs was established for the larger conurbations, while at the other end of the scale the barriers to the creation of parish councils were reduced. That new system did not prove robust, and the six metropolitan county councils, together with the Greater London Council (GLC), were all abolished in 1986 after a thirteen-year life (21 years for the GLC).

English local government went back into the melting pot in 1992 when the Major government established another new local government commission to simplify the structure outside the metropolitan areas with a pattern of unitary authorities. Many Conservatives had come to favour the unitary system as providing clearer accountability, relating local government structure more closely to local communities, increasing public interest in local affairs, and making for more responsible and representative local government.

Scotland was not covered by the Redcliffe-Maud inquiry. The Scottish Office had produced sweeping proposals for reform in 1963, but these were superseded by the appointment of the Wheatley royal commission on Scottish local government in 1966. In what many considered to be a better argued report than Redcliffe-Maud's, Wheatley proposed a new structure of regional and district councils which were largely embodied in the Local Government (Scotland) Act, 1973. The Thatcher and Major governments regarded the powerful regional councils with distaste, abolishing them in 1994.

At the end of the 20th century there were, then, 238 district councils, 34 county councils, 32 London boroughs (and the Corporation of the City of London), and 36 metropolitan district councils, together with the 46 new English unitary authorities. Scotland and Wales had uniform unitary systems with 32 and 22 councils respectively. *KY*

local option. Proposals for local authorities to vary the licensing laws over alcohol were a feature of temperance campaigns in the 19th century. By the late 19th century, such plans had become part of the Liberal Party's programme. Under the Temperance Acts of 1869 and 1904, areas of Britain could elect to limit their licensing hours and to make Sundays entirely 'dry' (though only areas of Wales ever voted to do so). Many of these provisions remained in legal force until the liberalization of licensing laws under both Conservative and Labour governments during the 1990s, though by then in no areas were Sundays still 'dry'. *JS*

Locarno treaty (1925), international agreement. The treaty is usually seen as the central achievement of the foreign secretaryship of Austen Chamberlain (1924–9), but it is important to note that Chamberlain adopted what began as a German proposal very much as a second best after his own preferred option of a bilateral Anglo-French pact was blocked by Baldwin's cabinet. Locarno was once seen as the most constructive diplomatic achievement of the whole inter-war period—the most promising basis upon which a lasting peace might have been constructed. Chamberlain described the treaty as marking the real dividing line between the years of war and the peace that would follow. Historical opinion is now rather more sceptical.

The treaties bound Britain, France, Germany, Belgium, and Italy to observe the demilitarization of the Rhineland, to defend the existing borders between Germany and France and Germany and Belgium, and to render military assistance to any signatory which fell victim to a flagrant violation of these agreements. But it was striking that, contrary to the universal spirit of the League of Nations, comparable guarantees were not given to Germany's eastern frontiers, despite France's existing treaty commitments to Poland and Czechoslovakia. Critics have therefore argued that Britain was advertising its unwillingness to get involved in the affairs of eastern Europe and opening the way for later, unscrupulous German leaders to challenge the Versailles treaty (see PARIS PEACE CONFERENCE) in this area without fear of British intervention.

More positively, it may be argued that Locarno represented Chamberlain's honest attempt to delimit the extent of Britain's commitment to continental Europe and thus confront the dilemma which faced all British policy makers in this period of reconciling Britain's obligations with its limited military capacity. At all events Locarno was violated with impunity in 1936 when Hitler remilitarized the *Rhineland. *DJD*

R. GRAYSON, *Austen Chamberlain and the Commitment to Europe: British Foreign Policy, 1924–1929* (London, 1997).

Lomé convention, a trade and aid agreement between the member states of the European Union and their former colonies. The original Lomé convention ran from 1975 to 1980 and was subsequently extended through Lomé II (1980–5), Lomé III (1985–90), and Lomé IV (1990–2000). It was preceded by the two Yaoundé conventions (1964–75) and, prior to that, Part IV Association (1958–64). However, Lomé marked a new departure and was driven by the perception of a 'new international economic order' and based on the concept of partnership between the European Union (EU) and the (then) 46 ACP (African, Caribbean, and Pacific) states. In addition to its institutional framework, the Lomé Conventions have contained three main elements: (1) trade concessions consisting of a free access for most industrial goods from the ACP to the EU, with much more limited concessions for agricultural products; (2) a multilateral aid fund—the European development fund (EDF); (3) export stabilization funds—STABEX (for general products) and SYSMIN (for minerals)—the purpose of which was to protect the ACP countries from fluctuations in their export earnings due, for example, to crop failure caused by poor weather.

Although the number of ACP countries has grown (to 70), Lomé remained the focus of strong criticism. The trade concessions were superficial because they were widely available to all other developing countries anyway and the ACP countries' main (agricultural) products continued to be excluded from EU markets. Moreover, the aid provided by the EDF and the stabilization funds proved to be inadequate and had been distributed inefficiently. These failures and the EU's preoccupation with central and eastern Europe meant that the future of Lomé became more doubtful in the late 1990s than ever before. *JR*

EUROPEAN COMMISSION, *The Lomé Convention: A Future after the Millennium?* (background report, Apr. 1997). | MARJORIE LISTER, *The European Union and the South* (London, 1997).

London, treaty of (1915). On the outbreak of the Great War in 1914, Italy remained neutral, adhering to the strict terms of its triple alliance with Germany and Austria-Hungary. Despite German encouragement, Austria-Hungary refused to make sufficient territorial concessions to purchase Italian belligerency. Turning to Britain, France, and Russia, Italy signed the treaty of London with them on 26 April 1915, denounced the triple alliance on 3 May, and declared war on Austria-Hungary on 23 May (though not on Germany until 19 August). Italy was deeply divided about intervention but the war appeared an opportunity to gain Great Power status. Sidney Sonnino, the Italian foreign minister, wanted significant territorial gains to join the entente but felt pressure to strike a bargain from apparent Russian success in Galicia and Anglo-French intentions in the Dardanelles. Sonnino secured most of his programme. Britain had over-optimistic hopes of Italian military capabilities and diplomatic influence in the Balkans, and overcame French and Russian reservations. The treaty promised Italy the South Tyrol, giving her a Brenner-pass frontier, Trentino, Trieste, Gorizia, Istria and much of Dalmatia, the Dodecanese islands, a share of Albania, and some rather indeterminate claims on Ottoman territory and German colonies, together with a loan of £50 million and a share in any war indemnity, but it did not promise Fiume. The treaty exemplified two of American President Woodrow Wilson's chief hatreds, secret diplomacy and the balance of power, thus embarrassing Entente–American relations. It denied national self-determination to the German-speaking inhabitants of the South Tyrol and the Slavs in the Balkans. In 1919, Italy gained Trentino, Tyrol, and Trieste but, feeling cheated in imperial and Balkan matters and especially over Fiume, declared Versailles a 'mutilated peace'. *AS*

René Albrecht-Carrié, *Italy at the Paris Peace Conference* (New Haven, 1966). | David Stevenson, *The First World War and International Politics* (Oxford, 1988).

Londonderry, 7th marquess of (1878–1949), Conservative politician, MP for Maidstone, 1906–15, when he succeeded his father. After a brief period at the Air Ministry, 1920–1, he joined the government of Northern Ireland, 1921–8. He returned to Westminster under Baldwin and was air minister, 1931–5, during which time he had to balance financial restrictions with the growing international menace, but failed to satisfy his critics. Out of office he pursued a private mission to reconcile the Nazis' ambitions with Britain's world position. Londonderry House was a key political salon of the period. *NJC*

London local government. The modernization of inner-London local government was completed by the London Government Act, 1899, which created the metropolitan borough councils (MetBCs) as a counterbalance to the London County Council (LCC). The ancient Corporation of the *City of London remained untouched. From the turn of the century until 1965, the LCC operated the great majority of local government services, and almost all those of importance. The sole exception was control of the police, where the home secretary remained the police authority for the wider Metropolitan Police Area. From its inception until 1907, the LCC was controlled by the Progressive (Liberal) Party; from that year until 1934 by the Municipal Reform (Conservative) Party; and thereafter by Labour.

The greatest political and governmental problems of London centred on the relations between the LCC area and the rapidly growing suburbs beyond its boundary. By 1938, more 'Londoners' lived outside the LCC area than within it, partly as a result of outward movement from the county to the suburbs. Population movement from the LCC area to outer London was accelerated by the Second World War, exacerbating the governmental problems of the region. Proposals to integrate the government of the metropolis under a single authority had been first aired in 1906, and were hotly opposed by the suburban authorities. A committee of inquiry into London government under the marquess of Reading was established by the coalition government in 1945, but its terms of reference were narrow, and it did not report. The intensity of conflicts in outer London precluded an evolutionary approach to reorganization, and in 1957 Henry Brooke established a royal commission on local government in greater London under Sir Edwin Herbert. The Herbert commission reported in favour of a new two-tier structure for the built-up area of London, with 52 London borough councils (LBC) as the 'primary units' of local government (the term was to prove a fruitful source of dispute) and a directly elected Council for Greater London (GLC). The Macmillan government largely accepted these proposals, which also appeared likely to restore Conservative fortunes in the capital city, but reduced the number of LBCs to 32 so as to enhance their powers, particularly in education. Inner London education was, however, retained undivided as the responsibility of a special inner London education authority (ILEA), a temporary measure that in 1967 was confirmed in its permanency by Labour.

Thereafter, uncertainties and conflicts over responsibility bedevilled the relations between the GLC and the boroughs. Against prediction, the first GLC election in April 1964 was won by Labour, which won again in 1973 and 1981. This last election sharpened the conflict between Margaret Thatcher's government and the GLC which, under Ken Livingstone's leadership, saw itself as the flagship of the non-parliamentary opposition. The Conservative majority on the London boroughs association called for GLC abolition, leading to almost all Labour LBCs leaving to form their own association of London authorities. Abolition attracted Thatcher and, despite being favoured by few of her senior ministers, was pressed home against strenuous opposition within and without parliament. After 1986, a complex web of joint arrangements evolved to deal with pan-London problems, while the remaining powers of the GLC (including education in inner London) were devolved to the boroughs. Labour had consistently opposed the dissolution of metropolitan government, and in 1998 the Blair government introduced a London Government Bill to create a greater London assembly and—a novel move for English local government—a directly elected mayor for the metropolis, to which post Livingstone was elected in May 2000. *KY*

London Municipal Society (LMS), local government front-organization for the Conservative Party, 1894–1963. The LMS was established to restore Conservative fortunes in London after the Progressive Party's decisive victories in the London County Council elections of 1889 and 1892. Being an arms-length organization proved initially advantageous in maintaining Liberal Unionist support, but led in time to frictions with the Conservative Party machine. The LMS had pretensions to orchestrate the anti-socialist movement in local government and to that end established the National Union of Ratepayers' Associations (NURA), of which it lost control in 1938. Largely irrelevant once Conservatives fought local elections openly after 1946, the LMS turned to the promotion of London government reform but succumbed to a reorganization of party organs after the creation of Greater London Council in the early 1960s. *KY*

London naval conference (1930). While the *Washington naval conference of 1920 had been held in the aftermath of a victorious war, but had nevertheless imposed serious restrictions on the Royal Navy, its successor in London took place amid early fears of another world war, and within the Labour government's strenuous efforts to secure disarmament on a worldwide scale. Under the terms of the agreement reached in London, the maximum number of cruisers permitted to the Royal Navy was reduced from 70 to 50 (which the first sea lord thought to be 'a starvation number', inadequate for the protection of British trade and imperial possessions around the world). The limit was more apparent than real, however, for actual cruiser strength at the time of the conference was only 54 (under half the figure for 1914) and modernized battleships were also below the level permitted at Washington. The London treaty can therefore be seen as much as a symptom of the navy's neglect as it was a cause, though its signature did then make later naval-building more problematic, hence Britain's readiness to accept a naval deal with Hitler in the 1935 *Anglo-German naval agreement, once British rearmament at sea was beginning. *JAR*

London School of Economics and Political Science (LSE), founded in 1895 by Sidney Webb, became a college of the University of London. Despite the socialist views of its founder, the LSE developed into a world-famous research and teaching organization without undue political bias, not least since its first director was the geographer and future Conservative MP Halford Mackinder (1903–8), a keen advocate of Empire and imperial preference. Between the wars, however, it became a bastion of the left, its staff including Harold Laski and Hugh Dalton and its pupils several future campaigners for colonial freedom from British rule. The LSE had an uncomfortable time in the 1960s, as the central location for British student radicalism, though this owed something to an insensitive management, a situation remedied during the directorship of the German Social Democrat and former LSE student Ralf Dahrendorf, 1974–84. *JAR*

Long, Walter Hume (1854–1924), Conservative politician. Long was the scion of a great Wiltshire family which had represented the county in parliament for four centuries. Understandably, he was an unshakeable advocate of the agricultural interest throughout his long political career. It is an unhappy irony that an excess of generosity as well as inattentive management during his young manhood led to the eventual sale of the ancient family estate, Rood Ashton. After Harrow and Christ Church, Oxford, Long entered the Commons for East Wiltshire in 1880. Never a facile or charismatic speaker, his political hopes rested on his diligence and unflagging party loyalty, and he gained junior office in 1886. He joined Salisbury's cabinet in 1895 as agriculture minister and in 1900 took charge of the Local Government Board, continuing successfully in this office under Balfour. Always a passionate champion of the Irish Union, Long in 1905 became chief secretary, and his political attention seemed thereafter seldom to stray from the Irish question. During the intense struggle over home rule preceding the Great War (particularly following the passage of the *Parliament Act, 1911), Long became one of the most outspoken defenders of Irish unionism, in and outside Ulster. He formed the *Union Defence League and worked closely with the Unionist movement in Britain and in Ireland. As the Third Home Rule Bill drew closer to reality in 1914, Long joined certain other Unionists in promoting, unsuccessfully as it turned out, consideration of a federal United Kingdom of semi-autonomous units, an idea he had once reviled.

Long again took the Local Government Board during Asquith's wartime coalition and was colonial secretary, 1916–18, and then first lord of the Admiralty, 1919–21, under Lloyd George. During this period, from the time of the *Easter Rising until the eve of the signing of the 1921 *Anglo-Irish treaty, Long was closely consulted on Irish policy; he abandoned the rigid unionism of his early career in favour of a search for compromise which would create an autonomous Ireland within the Empire and an Ulster separate of any Dublin government and firmly within the United Kingdom.

Long was much loved among Conservative traditionalists, but his indifferent health and ready, often roughly spoken, opinions—often followed by remorse and abject apologies—kept him from the topmost places in politics. He contested the party leadership in 1911 but, along with Austen Chamberlain, withdrew in favour of Andrew Bonar Law, rather than divide his party.

NJC

Walter Long, *Memories* (London, 1923). | John Kendle, *Walter Long: Ireland and the Union. 1905–1920* (Montreal, 1992). | Sir Charles Petrie, *Walter Long and his Times* (London, 1936).

Longford, 7th earl of (1905–2001), Labour politician and philanthropist. Frank Longford was renowned for Christian-motivated work on behalf of prisoners, including Myra Hindley. Though he worked in the 1930s for the Conservative Research Department, he served in a series of posts in post-war Labour governments, for example at the War Office, 1946–7, and civil aviation, 1948–51. He was in Wilson's cabinet as lord privy seal, 1964–5; secretary for the colonies, 1965–6; and leader of the Lords, 1966–8, resigning from the government in 1968 in protest at the postponement of the raising of the school leaving age to 16.

BJE

Looking Ahead (1924), Conservative policy statement. Drafted by Neville Chamberlain, it provided the basis for the 1924 election manifesto and much of the Conservative domestic legislation, 1924–9. The pamphlet was a summary of work done by the new shadow cabinet secretariat. Authorship was unattributed and there was some press speculation that it was the creation of Curzon. This was the first time ever that the party had officially a comprehensive and practicable statement of policy.

NJC

lord chamberlain, a senior court official who presides at most state ceremonies and formal social occasions where the sovereign is present. His office in St James's palace issues the invitations and organizes the ceremonial, for example at dinners for visiting heads of state and the weddings of the sovereign's children. The lord chamberlain is always a hereditary peer appointed by the sovereign and he attends these functions holding his white stave of office. The most formal occasions of all are the coronation and funeral of a sovereign. The duke of Norfolk organizes these in his hereditary capacity as earl marshal but the earl marshal's office, staffed by heralds of the College of Arms, only comes into being rarely as one reign is ending and the next beginning. In practice, the lord chamberlain's office in collaboration with the earl marshal's staff does much of the work. At the turn of the century, the lord chamberlain blamed bungles at coronations and funerals on the earl marshal, who in turn suggested the lord chamberlain had been uncooperative. Similar tensions between the two officials exist today. In a quaint survival from the days of personal rule by kings, theatrical stage *censorship continued to be carried out in the name of the lord chamberlain until the 1960s.

WMK

William M. Kuhn, *Democratic Royalism: The Transformation of the British Monarchy, 1861–1914* (Basingstoke and New York, 1996).

lord chancellorship, the most ancient continuously existing office in the British system of government, and an office of very high status: only senior members of the royal family and the archbishop of Canterbury have precedence over him in England. The lord chancellor had already developed by 1900 into a curious hybrid: he (there has not yet been a female lord chancellor) is a cabinet minister chosen by the prime minister, he chairs debates as Speaker in the House of Lords when he wishes (in practice rarely), and he exercises on behalf of the crown the prerogative to appoint judges and magistrates. This is the most extreme case of the British constitution not providing for the 'separation of powers' as in the USA and other democracies, for the lord chancellor is simultaneously a key figure in the executive, the legislature, and the judiciary. In political terms, lord chancellors have interpreted their role in very different ways, some (Birkenhead, 1st Lord Hailsham, Irvine) giving priority to political duties as a senior cabinet minister, for example by chairing numerous cabinet committees, others (notably 2nd Lord *Hailsham, Mackay of Clashfern) prioritizing the legal side and rarely making a party-political speech during their tenure; most have striven to maintain a balance. In a few cases, notably Lord *Halsbury, the legal and the political came dangerously close together, when the post was used to politicize the judiciary and to influence key judgements when the Lords was sitting as a court. The lord chancellor's office manages the legal system, for which he and the law officers in the Commons answer to parliament, and he is personally responsible for the appointment of judges and magistrates, though by the 1990s this power was exercised only with formal advice from representative groups. Since 1701, however, he could not remove a judge from office when once appointed, except by securing a formal parliamentary resolution (and in practice only on grounds of impropriety or incompetence would that issue ever arise).

JAR

Lords, House of, the upper house, or second chamber of the UK parliament. The Lords is one of the oldest parliamentary chambers in the world and exists by prescriptive right and slow evolution over 800 years and more. In the later Middle Ages the Lords was the dominant partner of the two chambers but slowly the Commons became more powerful. Following the Great Reform Act of 1832, with the advent of popular elections, and disciplined political parties, the Lords became a reviewing and suspending body. In the 1880s the Liberal government's espousal of Irish home rule resulted in a large Unionist majority in the Lords. Thereafter, when the Liberals were in power, repeated clashes between the Houses occurred which culminated in the struggle over the 'People's Budget' of 1909. The decision by the Conservative leadership to use their majority in the Lords to throw out the budget precipitated a crisis between the two Houses, and a bill was introduced which became the Parliament Act, 1911, limiting the Lords' legislative powers. The preamble of the Act stated, 'And whereas it is intended to substitute for the House of Lords as it at present exists a second Chamber constructed on a popular instead of hereditary basis, but such substitution cannot be immediately brought into operation'.

Since 1911, three significant, albeit abortive, attempts at comprehensive reform by agreement between the parties have been made. The first was in 1917, when the *Bryce report proposed a House three-quarters elected indirectly by MPs on a regional basis and one-quarter chosen by a joint standing committee of both Houses, with certain proportions of hereditary peers and bishops. The scheme was not proceeded with. The second attempt was in 1948–9 (for which see PARLIAMENT ACT, 1949). After 1949, changes were made to give effect to the principles agreed at the 1948 inter-party conference. The Life Peerages Act, 1958, allowed life peerages. Resolutions of the two Houses in 1957 enabled peers to recover, within limits, parliamentary expenses, and a leave of absence scheme was introduced in 1958. The Peerage Act, 1963, allowed peers by succession to renounce their peerages, and also removed anomalies within the peerage by opening membership of the House of Lords to peers of Scotland and peeresses in their own right by succession and by removing the disqualification of peers of Ireland from voting in parliamentary elections or standing for election to the Commons.

The third attempt to reform the House by agreement took place in 1968–9, again at the initiative of a Labour government with a mandate for Lords reform. Again an inter-party conference reached a large measure of agreement: the second chamber was to complement but not rival the Commons; the existing hereditary basis for membership should be eliminated; no one party should possess a permanent majority; the powers should be restricted, in particular in relation to subordinate legislation; and membership should be divided between voting and non-voting peers. Thereafter there was a breakdown of inter-party cooperation on Lords reform caused by the Lords' decision to vote down the Southern Rhodesia (UN Sanctions) Order 1968. The government's proposals, based on the inter-party talks, were welcomed in the Lords and the white paper *House of Lords Reform* (Cmnd 3799) was approved by 251 to 56. However, in the Commons the reception was less favourable, and the Parliament (No. 2) Bill was withdrawn after a filibuster mounted by an alliance of left- and right-wing members. In the years that followed, some of the functional and procedural reforms presaged in the 1968 white paper were quietly effected by the House itself. The Labour government elected in 1997 pledged itself in its manifesto to abolish the rights of hereditary peers as a first step towards reform (see LORDS, HOUSE OF: COMPOSITION OF).

The Lords has the following principal functions:

- A forum for debate on matters of public interest, on which the House spends some 28 per cent of its time, especially on Wednesdays, when debate takes precedence over legislation. Most debates are now time-limited.
- Revision of public bills brought from the Commons, which occupies more time than any other function, and has become increasingly important, with the weight of legislation, much of it little considered in the Commons. Lobbyists have learnt that it is easier to secure amendments in the Lords than in the Commons, because the importance attached to 'government credit' is less manifest.
- Initiation of public legislation, including private members' bills and government bills, and technical, legal, and other bills where the chief arguments will centre on expert considerations and are largely uncontroversial in party-political terms. These include Consolidation and Law Commission Bills. Private members possess an unfettered right to introduce bills, and the absence of constituency pressures has caused many bills on social and private morality to be pioneered in the Lords, for example on abortion, homosexuality, sexual discrimination, and euthanasia.
- Consideration of subordinate legislation, on which the Lords have full powers but use them with restraint. Technical and legal scrutiny is carried out by a joint committee. The Lords' Delegated Powers and Deregulation Committee has since 1992 established a reputation as the watchdog of both Houses in relation to delegated powers.
- Scrutiny of the executive, by oral questions, ministerial statements, private notice questions on matters of urgency, questions for written answer, and unstarred questions (that is questions with debate).
- Private legislation, on which both the powers and the workload of the two Houses are equal.
- Select committees of the Lords.
- Supreme Court of Appeal (see LORDS, HOUSE OF: AS COURT OF LAW). *MWB*

Lords, House of: committees. Lords' committees have proliferated recently as law-making and administration has increased, in four areas: legislation, sessional, domestic, and select. The Lords currently sits longer than any other parliamentary assembly in the world (except the Commons), and to save time in the House, a number of expedients in committee work off the floor have been tried. The House transacts the committee stage on most bills in committee of the whole House and has no legislative standing committee procedure like the Commons. Other committee procedures are used to consider legislation. In grand committees, where procedure is like that of the House, with no divisions, all members can attend and participate, and other business may be conducted simultaneously in the chamber. A 'public bill committee' is a select committee; the procedure is similar to that in the House: non-members may attend and speak but not vote. A 'special public bill' committee permits written and oral evidence to be taken, over 28 days, excluding recesses, and thereafter the committee takes the form of a public bill committee, and considers the bill clause by clause. Sessional committees regularly appointed for judicial and legislative purposes include appeal and appellate (two each); standing orders (private bills); personal bills; hybrid instruments; and delegated powers and deregulation. Domestic committees governing the internal working of the House include the committees for privileges; procedure; selection; liaison; offices, with subcommittees on finance and staff, administration and works, library and computers, refreshments, and works of art; and broadcasting. *MWB*

Companion to the Standing Orders (London, 1994 edn.).

Lords, House of: composition of. The House of Lords is composed of the lords spiritual and lords temporal who sit together in one chamber. The lords spiritual have been members of the House of Lords since its origins in the early Middle Ages, when they formed a majority of the House, but with the dissolution of the monasteries in 1536–9 the abbots went and the temporal lords became the majority. Since 1847, there has been no alteration in the number of bishops summoned: the archbishops of Canterbury and York, the bishops of London, Winchester, and Durham, and the 21 senior diocesan bishops, who retain their seat while bishops and retire at 70, but may resign earlier.

The lords temporal comprise three categories: the hereditary peers and peeresses in their own right of England, Scotland, Great Britain, and the UK; life peers and peeresses created for life under the Life Peerages Act, 1958; and the salaried lords of appeal in ordinary created life peers under the Appellate Jurisdiction Act, 1876 (as amended). The hereditary peerage has always been a constituent of the House, and consists of five degrees: dukes, marquesses, earls, viscounts, and barons, but the distinction is one of rank and does not affect their rights in the House as equal members. Under the Peerage Act, 1963, a person succeeding to a peerage may disclaim it for life by making an instrument of disclaimer which divests the person disclaiming of all rights or interest in the peerage for his lifetime, though it does not affect the devolution of the peerage on the death of the disclaimer. This allowed Anthony Wedgwood Benn to remain an MP, and Lords Hailsham and Home to return to the Commons, the latter becoming prime minister as Sir Alec Douglas-Home in 1963.

All temporal members of the House remain members of the House for life. They may not receive a writ of summons in right of their peerage until reaching the age of 21. There is a leave of absence scheme for Lords who do not wish to attend. Members receive no salary, but only reimbursement of expenses within specified limits, incurred in undertaking parliamentary duties.

In January 1999, the total membership of the House was 1,295, of whom 63 were on leave of absence and 67 were without a writ of summons. Of the reduced total of 1,165, 26 were bishops, 750 were peers by succession, 9 were hereditary peers of first creation, 28 were Law Lords, and 482 were life peers. Party allegiance in January 1999 was 476 Conservatives, 175 Labour, 69 Liberal Democrats, and 445 were 'cross-benchers' or independents, including the Law Lords and bishops. Of these totals, the hereditary peers were 304 Conservative, 18 Labour, 24 Liberal Democrat, and 290 cross-benchers.

The Labour government elected in 1997 had a mandate to reform the House of Lords and in January 1999 the House of Lords Bill was introduced into the Commons as part of a gradual approach to reform. Its purpose was to remove the right of hereditary peers to sit and vote in the Lords, and remove the disqualifications of hereditary peers to vote in general elections or stand as candidates for the Commons. When enacted, the bill created a transitional House of Lords. A white paper, *Modernizing Parliament: Reforming the House of Lords* (Cm 4183) which accompanied the bill stated that the government might accept an amendment to allow a limited number of hereditary peers (91 was the number later agreed) to sit temporarily in the transitional House. These new provisions came into force in the summer of 1999, with the 91 surviving hereditary peers elected proportionately by each party and (independent) group. It is also intended that in the transitional House no one party should have a majority. An independent appointments commission is appointed to recommend non-political appointments to the transitional house. The prime minister has undertaken to reduce his powers of patronage, by agreeing not to veto recommendations for independent members, or those of the other party leaders. The government also set up a royal commission to consider and report on the future role, functions, and composition of a reformed second chamber. When it reported in favour of an upper house composed of a mixture of elected and nominated members, its report was poorly received, and there seemed to be no inclination on the government's part to take any early action. *MWB*

Lords, House of: as court of law. The House of Lords is the final court of appeal in all matters from the High Courts and Courts of Appeal of England and Wales, and from Northern Ireland, and in civil matters from Scotland. This is one of two vestiges of the former jurisdiction of the 'High Court of Parliament'. The other, the trial of peers, was abolished in 1948. There are currently twelve Law-Lords, life peers, appointed by the queen on the advice of the prime minister, usually from judges of the English and Scottish appeal courts. The lord chancellor presides when available. Normally five sit, but as a committee (or two simultaneous committees) of the House, giving their judgements ('speeches') in writing and formally reporting the result to themselves ('voting') later in the Lords chamber. The two-tier appeal structure has been much criticized as expensive and slow, and for the tendency for the oldest and most conservative-minded judges to staff the Lords. The court is out of the reach of ordinary litigants and since it can undertake only a very small caseload, would-be appellants have to surmount a further hurdle by getting 'leave to appeal'. However, the advantage of the system is in the Lords' ability to overview a whole area of law and to give an authoritative wide-ranging decision, something the Court of Appeal rarely has the time to undertake. The Law Lords as peers may take part in the debates and ordinary work of the House, but by convention they do so from the cross-benches and only on matters connected with the administration of justice. *VT*

Lords, House of: and Europe. When the UK was negotiating to join the European Community (EC) in 1971, one of the conditions of EC membership was that the accumulated agreed institutional framework should be accepted as it then stood by the applicant country. As a consequence, the UK joined a community whose legislation, when agreed at the Council of Ministers, would thereafter have the force of law domestically with direct effect, without any necessary part being played by the national parliament in the process. To meet the challenge this posed to the traditional role of parliament in law-making, the Lords, on the recommendations of the Maybray-King committee, set up in 1974 a select committee on the European Communities to consider community proposals, with wide terms of reference. The committee has six subcommittees covering defined policy areas (agriculture, law, institutions, trade, and so on) and appoints ad hoc subcommittees as required. The committee co-opts to subcommittees, appoints specialist advisers, has a legal adviser and other staff, and receives copious evidence from home and abroad. The Lords' system is of pre-legislative specialist committee enquiry into selected important community initiatives at an early stage. The government has undertaken, unless in exceptional circumstances, not to agree to an EU proposal before the Scrutiny Committee have reported and the proposal and the report thereon have been debated in the House. About twenty such major reports are made annually. The House and its EC committee play an important role in scrutinizing European legislation, whose impact under the Amsterdam treaty will extend as the provisions of the treaty come into force.

MWB

Vernon Bogdanor, 'The House of Lords', in J. Jowell and D. Oliver (eds.), *The Changing Consitution* (3rd edn. Oxford, 1994).

Lords, House of: officers. The officers of the House of Lords comprise those members who act as speakers or chairmen and the senior officials who provide the permanent administrative substructure to the House. The lord chancellor is speaker ex officio, but does not possess powers to maintain order. As a minister he speaks and votes, but other duties entail frequent absence, when his speaker's duties are performed by deputies. The first deputy speaker is the chairman of committees or 'Lord Chairman' who supervises private legislation and chairs domestic committees. His principal deputy chairs the EC committee; there are other unpaid deputy speakers and chairmen. Of the permanent officers, the clerk of the parliaments is head of Lords' administration, accounting officer, procedural adviser, and corporate officer. He is assisted by a clerk assistant, reading and other clerks who form the parliament office. Black Rod is responsible for accommodation, services, and security, and he is also assisted by a department.

MWB

Lords, House of: peers' interests. Until 1995, the House's practice was governed by the principle that Lords should speak and act on their personal honour. In 1995 the Griffiths report strengthened and clarified previous practice. The House resolved (7 November 1995) that Lords should act always on their personal honour and should never accept any financial inducement or an incentive or reward for exercising parliamentary influence. Lords who accept payment or other incentive for providing parliamentary advice or services, or have any financial interest in any business involved in parliamentary lobbying, are not to speak, vote, lobby, or otherwise take advantage of their position as members of the House on behalf of their clients. This prohibition does not extend to members' outside employments or directorships where the interest does not arise from membership of the House. On private bills, Lords may not vote or speak where they have a direct pecuniary interest. On other matters, the decision rests with the member, but those with a direct financial interest must declare it and non-financial interests where relevant. In 1995, a public register of Lords' interests was established.

MWB

Lords, House of: powers. Until 1911 the Lords had the same rights to pass, amend, or reject proposed legislation as the Commons, subject to the Commons' financial privilege. Under the Parliament Acts, 1911 and 1949, public bills, with certain exceptions, may be presented for royal assent if passed by the Commons without the consent of the Lords. The exceptions are bills originating in the Lords, bills to extend the life of a parliament beyond five years, provisional order bills, private bills, and delegated legislation. With these exceptions, if the Lords reject a public bill sent up by the Commons in two successive sessions, whether in the same parliament or not, it is presented for royal assent without the consent of the Lords, unless the Commons direct to the contrary. The bill must be sent up to the Lords at least one calendar month before the end of each session and one year must elapse between the second reading in the Commons in the first session and the passing of the bill by the

Commons in the second. The Lords are deemed to have rejected the bill if they do not pass it without amendment or with such amendments only as are acceptable to the Commons. The effect of the Parliament Acts is that the Lords have power to delay enactment of a public bill until the session after that in which it was first introduced and until not less than thirteen months and one day have elapsed from the date of second reading in the Commons in the first session.

In the case of 'money bills', the Lords' power of delay is restricted to one month. A money bill is a bill certified by the Speaker of the Commons that it contains only provisions dealing with national, but not local, taxation, public money, or loans or their management. The certificate of the Speaker is conclusive.

The use made of the powers under the Parliament Act has been sparing; only five bills have been passed under its provisions, 1911–99. The essential point is that the existing House is unable to make much use of its powers because of its composition and one-party domination, and therefore the Lords have exercised restraint, notably by the Salisbury convention. Lords' powers over subordinate legislation are unlimited and are the same as the Commons, namely they may accept or reject an instrument, but cannot amend it. Recently they have evolved procedures for opposing instruments whereby they call on the government to delay or amend delegated legislation, without voting to reject it.

In addition to the legislative powers, the Lords is the ultimate court of appeal in the UK in all cases except Scottish criminal cases. Its concurrence is needed for the dismissal of a judge.

MWB

Lords, House of: procedure. Until the later 19th century, the procedures of the Lords and Commons were not dissimilar, and gave great latitude to private members and minorities. After 1870 the determined filibustering by Irish nationalist MPs forced the Commons to restrict their ancient procedures. In the Lords in the absence of Irish nationalist members there was no occasion for such restrictive changes. Lords' procedure has evolved slowly to permit a bigger workload, but without major restriction of private members' rights: it remains free, flexible, and self-regulating. It is the only chamber whose speaker—the lord chancellor—has no power or duty (under Standing Order 16) to maintain order. This is instead the responsibility of each of the individual members, who as 'peers' (meaning equals) share the duty of keeping order. The leader of the House (the leader of the government party and a cabinet minister), aided by the clerk of the parliaments, has the duty of advising the House on matters of procedure and order.

There are relatively few standing orders, and the procedure of the House is laid down by the *Companion to the Standing Orders*, as recommended by the all-party procedure committee. There continues to be no guillotine, no selection of amendments, and no fixed time for adjournment, and with few exceptions no time rules and no government priority. It is too early to say what effects the passing of the House of Lords Bill (1999) into law may have on Lords procedure.

MWB

Lords, House of: select committees. Since 1972, there has been a large increase in Lords select committee activity. Since then, select committees have been set up in response to particular needs ad hoc, rather than being the product of a systematic reform, as in the Commons in 1979. Sessional select committees were established in 1974 on the European Communities, and on science and technology (1980), which function by subcommittees, taking evidence and producing reports, for subsequent debate, in a steady stream. Since 1971, a series of ad hoc select committees, which consider and report on a single major topic, or on a public bill, have been established. Influential reports have included those on the Anti-Discrimination (No. 2) Bill (1972), Hare Coursing Bill (1976), the Bill of Rights (1977–8), overseas trade (1985), murder and life imprisonment (1988–9), and the public service (1996). In addition, there have been a series of ad hoc domestic select committees, to consider the internal affairs of the House; including televising the House (1966–7 and 1984–6) and a joint committee on private legislation. As well, there have been informal working groups, set up by the leader of the House, on issues such as the working of the House (1971, 1986–7, and 1998), and the library (1976).

MWB

Lothian, 11th marquess of (1882–1940), Liberal politician and journalist. Born Philip Kerr, he succeeded his cousin as Lord Lothian in 1930. A disciple of Lord Milner, Kerr was founding editor of the **Round Table* (1910–16) and private secretary to Lloyd George (1916–21). He achieved notoriety as a supporter of appeasement in the 1930s, but by the time of Munich had changed his mind. A lifelong advocate of Anglo-American cooperation, he was ambassador to the

USA during the critical early stages of the Second World War (1939–40). *ACM*

J. R. M. Butler, *Lord Lothian, 1882–1940* (London, 1960).

Low, Austin Richard Wilson ('Toby') (1914–) Conservative politician and businessman. Elected to parliament in 1945, Low was a minister, 1951–7. In 1959 he became deputy party chairman, serving in a backroom capacity under Butler and Macleod, and sparing them ministerial conflict of interest by taking responsibility for party finance. In 1962 he became Lord Aldington and the following year unsuccessfully supported Butler for Tory leader. He left politics but remained a confidant of Heath, his retirement darkened by a libel action concerning his staff-officer role in 1945, in repatriating prisoners of war to a grim fate in Stalin's Soviet Union and Tito's Yugoslavia. *RJS*

Low, David (1891–1963), the most celebrated political cartoonist of his era. Born in New Zealand, he worked in Australia and from 1919 in London, joining Lord Beaverbrook's *Evening Standard* in 1927. He won worldwide fame for his hostility to appeasement, his ridicule of the fascist dictators, his invention of 'Colonel Blimp', and his *New Statesman* caricatures. Beaverbrook rarely interfered with his left-leaning opinions. Low joined the *Daily Herald* in 1949 and the *Manchester Guardian* in 1953. *CKSU*

'lower than vermin' (1948), quip used by Aneurin *Bevan in a speech in Manchester, on 4 July 1948, to describe the highly orchestrated campaigners of the Tory opposition to the introduction of the National Health Service. It led some Tories to form a mockingly named vermin club. *KL*

Lubbock, Eric Reginald (1928–), Liberal politician. Lubbock was an industrial manager, ex-guardsman, and local councillor who shot to fame in 1962 when he snatched the *Orpington by-election from the Conservatives, holding the seat until 1970. He was his party's whip, 1963–70, but made only a limited parliamentary impact. He succeeded a cousin as 4th Lord Avebury, 1971. *JAR*

Lugard, Frederick John Dealtry (1858–1945), soldier, colonial administrator, and writer. As a senior administrator in Nigeria, 1900–6 and 1912–19, Lord Lugard developed the system of indirect rule, whereby British colonial control was exercised through indigenous institutions. Due to his advocacy, the system became widely adopted. His concern with the principles that should govern colonial rule were expounded in his influential *The Dual Mandate in British Tropical Africa* (1922). He became a respected member of the League of Nations' permanent mandates commission, 1920–36. *LL*

Marjorie Perham, *Lugard: The Years of Adventure* (London, 1956). | Marjorie Perham, *Lugard: The Years of Achievement* (London, 1960).

Lynch, Jack (1917–99), taoiseach of the republic of Ireland, 1966–73 and 1977–9. Although leader of the once militantly republican Fianna Fáil party, he pursued consensual policies which took his country into the European Community in 1973. In 1979, he ended the Irish currency's link with sterling. In 1969, he moved troops to the border with troubled Northern Ireland, but thereafter deprecated any military solution, duly dismissing two ministers after they had been accused of gun-running in 1970. *DRB*

Lynskey tribunal (1948), tribunal of inquiry appointed to investigate allegations of corruption against ministers. The inquiry focused on attempts by businessmen, especially Sidney Stanley, to subvert ministers through gifts in order to win considerations connected with the wartime economic controls that persisted at the time. Ministers Dalton, Key, Glenvil Hall, and their aides were questioned. Only John Belcher, parliamentary secretary to the Board of Trade, was found to have acted improperly—in a minor way—and resigned from parliament. *KMT*

Lyttelton, Alfred (1857–1913), Liberal Unionist minister. A brilliant athlete, Lyttelton was throughout his life a legend of the cricket pitch and lawn tennis court, playing both cricket and football for England. He was called to the Bar and elected to parliament in 1895. Close to both Joseph Chamberlain and Arthur Balfour, in 1903 he succeeded the former as colonial secretary in the cabinet of the latter. Though called 'the best-liked man in the House', his career was irretrievably damaged by the *'Chinese slavery' affair in South Africa, his early death allowing him no time to make up the lost ground. *RJQA*

Edith Lyttelton, *Alfred Lyttelton: An Account of his Life* (London, 1917).

Lyttelton, Oliver (1893–1972). Conservative politician and businessman, son of Alfred *Lyttelton. Having been successful in the metal business after the Great War, Lyttelton was made controller of non-ferrous metals when the Second World War started. Appointed president of the Board of Trade in 1940, becoming MP for Aldershot, Lyttelton joined the war cabinet in 1941 as minister resident in Cairo and in 1942 production minister. He did not keep to politics after the war and became chairman of Associated Electrical Industries (AEI), but by 1951 he was senior Conservative finance spokesman. Churchill, however, made Butler chancellor of the exchequer and appointed Lyttelton to the Colonial Office, a post once held by his father. Faced with emergencies in Malaya and Kenya, Lyttelton put security before reform, although in practice Malaya moved towards independence and, despite revulsion at the *Mau Mau insurgency, he told Kenya's whites of their need for African consent. He also accepted the inevitability of African rule in the Gold Coast (Ghana). Lyttelton, however, was dismissive of African opposition to the Central African Federation that he created to acclaim in Britain. In 1954 he returned to AEI and became Viscount Chandos, his public service in the arts being commemorated by the naming after him of one of the theatres within the National Theatre. *RJS*

Viscount Chandos, *The Memoirs of Lord Chandos* (London, 1962).

M3, one definition of a country's money supply. Many different definitions are possible, ranging across a spectrum from highly liquid to ever less liquid. The narrowest definition is that of the monetary base or Mo (sometimes called high-powered money) which is made up of notes and coins plus bankers' balances at the central bank. M3 is a relatively broad definition, and in Britain it comprises notes, coins, and public and private sector bank deposits (both sight and time) whether these are denominated in sterling or other currencies. *FHC*

Maastricht treaty (1992), major treaty revision of the European Union (EU) consisting of three main 'pillars': (1) the new European Community which builds on existing treaties and includes economic and monetary union; (2) the common foreign and security policy; (3) justice and home affairs (police and judicial cooperation, immigration and asylum policy). Whilst pillar (1) retained and extended the supranational element of the European Community, pillars (2) and (3) explicitly specified intergovernmental cooperation. Within this framework, the treaty also extended the powers of the European parliament, established a committee of the regions and a new cohesion fund to assist poorer regions within the EU, and adopted the principle of subsidiarity (which requires policy decisions to be taken at the appropriate level—local, regional, national, or European). The treaty was only narrowly ratified in France and needed a second referendum in Denmark, whilst the British required an *opt-out from economic and monetary union and from social policy before accepting it. Nevertheless, the agenda set by the treaty remained firmly in place, although far from complete by the end of the 1990s. *JR*

C. H. Church and D. Phinnemore, *European Union and European Community: A Handbook and Commentary, on the 1992 Maastricht Treaties* (2nd edn., London, 1995).

McAliskey, (Josephine) Bernadette (née Devlin) (1947–), Irish civil rights activist and republican. A Co. Tyrone-born 1960s civil rights campaigner in Northern Ireland, Devlin was a member of the radical People's Democracy movement. In 1969 she became the youngest woman ever elected to Westminster, and was MP for Mid-Ulster between 1969 and 1974. In 1974 she helped found the Irish Republican Socialist Party. Prominent in the anti-H-block campaigns of the early 1980s, she was shot and seriously wounded by loyalists in 1981. *RE*

Bernadette Devlin, *The Price of My Soul* (London, 1969).

McAlpine, Lord (1942–), political money man, publicist, eccentric. Alistair McAlpine was from the building family, early hired by Thatcher as a (successful) fund-raiser and party treasurer. Leader of the hedonistic tendency among Tories, he was known for lavish, champagne-and-lobster conference parties, later for marked anti-Europeanism. Highly critical of Major, he finally tranferred to the *Referendum Party. Author of vinegary memoirs and also of a curious study of Machiavelli. *EP*

Alistair McAlpine, *Once a Jolly Bagman* (London, 1997).

Macarthur, Mary (1880–1921), leader of women trade unionists. From a Glasgow background that was Conservative and well-to-do (her father owned several drapery shops), Mary Macarthur took up trade unionism and then, encouraged by Margaret Bondfield and Robert Smillie, socialism. She became secretary of and revitalized the Women's Trade Union League in 1903, founded the National Federation of Women Workers in 1906, and launched the *Woman Worker* in 1907. An attractive personality who married the Labour MP Will Anderson, her death from cancer at the age of 40 was widely mourned. *DEM*

M. A. Hamilton, *Mary Macarthur* (London, 1925).

MacBride principles, formulated as a result of a campaign conducted in the USA by Séan MacBride (1904–88), the son of Maud Gonne and Major John MacBride. His principles, which were adopted by several states of the Union, were designed to discourage and prevent American investment in Northern Ireland companies identified as discriminating against Catholic employees. *DGB*

McCaffrey, Thomas Daniel (1922–), prime minister's chief press secretary, 1976–9. A career civil servant who had handled James Callaghan's press relations at the Home and then Foreign Offices, Tom McCaffrey became one of Callaghan's most trusted Downing Street advisers. He immediately reinstated the lobby briefings ended by Joe Haines. Normally a safe pair of hands, he was embarrassed by reports of his remark that the outgoing ambassador in Washington was a snob (1977). He left Whitehall with Callaghan to become his chief of staff in opposition. *CL*

MacCormick, John MacDonald (1904–61), Scottish politician. 'King John', as he was known in Scottish nationalist circles, started his political career as the leader of the Glasgow University Scottish Nationalist Association. He took part in the formation of the National Party of Scotland in 1928 and the Scottish National Party (SNP) in 1934. Disillusioned with the SNP's drift towards 'extremism' in 1942, he left to found the Scottish Convention (see Scottish home rule conventions) which collected more than two million signatures in favour of Scottish home rule in 1949. In 1950 he was elected lord rector of Glasgow University. *RF*

MacDiarmid, Hugh (real name Christopher Murray Grieve) (1892–1978). First and foremost a poet and artist, MacDiarmid had little time for conventional politics. Although he always claimed to be a Scottish nationalist, MacDiarmid would flirt with whichever political philosophy caught his fancy or would annoy his detractors. In the inter-war period he was associated with Scottish nationalism, communism, fascism, and the social credit movement. In 1956, he joined the Communist Party when many were leaving in protest at the invasion of Hungary and was subsequently expelled for his Scottish nationalism. *RF*

MacDonald, Malcolm John (1901–81), politician and diplomat. Son of Ramsay *MacDonald, he entered parliament in 1929 as Labour MP for Bassetlaw, but followed his father into the *National Government in 1931. He secured cabinet status, 1935–40, with posts at the Dominions and Colonial Offices, becoming closely involved in the partition of Palestine and in policy towards Eire and the West Indies. He was minister of health, 1940, before a career as a senior Commonwealth diplomat and governor in Canada and Malaysia. *NJC*

MacDonald, Margo (1943–), Scottish nationalist politician. Victor of the 1973 Glasgow *Govan by-election, MacDonald was associated with those on the radical left of the Scottish National Party (SNP). Although she lost her seat at the 1974 general election, she remained an active figure within SNP politics. In 1979, following the collapse of the nationalist vote at that general election, MacDonald chaired the '79 Group' which had the objective of pushing the SNP further to the left. In the 1980s, she quit politics for a time to concentrate on broadcasting and journalism, although she rejoined the party in the late 1980s and was elected as a member of the Scottish parliament in 1999. *RF*

MacDonald, (James) Ramsay (1866–1937), Labour leader and prime minister. No 20th-century British political leader has been more reviled than Ramsay MacDonald, Britain's first Labour prime minister in 1924 and 1929–31. His decision to offer the resignation of the second Labour government but then to accept the king's commission to form a *National Government during the financial crisis of August 1931 provoked much animus among his former supporters and sustained the view that he had planned to ditch the second Labour government all along. It has long been an axiom that his actions in 1931 marked him as a traitor. To many Labour activists, the man who created the Labour Party had helped to undermine it.

MacDonald was born in Lossiemouth in Scotland, educated at a local school, and expected to become a teacher. However, in the 1880s, he took up various clerical posts in Bristol and London, where he acquired wide political experience between 1885 and 1892. He joined the Social Democratic Federation, a quasi-Marxist organization, while in Bristol; was employed by Thomas Lough, a Liberal radical MP; and circulated in socialist circles. He had ambitions of becoming a Liberal MP but his candidature for Southampton was thwarted in 1894 and he turned, instead, to the Independent Labour Party (ILP) in July 1894, becoming the unsuccessful ILP and Labour electoral association candidate in Southampton in the 1895 general election. During the early 1890s MacDonald was introduced to Sidney Webb and joined the Fabian Society. He was also a member of the Rainbow Circle, which first met in the Rainbow Tavern, Fleet Street, London, and brought together some collectivist Liberals such as Herbert Samuel, who believed that the old Liberal Party was about to disintegrate. The group published papers and, briefly, the *Progressive Review* in the hope of encouraging the formation of a new centre party in British politics. This desire, as well as his interest in foreign policy, were two abiding passions of MacDonald pursued throughout his political career.

Financial security came with his marriage to Margaret Gladstone in November 1896, and their home at 3 Lincoln Inn Fields, London, later became a base for the Labour Representation Committee in its formative years. Soon MacDonald's career began to blossom. He joined the executive committee of the Fabian Society in 1894 and was on the national administrative committee of the ILP in 1896. He remained a prominent member of the ILP until the Great War, but was more wedded to the Labour Party. The Labour Representation Committee (LRC) was formed in February 1900 and formally changed its name to the Labour Party after the 1906 general election. MacDonald was its secretary and chairman through to 1914 and was also chairman of the Parliamentary Labour Party (PLP), 1911–14. From the start he was committed to winning trade-union support for the embryonic organization and was helped in this respect by the attack upon trade unions funds represented by the Taff Vale judgement. Yet such support only emerged slowly and MacDonald embarked upon eight secret meetings to arrange the crucial *Lib-Lab pact (1903). This allowed Labour Party candidates a straight run against the Conservatives in about 30 parliamentary seats in return for a similar arrangement for the Liberals. In the 1906 general election only five of the 29 successful LRC candidates faced Liberal opposition, so the arrangement had clearly worked for Labour.

MacDonald also helped to direct the party towards a gradualist, and eventually socialist, direction by creating a socialist library to which he contributed his own books, such as *Socialism and Society* (1905). The dominating theme of his work was that a form of Social Darwinism ensured that private organizations would get bigger, that the state would have to intervene, and that socialism would emerge from the success, not the failure, of capitalism. During the Great War, these essentially Fabian views became the defining influence in the socialism the Labour Party espoused from 1918. From 1906 to 1918, MacDonald was MP for Leicester, and was strongly criticized for helping lead the Labour Party and the PLP into alliance with the Liberal Party, though his reputation for radicalism was restored, briefly, by his opposition to the Great War, which led to his loss of the party leadership in 1914 and ultimately to the loss of its parliamentary seat at Leicester in the 1918 general election.

In the immediate post-war years, relieved of his parliamentary duties, MacDonald concentrated his efforts in building up the party. However, he was returned as MP for Aberavon in 1922 and, shortly afterwards, became again leader of the PLP. When Stanley Baldwin failed to win support for his protectionist measures in the 1923 general election, MacDonald was invited to form the first Labour government in January 1924, though a minority government that lasted little more than ten months. Yet, in the May 1929 general election, MacDonald was returned for Seaham and, this time at the head of the largest party, formed his second, minority, Labour government in June. Unfortunately within six months of its return the Wall Street crash had occurred and, as a result of the world recession, British unemployment rose from about one million to three million in less than two years. The Labour government grossly overspent its budget and faced a financial crisis in August 1931, in which the cabinet attempted to find the spending cuts demanded by the opposition parties and the bankers. The cabinet split on the decision to cut unemployment benefit cuts by 10 per cent, and MacDonald offered the resignation of his government to King George V, but returned with a mandate to form a National Government, with the Liberals and Conservatives. These actions led L. MacNeill Weir, in *The Tragedy of Ramsay MacDonald* (1938), to suggest that MacDonald was never a socialist, rather an opportunist who had schemed to ditch the Labour government and was guilty of betrayal. However, David Marquand has suggested that such accusations are, at best, half-truths. Indeed, MacDonald was probably as good a socialist as any other leading figure in the Labour Party; he was a principled opportunist (after all he gave up the Labour leadership to oppose the Great war), who did not scheme to ditch the Labour government but may be guilty of betraying his former Labour supporters.

During the years 1931–5 MacDonald was prime minister of a National Government which won a landslide victory at the 1931 general election, although his position now depended upon the Conservatives. During this period, MacDonald indulged himself in foreign policy and was very much involved in two conferences in 1932: the Geneva disarmament conference and the Lausanne conference, which was concerned with German reparations. Thereafter, he went into physical and mental decline and was forced to resign as prime minister on 7 June 1935. He then lost his Seaham seat at the 1935 general election to Emanuel Shinwell who had proposed him as PLP leader in 1922. He was found a seat for Scottish Universities, but thereafter played a diminishing role in the activities of the government. MacDonald died of heart failure on 9 November 1937 whilst cruising in the Caribbean on the *Reina del Pacifico*. His body was returned to Britain, cremated, and then his ashes were interred in the Spynie graveyard, near Lossiemouth, next to those of his wife. *KL*

DAVID MARQUAND, *Ramsay MacDonald* (London, 1977).

MacDonald-Gladstone pact. See LIB-LAB PACT (1903).

MacDonnell, Anthony Patrick (1844–1925), civil servant, under-secretary for Ireland, 1902–7. An independent-minded civil servant, with 40 years' experience in India, he was appointed by George Wyndham to bring an imperial reforming zeal to bear on Irish social and administrative conditions. He was particularly associated with two abortive schemes of Irish devolution, both involving the establishment of councils, part-elected, part-nominated, to oversee educational and administrative concerns. The first provoked Wyndham's resignation in 1905 under Ulster Unionist pressure, while the second soured Liberal–nationalist relations in 1907. *DRB*

MacDonnell royal commission (1912–14), established to examine biases in civil service recruitment in response to parliamentary concerns and chaired by Anthony *MacDonnell. It examined the education provisions which fed recruitment and the pay and grading systems intended to retain officials once recruited. It urged the creation of a special section within the Treasury to control personnel matters across the civil service as a whole. A pedestrian and inward-looking examination, it had a very limited impact compared to the Haldane report of 1918 or the *Lloyd George/Bradbury/Warren Fisher reforms after the Great War. *PJH*

RICHARD CHAPMAN and J. R. GREENAWAY, *The Dynamics of Administrative Reform* (London, 1980). | PETER HENNESSY, *Whitehall* (London, 1989).

Macdougall, (George) Donald (1912–), economist. For many years Macdougall was an Oxford University economist. His Whitehall service started with work for Churchill in the prime minister's statistical branch, 1940–5 (and later in 1951–3). From 1962 to 1964, he was economic director of the National Economic Development Office, moving to become director-general of the Department of Economic Affairs (1964–8) and then chief economic adviser to the Treasury and head of the Government Economic Service, 1969–73. He was chief economic adviser to the CBI, 1973–84. *KT*

McGovern, John (1887–1968), Labour and Independent Labour Party (ILP) politician. Until McGovern was elected to the Commons as Labour MP for Glasgow Shettleston in 1930 (holding the seat until he retired in 1959), his political activity mainly revolved around the ILP, interrupted by a brief flirtation with Guy Aldred's anarchist anti-parliamentary communist federation. McGovern had a forthright and controversial political career, including vitriolic attacks on the Communist Party, expulsion from the Labour Party following an election scandal, regular suspensions from parliament, and being arrested and fined in defence of the principle of free speech. He was one of the signatories to the 1931 Mosley memorandum, though he later withdrew his support when Mosley deserted Labour for the New Party. McGovern took his battle with the Communists into the hunger marches and the National Unemployed Workers' Movement, where he sought to challenge Communist control. From an initially strong left-wing position in the prewar period, albeit anti-Communist, McGovern's views in the post-war years were marked by an increasing conservatism, linked with both his Roman Catholicism and his support for moral rearmament, and his anti-communism took on an ever more passionate dimension. *DWM*

John McGovern, *Neither Fear nor Favour* (London, 1960).

McGuinness, Martin (1950–), Irish paramilitary and politician. In July 1972 McGuinness was a member of the Provisional IRA (PIRA) delegation which met the British government in London. Although he was subsequently to deny membership of the PIRA, McGuinness was twice convicted of membership in Eire. In 1973 he told an Irish court: 'For over two years, I was an officer in the Derry Brigade of the IRA . . . I am a member of Oglaigh na Eireann (IRA) and very proud of it.' As Northern Ireland's peace process evolved in the 1990s, McGuinness's support was seen as crucial in placating republican hard-liners. In 1990–3, he was one of the key contacts from the republican movement who secretly met a British government representative from the security services. In 1997, McGuinness was elected MP for Mid-Ulster, becoming Sinn Fein's chief negotiator in multi-party talks in Belfast, 1997–8. *TWH*

Mackay of Clashfern, Lord (1927–), lawyer and lord chancellor. James Mackay's Conservative affinities were tenuous: when appointed lord advocate, Mackay, congratulated by John Smith, 'James, I didn't know you were a Tory', allegedly answered, 'Who said I was?' A Highland signalman's son and Free Presbyterian, Mackay proceeded brilliantly in mathematics through Glasgow to Cambridge, switching to law and acquiring a superb professional reputation. No party hack, this Scottish lawyer, when asked to govern the English Bar, tried to reform its union practices and was foreseeably rebuffed. *EP*

McKenna, Reginald (1863–1943), Liberal politician and financier. McKenna was a barrister and Liberal MP, 1895–1918. He held junior office at the Treasury; was president of the Board of Education, 1907–10; first lord of the Admiralty, 1910–11; home secretary, 1911–15; and chancellor of the exchequer, 1915–16. As the range of his posts suggests, he was a safe all-rounder rather than a spectacular performer, but he built up a reputation in his eighteen months at the Treasury that made him much respected post-war. Baldwin sought to make him chancellor again in 1923, but by then he preferred to remain chairman of the Midland Bank. The 'McKenna duties' of 1915 were tariffs on luxury goods raised to produce wartime income. Their continuation into peacetime therefore became symbolic of the deeper debates over tariffs and free trade; they were removed by Labour in 1924 but restored by the Conservatives in 1925 and subsumed into general tariffs from 1932. *JAR*

Mackenzie, Compton (1883–1972), novelist and political activist. A founder member of the National Party of Scotland (NPS), Mackenzie stood as a nationalist candidate for lord rector of Glasgow University in 1928 and was narrowly beaten into second place by the prime minister, Stanley Baldwin. Like many other cultural nationalists, he withdrew from active politics in the mid-thirties as the Scottish National Party, the NPS's successor, became bogged down in sectional infighting. *RF*

McKenzie, Robert Trelford (1917–81), political scientist. Bob McKenzie was a Canadian from British Columbia, who, staying in England after war service, made himself a national figure as a TV interviewer and election night commentator. He is especially remembered for a confrontation with Lord Hailsham over the Profumo affair in 1963, and for a series of retrospective discussions with Harold Macmillan in the 1970s. But his most substantial achievement was his LSE thesis, published in 1955 as *British Political Parties; The Distribution of Power within the Conservative and Labour Parties.* Much influenced by Robert *Michels and his 'iron law of oligarchy', this revisionist work made an enormous impact with its central argument that power in British parties rested with their parliamentary sections. He shocked his Labour friends by arguing that the Conservatives were in practice more democratic than Labour, being far more ready to throw their leaders out when they lost touch with the party. In 1968 he published, with Allan Silver, *Angels in Marble: A Study of the Conservative Working Man.* From 1949 to his death he taught in the sociology department at the LSE and was dedicated to the interests of the school and of his pupils, but he never lost his Canadian accent or his enthusiasm. *DEB*

Mackenzie, William James Millar (1909–96), political scientist. Bill Mackenzie represented a characteristically British scepticism towards the scientific aspirations of the professionalized study of politics spreading from mid-century USA. While he conceded that American political scientists were better trained at organizing their material, Mackenzie accurately predicted in *Politics and Social Science* (1967) that the British emphasis on the state marked 'the revival of an old fashion which is due to come round again' (pp. 323–4). Against ambitious transatlantic claims to propound 'overarching theory', Mackenzie argued that methodology came after, not before, practice. A classical philologist by training, Mackenzie switched to being a politics fellow in Oxford in 1936. He became professor of government in Manchester after wartime service in government. (His period, 1939–44, in the Air Ministry led him to write an unpublished history of Special Operations Executive activity in France before moving to Manchester in 1949.) He created in the 1950s and early 1960s the seedbed for young political scientists that were to occupy many of the chairs in Britain's expanding universities of the subsequent decades, partly because he had an instinctive sense of where the study of politics was heading. He resisted the tendency to narrow specialization, favouring the interdisciplinary approach, with politics as part of a cluster of social sciences, both contributing to and drawing sustenance from them. He was constitutional adviser to the new states of Tanganyika and Kenya, leading him to write an excellent little book on *Free Elections* (1958). His indirect personal influence was far greater than that of his writings. *JH*

W. J. M. Mackenzie, *Explorations in Government* (London, 1975).

Mackinnon Wood, Thomas (1885–1927), Liberal politician. Mackinnon Wood was a prominent member of the Edwardian Scottish Liberal Party, after he won Glasgow, St Rollox, in 1906. He was regarded as an outsider by many Scottish colleagues and his private diary reveals a man with many insecurities. An assiduous worker, he was appointed financial secretary to the Treasury in 1911, before moving to be Scottish secretary, February 1912–July 1916. He was responsible for helping to pilot Sir Henry Cowan's Home Rule Bill as far as a second reading, though it was soon shelved after the outbreak of war. He had to deal with wartime worker agitation on 'Red Clydeside' before being moved back to the Treasury in 1916, a post he lost with the advent of Lloyd George's coalition. His close affiliation with Asquith cost him his seat in the 1918 election. *RF*

Maclay, John (1905–92), Scottish politician. Maclay was National Liberal and Conservative MP for Montrose burghs, 1940–50, and for Renfrewshire West, 1950–64. After various junior posts, he entered the cabinet as secretary of state for Scotland in 1957, serving until 1962. His tenure of office saw a decline in Conservative electoral fortunes in Scotland, but a series of modernizing initiatives including the Toothill report on the Scottish economy, and the establishment of the Scottish development department. He was created Viscount Muirshiel in 1964. *MJK*

Maclean, Donald (1864–1932), Liberal politician. A solicitor, Maclean was Liberal MP for Bath, 1906–10; Peebles, 1910–22; and North Cornwall, 1929–32. Having been Deputy Speaker, 1911–18, he took a more partisan role in the Asquithian Liberal Party in parliament, acting as its chairman, 1919–22. He was briefly the president of the Board of Education in the National Government, 1931–2. Father of the spy Donald Duart *Maclean. *JAR*

Maclean, Donald Duart (1913–83), diplomat and Soviet agent. The son of the Liberal cabinet minister Sir Donald *Maclean, Donald Maclean was educated at Gresham's School and Trinity Hall, Cambridge, where he read modern languages, graduating in 1934 with a first. He joined the university socialist society, became friends with Guy Burgess, Anthony Blunt, and 'Kim' Philby and was recruited as a Soviet agent. After graduation, Maclean, who was a strikingly tall, handsome man, apparently abandoned left-wing politics for a career in the diplomatic service. He worked in the League of Nations and western department of the Foreign Office before service at the embassy in Paris, where he met and married Melinda Marling, an American. He served in London until 1944, when he was posted to Washington as first secretary. For a while in 1946, he even acted as head of the Foreign Office's chancery. In the years between 1935 and 1951, Maclean provided Russia with reams of Foreign Office documents. In this role, he did lasting damage both to the integrity of the atomic bomb programme and to Anglo-American relations. In 1948 he was made head of chancery in Cairo, but suffered a severe breakdown. Recovered, the Foreign Office made him head of their American department, but meanwhile evidence of his treachery was mounting, and in May 1951, as a result of a tip-off from Philby, he defected to Moscow, his wife and family later joining him. Unlike other defecting agents Maclean led an active life in Moscow, teaching and writing. By 1979 he was alone, his wife and family having returned to the West. *PM*

Maclean, John (1879–1923), Scottish socialist and educator. A leading member of the Scottish Social Democratic Federation, Maclean is recognized by all shades of opinion as an outstanding educator who influenced a whole generation of labour activists through his Marxist economics classes. His political legacy, however, is controversial. For those who subscribe to the legend of *'Red Clydeside' he was a heroic figure, the leading campaigner against the Great War and the most active supporter of the Bolshevik revolution. His importance was demonstrated both by the authorities, who imprisoned him, and by Lenin who appointed him Soviet consul in Glasgow. Walter Kendall has seen him as the leader of a revolutionary left which was tragically marginalized by the artificial creation of the Communist Party. To others he was marginal, unimportant, and sectarian, isolated from the workers whose cause he espoused, both by his uncompromising revolutionary beliefs and by his apparent espousal of Scottish nationalism. Certainly by any conventional standards Maclean was a failure, but the courage and integrity of a man who, literally, gave his life for the cause cannot be doubted. *MC*

THOMAS BELL, *John MacLean: A Fighter for Freedom* (Glasgow, 1944). | W. KENDALL, *The Revolutionary Movement in Britain 1900–1921* (London, 1969). | B. J. RIPLEY and J. MCHUGH, *John Maclean* (Manchester, 1989).

Maclean, Murdo (1943–), civil servant. Maclean served in the Board of Trade (1964–7), the prime minister's office (1967–72), and the Department of Industry (1972–8), before succeeding Freddie Warren as private secretary to the government chief whip in 1979, advising government business managers on legislative timetabling and procedural arrangements in parliament, and linking the parties behind the scenes. Maclean is only the third holder of this key, but low-profile, post in the British parliamentary system since 1931. *KT*

Maclennan, Robert Adam Ross (1936–), centrist politician. Maclennan was president of the *Liberal Democrats from 1994, having been the last leader of the *Social Democratic Party (SDP) in 1987–8 before its merger with the *Liberal Party. Elected to parliament for Labour in 1966, he served as a junior minister in the Callaghan government but joined the Council for Social Democracy in 1981 and retained his seat in 1983 and 1987. Although he opposed the merger of the SDP with the Liberals, he accepted the leadership of the party on David Owen's resignation in August 1987 and abided by the decision to merge taken by the membership in 1988. *JS*

McLennan, William Patrick (1942–), statistician and civil servant. An Australian, McLennan joined the Australian Bureau of Statistics (ABS) in 1960, rising to be its deputy director, 1986–92. Headhunted by Whitehall, and given the task of improving the quality of key economic indicators at a time when the Central Statistical Office (CSO) was the target of criticism, he was director of the CSO and head of the UK Government Statistical Service, 1992–5. He returned to Australia to become head of the ABS in 1995. *KT*

MacLeod, George, of Iona (1895–1991), founder of the Iona community. George MacLeod was the son of a Unionist MP. Though decorated in the Great War, in the 1930s he became a sponsor of the Peace Pledge Union. A Church of Scotland minister in Govan, in 1938 he founded the Iona community to witness to his Christian Socialist ideals, only ceasing to be leader when appointed a Labour life peer, as Lord MacLeod of Fuinary in 1967. *PPC*

Macleod, Iain Norman (1913–70), colonial secretary, chancellor of the exchequer, and the best Tory speechmaker of his generation. Macleod was born in Skipton, Yorkshire, but his parents were from the Isle of Lewis. His radical, romantic Toryism reflected his Western Isles' roots, while his pragmatic views on social policy were influenced by being the son and grandson of doctors. Educated at Fettes and Cambridge, Macleod became an international bridge player and made money at cards before finding his purpose in life during the war. He stood for the Western Isles in 1945 and the following year joined the Conservative Parliamentary Secretariat (later merged with the *Conservative Research Department), specializing in health and social policy. Elected MP for Enfield West in 1950, he became a founder-member of the One Nation group and co-edited its first book. In 1952, he published *The Social Services: Needs and Means* with Enoch Powell.

Macleod made his reputation as a debater in March 1952 with a brilliant, impromptu attack on Bevan that was heard by Churchill. Within two months he was appointed health minister and sought to repair the Tories' reputation on the new National Health Service by undogmatically making it work. Courageously he broke the taboo on publicizing family planning. Macleod also had to contend with personal and family illness. His wife, Eve, was left partially disabled by polio, and he suffered from ankylosing spondylitis, a degenerative back condition. Having entered the cabinet in 1955 as labour minister, his defeat of the left-wing union leader Cousins in the 1958 London bus strike revived Tory morale. He led the policy groups that prepared the 1955 and 1959 Conservative manifestos. In 1957 Macmillan, who regarded Macleod as having 'political genius', appointed him to the Steering Committee on Tory strategy.

Macleod's greatest achievement came as colonial secretary after 1959 when he resolved the grave crisis in British east and central Africa by accelerating the timetable for African rule. His radicalism antagonized white settlers and infuriated Tory right-wingers, whose leader, the marquess of Salisbury, woundingly caricatured him as being 'too clever by half'. Macleod has justifiably been described as the greatest colonial secretary since Joe Chamberlain and as Africa's Mountbatten. His credo on the 'brotherhood of man' at the 1961 Tory conference was one of the finest speeches of the century.

In 1961 Macmillan, who had tired of ministerial bickering over Africa, made Macleod leader of the House, party chairman, and chancellor of the duchy of Lancaster. Macleod's standing suffered, however, as the government stumbled from one crisis to another, and when Macmillan resigned in 1963 he backed Butler for the leadership. His refusal to serve Douglas-Home, and his sensational exposé in 1964, as editor of the *Spectator*, of the Tory 'magic circle' that had preferred Douglas-Home to Butler, angered many Tories. Although Macleod returned to the front bench as steel spokesman in October 1964, he did not contest the leadership in 1965. Appointed shadow chancellor by Heath, Macleod planned to become a great, reforming chancellor. In July 1970, however, only a month after entering the Treasury, he died suddenly at Number 11. His tragically early death was a grievous loss, since he had great acumen and was unrivalled as a Tory trumpeter.

RJS

Nigel Fisher, *Iain Macleod* (London, 1973). | Robert Shepherd, *Iain Macleod* (London, 1994).

Macmillan, (Maurice) Harold (1894–1986), Conservative politician and prime minister who dominated politics during the late 1950s and early 1960s. Macmillan's Edwardian manner and showmanship never entirely disguised his opportunism and ruthlessness, earning him the epithet 'actor-manager'. His theatricality and political skills, however, persuaded the Tories to accept a new, post-imperial role for Britain.

Born into the Macmillan publishing family, Macmillan took pride in his western Highland roots and his American connection through his Indiana-born mother. After Eton he went up to Oxford, but was badly wounded during the Great War. Serving with men of all classes was a formative experience and, 70 years later, in his maiden Lords' speech during the 1984 miners' strike, he described the miners as 'the best men in the world'.

In 1919 Macmillan became aide-de-camp to the duke of Devonshire, then governor-general of Canada, and married the duke's third daughter, Lady Dorothy Cavendish. He stood for the Conservatives in 1923 in Stockton-on-Tees, won the seat the following year, and except during 1929–31 held it until 1945. In 1929 his wife began an affair with Bob *Boothby that lasted in one form or another until her death in 1966, but this humiliation transformed Macmillan from being dull and earnest into a tougher, more cynical character and strengthened his determination to succeed in politics.

Tory Rebel

During the Depression Macmillan's detestation of heavy unemployment in Stockton gave his Toryism a radical edge. Seeking a course between free-market capitalism and egalitarian socialism, he supported Keynes's economic policies. In *The *Middle Way*, the 1938 book that was his political credo, Macmillan proposed economic planning, a mixed economy, and a minimum wage. Together with Churchill, he opposed the appeasement of Hitler and in 1936 resigned the whip for a year. In 1938, he voted against the Munich deal (see Munich crisis) and supported an anti-Munich candidate, A. D. *Lindsay, against the Conservative, Hogg, in the Oxford by-election. Macmillan was one of 30 Tory rebels who in May 1940 forced Neville Chamberlain to resign.

Disappointed at being given only junior ministerial posts after 1940, Macmillan's appointment as resident minister in Algiers in 1942 marked a turning point. He wielded independent power and established a lasting relationship with the Allied commander General Eisenhower. In the classical allusion that became his trademark, he likened Britain's role vis-à-vis the Americans to that of the Greeks in the Roman Empire, namely to act as a civilizing influence. In 1943 he was moved to Italy, where his responsibilities expanded to cover Greece, Yugoslavia, Lebanon, and Syria. He was air secretary in the 1945 Caretaker Government before losing Stockton in the Labour landslide.

An Opportunist in Office

Macmillan quickly returned as MP for Bromley and served on the committee that produced the

Industrial Charter. The shift in Tory policy towards Keynesian economics and acceptance of a mixed economy was welcome to Macmillan, but politically he was eclipsed by Butler. As housing minister from 1951, however, Macmillan ensured that within two years the Tories met their ambitious pledge to build 300,000 new houses a year. He was promoted to defence in 1954, but his tenure was brief and probably his most courageous act was to tell Churchill to retire. In April 1955 Eden appointed him foreign secretary, but wanted to continue running foreign policy himself. After barely six months Macmillan was moved to the Treasury, where he showed flair in his 1956 budget by introducing premium bonds.

Macmillan's role during the *Suez crisis, however, was problematic to say the least. From the outset he strongly advocated military force, but he was converted from a hawk into a dove following the threat of an oil embargo and a run on sterling. His advice to the cabinet on 6 November to agree a ceasefire proved decisive and was the justification for Wilson's jibe that Macmillan had been 'first in, first out' over Suez. In a striking omission as chancellor, Macmillan had failed to guard against a run on sterling by drawing out funds from the IMF in advance of any crisis. And, given his understanding of Eisenhower, it is extraordinary that after visiting Washington in late September he was convinced that the president would not make trouble for Britain.

The Rise of 'Supermac'

In the wake of Suez, Macmillan outmanoeuvred Butler to succeed the ailing Eden. His upstaging of Butler when they both addressed the *1922 Committee was regarded by Enoch Powell as having 'verged upon the disgusting'. The cabinet overwhelmingly favoured Macmillan. When he became prime minister on 10 January 1957, he warned the queen that his administration might not last six weeks. He concentrated initially on mending fences with the Americans, while pursuing a cautious economic policy, since another sterling crisis after Suez would have been disastrous. His 1957 call for pay restraint was misconstrued when he said that people had 'never had it so good'. Nonetheless, greater prosperity was transforming people's lives and he ensured that the Tories were the political beneficiaries.

Macmillan established his authority by calling Salisbury's bluff in March 1957 when he accepted the latter's resignation over the release from detention of the Cypriot leader Archbishop Makarios. In January 1958 he picked up the gauntlet thrown down by his Treasury ministers when they quit on the eve of his Commonwealth tour, magisterially dismissing their resignations as *'little local difficulties'. His unflappable image and his showmanship, as when he visited Khrushchev and entertained Eisenhower during an election year, proved irresistible. *'Supermac' was born. With a booming economy fuelled by an electioneering budget he won a landslide victory in October 1959, delivering the Tories their third successive electoral triumph.

Seeking a New Role for Britain

Armed with a Commons majority of 100, Macmillan began recasting Britain's role in the world. His response to grave crises in British Africa was to signal the end of empire by appointing Macleod colonial secretary, and in February 1960 he warned the South African parliament of the *'winds of change' blowing through their continent with the rise of African nationalism. When his summit diplomacy with Khrushchev and Eisenhower collapsed in 1960, he saw Britain's future lying in Europe as part of a 'grand design' to organize the Western world against the communist threat. His European conviction was reinforced by a 1960 study of Britain's economic prospects that he had commissioned from the Joint Intelligence Committee, which was so alarming that he dared not show it to the cabinet. Macmillan's modernizing strategy for Britain combined the 1961 application to join the European Economic Community (EEC) and economic intervention, including the National Economic Development Council ('Neddy'), that was intended to make the leaders of industry and the unions share responsibility for the economy. In an attempt to maintain full employment by preventing pay increases continually outstripping what the country could afford, Macmillan replaced the 1961 pay pause (the attempt to hold down wages, especially in the public sector) in 1962 with a permanent incomes policy (albeit on a voluntary basis) by establishing the National Incomes Commission. He further embraced the state's modernizing role by introducing earnings-related pensions and contracts of employment, and by planning new hospitals and universities.

Demise

The unpopularity of the pay pause contributed to a series of by-election defeats, and when he was prompted by the prospect of further humiliation in July 1962 to sack seven of his cabinet in the *'Night of the Long Knives', it seemed that he had lost his nerve. Yet his special relationship with President Kennedy made him a trusted sounding board during the 1962 Cuban missile crisis and enabled him to persuade Kennedy to preserve Britain's nuclear deterrent by substituting Polaris missiles for the cancelled Skybolt. The Polaris deal, however, confirmed de Gaulle's suspicions about Britain's Atlanticism, and in January 1963 the French president vetoed Britain's EEC application.

Macmillan's 'grand design' lay in ruins. He seemed to be at the mercy of events as unemployment reached its then post-war record of 878,000 (3.9 per cent). This impression was reinforced by the *Vassall and *Profumo cases, and as his Edwardian manner became a handicap he was prey to satirists. He realized a long-standing ambition, however, by initiating the 1963 nuclear test ban treaty and would probably have led his party at the next election had he not had to resign on health grounds during the 1963 Conservative conference. From his sickbed, Macmillan did all in his power to deny Butler the succession, first backing Hogg before switching to Douglas-Home. The controversy caused by his manipulation of the *'customary processes' led the Conservatives to introduce leadership elections.

Macmillan published six volumes of memoirs and in 1984 was created earl of Stockton. He never disguised his dislike of 'Thatcherism'. Among advocates of market economics and monetarism his name is synonymous with state intervention, excessive public spending, and inflation, but his government's record on growth, inflation, and unemployment, when taken together, was unsurpassed during the rest of the century. *RJS*

Alistair Horne, *Macmillan*, 2 vols. (London, 1988 and 1989). | John Turner, *Macmillan* (London, 1994).

Macmillan committee on finance and industry (1929–31), established under the chairmanship of the judge Lord Macmillan. Its remit was to examine the domestic and international financial system and to make recommendations as to how this could play an increased role in promoting trade and employment. At the core of this was the need to explain the British economy's poor performance during the 1920s, and this led to a detailed and often heated academic debate between orthodox economists such as Montagu Norman and radicals such as J. M. Keynes. In general, the evidence presented to the committee suggested a divergence between the natural self-adjustment of the market predicted by orthodox economic theory and the reality that this adjustment was not taking place. As Keynes put it, the mechanism seemed to have become jammed halfway through. A good example of this was the failure of British wages to fall, following the return to the gold standard at pre-war parity with the dollar. The higher value of the pound made British products more expensive and, according to classical theory, should have led to a fall in wages as a means of maintaining competitiveness. In reality, barriers such as trade-union bargaining power prevented this. Keynes argued that the return to the gold standard at too high a level had created a conflict between international and domestic economic policy, and the committee considered various solutions, including both protection and public works, as means of resolving this conflict. Agreement on a package of solutions was not reached and the report, published in July 1931, was quickly overtaken by the burgeoning financial crisis. Despite this, the proceedings of the committee remain of great value as a guide to the development of economic theory in the inter-war years. *WF*

Peter Clarke, *The Keynesian Revolution in the Making* (Oxford, 1988).

McNally, Tom (1943–), prime minister's political adviser, 1976–9. A Labour Party international relations specialist who advised Jim Callaghan at the Foreign Office (1974–6), McNally was Callaghan's closest adviser in Downing Street, involved in a wide range of policies. Charged with the task of maintaining good relations with union leaders and the party at a difficult time, perhaps his most significant role was in offering personal support to Callaghan as Labour's majority evaporated. A Labour MP from 1979, he defected to the Social Democratic Party in 1981. *CL*

McNeil, Hector (1907–55), Labour politician. McNeil, MP for Greenock, had a swift rise in the Attlee government, serving as parliamentary under-secretary, 1945–6, and minister of state, 1946–50, at the Foreign Office. In 1950, in the aftermath of Labour's difficulties with the Scottish Convention movement, he was promoted to cabinet as secretary of state for Scotland. In opposition he renewed his interest in international affairs and died while still an MP in 1955. *MJK*

Macneill, Eoin (1867–1945), scholar-revolutionary. Macneill was a Catholic from Co. Antrim and one of the founders of the Gaelic League in 1894. In 1913 he founded the Irish Volunteers in direct response to the Unionist Ulster Volunteer Force. He was involved in preparations for the Easter Rising, being deceived by one of the plotters that Dublin castle was about to suppress nationalists. On discovering the lie, he countermanded the order to rise. Nonetheless, he was imprisoned in 1916–17, and on release he became a minister in the Dáil underground government. Macneill supported the Anglo-Irish treaty of 1921, and was minister of education in the Free State executive, 1922–5. His political career ended in controversy when he served on the commission to delimit the boundary of Northern Ireland, which recommended only minimal changes on each side of the border. *DGB*

MacQuisten Bill (1925), private member's bill on trade union law, introduced by Scottish Conservative backbencher F. A. MacQuisten, which had widespread party support. It proposed the abolition of the political levy system whereby trade union members donated a percentage of their subscription to the Labour Party. Baldwin, concerned about the bill's impact upon industrial harmony, decided to impose his authority upon his party, and with cabinet support, killed the bill with one of his most successful parliamentary speeches, on 6 March. *NJC*

Mafeking, insignificant town in the Northern Cape colony, South Africa, besieged by the Boers from the outbreak of the Boer war on 10 October 1899. Its defence by a small garrison commanded by Colonel Robert Baden-Powell evoked great admiration, and made him a national celebrity. Its relief by the British army led to wild scenes of rejoicing in London on 'Mafeking night' (18 May 1900), and briefly to the use of the word 'Mafficking' to mean riotous behaviour of a good-humoured type. *JAR*

magistrates (England and Wales), laymen and -women who sit in groups as judges in the lowest criminal courts in England and Wales, reaching verdicts and imposing penalties (currently up to six months' imprisonment) for lesser crimes and committing more serious offenders for trial in higher courts. Justices of the peace (JPs) existed from medieval times, appointed by the lord chancellor on the advice of the lord lieutenant and his deputies in each county, and were formally enrolled in a separate commission for each county; in some urban areas, the lay magistracy is supported by professional 'stipendiary' magistrates who are in effect junior judges. Some local officials, such as mayors of towns, were ex officio magistrates until 1968, reflecting the origins of the position in local self-government. The 30,000 magistrates have no legal qualifications (though they must sit with and take advice from a legally qualified clerk), their lay status roughly equating to the citizen input of juries in more serious cases but, as the law has become more complex and the focus of media attention on judicial decisions sharper, they are obliged to undergo initial training when appointed, and periodic updates, under the auspices of the Judicial Studies Board. There have been criticisms of the system in the later part of the century, mainly on the ground of the magistracy's unrepresentative nature—too many JPs being over 50, white, middle class, and male—so that governments were obliged to take measures to include more women and ethnic minority magistrates, partly by allowing nominations directly from the public as well as from the 111 local advisory boards. *JAR*

H. Parker et al., *Unmasking the Magistrates* (Milton Keynes, 1989).

Maitland, Donald James Dundas (1922–), prime minister's chief press secretary, 1970–3. Maitland, a career civil servant without journalistic experience, had worked with Heath during the latter's abortive negotiations over British membership of the European Economic Community in the early 1960s. His appointment reflected the importance Heath attached to Europe. Maitland combined a politically neutral approach to his work with a role as an influential adviser. Having tried unsuccessfully to introduce 'on the record' lobby briefings, he was experimentally issuing press releases as an alternative when his posting ended. *CL*

Major, John (1943–), Conservative politician and prime minister. John Major inherited a party brought to both of Kipling's impostors of triumph and disaster by his predecessor, and had to govern a country and conciliate that party reduced to breakdown by triumph and disaster. He was the son of a 66-year-old ex-theatrical, Tom Major, and left school at 16 during a family financial crisis, working for two years like no other British premier, as a general labourer, but after joining the Standard Chartered Bank rose to head corporate affairs. Engaged in Conservative politics, he won election to Lambeth council on a freak swing, 1968, making a good name as chairman of housing. Inevitably defeated in 1971, Major pursued his banking career, contesting safe Labour St Pancras, 1974, but elected at Huntingdon in 1979.

Rising slowly but spotted for the elite Blue Chip Club by Tristan Garel-Jones, he rose through the Department of Health and Social Security before becoming Treasury whip. Chancellor Lawson, after the 1987 election, chose him as chief secretary, the cabinet minister restraining public spending, but he avoided the customary recourse to prime ministerial adjudication. His ascent had been brilliant, accelerating as Thatcher's quarrels gouged glittering holes ahead of him. He was briefly foreign secretary, then a competent chancellor: Tessas, the 5p piece, a sustained anti-inflationary stance, and support for entry to the Exchange Rate Mechanism (ERM). His leap to the premiership, though surrounded by conspiratorial chatter, was another example of a gratuitous vacuum before his feet. Thatcher had imposed the suicidal *poll tax (with Lawson and Major both against the idea), suffering terrible by-election results culminating at Eastborne. When she fell in November 1990, the party's right wing had no credible candidate and, wanting to stop Heseltine, found Major embodying negative virtue.

Prime Minister

Once prime minister, he and Heseltine replaced the poll tax with council tax, with no great political trouble. He was also early engaged in the Gulf war, with no Thatcherite inclination to rejoice and, after initial flinching, proposed Kurdish safe havens. Electorally, the change of leader reconciled voters by 1992, helped by Neil Kinnock's failings and John Smith's meagre (and very Scottish) definition of 'rich' and therefore surtaxable. Major returned from the 1992 election losing only 0.1 per cent of the 1987 vote, but his Tory majority of seats was seriously cut by Labour targeting voters; by-election defeats could—and did—now undermine him in the Commons. Meanwhile Major made a key mistake, having already made one in appointing Norman *Lamont—a model of dogmatic, hysterical chancellors—in refusing to realign a doomed sterling exchange rate. Replicating Wilson in 1964, Major would be compelled to devalue later in 1992. Blaming the debacle upon Europe and the ERM gave a green light to Eurosceptics, ahead of negotiating and ratifying the Euro-integrationist *Maastricht treaty. Despite British opt-outs neatly negotiated by Major, a Danish referendum 'No' foreclosed the guillotine during ratification, turning the debate into a drawn-out nightmare. Disloyalty of right-wing backbenchers and cabinet colleagues, dubbed 'the bastards' by Major himself, was reinforced by a venomous campaign in the Murdoch press, the *Mail* and the *Telegraph*. They believed European development could be stopped by destroying Major, replacing him with Michael Portillo, while rightists (mourning Thatcher and conspicuously disloyal to Major) virtually seceded, briefing, denigrating, conspiring while Tory newspapers applauded. Major in June 1995 offered resignation and a challenge, which Portillo ducked. Redwood resigned and stood against Major but the leader was comfortably re-elected. Nevertheless, denigration barely faltered, even though Britain's intrinsic economic performance was now outstanding: falling inflation, heavy inward investment, and growth followed devaluation and the low interest rate policy of Kenneth *Clarke.

There was also an effective attempt to rescue education from dismal standards. Reform plans were written off when first rebuffed, but Major returned with a new and effective secretary, Gillian *Shephard, pursuing a policy later accepted by Labour as well as Conservatives. Major also responded to the Hume initiative for an Ulster *ceasefire, which, despite dependence on Ulster Unionists and a limited resumption, did come about. But recession, deepened by the absurd interest rates in 1992, was never forgiven, Right-wing mavericks' antics, press malice, and a spate of *sleaze and corruption cases involving Aitken, Hamilton, and others, proved ruinous. The Tory defeat in May 1997 was unprecedented, ironically wiping out many of Major's party enemies, notably the widely detested Portillo. Major resigned immediately, though remaining in the Commons until 2001, and was then viewed and heard with renewed respect.

John Major, unfashionable, a rotten butcher, too dedicated a Treasury man, saner than most people who become premier, made a central mistake. But his destruction, sedulously sought by the press, may have destroyed for a generation the Tory party in a country innately moderate. Liked to the end, he was thought unable to control his extremists. Unwisely accommodating party before country, humane, courteous, and with great achievements, he lacked the authority to become the non-authoritarian figure necessary for Britain to elect the Conservatives.

EP

John Major, *The Autobiography* (London, 1999). | Anthony Seldon, *John Major* (London, 1997).

majority, age of. See voting age.

Makins, Roger Mellor (1904–96), later Lord Sherfield, diplomat and public servant. Makins was ambassador in Washington, 1953–6; joint permanent secretary at the Treasury, 1956–9; and chairman of the UK atomic energy authority, 1960–4. Constitutionally powerful and intellectually formidable, a fellow of All Souls, Oxford, at 21 and of the Royal Society at 82, Makins specialized in matters atomic and economic. He wanted to be remembered as a giver of good advice. The record is mixed, but a full assessment awaits. *AD*

Malaysian confrontation (1963–5). The federation of Malaysia, consisting of Malaya, Singapore, Sarawak, and Sabah (British North Borneo) was inaugurated in September 1963, but had already earned the enmity of neighbouring Indonesia, which stepped up its campaign of 'confrontation' by severing diplomatic relations and trade links, and continued the guerrilla raids across the Kalimantan border into Sarawak and Sabah, begun earlier in the year. Malaysia had been viewed in Whitehall as a way to scale down Britain's residual commitments in the Far East and relinquish the last vestiges of unpopular formal empire, but the retention of the Singapore base and the transfer of the Borneo territories to Kuala Lumpur's federal control brought Indonesian accusations of neo-colonialism. Committed to the defence of Malaysia by treaty, the British government deployed troops to Borneo, and maintained significant naval and air forces in the region. Escalation of the conflict was always a possibility, particularly in August–September 1964, when Indonesia staged several amphibious and parachute raids on peninsular Malaya, but low level attrition was the dominant pattern of confrontation. The counter-insurgency campaign was conducted with great skill and effectiveness, with gurkha forces playing a prominent role, and by late 1964 the Labour government was authorizing so-called 'Claret' raids back across the Kalimantan border. Nevertheless, serious doubts over how long Britain could maintain such a commitment had been raised in 1964, while relations between London and Kuala Lumpur were strained by differences over tactics to follow in the dispute. In August 1965 overwhelming Whitehall pressure for a negotiated settlement arose in the confusion of Singapore's departure from Malaysia, only to be quelled when the Americans made clear their strong opposition. Domestic upheaval in Indonesia from October 1965 signalled the end of a serious threat to Malaysia, and in August 1966 relations were normalized between the two countries. *MCJ*

Malmesbury, 5th earl of (1872–1950), Conservative politician. James Edward Harris succeeded his father as earl at the age of 27 and in a long partisan career championed tariff reform and Conservative social reform, but he was also an outspoken diehard throughout the constitutional crisis of 1909–12. A ready joiner of Tory organizations, Malmesbury was a mainstay of Page Croft's secret *Confederacy, of the Tariff Reform League, the Primrose League, the Navy League, and the Anti-Socialist Union. *RJQA*

Malvinas. See FALKLANDS WAR.

management. See BRITISH INSTITUTE OF MANAGEMENT.

Manchester bombing (15 June 1996), Provisional *IRA (PIRA) outrage. Following the collapse of the PIRA *ceasefire of 1994, the terrorist organization detonated a large bomb in Manchester city centre. It exploded in a van at 11.20 a.m. near the city's busy Arndale shopping centre, injuring more than 220 people, four of them seriously. Nearly 75,000 people had to be cleared from the city centre. The bombing was seen as a setback to the peace process when a new PIRA ceasefire was anticipated. *TWH*

***Manchester Guardian*.** See *GUARDIAN*.

mandate, term used to denote either a government's authority to govern or its authority to implement certain specified programmes. By virtue of popular election, a government is deemed to have the authorization—the 'mandate'—to govern. This interpretation of the term was the dominant one among the Conservative and Liberal parties in the 19th and early 20th centuries. One variant was the belief that this authority did not extend to a major change of policy and that such a policy would require the consent of the electorate at a subsequent election. The second interpretation—the authority to implement a stipulated programme of measures—has become the dominant one in the 20th century. It was championed by the Labour Party, deriving from the belief that it had particular objectives to achieve and that those who were elected were delegates, there to pursue policies endorsed by those who elected them (Birch, 117–18). The party issued programmatic election manifestos and the other parties followed suit. The two uses of the term can cause confusion. A government introducing a measure that it has not promised in its manifesto may be accused of lacking a mandate to introduce it. However, it may fall back on the original use of the term and claim a mandate to introduce it by virtue of the fact that it is the elected government. Critics argue that too much weight should not be accorded to the concept of the mandate in its now dominant interpretation, for there is little evidence that many electors read manifestos. Various studies have shown that electors are frequently unaware of what a winning party has promised and that the fit between the promises embodied in a party's manifesto and the beliefs of that party's supporters is not always a close one. *PN*

Anthony H. Birch, *Representative and Responsible Government* (London, 1964). | Richard Rose, *Do Parties Make a Difference?* (2nd edn., London, 1984).

mandates, colonial. In 1919 the American president, Woodrow Wilson, would not allow the victors of the Great War to annex the colonial territories of two defeated states, Germany and the Ottoman Empire. Instead, he took up the novel idea of South Africa's prime minister, General Smuts, that they become mandates under the League of Nations, and this was done. According to article 22 of the League's covenant, the well-being of peoples 'not yet able to stand by themselves under the strenuous conditions of the modern world', formed 'a sacred trust of civilization' to be entrusted to 'advanced nations' under League supervision. There were three categories of mandates. The 'A' mandates needed only 'administrative advice and assistance' and by 1945 were all independent or about to become independent: these were Iraq, *Palestine, and Transjordan (administered by Britain), and Syria and Lebanon (France). 'B' mandates needed colonial administration to guarantee freedom of conscience and religion, subject to certain safeguards: these were Tanganyika (Britain), the Cameroons and Togoland (both divided between Britain and France), and Ruanda Urundi (Belgium). 'C' mandates were deemed—because of their size, 'remoteness from the centres of civilization', or geography—best administered as integral portions of the mandatory power: these were south-west Africa—now Namibia (South Africa), Western Samoa (New Zealand), German New Guinea (Australia), Nauru (Britain, Australia, and New Zealand, but administered just by Australia), and the Mariana, Caroline, and Marshall Islands (Japan.) Criticisms of the system were that it was paternal and patronizing; that the objectives for 'B' and 'C' mandates were unclear; and that the machinery of supervision (by the permanent mandates commission on behalf of the League council) was weak, resulting in inadequate protection for the inhabitants. On the other hand, the system established the principle of international supervision of colonial territories, and opened their government to public view. This helped to transform attitudes towards colonialism, and eventually contributed to its demise. *LL*

William Roger Louis, *Great Britain and Germany's Lost Colonies 1914–1919* (Oxford, 1967). | Fred Northedge, *The League of Nations: Its Life and Times 1920–1946* (Leicester, 1986).

Mandelson, Peter Benjamin (1953–), Labour politician. Grandson of Herbert *Morrison, Mandelson was Labour Party communications director, 1985–90, organizing the skilful, much-praised election campaign in 1987. Labour MP for Hartlepool from 1992, he was close to Blair, becoming minister in the Cabinet Office, 1997–8, and secretary for trade and industry, 1998, where he was praised for his support for business competitiveness. Mandelson had to resign after revelations about an inappropriate house-purchase loan from another Labour MP, but was soon back in office as Northern Ireland secretary. A major influence on *New Labour's political strategy, he was seen as an expert on 'spin', the presentation of political issues to the public, but ironically became the victim of it himself in 2001, when he was forced to resign again in mysterious circumstances over a call placed to the Home Office over a passport application. *BJE*

Donald Macintyre, *Mandelson* (London, 2000).

manifestos, electoral, documents issued by political parties during election campaigns, outlining the measures they propose to introduce if elected to office. Manifestos offer a guide to electors as to what the political parties will do in office and are thus deemed useful in helping them make their choice in deciding how to vote. They are essentially a 20th-century phenomenon. At the beginning of the century, Conservative and Liberal leaders continued the 19th-century practice of issuing personal statements, often in the form of letters or statements to their own constituents. The Labour Party broke the mould in 1906 by issuing a policy programme in its own name, and the other parties followed suit in the inter-war years. The 1935 election 'was the first time the [Conservative] Party used a centrally printed manifesto in this form and the pattern has been followed ever since' (Block, 72). Manifestos have grown in size as the documents have become more detailed: they tripled in length in the first half of the century and almost doubled in length in the third quarter. Critics point out that few electors read manifestos and that manifesto promises can be overtaken by events. There is empirical evidence that the policies embodied in a party's manifestos do not always enjoy the complete support of that party's voters. However, parties have a good track record of implementing manifesto promises once returned to office. *PN*

GEOFFREY D. M. BLOCK, *A Source Book of Conservatism* (London, 1964). | F. W. S. CRAIG, *British General Election Manifestos 1900–1987* (3rd edn. Chichester, 1989). | RICHARD I. HOFFERBERT and IAN BUDGE, 'The Party Mandate and the Westminster Model: Election Programmes and Government Spending in Britain, 1945–1985', *British Journal of Political Science*, 22 (1992).

Mann, Thomas (1856–1941), socialist politician. Tom Mann was one of the most important figures in the British socialist movement and became an international socialist of renown. Born in Coventry, he began work in a coal mine at the age of 10, later moving to Birmingham to become an apprentice toolmaker and joining the Amalgamated Society of Engineers in 1881. He left for London and joined the quasi-Marxist Social Democratic Federation in 1885, becoming a lecturer for the organization and producing for it his influential pamphlet *What a compulsory eight-hour day means to the working man* (1886). He led the famous London dockers' strike in 1889 and became president of the Dockers' Union in 1891. His industrial prominence led to his appointment to the royal commission on labour, 1891–4. However, at this time he moved into political as well as industrial activity. He joined the Independent Labour Party (ILP), became its secretary in 1894, and unsuccessfully contested three parliamentary seats as an ILP candidate before resigning in 1897 to become president of the International Federation of Ship, Docks, and River Workers and emigrating to Australasia in 1901. On his return to Britain in 1910 he led the industrial syndicalist movement, editing the *Industrial Syndicalist*, and organizing industrial action. He was a founder member of the Communist Party of Great Britain in 1920 and became chairman of its National Minority Movement in the trade unions, 1924–32. *KL*

TOM MANN, *Memoirs* (London, 1923, repr. 1967).

Manningham-Buller, Reginald Edward (1905–80), lord chancellor and Conservative politician. Manningham-Buller was called to the Bar in 1927 and in 1943 became MP for Daventry (from 1950, South Northamptonshire). He served in Churchill's 1945 Caretaker Government as a works minister, and in 1951 was appointed solicitor-general. Three years later, he became attorney-general. Manningham-Buller's right-wing views and imposing bulk earned him the nickname 'Bullying-Manner'. He was criticized in parliament for his incompetent handling of the prosecution of the alleged murderer Dr Bodkin Adams. The trial judge had been Sir Patrick *Devlin and, whether or not this was a factor, Manningham-Buller later made a deplorable attack on Devlin in 1959 during the Commons debate on the latter's judicial inquiry into the Nyasaland riots. His promotion in 1962 to become lord chancellor, as Lord Dilhorne of Towcester, following the *'Night of the Long Knives', made a mockery of Macmillan's claims about bringing in new blood. In 1963 Dilhorne polled the cabinet and apparently found a majority in favour of Douglas-Home as Macmillan's successor, but he had counted Macleod and Boyle as Douglas-Home supporters when they both backed Butler. Dilhorne accepted a viscountcy in 1964. A possible model for Kenneth Widmerpool in Anthony Powell's *Dance to the Music of Time* novels. *RJS*

Manpower Services Commission (MSC) (1973–88), created by the Employment and Training Act, 1973, receiving a grant-in-aid from the Department of Employment. The MSC was tasked with comprehensive manpower planning in order to help reverse the UK's ongoing relative economic decline with special emphasis on new technology. It was transformed in 1988 into the short-lived Training Commission. *JD*

PATRICK AINLEY and MARK CORNEY, *Training for the Future* (London, 1990).

marching season, term used to describe the period of annual parades in Northern Ireland. The organizations involved belong mainly to Protestant loyal orders, such as the *Orange Order (Ulster). There are also a smaller number of nationalist and republican parades. The volume and range of parades has grown in recent years. Until the late 1960s the marching season was the July/August period, but it now stretches from March to September. *BMW*

T. G. FRASER (ed.), *The Irish Parading Tradition: Following the Drum* (London, 2000).

'march towards the sound of gunfire', confident phrase used by Jo *Grimond, leader of the Liberal Party, at the 1963 Liberal Assembly, following victory in the *Orpington by-election: 'In bygone days, commanders were taught that when in doubt, they should march their troops towards the sound of gunfire. I intend to march my troops towards the sound of gunfire.' *JS*

Marconi scandal (1912), major political corruption case involving Liberal ministers. The Marconi company was awarded in March 1912 a government contract for building radio stations around the Empire. Partly as a result of this, the value of Marconi shares more than doubled. It then transpired, mainly through revelations in *Eye-Witness* (owned by Hilaire *Belloc), that David *Lloyd George, chancellor of the exchequer; Rufus *Isaacs, attorney-general; and the Master of *Elibank, Liberal chief whip (in the latter case using the party's funds as well as his own), had all made investments in the related American Marconi company, and thus made profits from the general rise in Marconi shares (collective profits alleged to amount to about £100,000, a huge sum for the time). There was therefore a strong probability that they had used confidential information available to them as ministers in order to benefit themselves and their party financially. Elibank's flight to Bogota in South America ('fourteen days hard mule-riding from the nearest wireless telegraphy office', as a Tory paper sneered), added much to the general suspicion of corruption. The fact that Isaacs was the government's chief negotiator with Marconi, Lloyd George the man who would have to finance the contract from public funds, and Elibank the one who would push it through the Commons, made their collective personal involvement in trading Marconi shares even more suspicious.

Conservatives were rapidly onto the warpath, with the unshakeably upright Lord Robert *Cecil taking the lead in relentless questioning in the Commons. Since these debates coincided with the bitterest disputes over Irish home rule, the temperature rose steeply; it was, for example, hinted by Liberals that the Conservatives' glee at Isaacs's discomfiture was at least in part motivated by anti-Semitism. Polarization and partisanship was in the end what saw the Liberals through, for it was precisely because of antagonisms over other issues that Liberal, Labour, and Irish MPs refused to break ranks and support the Conservatives in bringing down the government. The demand for an investigatory select committee had to be conceded, but the government majority on the committee made sure that the implicated ministers were exonerated, largely by insisting on the technical separateness of British and American Marconi (the first having the contract, the second being the one in which the shares were traded), and by accepting assurances given on oath by Isaacs and Lloyd George. Tories thought this only proved them to be liars and perjurers as well as cheats.

The Liberals therefore weathered the storm and, though Elibank was replaced as chief whip and did not hold office again, Lloyd George went on to become prime minister four years later, and within a year of the scandal Asquith even made Isaacs lord chief justice. This last produced predictably irate reactions from the Tories (notably in Kipling's scathing poem 'Gehazi'), arguing that the country now had as its senior judge a man who ought to be in gaol himself. But Asquith really had little choice; it was customary for the attorney-general to become lord chief justice, so that not appointing Isaacs in 1913 would have been tantamount to accepting his guilt over Marconi in 1912. In the longer run, the whiff of corruption was never after 1912 absent from perceptions of Lloyd George, with damaging consequences for his career. Though making in 1916 and renewing in 1918 their coalition with Lloyd George (when, even then, Neville Chamberlain thought him to be a 'dirty little Welsh attorney', while others dubbed him 'the Welsh Walpole'), Conservatives were quick to cite the memory of Marconi when in 1921–2 the *honours scandal again tarnished Lloyd George's moral reputation, this time leading to his final ministerial downfall in 1922. *JAR*

Frances Donaldson, *The Marconi Scandal* (London, 1962).

Margesson, David (1890–1965), Conservative politician. Enjoying the patronage of Baldwin and Eyres-Monsell, Margesson secured the 'safe' Rugby seat in 1924 and immediately joined the Whips' Office. In 1931 he became chief whip, serving an ex-Labour prime minister leading an overwhelmingly Conservative 'national' coalition, but served four successive prime ministers. He quickly established a reputation as a strict disciplinarian, marshalling his parliamentary majorities by a mix of political patronage and threats. He was faced with a serious number of challenges: the passage of the 1935 India Act, continued disaffection with Baldwin's leadership, criticism of appeasement, and the initial months of Churchill's leadership. His greatest failure was to underestimate the strength of party dissatisfaction with the conduct of the war which culminated in the infamous May 1940 Norway debate. Critics listed Margesson's conduct as one of their principal complaints, but Churchill felt obliged to retain his services, conscious that a considerable proportion of the party remained faithful to Chamberlain. Only in December 1940 was Churchill secure enough to move Margesson to the War Office. This was Margesson's first ever departmental responsibility and, when combined with 1941's army reverses on several fronts and criticisms from the 1922 Committee, it hardly made for a successful tenure. He was sacked in February 1942. *NJC*

marginal seats, parliamentary constituencies in which the party holding the seat has a small majority and is thus considered vulnerable to defeat at the next election. Most post-war studies have defined as marginal a seat in which the winning candidate's majority constitutes 10 per cent or less of the poll, and as such vulnerable to a conventional swing of five per cent or more to the second-placed party. The number of marginal seats declined from 172 in 1955 to 80 in 1983, leading David Butler to conclude that 'Far fewer seats are now at risk from any given swing' (1983: 21). The number of marginal seats increased in 1992 though the swing of 10.3 per cent from Conservative to Labour at the 1997 general election was such as to render the term largely redundant. The Labour Party in that election concentrated its resources on 90 essentially marginal Conservative seats: not only did it win all but one of these seats, it also won 68 other seats, previously classified as 'safe' Conservative seats. Given the widespread assumption that the Labour Party would have difficulty improving on its performance at the next general election, those seats which were won by Conservatives in 1997 with majorities representing less than 10 per cent of the poll were no longer automatically considered marginal. Conversely, not all Labour seats won with majorities representing more than 10 per cent of the poll were treated as safe. The two most marginal seats in the 20th century, in terms of the actual majority, were Ilkeston in 1924, and Winchester in 1997: the winning candidate in each won by just two votes. *PN*

DAVID BUTLER, *Governing without a Majority* (2nd edn., London, 1983). | DAVID BUTLER, and DENNIS KAVANAGH, *The British General Election of 1997* (London, 1997).

Marples, (Alfred) Ernest (1907–78), Conservative politician. Elected in 1945, Marples was ideally qualified as a self-made building entrepreneur to ensure that the Tories kept their 1951 promise to construct 300,000 houses a year, and he became Macmillan's deputy at housing. By appointing Marples postmaster general in 1957 and transport minister in 1959, Macmillan harnessed his energy and skills as an innovator and self-publicist to modernize Britain's postal service, telephones, roads, and railways. Marples became a life peer in 1974. *RJS*

Marquand, David Ian (1934–), Labour and Social Democrat politician, the son of Hilary *Marquand. He has been a prominent pro-European intellectual and supporter of Roy Jenkins, joining the *Social Democrat Party in 1981 and subsequently the *Liberal Democrats. During the 1990s, he transferred his allegiance to Blair's Labour Party, but retaining his progressive and centrist leanings. *JS*

Marquand, Hilary Adair (1901–72), academic, author, and Labour politician. He served as professor of industrial relations at University College, Cardiff, 1930–45, and was the director of the notable industrial surveys of south Wales. Marquand was then the Labour MP for Cardiff East, 1945–50, and for Middlesbrough East, 1950–61. He held several high offices including secretary for overseas trade, 1945–7; paymaster general, 1947–8; minister of pensions, 1948–51; and minister of health, January–October 1951. Following his resignation, he was the director of the International Institute at Geneva, 1961–5. Father of David *Marquand. *JGJ*

Marsh, Richard William (1928–). Labour politician. After working in trade unions, Marsh became an MP in 1959 and a minister in 1964. Described by Wilson as a disloyal lightweight, Marsh was at one time the rising star of the 1964–70 Labour cabinet. His mixed record as a minister, especially at transport, and his opposition to Barbara Castle's *In Place of Strife* proposals, led to his sacking in 1969. He resigned his seat in 1971 and became chairman of British Railways, 1971–6, and subsequently of various other quangos, including the newspaper publishers' association. He received a life peerage in 1981 and supported Thatcher in government. *BB*

Marshall aid. On 5 June 1947, US Secretary of State George Marshall made a speech about the 'hunger, poverty, desperation and chaos' then rife in Europe, and the need to find 'a cure rather than a mere palliative' for this condition. In reality, the Marshall plan was less a plan than a speculation. American diplomat George Kennan summarized American thinking thus: 'We have no plan. The Europeans must be made to take responsibility.... Our main object: to render principal European countries able to exist without outside charity. Necessity of this: (a) so that they can buy from us; (b) so that they will have enough self-confidence to withstand outside pressures', chiefly the bogey of communism, masterminded (so they thought) from Moscow. In conception, and certainly in execution, Marshall aid served to solidify the emerging *Cold War.

Under the firm tutelage of Oliver *Franks, the Europeans did what was required of them. A Western, democratic bloc of sixteen nations concocted what became the European Recovery Programme. They were promised a substantial $17 billion over a four-year period. The first tranche of $5 billion was made available in 1948. Of this the British received no less than $1.24 billion. If Marshall aid was indeed a pork barrel, as Washington sometimes feared, then it was the British who were most adept at pork barrel politics. Though by no means the most deserving, they became the biggest beneficiaries of the whole programme, receiving some $2.7 billion of the $12 billion disbursed between April 1948 and December 1950, when the appropriations ceased. At once statesmanlike and self-regarding, Marshall aid was quite as unsordid as *Lend-Lease, its material effect considerable, its political and psychological effect immeasurable. *AD*

MICHAEL J. HOGAN, *The Marshall Plan* (Cambridge, 1987). | ALAN S. MILWARD, *The Reconstruction of Western Europe* (London, 1987).

Martell, Edward (1909–89), ex-Liberal who moved to the far right in the 1950s and 1960s, exercising a volatile influence on public opinion during periods of government unpopularity. He was an expert self-publicist, operating initially through his *People's League for the Defence of Freedom, later creating the Freedom Group, and influential through his 'free labour', anti-trade union newspaper the *New Daily*. He joined the Conservatives in 1962 but made little impact within a real political organization. An extreme libertarian rather than a neo-fascist, he foreshadowed similar activists later in the century. *JAR*

Marten, (Harry) Neil (1916–85), Conservative politician and anti-EEC campaigner. Elected in 1959, Marten became an aviation minister in 1962. As a supporter of the Commonwealth, however, he grew increasingly out of step with his party over membership of the European Community. Having made his mark as a courteous but determined opponent of British entry, he chaired the 1975 national referendum campaign for a 'No' vote. In 1979 he was appointed Foreign Office minister for overseas development. He retired in 1983. *RJS*

Martin, John Miller (1904–91), prime minister's principal private secretary, 1941–5. A former Colonial Office official, Martin may have owed his appointment to the recommendation of Brendan Bracken, who was impressed by his work as secretary of the Palestine Royal Commission. Brought to Downing Street in 1940 as part of Churchill's purge of his predecessor's private office, he soon won Churchill's trust and, following his promotion, he accompanied the prime minister to several conferences, including Yalta in February 1945. *CL*

SIR JOHN MARTIN, *Downing Street: The War Years* (London, 1991).

Martin, (Basil) Kingsley (1897–1969), socialist journalist. Conscientious objector and one-time chairman of the Union of Democratic Control, Martin edited the *New Statesman*, 1931–60. He combined political comment with a high standard of literary criticism to transform it into the country's most influential left-wing journal. After the Second World War, Martin was a member of the 'Europe Group', which argued for a democratic socialist third force to balance the two superpowers, and one of the founders of Campaign for Nuclear Disarmament in the late 1950s. *MC*

Marxism, political ideology derived from the works of Karl Marx (1818–83) and Friedrich Engels (1820–95) who claimed to demonstrate that advanced societies would inevitably become communist societies. Their argument (called 'historical materialism') amounts to a form of technological determinism: the development of the forces of production (technology, skills, equipment, and so on) would, they said, transform the relations of production (the relations between social classes based on ownership of property), and these in turn would transform cultural, religious, legal, and political institutions (the superstructure). In the past such developments transformed feudalism into capitalism and absolute monarchy into democracy; in the future they would transform capitalism into socialism, and representative democracy into a participatory or direct democracy. In modern society, they argued, the growth of the factory inevitably creates a new impoverished working class, and consequently the conditions for revolution. With *The Communist Manifesto* (1848) and the political movement called the First International (1864) they sought to bring this revolution about. In *Capital* (vol. 1, 1867) Marx also claimed to provide a theoretical analysis of the nature of profit (as deriving from 'surplus value'), and to demonstrate that the working class must of necessity be increasingly exploited and impoverished, for profits have a natural tendency to fall as wages diminish as a proportion of the costs of production.

In the late 19th and early 20th century the most influential followers of Marx were in the German Social Democratic Party, which was a member of the Second International (1889), and which increasingly adopted the reformist and gradualist ideas of Kautsky and Bernstein. This tradition transformed into the modern social democratic and labour parties, particularly after the parties in the Second International supported their national governments, not the principle of socialist internationalism, in the Great War.

Lenin (1870–1924) maintained, in *What is to be Done?* (1902), that it was necessary to construct a disciplined, professional, clandestine revolutionary party (at least wherever communist ideas and organization were illegal—the book was originally intended to address specific problems of organization in Russia), a view which resulted in a split in the Russian Social Democratic Party and the founding of the Bolshevik Party. In *Imperialism* (1916) he argued that capitalism must now be understood as a global system within which the working classes of the advanced countries had been bought off with higher standards of living. Revolution was now likely to take place in newly industrializing countries such as Russia. The Russian revolution of 1917 appeared to confirm this analysis, but Lenin had expected revolution in the periphery to be followed by revolution in the heartlands of capitalism. The failure of communist uprisings in Germany in 1919 proved him to be wrong in this key respect.

Lenin's *State and Revolution* had presented a picture of the new socialist society as founded in popular self-government, with the rapid withering away of the old state apparatus. Instead Bolshevism in Russia developed a one-party state exercising totalitarian control over the whole society. The Bolshevik model of party organization was adopted by the other communist parties in the Third International (1919), and Lenin's successor, Stalin (1879–1953), propounded the view that it was possible to build 'socialism in one country' (1924), thus enabling Russia to claim to be a communist society despite the failure of the revolutionary movement in the West, and justifying the Third International in sacrificing the interests of other national parties to those of the Russian state.

In 1929 Trotsky (1879–1940), whose ideas and actions in 1917 had closely paralleled Lenin's, fled into exile, and went on to found the Fourth International in 1934. This was dedicated to the principle of international revolution, and attacked Stalinism for betraying the cause of revolution. However, it was the parties of the Third International which were to successfully carry out revolutions through guerrilla warfare in China (1949) and Cuba (1959), while Eastern Europe fell under Russian control with the defeat of Hitler in 1945. *DRW*

Leszek Kolakowski, *Main Currents of Marxism*, 3 vols. (Oxford, 1978).

Marxism Today, a theoretical journal of the Communist Party of Great Britain (CPGB), launched in 1957. Martin Jacques, editor from 1976, made it the rallying point for the organization's Eurocommunist wing, and it signalled the retreat from class politics which eventually split the party. Derided by traditional communists as a purveyor of 'designer socialism', *Marxism Today* became one of the left's few publishing successes of the 1980s, leading the critique of Thatcherism. It ceased publication in 1991 when the CPGB also came to an end. *MC*

Mary, Queen Consort of George V (1867–1953). The daughter of a penniless Continental prince who was supported by Victoria, she married the future *George V in 1893. More interested in history and antiquities than her husband, she nevertheless submitted herself to his unintellectual tastes. Her toque hats, pearl chokers, and long skirts, worn decades beyond their season, were tokens of a more formal and certain era. She lived to see the revival of interest in Victorian certainties, which began during the Second World War after it had been rejected by Bloomsbury during the Great War. *WMK*

Mason, Roy (1924–), Labour politician. MP for Barnsley, 1953–87, Mason was a former miner and NUM branch official, 1947–53. In the Wilson government, 1964–70, he was junior minister for shipping, defence equipment, and power, postmaster general, and then reached cabinet as president of the Board of Trade, 1969–70. Defence secretary in 1974–5, Callaghan appointed him Northern Ireland secretary, 1975–9. He made little progress in resolving the political stalemate in Northern Ireland, concentrating on security matters and devoting his efforts to the containment of the IRA. *DLM*

Mass-Observation. Unofficial survey organization formed by Tom Harrisson, Humphrey Jennings, and Charles Madge in 1937. Its emergence reflected the increased importance attributed in the 1930s to public opinion and to the views and lives of ordinary people—a sort of domestic anthropology. But while opinion polls, emerging from the same mood and at the same time, sought to sample scientifically and hence to measure opinions statistically, Mass-Observation was more concerned to note down people's own conversation and hence to record the feel and the quality—rather than the quantity—of attitudes to contemporary events that this revealed. It used volunteers, enthusiasts who went among ordinary people, asked them questions, and reported what they saw and heard. Mass-Observation was sometimes resented as a bunch of snoopers in that age of *means testing: the *Daily Mirror* in December 1937 called it 'Public Busybody No. 1'. Much was left to local decision (for example in programmes to assess opinions on films and film stars), but coordinated national investigations were also undertaken, initially to record activities all over the country on coronation day 1937 (published in book form as Jennings and Madge, *May the Twelfth: A Mass-Observation Day-Survey, 1937*, 1937). The government employed Mass-Observation as part of its wartime investigations into public morale, it correctly picked up the swing of opinion to the left in 1942–5, and produced ten further books in 1945–50, but the greater sophistication of opinion polls after 1945 led to its withering away. Its archive at the University of Sussex has, however, proved of considerable value to historians investigating public attitudes in the 1937–50 period. *JAR*

ANGUS CALDER and DOROTHY SHERIDAN, *Speak for Yourself: A Mass-Observation Anthology, 1937–1949* (London, 1984).

Masterman, Charles Frederick Gurney (1874–1927), Liberal politician. A journalist by trade, Masterman was Liberal MP for West Ham, 1906–11, and Bethnal Green South West, 1911–14. He held junior office at the Local Government Board and Home Office, and was in the cabinet as chancellor the duchy of Lancaster, 1914–15, responsible for Britain's early war propaganda (he also launched the war artists' scheme). A keen Liberal progressive, his *The Condition of England* (1909) was a stout defence of *New Liberalism, and a warning of the dire consequences of not ameliorating working-class social grievances. *JAR*

maternal mortality. See POPULATION CHANGE.

Matrix-Churchill case, administrative and legal outrage, the infamous occasion of the Scott report, annihilating the Major government's credit. Four Coventry businessmen, including Matrix managing director Paul Hamilton, were prosecuted for illegal arms trading to Iraq, despite encouragement by civil servants, with ministers at least broadly informed. The initiative of officials at Trade, zealous to trade, was ignored by solicitor-general Sir Nicholas Lyall, narrowly bent on prosecution. The judge stopped the case after the candid evidence of Alan *Clark let the side (some would say the conspiracy) down. *EP*

Maud, John Primat Redcliffe (1906–82), public servant. An Oxford don, Maud became a temporary civil servant during the Second World War and enjoyed a meteoric rise in the Ministries of Food and of Reconstruction, being appointed permanent secretary at the Ministry of Education in 1945. In 1952 he became permanent secretary at the Ministry of Fuel and Power, and later served as British high commissioner to South Africa (1959–63). As Lord Redcliffe-Maud he chaired the royal commission on English local government, 1966–9 (see REDCLIFFE-MAUD COMMISSION). *KT*

Maud committee (1964–7), departmental committee on the management of local government. During the early 1960s, concern about the ability of local government to attract individuals of ability, both as councillors and as officials, led to pressures for a wide-ranging inquiry. At the behest of the local authority associations, two committees, under Sir John Maud and Sir George Mallaby respectively, were established. Maud's committee on management was appointed in 1964, its 1967 report being accompanied by substantial volumes of original research studies. The most important of the committee's many proposals was the relegation of hitherto decision-making committees to a merely deliberative role, with executive powers concentrated in a small 'management board' of five to nine members. This attempt to override politics with managerialism was ill-received, although it has been periodically revived since. *KY*

Maude, Angus Edmund Upton (1912–93), Conservative politician and journalist. Despite his *One Nation connections, Maude was a right-winger, notable as a *Suez Grouper and Beaverbrook journalist, joint author with Enoch Powell of *The Middle Classes*, director of the *Conservative Political Centre, 1951–5. He was an MP, 1950–8, but after Suez fled to Australia and editorship of the *Sydney Morning Herald*. Maude returned after the Profumo affair to win Profumo's vacated seat, Stratford-upon-Avon. Sacked from the front bench in the Heath era, his career revived mildly under Thatcher, heading the Conservative Research Department, 1975–9, and paymaster general, 1979–81. Father of Francis Maude, Conservative front-bencher in the 1990s. *EP*

Maudling, Reginald **(1917–79)**, Conservative politician, who championed Keynesian economic policies and whose easy, relaxed manner disguised a quick, first-class brain. Educated at Merchant Taylors' School and Oxford, 'Reggie' Maudling spent the war in RAF intelligence and the air secretary's private office. After standing for Heston and Isleworth in 1945, he joined the Conservative Parliamentary Secretariat (later merged with the *Conservative Research Department), where he briefed Churchill and Eden. He worked on the **Industrial Charter* and moved its acceptance at the 1947 Tory conference. Elected for Barnet in 1950, he joined the *One Nation group in 1951 and was promoted to the front bench as a civil aviation minister in April 1952. The following December he was appointed economic secretary to the Treasury, where he again worked with Butler, and in 1955 became supply minister. As paymaster general Maudling joined Macmillan's cabinet in September 1957. After his negotiations for a free trade area with the European Economic Community (EEC) (the so-called 'Plan G') failed, he was instrumental in establishing the *European Free Trade Association of seven non-EEC countries in 1959. Having spoken against British membership of the EEC, he changed his mind in 1961 but never supported a supranational Europe.

At the Board of Trade from October 1959 Maudling pursued a regional policy for industry and recognized the importance of boosting exports. In 1961 he succeeded Macleod at the Colonial Office, where, to Macmillan's dismay, he was just as radical, pushing through an independence constitution for Northern Rhodesia (Zambia) and devising Kenya's land resettlement scheme. In July 1962 his appointment as chancellor of the exchequer, aged 45, heralded the peak of his career. His chancellorship became controversial because of his 'dash for growth', but his 1963 budget was less reflationary than Macmillan (and many commentators) had suggested. He sought union support for an incomes policy that he believed was indispensable if the 4 per cent annual growth target set by the tripartite National Economic Development Council was to be sustained. By 1963 many younger Tories wanted him as leader, but when Macmillan resigned Maudling's poor conference speech dashed his hopes. After 1964 the Labour government's repeated claim that they had inherited an '£800 million deficit' tarnished Maudling's reputation. His defeat by Heath, who had succeeded him as shadow chancellor, in the July 1965 Tory leadership election shocked him, and although he became deputy leader he never fully recovered his confidence. In 1970 Maudling became home secretary but failed to get to grips with Ulster's troubles and resigned in 1972 when the Metropolitan Police, for whom he was responsible, investigated the bankruptcy case of John Poulson, with whom he had had a business association. Maudling served briefly as Thatcher's shadow foreign secretary, but doubts raised by his business judgement continued to mar his final years. His death in 1979 robbed parliament and his party of an intellectually formidable champion of Keynesian economics and the post-war commitment to full employment. *RJS*

Reginald Maudling, *Memoirs* (London, 1978).

Mau Mau insurgency (1952–6), term given to the uprising among Kenya's Kikuyu tribe, against the loss of tribal land and the breakdown of Kikuyu society. Although some European families were massacred, in essence the insurgency was a Kikuyu civil war, as Mau Mau terrorists targeted those collaborating with the British, including women and children. British troops, white settlers, and Kikuyu levies eventually defeated the insurgents, but not before 10,000 Kikuyu and about 100 Europeans had died. *KTS*

John Darwin, *Britain and Decolonisation* (London, 1988).

Maurice debate (9 May 1918), parliamentary confrontation, following the publication in the press on 7 May of a letter from General Sir Frederick Maurice, director of military operations at the War Office, in which he alleged that Prime Minister Lloyd George had misled the Commons in April about the number and adequacy of British troops in France (Lloyd George, seeking to avoid blame for the British defeats of March, had inherently therefore blamed instead the army command, which was deeply resentful). Lloyd George easily won the vote, mainly because few MPs wanted a new government at a crisis moment in the war, but the debate involved Asquith openly challenging him for the first time since falling from power in December 1916. Longer term, the government saw the challenge as necessitating preparations for an election in which it could confront its critics, and negotiations therefore began for an electoral pact between

Conservatives and National Liberals, duly implemented in the December *'Coupon' Election. *JAR*

NANCY MAURICE (ed.), *The Maurice Case* (London, 1972).

Mawhinney, Brian Stanley (1940–), Conservative politician. Mawhinney was a distinguished medical academic and also an Ulster Protestant, the first native-born Ulsterman to hold an appointment in the Northern Ireland Office. Responsible for education there, he promoted integrated, non-sectarian schooling. Close to John Major, he rose to become health secretary then party chairman in time to preside over the 1997 electoral debacle. In opposition he was shadow home secretary. *EP*

Maxton, James (1885–1946), Labour politician. Jimmy Maxton was a lifelong labour activist and propagandist in the west of Scotland, a *'Red Clydeside' Labour MP from 1922. Born in Glasgow, son of schoolteacher parents, Maxton became a trained teacher himself, interrupting his studies at Glasgow university to take up a teaching post. He later completed his MA part-time, graduating in 1910. He joined the university Unionist association before reading some of the socialist classics of the time and attending the university's socialist study circle. The influence of John Maclean and the Social Democratic Federation was also fundamental in establishing his socialist commitment. In 1904, he joined the Independent Labour Party (ILP) and held several offices at local and national level, including being chair of the Scottish ILP for the period 1913–19. He was a pacifist in the Great War and served a year's sentence following a conviction for sedition. He argued at a public meeting that workers should strike in protest at the deportation of David Kirkwood and other Clydeside labour activists. In 1918, he unsuccessfully contested Bridgeton, Glasgow, as an ILP candidate in the general election, but continued campaigning for the ILP and in 1922 was elected MP for Bridgeton, holding the seat until his death. His pacifism was challenged by the outbreak of the Spanish civil war and he was prepared to enlist in the International Brigade, but his poor health prevented any military involvement. He campaigned fiercely on housing and education issues both inside and out of parliament and was chair of the ILP between 1926–31 and 1934–9. He was almost universally recognized as an inspirational socialist orator and a man of immense political integrity. Robert Skidelsky writes that 'Maxton with his long black hair, and his cadaverous features, was the conscience of the left, highly emotional, unbalanced, but universally loved' (*Politicians and the Slump* (Harmondsworth, 1970), 92). *KJL*

G. BROWN, *Maxton* (Edinburgh, 1986). | WILLIAM KNOX, *James Maxton* (Manchester, 1987).

Maxwell, Alexander (1880–1963), civil servant. Maxwell's civil service career was spent in the Home Office, which he entered in 1904 and headed as permanent secretary, 1938–48. An efficient and humane administrator, and a strong believer in the abolition of capital punishment, Maxwell exerted a powerful liberal and liberalizing influence at the Home Office, even under the great security pressures of the Second World War (dealing with issues such as press censorship and detentions under Defence Regulation 18B). *KT*

Maxwell, (Ian) Robert (1923–91), businessman, publisher, and fraud. Born Jan Hoch in Ruthenia, he reinvented himself as Robert Maxwell and won the Military Cross in the Second World War. Maxwell built international business connections and developed the market for science publishing, through his Pergamon Press. Elected Labour MP for Buckingham in 1964, he quickly tired of backbench life. Flamboyant and increasingly overweight, he ran his companies as an impenetrable interlocking group, registered in Liechtenstein. He bought Oxford United football club and in 1984 achieved the ambition of gaining control over the *Mirror* group of newspapers. He played the impetuous, autocratic, self-publicizing, interventionist tycoon, helicoptering between residences. But he overextended himself financially, especially by buying the *New York Daily Post*. He sought to recover by fraudulently raiding the *Daily Mirror*'s pension fund. When possibly close to exposure, he drowned off his yacht near the Azores, in unexplained circumstances. *CKSU*

TOM BOWER, *Maxwell* (London, 1992).

Maxwell Fyfe, David Patrick (1900–67), lord chancellor, home secretary, and Conservative politician. Born in Scotland and educated at Oxford, Maxwell Fyfe became a barrister before being elected MP for Liverpool, West Derby, in 1935. Appointed solicitor-general in 1942 and attorney-general in the 1945 Caretaker Government, he continued in opposition as a prosecutor at Nuremberg (see NUREMBERG AND TOKYO WAR TRIALS). A supporter of the European Convention on *Human Rights, he also advocated European unity. During the war he deputized for Butler as chairman of the Tory *Post-War Problems Central Committee and after 1945 helped to produce the *Industrial Charter*. He headed the Conservatives' post-war inquiry into their organization but had little input into its proposed reforms although it is known as the 'Maxwell Fyfe Report'. Appointed home secretary in 1951, he faced the first post-war anxieties about rising crime. In what was to become one of the most controversial cases of the century, he refused to reprieve Derek Bentley, who had been convicted of murdering a policeman, although Bentley's accomplice, Christopher Craig, who was too young to be hanged, had fired the gun. (Bentley's conviction was quashed in 1998.) In 1954, Maxwell Fyfe was appointed lord chancellor as Viscount Kilmuir. After the Commons voted in 1956 for the abolition of capital punishment, in defiance of the government, Kilmuir proposed the compromise whereby the death penalty was retained only for certain types of murder. Advising Salisbury on selecting a successor to Eden as Tory leader in 1957, Kilmuir emphasized the preservation of the queen's prerogative in choosing her first minister. Sacked during the *'Night of the Long Knives' in 1962, Kilmuir accepted an earldom. He repeated in his self-important memoirs an earlier claim that loyalty was the Tories' 'secret weapon'. *RJS*

Earl of Kilmuir, *Political Adventure* (London, 1964).

May, Robert McCredie (1936–), scientist. Educated in Sydney, May's academic career included university appointments in Australia, the USA, and Britain. A leading scientific authority on bio-diversity, he took leave from his Royal Society research professorship at Oxford University and Imperial College, London, to become chief scientific adviser to the government and head of the Office of Science and Technology in 1995, responsible for advising the prime minister, cabinet, secretary of state for trade and industry, and the minister for science on scientific, engineering, and technology issues. *KT*

May committee (1931), established by the second Labour government to examine national expenditure. Its main finding was that spending was too high, and as such was hindering the efforts of the private sector and so restricting both employment and industrial growth. Using rigorously orthodox financial analysis the committee estimated that the following year's budget deficit would stand at £120 million, and called for spending cuts amounting to £97 million, the bulk of which were to be found from employment schemes and social services. Especially controversial was the stipulation that two-thirds of the economies should be found through cuts in unemployment benefit, as this attacked Labour's commitment to maintain an adequate social security system. The publication of the report coincided with a crisis of confidence abroad in the British economy, and the full implementation of the committee's recommendations came to be seen as the litmus test of the government's willingness to adhere to sound financial practice. The inability of the cabinet to agree upon a policy of retrenchment led to the collapse of the Labour government and its replacement by the National Government. *WF*

Philip Williamson, *National Crisis and National Government* (Cambridge, 1992).

Meacher, Michael (1939–), Labour MP. A veteran left-winger, Meacher was a junior minister during the 1974–9 governments and had the unique distinction of being elected to the shadow cabinet for fourteen years, 1983–97. He was offered only a junior position as environment secretary in the Blair government. Meacher was best known for his role in founding the Labour coordinating committee, champion of the Bennite left, which he chaired, 1978–83. *MC*

Meade, James Edward (1907–55), economist and government adviser. Oxford-educated, Meade was a fellow of Hertford College, 1931–7; worked for the League of Nations, 1931–7; and became an assistant in the economic section of the Cabinet Office, 1940–5, and its director, 1946–7. His post-war career included chairs at LSE, 1947–57, and Cambridge, 1957–68, and a fellowship at Nuffield College, Oxford, 1968–74, winning the Nobel prize for economics in 1977. He wrote widely on aspects of economic policy, notably *Principles of Political Economy* (4 vols., 1965–70). Meade was influential in establishing the Keynesian orthodoxy in British economic policy in and after the 1940s. *JAR*

Meadowcroft, Michael James (1942–), Liberal radical and activist and founder of the *Liberal Party (Continuing) in 1989. He joined the Liberal Party's full-time staff in 1962, becoming regional officer in Yorkshire and a Leeds councillor, and developed the community politics strategy, becoming MP for Leeds West in 1983 (but lost in 1987). His suspicions of the effects of a merger on traditional Liberal values led to him walking out of negotiations with the Social Democratic Party in 1988. In 1989 he announced the refounding of the Liberal Party with its base in West Yorkshire amongst pro-Meadowcroft Liberal activists. *JS*

means testing, restriction of benefits in accordance with 'means' or income, named after the means test of 1931, introduced by the *National Government in autumn of that year for those in receipt of unemployment insurance beyond the statutory period of six months under the National Insurance Acts. Under the new regulations, claimants had to undergo a 'household means test' carried out by the local public assistance committees, the successors to the poor-law guardians. Any form of income, including pensions, contributions from sons or daughters, lodgers, or charities, could be taken into account, as well as savings, furniture, or effects. These household enquiries aroused controversy because they were considered demeaning and officious. The means test remained in operation for the rest of the decade, although its operation was somewhat relaxed. It left a legacy of bitterness over any benefits not paid as of right and has become a generic term for any restriction on benefits according to income. As a result the aim for much of the post-war welfare state was *universality of provision earned through contributions. Increasing costs of welfare, however, have led to an increased number of benefits, such as *housing benefit and *family allowances being means tested. *JS*

Mebyon Kernow, Cornish National Party which flourished briefly in the 1970s alongside the Scottish National Party and Plaid Cymru in Scotland and Wales. It had been founded in 1951 to seek Cornwall's independence from the United Kingdom, but contested Cornish parliamentary constituencies only between 1970 and 1983—and with little effect. *JAR*

medium-term financial strategy. In 1980 the Conservative government introduced *monetarist policies based on the belief that these would improve the investing environment. Part of this was a five-year plan called the medium-term financial strategy in which the planned course of monetary variables was set out. In particular the money supply was targeted and government borrowing and expenditure were each planned (to be contained). This was to make clear what monetary policy was, and how it could be sustained, and at the same time influence expectations. *FHC*

Mellish, Robert Joseph (1913–98), Labour politician. Bob Mellish was MP for various London seats, 1946–82, becoming junior minister for housing and local government, 1964–7, and minister of public building, 1967–9. He became government chief whip, 1969–70, and was reappointed to instil discipline amongst MPs, 1974–6. Appointed by the Conservatives as chairman of the London Docklands Corporation in 1980, he supported an independent Labour candidate against the ultra-left Labour candidate Peter Tatchell, to become his successor as MP for Bermondsey. He received a life peerage in 1985. *BJE*

mercy, prerogative of, remaining specific power of the reigning monarch, the right to reduce a sentence after conviction on a criminal charge, but exercised only on the advice of (in practice, by) the home secretary. Free pardons or lesser sentences could in principle be applied after any offence, but the phrase was generally applied to the commutation of the death sentence for a capital crime to a term of imprisonment, and has therefore not applied since the death penalty for murder was finally removed in 1969. *JAR*

Meriden Cooperative, one of three workers' cooperatives (the others were Kirby Manufacturing and Engineering, and the *Scottish Daily News*) to receive the enthusiastic support of Tony *Benn when he was industry secretary, 1974–5. Benn forced financial support through a reluctant cabinet in the teeth of Treasury opposition, utilizing the provisions of the Tories' 1972 Industry Act. He saw them as exercises in industrial democracy. However, all were to illustrate the problems, notwithstanding the fervour of the secretary of state, besetting workers' attempts to protect their jobs by taking over failing concerns. The workers at the Norton Villiers Triumph (NVT) factory at Meriden near Coventry had blockaded the plant when they were made redundant. Keeping the plant open, however, alienated NVT workers at the Birmingham plant, fearful for their own jobs. Although the cooperative achieved higher productivity than before, the collapse of export markets and fierce domestic competition doomed the venture. None of the cooperatives lasted long. *PPC*

meritocracy, term coined by Michael Young in a book intended to satirize a British society that had been governed by an elite based upon birth and wealth, but was in transition to one based on merit as measured by examination performance. *The Rise of the Meritocracy, 1870–2033* (London, 1958) is subtitled 'An Essay on Education and Equality'. The choice of 1870 is clear, because 'Education was then made compulsory in Britain, patronage at last abolished in the civil service and competitive entry made the rule' (p. 17).

While equality of educational opportunity drained talent from the working classes, those who reached the upper class were promoted on merit not on seniority. This had led to a 'far-reaching redistribution of ability between classes in society, and the consequence is that the lower classes no longer have the power to make revolt effective' (p. 151). Young foreshadowed a populist revolt which he expected would fail. As he put it: 'Today we frankly recognize that democracy can be no more than aspiration, and have rule not so much by the people as by the cleverest people; not an aristocracy of birth, not a plutocracy of wealth but a true meritocracy of talent' (pp. 18–19). Democracy, like socialism, was a pious hope. The irony is that Young's pejorative neologism, meant to warn of a coming danger that was already well under way, was adopted as a favourable reflection on changes in British society. There is a double irony in that the trend that Young anticipated has not occurred to anything like the extent he sketched, because the old elite has managed to perpetuate traditional inequalities and thereby provide a more respectable educational veneer for privileges derived from birth and inherited wealth. We remain in matters of the distribution of wealth and power a long way from the socialist aspiration to a classless society in which equality and not just equality of opportunity would prevail. *JH*

Messina conference (1955). On 1–2 June 1955, the foreign ministers of the six European Coal and Steel Community (ECSC) powers (Belgium, France, Italy, Luxembourg, the Netherlands, and West Germany) met in Messina, Sicily. This was described by those in attendance and later commentators as the moment when European integration was relaunched after the failure of the *European Defence Community (EDC) (see also WESTERN EUROPEAN UNION). In fact, whether Messina represented a relaunch is a matter of debate, as some suggest that it was less of a relaunch and more of a redirection in the process of European unity away from the unsuccessful military sphere and back to the economic. The main task of the Messina conference was to discuss two proposals for future cooperation. First was the Beyen Plan, a Benelux proposal for a European customs union which was a response to the limited advances in European trade liberalization. Second was the suggestion promoted by Jean Monnet to make energy the focus of unity through the creation of an atomic energy community. From July 1955 a committee was convened, under the chairmanship of Belgian foreign minister Paul-Henri Spaak, to investigate these proposals and in May 1956 it produced a report which became the basis of the Treaty of Rome. Britain did not attend the Messina conference but famously sent a representative to the Spaak committee. Symbolically, this was a Board of Trade official rather than a minister, a move which struck one of the worst diplomatic notes in British–European relations either before or since. The death of the EDC had created an atmosphere of incredulity in London towards the Messina proposals, which for a brief but damaging period turned into active hostility in November/December 1955. The resilience of the six powers, together with American pressure, forced the British to rethink their policy and in 1956 they announced their own 'Plan G', a doomed proposal to complement the EEC with a European free trade area (see also ROME, TREATY OF). *JRVE*

Meston report (1936), springing from the *Liberal Reorganization Committee, chaired by Lord Meston. The report's main feature was the creation of the Liberal Party Organization to replace the old National Liberal Federation of 1877. It aimed to provide a single policy-making body for the party, although in practice this remained divided between the annual assembly, the party council, and the leader. The report also gave greater powers to the parliamentary party and the whips. Often seen as a largely top-down reshaping of the party, in contrast to the post-war grassroots activism of *community politics. *JS*

'methods of barbarism', resonant phrase used by the Liberal leader *Campbell-Bannerman on 14 June 1901, describing the British policy (including 'concentration camps') against civilians in the latter stages of the Boer war: 'When was a war not a war? When it was carried on by methods of barbarism in South Africa.' *JAR*

metropolitan authorities. See LOCAL GOVERNMENT STRUCTURE.

Metropolitan Police commissioner, the senior officer, equivalent to a chief constable in other forces, responsible to the home secretary for the management of police in London. The Metropolitan Police's direct link with government went back to the foundation of the force when Robert Peel was home secretary in the 1820s (hence, allegedly, their nickname as 'bobbies') but has been justified too on grounds of the special needs of the capital city (such as embassy and VIP protection), and the siting within London's police force (inevitably the largest in the country) of specialized units that could then be made available to other forces. The changes in London government after 1997 included provision for the setting up of its first police authority including elected local members. *JAR*

R. Plehwe, 'Police and Government: The Commissioner of Police for the Metropolis', *Public Law* (1974).

Meyer, Christopher John Rome (1944–), prime minister's press secretary, 1994–6. A former head of the Foreign Office news department (1984–8), influenced by his experience of working with Bernard Ingham, Meyer was a more forceful operator than his predecessor, Gus O'Donnell. Meyer tried to woo newspapers whose support for the Conservatives was wavering, with limited success. He attempted to give John Major a more statesmanlike image, stage-managing his foreign trips and encouraging him to be more reserved with journalists. *CL*

MI5. See Security Service.

MI6. See Secret Intelligence Service.

Michels, Robert (1876–1936), political scientist who was a German Jew by birth, initially a revolutionary Marxist by conviction, and an Italian from choice. He has been principally identified with the 'iron law of oligarchy' formulated in his *Political Parties: A Sociological Study of the Oligarchical Tendencies of Modern Democracy.* This generalization from his empirical study of the working of the German Social Democratic party appeared first in 1911 and was translated into English in 1915. Inspired by the Italian elitists Mosca and Pareto, Michels concluded his book with the assertions 'Leadership is a necessary phenomenon in every form of social life' and 'every system of leadership is incompatible with the most essential postulates of democracy' (p. 400). He goes on to formulate what he calls 'the fundamental sociological law of political parties'. 'It is organization which gives birth to the dominion of the elected over the electors, of the mandatories over the mandators, of the delegates over the delegators. Who says organization, says oligarchy' (p. 401). Socialists might seize power but social democracy could never triumph. This sweeping generalization from a case study became influential in the study not only of political parties but also of all large organizations, although it was directed at would-be democratic organizations, such as trade unions, rather than at big business. In Britain, it had a notable influence (together with Moisei *Ostrogorski's *Democracy and the Organisation of Political Parties,* 1902) on a pioneering study of *British Political Parties* (1955) by Robert *McKenzie, although he did not apply Michels's analysis uncritically to the British context, preferring Bryce's more optimistic view of the making of British party politics. *JH*

R. Michels, *Political Parties* (English edn., New York, 1959).

middle class. See class-consciousness; class-voting.

Middlemas, (Robert) Keith (1935–), historian, emeritus professor at Sussex, having taught there since 1966. Educated at Stowe and Pembroke College, Cambridge, Middlemas was a subaltern in the Northumberland Fusiliers (serving in Kenya, 1954–5, and a member of the UK national rifle team that toured Canada in 1958), and a clerk of the House of Commons, 1958–66. Having written *The Master Builders* (1963), *The Clydesiders* (1965), three edited volumes of the diaries of Thomas Jones (1969), and *Baldwin: A Biography* (with John Barnes, 1969), Middlemas established his niche with the 1979 publication of *Politics in Industrial Society,* a volume which through its identification of a 'corporate bias' helped to change perceptions of modern British politics, not least by enriching the emerging debate on consensus. His examination of the way in which Lloyd George's state sought 'to manage' Britain through links with employers and trade unions led to his notion of 'a political *Gleichschaltung*' in which 'governing institutions' came together to determine the range of political possibilities. Middlemas sustained his analysis in subsequent volumes which were welcomed for the way in which they encouraged historians to abandon their fixation on political parties and embrace continental social science. He regretted Margaret Thatcher's failure to understand his critique. *PS*

Middleton, Peter Edward (1934–), civil servant. From a northern grammar school and Sheffield University, Middleton started his career in the Central Office of Information and as a Treasury information officer. But he rose to the top of the Treasury, through the chancellor's private office (1969–72), as Treasury press secretary (1972–5), and as a senior official specializing in monetary policy. Picked out by Thatcher, he vaulted over several more senior officials to serve as permanent secretary to the Treasury, 1983–91. *KT*

Middleton, 'Captain' Richard (1846–1905), Conservative chief agent. Always addressed as 'Captain' or 'Skipper', this admiral's son retired from the Navy in 1877 with the actual rank of lieutenant of marines to become a local Tory organizer. He rose to chief agent, 1885–1903, and created and commanded from Central Office an efficient and highly successful electoral machine made up of regional agents working through the network of the *National Union of Conservative and Unionist Associations. A grateful party presented him with the colossal sum of £10,000 upon his retirement. *RJQA*

John Ramsden, *An Appetite for Power: A History of the Conservative Party since 1830* (London, 1889).

Middle Way, The (1938), book by Harold *Macmillan. Influenced by the experience of Soviet Russia, the Depression, and a desire for intellectual fulfilment, *The Middle Way* is seen as a precursor of much Conservative post-war thinking. Macmillan, at this time a backbench Conservative representing a northern industrial seat, advocated a centrist policy, government intervention, and the adoption of Keynesian economic ideas. The book was illustrative too of Macmillan's frustration with the economic policies of the National Government. *NJC*

Midleton, 1st earl of. See Brodrick, St John.

Mikardo, Ian (1908–93), Labour politician. Mikardo was a shrewd and popular left-winger who illustrated the old phrase that politicians are either bishops or bookmakers. For years he ran his own small-time business taking bets from colleagues in the Commons on political outcomes. His immigrant parents were Jewish refugees from Russia, and Mikardo maintained his father took his name from a poster for *The Mikado*, which was then wrongly spelled. He grew up and was educated in Portsmouth, like James Callaghan, and was one of that huge cohort of Labour MPs first elected in the 1945 landslide, representing Reading, 1945–59, and Poplar, 1964–87. Though he never held office, he was a prominent backbencher, active in **Keep Left* in the 1940s, a member of the Tribune group and later the *Campaign for Nuclear Disarmament, and close to other left-wingers such as Barbara Castle, at least when Labour was out of office between 1951 and 1964, and to the hard-left feminist MP Jo Richardson all the time. He was also noted for many close business contacts in central and eastern Europe when Communists ruled there. Interested in foreign affairs, he chaired the party's international committee, 1973–4, and was chairman of the Parliamentary Labour Party, March–November 1974, between Labour's rather unexpected return to power and re-election with a slightly larger majority. He was also vice-president amd then president of the Socialist International, 1978–83, and president of the Association of Scientific, Technical and Managerial Staffs, 1968–73. His publications included *Keep Left* (with others, 1947), *The Labour Case* (1950), and an autobiography, *Backbencher* (1988). *PRGR*

Miliband, Ralph (1924–94), political scientist who penned influential works, analysing British politics from a Marxist perspective. Born in Belgium, he moved with his father—a Polish Jew—to Britain in 1940. He studied at the LSE before enlisting in the Royal Navy, then returned there in 1946, graduating with a first and completing a PhD on French socialist ideas in the 1790s. He was then appointed a lecturer at the LSE and spent nearly a quarter of century teaching there. Miliband established his academic name with the publication in 1961 of *Parliamentary Socialism*, arguing that socialism was betrayed by Labour leaders in Parliament. He built a reputation as an articulate and independent writer of the left, was co-editor of *Socialist Register* and wrote regularly for journals such as *New Left Review*. Later publications included *The State in Capitalist Society* (1972) and *Socialism for a Sceptical Age*, published posthumously in 1994. He took up the chair of politics at Leeds University in 1972, retiring early in 1978. *PN*

Militant Tendency, Trotskyist organization. The Militant Tendency evolved out of the Revolutionary Socialist League (RSL), founded by Ted Grant in 1955. It adopted *entryism as a tactic from the outset, and became the most successful of all the groups operating inside the Labour party. The RSL launched its newspaper *Militant* in 1964 and thereafter claimed to be simply a trend within Labour, grouped around a newspaper. It dominated the Labour Party Young Socialists after 1970, and also the place on Labour's NEC offered to youth. Militant always claimed to be the true standard-bearer of Marxism and therefore refused to work with any other left faction, standing aloof from the radical movements of the 1960s and playing no part in the construction of left policy in the Labour Party in the 1970s. Nevertheless it was able to benefit from the growth of the constituency left, largely because of its relentless organizational zeal over many years. Nowhere was this more apparent than on Merseyside. There Labour won control of Liverpool council in 1983 for the first time in ten years, and a disciplined Militant minority was able to exercise a controlling influence. In the same year two Militant members were elected to parliament. These successes were achieved in spite of an internal Labour Party investigation into its activities, culminating in the Hayward-Hughes report and the expulsion from the party of five members of the *Militant*'s editorial board. For a time Militant enjoyed substantial mass support on Merseyside, but its cynical manoeuvring during the rate-capping crisis alienated much of this and provided Neil Kinnock with the ammunition to initiate a series of purges of Militant members. Forced to operate openly, the group now campaigns as Militant Labour; it organized anti-poll tax demonstrations in the early 1990s and has maintained some influence in Liverpool and Glasgow. *MC*

Milk Marketing Board, the largest and most successful of the organizations established under the *Agricultural Marketing Acts, 1931 and 1933. Created in 1934, it was placed under government control from 1939 to 1954, when it was re-established. (There were four separate boards before 1939, three after 1954: one for England and Wales, others for regions of Scotland and Northern Ireland.) The board was the sole agency for the wholesale milk trade, both as buyer from farmers and supplier to retailers and manufacturers. It entered into manufacturing itself, advertised milk, and also acted to promote better standards of dairy hygiene. In the 1980s the European Commission challenged the pricing policies and structure of the board on grounds of competition policies. The boards were wound up in 1994. *JHB*

Millan, Bruce, (1927–), Labour politician. Appointed as the successor to William Ross as secretary for Scotland in 1976, Millan had the arduous and thankless task of pushing the *Scotland Act, 1979, through the Commons. Furthermore, he had to paper over the divisions within the Scottish Labour Party which the devolution issue exposed. In spite of his best efforts, his bill was mangled by a number of amendments after the failure of a guillotine motion. Following the failure at the 1979 referendum and the victory of the Conservatives in the general election, Millan remained shadow Scottish secretary until his appointment as a European commissioner in 1983. *RF*

Mills, Percival (1890–1968), businessman and Conservative politician. Percy Mills was a self-made industrialist who made a vital contribution to the war effort at the Ministries of Production and Supply. In 1951, Macmillan, whom he had known at supply, made him an adviser at housing and in 1957 appointed him power minister as Lord Mills. 'Wise old Percy' was valued by Macmillan, becoming paymaster general, 1959, and minister without portfolio, 1961, but was sacked during 1962's *'Night of the Long Knives', receiving a viscountcy. *RJS*

Milner, 1st Viscount (1854–1925), statesman and imperialist. Born of British parents in Germany, Alfred Milner's political critics made much of his 'Prussianism'. Educated in England, he left a brilliant record at Oxford, was called to the Bar, and tried journalism before finding his place as an imperial administrator in Egypt in 1889 and then as chairman of the Board of Inland Revenue. In 1897 he became high commissioner in South Africa. His 'forward' policy and resistance to compromise with the Boer states played their parts in the coming of the 1899–1902 Boer war. Though the *'Chinese slavery' episode severely damaged his reputation, he was nonetheless much admired among imperialists and particularly by the circle of young men, his 'kindergarten' who served under him in Capetown. After returning home in 1905, Milner gave much of his time and energy to the tariff reform, conscription, and anti-home rule movements. His reputation as an administrator earned him a place in Lloyd George's unprecedented war cabinet in December 1916, and later he served as war and colonial secretary, 1918–21. An outspoken apostle of national organization and efficiency as well as of Empire, Milner's name long evoked strong reactions among the many who either admired or hated him. *RJQA*

A. M. Gollin, *Proconsul in Politics: A Study of Lord Milner in Opposition and in Power* (London, 1964). | John Marlowe, *Milner: Apostle of Empire* (London, 1976).

Mineowners' Association (1854–1947). The Mining Association of Great Britain was founded in 1854 as the national organization for colliery owners. It rose to public prominence after 1914 as a result of deteriorating labour relations and mounting governmental interest in the affairs of the coal industry. Dominated by exporting colliery owners, the association was noted for its extreme resistance to national negotiations over wages and hours of work. This stance was epitomized in the association's role in the General Strike and miners' lockout of 1926. Baldwin, who might have been expected to be sympathetic, remarked that he had thought the miners' leaders to be the stupidest men in the world—until he met the mineowners. *MWK*

miners' strikes Throughout the 20th century, coal mining has been the centre of much industrial conflict: there were major national strikes in 1912, 1921, 1926, 1972, 1974, and in 1984–5. In addition, by the 1950s and 1960s, up to half the 2,000 or so strikes per year that were recorded were connected with coal mining. Those were, of course, entirely unofficial strikes. It is, however, the national strikes that have attracted most attention.

The 1912 national strike by the Miners' Federation of Great Britain was a short-lived one in opposition to the Liberal government's National Minimum Wage Act. The 1921 dispute was equally short-lived and was a reaction to the wage cuts imposed by the coal owners who had just regained control of their industry on 1 April 1921, with the removal of the wartime control measures. The refusal of the railwaymen and the transport workers to support the miners on 15 April 1921, the infamous *Black Friday, led to the collapse of the Triple Alliance between them, by which they had agreed in 1915 to support each other in industrial disputes. The failure of the other unions to support the miners built up both a resentment by the miners and a guilt by other trade unions and the TUC, which meant that the TUC came out in their support when the miners were forced to strike again in a national dispute from 30 April 1926, resisting the attempt to reduce their wages. The resulting *General Strike lasted nine days before it was called off, but the miners continued to fight the dispute, led by Arthur James Cook and Herbert Smith, only to be driven back to work in November. Cook, Smith, and the miners felt betrayed and there was always a lingering sense of the need for revenge for 1926.

The opportunity did not come until 1972, the next national strike called by the national coal mining union, now called the National Union of Mineworkers (NUM). In the 46 years that intervened, the miner had been involved in thousands of unofficial disputes connected with the working of seams and payments. The fact that the coal industry had been nationalized in 1947 made little difference, for the miners' union ignored the appeal to serve on the newly formed National Coal Board, since it was felt that this might compromise its position in a dispute. The miners' disputes of the 1970s and 1980s were all fought against Conservative governments. In January–February 1972, the miners called their first official strike since 1926 in the teeth of the Heath government's attempt to impose wage restraint. They were demanding an increase of £9 per week for underground workers, £8 for surface workers. The National Coal Board replied with £1.75 (8 per cent) on all basic rates. Arthur Scargill organized the strike, arranged picketing at power stations, and arranged for flying pickets to operate. In the end, after there had been power cuts, Lord Wilberforce was asked to arbitrate, giving the miners most of what they had demanded. Yet the continued attempt to control wage rises forced the miners into another conflict in 1973. The Heath government imposed a three-day week and the union held a ballot which called for a strike from 10 February 1974. In this case the strike was overtaken by events when Heath announced a general election for 28 February 1974 and lost office to the Labour Party.

The last, and certainly the most protracted, miners' strike began in March 1984 and lasted until March 1985. It challenged the Employment Acts of Margaret Thatcher's Conservative government, designed to restrict trade union powers, but occurred as a result of the National Coal Board's closing pits in Scotland and Yorkshire. No ballot was held to legitimize the dispute and there was mass-picketing and violence, in Ollerton, in Nottinghamshire (a region where many miners continued to work), and at the Orgreave coke plant in Yorkshire. The NUM's funds were sequestrated by the courts. In the end, the strike petered out, without a settlement. Since then, with the collapse of the coal mining industry in Britain, and the continuing division of the union which began in 1984–5, the prospect of major official or unofficial strikes in coal mining has practically gone. *KL*

Keith Laybourn, *A History of British Trade Unionism c.1770–1990* (Stroud, 1992).

Mineworkers, National Union of (NUM). The NUM was formed in 1945 as successor to the Miners' Federation of Great Britain. Following nationalization in 1947, the coal industry expanded due to the economy's reliance on coal as the sole indigenous energy source and the NUM's membership grew from 533,000 in 1945 to 700,000 in 1955. However, between 1957 and 1970, hundreds of pits closed due to imports of cheap oil, and NUM membership fell from 681,000 to around 280,000. During 1969–70 a wave of unofficial strikes that expressed disillusionment with the coal industry's decline, persuaded many miners that industrial action was a viable weapon to pursue their grievances. In 1972 and 1974 the NUM called all-out national strikes which successfully challenged the pay restraint policies of the Heath government and sent the miners back to the top of the industrial wages league. The Thatcher government's pit closure programme in the early 1980s provoked (perhaps deliberately) the miners' strike of 1984–5. The miners' defeat was linked to a split in the NUM and the emergence of the rival *Union of Democratic Mineworkers. Later pit closures have reduced the NUM from 180,000 members in 1984 to 4,000 working miners in 1998. Over the last 40 years, the NUM has seen a steady decline in its bargaining position and numerical strength due to the contraction of manufacturing industry and the state-sponsored expansion of oil, gas, and nuclear power stations. From 1945, the NUM has been Britain's most militant trade union, its national strikes of 1972 and 1974 contributing to the defeat of Heath's government. However, the once mighty NUM was then effectively broken by Conservative governments as part of their campaign to subdue the British trade union movement. *DLM*

MICHAEL CRICK, *Scargill and the Miners* (London, 1984). | ANDREW RICHARDS, *Miners On Strike: Class Solidarity and Division in Britain* (Oxford, 1996).

minimum lending rate (MLR), term used to denote the penal rate of interest which the Bank of England imposed on joint-stock banks or discount houses for the unique position of always being able to borrow money by selling bills or giving bills as exchange. It acted as a safety valve to ensure their liquidity, irrespective of the financial strains they were enduring, MLR was the technical term used for these transactions between 1971 and 1981, before which it was referred to as the *Bank rate. *JFM*

ministers, appointment of by the crown. Although the prime minister selects his cabinet colleagues on the basis of their ability and standing in the party, the sovereign actually appoints them to office. New cabinet ministers receive their seals of office and 'kiss hands' during an interview with the sovereign shortly after they are named to their posts. This may be an empty, even a tiresome, ritual; but few former ministers forget it. *WMK*

Mitchell, Derek Jack (1922–), prime ministers' principal private secretary, 1964–6. The appointment of Mitchell, a Labour sympathizer, to Sir Alec Douglas-Home's private office reflected official expectations of a Labour victory in the 1964 general election. When it appeared a hung parliament might result, he hastily established the constitutional implications. He imposed a uniquely rigorous division between government and party work on Harold Wilson's Downing Street, leading to clashes with Marcia Williams, from which he generally emerged the victor, prompting Wilson to appoint a more pliant successor, Michael Halls. *CL*

Modernizing Government (1999), white paper. Intended in the words of cabinet secretary Sir Richard Wilson to be 'a key document which signals a change of course for the Civil Service for the next 10 years as important as *Next Steps* 10 years ago', the long-awaited and much-delayed white paper was couched in vividly Blairite tones (it bore the marks of important last-minute drafting by the prime minister's policy unit) and reflected Blair's growing preoccupation with 'delivery'. The 'Vision', outlined in an opening chapter carrying that semi-mystical title, manifested itself around the following key commitments:

- policy making would be forward-looking in developing policies to deliver results that matter, not simply reacting to short-term pressures;
- responsible public services would be delivered to meet the needs of citizens, not the convenience of service providers;
- quality and efficient public services would be delivered and mediocrity would not be tolerated;
- in the information age, government would use new technology to meet the needs of citizens and business, and not trail behind technological developments.

Such pledges reflected the preachy, aspirational tone of the white paper. But its content swiftly led to a development which raised concerns about the possible politicization of the senior civil service. *Modernizing Government* declared that 'We [the prime minister and the minister for the Cabinet Office] will ensure that permanent secretaries and heads of department have personal objectives, on which their performance will be assessed, for taking forward the government's modernisation agenda and ensuring the delivery of the government's key targets.' By the late summer of 1999, it was apparent that the performance-related pay of permanent secretaries would be affected by such objective-setting and that the prime minister had had a direct input into the final agreed versions of permanent secretaries' personal objectives. Mechanisms for the wider implementation of the white paper were entrusted by Sir Richard Wilson to four working groups of permanent secretaries on vision and value, diversity, performance and talent. *PJH*

PETER HENNESSY, 'The British Civil Service: The Condition of Mr Gladstone's Legacy as the Century Turns', *Stakeholder* (July 1999). | SIR RICHARD WILSON, 'The New Civil Service in the New Millennium' (Vice-Chancellor's Lecture, City University, May 1999).

Molyneaux, James Henry (1920–), leader of the Ulster Unionist Party, 1979–95. After service in the Second World War in the RAF, Molyneaux returned to run the family farm. He was elected to Westminster as the MP for South Antrim in 1970. He held this seat until 1983 when he became the MP for Lagan Valley until his resignation in 1997. In 1974 he became leader of the United Ulster Unionist Coalition and in 1979 he was elected leader of the Ulster Unionist Party. During the 1980s he opposed talks to bring about a devolved government in Northern Ireland, arguing that unionists would be better served by integration with the rest of the United Kingdom. The Anglo-Irish agreement was regarded as a serious threat to the Unionist position and he cooperated with other pro-Union parties in opposing it. He stepped down as party leader in 1995 and resigned his seat in 1997. *BMW*

ANN PURDY, *Molyneaux: The Long View* (Belfast, 1989).

monarchy, British. Britain is a constitutional monarchy, which means that the head of state is a hereditary ruler who in practice defers to and is ruled by a prime minister who commands the majority party in the Commons. Both head of state and prime minister are themselves ruled by a body of laws that they inherit and to which parliament adds or subtracts over the years. Although the head of state plays little or no role in the process by which the prime minister is elected or laws are passed, her life is a busy and movable one. A good idea of the nature and function of the monarchy can be had from looking at the places where Elizabeth II, who was sovereign for the greater part of the 20th century, spends most of her time.

Buckingham Palace

This is the queen's 'office', located in the centre of the most socially desirable postcode in London, SW1A 1AA. She lives here during the week and receives the prime minister for regular meetings when both are in town. People often mistake these meetings for the most important part of her work, but in fact sovereigns of the 20th century did not interfere much in politics (though few prime ministers would not welcome the advice of the most experienced 'politician' available). Their discussions together are about the visits she will make abroad as a tool of the government's foreign policy and on behalf of British trade, as well as her special interests, such as honours, church appointments, and relations with the Commonwealth. She meets a wide array of other government officials, including cabinet ministers, judges, ambassadors, and senior clerics. Her role is to encourage them and to take a sympathetic interest in their work. Personal contact with her is their reward for service to the state, for which they might be more highly paid in private industry.

Windsor Castle

The queen spends most weekends away from London in a castle on a hill overlooking the River Thames. The castle is now on the flight path to Heathrow, where millions of tourists debark every year in order to visit Ye Olde England. Windsor is on most of their itineraries and the monarchy is financially supported in part by the admission fees visitors pay to tour the castle's state rooms as well as see collections of porcelain and other works of art located there. In addition to tourists, the queen also receives visiting heads of state, politicians, and London opinion-makers at Windsor, where they are invited to 'dine and sleep'. They share a drink with the sovereign and eat a cutlet off the porcelain, but otherwise their brief experience of Windsor is not unlike the typical tourist's. Closer contact with the queen in her castle is an avenue into Britain's mystical past no less sought after by international celebrities than by farmboys from Ohio.

Balmoral Castle

The queen spends summer holidays in another castle, this one built by Victoria and Albert in the 19th century. Then, as now, the sovereign liked to get away from London and spend time in the Highlands. Latterly, this has been one way of linking the queen to the Scots who are fed up with being ruled by Englishmen and threaten to leave the UK. The hill-walking, fishing, and picnics that are fixtures of the queen's Scottish holidays also appeal to Englishmen who fancy themselves a countrified people, dream of rural idylls, and enjoy listening to pastoral symphonies.

Sandringham

The fourth of the queen's main residences is on an agricultural estate in Norfolk acquired by Victoria's son, Edward VII, as a place where he could get away from his mother's morbid influence.

The queen still farms this estate and has agricultural tenants who pay her rent. This too is a token of a bygone existence when noblemen made their money from agriculture rather than stock portfolios. She also raises racehorses at Sandringham. This is a sport she and her family have all enjoyed, but it too recalls the feudal knight's prestige, which came from his expertise on a horse. The queen's repeated appearance at celebrated races, like the Derby and Ascot, serves both to lead what remains of a hierarchical society and to recall the command medieval kings had over bands of mounted soldiers.

Planes, Trains, and Automobiles

She farms, raises racehorses, and lives in castles: all these illustrate the symbolic role of the monarchy, which is to highlight selected features of the nation's history. She is also frequently on the move. She travels on a fast train painted in the royal livery, goes abroad in Concorde, and drives about in bulletproof Range Rovers. She acts as a goodwill ambassador to provincial hospitals, where she comforts the sick and dying. She visits barracks to keep up the morale of soldiers. She encourages entrepreneurial and civic activities by visiting factories and opening new bridges. She leaves behind plaques as talismans of her sacred presence, though no one claims to believe in her divinity any more. She represents Britain abroad, forging new and less supercilious relationships with former British colonies, as well as promoting trade with economic superpowers where British businesses hope to invest and make money.

Television Screens

Above all the queen, increasingly since the 1970s, lives her life and spends time in front of television cameras; she appears constantly in the print and visual media both in Britain and abroad. The worldwide attention to the death of Diana, Princess of Wales, was partly a tribute to the princess's remarkable personality, but it was also a sign that, while the monarchy has lost political power in Britain, it has subjugated and saturated the world's airwaves. Managing this global interest in Britain's royal family, and learning to profit from it, will be the great challenge for British politicians, princes, and their private secretaries in the new millennium. *WMK*

VERNON BOGDANOR, *The Monarchy and the Constitution* (Oxford, 1995). | *Elizabeth R* (video) produced and directed by EDWARD MIZROEV (British Broadcasting Corporation and The Crown, 1992). | BEN PIMLOTT, *The Queen: A Biography of Elizabeth II* (London, 1996). | FRANK PROCHASKA, *Royal Bounty: The Making of a Welfare Monarchy* (New Haven, 1995).

Monckton, Walter Turner (1891–1965), confidant of Edward VIII and Conservative politician. Having served in the Great War, Monckton was called to the Bar and during the 1930s advised the Indian princes in negotiations for an Indian federation. As attorney-general to the duchy of Cornwall he became close to Edward VIII and represented him during the 1936 *abdication crisis. Monckton held various wartime government posts and was solicitor-general in the 1945 Caretaker Government. After 1945 he won the coal owners generous compensation for their nationalized pits and was involved in negotiations over Indian independence. At Churchill's wish, he succeeded Oliver Stanley as MP for Bristol West in 1951, and in October that year became labour minister. Churchill's appointee disproved predictions of industrial conflict under the Tories, but the cost of Monckton's conciliatory policy was excessive wage settlements. In 1955 Monckton became defence minister but, after vehemently challenging Eden in cabinet over the *Suez Crisis in 1956, was allowed to leave his post and become paymaster general. He left office in 1957 and accepted a viscountcy. In 1959 Monckton headed the commission on the development of the Central African Federation, but even his conciliatory skills could not save the federation. *RJS*

Mond, Alfred Moritz (1868–1930), industrialist and politician. Mond inherited his father's chemical business and expanded it through mergers and amalgamations to become the giant *ICI. A Liberal MP from 1906, he was typical of the businessmen-politicians who came into government during the Great War, often like Mond through association with Lloyd George. Mond joined the Conservatives in 1926 and conducted the *Mond-Turner talks of 1927 in an effort to lower the temperature of industrial relations after the 1926 General Strike. From 1928, 1st Lord Melchett. *JAR*

Mond-Turner Talks (1928–30/1). Sir Alfred Mond, of the Federation of British Industries, and Ben Turner, president of the general council of the TUC, entered discussions in January 1928. They were attempting to find common ground between the employers and the unions on matters such as unemployment, and outlined remedies for it such as a development fund, more liberal trade facilities, export credits, the raising of the school leaving age, and above all 'the substitution of modern plant and techniques for existing machinery and methods'—in consultation with the unions—and with 'measures... for safeguarding workers displaced by rationalisation'. Yet, although the leaders of both sides of industry worked hard to achieve a common agreement on policies, the talks, and the influence they exerted, began to wither away after a couple of years. They did, however, indicate a less confrontational attitude in industry than that which had produced the General Strike in 1926. *KL*

Chris J. Wrigley (ed.), *A History of British Industrial Relations, 2. 1914–1939* (Brighton, 1987).

Monday Club, right-wing grouping within the official Conservative Party with opposition to decolonization its original policy purpose. It was founded in 1961 and named after the day on which Macmillan made his *'winds of change' speech in Capetown. It grew in membership and importance during the 1960s, and in 1970 claimed 30 MPs as members, three of them ministers, and 10,000 members in the country as a whole. By then, it had adopted a whole raft of rightist policy positions, notably on trade union reform, race and immigration, support for the Rhodesian *UDI, and reducing public spending. It backed Enoch *Powell after his 1968 *'rivers of blood' speech in Birmingham, and made life difficult for more liberal Conservative MPs in their own constituencies, notably for Nigel Fisher in Surbiton; Monday Clubbers also helped to drive Sir Edward Boyle out of parliamentary life. It caused considerable difficulties for Heath in office, 1970–4, viewing a number of his policies (especially the admission of Ugandan Asian refugees) as a betrayal of promises made in opposition but, with the advent of Margaret Thatcher to the leadership in 1975, and the end of the decolonization period, the relevance of this essentially oppositionist grouping faded. *JAR*

Patrick Seyd, 'Factionalism within the Conservative Party: The Monday Club', *Government and Opposition*, 7 (1972).

monetarism, word coined in 1968 by the Swiss-American economist Karl Brunner, also one of its leading proponents. This was not a new theory, though its modern formulation was at that time fairly recent. The basis of monetarism is that money matters in the economy, that disturbances in monetary variables are the main cause of instability in the real economy. Changes in the stock of money lead to, and indeed are the main cause of, changes in money income. The theory has its roots in the quantity theory of the 18th century. It was formalized by Irving Fisher in *The Purchasing Power of Money* (1911). The essence of that theory was that in the long run the growth of the real economy (growth in the volume of output) was determined by real factors: by the physical inputs of land, labour, and capital, and improvements in the quality of these, and by ever more efficient means of organizing production. In the long run therefore what money did was to have an effect on the price level. If money grew in excess of output there would be a rise in prices; and if money growth were deficient in relation to output growth there would be price falls. This became known as the neutrality of money. These views were widely held by most economists, until around the middle of the 20th century, but were then challenged by Keynesian views on what best stabilized aggregate demand. The Keynesian view was that the consumption and investment functions were stable and that fiscal means could best be used to influence aggregate demand. Monetarists would argue that fiscal effects on aggregate demand were small. For one thing, if governments borrowed, that would simply replace private borrowing: in the jargon it would 'crowd out' the private sector. (Furthermore, they held that the interest elasticity of the demand for money was low.)

The academic arguments between the Keynesian and monetarist camps began to build in the 1960s following the work of Milton Friedman in 1956 ('The Quantity Theory: A Restatement') and Friedman and Anna Schwartz in 1963 (*A Monetary History of the United States 1867–1960*). These debates reached new heights in the 1970s when it appeared that Keynesianism had failed to explain the high and rising levels of inflation together with high and rising unemployment. For Friedman and his growing following, the money supply was superior to fiscal measures for stabilizing aggregate demand. These views rested heavily on the empirical support of *A Monetary History of the United States*, a work of enormous scholarship which analysed the behaviour of all agents but in particular that of government and the relatively recently founded Federal Reserve (1913). The American economy was a volatile one and the central explanation found in Friedman and Schwartz was that fluctuations in economic activity were caused by fluctuations in money. Friedman and Schwartz were careful to stress that this was particularly the case for large fluctuations. And of course a great deal of attention was devoted to the Great Depression of 1929–32 which in the USA was particularly acute.

Friedman and Schwartz laid the blame for the severe depression squarely at the door of the Federal Reserve: insufficient money tightened the contraction, then banks failed, and things got worse.

By the end of the 1960s these monetarist views were becoming accepted. It was also increasingly accepted that individuals' and firms' expectations of what would happen were important; particular 'rational expectations' began to prevail: economic agents learn to interpret events and policy actions and they begin to anticipate government action and take their own action accordingly. The policy implications of all this therefore became clear. For Friedman and for most monetarists, the desirable policy was to have constant growth of the money supply at a rate equal to the trend rate of growth of output in the economy (something that tended to be quite low and stable—in the region of 2–3 per cent per annum for modern industrial countries).

To some extent these views were being discussed in political circles in the early 1970s. There had been those such as Enoch Powell in Britain who had long ago accepted the monetarist argument. Nevertheless, the Conservative government of 1970–4, that of Prime Minister Edward Heath and Chancellor Anthony Barber, pursued an exceedingly lax monetary policy. In the course of one year up to September 1973 the money supply grew by almost 30 per cent and as predicted by the monetarists that was translated into high inflation in the following years. The policy was undoubtedly the consequence of advice from the Treasury which was overwhelmingly Keynesian in outlook—going so far as to deny that the money supply mattered at all, or at least that prices and incomes policy could contain any inflation that arose. However, the consequences of the 'Barber boom' were serious and the Labour government of 1974–9 came to accept the primary tenets of monetarism. Prime Minister Jim Callaghan and Chancellor Denis Healey effectively followed monetarist policies from 1976. *The Times* was influential in the education process.

The Thatcher government pursued essentially monetarist policies even if there were some obstructions to implementation along the way. For the monetarist view had by the end of the century become almost universally accepted. It was these views and their policy implication of stable monetary growth that were responsible for the giving of independence to central banks. This was so much the case that the Labour government of 1997, immediately on taking office, gave independence to the Bank of England in the setting of interest rates. Monetarism is associated with various attitudes to government. It is linked with laissez-faire in accepting that the real economy essentially looks after itself and does better without government interference. In other words it could be said that it is not politically neutral but rather goes with liberalism. *FHC*

Monopolies and Mergers Commission (1973–99). See Competition Commission.

Monster Raving Loony Party, fringe political party (or anti-party) led by pop singer David ('Screaming Lord') Sutch (1940–99). Starting in 1963 and using various names for his fringe parties, Sutch contested parliamentary seats 39 times. Largely mounted as publicity stunts, Sutch's contests cost him over £100,000 but gradually earned him respect for his dogged and flamboyant persistence. The party's last contest was in 1997 at the Winchester by-election, when it won 316 votes. *JS*

Montagu, Edwin Samuel (1879–1924), Liberal politician. Montagu was a Liberal MP from 1906 and parliamentary private secretary to the prime minister, Asquith, before joining his governments in junior posts at the India Office and the Treasury, 1910–15. He reached cabinet as chancellor of the duchy of Lancaster in 1915, and despite his association with Lloyd George when minister of munitions, 1915–16, left office with the Asquithians in December 1916. He had also by then married Venetia Stanley, Asquith's confidante. Montagu was, however, tempted back to office under Lloyd George soon afterwards, becoming secretary of state for India, 1917–22. Montagu was one of the most important ministers responsible for India, visiting the subcontinent himself for six months in 1917–18, and producing as a result the *Report on Indian Constitutional Reforms* (1918), which provided the blueprint for the post-war Montagu-Chelmsford initiatives to advance India towards eventual self-government through dyarchy. For this he could not easily be forgiven by Conservatives, whose ire was further raised by his sacking of General Dyer after the *Amritsar massacre and whose distrust of Montagu was (at least in some cases) reinforced by anti-Semitism. He eventually resigned over disagreements with colleagues over policy towards Turkey in March 1922, the ruler of India being all too conscious of the problems that would be created for Britain's proudest Asian possession from needlessly antagonizing Islam. *JAR*

S. D. Waley, *Edwin Montagu* (Bombay, 1964).

Montgomery, Bernard Law ('Monty') (1887–1976), soldier, Viscount Montgomery of Alamein from 1946. Monty commanded the Eighth army, 1942–3, and the Twenty-First Army Group, 1944–5, was chief of the imperial general staff, 1946–8, and deputy supreme allied commander, Europe, NATO, 1951–8. Montgomery provided Churchill with his long-sought decisive victory over Rommel. After serving with distinction in Palestine and in France in both world wars, Montgomery took over command in Egypt (only after the favoured candidate was killed), in August 1942 at a critical juncture. The Afrika Korps had been halted at *El Alamein by his predecessor, General Auchinleck, but was still poised to attack the Nile delta. Whether Auchinleck might have driven Rommel from Egypt for good had he not been sacked remains an open question, but what is apparent is that Monty was a more inspirational commander, less prone to take risks, and determined to build victories on the foundation of overwhelming resources—which were soon to hand. Denying Rommel the mobile warfare on which he thrived, Montgomery focused on the weak Italian sector of the Axis defences. Once breached, he drove the enemy back remorselessly following meticulous preparation. He repeated his formula for success with the Normandy landings and breakout. The failed Arnhem offensive of 1944 proved a costly miscalculation, but reflected Montgomery's frustration at Eisenhower's veto of his concept of a massive concentrated thrust for Berlin. After the war, the publication of his self-serving *Memoirs* (1958) provoked controversy. Perceived by his detractors as arrogant and aloof, Montgomery's successes at El Alamein and Normandy rank him as a great commander, notwithstanding his personality foibles. He was fortunate to take over major commands when the resources were there to favour his concept of cautious but sustained and decisive advances, an approach derived from his Great War experiences. At times, he may have foregone opportunities through overcaution, but he was concerned not to waste lives needlessly and, despite his harsh discipline, inspired a devoted following among his troops who appreciated his leadership qualities. *SM*

Michael Carver, 'Montgomery', in John Keegan (ed.), *Churchill's Generals* (London, 1991). | Nigel Hamilton, *Monty: The Making of a General, 1887–1942* (London, 1981). | Nigel Hamilton, *Monty: Master of the Battlefield, 1942–1944* (London, 1983). | Nigel Hamilton, *Monty: The Field Marshal, 1944–1976* (London, 1986).

Moore, Philip Brian Cecil (1921–), private secretary to Elizabeth II, 1977–86. He first came to the palace after civil service posts at the Admiralty and the Ministry of Defence, and in the high commissioner's office at Singapore. Thus, he had experience in two areas where the queen takes a special interest, the armed services and the Commonwealth, and this must have assisted the career of one who, unlike many previous private secretaries this century, had no family connections to the court. *WMK*

moral issues. Generally, overt moral and religious crusading has played a smaller part in 20th-century British politics than in some other countries, notably the USA. Nonetheless, the Liberal Party inherited moral positions from its links with the *Nonconformist conscience in areas such as temperance and civil and religious liberty. Over time, this was translated into support on the left generally (which earlier Nonconformists would have deeply resented) for reductions in *censorship, liberalization of the criminal code, and greater access to abortion (see Abortion Act) and *divorce. In reaction, the Conservatives have often found themselves defending traditional values and standards against the challenge of progressives and Liberals. The Labour Party has frequently found itself adopting a moral stand on issues of social reform, welfare, and racism. In practice though, there has been a great deal of common ground between the parties since 1945 on liberalizing areas which in earlier periods were taboo, such as *homosexuality and abortion. Opposition to reform has also frequently cut across party lines, often reflecting religious or moral positions held by minorities. Attempts to capitalize upon the reforms of the 1960s were made by Margaret Thatcher during the 1980s with her call for a return to 'Victorian values'. Such attempts, however, were frustrated by sex scandals and affairs concerning members of her own government. During the late 1990s Tony Blair attempted a similar moral positioning with a call for 'family values', but once again was undermined by the behaviour of members of his government. *JS*

Moran, David Patrick (1872–1936), Irish nationalist journalist. He was born in Waterford and moved to London in 1888, where he worked for the *Spectator*, but also became active in the Gaelic League and the Irish Literary Society. Moran returned to Ireland in 1898 to edit the *New Ireland Review* and founded the *Leader* in 1900 to promote national regeneration through the conversion of middle-class Irish Catholics to the Gaelic idea. He joined the Irish Volunteers in

1913, but played no part in the 1916 Easter Rising. His chief contribution to Irish nationalism was his uncompromising, but realistic, statement that nationalists regarded Ireland as a Catholic nation, and that the Orangemen of the north-east had the right to determine their own future.

DGB

Morant, Robert Laurie **(1863–1920)**, civil servant with a large influence over social policy in the 1900s and 1910s. Morant was a secretary of the 8th duke of Devonshire, much involved in the passing of the *Education Act 1902. As permanent secretary of the Board of Education, 1903–11, he then provided the crucial professional support for many of the Edwardian Liberals' welfare reforms, such as school medical services. In 1911–19, he became the first chairman of the commission which implemented the *National insurance Act, 1911, and in 1919–20 he set up, as permanent secretary, the new Ministry of Health.

JAR

Morel, Edmund Dene **(1873–1924)**, peace campaigner. Morel was an eloquent and influential opponent of Great Power diplomacy and the international arms race, which he passionately believed caused the Great War. He founded the *Union of Democratic Control (UDC) with H. N. *Brailsford, edited *Foreign Affairs*, and wrote scores of books and pamphlets. He was gaoled in 1917 for opposing the war and his health never recovered, though he was MP for Dundee 1922–4, having defeated Winston Churchill. *PRGR*

C. A. Cline, *E. D. Morel: The Strategies of Protest* (1980). | A. J. P. Taylor, *The Troublemakers* (London, 1957).

Morgan, John Vyrnwy **(1870–1954)**, author. The Revd J. Vyrnwy Morgan of Cwmafon belonged at various times to the Congregationalist, Baptist, and Anglican churches but he was to achieve a certain notoriety in Wales through his controversial racial judgements. At first he wrote biographies, then reference books on Welsh Victorian leaders, before turning to a denunciation of Welsh values. By 1925 he was calling for enforced birth control and sterilization to halt the moral deterioration he associated with communistic socialism.

PS

Morgan, Kenneth Owen **(1934–)**, historian and from 2000 a Labour peer. A London Welshman with strong roots in Cardigan bay, Morgan was educated at Oriel College, Oxford, before lecturing at Swansea (1958–66). He was a fellow at Queen's College, Oxford, 1966–89, and then principal and vice-chancellor at Aberystwyth, 1989–95, and senior vice-chancellor of the University of Wales, 1993–5. Since 1961 he has edited the *Welsh History Review* and his writings have greatly influenced the historical study of modern Wales. In *Wales in British Politics, 1868–1922* (1963), and over twenty later books, Morgan has demonstrated consistently the extent to which the radical parties and their leaders have determined the values of modern British politics. The careers of Lloyd George and Aneurin Bevan clearly inspired his work; he has emphasized both the constructive nature of Lloyd-George's post-war coalition government of 1918–22 and the utterly reasonable nature of Bevan's rebellion in 1950. In his *Oxford History of Britain* (edited, 1981) he argued that 'at key moments in British history society coalesced instead of divided', not least because many were 'deeply committed to an almost religious sense of the civilized essence of their country'. This analysis was sustained in a history of post-war Britain, *The People's Peace* (1990), and in *Callaghan: A Life* (1997). *PS*

Morley, John **(1838–1923)**, Liberal politician and guardian of Gladstonian standards in Edwardian Britain. A journalist, editor, and prolific writer who produced biographies of Voltaire, Rousseau, Burke, Cobden, Cromwell, Walpole, and Gladstone (the three-volume official life) among many other books, Morley entered active Liberal politics in the 1860s, though only became a Liberal MP in 1883. More effective as a writer than a speaker or committee man, he was close to Gladstone during his later career and much involved with the Liberals' attempts to legislate home rule for Ireland, for which he was chief secretary, 1886 and 1892–5. When the Liberals returned to office, he became a reforming secretary for India, 1905–10, though as a peer from 1908 he was heavily involved in the Lords' constitutional battles of those years and helped to steer through the 1911 Parliament Act. As lord president of the council from 1910, he took more of an elder statesman role, but resigned from the cabinet in August 1914 rather than accept that Britain should go to war, thus remaining faithful to his lifelong Gladstonian belief in peace, retrenchment, and reform. *JAR*

Morning Post **(1772–1937)**, influential right-wing newspaper in the first part of the century, though, following declining circulation and rising costs, it merged with the *Daily Telegraph* in October 1937. Edited by H. A. Gwynne from 1911, it maintained an extreme diehard Tory line towards both international affairs and domestic matters, aiming for the preservation and protection of Britain, British stock, and the British Empire. Strongly anti-communist. *NJC*

Moroccan crises (1905–6 and 1911), Franco-German diplomatic crises. The unstable kingdom of Morocco had become the object of colonial ambitions of various European powers since the late 1880s, although for Britain it mattered only with a view to the straits of Gibraltar. In terms of British foreign policy, Morocco acquired greater significance with the conclusion of the *Entente Cordiale with France in 1904, in which Britain pledged support for French ambitions in Morocco in return for French recognition of British predominance in Egypt. When in March 1905 Germany threatened to block France in Morocco, this was also a test of the Entente's strength. To maintain the Entente Foreign Secretary Lord Lansdowne and his Liberal successor, Sir Edward Grey, supported France in the ensuing diplomatic crisis and at the international conference at Algeciras (1906) at which Germany suffered a diplomatic defeat. Morocco, however, remained on the international agenda even after Algeciras. When in July 1911, in response to French efforts to establish a de facto protectorate over Morocco, Germany sent the gunboat *Panther* to the Moroccan port of Agadir, another Franco-German crisis erupted. As relations between the two countries deteriorated and a Continental war threatened, Britain could not remain aloof, and in a speech at the Mansion House Chancellor of the Exchequer David Lloyd George warned that no settlement could be tolerated in which Britain had no part. Grey had issued a similar warning to the German ambassador, but Lloyd George's public intervention transformed the crisis into an Anglo-German one. In the feverish atmosphere of late July 1911 war with Germany appeared a distinct possibility—the home fleet was even put on alert. Ultimately Germany climbed down, and settled her dispute with France. The Entente emerged strengthened from the crisis; indeed, by now, it was a firm element of British diplomacy. *TGO*

M. L. Dockrill, 'British Policy during the Agadir Crisis of 1911', in F. H. Hinsley (ed.), *British Foreign Policy under Sir Edward Grey* (Cambridge, 1977). | T. G. Otte, 'The Elusive Balance: British Foreign Policy and the French Entente', in Glyn Stone and Alan Sharp (eds.), *Discordant Neighbours: Anglo-French Relations in the Twentieth Century* (London, 1999).

Morris, John (1931–), Labour politician and barrister. MP for Aberavon since 1959, Morris was a junior defence minister, 1968–70, and in the cabinet as secretary of state for Wales, 1974–9. As a fervent supporter of devolution, its massive rejection by the Welsh electorate in 1979 was a personal blow. Memorably, he commented, 'When you see an elephant on your doorstep you know it's there!' His period as attorney-general in 1997–9 gave the Blair government a rare link with the Callaghan years. *PS*

Morris-Jones, John (1864–1929), scholar and poet. A native of Anglesey, Morris-Jones was educated at Jesus College, Oxford, where he was a founder member of Cymdeithas Dafydd ap Gwilym, the university's very successful Welsh society. As professor of Welsh at Bangor after 1895 he used his authority to establish not only the academic study of the Welsh language but also its more general literary grammar. Trained as a mathematician, he brought a similar rigour to his literary work as he cleansed the Welsh language of its 19th-century corruption. He was knighted in 1918. *PS*

Allan James, *John Morris-Jones* (Cardiff, 1987).

Morrison, Herbert Stanley (1888–1965), Labour politician. Alongside Attlee and Bevin, Morrison was one of the three most powerful political figures in the Labour governments of 1945–51. His real importance to Labour was as the organizer of the victory of 1945 and of the nationalization programme that emerged. He was also Attlee's deputy in what is considered the finest administrator that the Labour Party has ever produced. Morrison was born in London and became a shop assistant before he carved out a career in politics. Initially he joined the Social Democratic Federation in 1907 but left and joined the Brixton branch of the Independent Labour Party (ILP) in 1910. From 1910 to 1913 he was also chairman of the Brixton branch of the National Union of Clerks and became involved in local politics. During these years he developed a clear socialist perspective, advocating public works to deal with unemployment and supporting the women's suffrage movement.

During the Great War Morrison adopted an anti-war stance, became more closely involved in the ILP's peace activities and, though being blind in his right eye which would have exempted him from military service anyway, attended a military service tribunal and agreed to work on the land. Thereafter, he rose quickly in Labour circles, becoming a member of Hackney borough council and mayor in 1920 and 1921. He was also a member of London County Council, 1922–45, becoming its leader in 1939–40. Yet it was parliamentary activity that began to occupy his real interests. Morrison joined Labour's NEC in 1920; was MP for South Hackney, 1923–4, 1929–31, and 1935–45; for East Lewisham, 1945–1950; and for South Lewisham, 1950–9. He was also minister of transport in the Labour government of 1929–31 and minister of supply for a few months in 1940, before becoming home secretary and minister for home security, 1940–5, and a member of the war cabinet from 1942. Yet Morrison's finest hour came when he was lord president of the council and leader of the Commons, and deputy prime minister in Attlee's governments. In 1951 he became foreign secretary and, following Labour's defeat, continued to act as deputy leader of the Labour Party until 1955.

By any standards, Morrison's political career was impressive, whether as organizing the London Passenger Transport Board in the 1930s or in pushing forward bills nationalizing the coal industry and railways. He was, above all, a supreme party organizer. Yet he was thwarted by Attlee in his attempt to become party leader and was considered out of his depth as foreign secretary. He was raised to the peerage as Lord Morrison of Lambeth in 1959 and was president of the British Board of Film Censors from 1960 until his death. *KL*

Bernard Donoghue and G. W. Jones, *Herbert Morrison: Portrait of a Politician* (London, 1973). | Lord Morrison, *Herbert Morrison: An Autobiography* (London, 1960).

Morrison, John Granville (1906–96), Conservative politician. Born into great wealth, Major Morrison was a large, squirearchical figure whom Surtees might have invented. Elected for Salisbury in 1942, he never desired office and hardly spoke in parliament, but as chairman of the *1922 Committee from 1955 he wielded influence during three Tory premierships. The embodiment of traditional Toryism, he played an important role with fellow officers of 'the 22' in Douglas-Home's emergence as prime minister. He stood down in 1964. *RJS*

Morrison, William Shepherd ('Shakes') (1893–1961), Conservative politician and Speaker of the Commons. Morrison secured the safe parliamentary seat of Cirencester and Tewkesbury, 1929–59, and was chairman of the *1922 Committee, 1932–6, when the committee sought a more active role, before securing ministerial preferment as minister of agriculture, 1936–9. He kept private his doubts about the Munich agreement. Popularity amongst MPs contributed to his election as Speaker, 1951–9, after which he was governor-general of Australia. *NJC*

Moser, Claus Adolf (1922–). Professor of social statistics at the LSE (1961–70), Moser served as director of the Central Statistical Office and head of the Government Statistical Service, 1967–78, presiding over a great expansion of government statistical information in the economic field. He had earlier been statistical adviser to the Robbins committee on higher education (1961–4). Moser was also chairman of the Royal Opera House, 1974–87; a vice-chairman of Rothschild bank; and warden of Wadham College, Oxford, 1984–93. *KT*

Mosley, Oswald Ernald ('Tom') (1896–1980), politician. Mosley made a significant impact on virtually everyone who met him. To members of the British Union of Fascists (BUF), such as John Charnley, he remained the most inspiring, charismatic figure they ever encountered. To his political opponents in the 1930s he appeared as the peddler of a detestable ideology. To some members of the British political establishment 'Tom' Mosley was 'a wrong 'un', a representative of their class who had gone astray. The Mosleys had made their pile in Manchester before buying into landed property nearby, but Oswald Mosley was born in London. He chose to follow a military career and participated in the Great War, though a flying accident, in a moment of egotistical recklessness, meant he was sidelined after March 1916. He then served as a civil servant.

Thus far he had pursued a typical career path for someone from his background. He continued along that path, winning Harrow in 1918 for the Conservatives, but Mosley's impatience with established political structures soon emerged. He opposed the Lloyd George government's Irish policy and crossed the floor, but he held the Harrow seat in 1922 and again in 1923 as an independent. Then in 1924, he joined the Independent Labour Party and, though narrowly defeated (by Neville Chamberlain) at Birmingham, Ladywood in 1924, he was returned at Smethwick in 1929 and became chancellor of the duchy of Lancaster in MacDonald's government. But his links with Labour did not endure. The party's failure to support his Keynesian solutions as a cure for Britain's economic problems encouraged him to strike out and on 1 March 1931 he launched the *New Party. However, in the 1931 general election all 24 candidates were heavily defeated. Although he did not realize it, Mosley had taken the first step into the political wilderness.

In 1932, however, his intention to challenge existing political arrangements remained and the success of Mussolini in Italy encouraged him to form the *British Union of Fascists (BUF), but the BUF never achieved the degree of power which Mosley craved. Their *Olympia rally in June 1934, with its violent clashes between Fascists and anti-Fascists, marked an important turning point. Mosley found a haemorrhage of support, although there was some revival in his political fortunes in 1938–9, just before the war.

When war broke out Mosley was allowed to continue with his activities and members of the BUF were allowed to fight in the country's cause but in May 1940, along with significant supporters, he was interned under Defence Regulation 18B and detained until November 1943. After the war Mosley revived his political activities through the Union Movement, founded in 1948, with a new emphasis on European unity based on race. That theme, and his attempt to justify his earlier political career, as in his autobiography, *My Life*, filled his years of exile spent mainly in France. He ventured into parliamentary elections at North Kensington (1959) and Shoreditch (1966) and lost his deposit on both occasions. However, to the end he believed a great crisis would sweep him to power. He died at Orsay. *CH*

O. Mosley, *My Life* (London, 1968). | Robert Skidelsky, *Oswald Mosley* (London, 1975).

Mosley memorandum (1930) arose from a disagreement within the second Labour government over the best way to reduce unemployment, with a group led by Oswald *Mosley opposing the orthodox economic policies of Snowden and the Treasury. The memorandum called for high tariffs as a means of insulating the British economy from the vicissitudes of international finance, for government-led rationalization of the industrial system, and for a programme of public works to tackle unemployment. When it was rejected by the cabinet, Mosley resigned and continued his campaign from the backbenches. While his ideas proved popular with young politicians ranging from Harold Macmillan on the right to Aneuran Bevan on the left, his hopes of building a broad political coalition to carry through his programme foundered on the rock of party loyalty. This seeming failure of the parliamentary system was a major factor in his conversion to fascism. *WF*

Daniel Ritschel, *The Politics of Planning* (Oxford, 1997).

Mossadeq crisis (1951–3), dispute between Britain and Iran sparked by the radical government of Dr Mohammed Mossadeq in April 1951 and resolved by a CIA-inspired coup restoring the shah to power in 1953. Mossadeq threatened Britain's position in the Middle East by nationalizing the Iranian oil industry, thus relieving Britain of its majority share in the Anglo-Iranian oil company. This action humiliated the Attlee government and exposed Britain's dependence upon the USA. Despite calls within the cabinet for a defensive response, and Churchill's criticisms, Attlee sought a peaceful solution through the International Court of Justice. This reflected Britain's military limitations and, more importantly, the need to remain in step with the Truman administration. The Americans saw Mossadeq as a victim of British colonialism and feared that, unless the British were restrained, their pressure on Iran might lead to a communist-led revolt. That policy was not, however, maintained by Truman's successor. After a tour of the Middle East in May 1953, Secretary of State John Foster Dulles advised President Eisenhower that Western power in this crucial Cold War arena was under threat and warned of the dangers of Arab neutralism, or gravitation towards the Soviet orbit. As rumours of a Soviet loan to Iran grew, so too did American distrust of Mossadeq. The result was the CIA-engineered coup, with assistance from MI6, on 19–20 August 1953, to depose Mossadeq and restore the shah, who remained an ally of the West until the 1970s. Whilst these events restored British oil interests in Iran, they nevertheless confirmed that the USA, rather than Britain, was the leading foreign power in the Middle East. Anthony Eden's resentment at this influenced his policy leading up to the *Suez crisis of 1956. *JRVE*

Mount, (William Robert) Ferdinand (1939–), head of prime minister's policy unit, 1982–3. The aristocratic author of a book on the family which impressed Margaret Thatcher, Mount nevertheless failed to make much impression on social policy. A professional journalist, he was chiefly concerned with presentation before and during the 1983 general election, drafting the manifesto text and writing Thatcher's speeches. He then presided over an expansion of the prime minister's policy unit (following the abolition of the Central Policy Review Staff), laying the foundations for its more influential work under John Redwood. *CL*

Mountbatten of Burma, Earl (1900–79), admiral and last viceroy of India. Dickie Mountbatten joined the navy in 1913, rose fast (partly because of royal connections), and was a dashing, self-publicizing war-hero, eventually supreme allied commander in south-east Asia during the Second World War. He oversaw the reconquest of

Burma and Malaya from the Japanese, and this, alongside his apparent support for Asian liberty, prompted the Attlee government to appoint him viceroy of India in December 1946. As viceroy, Mountbatten secured Britain's withdrawal from the subcontinent and oversaw the transition to independence of *India and Pakistan on 15 August 1947. The rapidity of this process has been equally praised and condemned: critics blame him for the communal violence which caused thousands of deaths, while his admirers suggest that more would have died from any further delay. He has also been accused of being too partial to the Indian National Congress and interfering in the boundary settlement on India's behalf. Thereafter he returned to the navy, was appointed First Sea Lord in 1954, but fell out with Anthony Eden over the Suez crisis in 1956. Mountbatten was chief of the defence staff between 1959 and his retirement in 1965, and helped create a centralized Ministry of Defence. He was killed by an IRA bomb in 1979. *KTS*

PHILIP ZIEGLER, *Mountbatten* (London, 1985).

Mowat, Charles Loch (1911–70), historian. The son of professor R. B. Mowat and a relation of Charles Loch (whose work he was to examine in *The Charity Organisation Society, 1869–1913*, 1961), Mowat was educated at Marlborough and St John's, Oxford. In 1934 he went to the USA, did a PhD at the University of Minnesota, took American citizenship, and taught at the University of California at Los Angeles and the University of Chicago. His stand against McCarthyism led to his dismissal from Chicago, and he returned to Britain, where he was professor of history at Bangor, 1958–70. Mowat's reputation was established by *Britain between the Wars* (1955), for several decades the standard text on a then-recent period. The book's masterly overview owed much to the fact that it was written in Chicago although, as Mowat acknowledged, it was informed by the visits he had paid to 'factories, mills, steelworks, and coal mines', throughout Britain. Something of Mowat's independence and authority is captured in his summing up of the events of 1922 and the fall of Lloyd George: 'thus ended the reign of the great ones, the giants of the Edwardian era and of the war; and the role of pygmies, of the "second-class brains" began, to continue to 1940'. *PS*

Mowlam, Marjorie ('Mo') (1949–), Labour politician. Dr Mo Mowlam was elected MP for Redcar in 1987 and within two years was an opposition front-bench spokesman. When Labour came to power in 1997 she was appointed Northern Ireland secretary at a time when hopes were rising that the new government might be able to revive the peace process. She had an uncertain start when a senior official bitterly criticized her performance but she went on to gain great credit as one of the principal architects of the Good Friday agreement in 1998. Indeed, during the Labour conference that year a mention of her name by Prime Minister Blair during his speech drew a standing ovation. The following year, however, Mowlam lost the confidence of Northern Ireland's first minister, the Ulster Unionist David Trimble, and he called for her resignation. Blair reshuffled her to the Cabinet Office, but press speculation hinted that their personal relations were not good: she announced in summer 2000 that she would leave politics at the next election. *PR*

Moyne, Lord. See GUINNESS, WALTER EDWARD.

MPs. See COMMONS, HOUSE OF.

MPs, changing role of. During the 20th century, MPs became increasingly full-time as Members and only a minority earned a sizeable proportion of their earnings from other sources, notably as barristers, running their own businesses or as consultants, and, occasionally, journalists. At the beginning of the century, the House included a sizeable number of landowners, businessmen, and professional people who were part-time MPs, and were content to follow and not compete with a small core of more committed politicians who occupied the smaller number of front-bench posts. Even many of the first generation of Labour MPs were also busy as trade union officials. The shift in roles has reflected the changed social character of the House with the increasing domination by middle-class professionals, whether in the public or the private sectors, many of whom had been heavily or fully occupied in politics before their election. At the same time, the demands on Members increased, both via the extension of constituency work and, from the 1970s onwards, with the extension of the select committee system. This led in turn to demands for substantial increases in payments to reflect the heavier workload and commitment of Members. The biggest change has been in the constituency workload. Until the 1950s Members, whether Conservative or Labour, received few letters from constituents and seldom held surgeries to hear grievances, and some visited their constituencies only rarely unless they lived there. But the workload of Members in handling constituency problems rose steadily from the 1960s onwards. The rise in unemployment and the introduction of many discretionary welfare payments, notably housing benefit, led to more requests for help from Members. Moreover, an increasing number of MPs had previously been local councillors who were familiar with taking up local grievances. From the 1970s onwards, this was also linked with an increase in the size of MPs' offices and in their use of information technology to communicate with constituents. At Westminster, fewer MPs have been content to be 'backwoodsmen' and more have wanted to play an active role, whether as backbenchers, on select committees and the like, or on the front benches. One reason for the big expansion in the number of ministerial posts was to satisfy the ambitions of more MPs for advancement. The changing role of MPs can be measured by the increased number of questions asked. *PJRR*

MPs, payment of. MPs received payments from their shires and boroughs from the 13th until the late 17th century, but only started receiving payments from the taxpayer after 1911, when, in response to Labour pressure, the Commons approved by 265 votes to 173 an allowance of £400 a year. This was presented by Lloyd George, the chancellor of the exchequer, as 'not a recognition of the magnitude of the service, it is not a remuneration, it is not a recompense, it is not even a salary. It is just an allowance, and I think the minimum allowance, to enable men to come here, men who would render incalculable service to the state, and whom it is an incalculable loss to the state not to have here, but who cannot be here because their means do not allow it' (Hansard, vol. 29, col. 1383). The £400 was increased at irregular intervals and cut in 1931 to £360 but there was no regular machinery for review. The 1964 report of the committee on the remuneration of ministers and MPs established the principle that the pay was to enable Members 'efficiently to discharge the duties of the service, without undue financial worry and to live and maintain themselves and their families at a modest but honourable level'. In 1970, the Heath government announced that MPs' pay would be referred to the independent Top (later Senior) Salaries Review Body with the final decision resting with the House. The recommendations have not always been implemented in full or have been staged, largely because of the government of the day's desire to hold down general pay rises. Various attempts to link the pay of MPs to outside occupations, notably of senior civil servants, were never followed mechanically. In July 1996, the review body recommended an increase of about 26 per cent to £43,000 a year. The government proposed a 3 per cent rise but this was rejected by the Commons, which accepted the review body's rise. It took until April 1946 for the salary of an MP to reach £1,000 a year, and until June 1980 for it to reach five figures at £11,750. By April 1999, it was £47,008. MPs are also eligible for pensions via a compulsory contributory scheme, normally payable at 65 for both men and women, or later for those retiring from the Commons after 65. Members' pensions are based on their salaries in the year prior to leaving the House. MPs are entitled to an Office Costs Allowance for secretarial and research assistance expenses. This was introduced in October 1969 at an allowance of up to £500 a year and rose to £50,264 from April 1999. There are also a number of other allowances, including a supplement for London MPs, subsistence allowances, and allowances for second homes. MPs are also entitled to free stationery, postage, and inland telephone calls from within the Commons and to travel or car mileage allowances. *PJRR*

MPs, resignation of seats by. MPs can resign their seats between elections only by taking up a position which would disqualify them from office. By statute, people cannot serve as members of the Commons if they are aliens; aged under 21; certified as lunatics; peers of England, Scotland, Britain and the UK (until the 1999 House of Lords Act); bankrupts; those convicted of treason or corrupt or illegal practices; those sentenced to prison terms of one year or longer; clergymen of the Churches of England and Scotland or Roman Catholic priests; a wide range of office holders, including civil servants, members of regular armed forces, judges, ambassadors, and electoral registration officers. The main voluntary way of leaving the Commons is to be made a peer or via the traditional route of taking a largely honorary 'office of profit' under the crown, notably steward or bailiff of the three Chiltern Hundreds of Stoke, Desborough, and Burnham, or the Manor of Northstead. MPs who want to resign apply to the chancellor of the exchequer for appointment to one or other of the offices, and then cease to be an MP. The office ceases to be held when another MP applies or when the holder asks to be released. *PJRR*

MPs, social character of. The social background of the House of Commons changed twice during the 20th century. The first half saw the decline of the landed interest and the appearance of large numbers of manual workers with the rise of the Labour Party (particularly after the 1918 general election). Then, from the 1950s onwards, the number of manual workers dropped—from a peak of nearly three-quarters of Labour MPs in the 1920s and 1930s to less than 40 per cent by the mid-1950s and to just 13 per cent by 1997. Both sides of the House became increasingly dominated by middle-class professionals (private sector on the Conservative benches and public sector on the Labour ones), with a sharp increase during the 1990s in the number of full-time career politicians who were councillors, union officials, political consultants, or party researchers before being elected. The educational background of MPs also changed during the century, as an increasing number of Members of all parties have been to university. For the first half of the century, just over half of Conservative MPs had been to university, but this rose to nearly three-quarters during the 1980s and over four-fifths at the 1997 election. The proportion of university-educated Labour MPs has risen from none in 1906 to a third in 1945 and two-thirds in 1997. A large majority of Tory MPs have always been to public schools, with a peak of 85 per cent in 1950 before declining slowly in the 1980s to 66 per cent in 1997. The public school influence on Labour was highest in 1945 (23 per cent), before fluctuating thereafter in the mid-teens. The majority of the Commons has been both male (see WOMEN MPs) and white. Apart from occasional MPs with an Indian background from the 1920s onwards, the total of black and Asian MPs only rose from the late 1980s with nine, all on the Labour side, after the 1997 general election. *PJRR*

MPs, suspension of. The House of Commons has always exercised the right to discipline offenders without any involvement from the courts or other outside bodies. MPs can be suspended from the House in a variety of ways. The most common is for disorderly conduct, challenging the decisions of the chair, disrupting the proceedings of the House, and persisting in the use of unparliamentary language. If an MP refuses to apologize or back down, the Speaker or other occupant of the chair can request the MP to leave the House for the remainder of that day's sitting. However, in more serious cases—if an MP refuses to withdraw, or impugns the impartiality of the chair—the Speaker can 'name' the Member. The leader of the Commons or another minister then moves a motion calling for the suspension of the Member. Such a motion is put forthwith and cannot be amended or debated but it can be voted upon. Occasionally, members of the offending MP's party support him or her in a division but front benchers and whips usually abstain or support the chair. On the first occasion in a session, a Member is suspended for five sitting days. The suspension increases to twenty sitting days if a Member is named and suspended on a second occasion, and for the remainder of the session for a third offence. A Member is then required to leave the precincts of the House immediately. If the MP does not comply, the serjeant-at-arms ensures compliance and the Member is then suspended for the remainder of the session. Members can also be suspended following recommendations by the Privileges Committee (since 1995, Standards and Privileges Committee) (see COMMONS, HOUSE OF: COMMITTEE ON STANDARDS AND PRIVILEGES) about whether the rules and standing orders of the House have been breached. In these cases, the report of the committee is debated and the suggested penalty can be, and often has been, amended or rejected. Expulsion is the ultimate power available to the House, though has only rarely been used because of reluctance to interfere with the judgement of a constituency in electing a Member. Members have been expelled for crimes such as perjury, forgery, fraud, and corruption; an expelled Member may seek re-election. During the 20th century, three Members were expelled—Horatio *Bottomley in 1922 after his conviction for fraud and sentence to seven years' imprisonment; Gerry Allighan in 1947 for lying to a committee and gross contempt of the House after publishing an article accusing Members of insobriety and taking fees or bribes for the supply of information; and Peter Baker in 1954 after being sentenced to seven years' imprisonment for fraud. A person convicted of treason is disqualified from election or, if already a Member, from sitting and voting in the Commons. In 1903, Arthur Lynch, an Irish Nationalist, was convicted of high treason for fighting against the crown in the Boer war. After receiving a free pardon from the crown in 1907, he returned to the House in 1909. The House also has the right to punish non-Members (known as strangers) for disorderly or disrespectful acts against it. Offenders can be summoned before the Bar of the House and admonished by the Speaker (the last occasion being in 1957). The House has not fined any non-Member since 1666 and the last person imprisoned by the Commons was in 1880. *PJRR*

MPs, women. Women first obtained the vote

in 1918: initially just those aged over 30, and then from the 1929 election, all over 21. The first woman to take her seat was Nancy Astor. However, the number remained low for a long time thereafter, reaching 24 in 1945 and 29 in 1964. The big rise began in the 1990s when the Labour Party began a policy of discriminating in favour of women candidates, partly via all-women shortlists in target seats before this was ruled illegal by the courts. The Labour total rose from eleven in 1979 to 37 in 1992 and then leapt to 101 in the landslide victory of 1997. However, the number of Conservative and Liberal Democrat women MPs (and candidates) failed to rise. So the rise in the total number of women MPs from the two dozen of the 1960s and 1970s to 60 at the 1992 election and 120 in 1997 was entirely explained by the rising number of female Labour MPs. *PJRR*

Mr Balfour's poodle, description jestingly applied to the House of Lords by Liberal critics during the 1909–11 constitutional crisis, rejecting the Conservative claim that the Lords were 'the watchdog of the constitution'. Lloyd George had pointed out in 1907 that the upper house 'fetches and carries for him [Balfour, the Conservative leader]. It barks for him. It bites anybody that he sets it on to.' *JAR*

Muir, Ramsey (1872–1941), Liberal activist and thinker. Muir was a leading figure in the *Liberal Summer School movement and described by Sir Ernest Barker as 'the scholar-prophet of Liberalism', having resigned his chair in history at Manchester in 1921 in order to devote himself to politics. He established the Summer School movement in that year, attracting leading figures to consider international and domestic issues. Muir was briefly an MP in 1923–4, serving as chairman of the National Liberal Federation, 1931–3, and as its president, 1933–6. *JS*

Muirhead, Roland Eugene (1868–1964), Scottish politician. As a successful businessman, Muirhead devoted much time and money to the radical cause in Scotland. In 1906 he provided funds to start the socialist newspaper *Forward*, and played an important role within the radical Liberal group the Young Scots Society. He joined the Independent Labour Party in 1918, but its lack of commitment to Scottish home rule led him to take part in the founding of the National Party of Scotland in 1928. Muirhead's radicalism placed him at odds with endeavours to 'moderate' Scottish nationalism in the thirties and he increasingly found himself outside the mainstream of the Scottish National Party. In 1950 he founded the Scottish National Congress which had little success. *RF*

multiculturalism. As in the USA, Canada, Australia, and elsewhere, the multiculturalist movement first appeared in Britain in the 1960s, inspired by the belief that thanks to the post-war migration Britain now included several ethnic communities and should respect and cherish their identities. This involved such things as declaring Britain a multicultural society, suitably pluralizing its national identity, taking cultural differences into account in the enactment and application of laws and public policies, and teaching ethnic minority history, languages, and cultures in schools. Multiculturalism was advocated on three grounds. First, since human beings are culturally embedded and derive meaning and strength for their cultures, respect for them entailed respect for their culture. Second, cultural diversity added to the aesthetic and moral richness of British society. Third, knowledge of and cultivation of respect for other cultures helped weaken the roots of white racism and made Britain a more humane and equal society. One of the most eloquent and influential statements of multiculturalism was provided by Roy Jenkins, home secretary in 1966: 'I do not think that we need in this country a "melting pot", which will turn everybody out in a common mould, as one of a series of carbon copies of someone's misplaced vision of the stereotyped Englishman. I define integration, therefore, not as a flattening process of assimilation but as equal opportunity, accompanied by cultural diversity, in an atmosphere of mutual tolerance.' The Swann report (1984) gave the most systematic articulation to Jenkins's multiculturalist vision of Britain and worked out a coherent philosophy of multicultural education. The multiculturalist movement has not had an easy ride in Britain. The New Right, especially Enoch Powell and Margaret Thatcher, thought that it was divisive and diluted Britain's sense of national identity. Marxist and black activists argued that it did little to tackle the roots of white racism, divided the ethnic minorities, and detracted from the antiracist struggle. Postmodernists contended that multiculturalism froze existing cultures, took an unrealistic view of cultural authenticity, and needed to be replaced by the more cosmopolitan and individualist ideas of cultural hybridity and synthesis. Advocates of multiculturalism have responded to these criticisms with varying degrees of success and proposed more chastened and realistic versions of it. Thanks to Tony Blair's explicit commitment to some form of multiculturalism, it now enjoys considerable popularity that had been absent since the 1970s. *BPa*

Tariq Modood, Sharon Beishon, and Satnam Virdee, *Changing Ethnic Identities* (London, 1994). | Bhikhu Parekh, 'National Culture and Multiculturalism', in Kenneth Thompson (ed.), *Media and Cultural Regulation* (Milton Keynes, 1997).

Multilateral Nuclear Force (MLF). In 1961, America's Kennedy administration championed the idea of an MLF as part of its new view of US–European relations embodied in Kennedy's 'Grand Design'. The Americans hoped to reduce European, particularly French, resentment at its predominant nuclear arsenal, abate nuclear proliferation (a long-term American goal), and block the pressing issue of West Germany developing its own nuclear weapons. The MLF was abandoned by President Johnson, due mainly to British and French opposition. *JRVE*

multi-party politics, term applied to political competition between three or more parties. For part of the 20th century, Britain was characterized as a 'perfect' two-party system, enjoying what Sartori (p. 185) defined as the format and the properties of two-partyism. However, multi-party competition has been a feature at different times in the century at a parliamentary and, more frequently, at an electoral level. The early years of the century saw multi-party competition at a parliamentary level but two-party competition at an electoral level, the product of concentrated support for the Irish Nationalists (support that produced a significant number of Irish Nationalist MPs but made no major dent in the proportion of votes cast for the main parties). Multi-party competition took place in the inter-war years at both electoral and parliamentary levels as the Labour Party came to rival and then overtake the Liberals as the second largest party. Multi-party competition has also been a feature of electoral competition since the 1970s—the Liberal-SDP Alliance attracting almost the same proportion of the vote as the Labour Party in the general election of 1983—and multi-party competition existed at a parliamentary level in the period 1974–9. Since the 1970s, such competition has been a notable feature of electoral politics in Scotland and Wales. Various theses have been advanced to explain the shift from two-party politics in the quarter-century after 1945 to multi-party politics in the period since. Some ascribe it to structural dealignment (a dysfunctional party system, with a poor fit between what electors want and what the parties actually deliver), others to consensus politics (the pursuit by both parties from the 1950s to the 1970s of similar policies, denying voters a real choice and failing to address the nation's problems), and yet others to the end of consensus politics (parties in the 1980s and since pursuing extreme policies unacceptable to a centrist electorate). There tends to be a relationship between each thesis and the political stance of its proponents. *PN*

Vernon Bogdanor, *Multi-Party Politics and the Constitution* (Cambridge, 1983). | Philip Norton, 'Britain: Still a Two-Party System', in S. Bartolini and P. Mair (ed.), *Party Politics in Contemporary Western Europe* (London, 1984). | Giovanni Sartori, *Parties and Party Systems: A Framework for Analysis* (Cambridge, 1976).

Munich crisis (September 1938). This crisis had its origins in the ostensible demands of the German-speaking minority of Czechoslovakia, the so-called Sudeten Germans, for autonomy. The issue began to come to a head in the wake of the *Anschluss* of the preceding March which put Czechoslovakia under immediate strategic threat from Germany. For the British, Czech–German differences were problematic on two grounds. First, a war started in Czechoslovakia might extend into a world war; secondly, while the issue remained unresolved it would not be possible to engage the German government on the broader issues of a general European settlement, the real objective of British policy. The British premier, Neville Chamberlain, therefore determined to follow a policy that would avoid war by persuading the Czechs to compose their differences with the Sudeten Germans. On 5 September 1938, the Czech president Benes conceded the Sudeten demands almost in their entirety, but the rejection of this offer made it clear that the real objective of the Sudetens was union with the Reich, for which they had the backing of Hitler. It seemed as though Europe would collapse into war, but Chamberlain flew to Germany twice, finally conveying to Hitler Anglo-French agreement to the cession of the Sudetenland. Hitler, though, still seemed determined on war until 28 September when he invited Chamberlain, Mussolini, and the French premier, Daladier, to a conference in Munich. There, on 30 September, it was agreed that Germany should occupy the Sudetenland and that an international agreement should guarantee the rump Czech state. On returning to Britain, Chamberlain was greeted with euphoric relief, but his reputation was ultimately to suffer, when later the Munich conference became synonymous with cowardly surrender and this discredited the policy of *appeasement associated with him. *AJC*

KEITH ROBBINS, *Munich 1938* (London, 1968). | TELFORD TAYLOR, *Munich: The Price of Peace* (New York, 1979).

municipal socialism, catch-all term given to diverse strands of socialist thought and action, some of which extol the simple virtues of municipal enterprise, others the possibility of socializing society from the ground up. A number of urban councils established public utility operations in the 19th century, giving rise to the term 'gas and water socialism'. Sidney Webb in particular argued for municipal trading of this sort as a road to socialism, but municipal monopolies were opposed by commercial interests, and Conservative unease about municipal trading grew in the early years of the century, with select committee inquiries in 1900 and 1903. Following the 1906 general election, an Anti-Socialist Union (ASU) was established to campaign against socialist experiments which, at that stage, were most apparent at the municipal level. The ASU survived to 1940, but its role in combating municipal socialism was challenged by other right-wing bodies, notably the *London Municipal Society.

A second strand in municipal socialism was *Poplarism, named for the series of episodes in which the Poplar board of guardians and the metropolitan borough council respectively sought to pay high rates of poor relief, act as a high-wage employer, and retain local resources to meet local needs. For Conservatives, Poplarism became a catch-all term for electoral bribery with municipal resources, but it was sometimes convenient to abjure this as socialism. The revival of municipal (by now local) socialism came in the 1970s, with the rise of the new urban left in local government, and their novel extensions of local authority power and influence in the economic sphere. Local economic development policies aimed at promoting employment; procurement policies; contract compliance; industrial investment, sometimes using pension funds; and the establishment of local authority companies and enterprise boards were seen as ways of building socialism at the local level, though many leading practitioners conceded that these local experiments were not expected to be effective, but to serve as models or prototypes for future Labour government activities. Most had fallen foul of Conservative legislation long before that party left office in 1997. *KY*

Munitions, Ministry of (1915–21), pioneering department of state organized under the direction of David *Lloyd George in May 1915. Though a famous radical in August 1914, Lloyd George embraced the war effort and by early 1915 had taken up the question of arms supplies to the forces. By early 1915, after chairing several government committees to improve the production of warlike stores and encountering resistance from Kitchener and the war office, he concluded that advisory bodies could not materially improve the situation. With the creation of Asquith's coalition government, Lloyd George secured control of a new department of state endowed with broad powers to produce munitions of war. Relying on a series of Munitions of War Acts, the ministry gained temporary control of the factories of government contractors, built many new ones, and brought under its control skilled and unskilled industrial labour, 'diluting' the workforce (despite trade union regulations) with unskilled women and youths. It controlled profits, plant and equipment, raw materials, and distribution of all goods useful to the war effort and set precedents of control followed by all industrial powers in modern total war. *RJQA*

R. J. Q. ADAMS, *Arms and the Wizard: Lloyd George and the Ministry of Munitions, 1915–1916* (London, 1978). | *The History of the Ministry of Munitions* (London, 1922).

Munro, Robert (1868–1955), Liberal politician. Elected MP for Wick burghs in January 1910, Munro was appointed as lord advocate in 1913. He held this post until 1916, when he became Scottish secretary in Lloyd George's wartime coalition. As a National Liberal he was elected MP for Roxburgh and Selkirk in 1918 and resumed his post as Scottish secretary until the coalition collapsed in 1922. He served as lord justice clerk, 1922–34, when he was ennobled as Lord Alness. *RF*

Munro-Ferguson, Ronald. See NOVAR, VISCOUNT.

Murdoch, (Keith) Rupert (1931–), press-proprietor who typified the late 20th-century international multimedia entrepreneur. A brash capitalist risk-taker, admired and demonized, his worldwide empire started in Australia, where he turned a small newspaper inheritance into a major press and broadcasting chain. In 1969, he bought the British *News of the World* and the *Sun*, adding *The Times* and *Sunday Times* in 1979 and later the short-lived *Today*. These totalled about one-third of total national newspaper circulation. Murdoch earned the lasting hatred of the production unions in 1986 by moving to new premises overnight and hiring replacement labour. By the mid-1980s he owned major broadcast and publishing interests also in the USA and the Far East. At great financial risk, he launched the Sky satellite TV channel in 1989, swallowing the opposition. Later he led the move to digital TV. His politics were expediential, changing to serve his business interests. *CKSU*

W. Shawcross, *Rupert Murdoch* (London, 1992).

Murphy, John Thomas (1888–?), Communist. Murphy's life was marked by its progression from a Christian youth through revolutionary socialism to disillusionment with the communist path. Raised in a devoutly religious family, he first became actively involved in politics in 1910 when he joined the Amalgamated Society of Engineers. He found himself attracted by the emerging syndicalist movement and soon developed into one of the leading exponents of industrial unionism and industrial democracy. He played a key role in the wartime Sheffield shop stewards' movement and was a leading member of the Socialist Labour Party, formed as a result of a split in the Social Democratic Federation. He illegally travelled to Russia in 1920 to attend the world congress of the Third International and, by his own account, this experience transformed his life. Until his resignation in 1932, Murphy was a major figure in the Communist Party of Great Britain (CPGB), serving as secretary and representative on the executive committee of the Comintern. He unsuccessfully contested various parliamentary elections on behalf of the CPGB, 1929–31. He later joined the Labour Party, the Socialist League, and was an organizer for the People's Front Movement. *DWM*

John Thomas Murphy, *New Horizons* (London, 1941).

Murphy, William Martin (1844–1919), prominent Irish businessman and press baron. Closely associated with Tim Healy, he did much to undermine the Irish Parliamentary Party. His *Irish Independent* challenged the influence of its own newspaper, the *Freeman's Journal*, and he attacked Redmond's readiness to compromise over Ulster in the home rule debates of 1914, and again at the Irish convention of 1917–18. The Dublin lockout of 1913, initiated by his United Tramways Company, contributed to growing political extremism in Ireland. *DRB*

Murray, George Herbert (1849–1936), civil servant. Murray entered the Foreign Office in 1872 but transferred to the Treasury in 1880. He was private secretary to Gladstone and then Rosebery (1892–5) before becoming chairman of the Board of Inland Revenue (1897–9), secretary to the Post Office (1899–1903), and permanent secretary to the Treasury (1903–9). He vetoed a proposal to build a subway under Whitehall for the secret disposal of War Office archives in the event of an invasion on the grounds that 'the last objective of any intelligent invader of this country would be the war office'. *KT*

Must Labour Lose? (1959), Penguin book, by Mark Abrams, Rita Hindell, and Richard Rose, published in reaction to the Labour Party's third successive general election defeat. It was based on a survey conducted for *Socialist Commentary* by Mark Abrams (who before the 1959 election had done the first serious private polling). On the premiss that the Labour Party had failed to react to the change in the nature and attitudes of society in the post-war years, it explored attitudes towards parties and their leaders, trade unions, social class, and nationalization. It also explored the experience of the new consumerism, possession of washing-machines, refrigerators, television, cars, and housing. It put all these contributors to political loyalty in the context of age. Were young voters different from old? The lessons of the survey were drawn out by Rita Hinden, *Socialist Commentary*'s editor. Recognizing that Labour's historic appeal as a working-class, trade union, nationalizing party was fading, she urged it to move from its focus on standard of life to a focus on way of life, with an idealistic concentration on unselfish aims, whether it be aid to underdeveloped countries or increased taxes for social benefits: 'Socialism has stood for the generous impulses in man'. The irony of *Must Labour Lose?* is that Labour managed to win in 1964 without following most of its prescriptions. *DEB*

Mutual defense aid. This military assistance programme (some $7.3 billion expended, 1949–53) can be seen as the military analogue of *Marshall aid. Until 1949 Washington gave priority to economic recovery in Western Europe. From 1950 recovery jostled increasingly (and sometimes uncomfortably) with rearmament, especially after the outbreak of the Korean war. Like Marshall aid, military aid was made contingent on NATO countries agreeing an integrated defence plan. *AD*

Lawrence S. Kaplan, *A Community of Interests* (Washington, 1980).

N

Nabarro, Gerald David Nunes (1913–73), Conservative backbencher. After a career as a regular army officer, Nabarro became a journalist, company director, and broadcaster. He was a Conservative MP, 1950–64 and from 1966, a tireless self-publicist and self-confessed bounder, whose enormous moustache made him instantly recognizable and a cartoonists' favourite. His campaigns for clean air legislation and against taxation, his early Euroscepticism, and his championing of the rights of motorists, made him a very distinctive MP. He published two autobiographies, the first, *NAB 1* (1969), named after his car's characteristic registration plate. *JAR*

NACRO (National Association for the Care and Resettlement of Offenders), a charity concerned with ex-prisoners. Originally set up as the Central Discharged Prisoners' Aid Society in 1924, it changed its name to the National Association of Aid to Discharged Prisoners' Societies in 1960, taking its present name in 1966. *JS*

Nairne, Patrick Dalmahoy (1921–), civil servant. Nairne joined the Admiralty in 1947, switching to the Ministry of Defence (MoD) in 1964, where he shone as principal private secretary to the minister of defence, Denis Healey, 1965–7. In 1970 he became an MoD deputy secretary, moving to the Cabinet Office as a second permanent secretary, 1973–5. From 1975 to 1981 he was permanent secretary at the giant and complex Department of Health and Social Security. *KT*

'naked into the Conference Chamber', evocative phrase used by Aneurin Bevan on 3 October 1957 to explain his unexpected resistance to unilateralism. He told the Labour Party conference that 'if you carry this [unilteralist] motion ... you'll send the British foreign secretary, whoever he was, naked into the Conference Chamber'. *JAR*

Nassau conference (1962), summit between Harold Macmillan and US President John F. Kennedy in December 1962 which agreed close nuclear cooperation. Planned as a routine meeting, it became a crisis meeting, when in the preceding months Britain came to suspect that America wanted to prevent them remaining a nuclear power. In 1960 America had agreed to supply Britain with the *Skybolt air-launched nuclear missile, so prolonging the life of the British V-bombers. As an apparent quid pro quo, Britain agreed to the basing of US Navy submarines at Holy Loch. Macmillan had tried to secure agreement for Skybolt, or, if necessary the submarine-launched Polaris missile, but the Americans offered *Polaris only as part of a multilateral European force and so not an 'independent' British deterrent. However, the link between the agreements was unclear.

In 1962 Robert McNamara, Kennedy's defence secretary, announced the cancellation of Skybolt, failing to appreciate the intense political sensitivity of the issue for London. For America it was merely one of many nuclear systems, but Macmillan had staked his personal authority on prolonging Britain's independent nuclear deterrent force through Skybolt. At Nassau, Macmillan played on his good relations with Kennedy, rejected an offer to continue developing Skybolt alone, arguing that it was too late, and stated that he needed Polaris. Sensing the political crisis his close ally faced and accepting the moral obligation of Holy Loch, Kennedy agreed to supply Polaris on 'a continuing basis'. The favourable terms resulted in a stable British system for the next 20 years and its replacement with Trident essentially under the same terms. But Nassau also represented the end of true British independence in nuclear matters, leaving her dependent on America and Macmillan had to bounce his own cabinet rather more than Kennedy into accepting this change. France was also offered Polaris following Nassau, but de Gaulle rejected this, professing to see Nassau as evidence of continuing Anglo-American links and vetoing British entry to the European Community shortly thereafter, although it is questionable that Nassau was decisive in his decision. *JPSG*

IAN CLARK, *Nuclear Diplomacy and the Special Relationship: Britain's Deterrent and America 1957–1962* (Oxford, 1994). | LAWRENCE FREEDMAN and JOHN GEARSON, 'Interdependence and Independence: Nassau and the British Nuclear Deterrent', in K. Burk and M. Stokes (eds.), *The United States and the European Alliance since 1945* (Oxford, 1999).

Nation, prominent weekly Liberal periodical. The *Nation* attracted many of the leading spokesmen for *New Liberalism in the Edwardian period, including J. L. Hammond, Henry Brailsford, L. T. Hobhouse, C. F. G. Masterman, and J. A. Hobson. H. W. Massingham (1860–1924) served as its editor from 1907 to 1923. The *Nation* eventually merged with the *New Statesman* in 1923, its demise in itself indicating the party's decline. *JS*

National Assistance Act, 1948 provided, as of right, cash payments for those in real need. Intended to act as a safety-net and part of the *welfare state, it finally removed the last elements of the *poor law. Although anticipated to treat only small numbers of people because of the new welfare provisions made after 1945, in 1948 there were still about a million people who received National Assistance. Because welfare benefits often remained below those recommended by the *Beveridge report (1942) or were eroded by inflation, nearly three million people received national assistance by 1970. The system was increasingly superseded by the introduction of new benefits, notably supplementary benefit, family income supplement, housing benefit, and cash grants for emergencies. Many of these were revised and renamed under the Social Security Act of 1986 and subsequent legislation. Under legislation of April 1988, a social fund was set up to replace the original cash grants of national assistance with a system of loans and grants. *JS*

National Association of British Manufacturers. See NATIONAL UNION OF MANUFACTURERS.

National Chamber of Trade, organization which largely represented small retailers organized in local branches. This meant that many towns had a chamber of commerce and a chamber of trade. It was a founding member of the Retail Consortium in 1967. In 1995 it was merged into the British Chambers of Commerce, although separate organizations may survive at local level. *WG*

National Coal Board. See COAL INDUSTRY.

National Confederation of Employers' Organizations (NCEO), a 'peak organization' of industrial employers founded in 1919 to present a coherent employers' view to government and the trade unions. The origins of the NCEO lay in the debacle (from the employers' viewpoint) of the National Industrial Conference of 1919, at which trade unions and employers' organizations (including the *Federation of British Industries (FBI)) met, ostensibly to discuss a new industrial settlement for the cooperation of labour, capital, and government. A number of employers, led by Sir Allan Smith, who led the Engineering Employers' Federation (EEF), thought that the unions had had the better of the argument and that the employers, insufficiently organized, had been too ready to accept the conciliatory approach favoured by the FBI. The EEF had been suspicious of the FBI since its inception in 1917 because it had tried to combine the functions of a trade association, discussing and agreeing commercial matters, with those of an employers' association which dealt exclusively with labour matters. The NCEO soon attracted the support of the major employers' associations in heavy industry, and during the inter-war period was the most effective voice of capital in negotiations with government and the TUC. In 1942 (now called the British Employers' Confederation) it took the lead in expressing a sceptical view of any reform of the welfare system which would increase employers' costs. After the war it maintained a robust position, though it would often try to moderate the more extreme manifestations of anti-union expression by companies or by individual employers' organizations. In 1965 it merged with the FBI to form the *Confederation of British Industries. *JAT*

National Council for Civil Liberties. See LIBERTY.

National Council for One-Parent Families, pressure group formed in 1973 from the earlier National Council for the Unmarried Mother and her Child (1918). It campaigns for better childcare facilities and welfare rights for single-parent families. *JS*

national curriculum, part of an educational reform programme initiated by the Thatcher government with the intention of promoting higher standards of achievement in basic skills. Proposed by education minister Kenneth Baker, and influenced by the *Black Papers in education, the Education Reform Act of 1988 introduced a core curriculum in designated mainstream subjects to be followed by all pupils between the ages of 5 and 16, monitored by testing at 7, 11, 14, and 16. Both the choice of core subjects and the provision for testing aroused heated controversy, although most educationalists supported the need for greater rationalization of the curriculum. Under the Major and Blair governments the importance of core subjects and assessment was confirmed, with increasing emphasis on basic literacy and numeracy at primary school level. *JS*

national debt, the total amount owed at any time by the public finances as a result of previous and current expenditure. A permanent national debt has existed and been financed through the Bank of England since the 1690s, when the necessities of wartime under a popular Protestant monarchy encouraged parliament to accept that the nation rather than the king should bear the long-term costs. In the 18th century the existence of a permanent national debt, then overwhelmingly financed through government stock purchased domestically, was a bulwark against revolutionary change, since so many citizens depended on stability for the value of that stock and the prompt payment of interest. There were, and have continued to be, concerns voiced about the actual extent of the debt and the speed at which it was increasing in times of unusually high expenditure, for example in wartime, since the effect of borrowing to finance current spending is to place increased burdens (mainly of interest payments) on future generations. Governments have therefore mainly continued the Victorian practice of maintaining a 'sinking fund', annual payments to buy back a portion of the debt and hence reduce the cost of interest payments, though the temporary suspension of payments for this purpose, as in 1931, has been a favourite of governments trying to balance the books in difficult times. The existence of a permanent debt has, though, been largely unchallenged in 20th-century Britain, it being considered that there is nothing unreasonable in expecting posterity to help pay for capital investments like motorways from which posterity will benefit more than the present, or indeed for freedom from foreign domination achieved through war expenditure, where the same principles apply.

In 1900, Britain's total national debt stood at £629 million, about five times the annual income accruing to the Treasury (and almost a fifth of that income going to service the debt through interest payments); the total was, however, rather lower than it had been in 1815 when the last period of prolonged warfare ended. Expressed differently, the national debt at the turn of the century was just under a third of the total national income, the fruit of all economic activity. There were fluctuations but no major change to this pattern in the Edwardian period, but a veritable revolution occurred during the Great War: by 1920, the national debt was up to £7,828 million; revenue had increased at more or less the same rate and was still almost a fifth of that figure, but the real economy had not, and national debt now exceeded net national income by about half as much again; 40 per cent of all government revenue was now needed simply to pay interest on the debt. This pattern stabilized through the inter-war years, but only through maintaining the high level of taxation that had been unknown in 1914. The interest payments that were needed to service this much higher debt (and the need to borrow more and more regularly to refloat the debt as specific stocks fell in for repayment) help to explain the obsession of governments of the 1920s and 1930s both with keeping other expenditure down and with balancing the budget so as to maintain confidence and so lower interest rates. The net effect of their actions was to reduce the debt by about an eighth over twenty years, though in fact prices also fell during most of that period, so the gain was more apparent than real.

The Second World War produced a second step-change in an upwards direction. The national debt rose from £6,993 million in 1938 to £25,630 million in 1947, more than six times the government's annual income and nearly three times as much as net national income. Once again, the pattern stabilized in peacetime: despite continuous inflation, the national debt had risen only to £33,079 million by 1970 (now once again well under total national income for the year, and only twice the level of government income).

Higher inflation rates in the next quarter-century produced more rapid increases in the figures but a slow shift to a more favourable pattern as a result of economic growth without any prolonged periods of unbalanced budgets: the national debt stood at £248,626 million by 1993, but this was now only 1.4 times the government's annual income and 0.6 of national income. Though the deficit in the public finances run up by the Conservative governments in the early 1990s, as a consequence of recession, and the return to balanced budgets by the Blair government in better economic times after 1997, provided fuel for allegations of extravagance and overcaution respectively, the national debt was not playing a major part in the political debate at the end of the century. *JAR*

national deterioration, the idea that the country's population was becoming weaker and less pure, became a prominent concern at the end of the 19th century, and was treated as a very dangerous phenomenon because of prevailing *Social Darwinist assumptions. A declining birth rate amongst the better-off, heavy emigration overseas, and an inflow of poor immigrants from Ireland and eastern Europe caused alarm, as did the revelation that the majority of army recruits for the Boer war had to be rejected for overseas service as unfit. *Eugenic arguments suggested that there was declining quality in the genetic stock as a result of changes in population and environmental factors such as urban living conditions. An Interdepartmental Committee on Physical Deterioration which reported in 1904 found these fears to be exaggerated, though it led to 'national efficiency' measures to improve the urban environment, introduce *school medical services, and provide *school milk and *school meals. *JS*

National Economic Development Council (**'Neddy', NEDC**) (**1962–92**), the most important institutional outcome of the Macmillan government's efforts at 'indicative planning' after 1961. Unlike much of the novel economic machinery of that period, it survived Wilson and Heath and was finally dissolved, after a period of malign neglect by Mrs Thatcher's chancellors, in June 1992. As first conceived, Neddy had two important elements. The council itself was a tripartite body, with representatives from the TUC, the FBI and the government, meeting under the chairmanship of the chancellor of the exchequer. Associated with it was the National Economic Development Office (NEDO), a technical secretariat which was intended to supply the economic advice upon which the three parties could agree to act. NEDO also serviced sector working parties, known as 'little neddies', which were intended to agree each industry's contribution to the plan.

Reginald Maudling had mostly ignored the infant Neddy during his expansionist period at the exchequer, and it was not until Labour came to power in 1964 that tripartitism became dominant in economic planning. The joint statement of intent on productivity, prices, and incomes, signed in December 1964 by the TUC, the employers, and the government, committed all sides to voluntary planning. This was reinforced by the February 1965 *National Plan, which promulgated growth targets amounting to 4 per cent overall annual growth, and left it largely to the little neddies to apportion this within industrial sectors. Under Labour, the initiative in national target-setting and planning passed from NEDO to the Department of *Economic Affairs and did not return to it after Wilson closed down the latter, but NEDO retained a public stature by producing semi-independent reports which influenced public debate.

Edward Heath's government was at first suspicious of corporatist economic planning, but later embraced it as part of the 1972 *U-turn. Paradoxically this moved the initiative from Neddy to Downing Street where the prime minister himself held sway. Meeting monthly, Neddy provided an opportunity for conversation—once used by the TUC to try to avert conflict shortly before the February 1974 coal strike—but was never again to be the forum in which any party to the discussion tried to initiate economic or industrial policy. The 1974–9 Labour government made little use of Neddy and when the Conservatives returned to office in 1979 it was regarded by most ministers as no more than a talking shop. From March 1984 to the end of that year the TUC boycotted it because of the row over banning union membership at GCHQ and, although the CBI insisted on turning up to meetings, tripartism was patently over. Nigel Lawson tried to abolish Neddy after the Conservatives' 1987 election victory, but was prevented by Thatcher. Without any commitment to tripartitism, Conservative ministers grew impatient with meetings, which seemed an unnecessary opportunity for the trade unions to embarrass them. Neddy's demise in 1992 was predictable and overdue. *JAT*

National Enterprise Board (NEB), created by the Industry Act, 1975, inheriting and expanding the government's holdings in troubled firms such as Rolls-Royce and British Leyland and by 1979 having interests in 49 companies. The NEB also established a series of planning agreements, under which tripartite sector working parties reached a total of 39 by 1979, covering 40 per cent of manufacturing industry. The Thatcher years saw a change in role for the NEB as the fostering of free market ideals led to the disposal of the state-held assets. It was finally abolished in 1991. *JD*

Richard Coopey and Nicholas Woodward (eds.), *Britain in the 1970s* (London, 1996).

National Farmers' Union (NFU). The NFU (of England—there are sister unions for Wales and Scotland) was established in 1908 to represent farmers' interests in politics. Its membership, exclusively of farmers, grew rapidly from 10,000 in 1909 to 22,000 in 1916, by which time it was already a truly national organization. Membership reached 131,000 in 1939 and a peak of 210,000 in 1953, but in 1997 membership was down to 127,000. As a body representing farmers, the NFU was taken into government confidence during the Great War. After the repeal of the Agriculture Act, 1920, it was more distant from government but from 1933 onwards it was drawn back into a closer relationship by ministers anxious to encourage collaboration over the working of the *Agricultural Marketing Acts and other policies.

During the Second World War the NFU became one of the main instruments by which state control of agricultural production was put into effect. After the war, the union retained its position of close cooperation with government, a party to the government's annual review of agriculture. This activity made the union a very professional organization. With entry into the European Community in 1973, union and ministry continued to work in close cooperation on a more international scale. In the 1980s, agriculture and government faced new pressures to control expenditure under the common agricultural policy, pressures from environmental, consumer, and health interests putting strain on the Ministry of Agriculture, and weakening the links which the union had enjoyed. The NFU by the 1990s was returning to being a pressure group outside government. *JHB*

National Front (NF), right-wing political party. 'The formation of the National Front in 1967 was the most significant event in the radical right and fascist fringe of British politics since internment [during the Second World War]' (Thurlow, 275). The NF represented a merger between the League of Empire Loyalists and the British National Party (BNP). The first was dominated by A. K. Chesterton, whose political activities stretched back to Mosley's *British Union of Fascists. The BNP, founded in 1960, was presided over by Andrew Fountaine, a Norfolk landowner and former Conservative. The unified movement, which was 'anti-immigrant, anti-semitic, anti-American, anti-European Economic Community, anti-liberal and anti-Communist' (Thurlow, 292), drew especial strength from concerns about black and Asian immigration, an issue galvanized by the entry of Enoch Powell into the debate in 1968 and further stimulated during the next few years by the arrival of Asians from various east African states. The NF exploited this issue in Britain's inner cities where racial populism assumed an increasing salience. In this context John Tyndall and Martin Webster were able to make their presence felt. The messages they conveyed were powerfully presented in the NF journal *Spearhead*, and the movement also established links with certain Conservative MPs. The profile of the NF correspondingly increased although it was riven with ideological differences and almost constant personal intrigue. By the early 1980s, however, the NF was politically dead, partly because it met with strong opposition from the political left, partly because of state surveillance which limited its room for manoeuvre, but mainly because of the emergence of Thatcherism after 1975 and the consequent strong Tory policy on immigration which cut away a substantial plank in its ideology. Its days as a potential fourth political party, an emphasis heard in the 1970s, were at an end. *CH*

M. Billig, *Fascists: A Social Psychological Survey of the National Front* (London, 1978). | C. Husbands, *Racial Exclusionism and the City: The Urban Support of the National Front* (London, 1978). | S. Taylor, *The National Front in English Politics* (London, 1982). | M. Walker, *The National Front* (London, 1978).

National Government, coalition formed in August 1931 after the collapse amid economic crisis of Ramsay *MacDonald's second Labour government. The coalition initially comprised elements from the Labour, Liberal, and Conservative parties. Though envisaged as temporary, administrations calling themselves a 'national government' remained in power until 1945. It was obliged to introduce large public expenditure cuts and tax increases, and appealed for a *doctor's mandate at the 1931 general election, securing the most emphatic victory of the century (554 MPs out of 615). From 1932, the coalition became close to a Conservative government for MacDonald, though prime minister, had been disowned by his former Labour colleagues and Liberal members fragmented further over protection, only the Simonites (see LIBERAL NATIONAL PARTY) remaining in office. Viewed by some supporters as a means of keeping 'socialists' out of power and by others as a means of destroying Lloyd George, both the origins and record of the National Government continue to stir up historical debate. *NJC*

NICK SMART, *The National Government 1931–1940* (Basingstoke, 1999). | PHILIP WILLIAMSON, *National Crisis and National Government* (Cambridge, 1992).

national grid, established in 1926 by Baldwin's Conservative government, eager to see greater rationalization of electricity supply. Further co-ordination of resources took place under the Electricity Act, 1947, when the electricity system was fully nationalized. The national grid was privatized following the Electricity Act, 1989. For most of the century electricity delivered to homes and workplaces through the national grid has acted as catalyst for technological advance and has made possible great improvements in the standard of living. *WF*

National Health Service (NHS), set up by the National Health Service Act, 1946, which established a free comprehensive health service in England and Wales and was put into effect from 1948. Separate and equivalent acts were passed for Scotland and Northern Ireland. It was funded partly from national insurance (see NATIONAL INSURANCE ACT, 1946) contributions but mainly from taxation. It was *'free at the point of delivery', providing a general practitioner service and medical treatment, hospital care, and dental and optical services. The NHS was the result of extended campaigns by the left and parts of the medical profession to overhaul the piecemeal pre-war system of voluntary hospitals, local authority health services, and private provision. Given added impetus by the emergency measures of wartime, a comprehensive health service, was first recommended by the *Beveridge report (1942). The final Act was the result of skilful negotiation between Aneurin *Bevan and the doctors and consultants, many of whom opposed the scheme bitterly. Only by allowing doctors to continue with private practice was a compromise reached. Bevan resigned in April 1951 when Hugh *Gaitskell introduced prescription charges, thus breaking the principle of a completely free service.

During the 1960s a massive hospital building scheme was instituted, to bring the benefits of the latest medical equipment and post-operative care techniques. Politically, support for the NHS formed part of the so-called *post-war consensus over the welfare state. Public support for the service was also widespread and the service was popularly held to be 'the envy of the world'. The general health of the nation improved and old diseases such as tuberculosis and diphtheria were eliminated by improvements in treatment. Subsequently life expectancy increased and this placed an ever-increasing burden on the health service; rising costs steadily beset the service. Thus in 1989–90 Thatcher undertook a massive overhaul of the system in an attempt to reduce escalating costs. This highly unpopular scheme privatized elements of administration, introduced an 'internal market' where health authorities competed for resources, and created NHS Trusts where hospitals 'opted out' of health service control. Following a series of staff and bed shortages and rising hospital waiting lists, the future of the NHS became a key political issue in the 1997 general election. Committed to restoring the 'basic principles' of the NHS, Tony Blair's Labour government undertook a massive programme of investment and created a ten-year plan for a 'New NHS' which aimed to reduce bureaucracy, eliminate the internal market, and target specific diseases such as cancer and heart disease. Controversially, however, the Blair government also signed a 'concordat' with the private sector in 2000, whereby NHS patients could be treated in private hospitals. Despite attempts to reduce costs and improve services, by the end of the century the NHS remained a highly contentious issue generating considerable public debate and concern over its future. *JJN*

GEOFFREY RIVETT, *From Cradle to Grave: Fifty Years of the NHS* (London, 1998).

National Incomes Commission (1962–5) and **National Board for Prices and Incomes** (1965–70). The National Incomes Commission ('Nicky') was set up alongside the *National Economic Development Council ('Neddy') as part of the Macmillan government's efforts at indicative economic planning. Even more opportunistic than Neddy in its origins, the commission was conceived out of the collapse of Selwyn *Lloyd's 'pay pause', introduced in July 1961 to help control a run on sterling. The unpopular pause really affected only vulnerable and popular public sector workers such as nurses. Nicky, developed under Macmillan's direct supervision in the spring of 1962, was supposed to provide the element of wage control which was essential in a planned but expanding economy. The cabinet was grudging in its support for such an obviously interventionist policy, and the trade union movement equally suspicious. When Nicky's terms of reference were finally settled in November 1962 it was agreed within government that it would discuss specific proposed wage deals when asked by government, but would not discuss general policy, which was reserved to Neddy. Consisting entirely of 'independent' members, without trade union participation or cooperation, it could do little except proclaim a 'guiding light' for pay settlements, which it moved from 2.5 to 3.5 per cent under guidance from Neddy. Nicky struggled on, ignored, until the Wilson government replaced it in early 1965 by the National Board for Prices and Incomes. Under Aubrey *Jones, a former Conservative minister, the new board was an agent for imposing such control of both incomes and prices as the government dared. By using evidence and economic analysis of the relationship between wage costs, prices, and productivity, it contributed to a more reasoned policy of control than its predecessor had attempted. It was caught up in two historic conflicts, between the Treasury and the Department of *Economic Affairs and between the Wilson government and the trade union movement, and was abruptly disbanded by the incoming Heath government in 1970. *JAT*

National Industrial Relations Court (1971–4), created by the *Industrial Relations Act, 1971, to enforce a series of reforms of trade union practices. Neither the court's authority nor the provisions of the Act were ever recognized by the TUC, and by not formally registering (despite incentives to do so) the trade unions kept themselves outside most of the court's authority. On the rare occasions that employers took cases to the court, it strove to enforce its authority by making appropriate orders, by levying fines, and by sending strikers to gaol for contempt of court when its orders were ignored. When the last produced the threat of a general strike and political action to secure the release of those imprisoned, the court's authority was undermined. It was abolished by the Labour government in 1974, but had had little to do for most of its life anyway. Later trade union reforms after 1979 were more craftily drawn to bring offenders within ordinary courts (whose authority they could hardly deny), and to ensure that their funds rather than the individual members of unions were hit by the charge of contempt. *JAR*

National Institute of Economic and Social Research (NIESR), an independent non-profit-making body founded in 1938 which concentrates on investigating and quantifying the determinants of productivity and undertaking comparative research into the performance of British industry and other leading nations. It uses its own staff but also cooperates with other organizations, publishing the results of its findings in several series. NIESR was originally established as an independent check on Treasury forecasts. Using forecasting techniques first developed in the Treasury, NIESR was for many years part funded by the same department. The increasingly coherent and theoretically based econometric model of the UK first developed by NIESR in 1969 is used to produce the quarterly forecasts which are published in its quarterly *Review*. Treasury economists and NIESR economists have more in common with each other than any other group of laymen carrying out simulations. The April 1999 model incorporated nearly 400 variables and was able to carry out simulations up to the fourth quarter of 2029. It has *Keynesian properties since, in the short term, it assumes that fluctuations in output are determined primarily by changes in the components of aggregate demand. In the longer term, the model recognizes that the determination of output is underpinned by supply side influences. It also embraces the idea that inflation is a monetary phenomenon influenced by the monetary policy of the government. By the late 1990s, programmes of research funded through a consortium including the Bank of England and the ESRC have included work on productivity, education methods, trade and investment, European financial integration, labour markets, and economic statistics. Its investigations have also concentrated on the extension of productivity work to the service sector and studies of the relationship between productivity levels and different regulatory regimes. *JFM*

K. Jones, *Sixty Years of Economic Research* (Occasional Papers 52, NIESR, London, 1998).

National Insurance Act, 1911, cornerstone of the Edwardian Liberals' welfare legislation and foundation of the British welfare state, built upon piecemeal between the wars and systematically in the *National Insurance Act, 1946. Lloyd George as chancellor of the exchequer was the minister mainly responsible for driving the policy through, though the enthusiastic support of other reformers like Churchill and *Masterman, and of the prime minister, Asquith, was important too. A key influence was Germany, which had similar systems in place long before Britain (in order to counter the advance of socialism) and which British ministers visited in order to gather information: a radical Liberal MP urged LG to 'take a leaf from the book of Bismarck, who dealt the heaviest blow against German socialism not by his laws of oppression . . . but by that great system of state insurance'. British Liberals too had political as well as humanitarian motives in 1911.

The Act provided for a separate national insurance fund, financed by contributions relating to 'insured' workers coming differentially from the worker himself (fourpence a week, deducted at source), from his employer (threepence a week), and from the Treasury (twopence a week), producing LG's neat description of the scheme as giving the worker a benefit of 'ninepence for fourpence' invested, and hopefully allaying the suspicion of workers who had not previously seen the state make deductions from their pay packet. They would now have no choice but to contribute, but would receive in return guaranteed benefits if they fell ill. The Treasury contribution, derived from general taxation, thus guaranteed that employer and worker would not be alone in financing the scheme for their joint benefit, but beyond that it was intended to be a self-balancing 'insurance scheme' in the full meaning of the phrase. Initially, the scheme was limited to a few specific trades, and could not cover casual or seasonal workers who were perhaps most in need of its benefits. Later legislation, using the machinery set up in 1911, was able to repair these omissions.

Initially, there was bitter opposition to the scheme from the voluntary insurance and benefit companies who saw their trade disappearing, since they could not compete on equal terms with a state-subsidized scheme (but LG dealt with this effectively co-opting them into running his own scheme under state supervision), and from Conservatives who feared the public expenditure effects, and promised to repeal the Act when returned to power. Initially, it seems also to have been treated with suspicion by many workers, but over time, and especially as the Great War and then mass unemployment demonstrated the value of having a cushion against economic dislocations, there was no danger of it withering, and government became anxious rather to extend its provisions.

JAR

Bentley B. Gilbert, *The Origins of National Insurance in Great Britain* (London, 1966).

National Insurance Act, 1946, created the structure of the post-war *welfare state envisaged in the *Beveridge report (1942) and in the government white paper on national insurance in 1944. The Act provided for compulsory insurance for unemployment, sickness, maternity, widows', and old age pensions with contributions from employers, employees, and the state. It aimed at a comprehensive system of social security which, allied with the *National Assistance Act, 1948, the *National Health Service Act, 1946, and the *Family Allowance Act, 1945, provided a network of security 'from the cradle to the grave' as of right. Although additional benefits have been attached to its basic structure, it has remained the principle upon which the welfare state has been based since 1946.

JS

nationalism and **national identity**. Nationalism is a belief that a nation, usually ethnically defined, is the appropriate unit for political organization, and was central to the political activities of various far-right fringe parties (see, for example, the National Front). National identity is the feeling that one belongs to a nation. In Britain, the concepts of Scottish, Welsh, and Irish nationalism have been well defined; those of English or British nationalism powerful but ill-defined. English people are often unaware that 'English' and 'British' are not the same, whereas most Scottish and Welsh people identify themselves as both Scottish/Welsh and British, and are aware that these are not the same. The so-called 'Moreno question' inviting respondents to choose 'equally' (say) Scottish and British, more one than the other, or wholly one and not the other, is now extensively used in survey research. It is an excellent predictor of people's propensity to vote for one of the nationalist parties.

Most textbooks describe the United Kingdom as a multinational state. Scotland and Wales are nations with devolved institutions created in 1998 after earlier unsuccessful attempts. Northern Ireland is not a nation, but a forum where two apparently incompatible nationalisms, British and Irish, contend. Irish nationalism was expressed in the home rule and independence movements at the start of the century, which led to the creation of Northern Ireland in 1920 and independence for most of Ireland in 1921. The mutual incomprehension of Irish and English (or British, or imperial) nationalists made the achievement of Irish independence more long drawn out and painful than it need have been. Welsh nationalism has always been primarily a cultural and defensive movement, strongest in the areas of north and west Wales where Welsh speakers saw their language and way of life as under threat from assimilation (and sometimes, though not in the 20th century, outright persecution). Politically, it therefore has a strong but limited base. Scottish nationalism is more diffuse and not geographically concentrated within Scotland. Welsh and Scottish nationalism had some expression during the long crisis of Irish home rule, 1886–1921, but their link with the Irish did not help them. They faded after 1921, to re-emerge in the 1960s as protest movements against the perceived failure of the Labour governments. Scots and Welsh tend to find it easy to protest against perceived failure of a Conservative government by voting Labour; less easy to make the converse move. So Welsh and (especially) Scottish nationalism have been strongest under Labour governments.

British nationalism may be defined as a strong belief in Britain as a political (perhaps imperial) entity; English nationalism as either identification with specifically English symbols or a reactive desire to secure fair shares for England in the face of claims from the non-English parts of the United Kingdom. British nationalism was a potent force early in the century, and fuelled Unionist opposition to home rule. It was linked to support for the Empire and has inevitably faded somewhat with the transition to Commonwealth. The revival of the Commonwealth in the 1990s comes without 'British' in its title, and is unlikely to fuel British nationalism. However, it remains a potent force, which politicians and newspaper editors try to harness in opposition to the European Union. British nationalism as an inward-looking movement, however, was probably weaker in the 1990s than at any time earlier in the century, if 'nationalism' involves principled resistance to devolution on the grounds that it could lead to a break-up of the United Kingdom. The decline in the popularity of the monarchy in the 1990s is both a problem for British nationalism and a possible symptom of its fading away. However, reactive nationalism—in reaction both to attempts at further European integration and to the claims of Scotland, Wales, and Northern Ireland—will predictably grow in this millennium. *IM*

Paul Bew, *Ideology and the Irish Question: Ulster Unionism and Irish Nationalism* (Oxford, 1994). | Simon Heffer, *Nor Shall My Sword: The Reinvention of England* (London, 2000). | Christopher Harvie, *Scotland and Nationalism* (3rd edn., London, 1998).

nationalization. British socialists have often been attracted by the notion of government control of the nation's main industries. Such an idea was part of the policies of the Independent Labour Party and the Fabian Society at the end of the 19th century and became accepted by the Labour Party in its 1918 constitution, *Clause 4 (later 3d) of which committed Labour to the 'socialisation of industry'. Yet it was perhaps fortunate that the Labour Party was unable to form a majority government during the inter-war years, because it had obviously not properly thought out its policies in connection with nationalization. Indeed, in the 1930s, Hugh Dalton operated through various committees, publications, and party conference in order to produce a short list of industries which it was agreed, in *Labour's Immediate Programme* (1937), would be the basis of Labour's nationalization programme. This work had immediate relevance at the end of the Second World War when Attlee headed two post-war majority Labour governments, 1945–51. The 1945 party conference had insisted on a commitment to nationalization being placed in Labour's election manifesto, though party organizers like Morrison thought that this was a vote-loser that might even cost Labour the election.

There were already some state-owned industries and services in existence in 1945. Asquith's Liberal government created the Port of London Authority, and in 1914 provided £2 million for a more than 50 per cent stake in the Anglo-Persian Oil company (now British Petroleum). In addition, inter-war Conservative governments formed the Central Electricity Board to supervise the generation of electricity and to operate the national grid, and created the British Broadcasting Corporation, the London Passenger Transport Board, and Imperial Airways. The Attlee government built upon this base by implementing an extensive programme of nationalization. The main industries and services nationalized were the Bank of England (1946), civil aviation (1946), coal (1947), inland transport and railways (1947), electricity (1948), gas (1948), and iron and steel (1949). Labour felt that publicly owned industries could better serve the interests of the nation than private industry, largely on the basis that private industry was often wasteful. Indeed, this was partly recognized and it is clear that in most cases the Conservative opposition to nationalization in the 1940s was little more than ritual, except in the cases of road haulage and of iron and steel. Many coal owners were, indeed, happy to be bought out of their loss-making enterprises by the state. Nevertheless, the processes of preparation, legislation, and implementation for such a huge programme of state ownership in only five years were a very considerable achievement. In this process, the key figure was Herbert Morrison, and the model of organization adopted, a semi-independent body sometimes called 'the Morrisonian public corporation', owed much to his pre-war experience with London transport.

Having barely opposed these measures, post-1951 Conservatives did little to return nationalized industries back to private ownership until the 1980s. They privatized the iron and steel industry and the goods section of road transport but left the other industries much as they were before (though the introduction of commercial broadcasting in 1954–5 was a sort of privatization). Conservatives did, though, campaign against further nationalization, for example in 1959, and the impact they made helped persuade Gaitskell to seek the abandonment of Labour's commitment to Clause 4, but his party would not then accept the removal of the book of Genesis from Labour's bible (as Harold Wilson put it). The Labour governments of 1964–70 then extended the public sector in a minor way, most notably with the formation of the National Bus Company in 1968. The Heath government of 1970–4 partly nationalized the aero-engine business of Rolls Royce after the firm went bankrupt but privatized other small units like the Thomas Cook travel agent. In 1974–5 Wilson's government nationalized British Leyland in order to rescue the only surviving British-owned mass car producer from severe financial difficulties. There were some other small additions to the public sector.

By 1979 almost two million people were employed in nationalized industries, which accounted for about 10 per cent of British output. However, during the 1970s the financial burden on public finances of nationalized industries rose to about £3,000 million, largely in order to keep prices low and to maintain services, while the strikes of public sector workers against Heath and in the 'winter of discontent' did the idea of nationalization some damage too. When Margaret Thatcher came to power in 1979 it was obvious that the public sector would be reduced. Indeed, from 1981 real privatization began, if at first only tentatively and with the object of raising money to fund tax reductions. In 1981 Cable and Wireless and part of British Aerospace were sold. From 1983, British Airways, British Gas, British Leyland, British Shipbuilders, British Steel, British Telecom, the National Bus Company, and the water and electricity industries were all privatized. The pace of privatization gradually slackened but continued under John Major in the 1990s and had been accepted in advance as a fait accompli by Tony Blair's government, which came into power in 1997. This is not perhaps surprising, given that, in April 1995, a special Labour conference accepted a revised Clause 4 which effectively put an end to Labour's commitment to public ownership. *KL*

E. Eldon Barry, *Nationalisation in British Politics* (London, 1965). | Norman Chester, *The Nationalisation of British Industry, 1945–1951* (London, 1975). | Keith Laybourn, *The Rise of Socialism in Britain 1881–1951* (Stroud, 1998).

Nationalized Industries Committee, a select committee created in 1955, appointed on a sessional basis. It was established following the recommendation of the select committee of 1953 which had been established to investigate the relationship between parliament and the nationalized industries. When it initially met, Members from both sides of the House felt its remit was too narrow and the government agreed to expand it. The committee differed from previous select committees in being a tool for political accountability rather than to expedite legislation. Though it had no supervisory role, it did scrutinize the accounts of nationalized industries. Its role expanded at the time of the creation of the Crossman committees (see Commons, House of: 'Crossman select committees') in 1966–9. By 1967 it covered the Post Office and by 1969 the Independent Television Authority, Cable and Wireless Ltd, the Tote, and certain Bank of England activities. It was abolished in 1979 as part of the general reform of select committees. *KMT*

National Labour Party, supporters' club rapidly organized to provide organizational backing for those Labour ministers and MPs who backed Ramsay *MacDonald in the split occasioned by his formation of a *National Government in August 1931. In the ensuing general election, the group did well but on a narrow front, with thirteen of its twenty candidates being returned to the Commons, partly through the personal appeal of MacDonald, Snowden, and other National Labour ministers, though mainly because their candidates were spared contests against Conservatives and Liberals. From the 1935 election, when it elected only eight MPs and was unable to secure even MacDonald's own re-election in his former seat, the party existed mainly as window-dressing for a government that had become overwhelmingly Conservative, and both its survival and election campaigning were entirely at the Tories' behest. It still, though, had importance in retaining some working-class votes for the National Government of 1935–40. Hence, perhaps to enhance its visibility, six of its MPs held government posts and it had only a single back-bencher. The arrival of the Labour Party in office under Churchill in 1940 made National Labour's existence now largely pointless, and its star leaders had anyway all retired by that time. All of its seven remaining MPs either retired or were defeated in 1945. *JAR*

National Liberal Club, effective headquarters of the Liberal Party until the role was assumed by offices at *Abingdon Street, SW1, in 1910. After 1934, when Abingdon Street ceased to function as a party headquarters, the club remained the spiritual home in London of the Liberal Party. *JS*

National Liberal Federation, principal organization of the Liberal Party, founded in Birmingham in 1877, and so reflecting the provincial strength of Victorian Liberalism. Growing out of the Birmingham Liberal Association, it set up a general committee to provide a continuity of organization and summon an annual conference. Its offices were moved to London in 1886, but it was always considered an advisory body to the leadership and the parliamentary party. Loosely structured, it was felt to be a contributory cause of the Liberal Party's decline after the Great War and was wound up as a result of the *Meston report of 1936. *JS*

National Liberals (post-1931). See Liberal National Party.

National (Lloyd George) Liberal Party (1918–22), organization of those Liberals who supported David Lloyd George as prime minister, 1916–22, and who thereafter remained his supporters until the Liberal split formally ended in 1926, rather than going into opposition with Asquith. Because support was inherently tied up with the 1916–22 coalition government with the Conservatives (and after 1922 with the possibilities of renewed cooperation with Tories), the group has often been referred to as 'Coalition Liberals', and at the time was sometimes shortened by Liberal critics to 'Coalies'. A disparate group, united only in its support for Lloyd George as war leader and for peacetime reconstruction, the National Liberals ranged from political adventurers like their chief whip Freddy Guest and businessmen politicians like Sir Alfred Mond (both of whom eventually joined the Conservatives, the National Liberal Party effectively providing a bridge over which they could walk from left to right) to orthodox Liberals like H. A. L. *Fisher, Christopher *Addison and Edwin *Montagu (who either reverted to orthodox Liberalism in due course or (in Addison's case) joined Labour).

The party's continued existence owed much to an electoral deal with the Conservatives, which allowed 150 candidates (mainly sitting Liberal MPs) a contest without a Tory opponent in the 1918 *'Coupon' Election. As a result, 127 National Liberals were elected, dwarfing the 36 non-coalition Liberals, but themselves swamped on the government side by 382 Conservatives. Nevertheless, National Liberals were still extremely proud of their Liberalism, and could not be persuaded in 1920 to fuse with the Conservatives into a single centre party. National Liberal ministers also pressed ahead both with traditional Liberal policies (such as support for temperance) and with radical reforms, notably the *Addison Acts, 1919, Montagu's reforms in India, and Fisher's *Education Act, 1918. There was never, though, much institutional substance beneath the ministerial and parliamentary surface, and the need to finance local activities from central funds (since local memberships barely existed except in Wales), led Lloyd George down the slippery slope into selling honours for the *Lloyd George fund.

The rejection of fusion in 1920 left the National Liberals' future entirely at the mercy of their Conservative partners, and when Lloyd George was overthrown as prime minister at the 1922 *Carlton Club meeting, his party was cut adrift too. In the short term, the Conservatives' own needs ensured that a new pact could be made for the 1922 election, but this was more fragmentary than in 1918 and less effective (at least for the National Liberals, who held only 53 seats). Thereafter, the group was more a bargaining chip in internal Liberal battles than an effective force, and several leading members left to join other parties between 1922 and the final merging back into Liberalism when Lloyd George became leader in 1926. *JAR*

Kenneth O. Morgan, 'Lloyd George's Stage Army: The Coalition Liberals', in A. J. P. Taylor (ed.), *Lloyd George: Twelve Essays* (London, 1971).

National Minority Movement (NMM) (1924–33). The NMM was formed in January 1924 by Harry Pollitt, Tom Mann, and the *Communist Party of Great Britain, in order to press for industrial improvements for the workers. It aimed 'to organize the working class of Britain for the overthrow of capitalism'. By 1926 it was claiming that it had support from a million trade union members. From then onwards, however, it faced the opposition of the TUC and the fact that communism went through its 'class against class' period, during which the NMM found itself torn between building up its influence within the trade union movement and forming an independent movement. It also failed in its attempt to develop a broad-based Workers' Charter movement. It expired in 1933, with a mere 3,000 members, when the Communists reversed course and began their united front against fascism. *KL*

Keith Laybourn and Dylan Murphy, *Under the Red Flag* (Stroud, 1999).

national parks, areas of natural beauty and recreational value, set aside for special treatment under planning regulations. The first national parks were set up under the National Parks and Access to the Countryside Act of 1949, the outcome of lengthy campaigns to open the countryside to town-dwellers and to conserve areas of outstanding scenery. The idea of national parks (as wilderness areas such as Yellowstone) originated in the USA and, although this concept was inapplicable to Britain, the town and country planning movement supported tighter restrictions on specific areas of natural beauty than applied elsewhere. The 1949 Act set up a National Parks Commission to designate the areas concerned. The first to come into effect was the Peak District National Park (1951); followed by the Lake District, Snowdonia, and Dartmoor (1951); the Pembrokeshire Coast and North York Moors (1952); the Yorkshire Dales and Exmoor (1954); Northumberland (1956); and the Brecon Beacons (1957). Scotland has equivalent restrictions covering what are known there as regional parks. *JS*

National Party (1917–23), splinter group of right-wing Conservatives which, while not a true political party, did demonstrate the persistence of diehard and anti-coalitionist values within the greater party. Organized by Henry *Page Croft in 1917, the group ran a handful of candidates in 1918, of which only Page Croft was elected, and he had no official Conservative opposition. Their platform called for a renewed commitment to Empire, tariff reform, fiscal restraint, and probity in public life. In fact, what the party opposed was Lloyd George's reconstruction programme and his aggressive system of building up his political fund through the open secret of the sale of political honours. The National Party was yet another manifestation of the energetic, fearless, and independent-minded Page Croft rebelling against what he regarded as the compromise and impurity of his own party. As in the cases of the pre-war *Confederacy, Reveille, and Imperial Mission organizations, his normal reaction against the official Conservative policies which displeased him was to throw up an alternative organization to bring pressure to bear on the party leadership. Like these others, the National Party was soon dissolved, though the ending of the coalition had much more to do with backbench Tory loyalty than with such examples of revolt. Not to be confused with those MPs who in 1940–5 called themselves 'National' and were in fact non-party independents. *RJQA*

W. D. Rubenstein, 'Henry Page Croft and the National Party, 1917–1922', *Journal of Contemporary History* (1974).

National Party of Scotland. See Scottish National Party.

National Plan (1965), published in September, setting out Wilson's Labour government's plan to raise the British growth rate to 25 per cent between 1964 and 1970. The plan embodied the hopes of the early 1960s that Britain's economic growth, which lagged behind all other major Western European economies, could be increased with the help of a plan which would lay out the implications of such an acceleration. The plan was 'indicative', laying out forecasts and possibilities, rather than a Soviet-style plan with companies instructed on how much to produce. Such planning had been practised in France since the 1940s, but there the state had substantial control over the allocation of investment capital, which was not the case in Britain. The 1965 plan relied primarily on companies increasing their output in response to a more expansionary stance by the government. However, even by the time it was published, the Labour government had started to slow the rate of demand growth in order to help the balance of payments, and the plan's targets became wholly unrealistic with the sharp deflationary measures of July 1966. The plan was closely associated with George *Brown, as secretary for economic affairs. Its eventual failure was an important factor in Brown's declining role in the Labour Party in the later 1960s. For the Labour government, the failure of the plan is usually seen as a consequence of the unwillingness to devalue the pound in 1964, and hence the failure to break out of the 'stop-go' cycle of economic policy which Labour had so criticized in the 1950s and early 1960s. The actual rate of growth for the plan period was 2.6 per cent. *JDT*

The National Plan (Cmnd 2764, London, 1965). | Pamela Meadows, 'Planning', in Frank Blackaby (ed.), *British Economic Policy 1960–1974* (Cambridge, 1978).

national service. See conscription.

National Service League, pressure group. Formed in 1902 on the suggestion of Lord Newton, the league pressed for legal provision for men aged 18 to 22 to serve a compulsory two-month period of military training, followed by a fortnight's annual drill period in each of the following three years. The league ultimately enrolled more than 270,000 members on the eve of the Great War, largely through the efforts of its long-time president, Lord Roberts, and its organizational genius, Lord Milner. *RJQA*

R. J. Q. Adams and Philip P. Poirier, *The Conscription Controversy in Great Britain, 1900–1918* (London, 1987).

National Statistics, Office for (1996–). See Central Statistical Office.

National Trust, private charity and the leading conservation body in Britain. Founded in 1895 to preserve 'places of historic interest and natural beauty', its initial aim was to purchase threatened areas of scenery on the coasts and in areas such as the Lake district. Gradually, however, it also took on responsibility for historic houses and other buildings, especially from the 1940s onwards. In 1999, the National Trust had 2.6 million members (making it twice as large as any political party), owned over three hundred properties, and was one of the largest landowners in Britain with 667,000 acres (270,000 hectares), including 600 miles (940 km) of coast in England, Wales, and Northern Ireland. A National Trust for Scotland was set up in 1926 and now owns 125 properties and 185,000 acres (75,000 hectares). *JS*

David Cannadine, 'The National Trust: The First Hundred Years', in Howard Newby (ed.), *The National Trust: The Next Hundred Years* (London, 1995).

National Unemployed Workers' Movement (NUWM) (1921–40), formed by a number of unemployed London shop stewards and ex-servicemen on 15 April 1921. Walter *Hannington was appointed as its national organizer. From the start the NUWM was dominated by Communists who saw this organization as an agency for revolutionary change. Indeed, it was directly linked to the Communist Party of Great Britain (CPGB) by Hannington, who was often a member of its central committee. The NUWM organized six national hunger marches; produced a fortnightly paper, *Out of Work*; led local hunger marches, protest demonstrations against the means test, winter relief campaigns; and in the late 1930s fought more than 2,000 cases of appeal against the household means test benefits. Yet its influence was always limited, since its membership was constantly changing, as members gained jobs, and because of the opposition of both government and local authorities. Its members and leaders were frequently imprisoned, Hannington on three occasions. There were also difficulties with the CPGB and the international communist movement. In 1932, for instance, when Moscow called for revolutionary action, the NUWM became involved in drawing up a million-signature petition against the means test. This did not go down well with the CPGB and Hannington's arrest and imprisonment at the end of 1932 and early 1933 brought severe criticism of him and the NUWM leadership which led, unsuccessfully, to a CPGB attempt to widen the power base of the NUWM. It expired as an organization at the beginning of the Second World War when unemployment had effectively disappeared. *KL*

John Stevenson and Chris Cook, *The Slump: Politics and Society during the Depression* (London, 1977).

National Union of Conservative and Unionist Associations, Conservative federation of local party associations. Formed in 1867, following the first significant democratization of the franchise, the National Union (NU) was intended to be 'the handmaid' of the parliamentary party (as one of its founders admitted), effectively a supporters' club of activists grafted on to an existing parliamentary force. Already in the 1880s, though, Lord Randolph Churchill sought to use the popularity of his 'Tory Democracy' ideas among activists so that the NU could be his route to influence in the party. Similarly, when Joseph Chamberlain declared for tariffs in 1903, he was able to capture the NU, but he too found it to be an empty victory, for real authority lay with the leader and the Central Office machine. From 1911, harmony was restored, with the new post of party chairman encompassing the chairmanship of the NU's Executive Committee, its main channel of communication with the leader, while the principal agent became the NU secretary. A similar pattern was created in each region. In 1918–22, the NU became a platform for defence of the party's independence and integrity during the Lloyd George coalition, and it was again a focus of discontent against Baldwin's leadership in 1929–30. In a restructuring in 1930, however, the NU was freed to elect its own officers; indirect election of members to its upper-level committees reduced the role of nationally known dissidents, and the NU never again witnessed such highly charged politics within its committees. A small secretarial office for the NU has been housed within Central Office, and close cooperation has generally lowered the temperature, though NU representatives on the *Advisory Committee on Policy have continued to have leverage in policy development, while its participation in the examination and accreditation of agents and in the screening of parliamentary candidates has been vital in securing acceptance at the local level of national policies and practices.

The NU's role has mainly been to represent and coordinate federally the volunteer side of the party, representing regionally and nationally the ordinary members of constituency associations. Its annual autumn conference was the most important event of the party year, but it also organized meetings of Central Council, in effect a large subcommittee of conference, though recently more like a small representative conference that meets in the spring with specialist conferences for subsections of the party, women, Young Conservatives, councillors, and teachers. Its governing body was generally a national executive which tended to meet monthly early in the century, though the steady process of enlargement of that body to a membership of over two hundred led to fewer meetings and day-to-day decisions being devolved first to a general purposes committee and later to meetings of officers. The NU has from the 1970s been the forum for demands for a more democratic party, much of which were implemented in the later 1990s. While it has rarely backed radical proposals, it has generally defended the rights of ordinary members to play a part in the selection of the party leader and the development of the party's ideas and policies. *JAR*

Anthony Seldon and Stuart Ball (eds), *Conservative Century* (Oxford, 1994).

National Union of Manufacturers was formed in 1915 as the British Manufacturers' Association by Dudley *Docker and, after a brief but abrasive relationship with Docker's other creature the *Federation of British Industries (FBI) (in which the smaller body rejected the FBI's cautious approach to tariff protection), set itself up as the National Union of Manufacturers in 1917. Until the late 1950s it strove to present the view of the smaller manufacturer against trade unions, 'big government', and to a large extent 'big business' also. Shortly before merging with the FBI and the *British Employers' Confederation to form the *Confederation of British Industries in 1965, it changed its name again to the National Association of British Manufacturers, partly to avoid the confusion of its abbreviation with the National Union of Mineworkers. *JAT*

National Viewers and Listeners' Council, private broadcasting pressure group set up by Mrs Mary Whitehouse in 1964 to monitor broadcasting standards, especially the depiction of sex and violence. It has had an influence on the development of greater accountability on the part of broadcasters, including the setting up of the Broadcasting Complaints Commission, 1981, and the Broadcasting Standards Council, 1988 (the work of both bodies being subsumed into the Broadcasting Standards Commission from 1997). *JS*

NATO (North Atlantic Treaty Organization), security alliance established by the North Atlantic treaty of 4 April 1949. The founding members were Belgium, Canada, Denmark, France, Iceland, Italy, Luxembourg, the Netherlands, Norway, Portugal, the UK, and the USA. Greece and Turkey joined in 1952, the Federal Republic of Germany (West Germany) in 1955 and Spain in 1982. A product of the early Cold War, NATO's origins lay in Western European anxieties about Soviet expansion and a desire for American military support. Britain's policy towards the creation of NATO has been the centre of some historical debate. The argument revolves around two opposite interpretations. The first sees the foreign secretary, Ernest Bevin, set on tying the USA to Western Europe in a security arrangement from 1945 onwards, inspired by personal anti-communism. The second, more complex, explanation suggests that Bevin accepted the need for NATO only after his preferred course proved impractical. This would have been a *Western European Union, with an Anglo-French core, linked to European colonial possessions in Africa and the East. In the emerging superpower world, this Western bloc would be a third force between the USA and the Soviet Union. Steps along the road to the creation of the third force were the March 1947 treaty of Dunkirk (France and the UK) and the March 1948 Brussels treaty (Belgium, France, Luxembourg, the Netherlands, and the UK), both Western European defence agreements. According to the second interpretation, Bevin only abandoned his third force ideas to seek a North American–Western European security arrangement due to the heightening of the Cold War (particularly the Berlin crisis) and the weakening of the British economy.

At its core, the North Atlantic treaty's article 5 holds that 'The Parties agree that an armed attack against one or more of them in Europe or North America shall be considered an attack against them all', and includes a pledge to collective security. Crucially, collective security is dependent upon member states' constitutions, a principle established to protect the US senate's right to declare war. It took the Cold War's first hot war, in Korea (1950–3), before the USA made contributions in men and money to NATO, not least with the appointment of Dwight D. Eisenhower as the first supreme allied commander in Europe (SACEUR). The formal Soviet response came in May 1955, after the Federal Republic of Germany's accession to NATO, with the creation of the Warsaw pact.

Originally conceived from hostility towards the USSR, after 1967 NATO promoted détente with the Warsaw pact and in the early 1970s acceded to Soviet demands for a European security conference. Whilst a successful alliance over the long term, NATO also experienced internal divisions, especially with French withdrawal from its integrated military structure in March 1966. The end of the Cold War has seen a reappraisal of NATO's role, including moves towards enlargement to embrace former Soviet republics and Eastern European states and, for the first time, NATO forces were in action enforcing the UN no-fly zone over Serbia in 1994. For Britain, NATO has remained an organization where governments have sought diplomatic influence based upon military prestige and defence relations with the USA. *JRVE*

Sean Greenwood, *Britain and the Cold War* (London, 1999).

naturalization, the acquisition of British citizenship by foreign nationals, is governed by the terms of the 1981 British Nationality Act. Under it, naturalization is at the home secretary's discretion. Requirements include five years' residence, or three years if the applicant's spouse is a British citizen. Those who are not married to a British citizen are also required to have a sufficient knowledge of English, Welsh, or Scottish Gaelic; must also intend to have their main home in the UK; or be employed by the crown, by an international organization of which the UK is a member, or by a company or association established in the UK. In 1998, 54,000 people were granted British citizenship in the UK and nearly 3,800 applications were refused. Over one in four of all successful applications were from citizens of Indian subcontinent countries, with Africa accounting for almost one in four and the rest of Asia representing about one in five. *JS*

Natural Law Party, fringe political party in 1990s Britain, part of the worldwide Natural Law Party. Formed in 1992, it is dedicated to finding solutions to all problems through natural law, following the teachings of Maharashi Mahesh Yogi and through 'yogic flying'. The party put up 309 candidates in the general election of 1992 and 193 in 1997 but without any success. *JS*

Navy League, pressure group. Founded in 1894 under the guidance of Spencer Wilkinson, the former military correspondent of the *Manchester Guardian*, the league was slow to gain popularity. After hastily abandoning Wilkinson's specific ideas of naval reform in favour of general propaganda and support for increased naval building and for a continued reliance on 'blue water' defence thinking, the league prospered. Despite competition from the rival Imperial Maritime League, it numbered more than 120,000 members by the eve of the Great War. *RJQA*

Frans Coetzee, *For Party or Country: Nationalism and the Dilemmas of Popular Conservatism in Edwardian England* (London, 1990).

Neave, Airey Middleton Sheffield (1916–79), Conservative politician. A wartime escapee from the infamous Colditz prison and an intelligence officer, Neave entered the Commons in 1953. He was successively minister at transport and air during 1957–9, but made his greatest impact on politics in 1975 by masterminding Thatcher's election as Tory leader. He became head of her private office and Conservative Northern Ireland spokesman. He was assassinated when an Irish terrorist bomb exploded under his car shortly before the 1979 election. *RJS*

NEC. See Labour Party, National Executive Committee.

'Neddy'. See National Economic Development Council.

negligence, law of. See law of negligence.

Neill report (1998). In 1997 Lord Neill took over directly from Lord Nolan (see Nolan report). His report stated that, in contrast to previous occasions, governments must be neutral in referenda and provide equal funds for both camps. It advocated capping party expenditure in all campaigns, with a limit of £20 million for general elections, enforced by potential fines. It also recommended the naming of donors and ending gifts from overseas. It suggested the Elections Commission be given strong powers to police these systems. *KMT*

neo-colonialism, the exercise of undue influence within a former colony by its former colonial power. Despite the withering away of formal empires from the 1950s, in a process of rapid *decolonization, Britain was far from alone in seeking to retain close links with former colonies, hence the extensive efforts to persuade former colonies to remain members of the Commonwealth. The Commonwealth could be seen as a valuable experiment in interracial culturalism, and as fostering diplomatic cooperation at such places as the UN, but the desire to retain links also had an economic side. Too rapid severing of trading patterns built up over a century would harm both the former colony and Britain, hence the desire for example to protect the interests of West Indian sugar-growers when Britain negotiated to join the European Economic Community. For newly independent states, however, generally ruled by regimes that had struggled for national freedom from British rule, economic links could seem suspiciously like imperialism by another name, as Kwame Nkrumah, first post-independence leader of Ghana, argued in *Neo-Colonialism: The Last Stage of Capitalism* (1965). Much the same could be argued of the 'informal empire' in South America achieved by British capital before 1914, in places where the union flag was never planted, or indeed of the huge influence wielded by such businesses as American Fruit in the same continent throughout the century. By 2000, indeed, the entire debate was subsumed in wider concerns about multinational capitalism in a globalized economy. *JAR*

neo-corporatism. See CORPORATISM AND NEO-CORPORATISM.

Ne temere decree (1907), papal ruling which tightened up the rules for Catholic marriage. None were to be valid unless celebrated before a parish priest or ordinary. Protestant opinion in Ireland was greatly exercised by a case in 1910–11 when a Catholic husband left his Presbyterian wife, taking their children with him, on the grounds that his marriage was not valid. It seemed a papal encroachment into the civil affairs of the UK, and stiffened Unionist resolve for the approaching battles over devolution. *DRB*

'never had it so good'. Macmillan's use of this phrase at Bedford on 20 July 1957 echoed Harry Truman's words during the 1952 US presidential election, 'you never had it so good'. The catch-phrase 'You've never had it so good' became identified with Macmillan, notably in *'Vicky''s cartoons. But, while proclaiming that 'most of our people have never had it so good', Macmillan warned that the new prosperity might be 'too good to last' unless inflation could be controlled. *RJS*

new institutionalism, an analysis drawing on economics, rational choice theory, sociology, and organizational theory which sees institutions as a central feature of political life, offering an alternative to the rationalistic and individualistic approaches which dominate much of contemporary political science. Derived from the economic institutionalism of Nobel laureate Douglas North's *Institutions, Institutional Change and Economic Performance* (1990) and the work of the organizational theorists J. G. March and J. P. Olsen among others, it has come to pervade almost all areas of the social sciences. Here, an institution can be 'understood as a set of formal and informal rules, norms, expectations and conventions which govern human behaviour, maintaining the regular routines through which society is ordered. Institutions provide, therefore, for continuity and predictability in everyday life, setting frameworks for action, inaction and innovation' (Christine Bellamy and John Taylor, *Governing in the Information Age* (Buckingham, 1998), 157). Institutions create a predictable environment in which policy making takes place, but they provide decision makers with accessible patterns of behaviour based on past experience rather than current needs, and can act to reinterpret the intentions of policy makers, often in unexpected and unintended ways. In the longer term, institutions can create significant obstacles to attempts to secure radical economic, political, and organizational change. *CPS*

B. GUY PETERS, *Institutional Theory in Political Science: The New Institutionalism* (London, 1999).

New Ireland Forum. Following Sinn Fein's electoral breakthrough in the 1982 Northern Ireland Assembly election, the Irish government announced its intention in March 1983 to follow a suggestion from the Social Democratic and Labour Party to establish a forum representing

Irish constitutional parties (thereby excluding Sinn Fein) which would provide an agreed approach to a settlement in the North. Although invited to participate, Unionist parties refused to take part. Published in May 1984, the forum's report restated many traditional Nationalist arguments but also completely rejected violence as a means of effecting political change. The forum's report noted that Nationalists desired a unitary Irish state although the options of a federal state and joint authority over Northern Ireland were also mentioned. Later, in November 1984, Margaret Thatcher caused outrage among Nationalists by stating that each of these options was 'out'. The report did, nevertheless, provide constitutional Nationalists with a more focused perspective in the negotiations which would lead to the *Anglo-Irish agreement (1985). *GG*

Paul Bew and Gordon Gillespie. *Northern Ireland: A Chronology of the Troubles 1968–1999* (Dublin, 1999).

New Labour (1994–), the phrase used to describe the policies of Labour that have emerged under Tony Blair's leadership of the party and the Labour government (1997–). It refers to the third-way idea in which emphasis is placed upon combining both state activity and private enterprise in the development of the British economy, and is not unlike Harold Macmillan's *Middle Way* of the 1930s. *KL*

New Left. The New Left emerged from a group of Marxist intellectuals who left the Communist Party of Great Britain in the wake of Khruschev's denunciation of Stalinism and the Hungarian crisis of 1956. Grouped around the *New Reasoner*, they rejected both communism and labourism in favour of a socialist humanism which drew heavily on the earlier traditions and concerns of socialists such as William Morris. The *New Reasoner* amalgamated with the *Universities and Left Review* in 1960 as the *New Left Review*, which spawned a network of left clubs and discussion circles. Attempts to form a more permanent organization foundered, but in spite of its ephemeral character the New Left was important. Leading figures such as E. P. *Thompson and Raymond Williams raised fundamental questions about the nature of industrial society and its power structures, providing a cultural critique which extended the horizons of the left beyond its tradtional concern with class. *MC*

New Liberalism, Edwardian reformulation of Liberal political philosophy to move it away from the minimal intervention of classical Victorian liberalism and laissez-faire, acknowledging the need for greater government involvement in social issues. The restatement was required with the expansion of the electorate in 1867 and 1884, and the highlighting of a range of social problems which had not proved susceptible to eradication by the application of Gladstonian principles of self-help and free trade. The social enquiries of Charles Booth in London and Seebohm *Rowntree in York had demonstrated the persistence of urban poverty, while considerable attention was devoted to the issue of *national deterioration following the revelation of the poor quality of recruits for the *Boer war. At the centre of the movement were a group of writers associated with the **Nation*, including J. L. Hammond, H. N. *Brailsford, L. T. *Hobhouse, C. F. G. *Masterman, and J. A. *Hobson. Backed by Lloyd George and Winston Churchill in the 1906–14 Liberal governments, New Liberal policies included the introduction of old age *pensions, labour exchange, wage boards, and national insurance. As state assistance required extra spending, New Liberal policies were directly responsible via the *'People's Budget' of 1909 for precipitating the constitutional clash with the House of Lords which led to the Parliament Act of 1911. Lloyd George's reconstruction planning after the Great War owed a considerable debt to new liberal thinking, seeking to extend national insurance and the range of state spending into areas such as *council houses (see Addison Acts, 1919). *JS*

Freeden, Michael, *The New Liberalism: An Ideology of Social Reform* (London, 1978).

New Party, neo-fascist fringe party. 'Oswald *Mosley's New Party was surely the most bizarre episode in modern British politics. It started on 28 February 1931 when Mosley staggered to his office with pneumonia, appealed briefly for volunteer workers and funds, promised to run 400 candidates at the next election, and then went to bed for a month with pleurisy.' (Skidelsky, 247). Mosley hoped to implement changes which would stem Britain's relative economic decline. The earliest recruits consisted of former members of the Independent Labour Party (Robert Forgan was one), but the New Party faced both Labour and Communist attacks. Its first big test was the 1931 general election. To overcome press hostility the party produced its own newspaper, *Action*, from October 1931, edited by Harold Nicolson. The New Party fought on the following programme: (1) The reform of Parliament; (2) the need for scientific protection in economic policy;

(3) national planning; (4) imperial cooperation; (5) a General Powers Bill for government. All New Party candidates were heavily defeated. However, Mosley had put down a political marker. He said the New Party was fascist in theory but not in action. A fully fledged fascist party was his next step. *CH*

Robert Skidelsky, *Oswald Mosley* (London, 1975).

Newport by-election (18 October 1922), held on the day before the meeting of Conservative MPs at the *Carlton Club which had been called by Austen Chamberlain to crush an anti-coalitionist revolt among his followers. The morning press reported that in the by-election the Conservative Reginald Clarry had defeated his Liberal and Labour rivals. Though much concerned with local issues, the by-election was a boost for Tory confidence, and encouraged MPs to follow Law's advice and end the coalition. *RJQA*

Chris Cook and John Ramsden (eds.), *By-Elections in British Politics* (2nd edn., London, 1997).

Newsam, Frank Aubrey (1893–1964), civil servant. Newsam joined the Home Office in 1920, rising to be its permanent secretary, 1948–57. He was an influential and long-serving private secretary, 1924–33, first to permanent secretary John Anderson and then to successive home secretaries. A formidable and powerful permanent secretary, who dominated his department, Newsam was more an effective 'doer' than an original thinker or policy-initiator, though he pushed through significant reforms in the field of criminal law and police organization and training. *KT*

News Chronicle, Liberal newspaper. The *News Chronicle* was created in 1930 as a result of the merger of the pro-Asquith *Daily News* and the pro-Lloyd George *Daily Chronicle* but, with the decline of the party and social constituency that its predecessors had represented, it was always struggling. It still had one and half million readers in 1945, but this figure then fell fairly steadily and it was absorbed by the *Daily Mail* in 1960. *JAR*

newsreels. In the 1920s, and especially in the 1930s and 1940s after the coming of sound film, newsreels were shown in almost all cinema programmes and reached a high proportion of the electorate, offering both news and comment to viewers. By 1939, 6,000 cinemas in Britain sold 20 million tickets a week, and most adults were making at least one weekly visit. Labour took little interest in the new medium, turning down the TUC's offer to buy a cinema van to show party films, but the Conservatives seized the new medium with enthusiasm. Their party vans showed films (made to look like newsreels) and attracted big audiences; a Conservative and Unionist Films Association funded and made films; sympathizers in the industry ensured favourable coverage of party events and leaders, especially Baldwin. During the Second World War, BBC radio's ability to produce daily news during a national emergency enhanced its role and, from the 1950s, cinema was gradually eclipsed by television as a political medium. *JAR*

New Statesman, weekly radical journal. Launched by the Webbs in 1913 to publicize the work of the Fabian research department, the *New Statesman* became the country's leading left-wing journal during Kingsley *Martin's editorship, 1931–60. Circulation peaked at over 80,000 in 1960, but by the 1990s public perception was of a dull and irrelevant journal which had abandoned radical politics. It was rescued in 1996 by the controversial Labour MP Geoffrey Robinson and has since undergone a modest revival. *MC*

'new style of government', promise that became the keynote of Heath's 1970 election campaign. His foreword to the Conservative manifesto, *A Better Tomorrow*, condemned Labour's 'cheap and trivial style of government', in which 'short-term gain counted for everything'. Heath promised instead that decisions and policies would be based on the best advice, adding that the prime minister and his colleagues should have the 'courage' and 'intellectual honesty' to stick to them. These words were to haunt him after the U-turn of 1972. *RJS*

new towns. The New Towns Act of 1946 aimed to provide new focuses of urban development and relieve urban congestion. Several 'model' villages and towns had been built during the 19th century by philanthropic employers, notably at New Lanark, Saltaire, Bourneville, and Port Sunlight, while the ideas of Ebenezer *Howard for garden cities inspired the creation of the privately run Letchworth (1903) and Welwyn Garden City (1920). Growing concern about urban conditions and the need to provide new housing coincided after 1939 with wartime plans for reconstruction, resulting in the proposal to build an outer ring of 'overspill' towns around London under *Abercrombie's Greater London plan of 1944. The 1946 Act set up new town development corporations with sweeping powers to create whole new communities. Eight new towns in the London ring, including Harlow and Basildon, were designated by 1948 and more than twenty elsewhere in the country by 1970, including Peterlee (1948), Cumbernauld (1956), Skelmersdale (1962), and Milton Keynes (1967). Although affected by their share of economic and social problems, the new towns have been widely regarded as one of the most successful and imaginative schemes of British social policy since the war. *JS*

new universities. See HIGHER EDUCATION.

Next Five Years Group, cross-party movement preaching the virtues of economic planning. Founded by Lord Allen of Hurtwood following the March 1935 publication of *Planning for Employment*, it included Harold *Macmillan, Arthur Salter, and Geoffrey Crowther. Despite publications such as *The Next Five Years* (1935) and a journal *New Outlook*, its impact upon policy was limited, with government unwilling to abandon the defence of sterling and balanced budgets. Macmillan's biographers disagree over the extent of his influence on the movement's economic ideas. *NJC*

ALASTAIR HORNE, *Macmillan, 1894–1956* (Basingstoke, 1988).

Next Steps executive agencies. By the mid-1980s attempts to develop a more cost-effective and efficient civil service appeared to have become stymied. The Cabinet Office's efficiency unit, backed by the prime minister, analysed the reasons for the slow pace of change. The team appointed interviewed numerous civil servants across the country. This resulted in March 1987 in the so-called Ibbs report, *Improving Management in Government: The Next Steps* written by Kate Jenkins, Karen Caines, and Andrew Jackson. The report, published in February 1988, argued that the bulk of the civil service's work was in providing services for the public and that this could be done better by breaking up the unitary civil service into agencies. The agencies' work, in particular performance targets, would be determined by framework agreements. The agencies would remain accountable to parliament through their chief executives and a responsible minister but would gain far greater autonomy in their work, for example with pay scales. The government emphasized that creating agencies was about efficient services rather than a stage towards privatization. The report's recommendations were carried out briskly. By the end of 1988, three agencies had been created. Agencies were then created by most departments. In the first two years they tended to be similar to the initial ones, such as the Stationery Office and Companies House. They were generally small, discrete units, often with the potential to trade commercially. However, the process gathered momentum in 1991 when the Benefits Agency was created and the Customs and Excise was organized into agency-style executive units. The following year the Inland Revenue adopted similar executive offices. The addition of such large units meant that by 1993 half of all civil servants were working in agencies. The most controversial proved to be the Child Support Agency established from scratch in 1993 rather than being converted from a civil service unit. This, though, was attacked more for the policy it executed than for its status as an agency. Between 1993 and 1997, nine commercially viable agencies were privatized, though agencies continued to be created and by 1999 over three-quarters of civil servants worked in one of them. *KMT*

Nicholas, Herbert Richard ('Harry') (1907–97), trade union official and Labour organizer. A right-wing TGWU official (assistant general secretary, 1956–68), many favoured him as the successor to the left-wing general secretary Frank Cousins. In the event he was drafted by the right of the party to replace Len Williams as Labour's own general secretary in what was regarded at the time as part of a plot to unseat the prime minister, Harold Wilson. The plot failed, Nicholas proved an obedient general secretary, 1968–72, and his absence allowed the left to keep control of the TGWU under Jack Jones. *BB*

Nicholson, Robin Buchanan (1934–), scientist and government adviser. Nicholson was appointed professor of metallurgy at the University of Manchester in 1966. He became director of research at Inco Europe Ltd. in 1972, and managing director, 1976–81. Appointed chief scientist in the *Central Policy Review Staff in 1981, he and his small team were kept on after the think-tank was abolished in 1983, Nicholson becoming chief scientific adviser to the Cabinet Office, 1983–5. *KT*

'Nicky'. See NATIONAL INCOMES COMMISSION.

Nicolson, Arthur (1849–1928), diplomat. Nicolson entered the Foreign Office in 1870 and his hitherto largely uneventful career took a turn when he found himself, by now ambassador at Madrid, Britain's representative at the Algeciras conference (1906). In his subsequent postings as ambassador at St Petersburg and permanent secretary at the Foreign Office, 1910–16, Nicolson worked steadily for a strengthening of Britain's ties with France and Russia in the face of German attempts to wreck the *ententes.* Although a skilful diplomat he was a poor administrator and perhaps not the most suitable choice for the post. He failed to establish the rapport with the foreign secretary, Sir Edward Grey, that his predecessor, Sir Charles Hardinge, had enjoyed. *TGO*

HAROLD NICOLSON, *Sir Arthur Nicolson, Bart, First Lord Carnock: A Study in the Old Diplomacy* (London, 1930).

Nicolson, Harold **(1886–1968)**, diplomat, politician, and author. On resigning from the diplomatic service and after a journalistic interlude, Nicolson turned to politics, briefly flirting with Mosley's New Party. He eventually entered parliament as a National Labour member (1935–45). He was a constant and bitter opponent of appeasement. His hopes for office remained unrequited, confined to a short spell at the Ministry of Information (1940–1), and he unsuccessfully contested a by-election in 1948 in the Labour interest. He remained active as a political commentator, but was relegated to the fringes of postwar politics: he was 'a nineteenth-century character... living an eighteenth century life in the midst of the twentieth century' (Sparrow, 6). *TGO*

NIGEL NICOLSON (ed.), *Harold Nicolson: Diaries and Letters, 1930–1968,* 3 vols. (London, 1966–8). | JOHN SPARROW, *Harold Nicolson and Vita-Sackville-West: An Address Delivered... at a Memorial Service at St. James's, Piccadilly, 16 May 1968* (London, 1968).

Nield, William Alan **(1913–1994)**, civil servant. Nield had an illustrious career following his initial work for the research and policy department of the Labour Party, 1937–9. During the war he served in the RAF, and was mentioned in despatches in 1944. His subsequent appointments included working for the Ministry of Food and the Ministry of Agriculture, Fisheries, and Food, 1949–64, and under-secretary for a succession of key departments. He came into the public spotlight as deputy chairman of Rolls Royce Ltd during the turbulent period of its reorganization 1973–6. *JFM*

Niemeyer, Otto **(1884–1971)**, one of the most influential figures in the world of high finance during the inter-war period. At the Treasury he was in charge of the finance and budget divisions from 1919 until his promotion to deputy controller and subsequently controller of finance, 1921–7. This position gave him responsibility for the technical control of national finances, including the management of the national debt, conversion operations, settlement of war debts, and currency. He is best remembered for influencing the government's decision to return to the *gold standard at pre-war parity. His memoranda indicate that he had a tendency to argue only one side of the case and would on occasions abandon argument for assertion. Niemeyer, while recognizing the deflationary implications of the return to gold, considered that the policy could be carried out without any major long-term effects on the economy. In 1922 he also became a member of the financial committee of the League of Nations, a position he occupied for more than fifteen years, becoming its chairman in 1927. In the same year he took the unprecedented step of moving to the Bank of England as controller, becoming a director, 1938–52. *JFM*

D. E. MOGGRIDGE, *British Monetary Policy* (Cambridge, 1972).

Nigeria debate (8 November 1916). A Commons debate on the disposal of captured German property in Nigeria provided the excuse for a backbench Tory rebellion, in which half the party's MPs voted against the Asquith coalition government (which nevertheless won the vote). The rebellion helped to persuade Law to begin the talks with Lloyd George that led a month later to Asquith's replacement as prime minister. *JAR*

'Night of the Long Knives' (12–13 July 1962), popular description (after the name of Hitler's 1934 purge of the brownshirts) of Macmillan's dismissal of seven cabinet ministers following a series of by-election defeats. Alarmed by angry reactions to his sacking of Selwyn *Lloyd, the chancellor, and by the leaking of his planned reshuffle, Macmillan hastily dismissed Hill, Kilmuir, Mills, Maclay, Watkinson, and Eccles—the last of whose hope of becoming chancellor was rebuffed. Having acted so cynically, Macmillan never recovered his image of unflappability. *RJS*

NIMBY, acronym of 'not in my back yard', coined in the 1980s to describe those who supported freedom in building and commercial development, but only if it was kept away from their own property. *JAR*

Nineteen Sixty-Eight. Britain, like the USA and most of Western Europe, experienced a sudden upsurge of radical activism in 1968, predominantly among university students and other young people of the same age group, in imitation especially of events in Paris and in America.

Long-running disputes led to such direct action as sit-ins and occupations at the LSE and the University of Essex, paralleled by less serious disturbances on other campuses. The immediate result was the adoption by most British universities of concessions to student demands in such areas as amenities and student representation on decision-making boards, but without much long-term impact on the way in which the universities actually functioned. Although there were more serious civil disorders in the streets of some cities, notably *riots in Grosvenor Square in London, chosen because it was the site of the American Embassy and demonstrators were protesting about the Vietnam war, the British experience of '1968' was relatively limited by comparison with violence in the USA and the worker-student solidarity which almost brought down the French government. Disillusionment with the radical hopes engendered by the return of the Wilson government in 1964 was one local cause of tension, as was Wilson's refusal to denounce American activities in Vietnam (he was equally staunch in refusing to join the war, but got little credit for this). Briefly, the renewed disappointment with the hopes engendered by 1968's radical activity produced a youth terrorist activity, the Angry Brigade, which bombed the houses of a number of cabinet ministers in 1970, and more generally the radical pop culture that surfaced angrily in 1968 remained part of the lives of that generation of young people for long after the 1960s, but British institutions weathered the storm with remarkably little real trouble. *JAR*

ARTHUR MARWICK, *The Sixties* (Oxford, 1998).

1922 Committee, the official forum of the Conservative parliamentary party. It was initially formed by new MPs elected at the 1922 general election, but developed by 1925 into a weekly gathering which all Conservative MPs except ministers could attend. Hence in opposition it contained all Conservative MPs, and when the party was in power only backbenchers, though ministers would attend on occasion to explain and defend their policies, and there would usually be a whip in attendance to report on parliamentary business in the week ahead. Its chairman and its executive committee, elected annually, thus became a significant channel for the transmission of backbench grievances and opinion, as for example when Edward *du Cann, a critic of Heath, was elected chairman during the Heath government and contributed to Heath's fall in 1975. It has also been the body that elected parliamentary representatives to National Union committees, the Standing Advisory Committee on Candidates, and the *Advisory Committee on Policy. Its officers conducted elections for the party leadership after 1965. Subcommittees dealing with specific policy areas were open to all interested MPs to attend, and elections for their officers were also conducted annually. On occasion, for example during the Suez crisis, its meetings could be stormy, but only rarely did information about them find its way into the media. *JAR*

STUART BALL, 'The 1922 Committee: The Formative Years', *Parliamentary History*, 9 (1990). | PHILIP GOODHART, *The 1922* (London, 1973).

'No, no, no!' Famous last words of Margaret Thatcher, ignoring a wiser text, on 30 October 1990, when responding to the suggestion of Jacques Delors that the European parliament should be the European Community's democratic body, the commission its executive, and the council its senate. She thereby provoked Geoffrey *Howe's resignation, and gave him the topic for his resignation speech. *EP*

Noble, Michael Alfred (1913–84), Conservative politician. Elected for Argyllshire in 1958, Noble won rapid promotion as a whip and in 1962 entered the cabinet as Scottish secretary. In opposition he was shadow Scottish secretary until 1969. Briefly president of the Board of Trade in 1970 before it was subsumed into the Department of Trade and Industry, he served as trade minister until 1972. He stood down in 1974, taking a life peerage as Lord Glenkinglas. *RJS*

Noel, Conrad le Despenser Roden (1869–1942), Anglican priest and social democrat. Noel, known as the 'red vicar of *Thaxted', was an active member of both church socialist groups and socialist organizations, such as the Social Democratic Federation. In 1910 he was offered a living by the 'red' duchess of Warwick, which he occupied until 1942. He wrote eighteen books and many articles on the Christian Socialist revival in Britain. *KL*

R. GROVES, *Conrad Noel and the Thaxted Movement* (London, 1967).

Noel-Baker, Philip (1889–1982), peace campaigner and Labour politician. Noel-Baker was a lifelong advocate of pacifism and multilateral disarmament. His major work, *The Arms Race: A Programme for World Disarmament* (1958), earned him the Nobel peace prize in 1959 but his uncompromising beliefs prevented him from achieving the highest offices. An Olympic athlete himself, he fervently believed in the value of sport for promoting international understanding and founded the International Council for Sport and Physical Recreation. *MC*

Nolan, Michael Patrick (1928–), judge. Nolan was a lord of appeal from 1994, and the first chairman of the committee on standards in public life. He began as a tax specialist (QC, 1968). A tall, modest, devout Catholic layman of great presence and charm, Lord Nolan helped create and enhance a sustained sensitivity towards political and public service values in the aftermath of a wave of sleaze scandals and allegations in the early 1990s. Commissioned by John Major in 1994 to set up an 'ethical workshop', the initial impact of his first report (and the continuation of his work by Lord Neill of Bladen (see Neill report)) ensured that Nolan's name would remain indistinguishable from the concept of ethics in public life. *PJH*

Nolan report (1995). The Nolan committee was established in October 1994 to monitor standards in public life following scandals over MPs taking cash for asking parliamentary questions. With seven principles of propriety as its basis the report advocated a parliamentary commissioner and select committee for public standards. It recommended codes on extra-parliamentary remuneration for MPs and the behaviour of senior executives of NHS bodies and hived-off government agencies. These recommendations were fulfilled, though, with more flexibility than originally suggested. *KMT*

Nonconformist conscience, term coined at the time of the campaign led by the Methodist minister Hugh Price Hughes against the adulterous Irish politician Charles Stewart Parnell in 1890. In the wake of the franchise reform of 1867, even as Nonconformist disabilities were dismantled through legislation such as the 1881 Burials Act, the public persona of the Free Churches came to be characterized by a pugnacious defence of their own interests and righteousness. It has been argued that much of this simply reflected social aggression by groups hitherto marginalized in English society, who suddenly found themselves able to flex their muscles. It reached a crescendo with the passive resistance against the 1902 Education Act, which was felt to have discriminated against Nonconformity by providing public support for Anglican Church schools. In spite of the difficulties the Asquith government then had in attempting to amend the 1902 legislation, the Nonconformist conscience was already in decline by 1914. Political issues changed, with education becoming less contentious. The Great War encouraged ecumenism and changed Nonconformity's relationship with the state and the established Church. By 1938 Lloyd George, whose 1934–5 Council of Action for Peace and Reconstruction has been portrayed by Stephen Koss as its last hurrah, was teasing that these changes had killed the Nonconformist conscience. In the inter-war years, the Free Churches moved to a more professional and less strident form of social witness. Perhaps the clearest sign of the Nonconformist conscience's decline, however, was that the charge of adultery may have done for Parnell, but was never used against someone seen as one of their own, Lloyd George himself. *PPC*

D. W. Bebbington, *The Nonconformist Conscience: Chapel and Politics 1870–1914* (London, 1982). | Stephen Koss, *Nonconformity in Modern British Politics* (London, 1975).

Nonconformity, collective term for non-Anglican Protestant denominations, including Methodists, Congregationalists, Baptists, Presbyterians, Quakers, Unitarians, and Pentecostalists. Their traditional witness for civic liberty against the religious disabilities they suffered had, by the late 19th century, aligned much of Nonconformity with the Liberals. This relationship peaked during the Nonconformist agitation against the 1902 Education Act. Through campaigning and by greatly increasing the number of seats contested by Liberals, Nonconformity assisted the 1906 landslide. It also helped the Liberals to find suitable candidates to defend free trade in 1923. By then, however, political Nonconformity was atrophying. The historic disabilities had largely been removed by 1900, whilst the tag 'Nonconformity' was increasingly replaced by the more positive label of 'Free Churches'. Welsh disestablishment in 1920 ended the main remaining grievance and took the force out of political Nonconformity in Wales. Meanwhile, new political issues altered the traditional Liberal allegiance. Opposition to home rule had already encouraged some Free Church Unionism. Subsequently patriotism and fear of inter-war class conflict was skilfully played on by Conservative leader Stanley Baldwin to draw Free Churchmen to his banner. Others, however, felt that having gained civic liberty they should now pursue economic liberty through Labour. In the inter-war years, a growing number of leading Nonconformist ministers supported Labour, and Nonconformist MPs were well represented in the Liberal and Labour parties. In the 1950s Labour's general secretary Morgan Phillips, himself a Methodist, avowed that the Labour Party 'owed more to Methodism than it did to Marx'. The number of Free Church MPs was, however, to decline rapidly in the post-war years. Furthermore, *pace* Phillips, come the 1980s most of them were in the Conservative Party, when another Methodist, Margaret Thatcher, was to see the Nonconformist virtues of liberty and individual responsibility in rather different ways.

PPC

non-proliferation treaties. Preventing the spread of nuclear weapons to non-nuclear states through arms control agreements has been an enduring concern of the atomic age. The first agreement, the treaty of Tlateloco (1968), was regional in focus and aimed to prevent the nuclearization of Latin America. The most significant agreement, however, the treaty on the non-proliferation of nuclear weapons (NPT), also of 1968, was universal in application. Agreed between the USA, UK, and USSR, it was an attempt to prevent nuclear powers sharing their weapons technology with allies, something both superpowers feared. Although signed by most of the world's states, its significance was blunted by those states which did not sign. Significantly, both China and France, which had already developed nuclear weapons, refused to accede. Similarly, many states considered likely to develop nuclear weapons (Argentina, Brazil, India, Israel, Spain, South Africa, and Pakistan) refused to sign. Other states who did sign, moreover, such as North Korea and Iraq, ignored the treaty in developing their own nuclear weapons programmes. In exchange for agreeing to nuclear abstinence, the non-nuclear weapons states were promised two reciprocal incentives. First, the nuclear powers would prevent further nuclear proliferation in the size of their own arsenals. While the superpowers simultaneously announced the start of *SALT, progress on this pledge was slow to materialize, Second, access was promised to civil nuclear technology, the peaceful use of which would be verified through the International Atomic Energy Agency. Signed initially for 25 years, at the review and extension conference in 1995 it was agreed that the treaty regime should continue indefinitely. Although recognized as imperfect, the NPT regime has contributed to the international norm of non-proliferation and since its inception the number of nuclear states has grown less rapidly than expected. *DHD*

Norman, Montagu Collet (1871–1950), long-time governor of the Bank of England. Norman, a director of the Bank since 1907, assisted the deputy governor during the Great War before being elected deputy governor in 1918 and governor in 1920. He thereupon transformed what had been a two-year part-time turn for senior directors into a full-time, permanent post by concentrating authority in his own hands and greatly extending the Bank's activities. Convinced that private enterprise could be safeguarded from socialist encroachment only by interposing the discipline of the gold standard, he worked indefatigably for its restoration at home and abroad. By 1926 the edifice seemed almost complete, but fissures soon appeared which he was helpless to repair. Britain no longer earned enough abroad to enable the Bank to act as international lender of last resort. Nor, despite his affinity with America, could he persuade US statesmen to coordinate policy with Europe. Persisting, he drew the Bank into the rationalization of British export industries, and went so far as to withhold support for the pound in order to bounce British governments into retrenchment. An intensely private man and prone to nervous illness, he acquired an aura of mystery by his Mephistophelean appearance and attempts to travel incognito under an assumed name; and despite his ostensible disdain for publicity, he carefully cultivated members of the press. He was abroad recovering from a nervous breakdown when Britain abandoned the gold standard in September 1931. He remained at the Bank for another thirteen years, but with monetary policy shifted to the Treasury his influence diminished along with the aura that surrounded him.

RWDB

Robert Boyce, *British Capitalism at the Crossroads, 1919–1932: A Study in Politics, Economics and International Relations* (Cambridge, 1987). | Andrew Boyle, *Montagu Norman: A Biography* (London, 1967).

North Atlantic Treaty Organization. See NATO.

Northcliffe, Viscount (1865–1922), newspaper and magazine publisher. More than anyone, Northcliffe (born Alfred Harmsworth) shaped the modern press. Developments he introduced or harnessed remain central: broad contents, exploitation of advertising revenue to subsidize prices, aggressive marketing, subordinate regional markets, independence from party control. In a newspaper world without electronic competition, Northcliffe controlled a larger proportion of total circulation than anyone since. After making capital from children's magazines and a trivia magazine, *Answers* (1888), and from reviving the London *Evening News* (1894), he set new standards of value for money with his *Daily Mail*—launched in 1896 as 'a penny newspaper for one halfpenny'. By force of personality and marketing flair (competitions, the '*Daily Mail* loaf', the Ideal Home Exhibition), he outreached competitors. He bought and modernized *The Times* in 1908. Too much a populist to be a good party man, he never commanded serious political office. *CKSU*

P. P. Catterall, Colin Seymour-Ure, and Adrian Smith (eds.), *Northcliffe's Legacy* (Oxford, 2000). | S. J. Taylor, *The Great Outsiders* (London, 1996).

Northern Ireland assembly (1974), established by the Northern Ireland Constitution Act 1973, with a power-sharing executive of protestants and Catholics. Opposition to the Council of Ireland contained in the *Sunningdale agreement of 1973 sealed the assembly's fate, after the Ulster Unionist Council split. The February 1974 general election saw anti-Sunningdale Unionists win eleven of Northern Ireland's twelve parliamentary seats, though with only 51.1 per cent of the votes (pro-Sunningdale Unionists polled only 13.1 per cent of the votes). In March 1974, the Ulster Workers' Council, a new Loyalist workers' group, called for a general stoppage, which began with power cuts and the closure of factories. The executive collapsed when Brian Faulkner resigned as chief executive of the assembly on the grounds that the degree of consent required to support the executive no longer existed. *TWH*

Brigid Hadfield, *The Constitution of Northern Ireland* (Belfast, 1989).

Northern Ireland Civil Rights Association (NICRA), organization, founded in January 1967, embracing a range of groups and individuals, which sought to secure political and social reform within the context of Northern Ireland. At the outset the NICRA had no active politicians involved and instead looked for inspiration to the apparent success of the peaceful and non-violent campaign by African-Americans to obtain basic human rights for their community. Abandoning the anti-partition approach which had characterized previous attempts to bring to a wider audience the problems faced by the minority community in Northern Ireland, the decision was taken to try to secure 'British rights for British citizens'. With the assistance of non-political organizations in Great Britain, such as the National Council for Civil Liberties, it sought to win a substantial reform package from the authorities at Stormont. This campaign, which involved an effective publicity campaign and marches, brought some success in securing reforms. Attempts to maintain peaceful protests were unsuccessful, however, because of the conflict between those taking part and not only the Royal Ulster Constabulary but also counter-demonstrators who believed the movement was under the control of republican elements. As a result of these clashes, culminating with major disturbances in Derry on 5 October 1968, the members of NICRA began to move in different directions. Those who sought to keep their efforts non-violent withdrew and as a result the organization itself became embroiled in the growing paramilitary unrest after 1969. *BL*

Northern Ireland Constitution Act, 1973. This was passed by the British parliament following the proroguing of the Northern Ireland parliament in 1972 and provided for the holding of elections to a unicameral Northern Ireland assembly elected by proportional representation. Section 1 of the Act, known as the 'constitutional guarantee', defined Northern Ireland as the unit of self-determination which would decide if Northern Ireland was to remain within the United Kingdom: 'It is hereby declared that Northern Ireland remains part of Her Majesty's dominions and of the United Kingdom, and it is hereby affirmed that in no event will Northern Ireland or any part of it cease to be part of Her Majesty's dominions and of the United Kingdom without the consent of the majority of the people of Northern Ireland voting in a poll held for the purposes of this section'. The Act established a Northern Ireland power-sharing executive presided over by a 'chief executive member'. Northern Ireland's Unionists and Nationalists would have to share political power in a cabinet. *TWH*

Brigid Hadfield, *The Constitution of Northern Ireland* (Belfast, 1989).

Northern Ireland Constitutional Convention, created by the Northern Ireland secretary, Merlyn Rees, in 1975, for all constitutional parties and aimed at producing a broad, intercommunal support for a settlement. The agenda was deliberately kept open, in contrast to the rigid method used in the *Sunningdale agreement that preceded the ill-fated power-sharing experiment of 1974. The United Ulster Unionist Council, a hard-line coalition, won 55 per cent of the vote in the May 1975 elections, and favoured

the restoration of Stormont. Unsurprisingly, the draft report of the convention in November 1975 proposed a return to majority (Unionist) rule, and ignored the nationalist demand for an 'Irish dimension' (cross-border links with the Republic of Ireland). The nationalist Social Democratic and Labour Party found this unacceptable, as did Westminster, and the search for a settlement in Northern Ireland lay dormant for some time.
DGB

Paul Bew and Gordon Gillespie (eds.), *Northern Ireland: Chronology of the Troubles, 1968–1993* (Dublin, 1993).

Northern Ireland Nationalist Party. In the years after partition until the emergence of the civil rights movement, the Nationalist Party was widely regarded as the main political representative of the minority community in Northern Ireland. This apparent position of strength, however, masked a series of problems which were ultimately to lead to its demise in the late 1960s. To begin with, it lacked any real organization and structure with individual MPs only coordinating their activity in the Stormont parliament, where a leader emerged to give the party a figurehead of sorts. The most prominent to assume this title were the veteran Nationalist politician Joe *Devlin up until his death in 1934 and Eddie McAteer who held the position from 1962 to 1969. Furthermore, the party was forced to operate during an era in which the Unionist domination at Stormont was seemingly unchallengeable and when opinion outside Northern Ireland was to show little interest in the alleged mistreatment that Northern Nationalists had to endure. Initiatives such as the decision to accept the title of Official Opposition in 1965 brought little reward, and the party had little to show for its efforts. As a result, the party was unable to match the vigorous and strident approach of the civil rights movement. In the end, the party failed to survive the political turmoil of 1969 and was eventually supplanted by the establishment of the *Social Democratic and Labour Party in 1970.
BL

Brendan Lynn, *Holding the Ground: The Nationalist Party in Northern Ireland, 1945–1972* (Aldershot, 1997).

Northern Ireland Office (NIO). The 1920 Government of Ireland Act which partitioned Ireland provided for a devolved government in Belfast, with authority over most internal matters. This arrangement lasted until 1972 when four years of violence prompted the prime minister, Edward Heath, to abolish it. Self-government for the province was replaced by direct rule from Westminster, a move which necessitated the creation of the security-orientated NIO. After several abortive attempts (notably 1974 and 1982), moves to a political settlement of the troubles led to the signing of the Good Friday agreement in 1998. This provided for a new Northern Ireland assembly which was elected in June 1998 with power devolved to this assembly along with its institutions in December 1999. The new assembly took over most of the NIO's functions.
JD

Peter Hennessy, *Whitehall* (London, 1989). | Northern Ireland Office website: *www.nio.gov.uk*

Northern Ireland parliament and parliamentary assemblies. The Northern Ireland parliament was established under the Government of Ireland Act, 1920. While empowered to deal with a wide range of internal affairs, the parliament, consisting of an elected 52-member house of commons and a 26-member senate, remained subject to the sovereign parliament at Westminster which also retained certain legislative powers. From 1921 to 1932 the Northern Ireland parliament met in different buildings until November 1932 when it became permanently based in the new Parliament Buildings, Stormont, Belfast. A system of proportional representation was used for elections to the parliament during the period 1921–8, after which the *first past the post system prevailed. Following extensive civil disturbances the Northern Ireland parliament was prorogued in 1972 and abolished in 1973. The Northern Ireland assembly, elected by proportional representation, was established in May 1973. With a *power-sharing executive, it ran until it was prorogued in May 1974 and then dissolved in March 1975. A *Northern Ireland Constitutional Convention, similar to the Northern Ireland assembly in number of seats and manner of election, sat between May 1975 and March 1976. A new Northern Ireland assembly was established in 1982 and continued in existence until 1986. This assembly failed to elect an executive but exercised influence on government departments through a number of assembly committees.
BMW

C. J. Woods, 'Parliament and Parliamentary Assemblies of Northern Ireland, 1921–1968', in T. W. Moody et al. (eds.), *A New History of Ireland*, vol. 9 (Oxford, 1984).

Northern Ireland (Temporary Provisions) Act, 1972 (30 March), resulted in the prorogation of the Northern Ireland parliament for a year. Under the same Act, by means of a statutory instrument of March 1973, it was prorogued for a second year. Finally the parliament was abolished as a result of the *Northern Ireland Constitution Act, 1973, which received royal assent on 18 July 1973. *BMW*

North Sea oil and gas. The exploitation of natural gas and oil on the UK continental shelf began in 1964. Early discoveries were of gas fields, but between 1967 and 1974 eighteen oilfields were located. The first oil was piped ashore in 1975. Ten years later, daily deliveries amounted to 2.65 million barrels, so that by that time the UK was self-sufficient in oil and the world's fifth largest producer. Governmental interest was registered at the inception of exploration. During the 1980s, however, institutional agencies were sold off as part of the Conservative government's privatization programme. The impact of North Sea oil on the economy as a whole provoked substantial debate among economists, with a majority pointing to the deleterious effects on manufacturing competitiveness as sterling aspired to the status of a petro-currency. The bulk of government oil revenues were used to reduce fiscal deficits and to pay back part of the national debt. *MWK*

T. S. Barker and V. Brailovstiy (eds.), *Energy, Industrialisation and Economic Policy* (London, 1981). | Department of Energy, *Development of the Oil and Gas Reserves of the United Kingdom* (London, 1983).

north–south divide, term denoting two types of division between the north of England and the south. One division is economic, the south of England being more prosperous than the north. The 'south' of England in this context is a fairly constricted part of the country, principally the south-east. The other division is political, seats in the south of England returning mostly Conservative MPs and seats in the north returning mostly Labour MPs. The dividing line between north and south in this context is a line drawn from the River Severn in the south-west to the Wash in the east. The regional divide is essentially a long-standing one, dating back at least to 1918, but has become more pronounced in the latter half the century. According to research by John Curtice and Michael Steed, the cleavage became marked in the period 1955–9. One explanation for the divide has been the greater concentration of working-class voters in northern constituencies, but the divide remains even when class is held constant. Research by R. J. Johnston and his associates suggests that the divide is linked to spatial variations in voter economic satisfaction and optimism. However, the concept has to be treated with caution. The electoral system exacerbates party leads in each region and in certain parts of the south the Conservative Party is under greater threat from the Liberal Democrats than from the Labour Party. In the 1980s, the Conservative Party made inroads into traditional Labour support: in the 1983 election it actually won a majority of seats in the north (130 as against 119 for Labour). In the 1997 election, Labour made inroads into Conservative support in the south, the greatest swing to Labour taking place in the Conservative Party's traditional heartland. However, what support the Conservatives did retain in 1997 in terms of parliamentary seats was heavily concentrated in the south of England. *PN*

John Curtice and Michael Steed, 'Electoral Choice and the Production of Government', *British Journal of Political Science*, 12 (1982). | Anthony Heath et al. (eds.), *Understanding Political Change* (London, 1991). | R. W. Johnston, C. J. Pattie, and J. G. Allsop, *A Nation Dividing?* (London, 1988). | Richard Rose, 'Britain: Simple Abstractions and Complex Realities', in his (ed.), *Electoral Behaviour* (New York, 1974).

Norway debate (7–8 May 1940), Commons debate that precipitated the fall of Neville Chamberlain's wartime administration. Conservative MPs, especially younger backbenchers on military service, vented their frustration with the conduct of the war after military reverses in Finland and Norway by adverse votes and abstentions. When Labour forced a vote of confidence, Chamberlain appealed to his 'many friends', but with a majority reduced from over 200 to 81 he felt obliged to try to bring Labour into his administration and, when they refused, had to resign. *NJC*

Norwood report, education report of 1943, entitled *Curriculum and Examinations in Secondary Schools*, which rationalized the concept of a tripartite system of secondary education with separate grammar, technical, and modern schools for different types of 'child mind'. The report underpinned the division of secondary education in the *Education Act, 1944. *JAR*

'no such thing as society, There is'. Margaret Thatcher said this in the early 1980s in response to wearisome use of the claims of 'society' by opponents. It was an assertion of individual rights, and an attempt to point out that only the members of society had tax resources to pay for social policies, but was seen as (or twisted into) contempt for care and community. *EP*

'Not a penny off the pay, not a second on the day', slogan of the miners in the run-up to the General Strike. Coal owners were demanding wage cuts and longer working hours in 1925. A. J. Cook, secretary of the mineworkers, coined this phrase to sum up the miners' uncompromising response. *BB*

Nott, John William Frederick (1932–), Conservative politician. Remembered as defence secretary (1982) whose economies withdrew a warship from Falkland waters (and sent the wrong signal to Argentina), though following collective responsibility. He had been an effective Treasury minister, 1972–4, sympathetic to the premier's economic views, but this former Gurkha officer was now required to fall on his own curly knife after the islands had been recovered. Nott, taking responsibility for failure, was denied credit as a member of the war cabinet for winning back the lost ground (see FALKLANDS WAR). *EP*

Notting Hill carnival (1957–). Held in late August in the Notting Hill district of London, an area of substantial Afro-Caribbean immigration, the Notting Hill carnival has become the largest street spectacle in Britain. In its early years it occasioned some violence between police and local people and it is now highly organized and policed, although relatively peaceful in recent years. *JS*

No Turning Back, political ginger group and dining club. In Margaret Thatcher's early days, when opposition made her policy and position seem insecure, younger right-wingers established this dining club for the like-minded. It included Peter Lilley, Francis Maude, and Neil Hamilton, affirming the premier personally and attracting both believers and later on the career-minded, part of the process by which a right-wing faction would (after Thatcher's fall, ruinously) organize for its domination of Conservatism. *EP*

Novar, Viscount (1860–1934). A noted Liberal Imperialist in Edwardian Scotland, Ronald Munro-Ferguson was MP for Ross and Cromarty, 1884–5, and for Leith, 1886–1914. He was private secretary to his mentor Lord Rosebery at the Foreign Office and his interest in imperial affairs led to his appointment as governor-general of Australia in 1914, a post he held until 1920. Always to the right of the Liberal Party, Viscount Novar (ennobled 1920) was considered a safe pair of hands by Law and Baldwin who made him Scottish secretary, 1922–4. *RF*

nuclear weapons. Developed jointly by British and American scientists during the Second World War as part of 'the Manhattan project', nuclear weapons came to dominate the military strategy of the Cold War. As part of *NATO, Britain hosted American nuclear forces and contributed to the deterrence of the Soviet Union with its own nuclear forces. Britain's own weapons were developed independently after further collaboration with the USA was prevented by the McMahon Act of 1946. Britain tested its first atomic bomb in 1948 and a hydrogen bomb in 1955. Long-range delivery of these weapons was provided for by the introduction of the V-bomber force in 1955 (mainly Vulcan bombers). In 1960, development of Britain's own land-based missile, *Blue Streak, was cancelled due to its mounting cost and its potential vulnerability to enemy attack. In 1962, though, Harold Macmillan negotiated the purchase from the USA of *Polaris submarine-launched ballistic missiles, and the first four Polaris submarines (each carrying sixteen missiles) entered service in 1968. The number of warheads per missile was reduced from three to two in the 1970s, as part of the Chevaline project which upgraded British warheads against enemy defences. Between 1994 and 1998, four Trident (D5) submarines were launched, replacing the obsolescent Polaris fleet. The decision to procure Trident, taken in 1981, was extremely controversial, being opposed by both the Labour Party and the Campaign for Nuclear Disarmament, on economic, ethical, and credibility grounds.

These strategic systems, while notionally at the disposal of NATO, also constituted Britain's independent nuclear deterrent. During the Cold War, Britain's strategy involved the maintenance of its capability to destroy the Soviet capital ('the Moscow criterion') as a deterrent against attacks on Britain. In the post-Soviet period, these systems have been justified as an insurance against the uncertainties of unforeseen and future threats.

During the Cold War, the UK also deployed its own tactical nuclear weapons, such as naval nuclear depth charges and the RAF's free-fall bombs. It also operated American short-range missiles, such as Lance, for battlefield use. With the end of the Cold War, however, all British tactical systems were withdrawn and the UK's total stockpile of operationally available nuclear weapons reduced to fewer than 200, all assigned to the Trident fleet. This was a reduction of more than 70 per cent in the explosive power of the stockpile since the Cold War ended. For the critics, however, this was still too many in the absence of any credible nuclear threat to the UK. *DHD*

Nuffield College, Oxford postgraduate social science college and research institute. It was founded in 1937, on the only remaining site in central Oxford (the disused canal basin), and endowed by William Morris, Lord Nuffield, the founder of Morris Motors and one of Oxford University's greatest ever benefactors. Morris had originally wanted to endow a college for engineering, but was reluctantly persuaded to turn it over to social science. The buildings were designed (to Morris's taste) before 1939, but built mostly in the 1950s. Nuffield is best known to students of politics for the research of David Butler and his successors on British elections and voting behaviour. It has also hosted important studies of industrial relations, social mobility, and econometrics. Lord Nuffield separately endowed the Nuffield foundation, which funds social science research, and is best known for having funded studies of the school curriculum, hence such terms as 'Nuffield science'. College and foundation have no connection, but 'Nuffield-funded' research from both endowments has been extremely important to understanding 20th-century Britain. *IM*

Nuffield College Election Studies. See Butler, David Edgeworth.

Nuremburg and Tokyo war trials. The Second World War resulted in 50 million casualties and suffering and misery on an unimaginable scale, one of the great horrors of the war being the fact that so many atrocities were carried out against both combatants and civilians. Japanese aggression led to 50 million Chinese losing their homes and 2 million being orphaned. The Russians lost about 3 million soldiers in German camps, where, as racial and political enemies and 'inferiors', they were not accorded any status. Seven million Russian civilians lost their lives, as did 6 million Poles, nearly half of them Jews, and 6 million Jews in total. Such a catalogue of horrors, inflicted deliberately and outside battle, demanded a response from the Allied governments, and at the end of the war they conducted war crimes trials. These were criticized for being conducted only by the victors and for punishing acts not rated illegal before the trials. In fact, the trials led to a comprehensive review of war crimes and the definition of new ones, made necessary by the fact that Japan and Germany in particular had carried out such shocking atrocities on conquered peoples and prisoners of war. The new term 'genocide' was coined in order to give the destruction of subject peoples a legal definition.

Trials of Nazi leaders began in Nuremburg in November 1945 and ended in October 1946. Twenty-one defendants were tried (Martin Borman in his absence) and five corporate bodies: the Reich cabinet, the leadership corps of the Nazi Party, the SS and Brownshirt units, the Gestapo, and the general staff. The charges laid against these individuals and bodies were one, or all, of the following: crimes against peace, war crimes, crimes against humanity. Two were acquitted, eight sentenced to prison terms, and eleven condemned to death. Hermann Goering avoided the hangman by taking poison on the eve of his execution but Kaltenbrunner (head of the SS following Himmler's suicide in the bunker), Frank, Rosenberg, Seyss-Inquart, Sauckel, Keitel, Jodl, Ribbentrop, Frick, and Streicher were all put to death.

The trials did not end with the sentencing of these high-profile cases. A series of lesser war criminals were also put on trial, resulting in a further 24 executions, 114 imprisonments, and 35 acquittals. Later, other war criminals were tried and sentenced in national courts of countries where (or against whom) they had committed their offences. Nuremburg set the precedent for the Tokyo war trials. The Allies arrested over 5,000 Japanese suspected of war crimes in their campaigns against the Allies, in China, and against subject peoples. The major cases were brought against 25 Japanese leaders, of whom seven were condemned to death, including Tojo, the former prime minister, and his successor Koiso. Konoye avoided this fate by taking poison. A further 900 were executed by the Allies, mainly for mistreatment of prisoners of war. *MLC*

Werner Maser, *Nuremburg: A Nation on Trial* (London, 1979). | Bernard Rowling, *The Tokyo Trial and Beyond* (London, 1993).

nursery schools. Private pre-school education has existed in Britain for many years. But, although advocated by many educational reformers as a necessary way of improving educational attainment and eradicating social disadvantages amongst deprived groups, it was only in the last two decades of the century that serious attempts were made to provide state support for nursery education. In 1995, the Conservative government introduced a voucher scheme to help parents pay for nursery education or childcare. In turn, Labour in 1998 launched a campaign to ensure free early education, at least part-time, for all 4-year-olds in England and Wales and to increase the percentage of 3-year-olds with free nursery education from 34 per cent in 1997 to 66 per cent by 2002. *JS*

Nutting, (Harold) Anthony (1920–99). Conservative politician. Elected in 1945, Nutting was a protégé of Eden's and in 1951 became his deputy at the Foreign Office. In 1956, however, he opposed Eden's policy over the *Suez crisis and resigned. Dissuaded from making the traditional resignation statement by Macmillan, who feared that it could bring down the government, Nutting kept quiet about 'collusion' with Israel for ten years. Dumped by his constituency association, he quit the Commons. *RJS*

Anthony Nutting, *No End of a Lesson: The Story of Suez* (London, 1967).

NUWM. See National Unemployed Workers' Movement.

Oakeshott, Michael (1901–90), political theorist. Oakeshott is best known for a collection of essays, *Rationalism in Politics* (1962), which is perhaps the most important work of conservative political philosophy written in the 20th century by someone born in Britain. He taught in Cambridge for many years, briefly in Oxford, and was professor of political science at the LSE from 1951 until he retired. His major philosophical treatise is *Experience and its Modes* (1933), and his edition of Hobbes's *Leviathan* (1946) was long admired. Many of his lectures have been published posthumously. At the heart of Oakeshott's political philosophy is the conviction that politics is an art not a science. Abstract reasoning and theoretical analysis cannot tell one what will work in politics, because politicians must work with existing traditions, practices, and prejudices. Politics, unlike chemistry or grammar, cannot be reduced to rules; but it does require expertise, which must be acquired through apprenticeship. Rationalists, in Oakeshott's understanding, are those who deny tradition and experience their proper place, and faith in rationalism leads to ideologies such as liberalism, socialism, and laissez-faire economics. In place of such ideologies, he offers a vision of politics as 'the pursuit of intimations; a conversation, not an argument'. Oakeshott advocates a conservative disposition or temperament in politics. The objectives of government must be limited: 'to restrain, to deflate, to pacify and to reconcile; not to stoke the fires of desire, but to damp them down'. Conservatism in government, he maintains, is compatible with radicalism in almost every other activity: thus he prefers Hobbes and Hume to Burke. *DRW*

Observer, newspaper. By 1900 the *Observer*, founded in 1791 and the world's oldest Sunday paper, was edited by Rachel Beer, co-owner with her husband. In 1905 Lord Northcliffe salvaged it when at a low ebb. He installed as editor in 1908 the independent-minded J. L. *Garvin who became famous for his five-column editorials, took circulation to 200,000 by the Great War, and stayed with the paper under Astor family ownership (from 1915) until 1942. As owner-editor, 1948–75, David Astor gave the paper a radical tinge, but lost advertising by opposing the 1956 Suez invasion: circulation slipped far behind the rival *Sunday Times*. Succeeding owners, a Californian oil company (1976) and the Lonrho conglomerate run by maverick Tiny Rowland (1981), did not stabilize the business. In 1993 the paper was sold to the Scott Trust and became the Sunday partner of the *Guardian*. At an unprofitable 400,000, circulation had halved to its 1950 level. *CKSU*

ODA. See INTERNATIONAL DEVELOPMENT, DEPARTMENT OF; OVERSEAS AID POLICY.

O'Donnell, Augustine Thomas (1952–), prime minister's press secretary, 1990–4. A Treasury economist who became chancellor Nigel Lawson's press secretary, Gus O'Donnell then served Lawson's successor, John Major. O'Donnell had a good relationship with Major, who took him to Downing Street on becoming prime minister. Instructed to maintain a lower profile than his predecessor, Bernard Ingham, and arguably too amiable with the press, O'Donnell was criticized for allowing Major to be too open, but few press secretaries have had a tougher task. *CL*

Official Secrets Act, 1911. The foundation of secrecy legislation for most of the century, this Act was rushed through parliament on a single afternoon, when the 1911 *Moroccan crisis seemed to threaten war, and was thus a part, along with the development of the *Secret Service Bureau, of planning for the Great War. The 1911 Act tightened up and made explicit powers contained in previous legislation of 1889, but its notorious section 2 provided a blanket ban on any public servant releasing without authority (which the Act made it difficult to give anyway) any information that came into his possession in the course of official duties. Civil servants were on appointment or transfer obliged to read and sign relevant parts of the Act, even if they were working in lowly positions where information of sensitivity or significance never came. The 1911 Act, which remained broadly in force until the interest in *freedom of information and support for *whistleblowing made it no longer sustainable in and after the 1980s, fostered a 'culture of secrecy' in British government. By the 1980s, indeed, it was generally thought that the 1911 Act and its successors had done more to protect civil servants and their political masters from the revelation of their errors and misjudgements than it had ever done for national security. *JAR*

Ofsted, Ofwat, and other regulatory bodies. The need for continued public sector regulation after the mass privatizations of the 1980s, along with increasing pressure for ever higher standards in the remaining public sector, led to the creation of several new regulatory offices in the 1980s and 1990s. Oftel, the regulator for the telecommunications industry, was created under the Telecommunications Act, 1984. The main way Oftel regulates is through monitoring, enforcing, and initiating modifications to telecommunications licences. The office of gas supply, Ofgas, was set up under the Gas Act, 1986, to regulate British Gas, the newly privatized monopoly supplier, and to promote competitive pricing to industrial customers. Under the amended Gas Act, 1995, domestic customers are also now protected. By the late 1990s, British Gas was in many areas no longer the monopoly supplier of gas and Ofgas became the body which issued licences to the new gas suppliers. Offer, the office of electricity regulation, began in 1990 following the Electricity Act, 1990. Offer encouraged competition in the electricity market and, where this was unforthcoming, laid down rules whereby electricity prices were tagged to the level of inflation. Ofgas and Offer were combined in 1999 with the creation of Ofgem, the Office of Gas and Electricity Markets.

The privatization of the water industry heralded the establishment of the Office of Water Services, Ofwat, in 1989 under the Water Act (superseded by the Water Industry Act, 1991). The aim of the office is to regulate the water and sewerage companies in order to provide fair pricing. The Office for Standards in Education (Ofsted) was set up in 1992. Officially the office of Her Majesty's chief inspector of schools in England, it is a non-ministerial government department independent of the Department for Education. Its remit is to improve standards in schools through regular inspection and public reporting. Another organization, the Office of the National Lottery (Oflot), was created in 1993. It regulates the lottery for fairness and propriety and seeks to maximize the funds given to good causes, attracting considerable public exposure and the resignation of its chairperson in 2000 over the allocation of a lottery contract. *JD*

Oftel website: *www.oftel.gov.uk* | Ofgem website: *www.ofgem.gov.uk* | Ofwat website: *www.open.gov.uk/ofwat* | Ofsted website: *www.ofsted.gov.uk* | Oflot website: *www.national-lottery.co.uk/inform/oflot.html*

oil crisis (1973). The outbreak of the Arab-Israeli Yom Kippur war in October 1973 had a number of consequences for Britain and the Heath government. First, the threatened OPEC oil embargo divided the members of the European Community (EC) over how to respond. Britain (and France), by denying the US facilities to fly military equipment to Israel and suspending military supplies to both sides, managed to ensure uninterrupted, though reduced, oil supplies during the war, but not all EC countries were so lucky. Nevertheless, the shortage proved manageable, and the coupons prepared for petrol rationing did not have to be used. Second, the temporary shortage of oil during the war was followed by a quadrupling of the price in the immediate aftermath. Third, quite apart from its impact on British industry and the government's inflation strategy, this increased Britain's reliance on coal for its energy needs at a time when the miners were gearing up for a renewed pay dispute. To conserve energy supplies a state of emergency was declared in November, public expenditure cuts were made in December, and the *three-day week introduced in January 1974. The need for a fresh mandate to deal with the consequences of the oil shock played a key role in Heath's fatal decision to call the February 1974 election. *PPC*

Oldfield, Maurice (1915–81), chief of Secret Intelligence Service (SIS). Born in Derbyshire, Maurice Oldfield was educated locally before winning a scholarship to Manchester University. He graduated in 1938 with a first in history and was elected to a fellowship. During the Second World War, Oldfield joined the intelligence corps, spending much of his time in Cairo with Security Intelligence Middle East (SIME). He ended the war a lieutenant-colonel and joined SIS as deputy head of counter-intelligence. In the early 1950s, Oldfield spent time in Singapore, first as deputy then head of SIS's regional headquarters for south-east Asia and the Far East. Between 1959 and 1964, he was SIS representative to Washington DC, with the task of building relations with the CIA. He enjoyed excellent relations with James Angleton, the head of the CIA counter-intelligence branch, which was based in part on their joint interest in medieval history. Back in London, Oldfield became first deputy head of SIS and then in 1973 head. He was the first head of SIS to cultivate the press and, until his retirement in 1978, developed good relations with both Labour and Conservative ministers and with overseas intelligence agencies. He retired weighed down with honours. The following year, Margaret Thatcher appointed him coordinator of intelligence in Northern Ireland, but within a year he lost his positive vetting after lying to cover up his homosexuality. *PM*

Old Queen Street, Georgian street of houses in Westminster, within the division bell area for the House of Commons, whose residents have included numerous politicians. Numbers 24 and 34 were occupied from 1946 to 1979 by the *Conservative Research Department which also published discussion documents as *Old Queen Street Papers*. *JAR*

oligarchy. Derived from classical Greek, oligarchy means literally rule by a few, as opposed, in Aristotle's schema, to aristocracy or rule by the best. As such, oligarchy has traditionally been applied to the organization of political regimes. The concern with oligarchy in 20th-century British politics has, in contrast, been with oligarchy within organizations in general and grass-roots political parties in particular. Here the work of Robert *Michels has been particularly influential. In 1912, Michels, a political scientist who ended his career as professor in the Fascist political science department at the University of Perugia, published *Zur Soziologie des Parteiwesens* (translated as *Political Parties*, 1915), in which, following an empirical study of the German Social Democratic Party, he argued that there was an 'iron law of oligarchy'. As the bureaucracy of political parties expanded and began to pursue complex goals, it relied heavily on technical expertise and leadership. Those who acquire such organizational resources become set aside from rank-and-file membership and begin to form an elite. Their position is reinforced by the control they acquire over the organization's form, aided by their understanding of its rules and regulations and the time they can devote to its management, and encouraged by the social advantages they derive from their position. Ultimately, they begin to see their continued position within the organization as more important than its original goals, and begin to shape policy accordingly. This view added to a suspicion of activists in both left-wing political parties and pressure groups, and contributed to the rational choice analysis of bureaucracy. *CPS*

Olivier, Sydney (1859–1943), Fabian socialist and colonial administrator. One of ten children of an Anglican clergyman (a brother was the father of Laurence Olivier the actor), Olivier became a Colonial Office civil servant in 1882, and held posts abroad for many years, including the governorship of Jamaica, 1907–13. In 1924, after his retirement from the civil service, he was created a peer in order to join MacDonald's cabinet as secretary of state for India. He wrote widely on colonial issues and was a contributor to *Fabian Essays in Socialism* (1889). *DEM*

Margaret Olivier, *Sydney Olivier: Letters and Selected Writings* (London, 1948). | Francis Lee, *Fabianism and Colonialism: The Life and Political Thought of Lord Sydney Olivier* (London, 1988).

Olympia rally (7 June 1934). This battle between Fascists and anti-Fascists marked an important turning point for British fascism. The monster rally, planned by the *British Union of Fascists (BUF) before an expected audience of 13,000 people, and described by Mosley as 'the largest outdoor meeting ever held under one roof in Britain', was soon interrupted by shouts of 'Fascism means Murder. Down with Mosley!' The ensuing violence with Oswald *Mosley's blackshirts dealing brutally with their well-drilled adversaries provided ammunition which his opponents could fire against the BUF's activities. *CH*

R. Skidelsky, *Oswald Mosley* (London, 1975).

ombudsman, officially the parliamentary commissioner for administration, a post created

in 1967 to examine allegations of maladministration, initially by central government. Ombudsman is a Swedish word meaning literally 'legal representative' and one existed there well before its introduction in Britain. Similar ombudsmen were appointed for Northern Ireland in 1969 and for the National Health Service (a post combined with the Parliamentary Commissioner) and for local government in England, Scotland, and Wales in the early 1970s. In the NHS, members of the public can approach the ombudsman directly, but otherwise complaints have to come through MPs. Many complaints concern delays in processing claims or applications or underpaying social and other benefits. The ombudsman has wide powers to obtain evidence from departments and his recommendations, both to remedy the particular grievance and to improve procedures, are normally acted upon by the departments concerned, though there have been a few cases where the government has refused to act. Matters concerned with armed forces and personnel are outside his remit. The ombudsman makes regular reports to parliament and these are considered by a select committee (up to 1995 a special one on this issue and, after 1997, the select committee on public administration). In the mid-1990s, the ombudsman took on responsibility for the Open Government Code.
PJRR

O'Neill, Terence Marne (1914–90), prime minister of Northern Ireland. Captain O'Neill came from a distinguished Ulster landed and military background. After military service during the Second World War, he was elected to the Northern Ireland parliament in 1946. He served as minister of finance, 1956–63, and succeeded Lord Brookeborough as prime minister in 1963. Soon after his accession as premier, he made clear his intention to make Northern Ireland more prosperous and to improve community relations. The following years saw a considerable improvement in the local economy for which O'Neill is due much of the credit. He also sought to improve community relations by making reconciliatory gestures to the Catholic community. The first meeting of prime ministers of Northern Ireland and the Irish Republic occurred in 1965 in Belfast to be followed by a return visit in Dublin in 1966. In 1968, he introduced some reforms to the electoral and educational systems, but these were insufficient to satisfy the growing demands from the new civil rights movement, in response to which he introduced a number of additional reforms in late 1968 and 1969. In face of dissension within Unionist Party ranks and also opposition from loyalist protesters, however, he was forced to resign in April 1969. With a rather distant manner he was unable to relate well either to fellow cabinet members or to the grass-roots Unionist voters. He became Lord O'Neill of the Maine in 1970.
BMW

TERENCE O'NEILL, *Ulster at the Crossroads* (London, 1969). | JONATHAN BARDON, *A History of Ulster* (Belfast, 1992).

One Nation, book and discussion group. One Nation characterizes the philosophy of post-war, moderate Conservatism. Originally chosen as the title of a book published in 1950 by nine new Tory MPs who proposed reforming the welfare state, One Nation encapsulated their support for moderate Toryism of the kind advocated by Rab Butler. In their view, such an approach would encourage social cohesion and prevent the divisiveness of either laissez-faire liberalism or class-based socialism. The group's founding-members were Cub Alport, who had conceived the idea, Robert Carr, Richard Fort, Edward Heath, Gilbert Longden, Iain Macleod, Angus Maude, Enoch Powell, and John Rodgers. The choice of *One Nation* as a title is variously attributed to either Macleod or Maude, joint editors of the group's first book, and derives from Disraeli's novel *Sybil, or the Two Nations*, which had attacked the extreme inequality between rich and poor under laissez-faire capitalism. After the immediate impact made by their book, they became known as the One Nation Group. The group continues as a backbench discussion group and there have been occasional publications. By 1997, however, the reduced influence of 'One Nation' Toryism after the Thatcher period prompted Tony Blair to claim that Labour were now the party of 'One Nation'.
RJS

open government. See FREEDOM OF INFORMATION.

Open University. Originally proposed as a 'University of the Air', the Open University was set up by Wilson's Labour government and began functioning in 1969–70. Its aim was to encourage people without a formal educational background to take part-time university degrees through correspondence courses, short residential study programmes, and televised lectures. One of the notable successes of the 1964–70 government, the project was closely associated with arts minister Jennie *Lee. About 200,000 first degrees have been awarded in the 30 years since the university opened.
JS

opinion polls, surveys used to elicit the collective opinions of citizens. The use of systematic means of questioning people, typically through a sample chosen at random in the street or by the selection of people in an electoral register or telephone book, was first developed in the USA and employed throughout the 20th century. The use of opinion polls developed in Britain in the late 1930s and more especially after 1945. In 1937, Dr Henry Durant founded the *British Institute of Public Opinion as part of the international chain of Gallup organizations, and this institute began carrying out polls during elections, first during the 1938 Fulham by-election and then during the 1945 general election, in which it came close to identifying the precise share of the poll won by each party. Opinion polls were more extensively used in the 1950s and 1960s as more polling organizations came into being. By the 1970 general election, five major polling organizations existed.

Opinion polls have been used to chart the support of political parties between and during election campaigns and also, increasingly, to assess opinion on a range of political issues. Polling organizations such as Gallup and MORI carry out regular polls, allowing for time-series data on opinion to be created. The range of issues covered has increased, as has the sophistication of polling techniques. Different organizations will sometimes commission extensive polling exercises, such as the MORI 'State of the Nation' polls commissioned by the Joseph Rowntree Reform Trust in 1991 and 1995. The use of opinion polls has never been free from controversy. Some politicians have objected to publication of polls during election campaigns, fearing they may influence electors' voting intentions, and critics have queried the weight placed on them. They have mainly been used to predict the outcomes of general elections. In most elections, the principal polling organizations have predicted the share of the poll won by each party within a small margin of error. However, in two elections, 1970 and 1992, there was a marked discrepancy between the estimates of polling organizations and the actual share of the poll won by each party. Labour strength was overestimated in both (as it was by National Opinion Poll in October 1974), leading to post-mortems by the polling organizations. Not all opinion polls measure depth as well as breadth of opinion. Some do ask how strongly people feel about an issue and, as in the MORI State of the Nation Poll, how much they know about a subject. There is also a normative debate as to the use made of polls by political parties, especially when in government. The Labour government elected in 1997 was criticized for its reliance on survey data and focus groups. According to one study, the most important regular meeting the prime minister had was with his principal pollster, Philip Gould. *PN*

Market Research Society, *The Opinion Polls and the 1992 General Election* (London, 1994). | MORI, *State of the Nation 1995* (London, 1995). | Robert Worcester, *British Public Opinion: A Guide to the History and Methodology of Political Opinion Polling* (Oxford, 1991).

opt-out clause, formal protocol to a European Union (EU) treaty which enables a member state not to participate in a particular activity within the treaty's provisions. An opt-out was most famously secured by the prime minister, John Major, who, at the *Maastricht European Council in December 1991, negotiated Britain's exclusion from the social chapter. Both Britain and Ireland later opted out of frontier decontrol legislation in the treaty of *Amsterdam. *JRVE*

Orage, Alfred Richard (1873–1934), editor, writer, and guild socialist. While a Leeds schoolteacher in the 1890s, Orage became an idealistic, even mystical, socialist, influenced by the ideas of William Morris, Edward Carpenter, and Nietzsche. Partly financed by a loan from Bernard Shaw, he acquired the weekly *New Age*, which under his editorship (1907–22) became celebrated for creative and critical writings on politics and culture. For some years he advocated guild socialism, but after 1919 fell in with C. H. Douglas and his social credit nostrums, which Orage also favoured in the *New English Weekly*, a paper he launched in 1932. *DEM*

Wallace Martin, *The* New Age *under Orage* (Manchester, 1967).

O'Rahilly, Michael Joseph ('The O'Rahilly') (1875–1916), Irish nationalist. From a prosperous, Catholic, Co. Kerry background, O'Rahilly was an associate of Arthur Griffith, and was involved with Sinn Fein and the Gaelic League. A founder member of the Irish Volunteers in 1913, he was involved in their Howth gun-running the following year. Not privy to the conspiracy behind the 1916 Easter Rising, he aided attempts to call it off, but nevertheless participated in the rebellion and was killed in the fighting in Dublin. *RE*

Aodogán O'Rahilly, *Winding the Clock: O'Rahilly and the 1916 Rising* (Dublin, 1991).

Orange Book. See *We Can Conquer Unemployment*.

Orange Order (Ulster), Protestant organization formed as a result of agrarian conflict between Protestant and Catholic groups in North Armagh, culminating in the battle of the Diamond at Loughgall, Co. Armagh, in 1795. It took its title from King William of Orange, and its annual July marches focus around the anniversary of his victory at the battle of the Boyne in 1690. Between its founding and the 1880s, the Orange Institution enjoyed fluctuating fortunes, including a period of voluntary suppression in the 1830s. Its important role in Ulster politics and society was only achieved in the 1880s with the emergence of Unionist/nationalist conflict. Many Protestants, from across the social and denominational spectrum, now joined the institution as a common defence movement and its numbers grew considerably. Post-1921, it remained an influential body as all the Unionist prime ministers and many MPs belonged to it. In recent decades there has been a reduction in its numbers and influence, but at present about 50,000 active members belong to it. There is considerable debate within the order as to whether it is a religious or political movement. Since 1904 it has been able to elect 120 members to the Ulster Unionist Council, but this right has been questioned recently within both the Orange Order and the Unionist Party. *BMW*

Dominic Bryan, *The Orange Order* (London, 2000).

Orange Order in Scotland. Originally imported from Ireland in the 18th century, Orangeism grew in Scotland as a result of widespread Irish immigration in the 19th century. Largely confined to the west central belt, the order was an organization composed mainly of the skilled working class whose activities were more of a social rather than political nature. Orangeism was fairly prominent in the Clyde shipbuilding industry which was reinforced by frequent contacts with the Belfast industry. Orange culture is one reason mooted to explain the perseverance of the west of Scotland, Protestant, working-class Tory into the 1950s. As the industries which harboured sectarian practices declined in the 1960s, so too did the Orange Order. *RF*

Organization for Economic Cooperation and Development (OECD), intergovernmental economic organization created in 1960. It aimed to promote economic cooperation between industrialized states, coordinate development aid to third world countries, and provide a forum for the resolution of trade disputes. It generated economic intelligence and its reports on member states' economies and on world economic trends are valued internationally. The OECD was originally the *Organization for European Economic Cooperation (OEEC) founded in 1948.

The creation of the EEC and EFTA divided the OEEC's membership and thus in 1960, under the supervision of its associate members, Canada and the USA (who now became full members), the OEEC became the OECD. As European economic cooperation was now firmly within the remits of the EEC and EFTA, the OECD's membership was widened to non-western European industrial countries (Japan, 1964; Finland, 1969; Australia, 1971; New Zealand, 1973). Its scope also now included relations with developing countries. The OECD remains an influential economic organization with 24 members, which has been instrumental in the creation of such organs as the Group of Seven (G7) and the European Bank for Reconstruction and Development (EBRD). *JRVE*

Organization for European Economic Cooperation (OEEC) (1948–61), intergovernmental organization founded as a response to American secretary of state George Marshall's famous speech in June 1947, offering American financial assistance to post-war Europe: Marshall aid. Its founding members were Austria, Belgium, Britain, Denmark, France, Greece, Iceland, Ireland, Italy, Luxembourg, the Netherlands, Norway, Portugal, Sweden, and Turkey (as well as the three Western-administered zones of Germany). Largely because of the pugnacious diplomacy of British Foreign Secretary Ernest Bevin, OEEC did not embrace the Soviet Union, which in turn blocked the membership of any East European countries, so OEEC both contributed to, and symbolized, the Cold War division of Europe. OEEC's brief was to administer American aid through a four-year programme to increase agricultural and industrial production, ease the dollar gap by increasing European exports, ensure financial stability, and control inflation. OEEC payments encouraged West European economic recovery, and the freeing-up of trade restrictions through the European Payments Union. After 1950, the Americans allowed Marshall aid money to be used for rearming Western Europe. Roughly $13 billion of payments were authorized through OEEC, nearly $7 billion of these going to Britain. Its intergovernmental character appealed particularly to the British, who favoured it as the forum for free trade area negotiations in the 1950s. In 1961, OEEC was transformed into the *Organization for Economic Cooperation and Development (OECD), and the USA and Japan became full members. *ADe*

Alan S. Milward, *The Reconstruction of Western Europe* (London, 1984).

Orgreave, scene of a violent confrontation between miners' pickets and the police during May and June of 1984. Over 8,000 police prevented mass picketing from closing down the Orgreave coke depot near Sheffield. More than 32,500 pickets went to Orgreave, of whom 273 were arrested, while hundreds of miners and police were injured. Orgreave was a watershed in the 1984–5 miners' strike. Mass picketing, as an offensive tactic to spread the strike, began to tail off following the defeat at Orgeave. *DLM*

Ormsby-Gore, William. See Harlech, Lord.

Orpington by-election (14 March 1962), most sensational *Liberal Party by-election victory of the 1960s when a safe Conservative majority in a London commuter seat was captured. Following promising results in other Conservative seats, the Liberals capitalized on growing disillusion with the Macmillan government and confirmed the revival of the Liberal Party as a party of anti-Conservative protest. Eric *Lubbock overturned a majority of 14,760 to give a Liberal majority of 7,855. As well as marking a fresh Liberal revival following the disappointment of the 1959 general election, it appeared to promise a breakthrough in mainstream areas outside the *Celtic fringe, offering a genuine prospect of enlarging the party's base of support to a classless 'Orpington man' in southern England. Fleetingly, at the end of March, a National Opinion Poll in the *Daily Mail* showed the Liberals as the most popular party in the country with 30.0 per cent, Labour on 29.9 per cent, and the Conservatives on 29.2 per cent. But there was also hard evidence that grass-roots Liberal support was rising: there was a favourable result at Middlesbrough East on the same day as Orpington, pushing the Conservatives into third place. Further good results followed at Stockton-on-Tees and Derby North in April where the Liberals took almost a quarter of the votes. Liberal advance was confirmed in the municipal elections in May 1962 with considerable gains from the Conservatives, especially in the home counties. But, as in the aftermath of the *Torrington by-election in 1958, the revival was not sustained. By October 1962 Liberal support had dropped below 20 per cent in the opinion polls. In the subsequent general election of 1964, the Liberals doubled their vote, but still took only nine seats. Orpington was retained until 1970 but was until 1969 the only Liberal seat outside the Celtic fringe. *JS*

Ken Young, 'Orpington and the "Liberal Revival"', in Chris Cook and John Ramsden (eds.), *By-Elections in British Politics* (London, 1997).

Orwell, George (real name Eric Arthur Blair) (1903–50), journalist and writer. Orwell was born in India in 1903. After education at Eton he was a police officer in Burma, only becoming a writer in 1927, adopting the pseudonym 'Orwell' after the name of the river in Suffolk. His early books were *Down and Out in London and Paris* (1933), *Burmese Days*, based upon his policing experience in Burma (1934), *A Clergyman's Daughter* (1935), and *Keep the Aspidistra Flying* (1936). His account of the experience of living in poverty shot him to fame with *The Road to Wigan Pier* (1937), and his ability as a novelist was further confirmed by *Coming Up for Air* (1939) and by numerous essays and shorter pieces for the press. Orwell really found his voice, though, with his conversion to a highly independent type of socialism, which arose from his experience in the *Spanish civil war. He had gone to Spain to report on the war but found himself drawn into fighting, joining the semi-Trotskyist militia, and later wrote up his experiences in *Homage to Catalonia* (1938). During the Second World War Orwell worked for the BBC and wrote articles for the socialist journal *Tribune*. He also worked on other books and collections of essays, the most important being the allegorical *Animal Farm* (1945) where he represented communists as having betrayed the socialist dream of revolution. This made him an internationally known author, which was further emphasized by *Nineteen Eighty-Four* (1949), in which a future Britain is presented as an outpost of the West in its conflict with the East and controlled by the totalitarian 'Big Brother' and his 'thought police'. At the height of his fame, perceived as a teller of unfashionable truths, he died of tuberculosis in 1950. *KL*

Bernard Crick, *George Orwell* (London, 1980).

Osborne judgement (1909), legal decision which prevented trade unions from using funds for political purposes. The House of Lords (acting as a court) upheld the case brought by W. V. Osborne, a member of the Amalgamated Society of Railway Servants, which contended that his union had no right to use its funds for the purpose of supporting the Labour Party, nor had they the right to impose a levy on members for this purpose. The decision threw the party into a financial crisis but encouraged introduction of the payment of MPs in 1911, prior to the only-partial reversal of the judgement in the 1913 *Trade Union Act. *BB*

OSCE. See HELSINKI CONFERENCE/CSCE.

Ostrogorski, Moisei (1854–1919), Russian scholar, educated in Russia and France, who penned an influential and highly critical work on the development of party organization. He wrote a number of articles on party organization, based on extensive research and observation, before publishing a two-volume work, *La Démocratie et l'organisation des partis politiques* in 1902 (an English translation, *Democracy and the Organisation of Political Parties*, was published later the same year). Ostogorski analysed party development in the latter half of the 19th century in the USA and Britain. In his study of Britain, he concentrated on the party responses to the 1867 Reform Act, attacking the growth of party caucuses and arguing that they served to create powerful leaders rather than vesting power in party members. He claimed that the growth of party government was a challenge to, rather than a development of, representative government. He was, wrote Rodney Barker, 'the first liberal to face the party system and to attempt to judge it by traditional liberal values'. His work constituted one of the first major studies of party government and he influenced many subsequent writers in viewing party government in pejorative terms. Ostrogorski's pessimistic view of parties was not borne out in practice and his own prescription—a league of voters created for particular elections but without any formal organization—had little impact. He also published books on the rights of women and the political system in the USA. He served briefly as a member of the Russian Duma. *PN*

R. BARKER, 'Introduction', in his (ed.) *Studies in Opposition* (London, 1971).

Ottawa conference (1932). Every few years from the late 1880s onwards, British imperial conferences were held, providing a forum for discussion on all matters imperial. There were conferences in 1923 and 1926; and at the initiative of the Canadian government one was planned for 1930 to consider the pressing issue of tariffs, preferences, and, something that concerned Canadians greatly, wheat. That conference was held but little progress made. A conference was then proposed for 1931 but lack of agreement on timing saw it postponed until 1932. By 1932 when the world economy had collapsed, the agenda for the conference largely wrote itself: it was about Empire trade. There had been some growing interest in the protectionist 1920s in making arrangements for a self-sufficient empire and of turning this into a customs union, with free movement of goods and some factors of production within Empire but with tariffs against outsiders. Following Ottawa, imperial preference was introduced by some countries and, where it already existed was extended by others. Britain had left the gold standard in September 1931 and introduced a general tariff in April 1932. (This was perverse, since under a floating exchange rate a tariff loses its effect.) When the countries met in the summer of 1932 there was much to consider. Many Empire countries (and some others) had simply followed Britain in these actions. The negotiations at Ottawa were largely about trade and preferential trading arrangements, with a large number of bilateral agreements signed. There were some beneficiaries of Ottawa, perhaps British farmers and New Zealand and Australian meat producers, but overall the conference can hardly be considered a success. For one thing, it greatly annoyed the USA and damaged Anglo-American relations. It also upset many other countries too, such as Argentina, where the longer-term consequences of damaged trade, while difficult to measure, contributed to that country's deteriorating economic performance. *FHC*

OutRage, pressure group formed in 1990 to fight homophobic discrimination and to campaign for *homosexuality. Controversially, it used the tactic of 'outing' (revealing the homosexuality of prominent public figures) to highlight anti-gay hypocrisy. Most famously it 'outed' twelve Anglican bishops in 1994, in protest at anti-gay sentiment within the Church of England. Following the election of Tony Blair's Labour government in 1997, OutRage has campaigned vigorously for the repeal of Section 28 (part of a Local Government Act passed by the Thatcher government which had prohibited the 'promotion' of a homosexual lifestyle, and thus legitimated discrimination) and equalization of the gay age of consent. *JJN*

Overlords. The 'overlords' experiment of 1951–3 represented Churchill's attempt to adapt for peacetime use some of the methods of the 1940–5 war cabinet, in particular appointing a smaller cabinet (of sixteen members) and relying on a number of coordinating and supervising ministers to oversee the work of several departments. Lord Woolton, as lord president, coordinated the then separate ministries of agriculture and food; Lord Leathers was given the post of secretary of state for the coordination of transport, fuel, and power; Lord Cherwell (paymaster general) supervised atomic energy projects and nuclear research; Earl Alexander of Tunis, as minister of defence, was overlord of the three service ministries. The experiment soon broke down. The blurring of administrative and policy responsibilities was unpopular in Whitehall, and the constitutional issues around ministerial responsibility to parliament were criticized by the Labour Party (the fact that the coordinating ministers were all in the Lords was a special gripe). After 1953, the Conservative government reverted to the usual system of coordination through *cabinet committees. *KT*

overseas aid policy. British international aid provision can be traced back to the Colonial Development Act of 1929 which acknowledged that it was the responsibility of the British government to oversee the development of its colonies. Overseas aid policy did not acquire formal machinery within the British government until 1964 when Harold Wilson created the Ministry of Overseas Development. This reflected the growing political support for overseas aid which had developed, especially on the left, in response to post-war decolonization. Non-governmental organizations had also received growing public support most notably through the charity *Oxfam (the Oxford Committee for Famine Relief) which from 1942 worked to relieve suffering and promote long-term development throughout the world. Early lessons in overseas aid policy were learnt when the Labour Party's commitment to allocating 1 per cent of Britain's GNP to overseas aid was soon defeated by the hard truths of the British economy during the 1960s. This clash between plans for aid provision and pressures on public expenditure has remained a constant. Overseas aid policy has nevertheless grown in importance during the past 35 years. Since 1979 the Overseas Development Administration (ODA), a wing of the Foreign Office, has administered a growing budget which in 1995 was in excess of £2 billion. About 55 per cent of this was given directly to individual states and 45 per cent was channelled through international organizations such as the European Community (now European Union), the UN, and the World Bank. Britain's priorities are to relieve poverty, to promote sustainable development, and political stability. Much of the impetus given to overseas aid policy has derived from non-governmental organizations, some of which receive government support through the ODA. At the close of the 20th century, through globalization and the mass media, public opinion is more aware of the plight of the developing world and of humanitarian disasters. As a consequence aid has become an important political issue. *JRVE*

overseas development. See INTERNATIONAL DEVELOPMENT, DEPARTMENT OF.

Owen, David Anthony Llewellyn (1938–), Labour and centrist politician, leader of the *Social Democratic Party (SDP). Educated at Cambridge and trained as a doctor, Owen served as a Labour MP, 1966–81, and SDP MP, 1981–92, for Plymouth Sutton and then Plymouth Devonport. A successful under-secretary for defence, 1968–70, Owen then served as junior minister at the Department of Health and Social Security, 1974–6, but rose to the front rank of politicians with his appointment as Callaghan's foreign secretary, 1976–9. Following the Labour Party's defeat in 1979, his disillusionment with the leftward drift of the party under Michael Foot led him to joining with Roy *Jenkins, William *Rodgers and Shirley *Williams in founding the Social Democratic Party. He became the leader of the SDP during the 1983 election campaign and advocated distinctive SDP views on defence and the social market within the Liberal–SDP *Alliance. Although he campaigned as joint leader of the Alliance campaign with David *Steel in the 1987 election, differences on defence policy and the presentational difficulties of the two-leaders strategy limited their impact. He opposed calls for a merger following the election and resigned the leadership of the SDP when a majority of the party voted in favour. Owen then became leader of the non-merger SDP until its final demise in 1989. A staunch supporter of the independence of the SDP, he was widely regarded as hindering the emergence of an effective, merged party earlier than occurred. He left the Commons in 1992 and was given a peerage by John Major following discussion about a possible role in the Conservative Party. Owen was European Union peace negotiator in the former Yugoslavia from 1992, resigning in 1995 after working tirelessly for a settlement. Though earlier a strong pro-European, he has latterly lent his support to the campaign against Britain joining the Euro. *JS*

Oxbridge. See HIGHER EDUCATION.

Oxfam, major charity organization for overseas aid and food programmes, founded in 1942. Its name comes from its inception as the Oxford Committee for Famine Relief, and it still has its headquarters in Oxford. *JS*

Oxford by-election (27 October 1938), first of series of contests in the aftermath of the *Munich crisis. It was seen as a referendum on Chamberlain's *appeasement policy, especially when opposition parties united behind the candidature of an independent, A. D. *Lindsay. The Conservative candidate Quintin Hogg, despite contending with slogans such as 'A vote for Hogg is a vote for Hitler', managed to retain the seat for the government. In similar contests later in the year, the government lost at Bridgwater but won in Kinross and West Perthshire, suggesting a mixed public response to Munich. *NJC*

pacifism. When the French peace activist Émile Arnaud coined this word in 1901, he was labelling the programme of the peace movement as a whole: it therefore initially referred not merely to the unconditional rejection of military force by that movement's absolutist minority but also to the proposals for abolishing war—for example, through arbitration, multilateral disarmament, or economic interdependence—offered by its reformist majority. In the Great War, however, it was applied more to conscientious objectors than to those opposing secret diplomacy or proposing a league of nations. By the mid-1930s, in the English-speaking world at least, the term had attached itself firmly to those denying that any war, even a defensive one against Hitler, was justifiable.

British pacifism in this absolute sense dated back to its espousal by the Quakers in 1661, and was adopted by some mainstream Christians from the 1790s. Britain's first pacifist association, the Peace Society, was created in 1816 and was still operating, albeit in a doctrinally compromised way, when the outbreak of the Great War reinvigorated organized pacifism. In November 1914 the No-Conscription Fellowship was formed by members of the Independent Labour Party; wound up in 1919, it was reborn in 1921 as the No More War Movement. In December 1914 the Fellowship of Reconciliation was established by Christians: a mainly quietist body, it still exists. These were small bodies of not more than 3,000 members. Pacifism attracted a significant following only in the second half of the 1930s when the League of Nations, on which the peace movement's main hopes had been pinned, became discredited, particularly by its failure to stop Italy conquering Abyssinia (now Ethiopia). In May 1936 the Revd H. R. L. ('Dick') Sheppard formed the Peace Pledge Union, which not only attracted a remarkable group of intellectuals, including Vera Brittain, Aldous Huxley, John Middleton Murray, and Bertrand Russell, but for a time seemed to have the potential to become a politically significant movement. Its pacifism was largely of a humanitarian or utilitarian kind. Having absorbed the No More War Movement in 1937, it peaked at 136,000 members in April 1940, but thereafter was undermined by Hitler's military breakthrough. Although it still exists, pacifism has made virtually no political impact since 1945. *MEC*

Martin Ceadel, *Pacifism in Britain 1914–1945: The Defining of a Faith* (Oxford, 1980). | Martin Ceadel, *The Origins of War Prevention: The British Peace Movement and International Relations, 1730–1854* (Oxford, 1996).

pacts, electoral. The UK's *first-past-the-post electoral system militates against all but the two largest parties, encouraging electors to feel that votes cast for weaker parties would be *wasted votes. In times of political realignment then, or when there was strong convergence of interest between two or more parties (often coming together negatively to resist another stronger party), pacts have been made so that the parties participating would each be able to elect more MPs by relying on mutual support. The habit of cooperation has sometimes, as in the cases of the *Liberal Unionists and the *Liberal Nationals, been the precursor to merger with the partner, in these cases the Conservative Party. Sometimes, though, the difficulty of agreeing on the duration and mechanics of an electoral pact have eventually driven the partners to part, as in the case of the National Liberals and Conservatives in 1918–22.

The Liberal Unionist pact with the Conservatives, made in 1886 under the stress of the Irish home rule crisis, provides an exemplary model of a pact that worked. So keen were both groups to prevent Gladstone from getting a Commons majority for home rule that they were able to decide easily on a pact whereby neither would oppose the other's sitting MPs at the 1886 election; the choice of a single candidate to oppose home rule in seats not held by either party proved equally straightforward, and the pact thus converted a small majority of the national vote into a large majority in the Commons. Cooperation rapidly extended to supporting each other on the platform, in the parliamentary lobbies, and from 1895 around the cabinet table. Since home rule remained a topical issue, motivation for the pact remained high right up to the merger of the parties in 1912.

The *Lib-Lab pact (1903) was motivated more by the general desperation of Liberals and Labour after nearly twenty years of Tory dominance (much as in the 1990s, with a similar effect). The pact helped to give Labour its first parliamentary foothold, but also to reinforce Liberal strength, especially in the difficult elections of 1910. It did not, however, work especially well between general elections, for the partners were in the longer term rivals for the same progressive vote. It broke down locally in 1907–8, as a result of which the Liberals lost by-elections, for example to Victor *Grayson in Colne Valley; was put back in place for 1910; but then fell apart completely in the by-elections of 1911–14. It is unclear whether the pact could have been patched up for a general election due in 1914–15, for losses of both Liberal and Labour parliamentary seats in 1911–14 had soured relations between the partners. The intervention of war in any case made it unnecessary, and by 1918 the Labour Party felt confident enough to go it alone.

Pacts between the wars were all to do with gathering together the anti-socialist forces so as to prevent Labour winning. This happened most notably in the National Liberal–Conservative pact of 1918, for the *'Coupon' Election, and was partly revived in 1922. Similar deals were done all across local government to resist Labour in council elections, and the National Government of 1931 rested heavily on the similar foundation of Liberal–Tory cooperation, though in this case the Conservatives used the machinery of an electoral pact only to back Liberals who would support tariffs, so both improving the chance of getting tariffs through and accelerating another Liberal split. Since 1945, pacts have been much rarer, though limited Conservative–Liberal cooperation in Bolton and Huddersfield in the 1950s did deny three or four seats to Labour. Where cooperation between parties at the polls has existed, it has been through nods, winks, and hints to the voters (or by simply not really trying very hard in a local campaign, so as to allow the partner that might win the seat to pick up your vote) rather than by the mutual withdrawal of candidates, as was evident in the Liberal–Labour cooperation of 1997. The post-war expectation has been that any party claiming that it should govern the country must put up candidates in all constituencies—hence the disappearance in the 1950s of uncontested elections, and this makes formal electoral pacts impossible.

However, the increasing likelihood of some form of proportional representation being introduced for parliamentary elections, at the start of the new century, hints at a future in which electoral pacts would become pointless (since votes could not be 'wasted') but, if particular systems like the *alternative vote were to be adopted, in which there were deals between parties over how second and third preference votes were to be cast, they would become routine and absolutely crucial. *JAR*

Page Croft, Henry (1881–1947), Conservative backbencher, imperialist, and political organizer. A descendant of warriors and parliamentarians on his father's side and of prosperous tradesmen on his mother's, Page Croft quite appropriately divided his life between soldiering, politics, and business. He entered parliament in January 1910 and immediately sought a place among his elders on the right wing of his party. Enthralled by Chamberlain's programme for tariff reform and Empire unity, he became an uncompromising critic of the Conservatives who failed to embrace fully the new orthodoxy, including his leader, Balfour. In this interest he led the *Confederacy, Reveille, and Imperial Mission organizations, 1910–14, to drive the party and the nation into the arms of tariff reform and Empire. In the Great War, Page Croft served gallantly, rising to the rank of brigadier. After service, and unhappy with the coalition alliance with the Lloyd George Liberals, he organized the *National Party in opposition to it. In the inter-war years, neither his independence nor his energy flagged, and he finally achieved office in Churchill's wartime coalition as under-secretary at the War Office. He died as he had lived, a crusader for what he believed in: principle over party. *RJQA*

Lord Croft, *My Life of Strife* (London, 1949). | Larry L. Witherell, *Rebel on the Right: Henry Page Croft and the Crisis of British Conservatism, 1903–1914* (Newark, Del., 1997).

Paisley, Ian Richard Kyle (1926–), Northern Ireland politician and preacher. A Protestant fundamentalist, the Revd Dr Paisley became prominent when he led street demonstrations against the moderate reforms of Northern Ireland Prime Minister Terence O'Neill. The son of a Baptist minister, he was reputed to have started preaching at the age of 16. In 1951, he started a Free Presbyterian Church in the Ravenhill Road area of Belfast. In 1963 he organized a march to protest against the decision to lower the Union flag to half-mast to mark the death of Pope John XXIII. The *Scarman tribunal blamed Paisley's speeches for heightened tensions which led to intercommunal rioting in 1969. In 1971, Paisley formed the *Democratic Unionist Party (DUP), and since 1970 has been DUP MP for North Antrim. Paisley opposed the 1974 Northern Ireland executive on the grounds that Unionists could not share power with nationalists who wanted to destroy the province's position within the United Kingdom. Paisley believed that they would use their position within a cabinet and in cross-border bodies to lead Northern Ireland towards Irish unity. He demanded a return to Protestant majority rule in Northern Ireland. Following the commencement of Anglo-Irish talks in 1980, Paisley held a series of marches—the 'Carson trail'—and was associated with the *Third Force. He and the Ulster Unionist party leader James Molyneaux worked closely together in their opposition to the Anglo-Irish intergovernmental conference established by the British and Irish governments in 1985. Paisley boycotted the 1997–8 talks process and opposed the resulting Belfast agreement. He was first elected to the European parliament in 1983, and in 1999 for the fifth successive time he topped the Northern Ireland poll for the European parliament. *TWH*

Steve Bruce, *God Save Ulster! The Religion and Politics of Paisleyism* (Oxford, 1986).

Palace Chambers, the offices of the Conservative Central Office in Bridge Street, 1922–41, and often therefore used in conversation as a synonym for Central Office. *JAR*

Palestine. A League of Nations *mandate over this former territory of the defeated Ottoman Empire was awarded to Britain at the San Remo conference of 1920. Operation of the mandate was complicated by Britain's alignment with the Zionist cause through the *Balfour declaration of 1917, involving the establishment of a 'national home' for the Jewish people in the territory, while at the same time protecting the existing rights of the indigenous Arab population. The 1930s saw greatly increased Jewish immigration and communal tensions occasionally spilled over into violence, culminating in the Arab rebellion of 1936, fuelled by awareness of the erosion of their position and demands for immediate independence from British colonial controls. The Peel commission, set up to examine the causes of the rebellion, concluded in 1937 that the mandate was unworkable and the aims of the two communities contradictory, recommending partition as the least bad solution. While Jewish leaders were prepared to accept such an arrangement, Palestinian Arab opinion firmly rejected any departure from a unitary state and pressed for the speedy departure of the British. The following year, the British government also abandoned partition, and in May 1939 issued a white paper which placed ceilings on Jewish immigration and promised a grant of independence in ten years. This major reversal of policy was bitterly resisted by many Jewish groups, and before the end of the Second World War a terrorist campaign was being directed against the British presence. Tired of the intractable and costly problems generated by the mandate, in February 1947 Ernest Bevin placed responsibility for finding a solution in the hands of the unfortunate UN. In May 1948, the last British troops left Palestine as David Ben-Gurion announced the formation of the state of Israel, amid Arab nationalist recriminations over Britain's perfidious role. *MJC*

Palliser, (Arthur) Michael (1922–), diplomat, permanent secretary, Foreign and Commonwealth Office, and head of the diplomatic service, 1975–82. Appointed first head of the Foreign Office planning department in 1964, he instituted close consultations with the US state department which were greatly valued by both sides. In 1966 he was private secretary to the prime minister, Harold Wilson An enthusiastic pro-European, from 1973 to 1975 he was ambassador and UK permanent representative to the European Community. During the Falklands war he played a key role in the Cabinet Office. *DHD*

Pankhurst family, *suffragette campaigners. In 1879 the Manchester barrister Richard Marsden Pankhurst (1834–98) married Emmeline

Goulden (1858–1928), a daughter of the owner of a calico printing and bleach works. Both fervent characters and radical reformers, Richard and Emmeline Pankhurst had five children: two sons, one who died in infancy and Harry (1889–1910), and three daughters, Christabel (1880–1958), Sylvia (1882–1960), and Adela (1885–1961). The children were brought up in an atmosphere of radical politics, in which their parents moved from advanced Liberalism to Fabianism, and then to the socialism of the Independent Labour Party. Their parents' formation in 1889 of the Women's Franchise League, to ginger up the older suffrage societies, hinted at what was to come. Some five years after her husband's death, Emmeline, with the support of Christabel, founded the Women's Social and Political Union (WSPU), which in 1905 began to espouse a militant strategy to obtain votes for women. Sylvia, Adela, and Harry also worked for the WSPU, although Harry died young and in 1914, after disagreements with Emmeline and Christabel, Adela emigrated to Australia, where she continued her feminist activities. Sylvia too was to break away from her autocratic mother and older sister, although before then she shared with them several years of campaigning in which the militancy of the women was matched by the repression of the authorities. All three suffered periods of imprisonment: Sylvia was forcibly fed, while in 1912 Christabel escaped to Paris from where, as an inspired organizer, she directed operations. The methods employed by the Pankhursts and their followers put into the shade the larger, constitutional movement to enfranchise women. The outbreak of war in 1914 brought an end to militancy and Emmeline and Christabel became enthusiastic patriots. In 1917 the WSPU was renamed the Women's Party; its leader was Christabel who, in spite of Lloyd George's support, narrowly lost at Smethwick in the general election of 1918. Sylvia, an intimate of the Labour leader Keir Hardie, had opposed the war. In 1919–20 she was involved in the creation of the Communist Party of Great Britain, from which she was expelled when she refused to let the party take control of her paper, the *Workers' Dreadnought*. Among her later causes was that of Abyssinia (now Ethiopia), and she died in Addis Ababa. In the 1920s Emmeline joined the Conservative Party, becoming a prospective parliamentary candidate. Christabel, who was created a Dame of the British Empire in 1936, adopted the Second Adventist faith, which she sought to advance in the USA between 1939 and her death in Santa Monica. *DEM*

David Mitchell, *The Fighting Pankhersts: A Study in Tenacity* (London, 1967). | David Mitchell, *Queen Christabel* (London, 1977). | Christabel Pankhurst, *Unshackled: The Story of How We Won the Vote* (London, 1955). | Sylvia Pankhurst, *The Life of Emmeline Pankhurst* (London, 1935). | Sylvia Pankhurst, *The Suffragette Movement: An Intimate Account of Persons and Ideals* (London, 1931). | Patricia W. Romero, *E. Sylvia Pankhurst* (New Haven and London, 1987). | Andrew Rosen, *Rise Up, Women! The Militant Campaign of the Women's Social and Political Union 1903–1914* (London, 1974). | Barbara Winslow, *Sylvia Pankhurst: Sexual Politics and Political Activism* (London, 1996).

Pardoe, John (1934–), Liberal politician. Pardoe was a community activist who won North Cornwall for the Liberals in 1966. One of the most prominent MPs in the 1970s, he contested the leadership with David *Steel in 1976 (claiming to be 'an effective bastard'), but unsuccessfully, and although retaining a high profile in the late 1970s, he lost his seat in 1979. A supporter of the Alliance and the Liberal Democrats, he effectively retired from politics after the 1987 election. *JS*

parish councils. See local government structure.

Paris peace conference (1919), meeting of the victorious powers convened to put a formal end to the *Great War. Its principal outcome was the treaty of Versailles with Germany (June 1919) but there were also settlements with Austria (treaty of Saint-Germain, September 1919), Bulgaria (treaty of Neuilly, November 1919), Hungary (treaty of Trianon, June 1920), and Turkey (treaty of Sèvres, August 1920). Proceedings were dominated by the heads of the five Allied delegations (France, Great Britain, Italy, Japan, and the USA) and their foreign ministers, together making up the Council of Ten, before whom representatives of smaller nations made their territorial and other claims. The British delegation was led by the prime minister, David Lloyd George. Together with Woodrow Wilson (American president) and Georges Clemenceau (French prime minister) he constituted the 'Big Three' whose often conflicting aims did most to shape the peacemaking process.

The attempt to reconstitute Europe on the principle of national self-determination established by Allied acceptance of Wilson's Fourteen Points (8 January 1918) was complicated by the need to fulfil wartime pledges of territorial expansion, the intractable nature of the 'minorities' problem, French determination to establish long-term security against Germany, and fear of Bolshevism.

Frontier changes in western and southern Europe were relatively small. Alsace-Lorraine was returned to France. Belgium, Italy, Romania, and Greece enlarged their territories. Germany and Bulgaria were reduced in size. But in eastern Europe the maps were completely redrawn. The Baltic states of Estonia, Latvia, and Lithuania were carved out of the old tsarist empire. The fragmentation of Austria-Hungary into much smaller successor states was confirmed. New states of Czechoslovakia and Yugoslavia were created and the old state of Poland regained its independence. French fears were assuaged by German disarmament, the imposition of financial indemnities (*reparations), and temporary occupation and permanent demilitarization of the *Rhineland. Wilsonian idealism resulted in the creation of a *League of Nations, an international organization charged with preserving the peace by settling disputes through arbitration and conciliation.

Although a greater degree of ethnic self-determination was achieved than that which existed before the war, potentially destabilizing problems of ethnic minorities remained in many countries. The 'bastion' successor states were often consumed by mutual distrust and ambition and offered a poor bulwark against the threat of Soviet or renewed German power. Germany was not dismembered, but the imposition of reparations, the occupation of the Rhineland, and the generally triumphalist tone of the settlement permanently alienated German opinion and provided a fertile breeding ground for extreme nationalism. The prospect of future arbitration and amendment of the settlements was damaged from the outset by the American Congress's repudiation of the League of Nations. Within a few years opinion, not least in Britain, had turned against the peace settlements, making it more difficult for the liberal democracies to take a tough line against the rise of revanchist regimes in Germany and Italy. *JMB*

Alan Sharp, *The Versailles Settlement: Peacemaking in Paris* (Basingstoke, 1991).

Paris resolutions (1916). The Allied economic conference in Paris in April 1916 was an attempt to unify the Entente belligerents on an economic policy after the war which would punish Germany for its aggression and protect the interests of the hopefully victorious allies. Pressure came mostly from the French, whose pre-war economic policy had been protectionist. In Britain, it aroused great tensions within the Asquith coalition government. The Conservative minority, led by Andrew Bonar Law, regarded a punitive tariff policy as natural and appropriate. The Liberals, with Reginald McKenna at the exchequer and Walter Runciman at the Board of Trade, were much less comfortable. In the event, Britain supported a strong form of the resolutions, with measured support from Liberals in the cabinet. This alienated a number of backbench Liberals and contributed to the collapse of the Asquith coalition in December 1916. The Asquithian ex-cabinet ministers were only rehabilitated as free-traders in 1919. The resolutions themselves inspired the Committee on Commercial and Industrial Policy (see Balfour of Burleigh Committee (1916–18)), and were the basis of the *safeguarding policy adopted by the Lloyd George coalition immediately after the war, but economic events in the post-war slump soon outran the reach of the Paris policy. *JAT*

Parker, Hubert Lister (1900–72), judge. Called to the Bar in 1924, Parker was a High Court judge from 1950, lord justice of appeal, 1954–8, and lord chief justice, 1958–71. Though criticized for leniency in criminal cases heard on appeal, he was an innovative lord chief justice, introducing for example seminars at which judges, probation officers, and other interested parties could debate hypothetical cases and agree on common principles for sentencing. He chaired the inquiry into allegations of a leak concerning the raising of the Bank rate in 1957, reporting that Harold Wilson's claims were 'wholly false and altogether unsubstantiated'. *JAR*

Parkinson, Cecil Edward (1931–), Conservative politician. Although by no means a bad penny, Cecil Parkinson had a way of turning up: party chairman, displaced person, energy, then transport secretary, and then, after further exile, again party chairman—history repeating itself as *schadenfreude*. Originally at the Board of Trade, flitting as junior between continents, proud to be a first-rate salesman, he was, like his then friend, Norman Tebbit, an early Thatcher promotee. Moving steadily up from trade to the party chairmanship and the dream 1983 election, which he conducted gracefully and professionally, he was intended for a great office, probably foreign secretary, but was struck down by a woman that he had not only scorned but impregnated, Sarah Keays, to whom he would, when pressed, prefer his wife. After a dangerous hesitation, Thatcher accepted his resignation, appointing the most ostentatiously moral figure to hand, his deputy, John Gummer. Always looked to wistfully by the far from puritanical Thatcher, Parkinson might have returned sooner but for his personal dragon (and the cool dislike of William Whitelaw). After Whitelaw's retirement and another election victory in 1987, he returned at energy, conducting perhaps the most successful of all the privatizations, electricity. He succeeded, after a running wrangle, in getting his own way and excluding most nuclear energy from the deal, getting a less eccentric price than other privatizers and seeing the companies later thrive. He had backers for further advancement, including some surviving Thatcherian *tendresse*, but not enough for the Foreign Office or Treasury, successively taken by Major, enough for transport where stringency barred coups or projects and a lame conference speech put him out of further running. He sat out the Major era rather sourly, but was then William Hague's surprise choice for a transitional party chairman in 1997, in which post, once his springboard, he was thought hardly to have bounced.

EP

Cecil Parkinson, *Right at the Centre* (London, 1992).

parliament, broadcasting of. Ever since the appearance of radio, the House of Commons from time to time debated whether its proceedings should be broadcast. An experiment in sound broadcasting on a closed circuit network was undertaken in April and May 1968, and again in June and July 1975, but it was not until February 1978 that both the Commons and the Lords agreed to allow the BBC to provide a sound signal from the chambers and committee rooms. On Monday 3 April 1978, a permanent sound broadcasting system was launched. The televising of parliament was lengthily debated during the 1980s, with worries over changes to the traditional character of the chamber. The Lords was in the vanguard with a six-month experiment in January to June 1985, which was continued in July 1985 and authorized in May 1986 on an indefinite base. A motion on televising the Commons was defeated by 275 votes to 263 in November 1985, but, in February 1988, the principle of an experiment was approved by 318 votes to 264 with the creation of a select committee to consider the matter. The experiment began with the state opening on 21 November 1989, initially to continue until July 1990, when the proceedings were effectively made permanent. Tight rules were applied to coverage, limiting the type of shot which might be used, to protect the dignity of the House. These rules were gradually relaxed to allow reaction shots and wider views of the House. Live broadcasting has been largely limited to prime minister's questions and big occasions like budgets and emergency debates, though excerpts have been shown on, generally late night, programmes. Like C-Span in the USA, a dedicated Parliament Channel has since 1992 provided continuous unedited coverage of debates in the Commons chamber, showing proceedings of select committees and the House of Lords when the Commons is not sitting.

PJRR

Parliament Act, 1911. The House of Lords had theoretically equal legislative powers with the Commons until early in the 20th century, though by convention it did not reject 'money bills', those relating to the provision of funds for the carrying-on of government, the prerogative of the Commons since the 17th century. The Lords had, however, continued to thwart Liberal reforms in other areas, notably in summarily rejecting Gladstone's second Irish Home Rule Bill in 1893, which had already passed the Commons.

The Liberal governments of Campbell-Bannerman and Asquith after 1905 found themselves in continuous conflict with the Lords: Campbell-Bannerman spoke darkly of *'filling the cup' of Liberal grievances, while David Lloyd George dubbed the upper house *Mr Balfour's poodle, so tamely did it seem to follow the Conservative leader's instructions. The rejection of the *'People's Budget' in 1909, however, provided Liberals with a pretext for a showdown. The Liberal government won a general election in January 1910, so getting a mandate for its budget, which then passed the Lords, and after the failure of the *constitutional conference, Asquith then won a second general election in December, thereby getting a mandate also to end the Lords' veto powers.

A Parliament Bill was introduced on 21 February 1911 and passed its second reading in the Commons by 368 votes to 243. *George V had by then reluctantly agreed to coerce the Lords if necessary, by creating enough Liberal peers to pass the bill (since the Lords could only be shorn of their powers by a bill that the Lords as well as the Commons had agreed to pass). The large Conservative majority in the Lords raged, fretted, and eventually split (into *hedgers and ditchers) over the tactics of resistance. In the end, in a dramatic vote on 10 August, enough Conservative peers sided with the bishops and the Liberals (or abstained) to allow the bill to pass by 131 votes to 114. (See also LORDS, HOUSE OF: POWERS.) *JAR*

Parliament Act, 1949. In 1945, the Labour government had pledged not to permit its programme to be obstructed by the Lords. In 1947, a government bill was introduced to restrict the powers of the Lords under the *Parliament Act, 1911. Its effect was a reduction from three to two sessions in which a disputed bill must be passed by the Commons and from two years to one in the period of delay from second reading in the Commons. The bill was passed by the Commons in 1947, but debate in the Lords was adjourned to allow an inter-party conference between the party leaders. The conference (report published as Cmd 7380) did not agree on powers: the dispute over three months' extra delay was essentially whether it should be possible to pass controversial legislation introduced in the fourth year of a parliament. In default of agreement the bill as originally introduced was enacted under the provisions of the Parliament Act, 1911. On composition, there was agreement on certain principles, many of which were subsequently put into effect by the Conservative governments between 1951 and 1964. *MWB*

parliamentary commissioner, select committee on the, established in November 1967 to scrutinize the work of the parliamentary commissioner for administration appointed that April. It is chaired by a member of the opposition. The select committee's function is *post facto* scrutiny of the commissioner's work. Though it modelled itself on the Public Accounts Committee, its powers were initially more limited. Despite recommendations by the Procedure Committee in 1978 the committee continued and retained the power to study cases affecting any department. *KMT*

parliamentary commissioner for administration. See OMBUDSMAN.

Parliamentary Labour Party (PLP) (1906–), the collective body including all MPs taking the Labour whip. The PLP was initially subservient to the party's annual conference as the party's sovereign body. Historically, the PLP has been more moderate than the mass membership, as it represents the voters who elected Labour MPs rather than party members; MPs thus develop an 'electoralist' perspective not shared by the wider party. The PLP elects a twelve-member parliamentary committee, who become members of the first cabinet when Labour is in power. Attempts to re-establish a subservient PLP were made by reforms introduced in the 1970s which allowed constituency parties to deselect MPs, and set up an electoral college to elect the party leader, in which the electorate was widened to include trade unions and individual members. In practice deselection proved difficult to use, and the wider constituency to elect the party leader, beginning with Kinnock in 1983, has increased the parliamentary leader's legitimacy and made any challenge the more difficult. *BJE*

'parliamentary leper'. See SMETHWICK.

parliamentary lobby. The group of journalists covering the main political stories and behind the scenes developments. The term 'lobby' comes from their special access to the Members' lobby immediately outside the chamber and the adjoining Ways and Means corridor, not open to the public. Lobby journalists have been accredited on a list kept by the serjeant at arms since the 1880s when access to the palace of Westminster was restricted following a series of Irish terrorist attacks. Lobby journalists are distinct from the gallery reporters who cover what is said on the floor of the House and from parliamentary sketch writers who provide an often amusing flavour of a debate or exchange. The number of lobby journalists increased by more than a half from the 1960s onwards—up to around 220—following an expansion in the number of broadcasting stations and with the decline in gallery reporting of debates from the 1970s onwards. Separate from their access, lobby journalists can attend briefings held every day when parliament is sitting, in 10 Downing Street in the morning and in the lobby room in the palace of Westminster in the afternoon. These briefings started in the 1930s and were formalized in the 1950s. *PJRR*

parliamentary questions. The questioning by Members of ministers is one of the longest features of parliament. In 1900, more than 5,000 written or oral questions were asked per session, or roughly 41 a day. The total rose to an average of 13,200 in the 1920s, of which four-fifths were oral. After stabilizing in the inter-war period, the number of questions asked rose by two and a half times by the 1950s. By the early 1990s, the annual average was around 50,000. Questions come in various forms, not just oral and written but also questions to ministers, for the first hour of sitting from Monday to Thursday, and to the prime minister (see PRIME MINISTER'S QUESTIONS). In addition, MPs and opposition spokesmen occasionally table 'private notice questions' on the day about urgent topics which have suddenly arisen, such as a serious accident or foreign policy crisis. Whitehall departments are allocated question times of varying length on a monthly rota. Members have to table oral questions two weeks before each question time. The questions are then shuffled to fix the order in which they are put on the order paper and called by the Speaker. The Member asking the question is entitled to put a supplementary to the minister. Sometimes questions on the same topic are grouped together and opposition spokesmen are called on a number of questions. The Speaker alternates questioners from either side of the House and varies the amount of time allotted to a particular question depending on the interest and number of MPs rising. A large number of written questions are answered every day. *PJRR*

parliamentary session. For most of the century, parliament sat for around two-thirds of the year. By the second half of the century, the pattern was for the session to start with the *Queen's Speech in November, lasting until the following October or November, with a three-week recess at Christmas, from ten days to two weeks at Easter, one week in late May or early June, and roughly two and a half months in the summer and early autumn. From 1900 until 1930, the session lasted from February until July or August, and occasionally through the summer, but rarely during the autumn. In 1930, both Houses agreed to shift to a pattern nearer the academic year with sessions starting in the autumn. However, the increasing workload of legislation and an increased reluctance to sit long into August meant that the two Houses increasingly returned for an 'overspill' session to complete business in October with the state opening and Queen's Speech in November. The House of Commons has sat from the early afternoon until the late evening from Monday to Thursday (initially 2 p.m., then 2.45 p.m., and then 2.30 p.m. after 1945, with earlier starting times during the Second World War). The time for the adjournment of the House has varied depending on how many votes there are at 10 p.m. after the main debate and on how much additional business there is. Sittings lasting beyond midnight were common until the 1980s before a deliberate attempt was made to end between 10.30 p.m. and 11 p.m. On Fridays, the House sat from mid-morning until mid-afternoon: after 1939, from 11 a.m. until 4.30 p.m.; then from 1980, 9.30 a.m. until 3 p.m. Various experiments have been held with midweek morning sittings: for instance in 1969, and then on a more sustained basis on Wednesday mornings from the 1993–4 session (until the start of the parallel chamber in the Grand Committee room off Westminster Hall from November 1999). From the 1997–8 session, Thursday sittings began at 11.30 a.m. and lasted until 7.30 p.m. These changes in the late 1990s were accompanied by an increased number of constituency or non-sitting Fridays. *PJRR*

Parmoor, Lord **(1852–1940)**, Labour politician. Charles Alfred Cripps was a lawyer who stood as a Conservative before the Great War before crossing to Labour, becoming as Lord Parmoor Labour's lord president of the council, 1924 and 1929–31, but with little discernible impact. He was the brother-in-law of Beatrice Webb and the father of Stafford Cripps. *BB*

Parole Board, set up in 1967 to advise on the early release of prisoners still technically under sentence. The increasing use of parole indicated a shift in penal philosophy from retribution towards reform, since the supervised conditional release of prisoners, whose progress would continue to be monitored and reported on, was expected to improve the chances of rehabilitation, and to ease the transition from prison to civilian life, and so reduce the proportion who would reoffend. The board advised the home and Scottish secretaries (now Scotland's first minister) who issue actual licences authorizing early release. *JAR*

Parsons, Anthony Derrick **(1922–96)**, diplomat, writer, and commentator. Ambassador in Tehran from 1974 to 1979, Parsons was then permanent British representative to the UN, 1979–82, and special adviser on foreign affairs to the prime minister, 1982–3. He was instrumental at the UN during the Falklands war in securing the passage of resolution 502, condemning the Argentinian invasion, and in persuading Prime Minister Thatcher to enter preliminary negotiations. As a commentator on the UN and current events, his publications include *The Pride and the Fall* (London, 1984) and *From Cold War to Hot Peace* (London, 1995), *DHD*

Part, Antony Alexander **(1916–90)**, civil servant. Part entered the Board of Education in 1937 and, after a wartime stint in the Intelligence Corps, first made his mark as joint head of the school building branch of the Education Ministry in the late 1940s. By 1960 he had risen to be deputy secretary at education, but in 1963 was switched to the Ministry of Works, becoming permanent secretary, 1965–8. He was then, successively, permanent secretary at the Board of Trade (1968–70), Department of Trade and Industry (1970–4), and Department of Industry (1974–6). *KT*

party conferences. See under names of individual parties.

party finance, the means by which political parties obtain their funding. Michael Pinto-Duschinsky (1981) has identified three stages of party funding: the aristocratic era, the plutocratic era, and the modern era. The first of these lasted up to 1880 and the second until early in the 20th century. The modern era had its origins in the formation of the Labour Party. The aristocratic era was marked by bribery and high costs. The plutocratic era was characterized by the parties building up central funds through the largesse of businessmen, often in return for some public honour. The modern era has been characterized by a reliance on a wider spread of supporters. The newly formed Labour Party was funded by money from affiliated trade unions and, after 1918, by subscriptions from individual members (though the latter income was small compared to income from the unions). After the Great War, the Conservatives began to rely less on money from patronage-seeking businessmen and placed greater emphasis on donations from corporations and fund-raising by local party associations. The change occurred slowly and was not fully completed until the 1940s. By then the main pattern of modern party financing had emerged. 'Institutional sources of support had become (or were becoming) the mainstay of both major parties at national level. Labour headquarters relied almost entirely on trade union political levies and, on the Conservative side, company donations to the Central Office were gradually replacing payments by individuals. Constituency finance in both the Labour and the Conservative parties was becoming more dependent on small-scale fund raising by ordinary party members' (Pinto-Duschinsky, 126).

The quarter-century following the Second World War was characterized by this pattern, the Conservative Party in particular benefiting from an increase in party membership in the late 1940s. However, the closing decades of the century saw a crisis in party funding. Increases in costs outstripped increases in income. Membership of the Conservative Party declined in successive decades. The Labour Party had difficulty sustaining large and active constituency parties, the local parties relying on trade union funding. Trade union membership declined. In the 1990s, the Conservative Party had difficulty in attracting company donations on the scale to which it had been accustomed, though Labour was receiving more corporate contributions then ever before. Fears that the political parties would atrophy, and not be able to fulfil the tasks expected of them in a democracy, began to be expressed in the 1970s and in 1974 the Labour government announced the appointment of a committee on financial aid to political parties. The committee reported in 1976 with the majority recommending state aid for political parties based on the parties' electoral performance. A commission set up by the Hansard Society (1981) also recommended some measure of state aid based on matching funds for those donated by members. Neither set of recommendations has been implemented. Political parties receive effective state subsidies in the form of free distribution of election literature, the provision of rooms for public meetings and election broadcasts (and, in the case of opposition parliamentary parties, direct state aid to enable them to fulfil their parliamentary duties), but the issue of direct funding from the public purse remains controversial (see Ewing). By the end of the century, attracting sufficient funding to meet their needs remained a serious problem for both main political parties. *PN*

Keith Ewing, *The Funding of Political Parties in Britain* (Cambridge, 1987). | Hansard Society, *Paying for Politics: The Report of the Commission upon the Financing of Political Parties* (London, 1981). | Michael Pinto-Duschinsky, *British Political Finance 1830–1980* (Washington, 1981). | *Report of the Committee on Financial Aid to Political Parties* (Cmnd 6601, London, 1976).

party identification, long-term affinity felt toward a political party by an individual. The concept is essentially a psychological rather than a behavioural one. A person may feel an attachment to a particular party even though not necessarily voting for it in each and every election. The concept was first developed and subjected to empirical research in the USA but has since been employed by researchers in the UK. Party identification is often acquired through parental influence and is an important, but not necessarily an exclusive, influence on voting behaviour. In recent decades it has shown a notable decline, especially in terms of strong identification. In 1964 about 80 per cent of voters had a partisan identity. By 1983 the proportion had dropped to around 70 per cent. However, those expressing a strong identity virtually halved in number, from 43.4 per cent in the period from 1964–70 to 22.8 per cent in the period 1974–92. Unlike in the USA, where a decline in party identification was marked among young voters, the decline in the UK has been fairly uniform across the electorate. As class has declined in significance (though some political scientists, notably Heath, Jowell, and Curtice, 1985, have contested this), so class *dealignment appears to have contributed to partisan dealignment. Voters no longer associate strongly with their natural class party. Parties can no longer take for granted to the extent that they did in the middle decades of the century the support of a large block of strong party identifiers. As voters become more sensitive to more transient influences, so parties have to work harder to retain or improve upon existing levels of support. The extent of partisan dealignment is reflected in greater electoral volatility, apparent in voting behaviour since the 1960s. The concept of party identification has some utility but has a number of limitations. Nonetheless, it remains a useful concept. 'The *concept* of party identification provides a precise measure of dealignment and an initial explanation of volatility. It provides the simplest measure for distinguishing short-term and long-term electoral trends. It explains much about how voters interpret political information. Above all it explains why even in an age of dealignment most voters go on supporting the same party at election after election' (Harrop and Miller, 145). *PN*

Martin Harrop and William L. Miller, *Elections and Voters: A Comparative Introduction* (London, 1987). | Anthony Heath, Roger Jowell, and John Curtice, *How Britain Votes* (Oxford, 1985).

'party's over, the'. This phrase of Environment Secretary Crosland, to a local government conference in 1975, encapsulated the change in government policy from increasing to reducing local government revenue expenditure. As a known advocate of public expenditure, Crosland's statement forcibly signalled the scale of the emerging economic crisis of the mid-1970s. *BJE*

party systems, the different configurations of relationships between parties. A wide variety of relationships exists in different countries, and attempts have been made to categorize them, the most frequent basis of categorization being the number of parties. The simplest categorization has been trichotomous: one-, two-, and multi-party systems. Various studies have sought to refine this classification, such as multi-party systems with a dominant party and multi-party systems without a dominant party. La Palombara and Weiner offered a new typology for competitive party systems: hegemonic ideological, hegemonic pragmatic, turnover ideological, and turnover pragmatic. Sartori criticized this typology for being too sweeping and devised a classification that drew on the number of parties but also went beyond numbers to look at relevance. He produced a sevenfold classification: one party, hegemonic party, predominant party, two-party, limited pluralism, extreme pluralism, and atomized. Britain, he recognized, was offered as the archetypical two-party system, characterized by two parties being in a position to compete for the absolute majority of seats, one of the two succeeding in winning an absolute majority, the winning party being willing to govern alone, and alternation or rotation in office remaining a credible expectation. He acknowledged that in the first half of the century the country deviated from these properties. Though there was usually a party winning an absolute majority, there were periods when a governing party relied on support from another party, the Liberals relying for a time on Irish Nationalist support and the Labour Party in government being dependent on Liberal support, or at least acquiescence. In Sartori's classification, Britain appeared to hover on the border between a two-party system and—for periods when no one party had an absolute majority of seats—one of limited pluralism. Sartori's classification is based on competition at the parliamentary level (the number of seats won). If electoral competition (the number of votes won) is taken into account, Norton argued that the picture becomes more complex, with different configurations emerging. Only in the period from 1945 to 1974 can it be said that Britain exhibited the form and properties of Sartori's two-party system. Third parties existed but, in Sartori's terms, were not relevant: they were not needed for coalition purposes and did not affect the direction taken by other parties. The latter half of the 1970s was characterized by a form of limited pluralism. The extended period of Conservative government after 1979 led some commentators to argue, especially after the fourth consecutive Conservative election victory in 1992, that a predominant party system was emerging. The election of a Labour government in 1997 and 2001 served to swing the system back to a two-party one. The size of the government's overall majorities—among the largest of all time—suggested that there could be a new predominant system emerging. Conversely, the electoral performance and parliamentary representation of the Liberal Democratic Party also lent itself to the view that moderate pluralism could be a feature of the new millennium. *PN*

Jean Blondel, 'Party Systems and Patterns of Government in Western Democracies', *Canadian Journal of Political Science*, 1 (1968). | Anthony King, 'The Implications of One-Party Government', in his (ed.) *Britain at the Polls 1992* (Chatham, NJ, 1993). | Helen Margetts and Gareth Smyth (eds.), *Turning Japanese? Britain with a Permanent Party of Government* (London, 1994). | Philip Norton, 'Britain: Still a Two-Party System', in S. Bartolini and P. Mair (eds.), *Party Politics in Contemporary Western Europe* (London, 1984). | Giovanni Sartori, *Parties and Party Systems: A Framework for Analysis* (Cambridge, 1976).

patent legislation. Britain's modern patent system has its origins in the Patents, Designs and Trade Marks Act, 1883. The system, however, has been under constant review ever since, with major updates occurring in 1888, 1902, 1919, 1932, 1949, and 1977. The most important of these was the Patents Act, 1977, which brought British law into line with the various international agreements to which the UK had become a signatory, most notably the Patent Cooperation treaty (1970) and the European Patent convention (1973). *GBM*

Paton, John (1886–1976), Labour politician. A Scotsman, Paton was appointed Northern organizer for the Independent Labour Party in 1919 and became general secretary in 1927. He resigned in 1933 as a result of the adoption of a 'united front' policy and broke with the party shortly after. In 1945 he was elected as Labour MP for Norwich, serving until 1964, and was married to Florence Paton, also a Labour MP, 1945–50. He was active in matters relating to social security, housing, and education, but is best remembered for his campaigning on behalf of penal reform and for his expertise on the Far East. *DWM*

John Paton, *Proletarian Pilgrimage: An Autobiography* (London, 1935). | John Paton, *Left Turn! the Autobiography of John Paton* (London, 1976).

Patten, Christopher Francis (1944–), Conservative politician, colonial governor, and European commissioner. The natural choice as leader, for many, of a Conservative Party wanting to win, Chris Patten was a product of the politics of Heath and Macleod, a liberal, humanitarian, unostentatious Catholic Christian, grudgingly liked by right-wingers. He had been director of the *Conservative Research Department, but advanced slowly under Thatcher, who was variously perplexed, irked, and charmed, and needed his speechwriting talents. On the backbenches, Patten opposed many Thatcher measures, such as heavier lorries, cuts in housing and unemployment benefit, and wrote pamphlets against monetarism. He was, though, sent to Northern Ireland as a token Catholic minister, authorizing the explosive name change of Derry for Londonderry, and was then a junior minister successively at education and overseas development before becoming in 1989 secretary for environment. As a friend of John Major, he took the party chairmanship in 1990, a post too far for the voters of Bath who deprived him of his own seat in 1992, even when the campaign he had run had seen Major re-elected. Patten received the doubtful consolation of the governorship of *Hong Kong to supervise a decolonizing retreat before the mainland Chinese regime. Giving the colony representative institutions, he was roundly abused by Chinese Communists and their British apologists. It all ended with a midnight shipboard party, lowered flags, a royal presence, and symbols all round. Patten returned to be sent to Brussels as a European commissioner by Blair, a more congenial posting for a strong pro-European. *EP*

Paynter, Thomas William (1903–84), trade unionist and communist. Will Paynter was actively involved in inter-war communist political activity and he served briefly as a Comintern courier to the communist underground in Nazi Germany, 1933. He was president of the south Wales area of the National Union of Mineworkers (NUM), 1951–9, and was secretary of the NUM, 1959–68. Despite his communism, he had the reputation of a moderate trade union leader. *DWM*

T. W. Paynter, *My Generation* (London, 1972).

'peace for our time', declaration by Neville Chamberlain upon return from the Munich conference, 1938 (see Munich Crisis), indicating his relief at having averted an imminent European war. The phrase was borrowed from his predecessor, Benjamin Disraeli, in 1878 and Chamberlain immediately regretted using it, realizing that it might be prematurely euphoric, as indeed it was. *NJC*

Peace process, mark I. In 1991, in the face of increasing violence (especially from the Loyalist side), the Dublin and London governments evolved the idea of three 'strands' of a settlement plan: Unionist–Nationalist relations in Northern Ireland; north–south relations in Ireland; and Anglo-Irish relations. Nothing would be agreed until everything was agreed. From the later 1980s the Social Democratic and Labour Party leader, John Hume, embarked on talks with the Sinn Fein leader, Gerry Adams, to draw Sinn Fein into the political process. In November 1990, the Northern Ireland secretary, Peter Brooke, declared that Britain had 'no selfish, strategic or economic interest' in Northern Ireland. In October 1991 Hume produced his 'Strategy for peace and justice in Ireland' which spoke of 'self-determination', but with partition remaining 'for the moment at least'. In January 1992 the Irish prime minister, Albert Reynolds, took a hand, and in April 1992 Sinn Fein produced its proposals for a 'lasting peace', with the aspiration for a united Ireland taking precedence over the demand for one. The IRA army council approved the Hume-Adams initiative. When Reynolds met Major at an EU session in October 1993, they agreed to move forward, but Major did not accept the Hume-Adams document as a basis from which to work. On 28 November it was revealed that the British government had itself had regular communications with Sinn Fein and the IRA. The two governments made a joint declaration on 15 December 1993, reiterating the British lack of selfish interest in Northern Ireland and affirming the Irish right to self-determination, but with the Irish government accepting that this must operate only with the consent of a majority in Northern Ireland. The British would promote and facilitate any agreement arrived at. This document was not to the liking of Unionists, but Sinn Fein took encouragement from it, ceasing to demand a British withdrawal as a precondition of a settlement. The IRA thus called a *ceasefire on 31 August 1994, and Loyalist paramilitaries responded on 10 October. The British government was, though, losing its parliamentary majority, and there were suspicions that it was dragging its feet because of increasing reliance on the Ulster Unionists at Westminster, but it did authorize talks at ministerial level with Sinn Fein. The process ran into trouble over the question of 'decommissioning' terrorist weapons. The British accepted the idea of an international commission led by Senator George Mitchell, but the IRA ceasefire ended on 9 February 1996 with a huge IRA bomb in *Canary Wharf, London.

DGB

PAUL BEW and GORDON GILLESPIE (eds.), *Northern Ireland: Chronology of the Troubles, 1968–1993* (Dublin, 1993). | EAMONN MALLIE and DAVID MCKITTRICK, *The Fight for Peace: The Secret Story behind the Irish Peace Process* (London, 1996). | BRIAN ROWAN, *Behind the Headlines: The Story of the IRA and Loyalist Ceasefires* (Belfast, 1995).

Peace process, mark II. In September 1996 the IRA offered a new *ceasefire, with no decommissioning of arms until a settlement was reached, and with 'confidence'-building measures such as the release of prisoners. The Labour Party's overwhelming victory in the general election of May 1997 brought matters to a head once more. Prime minister Tony Blair sought to balance reassurances to Unionists that the union was safe, with overtures to Sinn Fein to enter the negotiating process—not least because, in the elections of 1997 it won 40 per cent of the nationalist vote. The Irish Republic experienced a change of government as well, with the return of Fianna Fáil to power, led by the pragmatic Bertie Ahern. On 9 July the British government thus declared that Sinn Fein could enter talks without decommissioning, providing that it committed itself to the Mitchell principles of non-violence, and on 20 July 1997 the IRA began another ceasefire. David Trimble led his Ulster Unionists into the talks in September, while the Revd Ian Paisley's Democratic Unionists stayed firmly away; small Loyalist parties with links to terrorist groups also entered the process. Negotiations were protracted, and often seemed to be on the point of failure, but on Good Friday, 10 April 1998, agreement was reached between the parties, although only after Trimble received some concessions, including a handwritten letter from Blair stating that decommissioning of arms 'should begin straight away'. The settlement plan envisaged devolved government in Northern Ireland, cross-border institutions, and institutional links between the nations of the British Isles. A referendum held on 22 May produced a 'yes' vote in both parts of Ireland (71.12 per cent in the North, 94.39 per cent in the South). As a result of Assembly elections on 25 June, Trimble emerged as chief executive, with the other posts going to the Ulster Unionist Party (3), Social Democratic and Labour Party (3), and Sinn Fein (2). Cross-border institutions were agreed on 18 December 1998, but the handing over of powers to the executive was held up by the refusal of the IRA to begin decommissioning weapons, which Trimble insisted upon as a precondition to Sinn Fein entering government. Meanwhile, the fragile nature of peace in Northern Ireland was illustrated by the continuing confrontation between members of the Orange Order and nationalists over the right of the order to march on its traditional route down the Garvaghy road, near Drumcree, Portadown, by the Omagh bombing on 15 August 1998, and by Loyalist and IRA 'punishment beatings' and the Loyalist murder in

March 1999 of a solicitor who represented nationalists and republicans. *DGB*

Peacock report (1985), on financing the BBC, advocated steps towards a free television market including privatizing Radio 1 and 2. Following its recommendations ITV franchises were given to the highest bidder, the Independent Broadcasting Authority was dissolved into new regulatory authorities, and BBC and ITV had to purchase more independently made programmes. *KMT*

Pearse, Patrick Henry (1879–1916), Irish writer and nationalist. A Dublin-born Irish cultural nationalist, Pearse was educated by the Christian Brothers, involved with the Gaelic League, and editor of the latter's journal, *An Claidheamh Soluis*, 1903–9. A committed educationalist, he established St Enda's bilingual (Irish and English) secondary school in Dublin in 1908. A supporter of home rule, he then became more militant in his nationalism. Pearse was a founder member of the Irish Volunteers in 1913, became their director of operations, and was among the organization's more militant spirits. He joined the Irish Republican Brotherhood (IRB) and became a member of its supreme council. As a member also of the IRB's military council, he was heavily involved in the conspiracy behind the 1916 *Easter Rising. Pearse was commander-in-chief of the volunteers during that rebellion, and president of its provisional government. He was court-martialled and executed for his role in the rising. More than any other 1916 rebel, Pearse became an icon for subsequent Irish republicanism: his spiritual, idealistic, sacrificial, and essentially naive form of nationalism have exerted a profound and lasting influence. *RE*

Ruth Dudley Edwards, *Patrick Pearse: The Triumph of Failure* (London, 1977).

Pease, Joseph Albert ('Jack') (1860–1943), Liberal politician, from the prominent Quaker coal-owning and ironmaking family. Pease was successively MP for Tyneside, Saffron Walden, and Rotherham, 1892–1917, when he went to the Lords as 1st Lord Gainford. He was an effective chief whip, 1908–10, but his political success thereafter was limited, for he achieved only the junior cabinet posts of the duchy of Lancaster (1910–11), the Board of Education (1911–15), and the Post Office (1916). A Liberal loyalist, he left office with Asquith and did not serve under Lloyd George. He was the first chairman of the BBC, 1922–6. *JAR*

Cameron Hazlehurst and Christine Woodland (eds.), *A Liberal Chronicle: Journals and Papers of J. A. Pease, 1908–1910* (London, 1994).

Peel, 1st earl (1867–1937), Conservative minister. Son of a Speaker of the Commons and grandson of Peel the prime minister, 'Willie' Peel entered parliament in 1900, succeeding his father as viscount in 1912 (1st earl, 1929). He gained office in Lloyd George's coalition, was one of the few senior ministers to support Law after the *Carlton Club meeting in 1922, and became Indian secretary. He continued in cabinet under Baldwin. Despite his heritage, perhaps because of it, he was a confirmed party loyalist. *RJQA*

'Peers v. People' (1910), cry adopted by the Liberals in their political campaigning between the Lords' rejection of the *'People's Budget' in 1909 and the passing of the 1911 Parliament Act, for example in the speeches of David Lloyd George at *Limehouse and subsequently at Newcastle-upon-Tyne. This assertion of the rights of the Commons as the popularly elected chamber proved to be electorally most successful, and seriously inhibited the Unionists' counter-claims about Liberal revolutionary radicalism. *JAR*

Edward Pearce, *Lines of Most Resistance: The Lords, the Tories and Ireland* (London, 1999).

Pelling, Henry Mathison (1920–97), historian. Born on the Wirral and educated at Birkenhead and St John's, Cambridge, Pelling's undergraduate career was interrupted by military service, including fierce combat in Normandy. He was a fellow of Queen's, Oxford, 1949–66, and then of St John's, Cambridge. A reserved scholar known for generosity and a dry wit, he was particularly admired for continuing to work unrelentingly after a serious stroke in 1971. Latterly, Pelling concentrated on the career of Churchill and politics in the era of the war in which he had fought, but his reputation was made by pioneering work on the early years of the Labour movement. In *The Origins of the Labour Party* (1954) and subsequent volumes, he carefully demythologized his subject and thereby established the agenda and tone in what was essentially the new field of Labour history. He noted that the birth of the Labour Party in 1900 was 'hardly noticed by the outside world', and there had been only 'nine spectators in the gallery'. Ideas were less important than Hardie's homely voice. Twenty years of detailed research culminated in *Popular Politics and Society* (1968) in which he gave authoritative judgements on the various debates attending the emergence of Britain's highly distinctive working-class party. *PS*

Penhaligon, David (1944–86), Liberal politician. A Cornishman who built on the surviving Liberal tradition in the south-west and adapted it to *community politics, he won the Truro seat, not traditionally Liberal, in 1974. A powerful and down-to-earth voice in parliament, Penhaligon was president of the Liberal Party, 1985–6, and considered a possible future leader before his early death in a road accident. *JS*

Penkovsky, Oleg Vladimirovich (1919–63), deputy head of the foreign section of Soviet military intelligence and Anglo-American agent. Penkovsky attended the Kiev artillery school and joined the Communist Party in 1940. During the Second World War he worked for Russian intelligence and was a highly successful field officer, commanding an artillery anti-tank brigade, taking part in three campaigns, and ending the war a much-decorated officer. After the war, he undertook further studies and went to work for Soviet military intelligence (the GRU), where he had access to a broad range of strategic and tactical military information. However, in the 1950s the KGB discovered his father's background (as a tsarist officer) and Penkovsky was branded politically unreliable: this became the key reason for his defection. In 1960, Penkovsky's initial approach to American intelligence was rebuffed, but he was later recruited by British intelligence and then jointly run with the CIA. Thereafter, Penkovsky became the West's most important agent. The information he passed was of incalculable value to the West and personally to President Kennedy during his 1961 Vienna meeting with Khrushchev and during the Berlin Wall crisis. The information Penkovsky provided included manuals of Soviet nuclear missile site construction, which enabled the CIA to target its U-2 planes during the Cuban missile crisis. The main assessments during the crisis bear his code name 'Ironbark' (thus acknowledging their debt to the documents he had provided). In 1962, Penkovsky was arrested in Moscow with his British contact Greville Wynne. He was tortured and the following year the Soviet Union tried and executed him. His astonishing story was published in 1964 as *The Penkovsky Papers*. *PM*

Penney, William George (1909–91), scientist and government official. During the Second World War, Penney was engaged in work that led to the development of the atomic bomb. Working at the Ministry of Supply, 1946–52, he led the team which designed the first British A-bomb. Director of the atomic weapons research establishment at Aldermaston (1953–9), he then developed the British hydrogen bomb. Penney was then appointed deputy chairman (1961–4) and chairman (1964–7) of the atomic energy authority. He was made a life peer in 1967. *KT*

Penrhyn strike, the 'Great Strike' (as it was often called), was actually a lockout. It occurred in 1900–3 at the north Wales slate quarries belonging to Lord Penrhyn. The dispute, which first flared up in 1896–7, arose out of Lord Penrhyn's determination to cancel concessions made by his father and to destroy trade unionism amongst his workers. The clash between a feudal employer who lived in a castle and an impoverished and largely monoglot Welsh labour force was utterly dramatic. It was a tragic dispute both for the workers and for the industry which never recovered. *PS*

pensions, old age. State old-age pensions were first introduced by Asquith's Liberal government in 1908. This scheme provided small non-contributory pensions to a limited number of people over the age of 70 based on a *means test. It was a radical step, aimed at alleviating reliance on the poor law and reducing poverty. Until then, the majority of the elderly still worked in their old age. Following the Great War, a long campaign began for universal, tax-funded state pensions. The first limited contributory scheme was introduced in 1925 by Neville *Chamberlain, for those aged 65–70. Neither this nor the 1908 scheme, however, required recipients to be retired from employment. During the Second World War, in the spirit of greater equality, reconstruction, and planning, the *Beveridge report (1942) recommended a new universal, contributory scheme, with pensions conditional upon retirement from work. The *National Insurance Act, 1946, legislated for these proposals and they were introduced in 1948. In 1959, a state scheme of graduated pensions was introduced, based on salary levels.

From the late 1970s, though, state pensions began to suffer. In 1978 the Occupational Pension Act encouraged the rapid growth of non-state pensions. Many employers established occupational arrangements in which contributions were paid into income yielding assets. Successive Conservative governments further encouraged their growth by offering tax benefits to such schemes. At the same time, state pensions were subject to further legislation. In 1980, the recently established link between pension rates and general earnings was removed. By the 1990s, there was much discussion of the burden of future pension costs given the rapidly ageing profile of Britain's population. These concerns and the dwindling levels of state pensions disconnected from the earnings link led to considerable political disquiet. By the close of 2000, pensions were clearly set to become a burning issue for the next century. *JJN*

Penybeth. See Bombing School incident.

'People's Budget' (1909), controversial political initiative and turning point in public finance. The budget of 1909 was predictably important for many reasons; Asquith's Liberal government was in the doldrums after by-election defeats and its inability to get much of its reforming legislation through the Lords; the increasing cost of naval building as an arms race built up with Germany was putting considerable strain on traditional sources of public revenue, as were old age pensions; a vociferous opposition was proclaiming that only tariffs, to which Liberals were implacably opposed, could rescue public finance by providing new revenue sources; it would be the first budget of David *Lloyd George, who would try to strike an attention-grabbing blow both for the government and for his own career. In the event, the budget, on 29 April 1909, lived up to expectations both in content and in the language by which it was defended and attacked.

Lloyd George found many sources of revenue: new or increased taxes would be levied on motor vehicles, petrol, spirits, and tobacco; tax on larger incomes would rise and a super-tax would apply to incomes over £5,000; death duties would be increased; licensing duties (on licensed premises supplying alcohol) would rise sharply; there would be *land taxes on the 'unearned increment' in values (that which did not follow from investment in the property). All this would enable the government both to build up national defences and at the same time to declare a 'war on poverty' at home.

After a few days of stunned, astonished silence, Conservatives and their press supporters launched angry denunciations of the budget, describing it as a revolutionary set of proposals which would vindictively fleece the rich, the landowning class, and 'the trade' (all by and large Conservative supporters), generally for the benefit of the Liberals' own client-voters. They also saw it as a quite disgraceful use of budgetary procedures—the Lords could not by convention reject a 'money bill'—to push through a social revolution, which was far from limited to finance. It was this last assumption that led them into the constitutional crisis of 1909–11, by which the House of Lords lost its right to veto any bills permanently. It has therefore often been asked whether Lloyd George was in fact deliberately laying a trap for the Conservatives and the Lords, hoping that they would reject his budget and so provoke a crisis which the *'Peers v. People' cry (over what Lloyd George had already called his 'People's Budget') ensured that they could not win. The evidence suggests otherwise, but in fact the Liberals were likely to win either way: if the Tory majority in the Lords were to pass the budget, then the Liberal government would have a major success; if they were to reject it, it could go on to win an even bigger prize.

In the event, the Unionists harried the bill during many weeks of debate in the Commons, where eventually the Liberal majority was bound to prevail, and used a *Budget Protest League to stir up opposition in the country. When it reached the Lords, it was summarily rejected after a single debate on 30 November by 350 votes to 75. Unionist peers, by then incensed anyway by violent attacks on them of the sort that Lloyd George had made in speeches at *Limehouse and Newcastle, barely paused to consider the consequences, but their official defence of rejection was that the budget contained such far-reaching proposals that it ought to be decided at a general election. Therein lay their ultimate downfall, for, when Asquith sought and won a general election in January 1910, they had no option but tamely to pass the budget on 28 April.

By then, however, the issues in dispute had become much wider, and the Liberal dependence on Irish MPs to remain in office ensured (even if their own preferences had not) that they would now seek the permanent curtailment of the Lords' powers. This they duly did, after the *Constitutional Conference and a second election in December 1910, in the *Parliament Act, 1911, one of whose provisions formally prevented the Lords even from delaying for more than a month any money bill in future. *JAR*

Bruce K. Murray, *The People's Budget, 1909–1910* (Oxford, 1980).

People's Democracy, radical student movement emerged in Belfast in late 1968 in response to the growing conflict in Northern Ireland over civil rights and influenced by the worldwide student protest movements. It organized marches and meetings, culminating with the controversial Belfast to Derry march in late 1968–early 1969 which provoked Loyalist attack at Burntollet, Co. Londonderry, and served to destabilize attempts to build community support for reforms. Subsequently popular student support for the movement declined, although it survived until the early 1980s. *BMW*

PAUL ARTHUR, *The People's Democracy, 1968–1973* (Belfast, 1974).

People's League for the Defence of Freedom (PLDF), middle-class pressure group of the mid-1950s, led by Edward *Martell. It took an extreme liberal viewpoint (in the Continental sense which placed liberals on the extreme right) urging less state intervention, lower taxes, and the curbing of trade unions. The PLDF was briefly successful in attracting disaffected voters during the 1956–8 recession, but failed to achieve second place in the 1957 East Ham by-election and then faded quickly. Ancestor of Martell's Freedom Association that operated in the 1960s and other later right-wing fringe political groups. *JAR*

Percy, Lord Eustace (1887–1958), Conservative politician, diplomat, and educationalist. Conservative MP for Hastings, 1921–37, Percy was promoted to minor office at the Board of Education, but initial promise was not fulfilled, for he was hampered by dislike of the partisanship of party politics. He was overlooked for office, 1931–5, and labelled 'Useless Percy' by his critics. He returned to office as minister without portfolio in 1935 but resigned a year later complaining of a lack of authority. *NJC*

Percy report (1957), on mental illness, reflected changed attitudes since the previous legislation of 1930 away from a coercive approach handled by local authorities. The committee was appointed following cases of adolescents claiming unwarranted detention. Much focus was put on the rights of the mentally ill, leading to the release of thousands whilst the committee sat. In line with the report's recommendations, the 1959 Mental Health Act allowed voluntary admissions and passed the responsibility for other admissions to doctors. *KMT*

Perth, declaration of (May 1968). At the Scottish Conservatives' annual conference, the leader of the opposition, Edward Heath, issued a policy statement announcing that the party would support devolution. This was in response to the rise of the Scottish National Party which had won the Hamilton by-election in 1967 and made sweeping gains in local elections. Heath at that time believed that Scottish nationalism was the 'coming force' in British politics, but another important factor in his endorsement of devolution was the discomfort it would cause the Wilson administration which had just appointed a royal commission (see KILBRANDON REPORT) to examine the constitution. Heath's policy was unpopular with rank and file Scottish Conservatives and many resented the way in which it was imposed from the top. As the challenge from the nationalists waned in the early 1970s, the policy was forgotten during Heath's administration of 1970–4. It was briefly reactivated by Sir Alec Douglas-Home during the referendum campaign of 1979, when he urged Scottish voters to reject Labour proposals for a Scottish assembly on the basis that a Conservative government would offer something better. Conservative support for devolution was formally repudiated in late 1979. *RF*

Pethick-Lawrence, Frederick William (1871–1961), lawyer and Labour politician. Pethick-Lawrence was secretary for India, 1945–7. During the key trip to India during the process of granting independence he played second fiddle to Cripps but had an important mediating role and was trusted by the Congress Party. Though never a politician of the first rank he was the classic radical of the first half of the century, a committed feminist, Women's Social and Political Union campaigner, and social reformer; he might have been a character from an H. G. Wells novel. *BB*

petitions to the House of Commons. See COMMONS, HOUSE OF: PETITIONS TO.

Peyton, John Wynne William (1919–), Conservative politician. Elected in 1951, Peyton won prominence as Heath's transport minister by denationalizing Thomas Cook's and making motor-cyclists wear helmets. He unwisely entered the 1975 Tory leadership election, attracting only eleven votes. In 1979 his mortification at being the only shadow cabinet member whom Thatcher rejected for office led him to tell her some home truths. This traditional Tory entered the Lords in 1983. *RJS*

JOHN PEYTON, *Without Benefit of Laundry* (London, 1997).

Philby, Harold Adrian Russell ('Kim') (1912–88), Soviet agent. Born in British India, the eldest child of an Indian civil servant, explorer, and orientalist, Philby was nicknamed 'Kim' after the youthful spy in Kipling's eponymous novel. Educated at Westminster and Trinity College, Cambridge, he left with a degree in economics.

Whilst at Cambridge he joined the university socialist society and became a convinced communist. After Cambridge, Philby went to Vienna where he met and married Alice ('Litzi') Friedman, an Austrian communist who persuaded him to become a Soviet agent. Back in London, Philby was recruited and ordered to sever his links with his communist past and move to the far right. He became involved with pro-Nazi groups and reported the Spanish civil war for *The Times*. He returned to London, his right wing credentials established, and in 1940 he was recruited into SIS (the Secret Intelligence Service or MI6), soon joining the counter-intelligence branch, and in 1944 he became head of the Communist espionage and counter-subversion section. After the war, he was posted first to Turkey then to Washington, from where he kept Moscow informed of Anglo-American intelligence collaboration. He saw the net close around his fellow traitor Donald Maclean, and was seriously compromised when Guy Burgess, with whom he was living and on whom no suspicions lay, fled with Maclean to Moscow. He was recalled to London, where he underwent an informal trial, and, despite his supporters, few people believed his innocence. However, forced to leave SIS, he became a journalist based in the Middle East. In 1963 the evidence of a defecting KGB agent finally provided the necessary evidence to implicate Philby, who confessed to an SIS colleague and escaped to Russia where he believed he would be welcomed as a KGB officer. In fact his status proved to be no more than 'Agent Tom'. Thereafter, thoroughly disillusioned, he lived a life in the shadows. He was given Soviet citizenship and many Soviet honours. When Philby died in 1988 the KGB organized an elaborate funeral honouring their greatest agent. *PM*

Philip, Duke of Edinburgh (1921–), husband and consort of Elizabeth II. His uncle, later Lord Mountbatten, successfully pressed for his marriage to the then Princess Elizabeth, whom he met for the first time when she was 13. They married in 1947. Philip supported the queen on her travels throughout Britain and the world, and also achieved prominence as president of the World Wildlife Fund, as an encourager of industry through the Duke of Edinburgh's Awards, and as someone who made rather too many ill-judged remarks within hearing of the press. *WMK*

Phillips, Morgan (1902–63), Labour organizer. As general secretary, 1944–62, Phillips was the key bureaucrat of the Labour Party in this period, responsible for organization and discipline. He was the classic working-class right-wing Labour politician of the 1950s. Staunchly loyal to the leadership and the achievements of the Attlee governments, he firmly adhered to the principle that socialism was what the majority of the Labour Party said it was, especially if that majority were made up of block votes. Under his control the party machine exercised democratic centralism, which entailed adherence to conference decisions and policies, so long as those policies remained broadly social democrat. The organization of ginger groups, like Victory for Socialism, was condemned by Phillips, but when the leadership was defeated and the right began to organize, his model of party control was challenged. Organizationally, the party ossified in the 1950s and membership declined to the extent that Harold Wilson described his own party as a 'penny farthing organization', a damning comment on Phillips's record as general secretary for which Phillips never forgave him. Phillips's reputation never recovered from Wilson's assault and, following a stroke in September 1960, he retired in 1962. Significantly, it was Phillips who famously declared that the Labour Party 'owes more to Methodism than to Marx'. *BB*

Phipps, Eric Claire Edmund (1875–1945), diplomat. Phipps entered the diplomatic service in 1899 and was in 1928–33 minister in Vienna. In 1933 he was appointed ambassador in Berlin where he served until 1937. His caustic despatches reveal his scathing views of the Nazis, describing the method of Hitler's rise as 'per aspera ad astra' (through harshness to the stars), a play on the RAF motto 'per ardua ad astra' (through endeavour to the stars). From 1937 until 1939 he was ambassador in Paris, from whence he warned of the dangers of French demoralization. *AJC*

Pickford, William. See STERNDALE, LORD.

Pigou, Arthur (1877–1959), economist. A follower of Alfred Marshall, Pigou's seminal work was *Wealth and Welfare* (1912). This established him as the founder of the welfare theory branch of economics, and went through several subsequent and expanded editions as *The Economics of Welfare*. Although he served on both the Cunliffe committee (1918–19) and the Chamberlain committee (1924–5), Pigou spent most of his life as a Cambridge academic. He is remembered as a representative of *classical economics, against which the *Keynesians revolted. *HOJ*

Pilkington report (1962), on broadcasting. Though reinforcing the duopoly principle, it vindicated the BBC and criticized ITV for excessive profits and populist broadcasting. Its recommendations for reorganizing ITV were disregarded but the report paved the way for the adoption of 625-line television broadcasting and the launch of BBC2 in 1964. *KMT*

Piratin, Philip (1907–96), Communist politician. Phil Piratin was a leading member of the Communist Party of Great Britain, serving both as London organizer and as West Middlesex organizer. He played a key role in the struggles and clashes of the inter-war years, including organizing rent strikes in the East End, and was Communist MP for Stepney, Mile End, in 1945–50. Piratin also served as a member of Stepney borough council, 1937–49. *DWM*

PHIL PIRATIN, *Our Flag stays Red* (London, 1978).

Pitblado, David Bruce (1912–97), prime ministers' principal private secretary, 1951–6. A Treasury official and future permanent secretary, Pitblado joined Clement Attlee's private office shortly before Winston Churchill returned to power. Churchill wanted Pitblado replaced by the more junior John Colville, who had been his wartime private secretary, but was persuaded to accept them as joint principal private secretaries. Pitblado, concentrating on home affairs, won Churchill's trust and helped to keep the government operating following the prime minister's stroke (1953), but Colville, always closer to Churchill, took the lead. *CL*

Plaid Cymru, Welsh political party. Founded as Plaid Genedlaethol Cymru (the Welsh National Party), in August 1925 at the Eisteddfod in Pwllheli, Plaid Cymru was initially more a cultural group than a political party. In its first electoral contest in Caernarfon in 1929 the party gained only 609 votes—the pre-war years as a whole were to be electorally barren for the party. Direct action to secure its aims appealed to some within Plaid Cymru. The burning of the RAF *Bombing School at Penyberth in September 1936 has entered the folklore of the party. The three men charged with the fire, Saunders Lewis, Lewis Valentine, and D. J. Williams, were leading figures in Welsh society and in Plaid Cymru. Their trial caused a wave of sympathy for the three defendants and a surge of support for Plaid Cymru. During the war years Plaid Cymru performed respectably in several by-elections, winning 22.5 per cent of the vote in the University of Wales seat in 1943, almost a quarter of the votes cast in Caernarfon boroughs, and 16.2 per cent of the vote in the Neath by-election in 1945. Plaid Cymru showed that these results were not solely due to the wartime party truce when it fielded seven candidates in the 1945 general election and performed well in the Ogmore and Aberdare by-elections in 1946. From 1945 onwards the party also began to refer to itself simply as Plaid Cymru.

The late 1940s and early 1950s, however, saw the party fall back electorally and Plaid Cymru once again became involved in other forms of political activity. In the early 1950s, Plaid Cymru was involved in the parliament for Wales petition sponsored by Undeb Cymru Fydd. This petition gathered almost a quarter of a million signatures but had little effect. In 1955 Liverpool Corporation announced plans to build a new reservoir in Wales, flooding a substantial part of the Tryweryn valley. Plaid Cymru campaigned tirelessly to stop this scheme, winning support from scores of local authorities in Wales, dozens of leading Welsh organizations and figures, and all but one of the MPs representing Wales. All was in vain, however, and the reservoir opened in 1965. *Tryweryn was to enter Plaid Cymru mythology as proof of the impotence of Wales against the British establishment. It also pitched some within the wider Welsh nationalist movement over the edge into unconstitutional direct action.

The 1959 general election saw Plaid Cymru win 77,500 votes overall, its best performance yet. Also at this time, Plaid Cymru gained an important defector, Huw T. Edwards, a leading Welsh politician and former chairman of the Council for Wales, a government advisory body. However, in the wake of the Tryweryn campaign many within the party had hoped for better and there were renewed calls to engage in direct action to secure Plaid Cymru's demands.

Plaid Cymru was helped by two events. In 1962 Cymdiethas yr Iaith Gymraeg (the Welsh Language Society) was founded to campaign for improved status for the Welsh language. Its constitution explicitly accepted the use of non-violent direct action and this relieved the pressure on Plaid Cymru to engage in direct action itself. Secondly, Plaid Cymru's electoral efforts finally paid off when it captured Carmarthen in a by-election in July 1966, Gwynfor *Evans, party president since 1945, now also becoming its first MP. Plaid Cymru performed spectacularly well in two further by-elections in the late 1960s, in the Rhondda and Caerphilly, slashing Labour majorities. Coupled with the nationalist successes in Scotland the Wilson government established a royal commission to examine devolution and the constitution (see KILBRANDON REPORT).

Plaid Cymru's electoral success and higher profile forced the party for the first time to develop policies on a range of economic and social as well as linguistic and cultural issues. This task was fulfilled by Dafydd Wigley and other young figures in the party's research group. Buoyed by its successes in the late 1960s, Plaid Cymru decided in 1970 to contest all the seats in Wales for the first time. In the 1970 general election it won 175,000 votes, 10.5 per cent of those cast and its highest share in a general election to date, but lost the Carmarthen seat.

The party's fortunes were transformed in the February 1974 election when it captured the constituencies of Caernarfon and Meirionydd, seats the party has held ever since. In October 1974 the party also recaptured Carmarthen and Plaid's tally of MPs rose to three. Aided by the Scottish nationalists who won eleven seats in the October 1974 election, Plaid Cymru's MPs were able to put enormous pressure on the minority Labour governments of Wilson and Callaghan, 1976–8. Concessions came in the form of a Welsh Development Agency, the promise of a Welsh language television channel, and compensation for former slate quarry workers with pneumoconiosis. The greatest concession, however, was the Wales Act and its promise of an elected assembly for Wales. However, in a shattering setback for the party, the devolution proposals were rejected by Welsh voters in a referendum on 1 March 1979 by a margin of four to one. Shortly afterwards in the general election of May 1979 Plaid Cymru lost its seat in Carmarthen, and saw many of the gains it had made in local government during the 1970s fall away and its share of the vote across Wales fall back.

Plaid Cymru thus began the 1980s in an introspective mood. An internal commission of inquiry found the party organization and appeal deficient in many respects. The early 1980s also saw the party divided into left- and right-wing camps. The adoption of 'community socialism' as one of the goals of the party in its constitution was a victory for the left. Dafydd Elis Thomas's election as party president in 1984 also confirmed the leftward drift of the party. Outside parliament Plaid Cymru continued to campaign actively on a number of issues. The work of Plaid's members, especially the threat of its president Gwynfor Evans to go on a hunger strike, succeeded in convincing the new Conservative government that it should honour its pledge to establish a Welsh-medium television channel and Sianel Pedwar Cymru (S4C) began broadcasting in 1982. On the issue of water bills, which the party claimed were unfairly high in Wales, unemployment in Wales and particularly support for the miners in 1984–5, and nuclear disarmament, the party met with less success.

The party began to emerge from its electoral doldrums in 1987 with the capture of Ynys Mon (Anglesey). Also, in the European elections of 1989 Plaid Cymru performed well with a new positive emphasis on Wales's role in a 'Europe of the Regions'. The 1990s saw further advances: in 1992, in alliance with the Green Party, it won the seat of Ceredigion and North Pembrokeshire, and increased its share of the vote, reversing a twenty-year long decline. In the 1994 European elections Plaid Cymru gained 17 per cent of the votes cast and pushed the Conservatives into third place. During the 1992–7 parliament with only a small Conservative majority, Plaid Cymru MPs were again able to extract concessions on such issues as the size of the Welsh contingent to the committee of the regions. In the 1997 general election Plaid Cymru again increased its share of the vote slightly but won no more seats. In the devolution referendum campaign in September 1997, Plaid Cymru played a prominent role and finally secured its goal of a Welsh national assembly. In 1998, to broaden its appeal across Wales, the party officially changed its name to 'Plaid Cymru—The Party of Wales' and when assembly elections were held in 1999, the party polled strongly enough to seize second place and deny Labour a majority. *DG*

VERNON BOGDANOR, *Devolution in the United Kingdom* (Oxford, 1999).

Plan G. See EUROPEAN FREE TRADE ASSOCIATION.

Playboy riots. See IRISH LITERARY THEATRE.

Playfair, Edward Wilder (1909–), civil servant. Playfair's Whitehall career started in the Inland Revenue, 1931–4, but he was then switched to the Treasury where he remained until 1956 (except for a spell in the control office for Germany and Austria, 1946–7). He was permanent under-secretary at the War Office, 1956–9, and then at the Ministry of Defence, 1960–1. In 1961, still in his early fifties, he retired from Whitehall and subsequently held business and banking positions. *KT*

Plebs League, an appropriately and splendidly named educational and political organization which was set up following a strike by the students at Ruskin College, Oxford, in 1909. The strike arose over the place of Marxist ideas in the curriculum offered to the adult students. The rebels were able to establish a new institution which became the Central Labour College and in the meantime they set up the Plebs League and printed *The Plebs* magazine in an attempt to establish a national movement. In all of this the leading influence was Noah Ablett from the Rhondda. In the short term the Plebs undoubtedly helped in giving a Marxist and syndicalist flavour to the union militancy of the 1910–12 era but in the long term the Marxism of the subsequent National Central Labour College classes is best examined within a wider tradition of working-class education. *PS*

RICHARD LEWIS, *Leaders and Teachers: Adult Education and the Challenge of Labour in South Wales* (Cardiff, 1998).

Pliatzky, Leo **(1919–99)**, civil servant. A former Fabian Society researcher, Pliatzky joined the civil service in 1947, becoming Treasury second permanent secretary in 1976. At the centre of Whitehall's attempts to manage the economic crises of the 1970s, he saw the Treasury as the voice of reality and strengthened its ability to resist departmental spending demands. As permanent secretary of the Department of Trade, 1977–9, he carried out a review designed to reduce the number of *quangos. *CL*

LEO PLIATZKY, *Getting and Spending* (Oxford, 1982).

'plough my furrow alone', phrase used by ex-prime minister *Rosebery on 19 July 1901, when his views had been repudiated by other Liberals: 'For the present, at any rate, I must proceed alone. I must plough my furrow alone, but before I get to the end of that furrow it is possible that I may not find myself alone.' *JAR*

Plowden report (1962) and **Public Expenditure Survey** (1959). A mixed committee of Whitehall insiders and outside figures from business and the City was established under the insider/outsider businessman and economic administrator Lord Plowden in 1959, following criticisms of the existing system of public expenditure allocation by the House of Commons Estimates Committee. It sat for two years and produced a report, *Control of Public Expenditure*, which led the Macmillan government to establish a system, the Public Expenditure Survey (PES), which survived with modifications until 1981. Macmillan also created a second Treasury minister of cabinet rank, the chief secretary (though not all of the postholders sat in the full cabinet), to oversee the system and ease the burdens on the chancellor of the exchequer. At the heart of the PES lay the concept of financial planning over five years in real terms, totals being automatically upgraded annually in line with inflation, largely the brainchild of Sir Richard Otto Clarke, the Treasury's 'assessor' on the Plowden committee. The aim of greater efficiency and consistency in resource allocation became increasingly difficult to achieve once inflation began to gather pace in the late 1960s. In the midst of a severe financial crisis in 1976, the Treasury subjected PES totals to strict cash limits. As the architect of cash limits, the senior Treasury official Sir Leo Pliatzky later wrote: 'The method of adjusting to rising pay and prices offered no resistance to general inflationary pressures, and no incentive to economise in or switch from those items of expenditure which were particularly swollen by relative inflation. Cash limits had been applied by the Labour administration of Jim Callaghan, but the incoming Conservatives in 1979 were seriously critical of the whole idea of forward planning in "funny money".' Sir Geoffrey Howe's Treasury team instructed officials to replace it with an unfunny arrangement based on real cash, rather than notional resources. This was introduced by Sir Geoffrey Howe in his 1981 budget. *PJH*

R. W. B. CLARKE, *Public Expenditure, Management and Control* (London, 1978). | *Control of Public Expenditure* (Cmnd 1432, London, 1961). | LEO PLIATZKY, *Getting and Spending* (London, 1984).

Plowden report (1979), into the public's relations with the police, recommended the setting-up of an independent police complaints authority as a means of increasing public confidence. The deputy chair of the committee of enquiry, Lord Plowden, was also the chair of the authority, 1976–81, overseeing the transition to the new regime. *JAR*

Plunkett, Horace Curzon **(1854–1932)**, Anglo-Irish politician. Plunkett founded the Irish agricultural organization society in 1894, was made vice-president of the Department of Agriculture in Ireland, 1899–1907, and knighted in 1903. He became a moderate home ruler by 1913, and chaired the *Irish Convention of 1917–18 which sought to reach agreement between the contending parties in Ireland. In 1919 he founded the Irish Dominion League to advocate dominion home rule for Ireland. *DGB*

pluralism, concept in political philosophy. Pluralism has been discussed without use of the actual term and as very different concepts under the label itself. It has been repeatedly rediscovered but, as Gunnell puts it in an understated way, 'the continuities are less evident than often assumed' (p. 254). The implication (if not terminology) of the discussion of Madison and Hamilton in the Federalist Papers is decidedly pluralist: for them good policy arose through encouraging diversity and competition. At the turn of the 20th century there was a philosophical reaction against the monistic state (see Hsiao). This concern about absolute power/sovereignty is a thread through different variants of pluralism. Philosophical reservations were turned by *Laski in particular into a political pluralism that defended the role of associations against the state. Later, in the USA, there developed a pressure group pluralism/conventional pluralism from Peter Odegard and J. Pendleton Herring to David Truman's *The Governmental Process* (1951) that looked at empirical practice and found groups active; Robert Dahl (*A Preface to Democratic Theory*, 1956) developed this orientation into a sort of empirically derived democratic theory (see also Dahl, 1989). Strangely, key texts of pluralism often address the term only tangentially, for example, Charles Lindblom's *The Intelligence of Democracy* (1965) and Dahl's *Polyarchy* (1971). (Connections between such mid-century work and A. F. Bentley's *The Process of Government* (1908) are easily exaggerated.) The positive vein of pluralism dried up and pluralism was used as a convenient target by a series of different approaches. Before that, however, a vital qualification emerged that stressed a sort of 'segmented pluralism' rather than 'competitive pluralism': this did not necessarily value iron triangles, group subgovernments, or the other closed policy-making arrangements that they described (see Jordan).

Pluralism was embroiled antagonistically with elitism in the 1960s and McLennan notes that 'American pluralism was taken by many radicals as representing little more than an apology for corporate capitalism, a western cold war ideology parading as mature social science' (p. 1). In the 1970s and 1980s a simplified form of pluralism was used to suggest there was in the corporatist description a novel discussion of interest group/governmental cooperation: this was less than distinctive when judged against the subgovernment approach. Sources making different qualifications adopted a label of 'critical pluralism'.

Latterly pluralism has been rediscovered by sources prepared to acknowledge that 'Striking similarities exist between the new theories of difference and identity... (and) the tradition of political pluralism' (Eisenberg, 1). This updating is well covered by Eisenberg and McLennan (1995). There is significant interest in the issue in international relations (for example, Grillo) and normative (multicultural) accounts. Ironically there has been a recolonization of the topic by those with philosophical rather than empirical interests. Pluralism has a renewed popularity, but at the cost of marginalization of the empirical thrust that distinguished it in the third quarter of the century. *GJ*

Robert Dahl, 'Polyarchy, Pluralism and Scale', *Scandinavian Political Studies*, 7/4 (1990). | Robert Dahl, *Democracy and its Critics* (New Haven, 1989). | Avigail Eisenberg, *Reconstructing Political Pluralism* (Albany, NY, 1995). | Ralph Grillo, *Pluralism and the Politics of Difference* (Oxford, 1998). | John Gunnell, 'The Genealogy of American Pluralism', *International Political Science Review*, 17/3 (1996). | Kung Chuan Hsiao, *Political Pluralism* (London, 1927). | Grant Jordan, 'The Pluralism of Pluralism', *Political Studies*, 38 (1990). | Gregor McLennan, *Pluralism* (Buckingham, 1997). | Nelson Polsby, *Community Power and Political Theory* (enlarged edn., London 1980).

Polaris, American submarine-launched nuclear missile. The crisis in Anglo-American relations after the cancellation of *Skybolt was only resolved by the Kennedy administration's agreement at the Nassau summit of December 1962 to sell Britain Polaris. Coinciding as it did with Britain's attempt to join the European Economic Community, this Polaris deal gave de Gaulle a reason to block British membership. It also ensured Britain's dependence on American nuclear technology, and consequently lasting political controversy, sustained when Thatcher purchased the next-generation deterrent, Trident. *JRVE*

Police and Criminal Evidence Act, 1984, increased but also regulated police powers of stop and search; road blocks; entry on premises, search and seizure of evidence; arrest, detention, interrogation, and treatment of suspects. Codes of practice guide the police on the detailed exercise of these powers, requiring a written record of compliance. Induced confessions were made less subject to exclusion. Judges were given a discretion to reject improperly obtained evidence which would otherwise make the trial unfair. A Police Complaints Authority was established. *VT*

Michael Zander, *The Police and Criminal Evidence Act, 1984* (3rd edn., London, 1995).

policing underwent a series of major changes over the century, as recorded crime increased dramatically, and the police's own image suffered both as a consequence of this and as high-profile cases indicating corruption or partiality among police officers damaged public confidence. In 1900, Great Britain (the UK excluding Northern Ireland) had about 46,000 officers, fragmented into 235 separate police forces, each under the management of its own chief constable responsible to the 'watch committee' of the local authority, counties, and county boroughs. By the middle of the century, however, the number of officers had risen by about half, now organized into 162 forces, while by the 1990s the processes of further force rationalizations meant that there were only 51 police forces, but the number of officers exceeded 140,000 (a growth in numbers rather greater than the rise in population over the century) (for (Northern) Ireland, see ROYAL IRISH CONSTABULARY; ROYAL ULSTER CONSTABULARY). Though management was initially localized, reflecting the local elites on which law enforcement depended when the police forces emerged in the 19th century, there had always been some powers of central involvement through the home secretary, not least because of the government's own duty to promote public order, while the specialist detection services pioneered by the London Metropolitan Police's 'Scotland Yard' could be and were called on for assistance by other local forces for much of the century. Nevertheless, such power to interfere and control did increase during the course of the century, as the home and Scottish secretaries provided funding for certain police functions throughout the country, and as they sought to maintain 'efficiency' through powers of inspection and direction.

The police's public image was predominantly positive in the early years of the century, and there was a determined effort in the media to keep it that way. Policemen did not always behave well under pressure, in such industrial disturbances as *Tonypandy, or in the strikes of 1919–20, during which the police themselves briefly went on strike, resulting in strike action by the police being made specifically illegal and the police's short-lived trade union evolving uneasily into a professional organization. It was more generally remembered, though, that Britain's unarmed police force had managed to keep violence to a minimum during the General Strike of 1926 (this being a rather selective memory from which several northern cities were excluded) and had actually played a 'police v. strikers' football match in Plymouth, popularly regarded as a fine example of British good sense. Even the greater street disturbances that accompanied mass unemployment and Fascist politics in the 1930s did not seriously impair this positive view of the 'the bobby on the beat', and it was considerably reinforced by the police's protective role on the home front in 1940–5. The epitome of this positive view came with the 1949 film *The Blue Lamp*, in which a reassuringly ordinary and selfless policeman, George Dixon, was stabbed to death by a desperate criminal, only for the whole local community, including petty thieves and gamblers, to rally to the police and help catch the villain. This message was then carried forward for the best part of twenty years, when a resurrected George Dixon presided over his own BBC television show as *Dixon of Dock Green*.

There was therefore a serious public shock when the crime figures, relatively static in the first half of the century, began to rocket from the 1940s, and there were increasing demands for the modernization of the force and its methods. In place of *Dixon of Dock Green* came the gritty Merseyside police saga *Z Cars*, ancestor of countless later 'cop shows' (many influenced by American equivalents) which showed individual policemen as all too human and fallible, and the forces as achieving a success rate no better than barely acceptable. Well-publicized cases of police corruption and equally well-known police resistance to attempts to modernize the force did little to help. In reality though, the arrival during the 1960s of graduate-recruitment, fast-track promotion for high-flyers, and the establishment of a police staff college (all of which was much resented by many policemen, conscious that theirs had always been a service without an 'officer class') did bring significant improvement in management. Unfortunately, the next two decades also pitted the police against sections of the public in riots (such as Brixton, 1981), demonstrations (*Grunwick, and outside the offices of *The Times*), and major strikes (notably three by the miners). In these confrontations, the police could not win, for if they kept control (as, eventually, at *Orgreave in 1984) they were accused of brutality, and if they did not they were accused of weakness, poor intelligence, and ineffective management (Trafalgar Square, 1990). The police were subjected to a series of damaging independent reports after enquiries into serious incidents of poor crowd control (Hillsborough football stadium) and allegations that racism was endemic in the force (the Stephen Lawrence enquiry). Meanwhile, the statistics for recorded crime continued to rise (however misleadingly) and each year's statistics produced a renewed debate on policing policy and a string of polls showing serious public concern.

JAR

R. Geary, *Policing Industrial Disputes* (Cambridge, 1985). | R. Mark, *A History of Policing in England and Wales* (London, 1978). | Charles Townshend, *Making the Peace: Public Order and Public Security in Modern Britain* (Oxford, 1993).

policy analysis, a multi-discipline academic area drawing on political science, organizational behaviour, social theory, economics, and statistics. At its broadest, it seeks to understand how societies develop and pursue policies. As such, it is as concerned with how policies can be constructed which reflect social values and the democratic will, as with the mechanics of policy making. However, it is this narrower field of enquiry that has dominated much of the literature since the 1960s. In this second form, the subject has both descriptive and prescriptive elements; although, in practice, both are intertwined. The former seeks to show how policy is made; while the latter offers ways of improving its formulation and delivery.

As an academic discipline, policy analysis developed in the USA and, at the outset, it was seen as broadly synonymous with the study of decision making. Here, the still unresolved debate between Herbert A. Simon, who argued that decisions were best made comprehensively, and Charles E. Lindblom, whose preference was for policy change to occur incrementally, came to dominate the literature. The attractiveness that this controversy had for textbook writers meant the overshadowing of the equally important and arguably more sophisticated study of decisions in a systems framework by Sir Geoffrey Vickers, in *The Art of Judgement: A Study of Policy Making* (1965).

From the late 1970s, emphasis began to shift towards the study of policy implementation. Implementation could no longer be seen as merely something that followed a decision; and successful implementation could no longer be seen as something that depended on the quality of the decision which preceded it. Instead, decisions and implementation could be conceptualized as having a dialectic relationship, with some arguing that a decision should be seen as no more than an intention which only becomes policy once implementation had been undertaken. The significance of this relationship became palpable as a result of two interrelated developments. The first was a new emphasis in the academic literature on *new institutionalist approaches which stress the impact of organizational culture on policy intention. The second was the increased fragmentation of the UK public sector in the 1980s which created an awareness that policy had to be implemented through networks of interdependent organizations over which it often had none or only notional hierarchical control. In addition, the interdependence of these organizations meant that a process often took place through which policy intention was renegotiated in mutually beneficial ways.

Finally, the 'new public management' paradigm which emerged in the 1980s saw the accent move towards policy evaluation and performance review, as governments began to seek to assure themselves of programme efficiency and effectiveness. Prescriptive analysis of policy making as a means-ends process has led to a number of interesting developments in UK government. These have included the use of programme-planning budgeting systems in central and local government, programme analysis and review, used by the Heath government from 1971, the development of corporate management strategies in local government following the Bains committee of 1972, and other new initiatives in the early 1980s.

CPS

Charles E. Lindblom, 'The Science of Muddling Through', *Public Administration Review*, 19 (1959). | H. A. Simon, *Administrative Behaviour* (New York, 1945).

policy unit, prime minister's. See Central Policy Review Staff.

Political and Economic Planning (PEP), policy research organization. PEP was founded in 1931 in response to the inspirational article 'A National Plan for Britain' by Gerald Barry in his new periodical *Weekend Review*. In the context of the apparent polarization of politics and calls for progressive state action, PEP funded research groups to gather data on industries and public services and promote the principles of planning by permeating elite opinion. They contained managers and experts but excluded trade unionists. PEP was led by the banker Basil Blackett, whose advocacy of a centralized economy originated in the Hegelian precept 'the Altogetherness of Everything' which, he argued, should be emblazoned on the wall of the cabinet room. This elite technocratic statist group included the economist Arthur Salter and the zoologist Julian Huxley. Initially, it was dominated by industrialists, favouring corporatist solutions, whose rhetoric of the self-government of industry thinly disguised demands for the extension of market control by restrictive trading agreements. In staple industries it called for structural reform through amalgamations. In the early 1930s PEP had little 'middle way' moral fervour and could not be described as a centre organization. However, Blackett, Salter, and Huxley did join the social planners and philanthropists in the *Next Five Years Group (1935). During the Second World War, PEP was quick to recognize the close correspondence between the state regulation of manpower and materials and the use of such statutory instruments for post-war reconstruction. It participated in J. B. Priestley's 1941 Committee and supported the Beveridge plan. PEP reports on the problems of economic reconstruction were widely circulated in wartime Whitehall and contributed to the bureaucratic expectation that planners would design the 'people's peace'. *KG*

P. ADDISON, *The Road to 1945: British Politics and the Second World War* (rev. edn., London, 1994). | JOHN CAMPBELL, 'The Renewal of Liberalism: Liberalism without Liberals', in G. Peele and C. Cook (eds.), *The Politics of Reappraisal 1918–1939* (London, 1975). | A. MARWICK, 'Middle Opinion in the Thirties, Planning, Progress and Political Agreement', *English Historical Review*, 79 (1964).

***Political Change in Britain* (1969)**, influential book subtitled 'Forces Shaping Electoral Choice' by David Butler and Donald Stokes. It reported the results of the first-ever nationwide surveys of the British electorate focusing on electoral behaviour, which were carried out in 1963, 1964, and 1966. The second edition (1974) extended coverage to include voting in the 1970 general election. What came to be known as 'the Butler-Stokes model' of voting behaviour emphasized the role of long-term forces, especially social class and party identification, in influencing the party choice of electors. Psychological attachment to a party ('partisan self-image', in the words of Butler and Stokes) was common among voters and was a product of socialization processes involving mainly the family and local community. This was buttressed by a strong alignment between class and party. Voters had a 'standing decision' to vote for a party in elections and rarely deviated from their normal choice. Short-term influences such as opinions on issues, political attitudes, and evaluations of party leaders had only a marginal impact. According to this model, electoral change would be slow and gradual, resulting from demographic trends and changes in the social structure and patterns of socialization. Although Butler and Stokes detected signs of change in the second edition of the book, the elections of the 1970s and after cast serious doubt upon their basic model. Their work remains, nonetheless, the essential starting point for all subsequent survey-based electoral analysis in Britain. *DD*

political correctness, one of the most extraordinary phenomena to sweep the Western world. It has established itself both as a term of approbation and disapproval, even ridicule. It springs from a kind of relativism, which holds that all societies, groups, and communities have their own special codes which are misunderstood by others who stand outside the group. Those who stand outside can never appreciate the sensitivity of such groups. Thus, to use an extreme example, the word 'black' is outlawed because people from that ethnicity must find it denigrating. This can be taken to the limits of common sense, when, for example, 'golliwogs' are to be removed from jam-jars because they seem to perpetuate a stereotypical ethnic image, but the principle that people should not suffer humiliation because of another group's sense of superiority, or simple insensitivity, is a very widely supported one. The problem goes deeper than the common-sense issue discussed above. It is that the decision of what is, or is not, politically correct, lies with the outside observer, who assumes that he or she knows how the group or individual in question feels. It is therefore highly subjective. For example, 'black', which can be a term of abuse, was promoted as something to be proud of in the USA in the 1970s and 1980s. The term 'British', which the Runnymede Trust claimed could give rise to racist connotations, has been embraced by many Asian and African citizens of the UK as the best means of combining their ethnic and citizen identities. *DGB*

political culture, overall term for the inherited assumptions and conventions within which a nation's political life takes place, and therefore bound up with a sense of political self-identity. Political culture is not therefore a fixed entity but a shifting platform on which politicians take their stance: Britain's political culture in relation to taxation, or public ownership, for example, was very different by 1950 from what it had been before 1914, but it was also different again (and in some ways more like 1914) by the 1990s. Within the UK, it can be argued that there are many different political cultures and self-identities, nationally (in respect of Scotland and Wales), regionally (in respect of certain parts of each country), and ethnically (black British voters will have had in many cases different perceptions of the country and its political system from white voters). Much research attention has been given to the study of the core values of the political elite, since these can be thought to provide conditioning both for newer members of the elite (as in Martin *Wiener's argument that the British elite was inherently anti-industrial) and as having a disproportionate significance for the country as a whole. It is, however, difficult to study such things in ways other than empirically and, as the reaction to Wiener's work showed, this can frequently lead to assertion and counter-assertion rather than agreement. Political culture, while useful for comparing different societies, is of limited value for the study of one, for it cannot be seen as culturally determinist: two politicians from the same background and conditioning may well in the end act differently in the same circumstance. Nevertheless, the assumption of many British politicians that Britain is exceptional, especially in the context of the debate about Britain's membership of the European Community since 1973, suggests that political culture has real salience, as it did when Churchill summoned up the British people's idea of themselves as a people with a historic specialness in 1940. *JAR*

political interviewing. See INTERVIEWING, POLITICAL.

Political Man (1959), an influential text in political sociology written by Harvard professor Seymour Martin Lipset. After initial publication in the USA, it appeared in Britain in 1960, bringing together some previously published essays with original work. It explored the social requisites of democracy and argued that there was a correlation between democracy and economic development. Wealth, industrialization, education, and urbanization were taken as indicators of such development: increased wealth and education reduce extremism among the working class; modernization induces a more emollient attitude on the part of the middle class as well as encouraging a more pluralist political society. Lipset argued that 'the chances for stable democracy are enhanced to the extent that groups and individuals have a number of crosscutting, politically relevant affiliations'. Stable Western democracies, he argued, were in a 'post-politics' phase, with little difference between left- and right-wing parties. The work was notable for the extensive use made of voting data and public opinion polls. It received mixed reviews when first published. 'Haste in theoretical formulation and in the interpretation of findings is his occasional weakness', noted Gabriel Almond in the *American Sociological Review* (July 1900), a criticism levelled by a number of other reviewers. Lipset was also criticized for accepting the reliability of data derived from different sources and for adopting a simple dichotomy between democratic and non-democratic countries. The work nonetheless constituted a path-breaking work, providing—as W. H. Greenleaf recorded in *Political Studies* (July 1900)—'an excellent introduction to what political sociology is about'. *PN*

S. M. Lipset, *Political Man: The Social Bases of Politics* (London, 1960).

Political Studies Association of the UK (PSA), established in 1950 at the prompting of the International Political Science Association. The need for an external stimulus was indicative of the rather sceptical attitude of the founding fathers, divided between a concentrated pro-political science LSE faction and a dispersed Oxford political studies faction. The initial membership was scattered in its disciplinary loyalties, hence the appellation 'studies' corresponded more accurately to a relaxed community of 100 scholars, some of whom had recently worked in wartime administration. It quickly published a journal *Political Studies* and organized an annual conference.

University expansion from the 1960s led to a rapid growth in membership and the acquisition of a separate identity from contemporary history, constitutional law, economics, and philosophy, as independent departments of politics came into existence. However, politics accounted for only 2 per cent of total academic staff spread over some 80 institutions. In 1969, a politics association of schoolteachers of politics was launched but has not succeeded in establishing civic education for democracy such as has existed in America and France. A shift towards a less professionally inert PSA came after its twenty-fifth anniversary in 1975, marked by the publication of a more self-congratulatory than self-critical commemorative issue of *Political Studies* by the outgoing executive, and the election of an entirely new one. The shock of the contested election marked a pervasive sense that if political science wished to be taken more seriously by others, inside and outside academia, it would have to provide more authoritative analysis of political problems even if it was seldom in a position to prescribe confidently. The subsequent expansion in the PSA's annual conference, its range of publications and specialist research groups, has undoubtedly made it a much more self-consciously professional association.

However, political studies in Britain continue to lack the mass constituency socialized at school to think in politically literate terms or to be solicited for advice by the political and administrative elites except on an occasional and ad hoc basis. The state-sustaining function that elsewhere has been an implicit purpose of political science has been largely absent because practical men of affairs in Britain usually think they have little to learn from academics, apart from the interpretation of opinion polls or information about the politics of remote countries. *JH*

Pollitt, Harry **(1890–1960),** Communist politician. Pollitt was the charismatic general secretary of the Communist Party of Great Britain (CPGB), 1929–56. By 1918 he was already a leading figure in the shop stewards movement, and was appointed organizer of the 'Hands off Russia' movement in 1919. His agitational work in this movement contributed to the *Jolly George* incident when London dockers refused to load munitions destined for use against Soviet Russia in 1920. A founder member of the CPGB, he was also an executive member of the Communist International (Comintern) in the 1920s. While he was secretary of the National Minority Movement (1924–9), it became an influential body, and in 1925 he was arrested with eleven other Communist leaders under the Incitement to Mutiny Act of 1797 and incarcerated for twelve months, preventing him from participating in the 1926 General Strike. Appointed CPGB general secretary in 1929, he stood for parliament on eight occasions, always unsuccessfully. A fervent supporter of the Spanish republicans, he visited the International Brigades five times. Pollitt resigned as general secretary in October 1939 following his opposition to the Comintern's anti-war policy, but was reinstated in 1941 and helped draft the CPGB's post-war programme *The British Road to Socialism*, which emphasized the parliamentary road to socialism. He again resigned his post in 1956 but remained politically active until his death. An outstanding propagandist and one of the labour movement's most gifted orators, under his leadership the CPGB orientated itself towards the trade unions and gained considerable influence. Despite his support for Stalin's purges his name became synonymous with the struggle against fascism in the 1930s. A great admirer of Stalin, he was a guard of honour at Stalin's funeral in 1953 and resigned his post after Khrushchev denounced Stalin in 1956. *DLM*

KEVIN MORGAN, *Harry Pollitt* (Manchester, 1993). | HARRY POLLITT, *Serving My Time* (London, 1940).

Pollock, Ernest Murray **(1861–1936),** judge and Conservative MP. Pollock was a member of the most eminent legal family of his time. He was elected MP in 1910 and thereafter held the office of solicitor-general (1919–22) and attorney-general (1922) in the Lloyd George government. Pollock did not support his party's withdrawal from the coalition in 1922, and his career appeared to be over after he refused Law's offer to become one of the law officers in the new government. However, in 1923 he accepted Baldwin's controversial offer to become master of the rolls, a position he held until 1935. *ML*

poll tax (1986–91), flat-rate tax levied on every citizen (or every citizen within a given category). The poll tax did not work in 1377 or in 1641 when it was tried in Britain. It proved a disaster when in 1986–90 it was implemented again in order to facilitate the abolition of *rates. The Thatcher government, unhappy at the reaction to rates revaluation in Scotland in 1986, legislated for a flat-rate poll tax on all electors in Scotland in 1989 and for a similar tax in England and Wales in 1990. The implementation of the poll tax revealed many anomalies and widespread public protest. On 31 March 1990 there was a very violent demonstration in Trafalgar Square which spread to the gates of Downing Street and was reported internationally. Many people refused to pay the tax and the whole affair was seen as a major factor in the disillusion with Thatcher which led to her downfall in November 1990. In 1991, John Major and Michael Heseltine agreed on an Act which substituted a 'council tax' on house values for the poll tax and which was generally if unwillingly accepted. *DEB*

D. E. BUTLER, ANDREW ADONIS, and TONY TRAVERS, *Failure in British Government: The Politics of the Poll Tax* (Oxford, 1994).

polytechnics. See HIGHER EDUCATION.

Ponsonby, Arthur **(1871–1946),** Labour politician. Born at Windsor castle (his father, Sir Henry Ponsonby, was Queen Victoria's private secretary), Ponsonby was a Liberal MP of advanced views, a critic of Edward Grey's foreign policy, and a leading figure in the Union of Democratic Control. Defeated in the general election of 1918, he returned to the Commons as a Labour MP in 1922, held ministerial posts in the governments of 1924 and 1929–31, and, having been created a peer in 1930, was Labour leader in the Lords, 1931–5. *DEM*

RAYMOND A. JONES, *Arthur Ponsonby: The Politics of Life* (Bromley, 1989).

Ponting, Clive. See WHISTLEBLOWING.

Poole, Oliver Brian Sanderson **(1911–93),** Conservative organizer. After distinguished service in the Second World War, Poole became MP for Oswestry in 1945. He undertook organizational and policy tasks for Butler and, despite returning to the city in 1950, became an influential figure in the party. In 1952, he was appointed joint party treasurer, and in 1955 Eden made him party chairman. Poole was the only Conservative Party chairman to serve without sitting in either House. After Hailsham succeeded him in 1957, Poole continued as his deputy and is credited with developing the innovative use of political *advertising prior to the 1959 Tory election landslide. He had been cleared by the *Parker tribunal after his name was linked with an alleged leak over the Bank rate in 1957, and in 1958 he accepted a hereditary peerage. In 1963 Macmillan appointed Poole joint party chairman with Macleod. Poole told Hailsham that Hailsham was Macmillan's chosen successor, and urged Macmillan to reach an early decision about whether or not he would continue as leader. After Macmillan resigned, Poole supported Butler but was persuaded by Macmillan to serve Douglas-Home and was vice-chairman until 1964. *RJS*

poor law, social legislation inherited from the Tudor and Stuart period and modified in the 19th century (mainly through the 1834 Poor Law Amendment Act, or 'new poor law'), was the backbone of British social policy prior to the 20th century. The inception of state-organized welfare, such as old age *pensions in 1908 and the *National Insurance Act, 1911, diminished the role of the poor law institutions which were, by the 1920s, mainly concerned with the elderly infirm. Under the Local Government Act, 1929, boards of guardians, the local poor law authorities, were abolished. The powers of the guardians were transferred to local authorities, such as county councils or county boroughs. Local boroughs were encouraged to convert their workhouses into infirmaries. A reform of the Conservative government of 1924–9, the end of the workhouse (incarceration in which was regarded as a terrible stigma by poor people) was a significant liberalizing political achievement, though the effective work had already been done by the extension of national insurance and old age pensions. *JS*

Poplarism, term that entered the political vocabulary following the Poplar rates rebellion of 1921. Defending their deprived East End community, 30 Poplar councillors, led by George Lansbury, were imprisoned in Brixton and Holloway prisons after High Court proceedings. The newly elected Labour-controlled Poplar council defied the government by refusing to levy the precepts (rates for services) for the London County Council and other Metropolitan bodies to demand action on unemployment and the equalization of the rates with wealthier West End boroughs. *JSS*

Noreen Branson, *Poplarism, 1919–1925: George Lansbury and the Councillors' Revolt* (London, 1979).

Popper, Karl Raimund **(1902–94),** Austrian philosopher and logician who came to the LSE in 1946. His *The Open Society and its Enemies* had recently been published (1945) with its vehement attacks on Plato, Hegel, and Marx inspired by Popper's wish to strike a resounding intellectual blow against fascist and communist totalitarianism. Together with his attack on historical determinism in *The Poverty of Historicism* (the 1957 book adding to earlier articles), this constituted his argument for methodological individualism and piecemeal social engineering, rather than the holistic planning of which his LSE colleague Hayek was an even more trenchant critic. These books had an immediate impact in the USA and Western Europe and a delayed impact in the countries beyond the iron curtain, where the liberalism he expounded enjoyed an undiminished subversive force.

Popper's philosophical reputation derived from his *The Logic of Scientific Discovery* (1934) whose rationalist argument he extended from the natural to the social sciences. The open society was one that engaged in an endless experimentation, with trial and avoidance of error being the 'fallibility' and probabilist basis of his scientific method. Totalitarianism was identified with the claim to dogmatic certainty that encouraged comprehensive coercion. His polemical caricature of the enemies of open society has not worn well. However, Sir Karl's critique of historicism remains a salutary antidote to attempts to extrapolate trends into laws of inevitable development, thereby allowing political actors freedom of choice in an unending experimental quest. *JH*

K. R. Popper, *The Poverty of Historicism* (London, 1957). | J. Shearmur, *The Political Thought of Karl Popper* (London, 1996).

Popplewell report (1986) on safety at sports stadia followed deaths at the Bradford and Heysel Stadium grounds. It recognized new developments in hooliganism and recommended new public order offences, training for stewards and police, safety monitoring at a wider range of sites, and consideration of a football membership scheme. *KMT*

popular front (1930s), new strategy adopted by the Communist International (Comintern) at its congress in 1935, aimed at anti-fascist unity between communists, socialists, and liberals. During 1934–9 the popular front strategy was linked with, and subservient to, the requirements of Russian foreign policy. Communist parties were expected to form popular front alliances with other anti-fascist groups regardless of their political persuasion, with the ultimate objective of forming coalition governments favourable to a military alliance with the Soviet Union. In Britain, the popular front campaign initiated by the Communist Party of Great Britain (CPGB) went through several stages. Failure to involve the Labour Party in a popular front during 1936–7 led the CPGB to change tack and begin to campaign with sections of the Liberal Party for a popular front government committed to a military alliance with the Soviet Union, and then during 1938–9 the popular front movement tried to form an electoral coalition of all anti-fascist opinion to defeat the National Government. This failed primarily due to the opposition of the Labour Party, which saw the popular front as an attempt to subvert its political independence and compromise its socialist programme, and individuals like Cripps who backed the popular front idea were expelled. Despite the election of popular front governments in France and Spain, the popular front failed to bring about an international anti-fascist front, partly because of the negative effect on Western public opinion of Stalin's purges in the Soviet Union, and partly because of the difficulty of reconciling politically opposed parties. The failure of the popular front to halt the rise of fascism in Europe led Stalin to conclude the Nazi-Soviet pact in August 1939, which cleared the way for Germany's attack on Poland in September 1939. *DLM*

Kevin McDermott and Jonathan Agnew, *The Comintern: A History of International Communism from Lenin to Stalin* (London, 1996). | Ben Pimlott, *Labour and the Left in the 1930s* (London, 1977).

population change. At the beginning of the 20th century, the population of the UK was 38 million and had risen to over 59 million in 1999. The distribution of the population in 2000 across the different parts of the UK was 53.3 million in England and Wales, 5.1 million in Scotland, and 1.7 million in Northern Ireland. Existing population totals are the result of a shifting balance between births, deaths, and migration. High rates of *infant mortality early in the century meant that, of the million or so children born around 1901, one in seven did not survive until their first birthday. The fall in infant mortality to its level in 2000 of around one in twenty has been accompanied by a fall in death rates overall. Birth rates have been falling throughout the 20th century, from around 28 births per 1,000 population in 1901–5 to just over 12 births per 1,000 population in 1998. This relatively low birth rate compared with the past reflects a preference for smaller families and the widespread practice of birth control (see FAMILY PLANNING).

For the past twenty years, population growth by natural replacement has fallen below the level needed to maintain the population. Britain has also had a net outflow of population by migration for much of the post-war period, in spite of substantial immigration. In the last twenty years, however, there has been a small surplus of immigrants over emigrants. Between 1988 and 1997 net immigration increased the population by about 300,000. Overall, the population of the UK has increased by 12 per cent since 1961 (when Commonwealth immigration began to be regulated) although the four constituent countries of the UK have experienced different rates of change. The population of Northern Ireland has increased by 18 per cent in the period, while for England and Wales the increase has been 14 per cent and 11 per cent respectively. The population of Scotland has declined by 1 per cent in the same period.

Britain's population is also ageing. The proportion of the population aged over 50 has almost doubled in the course of the 20th century, from approximately one in six in 1901 to one in three in 1998. There has also been a significant increase in the number of people living into their eighties, with current projections suggesting that by 2021 there will be three million people over 80 years. At the same time, the number of young people in the population is falling. It is estimated that by 2021 there will be more people aged 65 and over than under 16 years. The population balance between the sexes means that there are currently more than a million more women than men in the population, with an even larger concentration of women in the age group over 50.

The structure of households has also changed substantially over the course of the century. In 1900, the overwhelming majority of births occurred within marriage, divorce was uncommon, and the average household size was 4.6 people in England and Wales (1901). In 1998 almost 38 per cent of all births occurred outside marriage, although the majority were jointly registered by the parents who were usually living at a common address. *Divorce is, however, far more common than in the past, more than 150 times more so than in 1901. Average family size at 2.1 or just under has fallen to less than half of what it was in 1901. The number of households in Great Britain has risen ever since 1961 from 16.3 million to 23.6 million in 1998 and is projected to rise still further in the future. These changes are the product of the rapid increase in one-person households and an increase in single-parent households with dependent children. *JS*

populism, political stance which places authority and the source of wisdom in the people. Populism has not been popular in Britain, with its strong and stable tradition of representative government and—until recently—a greater willingness to trust and defer to elites and leaders than in most other countries. Whereas ancient republics were susceptible to demagoguery, populism is a modern phenomenon, a debased derivative of mass democracy. What they share is the recourse to direct democracy, not mediated by the representative liberal institutions that restrain the effects of ill-informed mass passion and prejudice. While the emergence of charismatic dictators in the 20th century, such as Mussolini, Hitler, and Peron, have been the extreme exemplars of the populist phenomenon, liberal democracies have not been immune to anti-elitist appeals to mass hysteria, especially when this is associated with xenophobia. Oswald Mosley's attempt to import such populism into Britain in the 1930s was a conspicuous failure, but where elites have been willing to engage in European integration by stealthy negotiation and faits accomplis there is scope for populist exploitation of latent public resentment, of which Sir James Goldsmith's Referendum Party was a rather pathetic manifestation in the 1990s.

The political expression of public opinion can take many forms. The crucial issue is whether public opinions are shaped by free discussion rather than mass manipulation. The opportunities for such manipulation and mobilization have been greatly increased through the capacity to control the media of mass communication, hence the importance of retaining a plurality of autonomous channels of elite and mass communication. In a diluted form, recourse to populistic methods is a temptation to leaders in the most liberal democracies, but propaganda based upon conspiracy theories has been a feature of extremist movements and of parties on both the left and right, which mercifully have been relatively weak in their popular appeal in Britain. Why is this so?

The survival of a long-established ruling class, based upon gentlemanly breeding, property, and power, coupled with institutional bulwarks that impede unruly surges of mass emotion, has for centuries prevented populist potentialities from getting out of hand in Britain. However, tabloid flattering of the mass public's self-esteem and the belief that they are not merely as good as but better than their rulers, are threatening the autonomous institutions that have provided secretive havens for the high and mighty. Elite propensity to indulge in arrogant complacency and collusive activities exposes them to the diatribes of the muck-raking popular press. The resulting discredit of the political class in particular and of all elites in general offers ample scope for pillorying them.

Margaret Thatcher was able to develop in the 1980s a successful populist onslaught on a variety of established British institutions, conveying the impression that she was an outsider because she was seeking to break the stranglehold of entrenched practices, hostile institutions, and interest groups. Opposed by elitists both outside and inside the Conservative Party she led, her appeal to the need to reverse national decline resembled in style the mass mobilization more characteristic of developing countries. However, in the British context, she was not able, ultimately, to resist the resentment of the parliamentary party over whom she had ridden roughshod with such delectation. Those she had led to three successive electoral victories abruptly removed her from power. Such is the enduring force in Britain of representative democracy, despite the inroads made by populist appeals to the mass public. *JH*

M. Canovan, *Populism* (London, 1981). | G. Ionescu and E. Gellner (eds.), *Populism: Its Meaning and National Characteristics* (London, 1969).

Portillo, Michael Denzil Xavier (1953–), Conservative politician, whose Southgate defeat was the emblematic event of the 1997 election. He was leadership candidate of the risen Tory right, with a tendency to nail-curling conference rants at foreigners, dismissive of Major and John Smith as like bank managers. An effective chief secretary and a ministerial supporter of the *poll tax,

Portillo dithered during the 1995 party leadership crisis, assembling banks of telephones for the second round, but refusing to risk anything on the first. He was then demoted to defence. Having lost his seat, he stressed his humility in among other things a Spanish television travelogue, but remained the darling of the right and was thus able to return quickly to parliament, becoming shadow chancellor in 1999. He stood for the party leadership in 2001 but failed to make the final round. *EP*

positivism, a position which holds that reality exists and comprises a series of causes and effects which can be understood empirically, that enquiry can be value-free, and that hypotheses can be tested. Attention is therefore concentrated on observable facts rather than on theoretical analysis. Positivism is used to describe policy analysis which disregards the social and political foundations of policy making, which require an extended theoretical analysis, in favour of concentration on the observable workings of the policy process. *CPS*

postal votes, system whereby an elector who is unable to go to a polling station to cast a vote personally can vote by sending in a ballot paper by post. They were introduced for the first time in 1949 (after their use for servicemen in the 1945 election), initially limited to those who were ill or disabled (a claim form for this requiring the signature of a doctor), had moved their residence to another constituency, or were obliged to travel because of their employment, but later extended to include those on holiday on election day, and even some British citizens living abroad. A postal vote has to be claimed well in advance and must be returned by the day before the election, but the numbers involved have become quite significant, already exceeding 600,000 actual votes in the 1970s, and three-quarters of a million in the 1990s. It was generally believed that the postal voter helped the Conservatives to win a few tight constituency contests, partly because their better organization enabled them to trace removed electors, partly because their middle-class supporters were more likely to claim their rights without being reminded of them. Postal votes may even have given Churchill his small parliamentary majority in 1951, but declining Tory organization since the 1950s has probably limited their impact. *JAR*

post-colonialism, concept that refers to the examination of Western modes of domination over colonial and post-colonial societies through theories based on literary texts and other theoretical works. The seminal text of post-colonial theory is Edward Said's *Orientalism* (1978). Said suggested that Western knowledge of the Orient, particularly the Middle East, was used to justify and reinforce Western imperialism. Moreover, this form of intellectual subjugation continued beyond the period of decolonization and is evident in modern scholarship. It is this aspect particularly which makes the work of Said and others 'post-colonial'. Historians have criticized post-colonial theories in several ways, for example, for failing to place literary texts in their historical context; and for seeing the West and the colonized as too monolithic. So far, common ground between post-colonial theorists and historians is rare. *KTS*

Dane Kennedy, 'Imperial History and Post-Colonial Theory', *Journal of Imperial and Commonwealth History*, 24 (1996).

postmodernism has been understood as describing both a philosophical position and a historical moment. For a philosopher such as Jean-François Lyotard the postmodern refers to cultural practices and philosophical systems that challenge the notion of totality and foreground 'the unpresentable' within existing systems of representation. Postmodernism on this model avoids nostalgia for organic cultural forms and foregrounds instead multiplicity, instability, and diversity. Its central political problematic is the question of legitimacy and the viability of overarching narratives of identity, of history, or of scientific knowledge. For Fredric Jameson, however, postmodernism is the articulation of the cultural logic of late capitalism and as such the inescapable 'cultural dominant' of the late 20th century. Jameson's reading of postmodern culture involves a mapping of its departures from the aesthetic, psychological, and historical parameters of high modernism. He thus stresses its fascination with surfaces, its lack of historical consciousness (which is replaced by a diffuse nostalgia), its deployment of pastiche, and the displacement of the temporal by the spatial and the synchronic. Jameson's account of postmodernism's suspicion of the referent is pushed much further in the work of Jean Baudrillard whose investigations of the social reproduction and circulation of images unpack the psychic and social consequences of the 'simulacrum' as representation with no originating referent. Postmodernism in its diverse cultural, political, and philosophical manifestations articulates a loss of confidence in organic forms, in fixed identities, and in founding narratives, and has thus spoken particularly to political constituencies who feel themselves to be marginal to the political and philosophical project of modernity. Its has contributed significantly to the imaginative and philosophical redrawing of cultural categories of sexuality, ethnicity, and class. It has also engaged directly with the particularity of a cultural and political moment marked by an increasingly rapid circulation of images, by the erosion of the boundaries between the mechanical and the organic, and by the new philosophical and psychic challenges of 'virtual' reality. *MES*

Post Office. The Post Office has taken responsibility for many tasks during the 20th century. In 1912 it took over the national telephone company in order to offer a unified telephone system throughout most of the UK. This was eventually hived off in 1981, when the British Telecommunications Act created British Telecom. The Post Office established a banking service, National Giro, in 1968, which was eventually sold to the Alliance and Leicester building society in 1990. In terms of organization, 1969 saw the Post Office cease to be a government department and become a nationalized industry. In 1986, it was reorganized into three separate businesses: Royal Mail Letters, Royal Mail Parcels, and Post Office Counters. The Blair government issued a white paper in 1999 on Post Office reform which allowed it greater commercial freedom. *JD*

Post Office website: *www.postoffice.co.uk*

post-war consensus. The idea of a post-1945 consensus derives from Richard *Titmuss's argument that common wartime suffering led to a common acceptance of the need for universal welfare provision, and from political historians' assumption that the Conservative Party responded to the 1945 Labour landslide by adopting Labour's policies. The concept was sharpened by political controversy after 1975, when the resurgent right tended to argue that *Thatcherite Conservatives had broken free of an egalitarian and corporatist consensus to restore the vigour of the market and roll back the boundaries of the state. Recent scholarship has emphasized the strong ideological content of post-war economic and welfare policies, as well as the compromises made, for pragmatic political reasons, by Labour politicians who administered them. Within the Conservative Party, many argued that electoral logic demanded an acceptance of the welfare state, encapsulated in their 1947 **Industrial Charter*; others insisted that the electorate had revolted in 1945 against the party's pre-war indifference to the consequences of unemployment. Pragmatically, Labour could not completely deliver an egalitarian, state-managed universalist welfare system with a large nationalized sector of the economy, and for electoral reasons the Conservative Party in government after 1951 could not completely dismantle Labour's legacy. Nevertheless the ideological tension and class antagonism of the immediate post-war years, in which Conservatives sought and gained the support of an embattled middle class and Labour flexed the muscles of the state to deliver benefits to the working class, bespeaks an armed truce rather than a political consensus. *JAT*

Harriet Jones and Michael Kandiah (eds.), *The Myth of Consensus: New Views on British History, 1945–1964* (Basingstoke, 1996).

Post-War Problems Central Committee, Conservative policy committee. Created in 1941 under the chairmanship of R. A. *Butler, with a membership drawn from the party's parliamentary, professional, and voluntary wings, the committee was intended to research and draw up reports on different aspects of the national life. Compared to its rival the unofficial *Tory Reform Committee, it failed to make much impact, and its reports rarely gained Churchill's official support, whilst many of its proposals were compromises that had little hope of rivalling the Beveridge report (1942) with the public. *NJC*

Potsdam conference (1945), last of the wartime meetings of the heads of the Grand Alliance, held in Berlin in the second half of July 1945 after the capitulation of Germany but before the surrender of Japan. Churchill was accompanied by Foreign Secretary Eden and also by the Labour leader, Clement Attlee, as the result of the British general election which had yet to be declared and might result in a Labour victory. The prime minister, increasingly suspicious of Soviet good faith, had been pressing for a heads of government meeting for some weeks and now had the opportunity to meet the new American president, Harry S. Truman, for the first time. Negotiations centred on three issues: reparations, the former German satellite states, and the borders of Poland. In an atmosphere of suspicion and bickering, little progress had been made by 25 July when the conference was suspended to allow the British delegation to return to London for the election results. Outside the formal sessions, however, Churchill had been informed on 17 July of the successful detonation of an atomic bomb at the American test site in New Mexico. Churchill noted that Truman was 'a changed man' after this event. As a result of Labour's victory it was Attlee and Ernest Bevin who returned to Potsdam on 28 July. The change had little obvious impact on British policy, though Bevin surprised some observers with his combative bluntness. It was the American secretary of state, James Byrnes, who ensured that the conference would not dissolve in a state of acrimony. In return for Soviet agreement that each ally should extract reparations from its own zone in Germany, he agreed to give ground over Poland's western frontier. The British had little option but to follow the American lead. But the conference ended without the mood of optimism which had characterized the meeting at *Yalta. *DJD*

C. L. Mee, *Meeting at Potsdam* (London, 1975).

'pound in your pocket', phrase used by Harold Wilson during his broadcast explaining the government's decision to devalue the pound in 1967. A bizarre attempt to persuade 'the British housewife' that her real purchasing power would be unaffected, the speech was a public relations disaster and permanently damaged Wilson's reputation. *MC*

poverty. Despite rising living standards for most British people, poverty is a problem which has continued to draw the attention of politicians and social commentators. Before 1914, Seebohm Rowntree (*Poverty: A Study of Town Life*, 1901) and others showed that most of the poor were victims of economic circumstances such as underemployment and low wages and were blameless for their situation. Rowntree also highlighted a minimum income level needed to maintain physical efficiency, and a dynamic poverty cycle whereby members of a family could fall into and rise out of poverty according to stages in their life. His study and investigations by others influenced the New Liberal government of 1906–15 which introduced old age pensions and free school meals for poor children. Poverty seemed to disappear with the full employment of the Great War, but in the 1920s it re-emerged as a major concern as the staple industries declined. Unlike the period before 1914 when the poor tended to be drawn from the unskilled, disabled, and elderly, now they included many adult males such as miners and shipbuilders who had enjoyed good wages and high status in their communities. In another difference, the main cause of poverty was recognized as unemployment. The concentration of structural unemployment in south Wales, central Scotland, and the north of England gave powerful regional and national dimensions to poverty and led to hunger marches and the emergence of the National Union of Unemployed Workers, associated strongly with the Communist Party. Still, most of the unemployed either retained their loyalty to established parties or were politically apathetic and did not turn to either the Communists or the British Union of Fascists. Yet poverty and unemployment did have serious political repercussions in 1931 when the Labour government split and fell over proposals to cut unemployment benefit. The subsequent National Government introduced the widely hated means test, administered by public assistance committees which had succeeded the poor-law guardians. The Second World War drove down unemployment and was followed by a Labour government which implemented the Beveridge report (1942) and introduced the welfare state, With work plentiful in the 1950s, poverty seemed to have been defeated, but in the next decade it was rediscovered by investigators such as Abel Smith and Townsend (*The Poor and the Poorest*, 1965). Increasingly, commentators such as these focused on the concept of relative poverty as opposed to absolute poverty. This concept became an especially contentious political issue in the early 1980s when manufacturing industry slumped and unemployment rose along with the number of low-paid and irregular jobs. Many Thatcherite Conservatives stressed not only the difficulties in defining poverty and a minimum quality of life but also their belief that personal failings were a major cause of poverty—if it did exist. By contrast Labour politicians emphasized the persistence of poverty, the importance of external factors in its causes, and the need for it to be eradicated by government action. Poverty remains not only a social matter but a political battleground. *CC*

Powell, Charles David (1941–), prime ministers' foreign affairs private secretary, 1984–91. A career diplomat until 1984, Powell became Margaret Thatcher's closest aide. By 1990, his influence, which extended beyond foreign affairs, appeared to some to have eclipsed that of her ministers, contributing to her isolation and subsequent fall. Their views often seemed indistinguishable, particularly on Europe, but the extent to which he actually affected policy is difficult to gauge. Powell remained at Downing Street long after his secondment would normally have ended, despite offers of ambassadorships and attempts to persuade Thatcher to replace him; and he was accused of allowing his loyalty to her to stray beyond the bounds of civil service propriety, particularly during the Westland affair (1986). He drafted Thatcher's *Bruges speech on the future of Europe (1988), and encouraged her positive view of Mikhail Gorbachev. Theoretically the Foreign Office's man in Downing Street, Powell fuelled Thatcher's suspicion of his former department, and his role may have damaged her relationship with Foreign Secretary Sir Geoffrey Howe. When Thatcher fell, on the eve of the Gulf war, Powell was considered too important to be replaced immediately. He left Whitehall when the war ended in March 1991. *CL*

John Ranelagh, *Thatcher's People* (London, 1991). | Hugo Young, *One of Us* (London, 1989).

Powell, (John) Enoch (1912–98), Tory and Ulster Unionist politician, anti-immigration campaigner, and Eurosceptic. Powell's intellectual arrogance and his dogmatic assertion of market economics and nationalism (or imperialism until the early 1950s) put him at odds with pragmatic Conservatives. The paradox of Powell was his application of cold logic to politics, while holding passionately to beliefs that were rooted in emotion and tradition.

Educated at King Edward VI school, Birmingham, and Cambridge, Powell became a classical scholar and wartime brigadier. In 1946 he joined the Conservative Parliamentary Secretariat (later merged with the *Conservative Research Department), fought the 1947 Normanton by-election, and became MP for Wolverhampton South-West in 1950. A founder-member of the One Nation group, he rebelled in 1950 against British involvement in the *European Coal and Steel Community, declined Churchill's offer to become Welsh minister in 1952, and joined the dissident *Suez Group. Having finally entered office as housing minister in 1955, he introduced the legislation to decontrol rents. Appointed financial secretary to the Treasury in 1957, Powell developed, together with Birch and Thorneycroft, the monetarist view that governments caused inflation by printing money to fund their borrowing. By stiffening Thorneycroft's resolve over government spending, Powell was instrumental in the 1958 Treasury team's resignations that Macmillan dismissed as 'little local difficulties'.

Although Powell rebelled against the 1958 introduction of life peers and attacked the executive's failure to take responsibility for the Hola Camp massacre in 1959, he returned to office in 1960 as health minister. In 1962 he entered the cabinet, despite the antipathy between him and Macmillan. Defying his aversion to state planning, Powell instituted the network of district general hospitals, but the 1961 pay pause brought him into conflict with the nurses. During the 1963 Conservative leadership crisis he hosted a 'midnight meeting' of Butler's supporters, but only he and Macleod eventually refused to serve Douglas-Home.

Powell received only fifteen votes in the 1965 Tory leadership election, but his espousal of free-market economics and English nationalism became known as 'Powellism', which was the clear precursor of 'Thatcherism'. Heath appointed him defence spokesman, but Powell's iconoclasm extended to criticizing nuclear deterrence. When Powell's increasingly outspoken attacks on immigration culminated in his 1968 (so-called) *'rivers of blood' speech, Heath sacked him for his 'racialist' tone. Powell's life was transformed; he was acclaimed by some, but vilified by others.

Nonetheless, the following year Powell's role in defeating Lords' reform established his reputation as a parliamentarian. He also declared his opposition to British membership of the European Community, despite having supported attempts to join during the 1960s, and he bitterly fought British entry. Having condemned as 'fraudulent' Heath's decision to call the February 1974 election he declined to stand but, by intervening to urge support for Labour's promise of a referendum on Europe, he contributed to Heath's downfall. Despite believing that EC membership stripped parliament of its independence, Powell became Ulster Unionist MP for Down South in October 1974. He was instrumental in increasing the province's representation at Westminster, but his opposition to devolution put him out of step with many Unionists. After losing his seat in 1987 he remained a compelling controversialist. *RJS*

Simon Heffer, *Like the Roman: The Life of Enoch Powell* (London, 1998). | Robert Shepherd, *Enoch Powell* (London, 1996).

Powell, Jonathan (1956–), prime minister's chief of staff since 1997. A former Foreign Office official, Powell became Tony Blair's chief of staff in 1995. In 1997 the proposal that he become Blair's principal private secretary (a post held by career civil servants since 1928) was abandoned following criticism that it was unconstitutional. Nevertheless, he has remained influential at the centre of Blair's Downing Street, with access to security papers and acting as the prime minister's envoy in an attempt to ease tensions in Northern Ireland in 1998. *CL*

Powell, Richard Royle (1909–), civil servant. Powell joined the civil service in 1931 and spent the bulk of his career in the defence field, working in the Admiralty and the Ministry of Defence (MoD), with a wartime spell in North America. In the 1950s, he was the key civil servant in the MoD, first as deputy secretary (1950–6) and then as permanent secretary (1956–9). He switched to permanent secretary at the Board of Trade, 1960–8. *KT*

power, one of the core concerns of political analysis. As such it includes such things as coercion, influence, authority, force, and manipulation. The initial assumption, which came to be associated with pluralism, was that power was an open and empirically determinable transaction in which an actor or group of actors stopped others from achieving their interests, either by forcing them to do something they did not wish to do, or preventing them from doing something they wished to do. Thus, the Harvard academic Robert Dahl argued, in a celebrated study of politics in New Haven, Connecticut, *Who Rules* (1961), that by observing whose interests dominate the decision-making process, one can detect the locus of power. In the case of New Haven, Dahl argued that he had shown empirically that decisions were not being taken systematically in the interests of the political elite. By the 1960s, this formulation had become inadequate. The political scientists Peter Bachrach and Morton S. Baratz argued that power had two faces. Not only was power exercised openly, but powerful actors could shape the agenda and prevent the interests of others from reaching the political process. In addition, they argued, social and political structures played a role in organizing the interests of some into the political process and the interests of others out of it. Political actors can therefore seek to wield power over others by reinforcing some structures and weakening others. Usually, but not always, they argued, the effect of this was to mobilize bias in favour of the interests of the political elite, and against the interests of the general population. Dahl, it followed, had not shown that decisions were made democratically, because the elite might have acted to keep issues which affected their core interests from getting on to the political agenda at all. The problems of investigating this phenomenon empirically led Bachrach and Baratz to play down this part of their analysis in favour of a second face of power which was observable. However, its insights formed the core of Steven Lukes's three-dimensional view of power. Whereas both the first and second faces of power are behavioural and observable, Lukes argued for a view of power in which the dominant political grouping acts to shape the values of others to prevent them understanding their real interests. This configuration of power has come to dominate the literature. However, while as an exercise in the social and political analysis of capitalism, it offers some considerable insights, as an analysis of power relations it presents some significant problems. Lukes insists that those unaware of their real interests must be able to begin to appreciate them when faced with the counterfactual. This leaves open the possibility that all the disempowered are being offered is an alternative false consciousness; and indeed it might follow that there are no real interests at all: merely subjective interests. This in itself does not invalidate broader elements of the analysis; it merely emphasizes the extent to which manipulation of subjective interests becomes the battleground. *CPS*

Steven Lukes, *Power: A Radical View* (London, 1974).

power-sharing executive, Northern Ireland. A government white paper of March 1973 proposed that there should be a new Northern Ireland assembly, that there should be a power-sharing executive, and that there should be an Irish government dimension. In the ensuing assembly elections, a majority emerged in favour of the white paper, consisting of the *Alliance Party of Northern Ireland, the *Social Democratic and Labour Party (SDLP), and the Ulster Unionist Party (see Ulster Unionist Council). Discussions between these parties led to the agreement to set up a government by the end of the year. In December a tripartite conference at Sunningdale between the Northern Ireland parties and the British and Irish governments led to agreement on a Council of Ireland. On 1 January 1974 the new executive took office, Unionist leader Brian Faulkner was chief executive while SDLP's Gerry Fitt was deputy. During the next five months, members of the executive worked well together but before they could deliver much of consequence the executive was overthrown. Its position was undermined by continued IRA violence and by objections from a range of Unionist opinion against power-sharing and the Council of Ireland. Faced with a widespread strike organized by the *Ulster Workers' Council the British government failed to restore order and the executive resigned at the end of May 1974. *BMW*

Paul Bew and Gordon Gillespie, *Northern Ireland: A Chronology of the Troubles, 1968–1999* (Belfast, 1999).

pragmatism. In its philosophical sense, pragmatism refers to the belief that politics is about the pursuit of power rather than the furtherance of justice and virtue and that the basis of action should be self-interest rather than duty and rights. Politically, therefore, pragmatism has come to mean a willingness to set aside entrenched political values in the interest of winning and/or maintaining power, as applied by his critics to the premierships of Harold Wilson. The Conservative Party is the obvious example of the last tendency, having seemingly trimmed its political values in order to recover power after its 1945 election defeat. The Conservative response to this accusation is varied. Some argued that post-war Conservative policy is fully compatible with the party's paternalist, collectivist, and one-nation strands; others that pragmatism has always been a hallmark of Conservatism, as a pragmatic response to the shifting policy needs of a complex modern society is the most appropriate means of managing a representative democracy. Influenced here by the ideas of conservative political thinkers, from the Whig Edmund Burke to Michael Oakeshott, the Conservative Party has contrasted its organic approach to political change with the dangerous attempts to impose the human mind on society which comes about as the result of an ideological stance. The debate re-emerged in reverse in the late 1980s and 1990s in response to a perceived ideological strand in party policy due to the influence of Margaret Thatcher. This led the former Thatcherite John Biffen to call for a policy of consolidation prior to the 1987 election, and fears, expressed most cogently by the political philosopher John Gray, that Conservative attempts at social constructions were damaging the social fabric in general and the Conservative political base in particular. If the succession of John Major to the party leadership in 1990 led some to see this as heralding the re-emergence of one-nation, pragmatic Conservatism, they were largely disappointed. Whereas the party under Major and (to a lesser extent) his successor William Hague acquired an inclusiveness that it lacked under their predecessor, the accusation continued that the pursuit of political absolutes which characterized the dominant, Thatcherite wing of the party was preventing the leadership from responding pragmatically to the political impulses and the policy needs of the electorate.

The concept has also been widely applied to Labour. Harold Wilson as prime minister prided himself on his practicality, and hence was proud to accept the label 'pragmatic' during the 1960s, but the actual record of his premierships added weight to the word's negative connotations. More recently, the *New Labour determination of Tony Blair to ditch policies that were a barrier to the party's election to office (and re-election after 1997) renewed the association. *CPS*

Prayer Book debates (1927–8). On a free vote, the attempt to modernize the 1662 Prayer Book was twice rejected in parliament in 1927 and 1928. The result of some twenty years' deliberation over revision of the Church of England's liturgy, the proposals roused suspicions that it conceded too much to Anglo-Catholicism, especially on matters such as the reservation of the sacrament. Its presentation in the Commons occasioned some of the most celebrated set-piece debates of the century. Particularly effective speeches against the measure were made by the Anglican evangelical Sir Thomas Inskip and by the home secretary, Joynson-Hicks. Evangelicals combined with Scottish Presbyterians, Nonconformists, and assorted others, including the Parsee Communist who sat for Battersea, to defeat a measure which had passed the Lords without difficulty. The rejected Book was nevertheless illegally used in some parishes, whilst leading laymen like Lord Selborne concluded that its parliamentary defeat demonstrated the need for greater independence for the Church. *PPC*

Prebble, John (1915–), writer of popular Scottish history. Prebble contributed much to the growing sense of Scottish cultural identity which emerged in the mid-1960s. Highly readable and accessible, such books as *The Highland Clearances* (1963) helped to foster an appetite for the study of Scottish history at all levels of society. *RF*

Prentice, Reginald Ernest (1923–), politician, Reg Prentice was Labour MP for London seats, 1957–77; then Conservative MP for Newham 1977–9, and Daventry, 1979–87. He was famous for a rapid trajectory to the right in the Labour Party in the 1970s, accelerated in his decision by a left-wing faction in his constituency Labour Party which led to his crossing the floor to the Conservatives in 1977. He was minister for public building, 1966–7, and for overseas development, 1967–9 and in 1975–6, and secretary for education and science, 1974–5. *BJE*

'prepare for government', David *Steel's famous oratorical flourish at the Liberals' Llandudno conference in September 1981 in the wake of the ratification of the Liberal-SDP *Alliance and euphoric support for a new party: 'Go back to your constituencies and prepare for government.' It captured the exultant early Alliance conviction that it was possible to sweep to power on the current (and short-lived) tide of opinion. *JS*

'prerogative of the harlot through the ages, power without responsibility', phrase used by Baldwin (though coined by his cousin, Rudyard Kipling) in a speech during the St George's by-election campaign, 17 March 1931. It was a castigation of the *press barons Rothermere and Beaverbrook, for using their newspapers for irresponsibly propagandist purposes. It reflected Baldwin's frustration at continued attacks on his leadership. *NJC*

Prescott, John Leslie (1938–), Labour politician. Prescott rose to be deputy leader in 1994 largely because, in the struggle over modernizing the party, he acted as a vital link between old Labour and *New Labour. A cheerful, engaging trade unionist, born on Merseyside, he was a trainee chef and served in the merchant navy, 1953–63, when he won a scholarship to Ruskin College, Oxford, 1963–5, and took his degree at Hull University, 1965–8. A full-time official for the National Union of Seamen, 1968–70, he was Labour MP for Hull East from 1983. Linked to the left in the 1960s, he wrote *Not Wanted On Voyage* (1966) and climbed steadily up the Labour ladder to become member of the select committee on nationalized industries, 1973–9, and the European parliament, 1975–9, leading the party delegation, 1976–9. He was parliamentary private secretary to the secretary for trade, 1974–9, and when Labour lost office became opposition spokesman on transport three times, 1979–92; on regional affairs and devolution, 1981–3; and on employment, 1984–7 and 1992–7. In the shadow cabinet from 1983, he ran for leader of the party when John Smith died suddenly in 1994 only to be defeated by Tony Blair, but he defeated Margaret Beckett for deputy leader in the same election. When Labour took office in 1997 Prescott became deputy prime minister with special responsibility for orchestrating the crucially important integrated transport policy, by which the government aimed at reducing car use, encouraging a switch from private to public transport, and thus reducing greenhouse gas emissions, atmospheric pollution, and global warming. Not judged a great ministerial success, he became non-departmental deputy prime minister in 2001. *PRGR*

Colin Brown, *Fighting Talk* (London, 1997).

presidentialization debate In 1960, R. W. K Hinton spoke of the 'prime minister as an elected monarch'. In 1998, Lord McNally stated that in his view the Blair government had moved us 'more closely along the lines of presidential government'. The demise of cabinet government in the face of autocratic prime ministers is an oft-heard lament, perhaps most famously espoused by Crossman in his introduction to Walter Bagehot's *The English Constitution* (1964 edn.). However, despite the eminence of its advocates it is a somewhat sterile argument since it is merely definitional. The prime minister is the centre of government, it is s/he who is charged with responsibility for the overall organization of the executive and this has been so since Peel (at least). G. W. Jones was much closer to the mark when he argued that presidential analyses exaggerate the power of premiers and that countervailing forces, particularly departments, restrain the exercise of the potential power a prime minister clearly has. In its simplest form the debate suggests that premiers used to respect collegiality and bow to the outcome of cabinet discussion, but latterly brook no discussion and simply lay down the law. This overestimates the power of modern prime ministers and underestimates that of their predecessors. It is no coincidence that since Walpole the office holder has been referred to as the 'prime' minister. They have never been *primus inter pares*, which in political terms is a nonsense. There is the number one and there are the others. Notwithstanding that distinction, the relationship between prime ministers and their cabinets is necessarily mutually symbiotic. Accepting that all power is relative, the real debate is about how individuals nurture or neglect the basic principles of management—and that is a question of style. *CAB*

G. W. Jones, 'The Prime Minister's Power', *Parliamentary Affairs*, 18/2 (1965).

press, royal commissions on the, chaired by Ross, 1947–9, Shawcross, 1961–2, and Finer/McGregor, 1974–7. As the *Calcutt report recognized, the press consistently fended off statutory legislation threatened by such inquiries by making small concessions. All the commissions were concerned about increased concentration of newspaper ownership. Each advocated a stronger regulatory body for the industry, recommendations which were only ever partially fulfilled. The Ross commission suggested a general council to safeguard press freedom, which was established, and also encouraged journalists to adopt a greater sense of public responsibility. Following the *News Chronicle*'s closure, the Shawcross commission focused on the financial aspects of the press rather than ethical issues, but noted that the general council did not report publicly as the Ross report had advocated. The commission did press for the inclusion of lay members on what became the press council but they were only allowed on its complaints committee. Rather than the separate body the Shawcross report had advocated, the Monopolies and Mergers Commission oversaw newspaper takeovers. The Finer/ McGregor commission, established against a background of problems in the Beaverbrook newspaper group and apparent overmanning in the press, had broader terms of reference than the previous commissions. It recommended improved training for journalists and that newspaper proprietors should be restricted in their ownership of other media. It found that the Press Council still had too few lay members and advocated further reform particularly in responding to complaints. The council subsequently re-formed as the *Press Complaints Commission. *KMT*

press barons. Some newspaper owners, such as Northcliffe and Beaverbrook, have literally been lords, as politicians sought to buy their loyalty with a peerage. Others, such as Murdoch and Maxwell, have simply been commercial 'barons' of the industry. A few have owned a single title, such as *The Times* (Lord Astor of Hever) or the *Morning Post* (Lord Glenesk). Others have owned newspaper chains (Lord Kemsley, Rupert Murdoch), often a combination of national and regional titles (Lord Thomson, Lord Rothermere). The baronial image fits the idea of a rich, cohesive enterprise, largely free of government and party control; having uncertain but possibly strong popular influence; and dominated by an outsize personality, ruling mercurially and autocratically, and perhaps more interested in politics and public office than maximizing profits. Northcliffe, Rothermere and Beaverbrook did indeed obtain ministerial rank. No successor did so after 1945, though Cecil King (*Mirror* group) apparently sought it. Most still determined their papers' politics, Thomson being a notable exception. Newcomers (Lord Matthews, Lord Stevens) seemingly acquired peerages for the asking. The term was increasingly supplanted by alternatives such as 'media baron', as newspapers joined broadcasting and leisure-based interests in diversified multinational conglomerates. *CKSU*

Matthew Engel, *Tickle the Public* (London, 1996).

Press Complaints Commission (1900–), non-statutory body financed by the press which investigates complaints by individuals about newspaper content and behaviour. It can also initiate complaints, for instance about treatment of the royal family. Lacking sanctions, it has relied since 1991 on a voluntary code of ethics and on papers' readiness to publish apologies. Founded in 1953 as the Press Council, the commission later acquired a non-industry chairman and a majority of lay members. *CKSU*

Press Office, Downing Street, that section of the prime ministerial staff which is responsible for dealing with all aspects of the relationship between the Number Ten staff and the media. The office is headed by the prime minister's press secretary, and additionally has a deputy and as many press secretaries as is deemed necessary. In recent years that number has grown with the increased significance accorded to media relations, especially by the Blair government elected in 1997. With this increased significance has come an increased profile of the post; Bernard Ingham under Margaret Thatcher and Alastair Campbell under Tony Blair became major media figures in their own right, not always to the advantage of their office. The press secretary performs the tasks of being the first point of reference for the media, a spokesman for the government, an adviser to Number Ten on media issues and relations, the intermediary between the premier and the media, and finally the coordinator of government information services. The natural tension between cabinet and prime ministerial imperatives means that the profile of the press secretary will fluctuate according to the personality of each prime minister though the increasing intrusiveness and influence of the modern media may mean a permanent position of high profile importance for the press secretary. *CAB*

press partisanship. Whereas commercial as well as public-sector broadcasters have been obliged to show balance in their coverage of politics, no such restriction has applied to the press. Throughout the century, the ownership, readership, and political management of the press has therefore been a subject of constant concern to the politicians.

In 1900, there was no very decisive advantage to either Liberals or Conservatives in the press, the Conservatives having by then recovered from their very weak press position in the mid-19th century, but not yet forged ahead. There was rough balance in the quality papers read by the elite (the Conservative *Times* and *Morning Post* set against the Liberal *Manchester Guardian*) and no decisive lead for either party among the mass-circulation papers either. Outside London, most regions and large cities had a Liberal-supporting paper and a Conservative one. By 1930, alongside the decline of the Liberal Party there had been a serious decline of the Liberals in the press. *The Times*, along with other Tory papers, easily dominated the quality end of the market, while the *Express* and *Mail* sold about 3.5 million copies a day, compared to less than half that for the Liberals' *News* and *Chronicle*. Meanwhile, many Liberal papers in the provinces had been quietly absorbed by their Conservative rivals. By 1960, when the last Liberal mass-circulation national daily folded, the Conservative papers largely dominated the market. Despite the rise by then of the Labour-leaning *Daily Mirror*, and the staggering-along survival of its *Daily Herald*, the Conservatives were supported by papers selling almost nine million copies a day, compared to barely half that for the other parties. The Conservative position then strengthened further, when the *Herald* was transformed into Rupert Murdoch's Thatcherite *Sun*: by the 1980s, Tory-supporting papers sold almost ten million copies a day, with Labour backed by papers selling under four million. These patterns for national dailies were fairly closely matched in Sunday papers and regional papers, while the only paper in the vital London region evening market was a Conservative one.

Royal commissions on the press wrestled with this pattern of partisanship as a potential problem for the democratic process, but did not manage to offer plausible solutions, it being after all hard to imagine taking the 'free press' within state ownership or regulation. The development of procedures for making complaints to a semi-independent press complaints authority might do something to protect individual rights from intrusion (even this being dubious) but it could do nothing to constrain the editorial and proprietorial influences which shaped what most British readers saw at their breakfast tables. There was plenty of academic research into patterns of distortion and types of influence: **Political Change in Britain* demonstrated the importance of the chosen family newspaper in socializing young people into support for a particular party, while the Glasgow University Media Group tirelessly analysed the ways in which the press (and broadcasters too) distorted news in subtle ways, by for example choosing a vocabulary and headlines that hinted that trade unions were always the cause of strikes.

In the last third of the century, the press had to operate within a world in which television took the lead in providing voters with news, and in ways that were not so susceptible to bias and partisanship. But there was, anyway, no simple equation between press support and voter attitudes, for while the Conservative papers achieved market dominance after 1950, the party lost as many elections as it won in the next 30 years. In some cases, there was no very reliable relationship between parties and their press supporters either. Lord Beaverbrook, having originally bought the *Daily Express* with Conservative Party money, turned it into a personal mouthpiece for his own right-wing causes, and almost managed to drive Baldwin out of the party leadership by doing so. Though a keen Labour-supporting paper, the *Mirror* also called for Wilson's resignation (and indeed described him in an editorial as being 'about as straight as a bent corkscrew'), while the *Sun*, hugely supportive of Thatcher (and of her trade union policies, from which press managers and owners benefited greatly), deserted Major after 1992 and helped to generate the Tory collapse in 1997 (an election at which only two national papers told their readers to back the Conservative government). Politicians by then needed to treat almost all newspapers as floating voters, always to be wooed, never to be won. *JAR*

Stephen Koss, *The Rise and Fall of the Political Press in Britain, 2. The Twentieth Century* (Chapel Hill, NC, 1981).

pressure groups. See interest groups.

Prevention of Terrorism Act, 1974, legislation rushed through parliament immediately after the November 1974 IRA Birmingham pub bombings. It possessed two main features: the power to exclude from Great Britain, Northern Ireland, or the United Kingdom as a whole, people allegedly involved in Northern Irish terrorism; and the power to arrest suspected terrorists and detain them for 48 hours, with the possibility of extending such detention by a further five days. Subsequent renewals of the legislation extended available powers to cover the funding of terrorism and the withholding of information on terrorism, and to allow the Northern Ireland secretary to proscribe organizations connected with terrorism and to issue exclusion orders from Northern Ireland. *RE*

Prevention of Unemployment Bill, 1926. This was the conclusion of a long and unsuccessful campaign, beginning before the minority report of the 1909 royal commission on the poor law, to make operational the Labour movement's rallying cry of 'work or maintenance' in legislation. The bill sought 'to make provision for the prevention of unemployment' by a variety of devices including large-scale public works to reduce average unemployment and the amplitude of the business cycle. *RM*

Parliamentary Debates (HC), 5th ser. 192, 5 Mar. 1926, cols. 1793–1878.

Prices and Incomes Board. See NATIONAL INCOMES COMMISSION.

Prices Commission. See COUNTER-INFLATION POLICY.

Priestley report (1955), produced by the royal commission on pay and conditions of the civil service, established by the Churchill administration in 1953 to advise on improvements to existing piecemeal arrangements. Its recommendation of a system of pay research based on the principle of fair comparisons with comparable jobs in the private sector was accepted. In 1955, equal pay was also established for women civil servants and a five-day week became the norm. The pay research system was abolished unilaterally by the Thatcher administration in 1980, precipitating the 21-week civil service strike of 1981, which did not, though, succeed in restoring the Priestley system. *PJH*

KEVIN THEAKSTON, *The Civil Service since 1945* (Oxford, 1955).

primary education, usually defined in relation to post-11-year-old or 'secondary' education, though in practice the boundaries between the two were much more fluid until the *Education Act, 1944. After 1870, education for all over the age of 7 was introduced and made compulsory in the 1880s. Progressive enactments tended to lengthen school attendance at elementary schools which after 1918 catered to most children up to the age of 14 (the *school leaving age). Only with the Hadow report in 1926 was the clear separation of 'primary' and 'secondary' education recommended, with the idea of a break in schooling at the age of 11 and the separation of pupils into academic and non-academic schools thereafter. These proposals were taken up in Butler's Education Act, 1944, which accepted the age of 11 as the critical one for the determination of what kind of secondary school children should attend. Primary education up to age 11 was to remain unaffected. In the processes of comprehensivization, though, some local authorities sought a different demarcation, with 'middle schools' (from the ages of about 10–12) coming between the primary and secondary stages.

In the post-1945 period, primary education underwent a revolution with the introduction of child-orientated methods of teaching and the development of a much more relaxed environment. In turn, these innovations have been challenged in the education debate of the 1970s and by concern about falling standards. This resulted in the introduction of the *national curriculum in 1988 and the testing of primary school children at ages 7 and 11. Essentially, these changes have been accepted by the Labour government of 1997, which has reiterated the need for better education at pre-11-year-old level. *JS*

prime ministership, development of. The history of the development of the prime ministership is largely the history of the interpretation and conduct of the position by those who have held it. Until the time that parliamentary power began to increase the crown had used advisers on a relatively ad hoc and disorganized manner. Gradually kings realized that in order to secure approval for legislation and, more importantly, for financial appropriations, they needed a group of advisers who had influence within parliament. Thus the embryonic cabinet began to emerge. When the first Hanoverian king, George I, ascended the throne of England, he was relatively uninterested in English politics and ceased to attend meetings of the cabinet in 1717. Once the nominal head of the cabinet had been removed, natural group dynamics demanded that a leader would emerge. The first to so emerge was Walpole. Although recognized as the first 'prime minister', Walpole still needed the aid of the king in order to develop a parliamentary majority. He was also unable to choose his own colleagues and as such his power was limited. Nevertheless, he was the primary figure in that small group of senior advisers.

Pitt the Younger was able to select his cabinet without royal intervention, with the exception of the lord chancellor, but he still did not feel confident enough to push through policies without the acquiescence of George III. Even George IV was not averse to offering cabinet posts to his favourites and the prime minister felt compelled to accept them. As late as William IV (1830–7) there was an accepted notion of a royal veto on cabinet decisions. The real change in the role and power of the prime minister came after the 1832 Reform Act, which shifted the balance of power away from the crown towards parliament and from the Lords to the Commons. It also began to change the nature of elections so that they became simultaneously constituency elections and an election for the person of the prime minister; Peel's 1834 Tamworth manifesto was surely a realization of this new situation. While the manifesto purported to be aimed at the electorate of Tamworth, its real target was clearly the national electorate, and although Peel failed to carry that national electorate in 1834 he did succeed in 1841. It is generally agreed that the 1841 election was the first to be fought on the principle of voting for the prime minister. From this moment onwards premiers were as pre-eminent as their personal attributes permitted. Their most significant relationships were no longer with the crown and their peers but with their cabinet, their party, their parliament, and their public. They came to embody the government. Peel, for example, used to call himself 'the country's minister'. In that sense then, the role of the prime minister had altered irrevocably.

In the sense of the individual's ability to manage the cabinet and the government the change was less significant. The success or failure of prime ministers in that role depends solely upon their personal status and managerial qualities, just as it always has. Thus while Balfour and MacDonald were not even considered the most powerful men in their own cabinets, others such Lloyd George, Churchill, Thatcher, and Blair have been seen as autocratic giants. Attlee, by contrast was an unobtrusive power-broker who considered himself to have been the chairman, someone whose task it was to get others to work. In Attlee's case it is argued that without the benefit of Bevin's loyalty he would never have survived. That may well be true but he must be credited with the perception to have recognized that fact and to have handled it, another facet of the job. Macmillan handled a deterioration in his government's fortunes by sacking a third of his cabinet in the 1962 'Night of the Long Knives', and it is instructive that nobody who survived bothered to resign and nobody offered advancement declined. Prime ministerial power had been drastically demonstrated. However, the executioner himself was not untouched. His reputation was further diminished because it appeared that he had picked easy targets as scapegoats and allowed his enemies to remain in the cabinet where he could keep an eye on them. Ultimately the ploy failed to increase Macmillan's popularity. John Major employed a similarly audacious strategy when he called the 1995 leadership election during his premiership. Again the ploy was initially successful but only delayed the inevitable. Thus while prime ministers can appear to be acting in a powerful manner, it is often an indication that their power is waning. Prime ministers' reputations are, therefore, the product of their style.

The circumstances against which their style is measured have changed and, as such, different styles will be judged as more or less appropriate. The effect on the prime minister of the resignation of a minister is just such an event. Until quite recently ministers would resign on principle, make a relatively innocuous resignation speech, and then slip quietly into political oblivion. The likes of Geoffrey Howe, Nigel Lawson, and Frank Field, among others, have changed those particular rules and with them the manner in which prime ministers must manage their colleagues.

The prime ministership remains a balancing act between a set of variables; it is simply that some of the variables have changed. The crown is now almost an irrelevance, as is parliament to a large extent. The media are enormously relevant and image is all. The prime minister who ignores this reality is as vulnerable as those who ignored the power of the crown in an earlier time. *CAB*

Peter Hennessy, *The Prime Minister: The Office and its Holders since 1945* (London, 2000).

prime minister's office, group of civil servants, official and unofficial political advisers gathered around prime ministers in order to enable them to carry out their duties. The staff is effectively divided into five separate sections: the political office, the prime minister's policy unit (see Central Policy Review Staff), the private office, the *press office, and a group of informal advisers (the last of which expanded considerably after the Blair government was elected in 1997). Despite this expansion, and indeed the general expansion of the prime minister's staff, the establishment is smaller than most comparable heads of government, being less than half that of its American and German counterparts. The prime minister's office is physically linked to the prime minister's room in the Commons with a fully integrated communications system. The private office is both the primary access portal to the prime minister and the transmitter of information to the cabinet and to the office. It is staffed by senior, upwardly mobile civil servants on secondment from their departments. The political office, usually a small unit, consisting of political secretary and the prime minister's parliamentary private secretary, is responsible for dealing with party-political issues, most often, therefore, with backbenchers and whips. It also deals with other relevant party matters, most obviously with party headquarters. The final formal section of the prime minister's office is the prime minister's policy unit, formed in 1974 by Harold Wilson in response to the

*Fulton report's recommendation that there was a need for policy advisers in both the prime minister's and the cabinet offices. It is staffed either by career civil servants or by outsiders employed as civil servants for the duration of their tenure, and functions entirely in line with the vision of the incumbent premier. In its early days it was tasked to concentrate on medium- to long-term policy analysis, under Thatcher it tended to be more departmentally focused, while under Major it took a more evaluatory role. As a unit, therefore, it reacts to prime ministerial imperatives. *CAB*

prime minister's questions. The 30-minute session every Wednesday from 3 p.m. until 3.30 p.m. has become the best-known feature of parliament, particularly since the arrival of the television cameras in 1989. The session has often become heated and at times rowdy, prompting protests to the Speaker from members of the public. However, it is a relatively recent development. Until 1961, questions to the prime minister came at 45 on the order paper, then at 40, latterly on two days a week. But during the 1950s, this number was often not reached or the prime minister was only questioned for five or ten minutes. In July 1961, as an experiment, Harold Macmillan proposed having two fifteen-minute sessions a week, on Tuesdays and Thursdays. This lasted until May 1997, when the incoming Blair government introduced one 30-minute session on Wednesdays. The format of prime minister's questions evolved from predominantly asking about substantive issues to open-ended ones about the prime minister's official engagements or whether the prime minister will visit the questioner's constituency. These are intended to permit the MP to raise a topical issue in a supplementary question. During the 1960s, the leader of the opposition sometimes did not intervene or just asked one question. But from the 1970s onwards the leader of the opposition invariably asked a number of questions. Following the consolidation into one day a week, the convention developed that the leader of the opposition could ask six questions, either about one topic or spread over two during the 30 minutes, while the leader of the Liberal Democrats could ask two questions. *PJRR*

Prior, James Michael Leathes (1927–), Conservative politician, long-suffering friend and lieutenant of Edward Heath in the 1960s opposition, their relationship once described as 'marsupial'. An agricultural specialist with a first in estate management from Cambridge, rooted in East Anglia and MP for Lowestoft, he supported Heath's crypto-free market abolition of resale price maintenance in 1964, becoming party vice-chairman in 1965 and thereafter was entirely identified with Heath. After election victory, he became minister of agriculture, 1970–2, then leader of the Commons, 1972–4, supported an early election in late 1973, but told Heath after two defeats in 1974 that the game was up. When Heath fought on, Prior offered loyal support in the first 1975 leadership ballot, then stood himself (achieving only a thin showing, nineteen votes) in the second. In the early tentative Thatcher opposition, Prior as employment spokesman kept the party to a moderate course, making excellent contacts with trade unionists, accepting the closed shop, supporting Labour's wage controls, and supporting proportional representation for Euro-elections—so was much murmured against by the right. In office from 1979, Prior was an honourable but unhappy servant of Thatcher for five years. He delayed anti-union legislation and disliked 1981's deflationary budget but, like Carrington, Pym, and Gilmour, failed to resign. Prior was then moved against his wishes to Northern Ireland, not being good at resistance, and given a hard time by militant Ulster Unionists, even being mobbed at a funeral. He responded with harmonization of law for Ulster's homosexuals and rejection of the death penalty for terrorism, his attempt to get an assembly going denounced by Enoch Powell. Prior was retired from office in 1984, passing to the more agreeable haven of the chairmanship of GEC (government defence contractors). Prior was the sort of moderate, conciliatory politician natural in Tory politics from Baldwin onwards, but was never a Thatcherite 'one of us', seeing the other side's point of view only too well, so was a falling stock after 1982, as Thatcher achieved closer control of her party. *EP*

JAMES PRIOR, *A Balance of Power* (London, 1986).

prisons and penal policy. For much of the 20th century prisons and penal policy were treated as non-party matters. Escapes or institutional scandals scarcely ruffled the bipartisan approach, and it was agreed that these were difficult areas of public policy and administration from which little political advantage could or should be derived. The consensus even survived upheavals in 1966, when a number of sensational escapes showed prisons to be operating in a poor state of security. More recently, however, escapes of IRA and other high-security prisoners caused sharp political divisions. In 1994 calls for the resignation of Conservative home secretary Michael *Howard were met by his argument that ministers were responsible for policy, not operations. This doctrine continues to be contentious.

Penal policy shifted in the last quarter of the 20th century: it had been a backwater, broadly reformatory in orientation, and in some respects overlapping social and health policy. The sense that crime levels were a product of wartime upheavals and post-war social disorganization and deprivation, dominated penal policy well into the 1960s. From about 1965 sentences—both custodial and non-custodial—began to come under the critical scrutiny of a group of criminologists whose evaluation studies established that penal measures did not appear to deter crime or to reform the offender.

The political mood was ripe for a more sceptical and hard-nosed approach, and politicians began to sense the advantage that might be gained from wrong-footing their opponent on criminal and penal policy. British politicians may have been influenced by American examples, particularly the realization that votes were to be gained (or lost) on crime and punishment issues. The liberal Republican Nelson Rockefeller, in his 1973 campaign, called for life sentences for drug dealers; Richard Nixon had made effective use of this and similar issues in the 1968 presidential campaign. By the 1980s no candidate could ignore criminal and penal policy; and to be seen to be 'soft on crime' was fatal.

In Britain, Labour had generally adopted a more socially ameliorative approach to crime than the Conservatives: hanging and flogging demands were as much a cliché at one set of party conferences as nationalization was at the other. Crime and punishment were mentioned in most election manifestos, and supported a modest amount of inter-party sniping. It was not, however, until the 1997 election that those issues came fully centre-stage. In 1994, after fifteen years out of office, and keenly aware of polling data on crime, Tony Blair (then Labour's shadow home secretary) determined not to be outflanked by his opponents. The resultant slogan *'tough on crime, tough on the causes of crime' safeguarded Labour's position and contributed to its election victory. The Conservatives countered with 'Prison Works'. These two slogans benchmarked and continued to dominate British penal policy. An armed truce supports a new bipartisanship: longer, mandatory, and semi-custodial sentences, and house arrest are supported by both parties, as is acceptance of the private sector as an active participant in penal expansion.

By the most accurate means of assessment (the US National Crime Survey and the British Crime Survey) most forms of crime have been static or in decline for the last decade. Public fear of crime still remains high, however, and is periodically inflamed by notorious and high-profile crimes. Competitive party politics and policy making by polling make it unlikely that there will be a return to an elite- or expert-dominated consensus in the development of criminal and penal policy. Equally, the incumbent party, of whatever hue, is daily and somewhat unpredictably at risk of electoral damage for failures in penal policy and the administration of punishment. *SMcC*

IAN DUNBAR and A. LANGDON, *Tough Justice: Sentencing and Penal Policy in the 1990s* (London, 1998). | MICHAEL TONRY (ed.), *Handbook of Crime and Punishment* (Oxford, 1998).

Pritt, Denis Nowell ('Johnny') (1887–1972), lawyer and socialist. Pritt became Labour MP for Hammersmith North in 1935, but the Labour Party expelled him in 1940 for defending the Soviet Union's invasion of Finland. However, he was returned to parliament as Labour Independent at Hammersmith, 1945–50, and continued to engage in various high-profile political cases. He received a Lenin peace prize, 1954, and doctorates from various universities in the Soviet bloc. He retired in 1960 but served, 1965–6, as presidential professor of Law at Ghana University. *CH*

D. N. PRITT, *From Right to Left* (London, 1965). | D. N. PRITT, *Brasshats and Bureaucrats* (London, 1966). | D. N. PRITT, *The Defence Accuses* (London, 1966).

Private Eye. Founded by Oxbridge graduates in 1962, the magazine thrived in the 'satire boom' of the Macmillan/Wilson era. Surviving a stream of libel actions and outgrowing its undergraduate humour, it developed factual commentary alongside cartoons and satire. Read and fed by Fleet Street, and developing a commitment to exposure journalism, it became financially secure in the 1970s and achieved a difficult generational transition from its founding editor, Richard Ingrams, to a successor, Richard Hislop. *CKSU*

private members' bills. See COMMONS, HOUSE OF: PRIVATE MEMBERS' BILLS.

privatization, sale of shares in nationalized industries since the 1980s. The idea of privatization was one of Britain's most successful exports from the mid-1980s. In Europe, America, Asia, and Africa, governments implemented an idea originating in the Thatcher government. Yet, the precise origins of the idea remain unclear. If anything, it appears to have been the surprising popularity of the sale of 600,000 council houses between 1979 and 1983 which alerted politicians to the potential political and financial benefits of privatization.

The privatization of nationalized industries provided an opportunity to change both their ownership and monopoly structure. For some commentators, often politicians, changing ownership would of itself encourage greater efficiency, as managers responded to the carrot of higher financial rewards and to the stick of potential takeovers. Other commentators, often economists, saw the introduction of competition as providing additional and greater incentives for efficiency. In large utilities like telecommunications, gas, and electricity, competition would occur in the production and distribution sections of the industry, but not in the separate natural monopoly grid network. However, while attracted by such aspects of privatization as the greater freedom to raise capital, managers and unions in nationalized monopolies were less keen to expose themselves to the uncertainties of competition. Knowing that their technical cooperation and goodwill was essential to any smooth process of privatization, the managers of the gas and telecommunications utilities ran a successful lobbying campaign which emphasized the benefits of changing ownership and exaggerated the extent of natural monopoly in their industries. In 1984, the privatization of the telecommunications utility transferred a public monopoly into a semi-private duopoly, while the privatization of the gas utility in 1986 preserved the industry as a monopoly.

The failure to provide for greater competition in these early privatizations attracted the ire of economists but the money of investors. The sale of 49 per cent of the shares in British Telecom raised £3.9 billion, was five-times oversubscribed, and dwarfed the £1.4 billion raised from all the other private-sector new equity issues combined in that same year. In all, the government raised £37 billion from privatization issues, 1984–9, and the incidence of share ownership among the adult population increased from 7 per cent in 1981 to 22 per cent in 1992. New share owners warmed themselves in the glow of rising share prices until the 'Black Monday' stock market collapse on 19 October 1987. In the morning after the night before, the government found itself with time in which to attempt to introduce greater competition in the next major privatization, that of the electricity industry. This privatization proved arduous and acrimonious, with alarm at the potential cost of decommissioning nuclear power stations forcing their withdrawal from the privatization plans. Politically most successful, when economically most disappointing, privatization brought immediate political benefits but often left the longer struggle to introduce competition to the later regulators.

MCh

John Vickers and George Yarrow, *Privatisation: An Economic Analysis* (Cambridge, Mass., 1988).

Privy Council, a survival from earlier periods of British government which retains some powers related to the monarch's prerogative powers but can also provide practical flexibility in the exercise of other governmental functions. The Privy Council was itself effectively a subcommittee of the larger and older royal council, which developed in the 16th century (hence 'privy', as relating to the dispatch of the more confidential business), while the cabinet developed in due course as its own subcommittee and eventually took over most of its powers. Cabinet ministers are usually made members of the Privy Council, membership of which is the distinction which entitles them to be called 'Right Honourable', while the award of membership to non-departmental ministers is therefore seen as a particular distinction—often indeed as a signal of promotion to come. Since the Privy Council does not change with the coming and going of party governments, membership is for life, though in cases of a political resignation as a result of improper conduct (for example John *Profumo in 1963), Privy Council membership can be withdrawn. The leader of the opposition (if not already a member) is invariably made a privy councillor, as are leaders of other parliamentary parties with significant numbers of MPs. This means that, since they have all sworn (literally on bended knee before the monarch) the privy councillor's lifelong oath of secrecy and loyalty (whereas ministerial oaths expire with a term of office), they can then be informally briefed 'on privy councillor terms', as for example Churchill was by Attlee on defence matters in the late 1940s. This is not always an advantage, for the possession of information to which an opposition politician cannot refer in public is just as likely to be inhibiting as beneficial to his party. Others can also be brought into the sworn circle of secrecy to facilitate their receipt of confidential government information, as was Len Murray of the TUC by the Labour government of 1974–9.

The presiding officer, the lord president of the council, is usually a senior member of the cabinet, but meetings tend to include only those few current ministers who can be dragged away from more urgent duties to attend and advise on the Privy Council's remaining routine business. The Privy Council, for example, 'advises' the monarch (in the same way that a cabinet offers binding advice), but on such non-party issues as the granting or revision of royal charters to bodies like universities and cities. *JAR*

Privy Council, Judicial Committee of (JCPC). The JCPC is a relic of the old royal conciliar jurisdiction, lost to the ordinary courts centuries ago. Only appeals outside the cognizance of the ordinary courts were left to it, for example from offshore islands and church courts. With the expansion of the Empire, its jurisdiction grew greatly and it was formally constituted by statute in 1833. However, most of the independent Commonwealth countries have now abolished appeals to the JCPC. In recent years it has been given statutory jurisdiction in appeals from the various medical disciplinary tribunals. The Law Lords are the regular judges, sometimes sitting with distinguished Commonwealth judges. Three is a quorum but usually five sit. It observes the style of a board of advisers rather than a court, its judgements expressed as 'advice to Her Majesty'. Not being a court, its decisions are not binding on UK courts. but may have highly persuasive authority. *VT*

Pro-Boers, label attached by Conservatives to Liberal and Irish critics of the South African war of 1899–1902, the objective being to make them seem unpatriotic. The leading 'Pro-Boer' was David Lloyd George, whose determination to press on with the case against the government led to his stormy meeting in Birmingham on 18 December 1901, from which he had to escape from a mob disguised in a policeman's uniform. *JAR*

Profumo, John Dennis (1915–), and **Profumo case**. Profumo is indelibly linked with the scandal that marked a sea change in attitudes towards secrecy about the private lives of public figures. John Profumo was MP for Kettering, 1940–5, had a distinguished war record, and married a film star, Valerie Hobson. In 1950 he became MP for Stratford-upon-Avon and was a minister at transport and the Colonial and Foreign Offices before Macmillan appointed him war secretary in 1960. The following year he began an affair with 19-year-old Christine Keeler, who was also involved with Yevgeny Ivanov, an attaché at the Soviet embassy. In March 1963 Labour MPs repeated rumours of the affair in the Commons. Pressed by ministers at a late-night meeting to repeat his denial, Profumo assured MPs the following morning that there had been no impropriety between him and Keeler. In June, however, he confessed to having lied and resigned. Macmillan's acceptance of Profumo's word probably reflected his regret at *Galbraith's treatment during the earlier *Vassall case, but his maladroit handling of the scandal brought his leadership into question. With rumours rife of sexual peccadilloes among other public figures, Macmillan commissioned a judicial inquiry by Lord *Denning, whose report became a best-seller. *RJS*

progressivism, doctrine of *New Liberalism which abandoned the Gladstonian prescriptions of minimum government and laissez-faire for greater state involvement and government spending. The 1905–14 Liberal government is credited with establishing the need to tackle deep-seated social problems such as poverty and low wages. Its policies of old age *pensions, wage boards, national insurance (see NATIONAL INSURANCE ACT, 1911), and *labour exchanges have been seen as enshrining progressive ideas and laying the foundations of the *welfare state. Progressives, fundamentally, believed in the appropriateness of state action to assist those unable to practise 'self-help', while retaining a belief in individualism and the voluntary principle. The Lib-Lab electoral arrangements underpinning these policies, which were equally acceptable to Labour, were sometimes called 'the progressive alliance'. *JS*

property-owning democracy, phrase that originated in Noel Skelton's book *Constructive Conservatism* (1924) as one of the ways by which moderate Conservatives of the *YMCA tried to project a sympathetic party image in response to Labour's arrival as a major party. It was taken up officially by Anthony *Eden in 1946 when the party's deputy leader, and then officially trumpeted as the party's central aspiration in domestic policy. Conservatives sought to show that they would diffuse ownership of property in contrast to Labour's centralizing through nationalization. In the generations of the 1920s–50s, only car- and home-ownership was actually much widened across class boundaries and no effective programme was adopted to extend ownership of industry until the 1980s' sales of public sector shares. *JAR*

proportional representation (PR), term used to denote electoral systems that seek to ensure that, in an election to an assembly, the proportion of seats won by a party corresponds as closely as possible to the proportion of votes received by the party in that election. The term is a generic one and encompasses a wide range of systems. There have been various attempts to replace the non-proportional first-past-the-post plurality system used in parliamentary elections in Britain with a system of proportional representation. A Speaker's Conference in 1918 recommended the use of the *single transferable vote in boroughs returning three or more Members. Disagreement between the two Houses, coupled with cabinet caution, resulted in a failure to implement the recommendation. Various attempts to introduce the non-proportional *alternative vote (AV) also failed. Pressure for a new electoral system increased in the 1970s as economic and political problems became more acute and the electoral system failed to produce a decisive winner, necessitating two general elections in a single year (1974). The Liberals and the Electoral Reform Society were long-standing advocates of reform. They were joined by Conservative Action for Electoral Reform in 1974 and the Labour Study Group on Electoral Reform in 1976. Labour support for electoral reform increased in the 1980s and early 1990s: shortly after his election as Labour leader in 1992, John Smith committed his party to a referendum on reform of the electoral system, a commitment maintained by his successor, Tony Blair. After the return of the Labour government in 1997, it appointed an independent commission on the voting system to recommend an alternative to the existing electoral system. The commission, chaired by Liberal Democrat peer Lord Jenkins of Hillhead, reported in October 1998, recommending the use of 'AV Plus' or 'AV Top-Up', using the alternative vote in single-member constituencies, with an additional member in each small geographical region (such as a county) to provide for some element of proportionality. The extent of the 'top-up' through additional members would not be such as to ensure exact proportionality. The government did not move to hold a referendum, indicating that it would be put off until after the subsequent general election. Though not embracing proportional representation for elections to the Commons, the Blair government did introduce legislation providing for new electoral systems for the election of members of the Scottish parliament, Welsh assembly, Northern Ireland assembly, the London assembly, and for members of the European parliament. A regional list system was employed for the European parliament, except in Northern Ireland where the single transferable vote was retained. For the Scottish parliament and Welsh assembly, an additional member system was employed. The debate over PR for parliamentary elections was a hotly fought one. Supporters contended that it was a fairer system, eliminating *'wasted votes', and the partisan see-saw and single-party dominance of adversary politics. Opponents argued that it would give disproportionate power to one or more small parties and destroy the accountability facilitated by the existing system. *PN*

V. Bogdanor, *What is Proportional Representation?* (Oxford, 1984). | P. Dunleavy, H. Margetts, B. O'Duffy, and S. Weir, *Making Votes Count* (Colchester, 1997). | P. Norton, *Power to the People* (London, 1998). | *Report of the Independent Commission on the Voting System* (Cm 4090, London, 1998).

protective tariffs, import duties levied in order to protect domestic industry. A distinction is sometimes made between protective tariffs and revenue tariffs. The latter are imposed on imports for the purpose of raising revenue. Sometimes, as will be readily seen, tariffs are said to be for revenue purposes as a guise for extending protection. The difference between the two is that if tariffs are genuinely imposed for revenue purposes, an equivalent excise duty is imposed on the domestic product. At the outbreak of the Great War the chancellor of the exchequer announced a range of revenue tariffs, but no excise duties were imposed and the conclusion must be that these tariffs were for other purposes. Protective tariffs are frequently the outcome of governments giving in to business pressure. Businessmen or producers are usually in favour of protecting the market they have against foreign competition. Arguments are often framed in terms of employment and backed up by business support for government.

Britain pursued a free trade policy for the second half of the 19th century but economic performance faltered and the pressure for protective tariffs began to grow from the 1880s onwards. The pressure made little headway until the Great War and in the 1920s there was evidence of further 'progress'. In 1921, 'Safeguarding duties' were imposed on a large list of items (argued to be in some way vital to the health of the economy—technological for example), even if the share of trade that they covered was very small. But protection was a big political issue in the 1920s with the Conservative Party its greatest advocate and Labour and the Liberals the parties of free trade. The big change came in the recession of 1929–32, when those sympathetic to protection argued that it was now necessary, and many were influenced by the fact that other countries were increasingly resorting to protection. Some emergency measures were taken late in 1931 when what were called 'Abnormal Import duties' were introduced, and a general tariff was then introduced in April 1932. This imposed a 10 per cent tariff on most manufactured goods. In the year following most tariffs were raised to 15 per cent and 20 per cent, but on some items were as high as 33.3 per cent. Raw materials and goods from the Empire remained largely exempt. But Britain had, like most other countries, become protectionist.

Although the period after the Second World War is generally characterized as one of liberalizing trade, it should not be forgotten that it took some time for tariffs to be reduced. As late as the mid-1960s there were 10 per cent tariffs on machine tools and 80 per cent tariffs on some man-made fibres. Although economists are almost universally agreed that tariffs are damaging to economic performance, they continue to be found and the pressure for them abounds. The reason is that they are difficult for politicians to resist. Politicians stand to gain from granting the legislation either from votes from their constituents to protect a local industry, or from donations to the party from the businesses protected.

FHC

Protestantism. As a political force, Protestantism in 20th-century Britain was largely confined to those areas where Catholicism was strong, such as Northern Ireland, Lancashire, and the west of Scotland. Working-class Protestantism helped to sustain the Conservatives electorally in both Liverpool and Glasgow until the 1960s, as well as underpinning Unionism in Ulster, where it also spawned Revd. Ian Paisley's *Democratic Unionist Party. Despite the embarrassment it caused to Conservative Central Office, local party bosses therefore continued to allow religious discrimination in Conservative clubs on Merseyside as late as the 1940s. Liverpool (in the 1920s) was also the only place in England where Protestantism emerged as an organized political organization, led by Harry Longbottom, pastor of the Protestant Martyrs' Memorial church, though Alderman *Salvidge's hold on the city had involved a strong Protestant flavour within the Conservative appeal. Though housing development, declining church attendance, and bomb damage all tended to destroy Liverpool's discrete communities of Catholic and Protestant and with them the intensity of sectarian feeling, his party retained some seats on the city council into the 1960s. Growing Catholic–Protestant cooperation in the face of economic decline by the 1970s had, however, undermined militant Protestantism on Merseyside. At the time of the pope's 1982 visit it was noted how feeble the protests were.

PPC

psephology, the study of elections. The word derives from the Greek *psephos*, the pebble which the ancient Athenians dropped into an urn in order to vote. The word was coined in Oxford and first appeared in print in 1952. It has been used to cover the whole field of election analysis—legal framework, political history, electoral sociology—but in popular parlance it is most often used to apply to polling and forecasting, often satirically. Five academic traditions may be distinguished.

1. History. Elections are landmarks in history, so the exact recording of their background and their campaigns has become a major activity. The *Nuffield College series on each British general election since 1945 stands out, together with Theodore White's work on each US presidential contest, 1960–76; the ... *at the Polls* books produced by the American Enterprise Institute cover elections in many countries from the 1970s, including Britain.

2. Political Science. Elections see political activity at its most intense and provide an opportunity to study the structure of parties and the nature of political communication. New developments in communication and campaigning have stimulated psephological research.

3. Mathematics. Votes are the most quantifiable units in political science. The relation between votes cast and seats won under different electoral systems has been the subject of extensive analysis, pragmatically by politicians and journalists and, at a more abstract level, by game theorists.

4. Sociology. Sociologists and social psychologists have found in elections an admirable ground for the study of attitudes and behaviour. Since Lazarsfeld's *The People's Choice* (1946), there has developed a vast literature on the correlates of voting. The British Election Survey, initiated in 1963 by Butler and Stokes (**Political Change in Britain*, 2nd edn. 1974) and continued

by Crewe and then Heath and their collaborators, provides a major archive on voting behaviour in the UK. It follows in the tradition of the comparable US archive at the University of Michigan, started in 1948.

5. Geography. Election results lend themselves to map-making. In 1913, Andre Siegfried started a widely copied tradition by plotting the relationship between left or right voting and church-going. The need to modify constituency boundaries has in recent years inspired the elaborate use of computers to assess party advantage under different solutions. *DEB*

Public Accounts Committee, established in 1861. Its membership of around fifteen specialist MPs reflects the party balance in parliament. The chair is held by a prominent member of the opposition. Since 1866 it has been assisted by the comptroller and auditor general who brings irregularities in government expenditure to the committee's attention, from 1978 taking evidence in public. The committee receives accounts of government departments and bodies receiving public funds such as universities and the NHS from the comptroller and auditor general's office (since 1983, the larger National Audit Office). It selects a few areas for particular scrutiny. Its distinctive power has been its ability to summon civil servants. It has proven difficult, though, for the committee to tackle more than a few areas or to identify incorrect behaviour especially in years when many departments have overspent. Two reports in 1984, however, revealed serious misuse of public funds by the property services agency and the De Lorean car company. In 1991 it reprimanded Treasury officials over concealed payments to the chancellor of the exchequer. With its 1994 report on public bodies it signalled the extension of its interests into the question of public service ethos beyond simply finance issues. *KMT*

Public Administration, Royal Institute of (RIPA). The RIPA was founded in 1922 as an independent organization committed to promoting the expert study of public administration and to developing the civil service, and other (national and local) public services, as a recognized profession. Its publications (including its quarterly journal *Public Administration* and the 'New Whitehall' series of books) and its conferences and lectures cemented its reputation as an active and impartial learned society. But the scepticism of higher civil service towards the 'scientific' study of public administration, and the Whitehall preference for the generalist, non-expert, all-rounder, meant that the institute never developed into a proper professional society. Civil service training developed separately, with the creation of the civil service college in 1970. In the 1970s and 1980s the RIPA greatly expanded its international consultancy and training programmes, but it encountered serious financial problems and went into receivership in 1992—apparently unmourned by ministers and mandarins, and at a time when the public service values for which it stood had become unfashionable. *KT*

public corporations, 'Morrisonian'. The 1945–51 Labour government's programme of nationalization of several substantial industries and utilities required tremendous effort, for nothing on such a scale had been attempted before. And since so many of the commitments to nationalize were politically partisan, the civil service was not allowed to plan for it in advance. There had previously been some smaller examples of nationalization (or municipalization). In 1931, the London Passenger Transport Board had been established by Herbert Morrison, minister of transport, bringing the underground trains and buses of London under a single authority. He was subsequently to run it when he became leader of the London County Council. Morrison not only presided over his transport creation, but municipalized organizations like the London port authority, schooling, housing, public health, and much of the hospital service. In appointing Morrison lord president of the council in 1945, the prime minister, Clement Attlee, made him co-ordinator of the government's public ownership programme due to his unique experience and he was successful in solving the problems it threw up. There has built around Morrison's stewardship of the nationalization two myths. One is that he was a fervent advocate of nationalization, when it is clear that he wasn't—as early as 1947 he realized that nationalization across the board was problematic. The other is that he was only interested in one solution to the problems, that based on his own London Passenger Transport Board model. Again this is false as he was very keen on variety and experiment. Therefore the idea of a Morrisonian model is too simplistic an idea. Nevertheless, the semi-independent board, appointed by a responsible minister but with day-to-day freedom to manage its industry without political interference, was a common factor in the bodies that Morrison saw through to public ownership. *JD*

Peter Hennessy, *Never Again* (London, 1992).

public expenditure, spending by general government, being a composite of current and capital expenditures by central government, local authorities, and the public corporations. Before the integration of the budget and national income accounts, beginning in the mid-1960s, public expenditure typically referred only to central government although this included grants to local authorities and some but not all public-sector capital formation.

For most economists and politicians, the most dramatic change in the 20th-century British economy, as elsewhere, has been in the proportion of national income appropriated by the state. Two standard indicators provide a measure of this transformation. First, the ratio of general government expenditure to the GDP rose from approximately 13 per cent to 40 per cent between 1900 and 1997, although the peacetime peak had been in the mid-1970s at closer to 50 per cent, at which point a reaction against leviathan set in. Second, between 1900 and 1997, real expenditures per capita rose from approximately £335 to £5,375 at 1997 prices, a sixteenfold rise.

Table 3 provides long-run estimates for selected years of the expenditure ratio and the composition of expenditure by economic category and by function. These two standard approaches to the economic significance of public expenditure and of the priorities of government are indicated by the scale and distribution of its spending activities. Final consumption by government plus capital formation (items 1–2 of panel A), the measure of the direct economic impact of the public sector on the economy, increased from 11.1 to 20.4 per cent of GDP, 1900–97, far less than the overall increase in the expenditure ratio which was therefore dominated by the growth of transfer payments, especially current grants to the personal sector (item 3). The rise to prominence of this broad category is confirmed by panel B of the table which exhibits two principal developments: the relative decline in the defence effort, the largest budget item in 1900; and the dominant growth of expenditure on social functions (item 13) which had become the most significant category as early as the 1930s.

There is an enormous literature which attempts to explain the growth, timing and pattern of public expenditure (surveyed in Middleton, chapter 3). This has produced few settled conclusions and a number of distinctive approaches: the historical, which stresses the role of war, technology, the advent of democracy, and searing influences such as the inter-war depression and the stagflation of the 1970s; short- and long-term forces, which differentiate over time and can be used to distinguish between policy and non-policy determinants; and in terms of the demand for public services and supply conditions. At the aggregate level, there are clear demographic factors underlying public expenditure growth

TABLE 3. **Total public expenditure as %age of GDP at current market prices, by economic category and functional classification, selected years, 1900–1997**

	1900	1913	1920	1937	1948	1964	1979	1997
A. Economic category:								
1. Current goods and services	9.3	8.1	8.2	11.7	15.0	16.4	19.9	18.4
2. Gross capital formation	1.8	1.2	1.7	3.3	5.7	9.0	6.6	2.0
3. Current grants to personal sector	0.5	0.9	2.7	5.0	6.0	7.2	10.9	14.9
4. Subsidies	0.0	0.0	2.1	0.6	4.9	1.6	2.3	0.6
5. Current grants paid abroad	0.1	0.0	0.2	0.1	0.3	0.5	1.1	0.0
6. Debt interest	1.6	1.7	5.7	5.4	5.1	4.2	5.1	3.8
7. TOTAL	13.3	11.9	20.5	26.0	37.0	38.9	45.9	39.7
B. Functional classification:								
8. Public administration and other	0.7	0.8	0.8	1.0	1.2	0.9	0.9	1.8
9. Debt interest	1.6	1.7	5.7	5.4	5.1	4.2	5.1	3.8
10. Law and order	0.4	0.6	0.2	0.5	0.5	0.8	1.2	2.0
11. External services	0.0	0.0	0.0	0.0	0.2	0.8	1.2	n.a
12. Defence	6.0	3.1	6.1	4.9	6.3	6.1	4.7	2.8
13. Social services	2.3	3.7	4.9	10.5	17.6	16.5	23.9	26.1
14. Economic services	1.6	1.4	2.4	2.7	4.8	7.1	5.7	2.1
15. Environmental services	0.5	0.6	0.3	0.9	1.3	2.5	3.1	1.2
16. TOTAL	13.3	11.9	20.5	26.0	37.0	38.9	45.9	39.7

Sources: Middleton, table 3.2; author's calculations.

but beyond this there has been much debate about the determinants of the trend behaviour of the expenditure ratio:

1. The displacement and inspection effects. Following upon the observation that after the two world wars the expenditure ratio never fell back to its pre-war levels, the hypothesis was advanced that wars resulted in a permanent upward shift in society's tolerance of higher tax rates and revealed information about social conditions which were not previously available, with this new knowledge producing a consensus in favour of additional public expenditures, these being possible because of the increment to revenue permitted by the displacement effect. However, what Peacock and Wiseman were unable to explain was why the expenditure ratio continued to grow on trend between the wars and from the end of the Second World War until the mid-1970s.

2. Wagner's law: that the demand for public services and willingness to pay is income-elastic, and therefore bound to increase with affluence. Extensive econometric work has been unable to confirm this, but for Britain there is evidence that, excluding the wars and immediate post-war periods, government expenditure has been remarkably stable over the course of the century, with its current value in any one year almost entirely explained as a linear function of its value in the previous year, and that the trend in expenditure over 1958–76 is an exact extrapolation of that established in 1907–13.

Such econometrics, however, leave much unexplained for the historian and political scientist and accordingly there is a rich but inconclusive literature which locates public expenditure growth in a composite of forces: political competition, with politicians attracting votes through spending promises; the actions of bureaucracies seeking to extend their influence through expanding their budgets; the impact of lobbying by sectional interests; the demonstration effect of other countries, feeling obliged to match services available elsewhere; and faulty control mechanisms—among others.

What stands out for the British case is that the forces making for the growth of social expenditures originate before the Great War in efforts to adjust the employment and distribution of income consequences of the market (social market failure); that these forces were strengthened between the wars, with the mass unemployment of the 1930s resulting in the British expenditure ratio moving in advance of other OECD economies; and that after the Second World War British public expenditure was noticeable for its slow growth relative to these other economies who were catching up on big government; and that the trend to expenditure, but less so its pattern, was largely invariant to the party of government until the reaction against leviathan of the 1970s. This development, whilst associated with the crisis of *Keynesianism and with the identification of government itself as the source of Britain's relative economic decline, was the culmination of there being no stable agreement in British politics of the purpose of government in relation to the market economy, and therefore of the appropriate size and scope of public expenditure which was viewed alternately as parasitic or as a panacea. Whilst the former view dominated in 1979–97, it is noteworthy that the Conservative governments who were so vocal about public expenditure as the source of Britain's economic problems, and tried so hard to contain its growth, left office with an expenditure ratio only 6 per cent lower than that they inherited. *RM*

R. Middleton, *Government versus the Market* (Cheltenham, 1996).

Public Expenditure Survey. See Plowden report (1962) and Public Expenditure Survey (1959).

public opinion, term used to denote the collective views of citizens. These views may be discerned by some form of structured or rigorous measurement, for example *opinion polls, or by observation and intuition. Systematic methods of collecting opinions developed especially after 1945. Prior to then, attempts at measurement were generally crude, though sometimes influential. In 1934–5, a massive 'ballot' was conducted, based on house-to-house surveys, eliciting the views of 11.5 million people. Dubbed the Peace Ballot, it produced majorities in favour of Britain remaining a member of the League of Nations, of a reduction in armaments by international agreement, and of the abolition of military aircraft by international agreement. Though a majority supported the use of collective military measures to stop one nation attacking another, the poll influenced government in favour of pursuing collective action through the League of Nations. Generally, though, in the absence of any form of structured measurement, politicians and others had to rely on anecdote, limited observation, and surmise. Geoffrey Dawson, editor of *The Times* in the 1930s, mixed in a limited social and political circle: Eton, All Souls, London clubs, the *Round*

Table, and the offices of ministers in parliament or Downing Street. 'He took the views of this circle to represent "average British opinion", and followed and encouraged them' (C. L. Mowat, *Britain between the Wars 1918–1940* (London, 1955), 536–7). Others were prepared simply to assert what they thought opinion was, or to infer that the views expressed by national newspapers reflected, or influenced, the opinions of their readers. The opinions of newspaper owners—the 'press barons'—carried considerable political clout. The years after 1945 saw the development of structured, though not necessarily infallible, means of finding and measuring the views of citizens. Opinion polling became more sophisticated and extensive. In the 1990s, the use of focus groups—small groups used to test reaction to particular ideas—became more common, especially by the principal political parties. Attempts to discern public opinion were accompanied by debate as to whether politicians should follow such opinion or seek to give a lead. One view was that, in a representative democracy, politicians should follow the views of citizens. Another was the more Burkean view that politicians should give a lead, and offer electors their judgement. Others took a more cynical view, echoing Key's definition of public opinion as 'those opinions of private persons which governments find it prudent to heed' (V. O. Key, *Public Opinion and American Democracy* (New York, 1961), 14). *PN*

G. C. Moodie and G. Studdert-Kennedy, *Opinions, Publics and Pressure Groups* (London, 1970).

Public Opinion, British Institute of, the title assumed by the Gallup poll in 1937 when Dr Henry Durant (1902–82) launched the first commercial polling company in the UK. He continued as chairman until 1971. In 1945 the Gallup poll, in the first sample survey prediction of a British general election result, predicted a 6 per cent lead for Labour, against all popular expectation—and was only 2 per cent out. In 1952 the company's name was changed to Social Surveys (Gallup Poll) Ltd. Until the late 1950s it had a virtual monopoly in political polling. But, with the arrival of competition, it held its own amongst the four or five firms that regularly publish political polls, although, like its rivals, its main activities were in market research. Its political findings were published exclusively in the *News Chronicle* until October 1960. Since 1961 they have appeared regularly in the *Daily* and *Sunday Telegraph*. *DEB*

public opinion polls. See opinion polls.

Public Order Act, 1936. The 'battle of *Cable Street' (4 October 1936), when large crowds blocked the intended march of the British Union of Fascists into Jewish areas of East London, assisted the introduction of the Public Order Act (effective from January 1937). It reflected 'police concern about the use of uniformed paramilitary groups which might challenge their monopoly of law enforcement and maintenance of public order, together with more general worries about the necessity of maintaining social control and of preventing provocative behaviour against law-abiding citizens' (Thurlow, 113). The Act gave the police powers to ban political demonstrations likely to lead to a breach of the peace. *CH*

R. Benewick, *The Fascist Movement in Britain* (London, 1972). | R. Thurlow, *Fascism in Britain: A History 1918–1985* (Oxford, 1987).

public prosecutions, director of (DPP), officer responsible since 1879 for managing the crown's part in the legal processes of criminal prosecution. The post had until recently a low profile, occupied generally for long periods (there were only ten DPPs in the period 1894–1998) by career civil servants with legal training. The DPP's staff liaised with the police over the preparation of evidence for courts above the level of local magistrates and took the decision whether to prosecute: the DPP could decline to prosecute if it seemed unlikely that a conviction would be achieved or if on other grounds it was deemed not to be in the public interest. There was always—and still is—a discretion not to prosecute, exercised by the police for the most minor offences, by the DPP for the bulk of crimes, and by the attorney-general in some of the most serious crimes (such as treason). Once a decision to prosecute had been taken, the DPP's office would employ and brief barristers (who would then receive 'Treasury briefs'), effectively taking the solicitor's part in managing the case (the DPP was originally the 'solicitor' for public prosecutions) when it came to court, but still therefore requiring the employment of barristers actually to plead the crown's case. From 1985, the police's role in preparing for trials was reduced, with the introduction of the Crown Prosecution Service (CPS), whose staff have had greater discretion. Initially, the CPS had severe problems both of underfunding and of a shortage of qualified lawyers prepared to work for civil service rates of pay, and it was not until 1993 that it approached its full staff establishment.

Nevertheless, the poor conviction rates that had led to the CPS's creation in the first place, did not improve after its appearance, and there continued to be mutual recrimination between the CPS and the police as to the cause of this. The publication of an extremely critical report on the CPS by Sir Ian Glidewell in 1999 led to a further restructuring, so that most CPS area offices now work with only a single police force, and personal contact and mutual trust ought to improve. The CPS published in 1994 a *Code for Crown Prosecutions* in the hope of improving public knowledge of the reasoning that lies behind its decision to prosecute or to drop a case. *JAR*

public records, reports on the, produced by the Pollock commission, 1910–18; the Grigg committee, 1952–4; and the Wilson committee, 1978–81. The Pollock commission's three reports on the Public Record Office (PRO), governmental records, and local records found storage, weeding of files, staff training, and research facilities to be poor. It recommended improvements in all these aspects. The Grigg committee focused on the vast amount of records arriving annually at the PRO. Its concerns included wartime service records, ships' logs, photographs, and films. Its recommendations were implemented by the 1958 Act. More records officers were introduced into government departments and conducted staged reviews of documents. Public records became the lord chancellor's responsibility. In 1967 the delay before records passed to the PRO was reduced to 30 years. The Wilson committee, reinforcing previous reports, advocated further development of the PRO's role, and allowed early access to certain documents. *KMT*

Public Records Act, 1958, introduced a rule that government records would normally be open to the public after 50 years, with government discretion to extend this period. The closed period was reduced in 1967 with the introduction of the '30-year rule'. There remained exceptions to these general principles (for example, on matters relating to the royal family or national security) but, under the 'Waldegrave initiative' in 1992, the criteria for extended closure and the retention of documents were specified more closely. The Blair government's freedom of information reforms retained the 30-year rule, but it was envisaged that fewer records would be withheld for the full 30 years. *KT*

public schools, fee-paying schools. Public schools have a long history in Britain, many being ancient foundations, some like Eton and Winchester even to medieval times. In the 19th century many more were established and older ones reformed to cater for a broader and more commercial elite. Their existence was widely attacked on the left in the 20th century for being bastions of outdated values and elite culture. Writers such as R. H. *Tawney in *Equality* (1929) complained of their overweening dominance of the 'establishment'. Little attempt at reform was undertaken, though, and the Fleming report of 1944 merely suggested that the public schools become more accessible to state candidates through scholarships. After 1945 public schools were often the butt of Labour and Liberal criticism for maintaining social elitism in British education, but no effective attempts at abolition have taken place. The independent sector continues to enjoy strong parental support and achieve high academic standards. There are now approximately 2,500 independent schools in the UK, catering for approximately 7 per cent of all children in education and 615,000 pupils in total. The leading public schools commonly head academic league tables, resulting in disproportionate (in population terms) access to elite universities. *JS*

public sector borrowing requirement (PSBR), the principal indicator since 1969 of the state of Britain's public finances, being the accounting identity which measures the difference between the receipts of the public sector (central government, local authorities, and public corporations) and its current and capital expenditure, including financial transfers. The PSBR, and earlier measures of the government's budget balance, are both a target of policy and, subject to certain important reservations, an indicator of its fiscal policy stance.

Figure B shows the PSBR since 1966 and a comparable longer-run measure of the budget balance since 1900. High public borrowing is unsurprisingly associated with the world wars, but has also been evident since the mid-1970s at which point concerns that the PSBR was excessive (it peaked at 9.6 per cent of GDP in 1975) contributed towards the crisis of *Keynesianism and the subsequent *monetarist policy experiment of the Conservatives, 1979–83. Budget deficits, however, were not uncommon in the pre-Keynesian era, and throughout the 20th century the limits to public borrowing have been set by two concerns: first, that it crowded out private investment with potentially deleterious effects on inflation and economic growth; second, that if unchecked, the resulting enlarged national debt would require additional taxation for its

FIGURE B. Public-sector budget balance and PSBR as a %age of GDP at current market prices, 1900–1998

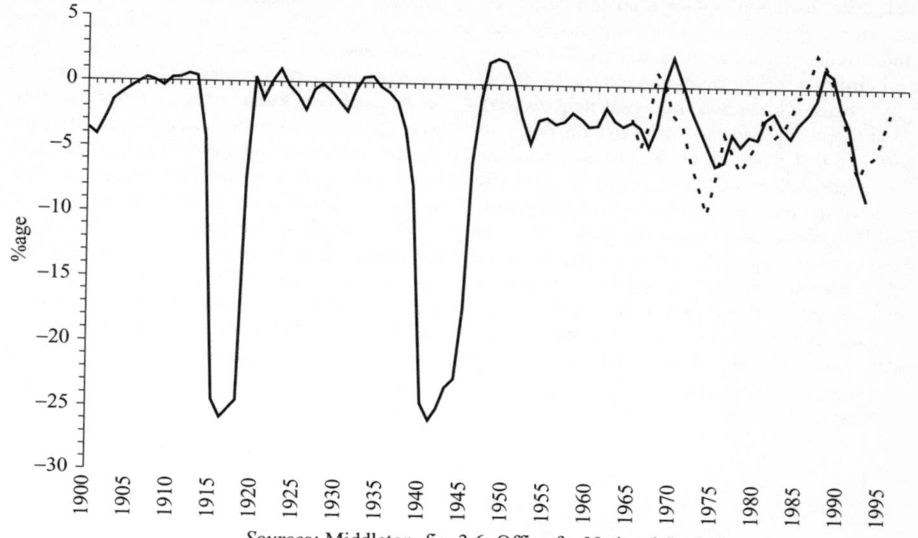

Sources: Middleton, fig. 3.6; Office for National Statistics.

—— Public-sector budget balance - - - PSBR (inverse sign)

servicing. These connect with the twin methods of financing the PSBR either by money creation and/or by debt issue, with the former increasing the money supply and the latter raising interest rates. Whilst public borrowing gave governments and money markets some anxious moments in the 1930s, and more regularly since the 1970s, at the end of the century the ratio of outstanding national debt to GDP was approximately one-third, as it had been in 1900, with the effects of war and peacetime borrowing nullified by a century of economic growth and inflation. *RM*

R. MIDDLETON, *The British Economy since 1945* (London, 1999).

purchase tax was introduced as an item of war finance in 1940 but because of its success became an important part of the post-war tax system. It was intended to absorb the purchasing power flowing towards non-rationed and price-controlled goods, to prevent inflation and distortions in production. It had to be regressive in order to absorb working-class consumption, but also to have minimal impact on the cost-of-living index from whose increases wage demands flowed. By 1942, the tax had three rates for different types of goods in addition to an exempted goods category, with the heaviest rate on luxury items. Its continuation after the war was attractive both as a restraint on consumption and as a source of revenue from those still willing to spend. Anxieties about its regressive effects shifted from early opposition to the tax to arguing about the rates to be applied to particular items and which might be exempt. Its wartime rates—23 per cent, 66 per cent and 100 per cent—were far higher than those of conventional sales taxes and were only reduced in 1953. It was eventually replaced in 1973 by *value added tax, which, although more costly to administer, has produced far more revenue than purchase tax would have done had it continued. *RCW*

U. K. HICKS, *British Public Finances* (London, 1954). | R. S. SAYERS, *Financial Policy 1939–1945* (London, 1956).

Putting Britain Right Ahead **(1965)**, the Conservative Party's key policy document in opposition during 1964–70. Published for the October 1965 party conference, it was the result of the policy review masterminded by Heath after 1964. With the expectation of an early election, the Tories had gone straight to detail in policy making. This approach suited Heath, who was happier dealing with specific proposals than principles. The publication of *Putting Britain Right Ahead* little more than two months after Heath won the Tory leadership in July 1965 reinforced his call for a radical break with the past. The document highlighted five priorities: tax reform, greater competition in industry, trade union reform, selectivity in the social services, and entry to the European Economic Community. The economic and industrial reforms were justified by the need to make Britain ready to compete in Europe, but the failure to say how the Conservatives would manage the economy reflected the party's divisions on incomes policy. Heath's technocratic language prompted *The Economist* to suggest that he had stolen Wilson's 'efficiency consultant's coat', while his eulogy to society's 'pacemakers' prompted the irreverent epigram in the Conservative Research Department, 'blessed are the pacemakers'. *RJS*

John Ramsden, *The Making of Conservative Party Policy* (London, 1980).

Pym, Francis Leslie (1922–), Conservative politician and whip. 'Francis, I need a new foreign secretary'. Thus Thatcher in 1983 annihilated a well-liked old-school, gentlemanly Tory. Pym was a landowner, lancer, Lloyds' member, before becoming Heath's chief whip and Northern Ireland secretary, Thatcher's agriculture minister, defence secretary and finally foreign secretary. He was chief whip for the 1972 European Communities Bill (see European Communities Act, 1972), at Northern Ireland for the Sunningdale agreement. Reluctance to carry on the Falklands war outside the exclusion zone and quoted election-time support for only a modest majority in 1983 led to the killing of his career that marked Thatcher's sense of omnipotence. *EP*

Francis Pym, *The Politics of Consent* (London, 1984).

quangos. The term quango emerged in the early 1970s as a shorthand for quasi-non-governmental organization, but was corrupted over the following decade to mean quasi-autonomous non- (or sometimes national-) governmental organization. Generally, a quango consists of appointed members and is responsible for spending or allocating public money. However, this definition, which covers bodies ranging from the Spongiform Encephalopathy Advisory Committee to the Atomic Energy Authority via the Child Support Agency and the Tote, is so broad that one key commentator has concluded that 'as a means of describing anything . . . the word is useless' (Barker, 3). The difficulty of defining a quango has led to disputes over their numbers; however, only a handful existed in 1900 and they have proliferated since 1945. Critics of quangos have focused on the power of ministers to appoint members, the lack of public accountability (the democratic deficit), and their expenditure. These concerns first reached a peak in the late 1970s, led by the Conservative MP Phillip Holland.

In 1979, this concern led Prime Minister Margaret Thatcher to ask former permanent secretary Sir Leo Pliatzky to conduct an inquiry into quangos. Pliatzky's *Report on Non-Departmental Public Bodies* (NDPBs) (Cmnd 7797, London, 1980) excluded bodies related to local government, the NHS, the BBC, and the nationalized industries. Pliatzky identified three kinds of NDPB: 489 executive bodies; 1,561 advisory bodies, and 67 tribunal systems. His report led to the abolition of 30 executives, 211 advisory bodies, and six individual tribunals saving some £11.9 million a year—a small sum given the level of concern which prompted the cull. By 1996 the number of executive NDPBs had fallen by 183 since 1979 and the number of advisory NDPBs by 811. However, by this time Pliatzky's criteria had been overtaken by events. Reform of the civil service and local government had led to a huge growth in quangos which were not NDPBs; for example, NHS trusts, training and enterprise councils, and grant-maintained schools.

In 1996 nearly 12,000 appointees served on advisory and executive NDPBs but another 4,000 served on NHS bodies and a further 60,000 on other non-NDPB quangos. The members of these new bodies have been termed the new magistracy, reflecting the view that their creation reverses the 19th-century trend of removing power from appointed elites to elected authorities. The 1990s saw renewed concern over quangos. The first report of the committee on standards in public life (Cm 2850, London, 1995) included recommendations on appointments to quangos and its second report (Cm 3270, London, 1996) examined local public spending bodies. The committee advocated improved codes of conduct, appointment and accountability procedures, and auditing arrangements, and led to the appointment of Sir Len Peach as the first commissioner for public appointments (December 1995). However, the commissioner's powers were not as great as had been recommended and the debate over the powers of appointed bodies continues. *CL*

Anthony Barker (ed.), *Quangos in Britain, Government and the Networks of Public Policy Making* (London, 1982). | Chris Skelcher, *The Appointed State: Quasi-Governmental Organisations and Democracy* (Buckingham, 1998). | Stuart Weir and W. Hall, *EGO-Trip: Extra-Governmen-*

tal Organisations in the United Kingdom and their Accountability (London, 1994).

Quebec agreement (1943), Anglo-American agreement on atomic collaboration, 19 August. In 1941, Churchill rejected Roosevelt's offer of a joint Anglo-American atomic project and instead agreed to information exchange. The British hoped to maintain an early lead in atomic technology and thus continued with their work code-named 'Tube Alloys'. Rapid American advances through the 'Manhattan project' forced a British rethink and the Quebec agreement established atomic partnership. This was shortly broken by the McMahon Act of 1946, prohibiting the disclosure of American atomic information to other countries. *JRVE*

Queen's Speech, delivered by the monarch from the throne in the House of Lords at the state opening of each parliamentary session, usually in November. The speech, written by the government of the day, sets out the legislative programme for the coming session and lasts up to ten minutes. The state opening is the grand ceremonial occasion of the parliamentary year with peers in their robes. The monarch commands Black Rod, the principal usher of the Lord Chamberlain's department, to summon the Commons to attend. The door to the chamber of the Commons is, by tradition, shut in his face, and he knocks three times before being admitted. The Speaker and Members of the Commons then walk across to the Lords to stand at the bar to hear the speech. This is followed by a debate of usually around five days opened by the leader of the opposition and the prime minister. *PJRR*

Quelch, Harry (1858–1913), socialist politician. An outstanding example of a self-taught worker-intellectual, Quelch was a leading member of the Social Democratic Federation, editor of its newspaper *Justice*, manager of its press, and a parliamentary candidate on four occasions. He also played an active role in London trade unionism. Quelch achieved notoriety in 1907 when he was expelled from the Stuttgart conference of the Socialist International by the Württemberg government for referring to The Hague peace conference as a 'thieves supper'. *MC*

Quinlan, Michael Edward (1930–), civil servant. A notably cerebral official, Quinlan spent most of his Whitehall career in the Ministry of Defence (MoD), though with stints as a senior official in the Cabinet Office (1974–7), the Treasury (1981–2), and as permanent secretary at the Department of Employment (1983–8). When deputy secretary responsible for policy at the MoD (1977–81), he impressed Margaret Thatcher with his work on strategic nuclear weapons and deterrence theory. He served as MoD permanent secretary, 1988–92. *KT*

Race. The question of race has been the subject of extensive study and debate in modern British politics. In the main, interest has focused on the political developments surrounding the historic transformation of Britain into a multiracial, multicultural society from the mid-20th century onwards. This change was associated with three important debates about the nature, responsiveness, and functioning of the British political process. Each raises important questions about the extent to which race is to be treated as a 'normal' party-political matter that fits into long-standing accounts of political change.

First, there is considerable doubt over the efficacy of the major parties' track record in tackling racial sensitivities. Opinion poll data between the 1960s and 1980s consistently showed hostility in public attitudes towards progressive race relations measures and liberal immigration regimes. The structure of these attitudes showed resentment and scepticism located amongst both ideological left- and right-wing voters. In essence, the issue cut across traditional, class-based political identities and voting loyalties. Race, therefore, exhibited many of the characteristics of other cross-cutting issues such as European integration and devolution. In the early phase, whilst race remained highly salient, it was clear that the issue did not fit into the established mould of issue management in British party competition.

Second, analysts have sought to throw light on the political integration of Britain's ethnic minorities. Voting studies have consistently shown a strong bias towards Labour support amongst minority electors (with around four in five backing Labour through all general elections, beginning in October 1974, for which reliable data has been gathered). Moreover, such loyalty has remained virtually untouched by major ebbs and flows in the Labour Party's national fortunes in the post-war period (support levels in 1983, Labour's nadir, were very similar to those in 1997). The evidence suggests that for British ethnic minorities, following the American case, race has trumped class in shaping voting choice. Indeed, exceptionally high levels of Labour support across all social classes have tended to conceal any underlying patterns that may have existed. Analysis based on the 1997 British Election Study challenges aspects of this conventional wisdom, however. By testing for the relative chances of non-Labour voting, putting aside saturation levels of Labour support, it is apparent that a relationship between class and vote does exist. This is pioneering finding, suggesting that class indicators, based on occupation, housing, and education, may have a larger pull on ethnic minority voting choice than previously thought. The consequences are potentially great for understanding the sources of political difference across ethnic groups.

Finally, the racial issue has also raised major questions about means and ends in social integration policy. The post-war political consensus was relatively quick to establish a liberal policy framework for managing race relations and fostering tolerance and harmony. This framework yielded three major *Race Relations Acts in 1965, 1968, and 1976, as well as considerable central support for local (public and voluntary) action to promote integration, such as through the Section 11 funding programme in education. However, the liberal approach has attracted criticism, both principled and tactical, from radical and conservative circles. The former has suggested that discriminatory immigration laws governing rights of settlement at the point of entry have undermined the moral and intellectual basis of integration policy. A form of double standards has resulted, it is argued, with potentially fatal consequences for liberal agendas to promote anti-discrimination in domestic affairs. Meanwhile, conservative opponents, spearheaded in the early years by Powellites, have dwelt on two themes. To begin with, they have publicly doubted the proposition that integration policy could work without highlighting the need to 'integrate' immigrants and their offspring to British norms and mores. In addition, scepticism has been aired regarding the moral relativism that has tended to underpin the strategy of multiculturalists, with the implication that this has led, however unwittingly, to an incohesive society in which contestation of basic values has become routine. These criticisms, not surprisingly, have brought conservatives into direct conflict with pluralist voices in favour of greater acceptance of ethnic and cultural diversity. *SS*

H. Gouldbourne, *Race Relations in Britain since 1945* (Basingstoke, 1998). | S. Saggar (ed.), *Race and British Electoral Politics* (London, 1998).

Race Relations Acts, 1965, 1968, 1976. The Race Relations Act of 1965, extended in 1968, sought to make overt racial discrimination unlawful. A Race Relations Board in 1965, supplemented by the Community Relations Commission in 1968, set out to promote 'harmonious community relations'. These were strengthened in 1976 as the Commission for Racial Equality. *JS*

Race Relations Board. Mass *immigration to the UK from the Commonwealth in the years after the Second World War created new problems and tensions in the field of racial equality. To counter these issues, the first Race Relations Act in 1965 created a Race Relations Board which was reconstituted three years later under the Race Relations Act, 1968. The main difference was that in its second incarnation, the board could investigate a suspected discriminatory matter even if there had been no complaint, and could institute civil proceedings if appropriate. The 1968 Act also created the Community Relations Commission to promote race harmony and advise the home secretary on racial matters. The 1976 Race Relations Act merged these two bodies and strengthened their powers, creating the Commission for Racial Equality. *JD*

Commission for Racial Equality website: *www.cre.gov.uk*

Rachmanism, practice of intimidating tenants or charging extortionate rents so as to secure their removal, associated with the 1960s' property developer Peter Rachman. Shortage of rented accommodation and the ability to charge higher rents after decontrol of rents in the 1957 Rent Act were widely blamed for 'Rachmanism' and other aspects of malpractice. The Labour government elected in 1964 brought in a Rent Act in 1965 which reintroduced controls over most privately owned unfurnished accommodation. *JS*

Racial Equality, Commission for. See Community Relations Commission; Race Relations Board.

radar, system which measures range, direction, and velocity electronically. Radio direction finding, as the British called it, had had a long gestation, but it was a British scientist, Robert Watson-Watt, who made the most dramatic breakthroughs in the mid-1930s, allowing the establishment of the Chain Home stations which gave the RAF a crucial advantage in the battle of Britain. Since then scientists have worked ceaselessly to improve, and avoid detection by, radar. *MLC*

Radcliffe, Cyril John (1899–1977), judge. A law lord, 1949–64, Lord Radcliffe was best known as the pre-eminent committee chairman of his day. A brilliant intellect and a lucid orator, a fellow of All Souls College, Oxford, 1922–37, he was called to the Bar in 1924. After an outstanding career at the Chancery Bar, he was, exceptionally, appointed directly to the House of Lords. His public service began during the Second World War in the Ministry of Information, where he became director-general in 1941. Although he returned to the Bar, his public service resumed in 1947 as the chairman of two boundary commissions established to partition India and Pakistan. Imbued with a great sense of duty, Radcliffe continued for the next 30 years to chair committees involving complex and confidential issues: the royal commission on the taxation of profits and income, 1951–5; the constitutional commission for Cyprus, 1956; the inquiry into the monetary system, 1957–9; the committee on security procedures and practices in the public service, 1961; the inquiry into the Vassall case, 1962; the committee of privy councillors investigating the *Daily Express* and D-notices, 1967; the committee on ministerial memoirs, 1975–6. *CAM*

Edmund Heward, *The Great and the Good* (Chichester, 1994).

Radcliffe report on the working of the monetary system (1959). The setting-up of this committee, under Lord *Radcliffe, reflected growing government concern with the post-war level of inflation, with prices in 1958 50 per cent higher than ten years earlier. Macmillan's Conservative government was divided on how to approach this problem, with some focusing on the need for a more deflationary policy, even at the price of higher unemployment, while others sought a solution less likely to alienate trade union opinion. These disagreements came to the surface in 1957 with the resignation of the chancellor of the exchequer, Thorneycroft, and his two junior ministers. The committee's report came down against the view that monetary policy should be used more actively to combat inflation. Rather, they suggested, monetary policy should be deployed as just one instrument amongst several. The committee also did not accept the idea that monetary policy should aim at controlling 'the supply of money'. Their view was that such an entity could not be effectively isolated and measured, and that monetary policy should instead be concerned with overall liquidity in the economy, and with the level of interest rates. Radcliffe represents the high water mark of post-war rejection of monetary policy from a broadly Keynesian perspective, which put the overall level of demand at the centre of concern. The Conservatives in the 1950s had used monetary policy more actively than Attlee's Labour governments but, after Radcliffe, anti-inflationary policy in the 1960s was dominated by the pursuit of incomes constraint. Amongst economists, the Radcliffe view was controversial, and advocates of tight control of the money supply decried what they saw as its rejection of established truths about the link between the money supply and the price level. *JDT*

Report of Committee on the Working of the Monetary System (Cmnd 827, London, 1959). | David Croome and Harry Johnson (eds.), *Money in Britain 1959–1969* (Oxford, 1970).

Radnor report (1908). Produced amongst rising concern over racial degeneration, this was the result of a 1906 royal commission originally chaired by the earl of Bath. It advocated that mental deficiency be handled distinctly from poverty or crime. Furthermore it called for more data and uniform supervision of the mentally ill with the local authorities assuming responsibility. The Lunacy Acts were not replaced as it suggested and controversy in parliament over eugenics delayed legislation on the lines of the report until the Mental Treatment Act of 1914. *KMT*

Ragged-Trousered Philanthropists, The (1908), socialist novel. Robert Tressell's semi-autobiographical account of working-class life during the Edwardian era is one of the most significant novels of the century. It relates the story of 'twelve months in hell', the subjection and destitution of a group of decorators in Mugsborough (based on Hastings).The first British political novel to compare with those of Upton Sinclair or Jack London, it was for long ignored by literary critics and historians and relied upon the labour and socialist movement for its circulation. *MC*

railways. See TRANSPORT POLICY.

Raison, Timothy Hugh Francis (1929–), Conservative politician. Raison edited the Bow Group magazine *Crossbow* and in 1962 became founding editor of the social policy weekly *New Society*. A moderate Tory, he was elected in 1970 and was Whitelaw's parliamentary private secretary at Northern Ireland before becoming an education minister in 1973. Despite Raison's 1976 sacking from Thatcher's shadow cabinet, he became Whitelaw's Home Office deputy in 1979 and was overseas development minister, 1983–6. He left politics in 1992. *RJS*

Rank, Joseph (1854–1943), flour-miller and philanthropist. Rank pioneered roller-milling in the 1880s. An astute businessman, he established strategically placed mills at Hull. In 1899 his business was incorporated into Joseph Rank Ltd, the headquarters of which moved five years later to London. After the Great War, new mills were built at Belfast and Southampton whilst existing mills were enlarged. In 1933 the firm acquired London Flour Millers Ltd before becoming a private company. During the Second World War, Rank played a key role in coordinating the purchase of large quantities of foreign wheat for Britain. His son, also Joseph Rank, diversified the family business first into film production and then more widely into entertainment and leisure. *JFM*

Rapid Reaction Force, generic term for highly mobile military intervention forces. President Carter created a Rapid Deployment Force (RDF) in 1980 to guarantee Persian Gulf security following the Soviet invasion of Afghanistan, and in 1981 Thatcher indicated Britain's preparedness to contribute to such a force. It was the RDF's successors, US Central Command, which initially responded to Kuwait's invasion in 1990. In 1992 the Allied Command Europe Rapid Reaction Corps was created under British command as part of NATO's post-Soviet re-organization. *DHD*

rates, the principal source of local authority finance to 1992. Originating in 1601, but taking their modern form under the Rating and Valuation Act, 1925, rates were a tax levied by local authorities upon the occupation and use of immovable property. The 1925 Act swept away a complex patchwork of rates and administration which had developed from centuries of piecemeal legislation. Rating authorities were now obliged to establish assessment committees, whose purpose was to ensure uniformity in local valuation. Outside the county boroughs, the work of assessment was overseen by county valuation committees, who sought consistency, although their powers were merely advisory, and local sentiments, preferences, and interests militated against objective valuation.

Meanwhile, the National Government's concern to protect agriculture and industry led to the full derating of the former, and the partial derating of the latter in 1929, shifting the burden of local finance onto the domestic ratepayer. In the hope of achieving equity and uniformity, responsibility for valuation was passed to the Inland Revenue under the Local Government Act, 1948. The post-war periodic revaluations were much delayed, and the effects of modernizing the basis of this highly visible tax—particularly in 1963 and 1973—politically unwelcome. The indefinite postponement of that due in England in 1983 (the Scottish revaluation went ahead the next year) indicated that the electoral costs of updating the system were too great to bear. The Conservatives struggled to find a new and more workable system of local government finance, which culminated in the abolition of rates under the Local Government Finance Act, 1988, and their short-lived replacement by the community charge, or *poll tax. *KY*

Rathbone, Eleanor Florence (1872–1946), feminist, social reformer, and pioneer advocate of *family allowances. Born into a Liverpool family with a strong philanthropic tradition, after her education at Oxford she returned to Liverpool to pursue social investigation, producing studies of working conditions, the operation of the poor law, and women's wages. In 1909 she became the first woman to be elected to Liverpool city council (remaining until 1935), and she was MP for the Combined English Universities, 1929–46. Although best known as one of the founders of the Family Endowment Society, created in 1917 to campaign for family allowances, as advocated in her book *The Disinherited Family* (1924), she was also prominent in many other areas. A strong supporter of women's suffrage, she became president of the National Union of Societies for Equal Citizenship in 1919. She worked on behalf of Indian women and for refugees. A former member of the 'pro-war' wing of the suffragette movement, she was a strong opponent of appeasement during the 1930s. She gave evidence before the Beveridge committee and lived to see the Family Allowances Act passed in 1945, working to ensure, shortly before her death, that the allowances be paid directly to women. *JS*

Susan Pederson, 'Eleanor Rathbone, 1872–1946', in Peter Mandler and Susan Pederson, (eds.), *After the Victorians: Private Conscience and Public Duty in Modern Britain* (London, 1994).

rationalization. Although there was a growing trend towards industrial consolidation after the joint-stock legislation of the mid-19th century, much of British industry remained fragmented and undercapitalized on the eve of the Great War. After the war, not only were there incentives to move towards fordist techniques and economies of scale, but also a need for industrial reconstruction. The first major example of rationalization in British industry was the creation of *ICI in 1926 from a number of smaller chemical firms. By the 1930s, the government was actively encouraging consolidation in badly hit industries like coal or textiles. The supposed fruits of rationalization included economies of scale and potential for higher investment. This could appeal to both sides of industry, as reflected in the 1928 *Mond-Turner talks. Walter Citrine, the TUC general secretary, was later to remark that rationalization was similar to and might pave the way for nationalization. Indeed, arguments for coal nationalization in the 1930s often focused principally on efficiency grounds. Though the term rationalization was dropped, the principle remained in the post-war years. Governments, especially in the 1950s and 1960s, sought consolidation in industries from aircraft to computers, latterly through the Industrial Reorganization Corporation, as a means of promoting efficiency and also 'national champions'. This perhaps demonstrates how close to nationalization the practice was, as one key characteristic of the industries affected in the post-war years was the importance of the government as a customer. By the 1970s, however, concerns that government involvement encouraged counter-productive overmanning and skewed investment strategies were undermining enthusiasm for rationalization, and paving the way for the Thatcher government. Although industrial consolidation continued into the 1990s, it reflected more the need to slim down suppliers in a globalizing economy than the workings of government policy. *PPC*

rationing was introduced in Britain during both world wars, to cope with shortages caused by enemy action against food supplies brought by sea. As a major food importer in peacetime, Britain was desperately vulnerable to any interruption of supply, while rationing also offered a visibly fair way of distributing what was available. Sugar was the first foodstuff to be rationed during the Great War but was followed in 1917 by a more extensive system of rationing, covering most major foodstuffs, as the Germans stepped up their submarine campaign. In the Second World War, rationing was introduced from the outset for many foods, clothing, and other items in short supply. A system of 'points' allocated to each ration book holder limited the amount that could be obtained. The system worked reasonably fairly, and with a minimal number of complaints (if also with a lot of low-level grumbling), but incurred greater unpopularity when it was continued into peacetime under the austerity programme of the Attlee government—when bread was rationed for the first time. Rationing controls were almost entirely removed between 1950 and 1953. In 1956, petrol rationing was introduced during the Suez crisis and was again planned during the Arab oil boycott of 1973–4, but not implemented. *JS*

Rawlinson, Peter Anthony Grayson (1919–), Conservative politician and law officer. With a distinguished accelerated career, Rawlinson reasonably expected the lord chancellorship (and constitutional adjustment to accommodate a Catholic—which was, incredibly, still technically barred). Mentioned in despatches, taking silk after thirteen years, MP for Epsom and Ewell 1955–78, solicitor-general at 43, Heath's attorney-general on Tory return 1970, chairman of the Bar 1975–6, leader of the western circuit, Rawlinson was much talked of for Woolsack, but was not close to Thatcher's politics and was then victim of Lord Hailsham's sempiternal tenacity. *EP*

Peter Rawlinson, *A Price too High* (London, 1989).

Rayner, Derek George (1926–98), business executive and government adviser. Rayner had two, interrelated, careers. The first was as a successful business manager in the Marks & Spencer retail empire, which he joined in the 1950s, rising to become managing director in 1973, chief executive in 1983, and chairman, 1984–91. The second was as an imported business adviser to the Heath and Thatcher governments in the 1970s and 1980s. Recruited to the team of businessmen advising the Conservatives in opposition in the 1960s, Rayner drew up the plans for what became the defence procurement executive, serving as its first chief executive, 1971–2. As Thatcher's efficiency adviser, 1979–82, and head of the efficiency unit of 'Rayner's raiders', he played a crucial role as an agenda-setter and change-agent in the design and promotion of innovative managerial reforms in central government (his programme of 'efficiency scrutinies' leading to cost-savings of hundreds of millions of pounds and stimulating an important change in Whitehall's management culture). *KT*

Rayner Scrutinies and **Financial Management Initiative** (1979–82). As one of her first acts as prime minister, Margaret Thatcher invited Sir Derek *Rayner, joint managing director of Marks & Spencer, to become her efficiency adviser and run part-time a small efficiency unit which would be attached to the prime minister's office. 'The two of us', she recalled, 'used to say that in politics you judge the value of a service by the amount you put in, but in business you judge it by the amount you get out. We were both convinced of the need to bring some of the attitudes of business into government. We neither of us conceived just how difficult this would prove' (Thatcher 1993: 30–1). Rayner developed a three-pronged strategy. He would find and empower reformers within the civil service as his instruments rather than seek business people or consultants from outside; he would go for quick and visible results from a series of 90-day efficiency scrutinies across a wide range of state activity carried out by insiders who came to be known as 'Rayner's Raiders'; from the wider lessons such scrutinies threw up he would develop longer-term, lasting reforms to be put before Thatcher and her cabinet. By 1980 the first fruits of this approach were visible (and Mrs Thatcher described him publicly as 'a remarkable and wonderful person') and, in private, he circulated a paper on *The Conventions of Government* to the cabinet urging a reduction in paperwork, an improvement in the quality of the management of the state, and a transformation in the culture of the senior civil service with a far greater emphasis on the effective management of people and money.

During 1981 these longer-term ideas were converted into what became the Financial Management Initiative (FMI), which sought to end the divide between policy and management, design and implementation. Rayner's central notion, accepted by the cabinet and promulgated in the spring of 1982 as the FMI, was 'a system in which managers at all levels have: (a) a clear view of their objectives; and assess and wherever possible measure outputs or performance in relation to these objectives; (b) well-defined responsibility for making the best use of their resources including a critical scrutiny of output and value for money; (c) the information . . . , training and access to expert advice which they need to exercise their responsibilities effectively'. Throughout his four years serving Thatcher, Rayner made an ally of the Commons select committee on the Treasury and the civil service (and of selected journalists, including the author).

With Mrs Thatcher's powerful backing, her cabinet (with varying degrees of enthusiasm) adopted ministerial information systems which increased their knowledge of the deployment of resources within their departments, though the application of *Next Steps* principles and the creation of executive agencies after 1988 somewhat prised policy and management apart once more. During Thatcher's first two terms, over 300 efficiency scrutinies generated savings of over £1 billion (the cost of the M25 motorway or 22 new hospitals at current prices) and a series of continuing economies worth £325 million a year. Rayner won praise from a source not known for his fulsomeness, Nigel Lawson, for introducing 'into the public service for the first time in any systematic way such useful disciplines as the clarification of specific objectives, the assignment of individual responsibilities, the delegation of authority and a detailed awareness of costs' (Lawson, 390–1). *PJH*

Financial Management in Government Departments (Cmnd 9058, London, 1983). | Peter Hennessy, *Whitehall* (London, 1989). | Nigel Lawson, *The View from Number Ten* (London, 1992). | Margaret Thatcher, *The Downing Street Years* (London, 1993).

Reading, marquess of. See Isaacs, Rufus.

reciprocity, mutual forgiveness of tariffs between nations. A reciprocity agreement between Canada and the USA was initialled in 1911. This outraged imperialists in both Britain and Canada, and the treaty was abrogated after the victory of the Canadian Conservatives in an election later that year. This encouraged British tariff reformers, including the Conservative leader Law, to press ahead with the Chamberlainite programme to unite the Empire through *protective tariffs on non-imperial goods. *RJQA*

reconstruction planning (1917–18). As the Great War dragged on into its third and fourth years, bringing increasing war-weariness and more and more casualties from battles of attrition, the Lloyd George government announced that it would make definite plans for a better society after the war, to sustain national morale and to demonstrate that the real social weaknesses (such as the physical unfitness of many conscripts) revealed by the war were being tackled. Plans were thus made by 1918 for the extension of national insurance, state-subsidized housebuilding, educational opportunities, and pensions. Planning was coordinated by the National Liberal reconstruction minister Christopher *Addison, who went to the new Ministry of Health to drive through his reforms in January 1919.

By that time the stakes had been raised considerably by the rhetoric of the *'Coupon' Election campaign of 1918, in which Lloyd George had promised that if returned he would build 'a land fit for heroes to live in', and more specifically 'homes fit for heroes'. There were successes that could be pointed to in the first years of peace, notably the *Addison Acts, 1919, for housing, extensions of national insurance cover and of pensions, and the implementation of the *Education Act, 1918. Liberal ministers responsible for social policy had to contend, however, with constant barracking from Conservative supporters of the government, for whom reducing taxation (at an all-time high because of the war) was a higher priority than raising public expenditure. When in 1920 the economy went into a recession, so reducing tax yields anyway, and when 'anti-waste' candidates from the right began doing well at by-elections, the reconstruction programme was first slowed down and then halted. By the *Geddes axe of 1922, much of it went into reverse, with damaging effects on the government's standing among working-class voters and for Lloyd George's reputation generally.

Memories of these disappointments were important during the Second World War, in the urgings of Labour MPs and progressive newspapers that the wartime government should give specific assurances that reconstruction proposals like the *Beveridge report (1942) would be carried out when hostilities ended. In helping to promote the return of a Labour government in 1945, such campaigns achieved their purposes. *JAR*

PAUL B. JOHNSON, *Land Fit for Heroes: The Planning of British Reconstruction 1916–1919* (Chicago, 1968). | LAURENCE ORBACH, *Homes for Heroes: A Study of the Evolution of British Public Housing, 1915–1921* (London, 1977).

redbrick universities. See HIGHER EDUCATION.

Redcliffe-Maud, John Primat. See MAUD, JOHN PRIMAT REDCLIFFE.

Redcliffe-Maud commission (1966–9), an unsuccessful attempt to rewrite the structure of local government. Its remit was to consider the structure of local government, outside Greater London, in relation to its functions, and to recommend a structure that would 'sustain a viable system of local democracy'. Local government finance, however, was not addressed. The commission's report in 1969 offered a vigorous criticism of the existing structure as one in which local government areas no longer corresponded to the pattern of life and work, ignored the interdependence of town and country, divided responsibilities in an unsatisfactory manner, and were based on too many units of inadequate size. The commission warned that fundamental reform was the only alternative to further creeping centralization. It concluded that all the major functions should be in the hands of a single authority, and they accordingly recommended a unitary structure. The exceptions would be the three metropolitan areas of Greater Manchester, Merseyside and West Midlands, where a Greater London Council-style metropolitan county would complement district councils. England would also be divided into eight provinces, each under the purview of a provincial council. The Labour government largely accepted the report in their white paper of 1970. The change of government in that year, however, consigned the report to oblivion, and Peter Walker's Local Government Act, 1972, embodied only the metropolitan county proposals, retaining a two-tier system throughout the rest of England. *KY*

'Red Clydeside', term given to the wave of industrial protest which swept the Clyde area in the period after 1915, eventually culminating in Labour's 'Clydesiders' winning nine of the ten Glasgow parliamentary seats in the general election of 1922. Although fuelled by social and economic grievances, the prominence of socialists in leading the protest led many to believe that the area was ripe for a Bolshevik-type revolution. Although this notion has been discredited by subsequent historical research, it did have the effect of galvanizing Scottish middle-class opinion into staunch anti-socialism. *RF*

Red Friday (31 July 1925), when Stanley Baldwin's Conservative government agreed to intervene to prevent a threatened coal lockout and strike by offering a nine-month subsidy to the coal industry and by setting up the royal commission on coal under the chairmanship of Sir Herbert Samuel. This seeming victory for the coal miners and the TUC effectively delayed the *General Strike for nine months. *KL*

redistribution of constituencies, the creation, modification, or abolition of parliamentary seats as a result of the redrawing of constituency boundaries. There have been major boundary redistributions in 1918, 1948, 1955, 1974, 1983, and 1995. Of these, the most radical was that of 1983, which left untouched less than 15 per cent of existing constituencies. The recommendations for redistribution are now made by the Parliamentary *Boundary Commission, which is enjoined to ensure that as far as practicable there is equality in the number of electors in each seat, though it may deviate from this for special geographic reasons or because of local ties or in order to keep within existing local government boundaries. It is a non-partisan body but its work attracts close political attention. A redistribution has potentially significant implications for political parties and for individual MPs. Local political parties will make representations to local inquiries conducted by the commission and national parties may seek to challenge the recommendations of the commission in the courts. Labour politicians objected to the Boundary Commission's recommendations published in 1969—Labour MPs voted them down, thus delaying their introduction until the following parliament—and those implemented in 1983, which the party had sought unsuccessfully to challenge in the courts. It was estimated that the review undertaken in the 1992–7 parliament would benefit the Conservative Party by between 20 and 50 seats, reflecting a shift in population from urban to rural areas. However, the effect of well-planned presentations by constituency Labour parties to local inquiries—not matched by local Conservatives—was largely to negate the advantage to the Conservative Party. The effect of redistribution for some MPs is that their seats disappear, thus forcing them to seek new constituencies, a quest in which they are not always successful. Robert Blackburn has argued for the existing rules governing redistribution to be rationalized and to be within the remit of an electoral commission. *PN*

ROBERT BLACKBURN, *The Electoral System in Britain* (London, 1995). | H. F. RAWLINGS, *Law and the Electoral Process* (London, 1988). | *The Redistribution of Seats*, second report from the Select Committee on Home Affairs, House of Commons, Session 1986–7, HC 97–I. | D. J. ROSSITER, R. J. JOHNSTON, and C. J. PATTIE, *The Boundary Commission: Redrawing the United Kingdom's Map of Parliamentary Constituencies* (Manchester, 1999).

Red Lion Square riots (15 June 1974), disturbance in which a demonstrator, Kevin Gately, died. The *National Front had intimated its intention to hold a march and then a meeting to protest against the government's immigration policy. Allegations were made that the police deliberately broke up anti-National Front protests, to which Gately belonged. Lord Scarman's report, however, described the police responses as 'forceful' but 'with some possible exceptions disciplined and necessary' (Cmnd 5919, p. 43), considering the behaviour of protesters from the International Marxist Group. *CH*

White Paper, *The Red Lion Square Disorders of 15 June 1974* (Cmnd 5919, London, 1975).

Redmayne, Martin (1910–85), Conservative politician. Elected to parliament in 1950, Redmayne spent eleven years in the Whips' Office from 1953. Appointed chief whip in 1959, he operated in military fashion, as befitted a man with a distinguished war record. Regimented efficiency, however, was no substitute for political sensitivity, especially when he was advising Macmillan during such difficult crises as the *Profumo case and the 1963 leadership struggle. Redmayne lost his seat in 1966 and took a life peerage. *RJS*

Redmond, John (1856–1918), Irish politician. Redmond was leader of the Irish Parliamentary Party between 1900 and his death in March 1918. He came from a comfortable Catholic gentry background in Co. Wexford, supported Charles Stewart Parnell in the divorce controversy that split the party in 1890–1, but presided over its reunification in January 1900. Redmond supported the Liberal government in its conflict with the Lords which culminated in the ending of the Lords' veto on Commons' legislation. H. H. Asquith then introduced the third Home Rule Bill in April 1912, but Ulster Unionist resistance blocked the way. When the Great War broke out in August 1914, Redmond threw nationalist Ireland's support behind the war effort, hoping thereby to guarantee that the bill, which reached the statute book in September 1914, would be implemented. The 1916 Easter Rising undermined this strategy, as did the failure of the post-Rising settlement plan. Redmond felt he had been deceived by Lloyd George over the question of whether the exclusion of six Ulster counties from home rule was permanent or not, but he reluctantly agreed to enter the Irish Convention in 1917. He died on 6 March 1918, before the Convention report, which failed to reach consensus, and before the party that he led was roundly defeated by Sinn Fein in the general election of December 1918. *DGB*

PAUL BEW, *John Redmond* (Dundalk, 1996). | STEPHEN GWYNN, *John Redmond's Last Years* (London, 1919).

Redwood, John Alan (1951–), Conservative politician, one of John Major's *'bastards'. As head of Thatcher's research unit in the early 1980s, Redwood was a systemic rightist, favouring NHS opt-outs, but made enemies by interfering in departments. A man of high IQ, elected fellow of All Souls, he was sometimes shaky on statistics, for example arguing that British benefit payments were the most generous in the world, which they were not. Welsh secretary under Major, he returned a small surplus to the Treasury, and never slept a single night in Wales. In the 1995 leadership challenge, Redwood struck when Portillo hesitated, but got too few votes to make the attack worth the surrendering of his cabinet post. After 1997 he returned intermittently to the shadow front bench, treated warily by Hague. *EP*

Rees, Merlyn (1920–), Labour politician. Merlyn Rees was one of the dominant politicians of the Labour governments of the 1960s and 1970s. Educated at Harrow Weald grammar school and London University, he was MP for Leeds South, 1963–83, and for Morley and Leeds South, 1983–92. He rose quickly in government circles, becoming a junior minister in the Home Office, 1968–70; secretary for Northern Ireland, March 1974 to September 1976; and home secretary until May 1979. A Welsh loyalist moderate, he has been described both as 'Labour's respected elder statesman' and as a 'fountain of ineffectual wisdom'. Whilst dealing with Northern Ireland, he secured a ceasefire and ended detention without trial and special status for political prisoners.

He was also Jim Callaghan's campaign manager in the Labour leadership contest of March 1976. An elder statesman of the Labour Party by the late 1980s, he became a life peer in 1992, as Lord Merlyn-Rees. *KL*

referendum, term used to cover both the process of polling the public on a particular issue and a particular device used to conduct that poll. The plural of the former, the process of consultation, is usually taken to be referenda, with referendums used for the plural of the latter. In definition, a referendum is no different from a plebiscite; but is merely more attuned to the modern idiom. Some use the term plebiscite to refer to a public poll on a change of political regime, with referendum used for policy consultation. However, this distinction, though superficially appealing, is essentially anachronistic. Although the term plebiscite came to be associated with regime change in the 19th century, its initial use was not limited in this way. Referendums offer a limited form of direct democracy as they consult only on the choice of policy options; not on the definition and refining of those options (see DEMOCRACY). Moreover, the precise question asked and the timing of the referendum are determined by the policy framers, allowing considerable leeway in securing the desired outcome. This limitation can be overcome to some extent if referendums become an automatic and continuous part of the policy-making process, as in Switzerland, where their use is the most common. In contrast to Switzerland, the UK uses referendums only rarely, for their use as a habitual tool of policy making is seen as problematic in two ways. First, it is inconsistent with the principle of parliamentary sovereignty, which it seems to undermine by suggesting a source of authority equal or superior to the process of political mandate, general election, and government formation. Second, it conflicts with the values underlying representative democracy. These are based on the rejection of the notion that there can be such a thing as a general will. Here the ideas of Joseph A. Schumpeter distil the issues: not only are there problems of lack of information and the intrusion of emotion and mob instinct, but a referendum is frozen in time, whereas policy needs might change. In contrast, political representatives are seen as well informed, rooted to coherent political interests, and playing an important role in mediating political needs and ensuring that policy is sensitive to fluctuating political needs. The one exception to this situation is on issues of fundamental political and constitutional change. Here, the nature of the change is deemed to transcend the process of parliamentary sovereignty; while the population is seen as being able to develop a well-rooted view of such issues. Thus, referendums have been used for the renegotiated terms of European Community membership in 1975 and for Scottish and Welsh devolution in 1979 and 1998 and were proposed for reform of the Lords in 1910–11 and for entry into European Monetary Union (by the Labour and Liberal parties) in 1997. In these cases, however, governments have been careful to draft the enabling legislation so as not appearing to be subverting the sovereignty of parliament. *CPS*

Referendum Party (RP), political pressure group in electoral form. With the rise of *Euroscepticism in various shades during the 1990s, some directed at currency integration, others like the UK Independence Party, opposed to the whole concept of European union, the most vigorous (and richest) group gathered around Sir James Goldsmith, multimillionaire, grocer and banker, earlier known politically for the failed weekly *Now* and for lawsuits against the 'Communist subversive' *Private Eye*. Ironically, though, the RP was created to obtain the promise of a referendum on entry into a single European currency, which John Major, to the regret of Kenneth Clarke, conceded. Goldsmith proceeded to finance candidates for the 1997 general election anyway, everywhere seen as an attempt to inflict maximum damage on the Tory party despite Labour being far more sympathetic to the European currency. Running several hundred candidates in 1997, the RP was responsible for the loss of a number of Tory seats (Harwich where the RP gathered 4,000 votes for a local undertaker and saw a 17,000 majority disappear being one example), but probably no more than five or six seats were directly lost like this. A loud screaming match between Sir James and David Mellor at the Putney declaration did not alter the RP's modest impact. *EP*

referendum pledge (1910). In an effort to lessen the electoral unpopularity of his party's tariff reform proposals, Arthur Balfour pledged in November 1910 that when the Conservatives next took office he would submit any such plan to a referendum before enactment. The ploy failed to win the ensuing election, and his successor as leader, Law, rescinded the pledge in late 1912, but was forced to backtrack after expressions of anxiety within the party that tariffs remained unpopular among voters. *RJQA*

R. J. Q. ADAMS, *Bonar Law* (London, 1999). | ALAN SYKES, *Tariff Reform in British Politics, 1903–1913* (Oxford, 1979).

Reform Club, leading London gentleman's club on the Liberal side of politics, dating back to the crisis over parliamentary reform in the 1830s. It was often at the centre of political discussion and debate in the pre-Great War era. *JS*

refugees. See ASYLUM, POLITICAL.

Regency Acts. Since 1937 statute has provided for a regent to do the duties of the sovereign in case of incapacity due either to youth or illness. The regent is usually next in line of succession to the throne. In case of the sovereign's absence abroad, counsellors of state are appointed to deputize for the sovereign. They are usually relations as well. Subsequent Acts have named persons other than those in direct line to the throne, for example, the duke of Edinburgh and Queen Elizabeth, the Queen Mother, as either regent or counsellor of state. *WMK*

regionalism, belief that a devolution of central government powers to elected regional bodies is both possible and desirable; not to be confused with the regional organization of central government. Sometimes argued from the premiss that regional inequalities of wealth would be better addressed were regional institutions to exist, sometimes from an assertion of existing regional consciousness, the regionalist case assumes that the devolution of power from Whitehall to elected bodies would make for better government. Regionalism was initially proposed in the form of 'provincial' government, the term province being more familiar in the early years of the century, after the Fabian Society published *Municipalisation by Provinces* in 1905. There was a surge of interest in provincial government in the home rule debates that followed the Great War. A Speaker's Conference on Devolution was established in 1919–20, while C. B. Fawcett's *Provinces of England* (1919) delineated possible boundaries. These strands were skilfully brought together in G. D. H. Cole's *The Future of Local Government* (1921), which remains the most powerful statement of the case for regionalism.

The regional issue assumed particular importance during the Second World War, when ten regional commissioners coordinated the central government presence in their regions, and stood ready to assume the powers of ministers in the event of invasion. Their work served to put the local authority associations on their guard, and it was early made clear that a system of regional government, necessarily at the expense of the local authorities, would be unacceptable in the post-war world. In the absence of any reform of local government structure, little more was heard of regionalism until the 1960s, when regional culture (particularly in the north of England) flourished, along with new concepts of regional economic planning. The Wilson government established (appointed) regional economic planning councils in 1965, supported by regional economic planning boards of civil servants, while in some regions, notably the north-east and south-east, local authorities had made their own collaborative regional arrangements, whose prescriptions conflicted with those of the planning councils. With the demise of the national plan in 1966, the councils withered.

The Redcliffe-Maud and the Kilbrandon reports (1969 and 1973 respectively) both dealt with regional elected government, though their various proposals only illuminated the complexities. The Labour Party consulted on schemes for elected regional authorities in 1976, partly in response to the multiplication of central government functions organized through ad hoc regional agencies, and partly in response to the raising of 'the English question' by the Scottish and Welsh devolution proposals, but no governmental action ensued. Regionalism languished under the Thatcher and Major governments, with hope sustained only by the EU's 'Europe of regions' concept. The election of the Labour government in 1997 reopened the question of English regionalism as both a concomitant of devolution and a means of democratizing government. *KY*

regional offices of government. The government offices for the regions (GOs) were formed in 1994, following the merger of the parallel regional offices of the Departments of Trade and Industry, Environment, Transport, and Employment. The broad objective of GOs is to advance the prosperity, competitiveness, and quality of life for each English region and to do this they integrate the programmes of their parent departments in dealings with individuals, businesses, and councils. There are nine GOs: for the north-east; Yorkshire and Humberside; north-west; west Midlands; east Midlands; south-west; south-east; east of England; and London. *JD*

Regional Offices of Government website: *www.local-regions.detr.gov.uk*

regional policy. Britain has a distinctive regional policy deriving from the *Town and Country Planning Act, 1947, which sought to restrict the development of London and the south-east, burgeoning in the inter-war years, and replace it with a more balanced growth favouring deprived and depressed areas. The Special Areas Act of 1934 was the first Act to specify areas which required special assistance: these were the rundown areas of south Wales, Tyneside, west Cumberland, and Scotland. This excluded other regions which were also badly affected by economic depression, notably Northern Ireland and Lancashire. The Barlow report of 1940 adopted the view that there was a need for planning legislation to promote growth in the regions and to limit London's expansion, and this became part of post-war planning policy which offered incentives to firms to relocate beyond the metropolitan south-east, imposing progressive restrictions via *green belt and town and country planning on what could be done elsewhere. Regional policy led in the 1960s to the development of new 'greenfield' manufacturing sites in south Wales, Merseyside, Scotland, and Tyneside. Not all were successful, with high profile failures such as the closure in the 1970s of the Linwood car plant in Scotland and Ford's later retreat from Halewood on Merseyside. Generally, Conservative governments have tended to close down or limit machinery for funding regional policy, while Labour governments have reinstated or extended it. There remains, however, a strong commitment to regional policy. As currently defined, regional policy is designed to promote 'economic growth and competitiveness in all areas of the UK' (*Britain, 2000*). Additional aid is focused on the Assisted Areas, which cover 34 per cent of the UK workforce. In 1998–9 the Department of Trade and Industry spent £112 million on regional selective assistance in England; total investment is expected to reach £115 million. Nine new regional development agencies became operative in 1999 to develop strategies and improve regional competitive performance. *JS*

Britain, 2000 (annual yearbook published by HMSO).

regnal years. In contrast to calendar years, regnal years begin from the succeeding anniversaries of the sovereign's accession. Until 1963, parliamentary legislation was dated according to its order within a particular parliamentary session in a given regnal year. As a parliamentary session often spread over more than one regnal year, the old system was complex and confusing. The occasional pruning away of such antique but troublesome traditions is necessary to sustain an ancient constitution. *WMK*

Reid, James Scott Cumberland (1890–1975), judge and Conservative MP. Reid entered parliament in 1931, earned a reputation as a formidable debater, and was later made lord advocate (1941–5). In 1948 he (reluctantly) accepted Attlee's offer to make him a lord of appeal in ordinary, remaining in the post until 1974. As senior Law Lord (1962–74), Lord Reid steered the judges of the House of Lords on a moderate course between radicalism and conservatism, delivering speeches characterized by their lucidity, precision, and generous humanity. *PPM*

Reith, John Charles Walsham (1889–1971), first director-general of the BBC. A Scottish-born engineer and veteran of the 1914–18 trenches, in 1922 John Reith became general manager of the British Broadcasting Company. He shaped its output according to his belief that broadcasting must be educational as well as entertaining and in 1926 became the first director-general of the public corporation, the *BBC. In 1938 he moved to the chairmanship of Imperial Airways. In 1940, as Neville Chamberlain's second minister of information, he helped to reinvigorate Britain's propaganda effort. In May 1940, Churchill moved Reith to transport and then works, making him a peer, but dropped him altogether in 1942. He completed the war as a lieutenant commander in the naval reserve, planning logistics for the D-Day landings. He felt painfully underused by the government, and spent the rest of his life waiting for a recall to high office that simply never came. *NC*

Andrew Boyle, *Only the Wind Will Listen* (London, 1972). | Charles Stuart (ed.), *The Reith Diaries* (London, 1975).

Relugas compact (September 1905), agreement reached at Relugas in Scotland by the *Liberal Imperialists Asquith, Grey, and Haldane, whereby they would each refuse to serve in the next Liberal government unless Campbell-Bannerman resigned the Commons leadership to Asquith and himself went to the Lords. When offered the premiership in December, Campbell-Bannerman outmanoeuvred the conspirators by refusing their terms but offering them office anyway. When Asquith accepted the exchequer, Grey and Haldane had to follow him into office. *JAR*

rent control, legislation primarily intended to govern rent levels in order to protect tenants from paying high costs to private sector landlords. Its origins go back to the Rent and Mortgage (War Restrictions) Act, 1915, which froze the rents of small, unfurnished properties. Once instituted in a period of rapid inflation, the controls proved almost impossible to withdraw without incurring deep political hostility from tenants, as the Conservative government discovered in 1923. After inter-war modifications, rents were again frozen in 1939. By 1950, a series of Acts, agencies, adjustments decontrols, and recontrols had produced a veritable hodgepodge of restrictions, exceptions, and variable rental levels, and abuses of the system demanded a tightening-up of the legislation in the 1957 Rent Act. A major landmark in the later period was the 1977 Rent Act, which introduced the concept of the 'fair rent', determined by local councils' rent officers and subject to appeal. Legal rent controls have been criticized for encouraging landlords to put housing property to other uses in order to increase their income, to reduce spending on maintenance, or to exploit loopholes in always complex legislation. Supporters of rent control argue that supply and demand for housing is highly inelastic and must therefore be subject to controls in order to guarantee equity. Rent control was extended to agricultural land by the Rent (Agricultural) Act, 1976. In that sector, controls, which apply only to long-term tenants whose security is enshrined in law, have encouraged landowners to introduce fixed, short-term tenancies exempted from the legislation. *JFM*

Rentoul, Gervase **(1884–1946)**, Conservative politician. MP for Lowestoft, 1922–34, Rentoul was founding chairman of the *1922 Committee, 1923–32. He developed a good relationship with Eyres-Monsell, the chief whip, ensuring during the 1924 parliament that 'the 1922' began to take on its modern form as a sounding board for the parliamentary party. Baldwin was persuaded to meet its representatives and a whip was sent along to its weekly meetings. Rentoul was parliamentary private secretary to Douglas Hogg, 1925–8. *NJC*

***Reorganisation of Central Government* (1970) (Cmnd 4506)**, white paper presented to parliament by Edward Heath four months after winning office, as the blueprint of the Whitehall end of his 'quiet revolution' (Campbell, 311). It was designed 'to change the structure of government', with a streamlined cabinet system as its centrepiece—a cause which 'engrossed' Heath as he 'was concerned that Ministers spent too much time on day-to-day matters, instead of a strategic thinking' (Heath, 314). It was also intended to reduce the problem of overload as government 'has been attempting to do too much', placing 'an excessive burden on industry, and on the people of the country as a whole, and has also overloaded the government machine itself', weakening 'the apparatus of policy formulation', and 'harming the quality of many government decisions over the last 25 years'. The white paper represented an attempt to attack the overload problem from several angles simultaneously:

- fewer and bigger ministries including a new department of the environment and another for trade and industry.
- the double advantage of slimming the cabinet down from 20+ to 18, thereby creating a body better placed for serious discussion and with fewer decisions cluttering its agenda, as more could be resolved within the ambit of the new super-ministries.
- departments themselves would be less burdened thanks to the hiving-off of certain executive functions, for example by the management of the government estate moving into a new property services agency and weaponry passing to an equally novel procurement executive.
- the slimmed-down cabinet would be a better-briefed cabinet as, in the words of the white paper, 'the necessary basis for good government is a radical improvement in the information system available to ministers'.
- information flow would be improved by the creation of a 'small multi-disciplinary central policy review staff [CPRS] in the Cabinet Office' which was 'to be at the disposal of the Government as a whole' and though 'under the supervision of the Prime Minister, it will work for Ministers collectively; and its task will be to enable them to take better policy decisions by assisting them to work out the implications of their basic strategy in terms of policies in specific areas, to establish the relative priorities to be given to the different sectors of their programme as a whole, to identify those areas of policy in which new choices can be exercised and to ensure that the underlying implications of alternative courses of action are fully analysed and considered.' The new CPRS would become a player in the annual public expenditure cycle and the quality of that process would be made more thoughtful and rational by a system called programme analysis and review (or PAR) for examining chunks of existing programmes to test their utility and efficiency, an idea developed by Heath's people in opposition after they had experienced the then novel techniques of zero-based budgeting practised in parts of the Washington bureaucracy.

Heath was keen, too, on the cabinet and its committees working from agreed sets of data, the preparation of which was another task for the CPRS. The aspirations of 1970 were subject to a severe battering as successive economic and industrial storms struck the Heath government from 1972 onwards. The giant Department of Trade and Industry was broken up and a separate department of energy spun off before Heath left office in March 1974. The Treasury, with Margaret Thatcher's authority, killed off PAR in 1979 (Hennessy, 236, 596). Thatcher disbanded the CPRS after winning her second general election in 1983. Yet Cmnd 4506 remains the most thoroughgoing attempt to apply reason to the structures and processes of central government since the Haldane report of 1918. *PJH*

John Campbell, *Edward Heath* (London, 1993). | Edward Heath, *The Course of My Life* (London, 1998). | Peter Hennessy, *Whitehall* (London, 1989).

Reorganization of Offices (Scotland) Act, 1939, gave effect to the recommendations of the *Gilmour report on the Scottish Office. The old boards which had previously managed Scottish administration were mostly abolished and replaced by departments coming directly under the secretary of state for Scotland and the permanent secretary of the Scottish Office. Initially there were four departments, for agriculture, education, health, and home affairs. In 1939 they were concentrated at St Andrew's House on Calton Hill in Edinburgh. *MJK*

reparations, payments of money and goods levied against Germany and its Central Power allies at the Paris peace conference of 1919. British demands for an indemnity to cover not just the physical damage wrought by the Great War but also the cost of waging the entire conflict, surfaced first in the Germanophobia that swept Britain at war's end. Promises to 'make Germany pay' were exploited by Lloyd George, amongst others, in the general election of 1918, for political gain and to avoid the domestic implications of paying for the war. But the economics of determining how much Germany could afford to pay were complex and negotiators at Paris balked at setting a final figure for German reparations. They passed the question on to a newly established reparations commission which in 1921 fixed German reparations at 132 billion gold Reichsmarks, some £33 billion. Despite claims that German capacity to pay had been 'scientifically determined', the findings of the London schedule, as the commission's report became known, were controversial. The long-established assumption that reparations irreparably damaged the Weimar Republic was a key theme in Kent (p. 1), but was challenged by Schuker (p. 16), who argued that, although Germany was plagued by temporary difficulties, in the long term the prospects for Germany's capacity to pay were excellent, given the economic record of the German Empire before 1913. According to Schuker's calculations, in real terms reparations amounted to 5.37 per cent of German national income in 1921. Reparations also provided a ready excuse for successive German governments to avoid bringing German inflation, already at dangerously high levels in 1918, under control. The issue was further complicated by Allied war debts owed to the USA. From the outset, Britain hoped to trade any reduction in the volume of German reparations for a reduction in their $4.7 billion war debts owed to the USA, but London was frustrated by the stance of the Americans, who refused to take what they called 'tribute payments' from Germany yet insisted on collecting the 'hired money' owed by their former allies. By 1923 the French occupation of the Ruhr and Germany's descent into hyperinflation prompted a committee of experts, led by the American general Charles G. Dawes and assisted by Sir Josiah Stamp, to propose a revised schedule for reparation payments and a German return to the gold standard. Announced in 1924, the Dawes plan also encouraged foreign investors to purchase huge volumes of German bonds, worth some 26 billion Reichsmarks—over 60 per cent of which were purchased by Americans, while British investors took around 12 per cent.

By 1929, however, the Dawes plan was in trouble. The foreign credit on which Germany, alongside much of central Europe, had become dependent, was drying up. In response Owen Young, the American chairman of General Electric, tabled a new scheme, dubbed the Young plan, designed to revive foreign investment in Europe. But negotiations were still underway when the American stock market on Wall Street spectacularly crashed and the Great Depression set in. To make up for the subsequent collapse in American investment, Germany increasingly turned to the City of London for short-term loans. When the German banking system disintegrated into chaos in July 1931 therefore, British banks had over $70 million frozen inside Germany under standstill agreements negotiated to shore up the German financial system. These came on top of similar arrangements made to cover the $27 million of British loans in Austria and played an important role in the sterling crisis of August 1931. Thereafter, the stability of the British financial system was increasingly equated with that of Germany—an important dynamic in appeasement—and the Treasury and the City advanced the view that British commercial loans to Germany would best be safeguarded by the complete abolition of reparations and war debts. Neville Chamberlain took the lead in negotiating the end of German reparations at a Lausanne conference in 1932, but again failed to secure a matching reduction in Allied war debts. By 1934, both Britain and France had defaulted on their obligations to America. Freed from reparations, Germany exploited Anglo-American disputes over war debts and commercial debts to further its expansionist foreign policy. *PC*

Bruce Kent, *The Spoils of War: The Politics, Economics and Diplomacy of Reparations, 1918–1932* (Oxford, 1989). | Steven Schuker, 'American "Reparations" to Germany, 1919–1933: Implications for the Third World Debt Crisis', *Princeton Studies in International Finance*, 62 (July 1988).

representation, concept that is widely employed but which has several meanings. It permits of at least four separate usages. First, it may denote acting to promote or defend the interests of some individual or group. Second, it may denote persons or assemblies freely elected. Though it is not axiomatic that the persons so elected will act to defend or pursue the interests of those who elected them, they will normally be expected to do so. Third, it may denote a person or persons who are typical of a particular group or class of persons. A 'representative' sample under this usage is thus one that reflects proportionally the socio-economic or other characteristics of the population under study. Fourth, it may be used to denote something that stands symbolically for a wider entity. An individual or object may thus stand for something: a flag, or a monarch, may symbolize the unity of the nation.

The first usage of the term is well established in British history, though it is only in the 19th and 20th centuries that the first two uses of the term have become inextricably linked, certainly in terms of members of public bodies. Before the 19th century, the concept of 'virtual' representation—with persons being able to recognize and speak on behalf of a particular group without necessarily having been chosen by that particular group—was well established, being articulated notably by Edmund Burke. Radical and liberal views became more prominent in the 19th century, forcing an extension of the franchise and a reform of constituency boundaries and electoral rules. More collectivist views have become prominent in the 20th century, placing more emphasis on political parties and the representation of groups and classes. The second usage of the term thus now underpins elections to public office—to be democratically legitimate, office holders have to be freely elected by those on whose behalf they speak and vote—and the third usage has also gained greater currency. The principle that elected bodies should be socially typical—that is, if 10 per cent of citizens are black, then 10 per cent of MPs should also be black—has never been fully embraced in the UK. Nonetheless, there is some general acceptance that each group in society should have some degree of representation—that is, members drawn from its own ranks—in public bodies. All main political parties are keen to ensure that more of their parliamentary candidates are drawn from women and from minority groups. The fourth usage of the term continues to be applied widely. If the queen is unable to attend a particular event—she normally does not attend funerals—she sends someone to represent her at that event. The growing acceptance of the concept of representation in its second sense—a body that is freely elected—has had significant implications for relationships between the three components of the queen-in-parliament, ensuring the dominance of the elected House, the Commons. *PN*

Anthony H. Birch, *Representative and Responsible Government* (London, 1964). | Anthony H. Birch, *Representation* (London, 1971). | Hanna Pitkin, *The Concept of Representation* (Berkeley, 1967).

Representation of the People Acts (1918 and since), a series of Acts modifying the franchise and the form of parliamentary representation. The Representation of the People (RP) Act, 1918, laid the basis for the modern franchise. It was introduced following a Speaker's Conference on Electoral Reform, which reported in 1917. The Act gave the vote to women aged 30 years and older. It stipulated that a period of six months' residence in a constituency (previously the period had been twelve months) was necessary and sufficient for having the right to vote in that constituency. It also provided for plural voting, businessmen occupying premises worth £10 or more in a different constituency having a vote (as did their wives) in the second constituency (the same also applied to women occupying business premises worth £5 or more). The RP Act of 1928 equalized the franchise, giving the vote to women aged 21 years and older. The RP Act of 1949 abolished university seats, double-member seats, and plural voting, and introduced postal votes. It is generally credited with bringing to fruition the principle of one person, one vote. The RP Act, 1969, lowered the voting age to 18 years. Subsequent Acts have covered, *inter alia*, disqualification for membership of the Commons (RP Act, 1981), barring anyone sentenced to more than one year in gaol from being elected during the period of imprisonment), campaign spending and protecting the secrecy of the ballot (RP Act, 1983), extension of postal and proxy voting, and increasing the deposit necessary for candidature (RP Act, 1985). Though changes to electoral law are normally covered by RP Acts, not all are. The age at which citizens are eligible for election to public office is not covered by such Acts. *PN*

ROBERT BLACKBURN, *The Electoral System in Britain* (London, 1995). | DAVID BUTLER, *The Electoral System in Britain since 1918* (Oxford, 1963).

republicanism. British republicans wish for a variety of reforms of the constitution, but they are all agreed on the abolition of the monarchy as a central plank of that reform. They think of the monarchy as a relic of the past when sovereignty lay in the king rather than in the people. They have always disliked Walter Bagehot's argument that the British constitution had, by the 19th century, already become a republic, though one cloaked in monarchical drapery. Republicans believe that there would be greater clarity and honesty, as well as a better guarantee of civil rights, in a written constitution than in the combination of medieval survivals, legal precedents, and pragmatic attitudes that make up the present, unwritten constitution. They also believe that a republic would be more egalitarian and less expensive than the monarchy, which they see as promoting class distinction and needless expenditure on ceremonial. There have been two occasions in the century when republicanism has been relatively strong. The first accompanied the social dislocations and labour unrest after the Great War. The second followed the divorce of the prince and princess of Wales. A fire at Windsor, which raised questions about whether taxpayers would have to pay for its restoration, also contributed fuel to this unhappiness with the monarchy late in the century. A strong republican movement in Australia in the 1990s may also have fortified English republicanism. Republican feeling is usually at its strongest when the cost of the monarchy can be shown to be excessive. It is at its weakest in times of prosperity and when individual members of the royal family are popular. *WMK*

CHRISTOPHER HITCHENS, *The Monarchy: A Critique of Britain's Favourite Fetish* (London, 1990).

Republic of Ireland Act, 1948. The inter-party government in Dublin passed the Republic of Ireland Act which ended the ambiguous relationship between Eire and the British Commonwealth. Eire remained the name of the Irish state but the status of that state was now formally that of a republic. The British government responded with the *Ireland Act, 1949, which enshrined the consent principle with regard to Irish unification but stated that Eire was not to be regarded as a foreign country. With reference to Northern Ireland, it affirmed that in no event would Northern Ireland or any part thereof cease to be part of His Majesty's dominions and of the United Kingdom without the consent of the parliament of Northern Ireland. The new republic's political leaders were angered by this as they believed it was, and should remain, in the Westminster parliament's power to unify Ireland without Northern Ireland's consent. *TWH*

resale price maintenance (RPM), or 'vertical price-fixing', a practice by which suppliers stipulate the prices at which the goods they sell will be resold by distributors. A form of forward vertical integration into distribution by manufacturers, its widespread adoption in Britain from the late 19th century is associated with the development of mass-produced, packaged, branded, and nationally advertised goods. Collective enforcement of RPM, whereby trade associations imposed collective boycotts and other penalties against price-cutters, was banned under the *Restrictive Trade Practices Act, 1956. RPM enforced by suppliers operating alone was first strengthened under the same Act and then banned under the Resale Prices Act, 1964, unless specifically exempted by category (as were, for example, drugs and books). Large-scale retailers benefited from the legislation which allowed them to compete in price with small retailers on the products affected. Heath forced through the change against intense opposition from within the Conservative Party, such opposition being based on the fear that the legislation would alienate the party's small business support. *HJM*

H. MERCER, *Constructing a Competitive Order: The Hidden History of British Antitrust Policies* (Cambridge, 1995).

research councils. The first of the research councils dates back to 1913 when the Medical Research Committee—renamed the Medical Research Council in 1918—was created, followed by the Department of Scientific and Industrial Research in 1916. Research councils were a key recommendation of the 1918 *Haldane report but the third did not appear until 1931 when the Agricultural Research Council—renamed the Agricultural and Food Research Council in 1983—was established. Before 1959, research councils were the responsibility of the Privy Council Office, but after then authority shifted to the newly created office of minister of science. In 1965, responsibility for research councils passed to the Department of Education and Science with the Department of Scientific and Industrial Research being split into three: the Science and Engineering Research Council; the Natural Environment Research Council; and the Social Science Research Council (renamed the Economic and Social Science Research Council in 1982). The year 1992 saw the creation of the Office of Science and Technology (OST) within the Cabinet Office. In 1993, a reorganization led to there being seven research councils: biotechnology and biological sciences; engineering and physical sciences; economic and social; medical; natural environment; particle physics and astronomy; and the council for the central laboratory of the research councils. The OST was transferred to the Department of Trade and Industry in 1996. *JD*

UK research councils website: *www.research-councils.ac.uk*

reselection of MPs, process by which sitting Members are chosen or not chosen by their local political parties to be candidates at the next general election. Once a party has chosen a candidate to replace a retiring MP, there is often little dispute as to who the candidate will be in succeeding elections. However, some MPs have run into trouble with their local parties, sometimes over policy stances and occasionally because of personality clashes or some indiscretion. Such clashes have occurred throughout the century. There were some high-profile clashes between Labour MPs and their local parties in the 1970s, and in 1981 the party adopted a policy of mandatory reselection: under this, sitting Members were subject to a full reselection process, with other candidates being considered, during the lifetime of each parliament. Between 1981 and 1986, fourteen Labour MPs were denied reselection. In 1989, a new procedure was introduced, in which electoral colleges were employed, reducing the influence of the activists who sometimes clashed with the MP. In the 1990s, a number of Conservative Members were denied reselection, and in 1999 controversy was stirred by a proposal that each Conservative MP be subject to what amounted to a reselection process, with the prospect of other candidates being considered, during each parliament. Disputes, though, are not specific to the 20th century. Edmund Burke had problems with his constituents in Bristol in the 1770s and his robust defence of the Member's independence has been cited since by Members under threat from their local parties. *PN*

Philip Norton, *Conservative Dissidents* (London, 1978). | Patrick Seyd, *The Rise and Fall of the Labour Left* (London, 1987). | Alison Young, *The Reselection of MPs* (London, 1983).

Restrictive Trade Practices Act, 1956, legislation that broke up the British cartel system as it had existed since the 1930s. It was the most far-reaching Act of competition policy in the post-war period, although its actual terms were dictated by business lobbying. All restrictive agreements were to be registered and could then be referred to the Restrictive Practices Court, which produced a series of hostile decisions. Collective enforcement of *resale price maintenance was banned but powers of individual resale price maintenance were strengthened. *HJM*

H. Mercer, *Constructing a Competitive Order: The Hidden History of British Antitrust Policies* (Cambridge, 1995).

Reveille, the, short-lived pressure group formed in 1910 by Henry *Page Croft and his small circle of Empire enthusiasts who had earlier formed the *Confederacy. Displeased with the leadership of Arthur Balfour, Croft called in the press for 'a Wellington' to lead Conservatives to an energetic programme of imperial integration, tariff reform, and stronger defence. A movement mainly of younger and uninfluential Tories, the Reveille like Croft's other organizations was born of frustration and achieved little success. *RJQA*

Larry L. Witherell, *Rebel on the Right: Henry Page Croft and the Crisis of British Conservatism, 1903–1914* (Newark, Del., 1997).

***Reversing The Trend* (1975)**, title of the book containing speeches made by Sir Keith *Joseph during 1974, in which he called for a whole new approach by the state (and his own Conservative Party) to the handling of economic policy. The chosen title reflected the belief of Joseph, and soon of the Conservative Party as a whole under Margaret Thatcher, that what was needed was a reversal of the entire 'consensus' on domestic policy which had characterized British government since 1945, but which had (in their view) simply meant that Conservatives accepted in office whatever Labour governments had done. The objective would be to make Labour now accept the New Right's agenda, and in this Joseph's book was both persuasive and deeply prophetic. *JAR*

Review of Overseas Representation (ROR) (1977). Commissioned by James Callaghan as foreign secretary in 1975, it was carried out by six members of the Central Policy Review

Staff (CPRS) under Sir Kenneth Berrill, who came to believe that his was the wrong team to undertake it. It inspired fierce internal resistance from the Foreign and Commonwealth Office and the defenders of the British Council. The CPRS investigators (the two women team members especially) endured sharp attacks in the media as they travelled the world. Its huge 442-page report appeared in August 1997 calling, as *The Times* put it on 4 August, for 'a smaller, more specialised, less hospitable Diplomatic Service containing fewer diplomats and more home civil servants'. A confidential section of the report on the work of the Secret Intelligence Service, MI6, has never been published. Its proposals were watered down in a cabinet committee specially convened for the purpose (GEN 89) and chaired by Callaghan, who was by this time prime minister. And the foreign secretary, David Owen, publicly repudiated the pessimistic assumptions, as the Foreign and Commonwealth Office saw them, of the CPRS's assumptions about the British economy and the UK's future place in the world. The Callaghan government did propose a few marginal changes as a result of the review (more interchange between the home civil and diplomatic services, an examination of training for commercial officers, British Council to be reviewed rather than abolished, more mini-diplomatic missions abroad). The CPRS's preferred option that the diplomatic service should be abolished as a separate entity and its functions grouped along with trade and overseas development as a foreign specialism within the home civil service was not (and never became) a runner. But, under the public expenditure pressure during the 1980s and 1990s, Britain's overseas capacities were trimmed and streamlined in a way that accorded with the ROR's spirit—though no such acknowledgement was made. *PJH*

Peter Hennessy, *Whitehall* (London, 1989). | Peter Hennessy, Susan Morrison, and Richard Townsend, *Routine Punctuated by Orgies: The Central Policy Review Staff 1970–1983* (Strathclyde Papers on Government and Politics, No. 31, Glasgow, 1985).

revisionism, term referring to the modification of an ideology or orthodoxy in general, but in particular to the rejection of Marxist-Leninism in the first three decades of the 20th century, theoretically by Eduard Bernstein and practically by Karl Kautsky. This was accompanied by a change in the use of the term 'social democratic'. Initially used as to embrace socialist and Marxist groups, it became linked to those left-wing parties which offered a parliamentary route to socialism. Thereafter, revisionism came to be associated with attempts to ensure that left-wing political parties offered policies that were compatible with the changed economic circumstances of post-war Europe. The most well known of these is the adoption of the 'Godesberg Program' by the West German Social Democrats in 1959 (see also Labour revisionism). *CPS*

Reynolds, Albert (1932–), Irish politician. In February 1992, Reynolds was elected leader of Fianna Fáil in succession to Charles Haughey, and was later ratified as taoiseach by the Irish parliament. Reynolds played a key role in persuading the Provisional IRA to declare a ceasefire in 1994 and also had secret contacts with Loyalist paramilitaries. He negotiated with John Major to produce the joint declaration in December 1993 which established the broad principles of the evolving Irish peace process. *TWH*

Rhineland crisis (1936). Under the treaties of Versailles (see Paris peace conference) and *Locarno, the Rhineland was demilitarized, but on 7 March 1936 Hitler violated this provision by remilitarizing it, so nullifying the guarantee of French and Belgian security contained in the Locarno arrangements. He took this action a year ahead of schedule because of the improvement in Italo-German relations attendant upon the *Abyssinian crisis and his perception of Anglo-French preoccupation with it. The Rhineland crisis occurred at precisely the point where, in its efforts to bring Germany into a general settlement, the British government had already privately conceded that the demilitarized zone could disappear. Moreover, it also considered that any violation of the demilitarized zone could not realistically be opposed by Britain and France by military means. As the French government would not take forceful action unilaterally, this meant that Germany would remain in military occupation of the Rhineland and that the crisis could only be resolved by diplomatic means. During the course of the next twelve months the British government took the lead in trying to renegotiate a western pact that would replace Locarno and act as the basis of a broader general settlement, but to no avail. Meanwhile, Belgium opted for neutrality. *AJC*

J. T. Emmerson, *The Rhineland Crisis, 7 March 1936* (London, 1977).

Rhodesian crisis (1965–80). This was caused by Rhodesian white settlers' illegal unilateral declaration of independence (UDI) in 1965, and remained unsolved for fifteen years. The

Rhodesian crisis proper began when the Central African Federation broke up in 1963. Two of its three component parts, modern Malawi and Zambia, soon obtained complete independence, but Rhodesia (formerly southern Rhodesia, now Zimbabwe) did not, for the British, with Commonwealth support, withheld independence from Rhodesia's white minority government.

In 1964–5, the uncompromising Rhodesian premier Ian Smith sought to reverse this situation but his attempts to solve the crisis by talks with Sir Alec Douglas-Home failed. It was then left to Harold Wilson's new Labour administration to try to settle the matter. Wilson met Smith several times during 1965, but no agreement was struck. Some members of the Commonwealth wanted Britain to use force to impose majority rule, but Wilson told Smith he objected to this idea. As a result of Wilson's indiscretion, Smith was confident in holding out if he had to. Wilson himself flew to Rhodesia on 25 October for further talks and also met some detained nationalist leaders. He was angered by their treatment and repeated earlier warnings that economic sanctions would be imposed if Rhodesia opted for UDI, but Smith remained obdurate and on 11 November 1965 declared UDI.

The British government therefore imposed economic sanctions immediately but these failed because Rhodesia continued to receive outside help. The British were especially embarrassed because they could do nothing to stop subsidiaries of British-owned companies in South Africa from exporting oil to Rhodesia. Wilson met Smith again in December 1966, on board HMS *Tiger* off Gibraltar, but again the talks resolved nothing. Nearly two years later, in October 1968, Wilson met Smith on board another British warship, HMS *Fearless*, but, yet again, Wilson failed to get Smith to agree to majority rule. With sanctions not working and nothing more to lose, Rhodesia declared itself a republic in March 1970.

Edward Heath as Conservative leader had been seriously embarrassed by Tory right-wingers' support for Rhodesia, and his new Conservative government tried in 1971 to reach a settlement with Smith. Basically, they agreed proposals which would have led to majority rule at some undefined future date. A royal commission, under Lord Pearce, was allowed by Smith to elicit the opinions of Rhodesia's Africans, who rejected any compromise with Smith's regime. Consequently, the British rejected the proposals and tried to ignore the Rhodesian problem.

From 1972, though, Rhodesia came under attack from nationalist guerrillas, supported by Zambia and Tanzania and, from 1974, also by the nationalist government in Mozambique. Eventually, South Africa, fearful of an escalating war on its northern frontier, and the USA, worried about the impact of the guerrilla fighting on the Cold War, pressured Smith into making reforms. In 1978 he accepted a form of majority rule which kept most white privileges intact. Subsequent elections, in which most Africans took part, brought the moderate bishop Abel Muzorewa into power. However, Muzorewa's government was unacceptable elsewhere and with the guerrilla war now destabilizing the entire region, the British stepped in once again in 1979. At *Lancaster House, a settlement was finally struck, with the whites accepting majority rule. The subsequent elections, in April 1980, were won by the nationalist Robert Mugabe's ZANU party, which then ruled Zimbabwe for the rest of the century. *KTS*

Brian Lapping, *End of Empire* (London, 1985). | Ben Pimlott, *Harold Wilson* (London, 1992).

Ribble Valley by-election (7 March 1991), heavy defeat suffered by the Major government in a Lancashire contest occasioned by the unnecessary promotion of David Waddington to the Lords. The Conservative share of the vote dropped by over a third, and there was a swing of well over 20 per cent to the Liberals who won the seat. *JAR*

Richard, Ivor Seward (1932–), lawyer and Labour politician. After serving as an MP, 1964–74, and as Britain's permanent representative to the UN, 1974–9, Lord Richard (life peer, 1992) led Labour in the Lords, 1992–7, becoming lord privy seal after the 1997 election. His main task was to prepare the ground for the reform of the Lords, beginning with the abolition of hereditary peerages. After conducting secret talks with Conservative peers he failed to deliver a deal. The lord chancellor replaced him in the talks and he lost his job in the government reshuffle of 1998. *BB*

Richards, Thomas (1859–1931), miners' leader. Tom Richards was general secretary of the South Wales Miners' Federation, 1898–1931, and MP for West Monmouthshire, 1904–18, and Ebbw Vale, 1918–20 (being returned unopposed three times). In his day he was the most powerful and respected trade unionist in Wales. His rise from working miner to privy councillor was archetypal, as was his transition from Lib-Lab to Labour after 1908. Essentially a bureaucrat, he withstood the challenge of militants and retained respect through his emphasis on the need to maintain the power of the union machine. *PS*

Richardson, Josephine **(1923–94)**, Labour politician. She joined the Labour Party in 1945, was secretary of the Tribune group, 1948–78, and fought to keep alive the socialist ideals of Labour's 1945 generation. She entered parliament comparatively late, succeeding another left-winger Tom *Driberg, 1974–94, as Labour MP for Barking, a London East End working-class overspill constituency, dominated by Ford Motors. Jo Richardson was opposition spokesperson on women's rights, 1983–92, and, though opposing Labour's leadership many times over many different issues, was elected to the NEC, 1979–91. *PRGR*

Riddell, Lord **(1865–1934)**, press baron and political intriguer. George Allardice Riddell was a solicitor by training, but moved in and out of the worlds of politics and the press as chairman of the *News of the World*, 1903–34. He was a particular intimate of David Lloyd George, used by him for several sensitive tasks including press liaison during the 1919 Paris peace conference. His diaries were published towards the end of his life (three volumes, 1933–4) but have not been found by historians to be a very reliable source. *JAR*

Ridley, Nicholas **(1929–93)**, Conservative politician. Close to Heath in his *'Selsdon mar' phase and an early free-marketeer, Ridley became an abrasive Thatcherite in the 1980s at transport, environment (infiller of the south-west, deriding *'NIMBYs'), and trade. A cultivated man, painter, and gardener, he could also be very rude, his career ending when in 1990 he described the ERM as a 'German racket', and an earlier joke about a fatal ferry disaster was also unappreciated. He was a strong supporter of an immediate *poll tax. Earlier, as Foreign Office junior minister, he had been keen on selling and leasing back the Falklands and his negotiating with the Argentinian president may have contributed to the impression of British indifference (see FALKLANDS WAR). *EP*

NICHOLAS RIDLEY, *My Kind of Government: The Thatcher Years* (London, 1991).

Rifkind, Malcolm Leslie **(1946–)**, Scottish Conservative politician. Moving alongside Robin Cook from Edinburgh High School to university to front bench, Rifkind made a noteless half-hour maiden speech. He was originally a Scottish devolutionist, later conforming to party resistance to the idea. In cabinet from 1986, he was secretary for Scotland, transport, and the Foreign Office. Leading desperate Scottish Tories while distrusted and carefully watched by Scottish Thatcherites, he made threats to resign, and advised 'consolidation and sensitivity' in 1989, but allowed the *poll tax experiment in Scotland. Rifkind personally saw off an SNP assault in 1992 but lost his seat in 1997, promising to fight again to regain it but lost it again in 2001. *EP*

***Right Approach, The* (1976)**, Conservative policy document, an ideological turning point. Margaret Thatcher wished to end interventionism and the acceptance of trade union power of post-1945 Conservatism. *The Right Approach* (1976) and its successor *The Right Approach to the Economy* (1997) involved Sir Keith Joseph, the more cautious Howe and Howell, and the leftish Prior. Despite right-wing criticism, these publications pushed the Tories towards monetarism, public spending restraint, and lower direct taxation, a key shift of policy. *EP*

***Right Road for Britain, The* (1949)**, Conservative policy document, the party's first full-length policy statement since 1945, and the first substantial document that involved the reformed *Conservative Research Department. Intended to consolidate the impact of the **Industrial Charter* and *The *Case for Conservatism*, it represented the development of a highly professional strain of administrative Conservatism that helped frame the political agenda for the 1950s. *NJC*

rights, bill of. See BILL OF RIGHTS.

right to buy. See HOUSING ACT, 1980.

Rimington, Stella. See SECURITY SERVICE.

Rio de Janeiro treaty (1947). The Inter-American treaty of reciprocal assistance established a permanent defensive alliance amongst all 21 American republics. Initiated by Washington as an attempt to create a continental anti-communist alliance, it has also been used by the USA to justify its intervention in other members' internal affairs. Used as a model for *NATO, the Rio treaty's article 3, 'an attack on one is an attack on all', is the basis of the North Atlantic Treaty's pivotal article 5. *DHD*

riots have been a relatively frequent occurrence in Britain during the 20th century, but over a wide range of different issues. At the beginning of the century, the most serious disturbances were those associated with industrial disputes. At *Tonypandy in 1910 troops were called out to disperse demonstrators during riots which accompanied the Cambrian Combine strike. The following year clashes between police and strikers in Liverpool on 13 August 1911, 'Bloody Sunday', led to the deaths of two strikers. In a dispute at Llanelli on 17 August, two more men were shot by police.

The Great War occasioned riots against Germans (and sometimes simply against foreigners) in London and other major cities in May 1915, following the sinking of the passenger liner *Lusitania* by a German submarine, causing the deaths of hundreds of passengers. In the immediate post-war period there were riots over demobilization amongst servicemen in Rhyl and London, and in 1919 a widespread strike in Glasgow led to clashes with the police, while the police strike later that year in Liverpool resulted in considerable looting in the city centre. During the inter-war years, marches of unemployed workers led to serious rioting in the early 1930s, principally in Belfast, Birkenhead, and London, but with smaller disturbances elsewhere. The British Union of Fascists occasioned violence when the route of their march through the East End in October 1936 was blockaded, leading to the 'battle of *Cable Street' between police and anti-Fascist demonstrators.

After the Second World War, there were anti-coloured riots at Notting Hill and Nottingham in 1958, but the largest number of disturbances were those associated with youth, with 'Mods' versus 'Rockers' fighting in seaside resorts in the early sixties and the development of *football hooliganism. Protests against the Vietnam war led to riots in universities and in Grosvenor Square, outside the American Embassy, in 1968 (see NINETEEN SIXTY-EIGHT). Anti-Fascist demonstrators were involved in a number of disturbances, at *Red Lion Square, London, in 1974, and Southall in 1979, in both of which people were killed. Sporadic disturbances between local inhabitants and the police at the *Notting Hill carnival, especially in 1976, foreshadowed the major outbreak of rioting in inner-city areas in the early 1980s. This began in the St Paul's district of Bristol in April 1980, and was followed by a wave of disturbances in 1981, the most serious at Brixton (London), Toxteth (Liverpool), and Moss Side (Manchester). These led to the appointment of the Scarman commission into relations between the police and inner-city communities, many of which have large ethnic minorities. The mid-1980s witnessed a recrudescence of violence occasioned by industrial disputes, including confrontations between police and strikers at *Orgreave, Yorkshire, during the miners' strike, and on London picket lines in the *Grunwick and Wapping disputes.

There remained, too, an undercurrent of inner-city violence, seen in the riots in Handsworth, Birmingham, in September 1985 and the following month at the Broadwater Farm Estate in Tottenham (London) where a policeman was murdered. The introduction of the *poll tax provoked riots in Trafalgar Square in March 1990. During the 1990s protests against road schemes at Twyford Down, Winchester, on the A30 near Devon, and over the Newbury bypass all occasioned violence. The largest and most expensive riot in recent years was the anti-capitalist protest by anarchists in the City of London in 1999, which caused £1 billion worth of damage. *JS*

Ripon, 1st marquess of (1827–1909), Liberal politician of remarkable longevity, the son of the Tory prime minister of 1827, Lord Goderich (subsequently 1st earl of Ripon). He was a Liberal MP from 1853 until succeeding his father in the Lords in 1859. Ripon first served in government under Palmerston and Russell, 1859–66, and was in three of Gladstone's four cabinets (missing the second as he was governor-general of India). As the elder statesman of Liberalism, he was leader in the Lords, 1905–8, Asquith thus being the eighth leader under whom he had served in a career spanning 55 years. *JAR*

Rippon, (Aubrey) Geoffrey Frederick (1924–97), Conservative politician. Rippon was mayor of Surbiton before he was 30 and entered the cabinet before he was 40. Despite belonging to the *Monday Club, he was strongly pro-European. Appointed chancellor of the duchy of Lancaster in 1970, he negotiated British entry into the European Community and during 1977–9 led the Conservatives in the *European parliament. Rippon was also environment secretary in Heath's cabinet, but he never subscribed to Thatcherism and did not serve under her. He received a life peerage in 1987. *RJS*

***Rise of the Meritocracy*.** See MERITOCRACY.

Ritchie, Charles Thomson (1838–1906), Conservative politician. As chancellor of the exchequer under Balfour, the veteran minister C. T. Ritchie rigidly opposed Joseph Chamberlain's desire to use the recently resurrected corn registration duty as a first step toward *imperial preference. Chamberlain opened his tariff reform campaign in mid-1903 and by September, with

Balfour's approval, left the cabinet to lead it. The prime minister, vainly hoping to save his government, was quick to accept Ritchie's resignation in order to placate the Chamberlainites. *RJQA*

Alan Sykes, *Tariff Reform in British Politics 1903–1913* (Oxford, 1979).

'rivers of blood', phrase used as a headline following Powell's Birmingham speech on immigration in April 1968. Powell actually said that, 'Like the Roman, I seem to see the River Tiber foaming with much blood'. This prophecy in Virgil's *Aeneid*, however, is the Sybil's, not the Roman's. *RJS*

roads. See transport policy.

Robbins, Lionel Charles (1898–1984), leading economist and author noted for his contribution to methodology, policy, and modern theory. His main areas of research were the general concept of the nature of economic science and political economy, economic problems in peace and war, and the economic causes of war. His most important work was *Essay on the Nature and Significance of Economic Science* (1932), which attributed high unemployment to high wages, and in the 1930s he opposed Keynes's advocacy of increased government expenditure to reduce unemployment. During the Second World War he moved towards a *Keynesian way of thinking about unemployment and the role of fiscal and monetary policies in alleviating it. As director of the economic section of the war cabinet, 1941–5, he was a delegate to the Hot Springs and *Bretton Woods conferences and a member of the team which negotiated the Anglo-American loan agreement in 1945. Robbins was professor of economics at the LSE, 1929–61; chairman of the *Financial Times*, 1961–70; and of the royal commission on higher education which produced the *Robbins report in 1964. *JFM*

J. R. Shackleton and G. Locksley, *Twelve Contemporary Economists* (London, 1981).

Robbins report (1963) into *higher education, set up in 1961 as a subcommittee of the University Grants Committee, chaired by Lionel *Robbins, an academic economist. The main findings supported a major increase in the numbers entering higher education, doubling the number of student places over the following decade with expansion in other areas of higher education, towards a target of half a million students by 1980. The Conservative administration of Sir Alec Douglas-Home accepted these recommendations, underpinning the development of the new universities already approved between 1958 and 1961. As a result of the Robbins report, the new universities were expanded more rapidly than anticipated and Oxbridge and the existing civic universities also greatly increased in size. By 1968 nearly 220,000 places in higher education were available. *JS*

Robens, Alfred (1910–99), Labour politician and industrial manager. Robens was a trade union official who entered the Commons in the Labour landslide of 1945, representing the Northumberland constituencies of Wansbeck, 1945–50, and Blyth, 1950–60. He held junior office under Attlee, and was briefly minister of labour in 1951. He had reached the cabinet when Bevan resigned, and continued to support right-wing causes in opposition during the 1950s. By 1960, as one of the few Labour survivors with cabinet experience, he was considered by a few as a potential party leader, but threw up his political career to become chairman of the National Coal Board, 1961–71, where he initiated a major rundown of the industry and managed to carry it through without a strike. After 1971 he was managing director of Vickers. *JAR*

Lord Robens, *Ten-Year Stint* (London, 1972).

Roberthall, Lord. See Hall, Robert Lowe.

Roberts, Frank Kenyon (1907–98), diplomat. He entered the Foreign Office in 1930 and remained there until 1968, European affairs dominating a career spanning the diplomacy of appeasement, war, peacemaking, and the construction of Britain's Atlanticist post-war foreign policy. He served with particular distinction as ambassador to Moscow (1960–2) and Bonn (1963–8). Slight, dapper, energetic, even combative, in his retirement he became a familiar and approachable figure at meetings, also working for the North Atlantic committee and the Königswinter conference. *ADe*

Frank Roberts, *Dealing with Dictators* (London, 1991).

Roberts, Lord ('Bobs') (1832–1914), military commander. At 19, the diminutive Frederick Roberts entered the Indian army, where his brilliant career (VC, 1858) saw him rise eventually to become commander-in-chief, 1885–93. He returned to Britain in 1895, was promoted field marshal, and burnished his legend further with his victorious command in the *Boer war. He served as the last commander-in-chief of the British army, 1900–4, his final years being spent leading the *National Service League and campaigning for mandatory military training. *RJQA*

David James, *Lord Roberts* (London, 1959). | J. A. Thompson and Arthur Mejia (eds.), *Edwardian Conservatism: Five Studies in Adaptation* (London, 1988).

Robertson, William Robertson (1860–1933), general. A rare example of a general officer risen from the ranks, 'Wully' Robertson was chief of the imperial general staff from December 1915 to February 1918. A prominent 'Westerner', he supported the concentration of British manpower on the western front. But he also bridled against political interference in military matters and alienated the prime minister, Lloyd George, so that he was forced to resign in 1918. His going demonstrated the extent to which civilian politicians increasingly asserted supremacy in modern, total war. *KJ*

David R. Woodward, *Lloyd George and the Generals* (London, 1983).

Robinson, (Edward) Austin Gossage (1897–1993), leading British economist. Robinson played a key role as economic adviser in the administration of the British war effort, 1939–45, holding positions in the economic section of the War Cabinet Office, 1939–42, and as head of production in the Ministry of Production 1942–5. He was instrumental in shaping post-war planning, as economic adviser to the Board of Trade, 1946, and as a member of the economic planning staff to the Treasury, 1947–8. Later he became chairman of the council of NIESR, 1949–62; professor of economics at the University of Cambridge, 1950–66; and adviser to the Ministry of Power, 1967–8. His numerous writings concentrated mainly on the problems of economic development. *JFM*

Robinson, Mary (1944–), president of the republic of Ireland, 1990–7. Labour's candidate, a liberal feminist lawyer, her election signified a sea change in Irish politics. As Sinn Fein also noted, old-style republicanism and nationalism were in retreat. Committed to human rights, and to reconciliation between Ireland's two historic communities, Robinson, unwilling to remain a purely ceremonial figure, used her high international profile to encourage the peace process, Eloquently she spoke of giving Ireland a fifth province, one in every Irish heart. *DRB*

ROBOT, the code name for a secret plan to introduce a flexible exchange rate for sterling in 1952, the code was derived from the names of Leslie *RO*wan and *OT*to Clarke of the Treasury. ROBOT called for the establishment of external current account convertibility at a variable exchange rate which would float around the par value of \$2.80 = £1, between unpublicized boundaries of \$2.40 = £1 and \$3.20 = £1. At the time, sterling was inconvertible for most holders and so this was a heroic plan. ROBOT was devised partly in response to pressure at the Commonwealth finance ministers' meeting at the beginning of 1951 for Britain to pursue freer trade and payments. The plan also reflected the views of those in the Treasury and the Bank of England who wished a quicker return to convertibility of sterling and the freedom to absorb external pressure on the economy through the exchange rate. The ROBOT plan was presented to cabinet by R. A. Butler on 28 February 1952 and then debated by ministers and officials in the Bank of England over the next two months. In the end, ROBOT was abandoned on several grounds. First, Churchill came to believe that devaluation would raise the price of imports more than it would affect the competitiveness of British exports. The result would be a worsening of the balance of payments and higher inflation. As the domestic price of imports rose, producers would be forced to lay off workers to cut costs. ROBOT thus threatened the two main Conservative government goals of price stability and full employment. Instituting a flexible exchange rate would also break the rules of the IMF and the European Payments Union, which would antagonize the Americans at a time when Britain needed their support. In the event, a floating exchange rate for sterling was not introduced until twenty years later. *CRS*

Rodgers, William Thomas (1928–), Social Democratic and Liberal Democrat politician. One of the original *'Gang of Four' who had fought for moderate causes in the party since the 1950s, and held cabinet office under Callaghan, he left the Labour Party to found the Council for Social Democracy and then the Social Democratic Party (SDP). Labour MP for Stockton South (from 1962), Rodgers lost his seat in the 1983 election. A leading figure in the SDP and in asserting its separate identity from the Liberals, he accepted the merger in 1988 and became leader of the Liberal Democrats in the Lords. *JS*

Roll, Eric (1907–), public servant and banker. An academic economist in the 1930s, Roll became a temporary civil servant during the Second World War (working in the British food mission to North America), and stayed on after 1945 to work variously in the Ministry of Food, the Treasury, and the Ministry of Agriculture; he was deputy leader of the UK delegation for the talks on entry to the European Economic Community, 1961–3. He served as permanent secretary of the ill-fated Department of Economic Affairs, 1964–6, leaving Whitehall for a career in banking. *KT*

Rome, treaty of (1957). On 25 March 1957 the six European Coal and Steel Community states (ECSC) signed two treaties in Rome. The first established the European Economic Community (EEC) and the second the European Atomic Energy Community (Euratom). The EEC became the dominant institution (hence the singular usage as 'the treaty of Rome'), building on the model of the ECSC to form a common market which became the foundation of the present-day European Union (see EUROPEAN INTEGRATION). Britain did not join the EEC but concurrently sought to complement it with an all-European free trade area (FTA). Known as Plan G in Whitehall, the FTA reflected Britain's recognition of the importance of cooperation with Europe but also its reluctance to accept the supranational elements and dirigiste economics of the EEC. Traditional ties with the Commonwealth and agricultural protection, both significant political issues for Macmillan's Conservative government, limited Britain's room for manoeuvre in the FTA negotiations and this, alongside French intransigence and the early strength of the EEC, led to the failure of the FTA proposal (see EUROPEAN FREE TRADE ASSOCIATION) and, in turn, to Britain's first application for membership of the EEC in 1961. *JRVE*

Rookes v. Barnard (1964), legal case involving trade union law. This was a House of Lords' judgement after Douglas Rookes took the Draughtsmen's and Allied Technicians' Association, from which he had resigned, to court for forcing a strike which led him to lose his job. He won £7,500 in damages from union officials and thus undermined the trade union immunity from legal action arising from industrial disputes as guaranteed under the Trades Dispute Act of 1906. The *Donovan commission was set up to deal with the problem this created but, by the time it recommended a reversal of the judgement in 1968, both the Conservatives (see *FAIR DEAL AT WORK*) and some Labour ministers (see *IN PLACE OF STRIFE*) wanted tougher action to restrain the unions. *KL*

Rose, Richard (1933–), political scientist. Born in St Louis, Missouri, Rose first came to Britain in 1953 and quickly had an impact on British political science. While still an Oxford doctoral student he co-wrote **Must Labour Lose?* with Mark Abrams (1960) and *The General Election of 1959* (1960) with David Butler. His *Politics in England* (1964) pioneered a behavioural approach and placed him at the heart of developments in the field internationally. His edited *Electoral Behaviour* (1974) remains a landmark in the field of comparative electoral studies. Rose's path-breaking work spanned the whole discipline and included books on territorial politics (*Governing Without Consensus: An Irish Perspective*, 1971); public policy (*Understanding Big Government*, 1984; *Lesson Drawing in Public Policy*, 1993); and political leadership (*The Postmodern President: The White House Meets the World*, 1988). After the collapse of the iron curtain, Rose produced a series of studies on citizen attitudes in post-communist systems including *Democracy and its Alternatives: Understanding Post-Communist Societies* (with Christian Haerpfer and William Mishler, 1998). Rose also built institutions for cross-national collaboration. He co-founded the European Consortium for Political Research (1970) and the British Politics Group of the American Political Science Association (1970) and was secretary of the Committee on Political Sociology of the International Political Science Association (1970–85). He set up the Centre for the Study of Public Policy at Strathclyde University in 1976 and co-founded the *Journal of Public Policy* in 1981. *ECP*

RICHARD ROSE, 'The Art of Writing about Politics', in Hans Daalder (ed.), *Comparative European Politics: The Story of a Profession* (London, 1997).

Rosebery, 5th earl of (1847–1929), Liberal politician and prime minister. Though Rosebery had held office effectively in all the Liberal administrations since 1881, as foreign secretary, 1886 and 1892–4, he was Queen Victoria's choice as Gladstone's successor in 1894 rather than the Liberal cabinet's. Never entirely at ease with the increasingly radical turn of Liberal politics in the 1890s and after, he was almost glad to lose office in 1895, and made no serious attempt to return. Rosebery devoted himself after 1895 mainly to making grand speeches on imperial themes, many of which did not go down at all well with the party he had recently led, as for example in his call for 'national efficiency' during the Boer war, his abandonment of home rule, and his rejection of the 1909 *'People's Budget'. In his later years he was both happier and more successful when writing than in active politics, producing valuable biographies of several 18th-century political leaders. He was a leading, most successful, racehorse owner whose horses won the Derby three times—but in politics a fish out of water. *JAR*

Ross, William (1911–88), Labour politician. As secretary for Scotland, 1964–70 and 1974–6, Ross was the only politician to have served two terms in this office since 1945. He set to work building up the economic arm of the Scottish Office and was merciless in both his denunciations of the Scottish National Party and his demands for more government spending north of the border. His no-nonsense approach and his cultural nationalism made him a popular figure in the party. Ross returned to the backbenches in April 1976, following the resignation of Harold Wilson. *RF*

Rothermere, 1st viscount (1868–1940), press baron. H. S. Harmsworth was co-founder of the *Daily Mail* in 1896 with his brother *Northcliffe, and over the following decades their Associated Press empire rapidly expanded. Lord Rothermere from 1914, he accepted minor ministerial posts during the Great War, but the grief of losing two sons led him to retreat from public life for a period. He took a direct editorial interest in the papers he ran, especially the *Daily Mail*, frequently instructing editors as to content for leaders and penning articles. Although his son Esmond took control of Associated Press in 1932, Rothermere retained direct involvement in the papers until 1938. He championed the cause of Hungary's lost territories, advocated air rearmament, and flirted with the *British Union of Fascists. Although the *Daily Mail* withdrew its official support for Mosley after the *Olympia rally, Rothermere remained in contact, including him in his propaganda organization the National League of Airmen. From the late 1920s Rothermere was driven by an almost pathological dislike of Baldwin and used both his press empire and personal fortune to challenge the authority of the Conservative leader, hence his joining with Beaverbrook in the *Empire Crusade. He saw much to favour in the regimes of Mussolini and Hitler and sought to promote better understanding between Britain and the dictators. *NJC*

N. J. Crowson (ed.), *Fleet Street, Press Barons and Party Politics: The Journals of Collin Brooks, 1932–1940* (Cambridge, 1999). | Sally Taylor, *The Great Outsiders: Northcliffe, Rothermere and the Daily Mail* (London, 1996).

Round Table, imperial movement and journal. Created in 1909 by committed British imperialists, the Round Table began as an organization dedicated to promoting an imperial federation, as a way of alleviating Britain's perceived economic and military weaknesses. In 1910, the *Round Table* journal was founded to publicize the movement's message, which in 1915 included the demand that India be given self-government. From 1920, the movement's founders either fell out or moved on and its initial zeal was lost. Hopes of an imperial union were never realized and instead the movement worked simply to keep Britain and the dominions in close contact. Some of their ideas were eventually taken up; for example, the British government created a separate Dominions Office in 1925. Although the journal still exists, it now deals with both international and Commonwealth affairs, a trend visible from the 1920s. *KTS*

John E. Kendle, *The Round Table Movement and Imperial Union* (Toronto, 1975).

Round Table conferences (1930–2), called in London by the British government and Lord Irwin, the viceroy of India, in an attempt to settle *India's constitutional development. On 31 October 1929, Irwin announced that India was to be given dominion status, in answer to the demands of Indian nationalists. All shades of Indian opinion were then invited to a Round Table conference to determine India's future government in November 1930. The British were represented by delegations from the three main political parties; while from India virtually every community and political persuasion took part, including the Indian princes. Only the Indian National Congress was missing. The main talking point was the establishment of a federal system in India. This appealed to virtually all concerned: the British felt federalism would undermine Congress and maintain a conservative, possibly pro-British interest in India; the princes would maintain authority over their own states and play a leading role in the central government; while for minorities, like the Muslims, their interests would be safeguarded. When the session closed on 19 January 1931, the British made it clear that they envisaged dominion status for India based on federalism. Irwin, however, realized that Congress participation was essential for a permanent solution and in March 1931 persuaded Gandhi to join the talks when they resumed in September. However, they soon broke down over the issue of reserved seats for minorities in the legislature. Attitudes hardened consequently and Irwin's successor, Lord Willingdon, was less inclined to conciliate Gandhi and Congress. By this time the Round Table idea was dead, and a third session in late 1932 achieved nothing. Thus it was left to the British to impose their own solutions. *KTS*

Rowan, Leslie (1908–72), prime ministers' principal private secretary, 1945–7. A Treasury official and former England hockey captain, Rowan was private secretary to Winston Churchill (1941–5). Following his promotion, he attended the Potsdam conference with both Churchill and his successor, Clement Attlee. He remained friendly with Churchill, who hoped to secure his services on returning to office in 1951. However, Rowan was now a Treasury second secretary and therefore too senior for the post. In 1952 he helped devise the *ROBOT plan for floating the pound. *CL*

Rowlands, Archibald (1892–1953), civil servant. Rowlands started his administrative career in the War Office in 1920. He had two stints in India, as a defence finance adviser (1937–9) and as coordinator of the wartime administration (1943–6). One of the dominant Whitehall figures of his day, he was permanent secretary of the Ministry of Aircraft Production (1940–3), and permanent secretary of the Ministry of Supply (1946–53), working to hold together these two very large and complex 'industrial' ministries. *KT*

Rowntree, (Benjamin) Seebohm (1871–1954), sociologist, businessman, and social reformer. Son of Joseph Rowntree the cocoa manufacturer and philanthropist, he joined the family firm in York in 1889, where he established welfare provisions for employees. Concerned about poverty, in 1897–8 he conducted (and published in 1901) a pioneering survey of working-class life in York. This was followed by two further York surveys in 1936 and 1950—important works of empirical sociology. In charge of welfare at the Ministry of Munitions (1915–18) he subsequently fought for improved welfare provision and better housing, being influential in the creation of the welfare state. *JJN*

Asa Briggs, *Social Thought and Social Action: A Study of the Work of Seebohm Rowntree* (London, 1961).

royal assent, the sovereign's approval of legislation passed by both houses of parliament. It is the last stage a measure goes through before becoming law, though the royal assent has not been withheld from legislation passed by both Houses since 1707. The sovereign could not now refuse to assent to legislation without bringing on a constitutional crisis. *WMK*

royal commissions, enquiries established by royal warrant, which meant that, unlike the similar departmental committees, once set up they could not be abolished by any government. They have the power to summon witnesses, to commission research, and to produce interim and final reports when they feel ready. The membership tends to be made up of renowned public figures to give a balanced view on the subject. Their strength lies in their ability to appear impartial so encouraging all of those with an interest in the topic to give evidence. Consequently royal commissions allow the government to make use of experts and also to gauge the opinions of interest groups and the broader public on a particular issue seen as important at the time.

Royal commissions tended to be reserved for broad social or political issues, though in the earlier part of the century they could be created to investigate very specific issues. From the 1970s the use of commissions dropped off sharply (only nine have reported since 1970, and only one since 1981, compared to an average of two a year in the first two-thirds of the century); departmental committees appointed by particular ministries have substituted for them. In addition the development of departmental select committees has effectively removed the need for royal commission scrutiny of the actions and policies of departments. The topics that commissions focus on have varied widely, but some have been returned to regularly, such as mental health, India, Ireland and Northern Ireland, local government, the police, the press and broadcasting.

Many, but not all, royal commissions aim to generate legislation on the issue they have investigated. Their success in doing this has been mixed. This reflects the fact that groups they have reported on often lie outside governmental control. In addition legislation has been prevented by the prevailing political climate, such as on trade union reform legislation. Conversely, for example, royal commissions on mental health have led to steady reform. *KMT*

royal family, the nearer descendants of the sovereign. George V ruled that the title 'Royal Highness' should be confined to the children and grandchildren of the sovereign. The group of persons entitled to use the 'HRH' (His/Her Royal Highness) is probably the nearest one can come to defining the royal family, though there is no distinct demarcation between the immediate family and more distant relations. Indeed, the use of the title 'HRH' has been controversial. The title was withheld from the duke of Windsor's wife after his abdication, a needless insult. After her divorce, Diana, Princess of Wales was also stripped of her 'HRH', which alienated millions who saw it as mean-spirited. The fact that Princess Anne has decided that, though entitled to it, her children would not take the title has earned her admiration. An egalitarian age is more content with a royal family that deprecates rather than displays its rank. *WMK*

royal household, the entourage of the sovereign, ranging from ladies-in-waiting at one end to housemaids at the other. The principal officers of the household were once appointed by the ministry and changed with the government of the day. After 1924, it was decided that only three officers of the household should change or be considered 'political', and these are essentially government whips. The four highest-ranking officials in the household all possess historic titles: the lord steward, the *lord chamberlain, the master of the horse, and the mistress of the robes. They are appointed by the sovereign personally, and are usually peers and friends. The most powerful person in the household is the sovereign's private secretary, another personal appointment. Private secretaries of the 20th century were often related to or descended from other private secretaries or members of the household. The royal family also prefers to employ servants who are related to or descended from other servants. So this is a world where, whether it concerns sovereign, lady-in-waiting, or housemaid, the hereditary principle counts a great deal more than it does in the world beyond. Hence, the risk is always that the household may become insular or isolated from the opinions and attitudes that circulate in the larger community. *WMK*

Royal Institute of International Affairs. See Chatham House.

Royal Irish Constabulary (RIC). Established in 1836 as the Irish Constabulary by the merging of the Peace Preservation Force and the Irish Constabulary, both created in 1822, it became the Royal Irish Constabulary in 1867 in recognition of its role in suppressing the Fenian rising. The RIC operated throughout Ireland except for Dublin, where the Dublin metropolitan police enforced the law. The main role of the RIC in the period before the great famine of the 1840s was to maintain public order. Thereafter, the RIC became more concerned with civil than military duties. During the Anglo-Irish war of 1919–21 it was a target for the IRA and proved unsuited for guerrilla warfare, and the predominantly Catholic force became increasingly demoralized as assassinations and ambushes took their toll. In January 1920 the IRA attacked a police barracks at Carrigtwohill, Co. Cork, which signalled an expansion of the terrorist campaign, and by June 1920 the IRA had killed 55 members of the RIC, sixteen occupied police barracks had been destroyed, and hundreds of others abandoned. Many constables resigned from the force, which was reinforced by British war veterans in the form of the *Black and Tans and the Auxiliaries (see Royal Irish Constabulary, Auxiliary Division), the RIC becoming involved in government-sanctioned official reprisals against the IRA. Confusion existed between the precise division of civil and military authority. Following the Anglo-Irish treaty of 1921 and the establishment of the Irish Free State in 1922 the RIC was disbanded. *TWH*

Charles Townshend, *The British Campaign in Ireland 1919–1921* (Oxford, 1975).

Royal Irish Constabulary, Auxiliary Division, one of the new forces raised by the British government to combat IRA terrorism in 1919–21, consisting of ex-officers of the regular army who were enrolled in the RIC as 'temporary cadets', divided into companies of 100 and sent to the most disturbed areas. They numbered about 2,200 men. They were undoubtedly brave, but their discipline was suspect and they were disbanded in 1922. *DGB*

Royal Ulster Constabulary (RUC), Northern Ireland police force. During the Anglo-Irish war, 1919–21, in the area which was to become Northern Ireland, the Royal Irish Constabulary were reinforced by an armed force of special constables, the Ulster Special Constabulary (USC), comprising three categories. Class 'B', or 'B-Specials' were part-time and unpaid and proved the most durable category, being required only in an emergency. The force which emerged was almost exclusively drawn from the majority Protestant community. The USC was to form an integral part of a new police force, the Royal Ulster Constabulary (RUC), which replaced the RIC in 1922. Its target strength was to be 3,000, with 1,000 places reserved for Catholics, but Catholics boycotted this like other institutions of the new administration. The Catholic proportion of the force declined from 21 per cent in 1921 to 17 per cent in 1927 but had stabilized at around 10 per cent by 1970. The RUC was an armed paramilitary police force associated with the defence of Northern Ireland against the IRA but, following the outbreak of communal violence in 1969, the British army played the dominant role in security. The B-Specials were disbanded by the British government and replaced by the Ulster Defence Regiment (UDR), a locally recruited regiment of the British army. In 1976, the British government increased RUC numbers with the RUC reserve, replacing the army and RUC in operations which required less specialized training. By the end of 1976, RUC strength increased by 1,000, and the RUC reserve was more than doubled. The use of the RUC and UDR in the forefront of the war against paramilitaries was commonly known as 'Ulsterization', concentrating on 'normal' policing activities rather than military operations alone. A central element of this new strategy was the policy of returning the primary responsibility for law and order, including security, to the police, with the army now operating in a support role, but the effect of this was to replace regular British army personnel with Ulster protestants. The main brunt of the Provisional IRA's terrorist campaign was borne by the RUC and UDR, most of their members being killed when off-duty. Out of 924 security force deaths in the Troubles, between 1969 and 1992, more than half, 486, were members of RUC, the RUC Reserve, and the UDR/Royal Irish Regiment. *TWH*

JOHN BREWER with KATHLEEN MAGEE, *Inside the RUC: Routine Policing in a Divided Society* (Oxford, 1991).

RSPCA See ANIMAL WELFARE.

Rucker, Arthur Nevil (1895–1991), prime minister's principal private secretary, 1939–40. Rucker was private secretary to several ministers of health (1928–36), including Neville Chamberlain. A loyal servant to Chamberlain at Downing Street, he continued to hope that fighting could be avoided as late as October 1939. He was removed from Number Ten (along with almost all the private office staff) when Winston Churchill became prime minister in May 1940, continuing to serve as private secretary to Chamberlain, now lord president of the council. *CL*

Runnymede Trust, pressure group opposed to racism, founded in 1968, and taking its name from the site at which Magna Charta was signed in 1215. *JS*

Rural England, Council for the Protection of (CPRE), pressure group set up in 1926 to campaign for the protection of areas of natural beauty. Early members included Patrick *Abercrombie. The CPRE was an influential part of the town and country planning movement, promoting conservation, access to the countryside, and *national parks. *JS*

Ruskin College, founded in 1903 in Oxford. It was named after the great prophet of Victorian culture, John Ruskin (1819–1900), and dedicated to adult education. A constituent member of Oxford University, its students are drawn from the trade union movement and many have risen to high office within trade union and Labour ranks. *JS*

Russell, Bertrand Arthur William (1872–1970), philosopher, radical, and peace activist. Russell was a brilliant Cambridge-educated mathematical logician with an incomparable Whig-Liberal pedigree: his grandfather was the Victorian prime minister Lord John Russell; his parents, Viscount and Lady Amberley, who both died young, held advanced views on politics and morality; and his secular godfather was the liberal theorist John Stuart Mill. Although Russell joined the Peace Society and stood as the first women's-suffrage parliamentary candidate (in a 1907 by-election), he concentrated on academic philosophy until the Great War, which he opposed. Though not himself a conscientious objector, he worked for the No-Conscription Fellowship, consequently losing his lectureship at Trinity College, Cambridge, and suffering imprisonment for sedition. During the 1920s he wrote popular books on politics, morals, education, and science from a left-wing and rationalist perspective, and from 1927 to 1935 ran an experimental school with the second of his four wives. Exaggerating the destructiveness of air power, he in 1936 declared on utilitarian grounds that modern war could never be justified, and became a sponsor of the Peace Pledge Union. However, he recanted his pacifism early in the Second World War, during most of which he lectured in the USA, and in 1945–8 was led by his utilitarianism to the opposite extreme of advocating preventive war against the Soviet Union if it opposed the international control of atomic weapons. He gained increasing public recognition as an intellectual, receiving the Order of Merit in 1949 and the Nobel prize for literature the following year. In 1954, he began warning of the destructiveness of the hydrogen bomb and, after the Campaign for Nuclear Disarmament was launched in Britain in 1958, he achieved considerable celebrity as both its president and the leading member of its direct-action offshoot, the Committee of 100, spending seven days in prison in 1961 after a mass sit-down protest. This militancy, and the extreme character of his opposition to American actions in Vietnam, reflected the hold which a young American Marxist, Ralph Schoenman, his private secretary, 1960–9, developed over him during his last decade. From 1931, he was 3rd earl Russell. His son Conrad (4th earl) Russell, a distinguished historian, was one of the Liberal peers elected to remain in the Lords after reform in 1999. *MEC*

RONALD W. CLARK, *The Life of Bertrand Russell* (London, 1975). | RAY MONK, *Bertrand Russell: The Spirit of Solitude* (London, 1996).

Russell, Thomas Wallace (1841–1920), radical, maverick Ulster politician, and temperance advocate. Elected Liberal Unionist MP for South Tyrone in 1886, he accepted junior office in Lord Salisbury's government, 1895–1900. Thereafter, he assumed an independent position, campaigning on behalf of, mainly Presbyterian, tenant farmers against Ulster's unionist establishment. By-elections, won by his candidates in East Down and North Fermanagh, helped force the passage of generous land purchase legislation in 1903, but he joined the Liberals in 1904, and in 1907 he again became a junior minister, remaining responsible for agriculture for twelve years under three prime ministers. *DRB*

Rust, William (1903–49), Communist. Bill Rust was born to working-class parents in Camberwell, and his first political attachment was to Labour, but he joined the Communist Party of Great Britain (CPGB) in 1920. His subsequent loyalty to communism never wavered, and moreover he could he relied upon to follow the Moscow line. He served as the first secretary of the Young Communist League and displayed an early interest in housing and unemployment issues. In 1925 he was one of the twelve British Communists charged with sedition and received a one-year prison sentence. In 1928 he travelled to Moscow to the fifth congress of the Communist Youth International and was elected to its executive committee. His links with Moscow continued to strengthen: in 1929, at the tenth enlarged plenum of the Communists International he presented a Moscow initiative and attacked fellow British Communists for their bourgeois outlook. In 1930 he was appointed first editor of the *Daily Worker.* His stage became wider in the course of the 1930s. He worked in Moscow, 1932–4, and served as a commissar in Spain, 1937–8. He resumed the editorship of the *Daily Worker* from 1939, and contested Hackney unsuccessfully in the 1945 general election. This Pickwickian-looking apparatchik with the 'Cox's Pippin cheeks' (*Daily Herald*, 4 February 1949) died suddenly in 1949. *CH*

W. RUST, *Britons in Spain: The Historv of the XVth International Brigade* (London, 1939).

Ryder, Richard Andrew (1949–), Conservative politician and chief whip, 1990–5. Margaret Thatcher's political secretary from her election as Conservative Party leader until 1981, Ryder entered parliament in 1983, rising via the Whips' Office to become paymaster general in 1989. His refusal to join Thatcher's team during the 1990 Conservative leadership election, was a blow she took particularly personally. As chief whip, his tough approach and chairmanship of the 'number twelve committee' on the coordination and presentation of policy, failed to dispel the impression of a divided party. *CL*

S

S4C (Sioned Pedwar Cymru), Welsh television channel. S4C, which operates as the fourth channel on Welsh transmitters, came into existence in 1982 following a bizarre political crisis. Welsh language activists had been pressing for an exclusively Welsh-language channel in a campaign in which many were either fined or imprisoned for refusing to pay for television licences. In 1979 the home secretary, William Whitelaw, reneged on an earlier pledge to establish a Welsh fourth channel and the result was further direct actions and a threatened hunger-strike by Gwynfor *Evans, president of Plaid Cymru. Again the government changed its mind, and S4C came into existence broadcasting Welsh language programmes at peak hours. At first there were many jibes about S4C being the most heavily subsidized television company in the free world, but all the while the channel was helping to sustain a new television and film culture in Wales, not least through the tremendous boost it gave to independent production companies. The great irony was that the subsidy from London and the programmes donated by BBC Wales and HTV were matched by a new entrepreneurial spirit. In 1998 it was awarded a digital strand. *PS*

John Davies, *Broadcasting and the BBC in Wales* (Cardiff, 1994).

Saatchi and Saatchi, advertising agency and political phenomenon. Maurice and Charles Saatchi provided Tories with *'Labour Isn't Working', marking the one million unemployed of 1978–9, so becoming the Thatcher Tories' favourite advertisers, until the struggle between Saatchis and Tim Bell during the 1987 election led to a split between Thatcher and party chairman Tebbit. Their work convinced Labour of the need for advertising men, implemented for Kinnock and Blair by Peter Mandelson. Maurice Saatchi offered Major 1997's 'Demon Eyes' and 'Weeping Lion' ideas, refusing any field testing. This time it proved a public relations disaster, though it is doubtful that any advertising could have helped in 1997. *EP*

safeguarding. Unable to find much economic common ground between its Liberal and Conservative backbench supporters, the post-1918 Lloyd George coalition declined to introduce *protective tariffs on all imported manufactured goods, as tariff-reform Conservatives demanded. Instead it passed in 1920 a Safeguarding Act which allowed tariffs to be imposed to protect 'infant' industries or those whose products were important in wartime but available mostly in Germany. The choice of industries to safeguard was somewhat bizarre, including lace gloves and gas mantles as well as optical glass. The legislation was a source of immense irritation to Liberals and pro-tariff Conservatives alike, until it was subsumed in the Import Duties Act of 1932. *JAT*

'Safety First', Conservative slogan for the 1929 general election. Devised by the advertisers Bensons, approved by Joseph Ball and party chairman Davidson, it was intended as an appeal to the electorate, especially the new female voters, not to gamble with socialism. Unfortunately it characterized instead an uninspiring manifesto and lacklustre campaign by Baldwin. *NJC*

St Audries, Baron. See Acland-Hood, Alexander Fuller.

St John-Stevas, Norman Anthony Francis (1929–), Conservative politician, writer, and constitutional reformer. St John Stevas was MP for Chelmsford from 1964, achieved junior office for education and the arts under Heath, and was briefly 'the blessed Margaret' Thatcher's leader of the House. In the latter capacity he somewhat surprisingly persuaded Thatcher to agree to set up House of *Commons' select committees to scrutinize government, so inventing therapy for despondent backbenchers and new self-esteem for remaindered ministers who chaired them. Earlier, he had been a lawyer and journalist, the scholarly editor of the collected works of Walter Bagehot. *EP*

Norman St John-Stevas, *The Two Cities* (London, 1984).

St Stephen's Chambers, the office address of the Conservative Central Office in Westminster, 1900–22. Often used as a synonym for Central Office itself. *JAR*

Saklatvala, Shapurji (1874–1936), Communist. A Parsee, Saklatvala was born in Bombay. In Britain he joined the Independent Labour Party and in 1920 became involved with the Communist Party of Great Britain. He entered parliament, 1922, as Labour member for Battersea, the third Indian member to sit in the Commons. He lost in 1923 but returned in 1924 to take a leading part (somewhat incongruously) in the rejection of the Church of England's revised Prayer Book in 1927. Saklatvala was often in difficulties with the authorities on account of his political views. *CH*

M. Squires, *Saklatvala* (London, 1993).

Salisbury, 3rd marquess of (1830–1903), Conservative statesman. Robert Cecil entered parliament for a family-controlled constituency in 1853 and from the first showed that he was a conservative in philosophy as well as Conservative by affiliation. Influenced by the Oxford Movement, he championed the Established Church throughout his long career. He believed in the aristocratic principle and the life of service through leadership and was forever sceptical of the growth of democracy. Nonetheless, he married without his father's permission in 1857 and resultantly for a time earned his living as a freelance journalist.

Cecil gained office as India secretary under Derby, 1866–7, predictably refused to support Disraeli's 1867 Reform Bill and resigned. He made his peace with Disraeli, however, and as marquess of Salisbury (after 1868) returned to the India Office, 1874–8, and then the Foreign Office, 1878–80, where he pursued a consistent 'forward' policy against Russian ambitions. After the Liberal interlude (1880–5) ultimately terminated by the Irish home rule controversy, Salisbury became prime minister, combining this with the foreign secretaryship. His quarrel with Lord Randolph Churchill resulted in the resignation and eclipse of the 'Tory democrat' and ensured Salisbury's unchallenged mastery of the party through the *Hotel Cecil until his retirement. His policies again reflected his own beliefs: firm support for the Church, the Irish union, the Empire, and the principle of individual responsibility and freedom. A second Liberal failure over home rule (1892–5) ensured Salisbury a third term as premier (1895–1902). Imperial and foreign policy matters dominated this final phase of his career, culminating in the *Boer war and the *Anglo-Japanese alliance. He retired following the death of Queen Victoria, handing over to his nephew, Arthur Balfour. Salisbury's life remained a monument for traditional Tories (hence the contemporary **Salisbury Review*), but his values had little real place in 20th-century politics. *RJQA*

Lord Blake and Hugh Cecil (eds.), *Salisbury, the Man and his Policies* (London, 1987). | Lady Gwendolyn Cecil, *Life of Robert, Marquess of Salisbury*, 4 vols. (London, 1921–32). | Andrew Roberts, *Salisbury: Victorian Titan* (London, 1999).

Salisbury, 4th marquess of (1861–1947), Conservative politician. Despite indifferent health, 'Jem' Cecil led a long life as soldier, churchman, and, above all, principal leader of the traditional right wing of his party in the Commons, 1885–1903, and then the Lords. He opposed the 1909 'People's Budget', the 1911 Parliament Act, home rule, Welsh Church disestablishment, and other movements which he thought debased British life. He was an indefatigable party warrior and enthusiastically supported Law after the Carlton Club meeting. *RJQA*

Lord David Cecil, *The Cecils of Hatfield House* (London, 1973). | Kenneth Rose, *The Later Cecils* (London, 1975).

Salisbury, 5th marquess of ('Bobbety') (1893–1972), Conservative politician and right-wing traditionalist. Viscount Cranborne (Robert Gascoyne-Cecil's courtesy title before he succeeded as marquess) failed to complete his degree at Oxford because of service in the Great War. Elected MP for South Dorset in 1929, he became *Eden's parliamentary private secretary in 1934, and was appointed to the Foreign Office in 1935.

Unsurprisingly, he resigned with Eden in 1938 and later savaged the Munich agreement. He was appointed paymaster general by Churchill before entering the cabinet in 1940 as dominions secretary. In 1941 he was created Lord Cecil of Essendon and dealt with foreign affairs in the Lords before being made leader of the Lords in 1942. As leader of the opposition in the Lords after 1945, Salisbury (as he became on the death of his father in 1947) fought the reduction of the Lords' delaying power. However, he advocated Lords' reform and formulated the 'Salisbury doctrine', whereby peers do not impede legislation that has been foreshadowed in a government's manifesto. In 1951 Churchill appointed him leader of the Lords and lord privy seal, and in 1952 he became Commonwealth relations secretary and lord president of the council. He supported Eden over Suez. When the queen sought his advice on Eden's successor he consulted the cabinet individually, asking each minister, 'Well, which is it? Wab [Butler] or Hawold [Macmillan]?' Salisbury's resignation in March 1957 over the release from detention of the Cypriot leader Archbishop Makarios failed to provoke any reaction and Macmillan called his bluff. Salisbury led right-wing opposition to *decolonization and in 1961 woundingly attacked Macleod, the colonial secretary, for being 'too clever by half'. Despite championing Africa's whites, Salisbury could not support the Rhodesian *UDI in 1965 because it was unconstitutional. *RJS*

Salisbury Review (1982–), polemical quarterly. The creation of its editor Roger *Scruton, it was run on minimal finance but attracted distinguished contributors like Hayek and Vaclav Havel, being wired into Eastern Europe. The title reflected Scruton's respect for Prime Minister Salisbury and his melancholy maxim 'Delay is life', while Burke was another hero. Its outlook favoured organic traditionalism—being pro-Union, the family, sexual continence, the classical order in art, and contemptuous of Blairism, finding it less custard than chaos. If there is a Zeitgeist the *Salisbury* is against it. *EP*

Salmond, Alexander Elliot Anderson (1954–), Scottish nationalist politician. MP for Banff and Buchan from the 1987 general election, Alex Salmond was leader of the Scottish National Party (SNP), 1990–2000. A former economist with the Royal Bank of Scotland, he did much to modernize the profile of Scottish nationalism. He was a consummate debater and skilled public performer, injected a degree of pragmatism into the SNP, and was instrumental in securing the support of the party in the referendum campaign for the Scottish parliament in 1997. *RF*

SALT (Strategic Arms Limitation Talks/Treaties). These superpower talks on a regime for nuclear weaponry were held from 1969 and continued through the 1970s and 1980s. They gave rise to the Antiballistic Missile Treaty (ABM, also called SALT I, 1972), and the SALT II Treaty (1979, not ratified in the USA). Both the development and the use of nuclear weapons had been under consideration since the 1950s, but only the limited *test-ban treaty (1963), and *non-proliferation treaty (1968) had been agreed in a multilateral context. The first SALT talks covered the questions of defence against nuclear attack, and the second dealt with levels and types of offensive strategic nuclear weapons. These talks took place in the context of superpower détente, and reflected the need for restraint in this field, although progress was slow and discussions very complicated. The SALT process fell into decline in the late 1970s. However, the Strategic Arms Reductions Talks (START) from the mid-1980s successfully addressed the goal of actually reducing the existing levels of nuclear weaponry while the Cold War was drawing to a close. Although remaining a nuclear power, the British played little part in these superpower talks. *ADe*

Salter, (James) Arthur (1881–1975) civil servant, politician, and academic. Entering the civil service in 1904, he transferred in 1911 to the staff responsible for administering the new national insurance scheme. During the Great War he served in the Admiralty with particular responsibility for merchant shipping and his expertise in shipping was utilized again in 1940–5. He then worked for the League of Nations, 1919–30. He was independent MP for Oxford University, 1937–50, and for Ormskirk 1951–3. As minister of economic affairs and an *overlord, he was credited with persuading the 1951 Churchill cabinet to reject floating sterling. *NJC*

Saltire Society, formed in 1936 to preserve and encourage Scottish culture, the society played an important role in the promotion of Scottish history, literature, and the arts. Throughout its history, the organization has stressed its non-political nature. *RF*

Salvidge, Archibald (1863–1928), local Conservative organizer. Salvidge was a brewer and Orangeman who was Tory political boss of Liverpool through his leadership of its Working Men's Conservative Association. Liverpool city alderman from 1898 and generally known as 'Alderman Salvidge', he made Liverpool a byword for effective party organization in the 1900s, and was consulted on organizational and political matters by national politicians as a result. A strong supporter of the Lloyd George coalition government from 1916, he helped to secure Tory acceptance of its Irish policy in 1921, so 'Salvidging Ulster'. A rare American-style political boss in Britain, but his power was largely overthrown by Liverpool's Conservative MPs in the 1920s. *JAR*

Samaritans, volunteer group dedicated to the prevention of suicide, set up in 1953, and deriving its name from the parable of the good Samaritan. The group has been credited with assisting the overall fall in the British suicide rate. Its counsellors man telephone lines to help people in personal crisis. *JS*

sampling, selection of a small body to represent a much larger population. Whereas interviewing or sending questionnaires to a whole population (inhabitants of a city, members of both Houses of Parliament) can be time-consuming and financially expensive, interviewing or sending a questionnaire to a carefully selected proportion of the population can save time and money. The value of sampling has been long recognized, though it was not until the 1930s that the system used to select the sample was recognized as being more important than the size of the sample. In order to ensure that the sample is typical of the whole population, those conducting surveys have to introduce rigorous checks. Selection criteria are devised to ensure that the sample replicates proportionately the whole population in terms, for example, of socio-economic characteristics, family size, marital status, gender, religion, and age. A frequently employed method is the random sample. The most rigorous type of random sampling is to take every *n*th name (the interval depending on the total sample to be generated) that appears in the electoral register. This avoids any bias that may otherwise creep in if one is relying on, for instance, random selection of individuals in the street. Assuming a less than 100 per cent response rate, responses have to be checked to ensure that they are representative of the total population. (Responses may come disproportionately from a particular section of the population, for example those with a university education.) Ensuring a representative sample is important to all polling organizations, especially those engaged on surveying voting intentions. Even a small bias can skew the survey results and hence the prediction of an election's outcome. *PN*

S. Arber, 'Designing Samples', in N. Gilbert (ed.), *Researching Social Life* (London, 1993). | William L. Miller, 'Quantitative Methods', in D. Marsh and G. Stoker (eds.), *Theory and Methods in Political Science* (Basingstoke, 1995).

Samuel, Herbert Louis (1870–1963), Liberal politician and leader of Jewish decent. Educated at Oxford, he entered parliament in 1902, serving in minor posts until 1909 when he became chancellor of the duchy of Lancaster, then postmaster general, 1910. Home secretary in Asquith's coalition cabinet in 1916, he had to deal with the Easter Rising. Samuel resigned when *Lloyd George supplanted Asquith in December 1916, lost his seat in the 1918 *'Coupon' Election, but was then the first high commissioner in Palestine, 1920–5. He headed the royal commission on the coal industry, 1925–6, whose report failed to prevent but formed the basis for ending the *General Strike. Samuel returned to parliament in 1929 and as acting Liberal leader supported the formation of the *National Government in August 1931, taking the post of home secretary, but resigned over the introduction of protection in 1932, leading the Liberal opposition until 1935. He was a committed Liberal whose career was gradually eclipsed by the decline of his party's influence between the wars. Samuel took a peerage in 1937 and led the Liberals in the Lords, 1944–55. *JS*

Viscount Samuel, *Memoirs* (London, 1945).

Samuel commission (1925–6). The royal commission on the coal industry was appointed in September 1925 to forestall the imminent prospect of a general strike, chaired by Sir Herbert *Samuel. The issue at stake—a reduction in miners' wages to enhance competitiveness—was central to the commission's deliberations, as was the future organization of the coal industry. But in recommending wage reductions and colliery amalgamations the commission pleased neither side in the dispute. The government's neutral stance contributed directly to the *General Strike and miners' lockout of 1926. *MWK*

Sandars, John Satterfield ('Jack') (1853–1934), prime minister's private secretary, 1902–5. A former barrister and civil servant, Sandars was Arthur Balfour's confidant throughout 1892–1911. During Balfour's premiership, Sandars dealt with political rather than departmental affairs, playing a vital role as the prime minister's eyes and ears when intrigues surrounding the party's divisions over tariff reform threatened its cohesion. Sandars appeared to exercise considerable influence and once convened a meeting of the shadow cabinet in Balfour's absence abroad. However, this appearance was the deceptive product of a close working relationship. *CL*

Sanders, Robert Arthur ('Peter') (1867–1940), Conservative MP, whip, minister, and diarist. Sanders entered the Commons in 1910, becoming a whip, 1911–14. After war service he was a junior minister and deputy party chairman, working for the overthrow of the Lloyd George coalition. A Harrow contemporary of Baldwin, he entered the Law/Baldwin cabinet of 1922 as minister of agriculture but had great difficulty with questions about food taxes during the 1923 general election. Losing his seat in 1923, he returned to the Commons in 1924 but did not hold office again. *JAR*

John Ramsden (ed.), *Real Old Tory Politics: The Political Diaries of Sir Robert Sanders, Lord Bayford, 1910–1935* (London, 1984).

Sands, Bobby (1954–81), Irish paramilitary. On 1 March 1981 Bobby Sands, the Provisional *IRA leader in the *H-blocks, led a hunger strike aimed at securing political status for republican prisoners. He was serving a fourteen-year prison sentence for firearms offences but was nominated for the Fermanagh and South Tyrone by-election and was (narrowly) elected an MP. On 5 May 1981 Sands, on the 66th day of his fast, was the first of ten hunger strikers to die. *TWH*

Sandys, Duncan Edwin (1908–87), Conservative politician. Elected to parliament in 1935, Sandys opposed *appeasement and supported Churchill, whose daughter Diana became his first wife. After wartime military service, he was a junior minister, 1943–5, but when he lost his seat in 1945 his belief in European unity made him a moving force in the European Movement. Returned to parliament in 1950, he was a moderate on denationalizing iron and steel as supply minister from 1951, but after entering the cabinet in 1954 as housing and local government minister he was more radical on rent decontrol. A tough taskmaster who only reached decisions after poring over every detail, Sandys's biggest impact came as Macmillan's defence minister in 1957 when he announced a strategic transformation by making the nuclear deterrent the basis of national security. As Commonwealth relations secretary from 1960 he clashed with Macleod over African decolonization but was also given the Colonial Office in 1962. He was dissuaded from resigning in 1963 at the height of the *Profumo case, when his name was linked with rumours surrounding the duchess of Argyll's divorce case. Dropped from Heath's shadow cabinet in 1966, the pro-European Sandys argued that tougher immigration control would preserve the British character of Britain. His tax-free payment as Lonrho chairman prompted Heath's attack on the *'unacceptable face of capitalism'. Sandys entered the Lords in 1974. *RJS*

Sandys white paper (1957). This major defence review, published as *Outline of Future Policy,* was conducted by Duncan *Sandys, defence secretary, and incorporated the strategic lessons of the *Suez crisis. Implementing the logic of a 1952 Global Strategy Paper, it argued that Britain could not afford large enough conventional forces to deter the Soviet Union alone and should therefore rely increasingly on allies and *nuclear weapons. Announcing severe cuts in defence expenditure and the end of conscription by 1962, it also predicted the imminent demise of manned military aircraft. *DHD*

San Francisco conference (1945). The 50 states that had declared war against Germany gathered at this venue in April 1945 to set up the *United Nations. They had before them the proposals of the major powers in the victorious alliance: Britain, the Soviet Union, and the USA, but the conference was far from a rubber-stamping exercise. In an unprecedented glare of publicity and popular demands for a vigorous attack on the evils of international life, 1,200 amendments were discussed (a two-thirds majority being necessary for adoption). As a result, the UN charter was in many respects different from what the 'Big Three' had had in mind. The general assembly (a deliberative body in which all members were to be represented) was given a bigger role, being empowered to make recommendations on any matter affecting world peace or the general welfare of nations. The role and status of two limited-membership bodies—the economic and social council and the trusteeship council—were enhanced and a 'declaration regarding non-self-governing territories' was included. But the scheme for the security council, which was to be responsible for the maintenance of international peace and security, was little changed. The major powers (the Big Three, plus China and France) refused to give up their individual rights to veto non-procedural decisions which they did not like. There was strong opposition to this proposal, but the major powers indicated that, if it were to be defeated, they would not join the UN, so the majority backed down. The final draft of the Charter (which was unanimously approved on 26 June) satisfied

Britain, which believed that it offered a realistic, powerful, and flexible scheme for maintaining international peace. The Charter was quickly ratified by the participants, plus Poland, and the UN came into being on 24 October 1945. *LL*

L. M. Goodrich, 'San Francisco in Retrospect', *International Journal*, 25/2 (Spring 1970) | *A Commentary on the Charter of the United Nations* (Cmd 6666, Misc. No. 9, London, 1945).

Sankey, 1st Viscount (1866–1948), lawyer and Labour politician. Sir John Sankey is chiefly remembered as the judge who chaired the commission which in 1919 inquired into the coal industry. The *Sankey commission favoured nationalization of the mines and Sankey was disappointed when Lloyd George's government ignored the report. A Labour supporter thereafter, he was appointed lord chancellor in the second Labour government from 1929, and was one of the few ministers to remain loyal to Ramsay MacDonald in 1931. He therefore remained as lord chancellor in the National Government until 1935. *MC*

Sankey commission (1919). The appointment of the royal (Sankey) commission on the coal industry in February 1919 was a successful attempt on the part of the Lloyd George coalition government to neutralize the miners' strong bargaining position inherited from the war. Equal division of membership between miners and colliery owners' representatives resulted in opposing recommendations on the future organization of the industry, thereby enabling the government to ignore the miners' case for joint control under a regime of public ownership. *MWK*

Saorstat Eireann. See Irish Free State.

Sargent, (Harold) Orme Garton (1884–1962). diplomat who became permanent secretary of the Foreign Office (1946–9). 'Moley' Sargent entered the diplomatic service in 1906, and established his reputation whilst in Paris, 1919–25. Thereafter, he resisted overseas appointments and spent his career at the Foreign Office. An anti-appeaser in the 1930s, Sargent was a proponent of British power. In his famous 'Stocktaking after VE-day' memorandum of July 1945, Sargent saw leadership of western Europe as the only means by which Britain could avoid second class status between the superpowers. *JRVE*

satire, political. Britain's 'satire boom' in the early 1960s signalled an end to the general post-war acceptance of the social order. It was a precursor, too, of more fundamental challenges proliferating at the end of the decade, and was led by young men (mainly), the products often of Oxbridge and public schools, and with only childhood memories of the war. The boom began with *Beyond the Fringe* (1960), a revue which launched the careers of Peter Cook, Dudley Moore, Alan Bennett, and Jonathan Miller. On television it started with **That Was the Week That Was* (1962), a weekly revue compèred by the unknown David Frost, who also worked at Cook's fashionable night club, 'The Establishment'. In print, Oxbridge graduates led by Richard Ingrams and Christopher Booker founded **Private Eye* (1962). Common to all these was a sharp, irreverent humour. Its roots were in the educated middle class more than in the showbiz, music-hall tradition which produced radio hits such as *ITMA*, *Take It From Here*, and *The Goon Show*. Its targets were broadly social: the allegedly outmoded, hypocritical, and inefficient institutions which entrenched Britain's class system and remained influential, despite Attlee's post-war Labour government. But the critique was political in the sense that, unlike an Ealing Studios movie or a Noel Coward comedy, it had a critical, reformist intent. It broke taboos by ridiculing actual public figures, including cabinet ministers, wartime heroes, and the royal family. Its humour distinguished it from the plays of 'angry young men' such as John Osborne and later authors such as Dennis Potter. The satirists were rebellious not revolutionary, fired neither by Marxism nor by any other vision originating in ideology, halucinogens, or the Vietnam war. Their influence especially on TV comedy, from *Monty Python* to the stand-up comedians of the 1980s and 1990s, was arguably immense. *CKSU*

Humphrey Carpenter, *That Was Satire That Was* (London, 2000).

Scanlon, Hugh Parr (1913–), trade unionist. Scanlon was the left-wing president of the Amalgamated Union of Engineering Workers (AEU), 1968–78. He was AEU divisional organizer for Manchester, 1947–63, and served on the AEU executive council, 1963–7. Scanlon was on the TUC general council, 1968–78, and was a leading figure in the campaigns that forced Wilson and Heath to back down over trade union legislation. With Jack Jones he was instrumental in healing the rift with Labour created by *In Place of Strife*. *DLM*

Scargill, Arthur (1938–), trade unionist. Scargill started work at Woolley colliery in 1953 and was elected to the Woolley branch committee of the NUM in 1964. An active member of the Young Communist League, 1955–62, he joined the Cooperative Party in 1963 before becoming a member of the Labour Party in 1966. He pioneered the tactic of *flying pickets that helped to bring victory in the miners' strike in 1972. This strike catapulted him onto the national stage, and his elevation to the NUM national executive in September 1972 was followed shortly by his election as president of the Yorkshire NUM. Following his election as NUM president in 1982, it was not long before the miners found themselves in a head-on collision with the Thatcher government: the miners' strike of 1984–5 which was the longest national strike in 20th-century Britain. Scargill served twice on the TUC general council, 1980–3 and 1986–8, and from September 1985 has been president of the International Miners' Organization. In January 1996 he set up the Socialist Labour Party (SLP) in response to the Labour Party's abandonment of *Clause 4. He has stood unsuccessfully for parliament in his capacity as SLP president, and remains a controversial miners' leader, demonized by the tabloid media and hounded by allegations of financial irregularities. Despite the failure of his syndicalist approach, Scargill's espousal of militant trade unionism won him a place in labour-movement mythology as an uncompromising opponent of capitalism and state authority. *DLM*

Michael Crick, *Scargill and the Miners* (London, 1984). | Paul Routledge, *Scargill: The Unauthorised Biography* (London, 1993).

Scarman, Leslie George (1911–), judge and public servant. After a career at the Bar, Scarman was a High Court judge, 1961–73; lord justice of appeal, 1973–7; and lord of appeal in ordinary, 1977–86. He also pursued a public career as the first chairman of the Law Commission, 1965–73, and of the Council for Legal Education, 1973–6, and served on the Arts Council for three years. His reputation for fair-minded forthrightness ensured that he was regularly used to chair public inquiries, including those into the Brixton riots of 1981, and he was a keen advocate of the need for a *bill of rights. *JAR*

Scarman report (1981), produced by Lord *Scarman, blamed social problems for the Brixton riots of that year. However, it felt policing practices had allowed minor incidents to trigger rioting. The report recommended changes in police training and greater contact with local communities. Whilst the committee sat, the 'sus' laws (stopping and searching on suspicion alone), blamed for much of the tension, were scrapped and water-cannon, CS gas, and plastic bullets were made available to mainland police. The report led to new procedures following the *Police and Criminal Evidence Act (PACE). *KMT*

Scarman tribunal (1969), inquiry into the outbreak of communal violence in Northern Ireland. The tribunal concluded there was no IRA conspiracy behind the Catholic-led civil rights movement, but that rioters were manipulated by opponents of the Unionist Northern Ireland government. It praised the Royal Ulster Constabulary's courage but found the police at fault on six occasions. The tribunal criticized Ian Paisley who, while not implicated in the violence, had inflamed the situation by his speeches. *TWH*

Scholar, Michael Charles (1942–), civil servant. Scholar held academic posts and was a philosophy lecturer at Leicester University before joining the Treasury in 1969. He was a private secretary to the Treasury's chief secretary (1974–7) and to the prime minister (1981–3). A Treasury deputy secretary, 1987–93, he was then permanent secretary at the Welsh Office, 1993–6, switching to become permanent secretary at the Department of Trade and Industry in 1996. *KT*

school-leaving age. The Education Act of 1880 made school attendance compulsory up to the age of 10, but the minimum age for ending full-time education was raised to 11 in 1893, 12 in 1899, and to 14 in 1918, though children who had reached a certain educational standard were allowed to work in factories half-time and to go to school for the rest of the day. The half-time system was abolished in Fisher's *Education Act, 1918. Raising the school-leaving age remained an objective of progressive educationalists but was always delayed by the inter-war depression and constraints on public finance. The leaving age was finally raised to 15 in 1944 and, again after further delay due to economic circumstances, to 16 in 1972. *JS*

school meals. In 1906 local authorities were permitted to provide school meals, initially concentrated in the poorest areas and only implemented by those with sympathetic, usually Labour, local councils. By 1939, half of education authorities provided school meals but provision was greatly extended during the Second World War to ensure adequate nutrition to young children and to facilitate women taking on war work. The school meals service continued after the war and by 1970 two-thirds of English and just under a half of Scottish children were taking school meals, many of them free. The proportion fell as the price of meals was raised from 1971, and in 1980 local education authorities were given greater discretion to plan and provide school meals, leading many to abandon them altogether. *JS*

school medical service, inaugurated in 1906 as part of the campaign against *national deterioration and to promote better health amongst schoolchildren. The service was maintained throughout the 20th century and up to the present day as a means of monitoring children's health. *JS*

school milk. The provision of *school meals was supplemented from 1934 when local authorities were permitted to provide a third of a pint of milk to schoolchildren at cost or free to poorer children. In 1946 free milk was provided for all children, but was ended in secondary schools in 1968 and for children over 7 in 1971 (earning Margaret Thatcher the epithet: 'Thatcher, milk snatcher'). The provision of free or subsidized milk played a significant part in improving the nutrition of schoolchildren, especially amongst the poor, and was supported by those concerned about the extent of child poverty before and after the Second World War. The importance of milk as a nutritional supplement was increasingly questioned with the rise of affluence in the post-war period. *JS*

Science and Technology, Office of (OST), created in 1992, an amalgamation of the science secretariat of the Cabinet Office, the science branch of the Department of Education and Science, and a group called the Advisory Council for Science and Technology. The fledgling OST was made part of the Cabinet Office but in 1995 was transferred to the Department of Trade and Industry. *JD*

Office of Science and Technology website: *www2.dti.gov.uk/ost/*

Scotland Act, 1979. Labour achieved power in 1974, committed to introducing devolved government in Scotland and Wales, but was unable to get its initial Scotland and Wales Bill through the Commons, where it met heavy backbench opposition from Labour MPs. The Scotland Bill was published in November 1976, designed to improve the government of Scotland by creating a directly elected assembly which would assume responsibility for the functions of the Scottish Office. The decision of the Callaghan government to implement the bill was not founded on a desire for improved government efficiency, however; rather, it was a political measure designed to halt the rise of the Scottish National Party (SNP). Given that the SNP had improved its position in both the general elections of 1974 and that opinion polls thereafter showed that nationalist support was catching up Labour, the primary focus of Labour Party strategy in Scotland was to find some way to diffuse SNP support. An elected assembly, it was argued, would give the Scots a greater role in their government but would not lead to separation from the United Kingdom, which was something that most Scots did not want. It was believed that most Scots wanted some form of devolution and were using the SNP as a means to achieve this. By giving the Scots what they wanted, but stopping short of independence, it was believed that the nationalist threat would subside. This pragmatic solution, however, encountered great hostility from devo-sceptics in the Scottish Labour Party who argued that, far from diminishing the nationalist threat, an assembly would act as a staging post to separation and make the nationalists' task easier. The party hierarchy had to coerce an unwilling Scottish section to accept the policy, although even then not without considerable protest. Devolution was one of the many crises faced by the minority Callaghan government which found it difficult to steer the legislation through the Commons. Almost immediately, the government was forced to concede that its bill would not become law unless endorsed by a referendum. Furthermore, it failed to impose a guillotine motion which left the bill vulnerable to various amendments. In January 1978 the 'Cunningham amendment' (proposed by George Cunningham, a Labour MP sitting for a London seat, though himself a Scot) was passed, stipulating that if less than 40 per cent of the electorate voted for the assembly, then the Act should be repealed. When the referendum came in early 1979, the 'Yes' campaign was hopelessly divided, with Labour and SNP supporting the bill for contradictory purposes. The 'No' campaign on the other hand, was well funded, tightly organized, and united. On 1 March the referendum was held: 51.6 per cent voted 'Yes', while 48.4 per cent voted 'No'. However, of the total electorate, only 32.9 per cent voted 'Yes' and the result fell short of the threshold imposed by the 'Cunningham amendment', so the Act fell. After 1997, the Blair government made sure to have the referendum before an equivalent bill was passed. *RF*

Richard Finlay, *A Partnership for Good* (Edinburgh, 1996). | James Mitchell, *Strategies for Self-Government* (Edinburgh, 1996).

Scotsman. Based in Edinburgh and serving as the quality daily for the eastern Lowlands, the

Scotsman was staunchly Unionist for most of the 20th century. In the late 1960s, under the ownership of Lord Thomson, the paper became more supportive of devolution, as reflected in its endorsement for the Scottish National Party (SNP) and Liberal Party in the 1970s, although by the late 1990s, while still officially supporting home rule, space was found in its columns for its Unionist critics. *RF*

Scott, Charles Prestwich (1846–1932), Liberal newspaperman. Scott was Liberal MP for Leigh, 1895–1905, which provided him with good contacts within parliamentary Liberalism, but was far more significant as editor for 57 years (1872–1929), and owner from 1905, of the *Manchester Guardian*. Under his editorship it developed into the leading quality Liberal paper, though never having more than a fraction of the readership of either the *Daily News* or the *Daily Chronicle*. Scott was a strong supporter of the Liberal–Labour alliance in Edwardian politics (which he sought unavailingly to get renewed after 1918) and a more qualified supporter of Lloyd George as prime minister. His diaries, kept as an aid to the writing of editorials, have proved an invaluable source to scholars. *JAR*

J. L. Hammond, *C. P. Scott of the Manchester Guardian* (London, 1934). | Trevor Wilson (ed.), *The Political Diaries of C. P. Scott, 1911–1928* (London, 1976).

Scott, Richard Rashleigh Folliot (1943–), judge, vice-chancellor of the Supreme Court from 1994. A South African-born lawyer (QC, 1975), who acquired a reputation as an independent-thinking, hunting, bicycling judge, Scott was brought to wider public attention by John Major's request that he investigate the arms-to-Iraq affair in 1992. His report in 1996 was an unwieldy, poorly written document which nonetheless caused great political inconvenience to the government, not least in a Commons debate in which it prevailed by a single vote. The only serious change to flow from Scott's report so far is the accountability resolution adopted by the House of Commons shortly before the demise of the 1992–7 parliament, which sharpened and clarified ministerial responsibilities to parliament. *PJH*

Scott, Robert Heatlie (1905–82), diplomat and home civil servant. Scott started his official career in the consular service in the Far East, serving in Japan, China, and Hong Kong. On the fall of Singapore, he was captured and imprisoned by the Japanese. After the war, he served as Foreign Office under-secretary of state responsible for Far Eastern affairs; in the Washington embassy; and as commissioner-general for the UK in south-east Asia. He was permanent secretary of the Ministry of Defence, 1961–3. *KT*

Scott affair, political scandal in the *Liberal Party, occasioned by Norman Scott's allegations of a homosexual affair with Jeremy *Thorpe and the mysterious death of a dog called Rinka. The affair forced Thorpe's resignation and unsuccessful prosecution, and, after an 'interregnum' leadership by Jo *Grimond and David *Steel, the election of Steel as party leader. *JS*

Scottish community councils, designed to ascertain, coordinate, and express the views of small communities to the various bodies of local government. Although Scottish district councils were obliged to set up a community council in an area where more than twenty electors requested one, these groups were dependent on local volunteers and participation and usually confined themselves to matters of specific local interest. By 1983, there were 1,131 community councils covering 80 per cent of the population. *RF*

A. Midwinter, M. Keating, and J. Mitchell, *Politics and Public Policy in Scotland* (Basingstoke, 1991).

Scottish Conservative and Unionist Party. During the long Liberal ascendancy in Scotland during the 19th century, the Conservatives remained very weak. The home rule crisis of 1886 and the alliance with the *Liberal Unionists, however, gave them powerful reinforcement. In 1912 the two merged into the Scottish Unionist Party, the name indicating the balance of influence. In the first half of the 20th century, the Unionists were an alliance of rural Conservatives, often local notables and landowners, and urban Unionist populists, mobilizing a Protestant working-class vote as well as that of the middle classes. Their high point came in 1955 when they won 50.1 per cent of the Scottish vote and 36 of the 71 Scottish seats. Since then they have been in almost continuous decline. Urban populism proved ever less effective, its last great exponent, Teddy Taylor, losing his Glasgow seat in 1979. The decline of Scottish-owned industry undercut the domestic bourgeoisie which provided an important element of support. Conservative MPs were increasingly upper-class landowners or ex-military officers, and highly Anglicized.

The Unionists had never contested local elections, leaving these to local anti-socialist coalitions variously described as moderates, progressives, or independents. In 1965, party organization was reformed: the name was changed to the Scottish Conservative and Unionist Party and right-wing local councillors told that they must join the party or face competition. The decline of Scottish-owned industry, however, caused financial problems and prevented an autonomous party emerging and so in the late 1970s, following the Fairgreave report, most of the party organization was merged with its English counterpart. A Scottish president and chairman remained as figures of some importance, appointed by the party leader. In 1974 the Conservatives lost seven rural seats to the Scottish National Party and, although they recovered these in 1979, they suffered further reverses in the 1980s, so that by 1987 the party had difficulty finding enough ministers to fill the posts in the Scottish Office. In 1997, they lost all their remaining parliamentary seats in Scotland and won back only one in 2001. While they had enjoyed considerable success in local government in the 1960s and 1970s, by the mid-1990s they controlled no local councils.

The Scottish Tories were long defined by support for the union with Ireland and then Northern Ireland, which had helped to win Protestant votes in Scotland, but they had also been opposed to Scottish nationalism. There was a rather weak Tory home rule tradition and in the 1940s the Unionists sought to use Scottish nationalism tactically against the Labour Party. In 1970, Edward Heath announced his support for a Scottish assembly but the policy was unpopular with the party rank and file in Scotland and was dropped by Margaret Thatcher in 1976. The party thereafter opposed legislative devolution, while continuing to build up the Scottish Office in the 1980s and 1990s. These years also saw efforts to revive the Scottish business community and the Conservatives' place in it, with the Conservative business group. Following the 1997 election rout, there were proposals for a new party, more Scottish in image, more independent of London, and with a new name, perhaps on the lines of the Bavarian Christian Social Union, but these came to naught. *MJK*

G. Warner, *The Scottish Tory Party: A History* (London, 1990).

Scottish Convention. See Scottish home rule conventions.

Scottish covenant. see Scottish home rule conventions.

Scottish economic conference. See Catto committee.

Scottish education. Established in 1872, the Scotch (rechristened Scottish in 1918) Education Department (SED) has had responsibility for the implementation of government education policy. The Education Act of 1918 brought most schools (including Catholic) within the state apparatus. Funded by local authorities, schools in Scotland were subject to SED regulation and policy. The 1945 Act (following Butler's *Education Act, 1944, for England and Wales) did not have much impact on Scotland as it merely formalized the system of free secondary education which had largely been achieved in 1918, mainly because the state sector of education in Scotland had a longer tradition. From 1965, selection was gradually abolished, with Scotland having a fully comprehensive state system by the late 1970s. The expansion of university education was another feature of the 1960s: new universities were established in Dundee, Strathclyde (Glasgow), Heriot Watt (Edinburgh), and Stirling, all of which adhered to the traditional Scottish four-year honours system. *RF*

Scottish Enterprise, established under the Enterprise and New Towns (Scotland) Act, 1990, was formed from the amalgamation of the former Scottish Development Agency and the (Scottish) Training Agency. The new integrated economic development agency began operating in 1991. It demonstrated substantial changes from the work of the training agency integrated into economic development and the delivery of services facilitated by local enterprise companies. *JD*

Scottish Enterprise website: *www.scottish-enterprise.com*

Scottish government, royal commission on (1954) ('the Balfour commission'). Appointed in 1952 and chaired by Lord Balfour, the commission was given the task of examining and reporting on the development of government agencies in Scotland as a result of the expansion of state services provided by the welfare state. A key factor in the Conservative government's decision was the desire to appease nationalist and home rule sentiment which had emerged in the late 1940s as a result of the Scottish Convention. Furthermore, Conservative election manifestos in Scotland had denounced Labour's policy of nationalization as 'socialist centralization'. The existing functions of the Scottish Office expanded after 1945, especially in the areas of health, housing, education, and economic development. The report recommended that, wherever practical, the Scottish Office should handle Scottish matters and be given the extra functions of transport and energy administration. To cope with these new duties, the Scottish Office was given three new ministers, and three new parliamentary committees were established to augment the work of the Scottish Grand Committee in scrutinizing Scottish legislation. The Balfour report provided the template for the expansion of the Scottish Office and the role of government in Scottish economic and social development in the post-war era. *RF*

Royal Commission Report on Scottish Affairs (Cmnd 9212, London, 1954). | T. M. Devine and R. J. Finlay (eds.), *Scotland in the Twentieth Century* (Edinburgh, 1996).

Scottish Grand Committee. See Commons, House of: Scottish Grand Committee.

Scottish Home Rule Association (SHRA), the first Scottish home rule group, set up in 1886, following Gladstone's initiative on home rule for Ireland. It was supported by radical Liberals, socialists, labour leaders, and Highland land reformers, and inspired a series of parliamentary bills before the Great War. The Liberals, however, gave priority to Ireland and the SHRA was unable to get more than token expressions of support from the parties of the left. In 1918, a second Scottish Home Rule Association was founded by Roland Muirhead, with Independent Labour Party, Cooperative, trade union, and Liberal support. The Labour Party regarded it with suspicion, although prominent Labour people were active. A rally on Glasgow Green in 1923 attracted a reported 35,000 people, including ten Labour MPs, and its activities culminated in 1924 with the Scottish National Convention, supported by many local authorities, a precursor of initiatives in the 1940s and the 1980s. Following disappointment with the lack of support from the Labour Party leadership and the failure of James Barr's Home Rule Bill in 1927, the SHRA declined. In 1928 Muirhead finally broke with Labour by contesting the West Renfrewshire by-election as an independent nationalist. The nationalists in the SHRA went on to found the National Party of Scotland, itself the forerunner of the Scottish National Party (SNP). *MJK*

Scottish home rule conventions (1924, 1942, 1948, 1988). The driving force behind the establishment of home rule conventions was the notion that if a body representing Scottish popular opinion could be brought into existence, then it could demand on behalf of the Scottish people the creation of a parliament in Edinburgh. The creation of the first such Scottish National Convention (SNC) in 1924 was driven by the desire to establish a non-party forum which would unite different shades of political opinion in favour of Scottish home rule. It was believed that the best way to achieve a Scottish parliament would be to show that there was popular support for it and that a convention would demonstrate this, but without challenging the authority of existing political parties. Having demonstrated that home rule did have considerable support, it was expected that the established parties would then act on this, but the SNC failed to mobilize popular support. It contained within its ranks members of both the Liberal and Labour parties who, while committed to the establishment of a Scottish parliament, were not prepared to promote devolution if it was perceived to go against their party's best interests. By 1927, the convention was gripped by inertia, as Labour loyalists vetoed attempts by nationalists to promote a more vigorous policy. In 1928, the convention collapsed when nationalists decided to form their own political party, the National Party of Scotland (NPS).

The failure of the NPS and its successor, the Scottish National Party (SNP), to make any electoral inroads led some in the late 1930s to canvas the creation of a cross-party convention. The seemingly futile efforts to demonstrate the appeal of a Scottish parliament through contesting elections, led John MacCormick to propose that the most economical way to demonstrate the popularity of home rule was to use the method of a convention which would represent a consensus of Scottish opinion, but plans to call a convention in 1939 were shelved because of the war.

An upsurge of fundamentalism in the SNP in 1942 led to the resignation of MacCormick from the party and the creation of the Scottish Convention. Although Labour blew hot and cold on the idea of a Scottish parliament during the war, it was soon apparent that the Attlee government had no intention of pursuing a policy of devolution. In an endeavour to demonstrate the popularity of the home rule cause and bring pressure to bear on the government, MacCormick launched the Scottish Covenant in October 1949, which would eventually collect two million signatures in favour of a Scottish parliament. Impressive as this might seem, the Scottish secretary, Hector McNeil, simply challenged the convention to demonstrate the popularity of home rule by contesting elections. The absence of an electoral mandate effectively discredited the convention and left the SNP as the sole carriers of the nationalist flag.

The Constitutional Convention of 1988 was formed as a result of the persistent refusal of the Thatcher government to accept that there was a case for devolution. The fact that Conservative support was declining north of the border and that the opposition parties, which were all committed to some form of constitutional change, had secured a majority of electoral support, was further grist to their mill. Their position was outlined in *The Claim of Right* (1988), which was endorsed by the Labour and Liberal Democrat parties, the Scottish churches, the convention of Scottish local authorities, and the Scottish Trade Union Congress. *The Claim of Right* was the template for the Labour government's Scotland Act of 1998. *RF*

J. Mitchell, *Strategies for Self-Government: The Campaign for a Scottish Parliament* (Edinburgh, 1996).

Scottish Labour Party. The first Scottish Labour Party was founded by Keir Hardie in 1888 as a party for working people, with a home rule commitment. In 1900, the Scottish Workers' Representation Committee was formed, in uneasy partnership with the London-based Labour Representation Committee but gradually ceded ground to the latter. Labour representation continued to be weak in Scotland and in 1915 the Scottish Advisory Council of the Labour Party was founded, clearly subordinate to London. Since the main basis for Labour constituency organization in Scotland was the Independent Labour Party (ILP), it suffered a serious blow when the ILP disaffiliated in 1932. Organization was slowly rebuilt but through the 1940s Labour was weaker in Scotland than in England. During the entire period of Conservative government, 1951–64, only one Scottish MP was elected to the shadow cabinet. Scottish Labour conferences attracted little attention and Scottish Labour MPs were predominantly locally oriented former councillors. In the large cities, machine politics emerged, based on the distribution of jobs and housing.

Labour in Scotland has been in favour of home rule for almost its whole existence, but after the Great War the issue languished and neither the MacDonald nor the Attlee governments were prepared to move on the issue, and in 1958 the Scottish Council of the Labour Party officially disowned the policy. In the 1960s, despite Labour's electoral advance in Scotland and a series of policy initiatives, party organization was increasingly moribund and ill-equipped to face a growing challenge from the Scottish National Party (SNP). Support for a reversion to home rule had been growing slowly for some years when the London leadership, apprehensive at the SNP success in the February 1974 election, effectively forced the hand of the Scottish party. Devolution remained a divisive issue until the fall of the Labour government in 1979, provoking a breakaway in 1976 of Jim Sillars' short-lived 'Scottish Labour Party'. Despite the Labour government's plans for devolution, Labour headquarters never accepted that its Scottish wing should make policy independently. In the 1980s, the devolution commitment strengthened, Scotland became an important base of support for Labour, and Scottish MPs rose to prominence in the shadow cabinet. After the 1987 election, Labour entered the Scottish Constitutional Convention with the Liberal Democrats, laying the basis for a Scottish parliament. In a reversion to historical form, Scottish Labour was now pressing for home rule and tensions with London resurfaced in 1996 when Tony Blair imposed a referendum requirement. In the mid-1990s the Scottish Council officially became the Scottish Labour Party (in 1997 'Scottish New Labour') but Labour Party headquarters in London continued to exercise a close control over policy and candidate selection. A number of prominent figures suspected of being too nationalist or too left-wing were kept off the candidates' list for the first Scottish parliament election. Conflicts between 'old' and 'new' Labour have been acute and the leadership in the 1990s appeared determined to root out the vestiges of the old urban machine politics. *MJK*

Scottish law. A major difficulty in legislating for the United Kingdom in the 20th century has been the fact that Scotland has a different system of law, based on the European system of Roman law in which cases are determined from principles, rather than the English common law which is based on precedent. The chief officer of law in Scotland, the lord advocate, is a political appointment and a member of the government. The fact that Scotland has a separate legal system means that legislation passed at Westminster for the United Kingdom must be adapted to fit the peculiarities of Scottish law. Much of the responsibility for this is handed to the Scottish Grand Committee of the Commons which has the remit of scrutinizing proposed Scottish legislation. A consequence of this is that all major British Acts of Parliament usually have to have separate Scottish Acts which are normally given the same name as the British Act but with Scotland added in brackets afterwards; as, for example, the Education Act (Scotland), 1918. *RF*

Scottish Liberal Federation. The Liberals were the dominant party in Scotland for much of the 19th century, but suffered badly with the defection of the Liberal Unionists after 1886. They regained their commanding position between 1906 and 1922 but declined with the renewed splits after the Great War. During the 1950s, their sole MP was Jo Grimond. In the 1960s and again in the 1980s they revived in the Borders, the Highlands, and the north-east, at the expense of the Conservatives, these all being areas where personal standing is important. The Scottish Liberals and their successors, uniquely in the UK, also benefited from the electoral system: in 1997, the Liberal Democrats gained the second largest number of seats, despite coming fourth in the popular vote. Apart from the case of Greenock, relationships between the Liberals and Social Democrats were free of the tensions found in England and the merger of the parties was quite easy. The Scottish Liberal Democrats are now a separate party, with a federal relationship with their counterparts in England and Wales and the Federal (British) Party itself. Liberals have always supported Scottish home rule and from the late 1980s cooperated with the Labour Party in the Scottish Constitutional Convention. *MJK*

Scottish local government. Local government in Scotland, because of the survival of a separate civic society, developed in different ways from its English counterpart. After reform in 1929, there were four all-purpose authorities which dealt with the cities of Aberdeen, Edinburgh, Glasgow, and Dundee; 21 large burghs; 176 small burghs; and 33 county councils. With the exception of the cities, which had the power to deal with all aspects of local government, functions were divided between the county council and the burghs, with the latter responsible for education and valuation and the former responsible for services like housing, sanitation, licensing, and street cleaning, although there was a mixture of responsibilities between the small burghs and the counties. In addition to this, there were some minor powers delegated to the 196 district councils. Local authorities combined to make up separate boards for police, fire, and water services. It was in an endeavour to streamline and rationalize the functions of local government that the Wheatley reform was implemented in 1975. This proposed a two-tier system, with nine large regions taking responsibility for services such as police, social work, and education, and 53 smaller districts which would administer housing, building regulation, and licensing. The Wheatley recommendations were subject to a number of amendments, largely designed to appeal to various interest groups in the Highlands and Islands. This division lasted until 1997 when local government was again reorganized into a single-tier system of 33 councils. *RF*

James Kellas, *The Scottish Political System* (Cambridge, 1986).

Scottish National Party (SNP), organization formed in 1934 as a result of a merger between the National Party of Scotland (NPS) and the Scottish Party (SP). The former was more left wing and the latter was decidedly right wing. The impetus for the formation was the belief among moderates in the NPS that there was a section of republicans and extremists in their own party which was bringing the movement into disrepute. It was believed that a Scottish parliament could only be attained once 'moderate' opinion was won over. The Scottish Party contained a number of former Liberals and Tories, which seemed to suggest that the organization was of a more respectable hue and would be more appealing to the electorate. The merger was basically a trade-off in which the NPS would provide the members and organization, while the SP would provide the figureheads and respectability. The SNP, however, was fraught with divisions, more or less from its inception. The party contained elements from both the right and left, those who were committed to independence, those who wanted devolution, those who wanted to contest elections and establish a fully functioning political party, and those who believed that the organization was primarily a pressure group. Throughout the 1930s, the SNP was divided between rival factions which each sought to establish its preferred political objective (independence or devolution) and strategy (contesting elections or pressure group campaigning) as party policy. Given such divisions, it should come as no surprise that the party was not able to contest more than a handful of seats and usually struggled to take more than 10 per cent of the votes in such contests. Furthermore, a collapse of party discipline in the mid-1930s meant that each section of the organization was more or less free to pursue its own agenda. On the eve of the Second World War, the party was simultaneously pursuing policies of promoting a cross-party convention, advocating an anti-conscription policy, and selective intervention in by-elections.

Although the SNP was to achieve a good result in the Argyll by-election of 1940, this was due to the lack of an official opposition candidate as a result of the wartime by-election truce between the main parties and popular resentment against the National Government which the nationalist candidate was able to monopolize. By 1942, however, years of bickering, declining membership, confused policies, an appalling and humiliating by-election performance in Glasgow, Cathcart, and an out-of-touch leadership led to a split at the party's annual conference. The moderate leadership was ousted and replaced by a more radical element which made contesting elections to secure a popular mandate for independence the cornerstone of SNP policy. Despite improvements during the war when the party won the Motherwell by-election in April 1945, only to lose the seat at the general election a month later, the SNP faced an uphill struggle in the 1940s and 1950s. The appearance of the Scottish Convention movement (see SCOTTISH HOME RULE CONVENTIONS) in the late 1940s, which organized a massive petition in favour of home rule, detracted attention away from the SNP. Furthermore, and more injurious to the SNP, this period saw the beginning of extensive government intervention in the Scottish economy and social infrastructure. With full employment, rising living standards, and memories of the hungry 1930s close at hand, few took the SNP's call for independence seriously. Most Scots associated social and economic well-being with Britain.

The electoral breakthrough of the mid-1960s was thus largely determined by economic failings, although an influx of new and gifted members meant that the SNP was organizationally in better shape than Labour, which had ossified into local government fiefdoms. Improvements in the numbers of seats contested in the general elections of 1964 and 1966, and good results in the Pollok by-election in March and the local elections of May 1967, showed that the SNP was growing in strength. Devaluation of the pound, rising unemployment, and a perception that Scotland was trailing the rest of the UK in standards of living, combined with Labour complacency, gave the nationalists electoral victory at the *Hamilton by-election in November 1967. The resultant publicity and continued economic problems meant that the nationalists were able to pocket 30 per cent of the vote in local elections in 1968. Although by 1969 the bubble had apparently burst, by the early 1970s the party seemed again on the way up. In November 1973, the party won the Glasgow *Govan by-election and in the first general election of 1974 was able to contest all but one of the Scottish seats, winning 21 per cent of the vote and nine seats. The new Labour government's continuing economic problems meant that the party was able to boost its share of the vote to 30 per cent and increase its seats to eleven in the second general election. However, although the SNP was committed to independence, not all who voted for the party believed this. Opinion poll evidence from the time showed that those in favour of severing ties with the United Kingdom were only about 12 per cent, which tends to suggest that the majority of nationalist voters were using the party as a means of protest against London government. The fact that the issue of devolution was so divisive, as evidenced by the 1979 referendum result which showed that those for or against or indifferent commanded almost equal numbers, and the fact that the SNP lost over a third of its vote in the general election of 1979, demonstrated that the party's support was very soft indeed.

The failure of devolution and electoral collapse in 1979 launched the party into a period of introspective infighting with traditionalists fending off left-wing encroachments. The effect of this was to damage the party's electoral credibility and at the 1983 election the nationalist share of the vote dropped to 11 per cent and the party lost 53 deposits. Improvements in the 1987 election, when the party gained three seats but lost two to Labour were due more to anti-Tory tactical voting. The victory at another by-election in 1988 at Glasgow *Govan and the party's stand against the poll tax, together with Labour's seeming impotence to win a British general election, did help to boost nationalist credibility in the late 1980s, although the party was unable to improve its performance in the 1992 general election. Under the leadership of Alex Salmond, the SNP moved to promote a 'positive case' for independence which sought to highlight the nation's good economic performance. Although the party's share of the vote moved up slightly in the 1997 general election, the first-past-the-post system kept its number of MPs down to five. Proportional representation in the Scottish parliament, however, ensured that the SNP became the principal opposition party in Scotland. *RF*

R. J. FINLAY, *Independent and Free: Scottish Politics and the Origins of the SNP* (Edinburgh, 1994). | J. MITCHELL, *Strategies for Self-Government: The Campaign for a Scottish Parliament* (Edinburgh, 1996).

Scottish Office. Prior to the opening of the Scottish parliament in 1999, the Scottish Office, located in both London and Edinburgh, handled virtually all policy areas affecting Scotland apart from foreign affairs, defence, and fiscal matters. With the 1997 referendums, the 1998 Scotland Act, and the eventual establishment of the parliament, the Scottish Office lost most of its duties. The UK parliament reserved some powers, though, with defence and foreign policy, economic and monetary policy, social security, some trade and industry functions, employment, consumer protection, broadcasting, abortion, energy, and the constitution continuing to reside in London. *JD*

PETER HENNESSY, *Whitehall* (London, 1989).

Scottish referenda on devolution (1979 and 1997). The referendum on a Scottish assembly in March 1979 was subject to a clause which stipulated that at least 40 per cent of the Scottish electorate had to vote in favour in order to implement the Scotland Act and bring an assembly into existence. The campaign between the 'Yes' and 'No' protagonists was very bitter. From its inception the 'Yes' campaign was racked with division. The SNP half-heartedly gave its support on the pretext that devolution would lead to independence, while Labour proponents, who had to tackle virulent anti-devolutionists within their own ranks, argued that an assembly would stave off demands for separation. Badly organized, divided, poorly funded, and politically incoherent, the 'Yes' campaign was not a particularly appealing advert for the virtues of Scottish self-government. The 'No' campaign, on the other hand, was united in its opposition to the scheme, well funded by business, and adept at exploiting the divisions within the 'Yes' camp. The referendum took place on 1 March, after the 'winter of discontent', when the Labour government was unpopular and whose sponsorship of the scheme was unlikely to garner extra support. In the event, 51.6 per cent voted Yes and 48.4 per cent No, revealing that Scots were almost evenly divided on the issue. The fact that a third of the electorate did not vote, as well as demonstrating considerable apathy, meant that the 'Yes' campaign came nowhere near the necessary 40 per cent endorsement. The campaign in 1997 on the other hand was conducted in the immediate aftermath of the return of a popular Labour government. With the SNP, Labour, and the Liberal Democrats forming a united coalition in the 'Yes' campaign, which was largely free from party-political infighting, it was left to the electorally unpopular Conservatives to carry the 'No' mantle alone. The results on 11 September showed 74.3 per cent voting Yes, with 63.5 per cent voting for tax-raising powers for the new assembly. *RF*

J. MITCHELL, *Strategies for Self-Government: The Campaign for a Scottish Parliament* (Edinburgh, 1996).

Scottish TUC (STUC). Founded in 1888, the STUC jealously guarded its independence from its sister British organization until the mid-1920s. The impact of post-war economic dislocation and the effects of the failure of the 1926 General Strike initiated a major reassessment of the importance of STUC independence. As Scottish unions were smaller and weaker than their British counterparts, it was believed that they would be more vulnerable to predatory Scottish employers. Also, the STUC feared that different working conditions and wages could be imposed on Scottish industries. The solution to these perceived threats was to take shelter in the safety of greater British numbers. Such fears were evidenced in the STUC's attitude towards Scottish home rule. In the early twenties, it had been very supportive, but began to blow cold as the impact of recession hit hard. The fact that after 1945 the British state was expected to look after the moral, social, and economic well-being of its members, meant that the STUC was opposed to devolution on economic grounds. Since the early 1970s, however, largely as a means to check the power of government economic agencies such as the Highlands and Islands Development Board and the Scottish Development Agency, the STUC has favoured devolution. *RF*

Scruton, Roger Vernon (1944–), philosopher and Conservative thinker. Scruton has been hugely productive, writing on Spinoza, aesthetics, music (composing it too), a guide to modern philosophy, and novels—over twenty books. Former holder of a Birkbeck chair and eight visiting professorships, he was a contributor to *The Moral Maze*, a discussion programme on BBC Radio, but Scruton was an intellectual phenomenon. He also riskily explored Czechoslovakia under Communist rule. Appalled by mass taste, unguilty about high intelligence, liking the idea of authority, and repelled by actuality, remote from corporate free-marketism, fierce but tentative, he was a profound pessimist—an anti-populist. *EP*

Seal, Eric (1898–1972), prime minister's principal private secretary, 1940–1. A trained engineer who educated himself to pass the civil service entrance exam, Seal became principal private secretary to successive first lords of the Admiralty, including Winston Churchill. He moved to Downing Street with Churchill (who wanted to replace Neville Chamberlain's officials), where he presided over a close-knit team during the bleakest days of the Second World War. In 1941 he was sent to the new Admiralty delegation in Washington as deputy secretary. *CL*

secondary education and **secondary modern schools**. Secondary education was defined in the Hadow report of 1926 as the education of those over 11 years of age. The previous category of 'elementary' education left little room for specialization amongst teenagers. One of the major thrusts of educational policy between the wars was to distinguish 'primary' from 'secondary' education, so that young adults could receive an education after the age of 11 or 13 most appropriate to their potential. As a result of the *Education Act 1944, secondary education was made free, but divided between different categories of school according to educational potential. This was to be determined by the *eleven-plus examination which remained the major means of deciding which children attended secondary schools of different types into the 1960s. The comprehensivization campaign after 1964 sought to make the comprehensive school the norm and thereby abolish the 'secondary modern' school. These last were schools established under the 1944 Education Act to provide education for non-academic and non-technical pupils. Although promised 'equality of esteem', the secondary schools frequently were seen as a second-class educational system and this provided ammunition for those who advocated the comprehensive model instead of the tripartite system. *JS*

second front. With the entry of the USA and the USSR into the war in 1941, pressure was mounted on the British government to open a second European front by invading western Europe, pressure coming mainly from the left but also from the Beaverbrook papers. Churchill was keen to postpone such a tricky operation until Anglo-American material strength and operational expertise reached a decisive level. He therefore advocated the strategic bombing offensive as a 'second front' and operations in the Mediterranean. This bought the necessary time for preparation in 1942–3, culminating successfully in D-Day in 1944. *MLC*

Second World War (1939–45). The origins of the Second World War lay in the unsatisfactory peace treaties drawn up at the end of the Great War. Europe saw the rise of aggressive undemocratic governments in Germany and Italy. A similar situation arose in Japan where a militaristic government took on a distinctly anti-occidental stance, determined to expand Japanese influence across China and south-east Asia. In the 1930s, these governments consistently contravened the 1919 peace treaties and the conventions of the League of Nations. In Europe the actions of Germany caused most concern and, after the failures of appeasement, Britain and France made in 1939 a joint commitment to deter further aggressive expansion by the Nazi regime. On 3 September 1939 they declared war after the German invasion of Poland, an invasion made possible by a Nazi-Soviet non-aggression pact of August.

Unable to help Poland, Britain and France drifted into 'the phoney war', but this was brought to an end by Hitler's invasion of Denmark and Norway in April 1940, followed swiftly by his western campaign against the Low Countries and France. Using the highly efficient blitzkrieg technique, German armies overran all in their path, and in Britain Neville Chamberlain's government fell in May as a result of the obvious unpreparedness of the country for war. France fell but the British army was rescued in the Dunkirk evacuation. Britain now stood alone against the vast German and Italian empires but, inspired by new premier Winston Churchill's gutsy leadership and by his radio oratory, the nation united as rarely before in its history. During summer 1940 the Germans sought to gain aerial superiority as a prelude to invasion. Unable to achieve this in the battle of Britain, they turned instead to the bombing of British cities in the *Blitz, but this too failed to do more than kill civilians and strengthen British morale.

Churchill, realizing that Britain could not reinvade Europe alone, decided to take on the enemy in the Mediterranean, and campaigns were therefore waged in this theatre. By the end of 1941 these efforts seemed foolish, for the Germans and Italians controlled Greece, Crete, and were pushing back the British in North Africa. In 1941 also the war exploded eastwards, for it witnessed the German invasion of the USSR, which began on 22 June, using the well-tried blitzkrieg. The Germans advanced at a stunning rate, capturing vast numbers of men, material, and land. By winter the Ukraine had been occupied, Leningrad was under siege, and Moscow was only 200 miles (322 km) away. Hitler believed victory would be his in the following spring.

At the same time a desperate struggle was fought out at sea, where Germany launched her submarine fleet against vital British supply lines. By a slim margin, the Allies held on, and without victory in this battle of the *Atlantic there could have been no reinvasion of France. In the Far East, Japan now launched its bid for supremacy. On 7 December 1941 Pearl Harbor was attacked and America dragged into the war, while a week later Germany also declared war on the USA. Complacency about the fighting qualities of the Japanese led to the rout of the British in Malaya and Singapore, the Dutch in the East Indies, and the Americans in the Philippines. Japanese expansion was checked, though, in mid-1942 by American naval victories at Midway and Guadalcanal, while British and Indian troops made a fighting retreat to the Indian frontier. On the eastern front, 1942 saw further German advances but their overextended drive south produced the encirclement of a huge German force near Stalingrad. At the end of January 1943 that army was forced to surrender, a crucial defeat for the Third Reich. Hitler's last chance in the east came at the battle of Kursk in July 1943, the biggest tank battle in history, but the Germans were driven back. From this moment the Germans were in retreat.

Unready to open a *second front in 1942–3 the British and Americans launched a strategic bombing offensive and conducted extensive operations around the Mediterranean in 1943, following Montgomery's desert victory at *El Alamein in October 1942. From this springboard, the Allies attacked Italy, causing Mussolini's government to collapse. By summer 1944 the western allies were ready to invade north-western Europe: on 6 June, D-Day, the Normandy landings took place, and after an initial bitter struggle German resistance was broken. Within three months the British and American armies were in Belgium and facing the Franco-German border. Despite a brief German winter success in the Ardennes, in the spring the Allies crossed the Rhine and advanced into Germany itself. In the east, the Russians raised the siege of Leningrad, cleared Russia itself, and plunged westwards into Poland. By spring 1945 Russian artillery was shelling Berlin and, after a vicious assault, the city fell. Just before this Hitler committed suicide and on 8 May hostilities came to an end in Europe.

While these events were unfolding in Europe, the war against Japan continued. By the end of 1943 British and Indian troops went onto the offensive in Burma, recapturing Rangoon in May 1945. Further east, US General Macarthur executed his 'island hopping' operations, designed to bring US forces within striking distance of Japan. Each of these tiny Pacific islands required savage fighting to wrest them from Japanese hands, but in the spring of 1945 Iwo Jima and Okinawa fell, and it was now possible to bomb Japan, where cities were razed by continuous fire-bombing raids. The Allies were now in a position to invade Japan. Although Russia now also entered the war against Japan, no further conventional operations were needed, for the Americans decided to use their new secret weapon: Hiroshima and Nagasaki were attacked with atomic bombs on 6 and 9 August respectively, forcing the surrender of the Japanese government on 14 August.

The war had cost the lives of over 50 million people, there was devastation all across Europe and parts of the Far East, the map of the world was vastly different, and the Allied governments began trials at *Nuremburg and Tokyo for the awful war crimes of the Nazi and Japanese regimes. On the home front, the leftward drift of public opinion during the war years, the combined product of the radicalizing effect of shared sacrifice, a growing demand for fairness after years of rationing and deprivation, increasing respect for Labour's wartime work in government, and retrospective disillusion with the Conservatives' record in the 1930s, swept Clement Attlee into office in 1945 as the first Labour prime minister with a parliamentary majority. This ensured that wartime government policy-making, as in the Beveridge report (1942) and a 1944 full employment white paper, would bear fruit in the late 1940s transformation of Britain into a country with a large nationalized industrial sector and a welfare state. *MLC*

John Keegan, *The Second World War* (London, 1989).

Second World War, and Whitehall. The 1939–45 war had an impact on Whitehall more than three years before its outbreak when Warren Fisher and Maurice Hankey began to plan for a rejigging of Whitehall departments if war came and for the recruitment of a wide range of skilled outsiders to help staff them. The initial search for highly qualified scientists and technologists was later extended to business people necessary for the successful installation of a wartime command economy and to promising administrators. By 1941 a dramatic transformation had taken place in the size, scope, capacity, and competence of Whitehall and in its policy-making and personal practices. Mixed teams of generalists and specialists became standard. The role of scientific advice to ministers was greatly enhanced. Concentrations of experts, such as the economic section of the War Cabinet Office, exerted an influence out of all proportion to their numbers. Promotion could be very rapid. Oliver Franks, recruited from Glasgow University to join the then fledgling Ministry of Supply in 1939, became permanent secretary of that by now vast department in 1945 at the age of 40.

With some justification the years 1939–45 have come to be regarded as the apogee of the British civil service. As the career official Sir John Winnifrith later said of the wartime temporaries, they were 'very unlike the Great and Good. They really were winners'. And the *Rayner scrutinies in the 1980s looked back to this period as in some ways exemplary. Clive Priestley, Rayner's first chief of staff, believed: 'The War showed that the Civil Service could manage against objectives in time of crisis.' Increasingly from the publication of the Beveridge report in 1942 onwards, efforts turned towards post-war reconstruction in which the new mixed-team approach—and the temporary economists and statisticians—played a central part. Michael Young, author of the 1945 Labour manifesto, would stress the relative ease with which those aspects of the Attlee programme planned for by Whitehall pre-1945 were implemented (education, National Health Service, national insurance) with those (nationalizations) that had not received such treatment for lack of agreement between the parties in the wartime coalition.

Inevitably and properly, the bulk of the wartime 'temporaries' wished to return to their laboratories, seminar rooms, and boardrooms. Whitehall was aware that a different level of expertise would be necessary for the overseeing of a full-employment state as envisaged in the 1944 white paper (and it was plain that wartime creations such as the Central Statistical Office would remain as permanent fixtures). But, as the war ended, it remained an open question as to whether lessons could be learned by the career civil service from the Whitehall-of-all-the-talents which Hitler had obliged them to create, for application to the permanently extended state which it was plain that the world war experience would bequeath to the post-war nation (see BRIDGES REVIEW). *PJH*

PETER HENNESSY, *Whitehall* (London, 1989).

secret ballot, an election in which voters cast ballots without anyone else knowing how they have voted. Before 1872, elections were conducted on the basis of open ballots; there was a show of hands or else a poll was held in which the voter's name was written down and his vote recorded as he called it out, a method that encouraged intimidation and bribery. It was ended by the Parliamentary and Municipal Elections Act (the 'Ballot Act') of 1872. This provided for secret ballots, a voter being able to mark a ballot paper in private, and the provision for privacy has been maintained ever since. There are strict rules governing the conduct of elections, the most recent set being embodied in the Representation of the People Act, 1983. Critics object to the fact that how an individual has voted can in fact subsequently be traced. Each voter is handed a ballot paper, which has a number on it, and the electoral registration number of the voter is written on a counterfoil to the ballot slip. It is thus possible to compare the number on the ballot paper with that on the counterfoil. The papers and counterfoils are retained for a period of one year, but may be studied only by order of a court or of the Commons. Critics point out that it is virtually impossible to demonstrate malpractice, such as impersonation, from looking at the ballot papers and advocate ending the practice of recording the electoral registration number on the counterfoil. *PN*

R. J. CLAYTON (ed.), *Parker's Conduct of Parliamentary Elections* (London, 1990). | H. F. RAWLINGS, *Law and the Electoral Process* (London, 1988).

Secret Intelligence Service (MI6). The Secret Intelligence Service, unlike MI5, has no policy of releasing historical documents and so its history, which goes back to the formation in 1909 of the Secret Service Bureau, is more difficult to unravel. However, memoirs, a biography of its founding chief Mansfield Smith Cumming that used previously unseen MI6 diaries, correspondence and contemporary files, together with documents obtained from other sources have helped to understand and place MI6 into some kind of context. The agency began in 1909 as one of the two Secret Service Bureau sections. It was concerned with naval intelligence and, headed by Mansfield Smith Cumming, became responsible for external and imperial intelligence, effectively collecting intelligence about the German navy. By the outbreak of war MI6's activities yielded important details concerning the German navy together with profiles of leading Germans. During the war MI6 ran a number of successful operations including the 'La Dame Blanche' network.

MI6 operations in pre-revolutionary Russia were also important, and in 1915 future foreign secretary Sir Samuel Hoare became station chief in St Petersburg. He obtained valuable intelligence from Russian agents operating in Germany, including details of Germany's food shortages. After the Bolshevik revolution there were important espionage opportunities for agents like Sidney Reilly but little by way of concrete results.

The Great War established MI6's reputation as an intelligence agency and by its end many regarded it as an essential bulwark against Bolshevism. Post-war financial and personnel cuts were blunted by Cumming's success in entrenching MI6's role in external espionage and counter-intelligence, and by the Foreign Office agreeing to station a network of officers under diplomatic cover in British consulates, ostensibly acting as passport control officers. The agency severed its War Office connections, becoming responsible to the Foreign Office and taking the new name Secret Intelligence Service (SIS). During the 1920s cuts reduced SIS to a shadow of its wartime self. Cumming died in 1923 and his successor Admiral Sir Hugh 'Quex' Sinclair oversaw SIS's inter-war rundown. It was not just financial retrenchment, for the organization suffered because of a policy of recruitment based largely in the bars of gentlemen's clubs and a steady supply of ex-Indian policemen. Poorly paid recruits were expected to supplement their income from private resources. It was in every way an old boy's network. Hugh Trevor Roper, a wartime SIS recruit, considered the hierarchy 'of limited intelligence' and the professionals 'by and large pretty stupid—and some of them very stupid'. Furthermore, the old boy recruitment policy enabled Soviet penetration agents Philby, Burgess, and Maclean to gain positions of power within the organization.

During the inter-war period, SIS engaged in counter-subversion activities against Russian communism and largely ignored the threat posed by European fascists. Whilst reports indicated another world war, Sinclair refused to take them seriously, and when war came MI6 was unprepared and at a low ebb. The infamous 1939 Venlo affair (when British agents were arrested near the Dutch border) showed how easy it was for German military intelligence to deceive the British government into believing it was negotiating with peace groups within the German army. The subsequent sting, which resulted in the spiriting across the Dutch-German border of two experienced SIS officers, indicated the paucity of talent in the agency and government. Sinclair died just before this episode and was succeeded by Stewart Menzies After the Nazi conquest of western Europe in 1940, SIS's most important intelligence liaison became the USA. The appointment that year of William Stephenson as New York station chief marked the turning point. His personal links gave SIS direct contact with J. Edgar Hoover of the FBI and the Roosevelt administration. He was also central to the creation of the first informal intelligence co-operation between Britain and the USA. SIS's main wartime prize was the joint 'double cross' system with the Security Service, turning captured German agents and feeding their controllers with false information.

Because of the shortage of evidence, the post-war history of SIS is difficult to chronicle, and any attempt must rely heavily on conjecture. However, it is clear that the war's end saw SIS unreformed, the pre-war old gang still in charge, and Soviet penetration agents gnawing at its vitals. The Cold War saved SIS from the rapid rundown it experienced after 1918 and it acquired responsibility for covert action from Special Operations Executive. However, the unreformed SIS was pitched into the Cold War with a cast of mind wholly unsuited to the times. In these circumstances, Kim Philby and his Soviet controllers confidently bided their time, waiting for him to become chief. However, even as they dared to hope, Soviet codes were cracked, leading in 1950 to the arrest of atom spy Klaus Fuchs and later to the unmasking of Burgess and Maclean.

SIS maintained the closest possible links with the CIA after it was formed in 1946. Unfortunately Philby was SIS Washington liaison officer in the critical years 1949–51. He passed intelligence material to his controllers and did much to sabotage early CIA/SIS covert activities. When Soviet penetration of British intelligence and the atomic programme was finally revealed, it caused a souring of Anglo-American intelligence relations. Despite the flight of Burgess and Maclean there was no direct evidence linking them to Philby, though lingering suspicions cost him the top job and he was retired. Amazingly he was later rehired and used as a freelance agent in Beirut, although by this time George Blake, another Soviet agent, had penetrated SIS. The agency suffered further blows in 1956, when the foreign secretary discovered unauthorized plans for covert action in the Middle East, including a plot to assassinate Egypt's President Nasser (something Prime Minister Anthony Eden wanted but had not confided to his colleagues). That same year another unauthorized and bungled SIS action, this time an agent killed trying to inspect the hull of a visiting Soviet cruiser in Portsmouth harbour, resulted in important changes at the top. Sir Dick White, the head of MI5, became chief. He reformed SIS, forbidding assassination, tightening up the ground rules, and bringing it back under political control. White believed in Philby's guilt and found the proof from two Russian defectors. They also betrayed Soviet penetration agent George Blake and the Portland spy ring, who passed submarine warfare secrets to KGB controller Konon Molody alias Gordon Lonsdale.

Between 1960 and 1962, SIS gained the best Soviet intelligence in its history, when Oleg Penkovsky of Soviet military intelligence passed many thousands of classified Soviet documents. His intelligence proved critical to Western understanding of Soviet nuclear capability, and during the Berlin wall crisis and the Cuban missile crisis. During the midst of the Cuban crisis he was arrested by the KGB and subsequently executed. The success of these actions had by the early 1960s convinced SIS that the horrors of the immediate post-war years had been left behind. The invasion of Czechoslovakia by Soviet forces in 1968 alienated Soviet intelligence officer Oleg Gordievsky, who became SIS's most successful penetration officer between 1974 and 1985. An experienced officer, he passed vital information concerning the Soviet Union's fears of a NATO first strike policy and of the activities of KGB agents in Western capitals, as well as crucial information about the workings of the Soviet system.

In 1994, the British government placed SIS on a statutory footing with the enactment of the Intelligence Services Act. This Act also created a parliamentary intelligence and security committee to scrutinize its and the other security agencies' activities. However, unlike the Security Service, SIS has not sought to recruit from press advertisements, nor has it announced a programme of historical document release. *PM*

Secret Service Bureau (1909–14), forerunner of today's Security Service (MI5) and the Secret Intelligence Service (MI6), created in 1909 in response to fears of German espionage in Britain. Initially, the bureau was divided on service lines, with a retired army officer Vernon Kell responsible to the War Office and a retired naval officer Mansfield Cumming to the Admiralty. However, by 1911 Kell had taken responsibility for German espionage in Britain, whilst Cumming's operation was centred on Germany itself. Without the power of arrest, Kell was dependent on support from the Metropolitan Police special branch. Nonetheless, and despite meagre resources (by 1914 he employed only three officers, a barrister, and seven clerks), his agency identified and rounded up the entire German network of agents operating in Britain. By contrast, Cumming faced a more difficult task and, though unsuccessful in placing agents in Germany, he obtained valuable strategic information concerning the German fleet. Pre-1914 changes to security legislation, including new Official Secrets and Aliens Registration Acts, helped Kell develop effective counter-subversion measures that were invaluable when war broke out. The formation of the Secret Service Bureau institutionalized Britain's intelligence gathering capacity and the denial by the state of its existence and activities. *PM*

Security Service (MI5). The antecedents of today's Security Service, Britain's main internal security agency (popularly known as MI5) go back to the creation of the Secret Service Bureau. Its first head Vernon Kell remained in office until 1940 and during his time many of the service's basic functions were established. Before the Great War, the work of the fourteen staff who made up Kell's tiny agency was taken up searching for German agents. During that war MI5 grew in size and by its end employed around 850 staff and agents, and its activities shifted from counter-espionage to counter-subversion. The critical factors making for this refocus were the coordination of policy concerning aliens, the introduction of male conscription, and the Easter Rising in Dublin (both of which occurred in 1916), the outbreak of major industrial disputes in Britain's war industries, and the 1917 Bolshevik revolution. These events, particularly the Bolshevik revolution, politicized the service, which for some time after the war became overtly identified with the Conservative Party and hostile to the emerging Labour Party. At the end of the war, Kell lost an important turf war to his rival Basil Thompson, the head of Special Branch, who became director of intelligence. However, Thompson's triumph was short-lived, and his increasingly eccentric outpourings led to his removal in 1921.

During the inter-war years, MI5 suffered major cutbacks and the agency lost most of its staff. However, it also experienced important organizational and role changes, gaining responsibility for communist subversion in the armed forces and sabotage. In 1931, the agency lost its War Office affiliation, which was replaced by the

Home Office. At the same time it gained responsibility for countering threats to national security, it also became known by its present title the Security Service and assumed Special Branch's role countering Bolshevik/communist subversion in Britain. The 1930s saw the service suffer the consequences of out-of-date management and inadequate resources. That said, it had its successes, placing agents in the German embassy in London and monitoring Soviet penetration of trade unions and the Communist Party of Great Britain. However, the time leading up to the outbreak of the Second World War was one of lost opportunities. The veteran Kell and his deputy Holt Wilson appeared incapable of planning for the war or of creating a cadre of staff in readiness for the conflict: at the start of the war the agency employed just 30 officers.

During the war's first year, the Security Service's internal organization was in a state of virtual collapse. Poor pre-war planning greatly increased demand for departmental security clearances, enormously increased workloads, and other duties brought about a functional breakdown in the registry. When Churchill came to power in May 1940, he dismissed Kell and Holt Wilson and appointed Sir David Petrie as Kell's successor. Petrie undertook root and branch reform and in 1941 the agency came under the control of a newly formed security executive headed by a cabinet minister. However, the dissolution of the 1930s and the breakdown of the early war period took its toll, and the agency was penetrated by Soviet agents; most famously by the Cambridge spy and art critic Anthony Blunt. Blunt caused irreparable damage to MI5 by passing to his Russian control information concerning the agency's personnel, organization, and structure, together with any other secret information he could lay his hands on. Nonetheless, the Security Service's success in jointly operating the 'double cross' system with SIS, whereby agents turned by British Intelligence fed the Germans false information, demonstrated the agency's wartime effectiveness.

The end of the Second World War saw the Security Service at its peak. Petrie's reorganization and management had transformed it, as had the welding together of Britain's intelligence agencies by Churchill, who turned them into a coordinated Intelligence Community. However, almost as soon as war ended MI5 was faced with the Cold War, with Soviet Russia and its satellites around the world as the new enemy. Many of MI5's post-war successes were focused on Britain's retreat from Empire; it played an important role in Malaya where the Communist Party had embarked on a guerrilla war in 1948. The issue of Soviet infiltration of British intelligence raised its head in 1951 when the atom spies Klaus Fuchs and Nunn May, and two of the Cambridge spies Burgess and Maclean, were discovered. Thereafter MI5 was forced to take seriously the intelligence service's pre-war penetration. The agency also had to face a suspicious Labour government which, on Petrie's retirement, rejected internal candidates for his job and installed Sir Percy Sillitoe, a former chief constable: the appointment was not a success and Sillitoe soon found himself outmanoeuvred by the old guard. In 1952, the prime minister's personal responsibility for the Security Service was transferred to the home secretary. In 1953 Sillitoe retired and was succeeded by Dick White, a career officer who later became head of SIS. Further blows to the intelligence community came with the flight to Moscow in 1963 of SIS traitor Kim Philby. In the 1960s other spies including SIS officer George Blake, the Portland spy ring, and Admiralty employee John Vassall revealed the inability of the Security Service to prevent Soviet infiltration. During the 1960s, the Soviet Union developed the simple technique of building up numbers at the London residency to the point that MI5 could not keep track. The watershed came in 1971 when the British government expelled 105 Soviet embassy staff for spying; an action that seriously weakened Soviet intelligence activities in London. Around the same time a dissident Security Service officer, Peter Wright, claimed to have undertaken a wave of unauthorized activities including 'burgling their way across London' and attempting to destabilize the second Wilson government. An utterly unreliable witness, the Security Service has consistently denied its involvement in these activities, most notably in the current Security Service recruitment and information booklet. The overseas publication of Wright's colourful memoir *Spycatcher* in the late 1980s involved the government in protracted, embarrassing, and ultimately failed legal proceedings and led to the eventual reform of Britain's intelligence agencies.

Since 'the Troubles' erupted in the late 1960s, the Security Service has had some intelligence responsibilities for Northern Ireland. The lack of quality intelligence concerning both sides in the Troubles took years of patient work to overcome. The service's counter-terrorist efforts were extended to the growing problem of Middle East terrorists operating in Britain, including the Iranian embassy siege in 1980 and the Libyan people's bureau in 1984. However, the Cold War still dominated, and in 1983 Michael Bettaney, a member of the Security Service, was found offering the KGB information and later convicted of espionage.

With the end of the Cold War in the early 1990s, major changes have taken place within the service: whilst the threat from subversion and espionage diminished, terrorism remained a major problem. In 1992, after a major turf war with Special Branch, the Security Service took over responsibility for the intelligence effort against Irish terrorism in Britain, which has resulted in the prevention of many acts of terrorism and the conviction of terrorists. Its brief was also extended to include the fight against organized crime, subversion, and counter-terrorism; its current information and recruitment booklet claims that the agency has in recent years foiled upwards of eighty per cent of terrorist attacks.

The late 1980s saw the opening up of the Security Service to public scrutiny. The Security Service Act, 1989, placed it on a statutory footing and created accountability mechanisms. Around half the employees of the Security Service are now female, and in 1993 the agency became the first in the world to appoint a woman, Stella Rimington, as its director-general. Rimington broke with the past when she gave a public speech setting out the agency's remit and work and from that point an open recruitment policy has been developed. The following year parliament enacted the Intelligence Services Act, which established the parliamentary intelligence and security committee to examine the expenditure, administration and policy of the Security Service, SIS, and GCHQ. Finally, in 1997 the Security Service began a programme of releasing into the Public Record Office its surviving historical archives. *PM*

Selborne, 2nd earl of (1859–1942), Conservative politician and colonial administrator. The first *Liberal Unionist chief whip before being unwillingly elevated to the Lords in 1895, Selborne held a succession of key posts: under-secretary for the colonies, 1895–1900; first lord of the Admiralty, 1900–5; governor-general of the Transvaal and high commissioner for South Africa, 1905–10; president of the Board of Agriculture, 1915–16. Married into the great *Hotel Cecil political dynasty, Selborne had the opportunity to play a major role in Unionist politics. Portrayed as a diehard backwoodsman for his opposition to the *Parliament Act, 1911, Selborne saw himself as fighting to restore the political rights of the class (his own) with the best interests of the British people at heart. The Irish question played a significant part in his political quest: opposed to Irish home rule, he resigned from Asquith's wartime coalition government in 1916. Thereafter he sought to find an outcome to the Irish problem along Unionist lines, at one time advocating a federalist solution. Although he recognized Lloyd George's capabilities as a war leader, he distrusted his personal ambition. Consequently he opposed the decision of his party's leadership to fight the 1918 election in alliance with Lloyd George. His belief that the coalition could not last was vindicated by the 1922 Carlton club meeting, but he then withdrew from active politics in 1922. His central place in British administrative and political life was assured through his wide circle of friends and relatives and his strong sense of public duty. Although he began political life as a Liberal, his gradual transition through Liberal Unionism to diehard conservatism reflected the evolution of British politics during the opening decades of the 20th century. *NJC*

D. George Boyce (ed.), *The Crisis of British Power: The Imperial and Naval Papers of the Second Earl of Selborne* (London, 1990). | D. George Boyce (ed.), *The Crisis of British Unionism: The Domestic Political Papers of the Second Earl of Selborne* (London, 1987).

Selborne, 3rd earl of (1887–1971), Conservative politician, styled Viscount Wolmer until 1942. He represented south-west Lancashire, 1910–18, and Aldershot, 1918–40. Rewarded with minor ministerial office in the 1920s, he developed a particular interest in reforming the Post Office. Out of office from 1931 he opposed the 1935 India Act, urged speedier rearmament, and was a critic of the Munich agreement, consequently incurring the wrath of his local Conservative activists. In 1942 he became minister of economic warfare with political responsibility for the covert activities of *Special Operations Executive. *NJC*

selective employment tax (SET), the particular brainchild of Labour's notorious tax adviser Nicholas *Kaldor, was introduced in 1966 and repealed by the succeeding Heath government. SET was a payroll tax from which employers in manufacturing could gain relief in order to encourage labour to move from services to manufacturing, and so improve export performance. It was also a useful cover for raising more revenue when Labour had already increased income tax. Though some economists liked the tax, it was cumbersome to administer and politically unpopular. *RCW*

selectivity. See UNIVERSALITY.

Selsdon Group, ideological ginger group formed in the late seventies, its name alluding to Edward Heath's supposed commitment at the Selsdon Park conference in 1970 to a rigorous free enterprise approach to the economy, later rescinded after his 'Selsdon man' phase ended in 1972. Margaret Thatcher, despite obvious sympathies, had to tread very circumspectly, something she continued to do until 1981. The Selsdon Group were a free market faction loyal to her but at discreet arm's length. *EP*

'Selsdon man', phrase of Harold Wilson's on 6 February 1970 which encapsulated his attack on the Tories, whom he accused of having moved to the extreme right during their Selsdon Park conference. 'Selsdon man' (as in 'Piltdown man') implied that the Tories held primitive views and were narrowly based in the suburban home counties. Wilson's barb, however, backfired because it succeeded where Heath had failed by creating the impression that the Tories offered a clear alternative with new policies. *RJS*

Selsdon Park conference (January 1970), weekend meeting of Heath's shadow cabinet at the Selsdon Park Hotel in South Croydon. It was intended to finalize policy priorities for the election, but entered political folklore when Heath, who was unsure what to tell journalists on the Saturday when they arrived unexpectedly, briefed them about *law and order. Headlines about the Tories getting tough on crime and reports of a Tory shift to the right prompted Wilson's gibe about *'Selsdon man'. *RJS*

Serious Fraud Office (SFO), specialist investigative branch of the policing and prosecution system. It employed staff with skills in reading balance sheets and tracing commercial crime through such activities as money-laundering. Its director has had since 1987 the power to requisition books and financial records for analysis if he suspects that a fraud of over £5 million has taken place and, contrary to usual practice, can require statements from suspects even if they have already been charged, thus effectively removing their 'right to silence'. It has, however, proved difficult to find suitable jurors for such complex cases where the evidence is so very technical and the length of trials exceptionally long. The SFO has not generally had a happy record of success in the courts, the acquittals of George Walker of Brent Walker and Ernest Saunders of Guinness being well-publicized examples of its embarrassment. *JAR*

serjeant at arms. See COMMONS, HOUSE OF: SUPPORT STAFF.

SERPS (State Earnings-Related Pensions) are intended as a supplement to the basic state pension and have been encouraged by Labour governments, but challenged by Conservatives who generally favour private pension provision for this purpose. In practice, the Labour Party now also advocates a private 'stakeholder' pension and has relegated the state pension to a much-diminished role. The future of the SERPS scheme remains a matter of contention between the parties. *JS*

set-aside, a measure to control overproduction in agriculture by making payment to farmers to compensate them for taking land out of production. The policy originated in the USA, where an extensive system was established by the mid-1980s. Set-aside was introduced by the UK in December 1987, and a voluntary scheme for the European Community, affecting cereal crops, was introduced in 1988. Set-aside became compulsory under the MacSharry proposals for reform of the Common Agricultural Policy, and this was brought into effect in 1993–4. *JHB*

'Set the People Free', Conservative campaign slogan for the 1951 general election, intended to emphasize Conservative freedom from controls and rationing, consumer choice, and opportunity. It was epitomized by the Tate and Lyle advert of 'Mr Cube' waving the sword of freedom. The approach proved effective in suburban and commuter areas, less so elsewhere, but the party normally won. The phrase was reused by Heath when addressing the 1970 Conservative conference. *NJC*

Sex Discrimination Act, 1975, made discrimination between men and women unlawful in employment, education, training, and the provision of housing, goods, facilities, and services. Discriminatory advertisements were also made illegal. The Act also set up an Equal Opportunities Commission to assist in the enforcement of the Equal Pay and Sex Discrimination Acts. *JS*

Shackleton, David (1863–1938), Labour MP and civil servant. Though he had little formal education, Shackleton, a Wesleyan Methodist, became a full-time weavers' union official and, after the Clitheroe by-election of August 1902, joined Keir Hardie and Richard Bell as the third Labour Representation Committee MP. He took a leading role in the Labour Party after retaining his seat in the general election of 1906 but left the

Commons in 1910 when Winston Churchill offered him the post of senior labour adviser at the Home Office. Awarded a knighthood in 1917, at the time of his retirement in 1925 he was chief labour adviser at the Ministry of Labour. *DEM*

KENNETH D. BROWN (ed.), *The First Labour Party 1906–1914* (London, 1985). | PETER M. MARTIN, *Lancashire Giant: David Shackleton, Labour Leader and Civil Servant* (London, 2000).

Sharp, Evelyn Adelaide (1902–85), civil servant. A pioneering woman in Whitehall's top ranks who entered the civil service in 1926 (only the second year in which the exam for the administrative class was open to women), Evelyn Sharp was the first female permanent secretary, heading the Ministry of Housing and Local Government, 1955–66. She was widely recognized as one of the most formidable civil servants of her day, her unique specialist knowledge of the field of local government, housing, and planning (in which she spent virtually her whole career), and her forthright manner and tough-minded approach marking her out. The publication of the Crossman diaries in 1975 gave a vivid but incomplete picture of 'the Dame'. She believed passionately in local government and was its champion inside Whitehall; after retiring from the civil service, she was one of the dominant figures on the *Redcliffe-Maud commission on local government (1966–9). *KT*

Shaw, George Bernard (1856–1950), the most famous dramatist and Fabian socialist of his times, but largely self-educated. Born in Dublin, he read voraciously there and, after moving to London in 1876, at the British Museum. He made his name, 1885–95, as a music critic and, influenced by Karl Marx, was converted to socialism, joined the *Fabian Society in 1884, and edited the influential *Fabian Essays in Socialism* (1889). Fabianism aimed at diverting British socialism from Marxist paths and sending it down what Shaw called 'The transition to social democracy'. He had written five unpublished novels (1878–83) before his first play, *Widowers' Houses*, was performed at the Independent Theatre in 1892. Others followed steadily in the 1890s, then his first successful New York production, *The Devil's Disciple*, in 1902, launched a long and triumphant international career which made Bernard Shaw the most famous dramatist in the world and won him the Nobel prize for literature in 1925. The content of his plays *Major Barbara* (1905), *Pygmalion* (1916), *Saint Joan* (1923) and their long polemical prefaces was not overtly socialist. But his lifelong association with such pillars of Fabianism as Sidney and Beatrice *Webb, and his best-selling pamphlets like *The Intelligent Woman's Guide to Socialism and Capitalism* (1928) and *Everybody's Political What's What* (1944) were important in making socialist ideas acceptable. Shaw's influence was further enhanced by vast correspondence with a host of diverse world figures. He left £700,000 (perhaps £10 million in today's money), mainly to the British Museum, whose reading room had been his university, but it was not well used. Better managed, Shaw's estate, vastly enhanced by the success of *My Fair Lady*, the musical version of *Pygmalion*, might have yielded £400 million in the year 2000. *PRGR*

MICHAEL HOLROYD, *Bernard Shaw*, 3 vols. (London, 1988–91).

Shaw, Thomas (1872–1938), Labour politician, minister of labour in 1924 and (though a former pacifist) secretary for war, 1929–31. Tom Shaw was a textile worker who served the International Textile Federation all his life, learning French and German in the process. Elected for Preston in 1918, he served in the minority Labour governments and refused to join the 1931 National Government but lost his seat in that year's election. He headed the delegation which highlighted the plight of Indian textile workers in 1926. A bluntly spoken, logical man, he was not particularly popular at the War Office. *BB*

Shawcross, Hartley William (1902–), lawyer and Labour politician. Shawcross was Attlee's attorney-general, 1945–51, and briefly president of the Board of Trade in 1951. He was the chief British prosecutor at the Nuremberg trials, his other most important contribution as attorney-general being to support the implementation of the Rushcliffe commission which extended legal aid to all proceedings in civil courts and civil proceedings in magistrates' courts, with the exception of defamation. Shawcross became concerned with Communist unrest and evoked order 1305 against strikers leading to the prosecution of seven London dockers. He is mainly remembered for a single triumphalist phrase, uttered in 1946, *'we are the masters at the moment'. *BB*

Sheey-Skeffington, Hanna (1877–1946), Irish feminist. In 1903 she married the pacifist and journalist Francis Skeffington and they took each other's surnames as a commitment to equality. Both were founder members of the Irish Women's Franchise League in 1908. During the 1916 Easter Rising her husband was summarily executed by a British officer and thereafter Hanna

Sheey-Skeffington was involved in nationalist activity. She opposed the Anglo-Irish treaty in 1921 and the traditional role of women as defined in the Irish constitution of 1937. *TWH*

Shelter, pressure-group formed in 1966 to campaign on behalf of the homeless, one of a number of single-issue campaigning organizations formed in the 1960s. It has been a persistent campaigner to bring the plight of the homeless to public attention. *JS*

Shephard, Gillian Patricia (1940–), Conservative politician. Shephard was a former Norfolk councillor close to John Major, and promoted by him to cabinet. Herself a former schools inspector, she was minister of state at the Treasury from 1990, but best known as a strong education secretary, 1994–7, succeeding a battered John Patten, enforcing testing and close insistence on the core curriculum. She had the advantage of following, but where Patten was rebuffed by National Union of Teacher campaigns of non-cooperation by teachers, Shephard essentially got her way. She was later shadow leader of the Commons. *EP*

GILLIAN SHEPHARD, *Shephard's Watch* (London, 2000).

Sherbourne, Stephen Ashley (1945–), prime minister's political secretary 1983–7. Having run Edward Heath's private office (1975–6) and advised industry secretary Patrick Jenkin (1982–3), Sherbourne briefed Margaret Thatcher before her daily press conferences during the 1983 general election. As political secretary, he worked on the Conservative manifesto for the 1987 election, during which he had the difficult task of smoothing Thatcher's relations with Conservative Central Office and party chairman Norman Tebbit. He played a key role in John Major's 1992 general election team, writing speeches and handling the media. *CL*

Shinwell, Emanuel (1884–1986), Labour politician. 'Manny' Shinwell was the eldest of thirteen children of Polish-Jewish parents. From that traditionally humble background, he became one of the most respected and longest-living politicians of the 20th century and a life peer, remembered as much for his temper as for his ready wit. Shinwell's early political schooling was in the volatile cauldron of late 19th- and early 20th-century Glasgow. He was an early member of the Independent Labour Party and in 1919 was imprisoned for five months for his part in the notorious riots of 'Red Friday'. Following a period as a trade union organizer and as a member of Glasgow trades council and city council, Shinwell was MP for Linlithgow, 1922–4 and 1928–31. He was junior minister for mines and for the War Office in the first two Labour governments, 1924 and 1929–31, but did not support the National Government and lost his seat in the 1931 election. In 1935, however, he defeated Ramsay MacDonald for the constituency of Seaham and then remained a Durham county Member until 1970. He was a stern wartime critic of Churchill and appointed by Attlee as minister of fuel and power, 1945–7. Although he nationalized the mines, he was also widely condemned for ineffective handling of the 1947 fuel crisis. As a result, he was relegated from cabinet to the War Office, but by 1950 had returned as minister of defence, adopting a hawkish posture on the issue of rearmament. He retired from the shadow cabinet in 1955, having found himself isolated from both the left and right of the party, but he remained an active and outspoken backbencher, from 1970 in the Lords. He resigned the Labour whip in 1982 because of what he perceived as a drift to the left, but remained a member of the party until his death. *DWM*

E. SHINWELL, *Conflict without Malice* (London, 1955). | E. SHINWELL, *Lead with the Left: My First Ninety-Six Years* (London, 1981). | PETER M. SLOWE, *Manny Shinwell: An Authorised Biography* (London, 1993).

shop stewards' movement. The incorporation of trade union leaders into the machinery of state and the suspension of trade union activities for the duration of the 1914–18 war allowed a dissident shop stewards' movement to fill the vacuum, particularly in engineering. A strike on Clydeside in February 1915 led to the formation of the Clyde Workers' Committee (CWC), and Sheffield and other major industrial centres soon followed. Localized at first, a national shop stewards' and workers' committee was formed in the engineering industry in August 1917. The majority of the Clydeside leaders were members of the Socialist Labour Party. They and the amalgamation committee movement in England argued for workers' control of industry. Socialist ideology combined with the wave of industrial unrest which swept Britain in 1916–19 has led some to interpret the shop stewards' movement as an embryonic revolutionary movement, particularly on Clydeside, but such a view is difficult to sustain. The committees were initially concerned to preserve the craft status of their members. On Clydeside the major concern was the dilution of labour; in Sheffield the committee was formed in response to the calling up of an engineer belonging to an exempt category; the extensive strikes of May 1917 were a response to government plans to abolish the trade card scheme. Also, these wartime industrial struggles were never linked to the anti-war movement. What can be said, though, is that, as the movement spread, simple craft defensiveness gave way to a wider class-consciousness. The Sheffield committee outspokenly condemned both craft sectionalism and sexism, the CWC struck for the reinstatement of four sacked female workers, and cooperation with unskilled unions increased. The eventual beneficiaries of this, however, were the Independent Labour Party on Clydeside and the Labour Party elsewhere. Revolutionaries were in a minority and only a handful of shop stewards' leaders joined the Communist Party of Great Britain when it formed in 1920. *MC*

Shore, Peter David (1924–), Labour politician. Shore was head of the Labour Party research department before being a Labour MP, 1964–97. A protégé of Harold Wilson, dismissed by Denis Healey as his 'lapdog', Shore became a cabinet minister in 1967 and held both the trade and the environment ministries in 1974–9. He opposed Britain's entry into the European Community and has become the grand old man of Labour Euroscepticism. Shore served on the Nolan committee and was created a life peer in 1997. *MC*

Short, Edward Watson (1912–), Labour politician and deputy party leader, 1972–6. After a career as a schoolteacher and headmaster, Short was Labour MP for Newcastle-upon-Tyne Central, 1951–76, spending much of his time as a Labour whip, and as chief whip managing Labour's wafer-thin majority of 1964–6. Thereafter he entered the cabinet as postmaster general (1966–8), secretary for education (1968–70), and lord president, leading the Commons, 1974–6. As a centrist that hardly anyone disliked, he was elected deputy leader of the party when Roy Jenkins resigned over Europe, retaining the post until he and Wilson both retired in 1976. He went to the Lords as Lord Glenamara in 1977. *JAR*

EDWARD SHORT, *Whip to Wilson* (London, 1989).

short, sharp shock. Introduced in 1948, partly to replace corporal punishment for juveniles, detention centres provided short, rigorous, and supposedly deterrent custodial sentences for novice offenders. More recently British politicians have been influenced by the boot camps which emerged in the USA in the 1980s, imposing physically demanding high-pressure discipline as an alternative to prison. Boot camps produce vivid TV images, politically attractive in periods of concern about *law and order. *SMcC*

Shortt, Edward (1862–1935), Liberal politician. Shortt was a barrister who was Liberal MP for Newcastle, 1910–22. Taking Lloyd George's side rather than Asquith's when his party split, he was a tough chief secretary for Ireland as the post-war troubles began in 1918–19, and then home secretary dealing with industrial disturbances, 1919–22. After retiring from politics he applied the same approach as president of the British Board of Film Censors, 1929–35. *JS*

sick pay was established as a benefit under the *National Insurance Act, 1911, which ensured that weekly payments were received for up to six months while an insured person was sick. A new scheme was introduced in 1994 under the Statutory Sick Pay Act which implemented changes to the regulations for payment of sick pay by employers. *JS*

Sidney Street, 'Siege of' (3 January 1911), scene of a gun battle in East London between Russian anarchists and police (supported by troops), which acquired special notoriety because the home secretary, Winston Churchill, attended to direct operations personally. The house in which the anarchists were surrounded eventually caught fire, or was fired deliberately, and its inhabitants did not escape alive. *JAR*

Signposts for the Sixties (1961), Labour policy statement, generated under Gaitskell, but which set the scene for Harold Wilson's later initiatives. It announced that 'We live in a scientific revolution', and followed by suggesting that Britain needed to harness the forces of science for the community, in order to supervise the balanced growth of the economy and to ensure the fair distribution of wealth. It was besotted by the illusion that the scientific revolution would make everything possible. *KL*

Silkin, John Ernest (1963–87), Labour politician. Silkin was MP for Deptford from 1963 to 1987, and a whip in the 1964–6 government, becoming chief whip, 1966–9. He became close to Wilson and his political secretary, Marcia Williams, but was replaced as chief whip after a period of turmoil in the parliamentary party over Lords' reform and *In Place of Strife*. He was minister of public building and works, 1969–70 and 1974–6, and minister of agriculture, 1976–9.

He contested both the party leadership in 1980 and the deputy leadership in 1981, as a 'soft left' candidate but with no prospect of success. *BJE*

Sillars, James (1937–), Scottish politician. As Labour MP for South Ayrshire, Jim Sillars made his political reputation in the early 1970s as the foremost critic of the Scottish National Party (SNP). This earned him the sobriquet of 'the hammer of the Nats'. Although on the left of the party, Sillars was in favour of devolution and believed that Labour ought to prepare itself better for the realities of political life in a post-devolution Scotland. Frustrated at leadership inertia, he founded a 'Scottish Labour Party' in 1976 as an independent organization but, lacking a grass roots membership and strapped for cash, the party was doomed to failure. Sillars gravitated towards the SNP in 1980 after losing his seat in the 1979 election. He was committed to 'direct action', which led to his arrest in 1981 for breaking the windows of the proposed Scottish assembly. As author of the SNP's 'Independence in Europe' campaign which reconciled membership of the European Community with political separation from Britain, Sillars offered the template for modern nationalist strategy. He won the Glasgow *Govan by-election in 1988, but lost the seat in 1992, which led to his famous outburst that the Scots were 'ninety minute patriots'. *RF*

Silverman, Sydney (1898–1968), Labour MP. A civil rights lawyer and left-wing MP for Nelson and Colne, 1935–68, Silverman was responsible for the introduction of the private member's Murder (Abolition of Death Penalty) Bill in December 1964. The Labour government allowed the measure to be debated every Wednesday morning for as long as was necessary, and it was passed in 1965, suspending the death penalty until 1970. It was a remarkable constructive achievement for a man who was the classic left-wing Labour backbench rebel and a constant critic of Labour governments. *BB*

Simon, Ernest Darwin (1879–1960), Liberal, industrialist, and town planner. A second-generation Jewish immigrant, Simon became a leading figure in Manchester politics. Lord mayor of Manchester, 1921, and MP for Withington, Manchester, 1923–4 and 1929–31, he created the 'new town' of Wythenshawe and wrote extensively on town planning. He joined the Labour Party in 1946 and was chairman of the BBC, 1947–52. *JS*

Simon, John Allsebrook (1873–1954), Liberal politician and founder of *Liberal National Party in 1931. Trained as a barrister, Simon was a Liberal MP from 1900 and served under Asquith as solicitor-general, 1910–13, then attorney-general, 1913–15. He oversaw the introduction of the 'cat and mouse' Act (to deal with the suffragettes) and the Defence of the Realm Act at the outbreak of the Great War. Appointed home secretary in 1915, he resigned over the introduction of *conscription in 1916. He remained active in post-war politics, though, chairing an important commission on the Indian constitution, 1927–30. He headed in 1931 the Liberal group of supporters of the National Government, staying in office when the Samuelites resigned in 1932, and held the posts of foreign secretary, 1931–5; home secretary, 1935–7; and chancellor of the exchequer, 1937–40. By 1935, his group of 'Simonite' Liberals were effectively aligned with the Conservatives and resisted moves to rejoin the Liberal followers of Herbert *Samuel, leading eventually to their fusion with the Conservatives in 1948. He served as Churchill's wartime lord chancellor, 1940–5. *JS*

David Dutton, *Simon: A Political Biography of Sir John Simon* (London, 1992).

Sinclair, Archibald Henry MacDonald (1890–1970), Liberal politician, leader of the Liberal Party, 1935–45. Trained as a soldier, he was a friend of Winston *Churchill (with whom he served in the Great War and as his personal military secretary at the War Office, 1919–21), and MP for Caithness and Sutherland, 1922–45. Sinclair joined the National Government in 1931 as secretary for Scotland but resigned with the Samuelite Liberals in 1932. Liberal leader in succession to Samuel, he oversaw reorganization of the party in line with the *Meston report. An opponent of appeasement, Sinclair declined to serve in Neville Chamberlain's war cabinet in 1939, but joined Churchill's coalition as secretary for air, 1940–5. He lost his seat in the 1945 election and was succeeded by Clement *Davies as Liberal leader, becoming 1st viscount Thurso in 1952. *JS*

Gerard de Groot, *Liberal Crusader: The Life of Sir Archibald Sinclair* (London, 1993).

Sinclair, John (1860–1925), Liberal politician. Sinclair was a prominent member of the Edwardian Scottish Liberal Party, MP for Dumbartonshire, 1892–5, and Forfarshire, 1900–9. Sinclair was identified as part of the radical wing of the party and had close relations with Sir Henry Campbell-Bannerman. He was Scottish secretary, 1905–12, and helped to push through the Education Act of 1908 and the Landholders Act.

Sinclair was ennobled in 1909 as Lord Pentland and in 1912 appointed governor of Madras. *RF*

Single European Act (SEA) (signed 1986, in force 1987), the first major revision of the treaty of *Rome. The SEA was the product of a constellation of factors which created momentum in the European Community after paralysis in the 1970s and early 1980s. The solution to the prickly question of British contributions to the community budget in June 1984, the issue of enlargement, pressure for institutional reform, and the dynamic commission presidency of Jacques Delors all combined to create opportunity for an advance. Impetus was even provided by Margaret Thatcher, whose free market economic philosophy extended to the creation of the single market in Europe. Thatcher's government planned to capitalize on its comparative advantage in the service sector where liberalization was far from complete. However, Thatcher was also concerned lest the single market bring greater supranationalism. As she put in her memoirs, 'My aim had to be to ensure that we were not driven helter-skelter towards European federalism' (*The Downing Street Years* (London, 1993), 548). To mastermind the creation of the single market, Thatcher appointed the Tory peer Lord Cockfield as European commissioner for the internal market but, much to Thatcher's disdain, Cockfield's June 1985 proposals recommended the extension of qualified majority voting (QMV) in all areas to achieve the single market. Thatcher believed that Cockfield had 'gone native' whilst in the European Commission and feared that the extension of QMV would open the way to Delors's plans for *European Monetary Union (EMU) and a single currency. Ultimately, the SEA was a trade-off between extensions of QMV in two-thirds of the areas defined in Cockfield's white paper, placating both the British and the commission, and the liberalization programme. It led to the single market, advanced institutional reform, and for the first time incorporated procedures for European political cooperation. Most importantly, it also strengthened Delors's presidency and paved the way for EMU. *JRVE*

single transferable vote (STV), a form of election used for parliamentary elections in the Republic of Ireland and Malta, for the Australian senate, and for the return of three members of the European parliament from Northern Ireland. STV is a system traditionally favoured by the Electoral Reform Society and the Liberal Party for introduction in the UK. With STV, there are multi-member constituencies in which each elector lists preferences on the ballot paper (giving 1 to the first preference, 2 to the second, and so on). Under what is known as the Droop quota, the total number of votes cast is divided by the total number of seats plus one, with one being added to the resulting number, to determine the number of votes necessary for a candidate to be declared elected. If a candidate achieves that number once first-preference votes are counted, he or she is declared elected, and any surplus votes are then redistributed. If not all seats are filled on first-preference votes, then the candidate with the least number of votes is eliminated and the second preferences of that candidate are then taken into account. This process is repeated until all seats are filled. The system is treated as a proportional one, though one study suggests that it is best described as contingentially proportional, 'that is, one that will usually produce a fairly proportional result, but not invariably' (Dunleavy et al., 27). The study calculated that, if employed in the 1997 general election, the STV method would have deviated from true proportionality by 13.5 per cent. The Independent Commission on the Voting System (1998), set up to make recommendations on an alternative electoral system to the existing one, did not come out in favour of STV, preferring instead a variant of the *alternative vote. *PN*

Patrick Dunleavy, Helen Margetts, Brendan O'Duffy, and Stuart Weir, *Making Votes Count* (Colchester, 1998). | David M. Farrell, *Comparing Electoral Systems* (Hemel Hempstead, 1997). | *Report of the Independent Commission on the Voting System* (Cm 4090–1, London, 1998).

Sinn Fein, Irish political party. In 1905 Arthur Griffith published a weekly journal entitled *Sinn Fein* (Ourselves), the base from which the Sinn Fein political movement gradually crystallized in 1906. The movement preached the doctrine of Irish self-reliance, and adopted a policy of passive resistance to British rule in Ireland. It had as its chief objects the building-up of Ireland intellectually and materially, and the regaining of her political independence. Griffith's objective was to unite Catholics and Protestants on grounds of Ireland's inherent rights to great nation status. By 1902, Griffith had already devised a programme for the parliamentary withdrawal of Irish MPs to Ireland, the declaration of an Irish state, and passive resistance to the British state, using the existing powers and resources of Irish local government. Sinn Fein was to implement this during the Anglo-Irish War 1919–21. Griffith favoured the restoration of the Kingdom of

Ireland which had existed prior to the Act of Union with Great Britain in 1800.

Drawn into the Sinn Fein movement was the revolutionary Irish Republican Brotherhood (IRB) organization, a physical-force organization dedicated to securing Irish independence by force and advocating the creation of an Irish republic. Elements of the IRB used the Irish Volunteers, a paramilitary nationalist force set up to ensure the passage of the Third Home Rule Bill in 1914, to lead an insurrection against British rule in 1916. Although the Sinn Fein movement was not formally involved in the Easter Rising, many of the IRB's leaders, who were executed, were involved in Sinn Fein. Popular sympathy and support rose for a rejuvenated Sinn Fein, which now received the credit for the rising. Republicans, such as Eamon de Valera, and monarchists, such as Griffith, created an uneasy alliance, but by December 1918 Sinn Fein had attracted 112,080 members. The 1918 general election demonstrated the level of its support when it won 73 out of 105 seats in Ireland, although with under 48 per cent of the national vote. In January 1919, Sinn Fein MPs met in Dublin, constituted an Irish parliament—Dáil Éireann—which declared independence from Britain, and established an alternative system of administration.

Following the Anglo-Irish war a truce was agreed between the British and the IRA. This led to the Anglo-Irish treaty of 1921 which established the Irish Free State. Sinn Fein split between Griffth and Michael Collins, who supported the treaty, and de Valera who opposed it, leading to the Irish civil war, 1922–3. Following the anti-treaty side's defeat, what was left of Sinn Fein refused to acknowledge the legitimacy of the Free State. Instead, it recognized the second Dáil Éireann, elected in 1921 before the treaty, as the legitimate government of the Irish Republic set up in 1916. Sinn Fein split again in 1926 when de Valera left to form Fianna Fáil. It had already split from the IRA in 1925 but a reconciliation between them occurred in 1938 when the rump of the second Dáil which claimed to be the true Irish government transferred its authority to the IRA Army Council. This body, in doctrinaire republican eyes, now became the legitimate government of the Irish republic. The IRA declared war on Britain and conducted an unsuccessful bombing campaign in England and Sinn Fein briefly revived electorally during the IRA border campaign of 1956–62. Following another military failure, Sinn Fein moved to the left with the aim of building working-class support for an all-Ireland socialist republic. In 1969 this again led to a split in Sinn Fein and the formation of the Official (OIRA) and the Provisional IRAs (PIRA). During the 1980s, the PIRA's political wing, Provisional Sinn Fein, eventually came under the leadership of Gerry Adams. Following the 1981 hunger strikes it contested elections and sat in the Irish parliament. This led to a further split when traditionalists formed Real Sinn Fein in 1986. In 1997, Provisional Sinn Fein entered the Stormont talks process and supported, in 1998, the Belfast agreement, in due course taking two portfolios in the devolved government of 2000. *TWH*

Thomas Hennessey, *Dividing Ireland: World War One and Partition* (London 1998). | Peter Taylor, *Provos: The IRA and Sinn Fein* (London 1995).

Skelton, Noel (1880–1935), Conservative MP. Skelton's undistinguished ministerial career (under-secretary for Scotland, 1931–5) and early death belied his earlier great promise. He had been the political and intellectual leader of the left-leaning *YMCA group of Tory MPs in the late 1920s, and his 1924 book *Constructive Conservatism,* Harold Macmillan later thought, 'had a great effect on all the younger Members of the party' (*Winds of Change, 1914–1939* (London 1966), 178). His death cleared the way, though, for Macmillan himself to play a similar role in the later 1930s with *The *Middle Way.* *JAR*

Skybolt, abandoned American air-to-ground missile. The cancellation of *Blue Streak was made easier by American agreement to sell Britain the Skybolt missile in March 1960. In return, the Americans constructed a nuclear submarine base at Holy Loch. This deal, and Anglo-American relations in general, were thrown into crisis by the Kennedy administration's November 1962 decision to drop Skybolt. The situation was resolved at the Kennedy–Macmillan Nassau summit in December 1962 when the US agreed to sell Britain the Polaris missile instead. *JRVE*

sleaze, political accusation and for the Tories an election loser in 1997. John Major, while immaculately honest, saw his government battered by charges of rampant immorality and dishonesty. Operating after 1992 on a dwindling majority and with widespread right-wing disloyalty, he was badly placed to discipline minor misconduct and was anyway temperamentally forgiving. Increased *lobbying, US-style, through public relations companies, had given MPs tempting business opportunities as ministerial contacts, while the press, hostile for other reasons, joined the opposition in maximizing adverse publicity. The original 'cash for questions' case involved Graham Riddick and David Tredinnick, persuaded by an undercover reporter to accept £1,000 each for asking a parliamentary question for a bogus company. The failure to take this case beyond the Commons privileges committee's ruminations damaged the government, and later allegations of financial or sexual immorality were then all catalogued under the name 'sleaze'. Much more seriously, the illegal actions of a minister, Jonathan *Aitken, culminating in his withdrawal of a libel action against the *Guardian*, brought injurious publicity. The general problem was met by Major bringing in a judge, Lord *Nolan, who recommended sweeping restraints on the outside interests of MPs as well as compulsory and detailed declarations of interest. The *Nolan report was largely adopted, causing much resentment among Conservative MPs about whom the word 'sleaze' had never been used. They felt that a climate of accusation had taken toll of perfectly reputable work, but the high-profile personal defeat of Neil Hamilton by an independent in his normally safe Cheshire constituency in 1997 was more justified. *EP*

Sloan, Thomas H. (1870–1941), populist Irish Protestant politician. An evangelical and temperance advocate, he attacked the Unionist parliamentary leadership for its neglect of Protestant and working-class interests. In August 1902 he won a by-election in South Belfast, standing as an independent Unionist. A keen supporter of trade unionism, he was from 1903 associated with the Independent Orange Order. His career illustrated Ulster's political cross-currents. In January 1910 he lost his seat as Unionists began to close ranks against home rule. *DRB*

slum clearance. The replacement of unsanitary and unfit dwellings became a major feature of housing policy between the wars. Under the Housing Act of 1930 local authorities were given graduated subsidies according to the number of families rehoused and the cost of clearance, and were obliged to draw up five-year plans for slum clearance. The Housing Act of 1933 introduced fresh plans, aiming to clear 266,000 slum dwellings and rehouse one and a quarter million people, and by 1939 over two million had been rehoused. Further large-scale slum clearance took place after the war and over four million substandard properties were demolished by 1985. *JS*

'smack of firm government', phrase which appeared in a *Daily Telegraph* article on Eden's premiership in January 1956. Recalling Eden's habit of clenching his fist to smack into his palm—but without making the expected impact—most Conservatives were said to be 'waiting to feel the smack of firm government'. *RJS*

Smethwick, constituency, situated between Birmingham and the Black Country, which hit the headlines when immigration dominated its contest during the 1964 election. Despite Labour's national victory, Patrick Gordon *Walker, a senior front-bencher, lost the seat amidst protests at the alleged use by Tories of the slogan 'If you want a nigger neighbour, vote Labour'. The Tory candidate, Peter Griffiths, had not used the slogan himself but had urged tough measures against immigration. In the Commons, Wilson dubbed Griffiths a 'parliamentary leper'. *RJS*

Smith, Cyril (1928–), Liberal politician. Smith was born in Rochdale, Lancashire, and joined the Liberal Party in 1945, but subsequently made a career as a Labour councillor. Disillusioned with Labour he rejoined the Liberals in 1968 and won Rochdale at a by-election in 1972. A powerful figure in Liberal grass-roots politics, with a huge girth and an unaffected regional accent, he never sought high party office, retiring in 1992. *JS*

Smith, Frederick Edwin (1872–1930), Conservative politician. A product of modest Cheshire stock, 'F.E.' won a scholarship to Wadham College, Oxford, took the Union by storm (president, 1893), and began early to establish the reputation for reckless brilliance which would be his lifelong hallmark. He came down with a first-class degree, the Vinerian law scholarship, and a fellowship of Merton College. He was called to the Bar in 1899, practising successfully first in Liverpool and then in London, and the ambitious young man entered the Commons for Liverpool, Walton, in the Conservatives' disastrous year of 1906. His maiden speech only a month into his first session was brash, cuttingly clever, and bitterly provocative and remains perhaps the most famous example of its kind. He sat down amidst cheers from the Tories—a decimated parliamentary party hungry for warrior chieftains—and within five years he was a privy councillor and sat on the opposition front bench.

Smith enthusiastically allied himself with the more bellicose elements in his party, defending with outspoken vigour the causes of tariff reform and the Established Church in Wales, and attacking with equal abandon the Liberal government's legislative programme and particularly Lloyd George's controversial 'People's Budget' of 1909. He joined the Conservative diehards in the struggle over the Parliament Act and gained considerable notoriety as one of the most strident British supporters of Sir Edward *Carson and the Ulster Unionists in their opposition to Irish home rule. Yet, contrary to this warlike demeanour, he maintained close friendships with certain members of the Liberal Party, particularly with Winston Churchill. Furthermore, during the *Buckingham palace conferences of 1910 and 1914, he favoured compromise over party differences and even consideration of an inter-party administration to allow an honourable exit from the crises which threatened to bring the Commons to a complete halt. This dichotomy gave rise to suspicions of political opportunism among certain of his party colleagues.

With the coming of the Great War, Smith headed the press censorship apparatus, and with the formation of the two wartime coalitions he became solicitor-general (1915) and then attorney-general (1915–19). In 1919 Lloyd George astonished the legal community by appointing him lord chancellor (as Lord Birkenhead) at the youthful age of 46, an office in which he was remarkably successful. He was one of the negotiators of the 1921 Anglo-Irish treaty which separated the Irish Free State from an autonomous Northern Ireland. He remained loyal to Lloyd George at the Carlton Club meeting of 1922, thereby making himself intolerable to the backbench anti-coalition Conservatives who thought him vain and utterly immoral, and then went deep into the political wilderness. Baldwin rescued him and sent him (without particular success) to the India Office, 1924–8, whereafter he retired from active politics. Though commonly tipped in the years before 1914 as a future premier, there is about Birkenhead's story the scent of unfulfilled promise. Perhaps too nakedly ambitious and too clever—certainly too outspoken and too pleasure-loving—he often inspired admiration but seldom trust. His admirers saw him as a visionary, his enemies as an egotistical adventurer.

RJQA

Earl of Birkenhead, *F. E.: The Life of F. E. Smith: First Earl of Birkenhead* (London, 1959). | John Campbell, *F. E. Smith: First Earl of Birkenhead* (London, 1983).

Smith, Herbert (1862–1938), trade unionist. Smith was president of the Miners' Federation of Great Britain at the time of the 1926 General Strike, and was famous for his blunt opposition to wage cuts, most notably his Yorkshireman's statement that 'We've nowt to give'. He began working in a mine at the age of 10 and later filled various official positions for the miners. Eventually, he became an official to the Yorkshire Miners' Association in 1894, and was drawn to local politics, largely on behalf of the Independent Labour Party—he was mayor of Barnsley in 1931–2. Smith became vice-president of the Yorkshire Miners in 1904 and president in 1906. He was also a member of the executive council of the Miners' Federation of Great Britain, 1908–37, acting as president, 1922–9.

KL

Smith, John (1938–94), Labour Party leader. After training as a barrister, Smith was called to the Bar in 1967 and made a QC in 1983. A pro-European Scot who advocated multilateral nuclear disarmament, he joined the Labour Party in 1955 and became Labour MP for Lanarkshire North, 1970–83, and Monklands East, 1983–94. He was widely admired in parliament for his integrity and debating skills. In 1972 Smith refused to back Labour's anti-European stance and supported the Conservative government's proposal that the UK should join the European Community. He held a number of junior ministerial positions before achieving cabinet rank as secretary for trade, 1978–9. Thereafter, Smith was a key figure in Labour's shadow cabinet under Foot and Kinnock, serving as chief opposition spokesman on trade, prices, and consumer protection, 1979–82; on energy, 1982–3; on trade and industry, 1984–7; and on Treasury and economic affairs, 1987–92. As shadow chancellor, Smith supported membership of the Exchange Rate Mechanism (ERM) and full involvement in the single currency project. He also encouraged Labour's pragmatic acceptance of private ownership and the market economy, but his redistributive tax proposals reinforced middle-class suspicion of the party at the 1992 general election. Following Kinnock's resignation, Smith was elected party leader in July 1992 with 91 per cent of the vote. He continued his predecessor's policy of modernizing Labour and giving it a more centrist identity but proceeded in a cautious, piecemeal fashion so as to preserve party unity. At the 1993 Labour conference, he used his personal authority to push through reform of the trade union block vote. However, Smith's traditionalist instincts resisted calls to revise Clause 4 and he favoured strengthening trade-union rights in the workplace. He died suddenly, while still leader in May 1994, his place taken by Tony Blair. *AM*

ANDY MCSMITH, *John Smith: A Life 1938–1994* (London, 1994).

Smith Square, just off Millbank in Westminster, has at various times contained the head offices of all three major British parties. The Labour Party had offices within the Transport House headquarters of the Transport and General Workers' Union, 1928–80, prior to moving to *Walworth Road; the Liberal Party headquarters were briefly in the Square, 1965–8; Conservative Central Office has been at 32 Smith Square since 1958. *JAR*

smoking, politics of. Smoking attracted little attention prior to the Second World War as a health risk. Tobacco was always, however, a source of government excise duty. Since the 1960s, with greater concerns and clearer evidence about the risks of smoking to health, governments have targeted taxes on tobacco for even higher excise duties. These have been combined with public health campaigns against smoking, much amplified by recent governments. Smoking has also been restricted in many public places, such as underground stations, offices, and places of entertainment. There are proposals to ban smoking in public areas such as pubs and restaurants, although these remain controversial and unfulfilled. *JS*

Smuts, Jan Christian **(1870–1949)**, South African liberal leader and prime minister, 1939–48. Smuts was one of the Boer military leaders of the war of 1899–1902 who went on to a political career, but in his case to seek reconciliation both within South Africa and between South Africa and Britain. A lifelong friend of Winston Churchill, he was South African representative in the Imperial war cabinet during the Great War and consulted again by Churchill on military matters in the Second World War. *JAR*

Snowden, Philip **(1864–1937)**, Labour politician. Snowden was a profoundly controversial figure in the early years of the British Labour movement. Raised in a Liberal Nonconformist community in the West Riding of Yorkshire, he became involved in the activities of the Liberal Party and then the Independent Labour Party (ILP), in January 1895. Politically active in both local and parliamentary politics, Snowden was returned as MP for Blackburn in 1906 and twice again in 1910. However, his opposition to the Great War led to his defeat in 1918. Nevertheless, he was returned for Colne Valley in the 1922 general election, and held the seat at four general elections until he was raised to a viscountcy in November 1931.

Throughout his life Snowden adhered to radical Liberal sentiments. He opposed the Great War and thus mounted the ILP's peace campaign of 1917 as well as attending the workmen's and soldiers' council convention held at Leeds in June 1917, designed to bring international peace in the wake of the February 1917 revolution in Russia. From 1922, Snowden made the Labour Party, rather than the ILP, his political home. He was frustrated at Ramsay MacDonald's return as Labour's parliamentary leader in 1922 but served under him as both chancellor of the exchequer and shadow chancellor, 1922–31. In the former role he gave full vent to his Gladstonian economic notions of balancing the budget, reducing the national debt, and, if necessary, deflating the economy. It is clear, however, that his economic policies were inappropriate to the economic climate of 1929–1931. The Wall Street crash reverberated around the world and led to a rise in unemployment in Britain which increased government expenditure enormously and simultaneously reduced income. With a deficit of between £100 million and £170 million, there was downward pressure on the pound and a serious economic crisis. Snowden, concerned about sound finance, advocated the twin policies of a 10 per cent cut in unemployment benefit and increased taxation upon the middle classes, which was referred to as 'equality of sacrifice'. Yet the Labour cabinet was deeply divided on the benefit cuts on 23 August 1931, and this led to the resignation of the second Labour government and the formation of a *National Government on 24 August 1931. Snowden assumed the role of lord privy seal in that government and was somewhat alarmed when Britain was taken off the gold standard on 21 September, although he assured himself that it was only a temporary situation and not the basis of a move towards protectionism. He therefore campaigned vigorously for the new government in the 1931 election campaign, referring to Labour's policies as 'Bolshevism run mad'. But after less than a year, frustrated by the continued rise of protectionism, Snowden resigned from the National Government. Subsequently, although a spent force in British politics, he engaged in making personal attacks on MacDonald, who he felt had thwarted his political ambitions, and published vitriolic memoirs (1934). *KL*

COLIN CROSS, *Philip Snowden* (London, 1966). | KEITH LAYBOURN, *Philip Snowden: A Biography, 1864–1937* (Aldershot, 1988).

SNP. See SCOTTISH NATIONAL PARTY.

Soames, (Arthur) Christopher John (1920–87), Conservative politician, diplomat, and European commissioner. After Eton and Sandhurst, Soames served in the Second World War before becoming liaison officer with General de Gaulle's Free French. Having served as a military attaché in Paris from 1945, he was elected MP for Bedford in 1950. He had married Churchill's daughter Mary in 1947 and, as his father-in-law's parliamentary private secretary in 1953, he ensured that Churchill could remain prime minister despite a serious stroke. After the 1954 Conservative conference, however, he helped persuade Churchill to retire. Emerging as a politician in his own right, Soames served at the Air Ministry from 1955 and the Admiralty from 1957 before Macmillan made him war secretary in 1958. Promoted to the cabinet in 1960 as agriculture minister, Soames faced the Herculean task of harmonizing British farming with the policy of the European Economic Community, but de Gaulle's veto wrecked his efforts. After 1964 he was shadow defence secretary and foreign affairs spokesman but lost his seat in 1966. His defeat, however, brought an opportunity that was to make Soames's career. In 1968 Wilson appointed him British ambassador in Paris, where his rapport with the French paved the way for British membership of the European Economic Community. On Britain's entry in 1973, he became vice-president of the European Commission with responsibility for foreign affairs. In 1978 he entered the Lords and the following year Thatcher appointed this pro-European, patrician Tory to her cabinet as leader of the House of Lords, lord president of the council, and civil service minister. She later appointed him governor of Rhodesia, where he supervised Zimbabwe's transition to independence in 1980. The next year, following a clash over civil service pay, Thatcher sacked him, but the bigger surprise was that she had ever appointed him to her cabinet in the first place. *RJS*

Social Chapter, protocol on social policy in the *Maastricht treaty. The social chapter committed member states to the objectives of 'the promotion of employment, improved living and working conditions, proper social protection, dialogue between management and labour, [and] the development of human resources with a view to lasting high employment and the combating of exclusion' (Article 1). In June 1997 the British Labour government signed the protocol after Major's Conservative government had secured an opt-out in 1991. *JRVE*

social contract (1975), phrase from Enlightenment political theory reapplied to describe the deal between the Labour Party and TUC in February 1973. Under this accord, the trade unions accepted restraints on wage demands, to avoid conflict with a future Labour government, in return for promises of social benefits. The social contract was undermined by the world recession of 1974–5 and finally brought to an end by the massive strike wave against pay restraint during the 'winter of discontent', 1978–9. *DLM*

Social Credit, fringe political movement linked to the American variety of populism, which sought to limit the political and economic influence of the banking system, substituting a promise of the simple life in which individuals controlled their own destinies (in this it was also linked to such fieldcraft rural ideologies as Kibbo Kift, which effectively became its activist wing). Social Credit flourished for much of the century in western Canada, only fitfully in the 1930s achieving any significance in Britain. Its founder and prophet, Major C. H. Douglas, was a British engineer and economist who worked in Alberta. Its visibility in that decade of political uniforms was achieved by wearing green shirts, not unlike the Fascists' black shirts. On hearing the news in 1935 that Social Credit had taken power in Alberta, their forces marched through the City of London in triumph. Later that year, their candidate stood at the general election in Leeds, insisted on paying his deposit in coins rather than a banker's cheque, but nevertheless lost it. *JAR*

MICHAEL WHARTON, 'A Few Lost Causes', in John Raymond (ed.), *The Baldwin Age* (London, 1960).

Social Darwinism, bastardized concept derived from Charles Darwin's work on evolution. Darwin had demonstrated that animal and plant species had evolved competitively, so that by 'natural selection' only the 'fittest', those that had best adapted to changing environments, had survived. Some of his disciples (but not Darwin himself) applied this biological concept to different ethnic groups within the human race, and, even more crudely, this was popularized by the 1890s into assumptions about the inevitability of conflict between nations, and into claims that a nation that was not expanding was inevitably in decline—'decline' being taken to mean a descent towards racial subjugation or even extinction. The concept lent itself easily to arguments in favour of acquiring and holding colonies, and other manifestations of national virility such as armaments. In the Edwardian period, Social Darwinism was therefore at the heart of popular racial concepts like 'Pan-Anglo-Saxonism' (though the inability of British and American believers to agree whether or not German 'Saxons' were part of that same racial 'stock' indicates the extreme fragility of the idea when applied to anything actual). It also helped to motivate defenders of the British Empire like Joseph Chamberlain, in his desire to unite Britain more closely with the 'white dominions' through imperial preference. Within domestic politics, it stimulated a drive for 'national efficiency', through administrative and social reforms, the latter intended to bolster the quality of 'the race' through such initiatives as free milk for schoolchildren. Social Darwinism also fed into even darker sides of politics, in anti-Semitism and the brief flourishing of British interest in eugenics, the supposed science of racial improvement through sterilization and selective breeding. Its association with the origins of the terrible Great War, and with theories afterwards propounded by fascists both at home and abroad, indicates why Social Darwinism found few British adherents from the 1920s onwards. *JAR*

G. R. Searle, *The Quest for National Efficiency in Britain, 1900–1914* (Oxford, 1971).

social democracy. In the 19th century this term referred to Marxist socialism, as in H. M. Hyndman's Social Democratic Federation, founded in 1884 and merged with other parties to form the British Socialist Party in 1911. This in turn merged with others to form the Communist Party of Great Britain in 1920. As with Presbyterian churches, each merger produced splinters, comprising purists who could not accept the compromises involved in it. Some of the splinters have survived in a shadowy way for decades. However, by 1910 another usage of 'social democrat' and its cognate terms was overtaking the original one. In 1903, the Russian Social Democratic Party split (at a meeting in London) into its 'Bolshevik' and 'Menshevik' wings. The former advocated an elite vanguard of revolutionaries, such as the one that came to power in Russia in October 1917. The latter advocated a mass socialist party. This strategy became known, first in Russia and then elsewhere, as social democracy. The idea that social democracy means right-wing, rather than left-wing, socialism received a further boost when the German Social Democratic Party (SPD, where the 'S' stands for 'Sozialdemocratisches') dropped Marxist socialism from its programme in 1959.

In the internal struggles of the Labour Party from the 1950s to 1981, 'social democrat' and 'social democracy' were the rallying flags of the right. There was never a particularly distinctive social democratic programme—the nearest to such a thing being Crosland's *The *Future of Socialism* (1956). Those who broke away from Labour, an amalgam of right-wing socialists and libertarians, took the title *Social Democratic Party (SDP) in 1981. It was an uncomfortable amalgam: the socialists believed in Keynesian planning of the economy, while the libertarians supported free-market economics and a liberal approach to moral and social questions such as homosexuality and divorce. However, this was no more uncomfortable than the amalgams which go to make up the Labour and Conservative parties. What defeated the SDP was not so much the incoherence of its ideology as the British electoral system. In the 1983 general election, the SDP/Liberal Alliance came within 2 percentage points of Labour's vote share but won only 23 seats to Labour's 209 (the SDP taking only six of the 23). After a similar performance in 1987, the two parties agreed to merge, leaving splinters on each side just like their Marxist predecessors 70 years earlier. The merged party is now called the Liberal Democrats. Under Neil Kinnock and (especially) Tony Blair, the Labour Party has moved to occupy the political space of the social democrats, plus a swathe of territory to their right. The Keynesian wing of social democracy is dead; the libertarian wing survives in the Liberal and (less certainly) Labour parties. *IM*

Social Democracy, Council for (1981), centrist pressure group. This was the first stage in the formation of the *Social Democratic Party. The Council for Social Democracy was launched with the *Limehouse declaration on 25 January 1981, in which the *'Gang of Four' invited people to join them. It provided the interim stage for defection from other parties which by 2 March included twelve Labour MPs who declared they would not seek re-election for Labour. With the launch of the Social Democratic Party on 26 March 1981, the Council for Social Democracy was wound up. *JS*

Social Democratic and Labour Party (SDLP), Northern Irish political party. The origins of the party can be found in the political turmoil produced by the developments that arose out of the civil rights movement. In order to offer the minority community a credible alternative to the Unionist government at Stormont, various opposition MPs agreed to come together. The objective was to try to unite the various strands of Northern nationalism, from the more conservative elements in rural areas to working-class supporters in Belfast. The outcome of these negotiations was the SDLP with its main aim to introduce progressive social and economic policies within a reformed Northern Ireland, while at the same time working for Irish unification on the basis of securing the consent of the Unionist community. The tensions between those from the more 'nationalist' wing of the party and those who wanted to concentrate on 'bread and butter issues' came to a head following the collapse of the power-sharing executive in May 1974. This was to result in the departure of two of the original founder members, Paddy Devlin in 1977 and Gerry *Fitt, the party leader, in 1979, both of whom had strong labour backgrounds. Under its new leader, John *Hume, the party began to concentrate on ensuring that any future settlement in Northern Ireland would have a much greater input from the Irish government. This led ultimately to the signing of the *Anglo-Irish agreement in November 1985. Within Northern Ireland itself the SDLP continued to draw the bulk of its support from the nationalist community but the entry of the Republican movement into the political scene through Sinn Fein created a new rival to challenge the party's dominant position. In fact, such has been the success of Sinn Fein on the back of the evolving peace process that the gap has narrowed to the extent that there are indications that Sinn Fein stands on the verge of overtaking the SDLP. Consequently, as the SDLP celebrates its thirtieth anniversary a great deal of uncertainty surrounds its immediate future. *BL*

GERARD MURRAY, *John Hume and the SDLP* (Dublin, 1998).

Social Democratic Federation (SDF), Britain's first avowedly Marxist party. Most historians have chosen to dismiss the SDF as a political sect, dominated by its founder H. M. *Hyndman and attempting to foist an alien political tradition on to the working class, but such a negative image is ill deserved. The SDF drew on native socialist traditions as well as Marxism and sank deep roots in several areas, notably London and north-east Lancashire. SDF members played an important role in the founding conference of the Labour Party in 1900; they campaigned against the Boer war; their right to work campaign, which included the first unemployed hunger march, forced concessions at both local and national level; they organized adult education classes. Theirs was by no means a negligible achievement but the SDF's fatal mistake was its decision to withdraw from the Labour Party in 1901. This condemned it to a mere evangelical and propagandist role, acting as a kind of conscience for the wider movement. It championed socialist unity as an alternative to the alliance with the trade unions and came together with dissident Independent Labour Party members and sections of the Clarion movement to form the British Socialist Party (BSP) in 1911. For a short while the BSP seemed to offer a genuine socialist alternative to the Labour Party, but internal dissension soon reduced it to a largely SDF rump. The party was divided over its attitude to the Great War and it split in 1916. Those remaining in the BSP eventually merged into the Communist Party of Great Britain whilst Hyndman and the 'old guard' formed the National Socialist Party and reaffiliated to the Labour Party. They reverted to their traditional name in 1920 but the SDF was a declining force and was finally wound up in 1939. *MC*

MARTIN CRICK, *The History of the Social Democratic Federation* (Keele, 1994).

Social Democratic Party (SDP), originated on 25 January 1981 as the Council for *Social Democracy, an organization led by four disillusioned Labour politicians, sometimes dubbed the *'Gang of Four' (Shirley *Williams, David *Owen, William *Rodgers, and Roy *Jenkins). The broad aims of the new party were set out in the *Limehouse declaration, followed on 26 March 1981 by the setting up of the Social Democratic Party as a separate political party. Although its aims were to be decided by reference to its members, its leaders expressed support for electoral reform through proportional representation, continued membership of the European Community, multilateral disarmament, and a reflationary economic strategy with an incomes policy and inflation tax. In September 1981, the new SDP formed the *Alliance with the Liberals to fight the next general election and reach mutual agreement on the fighting of by-elections and local government elections. The first elected SDP MP, Shirley Williams, won the *Crosby by-election in November 1981. Roy Jenkins then won the Glasgow *Hillhead by-election in 1982 and subsequently became leader of the party.

In the 1983 general election, the SDP campaigned alongside the Liberals in the Alliance, each contesting approximately half the seats nationally. Although the Alliance took almost a quarter of the popular vote, its return in terms of seats was disappointing, just 23 MPs, and only six of these were from the SDP. Disillusion with Jenkins's performance in the election as de facto 'prime minister designate' led to David Owen becoming SDP leader in June 1983. In 1986, serious rifts with the Liberal Party developed over defence policy, but the Alliance was relaunched early in 1987 and the SDP and Liberals campaigned again under joint leadership in the subsequent general election. This time the SDP returned only five MPs, only David Owen of the 'Gang of Four' being retained in his seat.

Liberal calls for a merger in the wake of the election led to fierce controversy within the SDP and a ballot of SDP members about opening merger talks with the Liberals. A vote of 57 per cent to 43 per cent in favour of merger talks led to David Owen's resignation as leader and a major split within the SDP appeared imminent when he was succeeded by Robert *Maclennan. Early in 1988 though, the SDP voted in favour of a merger with the Liberals to form the Social and Liberal Democrats, launched in March, subsequently taking the name *Liberal Democrats and electing a new leader, Paddy *Ashdown.

The formation of the SDP was the most serious attempt to set up a new political party in Britain since the war, in a famous attempt at *'breaking the mould' of British politics. The SDP was not, however, able to do so. Although in alliance with the Liberals it took an unprecedented share of the vote for a third force in both the 1983 and 1987 elections, more than a fifth of voters opting for the Alliance, it failed to achieve the sweeping successes which its launch and early by-election victories suggested. Founded at a time when the Thatcher government was deeply unpopular and when the Labour Party appeared bent on a self-destructive lurch to the left, the SDP and its Alliance partners sought to capitalize upon the centre ground and remodel the traditional boundaries of party support in post-war Britain. In practice, Thatcher's popularity was restored, in part by the Falklands war of 1982, and only one Conservative MP was prepared to defect to the SDP (and lost his seat in 1983 anyway). Moreover, the Labour Party proved more resilient than expected. Major figures of the Labour right refused to defect, stemming the tide of Labour support. Quarrels over seat allocations between the SDP and the Liberals soon took some of the initial enthusiasm for a 'new politics' away, and there remained a feeling within some of the original SDP, particularly David Owen, that alliance with the Liberals had compromised the identity of the new party from the start. These divisions surfaced especially over defence policy and were reflected in the delay over merging the two parties which many saw as an inevitable and necessary step as early as the 1983 election. The effect was to reduce SDP and Alliance support below the critical level at which it could gain large numbers of MPs, given the fairly even distribution of its vote across the country. Even with only a small extra percentage of the popular vote, the Labour Party in 1983 and 1987 was able to win almost ten times the Alliance's number of MPs, through its greater concentration of voters in the industrial heartlands.

Thus the workings of the *'first past the post' system have been identified as a significant factor in the failure of the SDP and the Alliance to break the mould. It was also particularly embarrassing for the SDP that the Liberal Party had strong traditional support concentrated in some areas, allowing it to capture the majority of Alliance seats. The alliance with the Liberal Party did, however, witness substantial gains in local government and continuing spectacular by-election victories which maintained a momentum towards the formation of a credible merged party. Although the Liberal Democrats suffered from an initial setback in support, largely due to Owen's resistance to merger and his formation of a short-lived 'Continuing SDP', an effective new party was established. In the long term the formation of the SDP promoted the creation of a larger third party than has existed since the 1920s in the shape of the Liberal Democrats and provided their current party leader, Charles Kennedy, who began his career in the SDP. *JS*

IVOR CREWE and ANTHONY KING, *SDP: The Birth, Life and Death of the Social Democratic Party* (Oxford, 1995).

social imperialism, term referring to the movement among Conservatives in the early 20th century to combine a dedication to maintaining the Empire with a commitment to social reform, so as to improve the material lot of the working classes, and at the same time raise the physical fitness of the British to be an imperial people (see SOCIAL DARWINISM). It was clearly a response to the reality of political democracy, the keen competition among nations for world markets, the challenges to older empires from ambitious rivals such as Germany, and the need to offer a political alternative to the collectivist programmes of the *New Liberalism and of socialism. It had roots in the ideas of imperial theorists such as Milner, but the major thrust of the movement lay in the tariff reform programme of Joseph Chamberlain. This proposed a blueprint to pull together the disparate units of the Empire into a more cohesive, more secure whole, with a plausible scheme to raise sufficient money to fund old age pensions, national insurance, urban recovery, and social and economic security—all without ruinous domestic taxation. Buoyed up on Chamberlain's magnificent rhetoric, it proposed a design for imperial renewal, cloaked in the missionary zeal of 'British race patriotism' with the added promise of improved domestic prosperity: 'Tariff Reform means work for all'. Though tariff reform and imperialism continued to be subjects of national debate for many years, the social imperialism of this grand vision faded away in the drastically changed post-war world after 1918. Conservatism was left to contest with socialism for working-class votes on a narrower national basis. *RJQA*

MATTHEW FFORDE, *Conservatism and Collectivism, 1886–1914* (Edinburgh, 1990). | E. W. W. GREEN, *The Crisis of Conservatism: The Politics, Economics and Ideology of the British Conservative Party, 1880–1914* (London, 1995). | BERNARD SEMMEL, *Imperialism and Social Reform: English Social–Imperial Thought, 1895–1914* (Cambridge, Mass., 1960).

socialism, a practical and theoretical position which holds that the means of production, distribution, and exchange should be held communally, and that production should be geared towards collective rather than individual needs. In this form, therefore, socialism is based on mechanical rather than moral reform; and in some circumstances it maintains a commitment to revolution to overthrow the existing political and economic regime. Socialism in the UK, in contrast, has tended to differ in two ways. First, following the ideas of Eduard Bernstein and others, British socialism has been explicitly revisionist, abandoning notions of revolution in favour of a parliamentary route to change (see REVISIONISM). Second, socialism in the UK has been a broader movement than the one stated above, reflecting the commonplace that it owed as much to Methodism as to Marxism, and emphasizing notions such as brotherhood and co-operation, and moral reform as much as mechanical reform. As such, it drew on the British tradition of self-improvement through education, public libraries, and local association. Its Christian Socialist strand emphasized the moral obligation of the state, and Fabian socialists emphasized the need for the permeation of existing political parties and the gradual introduction of reforms to produce a consensus for collectivist arrangements. Third, a large number of socialists followed Bernstein's social democratic analysis which suggested that capitalism had ceased to be a system of class oppression, due to the expansion of share ownership; the growing number of professional, salaried, and technical staff; and the extension of legal protection and welfare benefits, a view echoed by Crosland, in *The Future of Socialism*. This, coupled with the growth of the mixed and regulated economy and economic expansion through Keynesian demand management, could be presented as an alternative path to socialism's traditional goal of equality. Socialists also disagreed about the extent to which democratic participation is essential for a healthy society. While Fabianism concentrated on the role of political leaders to the extent that it appeared to be proposing government by an enlightened administrative elite, and the Labour Party in general was disposed to see socialism as an activity to be carried out on a national basis by political organizations on behalf of their members, guild socialists, such as G. D. H. Cole, argued for the democratization and decentralization of industry.

The combination of these forces has produced a Labour movement which is influenced more by New Liberalism policy making, Fabian social democracy, and the interests of organized labour, than by socialism. In 1918, the Labour Party adopted, as Clause 4 of its new constitution, a commitment to public ownership compatible with socialism. However, in *The Evolution of the Labour Party* (Oxford, 1974), R. I. McKibbin puts this into context by arguing that the adoption of this socialist objective was accompanied by a specific rejection of socialist ideology. Thus, the Labour Party was in essence a trade union party, 'where class loyalty drove out socialist doctrine' (p. 244) and where union dominance was felt at all levels. Thereafter, Clause 4 remained a policy objective without any chance of being implemented and seen increasingly by revisionists as an electoral millstone around the party's neck. Once in government the party abandoned any commitment to central planning, as did the Swedish Social Democrats in the 1930s and the West German Social Democrats in 1959, and it pursued nationalization only by consent and where there was a pragmatic reason for it, as during its 1945–51 period of office. Common ownership remained the goal of sections of party activists up until the 1980s; but without much hope of success. *CPS*

Socialist Inquiry and Propaganda, Society for (SSIP) (1931–2). The SSIP was formed by a group of intellectuals and trade union leaders dissatisfied with the second Labour government. Leading figures included G. D. H. Cole and Ernest Bevin. During its short existence it produced a series of pamphlets, study guides, and reports which galvanized thinking within the Labour movement. Opposition to the amalgamation of the SSIP with anti-disaffiliation members of the Independent Labour Party in a new organization called the Socialist League led to its dissolution in November 1932. *MC*

Socialist Labour League. See Workers' Revolutionary Party.

Socialist Labour Party (SLP) (1903–22). A revolutionary breakaway from the Social Democratic Federation, the SLP was originally concentrated in Scotland but by 1919 had branches all over Britain. Although a small organization, membership peaking at 1,258 in 1920, it achieved considerable significance. The SLP was unique amongst British socialists in rejecting the capture of political power. Instead, strongly influenced by the ideas of the American Daniel De Leon, it favoured industrial unionism, the creation of new unions on an industrial rather than a craft basis. These would form the administrative machinery of the new socialist society, the 'industrial republic of labour'. The party's concentration on the industrial arena allowed it to exercise a significant influence on the Clyde Workers' Committee and the shop stewards' movement during the Great War. Its stress on the importance of independent working-class education made it the most important distributor of Marxist literature in Britain. The SLP wholeheartedly supported the Bolshevik revolution, indeed saw itself as the 'British Bolsheviks', although this meant a change in its own ideology, and many SLP members joined the Communist Party of Great Britain, thus signalling the demise of their own party in 1922. *MC*

Raymond Challinor, *The Origins of British Bolshevism* (London, 1977).

Socialist League (1932–7). The inter-war Socialist League (not to be confused with William Morris's League in the 1880s) was founded in 1932 by ex-members of the Independent Labour Party (ILP) in conjunction with the Fabian-style Society for Socialist Inquiry and Propaganda. Prominent Socialist Leaguers included G. D. H. Cole, Sir Stafford Cripps, Frank Wise, William Mellor, and Barbara Betts (later Castle). Though its membership was small, the league became the focus for socialist dissent and left-wing rebellion within the Labour Party. In 1937, it joined forces with the ILP and Communist Party in a so-called Unity Campaign, which simultaneously opposed rearmament and called for an Anglo-French alliance with Russia. The Labour Party NEC responded by disaffiliating it, and shortly afterwards the league disbanded. The Socialist League's most enduring legacy was the weekly paper *Tribune*, first published in January 1937 as part of the Unity campaign. *BP*

Socialist Party of Great Britain (SPGB) (1904–). This unique organization was founded by London members of the Social Democratic Federation who objected to its minimum reform programme. It is the oldest independent socialist group in Britain and the declaration of principles adopted by its founders remains unchanged to this day. The SPGB rejects all compromise and believes that socialism will come only when the mass of the people has been converted. Thus it opposed the Russian revolution on the grounds that it was premature and did not have the support of the majority and is against the welfare state because it blinds workers to their real interests. The SPGB spreads the gospel via its *Socialist Standard*, debates with rival groups, and stands candidates in parliamentary elections with a total lack of success. Nevertheless it still claims to be the true custodian of the socialist vision. *MC*

Socialist Workers' Party (SWP) (1977–), originally the Socialist Review Group and, from 1962, the International Socialists (IS). The group's distinctive analysis of Soviet Russia as 'state capitalist' and its theory of the permanent arms economy led it to break with orthodox Trotskyism in 1950. It operated within the Labour Party until 1965 and was remarkable on the revolutionary left for its relatively libertarian, non-sectarian attitudes. Indeed it owed more to the influence of Rosa Luxemburg than to either Trotsky or Lenin. Largely student-based in the late 1960s, the growth of shop steward militancy encouraged the leadership to attempt an industrial base. This was accompanied by a turn to Leninism after 1968 and the adoption of democratic centralism as an organizational model. Rank and file groups were established in a number of industries during the early 1970s and IS launched a successful right to work campaign in 1975. Journalists such as Paul Foot and Eamonn McCabe made *Socialist Worker* the best-read newspaper on the revolutionary left. In 1977 the party was relaunched as the Socialist Workers' Party, since when it has remained committed to developing a Leninist party and has been characterized by an almost syndicalist belief that trade union militancy is inherently political. Paradoxically the SWP's greatest successes came with the establishment of the Anti-Nazi League in 1977, a broad-based anti-fascist movement, and with the anti-poll tax campaign of the early 1990s. *MC*

social justice, an object of great concern in modern political life. It was given its most articulate expression by *New Liberalism and *socialism, which held that there is indeed such a thing as society, and that the nature of society, in which people are interdependent, must shape the whole purpose of politics. That purpose is to narrow the gap between individuals as far as possible, through the redistribution of wealth and the provision of social and welfare services. Benefits must be distributed equally, and this must involve state action, perhaps on an ambitious scale. At bottom, then, is the idea of equality between people as a moral imperative. To the left in politics, large gaps in wealth in a society are a big flaw, perhaps even a moral affront. The nature of social justice can conflict with another idea of justice: that which places emphasis on the individual's right to justice. The New Right in Britain and elsewhere began to argue strongly in the 1970s that social justice was a form of injustice to the individual, whose freedom to live his life and enjoy what he owned and earned were deeply compromised by the foolish search for social justice. Justice, in this view, was the individual coming to the market place as a buyer or seller. The right indeed criticized the whole concept as an 'enterprise culture', a culture which had a particular purpose which informed the politics of distribution; such goals were not even achievable by political means, and ended in imposing penalties, maybe even loss of freedom, on the individual. Margaret Thatcher was criticized by advocates of social justice when she said 'there is *no such thing as society'. Supporters of social justice hold that society does exist and that it is the object of concern. Society, therefore, has a will and purpose of its own. The modern political consensus stands somewhere between these two positions, holding that there are limits to the acquisition of property, which must not be held at the expense of the well-being of others, but that any more ambitious project of social justice is highly dubious, and probably incompatible with the creation of a healthy national economy. *DGB*

L. T. Hobhouse, *Liberalism* (London, 1919 edn.).

social security. See NATIONAL ASSISTANCE.

Social Security, Department of (1988–). See HEALTH AND SOCIAL SECURITY, DEPARTMENT OF.

SOE. See SPECIAL OPERATIONS EXECUTIVE.

Solemn League and Covenant. See ULSTER'S SOLEMN LEAGUE AND COVENANT.

Somme, battle of the (1916). A battle central both to the catastrophic historical reputation of the Great War and to the making of the modern Ulster Unionist identity. It was part of Douglas *Haig's use of the 'new armies' of volunteer recruits, and was the testing ground of the Ulster Volunteer Force, which mustered into the British army as the 36th (Ulster) Division. The battle began on what was for Irishmen a symbolic date, 1 July, the anniversary of the battle of the Boyne in the old-style pre-Gregorian calendar. The battle cost 20,000 British lives on the first day, for little gain of ground, though its five months of attrition also inflicted irreplaceable casualties on the Germans. Ulster Unionists saw the Somme as a blood sacrifice for Ulster which must not be betrayed, and in the post-1970 'Troubles' Loyalists cited it as an example of noble sacrifice which Britain now seemed ready to betray. For the rest of the UK, the 1 July anniversary has been used as a regular reminder of the Great War's apparently senseless waste of young lives. *DGB*

Martin Middlebrook, *The First Day on the Somme* (new edn., London, 1991). | Philip Orr, *The Road to the Somme: Men of the Ulster Division tell their Story* (Belfast, 1987). | A. T. Q. Stewart, *The Ulster Crisis* (London, 1967).

Soper, Donald Oliver (1903–99), Christian Socialist and pacifist, created a Labour life peer in 1965. Ordained to the Methodist ministry in 1926, by the late 1930s he was a leading figure in the Socialist Christian League and vice-chair of the Peace Pledge Union. In the late 1950s he was equally active in the Campaign for Nuclear Disarmament, and was instrumental in the setting up in 1960 of the Christian Socialist Movement, of which he was the first chairman. *PPC*

Soskice, Frank (1902–79), Labour politician. An internationally respected barrister, Soskice became solicitor-general (1945–51) and attorney-general (1951) under Attlee. He belonged to the shadow cabinet, 1951–64, and supported Gaitskell on economic and defence matters. As home secretary, 1964–5, Soskice sometimes acted indecisively but he also promoted useful penal reforms and introduced the 1965 Race Relations Act. Briefly lord privy seal afterwards, he was made a life peer as Lord Stow Hill in 1966. *AM*

South Africa. Following the *Boer war, the 1905 Liberal government sought rapprochement between English-speaking settlers and Boers in order to avoid renewed conflict in southern Africa and through fear that, in a war with Germany, Afrikaans-speaking South Africans could back Germany. Moderate Boers were co-opted into the overall government of South Africa, which duly became a self-governing dominion in 1911. The price of Boer acquiescence was a constitution with little entrenchment of native rights; the benefit appeared very real when in 1914 most South Africans supported the British war effort, thousands fighting and dying in the Great War. South Africa received a mandate to govern the former German colony of south-west Africa, but during the inter-war years increasing concern was voiced in Britain over the treatment of Africans within South Africa. This was much increased with the advent to power of the Nationalist Party, introducing their *apartheid policies during the 1950s. By 1960, Macmillan was warning South Africa of the Continental wind of change to which it must bend. In fact, the horror that greeted the massacre of protesters by security forces at Sharpeville shortly afterwards led rather to the withdrawal of South Africa from the Commonwealth, largely to pre-empt its expulsion. The next 30 years saw a steady build-up of support in Britain for African rights in South Africa, and the gradual ostracization of South Africa in the world community. This was always difficult for British governments, uneasily aware of the strategic importance of the Simonstown naval base during the Cold War, and of continuing support for white South Africans amongst sectors of the British population. Britain, especially when under Conservative governments, was generally therefore a reluctant supporter of UN sanctions intended to bring apartheid down, lest they produce a communist regime at the Cape or a widespread racial war engulfing Rhodesia as well as South Africa. The end of the Cold War and the coincident collapse of the white South African regime in the 1990s therefore occasioned considerable relief as well as genuine pleasure in London. President Nelson Mandela, for decades a hero of the British left, was now able to return South Africa to the Commonwealth and be received on visits to Britain with extraordinary warmth and affection. *JAR*

South East Asia Treaty Organization (SEATO), regional security alliance signed between the USA, Britain, France, Thailand, the Philippines, Australia, and New Zealand at Manila on 8 September 1954. Anthony Eden would only agree to discuss American proposals for the collective defence of south-east Asia against communist aggression after the Geneva conference of May–July 1954 had succeeded in securing a compromise settlement of the conflict in Indochina, leading to considerable friction with the US secretary of state, John Foster Dulles. Britain failed to convince India, and later independent Malaya, to join the grouping, and from its inception SEATO was unpopular with the non-aligned states of the region, who saw it as a way to maintain Western influence and a militarized presence. Over time, SEATO became an important public symbol to British policy makers of their determination to prevent further communist gains in south-east Asia, but it also allowed them to exercise some influence over US policy. This became vital as the situation in Laos deteriorated in the late 1950s and plans were readied for SEATO intervention, which the British feared could provoke Chinese intervention and the danger of US pressure for the use of tactical nuclear weapons. British policy was to urge restraint and to seek a diplomatic solution to the Laotian conflict, but they were forever wary of more belligerent voices in the Pentagon. Crises in Laos recurred in January–May 1961, and again in May 1962 when, despite sanctioning the deployment of some troops and Hunter aircraft to Thailand (which had appealed for SEATO support), Macmillan resolved not to make any further commitment in Laos. As the likelihood of British military action in Indochina waned, the US undertook its own unilateral effort in Vietnam and SEATO was increasingly bypassed as an important decision-making body. *MCJ*

Southern Ireland, parliament of (1921), final attempt at a home-rule settlement briefly established by the Government of Ireland Act, 1920. Sinn Fein's sweeping victory in the May 1921 elections left it effectively stillborn, for only four university members, and fifteen senators nominated by the lord lieutenant, attended its first session. It was revived fleetingly in January 1922 to ratify the *Anglo-Irish treaty, Britain insisting that this should be done by a legally constituted authority (set up under a Westminster Act of Parliament) rather than by the Dáil. *DRB*

South Wales Miners' Federation, Welsh trade union. 'The Fed' (as it was always known to its members) was the foremost trade union in the mining valleys of south Wales between its foundation in 1898 and its redefinition as the South Wales Area of the National Union of Mineworkers in 1945. Born out of a dispute, the Fed was to have a turbulent history in which it was often at the centre of national cases. It affiliated to the Miners' Federation of Great Britain in 1899 and at first was regarded as a moderate influence within that organization. Things changed dramatically after the Cambrian Combine dispute of 1910 and from the time of the 1912 national strike onwards British miners were effectively led by a new generation of Welsh militants, several of whom espoused syndicalist and Marxist ideas. This period culminated in the great post-war coal disputes and in particular the 1926 General Strike in which British miners were led by A. J. Cook from the Rhondda. At that time and in the subsequent depression, the intransigence of Welsh miners was berated in the London press and by writers such as Evelyn Waugh. In the early 1930s the Fed was in crisis with a membership of less than half of those employed. Under presidents James Griffiths, 1934–6, and Arthur Horner, 1936–46, the union fought back to recover members and bargaining power. Within its democratic framework there were many Communist-controlled lodges but the majority of members adhered to Labour and it was two Labour members of the Fed, Aneurin Bevan and James Griffiths, who consciously based Labour's post-1945 welfare state on the values and services which the Fed had developed in the 1930s. It had been the protection offered to its members, especially those who were unemployed, which had earned the Fed the gratitude and affection of a depressed community. *PS*

HYWEL FRANCIS and DAVID SMITH, *The Fed* (2nd edn., Cardiff, 1999).

sovereign bases, term used to describe Britain's naval and military bases on the island of Cyprus, which remain British, rather than Cypriot, territory (see CYPRUS CRISES). Both Akrotiri and Dhekelia were kept by Britain as part of the final settlement which led to Cypriot independence in 1960. *Gibraltar is a former sovereign base because it was under British jurisdiction whilst part of the Spanish mainland, but the base has been run down since 1988 and Gibraltar is now classed as a dependent territory. *KTS*

sovereign in parliament. The supreme power in the UK rests in the sovereign in parliament. Lords and Commons together pass legislation that receives the assent of the sovereign, and this legislative process settles all disputes. It enacts laws to which all citizens must give their consent and obedience. In fact, the sovereign plays very little role in the process, and the Lords have generally deferred to the Commons. The Commons has its business managed by the cabinet; the cabinet on the whole gives in to the wishes of the prime minister who, through a combination of principle, as well as astute financial, electoral, and media management, has gained the support of his or her political party. The true power in the state is therefore complex and cannot be located precisely in what occurs at the palace of Westminster. Likewise the legal sovereignty of parliament has been eroded (by parliament itself) in acceding since 1973 to European laws, regulations, conventions, and courts. *WMK*

sovereignty, the omnicompetent capacity to give orders to all and take orders from none. It is the legal omnipotence to impose one's will that absolute monarchs claimed at the time when modern states were being built. It is the embodiment of unlimited and arbitrary power. That this power was subsequently transferred from the monarch to the crown-in-parliament as parliamentary sovereignty did not change its nature. It is antithetical to Acton's liberal view that all power tends to corrupt and absolute power corrupts absolutely. The doctrine that law and order required there to be some single source of state authority has also made it repugnant to pluralists. British membership of the European Union has rendered the notion of a singular supreme coercive power located in Westminster untenable.

Reference to the constitutional lawyer A. V. Dicey's conception of parliamentary sovereignty is the indispensable starting point, as set out in his *Introduction to the Study of the Law of the Constitution* (1885). He defined parliamentary sovereignty as 'the right to make or unmake any law whatever; and, further, that no person or body is recognised by the law of England as having a right to override or set aside the legislation of Parliament' (10th edn., London, 1959: 39–40). However, over and above such legal sovereignty there was the political sovereignty exercised by public opinion through the electorate, which held the government to account through its representatives in the House of Commons. In the absence of a written constitution, Dicey attached great weight to the accumulated conventions that in practice informally restrained the exercise of power and curbed its abuse, as well as to the rule of law enforced by an impartial and independent judiciary. However, what Lord Hailsham (when in opposition) called in 1978 an *'elective dictatorship' (a phrase he did not repeat as Margaret Thatcher's lord chancellor) proved in the 1980s that a resolute prime minister did not need to exercise conventional self-restraint if she did not choose to do so.

It is since the UK government signed the treaty of accession to the European Economic Community in 1972 and passed the European Communities Act that the issue of sovereignty has come to the fore. Ironically, it was precisely because of parliamentary sovereignty that the UK by a few lines in an Act of Parliament was able to recognize the European Community institutions' capacity to make decisions and issue regulations overriding UK parliamentary legislation. The House of Lords in its judicial capacity recognized, notably in a 1991 judgement by Lord Bridges, that the supremacy of law made by the UK parliament must give way to the higher supremacy of European Community law, which it had voluntarily accepted in the 1972 European Communities Act. Limits on parliamentary sovereignty are enforced by British judges, a further extension of which has resulted from giving legal effect to the European Convention on *Human Rights and the jurisdiction of the European Court of Human Rights.

The power-sharing and judicial restraint that have occurred within the European Union have been extended since 1997 by devolution to Scotland and Wales as well as to Northern Ireland, so that the former British constitutional dogma of national sovereignty has been bypassed both within and without the UK in a liberal and pluralist direction. *JH*

V. Bogdanor, *Politics and the Constitution: Essays on British Government* (Aldershot, 1996). | A. W. Bradley, 'The Sovereignty of Parliament—in Perpetuity?', in J. Jowell and D. Oliver (eds.), *The Changing Constitution* (3rd edn., Oxford, 1994).

Soviet Union, recognition of (16 March 1921), came in the form of an Anglo-Soviet trade agreement. Britain agreed to grant de facto recognition of the USSR in exchange for the resumption of trade between the two countries. The Soviets agreed to accept in principle liability for debts incurred in Britain by the former tsarist regime, whilst both sides agreed that they would not carry out propaganda against the other. Relations were briefly suspended following the 1927 *Arcos raid. *NJC*

Spanish civil war (1936–9). Following the establishment of a republic in Spain in 1931, an election in 1936 returned a left-wing, popular front government. On 16 July 1936, the Spanish army, led by General Franco, rose in revolt, its anticipated early victory prevented by the resistance of armed factory workers. Subsequently, intervention by the German and Italian governments on the side of the nationalists, and by the Soviet Union on the side of the republic, ensured that the war would become the greatest cause célèbre of its time. It seemed that the ideological polarization of democracy and socialism pitted against reactionary, dictatorial nationalism and fascism within Spain reflected the developing European conflict. There was a real fear that the war in Spain might precipitate a full-scale European war, which was why the British government rapidly endorsed the French proposal that the powers should observe in Spain the principle of non-intervention. It was also perceived that Britain would need to retain good relations with whichever side won. Non-intervention was not intended as a friendly act to the Spanish republican authorities. On the contrary, it was hoped and anticipated that the nationalists would win, for there was an anxiety lest the victory of the popular front in Spain would result in the Bolshevization of France. The non-intervention committee first met in September 1936 but, containing, as it did, representatives from Germany, Italy, and the Soviet Union, it was from first to last a charade. The only genuine non-interventionists were the British, although they scarcely intended to create a level playing field. Within Britain, the war in Spain produced a crisis of opinion that drove the government and opposition further apart, and many individual Britons fought for the republic in the *International Brigades. Madrid finally fell to Franco in March 1939. *AJC*

G. Brenan, *The Spanish Labyrinth* (Cambridge, 1990). | Jill Edwards, *The British Government and the Spanish Civil War* (London, 1979).

Sparrow, John (1933–), merchant banker and head of the *Central Policy Review Staff (CPRS) 1982–3. A director of Morgan Grenfell, Sparrow was an informal adviser to Thatcher on 'city' and financial matters from 1977. In 1982 she picked him to head the CPRS think-tank, but its standing under his leadership was undermined by a spate of leaks and an inability to deliver the sort of political and policy advice she wanted, so after the 1983 election she abolished it. *KT*

Speaker's Conference on Electoral Reform (1916–17), all-party conference established to undertake an extensive review of the existing law governing the franchise and parliamentary elections. The Speaker of the Commons agreed to convene and chair the conference. It reported in January 1917 and offered an extensive set of recommendations, virtually all of which were the product of all-party agreement. It recommended that the basis for the franchise should be residence, rather than property ownership, but nonetheless proposed keeping the business vote and recommended an increase in the number of university seats. It proposed a radical overhaul of the procedure for electoral registration. It produced a compromise on the issue of female suffrage, recommending that the franchise be extended to women, though not making a definitive recommendation as to the age at which they should become eligible to vote: 'Various ages were discussed of which 30 and 35 received most favour' (*Report*, section VIII). It recommended that proportional representation should be introduced for parliamentary elections—remarkably, the recommendation was the product of cross-party agreement. Most of the recommendations were embodied in the Representation of the People Act, 1918, but the issues of votes for women and proportional representation were made the subject of free votes during the bill's passage. Votes for women aged 30 and over were approved; the use of proportional representation for parliamentary elections was not. One consequence of the Act was to more than double the size of the electorate. *PN*

Report of the Speaker's Conference on Electoral Reform (Cd 8463, London, 1917). | MARTIN PUGH, *Electoral Reform in War and Peace, 1906–1918* (London, 1978).

special advisers (SPADs), politically committed temporary civil servants, attached to ministers. Experiments involving the use of 'outsiders' within the bureaucracy were conducted by the Liberal administration returned in 1906 and the coalition governments of both world wars. Labour Prime Minister Harold Wilson created SPADs in 1964, but appointing less than ten. Under subsequent Labour and Conservative administrations, SPADs have proliferated. Between 1974 and 1997, up to 30 were employed; since May 1997, in Tony Blair's government, around 70 has been the norm. The prime minister's policy unit, established by Wilson in 1974, is predominantly staffed by SPADs. Special advisers can be loosely categorized as political aides, policy experts, or media managers. The possible tasks of SPADs include political functions which fall outside the jurisdiction of permanent civil servants. SPADs may brief their ministers on policy proposals, write their speeches, maintain their diaries, or chase policy implementation. SPADs are not integrated into the bureaucratic chain of command. However, in 1997, Blair's two senior SPADs were given the power to issue instructions to permanent civil servants. The use of SPADs controversially challenges civil service traditions of neutrality and generalism, and SPADs may also usurp the functions of junior ministers. They sometimes participate in scuffles between ministers. In the event of reshuffles, SPADs may become unemployed, follow their employer to a new department, or serve the successor. Changes in administration are accompanied by wholesale clear-outs of SPADs. In July 2000, under parliamentary pressure, Blair's administration committed itself to enacting a code of practice specifically to govern SPADs. *AB*

SIMON JAMES, *British Cabinet Government* (London, 1999).

Special Areas Reconstruction (Agreement) Act, 1936, marked a transitional stage in the development of government policy towards chronic long-term regional unemployment, from that of a social relief policy for derelict areas into an interventionist strategy for the promotion of more spatially balanced employment growth. This built upon an earlier 1934 Act, which had delimited four areas (in south Wales, north-east England, west Cumberland, and Clydeside–north Lanarkshire) and appointed two commissioners to promote their rehabilitation. However, this legislation had been forced upon a reluctant government by pressure of public opinion. Within government, both politicians and official advisers were unconvinced that there were any short-term remedies for such unemployment and as a consequence the 1934 Act granted few powers, showed little underlying resolve to spend significant sums, and was, in any case, in conflict with the continuation of the labour transference policy that had been pursued since the 1920s. The origins of the 1936 Act, therefore, lay with continuing public dissatisfaction with the regional policy effort, and in particular with the periodic reports of the outspoken first commissioner for England and Wales, who championed the cause of the unemployed and was viewed in Whitehall increasingly as a mistaken appointment. The most significant features of the 1936 Act were the beginnings of funds to attract private industry to the areas (strengthened in a further 1937 Act) and the establishment of trading estates, the latter the most visibly successful of the armoury of regional policy measures that had been developed by 1939, even if by then there was as yet only limited employment generation. Ultimately, it was more the high national level of unemployment, and less continued government inhibitions about measures which differentiated between private companies on grounds of their location, which perpetuated the regional problem. *RM*

special branches, police units entrusted with especially sensitive and political duties. The original Special Branch was created within the Metropolitan Police in the 1880s to handle Fenian terrorism in the capital, and responsibility for combating terrorism was not transferred to the Security Service (MI5) until 1992 after a considerable internal battle. Each police force has its own special branch. Duties included (during the Cold War years) the monitoring of subversive movements of both right and left and the surveillance of both individuals and organizations. MI5 has no powers of arrest, so the special branches have acted as its arm when action of this type has been required. Special branch officers are also responsible for protective security of public persons. *PJH*

T. Bunyan, *The History and Practice of the Political Police in Britain* (London, 1976).

special category status. See H-blocks.

Special Operations Executive (SOE). When Hitler overran western Europe in the summer of 1940, driving British military forces from Dunkirk, beleaguered Prime Minister Winston Churchill was enthused with the idea of taking the war back to Europe by creating an organization of irregulars capable of 'setting Europe ablaze'. Section D of the Secret Intelligence Service (SIS) had been formed in 1938 to undertake covert operations. However, its poor performance during the early phases of the war caused Churchill to look elsewhere. In July 1940 he appointed Labour minister Hugh Dalton to head his new organization, the Special Operations Executive. SOE's brief included the planning and execution of operations behind enemy lines and the organization and use of resistance groups across occupied Europe. Given the defeatist state occupied Europe was in, SOE proved something of a damp squib, and in 1941 its propaganda arm was lost to the newly formed political warfare executive (PWE). SOE became involved in turf wars with other branches within Britain's intelligence community and inevitably failed to fulfil its exaggerated sense of its own potential. When the USA entered the war in 1941, SOE worked closely with America's own covert agency, the Office of Strategic Services, carving out respective spheres of influence. When the war ended, there were debates as to SOE's future. These were resolved in 1946 when responsibility for covert operations was restored to SIS. *PM*

W. J. McKenzie and M. R. D. Foot, *The History of SOE* (London, 2000).

special relationship, See Anglo-American relations.

Spectator, minority weekly magazine by, for, and about people involved in politics, literature, and the arts. Founded by Robert Rintoul in 1828, it was one of the few to survive throughout the 20th century. Its viewpoint was generally centrist (and earlier Unionist). Crucial to its reputation were the editorships of St Loe Strachey (1897–1925) and Wilson Harris (1932–53). From 1963 to 1965 it was edited by a former cabinet minister, Iain Macleod. Ownership latterly lay with rich men, such as Ian Gilmour, Henry Keswick, and Conrad Black, for whom it was a hobby. Circulation varied widely with the popularity of conservative thought, declining in the Harold Wilson era and flourishing in that of Margaret Thatcher. Rarely as much as 50,000, and far less before the Second World War, circulation was to some extent reciprocal with that of the left-wing *New Statesman*. The magazine's influence was amplified via its appeal to a political and media elite. *CKSU*

Spencerism (1926–7). The phrase arises from the formation of the 'Spencer Union' in 1926, named after George Spencer MP, a former president of the Nottingham miners. Spencer was opposed to the *General Strike and the six-month coal strike and lockout that had led to it. As a result, he organized the return to work of many Nottinghamshire miners, who were given a pay rise of 4 shillings, and was expelled by the Miners' Federation of Great Britain. The Spencer Union was thus seen to be an anti-strike union, a contradiction in terms. Since then the term has been used polemically to describe any non-strike trade union organization. The phrase appeared once again after the 1984–5 miners' national strike when the *Union of Democratic Miners was formed in the Nottinghamshire and Derbyshire coalfields. *KL*

A. R. Griffin, *County under Siege* (Ashbourne, n.d.).

Spender, John Alfred (1862–1942), Liberal journalist. Spender was a committed radical Liberal who lived for a time at Toynbee Hall settlement in East London, writing in 1892 *The State and Pensions in Old Age*, which helped to focus debate on a coming issue. His key role, however, was as editor of the *Westminster Gazette*, 1896–1922, the chief London evening paper on the Liberal side. He was a relentless defender of Liberal causes, took Asquith's side against Lloyd George, and wrote the standard biographies of Campbell-Bannerman, Asquith, and Sir Robert Hudson. *JAR*

Spens report (1938), result of government-appointed educational inquiry. It recommended free secondary education for all, on the basis of a tripartite division of schools: the 'technical school' as well as the 'grammar' and 'modern' schools. The report acknowledged new methods of teaching which stimulated curiosity and demonstrated relevance. Widely supported, the report provided the basis for the *Education Act, 1944. *JS*

Spitting Image, popular TV programme, 1982–96, widely imitated abroad and with many merchandizing spin-offs. Ingenious latex puppets, often lifesize, were modelled from caricatures originally by Peter Fluck and Roger Law. Celebrities of all kinds—political, sporting, showbiz, the royal family—were guyed in a succession of fast-moving sketches. The scripts lacked malice and generally did not match the quality of the models, especially after the first few series. *CKSU*

spoiled ballot papers, voting slips in elections for public office which are disqualified because of markings which identify the voter or make the voting intention unclear. A voter is required to place a cross beside the name of the candidate for whom he or she wishes to vote. Votes are not necessarily disallowed if voters use some other means of identifying their preference if this preference is clear from the marking: on one occasion, a dot rather than a cross was allowed. However, any ballot paper that identifies the voter (for example, by way of signature or initials) is automatically disqualified. Markings that fail to make clear a preference for a candidate are also disallowed. In contemporary elections there are usually 40,000 or more spoilt ballots in a general election (a figure which, despite the decline in illiteracy, is rather higher than in the inter-war period). In the general election of 1979—when the general election coincided with local elections—the figure reached a historical high of 117,848. *PN*

sponsorship of MPs. Labour MPs have been sponsored by the trade union movement since the party's inception and until the 1950s many received an allowance to supplement their low parliamentary salaries. Maintenance payments have been replaced by contribution towards constituency election expenses. The party was born from 'the bowels' of the trade unions and when the Labour Representation Committee was formed in 1900, its chief purpose was to secure the election to parliament of trade union representatives. The claim that sponsorship provides trade unions with a disproportionate weight within the Parliamentary Labour Party is unjustified. In 1933, the Hastings agreement specified the supremacy of the party and sporadic attempts to turn sponsored MPs into delegates of the trade union, as, for example, with the Yorkshire area of the National Union of Mineworkers in 1975, have been obstructed by the Commons committee of privileges. The practice of sponsorship is more innocuous than commercial links between MPs and external organizations, and in practice the liaison between unions and their sponsored MP is limited. Thatcher's attacks on trade unions provoked an increase in sponsorship, which climaxed in the 1987 parliament when it involved three-fifths of all Labour MPs. The practice of unions 'co-opting' serving MPs has recently increased. This has changed the historic pattern of sponsored MPs being more right wing and less intellectual than other Labour MPs. The transport workers, miners, shopworkers, local authority workers, and railwaymen have been the most active sponsors of MPs. *BJE*

sport was regarded as a relatively uncontentious issue until the 1950s when the *Cold War made tensions within sport more evident. The promotion of sporting prowess within the communist countries had the paradoxical effect of making them vulnerable to boycotts and bans over issues of international tension. As a result the withdrawal from the Moscow Olympic games in 1984 by America marked an unprecedented incursion of politics into the political sphere. These issues were largely overcome by the fall of the Soviet empire, making sport far less contentious than before. Within Britain, protests against cricket games against South Africa during its *apartheid period resulted in the breaking-off of sporting relations between the two countries and may have done a little to increase white South Africans' sense of isolation. Tensions between states have often been ignored in the search for sporting success, but there is little evidence that sporting contact has made a significant difference to international relations. For example, India and Pakistan have been able to enjoy sporting relations in spite of a troubled diplomatic history, including war. Sport has sometimes played a 'proxy' role to encourage or facilitate diplomacy, but has rarely been decisive in itself. *JS*

sports councils. The English Sports Council was created under royal charter in 1997. Previously, responsibility for the development of sport in England was with the GB Sports Council, which also had a remit for the whole UK. The other nations of the UK had sports councils of their own long before, being established also under royal charter in 1972 (the Scottish Sports Council changed its name to Sportscotland in 1999). A new coordinating organization, UK Sport, took responsibility for issues that need to be dealt with at national level. *JD*

Sports Council for England website: *www.english.sports.gov.uk* | Sportscotland website: *www.sportscotland.org.uk* | Sports Council of Wales website: | *www.sports-council-wales.co.uk* | Sports Council of Northern Ireland website: *www.sportscouncil-ni.org.uk*

Spring-Rice, Cecil Arthur ('Springie') (1859–1918), diplomat. Spring-Rice entered the diplomatic service in 1882. As minister at Tehran (1906–8) he was strongly opposed to the Anglo-Russian entente and would have preferred a strong policy against Russia and Germany, but carried out the 1907 agreement with Russia. After the outbreak of war in Europe, when ambassador at Washington (1913–18), he occupied himself warding off US protests against British blockade practices and countering German propaganda, whilst simultaneously trying to bring America into the war on the Entente's side. With America's entry into the war in 1917 his diplomatic task was consummated. He is perhaps best remembered as the author of the hymn-lines 'I vow to thee, my country ...'. *TGO*

David H. Burton, *Cecil Spring-Rice: A Diplomat's Life* (London and Toronto, 1992).

Spycatcher. See Security Service.

'squeeze Germany till the pips squeak' was the phrase (used first by Sir Eric Geddes in Cambridge) frequently uttered during the 1918 general election by those who desired punitive *reparations from Germany for war damages. Though Lloyd George and Law had no such expectations, they could do little to curb popular vengefulness. *RJQA*

stagflation, economic phenomenon characterized by concurrently rising rates of unemployment and inflation. The best-known instance of British stagflation occurred between 1973 and 1975 when inflation rose from 9.1 to 24.1 per cent and unemployment from 2.6 to 4 per cent. This appearance of stagflation in the 1970s posed a considerable dilemma for existing economic theory and policy, not the least because orthodox *Keynesian theory not only precluded the possibility of stagflation, but actually stipulated that there be a trade-off between inflation and unemployment: the so-called Phillips curve. The breakdown of this hitherto stable relationship in the 1970s greatly undermined confidence in Keynesian demand management and aided the rise of *monetarism. The causes of this episode of stagflation are still much debated. Monetarists see its roots in successive governments' use of expansionary fiscal policy and abrogation of market mechanisms, while many Keynesians prefer to stress the impact of decentralized collective bargaining. *GBM*

stakeholding, one of the defining phrases of 'New Labour' after 1995, usually refers to a set of policies and associated attitude changes which will mobilize various non-state actors and elements in 'civil society'—trade unions, voluntary associations, industry, local government, and representatives of unorganized categories like consumers and hospital patients—to operate more cooperatively than they would under a command economy or individualistically in a free market, with the expectation that greater overall welfare will result. *JAT*

Stamfordham, Lord (1849–1931), private secretary to Victoria, 1895–1901, and to George V, 1910–31. The queen chose Arthur Bigge, as he then was, for her private office on the basis of his good looks and the moving narrative he gave of the death of the son of Napoleon III, with whom he had served in Africa. Henry Ponsonby trained him in the arts of hinting, suggesting, and thanking that all royal secretaries need to acquire. They also became good friends, though Ponsonby's instincts were liberal and Bigge's were conservative. Raised to the peerage by George V, Stamfordham's greatest achievements came at the time of the Great War and the appointment of the first Labour government in 1924. During the war and under Stamfordham's aegis, expenditure was reduced and large sums were refunded from the king's civil list to the exchequer. The dynasty's connections to Germany were severed and the royal family's name changed to Windsor on Stamfordham's advice. Ramsay MacDonald paid special thanks to Stamfordham for having so gently taught the new Labour ministers about what was required of them in the more formal aspects of their appointments. He was a private secretary who grew old with his sovereign, knew his mind, and failed the monarchy only in sharing his master's utter lack of confidence in the prince of Wales, the future Edward VIII.

WMK

Stamp, Josiah (1880–1941), statistician and expert on taxation. Stamp played a pivotal role in restructuring the British taxation system. His positions included railway company chairman, director of the Bank of England, 1928–41, member of the committee on national debt and taxation, British representative on the Dawes and Young committees, and member of the Economic Advisory Committee. Stamp's major achievement as a civil servant was the creation of the excess profits duty, which was responsible for procuring one-third of the total tax revenue raised during the Great War. He was also responsible for the index of profits introduced in 1932. His books concentrated on the problems of national income and capital, and on taxation.

JFM

Stanley, Oliver Frederick George (1896–1950), Conservative politician. Son of the 17th earl of Derby, he entered parliament in 1924, representing Westmorland. Junior office at the Ministry of Education and Home Office was followed by a period as minister of transport. His tenure as minister of labour, 1934–5, was inglorious as his department tried to adapt to the consequences of the creation of the Unemployment Assistance Board. However, Neville Chamberlain promoted him to the Board of Trade, 1937–40, and he was a surprise appointment as minister of war in 1940, an appointment not well received either in military or political circles and viewed as a sop to the French. This was a contributory factor in Chamberlain's fall from office in May 1940. After army service and brief period as a government critic, Stanley became secretary of state for colonies, 1942–5, a deliberate backwater appointment intended to silence a dangerous backbencher. In opposition in 1945–50, he proved a dashing speechmaker, specializing in financial affairs, for which he could draw upon his experiences as a stockbroker, and was chairman of the party's backbench financial and imperial affairs committees. During these latter years he was seen as the third man in the party after Churchill and Eden and his early death probably robbed him of appointment as chancellor of the exchequer in 1951. *NJC*

Star Chamber on Public Expenditure, a cabinet committee (MISC 62) set up in the early Thatcher period to conduct annual bilateral reviews of expenditure between departmental and Treasury ministers. The name derived from the Tudor monarchs' judicial instrument of arbitrary government, itself named after the room in which it met (decorated with a star on the ceiling), but the 1980s version hardly deserved the comparison.

JAR

state, an organization which claims a monopoly of legitimate force over a territory. This definition, which owes much to Max Weber, contains a crucial ambiguity. What does 'legitimate' mean? It means that the subjects of a state accept that their state has the right to enforce its laws, even when they are caught disobeying them. The definition is not problematic except when large numbers of people think that the state that controls their territory does not have that right.

Throughout the 19th century and up to 1921, the legitimacy of the British state in Ireland was questionable. By 1921 it was non-existent, and Irish independence was recognized in the treaty of that year that made Ireland a 'Free State' within the British Empire. Even that was bitterly controversial, leading to civil war in the infant Free State. Ireland declared itself a republic in 1937 and left the Commonwealth in 1949. Northern Ireland has always contained a large minority who saw themselves as Irish rather than British citizens, and who accordingly did not accept the legitimacy of the British state there. After 1921, however, this was quiescent until 1968, when sectarian and anti-state violence again erupted there. The British and Irish states both continued to claim legitimacy over the territory of Northern Ireland until 1999, when the Irish state, backed by an overwhelming referendum majority, abandoned its claim on northern Ireland. However, the crisis of state legitimacy in Northern Ireland is unlikely to end there. Scotland and Wales have also housed challenges to the British state in the

20th century, but the stakes have been less high and there has been little anti-state violence in either country. For English politicians, the main expression of statism has been unionism: the doctrine that the Irish, the Scots, and (especially at the start of the century) the dominions should be held as close as possible into the union of the United Kingdom. Unionism was a powerful ideology as recently as the 1970s but seems to be fading fast. London politicians (of both parties) in the 1970s resisted Scottish nationalism because it threatened the Union. The heat had gone out of that issue when it re-emerged after 1997.

Apart from issues of territory, political arguments have concerned the reach of the state into private and business life. Broadly, both conservatives and socialists favour a large state, while liberals favour a small one. Conservatives favour a large state because they believe the state has a right or a duty to promote public morality; socialists favour one because they believe the state has a right or a duty to plan, and to redistribute resources from rich to poor; liberals oppose one because they think people and businesses are best left to run their own affairs. The political parties with these words in their titles have only loosely followed these ideologies. From 1906 onwards, many Liberals helped to bring about the welfare state. From 1979 to 1990, Thatcher has been aptly characterized as standing for a 'free economy and a strong state'. Thatcherism, however it is characterized, was against state intervention in some areas of life and for it in others. *IM*

Vernon Bogdanor, *Devolution in the United Kingdom* (Oxford, 1999). | Andrew Gamble, *The Free Economy and the Strong State: The Politics of Thatcherism* (Basingstoke, 1988).

State Education, Campaign for (CASE). One of the axioms of 20th-century politics has been the need to provide all children with an education, but in Britain, state education arrived later than in much of continental Europe. The 1870 Education Act making educational provision virtually universal was crucial. A small amount of state aid became available for teacher training, and the educational budget of the state has increased significantly ever since. As provision has been made for religious schools via 'voluntary-aided' status, creating, for example, an entire framework of Roman Catholic schools in some parts of Britain, the overall tendency has been for education to remain within the state sector and not to separate out for religious reasons (except, predictably, in Northern Ireland). Nonetheless, a large *public school sector remains to provide private education for those who choose it. CASE has been a parent-teacher pressure group which lobbied for adequate budgets for state schools, and has also been active both in moves towards comprehensive schools and in calls to remove residual state support from the independent sector. *JS*

states of emergency. At moments of crisis during the 20th century, for example, during the two world wars, or the *General Strike of 1926, legislation conferred special powers on the government of the day, powers that allow the government to rule without reference to parliament. At these moments orders in council are sufficient to provide for anything necessary to preserve order or regulate supplies of necessities. Because the sovereign presides over the privy council, and his/her approval of orders in council is required, conservatives have sometimes imagined the sovereign reclaiming long-disused prerogatives in a state of emergency to save the state from an electoral dictatorship or to repel invaders. In fact, the palace is ill-equipped and unused to dealing with the fast-moving political events likely to surround a state of emergency. So it is unlikely that the sovereign personally would want to play such a role in a state of emergency, much less be relied upon to reclaim powers last wielded by the Tudors and Stuarts. *WMK*

Keith Jeffery and Peter Hennessy, *States of Emergency: British Government and Strikebreaking since 1919* (London, 1983).

Statute of Westminster (1931). Passed on 11 December, the statute finally clarified the constitutional relationship between Britain and the dominions. By bringing together certain decisions made during the 1926 and 1930 imperial conferences, the statute recognized the legislative independence of the dominions and the fact that Britain could no longer interfere in dominion internal politics. This left the crown as the last remaining legal link between Britain and the dominions, a major step towards the modern *Commonwealth of Nations. *KTS*

W. D. McIntyre, *The Commonwealth of Nations: Origins and Impact 1869–1971* (Minneapolis, 1977).

statutory instruments, committees on. Established as the select committee on statutory rules and orders in 1944, its title changed in 1947. Despite the creation of a joint committee for both Houses in 1972, a separate Commons' select committee has remained. It arose from concerns that delegated legislation gave the executive wide powers to detail or amend instruments. Its role is to alert the House to delays in notification, retrospective or unusual use of powers, or drafting defects of statutory instruments. *KMT*

Steed, Michael (1940–), political scientist and Liberal activist. An important figure in the Liberal revival from the 1950s, working mainly in the Manchester area, he was a major influence on the Alliance commission on constitutional reform, and in the talks between Liberal Democrats and the Labour Party over constitutional matters prior to the 1997 general election. As an academic, he has concentrated on psephology, providing the statistical material for Nuffield election studies for much of the past half-century. *JS*

Steel, David Martin Scott (1938–), Liberal politician and party leader. He was MP for the border constituency of Roxburgh, Selkirk, and Peebles from 1965 until his elevation to the peerage in 1997. The longest-serving Liberal leader since Asquith, Steel led the party from 1976 to 1988. His principal early contribution lay in sponsoring the Abortion Act (see ABORTION) which passed into law in 1967, demonstrating a safe pair of hands during the passage of the controversial private member's bill. In the wake of Jeremy *Thorpe's damaging resignation, Steel was elected leader in a contest against John Pardoe. He helped the party to recover credibility and negotiated the *Lib-Lab pact (1977–8), which maintained the Labour government of Callaghan in power. Steel's claims that he wanted the party to enjoy the experience of responsibility did not, though, satisfy his critics who felt the party gained little from a pact with a vulnerable government. Often at odds with some of the activist grass roots, Steel enthusiastically embraced the *Alliance with the newly formed Social Democratic Party (SDP) in 1981 and was instrumental in persuading Roy *Jenkins to launch the new party. His relationship with David *Owen, the SDP leader from 1983, was less cordial, though he still managed to cooperate sufficiently to bring the Alliance approximately a quarter of all the votes cast in the 1983 and 1987 elections.

However, following the failure of the joint leadership strategy in 1987 to achieve an Alliance breakthrough, Steel precipitated events by calling for a merger of the Liberal Party and the SDP within days of the announcement of the election result. His decision provoked a split in the SDP but the majority voted to join the new party and Steel received the backing of his own party at a special Blackpool conference early in 1988. He and Robert MacLennan jointly led the merged *Liberal Democrats until a new, sole leader could be elected, Steel having announced he would not stand for the leadership.

An internationalist and pro-European, Steel retained active interests in both areas, standing for a European seat in Italy in 1989 for the Liberal-Republican interest. He maintained his long-standing commitment to devolution by co-chairing the Scottish Constitutional Convention (see SCOTTISH HOME RULE CONVENTIONS) from 1989, campaigning actively for a Scottish parliament, and serving as presiding officer (Speaker) for the new Scottish parliament in 1999. *JS*

DAVID STEEL, *A House Divided* (London, 1980).

steel industry. The British steel industry was the classic victim of adversarial politics, being nationalized, largely denationalized, renationalized, and privatized over a period of less than 40 years. There had been substantial government intervention in the industry before the Second World War, through both protection and the government-inspired formation of the British Iron and Steel Federation. During the war the industry was run by an iron and steel control board with full powers over production and distribution. After the war, the leaders of the industry would have been prepared to accept public control without public ownership and for a time this seemed possible. However, in 1948 the Attlee government introduced its controversial bill for the nationalization of the industry, but it was not actually nationalized until February 1951 and a Conservative government then came into office in October. The task of selling the companies to private owners was given to the Iron and Steel Holding and Realizations Agency. By 1964, one large company (Richard Thomas and Baldwins) and several smaller ones remained in public ownership. An Iron and Steel Board was set up to supervise the industry, with powers to set maximum prices and veto development proposals and capital expenditure. It was generally agreed that a new strip mill was needed, but in 1958 the Macmillan government decided for regional policy reasons to approve and subsidize two, one in Wales and one in Scotland, the latter eventually closing. In 1967 the industry, by this time facing serious productivity problems, was renationalized, although a significant private sector remained. In 1970–1, the British Steel Corporation (BSC) produced a long-term development plan which envisaged that by 1980 British steel production would be more than 40 million tonnes (39.4 million tons) per annum. This plan was produced at a time when the global economy was becoming less steel-intensive and serious overcapacity problems were appearing as the result of the growth of productive capacity. The new industry minister, Peter Walker, was convinced that BSC's modernization plan was essential to the future industrial strength of Britain and in 1972 agreement was reached on an expansion programme with a target of 36–8 million tonnes (35.4–37.4 million tons) of steel to be produced by the early 1980s (in 1972 production was 22.9 million tonnes (22.5 million tons) and the trend growth in UK steel demand between 1955 and 1970 had averaged 1.7 per cent per annum). The modernization plan was accompanied by closures of older plants and these were reviewed by Lord Beswick when Labour returned to office in 1974, the effect of which was that the development plan was to be phased in over a longer period. As the BSC ran into inevitable financial problems, it told the new Conservative government in 1979 that 52,000 jobs would have to be cut. A thirteen-week strike of steelworkers followed early in 1980. Ian MacGregor was brought in to head up BSC in 1980, and a radical efficiency drive involving plant closures and job cuts returned BSC to profitability. It was privatized in 1988. *WG*

H. Abromeit, *British Steel* (Leamington, 1986). | K. Ovenden, *The Politics of Steel* (London, 1978).

Steel-Maitland, Arthur Herbert Drummond Ramsay (1876–1935), Conservative politician. Arthur Steel-Maitland was one of 'Milner's young men' at the turn of the century and returned from South Africa to Britain to take an active part in Joseph Chamberlain's campaign for imperial preference, entering the Commons as a Birmingham MP in 1910. Following the report of the Unionist Organization Committee in 1911 (of which he was a member), he became the first chairman of the party organization. He was an energetic party chairman whose tenure set the parameters of a key organizational post, and the party's recovery of activity between 1911 and 1914 owes much to his input at Central Office. The outbreak of war in 1914 brought this partisan phase to an end, though he remained chairman until 1917. In the coalitions that governed from 1915, he had only junior office and became steadily more embittered, resigning in 1919 to become a dangerous critic of the government within the *National Union of Conservative and Unionist Associations. Steel-Maitland had now become distrusted as an intriguer, and was passed over for office in 1922–3, but was at last brought into the cabinet as minister of labour, 1924–9. In that role, in a period in which labour relations were bad enough to produce a general strike, and most industrial relations issues were therefore dealt with personally by the prime minister, there were few opportunities to shine. Baldwin later thought that he should have sent him to the Board of Trade, where his energy and originality of mind could have alleviated trade depression rather than merely dealing with its symptoms. This is borne out by activity after he lost his seat in 1929, a setback from which his career never recovered. He soon returned to the Commons, though his health was never strong, but he researched and wrote widely on economic matters, becoming one of the first British politicians to urge that Britain learn from such interventionist policies as Roosevelt's New Deal in the USA. *JAR*

John Ramsden, *The Age of Balfour and Baldwin, 1902–1940* (London, 1978).

Steering Committee, informal committee of Conservatives set up by Harold Macmillan in 1957 to plan the party's fightback after Suez and the manifesto for the next election. Chaired by the prime minister, with Michael *Fraser, director of the Conservative Research Department, as secretary, it also contained three other cabinet ministers. Widely credited with helping the Conservatives to win re-election against the odds in 1959, a similar system was used before the next five general elections, but never as effectively as in 1959. *JAR*

Sterling Area, a group of countries defined in the Exchange Control Act of 1947, including all members of the Commonwealth (except for Canada), all colonies, Burma, Iceland, Ireland, Iraq (from 1952), Jordan, Libya, and the Persian Gulf territories. Members pegged their exchange rates to sterling, maintained a common exchange control against the rest of the world, and enjoyed free current and capital transactions with the UK. They also maintained their national reserves in sterling, which required pooling foreign exchange earnings in London. The aim of the Sterling Area system was to allow the most use of sterling as an international currency while ensuring that those who used it agreed not to exhaust Britain's foreign exchange reserves. The Sterling Area also allowed free trade over a large part of the world in a time that was generally characterized by high tariffs. The links between the members of the Sterling Area were closest in crisis years of the immediate post-war period, when the spirit of emergency promoted cooperation on trade and macroeconomic policies. After 1952, as the *dollar gap receded and developing countries began to aspire to industrial development, the goals of the members began to diverge. In particular, the overseas members of the Sterling Area began to pressure the UK to move toward convertibility of sterling. In 1958, sterling was made convertible for residents outside the Sterling Area for current account transactions. Britain's subsequent efforts to join the European Economic Community further estranged the Commonwealth members of the Sterling Area from the UK. Through the 1960s, members of the Sterling Area diversified their reserves, and their preferred access to the London capital market was gradually eroded. In 1967 sterling was devalued and Sterling Area countries negotiated exchange guarantee agreements with the UK. When floating exchange rates were introduced in 1972 the Sterling Area ceased to function. *CRS*

Sterndale, Lord (1848–1923), judge. Following a primarily commercial practice as a barrister, William Pickford became a judge of the King's Bench division in 1907 and in 1914 a lord justice of appeal. He became president of the probate, divorce, and Admiralty division in 1918 before returning to the Court of Appeal as master of the rolls, 1919–23. He supported the movement for a unified maritime law and was a member, and then chairman, of the Dardanelles Commission, 1916–17. *CAM*

Steward, George (1884–1952), prime ministers' press adviser, 1929–40. The first of his breed, recruited from the Foreign Office news department by Ramsay MacDonald to handle a generally Conservative press, Steward erected himself as a barrier between lobby correspondents and the ministers to whom they had previously had direct access. He later helped Neville Chamberlain bypass Cabinet and Foreign Office anti-appeasers. By no means the last press officer to muddy the waters of civil service neutrality, his links with the German embassy were particularly murky. *CL*

Stewart, Donald (1920–92), Scottish nationalist politician. Elected as MP for the Western Isles in 1970, Stewart held the seat for the Scottish National Party (SNP) until his retirement from politics in 1987. Located within the moderate, traditionalist wing of the nationalist movement, he had a large personal vote in his constituency, accounting for the failure of the SNP to hold the seat when he retired. *RF*

Stewart, Michael Maitland (1906–90), Labour politician. Stewart was a teacher and Workers' Educational Association lecturer who was MP for Fulham, 1945–79. A close confidant of Wilson, during the 1964–70 government he was secretary for education and science, 1964–5, and foreign secretary, 1965–6 and 1968–70, where he encouraged Wilson to try to act as a mediator over the Vietnam war. He replaced George Brown at the Department of Economic Affairs (DEA), 1965–8, where he was more congenial to the Treasury. His tenure reflected the demise of the DEA as an effective alternative source of economic policy to the Treasury. He was lord Stewart of Fulham from 1980. *BJE*

Stewart, William Duncan Patterson (1935–), scientist and government adviser. Stewart's career as an academic scientist led to his appointment as professor of biology at the University of Dundee, 1968–94. He was active on many official scientific advisory groups and committees, including the royal commission on environmental pollution (1986–8). He served as chief scientific adviser in the Cabinet Office, 1990–5, and as head of the Office of Science and Technology, 1992–5. *KT*

Stokes, Richard Rapier (1897–1957), Labour politician. Stokes joined the Labour Party in the 1930s. After winning the Ipswich seat in 1938, he never lost it. He took a keen interest in international affairs and was often critical of the wartime government, for example over tank designs. Stokes became minister of works in 1950, in charge of the completion of the Festival of Britain Exhibition and after 1951 shadow defence minister. A devout Catholic and a believer in social justice and international brotherhood, he showed constant loyalty to the Labour Party. *CH*

Stonehaven, Viscount. See Baird, John Lawrence.

Stonehouse, John Thomson (1925–1988), Labour politician. Stonehouse was a Labour idealist who went wrong. He graduated from the LSE in 1951. Keen on the Cooperative movement and Africa, he was an MP, 1957–76; minister, 1964–70; and made privy councillor in 1967. Passed over for office in 1974 he suffered an identity crisis, absconded with third world relief funds, and faked suicide in Florida. When he turned up in Australia, living under an assumed name with his secretary, he at first refused to resign as an MP but was eventually repatriated and gaoled for fraud. *PRGR*

John Stonehouse, *Death of an Idealist* (London, 1975).

Stone of Scone (Stone of Destiny). Originally captured as booty by Edward I in the Anglo-Scottish wars of the late 13th and early 14th centuries, the Stone was placed under the coronation chair in Westminster abbey. It was 'stolen' briefly by Scottish nationalists in 1951 and, although subsequently returned, there are some doubts as to its authenticity. In an endeavour to dampen down home rule demands and boost Conservative electoral appeal north of the border, the Scottish secretary, Michael Forsyth, brought the Stone home to Scotland on St Andrew's day, 30 November 1996, amid great pomp and ceremony. *RF*

Stopes, Marie Carmichael (1880–1958), pioneer advocate of birth control (see FAMILY PLANNING) and sexual fulfilment. Trained as a botanist and appointed lecturer at Manchester University, she published *Married Love* (1918) on sexual relationships and *Wise Parenthood* (1918), dealing with birth control. Stopes attracted an enormous public response for her discussion of hitherto taboo subjects, selling over 700,000 copies of her books by 1924. She fought a highly publicized and ultimately successful libel action in 1923 against a Catholic doctor who had accused her of 'experimenting on the poor', which helped to broadcast her opinions to a wider public. She opened the first birth control clinic in London in 1921 and helped to found the National Birth Control Council in 1930, which became the Family Planning Association in 1939. *JS*

stop-go, phrase used to describe post-war economic policy making, particularly between the 1950s and 1970s, notably used by Wilson to describe the Conservative record, 1951–64. An economy with full employment ran rapidly into capacity constraints whenever governments attempted to reflate, sucking in imports and driving up inflation, forcing the 'stop' through higher interest rates. *PPC*

Stormont. See NORTHERN IRELAND PARLIAMENT.

Strachey, (Evelyn) John St Loe (1901–63), socialist theorist and politician. In May 1929, as Labour MP for Aston, Strachey became parliamentary private secretary to Oswald Mosley, who had special responsibility for unemployment policy. In May 1930 they both resigned when Mosley's programme was rejected by the cabinet. Together they formed the New Party In February 1931, but Strachey left in July and began to promote the communist cause. In 1936 he was one of the founders of the Left Book Club and its most popular author. Having broken away from communism in April 1940, he became Labour MP for Dundee and under-secretary of state for air in Attlee's first government. In May 1946 he was appointed minister of food and, after the February 1950 general election, he was secretary for war. In opposition, after October 1951, he gradually moved to the right of the party. He was shadow commonwealth secretary when he died. Strachey's real strength was as a writer: books such as *The Coming Struggle for Power* (1932) and *The Theory and Practice of Socialism* (1936) were the most widely read popularizations of Marxism ever published in English, while *Contemporary Capitalism* (1956) was a major work of democratic socialist theory. *MDN*

Michael Newman, *John Strachey* (Manchester, 1989). | Hugh Thomas, *John Strachey* (London, 1973). | Noel Thompson, *John Strachey: an intellectual biography* (Houndmills, 1993).

Strakosch, Henry (1871–1943), banker, financial adviser, and chairman of *The Economist* newspaper (1929–43). A naturalized South African, Strakosch received his knighthood in 1921 for his singular role in the creation of the South African reserve bank, the first of its type in the British Empire outside London. Strakosch became a prominent figure in international financial institutions and was especially noted for his economic work in India where he acted as financial adviser to the secretary of state, 1937–42. *JRVE*

Strang, William (1893–1978), diplomat. Strang joined the diplomatic service in 1919 and eventually succeeded Orme Sargent as permanent secretary of the Foreign Office, 1949–53. Strang was present at Neville Chamberlain's meeting with Hitler at Berchtesgaden, and at post-war conferences with the USA and USSR. He was also witness to crucial developments in the early Cold War, the experience of which led him to conclude that strong Anglo-American relations had to be the centre of British foreign policy. *JRVE*

Strange Death of Liberal England, The. See DANGERFIELD, GEORGE.

Strategic Arms Limitation Talks/Treaties. See SALT.

Stresa front (1935). In March 1935 Hitler denounced the disarmament clauses of the treaty of Versailles (see PARIS PEACE CONFERENCE) by declaring the reintroduction of conscription and the expansion of the German army and revealing the existence of the Luftwaffe. In response, the British, French, and Italian governments met at Stresa, 11–14 April 1935, and there publicly condemned the unilateral abrogation of treaty obligations. This brief display of allied solidarity became known as the Stresa front, but collapsed during the ensuing *Abyssinian (Ethiopian) crisis. *AJC*

Stuart, James Gray (1897–1971), Conservative politician. MP for Moray and Nairn, 1923–59, he joined the Whips Office in 1935 before becoming deputy to David Margesson, 1937–40, and chief whip himself, 1940–8. Stuart was considered a formidable whip, able to combine a strong will, a gregarious nature, and managerial skills. His dealings with Churchill were often rocky, not least because he saw his leader after 1945 as an increasing electoral liability to his party. One legend claimed that he was able to bluff Churchill into appointing as a minister the Chamberlainite Lord Dunglass because he was unaware he had become the earl of Home. Stuart was secretary of state for Scotland, 1951–7, during a period when the traditional heavy industries of Scotland were in decline, but this was the heyday of the Conservative grip on Scotland, for they won over half the Scottish vote in 1955. He was known not to favour Eden's succession to the leadership, believing he lacked domestic experience, but stayed in office until Macmillan became premier. *NJC*

Viscount Stuart of Findhorn, *Within the Fringe* (London, 1967).

student politics were scarcely evident in Britain before the Second World War, not least because students were drawn overwhelmingly from elite social groups. From the 1950s, however, movements such as *Campaign for Nuclear Disarmament attracted a following amongst the young and this was translated in the 1960s into the campaigns against the Vietnam war which produced major demonstrations and confrontations with the police in *1968. Compared to the Continent, however, student protest was relatively muted. University expansion, while rapid in the 1960s, was carried out within a highly paternalistic tradition of low staff–student ratios and a communal ethos, which obviated much direct confrontation. Student politics since the 1970s have largely been concerned with issues of direct relevance to students with campaigns against the introduction of loans as the major form of student finance in the 1980s and against the introduction of tuition fees in the 1990s. While the student body as represented by the major student organization, the National Union of Students (NUS), reflects a range of concerns, it is still largely non-partisan, though holding one of its national officerships has been one route towards a political career on the left for such politicians as Jack Straw (NUS president, 1968–71). *JS*

Suez crisis (1956), diplomatic and military crisis following the nationalization of the Suez Canal Company by the Egyptian leader, Colonel Nasser, on 26 July 1956. Nationalization was unacceptable to the British government: the company was French in character, but Britain was the leading shareholder and the canal was vital to the transportation of goods to Britain, especially oil.

Though the cabinet endorsed the idea of military retaliation, it soon became clear that Britain, a nuclear power, was unable to respond immediately with conventional forces to a crisis in the Middle East. Delay, however, made it difficult to maintain the initial sense of outrage. Prime Minister Anthony *Eden has often been criticized for exaggerating the threat posed by Nasser, but parallels with the era of appeasement were widely proclaimed and a sufficient measure of agreement probably existed in the first days of the crisis to sustain an immediate military response. One element in the consensus absent from the start, however, was American support. Eden tended to misread the tortuous pronouncements of secretary of state Dulles and to ignore the outright opposition to force of President Eisenhower. The prime minister was slow to appreciate that the diplomatic processes of the summer, a maritime conference followed by the creation of the Suez Canal Users' Association, were seen by the Americans as the means of avoiding military action rather than a springboard for it as Eden hoped.

Eden was eventually obliged to submit the matter to the UN Security Council and it seems that Foreign Secretary Selwyn Lloyd was authorized to negotiate in good faith. Lloyd's negotiations led to an outline settlement in mid-October. Eden, however, under pressure from the Conservative right wing and perhaps suffering from ill health, unwisely agreed to go along with French plans for collusive action with Israel. An Israeli invasion of Egypt would give Britain and France the excuse for military intervention to 'protect' the canal. Despite a news blackout, the Americans were soon aware of what was going on. RAF bombing of Egyptian airfields began on the night of 31 October with airborne landings on 5 November. Though the military operation was relatively successful, worldwide opposition led by the USA compelled a ceasefire on 6 November. Britain was almost isolated at the UN, her moral standing badly damaged. Eden would have been unlikely to survive this humiliation even had ill health not forced his resignation in January 1957.

DJD

KEITH KYLE, *Suez* (London, 1991). | W. SCOTT LUCAS, *Divided We Stand* (London, 1991).

Suez Group, imperialist-minded Conservative MPs who rebelled against Britain's military withdrawal from Egypt's Suez Canal zone in 1954. Led by Charles Waterhouse, the group included Julian Amery, Legge-Bourke, Maude, and Powell. In December 1953, 41 Tories signed an early day motion rejecting Eden's negotiations with Egypt. Churchill, however, was persuaded that the hydrogen bomb rendered the Egyptian military base 'obsolescent'. Although he rallied his backbenchers, 28 Tories voted against the final treaty.

RJS

suffragists/suffragettes. On 10 January 1906 the *Daily Mail* devised the word 'suffragette', and within a few weeks it was widely used to describe those activists who employed militant means to win for women the vote in parliamentary elections. It emphasized the division that was growing deeper between those prepared to break the law and the 'suffragists', who continued to rely on traditional methods to persuade opponents of the case for women's enfranchisement. In 1897, the principal suffragist campaign was reorganized in the form of the National Union of Women's Suffrage Societies (NUWSS), with Millicent Garrett Fawcett as its most prominent figure. It had some 600 branches which supported the tactics of a constitutional pressure group—lobbying, letter-writing, the holding of meetings—but was felt by critics to be making little impact. Chief among these critics were members of the *Pankhurst family. In 1903 Emmeline Pankhurst had established the Women's Social and Political Union (WSPU) which within a few years had become associated with a series of dramatic and disorderly activities. From heckling at meetings of politicians who refused to support the women's case, the suffragette campaign developed into attacks on property—including breaking windows, burning post-boxes, and the bombing of a house that Lloyd George was having built. At Epsom on Derby Day 1913, Emily *Davison gave the suffragettes their greatest martyr after she was killed by the king's horse. Other women subjected themselves to prison hunger strikes, some of which were ended by forcible feeding and others by the 'Cat and Mouse' (or Prisoners' Temporary Discharge for Ill Health) Act of 1913. The Pankhursts were redoubtable personalities, but Emmeline and her daughter Christabel in particular had a ruthlessness that extended to fellow suffragettes. In 1912 Emmeline and Frederick Pethick-Lawrence, who since 1907 had done much to finance *Votes for Women*, the organ of the WSPU, were forced out of the organization. Relations with other groups and individuals were often strained. In spite of the heroic status that has often been accorded the Pankhursts, some historians argue that their militant tactics backfired by dividing the movement, alienating sympathizers, and giving their opponents added grounds for denying women the vote. By the outbreak of war in 1914, the NUWSS had adopted a policy of supporting the Labour Party in by-elections, in order to put pressure on the Liberal government, but Fawcett, like Emmeline and Christabel Pankhurst, soon moved to a pro-war position and suspension of their suffrage campaigns. By the election of 1918 many factors, not least women's role in the war, had persuaded most politicians of the need to include women (but only those who had reached the age of 30) in the parliamentary franchise. Votes for women aged 21 came only in 1928.

DEM

BRIAN HARRISON, *Separate Spheres: The Opposition to Women's Suffrage in Britain* (London, 1978). | SANDRA STANLEY HOLTON, *Feminism and Democracy: Women's Suffrage and Reform Politics in Britain 1900–1918* (Cambridge, 1987). | MARTIN PUGH, *Electoral Reform in War and Peace 1906–1918* (London, 1978). | CONSTANCE ROVER, *Women's Suffrage and Party Politics 1866–1914* (London, 1967). | DAVID RUBINSTEIN, *A Different World for Women: The Life of Millicent Garrett Fawcett* (London, 1991).

Summerskill, Edith Clara (1901–80), Labour politician who personified that generation of women enfranchised in 1918 who sought power with the Labour Party. Qualifying as a doctor in 1925, she married another and was on Middlesex county council, 1934–41. Labour MP for West Fulham, 1938–55, and then Warrington, she became junior minister at the ministry of food, 1945–50, and at national insurance, 1950–1, becoming a life peer in 1961. She was party chairman, 1954–5, and famous for her fierce campaign to get boxing banned.

PRGR

EDITH SUMMERSKILL, *A Woman's World* (London, 1967).

Sun, newspaper. Failing as a relaunched *Daily Herald* aimed at younger working-class readers, the *Sun* was sold in 1969 to Rupert Murdoch. Overnight, he turned it against its previous owners' flagship *Daily Mirror* and produced a brash, jokey, lively tabloid, which tripled its circulation and overhauled the *Mirror* by 1980. Under Australian influence and Larry Lamb's editorship, the paper was typified by its daily topless page three pin-up. Despite its 'natural' Labour readership, the paper supported the Conservatives at every election until 1997, except 1970 (Labour) and October 1974 (coalition). Especially under Kelvin Mackenzie's bravura editorship, 1981–94, it was the working-class expression of the Thatcher era's appeal to individual and material self-interest. Electorally important, it claimed of the 1992 Tory election win, 'the *Sun* it woz wot won it'. In the mid-1990s the paper faltered, like its competitors, with circulation down below four million. The change of mood was reflected in its enthusiastic support of Tony Blair in the 1997 general election. *CKSU*

Sunday trading. Throughout the 19th century, the Christian prohibition on Sunday trading had been enforced through the Sunday Observance Act of 1677. But even under this legislation Sunday trading had not been totally prohibited. As methods of trading became more sophisticated, anomalies inevitably arose. During the 1930s a renewed attempt was made to uphold sabbatarian traditions. An alliance of convenience sprang up between the Lord's Day Observance Society, sections of the trade-union movement, and mainly small retailers. The result was the Shops Act of 1936, a backbench measure which sought to revive the general prohibition on Sunday trading, but which was so hastily drafted that it proved a lawyers' paradise. Those with a conscientious objection to trading on the Jewish sabbath could still trade on Sundays, and many retailers took on Jewish 'sleeping partners' to exploit this concession. The Act never applied to wholesalers, so that retail shops could in principle open on Sundays if they proclaimed themselves wholesalers on that day. Yet Sunday trading remained an emotive issue. A bill to liberalize the law was narrowly defeated at its second reading in the Commons in 1986, and the reform was not enacted until 1994. By that measure, small shops were allowed to trade at any time on Sundays, though larger premises could only open for six hours between 10.00 a.m. and 4.00 p.m. The growth of internet shopping is likely, in time, to destroy this remaining restriction. *GA*

JOHN WIGLEY, *The Rise and Fall of the Victorian Sunday* (Manchester, 1980).

Sunderland South by-election (13 May 1953). Sunderland South was the only seat to change hands in 45 contested elections during the 1951–5 parliament, and the first occasion since 1924 on which a government had gained a seat in a by-election. Although it had been a marginal Labour seat and the Conservatives led in the national Gallup poll, the Tories had learned from *Hammersmith South in 1949 not to emphasize a by-election's national significance. Victory, though, helped to convince Conservatives that they had finally recovered from their 1945 defeat. *RJS*

Sunningdale agreement (December 1973), the culmination of the process to rebuild a Northern Ireland administration after the abolition of the Stormont regime in March 1972. In late November 1973, talks at Stormont castle led to agreement on the formation of a cross-community *power-sharing executive involving the Social Democratic and Labour Party, the middle-ground Alliance Party, and the Ulster Unionist Party. A structural relationship with the Irish Republic, however, to give substance to the 'Irish Dimension' of the settlement, was still to be negotiated. A four-day conference involving the British and Irish governments and parties which would participate in the executive was held at the civil service staff college at Sunningdale park in Berkshire. Despite the optimistic views expressed about the Sunningdale communiqué, reached on 9 December, details of the agreement signposted many of the difficulties which lay ahead – there were, for example, separate statements from the two governments on the status of Northern Ireland. Unionists were also suspicious that the council was an all-Ireland government-in-waiting and this would prove fatal to the Sunningdale agreement as a whole. *GG*

PAUL BEW and GORDON GILLESPIE. *Northern Ireland: A Chronology of the Troubles 1968–1999* (Dublin, 1999).

'Supermac', nickname for Harold *Macmillan which originated in the cartoon character by *'Vicky' that first appeared in London's *Evening Standard* in November 1958, showing Macmillan in Superman garb. Inspired by Stephen Potter's humorous book *Supermanship*, Vicky's creation was turned to Macmillan's advantage as 'Supermac' came instead to symbolize his political dominance. *RJS*

Supply, Ministry of (1939–59). The ministry's origins can be traced back to the establishment of the Ministry of Munitions in the Great War. It was formally established on 1 August 1939, under the Ministry of Supply Act, 1939, charged with the task of converting industry on to a war footing. It was responsible for the administration of the royal ordnance factories and for the design, inspection, research, and experimental work in relation to the War Office and the Air Ministry. The ministry was given powers to control the acquisition, disposal, manufacture, and price of raw materials. In September 1939 it also became responsible for the Board of Trade's supply organization, established under the Essential Commodities Reserves Act, 1938. In practice, however, the Admiralty insisted on maintaining its traditional independence over naval design and production and the RAF control over its aircraft. The ministry's immediate role became little more than that of a buying agent, being restricted to supplying the army and having a limited input to the other two services. In an effort to coordinate its work with the Ministry of Aircraft Production and the Admiralty, a single minister of production was appointed in February 1942. After the war the ministry's functions were redefined with the merger of the Ministries of Supply and Aircraft Production. The Atomic Energy Act, 1946, led to the ministry taking over the Department of Scientific and Industrial Research, which was responsible for promoting and controlling the development of atomic energy. In October 1959, the civil aviation functions of the Ministry of Transport were transferred to the ministry, which in turn was reconstituted as the Ministry of Aviation. *JFM*

swing, a measure of the movement of votes between parties in successive elections. The phrase 'the swing of the pendulum' goes back to 19th-century elections, but the mathematical concept only came into general use after 1945. Swing can be used to describe the change in percentage support for each party between one election and another in any electoral system, but works best when the same two parties come first and second in successive elections. It has been calculated in various ways, but it is most commonly applied in predominantly two-party systems with single-member constituencies. 'Total vote' (or 'Butler') swing averages the change in the percentage of votes cast for each of the two leading parties, and can formally be defined as

$$\frac{\begin{matrix}\text{Change in party A's} \\ \text{\% share of total vote}\end{matrix} - \begin{matrix}\text{Change in party B's} \\ \text{\% share of total vote}\end{matrix}}{2} \times 100$$

'Two-party' (or 'Steed') swing measures the movement solely from the two parties' shares of their own combined vote. 'Electorate' swing measures movement solely from the two parties' shares of the electorate. 'Indian' swing, because there has been so much discontinuity in the Indian parties, has until recently been measured simply in terms of changes in support for the Indian National Congress. Swing has been much used as an instrument in election prediction: on the assumption of uniform and equal swing in different constituencies, it is easy to translate any opinion poll's finding into a statement of the number of seats that each party is likely to win. *DEB*

Swinton, Lord. See Cunliffe-Lister, Philip.

Swinton College, political education establishment. Officially 'the Conservative College of the North', this was opened in 1948 in the home of Lord Swinton, near Ripon in North Yorkshire, and remained the Conservative Party's only political college (in succession to Ashridge in the inter-war years) until closed in 1984. Training courses for agents and activists, weekend conferences of the *Conservative Political Centre, and occasional front-bench meetings were held there. For a short time it also published as a party intellectual magazine the *Swinton Journal*. *JAR*

Sykes-Picot agreement (1916), Anglo-French imperial agreement concluded on 16 May. It allocated future spheres of Middle Eastern influence and control in anticipation of the collapse of the still-undefeated Ottoman Empire. Sir Mark Sykes for Britain and François Georges-Picot for France, both enthusiastic imperialists, allocated Baghdad and Basra to Britain; Cilicia, Syria and Lebanon to France; with the area between as an independent Arab state or states within agreed Anglo-French spheres of influence. A compromise international administration of *Palestine masked rival Anglo-French aspirations, and the agreement was overtaken by the *Balfour declaration of 1917. *AS*

Sykes report (1923) on broadcasting sought regulation of the income of the British Broadcasting Company established by radio manufacturers. Following its recommendations, advertisements were rejected and licence fees were collected by the government, which was uncomfortable doing this for a private company. The report was only an interim measure. *KMT*

syndicalism, political movement based on the use of the general strike. Georges Sorel's *Reflections on Violence* (1906) argued that the most powerful form of political intervention possible by organized labour was to use direct action. This should take the form of a general strike and other industrial unrest designed to undermine capitalist industries. The effect of the strike would be to destroy the economic power of capital and the trade unions would then take over industry. Each industry would be run by the trade unions and political institutions would be replaced by this workers' control through a federation of trade union bodies which would replace the state and become responsible for all civil control of society and education. Such ideas had their widest currency before and immediately after the Great War. In France, they permanently influenced the trade union movement and prevented the industrial wing of the French labour movement from organizing politically through parliamentary institutions, preferring direct confrontation with employers and government. In the USA the International Workers of the World were initially influenced by syndicalist ideas before becoming more conventionally communist. In Britain, these ideas were influential in key unions and played a role in the 1926 General Strike, but the parliamentary road had already been established much more firmly, so their influence was transitory. In Spain, syndicalism combined with anarchist ideas in conflict with Marxism. The anarchist overtones of direct workers' control were anathema to the Bolshevik conception of the vanguard role of the party, therefore the trade unions that followed syndicalism tended to break with Marxist or Bolshevik groupings. In many parts of Europe, the long-term influence of syndicalism has been in the movement for workers' control and industrial democracy, but in Britain the parliamentary road to socialism was preferred at least from 1926. *BB*

T

Taff Vale judgement (1902), legal decision. This judgement made unions liable for losses incurred as a result of strikes. In 1901, Ammon Beasley, the manager of the Taff Vale Railway in south Wales, sued the Amalgamated Society of Railway Servants for damages sustained during a strike, involving the picketing of Cardiff station, which the owners argued was a breach of contract under the Conspiracy and Protection of Property Act, 1875. The case went right up to the House of Lords, which decided that a trade union was a corporate body and could be sued and held liable for the acts of its members. The Law Lords led by Lord Halsbury awarded damages against the union of £23,000, a decision which meant that virtually any direct action by a trade union could result in its bankruptcy. Taff Vale was endorsed by the Conservative government, and so could only be reversed through legislation. The Labour Representative Committee received a large rise in union affiliations as a result of the decision, with membership increasing from 350,000 in 1901 to 850,000 by 1903. After the 1906 election, unions' immunity from prosecution for actions during a strike was reinstated by the Liberal government through the Trade Disputes Act of 1906. The lasting significance of Taff Vale was to build into the union movement a profound distrust of judicial involvement in industrial relations and confirmed many of the need for direct parliamentary representation. *BB*

Talbot, Lord Edmund (1855–1947), Conservative chief whip and Ireland's lord lieutenant. After a career as a soldier, Talbot entered parliament in 1894 and became a party whip and finally Law's able chief whip (1913–21). A scion of a distinguished Catholic family, he was ennobled as Viscount Fitzalan and appointed lord lieutenant (1921–2) during the final phase of Lloyd George's negotiations with Irish nationalism. He was the last to hold that ancient post. *RJQA*

Tariff Commission, research unit and pressure group. Producers never lose interest in trade protection. In Britain in the latter part of the 19th century that interest began to gain more adherents. There were a number of attempts to gain credibility and wider acceptance. Between 1880 and 1930 there were various groupings formed to promote protection—the Tariff Reform Campaign, the Fair Trade League, the Empire Industries Association, and so on—but of them all the Tariff Commission was perhaps the most impressive. It was established in 1904 by Joseph Chamberlain, the Birmingham manufacturer, politician, and keen imperialist. He believed deeply in the need to protect manufacturing and at the same time strengthen Empire ties. In spite of its name the commission was not an official body, though it attracted a large number of distinguished businessmen and some leading academic figures. Its purpose was to treat protection seriously and to investigate how it could best be used to help industry. At the time this was expressed as the desire to design a 'scientific tariff', a subject about which there was a great deal of discussion. To that end it produced a large number of studies of individual products and sectors. The commission has been described as one of the most theoretically innovative business groups that Britain has ever had. Yet by the beginning of the 1920s it seemed to be fizzling out when the real pressure for protection was just beginning to develop. Other bodies such as the Federation of British Industries, the British Commonwealth Union, and later the Empire Industries Association took up the cause and, some would argue, were successful, though it is always difficult to assess the success (in terms of achieving its own objectives) made by a body such as the Tariff Commission. *FHC*

tariff reform, grand design for economic, imperial, and party renewal launched by colonial secretary Joseph *Chamberlain in a great speech in Birmingham on 15 May 1903. Retaliatory tariffs had been suggested by the fair-trade movement of the 1880s, but the immediate origins of Chamberlain's plan to combine import duties and imperial unification were several, including free-trade Britain's uncompetitiveness in tariff-protected foreign markets, her poor performance in the Boer war, the advantage of safeguarding domestic manufacturing and agriculture, and the appeal of using indirect taxation to finance social reform and defence programmes. Convinced that 'little Englandism' precluded national greatness and prosperity in the 20th century, Chamberlain argued that only a closely united empire could maintain Britain as a world power and home of a prosperous people.

His plan stunned an unprepared political world. Liberals united behind free trade, while Unionists soon split between supporters and opponents of tariff reform. The latter, the *Free-Fooders led by Devonshire and the Cecil brothers and seeming at first to include Prime Minister Balfour, reasoned that tariffs would repel an electorate unwilling to support any plan which would raise the cost of living. Undeterred, the Chamberlainites spawned the Tariff Reform League, *Tariff Commission, and other organizations (including the secret *Confederacy) to force their agenda on the party as the path toward imperial unity and the only possible Unionist response to Liberal promises of social reform. Chamberlain resigned office to lead the campaign, while Balfour struggled to avoid commitment and to keep his troubled government and party together. By 1906 the Unionist parliamentary party and the party organization were firmly in the control of the tariff reformers. The *Valentine compact of February 1906 announced their agreement that fiscal reform was to be the 'first constructive work' of the party, but its lack of specificity meant that when Chamberlain was struck down by illness, Balfour could not be kept to the deal by the lesser tariff leaders who followed him.

After two further election defeats in 1910, Balfour was replaced as party leader by the tariff reformer Law, who in 1912 rescinded Balfour's *referendum pledge. The negative public reaction this elicited illustrates the dilemma in which MPs found themselves: though most endorsed tariffs, they were also aware that the electorate remained sceptical, particularly of food duties—stigmatized as 'stomach taxes' by opponents—and this made it unlikely that the programme could win a general election. Law backed down, and tariffs were shelved, for in 1912 the party turned to the more pressing issue of Irish home rule. Tariff reform won the general endorsement of the party after 1918, but its prominent place in Baldwin's 1923 election manifesto brought another defeat, and in 1924 it was again shelved. A limited system of tariffs and imperial preference was implemented in 1932 by Neville Chamberlain, though neither on the scale nor with the results that his father had sought. *RJQA*

E. H. H. Green, *The Crisis of Conservatism: The Politics, Economics and Ideology of the British Conservative Party, 1880–1914* (London, 1995). | Peter T. Marsh, *Joseph Chamberlain: Entrepreneur in Politics* (London, 1994). | Alan Sykes, *Tariff Reform in British Politics, 1903–1913* (Oxford, 1979).

tariffs. See protective tariffs.

Taverne, Dick (1928–), Social Democrat activist. Taverne was the pro-European, right-wing Labour MP for Lincoln from 1962 who, having fallen out with his local party, created his own new party, Democratic Labour, stood for re-election, and romped home at a by-election in 1972. He held Lincoln until 1974, and was predictably an early and active recruit to the *Social Democratic Party when founded seven years later. A Liberal Democrat peer since 1996. *JAR*

Tawney, Richard Henry (1880–1962), historian and socialist intellectual. Beatrice Webb described R. H. Tawney as a 'saint of socialism', and he exercised much influence within the British Labour movement. He set out his idealistic philosophy in academic works, including *Religion and the Rise of Capitalism* (1926), as well as in more political texts such as *The Acquisitive Society* (1921) and *Equality* (1931), aimed at a wider audience. He taught for the Workers' Educational Association in Lancashire and north Staffordshire and lectured at the LSE. A. L. Rowse thought that 'Tawney exercised the widest influence of any historian of his time, politically, socially and, above all, educationally' (*Historians I* *have known* (London, 1995, 92). He lies buried in Highgate cemetery. *CH*

J. M. Winter (ed.), *R. H. Tawney's Commonplace Book* (Cambridge, 1972). | R. Terrill, *R. H. Tawney and his Times: Socialism as Fellowship* (London, 1974).

taxation policy may be considered as having three functions: generating revenue, managing the economy, and redistributing income and wealth. The taxes levied by British governments have increased dramatically over the century, from just under 10 per cent of GDP in 1900 to just under 40 per cent in the 1980s, two world wars having stretched taxable capacity fundamentally. While the tax demands of British governments have not deviated markedly from those of other countries, the structure of taxation has, with a heavier reliance on personal income tax, and less on social security contributions, than in Europe. Taxation policy has, not surprisingly, been affected by political considerations and particular interests. Satisfying important interests (homeowners) and encouraging particular activities (industrial investment) meant the proliferation of allowances and reliefs (tax expenditures), which eroded the tax base. By the 1960s, governments relied upon a narrow range of taxes at high rates to meet revenue demands. Since then, tax reform, particularly by Conservative governments, has tried to reduce the effects of tax expenditures, to lower tax rates, and to broaden the tax base (for example, through *value added tax). The larger aim, in which there has been some success, was to remove taxation as an important determinant of economic behaviour.

Although historians have differed about precisely when, after the Second World War, governments adopted *Keynesian demand management techniques for controlling the economy, the possibility of avoiding either hapless inactivity or direct intervention in the economy was attractive. For a good deal of the post-war period, the problem was to curb inflation rather than avoid unemployment, although in 1959 the Conservatives lightened taxes in order to stimulate the economy. Public sensitivity to taxes and the need to win elections have certainly complicated fiscal policy. Difficulties of forecasting, and underlying problems in the economy, have also meant that fiscal management has not had a particularly impressive record. The use of heavy taxation by the Labour governments of 1964–70, the failure of reflation under Heath, and the coexistence of inflation and unemployment under Callaghan in 1974–9, further undermined the budget as an instrument of economic management. Subsequently taxation policy has had the difficult task of responding to public distrust about state spending in general yet sustaining stubborn levels of government expenditure.

The limited power of the state to moderate inequality through taxation of high incomes and wealth has disappointed those on the left. Although *death duties have had some effect on large estates, receipts from capital taxes and higher rates of income tax have usually lagged behind the growth of the economy. For much of the century it has been easier to hang on to riches acquired through inheritance rather than to gain them by work. However, the progressivity of the tax system—the conventional test of fairness—has increased since the 1960s, although somewhat reduced since 1979. Before the 1960s, the progressivity of income tax was offset by flat rate national insurance contributions and regressive indirect taxes. Since then, the former have become related to earnings and the latter less regressive. *RCW*

J. A. Kay and M. A. King, *The British Tax System* (5th edn., 1990). | Roger Middleton, *Government versus the Market: The Growth of the Public Sector, Economic Management and British Economic Performance, c.1890–1979* (Cheltenham, 1996).

Taylor, Alan John Percival (1906–90), historian and public figure. Unquestionably, A. J. P. Taylor was the best-known British historian of the century. The son of a wealthy Lancashire cotton merchant, he was educated at a Quaker school in York, and something of the awkwardness of Nonconformist radicalism was always part of his approach to life. Having flirted with communism as an Oxford undergraduate, studied in Vienna and lectured under Lewis Namier at Manchester, he was a fellow of Magdalen College, Oxford, 1938–76. A prolific author and charismatic teacher, Taylor was notoriously overlooked for Oxford's regius chair in 1957, it being assumed that the university establishment resented his burgeoning popularity as a journalist and television performer. Essentially a historian of central Europe, he was initially a devotee of the archives, but subsequently relied on intuition, his famous 'green fingers'. *The Struggle for Mastery in Europe, 1848–1918* (1954) was his masterpiece, closely followed by *English History, 1914–1945* (1965), in which a superb narrative is punctuated by pithy insights. Spurned by Oxford, Taylor cultivated his friendship with Lord Beaverbrook, for whom he had worked on the *Daily Express*, becoming director of the Beaverbrook library and author of a life, *Beaverbrook* (1975). Taylor gave all his books a controversial twist (none more so than *The Origins of the Second World War* in 1961, which caused a major national rumpus), but the man himself became as intriguing as his work. Countless memoirs, tributes, biographies, and studies of his relationships with three wives filled out our sense of a brilliant, idiosyncratic Englishman. *PS*

KATHLEEN BURK, *Troublemaker: The Life and History of A. J. P. Taylor* (London, 2000).

Taylor, (Winifred) Ann (1947–), Labour politician, one of several women prominent in *New Labour in the 1990s. MP for Bolton West, 1974–83, and for Dewsbury from 1987, she was parliamentary private secretary to the minister for education, 1975–6; to the minister of defence, 1976–7; and then assistant government whip, 1977–9, which made her unusual in the Labour cabinet of 1997 in having some government experience. Opposition spokesman on several domestic areas, including education, 1979–81 and 1992–4, she became leader of the House after Labour's landslide win in 1997 and chief whip in 1998. *PRGR*

Taylor, Peter Murray (1930–97), judge. Taylor was a barrister from 1954 and chairman of the Bar, 1979–80. He became a crown court recorder, 1972–80; a high court judge, 1980–8; lord justice of appeal, 1988–92; and lord chief justice from 1992. He was chairman in 1989 of the high-profile inquiry into the Hillsborough football ground disaster. *JAR*

Teachers, National Union of (NUT), principal teachers' union, which originated in the National Union of Elementary Teachers and became the NUT in 1870. It has always campaigned for the rights of teachers and reached a peak membership of 311,000 in 1970. Broadly to the left of the political spectrum and plagued from time to time by factional disputes, it has since the 1960s found itself challenged by smaller, sectional teaching unions which have undermined its authority and its claim to speak for the profession as a whole. *JS*

Tebbit, Norman Beresford (1931–), Conservative politician and bogeyman. Tebbit, facing selection in Epping with an eye to a predecessor, said 'I am not a lawyer, I am not a homosexual and I am not a gentleman'. Not being a gentleman has been indeed a lifelong commitment, and he rather relished his 'polecat' label. Lower middle class, the RAF, an airline pilot, clever, resentful, funny, prejudiced, right-wing, bitter, incorrect in spades, always loyal to Thatcher, Tebbit was ill-used by her but still loyal, someone in whom rage and engagingness contended. The early Tebbit, elected to the Commons in 1970, was given to bitter asides such as 'Why don't you drop dead?' (and worse), savagely hostile to the liberalism of privileged groups, not necessarily lawyers or homosexuals, but frequently gentlemen. Even under Thatcher, he was held back by the liberal and gentlemanly establishment but, on his best behaviour after 1979, he was smuggled in as junior at industry, then in 1982 made employment secretary. Despite an electric conference speech about his self-help dad getting on his bike to seek work, his act was smoother, gentler, and more effective. He coolly limited trade union powers, introducing ballots and excluding sympathetic strikes. By 1984 he not only rode high with Thatcher but had become a major figure. Then at *Brighton, he and his wife were victims of an IRA bomb: Margaret Tebbit's back was broken, Tebbit required three skin graft operations. Pain was bravely borne but bitterness returned. Made party chairman, he was ill-served by Thatcher panicking during the easy election of 1987, then blaming the sensibly confident Tebbit, who after victory resigned. His subsequent record, not least as demagogic opponent of Hong Kong immigration, restored the old Tebbit, and in the flavourless Blair era he was appreciated by those who took their tabasco with a hint of strychnine. *EP*

NORMAN TEBBIT, *Upwardly Mobile* (London, 1989).

technical schools. The *Education Act, 1944, made provision for technical schools for some of those children who were not of the highest academic standard and qualified for *grammar school education. Deemed to have skills more appropriate for a technical education rather than the 'modern' school, they were expected to attain higher standards. In practice, only a minority of local authorities ever provided the tier of technical education which the 1944 Act required. *JS*

Technology, Ministry of (1964–70). See TRADE AND INDUSTRY, DEPARTMENT OF.

Tehran conference (1943), first tripartite meeting of Churchill, Roosevelt, and Stalin during the Second World War. The conference, held between 28 November and 1 December 1943, marked the point at which Britain's influence within the Great Alliance began to decline. American strategic planning now came to prevail over British ideas, while Roosevelt made it clear that his future priority would be to secure a working partnership with Stalin, even if this meant compromising the USA's special relationship with Britain. *DJD*

KEITH SAINSBURY, *The Turning Point* (Oxford, 1985).

television. See BROADCASTING.

television, independent. See BROADCASTING; INDEPENDENT BROADCASTING.

temperance, abstinence from, or the limited use of, alcoholic beverages. The temperance movement began in the USA as a movement to ban or restrict the actual sale of alcohol. Organizationally, the British and Foreign Temperance Society (1831) and the United Kingdom Alliance (1853) took the lead in Britain, and had a strong influence on Liberal and Labour Party politics through its association with the Nonconformist (especially Methodist) churches. Temperance Acts were passed in 1853 (for Scotland), in 1869, and in 1904. The most significant issue in the late 19th century was *local option, which allowed local authorities to determine, to a degree, their own licensing laws, but Lloyd George was suspected of temperance as well as other motives when he raised licensing duties in 1909 and proposed nationalizing the drink industry during the Great War: the pubs in Carlisle, nationalized as an experiment at this time, were run by civil servants at the Home Office until the 1970s. The temperance movement remained important until the end of the 20th century, when parts of the *Celtic fringe remained 'dry' on Sundays and drink was frowned upon generally. In general, there was a significant reduction in alcohol consumption during the first part of the 20th century as a result of the restrictions on opening hours for pubs introduced in the Great War, higher excise duties, and a reduction of the alcoholic content of beers and spirits (mostly introduced to prevent wartime munitions workers from suffering from impaired output after lunchtime binges). Although concerns about alcohol and alcohol-related problems remain part of the public health agenda, there has been a radical relaxation of controls over alcohol, which has extended pub licensing hours, permitted more outlets for the sale of alcohol, and facilitated the growth of licensed premises. *JS*

Temple, William **(1881–1944)**, archbishop of York, 1929–42, and of Canterbury, 1942–4. Temple has been characterized as a Hegelian idealist who sought to reform the Church and to prepare it better to comment on social problems. He was instrumental in the Life and Liberty movement founded in 1917, which led to the creation of the Church Assembly in 1919, the 1924 interdenominational Conference on Politics, Economics, and Citizenship (COPEC) in Birmingham, and the Anglican conference at Malvern in 1941. The last made tentative suggestions about nationalization and the welfare state, as well as spawning Temple's widely read *Christianity and Social Order* (1942). Although Temple briefly joined Labour (1918–25), this work was not particularly a Christian Socialist tract. Its significance lay as much in chiming with wartime sentiment as in having an enduring, if somewhat opaque, influence on discussions of the role of Christianity in social problems and national life. When asked why he of all people had appointed a socialist to the top job in the Church, Churchill replied, 'because he was the only half-crown article in a sixpenny-halfpenny bazaar'. *PPC*

Templer, Gerald Walter Robert **(1898–1979)**, soldier and high commissioner of Malaya, 1951–4. A dynamic man with a flair for publicity, Templer took over the combined posts of director of operations and high commissioner of Malaya when it was under attack from Communist insurgents in 1951. He masterminded the 'hearts and minds' campaign designed to keep Malayans loyal while he dealt with insurgency using both British and locally raised forces. By providing welfare schemes and promising free elections and early independence, he won over the population. Malaya avoided communism and then became independent in 1957. *MLC*

Templewood, Viscount. See HOARE, SAMUEL JOHN GURNEY.

Tennant, Harold John **(1865–1935)**, Liberal politician. Elected as MP for Berwickshire in 1894, 'Jack' Tennant was his brother-in-law Herbert Asquith's private secretary until 1895. He was junior minister at trade in 1909, moving to the Scottish Office in 1912 as under-secretary. He was briefly Scottish secretary in 1916, but was replaced by Robert Munro in Lloyd George's administration. He lost his seat in the 'Coupon' Election of 1918. *RF*

terms of trade, phrase which usually refers to the prices or volumes of exports relative to imports for a particular country. It is most commonly measured as the ratio of an export price index and an import price index relative to a given base year. This ratio loosely describes the amount of resources that a country's exports command in the international market. The terms of trade of a country deteriorate when this ratio falls and improve when the ratio rises. Hence, when in the 1950s the relative world price of food and raw materials (which Britain mainly imported) fell, while the relative cost of manufactured goods (which Britain mainly exported) rose, then Britain's terms of trade improved.

CRS

tertiary education is defined as the students who are between compulsory secondary education and higher education. In practice, before the Second World War, the major forms of tertiary education were night school and apprenticeships. In recent years, the growth of further education colleges and the opportunity to study a wide range of courses after the age of 16 have expanded the sector considerably. Government support for post-16, non-university-based education has included the development of a range of new qualifications, especially the GNVQ (General National Vocational Qualification) available in many further education colleges. In 1997–8, there were 2,480,000 students in further education institutions, compared to 1,938,000 in higher education.

JS

test-ban treaty (1963). From the mid-1950s international concern developed about the effects of fallout produced by nuclear tests in the earth's atmosphere. In July 1958, American, British, and Soviet leaders agreed on nuclear test controls and in October, the superpowers began a test moratorium. In August 1961, however, the moratorium was broken by the Soviets and, in response, the Americans recommenced tests. This situation was only resolved after the Cuban missile crisis when American, British, and Soviet leaders signed a treaty which banned nuclear tests. (See also NON-PROLIFERATION TREATIES.)

JRVE

Thatcher, Margaret Hilda (1925–), Conservative politician and prime minister. If Margaret Thatcher had died at the hands of the IRA in October 1984, her historical standing would be outstandingly high, for her career accomplished a historic change of policy—if not one shown in economic growth. She had exceptional courage and resolution in pursuing privatization and anti-trade union policies against senior Conservative opinion and enjoyed a triumph in the Falklands war: she was a dominant personality. Survival that night in Brighton released her for quarrels with colleagues, obsessional causes, and a calamitous domestic enthusiasm, the poll tax, and finally to exhaust the patience of the country. Her party would, unprecedentedly, dismiss her as prime minister, the nearest parallel being Neville Chamberlain with whom and with whose father Joseph she would be compared for drive—and conflict. She achieved success and it eventually destroyed her.

Margaret Thatcher, daughter of Alfred and Beatrice Roberts, adored her father, at whose name she once publicly wept, despising her humbler mother. Proceeding via grammar school to Oxford she read chemistry and worked on the elasticity of ice cream before shifting to the law and the Bar. After contesting Dartford, she was elected at Finchley in 1959. A successful junior at social security, she interested then repelled Iain Macleod, who once remarked 'We made a mistake there'. Right-wing by temperament, she adhered loyally to the interventionism of Edward Heath and as his minister of education she closed more *grammar schools than either Crosland or Shirley Williams, if with less enthusiasm.

Party Leader

Thatcher's accession to the party leadership after the two 1974 Tory defeats was revolutionary and very brave. Discontent with Heath for his statism and ultimate failure ran beyond the right wing. Meanwhile free market argument had been emerging, from among others Peter Jay, Sam Brittan, and Sir Keith *Joseph, the last too fastidious and anxious for a leadership bid. Thatcher wasn't and followed a first round lead which killed Heath, by beating William Whitelaw. Thatcher's opposition years were not, though, successful and James Callaghan regularly won on points at question time. Narrowly elected in 1979 and entering Downing Street with a cod St Francis quotation, she was initially cautious, for example accepting the inflationary Clegg report on teachers' pay. Snobbish and fashionable opinion denigrated her, contrasting her with the elegant Lord *Carrington as the government star, and speculation envisaged the grandees forcing her resignation, but two moves committed Thatcher and achieved her domination. Following Alan *Walters, her economic adviser, she pushed Geoffrey Howe into the 1980 budget aimed at taking £5 billion from the economy. A mistake then broke in her favour: sterling being absurdly hoisted by petroleum assets. Manufacturing industry, unable to compete, lost 20 per cent of its production and massive unemployment after a 40-year trade-union dominance, latterly grossly abused, failed to distress the middle class. Reading's threshold of tolerance about unemployment in Sunderland being found so high would set Thatcher free. A September reshuffle in 1981 took out left-wing critics like Gilmour, marginalized Prior, and promoted the devotional Thatcherites Tebbit and Parkinson. The *Falklands war, for which her military economies could be blamed, provided instead a Roman triumph in 1982. This good fortune had been consolidated by Labour which, when choosing between a proven strong minister and a dishevelled littérateur in a corduroy jacket, chose wrong. Michael Foot's Labour Party was annihilated in 1983.

Ascendancy and Decline

Thatcher could now proceed to *Thatcherism: shifts to indirect taxation, sale of public enterprises (usually too cheap, with luscious capital gains), and union-disempowering legislation coupled with the humiliation of the miners. This last, a tricky affair taking all 1984, and loseable, was symbolic. Arthur *Scargill, a ranting buffoon but full-dress bogey, had beaten Heath twice and (in 1981) Thatcher once. The union died, as did most coal production, but the government had won and governments hadn't won like this before: a central irony for free market liberalism. Thatcher was able to fundamentally shift power to benefit investors and give trade unions no beer and sandwiches at Number Ten, no say. Actual economic growth was modest, 1.6 per cent against the 2.4 per cent under Wilson and Heath, not helped by Nigel Lawson's overreaction to a stock market fall, over-injecting demand into his 1988 budget. Under late Thatcher and Major this produced another overreaction and dire deflationary consequences. Thatcher, riding high, surviving the IRA bomb, deified by the Murdoch press she had early cultivated, began to stumble: *Westland (arrogance if not deception); Peter Wright (obsessive pursuit of an unstoppable publication exploding in Australia); Zircon (policemen breaking down the doors of BBC Radio Scotland); suppression of the Greater London Council; and, supremely, the *poll tax unavailingly billed as the community charge. Meanwhile, she quarrelled with ministers who were variously sacked (Biffen), walked away (Fowler), or resigned to mounting public attention (Lawson and Howe). Considerate and sweet to servants, she treated critical colleagues as enemies. Success and praise accentuated Thatcher opinions remote from liberal market economics: class warfare and a virulent bubbling nationalism. The first ignited the poll tax, more effective at punishing council tenants than raising revenue. The second created public quarrels with European leaders. 'Britain', she said in German Chancellor Kohl's hearing, 'will need forty years to forgive Germany.' Something close to hatred of Europe coloured her dealings and encouraged mischief-making for her successor. The distinction between Thatcher the economic liberalizer and Thatcher the suburban militiawoman bombing Bonn is essential.

Margaret Thatcher was politically very important for late 20th-century Britain and incontestably brave, but the class warrior was ugly, making changes too brutally, and backing questionable police conduct during the miners' strike. Nationalism blended with conceit, and influenced by the right in her adored America, induced self-parody. Certain phrases linger: 'we are a grandmother', or 'He is a marxist, a crypto-communist' (of Neil Kinnock—of all people), or 'drooling and drivelling' (of the poor). Whatever Thatcher achieved, she finally quite lost the country, including great parts of the moderate Conservative vote. The ultimate defeat inflicted in 1997 upon John Major who had won a respite in 1992, but was then undermined by the Thatcherites in his cabinet and party, was also a rejection of her. And it is entirely possible that with her other cloudy trophies may eventually be hung the destruction of the Conservative Party. *EP*

Margaret Thatcher, *The Path to Power* (London, 1995). | Margaret Thatcher, *The Downing Street Years* (London, 1993). | John Campbell, *Margaret Thatcher*, I. *The Grocer's Daughter* (London, 2000). | Hugo Young, *One of Us* (2nd edn., London, 1991).

Thatcherism, political outlook, sometimes regarded as a right-wing ideology in 1980s Britain. It is not historically accurate to describe free market economics, liberal capitalism with minimum regulation, and privatized industry, as Thatcherism, but the shift to such practices in Britain happened when and because Margaret Thatcher was prime minister. The Conservative Party after its massive defeat in 1945 resolved that it must accept the substance of Attlee's post-war settlement. Historians do not talk about 'Attleeism', but Churchill, Butler, and Macmillan practised it after 1951: leaving welfare alone, barely touching the nationalized industries, and accepting trade union power. Full employment was implicit and Conservative governments, when the economic cycle produced 600,000 or 700,000 unemployed, always reflated the economy. For the final inheritance from wartime and the Attlee government had been *Keynesianism which had first reached Labour thinking through Ernest Bevin's participation in the Macmillan committee of 1930–1. Tory voices raised against this consensus were very few and discounted, though among economists, F. W. Paish argued that without a modest pool of unemployment, control of inflation would be exceptionally difficult. *Hayek's defence of free markets and liberal institutions, *The Road to Serfdom* (1945), unfortunately titled and even more unfortunately dated, was treated as a brilliant anachronism. The *Institute of Economic Affairs was, against the fashion, a constant source of free-market argument through its Hobart pamphlets, but Conservative governments under Churchill, Eden, Macmillan, Douglas-Home, and Heath, remained dirigiste, Keynesian, and allergic to rising unemployment. The catchphrase then, of equal importance with Thatcherism later, was 'the mixed economy', though doubt did stir, from Enoch *Powell, from the example of the German social market, and at one stage from Heath himself for his Selsdon Park conference in 1970 was a false dawn of free market thinking (which in the mocking term *'Selsdon man' became Labour propaganda).

Heath retreated from such experiments as soon as unemployment hit an unprecedented million for the post-war period, but iconoclastic economic thinking resumed after his humiliation in 1974 at the hands of the miners. Indeed, so powerful was fear of union militancy that one might think of the reaction as 'anti-Scargillism'. Peter Jay in *The Times* was influential, Samuel Brittan in the *Financial Times* even more so, and they won a key convert in Keith Joseph who, with Thatcher, founded the *Centre for Policy Studies in 1974 to carry forward the cause. Neither a contributor to the thinking, nor a previous supporter, having been a mainly conventional politician, Thatcher was best known, bizarrely, for extending spending on education. She was, moreover, the holder of other opinions unrelated to free market economics, notably strongly nationalist and class-war antipathies. But, after initial caution, she had the political skill from 1979 onwards to push privatization and deregulation forward, steadily tilting and nuancing her cabinet to the right as she did so. Warned by James Prior that tight control of money would create three million unemployed, she apparently genuinely thought not, but found to her gratified surprise that this problem, though true, falling as it did in old industrial areas, did not damage Conservative support. She and Major were therefore able to govern as 'Thatcherites' for eighteen years, and despite subsequent and related Conservative unpopularity, the basic idea, particularly because of its side-effect of direct tax cuts, established itself as the new conventional wisdom, unchallenged by the opposition and pursued with equal enthusiasm by Labour when in power after 1997. *EP*

DENIS KAVANAGH, *Thatcherism and British Politics* (Oxford, 1987). | ANTHONY SELDON (ed.), *The Thatcher Effect* (London, 1989)

That Was the Week That Was, cult weekly BBC TV progamme of satirical sketches, songs, and political comment in 1962–4. 'TW3' outraged viewers steeped in the genteel and showbiz traditions of BBC comedy, but enjoyed large audiences and the protection of the director-general, Hugh Carleton Greene, whom it reminded of Berlin cabaret in the Weimar era. It offended politicians and lost its freshness, but spawned generations of successors. David Frost's TV career took off as its presenter. *CKSU*

HUMPHREY CARPENTER, *That Was Satire That Was* (London, 2000).

Thaxted, rural parish in Essex. Thaxted was a centre of Christian Socialism during the 32 years Conrad *Noel was its vicar. An Anglo-Catholic whose Catholic Crusade, founded in 1918, was the first British socialist organization to welcome the Bolshevik revolution, Noel was given to flying the red flag of socialism or the green flag of Sinn Fein from the church tower, whilst his politics veered from anarcho-syndicalism to communism. He died in 1942, being succeeded in the parish by another High Anglican and socialist, Jack Putterill. *PPC*

'There 'aint gonna be no war.' Taken from a music-hall song, this was Harold Macmillan's response after a meeting in Geneva in July 1955 between the Western powers and the Soviet Union to discuss the possible reunification of Germany. It reflected Foreign Secretary Macmillan's reassuring belief that the Soviets wanted peace with the West and not war. *KTS*

'There is no alternative', slogan. The phrase, once used by Margaret Thatcher, shortened to the acronym TINA. Her response to suggestions that mass unemployment might be met by lower interest rates or job creation through public spending, this was, like 'no turning back' (and all slogans), endlessly repeated. The riposte, 'there is a realistic alternative', or TIARA, never quite caught on. *EP*

think-tank. See CENTRAL POLICY REVIEW STAFF.

Third Force, Northern Ireland vigilante organization. Closely connected with the Democratic Unionist Party and Ian Paisley, the Third

Force was established in 1981 in response to Anglo-Irish talks and the security situation in Northern Ireland. A group of men led by Paisley also appeared on a hillside brandishing firearms certificates. Organized on a county basis it was reputed to have a strength of 15,000 to 20,000, but faded from public view after 1982. *TWH*

third-party squeeze. See WASTED VOTES.

38th Parallel. In June 1950, North Korean troops crossed the 38th Parallel to reunite the Korean peninsula by force. Within four months their armies had been destroyed. Attlee and Bevin agreed with the USA to reunite the peninsula, despite Chinese threats to intervene. UN forces advanced into North Korea and, in November, Chinese forces drove them back beyond the 38th Parallel. Not till July 1953 was peace made, with the peninsula again divided approximately at the 38th Parallel. *PAT*

Thomas, George (1909–97), Welsh Labour politician. Starting his working life as a schoolteacher, Thomas took part in the hunger marches before the Second World War. He was elected to parliament in 1945 as MP for Cardiff Central and after 1951 sat for Cardiff West. After junior ministerial positions at the Home, Welsh, and Commonwealth Offices he became secretary of state for Wales in 1968, when Welsh nationalism was experiencing its first real surge, and remained in this post until Labour's defeat in 1970. From 1976 to 1983 he was an authoritative and sonorous Speaker of the Commons, on his retirement accepting a hereditary peerage as Viscount Tonypandy. He was a devout Methodist throughout his life, but his Nonconformity did not stretch to his politics. At the time of his death, he was more associated with the ceremonies and traditions of parliament than with the hunger marches of his youth. *SB*

GEORGE THOMAS, *George Thomas, Mr. Speaker* (London, 1985).

Thomas, Godfrey John (1889–1968), left the Foreign Office to work for the prince of Wales (later Edward VIII) and became his private secretary in 1919. Thomas refused to carry on in the head post after the prince's accession in 1936. Perhaps he sensed difficulties to come, but he pleaded the need for a rest and served the king as assistant private secretary before leaving to work for the king's brother, the duke of Gloucester. *WMK*

Thomas, James Henry (1874–1949), Labour politician. Born in direst poverty, Jimmy Thomas rose to become a powerful trade union leader and cabinet minister, hated by the left as a 'labour faker'. Self-educated, he became a railway union organizer in Newport, leading his first strike while still in his teens. In 1898 he was delegate at the annual conference of the Amalgamated Society of Railway Servants (ASRS). Transferring to the important railway centre at Swindon in 1901, he became organizing secretary from 1906, moving to Manchester, Cardiff, and finally London as work demanded. Elected union assistant secretary 1910, he led Britain's first national railway strike, 1911, which brought him and the union to national prominence.

In 1913, he played a leading part in merging the ASRS with two other rail unions to form the National Union of Railwaymen (NUR), becoming general secretary and from 1919 to 1931 parliamentary general secretary. The NUR joined the miners and transport workers in April 1914 to form the 'triple alliance', which talked of united industrial action in defence of all three groups of workers. This was suspended during the Great War, which Thomas, unlike Ramsay MacDonald and the pacifist wing of the Labour Party, supported with enthusiastic patriotism. As reward he was sent to the USA and Canada in 1917 as part of the Balfour mission, and made a privy councillor. He led another national rail strike in 1919, but in 1921 played a key role in splitting the triple alliance when called upon to back a miners' strike, failed to support striking footplatemen in 1924, and finally was instrumental in calling off the 1926 *General Strike in a way disastrous for his own railwaymen, the miners, and trade unionism generally.

Yet Thomas continued as Labour MP for the railway town of Derby, which he first won in 1910, and was colonial secretary, 1924; lord privy seal (with the task of reducing unemployment), 1929–30; and dominions secretary, 1930–1. In October 1931 he and four cabinet colleagues joined MacDonald's *National Government when financial crisis brought down Labour. The NUR expelled him without pension. Yet what destroyed his credit with the working class was his making hay elsewhere and, buoyant as ever, he kept his dominions job and returned as colonial secretary, 1935–6. Then his part in a budget leak drove him from public life. An engaging character, unashamedly on the make with his taste for champagne, racetracks, and high living, the cartoonist David *Low dubbed him 'the Rt. Hon. Dress Shirt'. *PRGR*

GREGORY BLAXLAND, *J. H. Thomas, A Life for Unity* (London, 1964).

Thomas, James Purdon Lewes (1903–60), Conservative politician. Elected for Hereford in 1931, for most of the 1930s he served as parliamentary private secretary to J. H. Thomas, 1932–6, then to Anthony Eden, 1937–8. Jim Thomas was a close confidant of Eden, resigned alongside his master in February 1938 over Chamberlain's Italian policy, and opposed the Munich agreement. He joined Eden at the Dominions Office, 1939–40, and was a whip 1940–3, becoming an influential party vice-chairman for candidates in the late 1940s. He achieved major office as first lord of the Admiralty, 1951–5, before retiring to chair a Welsh television company. *NJC*

Thomas, Peter John Mitchell (1920–), Conservative politician. Thomas had served in RAF Bomber Command and was a barrister when he became MP for Conway in 1951. A minister at labour and the Foreign Office during 1959–64, he lost his Welsh seat in 1966. In 1970, however, he won Hendon South, whereupon Heath appointed him party chairman and Welsh secretary. Thomas's genial chairmanship ended in 1972, but he remained Welsh secretary until 1974. He became Lord Thomas of Gwydir in 1987. *RJS*

Thomas, Ronald Stuart (1913–2000), poet. A native of Cardiff but reared on Anglesey, 'R. S.' Thomas became a Church of Wales priest and then a poet. He published the first of many volumes in 1946, an autobiography in 1985, and his *Collected Poems* in 1993. He has long been regarded as the principality's most deeply challenging and complex poet and as its most significant contemporary literary figure. A fervent nationalist and lover of Welsh, which he learnt as a second language, he nevertheless wrote his poetry in English. In early poems he established a full sense of the poor hill-country of north Wales which he saw through the eyes of a peasant character Iago Prytherch. In later work he considers his insignificance in a cosmos in which he seeks a god even as he comes to terms with contemporary physics. In Wales he has prompted a formidable scholarly response but there are readers who were dismayed at his fierce denunciation of both non-Welsh-speaking natives and English immigrants. *PS*

Justin Wintle, *Furious Interiors* (London, 1996).

Thompson, Edward Palmer (1924–93). 'E. P.' Thompson is regarded by many not only as one of the finest historians since the Second World War, but also as in the top flight of socialist writers alongside such luminaries as Raymond Williams, Raphael Samuel, and Stuart Hall. He was also a socialist activist, being a key figure in the Campaign for Nuclear Disarmament (CND). Thompson was born into a Halifax Methodist family in 1924. In the Second World War he was in the Tank Regiment and this experience, with his concern about nuclear weapons, convinced him that there could be no winners in any nuclear war. After the war he was employed by the University of Leeds to teach history to adult education groups. He held this post until the mid-1960s, when he went to Warwick University, later becoming a freelance writer. During that period he wrote his excellent *William Morris: Romantic to Revolutionary* (1955). He also began to write for *Tribune*, the socialist journal, and was an active member of the Communist Party of Great Britain (CPGB). However, he resigned from the CPGB, along with many others, in November 1956 following the Soviet invasion of Hungary, but largely because of its reluctance to abandon Stalinism and introduce the free and open discussions which he demanded in the *Reasoner*, the paper he co-edited with John Saville. Pursuing his interest in British rather than European socialism, which the 1956 debate had been partly about, he began his study of English working-class history and socialism. This prompted his monumental *The Making of the English Working Class* (1962), which suggested that a revolutionary class movement had been emerging ever since the 1790s and that political issues were as important as economic ones in creating revolutionary class activity. Although he produced many other major works on political theory and crime during the rest of his life, no other work quite defined his work and approach so markedly. Through the 1960s and 1970s, Thompson was a strong supporter of CND and a determined supporter of the History Workshop movement, with its commitment to a 'history from below' approach to writing history. He was ill, though, for the last years of his life and his prodigious output declined. *KL*

Dorothy Thompson (ed.), *Essential E. P. Thompson* (London, 2001).

Thomson of Fleet, Lord (1894–1971), Canadian/British businessman and media tycoon. Initially noticed for his frank description of his pioneer Scottish ITV franchise in 1957 as 'a licence to print money', Roy Thomson epitomized the publisher who cares nothing for editorial policy, provided his papers make a profit. Thomson built from nothing a chain of radio stations and newspapers in Canada, which grew into a diversified worldwide conglomerate, including oil and travel businesses. Among his UK properties were the *Scotsman* (1953), *Sunday Times* (1959), *The Times* (1966), a large regional press group, and the phone-book Yellow Pages. The Thomson era was a profitable and journalistic heyday of the *Sunday Times*. Having given up Canadian citizenship in order sentimentally to accept a British peerage (1964), Thomson saw struggles with production unions turn the enterprise sour, especially at the loss-making *Times*, and his son sold up and refocused the business in Toronto. *CKSU*

RUSSELL BRADDON, *Roy Thomson* (London, 1968).

Thorne, William James (1857–1946), trade unionist. Will Thorne's claim to fame is that he was general secretary of the National Union of General Labourers of Great Britain and Ireland from 1889 to 1924, and held numerous other trade union posts. He was also a member of the Social Democratic Federation and the Independent Labour Party at various stages in his career, and Labour MP for Plaistow, 1918–45. *KL*

L. RADICE, *Will Thorne: Constructive Militant* (London, 1974).

Thorneycroft, (George Edward) Peter (1909–94), Conservative politician whose resignation as chancellor of the exchequer in 1958 is sometimes cited as a defining moment in economic policy. Thorneycroft's genial manner and dated upper-class cockney twang created a Woosterish impression, but he was a shrewd politician. Born into a family of Staffordshire ironmasters and soldiers, he entered parliament at the 1938 Stafford by-election. After wartime service in the artillery, Thorneycroft joined other backbenchers in the Tory Reform Committee to press for enlightened social policies. A junior minister in Churchill's Caretaker Government, he lost his seat in 1945 but soon returned as MP for Monmouth. By remaining on the backbenches after opposing the 1945 American loan agreement, he made his reputation as an outstanding debater, and in 1951 Churchill brought him into his cabinet as president of the Board of Trade. In 1954 Thorneycroft achieved a historic shift in trade policy by persuading his party finally to abandon protectionist imperial preference in favour of liberalization through the *General Agreement on Trade and Tariffs (GATT). Having supported Macmillan as Eden's successor in 1957, Thorneycroft became chancellor of the exchequer. Following a run on sterling he dramatically raised the bank rate from 5 to 7 per cent in his September 1957 measures. Influenced by his junior ministers Birch and Powell, Thorneycroft came to the then unfashionable monetarist view that inflation resulted from excessive borrowing by the government, financed by printing money. He demanded cuts of £150 million in planned spending, but when the cabinet offered only £100 million, all three Treasury ministers resigned in January 1958, prompting Macmillan's dismissive comment about *'little local difficulties'. Thorneycroft came to be seen by Powellites and Thatcherites as a monetarist martyr whose defeat culminated in the inflationary explosion of the 1970s. For his part, however, Thorneycroft later admitted that he had pressed his case too early, while published papers confirm that he was egged on by Powell. Thorneycroft returned to the cabinet in 1960, serving at civil aviation and defence and remaining strongly pro-European. He had become shadow home secretary when he lost his seat in 1966. He entered the Lords in 1967 but successfully returned to front-line politics in 1975 as Thatcher's party chairman. His steadying hand was invaluable during the 1979 election, but he was sacked in 1981 after confessing to 'rising damp', revealing that he had some sympathy for the 'wets'. *RJS*

Thorpe, (John) Jeremy (1929–), Liberal leader. Thorpe was one of the rising stars of the Liberal revival in the late 1950s. Oxford-educated and an accomplished performer on the platform and in the media, he was a natural successor to Jo *Grimond. As MP for North Devon, 1959–79, he had solid credentials in one of the *Celtic fringe heartlands of Liberalism. He was also the first post-war Liberal leader to have a real opportunity for office. Following the February 1974 general election he entered into discussions with Edward *Heath about maintaining a Conservative administration with Liberal support, and was offered the Home Office. The talks, however, proved abortive and Thorpe's career was soon afterwards ruined by allegations surrounding his relationship with Norman Scott. Although exonerated of the charges arising out of the *Scott affair, the suspension of his leadership in 1976 and the long legal proceedings which ensued left him excluded from an active political career. *JS*

JEREMY THORPE, *In My Time: Reminiscences of a Liberal Leader* (London, 1999).

'thousand years of history', phrase from Hugh *Gaitskell's 1962 speech at the Labour Party conference opposing Macmillan's proposal for British membership of the European Economic Community (EEC). Membership, he argued, would end a thousand years of separate

British history. The issue was made redundant by De Gaulle's veto but the speech was long remembered by anti-European campaigners. *BB*

three-day week (1974), introduced on 1 January by the Heath government. In the face of the disruption of supplies by the 1973 oil price shock and the miners' dispute, it was designed to try to prevent the total loss of energy which had repeatedly plunged homes and industry into darkness in the emergencies in 1970 and 1972. There were accompanying restrictions on the use of electricity and petrol. Predictions of massive unemployment proved unfounded. Wages and output were only marginally affected. However, this very success undermined the public's sense of crisis whilst persuading the miners to escalate the dispute, and perhaps helped to ensure that Heath lost the February 1974 election. The incoming Labour government settled with the miners and ended the three-day week. *PPC*

***Tiger* talks**. See RHODESIAN CRISIS.

Tillett, Benjamin (1860–1943), trade union organizer, MP, and socialist writer. Although born in Bristol, Ben Tillett rose to fame as a casual labourer at the London docks. He became a member of the Boot and Shoe Operatives' Union in the 1880s and secretary of the Tea Operatives' and General Labourers' Association, which was formed in July 1887. It was as leader of this latter body that he organized the London dock strike in the autumn of 1889, which successfully raised the wages of dockers to six pence per hour. At this time he also reorganized the union into the Dock, Wharf, Riverside, and General Labourers' Union of Great Britain and Ireland, of which he was secretary, 1889–1922. He played an active part in the work of the TUC and, in 1910, formed the National Transport Workers' Federation to revive militancy in the docks. Tillett was involved in many other national and international trade union activities, most importantly being a member of the special industrial committee of the TUC in 1925 to deal with the mining dispute, chairman of the TUC in 1928, and president of congress in 1929. Politically, Tillett was a member of the Independent Labour Party (ILP) and the Social Democratic Federation, and an alderman on the London County Council, 1892–8. In 1908, reflecting his political frustrations, he wrote *Is the Parliamentary Labour Party a Failure?* Having failed in four parliamentary contests, he was MP for North Salford, 1917–24 and 1929–31, active as an ILP socialist. *KL*

JONATHAN SCHNEER, *Ben Tillett: Portrait of a Labour Leader* (London, 1982). | E. TAPLIN, *The Dockers' Union: A Study of the National Union of Dock Labourers, 1889–1922* (London, 1985).

Times, The, newspaper. In its 19th-century heyday *The Times* (founded 1785) was a pioneer in printing and journalism. Under editors Thomas Barnes and John Delane it was 'the thunderer', a power in the land, but by 1900 it was living on its reputation. In 1908 Northcliffe bought control from the founding Walter family, cut the paper's price, and made it solvent, without popularizing it unduly. It remained non-partisan (though implicitly conservative), a 'paper of record': strong on parliament, law reports, and overseas news; weak on human interest. Northcliffe's successor, Colonel John Astor, bought the paper in 1922 to preserve its status above mundane politics. His non-involvement disastrously enabled editor Geoffrey *Dawson to lend support to the appeasement of Nazi Germany. After an unexpected post-war enthusiasm for Attlee's Labour government, *The Times* settled into a generally conservative mould. Lacking capital for modernization, the Astors sold out in 1966 to Roy Thomson. Bruised by industrial disputes, which kept the paper unpublished for eleven months in 1978–9, Thomson's son sold to Rupert Murdoch in 1981. The paper was saved but lost the last vestiges of its historic role as an institution beholden to no interest, public, private, or financial. *CKSU*

J. TUNSTALL, *Newspaper Power* (London, 1996).

TINA. See 'THERE IS NO ALTERNATIVE'.

Titanic. The *Titanic* was built in Belfast and launched on 1 April 1912. It struck an iceberg and sank on 14 April. Some commentators in the present generation have seen it as in some way symbolic of the blows dealt to Ulster Unionism: a great enterprise that, like the place which built it, suffered a grievous fate. *DGB*

Titmuss, Richard (1907–73), social policy expert. Titmuss was educated privately until the age of 15, never attended a university, but accumulated five honorary doctorates and a chair in social administration at the LSE, 1950–73. After a career in industry and commerce, he joined the Cabinet Office as an official historian, 1942–9, but had by then established his reputation through such books as *Poverty and Population* (1938), later reinforced by his *Birth, Poverty and Wealth* (1943) and *Problems of Social Policy* (1950). Titmuss was a tireless advocate of the rights of the underprivileged and of the necessity—in the national interest as well as for humanitarian reasons—to pursue social policies to improve their lot. *JAR*

Tizard, Henry (1885–1959), scientist and administrator. Tizard's service as an administrator of (particularly defence) scientific research and government advice spanned the period from the Great War to the early 1950s. In the 1920s he was a senior official in, and then head of, the Department of Scientific and Industrial Research. He was an influential air defence scientific adviser and committee man in the 1930s and in the early years of the Second World War, but famously clashed with F. A. Lindemann. From 1947 to 1952 he chaired both the Defence Research Policy Committee and the Advisory Council on Scientific Policy. *KT*

Todd, Ronald (1927–), London-born general secretary of Britain's most powerful union, the Transport and General Workers (TGWU), 1985–92. Ron Todd's union career took shape when he worked for the motor giant Ford, 1954–62, then the symbol of a new industrial age. He became a full-time paid official of the TGWU, 1962, and worked his way up through the union to become a member of the TUC general council in 1984, chairing the TUC international committee in 1985. He was supportive of the miners' strike, 1984–5, and fiercely opposed Thatcher's reforms of the trade union movement. Todd was honorary president of the Campaign for Nuclear Disarmament. *DMM*

Tokyo war trials. See NUREMBURG AND TOKYO WAR TRIALS.

Tomlinson, George (1890–1952), Labour politician. A former weaver with trade union and Methodist roots, Tomlinson was devoted to his native Lancashire and served as MP for Farnworth, 1938–52. He was appointed minister of works, 1945–7, and on the death of Ellen Wilkinson was promoted to education secretary and the cabinet, 1947–51. In his new post, Tomlinson proved to be a cautious reformer, resisting calls for radical change and adhering to the tripartite framework established by Butler's Education Act, 1944. *AM*

Tonypandy (8 November 1910). The Rhondda valley town of Tonypandy is for ever associated with the rioting which occurred during a dispute at the Cambrian Combine and marked the opening of a new era of militancy on the part of the *South Wales Miners' Federation. The events achieved a certain notoriety, largely through the involvement of the home secretary, Winston Churchill, who in the folk mythology is alleged to have 'sent in the troops'. In fact Churchill, in ordering the local authorities to rely on the police in the first instance, behaved both properly and cautiously. The anger which led to rioting, first at the engine house and then in the main street where shop windows were smashed, was occasioned by a high-handed management who were refusing to grant a minimum wage to miners working in 'abnormal places' and who called in blackleg labour when their 12,000 workforce came out in support. *PS*

DAI SMITH, *A Place in South Wales: A Question for History* (Bridgend, 1999).

'too clever by half', phrase used in March 1961 by the 5th marquess of *Salisbury about Iain *Macleod, the colonial secretary. Salisbury accused Macleod of having brought his card-player's bridge technique into politics and outfinessed Africa's whites. The attack damaged Macleod because it had a ring of truth. *RJS*

Tope, Graham Norman (1943–), local Liberal politician in South London, who won a sensational by-election victory against the Conservatives on 7 December 1972, and was MP for Sutton and Cheam, 1972–4. He remained active both in London politics and in the Liberal Party, becoming Liberal life peer in 1994. *JAR*

Topping, (Hugh) Robert (1877–1952), Conservative organizer. As general director, Topping was the professional head of the Conservative Party Organization, 1928–45. He had been one of the best of the younger agents that emerged during the 1900s and 1910s, then area agent for the north-west. In 1930, the 'Topping Memorandum' on the state of party morale almost toppled Baldwin as party leader, but he subsequently avoided visible involvement in such intra-party battles. Topping stayed on after retirement age to see the party through the Second World War but was unable to prevent the organization from disintegrating. *JAR*

Torrington by-election (27 March 1958), Liberal gain by Mark *Bonham Carter from the Conservatives during the unpopular early days of the Macmillan government. This was the first Liberal by-election gain for nearly 30 years, and widely seen as the harbinger of the Liberal revival. This duly came in the early 1960s, but by then the Conservatives had won Torrington back in 1959. *JAR*

Tory, political label deriving from an ancestor grouping of the modern Conservative Party from the 1680s to the 1830s. In the 20th century it was used by Conservatives as a badge of honour, particularly for those like Macleod or Powell who saw themselves as especially principled, and by opponents to describe Conservatives in a derogatory way. Effectively synonymous in normal usage with the label 'Conservative'. *JAR*

Tory Reform Committee (TRC), ginger group of young MPs on the left of the Conservative Party, led by Peter Thorneycroft, Quintin Hogg, Hugh Molson, and Viscount Hinchingbrooke. The TRC was formed in 1943 to persuade the party's leadership to accept the Beveridge report and other wartime reforms, attracting a membership of 41 MPs. Taking its inspiration from the old Tory tradition of state interventionism and adding some of the more recent radical ideas of the 1930s, as espoused in Macmillan's *The Middle Way*, the TRC presented a very contemporary vision of how the Conservatives should tackle social reform. It also took a thoroughly modern approach to its work, adopting professional methods: it met weekly to discuss parliamentary business, produced pamphlets, and retained a paid research staff (which was more than the official party could manage in wartime). The TRC provoked considerable hostility from the right of the party who saw them as quasi-socialists and, in wartime, had limited impact on the political debate and came nowhere near capturing the party. Many of the TRC's interests overlapped with the *Post-War Problems Central Committee and, whilst neither were especially successful in propagating their intentions, each helped contribute to the climate that would shape post-war party thinking. *NJC*

JOHN RAMSDEN, *The Age of Churchill and Eden, 1940–1957* (London, 1995).

'Tough on crime, tough on the causes of crime', slogan used by Tony Blair when shadow home secretary (1992–4). This effective Labour slogan affected public sentiment prior to the 1997 general election, by distancing New Labour from the party's traditionally 'soft' approach to law and order, rather blaming Conservative policies for rising *crime rates. Like all such slogans it gave hostages to fortune, for Labour's record in office after 1997 would be bound to be judged against it. *AM*

tower blocks. The tower block of flats became the symbol of the best—and more often the worst—of British council housing in the post-war era. Low-rise flats of up to five storeys had become common in the inter-war years as a solution to the need for new high-density housing in urban areas. Built without lifts, they were 'walk-up' flats similar to traditional Scottish tenements. New forms of prefabricated construction and lifts made it possible to build 'high-rise' tower blocks by the 1960s, and some, such as Sheffield's Park-hill flats, won international architectural prizes, but they were soon found to be difficult and expensive to maintain, hard to police, and highly unpopular with tenants (who missed the community of the street and could feel very isolated several storeys up). The collapse of the Ronan Point block in London in 1968 also raised questions about their safety and they became the focus of concerns about the quality and integrity of the new housing being built in Britain. Tower blocks, in practice, were never more than a quarter of all housing units built, though their stark appearance on the skylines of most towns made them seem more predominant than they were. Many have now been dynamited and replaced by low-rise housing of a more traditional character. *JS*

Town and Country Planning Act, 1947, first Act to control the use of and development of land and buildings in the interests of the nation as a whole, along the terms advocated by pre-war and wartime reports. County councils had to prepare development plans, revised quinquennially, and were given powers of compulsory purchase. Planning permission was required by property owners for changes of use or additions to buildings. It created the framework for post-war planning controls over land use and building, and remains operative in its essential elements. *JS*

Townsend, Peter Brereton (1928–), sociologist. Professor Townsend's studies of poverty in the 1950s and 1960s, beginning with *The Family Life of Old People* (1957), introduced the concept of 'relative poverty' and heralded the 'rediscovery of poverty' in the midst of affluence and despite the intended safety net provided by the welfare state. *JS*

trade, process that allows countries to take advantage of the gains from international specialization in production. Without trade, each country must produce all the goods it consumes, which would require the production of some products that might be more efficiently produced elsewhere, and would usually result in a low level of consumption and welfare. With international trade, producers in each country can specialize in the production of the good which they make most efficiently, and then exchange that good in the international market for other goods. When each trading nation uses its own resources most efficiently by specializing in what it does best, this allows the most efficient allocation of resources overall, and therefore the best prospects for growth. The increased production that arises from international specialization is known to economists as the 'gains from trade'.

Each country's comparative advantage in production may be due to a variety of factors. These include climate and natural-resource allocation, as well as factor endowment. For example, a country with a large population but little capital will have a comparative advantage in labour-intensive production because their labour is cheap relative to capital. This is known as the Hecksher-Ohlin theory of the source of comparative advantage and was developed in the 1920s. With trade, these factor prices will change. For example, labour costs may rise in the labour-rich country as employment expands in response to increased production of the country's goods for export. This will prompt managers to substitute capital for labour. Through time, therefore, a country's comparative advantage may shift in response to trade, from labour-intensive production to more capital-intensive production. The tendency for factor prices to respond to international trade is known as the Stolper-Samuelson theorem, which was developed in the 1940s. Although the gains from trade are intuitively obvious, most countries at some time have restricted international trade. Britain adhered to relatively free trade from the 1840s until the 1930s, although since then there have existed various barriers to trade. Barriers to trade, such as *protective tariffs or quotas, are most often erected to protect domestic producers from international competition. This has an economic rationale in the short term: to protect infant industries until they are of a size to compete in the world market. Protection is also a response to political pressure from industry leaders, or to protect the labour employed in an uncompetitive industry. A major target for protectionism in 20th-century Britain has been farmers, who have benefited from European Community policies which guarantee minimum agricultural prices by excluding cheap imports of food. Although barriers to trade may have economic and political benefits, they will also have costs in terms of welfare. Most importantly, the exclusion of cheap imports raises the price of these goods for domestic consumers. In the longer term, protection can also prolong the allocation of resources to an uncompetitive industry. The historical record of tariffs and quotas is that while they may be effective in the short term, they are costly to the economy overall and will not generate sustained growth. *CRS*

Trade, Board of. See TRADE AND INDUSTRY, DEPARTMENT OF.

Trade and Industry, Department of (DTI) (1983–). The greater willingness of the state to intervene in commercial and industrial affairs during the 20th century led to much specialization and separation of responsibilities from the late 19th-century configuration of the Board of Trade. Thus, in 1918 the Ministry of Labour was created, in 1920 the Ministry of Transport, and the Ministry of Food in 1938. Further change happened in 1942, when the Ministry of Fuel and Power was created, and the Ministry of Supply was created in 1939 in order to provide war *matériel*. In 1964 a Ministry of Technology was formed, partly by taking functions from the Board of Trade and partly by merging them with the Department of Scientific and Industrial Research which then ceased to exist. The Heath government formed the Department of Trade and Industry in 1970, merging the Board of Trade and the Ministry of Technology, with the intention of increasing economic competitiveness, especially once Britain joined the European Community in 1973. Energy resource functions were taken away in 1974 with the creation of the Department of Energy. Upon Harold Wilson's return to the premiership in March 1974, the Department of Trade and Industry was split into three: the Department of Trade, the Department of Industry, and the Department of Prices and Consumer Protection. The Thatcher government reintegrated the Department of Prices and Consumer Protection with the Department of Trade in 1979 and in 1983 merged the Departments of Trade and Industry once more. In the 1980s and 1990s, the DTI also shifted from directly sponsoring and overseeing nationalized industries to setting up and handling the politics of the newly privatized industries. The year 1992 saw the Department of Energy merged with the DTI and the functions of industrial relations were also given to DTI upon the merger of the Department for Education with the Department of Employment. *JD*

Department of Trade and Industry website: *www.dti.gov.uk*

Trades Disputes Act, 1906, reversed the *Taff Vale judgement, so that unions would no longer be liable for the damages incurred by employers during a strike. It reflected the Liberal government's attempt to prevent the development of a separate Labour party by delivering reforms demanded by the trade unions, but it served rather to underline for many trade unions the importance of separate parliamentary representation. *BB*

Trades Disputes and Trade Union Act, 1927, anti-labour legislation passed after the General Strike. The Act was designed to prevent another general strike and to restrict the political involvement of trade unions. After the Act, the political levy which went to the Labour Party could only be paid by those who 'contracted in' (actually decided to pay it), a provision reversed in 1946. Sympathetic strikes or lockouts were made illegal and civil service unions were separated from other union bodies. Though not as potentially restrictive as the Taff Vale judgement, the Act was a major source of disaffection on the left. *BB*

Trades Union Congress (TUC), central organization of affiliated unions. The TUC was founded in 1868 to bring trade unions together for an annual meeting, which takes place in the first week of September. Between meetings the organization is run by the general council (GC) of the TUC which is elected at each congress. The GC meets monthly and is the voice of organized labour in Britain. The TUC has generally been a moderating influence on militant trade unions and has been consistently anti-communist, but at times it has been strongly partisan and worked closely with the Labour Party and Labour governments. At other times, it had been more concerned with industrial questions and the needs of its members. In periods of Conservative government, notably 1951–64, the TUC pursued a policy of constructive engagement, thereby positioning itself to deal with governments of any colour. Its major industrial aim has been to ensure union recognition from employers and to maintain a framework of free collective bargaining. Though strongly linked with the Labour Party, the TUC contains non-affiliated unions and has at times clashed with Labour governments when they have tried to impose a prices and incomes policy, most notably during the winter of 1978, or to reform the powers of unions to use industrial disputes, most notably in response to the **In Place of Strife* white paper in 1969. In this instance the Labour government was forced into a humiliating climbdown and a meaningless voluntary guideline was introduced instead of legislation. However, since the General Strike of 1926 the TUC has been committed to an accommodation with business and limited confrontation, together with organized industrial disputes and the symbolic occasional day of action, for example against the Conservative government's trade union legislation in the early 1980s. That period was the darkest in its history: the Thatcher government, unlike all Conservative administrations since Baldwin, refused to deal with the TUC and abolished all tripartist bodies, such as the National Economic Development Council, through which government, unions, and employers cooperated. The TUC's response was to adapt to the changing times and adopt a 'new realism', though not without much resistance from left-wing unions, leading to the defection for a period of the leading modernizing union, the electricians, the first major defection in TUC history. After 1992 the TUC began to outpace even the Labour Party in its call for reform, most importantly on British involvement in the European Union. Slow to change and deeply conservative in nature, the TUC was portrayed as a carthorse by the cartoonist David Low and an ex-general secretary once commented that if the TUC were in a javelin-throwing contest it would elect to receive. *BB*

Trade Union Act, 1913, allowed political use of union funds. Passed at a time of increasing industrial unrest, this Act partially reversed the *Osborne judgement and outlined the conditions under which political involvement could be included in the rules of a trade union, with its members' consent. A partial response to the 'great unrest', 1910–14, the Act allowed moderate trade unions to engage more easily with democratic politics by having a separate political fund so long as members were allowed to 'contract out' of paying into it. In turn, this undermined the revolutionary road to socialism. *BB*

Trade Union Act, 1946, repealed the 1927 Trades Disputes and Trade Union Act. It allowed the political levy to be paid by all trade unionists except for those who 'contracted out' (specifically decided not to do so), and therefore increased the funds contributed to the Labour Party. It also reallowed the theoretical possibility of a general strike and the use of sympathetic strikes. *BB*

Trade Union and Labour Relations Act, 1974, repealed the Industrial Relations Act, 1971. It was designed to retain some features of the 1971 Act, for example the procedures in unfair dismissal, but abolished the National Industrial Relations Court and the Commission on Industrial Relations. The Labour movement's long-standing opposition to judicial involvement in industrial relations and distrust of the Conservative legislation were behind the Act, but it also made it virtually impossible for the 1974–9 Labour governments to do anything to deal with the excesses of the trade unions and clearly signalled the trade unions' influence over them. *BB*

trade unions, bodies which are prepared to organize strikes of workers in order to improve wages and conditions. Trade unions only received legal recognition of their rights in the 1870s, but by 1900 they had two million members and had begun a lasting political association with the Labour Representation Committee and the Labour Party. Throughout the 20th century, trade unions have normally been under severe industrial and political pressure, except perhaps in the period 1945–79. In 1901, for instance, they faced a challenge to their funds and their right to strike by the Taff Vale judgement, although in 1906 the new Liberal government granted them legal immunity for costs incurred in disputes. Similarly, the Osborne judgement (1910), which limited trade unions in providing political funds, was partially rescinded in 1913.

The deep industrial unrest between 1910 and the early 1920s raised serious issues about trade union power. There were concerns about revolutionary syndicalist activities. However, the sting of such events was drawn by the Munitions of War Act, 1915, which gave governments the right to control industrial relations and industries, and the Emergency Powers Act, 1920, which allowed governments to declare a national emergency in the case of industrial disputes, if they so wished. Nonetheless, trade unions were in a powerful situation at this time, with the demand for labour high. As a result, membership also increased from about four million in 1914 to eight million in 1920. Thereafter, the industrial depression of the inter-war years, the failed General Strike of 1926, and employer opposition, took its toll so that by the 1930s trade union membership fluctuated between four and five million. The biggest restriction was imposed by the Trades Disputes and Trade Union Act of 1927, which made picketing more difficult, banned general strikes, and made it difficult for public workers to strike. It was not withdrawn until 1946.

Since the Second World War, trade unions have had mixed fortunes. At first, from 1945 to 1970, they faced restrictions from time to time but were allowed to develop. Indeed, by 1979 the TUC could claim about thirteen million members. However, the *Rookes* v. *Barnard* case (1964) challenged the legal immunities which the trade unions had had since 1906. The Donovan commission report (1968) and the white paper *In Place of Strife* (1969), Heath's battles with the miners, and the 'winter of discontent' (1979) brought the whole position of trade union powers into sharp focus. As a result, when the Conservatives came to power, they introduced legislation between 1979 and 1992 which ensured that trade unions had to hold strike ballots to make certain that their funds were protected from seizure, and many other restrictions (see EMPLOYMENT ACTS, 1980–90). With membership slumped to around 8 million by the mid-1990s, trade unions became less militant, more diverse in their activities, and fewer in number, as mergers and amalgamations occur. *KL*

KEITH LAYBOURN, *A History of British Trade Unionism c.1779–c.1990* (Stroud, 1997). | ROBERT TAYLOR, *The Trade Union Question in British Politics: Government and Unions since 1945* (Oxford, 1993).

traffic in towns. See BUCHANAN REPORT.

Transport House, the headquarters of the Transport and General Workers' Union since 1928 and also of the TUC and the Labour Party, 1928–60. It was built in Smith Square as a result of the efforts of Ernest Bevin and symbolized the intimate connection between the political and industrial wings of the Labour movement. *KL*

transport policy. In 1900 the railways were the dominant transport mode in Britain and the only one experiencing substantial regulation. They were required to publish their rates, not to discriminate, to provide cheap trains, to limit the hours of employees, and to obtain official approval before raising rates. Fear of railway monopoly lay behind the policy of discouraging mergers, which needed parliamentary sanction. The 1914–18 war, however, demonstrated the advantages of unified control of the system, produced a ministry of transport, and brought nationalization close by 1919. A compromise solution, the Railways Act of 1921, returned the network to private ownership, but in the new form of four large territorial groups, subject to intensified regulation. This legislation failed to anticipate the powerful growth of road competition in the inter-war years. Road building had been encouraged by the road fund (the proceeds of car licences, officially the 'road fund licence', originally kept in a separate fund to pay for road building) in 1909 (raided by the Treasury from 1926 and wound up in 1937), and by the transfer of responsibility for trunk roads to the Ministry of Transport in 1937. The Road Traffic Act of 1930 introduced regulation of bus services and the Road and Rail Traffic Act of 1933 established a licensing system for goods vehicles. Despite these measures, more freight traffic was won by road carriers, especially for higher value goods and over shorter distances. Coordination was achieved only where railway companies operated their own bus services (after 1928) and in the congested London area, under the London Passenger Transport Board of 1933.

After a further period of wartime government control, the Transport Act of 1947 nationalized the mainline railways and minority parts of road transport, both passenger and freight (mainly long distance). The British Transport Commission (BTC), of which the Railway Executive was the largest component, was supposed to develop an integrated system of inland transport, but a retreat from this objective was soon under way. The Transport Act of 1953 largely reversed the limited nationalization of road haulage, and the Transport Act of 1962 abolished the BTC, conferring greater independence on the British Railways Board (BRB). Under the chairmanship of Dr *Beeching in the early 1960s and under growing pressure to reduce the railways' losses, the BRB made major reductions in the size of the network, with a view to concentrating on principal traffic flows. Legislation of 1968 introduced 'social service grants' to maintain unremunerative lines. The same purpose was served by six urban passenger transport authorities established in 1969 and 1972, with powers to subsidize and coordinate local bus and rail services.

Road transport, almost entirely in private hands, expanded strongly, encouraged by a programme of trunk road building, including motorways from 1959. The Ministry of Transport was widely regarded as a ministry for roads, which were given priority over railways. Road investment was sanctioned on a social cost-benefit basis, whereas railway projects were required to show a target rate of return (latterly 8 per cent). Between 1950 and 1990 the volume of road freight quadrupled, to reach two-thirds of the national total. Rail freight fell by more than half. The use of private cars continued to grow rapidly, with car registrations increasing from 2 million in 1950 to almost 20 million in 1990. Rail passenger volumes were merely stable over the same period and in 1990 represented only about 6 per cent of the total. Bus services, after several decades of expansion (partly at the expense of trams) declined from the late 1950s. The one remaining growth area, long-distance coaches, was deregulated by the 1980 Transport Act. Further legislation in 1985 derestricted remaining bus services and sold the National Bus Company.

One of the last measures in the Conservative programme of deregulation, privatization, and (within limits) competition, was the Railways Act of 1993. This was based on the separation of the railway infrastructure from the operation of train services. The former was sold to a new company, Railtrack, and franchises (about 25 for passenger services, four for freight) to provide the latter were awarded, subject to public regulation, to various successful bidders, some of whom were also large-scale bus operators. The newly privatized system was initially lubricated by a considerably higher level of subsidies than British Rail had received. One implication of the free market policies of the 1980s was the lengthy and embarrassing delay in building a fast rail link between London and the Channel Tunnel, since the government made a virtue of denying public subsidy to both projects. Although the tunnel was successfully opened in 1994, it remained financially fragile for some years. High-speed rail services had been running from the French end of the tunnel since 1994, but no progress had been made in Britain. After the collapse of two schemes and the abandonment of the original no-subsidy principle, the best expectation in 1999 was that the British private sector might have emulated the French public sector by 2007.

GC

S. Bagwell, *The Transport Revolution from 1770* (London, 1974). | S. Glaister et al., *Transport Policy in Britain* (London, 1998).

Treasury, the dominant British government department. A major reorganization of the Treasury in 1919 created three divisions, each headed by a controller: finance, both home and overseas; supply, to take care of public spending; and establishments, to deal with organization, manpower, and pay for the whole civil service. At this time it also became general practice for each government department to obtain Treasury acceptance from two divisions—staffing and all other expenditure—for its spending plans. Taken as a whole, these changes considerably reinforced the Treasury's control over other departments. The next big change to the Treasury's functions came in 1955 when the first survey of social service expenditure for the coming five years heralded the establishment of the public expenditure survey system, following a decade of rocketing state spending. This was formalized by the creation of the public expenditure survey committee (PESC), an evolution of a recommendation by the 1961 *Plowden report. The sense that British relative economic decline was linked to its lack of indicative planning in comparison with economies such as France's led to the creation in 1962 of the National Economic Development Council. The creation of the Department for *Economic Affairs (DEA) in 1964 was meant to counter what was perceived by some as the Treasury's entrenched support for stable prices above economic growth. The DEA was given the task of creating much higher than average growth, but the Treasury held all other economic levers. This dichotomy of functions was described by its creator, Prime Minister Harold Wilson, as 'creative tension'. Being more tense than creative, the experiment failed and in 1969 was quietly wound up, even though the prime minister had placed himself in charge in 1967. Another experiment, this time to remedy the problem of uncontrolled public expenditure projects, 'programme analysis and review', was created in 1970. In the very difficult economic times of the 1970s, this never became embedded and was abandoned in 1979. In 1968 the Treasury lost its civil service functions with the establishment of a civil service department (CSD) but on the abolition of the CSD in 1981 it regained these responsibilities. The year 1975 saw a major reorganization of the Treasury's departments concerned with the national economy into four sections: the chief economic adviser's sector, the overseas finance sector, the domestic economy sector, and the public services sector. A central unit was established to coordinate the policy and management of budgetary and any other issues spanning the responsibility of several groups. With the advent of the Labour government in 1997, there were some very big changes to the functions of the Treasury. Within the week of its election victory, the government gave the Bank of England operational independence as regards the setting of interest rates, with the proviso that it aimed for a 2.5 per cent inflation rate. As the government progressed, the Treasury began to assume ever more control over other departments, primarily through the creation of public service agreements, with Treasury funding tied to policy outcomes. *JD*

Peter Hennessy, *Whitehall* (London, 1989). | David Lipsey, *The Secret Treasury* (London, 2000). | Public Record Office website: *www.pro.gov.uk/finding/coreexec/data/T-main.htm*

Treasury view, term used to denote what is regarded as the prevailing view of the Treasury mandarins ensconced in Whitehall. The Treasury controls central government expenditure from the point of view of value for money and broad aggregates. Prior to the Great War, in conjunction with the Bank of England, it had the responsibility for managing the national debt, largely independently of the government. The 'Treasury view' was widely attributed as being a key factor in influencing the Baldwin government's ill-fated return to the *gold standard in 1925. During the 1920s, the prevailing view in the Treasury was that the overall supply of capital was fixed. *Classical economic orthodoxy, with which the Treasury was closely associated, assumed that when the government borrowed in the money markets, it did so in competition with industry, which invariably led to a rise in interest rates. The Treasury firmly believed that permanent employment could not be created by loan-financed public expenditure. As the guardian of financial frugality, its views were a major obstacle to the expansionary economic policies advocated by Lloyd George and Keynes. The Treasury at this time was cast in the role of *devil's advocate*, using arguments based on the availability of financial resources to counteract the merits of other departments' spending proposals. Its functions reflected the fact that its original development as a department was tied up with the advent of parliamentary control over expenditure.

In the Second World War, the power of the Treasury lapsed when the physical allocation of productive resources including manpower took priority over budgetary considerations. Post-war political changes, coupled with the enhanced importance of international financial negotiations through the work of the Organization for European Economic Cooperation (the agency for Marshall aid), helped to restore its position. The Treasury continued to be associated with the view that money was best left to fructify in the pockets of the people. Keynesian accounts in particular portrayed it as monolithic, obscurant, and an institutional impediment to effective demand management. The Treasury never had to formulate a theoretical defence of its view until the Gladstonian orthodoxy of minimal public expenditure was challenged during and after the Second World War. While there was no formal written-down 'Treasury view', for its views did evolve over time, there was a tendency for its civil servants to use accumulated departmental wisdom and practical philosophy to temper their individual enthusiasm for new ideas, while Treasury officials tended to be too sceptical by nature and training to be swayed by new economic remedies. The recruitment process, focusing on individuals from specific backgrounds coupled with the promotion system, effectively ensured that internal differences of opinion did not become major issues of controversy.

The degree to which the Treasury accepted the concept of demand management is rather a controversial issue, but it is probable that its conversion reflected Keynesian appreciation of the importance of finance. This gave the Treasury a central role in the post-war management of the economy. The subsequent adoption of econometric modelling techniques by the Treasury ensured that its officials exhibited a consensus view, particularly in the department's role of assisting the chancellor to formulate the budget. The advent of *monetarism in the late 1970s temporarily undermined its role in the management of the economy but its collective views have continued to play an important role in influencing the government's management of the economy. *JFM*

Henry Roseveare, *The Treasury: The Evolution of a British Institution* (London, 1969).

treaty of accession to the EEC. See EEC, TREATY OF ACCESSION TO THE.

treaty ports, three naval bases in Ireland—Queenstown/Cobh, Berehaven, and Lough Swilly—retained by Britain on Irish Free State territory after 1921. They were relinquished, during the era of appeasement, under the *Anglo-Irish agreement of April 1938. Churchill always regretted the surrender of such strategic assets, and during the Second World War the range of British naval operations was reduced by up to 400 miles (644 km), and Eire, as its prime minister had calculated, found it much easier to preserve its neutrality. *DRB*

Trenchard, Hugh Montagu (1873–1956), airman. Trenchard joined the royal flying corps in 1912 and rose to command it in 1915. Appointed first chief of air staff in January 1918, he resigned because of his poor relations with the minister Rothermere but was reappointed by Churchill in 1919, holding the post until 1929, defeating Admiralty demands for its own air service and establishing himself as professional equal of the heads of the other services. Trenchard was commissioner of the Metropolitan Police, 1931–5, where he staunchly opposed the British Union of Fascists and unsuccessfully attempted to create 'a police officer class'. *SJB*

Trend, Burke St John (1914–87), civil servant, secretary of the cabinet, 1963–73. Trend was an unobtrusive and discreet mandarin, a cautious and careful—but influential—adviser to chancellors of the exchequer and prime ministers. He had joined the Board of Education in 1936 with the inevitable first in classics from Oxford, soon switching to the Treasury where he was the chancellor of the exchequer's principal private secretary under Dalton and Cripps in the post-war Labour government. He later worked closely with Rab Butler as his chief of staff in the office of the lord privy seal, 1955–6. A spell as deputy to Norman Brook in the cabinet secretariat (1956–9) was followed by senior Treasury jobs before Trend became secretary to the cabinet at the start of 1963. A superb operator of the Whitehall machine, he was Harold Wilson's indispensable adviser and aide during the 1964–70 Labour government. Trend's influence with Wilson and his role in the government's defence and nuclear decisions, together with his links with the US authorities and the intelligence services, aroused the suspicion of some left-wing ministers. His relationship with Heath after 1970 was at times more strained: Trend preferred the 'socratic' approach in his briefings and advice, while Heath wanted a tougher, more proactive executive style. *KT*

Tressell, Robert. See *Ragged-Trousered Philanthropists, The.*

Trevelyan, Charles Philip (1870–1958), Liberal, later Labour, politician. Liberal MP for Elland, 1899–1918, Trevelyan held junior office under Asquith but resigned over the decision to go to war in 1914, and became a leading supporter of the anti-war and anti-conscription movements, later of the internationalism associated with the League of Nations. A Labour MP, 1922–31, he was MacDonald's president of the Board of Education in 1924 and 1929–31, but resigned in March 1931 in despair with the government's general inaction. *JAR*

Trevelyan, George Macaulay (1876–1962), historian. Trevelyan was blessed by family, Liberal connections, education, financial independence, and brains. Convinced that history must instruct and improve public and private life, he wrote 24 books and 58 chapters, essays, lectures, and pamphlets to reach the greatest audience of any historian in the 20th century: his *English Social History* (1944) was one of the biggest-selling books of the century. A committed Victorian altruist, he edited the *Independent Review*, lectured to the Working Men's College and the BBC, and served as a royal commissioner investigating Oxford and Cambridge. He was also a museum trustee, an active conservationist for the National Trust, and commander of a British Red Cross ambulance unit in Italy during the Great War. Disappointed by the tragedies of the 20th century, Trevelyan preferred to write about earlier times, great leaders such as Caribaldi and Grey of Fallodon, and happier endings. An admirer of Baldwin as an exemplar of politically sound liberal and conservative values, Trevelyan remained the last of the Whig historians, affirming the exceptional character of Englishmen, the excellence of the English constitution, and the possibility of progress. *RNS*

David Cannadine, *G. M. Trevelyan: A Life in History* (London, 1992). | Reba N. Soffer, *Discipline and Power: The University, History, and the Making of an English Elite, 1870–1930* (Stanford, 1995).

Trevethin, Lord (1843–1936), judge. Alfred Tristram Lawrence was a barrister from 1869 on the Oxford circuit, and recorder of Windsor, 1885–1904. He was a judge from 1904, and (as Lord Trevethin) lord chief justice, 1921–2. He also had the difficult task of presiding over the 1920–2 war compensation court. *JAR*

Tribune, newspaper. *Tribune* was founded in 1937 to provide a strong voice for the left within the Labour Party, and has generally had a high profile within the Labour movement as a whole. Under the editorships of Nye *Bevan (1942–5) and Michael *Foot (1948–52 and 1956–9) in particular, it was the weekly mouthpiece for the Bevanite wing of the movement, and thereafter for the 'Tribune group' of MPs that succeeded them as the main organization on the left in the Parliamentary Labour Party. It was associated in the 1940s and 1950s with campaigns for further nationalization and for *unilateralism, viewpoints that were not strongly represented in the press as a whole. *JAR*

Trident, American submarine-launched nuclear missile. Despite the Labour government's reluctance to replace the ageing Polaris in the 1970s, Callaghan entered into secret talks with the Carter administration for the purchase of Trident. In 1979 Thatcher energetically sought to renew Anglo-American nuclear ties and secured Trident in July 1980 amid the atmosphere of renewed tension, the 'second cold war'. This led to a resurgence in anti-nuclear pressure groups in Britain, particularly the Campaign for Nuclear Disarmament and the women's peace camp at the US *Greenham Common airbase (see CRUISE MISSILES). *JRVE*

Trimble, (William) David (1944–), first minister of the Northern Ireland Executive and leader of the Ulster Unionist Party. A barrister by profession, Trimble was elected to the Northern Ireland Convention as a *Vanguard Unionist in 1975 and supported the proposal for a voluntary all-party coalition. He joined the Ulster Unionists in 1978 and won the Westminster parliamentary seat of Upper Bann in a 1990 by-election. Initially viewed as a hard-line Unionist because of his support for Orange marchers at *Drumcree in 1995, he became leader of the Unionists in the same year. Despite his hard-line image, Trimble kept the Ulster Unionists in the talks which led to the Good Friday agreement of 1998, the year in which he was awarded the Nobel peace prize. Although a Northern Ireland executive with Trimble as first minister, which involved *Sinn Fein representatives, was established in late 1999 (suspended and re-established in early 2000), the issue of the decommissioning of IRA weapons continued to split the Ulster Unionists and to threaten to collapse the Good Friday agreement, leaving Trimble's position as Unionist leader still tenuous. *GG*

Henry McDonald, *Trimble* (London, 2000).

Truman doctrine (1947), espoused in an address to a joint session of the US Congress on 12 March 1947 by President Harry S. Truman, which led to American financial support for Greece and Turkey. On 21 February 1947, Britain informed the USA that its assistance to Greek royalists, who were fighting communist guerrillas, and to the Turkish government, which was resisting Soviet attempts to gain access to the Black Sea straits, would end. Economic weakness, worsened by the terrible winter of 1947, forced the Attlee government to accept realities: Britain had to reduce its international burdens. The Truman administration was, supposedly, surprised by this announcement. In fact, it had been prepared to replace Britain in Greece since September 1946. Affecting surprise, however, served Truman's objective of attaining congressional and public approval of his foreign policy of containment (resistance against Soviet expansionism). In his speech, the president proclaimed: 'I believe that it must be the policy of the United States to support free peoples who are resisting attempted subjugation by armed minorities or by outside pressures.' Setting Greece and Turkey against a backdrop of an international struggle for freedom ('nearly every nation must choose between alternative ways of life'), Truman rallied his country against Soviet communism. It worked. On 15 May 1947, Congress appropriated $400 million for Greece and Turkey and, within a year, extended containment from the eastern Mediterranean to Europe, with $4 billion appropriated for Marshall aid. These events ensured that containment would remain the foundation of American foreign policy until the late 1980s. For Britain, the 1947 withdrawals from the Near East (Greece, Turkey, and then Palestine) and from India signified a diminution of international status. Whilst British influence remained, especially in the Middle East, global power waned. From the Truman doctrine and the *Marshall plan onwards, British governments, often due to economic frailty, would depend upon the international power of the USA and search for ways to mould it. *JRVE*

C. J. Bartlett, *The Special Relationship: A Political History of Anglo-American Relations since 1945* (London, 1992).

trusteeships. The concept of 'trusteeship' was long regarded as the guiding principle of British colonial policy. The term was also applied to the eleven colonial territories which were placed under the supervision of the *United Nations' trusteeship council. This system operated from 1946 to 1994, generally resulting in better preparation for independence and encouraging diligence in safeguarding the interests of indigenous peoples. But it made little difference to the speed of Britain's departure from Togoland (1957), Cameroon, and Tanganyika (both 1961). *LL*

David R. Wainhouse, *Remnants of Empire: The United Nations and the End of Colonialism* (New York, 1967).

Tryweryn reservoir controversy. The drowning of the Tryweryn valley in Merionethshire was undoubtedly the most emotive issue in Welsh politics in the late 1950s and early 1960s. A Welsh community centred on the village of Capel Celyn was sacrificed in order to provide water to the English city of Liverpool. A broadly based opposition to the proposal was overcome by the government who pushed through a private bill, but the debate on Tryweryn was chiefly significant for the way in which it transformed the standing of Plaid Cymru. Gwynfor Evans, the party's leader, was particularly prominent in the agitation and his efforts effectively politicized many young Welsh speakers, some of whom attacked installations at Tryweryn. A new era opened in the politics of Wales. *PS*

Alan Butt-Philip, *The Welsh Question* (Cardiff, 1975).

Turnbull, Andrew (1945–), civil servant. Turnbull joined the Treasury in 1970 after having worked for two years as an economist in Zambia. He worked in Number Ten, 1983–5, and was principal private secretary to prime ministers Thatcher and Major, 1988–92. Second permanent secretary at the Treasury in charge of public spending, 1993–4, he was permanent secretary at the Department of the Environment (later Environment, Transport, and the Regions), 1994–8, and was then permanent secretary to the Treasury from 1998. *KT*

Turner, Benjamin (1863–1942), Labour and trade union pioneer in Yorkshire. Coming from Luddite and Chartist ancestry, Ben Turner's experience in the wool textile industry led to a lifetime involved with textile trade unionism. A trade union official from 1889, he was president of the General Union of Weavers and Textile Workers, 1902–22; of the National Union of Textile Workers, 1922–33; and of the National Association of Unions in the Textile Trade, 1917–29. He joined the Independent Labour Party on its foundation in 1893 and for seventeen years sat on the NEC of the Labour Party. MP for Batley and Morley, 1922–4 and 1929–31, he was in 1929 parliamentary secretary for mines. He was also a councillor, alderman, and four times mayor of Batley and a county councillor and alderman for the West Riding of Yorkshire, in a local government career which spanned 48 years. He served on the general council of the TUC, 1921–9, and was president of congress in 1928, when he collaborated with Sir Alfred Mond in the Mond–Turner talks which attempted to develop a conciliation procedure for industrial disputes—which proved abortive. *JAJ*

Benjamin Turner, *About Myself* (London, 1930).

turnout, the number or proportion (usually the latter) of those on the electoral register who cast their votes in a particular election. Turnout in British general elections for most of the century was usually well in excess of 70 per cent. It exceeded 80 per cent in the first three general elections of the century (1906, Jan. 1910, Dec.

1910) and in the two general elections in the middle of the century (1950, 1951). It reached a low point (57.2 per cent) in the unusual circumstances of 1918, even though (or perhaps, in part, because) the franchise had been extended to 19-year-old servicemen and to women aged 30 and above. In the remaining elections, the turnout ranged from a little over 71 per cent (1923, 1935, 1997) to 79 per cent (1959, Feb. 1974). Critics of the political and electoral system noted a decline in turnout after February 1974, arguing that this—along with a decline in the share of the vote being cast for the two main parties—indicated a decline in support for the two-party system. Supporters of the existing political system argue that the decline reflects a phenomenon that is not peculiar to the UK: that is, a move away from political parties to a greater involvement in single-issue politics.

Turnout in general elections notably exceeds turnout in elections to other public offices. Turnout in elections for members of the European parliament has been low since direct election was introduced in 1979 and is declining. Turnout for elections to local government has also been low, markedly so in comparison with other West European countries where turnout reaches or exceeds 60 per cent. In 1997, turnout in elections to both the European parliament and to local councils reached a historic low: the turnout in local government elections in May 1997 was 29 per cent (in some individual wards, turnout was less than 15 per cent); turnout in the European parliament elections the following month was 24 per cent. A Home Office study was begun in 1998 to see if ways could be found to increase voter participation. In 1999 a Representation of the People Act provided for a rolling electoral register, easier access to postal votes, and pilot schemes for alternative means of voting. The radical option of introducing compulsory voting was not included. Despite declining turnout, under 60 per cent in 2001, voting remains the most regular form of political participation by citizens. *PN*

R. Blackburn, *The Electoral System in Britain* (London, 1995). | D. Denver and G. Hards (eds.), *Issues and Controversies in British Electoral Behaviour*, pt. 1 (Hemel Hempstead, 1992). | G. Parry, G. Moyser, and N. Day, *Political Participation and Democracy in Britain* (Cambridge, 1992).

two-party system, competition between two dominant parties. According to Giovanni Sartori (1976), Britain was a 'perfect' two-party system in that it had both the format and the properties of two-partyism. Two parties are in a position to compete for the absolute majority of seats. One of the two parties actually succeeds in winning a parliamentary majority; that party is then willing to govern alone. Alternation or rotation of power remains a credible expectation. Critics have argued that Britain has not displayed the properties of a two-party system throughout the 20th century. For part of the century, party competition at a parliamentary level did not have the properties of a two-party system, notably so early in the century, a consequence of concentrated support for Irish Nationalists in Ireland and the overtaking of the Liberal Party by the Labour Party as the second largest party. At various times in the century, two-party competition was not a characteristic of electoral competition, including in the 1983 general election, when Labour and the SDP-Liberal Alliance competed vigorously for second place, Labour just squeezing ahead of the Alliance. Supporters of two-party politics contend that it has been the predominant mode of party competition throughout the century. The debate has focused on UK politics. Two-party competition has not been a characteristic of the 1998 elections to the Northern Ireland assembly and the 1999 elections to the Scottish parliament and Welsh assembly, in each of which multi-party competition has predominated. *PN*

P. Norton, 'Britain: Still a Two-Party System?', in S. Bartolini and P. Mair (eds.), *Party Politics in Contemporary Western Europe* (London, 1984). | G. Sartori, *Parties and Party Systems: A Framework for Analysis* (Cambridge, 1976).

Tyndall, John (1934–), racial nationalist. Tyndall served in the League of *Empire Loyalists and involved himself in other groups such as the National Labour Party, the *British National Party, and the National Socialist Movement, before gaining greater prominence in the *National Front (NF). He helped to form the NF (1967), developed its ideology of English nationalism, and played a key role in its general development. With its decline he founded the New National Front which became the British National Party (1982) and remains its leader. *CH*

J. Tyndall, *The Authoritarian State* (London, 1962). | J. Tyndall, *Six Principles of British Nationalism* (London, 1964).

Tyrrell, William George (1866–1947), diplomat. Tyrrell entered the diplomatic service in 1889 and was appointed private secretary to the new foreign secretary, Grey, in 1905. An astute operator behind the scenes, he supported the

Entente policy, but seems not have thought feasible a rapprochement with Germany before 1914. As head of the political intelligence department, 1916–19, he took a leading part in preparing for the Paris peace conference. As Foreign Office permanent secretary, 1925–8, and ambassador to Paris, 1928–34, he continued to work for a firm Anglo-French agreement. In retirement he brought the same diplomatic skills to the presidency of the British Board of Film Censors.

TGO

Edward T. Corp, 'Sir William Tyrrell: Eminence Grise of the British Foreign Office, 1912–1915', *Historical Journal*, 25 (1982).

U

UDI, Rhodesian, the illegal Rhodesian unilateral declaration of independence on 11 November 1965. Until then, Rhodesia was a self-governing British colony, but allowed only the minority white settlers and a few Africans to have the vote. By 1961, many white Rhodesians feared that Britain would impose majority rule and in April 1964, they elected Ian Smith as their prime minister and spokesman. After fruitless negotiations with the Conservative and then Labour governments, Smith declared UDI, provoking the fifteen-year *Rhodesian crisis. *KTS*

Brian Lapping, *End of Empire* (London, 1985).

UKASA, permanent agreement between the USA and the UK covering the full exchange of methods and results of signals intelligence acquired clandestinely. UKASA was thus an important collaboration over the decipherment and distribution of foreign signals intelligence beginning in 1941, before the USA entered the war, and proved of vital importance to the Allied war effort. Visits by cryptographic experts soon established mutual trust and confidence covering both confidentiality and priority, with the Americans concentrating on Japanese traffic, primarily diplomatic and naval, while the British handled Europe, especially German and Italian messages transmitted by the Enigma enciphering machine. Conferences at regular intervals between the heads of the Bletchley Park cryptographic code-breaking establishment and its American counterpart consolidated the collaboration, which led in the autumn of 1945 to a prolonged negotiation stretching through 1946. The reasons for the delay were twofold. One was the determination of the Americans to deal unilaterally with Canada, Australia, and New Zealand, opposed by the British. The other was that neither country had made much headway against high-grade Soviet codes and ciphers whose importance was highlighted by the Cold War. *RD*

Bradley F. Smith, *The Ultra-Magic Deals: and the Most Secret Special Relationship 1940–1946* (Novato, Calif., 1993).

UK Independence Party (UKIP), electoral pressure group. The UKIP, led by LSE historian Alan Sked, held anti-European views which were in theory rather more extreme than those professed by the *Referendum Party (RP), since it called for Britain to leave the European Union rather than merely to limit its federalization. While the RP fought every seat and frequently won 2,000 votes, the performance of the UKIP's handful of less-funded candidates was electorally invisible. *EP*

Ullswater report (1936) on broadcasting gave guidance on the oversight of the BBC and on union representation, a key issue of the time. It outlined a view of balanced programming, particularly on news and controversial issues. Though vague on financing broadcasting, it paved the way for the promotion of television. *KMT*

Ulster Defence Association (UDA) (1971–), Loyalist paramilitary organization established late in 1971, a year of rapidly increasing violence in Northern Ireland. The UDA aimed to protect the province's mainly Protestant population, apparently left vulnerable by the recent disbanding of the B-Specials and disarming of the Royal Ulster Constabulary. Stormont's suspension early in 1972 removed another restraining influence, and shortly afterwards the UDA established its own no-go areas in Belfast. These risked provoking a confrontation with the British army, but may also have impelled it to take action against the more notorious republican equivalents in July 1972. The UDA's biggest success came in May 1974 when it played a key role in organizing and enforcing the Ulster Workers' Council strike, resulting in the collapse of the power-sharing executive and the Sunningdale agreement. The UDA has remained ambivalent in its attitude towards conventional politics. In 1975 it flirted with the Vanguard Unionist Progressive Party and its campaign for an independent Ulster; but more extremist elements within it, known as the Ulster Freedom Fighters, preferred to concentrate on sectarian killing. The UDA has put much of its energy into housing allocation and residential segregation, its leadership remaining predominantly secular and urban working class. *DRB*

STEVE BRUCE, *The Red Hand: Protestant Paramilitaries in Northern Ireland* (Oxford, 1992).

Ulster Defence Regiment (UDR) (**1970–92**), a full- and part-time military force, under the control of the British army's general officer commanding in Northern Ireland, and liable only for service in that province. It was established in order to replace the 'B-Specials', discredited by their role in the riots of 1969, and, hopefully, also to attract more Catholic recruits. Early on, its members became obvious targets for the IRA, 24 for instance being killed in 1972, a peak year of violence in Northern Ireland. Often living in the community, UDR members were vulnerable, especially in the remoter rural areas west of the River Bann. At its maximum the regiment had 9,000 soldiers. Altogether, 40,000 men and women served in its ranks at various times, 188 of them being killed. It was never used for riot control, duties being confined to guarding, patrolling, and manning checkpoints. The UDR came under a cloud in the late 1980s, due to evidence of collusion with Protestant paramilitaries in carrying out sectarian murders. In 1992 it was merged with the full-time Royal Irish Rangers, itself 30 per cent Catholic in composition, to form the Royal Irish Regiment. *DRB*

JONATHAN BARDON, *A History of Ulster* (Belfast, 1992).

Ulster Freedom Fighters (UFF). Essentially the military wing of the contemporary Ulster Defence Association, UFF emerged in 1973 and since then has been responsible for many sectarian and politically motivated murders. In August 1992, following a series of UFF murders, the Ulster Defence Association, which had remained a legal organization, was banned. Although the UFF has claimed to support the peace process, the activities of some of its members in recent years have often served to undermine confidence in it. *GG*

STEVE BRUCE, *The Red Hand: Protestant Paramilitaries in Northern Ireland* (Oxford, 1992).

Ulster Special Constabulary (**1920–69**). Formed in November 1920 and funded by the British government as part of its campaign to defeat the IRA campaign in the North, it consisted of 'A', 'B', and 'C' class constables, with 'A' as full-timers, 'B' as part-timers, and 'C' as reserve. This was effectively the reconstitution of the pre-1914 Ulster Volunteer Force and few, if any, Catholics joined, then or subsequently. The 'B-specials' class was retained until its disbanding as part of a reform package in 1969 and on 30 April 1970 it was replaced by the Ulster Defence Regiment. *DGB*

Ulster's Solemn League and Covenant (**28 September 1912**) was signed by 471,414 men and women who could prove Ulster birth. It was a well-organized, highly publicized event which served to highlight opposition in Ulster to the passing of the Third Home Rule Bill which had received its first reading in parliament in 1912. In this covenant, people pledged themselves 'to stand by one another in defending for ourselves and our children our cherished position of equal citizenship in the United Kingdom and in using all means which may be found necessary to defeat the present conspiracy to set up a home rule parliament in Ireland'. Other steps were taken around this time by the leadership of the Unionist Party to organize a provisional government and an armed volunteer force for Ulster in opposition to the threat of rule by a Dublin parliament. *BMW*

JONATHAN BARDON, *A History of Ulster* (Belfast, 1992).

Ulster Unionist Council, ruling body of the Ulster Unionist Party (UUP), though in theory there is no such entity as the UUP. In 1885–6 a number of Ulster MPs from the Irish Unionist Party formed a loose group to resist Irish home rule. In 1905, a number of younger Unionist leaders urged reform of the administrative structure in Ulster to resist the divisive campaign on land reform and the growth of the Independent Orange Order. The result was the Ulster Unionist Council (UUC) in August 1905. The UUC united local Unionist associations, bound Ulster Unionist MPs and their constituents, contributed to the formation of parliamentary policy, and expressed the views of the wider movement. In 1912 the UUC devised plans for a provisional government, to militarily resist the Third Home Rule Bill coming into force for any part of Ireland, but in 1916 it accepted the wartime British government's proposals for a partitioned Ireland as a settlement of the Irish question. The UUC nominated delegates for negotiations at the Irish Convention during 1917–18 but rejected the convention's scheme for an all-Ireland parliament.

The UUC's significance then declined when a devolved Northern Ireland parliament was established in 1920–1. The UUP's monopoly of political power in Northern Ireland meant that the regional parliament and government became the centre of policy making, not merely for the party, but for the province as a whole. The UUC was enlarged in 1921, 1929, and 1944, and in 1946 a restructuring of the UUC resulted in the formation of an executive committee and a number of subcommittees. In the 1960s, the UUP buckled under the impact of the civil rights campaign, and the significance of the UUC increased with the proroguing of the Northern Ireland parliament in 1972, while the UUP became just another party in Northern Ireland's political landscape. In 1973, the British government attempted to establish a power-sharing Northern Ireland assembly. The UUC twice rejected by narrow margins proposals to oppose power-sharing, but it was the Sunningdale agreement's proposal for a council of Ireland taking all-Ireland decisions, which tore the UUP apart. In January 1974, the UUC rejected the Council of Ireland by 427 votes to 374 and Brian Faulkner the UUP leader was forced to resign and was replaced by Harry West. In 1979, West was succeeded by James Molyneaux, and under Molyneaux's leadership the UUP recovered its political dominance in Unionist politics, though its greatest challenge now came from Ian Paisley and the Democratic Unionist Party. In 1995, the UUC elected David Trimble to succeed Molyneaux as the leader of the UUP, and in 1997 Trimble surprised many commentators when he and his party remained in multi-party talks in Belfast following the admission of Sinn Fein to them. The resultant Belfast agreement, to which Trimble was one of the signatories, was endorsed by over 70 per cent of the UUC in April 1998, and it continued to support him, though more narrowly, in later disputes in 1999–2000. *TWH*

John F. Harbinson, *The Ulster Unionist Party, 1882–1973: Its Development and Organisation* (Belfast, 1973). | David Hume, *The Ulster Unionist Party 1972–1992: A Political Movement in an Era of Conflict and Change* (Lurgan, 1996).

Ulster Volunteer Force (1913–14) (UVF). In early 1913, the Ulster Unionist Council agreed to set up the Ulster Volunteer Force to create a military organization to oppose home rule, which now seemed a distinct possibility. By the end of the year, 90,000 men had been recruited for this force which was organized on military lines with ex-army officers providing a command structure. In April 1914 a large assignment of arms was brought into ports in Cos. Down and Antrim and distributed to units of the UVF. With the suspension of the Third Home Rule Bill following the outbreak of the Great War, the Ulster Volunteers were not required for action in Ireland. Instead, many members now volunteered to join the British army for the war in Europe. The bulk of the Volunteers became members of the 16th Ulster Division. While involved in a number of important European battles, the most important event for the division was the battle of the Somme in July 1916 when in the first two days of the battle 5,500 men of the Ulster Division were killed or wounded. After the war there were attempts to revive the UVF in face of republican violence but these did not materialize. *BMW*

Ulster Volunteer Force (1966–) (UVF). The name and the concept were both revived in 1966, in opposition to Terence O'Neill's liberalizing policies. Following two killings in mid-1966 it was proscribed, and remained an illegal organization for most of the period since. In early 1969 it helped to end O'Neill's premiership by mounting bomb attacks on public installations. Its notoriety increased especially after 1971, when it responded to the spate of IRA killings and attacks on property by often savage reprisals against Catholics. An early such example was the explosion at McGurk's bar, in December 1971, in which fifteen people were killed. Sectarian murders became commonplace during 1972–3, and in May 1974 the UVF extended its campaign to the Irish Republic, with bomb attacks in Dublin and Monaghan. During 1975–6 the activities of a UVF murder gang, known as 'the Shankill butchers', imposed a reign of terror upon much of Belfast. In these circumstances the conviction and sentencing, in March 1977, of 26 UVF men to terms of imprisonment totalling some 700 years represented a triumph for the security services and for the energetic secretary of state Roy Mason. In the early 1990s sectarian killings by the UVF increased once more, and may have been one factor encouraging Sinn Fein to explore the peace process. The UVF joined the Loyalist ceasefire in October 1994. *DRB*

Sarah Nelson, *Ulster's Uncertain Defenders: Protestant Paramilitary and Community Groups and the Northern Ireland Conflict* (Belfast, 1984).

Ulster Workers' Council (UWC). Formed in the autumn of 1973 the UWC was intended to coordinate Loyalist workers' opposition to the perceived weakness of government security policy. However, this was later overtaken by opposition to power-sharing and the Council of Ireland. Chaired by shipyard shop steward Harry Murray, the UWC attempted to remain free from the influence of politicians and paramilitaries but in the May 1974 strike which brought down the power-sharing executive the UWC was forced to rely heavily on both for support. *GG*

Ulster Workers' strike (1974). Despite political opposition to the Sunningdale agreement in early 1974 Unionist politicians appeared unable to prevent its continuing implementation. On 14 May a group of Loyalist workers, the Ulster Workers' Council (UWC), called a strike, nominally in favour of fresh assembly elections. With the support of Loyalist paramilitaries and politicians the UWC were able to bring many areas of Northern Ireland to a standstill through the use of power cuts, road barricades, and restrictions on petrol supplies. The extent of genuine support for the strike has remained a matter of dispute as has the question of whether the government might have taken a firmer line. It is clear, however, that by the end of the 'constitutional stoppage' it was widely supported by all shades of Unionism. On 28 May, with electricity and sewage services apparently on the brink of collapse, Brian Faulkner and his fellow Unionists resigned from the executive. On the following day the strike was called off, but the UWC failed to achieve their stated objective of fresh elections to the Northern Ireland Assembly. *GG*

Don Anderson, *14 May Days: The Inside Story of the Loyalist Strike of 1974* (Dublin, 1994).

***ultra vires*, in local government**, doctrine that an authority may not act outside the powers accorded to it by statute. Local authorities are said to be 'creatures of statute', in that they may act, and spend money, only insofar as they can cite legal authority. To act outside the law risks challenge from district audit, with surcharges levied against individual councillors implicated in unlawful decisions. It has often been argued that the *ultra vires* rule operates to make local authorities unduly cautious, and some have urged instead that they should have a 'general competence' to act in the interests of their area. This was bestowed in a limited fashion, and confined to the product of a penny rate, by the Local Government (Financial Provisions) Act, 1963. The *Redcliffe-Maud commission recommended a general competence, under which authorities would be limited only by the wishes of their electors, subject to the constraints of national expenditure. Section 137 of the Local Government Act, 1972, introduced some flexibility into the *ultra vires* regime by permitting such expenditure, to the limit of a 2p rate, providing the activity was not contrary to other statutory limitations. During the last quarter-century, the practice of judicial review has greatly extended the traditional doctrine of *ultra vires* to cover the ways in which decisions are taken, as well as the narrow statutory basis on which they are founded. *KY*

'unacceptable face of capitalism', phrase used by Heath in May 1973 to condemn undercover, tax-free handouts in the city when most people's pay rises were limited by his counter-inflation laws. Wrongly taken to imply that capitalism itself was 'unacceptable', it became one of Heath's most famous remarks. *RJS*

Underhill, (Henry) Reginald (1914–93), Labour Party organizer. A long-standing opponent of the left, Underhill was a national agent, 1972–9, particularly concerned about the activities of the Militant Tendency, and prepared a report on entryism in 1975. This was ignored by the NEC but after his retirement Underhill published it at his own expense. The resulting press coverage was acutely damaging to the Labour Party but the left-controlled NEC again refused to act, Tony Benn comparing the report to the Zinoviev letter. *MC*

unemployment. Classical political economy of the early 19th century taught that the broad equilibrium between supply and demand would ensure the full utilization of labour, except for marginal shifts towards more productive forms of employment. In the face of the cyclical downturns in trade and therefore employment in the more fully industrialized economy of the late 19th century, it was becoming clear that this was not so. From the 1880s, not only did economists such as Alfred Marshall seek to define unemployment and diagnose its causes, but it also became an issue of increasing salience for both politicians and policy makers. The Independent Labour Party (ILP), its journal later proclaimed, was formed in 1893 in 'an unemployment crisis'. With sharp swings in trade and employment driving the industrial crises of the late Victorian and Edwardian period, labour organizations began to call for 'work or maintenance at trade union rates', most notably in a series of bills presented by the new Parliamentary Labour Party, 1900–10. Many radicals, however, continued to focus, even into the inter-war years, on the land, the basic unit of production, as a possible cure for unemployment, favouring land settlement or *Empire emigration to the lands of opportunity in the dominions. Although their Edwardian protagonists claimed respectively that tariff reform or fiscal reform would provide a supply-side weapon against unemployment, direct measures before the Great War were confined to the largely ineffective permissive public works programme of the 1905 Unemployed Workman's Act and the *labour exchanges established in 1909.

The fear that dislocation of trade would bring mass unemployment during the Great War proved unrealized. After the short-lived boom that followed, however, it arrived with a vengeance. After 1921, unemployment remained at over 1 million of the insured labour force for the remainder of the inter-war years, but the 1929 general election was to be the first in which all three parties highlighted unemployment in their manifestos. The Liberal Yellow Book also published as **We Can Conquer Unemployment*, largely the work of J. M. *Keynes, drew on the theories that J. A. *Hobson had begun to elaborate since the Edwardian years, particularly that of under-consumption: the way to smooth the trade cycle and therefore the peaks and troughs of unemployment was through keeping up levels of consumption. Hobson had earlier articulated these views in the ILP's 1926 manifesto, *Socialism in Our Time*.

Whether such measures, or the public works envisaged in the 1930 *Mosley memorandum, would have curbed the unemployment which surged under the 1929–31 Labour government to more than 2.5 million insured workers, is unknowable. The fundamental problem of the inter-war economy was structural: high unemployment in declining areas of heavy industry contrasted with relative prosperity elsewhere. In some places such as *Jarrow, made famous by the march in 1936 and the book by the local MP Ellen Wilkinson, entitled *The Town that was Murdered*, unemployment exceeded 60 per cent of the insured population. Attempts to resolve this included incentives to move in the 1920s and, in the 1930s, the first stirrings of regional policy. The Treasury, however, remained sceptical about blunt instruments like public works, or the growing enthusiasm for planning, pointing to the variegated and seasonal nature of unemployment and the extent to which the figures concealed a wider problem of underemployment in its criticisms of, for instance, Lloyd George's 'new deal' proposals in 1934–5. The figures nevertheless remained high, surging to again exceed 2 million in 1939.

In 1939–45, war again provided a cure for unemployment. Its revival in the aftermath was, however, on this occasion avoided. Greater care over the demobilization of 4.5 million from the forces and 3.5 million from munitions factories ensured minimal impact on the unemployment statistics. The one surge was during the harsh winter of 1946–7, when disruption to supplies led to a temporary peak of unemployment at over 1.8 million. Otherwise, despite the persistence of relatively high unemployment in the north and particularly in Northern Ireland, full employment was more or less maintained for the quarter-century after 1945. Governments did much better than the 8 per cent ceiling on unemployment nominally aimed at by the 1944 **Full Employment* white paper. At the time Keynes had felt that 3 per cent ought to be the target, but would be difficult to achieve, 'because of the openness of the British economy to depressive influences from abroad'. In fact, it was rarely above 2 per cent until the late 1960s. This was perhaps because built-in rigidities undermined reflationary efforts such as Maudling's 'dash for growth' in 1963–4, as well as encouraging a higher inflation rate, but as this rarely passed 5 per cent it proved politically acceptable. Indeed, a figure of 500,000 or 600,000 unemployed was regarded as unpalatable by ministers who could remember the inter-war years.

From the late 1960s, however, a sustained rise in inflation was fuelled by the Vietnam inflation in the USA and the OPEC oil price shocks of 1973 and 1979. Unemployment passing 1 million in 1971–2 provoked demonstrations and the ill-fated 'Barber boom'. This failure contributed to a loss of faith in counter-cyclical measures, and accordingly in the pursuit of full employment, most famously expressed in James Callaghan's 1976 speech to the Labour conference. Sir Keith Joseph, in the meantime, had begun to speak of using the money supply to control inflation. Some Tories clearly assumed that the stability thus imparted to the system would allow rational and employment-boosting decision taking by companies, which would obviate the need for intervention. They were sadly mistaken. Applied in the wake of the second OPEC shock, the *Clegg awards, and the petro-currency status sterling acquired when North Sea oil came on stream, the result was instead a massive hike in unemployment. Despite repeated adjustments to the way the figure was calculated, the claimant count peaked at well over 3 million in 1986, and was again around the 3 million mark in the early 1990s. These were levels which would have been politically unthinkable twenty years earlier, but had become acceptable after the economic travails and humiliations of the 1970s. By the early 1990s, some pundits were querying whether mass unemployment had come to stay. The economy certainly seemed to have reached a higher natural rate of unemployment. However, the sustained growth from 1993 saw unemployment fall back, by the end of the century, to levels last seen in the early 1970s. *PPC*

Unemployment Assistance Board Act, 1934, legislation of the National Government intended to rationalize the administration and payments of unemployment assistance and the cause of serious protests in 1935. Part I of the Act set up in 1934 an Unemployment Assistance Board to take over payments to the unemployed. Part II, early in 1935, implemented new relief scales which caused widespread demonstrations and disorder when it was discovered that payments were sometimes lower than before, contrary to what had been promised. After considerable uproar the government was forced to issue a standstill order guaranteeing existing levels of benefit and phasing in its reform more gradually. *JS*

unemployment pay (widely called 'dole' payments) has been a part of British social welfare since the *National Insurance Act 1911, which gave an entitlement to six months' unemployment pay to 'insured' workers. These provisions were extended to almost 12 million workers by the National Insurance Act of 1920. The onset of prolonged mass unemployment unbalanced the provisions of the national insurance fund which was intended to be self-balancing. Originally the fund would have received enough contributions to balance the benefits paid out; in practice, the fund was in regular deficit once mass unemployment became semi-permanent after 1921. By 1931, the drain of unemployment pay was a significant factor in the budgetary deficit which in August destroyed the Labour government. Governments were reluctant to abandon the unemployed to the *poor law, and provided benefits even beyond the period to which people were entitled. Government economy in the 1931 financial crisis, however, led to cuts in unemployment pay and use of the 'means test' for those receiving benefits beyond their six-month statutory entitlement. Unemployment pay was incorporated in the general welfare provisions of the *Beveridge report (1942) and has become a standard item of benefits received under the *welfare state. In recent years, attempts have been made to target benefits and to ensure that unemployment pay is made conditional upon job-seeking after a fixed period. *JS*

Unilateral Declaration of Independence. See UDI, RHODESIAN.

unilateralism, doctrine that demands unilateral disarmament, a view current in the 1930s, but later especially relating to nuclear weapons. Unilateralists believed that renunciation of nuclear weapons by a single state would set a moral example to other nuclear powers and encourage them also to disarm. There was an associated argument which suggested that by expelling all foreign nuclear bases on its soil a state would be able to recover its lost independence and sovereignty over its own defence (and relieve itself of the threat of attack). Unilateralism grew as a political doctrine in Britain during the 1950s and was promoted by the birth of the *Campaign for Nuclear Disarmament (CND) in February 1958. CND attracted mass support, demonstrated by its annual march from the Aldermaston nuclear weapons research centre to London. It also attracted mainstream political support from the Labour Party which adopted unilateralism as official policy in 1960–1, and again in the 1970s, and unsuccessfully fought the 1983 general election on this issue of disarmament. *JRVE*

Union Defence League (UDL), founded by Walter *Long in 1907 in order to organize opposition at the constituency level to Irish home rule. For several years, the league gained little attention or membership but, by late 1911, after passage of the *Parliament Act made the threat of such a bill more credible, the UDL attracted both attention and numbers. The leaguers played important roles in all the Unionist mass meetings and demonstrations which characterized the remaining pre-war years. *RJQA*

John Kendall, *Walter Long, Ireland and the Irish Union, 1905–1920* (Montreal, 1992).

Unionist, adjective correctly used to describe those who favoured politically the United Kingdom: the union of England, Wales, Scotland, and Ireland; more specifically, the combined title of the Conservative and Liberal Unionist parties until 1925, though still used as a party label afterwards, especially in Scotland. In Ulster politics, the label defined a more specifically local political loyalty to the union with Britain. *JAR*

Unionist Social Reform Committee, Conservative Party pressure group. Formed in 1911, and chaired by F. E. *Smith, it continued until 1914 under the patronage of the party chairman, Arthur Steel-Maitland. It was meant to demonstrate that the Conservatives could offer programmes for social betterment as alternatives to the *New Liberalism or Labour. None of its ambitious plans for housing, agriculture, or public health reform became party policy, but several of its members, including Baldwin and Neville Chamberlain, became the principal authors of party policy after 1923. *RJQA*

Matthew Fforde, *Conservatism and Collectivism, 1886–1914* (Edinburgh, 1990).

Union Movement, fascist organization established on 8 February 1948, through which Sir Oswald *Mosley attempted to revive his political career. Its message was 'Europe: A Nation', with an emphasis on European racial unity. However, the movement, in which Mosley was 'Surrounded by familiar faces from his immediate past' (R. Skidelsky, *Oswald Mosley* (London, 1975), 490), achieved little political salience, despite exploiting issues such as black and Asian immigration. From the late 1960s, following Mosley's election defeat at Shoreditch, much responsibility for the movement fell on his faithful acolytes. *CH*

Union Movement, *The Coloured Invasion* (London, 1958). | G. Thayer, *The British Political Fringe: A Profile* (London, 1965).

Union of Democratic Control (UDC), peace association founded in August 1914 by Norman *Angell, Ramsay MacDonald, E. D. Morel, and C. P. Trevelyan, soon joined by Arthur Ponsonby (all critics of British entry into the Great War). It did not demand a halt to the fighting but advocated principles for a post-war settlement, notably that territory should not be transferred without a plebiscite and that foreign policy should be brought under parliamentary control. Because this approach enabled it to reconcile its pro- and anti-war wings, the Labour Party drew close to the UDC from 1917 onwards and recruited many of its formerly Liberal supporters. This closeness continued during the early 1920s when the UDC's attacks on the treaty of Versailles and French efforts to enforce it fitted Labour's needs as an opposition party. But after 1924, when fifteen of its leading members joined the first Labour government and its driving force Morel died, the UDC rapidly lost ground to the League of Nations Union, whose programme was more constructive. Though kept going for several decades by Dorothy Woodman and not wound up until 1967, the UDC had ceased to be of importance before the end of the 1920s. *MEC*

Marvin Schwarz, *The Union of Democratic Control in British Politics during the First World War* (Oxford, 1971).

Union of Democratic Mineworkers (1985–). Frustrated at the failure of Arthur *Scargill to hold a national ballot on the national miners' strike of 1984–5, a substantial proportion of the Nottingham miners, and some from Derbyshire, formed the breakaway Union of Democratic Mineworkers in December 1985. It was registered in 1986 and committed to industrial peace and the slogan 'Democracy Reborn'. With the overall rundown in the coal industry, the union now has fewer than 6,000 members. *KL*

unitary authorities. See local government structure.

United Empire Party, the political wing of the *Empire Crusade. Formed on 18 February 1930 by *Beaverbrook, disbanded 8 March, but then relaunched 3 April, this was a single issue party campaigning for the introduction of tariffs upon the goods from non-Empire nations. Its candidates contested by-elections, usually resulting in a split in the Conservative vote allowing a Labour gain. Their one election success was with Vice-Admiral Taylor's victory in South Paddington. *NJC*

United Europe Movement. See European Movement.

united front against fascism. Hitler's arrival as German chancellor in 1933 gave rise to demands for a united front of all communist and socialist organizations. On 7 February 1933, seven socialist parties appealed to the Communist International and the Labour and Socialist International (LSI) to form a united front against fascism. The LSI's response was to call on workers everywhere to unite against fascism, but the Comintern rejected a united front with the LSI while instructing all communist parties to approach their socialist counterparts for joint anti-fascist action. In Britain the Independent Labour Party and Communist Party of Great Britain formed a united front in March 1933, which the Labour Party refused to join. It organized demonstrations against fascism, provided relief for refugees fleeing Germany, and campaigned for the release of political prisoners incarcerated in Germany. Fascist ascendancy in Germany encouraged the growth of Fascist parties in other countries, and by mid-1934 the British Union of Fascists (BUF) had grown to over 50,000 members. Its growth was halted mainly by the united front activity organized by rank and file socialists and communists, and BUF support collapsed after the attacks upon anti-Fascist demonstrators at its Olympia rally in 1934. Its revival during 1936 was halted by the 250,000-strong counter-demonstration that led to the battle of Cable Street in October. Despite the failure of the LSI and the Comintern to conclude a united front, in several countries socialist and communist parties formed such alliances that temporarily halted the growth of fascism. In Britain, the much weaker BUF was sent into decline by the activities of rank and file socialists and communists (though also by the counteraction of the National Government, such as the 1936 Public Order Act). In several countries the united front prepared the way for the emergence of anti-fascist unity on a wider basis in the form of the *popular front—which also failed in Britain. *DLM*

Noreen Branson, *History of the Communist Party of Great Britain 1927–1941* (London, 1985).

United Irish League, established in 1898 by William O'Brien, home rule MP for Cork. The league agitated for the redistribution of grass ranches in the west of Ireland to small farmers. It was a key factor in reuniting the home rule movement which had divided after Charles Stewart Parnell's fall from power in the 1890s. O'Brien lost control of the league after 1903. During the Great War the influence of the league and the home rule movement itself stagnated. *TWH*

United Irishmen, revolutionary society, influenced by events in France, founded by Wolfe Tone in 1791. It engineered the unsuccessful insurrection of 1798, which, far from freeing Ireland, persuaded the British government to pass the Act of Union in 1800. Its commitment to ending sectarian divisions, and to establishing an Irish republic, if necessary with foreign aid, has inspired 20th-century nationalist movements, most notably in 1916. Tone's grave at Bodenstown remains a place of annual pilgrimage for Sinn Fein. *DRB*

United Kingdom Alliance. See TEMPERANCE.

United Nations (UN). The UN was established after the Second World War by the victorious powers, its basic shape agreed by Britain, the USA, and the USSR at wartime conferences, and its charter finalized by the 1945 *San Francisco conference. The UN came into existence on 24 October 1945, at which time it had 51 members; by January 1999 the number was 184. Switzerland is the only notable absentee, though between 1949 and 1971 China was represented by Taiwan. The UN's headquarters are in New York, where its secretariat is headed by a secretary-general. As almost all states belong to the UN and have permanent missions to it, headed by senior officials, New York is a hive of diplomatic activity. Much private diplomacy goes on, as well as the public debates in the UN's two main organs, the general assembly and security council. The assembly is a general deliberative body; the council has primary responsibility for the maintenance of international peace.

All states are represented in the general assembly, each member, whatever its size, having one vote. During its annual meetings, usually of about three months, most issues are thrashed out in committee (all members always being represented) before being submitted to plenary meetings. There, important resolutions need a two-thirds majority (others a simple majority), and the world's weaker states have used their numerical preponderance to pass resolutions calling for the rectification of international injustices. Such resolutions are only advisory; but they are widely seen as expressing international opinion. Britain was therefore in an uncomfortable position when there was regular criticism of colonialism, of her failure to bring a forceful end to Rhodesia's illegal declaration of independence, and of her refusal to support tough action against South Africa's apartheid regime. However, such resolutions did not alter her policies. By the mid-1980s the assembly was becoming more moderate following a cut in the USA's contribution to the

UN budget, reflecting her annoyance at many criticisms of her policies.

The other main organ is the security council, of which Britain is one of the five permanent members (the others being the USA, Russia, China, and France). There are also non-permanent members—ten since 1966—elected for two-year terms. Draft resolutions require nine votes to pass, but any permanent member can veto a non-procedural proposal. This is important because 'decisions' of the security council are binding on all members of the UN. However, the council cannot decide to make use of a member's armed forces against its will. During the Cold War, superpower disagreement prevented enforcement action—except during the Korean war (1950–3) when the Soviet Union was boycotting the council at the time of the crucial vote. However, the UN has played a valuable role both then and since by despatching impartial, non-threatening peacekeeping bodies to help disputants who wanted, at least for the time being, to live at peace. But peacekeeping, like the UN's other tools for dispute resolution, depends upon the willingness of the parties to accept its help.

The end of the Cold War in the late 1980s removed the barriers that had prevented the security council operating as originally intended. It thus assumed a central role in trying to settle conflicts, and was able to legitimize force to liberate Kuwait after Iraq had invaded in 1991. Britain was a major contributor both to the anti-Iraqi coalition and to the peacekeeping operations of the early 1990s. But then, because too much was expected of the UN, disillusion set in, which was not helped by the UN's own perennial financial crisis. Moreover, there were demands that membership of the security council be made larger and more 'democratic'. Because of Britain's decline in power, her permanent seat is threatened by any reform; but, as the charter requires her consent for changes, she still has a good bargaining lever.

There are two other important UN organs: the International Court of Justice (which sits at The Hague, and has always had a British judge), and the Economic and Social Council (ECOSOC) which consists of 54 members (Britain always among them). The court adjudicates legal disputes that states voluntarily submit to it. ECOSOC has manifold responsibilities over a huge range of activities. In theory it also coordinates the work of the eighteen 'specialized agencies', such as the International Monetary Fund and the World Health Organization, but, as each of them is a separate organization, there are limits to this process. In 1986 Britain withdrew from one of them, the UN's Educational Scientific and Cultural Organization, in protest at the way it was run. Reforms were swiftly introduced, but Britain only rejoined in 1997. *LL*

House of Commons, session 1992–3, Foreign Affairs Committee, third report, *The Expanding Role of the United Nations and its Implications for United Kingdom Policy*, vol. 1. Report together with Proceedings of the Committee (HCP 235–I); vol. 2. Minutes of Evidence and Appendices (HCP 235–II). | Jack C. Plano and Robert E. Riggs, The *United Nations: International Organization and World Politics* (Chicago, 1988).

United Nations, declaration of the, statement of military alliance, January 1942. On his visit to Washington in December 1941 after the American entry into the Second World War, Churchill found himself presented with a draft declaration designed to commit its signatories to the war aims which he had agreed with President Roosevelt in the *Atlantic charter. The declaration was important as a general statement of the principles expected to govern the relations of the countries fighting Hitlerism once the war was over. *DJD*

United States of Europe, an expression, and a cause, given currency by Churchill in 1945–8. 'We must build a kind of United States of Europe.... The process is simple. All that is needed is the resolve of hundreds of millions of men and women to do right instead of wrong and gain as their reward blessing instead of cursing' (speech in Zurich, 19 September 1946). Stage 1 was to be Franco-German rapprochement. This was magnanimous and far-sighted, but also detached—Britain would watch from the wings. *AD*

United Ulster Action Council (UUAC), formed in 1977 in an unavailing attempt to repeat the success of the Ulster Workers' Council strike or 'constitutional stoppage' of May 1974. Loyalist opinion was considerably exercised by the failure to re-establish majority rule in Northern Ireland, as recommended by the Constitutional Convention in 1975, and by the worsening security situation. In 1976 the death toll was the highest of the decade, apart from the peak year, 1972. Demanding a return to self-government, and an all-out offensive against the IRA, the UUAC, composed of Ian Paisley's Democratic Unionist Party and dissident members of the Vanguard Unionist Progressive Party, called for a strike which began on 2 May 1977. It commanded nothing like the same support as that of 1974, and was abandoned on 13 May, Most shipyard workers refused to strike, as did, crucially, those in the power stations. Increasing unemployment was one factor, but also many Unionist politicians opposed the stoppage, which lacked such a clear objective as that of 1974. Roy Mason, as secretary of state, proved more adept and resolute than his predecessor, direct rule from Westminster was starting to prove its worth, and the security situation was to improve markedly during 1977. *DRB*

Ed Maloney and Andy Pollak, *Paisley* (Dublin, 1986).

United Ulster Unionist Council (UUUC), formed in December 1973 by Ulster Unionist, Vanguard, Democratic Unionist, and members of the Orange Order to oppose the *power-sharing executive and the Council of Ireland. In the February 1974 Westminster general election the UUUC ran a single candidate in each of Northern Ireland's twelve constituencies. The result demonstrated the unpopularity of the Sunningdale agreement among unionist voters: eleven UUUC candidates were returned with 51 per cent of the vote. *GG*

Paul Bew and Gordon Gillespie. *Northern Ireland: A Chronology of the Troubles 1968–1999* (Dublin, 1999).

Unity Campaign (1937). Launched on 24 January in Manchester by the Socialist League, Independent Labour Party (ILP), and Communist Party of Great Britain (CPGB), its objective was to get the Labour Party to actively support the united front against fascism. Three days later, the Labour Party disaffiliated the Socialist League. Between February and May over 40,000 people attended campaign meetings, yet it failed to attract widespread support from the Labour movement. In mid-May, the Socialist League voted to dissolve itself to save its members from being expelled from the Labour Party, and on 1 June the National Unity Campaign Committee dissolved itself and the campaign's format changed. Labour supporters of the campaign formed local Labour unity committees to carry on propaganda in favour of unity; while the ILP and CPGB conducted their own propaganda on a separate basis. At the Labour Party conference in October, the united front was defeated by 2,116,000 to 331,000 votes. This was the last occasion before the war in which a unified left platform attempted to change the course of Labour Party policy. By the autumn, the organized left within the Labour movement was a substantially weaker force following the dissolution of the Socialist League and the continuing decline of the ILP, the exception being the CPGB which had emerged in a position of organizational and intellectual dominance over the rest of the left. The Unity Campaign foundered on the determined opposition of the Labour Party, which saw this extra-parliamentary movement as a diversion from its task of winning the next general election. It was further undermined by its association, through the CPGB, with popular frontism and Stalin's purges in the Soviet Union. *DLM*

Fenner Brockway, *Inside the Left* (London, 1942). | Ben Pimlott, *Labour and the Left in the 1930s* (Cambridge, 1977).

universality, concept which was a key component of the *Beveridge report's (1942) view of the *welfare state. Where earlier national insurance (see National Insurance Act, 1911) provision had been selective, the comprehensive system envisaged by Beveridge was only financially viable if everyone contributed, in return for which everybody could receive benefits in time of need. The counter-principle, selectivity or 'targeting', has been more used in the 1980s and 1990s, to channel benefits directly to particular groups. *JS*

university constituencies, seats which had electorates determined by education rather than by residence or ownership of property. University seats were first created in the 17th century, with Oxford and Cambridge each returning one MP, the electorate for each comprising the University's MAs. The number of seats was extended in the 19th century and increased in 1918 from nine to fifteen, with the provincial universities being accorded representation (though that number was reduced to twelve in 1920 with the disappearance of three Irish university seats). Under the 1918 Act, voting in two- and three-member seats was to be by proportional representation, though the use of the single transferable vote appears to have made little difference to the outcomes. An attempt to abolish the seats in 1931 was defeated in the Commons. The constituencies were eventually abolished by the Attlee government, under the provisions of the Representation of the People Act, 1948, so that the seats disappeared in 1950 when parliament was next dissolved. Supporters of university seats argued that they allowed independent-minded people to serve in parliament. Among those who represented university seats were the novelist A. P. Herbert, the wartime home secretary and chancellor of the exchequer Sir John Anderson, and the writer and academic Eleanor Rathbone. *PN*

David Butler, *The Electoral System in Britain since 1918* (Oxford, 1963).

University Grants Committee. See HIGHER EDUCATION.

unopposed return of MPs, the election of Members of Parliament without a contest. In the first half of the century, some seats were so safe for one party that the other parties did not bother to field candidates. In the general election of 1918, no fewer than 107 seats (15 per cent of the total) had unopposed returns. The number varied in subsequent elections—in 1929 there were only seven unopposed returns, whereas in 1931 there were 67—and then dropped substantially after 1935. In 1945 there were only three unopposed returns, in 1950 there were two, and in 1951 four: all of these were in Northern Ireland seats where the Ulster Unionist Party enjoyed hegemony. Unopposed returns were also a feature of by-elections, especially in the 1920s and then most notably during the Second World War, when agreement between the parties meant that the field was left clear for the incumbent party. There were five uncontested by-elections between 1945 and 1954, four of them in seats in Northern Ireland. The Armagh by-election of 20 November 1954 constitutes the last uncontested parliamentary election in the UK. Though it is deemed to be the convention that the Speaker of the House of Commons is not opposed if seeking re-election, in practice some independent candidates—and sometimes a candidate from one of the main parties—have stood to deny the Speaker an unopposed return. *PN*

F. W. S. Craig, *British Parliamentary Election Statistics 1918–1970* (2nd edn., Chichester, 1971).

Upper Clyde Shipbuilders (UCS), loss-making consortium put together by Tony Benn's Ministry of Technology in 1968. In 1971 the Heath government, consistent with its policy of not assisting *'lame ducks', ended subsidies to the company. A work-in organized by Communist shop steward Jimmy Reid and backed by Benn turned UCS into a symbol of working-class defiance. It was not this, however, but mounting unemployment and police fears of civil disorder which prompted the *U-turn involved in rescuing UCS the following February. *PPC*

urban development corporations were set up to regenerate rundown inner-city areas after the 1981 riots. The Urban Development Corporation has now been overtaken by the setting up of the Single Regeneration Budget (SRB) and the New Deal for Communities (NDC). The SRB provides resources to support regeneration initiatives in England, to which the government devoted £2.4 billion for the three years 1999–2002. A further £770 million will be directed to some of the most deprived areas of Britain. *JS*

Urdd Gobaith Cymru, Welsh youth organization. The Welsh League of Youth (always referred to in Wales as the Urdd) was founded in 1922 by Ifan ab Owen Edwards, an academic and son of the educationalist Owen M. Edwards. Initially the emphasis was very much on Christian ideals, the ideas of the League of Nations, and Welsh cultural values, but in time the Urdd became far more generally a non-sectarian youth movement receiving government support and sponsoring a wide variety of educational, cultural, and recreational activities. To a greater degree than any political party, it helped give the bilingual youth of Wales a sense of confidence and style, not least because of its emphasis on participation and entertainment. Particularly important in these respects were its itinerant annual Eisteddfod and its residential camps. With over 1,000 branches it has been a major force in shaping the Wales of the 1990s. *PS*

utopianism, an approach to social and political theory, named after the mythical country described in Thomas More's *Utopia* (1516), and based on identifying the lineaments of a perfect society, either to demonstrate what the good life should be like or to offer a yardstick by which to judge existing behaviour. The 20th century tended to produce dystopias, as a means of applying a *reductio ad absurdum* of the utopias of others (see, for example, Aldous Huxley, *Brave New World* (1932); George Orwell, *Nineteen Eighty-Four* (1949); and L. P. Hartley, *Facial Justice* (1960).) In a general sense, the term utopian is used to insinuate that the aims of a political philosophy are unrealistic or unrealizable. *CPS*

U-turns (1972). In 1972, Edward Heath's government reversed its policy in three key areas: industry, industrial relations, and prices and incomes. The context was the impending entry to the European Community, and the need to put Britain on a sustainable growth path against that eventuality, the floating of the pound and the rising level of unemployment. In contrast to the anti-interventionist (*'Selsdon man') rhetoric which had been deployed in the 1970 election, the 1972 Industry Act offered capital allowances on depreciation of new plant and machinery, a new system of regional aid, and resurrection under new names of devices abolished in 1970, to aid individual firms and to control prices. Second, aware of the need to win the support of the trade unions for the third leg of its new strategy, over the summer the government quietly shelved its flagship *Industrial Relations Act, 1971. The third leg, meanwhile, was a prices and incomes strategy to contain inflation and permit growth. All these shifts provoked merriment on the Labour benches, but it should be said that to a considerable extent they reflected a return to the kind of strategy Heath had been closely involved with in the early 1960s. That they were not blessed with success, however, shaped the way the idea of a 'U-turn' subsequently became embedded in the symbolic rhetoric of politics, not least in Thatcher's 'The *Lady's not for turning' at the 1980 Conservative conference.

PPC

Valentine, Revd Lewis (1893–1986), author and pacifist. A native of Denbighshire, Valentine interrupted his undergraduate career to spend three years performing non-combatant duties for the Medical Corps in the Great War. Subsequently he became a Baptist minister and both the first president and first parliamentary candidate of Plaid Cymru. In 1936 he was one of the three Plaid Cymru leaders who took part in the burning of the Bombing School. A successful magazine editor, he also published acclaimed accounts of both his wartime experience and his time in Wormwood Scrubs. *PS*

Valentine compact (14 February 1906), compromise between Unionist leader Arthur Balfour and Joseph Chamberlain, chieftain of the tariff reform movement. Their exchange of letters, published on St Valentine's day, stipulated that 'Fiscal Reform is, and must remain, the first constructive work of the Unionist Party' and that moderate tariffs on imported manufactured goods and corn 'are not in principle objectionable'. The agreement, however, did not terminate the quarrel within the party over tariff policy, which continued until the beginning of the Great War. *RJQA*

value added tax (VAT), introduced in 1973 when Britain entered the European Community, has been regarded as the tax innovation of the 20th century and is a major source of revenue for many countries. It is a general turnover tax on consumption. Businesses are charged VAT on the goods they buy as inputs and then charge their own customers with VAT. Because the 'input' can be reclaimed, it was much better than the 'cascade' sales taxes in France and Germany which distorted industrial organization in those countries. The attractions of VAT in Europe came from a tax context very unlike Britain's. VAT was relevant to Britain as a buoyant revenue source when it was widely assumed that the limits of income tax had been reached, but its introduction was still a tense issue because of fears that working-class living standards would suffer at a time of industrial unrest. Subsequent debate has concerned what should be included in VAT, whose success relies upon the breadth of its coverage. The inclusion of central heating fuel by the Conservatives in 1993 caused an outcry, and in the 1997 general election campaign Labour raised the spectre of Conservatives putting VAT on food. *RCW*

A. Tait, *Value Added Tax* (Oxford, 1972).

Vanguard Unionist Party, Northern Ireland political party. Led by William *Craig, Vanguard developed as a pressure group within the Ulster Unionist Party (UUP) opposing the party leadership's liberal reforms. It was launched as the Vanguard Unionist Progressive Party in 1973, opposing power-sharing and the Sunningdale agreement. Vanguard split over Craig's proposal for 'voluntary coalition' with Catholics in 1976. In 1978 it ceased to function as a political party, Craig and his deputy leader David Trimble returning to the UUP fold. *TWH*

Vansittart, Robert Gilbert (1881–1957), diplomat. 'Van' entered the diplomatic service in 1903. In 1930–8, as permanent secretary in the Foreign Office, he developed the reputation of an emphatic opponent of Nazi Germany. Nonetheless, despite his doubts about the long-term viability of an agreement with Hitler, he played a significant role in the formulation of the British policy of appeasement, although his doubts prompted Chamberlain to remove him to an honorific, advisory role in 1938. *AJC*

Ian Colvin, *Vansittart in Office* (London, 1965).

Varley, Julia **(1871–1952)**, feminist, suffragist, and one of the most important early female trade union leaders. At 15, she was secretary of the Bradford branch of the Weavers' and Textile Workers' Union and, in a long career of grassroots activism, led numerous strikes and was imprisoned during the women's suffrage campaigns. However, her early spontaneous militancy waned as her activities became more institutionally orientated in the 1920s. Varley was involved with the Women's Trade Union League and the National Federation of Women Workers, became the first women's officer of the Transport and General Workers' Union, 1929, and served on many government committees from the 1920s. *DMM*

Vassall case, scandal that followed the discovery in 1962 that John Vassall, a junior Admiralty official and homosexual, was a spy. Press speculation about Vassall's relations with *Galbraith, formerly civil lord at the Admiralty, prompted Macmillan to accept Galbraith's resignation. The Radcliffe tribunal subsequently exonerated Galbraith, but the imprisonment of two journalists for refusing to reveal their sources poisoned relations between press and government. Macmillan's regret at Galbraith's resignation had damaging repercussions during the Profumo scandal. *RJS*

Versailles, treaty of. See Paris peace conference.

'Vicky' (1913–66), pen name of the cartoonist Viktor Weisz. A Berlin-born Hungarian and Hitler refugee, Weisz was sent to 'learn' Britain by the *News Chronicle* editor in 1939. A committed socialist, he worked for the *Daily Mirror*, *New Statesman*, and most famously for the *Evening Standard* (1958–66). His cartoons combined clever caricature, often of Cold War leaders (notably Macmillan as *'Supermac'), with economy of detail and a distinct 'Oxfam style' for humanitarian subjects. Frequently depressive, he died from an overdose of barbiturates. *CKSU*

Vietnam wars. British governments were passive spectators of the French (1946–54) and American (1965–74) wars in Vietnam. General Gracey's British troops occupied the southern part of Vietnam in September 1945 and assisted the French in re-establishing themselves there. Thereafter, London watched with alarm as the guerrilla war intensified. During the siege of Dien Bien Phu in 1953, Britain discouraged the USA from using nuclear weapons to assist France and also played a major part in bringing French involvement to an end at the Geneva conference in 1954. In the 1960s, Harold Wilson's government resisted Washington's pressure to send British troops to Vietnam and demands by many Labour activists to denounce the conflict. The war led to student unrest in Britain and made it more difficult for the USA to support Britain financially in the various sterling crises. *PAT*

violence, the doing of deliberate physical harm, or acting with physical recklessness and so not avoiding such harm. The Nazis committed violent acts against those they regarded as foes, and the word here implies acting outside the law, acting improperly, acting brutally. But there are those who hold that the law, and the state that upholds that law, can act in a violent way, for example, in banning or suppressing demonstrations, that may be illegal, but are justified (for example, the civil rights movements in the USA and in Northern Ireland). Some would widen the definition even further, and include 'social violence' (where the state deliberately maintains groups and individuals in inferior status, discriminates against them, or otherwise oppresses them). The term 'force' is one that states prefer to use, implying as it does a certain restraint, a legal action, and, above all, an act which can be justified: thus the NATO intervention in Kosovo was the application of force, not of violence.

The question is raised in an acute form when groups or individuals resort to violence/force, claiming that all other means of political expression have been denied them. Thus the IRA in Northern Ireland, the Free Wales Army in the Principality, and countless similar groups across the world claimed that their use of force was not only politically but morally justified. Christianity has had particular difficulties with this issue, as it is reluctant to support or endorse illegal acts, yet has in recent times set its face against social and political injustice. Advocates of political violence seek to discredit the whole state structure, claiming that there is within it a form of 'institutionalized violence' that must be overthrown; anti-colonial movements have used this argument, as have the IRA and its supporters. Liberal democrats are loath to admit that violence is (a) ever justified or (b) is ever unjustified, and the debate becomes one of semantics: 'terrorism' is transformed into a 'liberation movement', and violence into an 'armed struggle'. Because of the linguistic politics involved, violence against the liberal state by terrorist groups has proved extraordinarily hard to defeat or undermine, and the state has at times resorted to means that are hardly compatible with its own principles (see, for example, BLACK AND TANS). It is also troubled by the difficulty of government and the law securing full control of its own security, and especially secret, services. Industrial disputes in Britain in the 1970s and 1980s gave rise to almost unprecedented scenes of violence, and the Conservative government in 1984 was much criticized for its robust stand against the miners' strike of that year (see ORGREAVE). It is hardly surprising that, when confronted with these dilemmas, politicians (and soldiers) prefer to look to 'clean' wars between states as force, legitimately and wisely used, and (within normal limits) humanely applied. But the recent NATO intervention in Kosovo threw a shadow over even that apparently clear-cut prospect. *DGB*

HANNAH ARENDT, *On Violence* (London, 1969). | L. MACFARLANE, *Violence and the State* (London, 1979).

Voluntarism has been a major feature of British social and philanthropic provision since the 18th century. Many of the longest-standing and most prestigious philanthropic bodies are private organizations, high-profile examples including the RSPCA (see ANIMAL WELFARE), the *National Trust, and *Oxfam. Britain's voluntarist tradition has often been contrasted with the more statist provision found elsewhere in Europe. In practice, although Britain has seen an enormous growth in its state-supported welfare provision in the course of the 20th century, it has also maintained a strong voluntary sector in many areas. According to the most recent estimates the charitable sector has an annual income of £20 billion and 188,000 charities are registered with the Charity Commission. *JS*

voting age, the age at which a citizen becomes eligible to cast a ballot in elections to public office. Until 1969, the age at which male electors became eligible to vote was, unless otherwise disqualified, 21 years. In 1918, after lengthy and intense political struggle, the case for extending the vote to women was conceded: the Representation of the People Act, 1918, extended the vote to women aged 30 years and over and the franchise was equalized in 1928 when the voting age for women was lowered to 21 years. In 1968, a Speaker's Conference recommended that the voting age be lowered to 20 years. The government, having agreed to lower the age of majority for other purposes to 18 years (Family Law Reform Act, 1969), decided to lower the voting age to 18 years. The Representation of the People Act, 1969, gave effect to the government's intentions. The voting age is distinct from the age at which citizens become eligible for election to public office. Twice during the century, the two ages were different. From 1918 to 1928, women aged 21 and over could seek election to public office but could not vote until they were 30 years old. Since 1969, 18–20-year-olds have been eligible to vote but not to stand for election. There is pressure to bring the qualifying age for candidature into line with the voting age. *PN*

vouchers, educational. These gave parents the right to 'shop around' for their children's education amongst local schools, and were one of the most radical ideas to emerge from the education debate of the 1970s. Although ideologically attractive to the Thatcher government of the 1980s, it was reluctantly recognized that the local and financial implications of such schemes might be counter-productive, producing impossible demands on 'good' schools and leaving others virtually unused. The last example of the voucher scheme was the one put into practice in *nursery schools in 1995 where these effects were less marked. *JS*

Waddington, David Charles (1929–), Conservative politician. A well-liked lawyer long in junior office before a sudden three-year explosion, Waddington might, by remaining a capable chief whip, have saved Margaret Thatcher from dismissal by popular demand in 1990, but in 1989, in the endless cabinet remaking of her last febrile years, he had been promoted home secretary from that useful post. Accordingly, in tears, he told her that she could not go on. His yaffling bark worse than his tender bite, and notably trusted by Labour Members, as chief whip he had saved Thatcher from a disastrous football identity card scheme. *EP*

Wade, Donald William (1904–88), Liberal politician. Wade was a solicitor who, benefiting from a Liberal–Conservative electoral pact, held Huddersfield West for the Liberals, 1950–64, throughout the period of the party's nadir. He was whip and from 1962 to 1964 deputy leader. When the local pact broke down, he lost his seat in 1964, going to the Lords as life peer. *JAR*

Wadsworth, Alfred Powell (1891–1956), journalist and historian. Wadworth edited the *Manchester Guardian* from 1944 to 1956, continuing the Liberal traditions of C. P. *Scott. Under his editorship circulation rose from 72,000 to 168,000, making it the most successful provincial daily newspaper, but also one with a strong national and international coverage. *JS*

wage freezes. Governments remained reluctant to intervene directly in wages policy before the Second World War. Wages and prices were subordinate to other macroeconomic considerations in the decision to return to the gold standard in 1925 or to devalue in 1931. Even during the Second World War, there was no direct control of wages, whilst the TUC sought to reassure Beveridge and others that the maintenance of free collective bargaining would not undermine full employment. After 1945, however, the commitment to full employment repeatedly forced governments to try to restrain wage increases in order to contain inflation. As early as February 1948, the white paper *Personal Incomes, Costs and Prices* stressed that 'there is no justification for any general increase of money incomes without at least a corresponding increase in the volume of production', as this would simply push up prices. Despite the lack of prior consultation, the TUC agreed to voluntary restraint, which successfully reduced the annual rate of money wage increase from nearly 9 to about 2.8 per cent. Wage restraint was only to collapse in the summer of 1950, in the face of rising inflation, though it is perhaps more remarkable that it held so long in such a tight labour market.

Union moderation nevertheless persisted after the return of the Conservatives in 1951, whilst governments, in their turn, continued to rely largely on exhortation to keep down prices and incomes. A deteriorating economic position in July 1961, however, obliged Selwyn *Lloyd to introduce his 'pay pause'. As the prime minister, Harold Macmillan, noted, 'the desire to consume started to outrun the willingness to produce'. The pay pause, however, remained voluntary. It was also unpopular, being breached most obviously by the power workers during its seven months' duration. The trade unions again only reluctantly acquiesced in the wage freeze—this time with statutory teeth—imposed by Wilson as part of the July 1966 measures, though this was not on this occasion tested by industrial action.

After the Conservative victory in 1970, the new government's rhetoric was initially resolutely opposed to such devices. In September 1972, however, Heath sought TUC agreement to no pay rises over £2 a week to support wider growth and inflation targets. Unable to reach agreement, he was instead forced in November to announce a statutory prices and incomes policy, including an initial 90-day wage freeze, followed by restrictions on increases in stages 2 and 3 of the policy. Although this strategy was eventually broken by the National Union of Mineworkers, by summer 1975 the new Wilson government was again trying to curb wage-push inflation by a, this time voluntary, wage restraint package. This was tightened in 1976 with the reluctant agreement of the TUC. There was, however, no renewal in 1977. The government, nevertheless, continued to seek a 5 per cent pay award limit into 1978. This, again, ran into the inability of the TUC to deliver. From Attlee to Callaghan wage freezes and controls were at best temporary expedients, which frequently ended by embarrassing the governments seeking to impose them. After 1979 Mrs Thatcher was to try a different approach. *PPC*

'wait and see', the repeated reply given by H. H. *Asquith, originally on 4 April 1910, to Conservative demands for an indication of what the government would do next in the constitutional crisis over the Lords. It was effective at the time but, as Asquith later—especially in wartime—acquired the reputation for procrastination, it became a dangerous phrase with which to be popularly associated. *JAR*

Wakeham, John (1932–), Conservative politician. A chartered accountant, Wakeham was MP for Maldon, 1974–92, his political career mainly in the Whips' Office, where he was Thatcher's chief whip, 1983–7. He then held a number of non-departmental posts, enabling him to chair cabinet committees and generally act as fixer in difficult times after 1987 (for example coordinating government information, 1990–2), and was secretary for energy, 1989–92 (privatizing electricity). A peer from 1992, he was in retirement chair of the British Horseracing Board and the first chair of the Press Complaints Commission (1995–). *JAR*

Waldegrave, William Arthur (1946–). Conservative politician. An adviser to Heath, 1970–4, Waldegrave entered parliament in 1979 and joined the leftist 'Blue Chip' Club. Nonetheless, from 1981 he served in Thatcher's government at education, environment, and the Foreign Office, where his role later made him a central figure in the arms-to-Iraq controversy. As a member of Major's cabinet, 1990–7, he implemented the **Citizen's Charter* and introduced more open government. He lost his seat in 1997. *RJS*

Walker, Peter Edward (1932–). Conservative politician and leading 'wet' during Thatcher's leadership. Walker took Leo Amery's advice and made money before pursuing his political career. A success in the city and MP for Worcester before he was 30 years old, Walker was recruited by Heath to fight Labour's 1965 finance bill and was soon running Heath's leadership campaign too. Walker personified the young, meritocratic modernizers who transformed their party's image. In Heath's shadow cabinet, he was spokesman on transport and later on housing and local government. Appointed to Heath's cabinet in 1970, Walker soon became environment secretary at a new 'super ministry', where he totally redrew the map of local government. From 1972 he was an interventionist trade and industry secretary. Following Heath's demise, Thatcher dropped Walker from her shadow cabinet but in 1979 appointed him agriculture minister. A leader of the 'wets', he remained in her cabinet for eleven years, periodically restating his moderate Toryism but never becoming more than a pragmatic departmental minister. As energy secretary he helped to avenge the Tory disaster of 1974 with the defeat of the 1984–5 *miners' strike. He was Welsh secretary, 1987–90, and entered the Lords in 1992. *RJS*

PETER WALKER, *Staying Power* (London, 1991).

Walker-Smith, Derek Colclough (1924–97), Conservative politician. Elected in 1945, Walker-Smith was chairman of the *1922 Committee from 1951 until he entered government in 1955. He became health minister in 1957 but left office in 1960 and was soon arguing against British membership of the European Economic Community because of the loss of sovereignty involved. In 1975, his nomination to the *European parliament caused surprise, but he acted responsibly and chaired Strasbourg's legal committee. In 1983 he took a peerage as Lord Broxbourne. *RJS*

Wall, Patrick Henry Bligh (1916–98), Conservative politician. Elected in 1954 after distinguished military service, Wall was an extreme right-winger. He bitterly opposed decolonization, was a member of the *Monday Club, and supported almost every anti-communist cause, including the white minority regimes in Rhodesia and South Africa. The '92 Group' of right-wing Conservative MPs took their name from his London house at 92 Cheyne Walk, where they first dined and plotted. He retired in 1983. *RJS*

Wall, (John) Stephen (1947–), prime minister's foreign affairs private secretary, 1991–3. Principal private secretary to foreign secretaries Sir Geoffrey Howe, John Major, and Douglas Hurd (1988–90), Wall became Major's trusted and influential aide at Downing Street. Arriving in the aftermath of the Gulf war, he helped develop proposals for Kurdish 'safe havens'. A specialist on Europe, he was part of the British team at the Maastricht negotiations. He encouraged Major not to resign after Britain's forced withdrawal from the European Exchange Rate Mechanism (ERM) in 1992. *CL*

Wallas, Graham. See *HUMAN NATURE IN POLITICS*.

Wall Street crash (1929), collapse of US share prices. This is normally dated from the first day of panic selling on 'Black Thursday', 24 October 1929, and had severe repercussions in Britain, although this was not immediately apparent. In contrast to New York, where leading US industrial shares rose over 80 per cent in the eighteen months before the crash, then declined by nearly a half in the next six months, British share price changes were much more modest. Meanwhile, once the crash ended demand for foreign funds to supply brokers' loans, the Bank of England was able to reduce interest rates from their historically high levels. However, optimism vanished as the crash gave way to an increasingly severe slump in America and unemployment in Britain climbed to record levels. British statesmen, favourable to closer Anglo-American relations, regretted the isolationist reactions that the crash provoked in Washington. To many British observers the crash seemed to be symptomatic of the frivolousness of American society. For increasing numbers, too, it illustrated the irrationalism of the international capitalist system and, as the slump worsened, demands for a policy of trade protectionism to insulate Britain from its uncontrolled gyrations arose from all sides including manufacturing industry, the trade unions, the City, and especially the Conservative Party. The crash is still widely credited with the breakdown of the interwar economic and political order, although it was probably just one among many causes—including the Wall Street boom that preceded it. *RWDB*

ROBERT BOYCE, *British Capitalism at the Crossroads, 1919–1932: A Study in Politics, Economics and International Relations* (Cambridge, 1987). | ROBERT SKIDELSKY, *Politicians and the Slump: The Labour Government of 1929–1931* (London, 1967).

Walters, Alan Arthur (1926–), influential British monetarist economist. Influenced by Milton *Friedman, Walters was an ardent economic liberal from the early 1960s and wrote frequently for the Institute of Economic Affairs. He played a key role in the popularization of monetarism in Britain in the 1970s. Briefly an adviser for the Heath administration, he soon became a fierce critic of Barber's economic policy. The force of his arguments made a deep impression on Margaret Thatcher in the mid-1970s, and he returned from a spell in the USA as her personal economic adviser in January 1981. Walters played a critical role in the landmark 1981 budget which, by raising taxes and reducing spending in the midst of a recession, overturned Keynesian economic orthodoxy. Along with many other monetarists, he left Whitehall after the 1983 election but was recalled briefly in 1989, his alternative advice to Thatcher playing a part in the resignation of Lawson as her chancellor. *HOJ*

RICHARD COCKETT, *Thinking the Unthinkable: Think-Tanks and the Economic Counter-Revolution, 1931–1983* (London, 1994).

Walworth Road, the collective popular name for numbers 144–52 of the street in south-east London where the sixth Labour Party headquarters were situated from January 1980 to January 1998. This was the first large Labour Party headquarters the party occupied on its own, without sharing it with the Transport and General Workers, Union. However, the party did not fully own the premises as it turned out to be a listed building and thus the purchase cost was more than was originally estimated. To pay for it the party had to lease back the purchase from a consortium of trade unions. After the death of the party leader John Smith in 1994, the building was named after him. In 1995, in anticipation of a coming general election, a campaign headquarters was set up at Millbank Tower on the banks of the Thames near the Houses of Parliament and the majority of the staff moved there. After the general election of 1997 the remainder of the staff joined them and a symbol of the Labour Party's eighteen years of parliamentary opposition came to an end. *SB*

war bonds. In two world wars growth in government expenditure required the selling of war bonds so that the tax burden of total war would be shared by following generations. The war loans raised in November 1914, June 1915, and January 1917 were focal points for expressions of patriotism, second only to recruiting, but, with returns of 3.5 per cent rising to 5 per cent, the appeal of National War Bonds to banks and wealthy investors hardly resembled the conscription of riches. Attempts to promote the purchase of War Savings Certificates by small investors were less successful, despite propagandist efforts including the transformation of Trafalgar Square into a ruined French village during the 'Feed the Guns' campaign in October 1918. War loan policy fuelled inflationary pressures and diminished the wealth-levelling consequences of waging attritional war. In 1941 the nation's savings were mobilized at 3 per cent interest and the government succeeded in borrowing more cheaply through tailored investment initiatives, including National Savings Certificates for small savers. *KG*

T. Balderston, 'War Finance and Inflation in Britain and Germany, 1914–1918', *Economic History Review*, 42 (1989).

war cabinets. During the Great War in 1916, Lloyd George set up a cabinet of five to control the war, only one of whom, the chancellor, retained any departmental responsibility. For the Second World War, Chamberlain formed a war cabinet of up to fifteen members which Churchill cut to eight, leaving them with departmental responsibilities; the responsibility for actually running the war was left to Churchill, with domestic matters the concern of the lord president's committee. For the Korean war the cabinet operated normally while the defence committee, headed by Attlee, and consisting of nine other members, ran the war. For Suez, the cabinet's Egypt committee was formed, originally consisting of Eden plus six of his closest advisers; this was an ad hoc crisis management device, which failed to manage the crisis, and as a result became a war cabinet. The Falklands war cabinet was an official subcommittee consisting of Thatcher plus four, meeting every day and controlling the strategic aspects of the war completely, referring to the full cabinet only on policy decisions (and even then it was for confirmation or veto, not discussion). The Gulf war, with minimal British involvement and control meant that the cabinet, defence and chiefs of staff committees dealt with the situation through a special subgroup. War cabinets are the cabinet system's method of managing emergencies. Their composition is such as to provide the leadership with the optimal level of trusted and expert advice. They appear and disappear with the crisis. *CAB*

Colin Seymour-Ure, 'British "War Cabinets" in Limited Wars: Korea, Suez and the Falklands', *Public Administration*, 62/2 (1984).

war crimes trials. See Nuremburg and Tokyo war trials.

war debts. See reparations.

Warnock report (1984) on human fertilization and embryos. The committee scrutinized the full range of techniques available for fertilization and, whilst recommending safeguards and legal rights, it approved them all. It did oppose experimentation on embryos. Following the report's recommendations surrogacy agencies were banned in 1985 and private agreements were made legally unenforceable. After two interim bodies, the Human Fertilisation and Embryology Authority was established in 1991. The authority oversees regulation of gametes and embryos in line with the report's suggestions. *KMT*

War Office. See Defence, Ministry of.

Warren, Freddie (1915–90), civil servant. For two decades Warren oiled the wheels of the parliamentary machine as (first assistant, then principal) private secretary to the government chief whip, 1958–79. He had earlier been an assistant private secretary to Norman Brook, the secretary of the cabinet, 1951–8. Shrewd and self-effacing, Warren worked behind the scenes to ensure workable timetables for government legislation, advise on procedural arrangements, and keep relations between the parties working as smoothly as possible ('the usual channels'). *KT*

Warrington by-election (16 July 1981), a triumph for the electoral credibility of the newly formed *Social Democratic Party (SDP). A safe Labour seat in which the Liberals had polled only 3,000 votes in 1979, Warrington was vacated when its sitting MP, Tom Williams, resigned to become a judge. Although a Liberal candidate was available, in an early show of pre-merger cooperation, the SDP was given a run at the candidature in the hope that the selection of one of its national celebrities would maximize impact. After some delay in which it was considered that Shirley Williams might contest the seat, Roy Jenkins put himself forward. In a popular campaign, Jenkins secured an important moral victory for the SDP and for the venture of *'breaking the mould'. The left-wing Labour candidate Doug Hoyle won as anticipated, but his majority was slashed from

10,274 to a mere 1,759 over Jenkins. With barely any organization, Jenkins had captured 12,521 votes and 42 per cent of the poll. The result was at once a further blow to Labour, almost displaced in its heartland, and a tremendous boost for the SDP. Seasoned political commentators began to take the prospect of electoral realignment seriously after Warrington, which launched the SDP–Liberal Alliance on a series of major by-election victories in 1981–2. *JS*

Ivor Crewe and Anthony King, *SDP: The Birth, Life and Death of the Social Democratic Party* (Oxford, 1995).

Warwick, Daisy, countess of (1861–1938). Francis Evelyn Maynard was a famous socialite, mistress of Edward VII when prince of Wales, but then converted to socialism. She married Francis Greville, later 5th earl of Warwick, in 1881 and was known as Lady Brooke until December 1893 when her husband succeeded to the earldom. In the late 1890s she was influenced by Robert Blatchford and H. M. Hyndman, and became an active socialist in 1904, attending the international socialist conference at Amsterdam in 1904. Initially drawn to Marxist ideas, she later joined the Labour Party and was defeated by Anthony Eden in the contest for Warwick and Leamington at the 1923 general election. For more than twenty years she entertained socialists at Easton Lodge on her estates, and in the early 1920s the Independent Labour Party often held an Easter conference there, the guests including H. G. Wells, Ramsay MacDonald, and Oswald Mosley. *KL*

M. Blunden, *The Countess of Warwick* (London, 1967).

Washington naval conference (1922). Lloyd George's government sought in 1921–2 reductions in expenditure through the *Geddes axe, and from this the navy was not exempt, but it also sought to safeguard the security of the Empire, especially in the Far East where naval power was at a premium. During the Great War, Britain's alliance with Japan had countered any threat in those distant waters, but that alliance could not now be renewed without antagonizing America, increasingly suspicious of Japan in the Pacific. The naval conference convened by the American government in Washington offered the opportunity to find a solution. In the treaty negotiated in Washington, Britain agreed to a 5:5:3 ratio between the total naval tonnages of America, Britain, and Japan, so abandoning her traditional claim to naval supremacy. The navy therefore had to plan after 1922 within an arbitrary overall tonnage total of 500,000 tons (508,000 tonnes), and with the added difficulty of an ageing British fleet that could not be easily replaced in view of the 'ten-year holiday' in naval building also agreed at Washington. Britain agreed to all this, partly to allow cuts in defence expenditure, partly to assuage American opinion, but without receiving any guarantee of American support in a future war in which Britain might face European and Japanese enemies at the same time. The conference was, however, hailed as the beginning of a new era of world disarmament, it being recognized that the naval-building race between Britain and Germany before 1914 had reinforced the mutual antagonism that spilled over into war. Few major British warships were therefore built in the 1920s; the few that were, like the *Nelson* class battleships, were themselves hampered by individual tonnage limits also agreed at Washington—a situation worsened by the 1930 *London naval conference. *JAR*

Wass, Douglas William Gretton (1923–), Treasury civil servant. A highly numerate official (having been a Cambridge mathematics wrangler), and thoughtful and donnish in style, Wass joined the Treasury in 1946. He served in the chancellor's private office, 1959–61 and was appointed permanent secretary in 1974, holding that post until he retired in 1983. During 1981–3 he was also joint head of the civil service, serving alongside Robert Armstrong in that role. A committed Keynesian, Wass got to the top just when the Keynesian economic orthodoxies were being questioned and challenged. He did not hide his scepticism about monetarism with the result that, after 1979, ministers in the Thatcher government effectively bypassed him and looked elsewhere for economic policy advice. But Wass was keen to uphold the Northcote-Trevelyan principles of a permanent civil service working professionally for the government of the day and to prevent the politicization of the higher civil service. *KT*

wasted votes, term given to votes cast for losing candidates in elections. The term is employed by critics of the first-past-the-post method of electing MPs, arguing that votes cast for losing candidates are wasted since those casting them have no effect on the outcome of the election. Recognition of the phenomenon of the wasted vote can also have a distorting effect on voter behaviour, through 'third-party squeeze'. Voters who prefer a third-party candidate may decide not to 'waste' their vote by voting for that candidate but instead vote for a main party candidate, either as a positive second preference or as a way of trying to keep out the least favoured candidate. For those who cast votes for losing candidates, 'the result is the same as if all those voters had stayed at home' (Lakeman, 29). Critics argue that a new electoral system, such as that of the single transferable vote (STV), is necessary to eliminate wasted votes. Supporters of the present system contend that the benefits of the system, such as accountability, outweigh the arguments for change. Some also contend that voting for candidates, even if they lose, has a symbolic value and explains why some voters engage in what otherwise appears an irrational activity. They also question why a third- or fourth-preference vote should carry the same weight as a first-preference one. What under the present system is a wasted vote could under STV become a disproportionately influential one. *PN*

ENID LAKEMAN, *How Democracies Vote* (4th edn., London, 1974).

Waterhouse, Ronald (1878–1942), prime ministers' principal private secretary, 1922–8. Brought to Downing Street by Andrew Bonar Law, Colonel Waterhouse was the last principal private secretary appointed from outside the civil service. Delivering Law's resignation, Waterhouse broke his master's confidence to tell the king that Stanley Baldwin was the prime minister's preferred successor. Having served Baldwin (1923–4), he became the first principal private secretary to serve prime ministers of different parties when Ramsay MacDonald retained his services (1924). Following MacDonald's fall, he served Baldwin again (1924–8) until resigning under the cloud of a divorce case. *CL*

Watkinson, Harold Arthur (1910–95), Conservative politician and industrialist. A businessman by background, Watkinson was elected in 1950, became a minister in 1952, and entered the cabinet in 1957 as transport and civil aviation minister. Appointed defence minister in 1959, his assessment that Britain could no longer afford both worldwide commitments and the nuclear deterrent put him at odds with Macmillan, whom he never forgave for his peremptory sacking in 1962. He accepted a viscountcy in 1964, again becoming an industrialist. *RJS*

HAROLD WATKINSON, *Turning Points* (Salisbury, 1986).

Wavell, Archibald Percival (1883–1950), soldier. Wavell was commander-in-chief, Middle East (1939–41) and India (1941–3), and remains a controversial figure. He is best remembered for Britain's first land victory of the Second World War—the spectacular defeat of the Italian threat to Egypt—but also for the failed intervention to save Greece and the first military reverses in the Western Desert against the Afrika Korps. A taciturn commander, his relationship with Churchill was problematic, contributing to his eventual dismissal. In mitigation, Wavell had a vast theatre to defend with few resources, especially lacking modern tanks and aircraft, yet still left a largely intact command on which his successors built. He was then viceroy of India in exceptionally difficult times, 1943–7. *SM*

JOHN CONNELL, *Wavell: Scholar and Soldier* (London, 1964). | HAROLD WAUGH, *Wavell in the Middle East 1939–1941: A Study in Generalship* (London, 1993).

Ways and Means, Chairman of. See COMMONS, HOUSE OF: PROCEDURE.

'We are the masters at the moment' (usually misquoted as 'we are the masters now'), line from a speech by Hartley Shawcross in 1946. Early in the life of the Attlee government of 1945–51, the unlikely figure of the attorney-general thus articulated the meaning of the election of the first majority Labour government. He went on, without much prophetic accuracy, to add: 'and not only for the moment, but for a very long time to come'. *BB*

Webb, (Martha) Beatrice (1858–1943) and Sidney James (1859–1947), influential, encyclopaedic Fabian socialists. Beatrice, the daughter of Richard Potter, an industrial magnate, was an 1876 debutante and striking beauty who was pursued by, amongst many others, Joseph Chamberlain. Sidney was the son of a small-time public accountant, educated in Switzerland, Germany, Birkbeck Institute, and City of London College, who looked like a foreigner and spoke like a cockney. Together they comprised 'the partnership', inexhaustibly probing every aspect of social policy and tirelessly proposing reform. 'We are both second-rate minds', Beatrice explained, 'but we are curiously combined. I am the investigator and he the executant; between us we have a wide and varied experience of men and affairs. We also have an unearned salary. These are unique circumstances. A considerable body of work should result if we use our combined talents with a deliberate and persistent purpose.' Their *History of Trade Unionism* (1894), the first to treat the subject seriously, was a masterpiece, widely translated. *Industrial Democracy* (2 vols., 1897) and *English Local Government* (9 vols., 1906–29) expected progress to come from an elite, an attitude Beatrice especially held, which rendered her curiously uncritical of Bolshevism. *Soviet Communism: A New Civilization?* which first appeared in 1935, but was reissued in 1937, at the height of Stalin's purges, with the question mark removed, has been described by the historian A. J. P. Taylor as 'despite severe competition, the most preposterous book ever written about Soviet Russia'. Bertrand Russell described Beatrice as 'prodigiously clever, prodigiously industrious and a prodigious prig'. Nevertheless, their part in spreading socialism, reform, and the growth of the Labour Party was enormous. G. D. H. Cole called Sidney's writing in *Fabian Essays* 'the most important single contribution in the history of British socialism' and their Fabian doctrine of the *inevitability of gradualness won wide acceptance. They helped found the LSE in 1895, and saw it grow into a great world institution, and the *New Statesman* in 1913, which became a leading journal of left opinion. Their most significant contribution was reforming the *poor law. Beatrice served on the royal commission on the poor law 1905–9, Sidney helped her draft the minority report, and together they played the major part in replacing the poor law over the years with something better.

First elected to London County Council for Labour in 1892, Sidney became convinced the party alone could advance collectivist ideals and drafted its celebrated 1918 socialist constitution, which survived until 1996. MP for Seaham in Durham, 1922–9, when he became Lord Passfield, he was president of the Board of Trade, 1924; secretary for dominions and colonies, 1929–30; and for colonies 1930–1. He was awarded the Order of Merit in 1944. Both are buried in Westminster abbey. No two people played a larger part in laying the intellectual foundations for Labour's eventual election to power for the first time in 1945. *PRGR*

ROYDEN HARRISON, *Socialism and the Intellectuals* (London, 1999). | N. MACKENZIE (ed.), *The Letters of Sidney and Beatrice Webb*, 3 vols. (London, 1978).

Weber, Max (1864–1920) German sociologist, renowned for his work in many areas of social science. Among these are

1. the connection between Protestant religion and the spread of capitalist ideology;
2. the distinction between class, as defined by Karl Marx in terms of relationship to the means of production, and status-group, which corresponds more closely to what we often think of as class—the market researcher's social groups, classified by lifestyle, the newspaper they read, and the way they tend to vote, are Weberian status groups, not Marxian classes;
3. bureaucracy, which Weber conceived of as the most 'rational' way of running a state or an organization.

The British civil service has often been hailed as an 'ideal type' (another of Weber's phrases) of Weberian bureaucracy. Since the Northcote-Trevelyan reforms in the mid-19th century, it has been organized along exactly the lines that Weber hails in his essay on *Bureaucracy*, but, this is a coincidence. Weber knew a great deal about ancient India but little about 19th-century Britain. *IM*

H. H. GERTH and C. WRIGHT MILLS, *From Max Weber* (London, 1948).

Webster, Martin (1943–), racial nationalist. Webster joined the League of Empire Loyalists in the 1950s, but he achieved greater prominence in the 1970s within the National Front (NF). Together with John Tyndall he provided much of the impetus behind the NF's political growth. He wrote under the pen-name 'Julius' in *Spearhead* and was active at meetings, marches, and rallies. His influence declined after the NF's failure in the 1979 election: he was expelled from the movement in 1982. *CH*

M. CRONIN (ed.), *The Failure of British Fascism* (London, 1996).

Webster, Richard Everard. See ALVERSTONE, 1ST VISCOUNT.

We Can Conquer Unemployment (1929), Liberal policy document. Derived from the Yellow Book **Britain's Industrial Future* of February 1928, *We Can Conquer Unemployment* was the product of a committee headed by David *Lloyd George, Lord Lothian, and Seebohm *Rowntree, and it provided the basis for the Liberal general election campaign of 1929. At its heart was a *Keynesian commitment to reduce unemployment by an emergency programme of road-building and housing. *JS*

Wee Frees, derogatory term (deriving from a Scottish religious sect more notable for its purity than its numbers) for the group of 'independent' or 'free' Liberals, supporters of H. H. *Asquith, who opposed the National Liberals led by David *Lloyd George in the 1918 election. Only 28 were elected in 1918 and their leader Asquith was defeated. They eventually reunited with the former National Liberals to fight the 1923 election, although by that time the division of the

Liberals into rival factions had done lasting damage to the Liberal Party. *JS*

'week is a long time in politics', phrase attributed to Harold Wilson and generally considered to have been uttered at a parliamentary lobby meeting in 1964 during the sterling crisis. Even if apocryphal, it is an important political myth, symbolizing the cynicism of Wilson in particular and of politicians in general. *BJE*

Weighell, Sidney (1922–), trade unionist. Sid Weighell was elected to the executive committee of the National Union of Railwaymen in 1953. The following year he was appointed a divisional officer before becoming assistant general secretary in 1965 and a moderate general secretary, 1975–83. Weighell was a Labour Party agent, 1947–52, and a member of the Labour NEC, 1972–5. *DWM*

SIDNEY WEIGHELL, *A Hundred Years of Railway Weighells* (London, 1984).

Weir, William Douglas (1877–1959), industrialist. Weir was managing director (1902) and chairman (1912) of his father's engineering firm G. & J. Weir, of Cathcart, and became an administrator of the war economy as director of munitions for Scotland (1915), controller of aeronautical supplies (1917), and secretary of state for air. He hastily resigned from ministerial office in 1919, but thereafter became a central figure in the rise of the corporate economy. In 1926 his committee advised a national grid for the electricity supply industry. In 1934 he negotiated the merger of Cunard and White Star, which ensured government funding for the construction of two luxury liners on the Clyde. As a member of the defence policy and requirements committee, 1935–7, and adviser to Lord Swinton, air minister, 1935–8, Weir became a powerful advocate of the large bomber force and the creation of shadow factories. The technical knowledge of this *éminence grise* connected grand strategy to manufacturing capacity. Habitually at the intersection of government, finance and industry Viscount Weir (ennobled 1938) embraced rationalization, anti-socialism, and cooperation between employers and trade union leaders on national economic policy, alongside the paramountcy of private enterprise. *WG*

L. HANNAH, *The Rise of the Corporate Economy* (London, 1976). | W. J. READER, *Architect of Air Power: The Life of the First Viscount Weir of Eastwood 1877–1959* (London, 1968).

Weisz, Viktor. See 'VICKY'.

welfare state, term used to describe the system of comprehensive welfare provision whereby a state uses government apparatus to prevent poverty and promote higher living standards. This can be achieved through cash benefits, services, and the regulation of the economy. The term, widely used since 1945, was first coined during the 1930s to contrast with the 'warfare state' devoting itself to armaments.

The origins of the Welfare State in Britain can be traced back to the creation of state-provided 'social services' in the aftermath of 19th-century industrialization. Concern about the appalling conditions in which the poorest members of society lived meant that central government came under increasing pressure at the start of the 20th century to extend welfare beyond the poor law's framework of provision. Thus, between 1906 and 1914, Liberal governments introduced a series of social welfare measures, including the Old Age *Pension Act, 1908, and the *National Insurance Act, 1911, providing a range of health and unemployment benefits. These were radical measures but were still limited in scope. Policies were extended in the inter-war period with the widening of national insurance in 1920 and the reorganization of unemployment insurance in 1934–5, along with limited state housing and state education. The Second World War reinforced the case for an extension of welfare and the *Beveridge report (1942) advocated a universal system of welfare provision. The Labour government elected in 1945 was committed to establishing such a system. *Family allowances were introduced in 1945, while the *National Insurance Act, 1946, established a comprehensive 'welfare state' along the lines advocated by Beveridge. Compulsory insurance thus provided for unemployment, sickness, and maternity benefits and for old-age and widows' pensions. The *National Health Service established a free medical service for all. There were also major improvements in housing, education, and community social services. It provided a system of support *'from the cradle to the grave'.

After initial opposition, the Conservatives accepted the notion of a 'welfare state'. Thus, throughout the 1950s and 1960 both Labour and Conservative governments supported and expanded welfare provision and spending increased, especially during the 1960s.

By the 1970s, however, a faltering economy and spiralling welfare costs saw this consensus break down. Right-wing critics attacked the welfare state for holding back economic growth. Backed by public concern at increasing expenditure and a belief in the emergence of a culture of dependency, Conservative governments from 1979 to 1997 undertook a systematic overhaul of the welfare state. Rates of welfare support were reduced, private insurance and private care were encouraged, and state services cut. The public eventually became concerned at the level of these cuts and in 1997 Tony Blair's Labour government was elected, initiating a debate on the future of the welfare state. Blair's administration accepted right-wing criticisms of dependency and escalating costs but set out to reinvigorate the welfare state. In 1998 a £5 billion 'Welfare to Work' scheme was introduced to tackle youth and long-term unemployment. Reform of national insurance also sought to improve incentives to work for the low-paid. At the close of the century, no new consensus on the scope and nature of the welfare state had emerged and it remained a highly charged political issue. *JJN*

welfare to work, policy of the Labour government since 1997 to tackle youth and long-term unemployment, promote employability, and develop skills. A key aspect of the policy is the single 'gateway' to welfare and, ultimately, to work. The scheme is being funded by a windfall tax on excess profits of the privatized utilities, totalling £5.2 billion. *JS*

Welsh Board of Health. See WELSH OFFICE.

Welsh church disestablishment. See CHURCH IN WALES, DISESTABLISHMENT OF.

Welsh counties, renaming of. The historic counties of Wales, which had been given formal recognition in the Act of Union of 1536, and which became the basis of democratic local government after 1888, enjoyed mixed fortunes at the end of the 20th century. In 1974 the thirteen traditional counties were reduced to eight. Anglesey, Caernarfon, and Merioneth were amalgamated to form Gwynedd; Denbigh and Flint formed Clwyd; Brecknock, Radnor, and Montgomery formed Powys; Cardigan, Pembroke, and Carmarthen formed Dyfed; Monmouthshire was renamed Gwent; and Glamorgan was divided into three. In 1996 local government was extensively reformed and a pattern of 22 new unitary authorities was established. This new dispensation allowed Anglesey, Denbighshire, Flintshire, Cardiganshire, Pembrokeshire, Carmarthenshire, and Monmouth to reassert their identity. *PS*

Welsh Development Agency, semi-autonomous government body created in 1976 to advertise opportunities in and foster investment in Wales (roughly equivalent to the Highlands and Islands Development Board in Scotland). It has had considerable success in attracting inward international investment into Wales, and came under the Welsh assembly from 1999. *JAR*

Welsh Grand Committee. See COMMONS, HOUSE OF: WELSH GRAND COMMITTEE.

Welsh language. The Welsh language, which is both older than English and one of the oldest written languages in Europe, was officially proscribed by Henry VIII's Acts of Union in 1536 and 1542. Remarkably, Welsh survived that loss of prestige not least because of the way in which a peasantry embraced a Nonconformity which was characterized by a magnificent Bible-inspired rhetoric. Even with the coming of towns and industry, the census of 1901 indicated that 40 per cent of the population spoke Welsh. Inevitably the new century brought a dramatic decline as schools and the media gave English a new power and teachers and parents deliberately chose not to inculcate what was thought of as a peasant language. By 1961 only 26 per cent spoke Welsh. It was at this stage that the fight back began, as Saunders Lewis and others argued that the saving of the language had to come now or never, and that it could only be achieved by giving the language a new official status. The vital steps in the recovery were the Welsh Language Act of 1967 which gave Welsh a new status in legal proceedings and on official forms, and a similar Act of 1993 which led to the setting up of the Welsh Language Board whose principal function is to 'promote and facilitate the use of the Welsh language'. The fight to save the language, during which many young people went to prison, was remarkably successful, not least in broadcasting, in education where the Welsh language is compulsory and bilingual education now generally available, and in politics where the Welsh assembly is fully bilingual. Welsh is still not permitted at Westminster, but simultaneous translation facilities are available at most official meetings in Wales. In 1991, Welsh speakers still constituted 18.7 per cent of the population, so the rate of decline has been halted and the principality has come to terms with its bilingualism. Certainly there was in 1999 far less evidence of that hostility to the Welsh language which had been a factor in the defeat of the 1979 devolution proposals. *PS*

JANET DAVIES, *The Welsh Language* (Cardiff, 1993).

Welsh language society. See CYMDEITHAS YR LAITH GYMRAEG.

Welsh League of Youth. See URDD GOBAITH CYMRU.

Welsh Nationalists, See PLAID CYMRU.

Welsh Office, government department which originated as a section of the Home Office but achieved independent status in 1964 when a secretary of state for Wales was first appointed. Initially it had responsibility for roads, housing, planning, water, tourism, and national parks, but gradually also acquired health and welfare, education, and agriculture. The office was located both in London and in Cardiff, its powers passing to the Welsh assembly in 1999. *JAR*

Welsh religious revival (1904–5). Great revivals were a feature of 19th-century Nonconformity but the memory of them was eclipsed in Wales by the dramatic revival of 1904–5, inspired by Evan Roberts of Loughor. A former miner and blacksmith's apprentice Roberts was training for the Calvinistic Methodist ministry when he underwent the religious and psychological experience which became the basis for the revival. His services were held at his church, Moriah, Loughor and then throughout Wales and in Liverpool. They were characterized by an intense spirituality which depended little on sermons and the spoken word. The emphasis was on spontaneous singing and personal testimony, and not surprisingly the Nonconformist establishment figures were sceptical. As the revival faded in 1906 attention switched to radical politics and James Griffiths somewhat too easily explained that men and women, having realized that religion had not changed things, turned to socialism. Other commentators have suggested that the revival gave Nonconformity a boost that allowed it to survive as an important influence on Welsh life throughout the first half of the 20th century. Roberts himself lived on in some obscurity until his death in 1951. *PS*

Western European Union (WEU). A diplomatic triumph for Anthony Eden, the WEU was conceived in 1954 as a means of keeping European cooperation alive after the death of the supranational European Defence Community. Through its establishment on 6 May 1955, the WEU achieved its primary task by facilitating West German rearmament, but became largely redundant after the *Messina conference. It was not until the 1990s that the WEU played a serious role in international relations. *JRVE*

Western Mail, daily newspaper published in Cardiff. The *Western Mail* was established in 1869 as the voice of the marquess of Bute. Firmly committed to the Conservative Party, in 1928 it was able to incorporate its hitherto Liberal rival, the *South Wales Daily News*. Hated by the South Wales Miners, Aneurin Bevan was said to have arranged bonfires for certain issues. Since the 1960s, it has become far more sympathetic to a range of Welsh aspirations, supported devolution in 1979 and 1997, and gives extensive coverage to sport, literature, and the arts. Trinity Holdings are the parent company. *PS*

Westland affair, government crisis (1986). Ostensibly rooted in jealousy between Michael *Heseltine supporting a European consortium bid for Westland helicopters, and Leon *Brittan supporting the American Sikorski, this became a three-sided battle for Margaret Thatcher detested Heseltine, as statist, pro-European, and rival, driving him to resign. Leak of the attorney-general's letter criticizing Heseltine then made the law officers threaten resignation, but blame fell on a civil servant and Brittan, who also resigned, but suspicion of Thatcher was general. But for Kinnock's ineptitude in debate Thatcher might have fallen then, with advantage to her reputation. *EP*

Westwood, Joseph (1884–1948), Labour politician. Westwood was a Fife miner and trade unionist who first entered parliament in 1922 for Peebles and South Midlothian, from 1935 representing Stirling and Falkirk. In 1945 he was appointed secretary of state for Scotland in the Attlee government, but retired in 1947 in a cabinet reshuffle. He was killed in a car crash in 1948. *MJK*

'wets and dries', catchphrases and terms of abuse going back (at least) to the 1940s, but popularized in the Thatcher period. Originally, when Thatcher called left-wing Conservatives 'wet', she intended the common, abusive sense as with 'drooling and drivelling', so it meant weak, cowardly, or feeble. But left-wing Tories rejoiced in the phrase, even calling themselves 'sodden wet', while someone provided an opposite, 'dry', as meaning anti-statist. The terms took on economic significance, free market against interventionist, *Thatcherite and anti-Thatcherite. *EP*

'We Want Eight, and We Won't Wait', slogan of critics of the Asquith govemment in early 1909, referring to the compromise fashioned among the cabinet's 'economists' and 'imperialists' to lay down four Dreadnought battleships and to build four more only if the rival Germans pressed their own building programme. The opposition Tories introduced this popular cry at the Croydon by-election in March, which was won handily by a supporter of naval expansion, ensuring that the four 'contingent' ships were authorized in July. *RJQA*

ARTHUR J. MARDER, *From the Dreadnought to Scapa Flow*, vol. 1 (London, 1961).

Wharf, The, H. H. *Asquith's home at Sutton Courtenay, Berkshire, from 1912 until his death in 1928. *JS*

What the Conservatives have done for the British People, leaflet first issued for the general election of 1880, listing the claimed social policy achievements of the second Disraeli government, and subsequently updated for almost every election in the appeal to working-class voters. From 1947, it was retitled less patronizingly as *Conservative Industrial and Social Reform* but had by then become a useful, if highly slanted, guide to past legislation for party activists and candidates, rather than an election leaflet. Apparently last published in 1977. *JAR*

Wheare, Kenneth Clinton (1907–79), academic and public administrator. An Australian, educated at Melbourne and Oxford Universities, Wheare spent his entire academic career at Oxford, as fellow of University College, 1939–44; Gladstone professor of government and public administration, 1944–57; fellow of All Souls, 1944–57; fellow of Nuffield, 1944–58; rector of Exeter College, 1957–72; and vice-chancellor, 1964–6. But Wheare combined an academic with a public life. He was constitutional adviser to the National Convention of Newfoundland, 1946–7, and to the conference on Central African Federation, 1951–3; president of the British Academy, 1967–71; a member of the Franks committee on administrative tribunals and inquiries, 1956–7; and the university's representative on Oxford City Council, 1940–57. Wheare's academic work was conventional, combining a practical approach to political institutions with a practitioner's feel for public administration. His writing was comparative and focused on the institutions of government and their constitutional underpinnings. It also evokes a sense of the role of the administrator within these structures. He is best remembered for three works, *Federal Government* (1946), *Government by Committee: An Essay on the British Constitution* (1955), and *The Constitutional Structures of the Commonwealth* (1960). *CPS*

Wheatley, John (1869–1930), Labour politician and journalist. Irish-born, Wheatley joined the Independent Labour Party (ILP) in 1907 and founded the Catholic Socialist Society, challenging the Church's hostility to labour politics. Active in local politics, he was involved in the rent strikes and labour agitation during the Great War. Elected as Labour MP for the Shettleston, Glasgow constituency in 1922, one of the Clydesiders, he was minister of health in MacDonald's 1924 Labour government and so was responsible for the Housing Act of that year, the government's most important domestic achievement. He suffered loss of reputation from a lawsuit in 1927, which may explain his non-inclusion in Labour's 1929 government. *KJL*

I. WOOD, *John Wheatley* (Manchester, 1990).

Wheatley Housing Act. See HOUSING ACT, 1924.

Whiggism, political attitude. For two centuries, the Whigs were one of the dominant British parties, though shrunk by the 1880s to a wing within Liberalism. In 1886, over Irish home rule, most Whigs deserted Gladstone's Liberals, crossing over to sit with the Conservatives. Whiggism had been led from the top of the social hierarchy, and the leader of 1886 's Whig seceders was the 8th duke of Devonshire. Unsurprisingly then, Whiggism was conservative in its core political attitudes, resistant to change in matters relating to the ownership of land and distribution of influence. Whigs had, though, been a group in opposition to 17th-century Stuart kings. Many had lost their lives and fortunes in constitutional struggle, but broadly triumphed in 1688's 'glorious revolution' and in the Protestant succession agreed in 1701, implemented and consolidated by Whig rule from 1714. Whigs did not therefore see themselves as conservative, but rather as heirs to a radical aristocratic tradition of resistance to monarchy. It was difficult to maintain so schizophrenic an identity in the 19th century, as the country changed into an urban, industrial entity, with the threat to dukes now coming not from the crown but from the workers (or at least from radical Liberals in search of working-class votes). Whiggism therefore became a tactic for political survival, the timely (or, critics said, unprincipled and selfish) making of minimal concessions that would allow the power structures themselves to remain intact. Once the last Whigs had merged into the Conservative Party in 1912, and political debates became more focused on economic than on constitutional issues by the 1920s, Whiggism had no remaining role to play and no separate group of politicians used the label. There remained, though, politicians dubbed 'Whigs' by their contemporaries for much of the century, generally not as a term of approbation. For his opposition to tariffs and resistance to domestic reform, Winston Churchill was dubbed 'an old-fashioned Whig' by Leo Amery, while Harold Macmillan, aristocratically aloof, cynical, a master-manipulator, and actually married into the Devonshire family, was called a 'Whig' by Enoch Powell. Related to Whiggism was the 'Whig interpretation of history', a dominant approach to the interpretation of Britain's past until mid-century. On this view, Britain's development towards liberal, parliamentary democracy, had been a seamless, sweeping progress that could be traced back at least to 1066, though especially to the 17th century. Whig historians took little interest in social, economic, or diplomatic history, and found in Britain itself a powerful object for admiration, so sharing much of the complacency of the real Whigs. *JAR*

whipping. See COMMONS, HOUSE OF: WHIPPING.

whistleblowing, the unauthorized disclosure of confidential information which relates to some danger, fraud, abuse, or other illegal or unethical conduct within an organization. The Public Interest Disclosure Act, 1998 (introduced as a private member's bill), encourages employees to raise such concerns internally in the first instance, and then regulates the situations in which they may make an unauthorized disclosure and raise the matter externally. Given that their primary duty is to ministers, whistleblowing by civil servants has traditionally been viewed as unacceptable and improper. However, in the 1930s Winston Churchill's attacks on the Chamberlain government's appeasement policies were based on confidential information leaked to him by civil servants. And in the 1980s a series of controversial cases, including the Ponting and *Spycatcher* affairs, raised the issue of the civil servant's 'right to leak'. The *Civil Service Code* introduced in 1995 laid down that officials believing that they were being required to act in a way which was illegal, improper, involved possible maladministration, was unethical, or in breach of constitutional convention could ultimately report the matter to the independent civil service commissioners, but were still bound by their overriding duty of confidentiality. *KT*

White, Dick Goldsmith (1906–93), chief of the British Security Service (MI5) and of the Secret Intelligence Service (SIS or MI6). Dick White was educated privately and at Christ Church, Oxford. He also spent time at American universities, beginning a lifelong association with that country. Thereafter, White had various jobs including that of schoolmaster. He joined the Security Service in 1935—their first ever graduate employee. Before the war he toured Nazi Germany, making important contacts with anti-Nazi dissidents, and was controller for German embassy penetration agent Klop Ustinov. During the Second World War, White ran the 'double cross' system, turning German agents and feeding their controls with false information. Once the USA entered the war he trained and inducted their intelligence officers in counter-intelligence. During these years he worked with individuals who later dominated America's post-war intelligence community. After the war, White became head of counter-espionage and was involved in the fallout surrounding Soviet penetration of the British intelligence community and atomic programme. In 1952, White was appointed director of MI5 and four years later became head of the Secret Intelligence Service. He reformed both institutions, professionalizing SIS and ending the policy of recruitment at the bars of gentlemen's clubs. White also worked closely with Alan Dulles and his successors at the CIA. He remained head of SIS until 1968, dealing with critical Cold War incidents such as the George Blake affair, the revelation of Philby and Blunt's treachery, the Berlin wall, and the Cuban missile crisis. On retirement he was persuaded to become the Joint Intelligence Committee's first intelligence coordinator until his final retirement in 1972. *PM*

White, Captain Jack (1879–1947), a somewhat eccentric British army officer who hailed from Ulster and was drawn into Irish politics through his left-wing ideas and his sympathy with the Irish Transport and General Workers' Union strike in Dublin in 1913. White formed the Irish Citizen Army to defend the strikers against attacks from the police, the first two companies formed on 23 November. He lost control of the army to James Connolly, who led it to destruction in the Easter Rising of 1916. *DGB*

'white heat of the technological revolution', paraphrase from speech by Harold Wilson in 1963 that summed up his positioning of Labour in the run-up to the 1964 election. Wilson argued that Labour's socialism would be in terms of the 'scientific revolution', and that Labour's Britain would be forged in the 'white heat' of that revolution. His main references were to

Soviet technology and the potential of planning, but the theme was effective in giving Labour a unified, defined, and modern identity in the campaign. *BB*

Whitelaw, William Stephen Ian (1918–2000), Conservative politician and deputy prime minister. A country gentleman very happy with mid-century moderate Conservative politics, he became the indispensable ally of the fiercely right-wing and lower middle-class Margaret Thatcher, and after he retired in 1987 she was never the same. Whitelaw rose through the chief whip's office which had never previously advanced anyone beyond four years running Scotland, but he was second successor to Edward Heath who had changed all that and, replacing the useless Martin *Redmayne, he proved a loyal, capable chief, self-derisively eccentric, capable of spluttering irk but more often of cajoling charm. Heath gave him the Northern Irish secretaryship, where he attracted Unionist hostility for initiating talks with republicans first in a northern hotel, then at *Sunningdale. Unhappy about Heath's 1974 election bid, he stayed loyal, resisting pressure to stand until Thatcher's showing in 1975 made him a too-late 'stop her' candidate. He then protected her effectively from his own friends, the wets. A natural conciliator and soft-liner, like many holders of the Military Cross, his style embodied the British self-conscious silly ass tradition, as when he complained that people were 'going around stirring up apathy'. A keen field sportsman, like Archbishop Abbot, he once shot a keeper, not though in this case fatally, to his own great distress. But the silly ass could kick: after a major Labour confusion. he said 'Wrong to gloat, thoroughly bad form, absolutely mustn't gloat. But I'm gloating like hell'. Part of his function under Thatcher was to be a Conservative that non-Thatcherites could like. Another part was to combine loyalty, against his own instincts, with the authority to restrain her wilder impulses; one story credits him with stopping Thatcher going to Leeds to take over personally the search for the Yorkshire Ripper. The editor of a Tory paper said when Whitelaw retired, 'I fear for the future. Now she has only the cabinet functionaries, creatures, and enemies. Willy was the only one who could put a hand on her wrist and say, "Margaret, *don't*".' Whitelaw himself, despite natural chivalry, called this undertaking 'hosing her down'. *EP*

William Whitelaw, *The Whitelaw Memoirs* (London, 1989).

Whitmore, Clive Anthony (1935–), civil servant. Whitmore entered the civil service in 1959, working in the War Office and Ministry of Defence. He was a tough-minded, dynamic, and influential principal private secretary to Prime Minister Thatcher, 1979–82. She appointed him to be permanent secretary at the Ministry of Defence at the early age of 48 in 1983. From 1988 to 1994 he was permanent secretary at the Home Office, retiring early but denying a rift with his political boss, Michael Howard. *KT*

Whitty, (John) Laurence (1943–), trade union and Labour Party official. After education at Latymer Upper School and Cambridge, Larry Whitty worked in the aviation industry and the Ministry of Education. In 1970 he started to work for the TUC and then moved to the General Municipal Boilermakers' and Allied Trade Union in 1973. During his time at this union he was made secretary to the organization Trades Unions for a Labour Victory where, in spite of the Labour Party's big election defeat in 1983, it was considered he did an able job in difficult circumstances. In 1985 he was made general secretary of the Labour Party, a post he held for nine difficult years, covering two election defeats, as the party began its long but slow recovery. For three years he was the Labour Party's European coordinator. In 1996 he was elevated to the House of Lords where, after the Labour election victory of 1997, he held government posts as a whip and at the transport ministry. His significance will always remain as the last major Labour Party official to work closely with the unions but lay the way for the more electable Labour Party. His career thus symbolizes the move from old to New Labour. *SB*

Whole-Hoggers, in the years 1903–14, those who in the debate over Joseph Chamberlain's tariff reform proposals rejected the idea of compromise. They were opposed to such as C. T. Ritchie and Lord Hugh Cecil who came to be called *Free-Fooders, and those, including Winston Churchill, who actually defected to the Liberals. Those who wished the party to embrace the full tariff plan were styled 'Whole-Hoggers' from a political phrase indicating support for the undiluted programme of a party, 'going the whole hog'. *RJQA*

'Whose finger on the trigger?' In the 1951 general election the *Daily Mirror* highlighted the threat of nuclear war with this theme and on election day a front-page spread reminded its five million readers, 'Today your finger is on the trigger', implying that there was a risk of war if

Churchill were to become prime minister. Incensed by this claim that he was a warmonger, Churchill (even though he won the election) successfully sued the paper for libel. *BJE*

Widdicombe committee (1985–6), attempt, which largely misfired, to curb the activities of Labour councils. The committee of inquiry into the conduct of local authority business was established under the chairmanship of David Widdicombe, QC, in response to Conservative concern about what were seen as politically corrupt practices on the part of 'new urban Left' authorities. Widdicombe's report, published in 1986, largely cleared Labour authorities of these charges, but made a number of proposals to restrain the impact of party politics on local government, most of which were embodied in part 3 of the Local Government and Housing Act, 1989. *KY*

Widgery, John Passmore (1911–81), judge. After war service in the artillery, Widgery was called to the Bar in 1946, becoming a judge, 1961–8; lord justice of appeal, 1968–71; and lord chief justice, 1971–80. Lord Widgery chaired the inquiry into the 'Bloody Sunday' killings in Londonderry in 1972, his broad exoneration of the army's role later being much criticized, and reopened by a new inquiry in 2000. *JAR*

Widgery report (1972), the result of the inquiry into the 'Bloody Sunday' shootings in Londonderry conducted by Lord *Widgery. After thirteen civilians were shot dead by British paratroopers in Londonderry following a banned civil rights march in January 1972, the prime minister, Edward Heath, announced an inquiry by Widgery, the lord chief justice. Widgery found that the tragedy would not have happened if there had not been an illegal march which created 'a highly dangerous situation'. Equally, if the army had maintained a low profile and not launched a large-scale operation to arrest hooligans, the deaths might have been avoided. The report concluded that the paratroopers had been fired on first and there was no reason to suppose they would have opened fire otherwise. However, some of the army's return fire 'bordered on the reckless' and it had not been proved that any of the dead or injured were shot while handling a bomb or gun. Widgery's conclusions were condemned as a whitewash by the nationalist community and Dublin called for an international investigation. After years of campaigning by nationalists and the bereaved, Tony Blair promised a fresh inquiry which began in 2000. *PR*

The Widgery Report (HC papers, 220/72, London, 1972). | JONATHAN BARDON, *A History of Ulster* (Belfast, 1992).

Widows', Orphans', and Old Age Contributory Pensions Act, 1925 provided pensions of ten shillings (50p) a week for widows and for insured workers and their wives at the age of 65, seven shillings and sixpence (37.5p) for orphan children. The scheme only applied to those covered by national insurance and contributions were raised to help to pay for it. Seen as an example of 'Tory socialism' and an attempt by the Conservatives to win over the mass electorate created in 1918 by franchise extensions. *JS*

Wiener, Martin Joel (1937–), historian. Educated at Brandeis and Harvard, Wiener has taught at Rice University in Texas since 1967. His first book was *Between Two Worlds: the Political Thought of Graham Wallas* (1971), and more recently he has worked on the history of crime in Britain, publishing *Reconstructing the Criminal, 1850–1914* (1990) and editing the 30-volume reprint series *Crime and Punishment in England, 1850–1922* (1984). Wiener's name and influence, however, will always be associated with *English Culture and the Decline of the Industrial Spirit* (1981). In these early Thatcher years, there was a widespread debate on the causes of British decline, and Wiener's timely and eloquent argument that the British had never been fully committed to industry anyway seemed very plausible. He began with the assertion that 'in the world's first industrial nation, industrialism did not seem quite at home'. Industrialists had been seduced by the values and lifestyle of the rural gentry, while intellectuals had always been antagonistic to the world of industry. In a spirited response, British historians accused Wiener of 'random quotation' and of a failure to examine the roles of banking and commerce. *PS*

B. COLLINS and K. ROBBINS (eds.), *British Culture and Economic Decline* (London, 1985).

Wigg, George (1900–83), politician and turf administrator. Wigg began his working life as a professional soldier, rising to the rank of colonel. In 1945 he was elected Labour MP for Dudley and not long afterwards became parliamentary private secretary to Emanuel Shinwell. From 1951 to 1954 he was an opposition whip, but he became well known as the leading parliamentary questioner during the Profumo affair in 1963. When Labour came back to power in 1964, Harold

Wilson made him paymaster general and a privy councillor. He held this post until 1967 when he resigned his seat to become chairman of the Horserace Betting Levy Board. At the same time he was elevated to the Lords and took the title Baron Wigg of Dudley. In 1972 he retired and published his memoirs. *SB*

Lord Wigg, *George Wigg* (London, 1972).

Wigley, Dafydd Wynne (1943–), Welsh nationalist politician, Wigley was MP for Caernarfon, from February 1974, the Plaid Cymru party president, 1981–4 and 1991–2000. As a member of Plaid Cymru's research group, 1966–70, he was influential in developing party policies in a number of areas. His experience as an industrial economist assisted the research group in preparing its *Economic Plan for Wales* (1970). In developing an economic case for Welsh nationalism in addition to the cultural and linguistic case, he made a significant contribution to the development of Plaid Cymru as a successful electoral force in Welsh politics. In addition to Welsh nationalist causes, he is interested in parliament, in genetic and embryo research, an interest borne of the death of two handicapped sons. He was a sponsor of the Disabled Persons Act and has been vice-chairman of the all-party disablement group since 1992. A lifelong pro-European, he contested the North Wales constituency in the 1994 European parliamentary elections, substantially reducing Labour's majority. In 1999 he contested the elections that he always wanted to fight, elections for the Welsh national assembly. *DG*

Dafydd Wigley, *Working for Wales* (Aberystwyth, 1996).

Wigram, Clive (1873–1960), private secretary to *George V, 1931–6. He was an army officer who served in India before coming to the palace in 1910. He spent most of his career as deputy to Lord *Stamfordham; contemporaries regarded him as less able but more approachable than his chief. Almost as soon as he took over as the king's principal private secretary he was faced with the most serious difficulty of his time in office. The worldwide Depression led the king, who distrusted Labour's ability to manage the crisis, to persuade Ramsay MacDonald to form a national government by bringing members of the opposition into the cabinet. This was bitterly resented by Labour and left a dangerous mistrust of the monarchy in Labour circles. A more assertive private secretary might have cautioned the king to proceed more slowly before such a significant intervention. *WMK*

Wilberforce, Richard Orme Wilkinson (1907–), judge. Wilberforce returned to the Bar in 1947, following war service, and specialized in commercial and civil rights cases, aviation, and international law. He was a High Court judge, Chancery division, 1961–4, and a lord of appeal in ordinary, 1964–82. Much used by government, he chaired the inquiry which in 1972 awarded the miners a generous pay settlement and humiliated the Heath government. *JAR*

Wilberforce inquiry (1972). Lord *Wilberforce had awarded a generous settlement to power workers in 1971. In 1972, with power supplies badly hit by the miners' strike, the Heath government turned to him again. His report, prepared in three days, was described by *The Times* as 'like a printed version of the arguments used by NUM leaders over the past six weeks'. The latter, however, still managed to extract further fringe benefits, which would cost £10 million to implement, before the dispute was called off. *PPC*

Wilkinson, Ellen Cicely (1891–1947), Labour politician. Ellen Wilkinson was one of Britain's most important female politicians, and one of the first women cabinet ministers. Born in Manchester into a respectable working-class family, she was raised as a Methodist, worked her way through school, and won a scholarship to the University of Manchester in 1910, where she obtained an honours degree and an MA. At university she joined the Fabian Society and was active in the University Socialist Federation. During these early years she gained a reputation for being a fiery personality, nicknamed 'Red Ellen', was active in the National Union of Women's Suffrage Societies, and in 1915 became national organizer of the Amalgamated Union of Cooperative Employees. She rose quickly in politics, becoming a Labour councillor in Manchester in 1923; MP for Middlesbrough, 1924–31; and for Jarrow, 1935–47. In 1936 she helped organize the *Jarrow march to bring unemployment in her constituency to national attention. She held several ministerial posts during the Second World War and became Attlee's minister of education in August 1945, a post she held until her death. *KL*

B. D. Vernon, *Ellen Wilkinson* (Manchester, 1982).

Williams, David James (1897–1972), trade unionist and Labour politician. He had worked as a coal miner, miners' agent, and checkweigher, and had attended the central Labour college prior to his election as the Labour MP for the Neath division of Glamorgan at a by-election in May 1945. A native Welsh speaker, Williams regularly participated in Welsh day debates and spoke often and authoritatively in the Commons on the problems besetting the coal industry in south Wales. He was a member of the miners' delegation to Russia. He was re-elected with large majorities until he resolved to retire from parliament in 1964. *JGJ*

Williams, Evan (1871–1959), coalowner. Educated at Christ College, Brecon, and Clare College, Cambridge, in 1892 Williams joined his father's Carmarthenshire-based coal company. In 1913 he was elected chairman of the South Wales and Monmouthshire Coalowners' Association, and served as a member of the 1919 Sankey coal commission. Sir Evan Williams, elected president of the Mining Association of Great Britain in 1919, was a prominent figure in the industrial troubles of 1919–21 and 1925–6. He was a skilled negotiator who succeeded in securing regional pay scales and hours of work. *JGJ*

Williams, Francis (1903–70), author, journalist, historian. Born in Middleton, Williams left the local grammar school for a career in journalism. At the age of 33 he became editor of the **Daily Herald*, and during the Second World War he was controller of news and censorship at the Ministry of Information (1941–5). After the war he became Prime Minister Attlee's press adviser and in 1950 wrote *Fifty Years March*, an official history of the Labour Party to mark its 50th anniversary. He also later assisted Attlee with his memoirs *As It Happened.* In 1962 he was made a life peer, taking the title Lord Francis-Williams. He wrote a number of novels and books on the press, as well as making television programmes. He came to represent, along with men Like Percy Cudlipp and William Connor, an observer of Britain in the decades that crossed the Second World War and beyond from a solid Labour Party perspective. *SB*

Williams, Marcia Matilda (1932–), prime minister's political secretary, 1964–70 and 1974–6. Harold Wilson's private and political secretary throughout 1956–83, Williams's influence on the prime minister, as the most prominent member of his 'kitchen cabinet', was a recurring source of criticism. Her appointment to head the newly established political office at Downing Street in 1964 led to her territorial struggles with officials (particularly Derek Mitchell). Her influence on policy was probably overestimated by her contemporaries and understated by her and Wilson. Her role was primarily that of confidante and socialist conscience, keeping him in touch with party feeling and able to say frankly that which others could not. From 1969 this position was increasingly usurped by Joe Haines and, after 1974, Bernard Donoughue. Attacks on Wilson's ennoblement of her as Lady Falkender (1974) and unsubstantiated allegations that she drew up his resignation honours list (1976) provided a characteristic coda to a controversial career. *CL*

MARCIA WILLIAMS, *Inside Number Ten* (London, 1972). | LADY FALKENDER, *Downing Street in Perspective* (London, 1983).

Williams, Shirley Vivien Teresa Brittain (1930–), Labour and Social Democrat politician. Daughter of the prominent feminist Vera Brittain (1896–1970), Shirley Williams was married first to the philosopher Bernard Williams and later to the American political scientist Richard Neustadt. She had been general secretary of the *Fabian Society, 1960–4; was a popular Labour MP, 1964–79; held several junior posts in the later 1960s; and reached Wilson's cabinet as secretary for prices and consumer protection, 1974–6. As secretary for education, 1976–9, she continued the process of requiring local authorities to introduce *comprehensive schools, but also began initiatives later followed up in the Thatcher period, towards more traditional teaching methods. A staunch Labour moderate and pro-European, she perhaps tried too hard to retain her broader party credentials, for example in joining the *Grunwick picket line while a cabinet minister, but her defeat at Stevenage was an emotional moment on election night in 1979, and generally viewed as a great loss to parliament. In opposition, Williams found herself increasingly out of step with Michael *Foot's Labour Party and naturally gravitated to the *'Gang of Four' which launched in 1981 first the Council for *Social Democracy and then the *Social Democratic Party (SDP). Her finest moment then came with the *Crosby by-election, in November 1981, when she stormed a safe Tory seat on Merseyside, becoming the SDP's first elected MP (all the others had defected from other parties) and seemingly showing that the *Alliance could sweep the country. The sequel was, though, disappointment for the Alliance and her own ousting at Crosby in the 1983 general election eighteen months later. She was president of the SDP, 1982–8, a supporter for merger with the Liberals, and subsequently a Liberal Democrat peer. *JAR*

Williams, Thomas (1888–1967), miners' official and Labour politician. The seventh son

and one of the fourteen children of a coalminer, Tom Williams was elected MP for the Don Valley in 1922, a constituency he represented for 37 years during which time he specialized in agricultural issues. He was minister of agriculture, 1945–51, under Attlee who, in a foreword to Williams's autobiography (*Digging for Britain*, 8), claimed his 'place in history is assured as the greatest British Minister of Agriculture of all time'.
DEM

Lord Williams of Barnburgh, *Digging for Britain* (London, 1965).

Williamson, Thomas (1897–1983), trade union leader. As general secretary of the National Union of General and Municipal Workers, 1946–61, he was an influential right-winger on both the TUC general council and the Labour Party NEC. A Labour MP, 1945–8, Tom Williamson was an active supporter of Hugh Gaitskell in the 1955 leadership contest. On retirement from union office he was created a life peer in 1962 and pursued a number of charitable and business interests.
DEM

Hugh Armstrong Clegg, *A History of British Trade Unions since 1889*, 3. *1934–1951* (Oxford, 1994).

Willink, Henry Urmston (1894–1973), lawyer, politician, and administrator. After a legal career, Willink won the 1940 Croydon North by-election and succeeded in retaining his seat in 1945. He became commissioner for rehousing in London in 1940 and minister of health, 1943–5. Whilst in opposition, 1945–8, he was responsible for shadowing Aneurin Bevan, but found it too difficult to combine opposition politics and the law and abandoned both in 1948 to become master of Magdalene College, Cambridge (see also Willink report).
NJC

Willink report (1962) into the police, set up by Rab Butler as home secretary, to defuse a political row over the Metropolitan Police's decision to settle a wrongful imprisonment case out of court in order to avoid embarrassment. The ensuing royal commission, chaired by a former Conservative cabinet minister, ranged widely over all aspects of the police's relations with the public. Among the commission's recommendations which were implemented was the legalization of betting on licensed betting-shop premises, the police's previous efforts to stamp out illegal street betting having proved fruitless and unpopular.
JAR

Wilmot, John (1893–1964), Labour politician. Wilmot turned a Conservative majority of 14,000 into a Labour majority of 5,000 at *East Fulham in 1933. The result shocked the National Government and was widely reported as an indication of pacifism. He used the Conservative candidate's call for rearmament against him, though the economic situation clearly also played a significant role. He lost the seat in 1935 but returned to the Commons in 1939 and served as minister of supply in the Attlee government until 1947, when he was dropped from the administration because of an antipathy to Cripps.
BB

Wilson, Des (1941–), Liberal activist. A New Zealander, Wilson became a prominent campaigner for a range of causes in Britain, including homelessness, the environment, and freedom of information. He served as president of the Liberal Party, 1986–7, and general election campaign director in 1992, but left active politics after the 1992 election.
JS

Wilson, Gordon (1938–), the father of Marie Wilson, a nurse killed in the IRA explosion at the cenotaph at Enniskillen, Co. Fermanagh, on 8 November 1987. A Methodist preacher, he impressed many by his Christian charity and forgiveness of his daughter's murderers, and was subsequently nominated to the Irish senate.
BMW

Alf McCreary, *Gordon Wilson* (Belfast, 1996).

Wilson, (James) Harold (1916–95), Labour prime minister. Wilson came from a lower middle-class family, and was profoundly influenced by the unemployment of his father, an industrial chemist in the 1930s and by the Nonconformist radicalism of his grandfather. It was this combination which pushed him towards the left in his prodigiously successful early academic career. The key to his prowess at Oxford was his amazing memory, a facility which, combined with a driving ambition rooted in part at least in social insecurity, carried him from research assistant to William Beveridge to president of the Board of Trade in a decade. His rapid rise did not give him deep roots in the Labour Party—he might just as easily have been a Liberal—and he attached himself to the champion of the left, Aneurin Bevan, in part out of genuine awe of the Welshman, in part to fill out the ideological gaps in his CV. When Bevan resigned from the government over the imposition of charges on teeth and spectacles in 1951, Wilson resigned with him. Thereafter he became a *Bevanite, though he was never socially or emotionally close to Bevan's intimate followers like Michael Foot. Having firmly established his credentials as a left-winger through the symbolic act of resignation, Wilson then resumed his rise by replacing Bevan on the shadow cabinet when the latter resigned in 1954. Such actions contributed to his reputation for blind ambition but also balanced the need to appear loyal, a virtue for the majority of the Parliamentary Labour Party, with the need to appear left of centre, a necessity, according to Attlee, in being leader of the Labour Party. Bevan died in 1960 and Wilson slipped into the position of leader of the left, indeed, their only credible candidate. When Gaitskell died in 1963, Wilson easily defeated a split right-wing vote to become leader.

The period from Wilson's election as leader of the party to the election of 1966 was the most successful of his career at the top of British politics. In a brilliant performance as leader of the opposition, Wilson positioned Labour as the party of the future. He turned a Conservative majority of 100 over all other parties into a Labour majority of four in 1964. But though the Conservative vote was lower than in 1959, the Labour vote also went down slightly and the final victory was much narrower than many had supposed it would be when the election had been called. Thus the new Labour government was beset with uncertainty from the start and a mix of high expectations from a pro-Labour intelligentsia and a party hungry for power after over a decade of opposition, made Wilson's task almost impossible. That he raised his majority from four to 96 at the 1966 election is testament to his presentational skill. That the government was almost immediately plunged into an economic crisis from which it never properly recovered until late 1969 is testament to his political weakness. As many have commented, Wilson's key mistake was not to devalue the pound in 1964. For a first-class economist like Wilson the case should have been unanswerable but, though the economic timing was right, the political timing was wrong. Given the result in 1966 it is difficult to challenge Wilson's political decision. The failure to devalue, though, caused a series of balance-of-payments problems which in turn created an image of crisis that plagued the remainder of the administration and is still attached to the era. Wilson's prime ministerial style also contributed to this air of chaos. He had been offered a job as a leader writer after graduating and he remained obsessed with the press for the rest of his life.

Wilson was also obsessed with the Gaitskellites and his supposed enemies within. Cabinet under Wilson was consensual but it also gave rise to Wilson's bouts of paranoia about leaks. Rather than trying to control the press by setting the news agenda, Wilson and his private office were constantly being reactive—and thus usually appeared to be dictated to by the day's headlines. When devaluation finally came in 1967, it had all the appearance of being forced on the government rather than being implemented through choice, and Wilson's own 'pound in your pocket' broadcast did not help much. The final crisis of the 1964–70 government exhibited all Wilson's weaknesses. Barbara Castle introduced a trade union reform white paper, *In Place of Strife*, designed to reduce industrial tension by legally controlling trade unions. It was bitterly opposed by the TUC and by some in the cabinet because it proposed reintroducing legal penalties into industrial disputes. Wilson neither supported the measure sufficiently to see it through to legislation, nor blocked it early enough to prevent a climbdown causing damage to the government. Instead, he allowed Castle to launch the white paper and was then relieved when it had to be dropped because of opposition. A similar, though more successful, fence-sitting by him during the debate on entry to the European Community (EC) in 1973 and during the referendum campaign of 1975, helped keep the Labour Party together.

Labour's victory in February 1974 was a little unexpected and the 1974–6 period of Wilson's second premiership was altogether more politically assured though less successful in policy terms. The period was dominated by the EC, towards which Wilson was intellectually ambivalent but emotionally opposed. He was anyway now exhausted and began to tell people, according to one biographer, 'that he had seen it all before, that when he saw old problems coming round, all he could think of was the old solutions' (Pimlott, 648). He had long ago decided to retire at 60, so there is no mystery about the decision, and he did so in 1976, though his actual going was disfigured by some unsavoury revelations about the award of honours.

Few prime ministers have disappeared from public consciousness as quickly as Wilson, swamped by the tide of Thatcherism and the division of his own party. Wilson's reputation declined steadily until the earlier 1990s, when a series of new biographies began a process of re-evaluation which continues. For Labour supporters, the era of Harold Wilson (1963–76) gets better with distance because many economic indicators, such as the level of unemployment, inflation, and the gap between the rich and the poor, reflected a more egalitarian and less free market economy. For opponents, the insularity of the British economy, its failure to modernize, and the way in which Wilson clung to outmoded collectivism and tripartism, in the face of rampant inflation and a collapse in manufacturing competitiveness, will for ever condemn these years as the age of British decline. But Wilson's personal stock continues to rise and the achievements with which he was most personally associated, the creation of the Open University for example, will stand as lasting achievements alongside the liberal moral legislation that he allowed to be passed during his first administration.

His contribution to the Labour Party was twofold: power and unity. He won four out the five general elections that he fought as leader and gave Labour half the years in office it has enjoyed in the century of its history to date. If the purpose of the Labour Party, as a democratic political party, was to gain and hold power, then Wilson's record must be judged favourably. He also did these things while keeping the party unified, and within five years of his retirement the party had split with the Social Democratic Party schism. However, his most significant legacy and the quality which marks him out from his successors was his ability to govern consensually through cabinet and maintain collective responsibility. At the time many criticized him for not running a 'command premiership'. After twenty years of politics dominated by such a style and the permanent change in the constitutional balance between the executive and the civil service on the one hand and the legislature on the other, Wilson's form of cabinet government is increasingly lauded as more democratic. Labour's longest-serving prime minister to date may well therefore be remembered longer for his style of government than for what those governments achieved. *BB*

Ben Pimlott, *Harold Wilson* (London, 1992). | Philip Ziegler, *Harold Wilson* (London, 1993).

Wilson, Henry Hughes (1854–1922), Anglo-Irish general and politician. Wilson was a brilliant staff officer who, under Lloyd George's patronage, rose to be chief of the imperial general staff, 1918–22. His strong Unionist sympathies contributed to a reputation for political intrigue, especially at the time of the *Curragh 'mutiny'. In 1922 he became chief security adviser to the new Northern Ireland government and was elected an MP for North Down, but he survived only five months before being assassinated by the IRA outside his home in London. *KJ*

C. E. Callwell, *Field Marshal Sir Henry Wilson*, 2 vols. (London, 1927).

Wilson, Horace (1882–1972), civil servant. Wilson's career took him from a humble background and state elementary school, through employment as a boy clerk in the Patent Office in 1898 and promotion to the executive ranks ('second division') of the civil service in 1900 (studying for a degree from the LSE as a 'night school student'), to the rank of permanent secretary, the headship of the civil service, and a controversial role as a prime ministerial adviser and confidant. His breakthrough to the top levels of Whitehall came in the Ministry of Labour during the Great War, Wilson making his mark in industrial relations and arbitration and becoming permanent secretary of that department in 1921. He was an influential government adviser during the 1926 General Strike. In 1930 Wilson was appointed chief industrial adviser to the government, and he played an important part in the preparation of the 1932 Ottawa tariff agreement. From 1935 to 1937 he was a personal adviser to Prime Minister Baldwin, playing a key role in the abdication crisis. Kept on by Neville Chamberlain, Wilson became that premier's right-hand man and centrally involved in the policy of appeasement—in a damagingly high-profile fashion for a career civil servant. Appointed permanent secretary to the Treasury and head of the home civil service in 1939, Wilson was effectively sidelined in the Churchill regime and retired in 1942. *KT*

Wilson, Leslie Orme (1876–1955), Conservative chief whip. After a distinguished military career, Wilson entered parliament in 1913. He served heroically when recalled to the colours during the Great War, returned to the House in 1918, and held junior office in the Lloyd George coalition. Wilson became chief whip in 1921, but split from his own leader, Austen Chamberlain, and supported Law and the backbench revolt against the coalition at the *Carlton Club meeting of October 1922. Thereafter he lost his parliamentary seat and his career. *RJQA*

Wilson, Richard Thomas James (1942–), civil servant. Wilson served in the Board of Trade and the Department of Energy, and was a senior Cabinet Office and Treasury official, before becoming permanent secretary at the Department of the Environment (1992–4) and the Home Office (1994–7). Picked by Tony Blair to be cabinet secretary and head of the civil service from January 1998, he was a reformer and in tune with Blair's own approach, reorganizing the Cabinet Office, strengthening the centre of Whitehall, and emphasizing the importance of better implementation of policies and 'joined-up' government. *KT*

Windlesham, 3rd Lord (1932–), Conservative politician. A leading light in the *Bow Group, Windlesham entered the Lords in 1962 after succeeding his father and published in 1966 an informed commentary on changing political campaign methods, *Communication and Political Power.* In Heath's administration, he was a minister at the Home Office and in Northern Ireland before becoming leader of the Lords and lord privy seal in 1973. After 1974, he resumed his career as a broadcasting executive and author on the media, politics, and responses to crime. He chaired the Parole Board, 1982–8. *RJS*

'winds of change' speech (3 February 1960), made by Harold Macmillan in the *South African parliament in Capetown. He warned the white-supremacist South African government that 'the wind of change is blowing through this continent'. The speech attacked the South African government's policy of apartheid and urged South Africans to take heed of individual rights and create a society based on equality. Although the speech created a stir outside South Africa, inside the white regime remained unmoved. *KTS*

Alistair Home, *Macmillan 1957–1986* (London, 1989).

'winter of discontent' (1978/9) was the media name for the industrial difficulties at the end of the Callaghan government. Callaghan's decision not to call a general election for October 1978 proved a disaster. After years of rapid inflation and pay restraint, public service unions struck that winter for high wage claims. Hospital emergency rooms closed, city rubbish piled up rotting and uncollected, and even the dead remained unburied. This was the definitive moment which finally discredited old Labour. The following May, the party lost heavily at the polls and was in opposition 1979–97, during which time unions lost much power. *PRGR*

Winterton, Lord (1883–1962), Conservative politician. As an Irish peer Eddie Winterton had no seat in the Lords and so was able to represent Horsham as MP, 1904–51. With a reputation as a diehard and a belligerent debating style, he was in the vanguard of his party's resistance to the Liberal reforms of 1906–14 and wartime coalitions. In 1922–9 he was under-secretary for India, but later opposed the 1935 Government of India bill (see India). Brought back to ministerial office to curb his potential for criticism from the backbenches, his inept performance during a debate on the air estimates in May 1938 stunted his ministerial career. *NJC*

Wintringham, Thomas Henry (1898–1949), socialist activist. Tom Wintringham's politics have been described as 'Socialism in the English tradition' (J. M. Bellamy and J. Saville (eds.), *Dictionary of Labour Biography*, vol. 7 (London, 1984), 263). The Communist Party captured his initial interest, but his experiences in the Spanish civil war, 'Two bullets and typhoid', ended that link. He then attached himself to the Common Wealth Party and stood as a parliamentary candidate in 1943 and 1945. He was one of the few socialists to become a recognized authority on military matters and assumed an important role in the Home Guard in the Second World War. *CH*

T. Wintringham, *English Captain* (London, 1939). | T. Wintringham, *The People's War* (Harmondsworth, 1942).

Wiseman, William George Eden (1885–1962), banker and intelligence officer. Head of station in New York from 1915 for MI1c, the British overseas secret service, he became a close friend of President Woodrow Wilson and an important channel for Anglo-American relations in 1917–18, enjoying remarkable access to American sources. He was chief British delegation adviser on America at the Paris peace conference in 1918–19 but lost his influence with Wilson, joining the bankers Kuhn, Loeb and Co in 1921. *AS*

Wolfenden report. See homosexuality.

Wolfson, David (1935–), chief of staff, Downing Street political office, 1979–85. The director of a mail order firm, Wolfson helped the Conservative Party deal with its mailings in the mid-1970s, before advising Margaret Thatcher on more weighty matters in opposition. He was secretary to the shadow cabinet, 1978–9. He acted as an unpaid confidant, emissary, and adviser in Downing Street, identifying policy priorities, supporting the views of John Hoskyns's policy unit, and ensuring that it had the prime minister's ear. *CL*

Wolmer, Viscount. See Selborne, 3rd earl of.

women in British politics. Until 1918, British women did not have the vote for parliamentary elections and could not be elected to parliament, so in that formal sense women's political careers could begin only after the 1918 Representation of the People Act. In practice, though, many women had been politically active in earlier generations, as part of the vibrant street culture that surrounded elections before 1832, as local government electors and with more direct involvement in such representative bodies as school boards, as the wives and daughters of politicians who expected them to play their parts as hostess (in some cases very actively in the grander Edwardian political salons and country houses), and as feminist campaigners for the suffrage. On an individual basis, a remarkable woman like Beatrice Webb had shown long before 1914 that she could be influential personally (through friendships with Joseph Chamberlain and Arthur Balfour) and by writing, in combination with her husband Sidney Webb and through the Fabian Society.

The year 1918 did, however, mark a milestone (see FRANCHISE), for women were now more directly involved in all the political processes, and on a legally equal basis from 1928 (from whence they were and remained the majority of the British electorate). Political parties therefore sought to recruit women as political activists, to appeal to women voters at elections, and to decide on their attitudes to women as MPs and in leading party posts. On the first count, the Conservatives were quicker off the mark, perhaps because they had more prior experience through the mass-involvement of women as 'dames' of the Primrose League, founded in memory of Disraeli in the 1880s and in effect a Conservative front organization, a well-oiled machine for electoral persuasion. During the 1920s, the Conservatives welcomed thousands of women formally into their party organizations at the local level, and women soon became in fact the party's major local workers and fund-raisers. In terms of electoral appeal, most male politicians were nervous of women voters in the 1920s, especially of the 'flapper vote', the 21–30-year-old women enfranchised only in 1928. All parties tended to emphasize family, and children's issues figured in leaflets and posters more than before 1914; once again, the Conservatives were the most energetic and innovative. In the absence of reliable information, it is impossible to know how women voted in these first decades, but the folklore of the party agents suggests that they did not vote very differently from men—which, if true, is hardly surprising, given the fact that most interwar debates were about economic issues on which women were not likely to have a separate collective opinion. In terms of candidacies and elections, the record was unimpressive. There were seventeen women candidates in 1918, only one of whom was elected (and she, being a Sinn Fein candidate, did not take her seat anyway). Not until 1919, when the idiosyncratic Nancy Astor was elected as Conservative MP for Plymouth (in effect inheriting her husband's seat when he went to the Lords), did a woman sit in parliament. Thereafter the number of women candidates rose, to about 65 in each of the last three elections before the Second World War, though fifteen MPs in 1931 was the largest number ever elected (and this was largely the result of the Tories winning so many seats in that landslide year, for women rarely got picked for winnable seats).

Things did not improve much after 1945 for, although the number of female candidacies averaged about 90 in the general elections of the 1950s and 1960s, the number elected only fluctuated at around 25, the 29 women MPs of 1964 being the highest figure for this period. Most women MPs sat on the Labour side, and it was also Labour that first provided for women to enter the cabinet: Margaret Bondfield in 1929–31, Ellen Wilkinson in 1945–7. The Conservatives followed suit with Florence Horsbrugh, 1953–4 (though it was noticeable that Wilkinson and Horsbrugh both held the education portfolio, often said to be a 'woman's job' anyway, because it involved children). The Conservatives' reluctance to give more political prominence to its women supporters is at first sight puzzling, for the opinion polls that began to be published from the 1940s found a steady pattern of differential behaviour; in almost every poll, women were more pro-Conservative than men. The explanation of the paradox seems to be that the women who were by now coming to occupy important positions at all levels of the party organization put their Conservatism before their gender when helping to select candidates (and most Conservatives still saw the woman's place as in the home). Even the undeniably talented Margaret Thatcher was turned down again and again, sometimes in favour of rather obscure male alternatives, by Tory selection committees, and when she entered the Commons in 1959 she too was appointed to 'women's jobs' at pensions and education. When she became Conservative leader in 1975, the first woman to occupy such a role in Britain (and still one of the first in the world), the Conservative MPs who elected her were exhilarated by the extreme radicalism of their choice. For years her male colleagues treated her with elaborate courtesy (much to their own later discomfiture in some cases), and much of the press comment centred on 'the woman question' (largely an excuse to discuss her clothes, her voice, her housekeeping, and her hairstyle).

By the time that Thatcher became prime minister in 1979, Labour had taken further steps towards the promotion of women, not only by running more women candidates and getting more MPs elected, but also by demonstrating in the careers of cabinet ministers like Barbara Castle (transport, employment, health), and Shirley Williams (prices), that women could now occupy with distinction any type of post (though even in 2000 no woman had yet held the exchequer, foreign, defence, or home offices). Thatcher herself was not at all inclined to promote women from among her backbenchers, the only other woman who sat in her cabinet coming from outside national politics with a peerage. Interestingly, Thatcher alone among Conservative leaders seems to have forfeited the favourable position among women voters enjoyed by her Conservative predecessors and successors; but then she was, as it was often said of her cabinet, 'the best man amongst them'. It could then easily be said in the 1980s about politics, as about business and the professions, that women still met a 'glass ceiling', an invisible wall of prejudicial assumptions (that even other women had come to share), and which prevented them from rising as far, or in equivalent numbers, as men.

By the last quarter of the century, however, the women's movement itself had become more insistent about the need for affirmative action of some kind to break that ceiling, and the success of women in other careers was already making politicians seem unduly backward in this regard. Campaigns and publications such as Elizabeth Vallance's *Women in the House* began at last to change awareness. The shift of attitude was mainly on the left, which was not winning many parliamentary seats in the heyday of Thatcher, but Labour's tally of women MPs did go up from 21 in 1979 to 37 in 1992. Shortly afterwards, the party adopted drastic measures to guarantee more women candidates in winnable seats, by insisting that some marginals drew up shortlists containing only women. That practice was subsequently declared illegal by the courts, but by then many selections had taken place, and Labour's landslide victory in 1997 was therefore marked too by a dramatic increase in the number of women MPs: there were 120 female MPs, 101 of them on the Labour benches, but their christening as 'Blair's Babes' by the media suggested that trivializing women's role in politics was far from a thing of the past. The shift was marked too in Tony Blair's appointment of more women to senior positions with seven in the cabinet by 2001. The century ended with women finally getting perhaps halfway towards an equal and fair share of political power. *JAR*

Christina Baron et al., *Fair Shares in Parliament, or how to elect more women MPs* (London, 1981). | Pamela Brookes, *Women at Westminster* (London, 1976). | Elizabeth Vallance, *Women in the House* (London, 1979).

Women's Freedom League (WFL), feminist group which split off from the *Women's Social and Political Union in 1907, following the transfer of its headquarters to London and in protest at the tight control over its activities exercised by the *Pankhurst Family. Under the presidency of Charlotte Despard, the WFL developed a more democratic structure and moved back towards the socialist and radical approaches to politics that the WSPU had shed in its efforts to woo 'respectable' opinion. Not sharing the WSPU's relatively narrow focus on the franchise, the WFL campaigned for 'full equality for men and women in every branch of our national and international life' and remained active long after the vote was won on equal terms in 1928. During the Second World War, it lobbied hard for *equal pay, and for similar issues relating to economic equality. Outflanked, though, by a younger generation of more radical feminists, the WFL was wound up in 1961. *JAR*

women's property rights were enhanced by legislation in 1882 and 1884 which allowed married women to own and administer their own property and gave them an independent legal status distinct from that of their husbands. In 1925, the Married Women's Property Act required husbands and wives to be treated as separate individuals in property transactions. *JS*

Women's Social and Political Union (WSPU), feminist organization, the most high-profile of the Edwardian groups that campaigned for the franchise for women. It was formed in 1903 in Manchester, largely on the initiative of the *Pankhurst family, whose members kept it under tight personal control. It was initially intended to combine a militant campaign for women's voting rights with a broader radical political platform, but its leaders soon fell out with the Labour movement, many of whose trade unionists at least were lukewarm on their main objective, and concentrated instead on direct action to win over elite opinion on their single issue. So, for example, campaigners interrupted election meetings in 1906 with 'votes for women' chants and banners and, following the Liberals' victory in that election, the party found itself the prime objective of WSPU attacks, which were concentrated on persuading the government to take up their cause.

Between 1906 and the outbreak of war in 1914, thousands of outdoor meetings were held, government candidates were harried at by-elections, while window-breaking and other street protests, and even cases of arson, took place, raising the emotional mood of the debate to very high levels. When protesters were gaoled, they gained the status of martyrs, some adding to the fury of their supporters by going on hunger strikes to protest at their detention; this effectively forced the government into sanctioning forced feeding rather than risk the greater danger of women dying in custody, passing the 'Cat and Mouse Act' (more correctly the Prisoners (Temporary Provisions for Discharge) Act) of 1913, whereby prisoners could be released if in danger of starvation but rearrested when their health recovered—as a cat might play with a mouse. The WSPU coordinated and encouraged such activities in a highly disciplined manner, making up in determination and discipline indeed for its relatively small numbers. Increasingly, however, the WSPU itself was criticized as overcentralized and too dependent on the personal whims of the Pankhursts, and factions began to secede, notably the *Women's Freedom League, though in due course Sylvia Pankhurst also left in the quest for working-class women's support in East London (a drift to the left that was to take her in due course into the Communist Party). When war came in 1914, the WSPU called off its campaign and rallied behind the war effort, helped to recruit women for munitions factories, and called insistently for women's wartime work to be recognized. The popular mythology of a heroic struggle long attributed the gaining of the vote for the majority of women in 1918 to the success of the WSPU's tactics of militancy to attract attention in peacetime and responsibility when the nation was threatened. But this view can now be seen to be flawed in two ways, or at least only a partial explanation for the women's movement's success in its battle for the franchise. First, it is at least possible that the long campaign of militancy actually delayed rather than hastened the winning of the vote, for it certainly irritated many potential MP-supporters who were reluctant to grant under coercion rights that they were beginning to see as inevitable in the near future (it irritated moderate feminists in much the same way, and hence split the movement). Second, most research into the suffragette movement until recently was only into the work of the WSPU, and this naturally helped to support the heroic myth that it was the vanguard of the overall campaign. More recent writing has, however, pointed to the less spectacular work, on wider issues of women's rights as well as the franchise, done by other campaigning organizations, which have generally been denied any recognition. *JAR*

SANDRA HOLTON, *Feminism and Democracy: Women's Suffrage and Reform Politics in Britain, 1900–1918* (Cambridge, 1986).

Wood, Edward Frederick Lindley (1881–1959), Conservative politician, minister, colonial administrator, and diplomat. Elected to parliament in 1910, Wood retained the Ripon seat until his elevation to the Lords in 1925. His first appointment was as a junior minister at colonies, but he distrusted Lloyd George and consequently voted to end the coalition in 1922. Law promoted him to the cabinet, but his opening years at education, 1922–3, and agriculture, 1924–5, were relatively unsuccessful, with Wood finding neither department to his personal taste. In 1925 he was appointed (as Lord Irwin) governor-general and viceroy of India, a post he retained for five years. He strove to end intercommunal tensions, arguing that this was a necessary precursor for any viceroy to consider the possibility of Indian self-government. In response to the Simon commission Irwin proposed a *Round Table conference to include all sides of the issue and personally suggested granting India dominion status. This provoked outrage from former colleagues in London, most notably Churchill, Birkenhead, and Reading. In an attempt to seek a compromise solution to the escalating violence, he ordered the release of Gandhi from prison and met him on eight occasions. Nevertheless, upon his return to London in 1931 his attempts at compromise appeared to have yielded little. Although agreeing to return to the education ministry, he accepted it only in order to assist Samuel Hoare in drafting the India bill. In 1935 he spent a brief few months as secretary of state for war, and thereafter he held a series of posts without departmental responsibilities, which enabled him increasingly to concentrate on foreign affairs, and on occasions of Eden's absence deputized at the Foreign Office. In November 1937, Halifax (the title he inherited in 1934) was invited to Germany, ostensibly in his capacity as a master of the Middleton foxhounds, although in reality to meet with the German leadership. Despite nearly mistaking Hitler for a footman, Halifax returned, believing he had gone some way to defining Germany's grievances. When Eden resigned in February 1938, Halifax was the automatic choice to succeed him. Because Halifax sat in the Lords, this left the explanation of foreign affairs in the Commons to the prime minister. Both Halifax and Chamberlain held a similar perspective of the threat from the dictators, believing that the Nazis were capable of reason and persuasion. However, any idea that Halifax was not his own man should be dismissed. He increasingly proved during the *Munich crisis, and later on in 1939, that he knew his own mind and would seek to impose this upon Chamberlain. With the outbreak of war in 1939, Halifax remained at the Foreign Office, concentrating upon persuading neutral nations to support the allied cause (or at least withhold assistance from Germany). Many Conservatives would have liked Halifax to succeed as premier in May 1940, but he himself was appalled at the prospect and concerned that no unified war effort could be led from the Lords. He thus supported Churchill's appointment, but for a time continued to support peacemaking initiatives from inside the war cabinet. From December 1940 until 1946, Halifax was British ambassador in Washington, where he concentrated his efforts, successfully so after a sticky start, on cementing Anglo-American relations. *NJC*

Lord Halifax, *Fulness of Days* (London, 1957). | Andrew Roberts, *Holy Fox: A Biography of Lord Halifax* (London, 1990).

Wood, Kingsley (1881–1943), Conservative politician and prominent Methodist. After a career in municipal politics, Wood was elected in 1918 to represent West Woolwich. His major opportunity came when he served under Neville Chamberlain at the Ministry of Health, 1924–9, where he gained his minister's respect and friendship. In 1930 he was elected chairman of the party's *National Union of Conservative and Unionist Associations. As postmaster general, 1932–5, he initiated an overhaul of the Post Office which included implementing such publicity campaigns to attract more custom as using cinema films to encourage use of the telephone. These skills in propaganda were recognized by appointing Wood to chair the party propaganda committee set up in general election year 1935. In 1933 Wood was elevated to cabinet, and in 1935 took over the Ministry of Health. As a consequence of his publicity skills, Wood was a 'recognizable' figure in the government and in some circles talked of as a future Conservative leader. In May 1938 Wood moved to the Air Ministry. In many respects he was lucky to inherit schemes inaugurated by his predecessors which made his tenure at this critical time slightly easier. He advised Chamberlain to resign in May 1940, and Churchill then moved him to the Treasury where he introduced the PAYE scheme, provided Keynes with an advisory role, and introduced Britain's first *Keynesian budget. *NJC*

Woodburn, Arthur (1890–1978), Labour politician. Arthur Woodburn was secretary of the Scottish council of the Labour Party, 1931–9, rebuilding party organization after the secession of the Independent Labour Party. Elected to parliament in 1939, he became secretary of state for Scotland in 1947 and was soon in confrontation with the Scottish Convention movement led by John MacCormick. Attacks by home rulers, and MacCormick's candidature in the 1948 Paisley by-election with Liberal and Conservative support, confirmed Woodburn's hostility to devolution. In 1950 he was replaced by Hector McNeil. *MJK*

Woodcock, George (1904–79), TUC leader. Woodcock's quiet, patient, and courteous manner hid the sharp mind that had won him prizes and a first at Oxford, following the traditional Labour movement route through Ruskin College. After a brief period in the civil service, he joined the TUC's small staff in 1934, and stayed there for the rest of his working life, becoming assistant general secretary to Walter *Citrine in 1947, and general secretary himself, 1960–9. Woodcock had to lead a trade union movement whose centre of gravity was shifting to the left, where the TUC leadership had few powers except to cajole and persuade, and in a decade in which governments and the media were increasingly coming to the conclusion that the trade unions could not be left to self-regulation. Woodcock himself did much to hold back the drift towards trade-union battles with government, through persuading the unions to accept control of prices and incomes, in his membership of the 1965–8 royal commission on the trade unions (which he had persuaded Wilson to set up, and which he steered towards non-interventionist recommendations), and by his own effective but deliberately unspectacular leadership of the TUC in a moderate direction. He was powerless, however, to prevent the confrontation between Wilson's Labour government and the unions over

Barbara Castle's *In Place of Strife* proposals of 1968–9 (on which the government ignored his advice). But once the government had been headed off he characteristically brokered the deal that enabled it to retreat with a few shreds of credibility intact, clutching the TUC's *Programme for Action.* Woodcock was probably lucky to have retired before the Heath government was elected in 1970, ushering in fifteen years of extremely heated industrial relations. Wilson had made him in 1969 the first chairman of the commission on industrial relations, a post from which he resigned in 1971 rather than accept its transformation by the Heath government into a body with legal powers. *JAR*

Woods, John (1895–1962), civil servant. After being severely wounded in the Great War, Woods entered the Treasury in 1920, serving as private secretary to Philip Snowden, Neville Chamberlain, and Sir John Simon in the 1930s. He was an influential permanent secretary, first at the Ministry of Production (1943–5) and then at the Board of Trade (1945–51), where he worked closely with Sir Stafford Cripps and then Harold Wilson, and was concerned to reduce the bureaucratic burden of controls. *KT*

Woodward, John Forster ('Sandy') (1932–), admiral. Woodward was senior task group commander during the *Falklands war, 1982. Given a complex network of command and constant psychological pressure—'only the land forces could win the war, but the Navy could always lose it', remarked his army opposite number—Woodward handled himself throughout with great professionalism, well conveyed, with an almost Alanbrookian blend of irascibility and sensitivity, in his wartime diary and post-war reflections. *AD*

Sandy Woodward, *One Hundred Days* (London, 1992).

Woolton, earl of (1883–1964), businessman and Conservative politician. Frederick Marquis came from humble beginnings in Manchester and, after work in boys' clubs in Liverpool, entered government war service for logistic supplies in 1914. He returned in 1918 to Lewis's department store in Liverpool and worked his way up to become well known nationally as one of the leaders in the distributive trade. When war approached again in 1937, he returned to government, first to reorganize fire brigades, then reviewing civil aviation and the mass-production of uniforms. As director-general of the Ministry of *Supply, he became Lord Woolton in 1939, and in April 1940 Neville Chamberlain gave him cabinet office as the first minister of food, a post retained under Churchill until 1943. In addition to his organizing genius, which greatly assisted the war effort in the supply crisis of the battle of the Atlantic, this posting allowed Woolton to display his communication skills. He was a popular radio broadcaster on food and rationing, demonstrating a populist ability to make people feel their sacrifices were crucial to the war effort: 'Woolton pie' was one initiative intended to alleviate families' shortages through the minister's communicative ingenuity. He was still, though, a businessman-technician rather than a politician, and it was in that neutral capacity that he was minister of reconstruction, 1943–5. When Churchill lost the 1945 election, Woolton's innate anti-socialism prompted him to join the Conservatives the day after their defeat. Within a year he was party chairman, using those formidable skills to bring its membership, its finances, and the effectiveness of its Central Office to their historic zenith in the early 1950s. After Churchill returned to office in 1951, Woolton held non-executive cabinet posts, but his health was now poor. He retired from all government and party posts in 1955. *JAR*

Earl of Woolton, *The Memoirs of the Earl of Woolton* (London, 1959).

Woolton-Teviot pact. See Liberal National Party.

Workers' Educational Association (WEA), adult education movement, founded in 1903 by Albert Mansbridge (1876–1952). Originally called an Association to Promote the Higher Education of Working Men, it changed its name to the WEA in 1905. Linked to the universities, it provided evening classes, often staffed by volunteer university teachers. An extremely influential self-help movement, it has been supported by many leading Labour and left-wing intellectuals such as R. H. *Tawney and E. P. *Thompson. *JS*

Workers' Revolutionary Party (WRP), one of three groups to emerge from the wreckage of the Revolutionary Communist Party in 1947. Originally 'The Club' and from 1958 the Socialist Labour League, the group operated within the Labour Party until 1964. By the early 1970s it had become the largest Trotskyist organization in Britain, boasting the movement's first daily newspaper and some trade union influence, especially at British Leyland's Cowley plant. Convinced of its vanguard status, it adopted the title of Workers' Revolutionary Party in 1973. From the outset the party was characterized by ultra-sectarianism and dominated by its founder Gerry Healey. It displayed all the characteristics of a religious sect, with punishments and beatings for deviation from an almost mantra-like political perspective which predicted the imminent collapse of capitalism and the onset of fascism. In 1974, Healey was confidently predicting a military coup in Britain, but its failure to materialize sparked off a series of rebellions and expulsions which severely weakened the party. Thereafter, it was kept afloat only by wealthy supporters such as Vanessa and Corin Redgrave and by aid from Libya and Iraq. Healey's expulsion in 1985 for alleged sexual misdemeanours caused the WRP to splinter into several competing sects. *MC*

working class. See CLASS-CONSCIOUSNESS; CLASS-VOTING.

World Bank, a group of institutions designed to channel investment funds from capital rich countries to poor countries. The first member of the World Bank Group was the International Bank for Reconstruction and Development (IBRD) created at the *Bretton Woods conference in 1944. It began operations in 1946 and is located in Washington DC. It was initially designed to assist European reconstruction after the Second World War, but once this task was taken over by Marshall aid in 1947, its attention turned to supporting developing countries. Two other institutions were created to provide loans on different terms to the IBRD: the International Development Association (IDA) in 1962 and the International Finance Corporation (IFC) in 1956. The IDA lends to the poorest countries on easier terms than the IBRD, and the IFC promotes private sector development. Together, these three institutions make up the World Bank group. The IBRD initially had authorized capital of $10 billion, subscribed by wealthy members of the UN. As the largest contributor, the USA commands the greatest influence in the decision making of the Bank. The IBRD was authorized to use its resources to help raise private capital for specific infrastructure development projects, by guaranteeing loans, issuing its own securities, and offering technical advice. The constitution of the IBRD requires that it pay due regard to the capacity of borrowers to service their debts. It therefore operates on a quasi-commercial basis rather than as an aid organization. In response to the balance of payments crises of the 1980s the World Bank changed its strategy from lending for specific projects and began increasingly to lend to support general structural adjustment such as tariff reduction, tax reform, and financial market liberalization. These activities now dominate the Bank's business. *CRS*

Worthington-Evans, Laming (1868–1931), Conservative politician. A successful solicitor, he retired in 1910 and devoted the next nineteen years to his parliamentary career, serving in both wartime coalitions and joining Lloyd George's cabinet as war secretary, 1921–2. He was one of the British negotiators who signed the 1921 *Anglo-Irish treaty which created the Irish Free State. At the *Carlton Club meeting, he favoured continued coalition but 'Worthy' was reconciled with his party and served as postmaster general under Baldwin, 1923–4. *RJQA*

Wyatt, Woodrow Lyle (1918–97) illustrates the classic journey from left to right in politics. After Oxford and a 'good war' he was Labour MP for Birmingham Aston, 1945–55, and Bosworth, 1959–70. A keen *Keep Left* journalist, he made his name exposing corruption in the Communist-led Electrical Trade Union in the 1950s. By the time Labour won office again in 1964 he had become a right-winger, and by the 1970s was so infatuated with Thatcherism that he left the party and was made a life peer in 1988. *PRGR*

WOODROW WYATT, *Confessions of an Optimist* (London, 1985).

Wyndham, George (1863–1913), talented Unionist chief secretary for Ireland (appointed in 1900), who fell foul of the ill-fated attempt by his under-secretary Sir Anthony MacDonnell to introduce in 1905 a devolution scheme which would have steered a path between absolute home rulers and absolute Unionists. When the storm broke in February 1905 Wyndham denied that he was aware of the devolution scheme, but there is evidence to show that he had at least indicated sympathy in August and September 1904. Irish Unionists seized the chance to attack the government's Irish record as a whole, which they regarded as soft towards nationalism. Wyndham was forced to resign, his departure marking the end of the policy of 'constructive Unionism' that the Conservative Party had offered in the 1890s. *DGB*

ALVIN JACKSON, *The Ulster Party: Irish Unionists in the House of Commons* (Oxford, 1989). | JOHN BIGGS-DAVISON, *George Wyndham: A Study in Toryism* (London, 1951).

Wyndham, John (1920–72), prime minister's private secretary, 1957–63. Wyndham had been

Harold Macmillan's private secretary in various wartime posts (1940–5) and at the Foreign Office (1955) before joining him at Downing Street. As an unpaid personal appointee to the private office, living on his inherited wealth, Wyndham was a unique, but uncontroversial, figure. He was chiefly concerned with party-political work, but was also involved in the general tasks of the office. Something of a surrogate son, he offered Macmillan humour and companionship. *CL*

Lord Egremont, *Wyndham and Children First* (London, 1968).

Y

Yalta conference (1945), wartime meeting of Churchill, Roosevelt, and Stalin, accompanied by their foreign ministers, held in the Crimea in February 1945. The conference took place against the background of Germany's imminent defeat and with Soviet forces already occupying much of eastern Europe. In the circumstances, Britain, very much diminished within the Grand Alliance, had some reason for satisfaction with the conclusions reached, especially as Roosevelt had rejected any notion of a common Anglo-American front in advance of the conference. The problem with Yalta was less the agreements reached than the fact that some of them were never honoured.

For Britain the key issue was Poland, for whose independence she had gone to war in September 1939. The dominant position of the Red Army made it inevitable that the Soviet-backed Lublin committee, rather than the Polish government-in-exile in London, would form the nucleus of Poland's post-war administration. The best that Churchill could do was to secure a commitment that the committee would be expanded through the inclusion of democratic elements from within Poland and outside. The country itself would lose territory in the east to the Soviet Union, but would receive compensation in the west at Germany's expense. Most important was Stalin's promise to hold free elections in Poland. Told by Roosevelt that the USA would withdraw American troops from Europe within two years of the end of the war, Churchill was particularly anxious to secure agreement on the recreation of France as a great power, to act as a barrier against possible future Soviet expansion. Here the prime minister was remarkably successful. France was granted a zone of occupation in Germany, together with permanent membership of the security council of the embryonic United Nations Organization. However, Roosevelt's agreement with Stalin, without consulting Churchill, about Soviet entry into the war against Japan, was more indicative of Britain's declining status. *DJD*

D. S. Clemens, *Yalta* (Oxford, 1970).

Yellow Book. See *Britain's Industrial Future*.

Yes Minister, series of satirical programmes about the relationship between British ministers and civil servants, written by Jonathan Lynn and Anthony Jay, produced by Sydney Lotterby and Peter Whitmore, and originally broadcast 1981–3. They featured a fictitious minister, Jim Hacker MP; the permanent secretary of his ministry, the department of administrative affairs, Sir Humphrey Appleby; and his civil service private secretary, Bernard Woolley, parts played respectively by Paul Eddington, Nigel Hawthorne, and Derek Fowlds. The theme of the programmes was the weaknesses and foibles of politicians and civil servants and their reactions to situations when their interests conflict. The series became very popular and was said to be the favourite television programme of the then prime minister, Margaret Thatcher. At a ceremony when the programme received the Mary Whitehouse award for television comedy, Thatcher took part in a sketch in which she played the prime minister with Eddington and Hawthorne. The series was followed by an equally successful sequel *Yes Prime Minister* in which Hacker had become prime minister and Sir Humphrey cabinet secretary.

The scripts were published (5 vols., 1981–7) and the programmes were issued on video. *RB*

Yesterday's Men **(1971)**, television documentary produced by Angela Pope which soured relations between the BBC and the Labour Party. The disparaging title, provocative interviews, and jokey theme song angered several Labour ex-ministers and especially the ex-premier, Harold Wilson. Wilson thought he was deliberately misled to expect a serious analysis of the predicament of ministers recently dismissed by the electorate. Instead he faced nosy questions from David Dimbleby about the earnings from his memoirs. *CKSU*

YMCA, nickname for a group of Conservative backbenchers in the 1924–9 parliament. Including Harold Macmillan, Gerald Loder, Noel Skelton, and Robert Boothby, they were generally not well regarded by the leadership, being viewed as too earnest and left-wing for mainstream Conservatism. The group collectively published the book *Industry and the State* (1927) which called for greater state intervention in both economic and social policies. *NJC*

Young, David **(1932–)**, industrialist and politician. Lord Young was one of the most prominent businessmen to reach high political office in the 1980s, one of 'Mrs Thatcher's Jews'. Related by marriage to Lord Wolfson of Great Universal Stores, he joined that company but then went into the property business where he prospered. In 1974 he joined Keith Joseph at the *Centre for Policy Studies, and entered the Thatcher government first as a special adviser and eventually as secretary for employment. He was prominent (and controversial) in his intervention in the 1987 election campaign when he seized the initiative late in the day from the party chairman, Norman Tebbit. His last political job was at the Department of Trade and Industry. Though a proponent of liberalization and small government, he was inclined in both his departments to mount high-profile interventionist initiatives which in the end had little provable effect. *JAT*

David Young, *The Enterprise Years* (London, 1990).

Young Conservatives ('YCs'), the post-war youth wing of the Conservative Party, successor to the Junior Imperial League. When the YCs were launched in 1945, there were only 50 surviving party youth branches, but by the end of 1946 there were already over 1,000. YCs took a leading part in the Conservatives' recovery of impetus in the late 1940s, claiming 200,000 members within five years and to be then the biggest political youth movement in the free world. They were integrated into the National Union structure at all levels and their under-30s provided a high proportion of the party's active canvassers, recruiters, and deliverers, but at heart the YC organization was always as much a social as a political body—to their critics a middle-class 'marriage market'. From the 1950s, there was a continuous battle to maintain numbers: the age limit was raised from 30 to 35, but by the 1970s most members were actually in their late teens and had limited political knowledge. By then the national total was under 40,000, and the party was having difficulty adjusting to the less deferential attitude of its youth wing too. In part the YCs' decline reflected the appeal of alternative social activities (which had not even existed in their heyday), in part a general decline in political partisanship, especially among the young. *JAR*

Younger, George Kenneth Hotson **(1931–)**, Conservative politician. Great-grandson of the party chairman Viscount *Younger, nephew of a Labour minister, and heir to a viscountcy, Younger stepped down in 1963 as Tory candidate at Kinross to provide a seat for Douglas-Home, but was elected for Ayr in 1964 and achieved junior office under Heath. Under Thatcher he ran Scotland on non-Thatcherite lines, asking for and getting money elsewhere refused, playing on the Nationalist threat and Conservative decline evident since 1959 as sweetly as Peter Walker did in Wales. Moving to defence after Heseltine's resignation in 1986 he himself resigned to Thatcher's displeasure in 1989. *EP*

Younger, 1st viscount **(1851–1929)**, brewer and Conservative organizer. A son of the great Scottish brewing family, George Younger entered parliament in 1906 and sat as MP for Ayr Burghs until 1922. He became the second chairman of the Conservative Party organization (1917–23) and was well known for understanding backbench and constituency party feeling. Younger loyally supported the Lloyd George coalition in the Great War and afterwards but grew concerned about the effect on his party of continuing the arrangement any longer than absolutely necessary. In 1922, alarmed at Austen Chamberlain's desire to lead the party into another election in cooperation with Lloyd George, the plain-speaking Younger in January took the unprecedented step of making public his opposition. This prompted Birkenhead to accuse him of acting like a 'cabin boy' attempting to seize the helm of the ship of state. Younger was vindicated, however, by many expressions of support, and Chamberlain's and Birkenhead's advice was rejected by Conservative MPs at the *Carlton Club meeting on 19 October. With Younger's blessing, the party then supported a Conservative administration under Law. After leaving the party chairmanship, Younger, by now a peer but ever the party's servant, became its treasurer until his death. *RJQA*

John Ramsden, *The Age of Balfour and Baldwin, 1902–1940* (London, 1978).

Young Liberals, the youth organization of the Liberal Party, technically open to anyone under 30. After the Second World War it provided a route through which party leaders such as Jo *Grimond and Jeremy *Thorpe emerged and assisted in the 1960s' Liberal revival. During the late 1960s, however, the Young Liberals also became a dynamic and sometimes troublesome element in the party. With an influx of new members encouraged by the party's by-election successes and its garnering of the protest vote, the Young Liberals became a radicalizing force within the party. By 1966, the Young Liberals were demanding the withdrawal of all American troops from Vietnam, workers' control of nationalized industries, non-alignment in the Cold War, British withdrawal from NATO, support for liberation movements in Rhodesia and Palestine, and a massive reduction in armaments (all of which were policies to the left of Labour). The party leadership was attacked for its caution and complacency. A high point of conflict came in January 1970, when the party's national executive 'requested' the Young Liberals to dismiss Louis Eaks, their chairman. Eaks's defeat in a leadership contest with Tony Greaves in March 1970 eased tensions somewhat. Greaves was more concerned with *community politics than high-profile international issues and used his influence to make grass-roots campaigning an intrinsic part of the Liberal Party's approach. As a result the Young Liberals became an important part of the next Liberal revival during the 1970s. Often in alliance with, indeed using the same personnel as, the Association of Liberal Councillors, they provided the activists who brought by-election and municipal success to the Liberals and the Alliance into the 1980s. *JS*

Young plan. See REPARATIONS.

Youth Training Scheme (YTS), introduced in September 1983. There was nothing new about concern about youth unemployment; indeed, this measure replaced the Youth Opportunities Programme (YOP) introduced five years earlier under Callaghan. It did, however, involve more explicit commitment to work-based training than YOP. YTS was nevertheless dogged by criticism that much of the training provided was low-grade, necessitated by the short time period, six months, over which it was made available. Furthermore, it never escaped the suspicion that anxieties about the social consequences of unemployed youth, fuelled by the riots of the early 1980s, predominated over supply-side concerns in framing of the policy. *PPC*

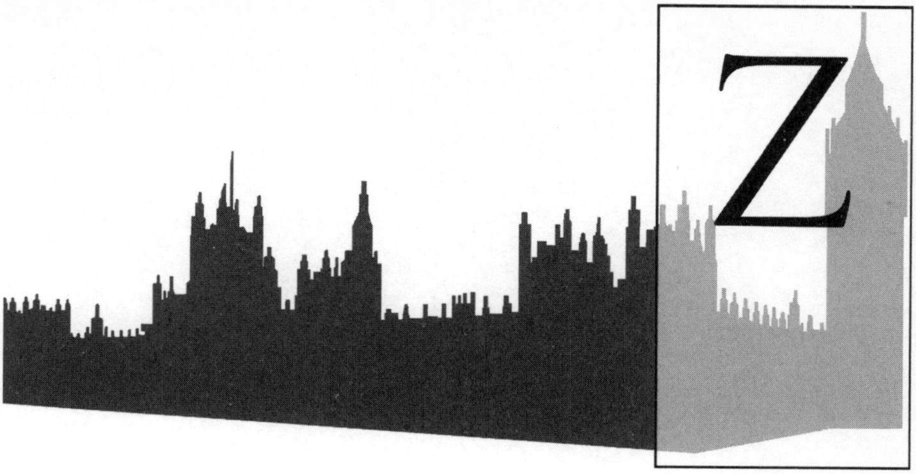

Zilliacus, Konni (1894–1967), Labour politician. 'It was impossible to fit Zilliacus into any known political category, whether an extreme left-winger, fellow-traveller, or crypto-Communist. In the eyes of some he appeared at times to be one or all of these things.' In reply he would say that 'Communists have sometimes been my fellow-travellers but I have never been theirs' (*The Times*, 7 July 1967). Zilliacus was born at Kobe in Japan to a Finnish-Swedish father and Scottish-American mother. He entered parliament in 1945 as Labour MP for Gateshead, having earlier served in the Royal Flying Corps in the Great War and as an intelligence officer. He worked later for the League of Nations and between 1939 and 1945 for the Ministry of Information. Once in parliament he clashed frequently with his party, notably over foreign policy, and was expelled in May 1949. Zilliacus stood unsuccessfully as an independent labour candidate in Gateshead East in 1950, but in 1952 the NEC reinstated him and he was successful at Manchester, Gorton in 1955. His party difficulties continued but Gorton returned him in 1959, 1964, and 1966. His writings influenced politicians in both Western and Eastern Europe and his contacts greased the wheels of politics across the Continent. *CH*

K. Zilliacus, *I Choose Peace* (Harmondsworth, 1949).

Zinoviev letter (1924), election stunt. The letter was probably a forgery (historians' opinions have differed on this), but purported to convey instructions from Zinoviev of the Communist International to British Communists, directing them to foment disaffection in the British army. It was published by the *Daily Mail* only three days before polling day in the 1924 general election, so contributing to the defeat of the Labour government by scaring pro-Liberal voters into supporting the Conservatives. The Labour vote rose by over a million, though mainly because the party put up 80 more candidates, while the 'red letter' provided a comforting alibi for losing office after just ten months (which would surely have happened anyway). *DLM*

Lewis Chester, Stephen Fay, and Hugo Young, *The Zinoviev Letter* (London, 1967).

Zuckerman, Solly (1904–93), scientist and government adviser. Zuckerman was one of the giants of the post-1945 Whitehall scientific advisory community. Born in South Africa, he published influential books on monkeys and apes and taught at Oxford from 1934 (he was later professor of anatomy at Birmingham, 1943–68). During the Second World War, he researched the effects of bombs and advised on strategic bombing. After the war, he was ubiquitous in the network of government advisory committees: a member of the Barlow committee on future scientific policy, 1946; deputy chairman of the advisory council on scientific policy, 1948–64; chief scientific adviser to the secretary of state for defence, 1960–6; and many other assignments. In 1964 he was appointed the first-ever chief scientific adviser to the government, with the rank of permanent secretary, serving in that post until 1971. He was a member of the royal commission on environmental pollution, 1970–4. Zuckerman was created a life peer in 1971. *KT*

APPENDIX ONE

DATES OF MINISTRIES

Prime Minister	Date of Formation	Party
3rd marquess of Salisbury	25 June 1895	Unionist
Arthur Balfour	12 July 1902	Unionist
Sir Henry Campbell-Bannerman	5 December 1905	Liberal
Herbert Asquith	5 April 1908	Liberal
Herbert Asquith	25 May 1915	Coalition[1]
David Lloyd George	6 December 1916	Coalition[2]
Andrew Bonar Law	23 October 1922	Conservative
Stanley Baldwin	22 May 1923	Conservative
Ramsay MacDonald	22 January 1924	Labour*
Stanley Baldwin	4 November 1924	Conservative
Ramsay MacDonald	5 June 1929	Labour*
Ramsay MacDonald	24 August 1931	National[3]
Stanley Baldwin	7 June 1935	National/Conservative
Neville Chamberlain	28 May 1937	National/Conservative
Winston Churchill	10 May 1940	National[4]
Winston Churchill	23 May 1945	National/Conservative[5]
Clement Attlee	26 July 1945	Labour
Winston Churchill	26 October 1951	Conservative
Sir Anthony Eden	6 April 1955	Conservative
Harold Macmillan	10 January 1957	Conservative
Sir Alec Douglas-Home	18 October 1963	Conservative
Harold Wilson	16 October 1964	Labour
Edward Heath	19 June 1970	Conservative
Harold Wilson	4 March 1974	Labour*
James Callaghan	5 April 1976	Labour*
Margaret Thatcher	4 May 1979	Conservative
John Major	28 November 1990	Conservative*
Tony Blair	2 May 1997	Labour

Notes

* Governments without a parliamentary majority for all or part of their duration

1. Asquith's coalition included Liberal, Unionist, and Labour members.
2. Lloyd George's coalition included Conservatives and National (Lloyd George) Liberals (but not Asquithian Liberals), Labour members only until 1918.
3. The 1931 National Government initially included all parties except the official Labour Party (but had 'National Labour' members). Many of its Liberal members resigned in 1932, and by 1935 it still called itself a National but was virtually a Conservative government.
4. Churchill's wartime coalition government contained members of all parties.
5. The Caretaker Government governed only between Labour's departure from office and the general election. It called itself a National Government but consisted almost entirely of Conservatives.

APPENDIX TWO

Dates	Prime Minister	Home Secretary	Foreign Secretary
1895–1902	Salisbury	White-Ridley (1895–1900) Ritchie (1900–2)	Salisbury (1895–1900) Lansdowne (1900–2)
1902–5	Balfour	Akers-Douglas	Lansdowne
1905–8	Campbell-Bannerman	Gladstone	Grey
1908–15	Asquith	Gladstone (1908–10) Churchill (1910–11) McKenna (1911–15)	Grey
1915–16	Asquith	Simon (1915–16) Samuel (1916)	Grey
1916–22	Lloyd George	Cave (1916–19) Shortt (1919–22)	Balfour (1916–19) Curzon (1919–22)

OFFICE HOLDERS

Chancellor of the Exchequer	Lord Chancellor	Other Major Offices
Hicks Beach (1895–1902)	Halsbury	*Chief Sec. For Ireland*: Wyndham (1900–2) *War*: Lansdowne (1895–1900) *Colonies*: J. Chamberlain *Lord President*: Devonshire
Ritchie (1902–3) A. Chamberlain (1902–5)	Halsbury	*Chief Sec. for Ireland*: Wyndham (1902–5) *Colonies*: J. Chamberlain (1902–3) *Lord President*: Devonshire (1902–3) *Admiralty*: Selborne (1902–5)
Asquith	Loreburn	*India*: Morley *War*: Haldane *Board of Trade*: Lloyd George
Lloyd George	Loreburn (1908–12) Haldane (1912–15)	*War*: Haldane (1908–12) *Admiralty*: Churchill (1911–15) *Chief Sec. for Ireland*: Birrell *War*: Kitchener (1914–15) *Attorney-General*: Isaacs (1910–13)
McKenna	Buckmaster	*War*: Kitchener (1915–16); Lloyd George (1916) *Admiralty*: Balfour *Munitions*: Lloyd George (1915–16) *Chief Sec. for Ireland*: Birrell (1915–16) *Colonies*: Law *Education*: Henderson
Law (1916–19) A. Chamberlain (1921–2) Horne (1921–2)	Finlay (1916–19) Birkenhead (1919–22)	*Privy Seal*: Law (1919–21); A. Chamberlain (1919–21) *Education*: Fisher *Health*: Addision (1919–21) *Board of Trade*: Baldwin (1921–2) *Reconstruction*: Addison (1917–19) *War*: Derby (1916–18); Milner (1918); Churchill (1918–21)

Dates	Prime Minister	Home Secretary	Foreign Secretary
1922–4	Law (1922–3) Baldwin (1923–4)	Bridgeman	Curzon
1924	MacDonald	Henderson	MacDonald
1924–9	Baldwin	Joynson-Hicks	A. Chamberlain
1929–31	MacDonald	Clynes	Henderson
1931–5	MacDonald	Samuel (1931–2) Gilmour (1932–5)	Reading (1931) Simon (1931–5)
1935–40	Baldwin (1935–7) N. Chamberlain (1937–40)	Simon (1935–7) Hoare (1937–9) Anderson (1939–40)	Hoare (1935–7) Eden (1937–8) Halifax (1938–40)
1940–5	Churchill	Anderson (1940) Morrison (1940–5)	Halifax (1940) Eden (1940–5)
1945	Churchill	Somervell	Eden
1945–51	Attlee	Chuter Ede	Bevin (1945–51) Morrison (1951)
1951–7	Churchill (1951–5) Eden (1955–7)	Maxwell Fyfe (1951–4) G. Lloyd George (1954–7)	Eden (1951–5) Macmillan (1955) Lloyd (1955–7)

Chancellor of the Exchequer	Lord Chancellor	Other Major Offices
Baldwin (1922–3) N. Chamberlain (1923–4)	Cave	*Health*: N. Chamberlain (1923)
Snowden	Haldane	*Health*: Wheatley
Churchill	Cave (1924–8) Hailsham (1928–9)	*Health*: N. Chamberlain *Labour*: Steel-Maitland *Colonies*: Amery *India*: Birkenhead (1924–8) *Lord President*: Balfour (1925–9)
Snowden	Sankey	*Labour*: Bondfield *Duchy of Lancaster*: Mosley (1929–30)
Snowden (1931) N. Chamberlain (1931–5)	Sankey	*Air*: Londonderry (1931–5) *Board of Trade*: Runciman (1931–5) *India*: Hoare
N. Chamberlain (1935–7) Simon (1937–40)	Hailsham (1935–8) Maugham (1938–9) Caldecote (1939–40)	*Air*: Cunliffe-Lister (1935–8) *Coordn. of Defence*: Inskip (1936–9) *Health*: Wood (1935–8) *League of Nations*: Eden (1935) *War*: Hore-Belisha (1937–40) *Admiralty*: Churchill (1939–40)
K. Wood (1940–3) Anderson (1943–5)	Simon	*Lord President*: N. Chamberlain (1940); Anderson (1940–3); Attlee (1943–5) *Privy Seal*: Cripps (1942) *Aircraft production*: Beaverbrook (1940–1) *Labour*: Bevin *Education*: Butler (1941–5) *Information*: Bracken (1941–5)
Anderson	Simon	*Labour*: Butler
Dalton (1945–7) Cripps (1947–50) Gaitskell (1950–1)	Jowitt	*Health*: Bevan (1945–51) *Lord President*: Morrison (1945–51) *Board of Trade*: Cripps (1945–7); Wilson (1947–51)
Butler (1951–5) Macmillan (1955–7)	Simonds (1951–4) Kilmuir (1954–7)	*Agriculture*: Dugdale (1951–4) *Housing*: Macmillan (1951–4) *Lord President*: Salisbury (1952–7) *Privy Seal*: Butler (1955–7)

Dates	Prime Minister	Home Secretary	Foreign Secretary
1957–63	Macmillan	Butler (1957–62) Brooke (1962–3)	Lloyd (1957–60) Home (1960–3)
1963–4	Douglas-Home	Brooke	Butler
1964–70	Wilson	Soskice (1964–5) Jenkins (1965–7) Callaghan (1967–70)	Gordon Walker (1964–5) Stewart (1965–6, 1968–70) Brown (1966–8)
1970–4	Heath	Maudling (1970–2) Carr (1970–4)	Douglas-Home
1974–9	Wilson (1974–6) Callaghan (1976–9)	Jenkins (1974–6) Rees (1976–9)	Callaghan (1974–6) Crosland (1976–7) Owen (1977–9)
1979–90	Thatcher	Whitelaw (1979–83) Brittan (1983–5) Hurd (1985–9) Waddington (1989–90)	Carrington (1979–82) Pym (1982–3) Howe (1983–9) Major (1989) Hurd (1989–90)

Chancellor of the Exchequer	Lord Chancellor	Other Major Offices
Thorneycroft (1957–8) Heathcoat Amory (1958–60) Macleod (1959–61) Maudling (1962–3)	Kilmuir (1957–62) Dilhorne (1962–3)	*First Secretary*: Butler (1962–3) *Lord President*: Hailsham (1960–3) *Colonies*: Lennox-Boyd (1957–9); Lloyd (1960–2) *Defence*: Sandys (1957–9) *Housing*: Brooke (1957–61) *Health*: Powell (1960–3) *Privy Seal*: Heath (1960–3) *Transport*: Marples (1960–3) *War*: Profumo (1959–63)
Maudling	Dilhorne	*Trade and Industry*: Heath
Callaghan (1964–7) Jenkins (1967–70)	Gardiner	*Economic Affairs*: Brown (1964–6) *Employment*: Castle (1968–70) *Defence*: Healey *Education*: Crosland (1965–7) *Technology*: Benn (1966–70) *Transport*: Castle (1965–8)
Macleod (1970) Barber (1970–4)	Hailsham	*Education*: Thatcher *Employment*: Carr (1970–2) *Environment*: Walker (1970–2) *Northern Ireland*: Whitelaw (1972–3) *Trade and Industry*: Walker (1972–4)
Healey	Elwyn-Jones	*Employment*: Foot (1974–5) *Environment*: Crosland (1974–6) *Energy*: Benn (1975–9) *Health*: Castle (1974–6) *Northern Ireland*: Rees (1974–6); Mason (1976–9)
Howe (1979–83) Lawson (1983–9) Major (1989–90)	Hailsham (1979–87) Havers (1987) Mackay (1987–90)	*Defence*: Nott (1981–3); Heseltine (1983–6) *Education*: Joseph (1981–6); Baker (1986–9) *Employment*: Prior (1979–81); Tebbit (1981–3) *Energy*: Walker (1983–7) *Environment*: Heseltine (1979–83); Jenkin (1983–5); Ridley (1986–9) *Health*: Fowler (1981–7); Clarke (1988–90) *Northern Ireland*: Prior (1981–3); King (1984–9)

Dates	Prime Minister	Home Secretary	Foreign Secretary
1990–7	Major	Baker (1990–2) Clarke (1992–3) Howard (1993–7)	Hurd (1990–5) Rifkind (1995–7)
1997–	Blair	Straw (1997–2001) Blunkett (2001–)	Cook (1997–2001) Straw (2001–)

Notes

Where no dates are given, the minister served in the office indicated for the whole period of the ministry.
Full titles of departments have been abbreviated.

Chancellor of the Exchequer	Lord Chancellor	Other Major Offices
Lamont (1990–3) Clarke (1993–7)	Mackay	*Agriculture*: Gummer (1990–3); Waldegrave (1994–7) *Education*: Clarke (1990–2); Shephard (1994–7) *Employment*: Howard (1990–2); Portillo (1994–7) *Environment*: Heseltine (1990–2) *Health*: Bottomley (1992–7) *Trade*: Heseltine (1992–7)
Brown	Irvine	*Education*: Blunkett (1997–2001) *Environment*: Prescott (1997–2001) *Northern Ireland*: Mowlam (1997–9); Mandelson (1999–2000)

APPENDIX THREE

RESULTS OF GENERAL ELECTIONS

Each cell in the table gives for each party: (1) the number of candidates; (2) the number of MPs elected; and (3) the number of votes in millions.

Date	***Conservative***	***Labour***	***Liberal***	***Other Major Parties***	
28 Sept. to 24 Oct. 1900				*Irish Nationalists*	
	579	15	406	100	
	402	2	184	82	
	1.79	0.06	1.57	0.09	
13 Jan. to 7 Feb. 1906				*Irish Nationalists*	
	574	51	539	87	
	157	30	400	83	
	2.45	0.33	2.76	0.035	
14 Jan. to 9 Feb. 1910				*Irish Nationalists*	
	600	78	516	104	
	273	40	275	82	
	3.12	0.51	2.88	0.12	
2 Dec. to 19 Dec. 1910					
	550	56	467	106	
	272	42	272	84	
	2.42	0.37	2.29	0.13	
14 Dec. 1918				*Nat. Lib.*	*Sinn Fein*
	449	388	253	158	102
	383	63	28	133	75
	4.16	2.38	1.29	1.45	0.48
15 Nov. 1922				*Nat. Lib.*	
	483	411	328	162	
	345	142	54	62	
	5.50	4.24	2.52	1.67	
6 Dec. 1923	540	422	453		
	258	191	159		
	5.54	4.44	4.31		
29 Oct. 1924	552	512	340		
	419	151	40		
	8.04	5.49	2.93		

Date	Conservative	Labour	Liberal	Other Major Parties	
30 May 1929	590	571	513		
	260	288	59		
	8.66	8.39	5.31		
27 Oct. 1931				*Nat. Lib.*	*Nat. Lib.*
	523	515	119	41	20
	473	52	37	35	13
	11.98	6.65	1.51	0.81	0.34
14 Nov. 1935	585	569	161		
	432	158	20		
	11.81	8.46	1.42		
5 July 1945	624	604	306		
	213	393	12		
	9.99	11.99	2.25		
23 Feb. 1950	620	617	475		
	298	315	9		
	12.50	13.27	2.62		
25 Oct. 1951	617	617	109		
	321	295	6		
	13.71	13.95	0.73		
26 May 1955	623	620	110		
	344	277	6		
	13.29	12.40	0.72		
8 Oct. 1959				*Pl. Cymru*	*SNP*
	625	621	216	20	5
	365	258	6	—	—
	13.75	12.22	1.64	0.08	0.02
15 Oct. 1964	630	628	565	23	15
	304	317	9	—	—
	12.00	12.21	3.09	0.07	0.06
31 March 1966	629	621	311	20	20
	253	363	12	—	—
	11.42	13.06	2.33	0.06	0.13
18 June 1970	628	624	332	36	65
	330	287	6	—	1
	13.15	12.18	2.12	0.18	0.31

Date	*Conservative*	*Labour*	*Liberal*	*Other Major Parties*	
28 Feb. 1974				*Pl. Cymru*	*SNP*
	623	623	517	36	70
	297	301	14	2	7
	11.87	11.64	6.06	0.17	0.63
10 Oct. 1974	623	623	619	36	71
	277	319	13	3	11
	10.46	11.46	5.35	0.17	0.84
3 May 1979	622	623	577	36	71
	339	269	11	2	2
	13.69	11.53	4.31	0.13	0.50
9 June 1983	633	633	633	36	71
	397	209	17	2	2
	13.01	8.85	7.78	0.13	0.33
11 June 1987	633	633	633	38	71
	376	229	22	3	3
	13.76	10.03	7.34	0.12	0.42
9 April 1992	645	634	632	38	72
	336	271	20	4	3
	14.09	11.56	5.60	0.15	0.63
1 May 1997	640	639	639	40	72
	165	418	46	4	6
	9.60	13.52	5.24	0.16	0.62
7 June 2001	640	640	639	40	72
	166	413	52	4	5
	8.36	10.74	4.82	0.19	0.46

Notes

Before 1950, and especially before 1918, the number of votes gained by each party was often considerably distorted by constituencies not contested.

Until 1918, constituencies voted on different days over a period of about four weeks.

In 1935 and 1945, candidates calling themselves Liberal National, National Labour, and National are counted as Conservatives.

Since 1983, all Alliance, SDP, and Liberal and Liberal Democrat candidates except those not supported by their national party are counted as Liberals.